About the cover

Paul End, *Maison et Deux Visages Féminins* (1949–50). Poorly educated and of a humble and submissive nature, End (b. 1895) worked for more than twenty years as a laborer in a factory. At the age of 38, he was admitted to a psychiatric hospital in Lille, France, where he began to create drawings and sketches. This drawing, done in colored pencil, skillfully combines fluid motion and patterns of geometric rigidity.

Abnormal Psychology and Modern Life

SEVENTH EDITION

Abnormal Psychology and Modern Life

SEVENTH EDITION

James C. Coleman
Emeritus, University of California at Los Angeles

James N. Butcher
University of Minnesota

Robert C. Carson
Duke University

Scott, Foresman and Company

Glenview, Illinois   Dallas, Tex.   Oakland, N.J.   Palo Alto, Cal.
Tucker, Ga.   London, England

Credit lines for the photos, illustrations, and copyrighted materials appearing in this work appear in the Acknowledgments section beginning on page LIV. This section is to be considered an extension of the copyright page.

Library of Congress Cataloging in Publication Data
Coleman, James Covington.
     Abnormal psychology and modern life.
     Bibliography: p.
     Includes indexes.
     1. Psychology, Pathological. 2. Psychotherapy.
I.   Butcher, James Neal, 1933-   . II. Carson,
Robert C., 1930-   . III. Title.
RC454.C6 1984   616.89   83-20038
ISBN 0-673-15886-1

2 3 4 5 6 7 8-RRW-88 87 86 85 84

Preface

This Seventh Edition of *Abnormal Psychology and Modern Life* is the current authors' second attempt to match and—if possible, beyond mere updating—to improve upon the classic *Abnormal* text James Coleman first introduced in 1950. That work, in its successive editions to 1976 (5th Edition), was the generally acknowledged premier text in undergraduate abnormal psychology, and we continue to be pleased at the numbers of our colleagues, many of them now leaders in the field, who tell us they "cut their abnormal psychology teeth" on the predecessors of the present volume. We readily acknowledge our debt to the history of this book and to the scholarly excellence of its originator, whose wise words continue to grace its pages in abundance in the Seventh Edition.

But all things that are truly alive change, and indeed they seem to change on an escalating curve of acceleration as we move into an exciting but still largely unpredictable future. In our judgment—and apart from certain astounding advances in the more technological sciences—the field of abnormal psychology is developing today at an unprecedented rate, one that far exceeds the rate of progress of virtually all of the "other" social sciences. Many readers will view the last statement skeptically, and may be inclined to retort that such progress as has been made is attributable to new *biologically based* technical advances—*not* to any greater understanding of people as biopsychosocial units. We can understand such reservations. Progress in areas of biology that intersect with abnormal behavior has indeed been impressive, even since the last edition of this text, and, as will be seen, we have amply documented that progress in the present edition.

However, although often less dramatic and, because of their complexity, less often given prominent "play" in the media, psychosocial and sociocultural advances in understanding abnormal behavior have also been noteworthy in recent years. Of course, the basic issue nearly always comes down to the nature of the interaction among the different approaches; and, as

again will be seen, we have tried to emphasize these very basic and difficult interactive issues in inviting the student to think along with us in trying to understand varied abnormalities.

We do not wholeheartedly salute the way in which "varied abnormalities" are at present officially differentiated from one another; that is, we—along with many others—have serious reservations about the American Psychiatric Association's (1980) *Diagnostic and Statistical Manual, Third Edition* (DSM-III) that is now the accepted taxonomy for the classification of instances of abnormal behavior. While we acknowledge that this document is in many ways an improvement over its predecessors (DSM-I and -II), we also think that it reflects nature (that is, the real behavior of persons) through distorted and in many ways artificial and arbitrary lenses.

Nevertheless, we have sought throughout to educate the reader about what the DSM-III *says*, and indeed the organization of the book is largely in keeping with DSM-III's major categories of disorder. At the same time, however, we have not been hesitant to raise fundamental questions about the decisions that were made in framing DSM-III; these reservations are discussed throughout the book, but particularly in regard to the specific clinical entities that are addressed in its central portions. For ready reference, the DSM-III is reprinted in full on the back endsheets of the text.

As in the Sixth Edition, we again made a valiant effort to shorten the book's length. And again, as in the Sixth Edition, we have made only modest inroads toward this goal. This text has been for years the standard in comprehensiveness and encyclopedic coverage, and we did not wish to tamper excessively with this image; on the contrary, we think that a text of this inclusive sort fulfills an important function at various educational levels. Clearly, most instructors, entirely appropriately, have their own ideas about what are the really basic and essential facts, ideas, and syndromes in the area of abnormal psychology, and they make assignments from this survey text accordingly. Partly in recognition of this reality, and as was attempted in earlier editions, we have tried insofar as feasible to make each chapter an independent and self-sustaining unit—*not* requiring for essential understanding material from other chapters in the book. Of course, there are limits to the degree to which this goal can efficiently be managed: we have done our best in making the required compromise. In general, the sequence of the Seventh Edition may be summarized as follows:

In response to reviewer input, Part I has been extensively revised and streamlined to consist of four chapters (instead of five). It begins by setting forth a framework for understanding *abnormal*, or *maladaptive*, behavior, including common misconceptions, accepted definitions, broader discussion of issues of classification, and a new section on issues in scientific research in abnormal psychology. A brief historical overview follows, which traces the changing views of mental disorders from ancient to modern times. This leads to a discussion of the development of contemporary biological, psychosocial, and sociocultural viewpoints. Included here is more coverage of the recent growth that has occurred in both biological and psychosocial viewpoints, particularly along the psychodynamic and cognitive-behavioral avenues. The reader is reminded of the continuing need for an interdisciplinary approach to understanding and dealing with abnormal behavior. Part I concludes with an overview of causal factors in abnormal behavior; it introduces the diathesis-stress model as a broad way of viewing human vulnerabilities and abnormal behavior. The crucial roles of both learning and life stressors in the development and maintenance of abnormal behavior are emphasized throughout, as well as the interaction of biological, psychosocial, and sociocultural factors. Within this context, maladaptive behavior can be viewed as involving not only individuals but also the physical, interpersonal, and sociocultural environments in which they live.

Part II details the clinical pictures, causal factors, and treatment and outcomes of maladaptive patterns. It begins with a discussion of the nature of stress and of adjustment disorders and more severe posttraumatic stress disorders. This is followed by chapters on the anxiety-based disorders, personality disorders, psychophysiologic

disorders, affective disorders, schizophrenic and paranoid disorders, substance-use disorders, psychosexual disorders, organic mental disorders and mental retardation, and, finally, behavior disorders of childhood and adolescence.

Part III deals with the areas of assessment, therapy, and current issues. The value of assessment as a continuing aid and check on progress is emphasized. The scope of therapeutic intervention on both biological and psychological frontiers is examined, critical legal and ethical issues related to abnormal behavior are presented in a new section, and ongoing efforts and future prospects toward prevention of maladaptive behavior are explored.

A number of efforts have been made to add to the instructional format of this edition. Expanded *chapter outlines* introduce each chapter and provide an overview of what is to come. *Chapter summaries* have been rewritten and expanded, too. For easy referral, *key terms appear in boldface type*, and the comprehensive *Glossary* has been thoroughly revised, with key terms page-referenced to the text. Again, as has been true of earlier editions, the Seventh Edition is sensitively illustrated, with new full-color illustrations throughout conveying in visual terms the reality of the many forms of human experience and behavior. A wide variety of case studies and **HIGHLIGHT** boxes enrich and enhance the reader's understanding of the field. The **HIGHLIGHT** are clearly set apart from the text proper but are cross-referenced within the text to indicate the opportune time for the reader to refer to them.

The *References* provide a rich source of both classic studies and the most recent research in the field; in this edition they appear in the new 1983 APA format and are also alphabetized for the entire text, rather than on a chapter-by-chapter basis as in previous editions. The *Name* and *Subject Indexes* are thorough and accurate as always. In addition, the *Student's Guide*, prepared by Mary P. Koss of Kent State University, presents the student with a useful aid in mastering essential materials contained in the text.

The current revision was an undertaking of considerably greater magnitude than was attempted in the Sixth Edition. Correspondingly, it imposed on the authors a level of demand that can probably only be truly understood and appreciated by other writers of textbooks. Exhausting and difficult as was the authors' task, it was undoubtedly at least matched in time and energy demands by our publishing colleagues, the editorial and production staffs of Scott, Foresman and Company. We owe a particular debt of gratitude to Joanne M. Tinsley, developmental editor, who kept our noses to the grindstone, with amazing equanimity, throughout the project—even when frustration-produced tirades were erupting with extraordinary frequency. We are likewise grateful for the sensitive and wise advice of our manuscript editor, Trig Thoreson, who, we regret to say, probably had not previously experienced author "expressiveness" on a comparable scale; he did a fine job.

We wish to thank the following colleagues from the University of Minnesota for the case material they generously provided: Carolyn Williams, Joseph Westermeyer, Rosa Garcia, and Gloria Leon. We must also thank the many colleagues who read and commented on both the previous edition and early drafts of the current one. Their help and advice, while not always (but, in fact, mostly) followed, was invaluable in pinpointing areas in which we needed greater currency and/or clarity in the discussion of particular issues. They include:

Linda M. Baskett
  University of Arkansas
Stewart R. Beasley
  Central State University
Douglas A. Bernstein
  University of Illinois
Edward B. Blanchard
  SUNY, Albany
Barbara E. Brackney
  Eastern Michigan University
Alan Button
  California State University, Fresno
Bruce Carpenter
  University of Tulsa
Tracey Potts Carson
  VA Hospital, Durham, N.C.
Richard A. Depue
  University of Minnesota
Alan S. DeWolfe
  Loyola University of Chicago
Juris G. Draguns
  The Pennsylvania State University
Thomas W. Durham
  East Carolina University

Norman L. Egger
  San Jose State University
Paul Ellen
  Georgia State University
Louis Gaffney
  Seattle University
John Gonsiorek
  Twin Cities Therapy Clinic
Joann H. Grayson
  James Madison University
W. Daniel Hale
  Stetson University
Robert Hogan
  University of Tulsa
Carl Insalaco
  Grand Valley State Colleges
Philip C. Kendall
  University of Minnesota
Marcel Kinsbourne
  Shriver Research Institute
Donald Klein
  New York State Psychiatric Institute
Sheldon J. Korchin
  University of California, Berkeley
Mary P. Koss
  Kent State University
Arnold LeUnes
  Texas A & M University
Leon H. Levy
  University of Maryland
Lawrence Lilliston
  Oakland University
Joseph LoPiccolo
  SUNY, Stony Brook
Brendan A. Maher
  Harvard University
Willard A. Mainor
  University of Louisville
Marco J. Mariotto
  University of Houston
Sharon M. McCordick
  San Diego State University
Denis Nissim-Sabat
  Mary Washington College
Martin M. Oper
  Erie Community College-North Campus
Chester C. Parker
  Middle Tennessee State University
Richard A. Pasewark
  University of Wyoming
Jeanne S. Phillips
  University of Denver

Timothy T. Pohmer
   Butler County Community College
Michael T. Prince
   University of Central Arkansas
Charles K. Prokop
   Texas Tech University
Michael M. Reece
   Wayne State University
Duane H. Reeder
   Glendale Community College
Lloyd K. Sines
   University of Minnesota
Jim Smith
   Chattanooga State Technical Community College
Patricia B. Sutker
   VA Medical Center, New Orleans, Louisiana
James A. Sutton
   Chattanooga State Technical Community College
Robert J. Thompson, Jr.
   Duke University Medical Center

June M. Tuma
   Louisiana State University
Edwin E. Wheeler
   Texas A & I University
Patricia A. Wisocki
   University of Massachusetts
Julian Wohl
   The University of Toledo
Janet P. Wollersheim
   University of Montana

Finally, we have retained the order of the authors' names as they appeared in the Sixth Edition for the reasons we stated at that time. James Coleman's appears first simply because this remains largely his book. The second and third authors' names appear alphabetically; our contributions in the preparation of the work were as near equal as we could make them.

J. N. B.
R. C. C.

Contents

Part 1
Perspectives on abnormal behavior 2

Part 3
Assessment, treatment, and prevention 580

18 Contemporary issues in abnormal psychology 672

Abnormal Psychology and Modern Life

SEVENTH EDITION

Part 1

Perspectives on abnormal behavior

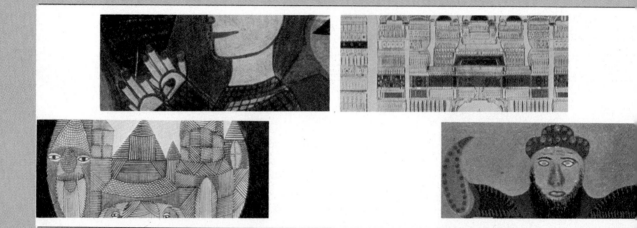

1

Abnormal behavior in our times

Augustin Lesage, Composition
Symbolique sur le Monde Spirituel
*(1913). Lesage (1876–1954) was a French
coalminer who, under the influence of
"spirit guides," became a painter.
Successful both as artist and medium, he
came to regard himself as the reincarnation
of a great painter of the past. His work
characteristically consists of symmetrical
and intricate design patterns reminiscent of
Egyptian or East Indian art.*

The seventeenth century has been called the Age of Enlightenment; the eighteenth, the Age of Reason; the nineteenth, the Age of Progress; and the twentieth, the Age of Anxiety.

Through technology and the advances of science, our understanding of the world has grown and with it a sense of the seemingly limitless opportunity and diversity that our environment makes possible for us. We Westerners have tended to regard this environment as something that can be controlled and conquered; now we are becoming more aware of how the environment can affect us in sometimes unforeseen ways.

Brilliant solutions to problems of production, communication, transportation, and so on have also provided us with a host of new problems. The speed and complexity of modern life—with its constant change and its demands for new knowledge, skills, and competencies—leave little room for either contemplation or complacency. Many of us find ourselves running at full tilt just to stay in the race. Breakneck technological advances confront us almost daily as we move from an industrial to a postindustrial society. We are threatened with the obsolescence of the skills we have developed to ensure our economic security. We are rapidly moving into a high-tech society for which many of us feel ill-prepared.

Even those of us who manage to remain productive and employable—a status increasingly dependent on advanced and specialized training—find that our futures are far from guaranteed. Worldwide economic fluctuations, inflation, unemployment, and discrimination take their toll in dislocation and poverty for millions of people. With the communications explosion, we grow ever closer to forces and events seemingly beyond the control of any one individual or, indeed, of any nation or alignment of nations. Meanwhile, in the background, we remain aware that all of us are potential competitors for the world's dwindling supply of vital natural resources.

The entire life of the typical college student of today has been spent under the shadow of thermonuclear threat. Even if we manage to avoid a nuclear catastrophe of some sort, we will continue to experience the fouling of our environment through the byproducts of "advancing" industry and technology, and we will continue to

5

hear almost daily reports of discoveries of hazardous substances in the food we eat and the air we breathe. The once great confidence of our people that solutions can and will be found to our environmental and health problems appears to have been shaken in recent years.

Similarly, the grand hopes for world peace felt by most following the adoption of the United Nations charter some forty years ago have been dashed repeatedly by the cruel realities of international armed conflict and civil unrest. There appears to be no end in sight to such outbreaks of violence, and young people in particular must live and plan with the uncertainty that they may be called at any time to serve in their country's defense.

Meanwhile, shifts in the structure and values of our Western culture deprive us of many of the supports enjoyed by those who came before us. The increasing number of divorces has taken its toll; for many, the stable nuclear family of mother, father, and children is a thing of the past. And only rarely can a child expect to grow to adulthood with an extended family nearby. Grandparents, so often wonderful sources of unconditional love, are now frequently many hundreds of miles distant, their relationship with their growing grandchild reduced to occasional brief visits. In addition, cultural values once regarded as permanent and sacrosanct are increasingly seen as relative rather than as firm guidelines for important life decisions. Religion, sex, marriage, the family, and long-standing social and political institutions and assumptions are subjected to unrelenting and often withering analysis by hosts of public critics—inspiring on occasion conservative overreactions that may themselves threaten other important cultural values. Much evidence indicates that human beings *need* to believe, even passionately, in things abstract, moral, and "spiritual." But there are so many divergent "moralities" from which to choose today that the choice itself can be a source of confusion.

Small wonder that on every side we see anxious, unhappy people who miss the realization of their potentialities because they cannot find adequate solutions or answers to problems that seem beyond them. The hassles of modern, postindustrial life are reflected in the incredible amounts of tranquilizing chemicals—alcoholic or otherwise, prescription and nonprescription—

we as a society consume. Other indications of widespread stress can be found in activities that are not related to the use of chemicals: involvement, among young people in particular, in strange religious cults; acts of suicide, which also have been on the increase among youths in recent years; and criminal or antisocial behavior, particularly involving assaults upon other individuals, often justified—contrary to much cross-cultural research evidence—as "normal" and "natural" responses to frustrating conditions.

Despite the stressful nature of modern life, most of us seem to "muddle through," although probably not without at least some psychological scars. Some of the more hardy among us even seem to thrive on the multiple challenges our situation presents. But for many of us, the test of our resources proves too great, and our attempts to cope become erratic and nonfunctional, perhaps even self-damaging. Mental impairments of one sort or another now afflict more people than all physical health problems combined. Furthermore, the Institute of Medicine of the National Academy of Sciences and certain other governmental agencies have increasingly called attention to the widespread influence of mental and behavioral factors in what were once thought to be purely *physical* diseases (Hamburg, Elliott, & Parron, 1982). Stress-related physical diseases are now seen as major medical problems.

President Carter's Commission on Mental Health concluded in its 1978 report that one person in seven living in the United States would at some time require professional treatment for emotional disturbances. These statistics have not improved over the last several years (see **HIGH-LIGHT** on page 7). In fact, they reflect only the tip of the iceberg: many people live their lives, or episodes of their lives, in quiet suffering and desperation, needing but never seeking professional intervention.

In studying abnormal psychology, we set our sights squarely on the worst that can happen when human beings find themselves confronted by challenges or internal demands that exceed their coping resources, by problems that are just too great. To an extent, then, we necessarily see a distorted picture, one emphasizing the *limits*, or failings, of psychological resourcefulness rather than the inspiring heights it probably more often attains in our difficult world. But in

looking at these limits, we also learn something of how they come about and how they may be prevented or reversed. We find that the events here are lawful: they are understandable and even, within reason, predictable and controllable. This knowledge in itself inspires confidence that we can continue to build on an already impressive rate of scientific progress in the field of abnormal psychology, and that one day we may be "masters of our fate."

Popular views of abnormal behavior

Examples of mental disorders that we have heard or read about are apt to be extreme cases that give us a chamber-of-horrors impression of abnormal behavior rather than the truer picture,

in which less spectacular maladjustments are far more common. Popular beliefs about abnormal behavior thus tend to be based on atypical and, often, unscientific descriptions.

A brief review of a few cases of mental disorders from history and literature will be of value in giving us a broader perspective, for most of the forms of severe mental disorder that we see today have been observed and reported in other ages too. Following that discussion, we shall look at some of the misconceptions about abnormal behavior that are common today.

Views carried over from history and literature

Some of the earliest historical writings—Chinese, Egyptian, Hebrew, and Greek—provide striking "case histories" of disturbed individuals. Saul, King of Israel in the eleventh century B.C., suffered from recurrent manic-

King Saul's mental disturbances were legendary. Here, in an illustration from a fourteenth-century English psalter, the boy David is shown playing music to soothe the troubled king. The demon thought to be responsible for Saul's condition is shown just above and behind Saul's upraised arm.

depressive episodes. During an attack of mania (excitement) he stripped off all his clothes in a public place. On another occasion he tried to kill his son Jonathan.

Cambyses, King of Persia in the sixth century B.C., was one of the first alcoholics on record. His alcoholic excesses were apparently associated with periods of uncontrollable rage during which he behaved "as a madman not in possession of his senses" (Whitwell, 1936, p. 38). On one occasion, without making any provision for the feeding of his army, he set out against the Ethiopians, who had greatly enraged him by calling the Persians "dung eaters." He was shortly forced to return to Memphis, where he found the people celebrating the feast of Apis. Furious at what he took to be rejoicing at his failure, he ordered that all the people taking part in the feast be killed. On another occasion he used his friend's son as a target for his arrows to demonstrate that his excessive drinking had not affected his skill. His aim was true and he killed the boy, proving his point, at least to his own satisfaction.

Greek mythology and history contain many descriptions of mentally disturbed persons that afford some insight into the nature of the real-life cases from which the descriptions must have been drawn. For example, Hercules seems to have been afflicted with convulsive seizures accompanied by a homicidal reaction. His attacks are graphically described by Euripides in the "phrenzy of Hercules": his eyes rolled, his consciousness clouded, he frothed at the mouth, showed violent fury, and attacked persons in his way, then fell, writhed, and finally fell into a deep sleep. Upon awakening, he had complete amnesia for the seizure. During the course of several attacks, Hercules killed two of his own children, two of his brother's children, his best friend, and his teacher.

Many of the notables of later Greece and Rome, including Socrates, Alexander the Great, and Julius Caesar, apparently suffered from mental disorders of one kind or another, and the ensuing period of the Middle Ages contains innumerable instances of abnormal behavior. The great Oriental conqueror, Tamerlane (1336–1405), for example, was particularly fond of building pyramids of human skulls. One of his architectural achievements is reported to have contained some forty thousand of them.

Some time later, the French philosopher Jean Jacques Rousseau (1712–1778) developed marked paranoid symptoms in the latter part of his life. He was obsessed with fears of secret enemies and thought that Prussia, England, France, the king, priests, and others were waging a terrible war against him. He believed that these enemies caused him to suffer indigestion, diarrhea, and other internal troubles, but their chief trick was to torture him by overwhelming him with benefits and praise, even going so far as to corrupt vegetable peddlers so that they would sell him better vegetables more cheaply. According to Rousseau, this was undoubtedly designed to prove his baseness and their generosity.

The names of other philosophers, writers, painters, musicians, and celebrities who suffered emotional disturbances would make a long list. Mozart, for example, during the time he was composing the Requiem, thought that he was being poisoned. Keats suffered from chronic tension and was subject to spells of uncontrollable laughter and crying. On one occasion Van Gogh cut off his ear and sent it to a prostitute, an action apparently performed in a state of

In Shakespeare's play Hamlet, *the heroine Ophelia—driven mad with grief upon learning of the death of her father—accidentally slips into a pool of water and "as one incapable of [not understanding] her own distress," sinks slowly to her death. Ophelia is one of a number of Shakespeare's memorable characters who suffer greatly from mental disorder and confusion.*

clouded consciousness resulting from his epileptic condition. Schopenhauer, Chopin, and John Stuart Mill suffered from attacks of depression. Rabelais, Samuel Butler, Burns, Byron, and Poe used alcohol excessively. Coleridge acknowledged using opiates before writing "Kubla Khan."

In reviewing these historical instances of abnormal behavior, it should be made clear that we are to some extent evaluating this behavior in the light of present-day concepts of mental disorder. In their own day, some of these people were looked on as perfectly normal, and others as only eccentric or unusual.

Mental disorders of one kind or another have been a favorite topic of writers for many centuries, and the public's changing conceptions of mental disorders have been strongly influenced by popular literary and dramatic works. Though certainly not the first to explore this area, William Shakespeare is especially notable for having created a number of unforgettable characters whose actions resemble certain behaviors we now associate with officially recognized clinical patterns—characters such as Lady Macbeth

(obsessive-compulsive behavior), King Lear (paranoia), Ophelia (depression/melancholy) and Othello (obsessive, paranoid jealousy). Shakespeare's gifts for observation and insight into the human personality are nowhere displayed with greater clarity than in his depiction of tortured and shattered minds.

The prominence of abnormal behavior in literature has continued to modern times. A significant amount of the modern work in this area has been autobiographical. Examples include the story of Chris Sizemore (Sizemore & Pittillo, 1977), subject of the original *Three Faces of Eve,* whose experiences dramatized the problem of multiple personality, a condition that is also the theme of the popular book *Sybil.* Equally well-known is Mark Vonnegut's *The Eden Express,* in which the author describes his own acute schizophrenic breakdown. Hannah Green's *I Never Promised You a Rose Garden* describes her treatment by a gifted therapist for a more chronic form of the same disorder. Stuart Sutherland, a distinguished British psychologist, presents an account of his own psychotic episode in *Breakdown.* An earlier autobiographical account of psychosis, *A Mind That Found Itself*, (1908/1970) by Clifford Beers, played a significant role in the development of the mental hygiene movement in the United States. The Beers book, in part a chilling account of the mental hospital environment around the turn of the century, foreshadowed equally chilling recent accounts by Mary Jane Ward in *The Snake Pit* and by Ken Kesey in his fictionalized (but in many ways poignantly accurate) *One Flew Over the Cuckoo's Nest*. Fortunately, the conditions described by these writers have been overcome in many contemporary mental hospitals, although a study by Rosenhan (1973) indicates that serious problems of dehumanization of patients may still occasionally occur.

Popular writings on mental disorders are being continually supplemented by dramatic presentations in the theaters, in the movies, and on television. In addition, the daily press regularly carries accounts of the behavior of seemingly demented persons and often seeks to lend legitimacy to its accounts by citing commentary by mental health professionals, who more often than not have never examined the offender. Such "armchair" diagnoses are probably useless, or worse, in the majority of cases. We seem to have an insatiable curiosity about bizarre behavior, and most of us avidly seek and devour the newspaper, radio, and TV accounts available on the subject. Though we surely learn some things from these accounts, we also may be narrowing our perspective: such accounts are written for the popular media; they are typically simplified and can appear to give answers when, in fact, they barely succeed in posing the correct questions.

As a result of such extensive exposure, readers of this text are likely to have a more than passing acquaintance with abnormal behavior. Many may already have reached conclusions about its causes and its proper management. In fact, however, we simply do not yet have in most instances sufficient information to permit valid conclusions in these areas, and much misinformation that is readily available can cloud one's perspective. Therefore, the reader will be wise to suspend any already formed beliefs about abnormal psychology until we move to a consideration of the evidence. The following section reviews briefly some of the more common *misconceptions* people are likely to have.

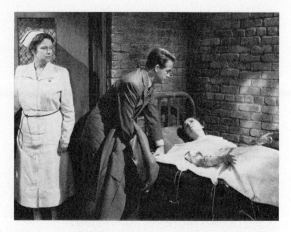

A scene from the motion picture The Snake Pit, *with Olivia de Havilland playing the part of an embattled mental patient. The dungeon-like atmosphere and the primitive restraining devices in evidence here were for many years (and to some extent still are) associated in the popular mind with mental hospitals and mental health care.*

Some popular misconceptions

Throughout most of history, as we shall see in Chapter 2, beliefs about mental disorders have been generally characterized by superstition, ignorance, and fear. Although successive advances in the scientific understanding of abnormal behavior have dispelled many false ideas, a number of popular misconceptions remain.

The belief that abnormal behavior is always bizarre. The instances of abnormal behavior reported in the mass media, like those reported in history and literature, are likely to be extreme ones involving murder, sexual assault, airplane hijacking, or other striking deviations from accepted social norms. Patients in mental hospitals and clinics are often pictured as a weird lot who spend their time ranting and raving, posing as Napoleon, or engaging in other bizarre behavior. In fact, most hospitalized patients are quite aware of what is going on around them, and only a small percentage exhibit behavior that might be labeled bizarre. The behavior of most mental patients, whether in a clinical setting or not, is indistinguishable in most respects from that of "normal" people.

Actually, the term "abnormal" covers a wide range of behaviors. Some types of abnormal behavior are bizarre; but, as we shall see, in the

In the eighteenth century, an entertaining diversion often involved a visit to the asylum to view the bizarre behavior of the lunatics, as the two "ladies of fashion" are doing here. Unfortunately, the belief that abnormal behavior is always bizarre persists among many to this day.

great majority of cases, abnormal behavior is so labeled because it is self-defeating and maladaptive. Such self-defeating patterns are a cause of concern, but they are well within the bounds of ordinary human experience.

The view that "normal" and "abnormal" behavior are different in kind.   A sharp dividing line between "normal" and "abnormal" behavior simply does not exist. There are not "normal" people on the one hand and "abnormal" people on the other—two different and distinct kinds of beings. Rather, adjustment seems to follow what is called a normal distribution, with most people clustering around the

center, and the rest spreading out toward the two extremes. Most people are moderately well adjusted, with minor maladaptive patterns; a few at one extreme enter mental hospitals or clinics; and a few at the other extreme lead unusually satisfying and effective lives.

We have probably all sympathized with someone who became severely depressed after the breakup of a romance or who began to drink excessively following a major occupational failure. These people were showing behavior that differed only in degree from that of patients in mental hospitals or clinics, on the one hand, and from that of "normal, well-adjusted" people on the other.

Not only does the behavior of different individuals range from normal to abnormal, but from time to time most of us shift our position somewhat along the continuum. For example, we may be coping adequately with our problems when some change—perhaps a divorce, a prolonged illness, a serious financial loss, or several problems at once—may increase the severity of the demands made on us to the point where we can no longer cope with them satisfactorily.

Both normal and abnormal behavior patterns are now seen as attempts to cope with life problems as the individual perceives them. Although people have different adaptive resources, use different methods of coping, and have differing degrees of success, the same general principles apply to both normal and abnormal behavior, however unusual the latter may be.

The view of former mental patients as unstable and dangerous. The common misconception persists that mental disorders are essentially "incurable." As a consequence, persons who have been discharged from mental hospitals or clinics are often viewed with suspicion as being unstable and possibly dangerous. Commonly they are discriminated against in employment or job advancement as well as in the political arena. While it is true that persons with certain forms of mental disorders—such as those associated with severe senile brain damage—will never recover completely, most mental patients respond well to treatment and later meet their responsibilities satisfactorily. Indeed, many feel they achieve a higher level of personality adjustment than before their breakdowns.

Although research on the rate of crime among former mental patients is inconclusive, it now appears that their overall arrest record is somewhat higher than that for the general population (Zitrin et al., 1976). This finding may reflect the recent trend toward earlier release of patients from mental hospitals into communities which often do not have sufficient resources to help the patients continue the readjustment process (Sosowsky, 1980; also see **HIGHLIGHT** on this page). We will address this critical problem in greater detail in Chapter 18.

Most persons who recover from even serious mental disorders, however, do *not* later engage in violent or socially disruptive behavior, especially if they had no history of arrest prior to

HIGHLIGHT

Patients in state and county mental hospitals from 1880 to 1978 (approximate figures)

At the end of 1977 there were 48 percent fewer patients in the state and county mental hospitals of the United States than there had been at the end of 1971, continuing a trend that had begun shortly after the peak year of 1955. The trend will undoubtedly continue, although perhaps at a slower rate, as we learn of an increasing number of problems associated with too early and insufficiently stringent releases of mental patients into communities ill-equipped to deal with them. The dramatic decline in occupied mental hospital beds has been due to several factors, including (a) introduction of a host of potent drugs that suppress severe mental symptoms; (b) recognition of the debilitating and antitherapeutic effects of long-term hospitalization and the attendant "deinstitutionalization" movement; (c) introduction of community mental health centers and related community facilities to care for individuals needing continued treatment on an outpatient basis; and (d) increased availability of alternate care facilities, such as nursing homes for the aged.

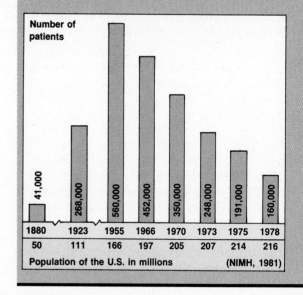

Number of patients							
41,000	268,000	560,000	452,000	350,000	248,000	191,000	160,000
1880	1923	1955	1966	1970	1973	1975	1978
50	111	166	197	205	207	214	216

Population of the U.S. in millions   (NIMH, 1981)

their hospitalization (Rabkin, 1979; Sosowsky, 1980). As we shall see in Chapter 18, "dangerousness" is quite difficult to assess or predict, and past history is by no means an infallible indicator of nonviolence in the future. Still, though care should be taken in releasing patients with a history of violence, less than 1 percent of all patients released from mental hospitals or clinics can be regarded as dangerous, and most of them are more likely to be a threat to themselves than to others. The unthreatening nature of most persons who have suffered mental breakdowns is difficult for the public to accept, owing to the extensive publicity usually given to this topic when it is presented as a background to reports of criminal behavior. Unfortunately, people in the media are as likely to adhere to certain prejudices and some misinformation as are members of the general public. Such prejudices are of course reinforced by the occasional "senseless" crimes that do occur; however, only a relatively small number of disturbed persons are ever attracted to such crimes.

The belief that mental disorder is something to be ashamed of. Many people who do not hesitate to consult a dentist, a lawyer, or other professional for assistance with various types of problems are reluctant to go to a psychologist or a psychiatrist with their emotional problems. Actually, a mental disorder should be considered no more disgraceful than a physical disorder. Both are adaptive failures.

Nevertheless, there is still a tendency in our society to reject the emotionally disturbed. Whereas most people are sympathetic toward a crippled child or an adult with cancer, they may turn away from the person suffering from an incapacitating mental disorder. Even many psychologists and medical personnel are both uninformed and unsympathetic when they are confronted with persons evidencing mental disorders (Langer & Abelson, 1974; Rabkin, 1972). Yet the great majority of persons suffering mental disorders are doing the best they know how and desperately need understanding and help.

Fortunately, treatment of mental disorders is becoming an integral part of total social and community health programs. But the stigma that has traditionally been attached to mental disorders still lingers in the minds of many people in our society.

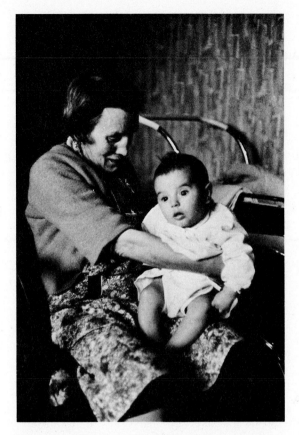

For centuries, the colony of Gheel in Belgium has recognized that the majority of mental patients are not unstable or dangerous. This mentally retarded woman, shown caring for an infant, is one of many mental patients who live in private homes and benefit from love, warmth, and interaction with family members.

The belief that mental disorder is something magical or awe-inspiring. In some societies people who had hallucinations or showed strange behavior were thought to be possessed by supernatural powers and were regarded with awe. This view lessened with the rise of scientific views but has never been completely abandoned in popular thought and periodically attracts new attention. Today, in fact, there is a "pop psychology" view in which those labeled "sick" are seen as actually having more accurate and insightful views than the "righteous" people who commit them to institutions. The following excerpt reprinted in *Madness Network News Reader* reflects this view—as does the existence of such a publication.

We are the aged
forbidden to pass among the young
we are the deceivers
caged in by the righteous
we are the insane
walled off by the sane

You, You are the young
the righteous
the sane,
If by some quirk
you must enter our colony
we will accept you

For we are the aged
we are the deceivers
we are the insane
and know full well
who we are

(Poem by Patrick George Harrison, *Visions of a Madman,* in Hirsh et al., 1974)

Such writings are critical of the traditional ways of treating disturbed persons. They see no need for therapy; rather they revel in the abnormal, which they see as closer to "truth." They ignore the reality that many people who show "odd behavior" are not simply expressing their individuality but rather are unhappy, confused, and incapacitated by their behavior. By idealizing psychological problems, such critics detract from the efforts of professionals to understand and help the people who experience them.

We may also take note of the fact that, although many individuals with mental disorders have made significant contributions to society and the shaping of history, it has been those men and women of more effective personality adjustment who have carried the major burden in the achievement of social progress.

An exaggerated fear of one's own susceptibility to mental disorders. Fears of possible mental disorder are quite common and cause much needless unhappiness. "Other people seem so self-assured and capable. They cannot possibly have the irrational impulses and fantasies I do, or feel the hostility or anxiety or despair that plagues me." Most people feel anxious and discouraged during difficult periods in their lives. Many notice with alarm that they are unreasonably irritable, have difficulty in concentrating or remembering, or even feel that they are "going to pieces." In one study, a representative sample of Americans were asked if they

had ever felt they were going to have a "nervous breakdown." Almost one out of five people interviewed replied "yes" (U.S. Department of Health, Education, and Welfare, 1971).

In this connection, it should be mentioned that medical students, in reading about various physical disorders, are likely to imagine that they have many of the symptoms described; the same reaction is likely among those reading about mental disorders and is reflected in the number of students from abnormal psychology classes who seek counseling.

The student who experiences a high level of distress in coping with the subject matter of abnormal psychology might well benefit from a few counseling sessions. However, it is important to remember that feelings of anxiety, crises of self-confidence, and concern about one's own irrational fantasies and actions are common experiences that we all have. In most cases they do not become pervasive or disabling: they are not "symptoms of disorder" but normal reactions. Their universality in human experience can help us see seriously disturbed individuals as less "strange" but need not be cause for personal alarm. A realization that other people have the same worries and self-doubts as we have can help reduce the feelings of isolation and of being "different" that often play a part in personal fears of mental disorder.

Abnormal behavior as the scientist sees it

There are currently several distinct but closely related professional fields concerned with the study of abnormal behavior and with mental health. The distinction among them is often hard to draw precisely, for even though each has its own functions and areas of work, the contributions in one field are constantly influencing and contributing to the thinking and work in others.

Abnormal psychology has long been referred to as that part of the field of psychology concerned with the understanding, treatment, and prevention of abnormal behavior. However, the term is now relegated largely to titles of courses in colleges and universities that cover the subject matter of abnormal behavior. In other contexts it has generally been replaced by the term *clinical psychology,* the professional field broadly concerned with the study, assessment, treatment, and prevention of abnormal behavior. *Psychiatry* is the corresponding field of medicine, and is thus closely related to clinical psychology. *Social work,* which evolved as a result of volunteer charities, is concerned with the analysis of social environments and with providing services which assist the adjustment of the patient in both family and community settings. *Psychopathology* is another term used to refer to the study of abnormal behavior.

In order to assess, treat, and prevent abnormal behavior in any of the specialty fields, professionals must work out definitions of "normal" and "abnormal," and develop criteria for distinguishing one from the other in real life. Unfortunately, this is not always easy.

What do we mean by "abnormal behavior"?

Since the word *abnormal* literally means "away from the normal," it implies deviation from some clearly defined norm. But what should be the norm? What is normal? In the case of physical illness, the norm is the structural and functional integrity of the body; here the boundary lines between normality and pathology are usually (but by no means always) clear. On a psychological level, however, we have no "ideal model" or even "normal model" of human functioning to use as a base of comparison. Thus we suffer considerable confusion and disagreement as to just what is or is not *normal,* a confusion aggravated by our changing values.

In the final analysis, any definition of "abnormal" must be somewhat arbitrary. Definitions tend to represent one or the other of two broad perspectives. One view maintains that the concepts of "normal" and "abnormal" are meaningful only with reference to a given culture: abnormal behavior is behavior that deviates from society's norms. The other view maintains that behavior is abnormal if it interferes with the well-being of the individual and/or the group.

Abnormal as deviation from social norms.
The concept of "abnormal" as deviation from societal norms has been well formulated by Ull-

mann and Krasner (1975), who maintain that *abnormal* is simply a label given to behavior that is deviant from social expectations. They maintain that behavior cannot be considered abnormal so long as society accepts it. As *cultural relativists,* they reject the concept of a "sick society" in which the social norms themselves might be viewed as pathological.

"A critical example is whether an obedient Nazi concentration camp commander would be considered normal or abnormal. To the extent that he was responding accurately and successfully to his environment and not breaking its rules, much less coming to the professional attention of psychiatrists, he would not be labeled abnormal. Repulsive as his behavior is to mid-twentieth century Americans, such repulsion is based on a particular set of values. Although such a person may be held responsible for his acts—as Nazi war criminals were—the concept of abnormality as a special entity does not seem necessary or justified. If it is, the problem arises as to who selects the values, and this, in turn, implies that one group may select values that are applied to others. This situation of one group's values being dominant over others is the fascistic background from which the Nazi camp commander sprang." (Ullman & Krasner, 1975, p. 16)

The acceptance of complete cultural relativism obviously simplifies the task of defining abnormality: behavior is abnormal if—and only if—the society labels it as such. But serious questions may be raised about the validity of this definition. It rests on the questionable assumption that it is social acceptance that makes behavior normal—that one set of values is as good as another for human beings to adopt. It then follows that the task of the psychotherapist is to ensure that patients conform to the norms their society views as appropriate, regardless of the values on which these norms are based.

This viewpoint was dealt a heavy blow following World War II when a number of Nazi leaders were convicted of genocide and other "crimes against humanity." The Nuremberg trials were based on the assumption that a whole society can develop maladaptive patterns and that there are standards which groups as well as individuals must follow for human survival and well-being.

Abnormal as maladaptive.
Some degree of social conformity is clearly essential to group life, and some kinds of deviance are clearly

harmful not only to society but to the individual. *However, the present text maintains that the best criterion for determining the normality of behavior is not whether society accepts it but rather whether it fosters the well-being of the individual and, ultimately, of the group.* By *well-being* is meant not simply maintenance or survival but also growth and fulfillment—the actualization of potentialities. According to this criterion, even conforming behavior is abnormal if it is *maladaptive,* that is, if it interferes with functioning and growth.

So defined, abnormal behavior includes the more traditional categories of mental disorders—alcoholism and schizophrenia, for example—as well as prejudice and discrimination against persons because of race or sex, wasteful use of our natural resources, pollution of our air and water, irrational violence, and political corruption—regardless of whether such patterns are condemned or condoned by a given society. All represent maladaptive behavior that impairs individual and/or group well-being. Typically they lead to personal distress, and often they bring about destructive group conflict.

In defining abnormal behavior as *maladaptive,* we are making two value assumptions: (a) that survival and actualization are worth striving for on both individual and group levels; and (b) that human behavior can be evaluated in terms of its consequences for these objectives. As with the assumptions of cultural relativism, such value assumptions are open to criticism on the grounds that they are arbitrary. But unless we value the survival and actualization of the human race, there seems little point in trying to identify abnormal behavior or do anything about it.

In assessing, treating, and preventing abnormal behavior, mental health personnel are concerned not only with the individual but also with the family, community, and general societal setting. Increasingly, therapy is defined not solely in terms of helping individuals adjust to their personal situations—no matter how frustrating or abnormal—but also in terms of alleviating group and societal conditions that may be causing or maintaining the maladaptive behavior.

The need for classification

Classification of phenomena is important in any science—whether we are studying plants, plan-

ets, or people. With an agreed-upon classification system, we can be confident that we are communicating clearly. If someone says to you, "I saw a collie running down the street," you probably have an accurate idea of what the collie looked like—not from seeing it but rather from your knowledge of the classification of dogs.

In abnormal psychology, classification involves the delineation of various types, or categories, of maladaptive behavior. It is a necessary first step toward introducing some order into our discussion of the nature, causes, and treatment of such behavior and in communicating about particular clusters of behavior in agreed-upon and meaningful ways. For example, we would hardly be in a position to do research on a given disorder unless we could begin with a more or less clear definition of the behavior under examination. There are also more mundane reasons for "diagnostic" classifications, such as enabling adequate statistical counts of the incidence of various disorders or meeting the needs of medical insurance companies (which insist upon having formal diagnoses before they will authorize payment of claims).

It is important to keep in mind that all classification is the product of human invention—that it is, in essence, a matter of making generalizations based on what has been observed. Even when observations are precise and carefully made, the generalizations go beyond them by making inferences about underlying similarities and differences. Nevertheless, granting the fundamental arbitrariness involved, some classification systems are immeasurably better than others in helping us organize our observations and talk about them.

There are basically two considerations here, those of *reliability* and *validity.* Reliability in this context refers to the extent to which different observers can agree that the behavior they observe does indeed "fit" a given diagnostic category. If observers cannot come to such agreement, it means that the classification criteria are not precise enough to determine whether the disorder is present or absent. By validity, we mean that a classification should be meaningful in the sense that it tells us something important or basic about the entity classified. For example, if we diagnose someone's behavior as "schizophrenic," then we should be able to infer some very important things about the person so diagnosed—things that differentiate him or her from other persons, including those whose behavior warrants placing the person in some other diagnostic category. Validity presupposes reliability.

Unfortunately, both reliability and validity have proven extraordinarily difficult to achieve in the classifications employed in abnormal psychology. This is due in no small part to our complexity as human beings. Psychology has made great strides in understanding human behavior, but a foolproof classification system that pigeonholes behavior—either normal or abnormal—remains elusive.

Current classification of mental disorders.
The most widely used classification scheme for mental disorders in the United States is the *Diagnostic and Statistical Manual of Mental Disorders*, devised by the American Psychiatric Association (1980). Currently in its third edition, it is referred to in brief as *DSM-III*. There also exists a worldwide classification system, called the *International Classification of Diseases, 9th Edition* (World Health Organization, 1979) or *ICD-9*, which covers all diseases and disorders, both physical and mental. Both the American Psychiatric Association and the World Health Organization have worked closely over the years to ensure compatibility between their two classification systems. With the publication of *DSM-III*, a "clinical modification" of the mental disorders section of the ICD-9 was written to accommodate many of the changes called for in DSM-III; some differences remain, however. For example, the ICD-9-CM (the new code was adopted to indicate the clinical modification) retains a number of categories that have since been dropped from DSM-III. These differences reflect to some extent the nature of classification as an ongoing search for a better, more effective system.

Each successive edition of DSM has sought to improve its clinical usefulness for professionals who diagnose and treat patients. Efforts have been specifically directed at overcoming the serious weaknesses in reliability and validity encountered with its predecessors. The distinctive feature of DSM-III is its attempt to use only "operational" criteria for defining the different disorders included in the classification system. This means that the DSM system seeks to specify the *exact* behaviors that must be observed for a given diagnostic label to be applied. In the typi-

cal case, a specific number of signs or symptoms from a designated list must be present before the diagnosis can properly be assigned. In other words, efforts have been made to remove, to the degree possible, subjective elements from the diagnostic process.

To the extent this goal can be achieved, reliability of diagnosis is substantially improved. On the other hand, the use of stricter criteria can cause much abnormal behavior to "fall between the cracks" and to be assigned to "wastebasket" or residual categories such as "psychotic disorders not elsewhere classified." When that occurs, validity suffers, since a category so broad can give only broad generalities about disorders within it. In fact, it may be too much to expect a *truly* valid system of categories until we have a better understanding of the origins or causes of the different forms of abnormal behavior. Preliminary evaluations of the DSM-III have suggested that reliability is indeed enhanced but have offered little reassurance on the question of validity (Eysenck, Wakefield, & Friedman, 1983; Mezzich, Coffman & Goodpaster, 1982).

DSM-III was released after extensive field trials. It evaluates an individual's behavior according to five dimensions, or *axes*.

The first three axes assess the individual's present condition:

I. The particular maladaptive symptoms, or clinical psychiatric syndromes, such as schizophrenia;

II. Any long-standing personality problems (adults) or specific developmental problems (children and adolescents);

III. Any medical, or physical, disorders that may also be present.

Note that more than one diagnosis may be recorded on Axes I and III and, in exceptional instances, on Axis II. A person may have multiple psychiatric symptoms or medical diseases (Axes I and III, respectively) and, much more rarely, may manifest more than one "personality disorder" (Axis II).

The last two axes are used to provide assessments of broader aspects of the individual's situation, one dealing with the stressors that may have contributed to the current disorder and the other dealing with how well the individual has been coping in recent months:

IV. Severity of psychosocial stressors;

V. Level of adaptive functioning.

Axes I and II, which list the categories of mental disorders, are provided in full on the endsheets of this book. These categories may be regarded for purposes of clarity as fitting into several broad groupings, each containing several subgroupings:

a) *Organic mental disorders* refer to disorders involving gross destruction or malfunctioning of brain tissue (as in Alzheimer's disease) and a wide range of other conditions based on brain pathology; these disorders are described in Chapter 13.

b) *Substance-use disorders* involve problems such as drug and alcohol abuse; these are discussed in Chapter 11.

c) *Disorders of psychological or sociocultural origin* have no known brain pathology as a primary causal factor, as in anxiety (Chapter 6), psychophysiologic (Chapter 8), psychosexual (Chapter 12), and personality (Chapter 7) disorders. The "functional" psychoses such as major affective disorders (Chapter 9) and schizophrenia (Chapter 10) are also traditionally included here, although it appears increasingly likely that certain types of brain dysfunction are implicated in their causation.

d) *Disorders usually arising during childhood or adolescence* include mental retardation (considered in Chapter 13) and special problems, such as early infantile autism, that may occur in children and that warrant separate categorization; Chapter 14 is devoted to these problems of childhood.

In referring to mental disorders, several qualifying terms are commonly used. *Acute* is a term used for disorders of relatively short duration, say under six months; in some contexts it also connotes behavioral symptoms of high intensity. *Chronic* refers to long-standing and usually permanent disorders, but the term can also be applied generally to low-intensity disorders since long-term difficulties are often of this sort. *Mild, moderate,* and *severe* are used in referring to the severity of a disorder. *Episodic* is used for disorders that tend to recur, as with some affective and schizophrenic patterns.

Axis III of DSM-III is often used in conjunction with the Axis I diagnosis of *psychological factors affecting physical condition.* This diagnosis, which requires a medical examination, would be used when the diagnostician has reason to believe that a psychological factor is contributing in some way to a physical disease. Axis III itself can be used for *any* physical disorder that accompanies a psychiatric one, whether or not the two are related.

Axes IV and V are dimensions new to the DSM-III classification. They provide a framework for assessing the individual's life situation (Axis IV) and recent degree of success in coping with it (Axis V). Axis IV (see **HIGHLIGHT** on page 19) has a seven-point scale for rating the severity of psychosocial factors that may have been placing the individual under stress and contributing to the current disorder. Examples are provided for both adult and child. Levels range from "none" at one end of the scale to "catastrophic" at the other. Axis V (see **HIGHLIGHT** on page 20) has a seven-point scale for rating the individual's highest level of functioning during the preceding year, again with adult and child examples. Here the levels range from "superior" to "grossly impaired." Both these scales can help assure that when different clinicians talk about either severity of stress or "good" adjustments, for example, they are talking about the same thing.

As an example of an extended DSM-III diagnosis, let us consider the plight of a man of dependent personality organization whose new supervisor at work is unsympathetic and demanding and who, as a result, has developed generalized anxiety and an alarming increase in blood pressure. The man's diagnosis might be as follows:

Axis I
   1. Generalized anxiety disorder
   2. Psychological factors affecting physical condition

Axis II
   Dependent personality disorder

Axis III
   Essential hypertension

Axis IV
   Level of psychosocial stressors: 3 (mild)

Axis V
   Highest level of adaptive functioning, past year: 4 (fair)

HIGHLIGHT

Axis IV scale for rating severity of psychosocial stressors

Code	Term	Adult examples	Child or adolescent examples
1	None	No apparent psychosocial stressor	No apparent psychosocial stressor
2	Minimal	Minor violation of the law; small bank loan	Vacation with family
3	Mild	Argument with neighbor; change in work hours	Change in schoolteacher; new school year
4	Moderate	New career; death of close friend; pregnancy	Chronic parental fighting; change to new school; illness of close relative; birth of sibling
5	Severe	Major illness in self or family; major financial loss; marital separation; birth of child	Death of peer; divorce of parents; arrest; hospitalization; persistent and harsh parental discipline
6	Extreme	Death of close relative; divorce	Death of parent or sibling; repeated physical or sexual abuse
7	Catastrophic	Concentration camp experience; devastating natural disaster	Multiple family deaths
0	Unspecified	No information or not applicable	No information or not applicable

From DSM-III (APA, 1980).

Axes IV and V are significant additions. Knowing what demands the individual has been trying to meet is important for an understanding of the problem behavior that has developed. Knowing the individual's general level of success in meeting adjustive demands in the recent past can help the clinician make an appropriate and realistic treatment plan and can give him or her an idea of what to expect. However, some clinicians object to the routine use of these axes for insurance forms and the like on the grounds that such use unnecessarily compromises the patient's right to privacy. As a consequence of such concerns, Axes IV and V are now considered optional for use in diagnosis.

Further limitations of DSM-III classification. Beyond the somewhat technical questions of reliability and validity, where the DSM-III has undoubtedly improved to some extent on its predecessors, there are certain other serious limitations it shares with them, some of which may be inherent in such classifications schemes. First, the categories *describe;* they do

HIGHLIGHT
Axis V scale for rating level of functioning

Levels	Adult examples	Child or adolescent examples
1 SUPERIOR Unusually effective functioning in social relations, occupational functioning, and use of leisure time.	Single parent living in deteriorating neighborhood takes excellent care of children and home, has warm relations with friends, and finds time for pursuit of hobby.	A 12-year-old girl gets superior grades in school, is extremely popular among her peers, and excels in many sports. She does all of this with apparent ease and comfort.
2 VERY GOOD Better than average functioning in social relations, occupational functioning, and use of leisure time.	A 65-year-old retired widower does some volunteer work, often sees old friends, and pursues hobbies.	An adolescent boy gets excellent grades, works part-time, has several close friends, and plays banjo in a jazz band. He admits to some distress in "keeping up with everything."
3 GOOD No more than slight impairment in either social or occupational functioning.	A woman with many friends functions extremely well at a difficult job, but says "the strain is too much."	An 8-year-old boy does well in school, has several friends, but bullies younger children.
4 FAIR Moderate impairment in either social relations or occupational functioning, *or* some impairment in both.	A lawyer has trouble carrying through assignments; has several acquaintances, but hardly any close friends.	A 10-year-old girl does poorly in school, but has adequate peer and family relations.
5 POOR Marked impairment in either social relations or occupational functioning, *or* moderate impairment in both.	A man with one or two friends has trouble keeping a job for more than a few weeks.	A 14-year-old boy almost fails in school and has trouble getting along with his peers.
6 VERY POOR Marked impairment in both social relations and occupational functioning.	A woman is unable to do any of her housework and has violent outbursts toward family and neighbors.	A 6-year-old girl needs special help in all subjects and has virtually no peer relationships.
7 GROSSLY IMPAIRED Gross impairment in virtually all areas of functioning.	An elderly man needs supervision to maintain minimal personal hygiene and is usually incoherent.	A 4-year-old boy needs constant restraint to avoid hurting himself and is almost totally lacking in skills.
0 UNSPECIFIED	No information.	No information.

From DSM-III (APA, 1980)

not explain. One must guard against the tendency to think something has been fully explained when in fact it has only been named.

A second limitation is that only individual behavior is covered. Disturbed families, delinquent subcultures, and violence-prone societies show maladaptive behavior that does not fit into a scheme made for classifying individuals. Yet classifying only individual behavior as abnormal implies that when individuals do not fit smoothly into their social milieu, it is the individuals who are at fault and must change. This attitude casts the mental health profession in the role of a force for preserving the status quo, no matter how "abnormal" the status quo might be. We shall deal further with this point later in the text, and in our discussions of particular disorders we shall consider not only disturbed individuals but also pathogenic families and larger groups that are implicated in the causation and maintenance of maladaptive behavior. Such behavior does not occur in a vacuum but is rather in part a response to factors of context, particularly social context (Weary & Mirels, 1982).

The problem of labeling.
In addition to the above limitations, we must never lose sight of the fact that psychiatric diagnosis is merely a label applied to a defined disorder from which a person is presumed to be suffering. It never describes the *person*, but rather some behavioral pattern associated with that person's current level of functioning. Yet once a label has been assigned, it may close off further inquiry. It becomes all too easy—even among professionals—to accept the label uncritically as an accurate and complete description of the individual rather than of the behavior. (See **HIGHLIGHT** on page 22.) It is then hard to look at the person's behavior objectively, without preconceptions about how he or she will act. Expectations, in turn, may affect interactions with the person and may influence decisions as to what kinds of treatment will be tried.

These expectations are also communicated to the individual, who may accept the new identity implied by the label and develop the expected role and outlook. This can be very harmful, especially because psychiatric diagnostic labels very often carry pejorative and stigmatizing implications. Acquiring such a label may transform

The man shown here is a tragic example of the dangerous effects of labeling. Born in a mental hospital to parents with mental problems, Jack Smith was assumed to be mentally retarded and received no formal schooling after age 12, in spite of the fact that he showed interest in learning. His early years were spent in a state orphanage, followed by 38 years in a mental hospital. In 1976, a Michigan judge declared that Mr. Smith was not mentally ill or dangerous, based on findings of a psychiatric evaluation. By that time, however, the 54-year-old man was considered "so impaired that it would be unwise to put him out on the streets" (New York Times, March 11, 1979, p. 26). Mr. Smith now lives in a nursing home.

one's social identity, so that one becomes "marked" as a person who is thought to lack a legitimate claim to full membership in the human community (Sarbin & Mancuso, 1970). Obviously, the effects on morale and self-esteem can be devastating.

For all these reasons, responsible professionals are very cautious in the diagnostic process, in their use of labels, and in ensuring confidentiality with respect to both. Somewhat related to this is a change that has grown throughout the decade regarding the person who goes to see a mental health professional. For years, the traditional term has been *patient*, which seems closely associated with a medical "sick" role and

HIGHLIGHT
Mental illness as a myth

Psychiatrist Thomas Szasz (1920 –   ) has been an outspoken critic of current practices and labels within the field of abnormal psychology (Szasz, 1961, 1970). In his writings, Szasz contends that mental illness is a myth and that traditional treatment can be more harmful than helpful.

According to Szasz, most of the disorders treated by psychiatrists and other mental health practitioners are not illnesses. Instead, he claims, they are simply individual traits or behaviors that deviate from what our society considers morally or socially normal. They are caused by "problems in living"—by unmet needs and by stressful relationships, for example.

Szasz believes that traditional psychiatric treatment harms such people by labeling them as ill. Not only does this labeling encourage them to fulfill soci-

ety's expectations and act in irresponsible ways; it also implies that they must become patients and accept treatment in order to change. In Szasz's view, this means that they are being encouraged to think and behave in ways considered normal by psychiatrists rather than to attack the social causes of their problems.

More recently, Sarbin and Mancuso (1980) have developed a related attack on the specific concept of *schizophrenia*, thought by many to be the most serious of the mental disorders. These authors liken this concept to that of the unicorn, a mythical animal of antiquity. Schizophrenia, they say, is not a proper medical diagnosis, but is rather a "moral verdict" rendered against persons who do not behave in prescribed ways.

the passive stance of waiting for the doctor to cure you. Today, many professionals prefer the term *client* because it implies more responsibility and active participation on the part of the individual for bringing about his or her own recovery.

Research in abnormal psychology

Virtually all of the facts and ideas that constitute the substance of this book are more or less direct products of the application of the powerful methods of science to phenomena associated with maladaptive human behavior. Doubtless the reader is already familiar with scientific methods in general and likely has also been exposed to their use in various areas of psychology. Certain special issues and problems arise in attempting to apply these methods to the understanding and control of abnormal behavior, and some review of these is appropriate before we move on. Our review will be organized around

the issues of (a) direct observation and constructs based on inference or hypothesis, (b) sampling and generalization, (c) correlation and causation, (d) methodological constraints, and (e) retrospective and prospective strategies.

Observation of behavior

The subdiscipline of abnormal psychology shares with psychology as a whole a focus on *behavior* as its observational base. Whether we are considering the overt actions of an organism, certain of its measurable internal behaviors (e.g., physiological processes), or, in the case of humans, verbal reports about inner processes or events, the focus of psychology is always on observing behavior. Of course, all of us are constantly observing both our own overt behavior and certain of our inner events such as thoughts and feelings. But self-observation of one's own inner processes has distinct limits as a data base for psychological science partly because the observations are one's own, forever hidden from direct observation by anyone else. They cannot be subjected to the confirmation by others that science normally demands. As might be guessed, this constraint has been a source of considerable difficulty for the discipline of psychology throughout its history.

Psychologists do, of course, make use of a subject's verbal reports of his or her inner experience on the reasonable assumption that in most situations people will be cooperative and truthful. But, even assuming an attitude of cooperation and sincerity, very often the person will be unable to *make* the crucial observations. The determinants of behavior are many and they operate at many levels of functioning; not all of them are by any means within the range of the behaving person's conscious awareness. Hence, to make sense of observed behavior, psychologists generate more or less plausible ideas—*hypotheses*—to help explain it. All empirical sciences employ hypothetical constructs, although the constructs tend to be less obvious as constructs and more closely tied to observable phenomena in the more mature of the scientific disciplines. For example, "electricity" is a hypothetical construct. All we ever observe are the effects of this presumed entity. But these effects are extremely reliable and predictable, and hence we believe in the real existence of electricity. Most people have less confidence in a construct such as the "ego."

These considerations are particularly important in the study of *abnormal* behavior. For the most part, we feel we *can* understand the behavior of most of the people we come in contact with, at least to the extent necessary to carry on ordinary social interactions. Even when we observe something unexpected in the behavior of someone else, we can usually empathize sufficiently to have a sense of "where they're coming from." Almost by definition, however, abnormal behavior is behavior that is *unintelligible* to the vast majority of persons observing it. It is behavior that seems not to be governed by the same principles we think we understand, and our minds are therefore attracted to extraordinary explanations of it—to extraordinary hypothetical constructs, if you will. Whether or not these hypothetical constructs can account satisfactorily for abnormal behavior is open to question. But it is clear that we will and do need hypothetical constructs of some sort in order to begin to understand. Behavior never explains itself, and that is as true of normal as it is of abnormal behavior.

In a relatively inexact field such as that of ab-

normal behavior, there may be several competing hypothetical constructs purporting to shed light on the meaning of the particular instance of abnormality. In fact, such constructs tend to cluster together in distinctive types of approaches, or "viewpoints." These general viewpoints are described in some detail in Chapter 3. For now, we wish merely to emphasize that all forms of psychological inquiry begin with observations of behavior, and that much of the subject matter of abnormal psychology is built on inferences which account more or less adequately for the observed behavior. The inferences made are not trivial, for frequently they determine the therapeutic approaches used to counter the abnormality. For example, suppose we are confronted with someone who washes his or her hands sixty to a hundred times a day, causing serious injury to the skin and underlying tissues. If we conclude that this behavior is a manifestation of subtle neurological damage, we would try to discover the nature of the individual's disease in the hope of administering a cure for it. If we view the behavior as the symbolic "undoing" of sinful thoughts, we would try to unearth and do away with the sources of the person's excessive scrupulousness. If we regard the hand-washing "symptom" as merely the product of unfortunate conditioning or learning, we would devise a means of counterconditioning the offending behavior. These are very different approaches, based on very different conceptualizations of what may be causing the abnormal hand-washing behavior. And yet, if limited merely to observing the behavior itself, we'd be left with *no* direction in which to move.

Sampling and generalization

In the normal course of scientific advance, some hypothetical constructs are found to be better than others in accounting for observed phenomena. Discoveries are made and our methods of observing are refined in such a way that new observations render certain hypothetical constructs implausible and, perhaps simultaneously, lend support to others. The refinement of methods of observation is at the heart of all scientific research.

Research in abnormal psychology is concerned with gaining enhanced understanding and, where possible, control of particular types of abnormal behavior. While we can occasionally get important leads from the intensive study of a single case of a given type of disorder, such a strategy rarely yields enough information to allow us to reach firm conclusions on the given disorder. The basic difficulty with the strategy is that we cannot know whether our observations pertain to the disorder, to unrelated characteristics of the person with the disorder, to some combination or interaction of both, or even to characteristics of the observer. It is also possible that the particular abnormality of behavior (e.g., excessive hand-washing) might arise from different internal sources in different people affected, a circumstance that could be detected only by studying a number of patients exhibiting the behavior.

For these reasons, we generally place greater reliance on research studies employing groups of individuals showing roughly equivalent abnormalities of behavior. Since the several people will share one characteristic (the problematic behavior) while varying widely on others, we can infer that anything *else* we discover they share in common, such as excessively punitive parents, may be related to the behavioral abnormality—provided, of course, it is not also widely shared among persons *not* having the abnormality. Should the common abnormality arise from different sources in different people (which might in itself be an important finding) we would probably have considerable difficulty identifying with precision the patterns underlying the abnormality. In fact, it does appear that difficulties of this sort are impeding our progress in respect to several of the disorders we'll be considering in later chapters. For example, it appears increasingly likely that the disorder known as schizophrenia has multiple patterns of causation that vary from one affected person to another.

If we wish to research the problem of compulsive hand-washing, for example, a first step would be to determine criteria for identifying persons affected with the alleged condition. Presumably, these criteria would cover such areas as the frequency of hand-washing and the degree of impairment in living caused by it. We would then need to find the people who fit our criteria. Obviously, we could never hope to study all of the people in the world who would meet our criteria as compulsive hand-washers;

we would need a *sample* of hand-washers that is *representative* in all important respects of the much larger group of compulsive hand-washers. A strict rule of "representativeness" is that every person in the larger group must have an equal chance of being included in the sample we intend to study. Usually, we can only approximate that degree of rigor in choosing research samples.

As we have learned from the results of poorly designed public-opinion polling, nonrepresentative sampling can produce markedly erroneous conclusions about the larger group we wish to study. For example, if in our study of compulsive hand-washing the distribution of socioeconomic statuses in the research sample were not adequately representative of compulsive hand-washers in general, we might attribute some characteristic to hand-washers that is in fact more true of persons of a given socioeconomic status.

Even if our study group *were* thoroughly representative, there is always the possibility that what we found to be true about, let us say, the family backgrounds of our hand-washers would also turn out to be true of *other* selected groups as well, or even of persons in general. If such were the case, we would have wasted our and our subjects' time. The proper way to proceed involves the use of a *control group,* a sample of persons who do not exhibit the particular disorder but who are comparable in all other respects to our *experimental group,* members of which do exhibit the disorder. Typically, the former group would be psychologically "normal" according to specified criteria. We could compare the two groups in certain areas—such as reported parental punishment practices—to determine if they differ. They would in fact almost certainly not come out exactly the same because of chance factors, but we have powerful statistical techniques to determine whether or not such factors are truly "significant." If we found, then, that the hand-washers had significantly greater severity of parental punishment in their backgrounds, as reported, than the "normals," we might be attracted to the hypothesis that parental punishment in childhood is associated with later compulsive hand-washing. This, of course, assumes that we could accept the reports of our subjects at face value, a sometimes dubious assumption.

Correlation and causation

The limitation just referred to illustrates a general point that is already familiar to most students of abnormal psychology but which is important enough to bear mentioning here. The mere *correlation,* or association, of two or more variables can never by itself be taken as evidence of a causal relationship. We could not legitimately conclude from the hypothetical results reported above that severe parental punishment practices are *causal* factors in the emergence of compulsive hand-washing among adults. There are simply too many alternative ways of accounting for such an association, including the possibility that hand-washers are for some reason more prone than others to report high levels of punitiveness in their parents.

Many studies in abnormal psychology show that two (or more) things regularly occur together, such as poverty and retarded intellectual development, or psychological depression and reported prior life stressors. Such variables may well be related to one another in some kind of causal context, but the relationship could take any of a variety of forms:

1. Variable *a* causes variable *b* (or vice versa).

2. Variable *a* and variable *b* are both caused by variable *c.*

3. Variables *a* and *b* are both involved in a complex pattern of variables influencing *a* and *b* in similar ways.

Coming from a "broken home," for instance, has been established as a significant correlate of many forms of abnormal behavior. Yet we cannot conclude that ruptured families *cause* abnormality because many other potential causes are statistically associated with parental separation or divorce, such as socioeconomic stress, marital disharmony, alcoholism in one or both parents, a move to a new neighborhood or school, the effort to adjust to the single parent's new love relationships, and so forth. Unfortunately, such complexity is the rule rather than the exception in attempting to understand how an abnormal pattern of behavior becomes established. Recently developed statistical techniques, such as *path analysis,* which take into account how variables are related to one another through time and how they "predict" one another, are fre-

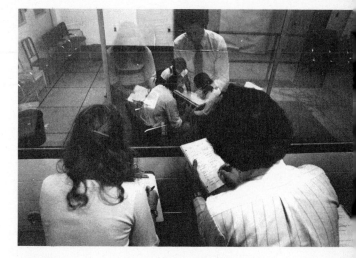

In applying the experimental method to human behavior, it is important to "control" for the various factors that may affect the behavior. When observing people in action, a researcher may find that his or her presence itself influences the behavior being assessed. In some cases, as shown here, special facilities with one-way mirrors or similar devices can be used to minimize the impact of the observer's presence.

quently helpful in disentangling complex arrays of correlated factors so that we may have greater confidence in our causal inferences.

Methodological constraints

Scientific research is most rigorous, and its findings most reliable, when the full power of the *experimental method* is employed. In such cases, scientists control all factors, except one, that conceivably could have an effect on a variable or outcome of interest; then they actively manipulate the presence or absence (or degree of presence or absence) of that one factor. If the outcome of interest is observed to change with changes in the manipulated factor, the factor can be regarded as a *cause* of the outcome.

Unfortunately, the experimental method cannot appropriately be applied to the solution of many of the problems of abnormal psychology. This is due to both practical and ethical constraints. Suppose, for example, we wanted to use the experimental method to determine whether parental punitiveness causes compulsive hand-washing. But for ethical constraints, our ideal approach would be to choose at random two groups of young children for a "longitudinal" study (a longitudinal study is simply one in which subjects are studied over an extended period of time). In one group the children's parents would be taught to be highly punitive in their child-rearing practices; the other group of parents would be left to their own devices. Our design would provide for carefully monitoring the two groups of children until they reached an age considered beyond risk for the development of new cases of compulsive hand-washing. At that point, we would seek to assess in some systematic way the prevalence of hand-washing compulsions in the two groups in the light of our hypothesis that the ill-treated children would have a significantly higher casualty rate for the disorder. This would be good—although logistically demanding—science, but it would of course be wholly unacceptable to treat people in this exceedingly callous and destructive way.

The experimental method has a limited role to play in the search for the causes of abnormal behavior among humans. On the other hand, the scientific method can be applied with great profit and without notable risk or expense to research concerned with the efficacy of one or another *treatment* for particular disorders. It is a relatively simple and straightforward matter to set up a study in which a treatment is given to a designated group of patients and withheld from another group of patients with the same behavioral abnormality and with similar other characteristics. Should the former group show significantly more improvement than the latter, we can have confidence in the treatment's effectiveness. Of course, special techniques must often be employed in such treatment research to ensure that the two groups are in fact comparable in every respect save that of treatment versus no treatment. Once the treatment has proved effective, it can subsequently be employed for members of the original control group, leading to improved functioning for everyone. The use of this "waiting list control group" has become a fairly standard feature of treatment research in abnormal psychology in recent years.

Despite the growing use of methods such as those described above, most instances of a given disorder are still studied individually, using the traditional clinical case-study method. In such cases, the clinical investigator, who is usually also the patient's therapist, intensively observes the individual's behavior and marshals background facts that may be pertinent in an attempt to arrive at an overall formulation of the case. The formulation consists of a set of hypotheses about what is causing the problem and a guide to treatment planning. The formulation may be revised as necessary based on the patient's response to treatment interventions. While much can be learned when skillful clinicians use the case-study method, the information thus acquired can also be seriously flawed, especially if one seeks to apply it to other cases involving an apparently similar abnormality. Where there is only one observer, and where the observations are made in a relatively uncontrolled context, there is a distinct possibility that erroneous conclusions will be drawn.

Fortunately, we have made great progress in the *statistical* control of variables which do not yield readily to the classic form of *experimental* control and in the precise measurement and modification of specific aspects of problematic behavior. Statistical controls, in effect, allow us to adjust for otherwise uncontrolled variables. For example, the incidence of certain mental disorders appears to vary with socioeconomic status. Using statistical controls, we can "correct" our results for any differences in socioeconomic status existing between our experimental and control (normal) groups. As an earlier example suggests, the same effect could be achieved by *experimental* control if we could ensure that socioeconomic statuses in our control group existed in exactly the same proportions as those in the pathological group we wish to study, but such a proportional distribution might be difficult to achieve.[1]

Retrospective versus prospective strategies

In one of the most important developments of recent years, the more or less standard "retrospective" research (that is, research that looks backward from the present) has been supplemented by research that focuses, *before* the fact,

---

[1]There is another problem here that could create difficulty. If we insist that socioeconomic statuses in our control group exactly mirror those in the experimental (or pathological) group rather than those in the general population, then our control group may no longer be "representative" of the general population.

on individuals who appear destined to become psychologically disordered. As we saw in our example of compulsive hand-washers, there are certain difficulties in attempting to reconstruct the pasts of the persons already experiencing a disorder; it is hard to disentangle the effects of the present disorder from the effects of past events and to trace a clear cause-and-effect relationship. Nevertheless, this has been the standard method of causal investigation: we observe the behavioral abnormality, and we comb the background histories of afflicted individuals for commonalities that might plausibly have caused it. Apart from the fact that a disordered person may not be the most accurate or objective source of information, such a strategy invites investigators to discover what they *expect* to discover in the way of background factors "theoretically" linked to particular forms of disorder.

We can have much more confidence in our causal explanations when they look ahead instead of backward, and when they correctly predict *which* individuals of a group *will* in the future develop a particular form of disordered behavior—or, alternatively, which of two groups will prove by subsequent events to have been *at risk* for it. It would be logistically difficult, of course, to follow various unselected groups of persons from childhood into adulthood in the numbers required to produce a suitable "yield" of adult disorder of one sort or another. Hence in the typical instance children sharing a risk factor known to be associated with relatively high rates of subsequent breakdown are followed up over the course of years. Those who do subsequently break down are compared with those who don't in the hope that crucial differentiating factors will be discovered. The method is not without certain difficulties, however, including an uncertainty about what constitutes risk and how the selected risk factor may interact with other factors. In addition, "prospective" studies have so far failed to produce striking results. Despite these reservations, however, the very invention of the method and its widespread deployment in many long-term ongoing research projects (Garmezy, 1978c) is probably indicative of a genuine maturing of the field. Serious researchers in abnormal behavior are aware of the magnitude of the challenges facing them, and as a group are no longer confident that easy or "cheap" answers are lying about ready to be picked up by the enterprising but impatient investigator. That level of confidence was probably never really justified in the first place, in that it seriously underestimated the complex nature of the functioning and malfunctioning of persons.

The orientation of this book

Throughout this book we shall be attempting to acquire a perspective on abnormal behavior and its place in contemporary society. Although we shall deal with all the major categories of mental disorders, we shall focus on those patterns that seem most relevant to a broad, basic understanding of maladaptive behavior. And while we shall not hesitate to include the unusual or bizarre, our emphasis will be on the unity of human behavior, ranging from the normal to the abnormal ends of the continuum.

This text is predicated on the assumption that a sound and comprehensive study of abnormal behavior should be based on the following concepts:

1. *A scientific approach to abnormal behavior.* Any comprehensive view of human behavior must draw upon concepts and research findings from a variety of scientific fields. Of particular relevance are genetics, biochemistry, neurophysiology, sociology, and anthropology, as well as psychology. Common scientific concepts such as causal processes, control groups, dependent variables, placebos, and theories will figure in our discussion. Special emphasis will be placed on the application of principles of learning to the understanding and treatment of mental disorders.

In this general context, students are encouraged to take a critical and evaluative attitude toward research findings presented in this text and in other available sources. When properly conducted, scientific research provides us with information that has a high probability of being accurate, but many research findings are subject to bias and open to serious question.

2. *An awareness of our common human concerns.* There are many experiences and problems common to human existence about which science as yet has had little to say. Included are such vital experiences as hope, faith, courage, love, grief,

despair, death, and the quest for values and meaning. Authentic insights into such experiences can often be gained from literature, drama, and autobiographical accounts that strike a common chord and relate directly to an understanding of human behavior. Material from such fields as art, history, and religion can also provide useful insights into certain aspects of abnormal behavior. However, information from the preceding sources will be distinguished from that obtained through scientific observation.

3. *Respect for the dignity, integrity, and growth potential of the individual.* A basic orientation of this book is well described in the opening statement of the *Ethical Principles of Psychologists,* formulated by the American Psychological Association:

"Psychologists respect the dignity and worth of the individual and strive for the preservation and protection of fundamental human rights." (1981, p. 1)

Implicit in this statement is a view of individuals not merely as products of their past conditioning and present situation but as potentially active agents as well—persons who can develop and use their capacities for building the kind of life they choose and a better future world for humankind.

In attempting throughout this volume to provide a perspective for viewing abnormal behavior, we shall focus not only on how maladaptive patterns such as schizophrenia are perceived by clinical psychologists and other mental health personnel, but also on how such disorders feel and are perceived by the individuals experiencing them. In dealing with the major patterns of abnormal behavior, we shall focus on four significant aspects of each: clinical picture, causal factors, treatment, and outcome. And in each case we shall examine the evidence for biological, psychological and interpersonal, and sociocultural factors.

Most of this volume will be devoted to a presentation of well-established patterns of abnormal behavior and to special problem behaviors of our time that are more controversial but directly relevant to any discussion of maladaptive behavior. Initially, however, we shall trace the development of our contemporary views of abnormal behavior from early beliefs and practices, sketch several attempts to explain what makes

human beings "tick," and review the general causes of abnormal behavior in modern life.

Later, after our discussion of the various problem behaviors, we shall devote four chapters to modern methods of assessment and treatment, including the potentialities of modern psychology and allied sciences for preventing mental disorders and for helping humankind achieve a more sane and harmonious world.

At the close of his journeys, Tennyson's Ulysses says, "I am part of all that I have met." It is the authors' hope that readers of this book, at the end of their journey through it, will have a better understanding of human experience and behavior—and that they will consider what they have learned as a meaningful part of their own life experience.

Summary

In our contemporary culture, people must constantly face a bewildering assortment of challenges and pressures, many of which sometimes get in the way of their efforts to live happy, fulfilling, and purposeful lives. Every psychologist is ethically committed to helping people succeed in these efforts, but the psychologist too must face certain obstacles, in particular those beliefs and preconceptions that impede progress in our understanding of mental disorder, its prevention, and its proper treatment.

The student beginning serious study of abnormal psychology is very likely to hold preconceptions about the field that are widely shared by people in general. In part this is due to certain popular images of mental disorders that have persisted over time; but it is also due to the great attention focused on the subject by the media in recent years and to the willingness of mental health professionals to supply offhand accounts of mental disorders and their management. Much of this exposure has accurately depicted limited aspects of the field, but much of it has also been distorted and misleading, causing widespread misconceptions about mental disorders and the people who suffer from them.

The most certain way to avoid misconception and error is to adopt a scientific attitude and approach to the study of abnormal behavior. This involves, among other things, a habit of suspending judgment until pertinent facts are known, the employment of objective and reliable methods of observation, and the development of a valid system for classifying the phenomena to be studied. Progress has been made in all of these areas, but the province of abnormal psychology continues to be complex and challenging; much work remains to be done. We still lack even a universally accepted definition of abnormality, although the authors argue for one which emphasizes outcomes of behavior in terms of the good that is accomplished for the individual or the group.

A scientific approach to abnormal behavior also involves a focus on research and research methods, including an appreciation of the distinction between what is observable and what is hypothetical or inferred. Much of the content of abnormal psychology falls into the latter category. Research on abnormal conditions, if it is to produce valid results, must be done on samples of persons who are truly representative of the pathological groups to which they purportedly belong—a requirement that is often difficult to satisfy. We must also constantly remain alert to the fact that mere correlation does not establish a causal relationship between the variables in question. The use of *experimental* methods and of *prospective* research designs are attempts to resolve questions of causality, but they are not always appropriate approaches and may not always be effective. The individual case-study method, despite its weaknesses, remains a frequently used investigative technique.

It will, no doubt, turn out that science does not have all the answers. Hence, any approach to the field must also recognize the significance of more simply human concerns, such as the feelings of despair or of hope that are such crucial elements in the total picture of normal and abnormal functioning.

2

Historical views of abnormal behavior

*Joseph Crepin, Composition No. 32
(1939). Crepin (1875–1948) was a well-
known medium and spiritual healer in the
Pas-de-Calais region of France. At the age
of 63, his hand "independently" began to
draw striking designs on spare sheets of
paper. His paintings express an austerity
and "antinatural" intellectualism through
their stark flatness and absolute symmetry.*

The history of our efforts to understand abnormal behavior is a fascinating one. Its beginnings are the subject of this chapter. Certainly many of our misconceptions about mental disorders have their roots in the past; but more importantly, many modern scientific concepts and treatments have their counterparts in approaches tried long ago. For example, the method of "free association"—a cornerstone of psychoanalytic therapy, designed to allow repressed conflicts and emotions to enter conscious awareness—is described by the Greek playwright Aristophanes in his play *The Clouds.* Interestingly enough, the scene in which Socrates tries to calm and bring self-knowledge to Strepsiades is complete with a couch.

In this chapter we shall trace from ancient times through to the twentieth century the evolution of popular views of psychopathology and ways of treating those afflicted. In a broad sense, we shall see an evolution from beliefs grounded in superstition to those based on scientific awareness, from a focus on supernatural causes to natural causes. The course of this evolution has not been a steady movement upward; on the contrary, it has often been marked with brief periods of great advancement or unique individual contribution followed by long years of inactivity or destructive backward surges.

As we shall see, our current views of abnormal behavior have been shaped by the prevailing attitudes of past times and the advances of science. Each has contributed to the growth—and often stagnation—of the other. For example, during certain periods in the history of ancient Greece, the body was considered to be sacred. Researchers were thus prevented from performing human autopsies, which did little to advance understanding of human anatomy or biological processes. Too, during a much later period, the belief that demonic possession caused abnormal behavior did little to foster investigation into psychological causes.

The great advances that have come about in the understanding and treatment of abnormal behavior become all the more remarkable when viewed against a persistent resurfacing of ignorance, superstition, and fear. And should we begin to think we have today arrived at an understanding and humane approach to treating the mentally ill, we should think again. We are still not free of many of the culturally conditioned constraints of our past and present; for many, attitudes toward people who are different are still formed, at least in part, by superstition and fear.

Abnormal behavior in ancient times

Although human life presumably appeared on earth some three million or more years ago, written records extend back only a few thousand years. Thus our knowledge of our early ancestors is very limited.

The earliest treatment of abnormal behavior of which we have any awareness was that practiced by Stone Age cave dwellers some half-million years ago. For certain forms of mental disorders, probably those in which the individual complained of severe headaches and experienced convulsive attacks, the shaman (medicine man) appears to have treated the disorder by means of an operation now called *trephining*. This operation was performed with stone instruments and consisted of chipping away one area of the skull in the form of a circle until the skull was cut through. This opening, called a *trephine*, presumably permitted the evil spirit that supposedly was causing all the trouble to escape—and incidentally may have relieved a certain amount of pressure on the brain. In some cases trephined skulls of primitive people show healing around the opening, indicating that the patient survived the operation and lived for many years afterward (Selling, 1943).

Much later, two Egyptian papyri dating from the sixteenth century B.C. were discovered, which have provided some of the earliest written evidence of treatment of disease and behavior disorders. The Edwin Smith papyrus (named after its nineteenth century discoverer) contains a detailed description of the treatment of wounds and other surgical operations; in it the brain is described—possibly for the first time in history—and the writing clearly shows that the brain was recognized as the site of mental functions. We may think this remarkable for the sixteenth century B.C.; it becomes even more remarkable once we realize this papyrus is

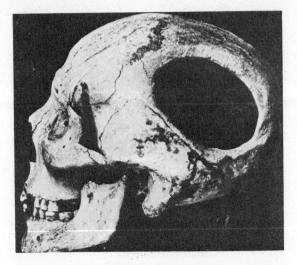

Above, a trephined skull from neolithic times. Trephination—perforating the skull with a sharp instrument—has long been thought to be a means of treating mental disorders. Presumably, by boring a hole in the patient's skull, the "evil spirits" causing the mental disturbances would be driven out.

believed to be a copy of an earlier work from about 3000 B.C. The Ebers papyrus provides another perspective on treatment: it covers internal medicine and the circulatory system but relies more on incantations and magic for explaining and curing diseases whose causes were unknown. This suggests that though surgical techniques may have been used, they were probably coupled with prayers and the like—which no doubt reflected the prevailing view of the origin of behavior disorders.

Demonology, gods, and magic

References to abnormal behavior in the early writings of the Chinese, Egyptians, Hebrews, and Greeks show that they generally attributed such behavior to a demon or god who had taken possession of the individual. This is not surprising when we remember that "good" and "bad" spirits were widely used to explain lightning, thunder, earthquakes, storms, fires, sickness, and many other events that otherwise seemed incomprehensible. It was probably a very simple and logical step to extend this theory to peculiar and incomprehensible behavior in their fellows.

The decision as to whether the "possession" involved good spirits or evil spirits usually depended on the individual's symptoms. If speech or behavior appeared to have a religious or mystical significance, it was usually thought that the person was possessed by a good spirit or god. Such individuals were often treated with considerable awe and respect, for it was thought that they had supernatural powers.

Most possessions, however, were considered to be the work of an angry god or evil spirits, particularly when the individual became excited and overactive and engaged in behavior contrary to religious teachings. Among the ancient Hebrews, for example, such possessions were thought to represent the wrath and punishment of God. Moses is quoted in the Bible as saying, "The Lord shall smite thee with madness. . . ." Apparently this was thought to involve primarily the withdrawal of God's protection, and the abandonment of the individual to the forces of evil. In such cases every effort was made to rid the person of the evil spirit. Jesus reportedly cured a man with an "unclean spirit" by transferring the devils that plagued him to a herd of swine who, in turn, became possessed and "ran violently down a steep place into the sea" (Mark 5:1–13).

The primary type of treatment for demoniacal possession was exorcism, which included various techniques for casting the evil spirit out of the body of the afflicted one. These varied considerably but typically included magic, prayer, incantation, noisemaking, and the use of various horrible-tasting concoctions, such as purgatives made from sheep's dung and wine. In extreme cases more severe measures, such as starving or flogging, were sometimes used in an attempt to make the body of the possessed person such an unpleasant place that the evil spirit would be driven out. The popularity of motion pictures and books on possession and exorcism suggest that these primitive ideas still have appeal today.

The task of exorcising was originally in the hands of shamans, but was eventually taken over in Egypt and Greece by the priests, who were apparently an interesting mixture of priest, physician, psychologist, and magician. Many of the cures remained based in magical rites. Although these priests in the main believed in demonology and used established exorcistic practices, many made a beginning in the more humane treatment of mental disturbances. For example, in the temples of the god Asclepius in ancient Greece, the priests had patients sleep in the temple; supposedly the dreams they had there would reveal what they needed to do to get better. The priests supplemented prayer and incantation with kindness, suggestion, and recreational measures, such as theatricals, riding, walking, and harmonious music.

Early philosophical and medical concepts

The Greek temples of healing ushered in the Golden Age of Greece under the Athenian statesman Pericles (461–429 B.C.), a time during which considerable progress was made in the understanding and treatment of mental disorders. Interestingly, this progress was made in spite of the fact that it was also a time during which little was learned of human anatomy or physiology because the human body was viewed as sacred and therefore not to be dissected. It was in this period that Hippocrates (460–377 B.C.), often referred to as the "father of modern medicine," received his training and made his substantial contributions to the field.

Hippocrates. Hippocrates denied the intervention of deities and demons in the development of disease, and insisted that mental disorders had natural causes and required treatment like other diseases. His position was unequivocal: "For my own part, I do not believe that the human body is ever befouled by a God" (in Lewis, 1941, p. 37). Hippocrates emphasized the view that the brain was the central organ of intellectual activity and that mental disorders were due to brain pathology. Hippocrates also emphasized the importance of heredity and predisposition and pointed out that injuries to the head could cause sensory and motor disorders.

Hippocrates classified all the varieties of mental disorder into three general categories—mania, melancholia, and phrentis (brain fever)—and gave detailed clinical descriptions of the specific disorders included in each category. He relied heavily on clinical observation, and his descriptions, which were based on the daily clinical records of his patients, were surprisingly thorough. Hippocrates considered dreams to be

Each of the four humors were thought to have a different effect on the body and personality, as shown in this page from a medieval illuminated manuscript. The individuals pictured here were intended to illustrate the types of maladies that could result from imbalances in the humors. The types are (clockwise from top left) melancholic (black bile), sanguine (blood), choleric (yellow bile), and phlegmatic (phlegm).

important in understanding the personality of the patient. On this point he not only elaborated on the thinking set forth by the priests in the temples of Asclepius but also was a harbinger of one of the concepts basic to contemporary psychodynamic psychotherapy.

The methods of treatment advocated by Hippocrates were far in advance of the exorcistic practices then prevalent. For the treatment of melancholia, for example, he prescribed a regular and tranquil life, sobriety and abstinence from all excesses, a vegetable diet, celibacy, exercise short of fatigue, and bleeding if indicated. But for hysteria,[1] which was thought to be restricted to women and caused by the wandering of the uterus to various parts of the body because of its pining for children, Hippocrates recommended marriage as the best remedy. He also believed in the importance of the environment, and not infrequently removed his patients from their families.

Hippocrates' emphasis on natural causes, clinical observations, and brain pathology as a cause of mental disorders was truly revolutionary. Like his contemporaries, however, Hippo-

[1]The appearance of symptoms of physical illness in the absence of organic pathology.

crates had very little knowledge of physiology. He wrongly believed in the existence of four bodily fluids or "humors"—blood, black bile, yellow bile, and phlegm. In his work *On Sacred Disease*, he stated that when the humors were adversely mixed or otherwise disturbed, physical or mental disease resulted: "Depravement of the brain arises from phlegm and bile; those mad from phlegm are quiet, depressed and oblivious; those from bile excited, noisy and mischievous." Although this concept went far beyond demonology, it was too crude physiologically to be of much therapeutic value. Yet in its emphasis on the importance of bodily balances to mental health, it may be seen as a precursor of today's focus on the need for biochemical balances in order to maintain normal brain functioning and good health.

Plato and Aristotle. The problem of dealing with mentally disturbed individuals who committed criminal acts was studied by the great philosopher Plato (429–347 B.C.). He wrote that such persons were in some "obvious" sense not responsible for their acts and should not receive punishment in the same way as normal persons: ". . . someone may commit an act when mad or afflicted with disease . . . [if so,] let him pay simply for the damage; and let him be exempt from other punishment." Plato also made provision for mental cases to be cared for in the community as follows: "If anyone is insane, let him not be seen openly in the city, but let the relatives of such a person watch over him in the best manner they know of; and if they are negligent, let them pay a fine . . ." (Plato, n.d., p. 56). In making these humane suggestions, Plato was addressing issues with which we are still grappling today—the issue of "insanity" as a legal defense when a crime has been committed and the proper treatment of persons whose public behavior is considered offensive or dangerous to the social order.

In addition to this emphasis on the more humane treatment of the mentally disturbed, Plato contributed to a better understanding of human behavior by pointing out that all forms of life, human included, were motivated by physiologic needs, or "natural appetites." Perhaps his most significant contribution was that he saw psychological phenomena as responses of the whole organism, reflecting its internal state. He also seems to have anticipated Freud's insight into the functions of fantasies and dreams as substitutive satisfactions, concluding that in dreams, desire tended to satisfy itself in imagery when the higher faculties no longer inhibited the "passions." In his *Republic,* Plato emphasized the importance of individual differences in intellectual and other abilities, pointing also to the role of sociocultural influences in shaping thinking and behavior. Despite these modern ideas, however, Plato shared the belief of his time that mental disorders were partly divinely caused.

The celebrated philosopher Aristotle (384–322 B.C.), who was a pupil of Plato, wrote extensively on mental disorders. Among his most lasting contributions to psychology are his descriptions of the content of consciousness. He, too, anticipated Freud in his view of "thinking" as directed striving toward elimination of pain and attainment of pleasure. On the question of whether mental disorders could be caused by psychological factors like frustration and conflict, Aristotle discussed the possibility and rejected it, and his influence was widespread. Aristotle generally followed the Hippocratic theory of disturbances in the bile. For example, he believed that very hot bile generated amorous desires and loquacity, and was also responsible for suicidal impulses.

Later Greek and Roman thought. Work along the lines that had been established by Hippocrates was continued by some of the later Greek and Roman physicians. Particularly in Alexandria, Egypt (which after its founding in 332 B.C. by Alexander the Great became a center of Greek culture), medical practices developed to a high level, and the temples dedicated to Saturn were first-rate sanatoriums. Pleasant surroundings were considered of great therapeutic value for the mental patients, who were provided with constant activities including parties, dances, walks in the temple gardens, rowing along the Nile, and musical concerts. Physicians of this time also employed a wide range of other kinds of therapeutic measures, including dieting, massage, hydrotherapy, gymnastics, and education, as well as certain less desirable measures, such as bleeding, purging, and mechanical restraints.

Among the Greeks and Romans who continued in the Hippocratic tradition were Asclepiades, Cicero, Aretaeus, and Galen. Asclepiades (born *c.* 124 B.C.) was the first to note the

difference between acute and chronic mental disorders, and to distinguish between illusions, delusions, and hallucinations. In addition, he invented various ingenious devices designed to make patients more comfortable. One of these was a suspended hammock-like bed whose swaying was considered very beneficial for disturbed patients. Asclepiades' progressive approach to mental disorders was also evidenced by his opposition to bleeding and mechanical restraints.

Cicero (106–43 B.C.) was perhaps the first to go on record as stating boldly that body ailments could be the result of emotional factors. A century later, Aretaeus saw certain mental disorders as merely an extension of normal psychological processes. He thought that people who were irritable, violent, and easily given to joy and pleasurable pursuits were prone to the development of manic excitement, while those who tended to be serious were more apt to develop melancholia. Aretaeus was the first to describe the various phases of mania and melancholia, and to consider these two pathological states as expressions of the same illness. His insight into the importance of emotional factors and of the prepsychotic personality of the patient was an extraordinary achievement for his day.

Galen (A.D. 130–200) was a Greek physician who moved to Rome. A devoted elaborator of Hippocratic tradition, he did not contribute much that was new to the treatment or clinical descriptions of mental disorders. Rather, he made a number of original contributions concerning the anatomy of the nervous system. (These findings were based on dissections of animals; human autopsies were still not done.) Galen also maintained a scientific approach to the field, dividing the causes of mental disorders into physical and mental. Among the causes he named were injuries to the head, alcoholic excess, shock, fear, adolescence, menstrual changes, economic reverses, and disappointment in love.

Roman medicine reflected the characteristic pragmatism of the Roman people. Roman physicians wanted to make their patients comfortable and used pleasant physical therapies, such as warm baths and massage. They also followed the principle of *contrariis contrarius* ("opposite by opposite")—for example, having their patients drink chilled wine while immersed in a warm tub.

Although historians consider the fall of Rome to the barbarians toward the end of the fifth century to be the dividing line between ancient and medieval times, the Dark Ages in the history of abnormal psychology began much earlier, with Galen's death in A.D. 200. The contributions of Hippocrates and the later Greek and Roman physicians were shortly lost in the welter of popular superstition, and, though some exceptions can be found, most of the physicians of later Rome returned to some sort of demonology.

Survival of Greek thought in Islamic countries.   During medieval times it was only in Islamic countries that the more scientific aspects of Greek medicine survived. The first mental hospital was apparently established in Baghdad in A.D. 792; it was soon followed by others in Damascus and Aleppo (Polvan, 1969). In these hospitals the mentally disturbed reportedly received humane treatment.

The outstanding figure in Islamic medicine was Avicenna (c. A.D. 980–1037), called the "prince of physicians" (Campbell, 1926) and author of *The Canon of Medicine*, perhaps the most widely studied medical work ever written. In his writings Avicenna frequently referred to hysteria, epilepsy, manic reactions, and melancholia. The following case shows his unique approach to the treatment of a young prince suffering from a mental disorder:

"A certain prince . . . was afflicted with melancholia, and suffered from the delusion that he was a cow . . . he would low like a cow, causing annoyance to everyone, . . . crying 'Kill me so that a good stew may be made of my flesh,' finally . . . he would eat nothing. . . . Avicenna was persuaded to take the case. . . . First of all he sent a message to the patient bidding him be of good cheer because the butcher was coming to slaughter him, whereat . . . the sick man rejoiced. Some time afterwards Avicenna, holding a knife in his hand, entered the sickroom saying, 'Where is this cow that I may kill it?' The patient lowed like a cow to indicate where he was. By Avicenna's orders he was laid on the ground bound hand and foot. Avicenna then felt him all over and said, 'He is too lean, and not ready to be killed; he must be fattened.' Then they offered him suitable food of which he now partook eagerly, and gradually he gained strength, got rid of his delusion, and was completely cured." (Browne, 1921, pp. 88–89)

Unfortunately, most Western medical men of Avicenna's time were dealing with mental patients in a very different way. The advances made by the thinkers of antiquity were having little impact on European approaches to abnormal behavior.

Demonology in the Middle Ages

During the Middle Ages in Europe (about A.D. 500–1500) there was a tremendous revival of the most ancient superstition and demonology, with only a slight modification to conform to current theological demands. (Similar revivals of superstition had occurred or were to occur in other parts of the world as well—see the **HIGHLIGHT** on page 38—though perhaps not to such an extreme degree.) Human beings became the battleground of demons and spirits who waged eternal war for the possession of their souls. Mental disorders were apparently quite prevalent throughout the Middle Ages, especially so toward the end of the period, when medieval institutions began to collapse. As Rosen (1967) has described it:

"The medieval world began to come apart in the 14th century, and the process of disintegration continued inexorably through the succeeding centuries. Fundamental changes took place in its institutions, its social structure, its beliefs and outlook. It was a period of peasant revolts and urban uprisings, of wars and plagues, and thus an age in which many felt acutely insecure and discontented. An emotional malaise was abroad." (p. 775)

"Mass madness"

The last half of the Middle Ages saw a peculiar trend in abnormal behavior, involving the widespread occurrence of group behavior disorders that were apparently mainly cases of hysteria. Whole groups of people were affected simultaneously.

Dance manias, taking the form of epidemics of raving, jumping, dancing, and convulsions, were reported as early as the tenth century. One such episode, occurring in Italy early in the thirteenth century, was recorded by physicians of the time whose records have been reviewed by the medical historian H. E. Sigerist. He has written:

"[It] occurred at the height of the summer heat. . . . People, asleep or awake, would suddenly jump up, feeling an acute pain like the sting of a bee. Some saw the spider, others did not, but they knew that it must be the tarantula. They ran out of the house into the street, to the market place, dancing in great excitement. Soon they were joined by others who like them had been bitten, or by people who had been stung in previous years. . .

"Thus groups of patients would gather, dancing wildly in the queerest attire. . . . Others would tear their clothes and show their nakedness, losing all sense of modesty. . . . Some called for swords and acted like fencers, others for whips and beat each other. . . . Some of them had still stranger fancies, like to be tossed in the air, dug holes in the ground, and rolled themselves into the dirt like swine. They all drank wine plentifully and sang and talked like drunken people. . . ." (1943, pp. 103, 106–107)

Known as *tarantism* in Italy, the dancing mania later spread to Germany and the rest of Europe, where it was known as *St. Vitus's dance.* Actually, the behavior was very similar to the ancient orgiastic rites by which people had worshiped the Greek god Dionysus. These had been banned with the advent of Christianity, but were deeply embedded in the culture and were apparently kept alive by secret gatherings. Probably considerable guilt and conflict were engendered; then, with time, the meaning of the dances changed, and the old rites appeared as symptoms of the tarantula's bite. The participants were no longer sinners but the unwilling victims of the spirit of the tarantula. The dancing became the "cure," and is the source of the dance we know today as the "tarantella."

Isolated rural areas were also afflicted with outbreaks of *lycanthropy*—a mental disorder in which individuals believed themselves to be possessed by wolves and imitated their behavior. In 1541 a case was reported in which a lycanthrope told his captors, in confidence, that he was really a wolf but that his skin was smooth on the surface because all the hairs were on the inside (Stone, 1937). To cure him of his delusions, his extremities were amputated, following which he died, still unconvinced.

These episodes of "mass madness" occurred periodically into the seventeenth century, but

The chaos set in motion by the collapse of medieval institutions was mirrored in the fears of individuals who believed themselves to be at the mercy of demons intent on inflicting divine punishment. This painting, Mouth of Hell, *from a fifteenth-century manuscript, is an expression of the terrifying reality of these unseen demons.*

HIGHLIGHT
Early views of mental disorders in China

Tseng (1973) traced the development of concepts of mental disorders in China by reviewing the descriptions of the disorders and their recommended treatment in Chinese medical documents. For example, the following is taken from an ancient Chinese medical text supposedly written by Huang Ti (c. 2674 B.C.), the third legendary emperor, but now considered by historians to have been written at a later date, possibly during the seventh century B.C.:

"The person suffering from excited insanity initially feels sad, eating and sleeping less; he then becomes grandiose, feeling that he is very smart and noble, talking and scolding day and night, singing, behaving strangely, seeing strange things, hearing strange voices, believing that he can see the devil or gods. . . ."570)

Even at this early date, Chinese medicine was based on natural rather than supernatural causes. For example, in the concept of Ying and Yang the human body, like the cosmos, is divided into a positive and a negative force which are both complementary and contradictory to each other. If the two forces are balanced, the result is physical and mental health, if they are not, illness will result. Consequently:

"As treatment for such an excited condition withholding food was suggested, since food was consid- ered to be the source of positive force and the patient was thought to be in need of a decrease in such force." (p. 570)

Chinese medicine apparently reached a relatively sophisticated level during the second century, and Chung Ching, who has been called the Hippocrates of China, wrote two well-known medical works around A.D. 200. Like Hippocrates, he based his views of both physical and mental disorders on clinical observations and implicated organ pathology as the primary cause. However, he also believed that stressful psychological conditions could cause the organ pathology, and his treatment, like that of Hippocrates, utilized both drugs and the regaining of emotional balance through appropriate activities.

As in the West, however, Chinese views of mental disorders were to regress to the belief in supernatural forces as causal agents. From the later part of the second century through the early part of the ninth century, ghosts and devils were implicated in "Ghost-evil" insanity, which presumably resulted from bewitchment by evil spirits. However, the "Dark Ages" in China were not so severe—in terms of the treatment of mental patients—nor did they last so long as in the West. And a return to biological, somatic (bodily) views as well as the emphasis on psychosocial factors were to occur in the centuries which followed.

---

apparently reached their peak during the fourteenth and fifteenth centuries—a period noted for oppression, famine, and pestilence. During this period, Europe was ravaged by an epidemic known as the "Black Death," which spread across the continent, killing millions—some estimates say 50 percent of the population of Europe—and severely disrupting social organization. Undoubtedly many of the peculiar manifestations during this period were related to the depression, fear, and wild mysticism engendered by the terrible events of the time. People did not dream that such frightening catastrophes were attributable to natural causes and thus would some day be within our power to control, prevent, or even create.

Interestingly, it was during the sixteenth century that Teresa of Avila, a Spanish nun who was later to be canonized, made an extraordinary conceptual leap that influences our thinking to the present day. Teresa, in charge of a group of cloistered nuns who had become hysterical and were therefore in danger from the Spanish Inquisition, argued convincingly that her nuns were not bewitched, but rather were "as if sick" (comas enfermas). Apparently, she did not mean they were sick of body. Rather, in the expression "as if," we have what is perhaps the first suggestion that a mind can be sick just as can a body. It was a momentous suggestion that apparently began as a kind of metaphor but was, with time, reified (viewed as real): *mental*

Madness has been a favorite subject for artists throughout history. Here (top), a fifteenth-century drawing by Pieter Brueghel shows peasant women overcome by St. Vitus's dance. And William Blake's eighteenth-century depiction of Nebuchadnezzar (bottom), the king of Babylon who suffered from lycanthropy, is a powerful work based on a biblical description: ". . . he was driven from men, and did eat grass as oxen, and his body was wet with the dew of heaven, til his hairs were grown like eagles' feathers, and his nails like birds' claws" (Daniel 4:33).

illness came to be seen as an entity and the "as if" dropped out of use (Sarbin & Juhasz, 1967).

Mass disorder is not unknown in the present day. Reports of so-called "mass hysteria" occur from time to time in the contemporary press; the affliction is usually one that mimics some type of physical disorder, such as fainting spells or convulsive movements. In 1979, for example, about one third of a Massachusetts elementary school student body was struck with a sudden wave of illness. While attending their last general assembly of the year, thirty-four children became extremely ill and were rushed to the hospital; another fifty were treated on the school grounds. In each case, the symptoms were similar and appeared suddenly: dizziness, hyper-ventilation, headache, chills, and nausea. The symptoms disappeared just as suddenly as they appeared. Health officials could find no cause. Two psychiatrists who studied the incident, however, hypothesized that fears associated with certain kinds of upcoming losses, including graduation, may have been stressful enough to trigger the mass hysteria (Small & Nicholi, 1982). A similar incident was reported in 1982 after a story broke nationwide concerning the poisoning of some Chicago-area residents by Tylenol capsules laced with cyanide. Shortly after news of the Tylenol poisonings became public, California health officials reported a sudden wave of illness among some two hundred people who drank soda at a high school football

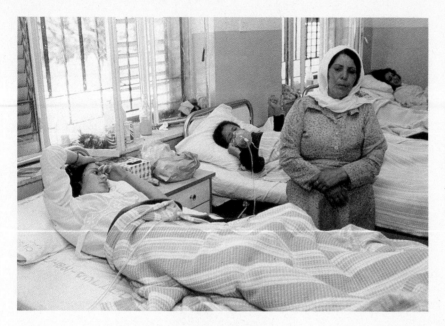

Mass disorders seem to occur during periods of widespread public fear and stress, such as that felt by these West Bank Palestinian schoolgirls, who developed the same mysterious physical symptoms in April of 1983. Although Arab leaders at first suspected the girls had been the victims of an Israeli poison plot, it was later thought that psychological factors had played an important role in the appearance of their symptoms.

game. No objective cause of the illness could be found, and officials speculated that the majority of sufferers had been experiencing a kind of mass hysteria related to the Tylenol incident (UPI, 1982). Even more recently, a case of apparent mass hysteria occurred among hundreds of West Bank Palestinian school girls in April of 1983. This episode threatened to have serious political repercussions for a time because some Arab leaders concluded that the girls had been poisoned by Israelis (*Time,* April 18, 1983).

Exorcism in medieval times

In the Middle Ages treatment of the mentally disturbed was left largely to the clergy. Monasteries served as refuges and places of confinement. During the early part of the medieval period, the mentally disturbed for the most part were treated with considerable kindness. Much store was set by prayer, holy water, sanctified ointments, the breath or spittle of the priests, the touching of relics, visits to holy places, and mild forms of exorcism. In some monasteries and shrines exorcism was performed by the gentle "laying on of hands." Such methods were often intermixed with vague ideas of medical treatment derived mainly from Galen, which gave rise to such prescriptions as the following: "For a fiend-sick man: When a devil possesses a man, or controls him from within with disease,

a spewdrink of lupin, bishopswort, henbane, garlic. Pound these together, add ale and holy water" (Cockayne, 1864–1866).

As exorcistic techniques became more fully developed, emphasis was placed on Satan's pride, which was believed to have led to his original downfall. Hence, in treating persons possessed by a devil, the first thing to do was to strike a fatal blow at the devil's pride—to insult him. This involved calling the devil some of the most obscene epithets that imagination could devise, and the insults were usually supplemented by long litanies of cursing:

". . . May all the devils that are thy foes rush forth upon thee, and drag thee down to hell! . . May God set a nail to your skull, and pound it in with a hammer, as Jael did unto Sisera! . . . May . . . Sother break thy head and cut off thy hands, as was done to the cursed Dagon! . . . May God hang thee in a hellish yoke, as seven men were hanged by the sons of Saul!" (From *Thesaurus Exorcismorum*)

This procedure was considered highly successful in the treatment of possessed persons. A certain bishop of Beauvais claimed to have rid a person of five devils, all of whom signed an agreement stating that they and their subordinate imps would no longer persecute the possessed individual (A. D. White, 1896).

Had this been the worst treatment the mentally disturbed person received during the Middle Ages, the world would have been spared some tragic chapters in its history. Unfortunately, however, as theological beliefs concerning abnormal behavior became widespread and were endorsed by the secular world, mild and gentle treatment was replaced by harsh and punitive action. It was generally believed that cruelty to people afflicted with "madness" was punishment of the devil residing within them, and when "scourging" proved ineffective, the authorities felt justified in driving out the demons by more unpleasant methods. Flogging, starving, chains, immersion in hot water, and other torturous methods were devised in order to make the body such an unpleasant place of residence that no self-respecting devil would remain in it. Undoubtedly many men and women who might have been restored to health by more gentle and humane measures were driven into hopeless derangement by such brutal treatment.

Witchcraft

During the latter part of the fifteenth century, it became the accepted theological belief that demoniacal possessions were of two general types: (a) possessions in which the victim was unwillingly seized by the devil as a punishment by God for past sins, and (b) possessions in which the individual was actually in league with the devil. The latter persons were supposed to have made a pact with the devil, consummated by signing in blood a book presented to them by Satan, which gave them certain supernatural powers. They could cause pestilence, storms, floods, sexual impotence, injuries to their enemies, and ruination of crops, and could rise through the air, cause milk to sour, and turn themselves into animals. In short, they were witches.

These beliefs were not confined to simple serfs but were held and elaborated upon by most of the important clergyman of this period. No less a man than Martin Luther (1483–1546) came to the following conclusions:

"The greatest punishment God can inflict on the wicked . . . is to deliver them over to Satan, who with God's permission, kills them or makes them to undergo great calamities. Many devils are in woods, water, wildernesses, etc., ready to hurt and prejudice people. When these things happen, then the philosophers and physicians say it is natural, ascribing it to the planets.

"[People] are possessed by the devil in two ways; corporally or spiritually. Those whom he possesses corporally, as mad people, he has permission from God to vex and agitate, but he has no power over their souls." *(Colloquia Mensalia [Table Talk])*

Those who were judged to have been unwillingly seized by the devil as punishment by God were treated initially in accordance with the established exorcistic practices of the time. As time went on, however, the distinction between the two types of possessions became somewhat obscured, and by the close of the fifteenth century, few were considered to be unwilling victims. "Possessed" individuals tended to be viewed as heretics and witches (though this point has been challenged by some scholars—see Allridge, 1979; Spanos, 1978).

More and more concern was expressed in official quarters over the number of witches roaming around and the great damage they were doing by pestilences, storms, sexual depravity, and other heinous crimes. Consequently, on December 7, 1484, Pope Innocent VIII sent forth his papal brief, *Summis Desiderantes Affectibus,* in which he exhorted the clergy of Europe, especially Germany, to leave no means untried in the detection of witches. This papal brief was theologically based on the biblical command "Thou shalt not suffer a witch to live" (Exodus 22:18).

To assist in this great work, a manual, *Malleus maleficarum (The Witches' Hammer),* was prepared by two Dominican monks, Johann Sprenger and Heinrich Kraemer, both Inquisitors appointed by the pope to act in northern Germany and territories along the Rhine. This manual, revered for centuries in both Catholic and Protestant countries as being almost divinely inspired, was complete in every detail concerning witchcraft and was of great value in witch-hunting. It was divided into three parts. The first confirmed the existence of witches and pointed out that those who did not believe in them were either in honest error or polluted with heresy. The second part contained a description of the clinical symptoms by which witches could be detected, such as red spots or areas of anesthesia on the skin, which were thought to resemble the claw of the devil ("devil's claw") and were presumably left by the devil to denote the sealing of the pact with him. The third part dealt with the legal forms of examining and sentencing a witch. To be convicted of witchcraft was a most serious

The basic assumption of exorcism was that the demons and spirits possessing an individual could be driven out if one found the right method, such as this physician's device for curing "folly and fantasy."

We do not intend to give the impression that most mentally disordered people were tried as witches during the Middle Ages or that the vast majority of the thousands of people who were executed as witches were insane. Rather, one must understand the context of European witchcraft in the Middle Ages. Russell (1972) described the period as one of great social change in which some people were branded and punished as witches for many reasons, including, for example, for simply having been successful in life. Others may have adopted witchcraft in the hope that they could gain power over death. As Russell pointed out,

"Most people expressed social discontent in forms other than witchcraft. One must therefore inquire why some chose such an extreme form of protest. We need not impose our own ideas of mental illness upon the Middle Ages to recognize that there were individuals then as now seriously impeded from functioning

matter. The penalty usually followed one of three general forms. There were those who were beheaded or strangled before being burned, those who were burned alive, and those who were mutilated before being burned.

In accordance with the precepts laid down in the *Malleus,* the accepted way to gain sure proof of witchcraft was to torture the person until a confession was obtained. This method was eminently effective. The victims of these tortures, writhing in agony, confessed to anything and everything. Frequently they were forced to give the names of alleged accomplices in their evildoing, and these unfortunate persons were in turn tortured until they, too, confessed.

Confessions were often weird, but this seldom deterred the learned judges. For example, James I of England proved, through the skillful use of unlimited torture, that witches were to blame for the tempests that beset his bride on her voyage from Denmark. A Dr. Fian, whose legs were being crushed in the "boots" and who had wedges driven under his fingernails, confessed that more than a hundred witches had put to sea in a sieve to produce the storms (A. D. White, 1896).

One of the accepted penalties for witchcraft, as described in the Malleus, *was to be burned alive, usually after a confession extracted through torture.*

in society by their idiosyncratic views of reality. Such persons, particularly during times of unusual change and stress, might have either embraced witchcraft or been seized by the unreasoning terror of witchcraft." (pp. 272–73)

There seems to have been little distinction between the Roman and the Reformed churches in their attitudes toward witchcraft, and large numbers of people were put to death in this period.

"A French judge boasted that he had burned 800 women in sixteen years on the bench; 600 were burned during the administration of a bishop in Bamberg. The Inquisition, originally started by the Church of Rome, was carried along by protestant churches in Great Britian and Germany. In protestant Geneva 500 persons were burned in the year 1515. In Trèves some 7000 people were reported burned during a period of several years." (Bromberg, 1937, p. 61)

The full horror of the witch mania and its enthusiastic adoption by other countries, including some American colonies, took place during the sixteenth and seventeenth centuries. And though religious and scientific thought began to change gradually, the idea of mental disorder as representing punishment by God or deliberate association with the devil dominated popular thought until well into the nineteenth century.

Growth toward humanitarian approaches

Any criticism or questioning of the theological doctrine of demonology during the Middle Ages was made at the risk of life itself. Yet during the latter part of the Middle Ages there were stirrings of scientific intellectual activity and the beginnings of a movement emphasizing the importance of specifically human interests and concerns—a movement (still very much with us today) which can be loosely referred to as "humanism." Consequently, the belief in demons and witches, which had retarded the understanding and therapeutic treatment of mental disorders, began to be challenged.

Scientific questioning in Europe

One of the first physicians to speak out against the code of the witch burners was Agrippa (1486–1535), who is best known as the teacher of Johann Weyer, discussed below. Paracelsus, a Swiss physician (1490–1541), was an early critic, too, who insisted that the "dancing mania" was not a possession but a form of disease, and that it should be treated as such. He also postulated a conflict between the instinctual and spiritual nature of human beings, formulated the idea of psychic causes for mental illness, and advocated treatment by "bodily magnetism," later called *hypnosis* (Mora, 1967). Although Paracelsus rejected demonology, his view of abnormal behavior was colored by his belief in astral influences (*lunatic* is derived from the Latin word "luna" or moon): he was convinced that the moon exercised a supernatural influence over the brain—an idea, incidentally, that persists among some people today. Paracelsus defied the medical and theological traditions of his time. Had he been more restrained and diplomatic in his efforts, he might have exerted more influence over the scientific thinking of his day. As it was, he became known more for his arrogance and lack of tact than for his scientific advances; to make his points, he often burned the works of Galen and others of whom he disapproved. As a result, he was hounded and persecuted until his death.

Johann Weyer (1515–1588), a German physician and man of letters who wrote under the Latin name of Joannus Wierus, was so deeply impressed by the scenes of imprisonment, torture, and burning of persons accused of witchcraft that he made a careful study of the entire problem of witchcraft and about 1563 published a book, *The Deception of Demons*, which contains a step-by-step rebuttal of the *Malleus maleficarum*. In it he argued that a considerable number, if not all, of those imprisoned, tortured, and burned for witchcraft were really sick in mind or body, and consequently that great wrongs were being committed against innocent people. Weyer's work received the approval of a few outstanding physicians and theologians of his time. In the main, however, it met with vehement protest and condemnation.

Weyer was one of the first physicians to specialize in mental disorders, and his wide experience and progressive views justify his reputa-

Johann Weyer (1515–1588) wrote against the prevalent beliefs in witchcraft and decried the persecution of the mentally ill.

tion as founder of modern psychopathology. Unfortunately, however, he was too far ahead of his time. He was scorned by his peers, many of whom called him "Weirus Hereticus" and "Weirus Insanus." His works were banned by the Church and remained so until the twentieth century.

Perhaps there is no better illustration of the spirit of scientific skepticism that was developing in the sixteenth century than the works of the Oxford-educated Reginald Scot (1538–1599), who devoted his life to exposing the fallacies of witchcraft and demonology. In his book, *Discovery of Witchcraft*, published in 1584, he convincingly and daringly denied the existence of demons, devils, and evil spirits as the cause of mental disorders.

"These women are but diseased wretches suffering from melancholy, and their words, actions, reasoning, and gestures show that sickness has affected their brains and impaired their powers of judgment. You must know that the effects of sickness on men, and still more on women, are almost unbelievable. Some of these persons imagine, confess, and maintain that they are witches and are capable of performing extraordinary miracles through the arts of witchcraft; others, due to the same mental disorder, imagine strange and impossible things which they claim to have witnessed." (in Castiglioni, 1946, p. 253)

King James I of England, however, came to the rescue of demonology, personally refuted Scot's thesis, and ordered his book seized and burned. But churchmen also were beginning to question the practices of the time. For example, St. Vincent de Paul (1576–1660), surrounded by every opposing influence and at the risk of his life, declared: "Mental disease is no different to bodily disease and Christianity demands of the humane and powerful to protect, and the skilful to relieve the one as well as the other."

In the face of such persistent advocates of science, who continued their testimonies throughout the next two centuries, demonology was forced to give ground, and the way was gradually paved for the return of observation and reason, culminating in the development of modern experimental and clinical approaches.

Establishment of early asylums and shrines

From the sixteenth century on, monasteries and prisons gradually relinquished the care of persons suffering from mental disorders to special institutions that were being established in increasing numbers. Although scientific skepticism was gradually undermining the belief that mental disturbance was the devil's work, most early asylums were not much better than concentration camps. The unfortunate residents lived and died amid conditions of incredible filth and cruelty.

Early asylums. In 1547, the monastery of St. Mary of Bethlehem at London was officially made into a mental hospital by Henry VIII. Its name soon became contracted to "Bedlam," and it became widely known for the deplorable conditions and practices that prevailed. The more violent patients were exhibited to the public for one penny a look, and the more harmless inmates were forced to seek charity on the streets of London in the manner described by Shakespeare:

". . . Bedlam beggars, who, with roaring voices . . . Sometimes with lunatic bans, sometime with prayers Enforce their charity." (*King Lear*, Act II, Scene iii)

Such hospitals, or "asylums" as they were called, were gradually established in other countries. The San Hipolito, established in Mexico in 1566 by the philanthropist Bernardino Alvares, was the first hospital for the care and study of mental disorders to be established in the Amer-

From the sixteenth century on, an accepted treatment for persons with mental disorders was confinement in asylums like this, the Bethlehem Royal Hospital in London. The hospital's name was soon contracted to "Bedlam," a synonym for the uproar and confusion within its walls.

icas. The first mental hospital in France, La Maison de Charenton, was founded in 1641 in a suburb of Paris. A mental hospital was established in Moscow in 1764, and the notorious Lunatics' Tower in Vienna was constructed in 1784. This was a showplace in Old Vienna, and the description of the structure and its practices makes interesting reading. It was an ornately decorated round tower within which were square rooms. The doctors and "keepers" lived in the square rooms, while the patients were confined in the spaces between the walls of the square rooms and the outside of the tower. The patients were put on exhibit to the public for a small fee.

These early asylums, or hospitals, were primarily modifications of penal institutions, and the inmates were treated more like beasts than like human beings. Selling gives a striking account of the treatment of the chronic insane in La Bicêtre Hospital in Paris. This treatment was typical of the asylums of this period and continued through most of the eighteenth century.

The patients were ordinarily shackled to the walls of their dark, unlighted cells by iron collars which held them flat against the wall and permitted little movement. Ofttimes there were also iron hoops around the waists of the patients and both their hands and feet were chained. Although these chains usually permitted enough movement that the patients could feed themselves out of bowls, they often kept them from being able to lie down at night. Since little was known about dietetics, and the patients were presumed to be animals anyway, little attention was paid to whether they were adequately fed or to whether the food was good or bad. The cells were furnished only with straw and were never swept or cleaned; the patient re-

mained in the midst of all the accumulated ordure. No one visited the cells except at feeding time, no provision was made for warmth, and even the most elementary gestures of humanity were lacking. (Modified from Selling, 1943, pp. 54–55)

In the United States, the Pennsylvania Hospital at Philadelphia, completed under the guidance of Benjamin Franklin in 1756, provided some cells or wards for the mental patients; the first hospital in the United States devoted exclusively to mental patients was constructed in Williamsburg, Virginia, in 1773. Yet treatment of mental patients in the U.S. was hardly much better than that offered by European institutions. The following is a vivid description of their plight in this country during colonial times:

"The mentally ill were hanged, imprisoned, tortured, and otherwise persecuted as agents of Satan. Regarded as sub-human beings, they were chained in specially devised kennels and cages like wild beasts, and thrown into prisons, bridewells and jails like criminals. They were incarcerated in workhouse dungeons or made to slave as able-bodied paupers, unclassified from the rest. They were left to wander about stark naked, driven from place to place like mad dogs, subjected to whippings as vagrants and rogues. Even the well-to-do were not spared confinement in strong rooms and cellar dungeons, while legislation usually concerned itself more with their property than their persons." (Deutsch, 1946, p. 53)

Some insight into the prevalent forms of treatment in the early American hospitals may be gained from a thesis on "Chronic Mania," written by a medical student in 1796 at the New York Hospital, in which cells or wards were provided in the cellar for the mentally ill patients.

He considered that restraint should be avoided as long as possible, "lest the strait jackets, and chains and cells should induce a depression of spirits seldom surmounted. He also doubted the propriety of "unexpected plunging into cold water," of "two to six hours in spring water or still colder," of the "refrigerant plan," of bleeding, purging, vomiting, streams of cold water on the head, blisters, and similar procedures (Russell, 1941, p. 230).

Even as late as 1830, new patients had their heads shaved, were dressed in straitjackets, put on a sparse diet, compelled to swallow some active purgative, and placed in a dark cell. If these measures did not serve to quiet unruly or excited patients, more severe measures, such as starvation, solitary confinement, cold baths, and other torturelike methods, were used (Bennett, 1947).

The Gheel shrine. There were a few bright spots in this otherwise tragic situation. Out of the more humane Christian tradition of prayer, and laying on of hands, or holy touch, and visits to shrines for cure of illness, there arose several great shrines where treatment by kindness and love stood out in marked contrast to generally prevailing conditions. The one at Gheel in Belgium, visited since the thirteenth century, is probably most famous—and the story of its founding is an interesting one.

"Somewhere in the dim past there lived a king in Ireland who was married to a most beautiful woman and who sired an equally beautiful daughter. The good queen developed a fatal illness, and at her death bed the daughter dedicated herself to a life of purity and service to the poor and the mentally bereft. The widowed king was beside himself with grief and announced to his subjects that he must at once be assuaged of sorrow by marrying the woman in his kingdom who most resembled the dead queen. No such paragon was found. But the devil came and whispered to the king that there was such a woman—his own daughter. The devil spurred the king to propose marriage to the girl, but she was appropriately outraged by this incestuous overture and fled across the English Channel to Belgium. There the king overtook her and with Satan at his elbow, slew the girl and her faithful attendants. In the night the angels came, recapitated the body and concealed it in the forest near the village of Gheel. Years later five lunatics chained together spent the night with their keepers at a small wayside shrine near this Belgian village. Overnight all the victims recovered. Here indeed must be the place where the dead girl, reincarnated as St. Dymphna, was buried, and here was the sacred spot where her cures of the insane are effected. In the 15th century pilgrimages to Gheel from every part of the civilized world were organized for the mentally sick. Many of the pilgrims remained in Gheel to live with the inhabitants of the locality, and in the passing years it became the natural thing to accept them into the homes and thus the first 'colony' was formed and for that matter the only one which has been consistently successful." (Karnosh & Zucker, 1945, p. 15)

The colony of Gheel has continued its work into modern times (Aring, 1974, 1975b; Belgian Consulate, 1982). Today more than two thousand certified mental patients live in private homes, work with the inhabitants, and suffer few restrictions other than not using alcohol. Many types of mental disorders are represented, including schizophrenia, affective disorder, antisocial personality, and mental retardation. Ordinarily, patients remain in Gheel until they are considered recovered by a supervising therapist. It is unfortunate that the great humanitarian work of this colony—and the opportunity Gheel affords to study the treatment of mental patients in a family and community setting—has received so little recognition.

Humanitarian reform

Clearly, by the late eighteenth century most mental hospitals in Europe and America were in need of reform. The movement toward humanitarian treatment of patients received its first great impetus from the work of Philippe Pinel (1745–1826) in France.

Pinel's experiment. In 1792, shortly after the first phase of the French Revolution came to a close, Pinel was placed in charge of La Bicêtre (the hospital for the insane in Paris to which we have previously referred). In this capacity he received the grudging permission of the Revolutionary Commune to remove the chains from some of the inmates as an experiment to test his views that mental patients should be treated with kindness and consideration—as sick people and not as vicious beasts or criminals. Had his experiment proved a failure, Pinel might well have lost his head, but, fortunately for all, it proved to be a great success. Chains were removed, sunny rooms were provided instead of dungeons, patients were permitted to exercise on the hospital grounds, and kindness was extended to these poor creatures, some of whom had been chained in dungeons for thirty years or more. The effect was almost miraculous. The previous noise, filth, and abuse were replaced by order and peace. As Pinel said: "The whole discipline was marked with regularity and kindness which had the most favorable effect on the insane themselves, rendering even the most furious more tractable" (Selling, 1943, p. 65).

The reactions of these patients when all their chains were removed for the first time is a pathetic story. One patient, an English officer who had years before killed a guard in an attack of fury, tottered outside on legs weak from lack of use, and for the first time in some forty years saw the sun and sky. With tears in his eyes he exclaimed, "Oh, how beautiful! (Zilboorg & Henry, 1941, p. 323). Finally, when night came, he voluntarily returned to his cell, which had been cleaned during his absence, to fall peacefully asleep on his new bed. After two years of orderly behavior, including helping to handle other patients, he was pronounced recovered and permitted to leave the hospital.

Pinel was later given charge of the Salpêtrière Hospital, where the same reorganization in treatment was instituted with similarly gratifying results. The Bicêtre and Salpêtrière hospitals thus became the first modern hospitals for the care of the insane. Pinel's successor, Jean Esquirol (1772–1840), continued his good work at the Salpêtrière and, in addition, helped in the establishment of some ten new mental hospitals, which helped put France in the forefront of humane treatment for the mentally disturbed.

It is a curious fact of history that Pinel was saved from the hands of a mob who suspected him of antirevolutionary activities by a soldier whom he had freed from asylum chains.

Tuke's work in England. At about the same time that Pinel was reforming the Bicêtre Hospital, an English Quaker named William Tuke established the "York Retreat," a pleasant country house where mental patients lived,

This painting shows Philippe Pinel supervising the unchaining of inmates at La Bicêtre hospital. Pinel's experiment represented both a great reform and a major step in devising humanitarian methods of treating mental disorders.

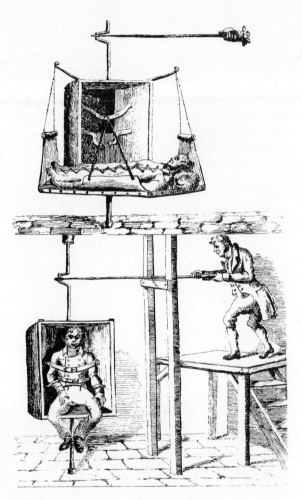

Even after reform of mental institutions had begun, various devices were used to control unmanageable patients: the crib (above), used as late as 1882 to restrain violent patients; the "tranquilizing chair" of Benjamin Rush (top left); and the circulating swing, used in the early nineteenth century to bring the mentally disordered back to sound reasoning (top right). It was said that "no well-regulated institution should be without one."

worked, and rested in a kindly religious atmosphere. This represented the culmination of a noble battle against the brutality, ignorance, and indifference of his time. Some insight into the difficulties and discouragements he encountered in the establishment of the York Retreat may be gleaned from a simple statement he made in a letter regarding his early efforts: "All men seem to desert me." This is not surprising when we remember that demonology was still widespread, and that as late as 1768 we find the Protestant John Wesley's famous declaration that "The giving up of witchcraft is in effect the giving up of the Bible." The belief in demonology was too strong to be conquered overnight.

As word of the amazing results obtained by Pinel spread to England, Tuke's small force of

Quakers gradually gained support from John Connolly, Samuel Hitch, and other great English medical psychologists. In 1841 Hitch introduced trained women nurses into the wards at the Gloucester Asylum and put trained supervisors at the head of the nursing staffs. These innovations, regarded as quite revolutionary at the time, were of great importance not only in improving the care of mental patients but also in changing public attitudes toward the mentally disturbed.

Rush and moral therapy in America.

The success of Pinel's and Tuke's experiments in humanitarian methods revolutionized the treatment of mental patients throughout the civilized world. In the United States, this was reflected in the work of Benjamin Rush (1745–1813), the founder of American psychiatry. While associated with the Pennsylvania Hospital in 1783, Rush encouraged more humane treatment of the mentally ill, wrote the first systematic treatise on psychiatry in America, *Medical Inquiries and Observations upon the Diseases of the Mind* (1812), and was the first American to organize a course in psychiatry. But even he did not escape entirely from the established beliefs of his time. His medical theory was tainted with astrology, and his principal remedies were bloodletting and purgatives. In addition, he invented and used a device called "the tranquilizer," which was probably more torturous than tranquil for the patient. Despite these limitations, however, we may consider Rush an important transitional figure between the old era and the new.

During the early part of this period of humanitarian reform, the use of "moral therapy" in mental hospitals became relatively widespread. This approach stemmed largely from the work of Pinel and Tuke. As Rees (1957) has described it.:

"The insane came to be regarded as normal people who had lost their reason as a result of having been exposed to severe psychological and social stresses. These stresses were called the moral causes of insanity, and moral treatment aimed at relieving the patient by friendly association, discussion of his difficulties, and the daily pursuit of purposeful activity; in other words, social therapy, individual therapy, and occupational therapy." (pp. 306–7)

Moral therapy achieved an almost incredible level of effectiveness—all the more amazing because it was done without the benefit of the antipsychotic drugs so prevalent today, and because, we must surmise, many of the patients so treated were suffering from the then-incurable neurological disease of central-nervous-system syphilis. In the twenty-year period between 1833 and 1853, Worcester State Hospital's discharge rate for patients who had been ill less than one year prior to admission was 71 percent; even for patients with a longer preadmission disorder it was 59 percent (Bockhoven, 1972).

Despite its relative effectiveness, however, moral therapy declined and was nearly abandoned by the latter part of the nineteenth century. The reasons were many and varied. Among the more obvious ones were ethnic and racial prejudice that came with the rising immigrant population and consequent distancing and impersonality between staff and patients; a failure of the leadership to train their own replacements; and the overextension of hospital facilities, reflecting the misguided belief that bigger hospitals would differ from smaller ones only in size.

Two other, less obvious, reasons for the demise of moral therapy are, in retrospect, truly ironic. One was the rise of the mental hygiene movement, which focused almost exclusively on the *physical* well-being of mental patients in hospitals. Thus, though the creature comforts of patients may have improved under the mental hygienists, the patients received no help for their mental problems and were thus condemned in a subtle way to helplessness and dependency.

An emphasis on the physical basis of mental illness was also characteristic of the other historical trend that contributed to the demise of moral therapy. Brilliant advances in biomedical science fostered the notion that all mental disorders would sooner or later yield to biological explanations and appropriate biologically based treatment. As such, the psychological and social environment of the patient was considered largely irrelevant in treatment; the best one could do was keep the patient comfortable until the biological cure was discovered. Needless to say, the anticipated biological cure-all did not arrive, and by the late 1940s and early 1950s, discharge rates were down to about 30 percent. We do better today, with discharge rates above 90 percent, but this is a very recent development due to a number of factors, including advances in drug therapy and a trend to release many patients for continued care in their communities.

Notwithstanding its negative effects on the use of moral therapy, the mental hygiene movement has accounted for many positive humanitarian accomplishments. Some of these are reviewed in what follows.

Dix and the beginning of the mental hygiene movement.   Dorothea Dix (1802–1887) was an energetic New England schoolteacher forced into early retirement because of recurring attacks of tuberculosis. In 1841 she began to teach in a women's prison. Through this contact she soon became acquainted with the deplorable conditions prevalent in jails, alms-houses, and asylums. In a "Memorial" submitted to the Congress of the United States in 1848, she stated that she had seen "more than 9000 idiots, epileptics and insane in the United States, destitute of appropriate care and protection . . . bound with galling chains, bowed beneath fetters and heavy iron balls attached to drag-chains, lacerated with ropes, scourged with rods and terrified beneath storms of execration and cruel blows; now subject to jibes and scorn and torturing tricks; now abandoned to the most outrageous violations" (Zilboorg & Henry, 1941, pp. 583–84).

As a result of her findings, Dix carried on a zealous campaign between 1841 and 1881 that aroused the people and the legislatures to an awareness of the inhuman treatment accorded the mentally ill. Through her efforts many millions of dollars were raised to build suitable hospitals, and some twenty states responded directly to her appeals. Not only was she instrumental in improving conditions in hospitals in the United States, but she directed the opening of two large institutions in Canada, and completely reformed the asylum system in Scotland and several other countries. She is credited with the establishment of some thirty-two mental hospitals, an astonishing record considering the ignorance and superstition that still prevailed in the field of mental health. She rounded out her career by organizing the nursing forces of the northern armies during the Civil War. A resolution presented by the United States Congress in 1901 characterized her as "among the noblest examples of humanity in all history" (Karnosh & Zucker, 1945, p. 18).

The foundations of twentieth century views

It is difficult to partition modern views of abnormal behavior into discrete, uniform attitudes or to trace their historical precedents without appearing somewhat arbitrary and overly simplistic. Also, as we shall see, much that has happened in the nineteenth and twentieth centuries becomes the subject matter of the next chapter. However, a brief, selective overview is in order here to bring us into the twentieth century and set the scene for Chapter 3.

Changing attitudes toward mental health

By the end of the nineteenth century the mental hospital or asylum—"the big house on the hill"—with its high turrets and fortresslike appearance had become a familiar landmark in America. In it mental patients lived under semi-adequate conditions of comfort and freedom from abuse. To the general public, however, the asylum was an eerie place, and its occupants a strange and frightening lot.

Little was done by the resident psychiatrists to educate the public along lines that would reduce the general fear and horror of insanity.[2] One principal reason for this, of course, was that the early psychiatrist had very little actual information to impart. As late as 1840 a German physician, Dr. Heinroth, was still advancing the theory that sin produced insanity and repentance a cure, and that piety was conducive to mental health (Lewis, 1941).

Gradually, however, important strides were made toward changing the attitude of the general public toward mental patients. In America, the pioneering work of Dix in educating the public about mental disorders was followed up by that of Clifford Beers, whose now-famous book, *A Mind That Found Itself,* was published in 1908. Beers, a Yale graduate, described his own

---

[2]It is of interest to note that psychiatrists were formerly called *alienists*—and in some places still are—referring to persons who treat the "alienated" or insane.

These three people contributed greatly to our contemporary views of mental disorders.
Teresa of Avila (1515–1582, left) argued that her hysterical nuns were "as if sick," paving
the way for the view that the mind can be just as sick as the body. Dorothea Dix (1802–
1887, center) was a tireless reformer who made great strides in changing public attitudes
toward mental patients. And Wilhelm Wundt (1832–1920, right) established the first
experimental psychology laboratory, which led others to use scientific methods to investigate
psychological processes including mental disorders.

mental collapse and told of the bad treatment he received in three typical institutions of the day, and of his eventual recovery in the home of a friendly attendant. Although chains and other torture devices had long since been given up, the straitjacket was still widely used as a means of "quieting" excited patients. Beers experienced this treatment and supplied a vivid description of what such painful immobilization of the arms means to an overwrought mental patient in terms of intensification of inner excitement. He began a campaign to make people realize that this was no way to handle the sick, winning the interest and support of many public-spirited individuals, including the eminent psychologist William James, and the "dean of American psychiatry," Adolf Meyer.

Growth of scientific research

At about the same time that the mental hygiene movement was gaining ground in the U.S. (during the latter years of the nineteenth century), great technological discoveries and advances were occurring both at home and abroad. These contributed to the beginnings of what we know today as a scientific, or experimentally oriented, view of abnormal behavior, and the application of this knowledge to bettering the situation of disturbed individuals.

Most immediately apparent were advances made in the study of biological and anatomical

factors underlying both physical and mental disorders. The biomedical breakthrough came with the discovery of the organic factors underlying general paresis, one of the most serious mental illnesses of the day. General paresis produced paralysis and insanity and typically brought about the death of the afflicted subject within two to five years. The investigation into the cause of paresis—syphilis of the brain—and of a cure—in essence, infecting the sufferer with malarial fever—stretched over a period of nearly one hundred years (see **HIGHLIGHT** on page 52.) Though today we have a far simpler treatment available through the use of penicillin, this early treatment represented, for the first time in all history, a clear-cut conquest of a mental disorder by medical science. We had come far from where we began—from a belief in demons to scientific proof of how brain pathology can cause a specific disorder. As we have mentioned, this raised great hopes in the medical community that organic bases would be found for many other mental disorders—perhaps for all.

Yet despite the emphasis on biological causation, scientific investigation into psychological factors and human behavior was progressing too. In 1879, Wilhelm Wundt (1832–1920) established the first experimental psychology laboratory at the University of Leipzig. While studying the psychological factors involved in memory and sensation, Wundt and his colleagues devised many basic experimental methods and

HIGHLIGHT

Events leading to the discovery of organic factors in general paresis

Scientific discoveries do not occur overnight; usually they require the combined efforts of many scientists over extended periods of time. And such discoveries rarely proceed sequentially from point a to point z. Rather, they often result from a very uncoordinated process in which many scientists pursue hypotheses that are later seen as dead ends, go off on tangents, refuse to accept "evidence," experience crises in their thinking, and so on.

Abbreviated descriptions of the events that have led to scientific discoveries often fail to capture the excitement, intrigue, and frustration that entered into the process. With this caution in mind, we identify below ten key steps in the long search to find a cure for general paresis.

1. Differentiation of general paresis as a specific type of mental disorder by the French physician A. L. J. Bayle in 1825. Bayle gave a very complete and accurate description of the symptom pattern of paresis and convincingly presented his reasons for believing paresis to be a distinct disorder.

2. Report by Esmarch and Jessen in 1857 of paretic patients known to have had syphilis and their conclusion that the syphilis caused the paresis.

3. Description by the Scot Argyll-Robertson in 1869 of the failure of the pupillary reflex to light (failure of the pupil of the eye to narrow under bright light) as diagnostic of the involvement of the central nervous system in syphilis.

4. Experiment by Viennese psychiatrist Krafft-Ebing in 1897, involving the inoculation of paretic patients with matter from syphilitic sores. None developed secondary symptoms of syphilis, which led to the conclusion that they must previously have been infected. This crucial experiment definitely established the relationship of general paresis to syphilis.

5. Discovery of the *Spirochaeta pallida* by Schaudinn in 1905 as the cause of syphilis.

6. Development by von Wassermann in 1906 of a blood test for syphilis. Now it became possible to check for the presence of the deadly spirochetes in the bloodstream of individuals before the more serious consequences of infection appeared.

7. Application by Plant in 1908 of the Wasserman test to the cerebrospinal fluid, to indicate whether or not the spirochete had invaded the patient's central nervous system.

8. Development by Paul Ehrlich in 1909, after 605 failures, of the arsenical compound arsphenamine (which he thereupon called "606") for the treatment of syphilis. Although "606" proved effective in killing the syphilitic spirochetes in the bloodstream, it was not effective against the spirochetes that had penetrated the central nervous system.

9. Verification by Noguchi and Moore in 1913 of the syphilitic spirochete as the brain-damaging agent in general paresis. They discovered these spirochetes in the postmortem study of the brains of patients who had suffered from paresis.

10. Introduction in 1917 by Wagner-Jauregg, chief of the psychiatric clinic of the University of Vienna, of the malarial fever treatment of syphilis and paresis. He inoculated nine paretic patients with the blood of a soldier who was ill with malaria and found marked improvement in three patients and apparent recovery in three of the others.

---

strategies that set the standard for later studies. Early contributors to the empirical study of abnormal behavior were directly influenced by Wundt; they followed his experimental methodology and also used some of his research strategies to study clinical problems. For example, a student of Wundt, J. McKeen Cattell (1860–1944) brought Wundt's experimental methods to the United States and made use of them to assess individual differences in mental processing. He and other students of Wundt established research laboratories throughout the United States. It was not until 1896, however, that another of his students, Lightner Witmer (1867–1956), combined research with application: he established the first psychological clinic in the United States at the University of Pennsylvania. The focus of Witmer's clinic was on problems of mentally deficient children, both in terms of research and therapy. Other clinics followed. One of note was the Chicago Juvenile Psychopathic Institute (later called the Institute of Juvenile Research), established in 1909 by William Healy (1869–1963). Healy was the first to describe juvenile delinquency as a symptom of the phenomenon of urbanization and not due to inner psychological problems. In so doing, he became the first to seize upon a new area of causation—namely environmental, or sociocultural, factors.

By the first decade of the twentieth century, psychological laboratories and clinics were burgeoning, and a great deal of research was being generated. Rapid and objective communication of scientific findings is perhaps as important in the development of a science as the collection and interpretation of research findings, and this period saw the origin of many scientific journals for the dissemination of research and theoretical discoveries. Two notable publications in the field of abnormal psychology were the *Journal of Abnormal Psychology,* founded by Morton Prince in 1906, and *The Psychological Clinic,* founded by Lightner Witmer in 1907. As the years have passed, the number of journals has grown. The audience has grown, too, so that today some magazines are directed specifically at the general reader. The many avenues available for communicating new findings ensures that important new discoveries will become widely known. Yet the very amount of information available can cause confusion and controversy, as we shall see in Chapter 3. We may have left supernatural demons behind, but we have moved into something far more complex in our view of the role of natural factors—be they biological, psychological, or sociocultural—that lie behind abnormal behavior.

Summary

The development of views of psychopathology from ancient times to the present has not followed a straight evolutionary path, though we *can* trace a general movement away from superstitious and "magical" explanations of abnormal behavior and toward reasoned scientific explanations.

Early beliefs in demonology and exorcism were followed by the emergence of early medical concepts in such places as Egypt and Greece; many of these concepts were developed and refined by Roman physicians. With the fall of Rome near the end of the fifth century A.D., most Europeans returned to the primitive concepts of demonology, and these views continued to dominate popular thinking about mental disorders for over a thousand years. In the fifteenth and early sixteenth centuries it was still widely believed that mentally disturbed people were possessed by the devil. Many individuals suffered inhumane treatment, including torture and death, as a result of official church policies on witchcraft and as a result of numerous efforts to rid the church of heretics.

During the latter stages of the Middle Ages, however, a spirit of scientific questioning reappeared in Europe, and several noted physicians spoke out against inhumane treatment, arguing that "possessed" individuals were actually "sick of mind" and should be treated as such. More humanitarian treatment of disturbed people came with the founding of various "asylums" for the mentally disturbed toward the end of the sixteenth century. In the eighteenth century, further efforts were made to help afflicted individuals by providing them with better conditions and kind treatment.

The nineteenth and early twentieth centuries witnessed a number of scientific and humanitarian advances. The work of Philippe Pinel in France, William Tuke in England, and Benjamin Rush and Dorothea Dix in the United States prepared the way for several later developments which have had notable impact on contemporary abnormal psychology. Among these developments were the gradual acceptance of mental patients as afflicted individuals who need and deserve professional attention; the success of biomedical methods as applied to disorders such as general paresis; and the growth of scientific research into the biological, psychological, and sociocultural roots of abnormal behavior.

Understanding this developmental sequence, with its forward steps and reverses, helps us understand the emergence of modern concepts of psychopathology and provides us with a perspective for understanding the advances that have come about and are yet to come.

3

Biological, psychosocial, and sociocultural viewpoints

Robert "Scottie" Wilson, Thinking About Houses. *Wilson (b. 1890) grew up in a poor family in Glasgow Scotland. An itinerant merchant by trade, he traveled extensively, making his home at various times in Scotland, London, and Canada. In his early forties, while living in Toronto, Wilson suddenly began to make complex sketches in ink on various surfaces. His stylized self-portraits and symbolic designs (sometimes, as here, depicting grotesque or cartoonish faces) reveal Wilson's originality and inward-looking vision.*

In the preceding chapter, we examined the widely varying interpretations used over the centuries to explain the sources of deviant behavior, from beliefs in supernatural possession to theories of naturally occurring biological, psychological, and sociocultural factors. In this chapter, we shall look at the several broad viewpoints that have developed from theories of natural causation. These viewpoints represent the state of the art as we know it today; they currently dominate professional approaches to understanding abnormal behavior and form the basis for the types of therapy we will discuss in Chapters 16 and 17. They are very much an outgrowth of the events described in Chapter 2, and, since we can expect them to continue evolving to meet new ideas and discoveries, they may well represent tomorrow's "history."

Students are often perplexed by the fact that, in the behavioral sciences especially, several competing explanations are advanced to account for the same phenomena—for example, the behaviors associated with mental disorders. The human mind evidently has a strong tendency to find explanations, to seek final answers. Even in the most "exact" of the scientific disciplines, however, final answers are rarely if ever achieved (see **HIGHLIGHT** on page 56). Usually we have only tentative approximations. Science does not seek or expect ultimate truth but only adequate ways of understanding nature.

In general, the more complex the phenomena being investigated, the greater the number of diverse viewpoints to emerge, all attempting to explain the phenomena, which, in our case, are abnormal behaviors. Inevitably, not all these viewpoints will be equally valid. As we shall see, the applicability of a viewpoint is often determined by the extent to which it seems helpful in understanding a given case.

In this chapter our survey of the major viewpoints of abnormal behavior will be *eclectic,* in the sense of being both comprehensive and, we hope, objective. We begin with a consideration of the biological viewpoint. From there we shall move on to the several psychosocial approaches, including the psychoanalytic, behavioristic, humanistic, and interpersonal perspectives; we shall look briefly, too, at the sociocultural viewpoint. Finally, we will investigate possible avenues toward an interdisciplinary approach to the study of abnormal behavior.

The biological viewpoint

Many professionals in the field, especially those with medical backgrounds, believe that most, if not all, abnormal behavior is the product of aberrant biophysical processes occurring chiefly in the brains of affected persons. This view represents the *biological viewpoint.* In its most extreme form, this perspective holds that a mental disorder is similar to a medical disease, except that the primary symptoms are behavioral rather than physiological or anatomical. In such a case, neither psychological factors nor the psychosocial environment of the individual is believed to play a causal role in the mental disorder; rather, mental disorder is viewed as a disease of the central nervous system whose rudiments are either acquired by pathophysiologic processes or inherited. A less extreme version of the biological viewpoint holds that, in most cases, at the root of causation are biochemical processes in the brain or elsewhere that become imbalanced (for whatever reason) and thereby disrupt the normal behavior of the individual.

To an extent, these two versions of the biological viewpoint mirror, respectively, the early and more recent developments in the field.

Roots of the biological viewpoint

As we have seen, we can look far back into our history and find individuals who suspected that organic factors played a role in psychopathology. However, to find the more direct roots of our current views, we need not look back very far.

Establishment of brain pathology as a causal factor.   With the emergence of modern experimental science in the early part of the eighteenth century, knowledge of anatomy, physiology, neurology, chemistry, and general medicine increased rapidly. These advances led not only to the further demise of lingering beliefs in demonology but more importantly to the gradual identification of the biological, or organic, pathology underlying many physical ailments. That is, scientists focused on body or-

HIGHLIGHT

Paradigm shifts—toward a new biological viewpoint?

The coexistence of several different viewpoints in a field of science, as we see in this chapter, is not at all unusual. The historian of science Thomas Kuhn (1962) has noted that, historically, theoretical orientations in science typically retain a strong hold over their adherents, even in the face of disconfirming evidence and equally plausible alternative explanations of observable phenomena. They do so until some new and fundamental insight is achieved that appears to resolve the problems left unsolved by the conflicting interpretations of the empirical data. These new insights constitute "paradigm shifts," fundamental reorganizations of how people think about an entire field of science; they parallel in certain ways the momentous cognitive shifts a child undergoes in gaining an adult understanding of the nature of the world, a process well described in the work of Piaget.

In general, our understanding of nature proceeds from a limited understanding of the particular to a broadened understanding of how individual particulars are aspects of a more encompassing and orderly system. Freud was responsible for a massive paradigm shift in abnormal psychology, although—as is the ultimate fate of all such shifts—we now see much of his system under severe attack. We cannot yet discern with any clarity the next of the major paradigm shifts in the field, although the ascendancy of the (modern) biological viewpoint in recent years indicates one possible direction. If the biological viewpoint is to become a truly dominant force, however, its adherents will have to find ways of incorporating into its tenets a variety of well-established findings in the psychosocial and sociocultural areas.

gans as being diseased and thereby causing physical ailments. It was only another step for these workers to rediscover the idea of *mental disorder as an illness based on pathology of an organ*—in this case the *brain.*

In 1757, Albrecht von Haller (1708–1777) in his *Elements of Physiology* emphasized the importance of the brain in psychic functions and advocated studying the brains of the insane by postmortem dissection. The first systematic presentation of this viewpoint, however, was made by the German psychiatrist William Griesinger

(1817–1868). In his textbook *The Pathology and Therapy of Psychic Disorders,* published in 1845, Griesinger insisted that all mental disorders could be explained in terms of brain pathology and that psychiatry should thus proceed on a physiological and clinical basis.

It was in this encouraging climate that scientists ultimately discovered the organic cause of general paresis, which we discussed in Chapter 2. Other successes followed. The brain pathology in cerebral arteriosclerosis and in the senile psychoses was established by Alzheimer and other investigators. Eventually, the organic pathologies underlying the toxic psychoses, certain types of mental retardation, and other mental disorders were discovered.

It is important to note here that, although the discovery of the organic bases of mental disorders may have addressed the "how" behind causation, it did not, in most cases, address the question of "why." This is still often true to this day. For example, although we know what causes presenile psychoses—brain pathology— we do not yet know why some individuals are afflicted with it and others not. Nonetheless, we can predict quite accurately the course of the disorder. This is due not only to a greater understanding of the organic factors involved but also, in large part, to the work of a follower of Griesinger, Emil Kraepelin (1856–1926).

Beginnings of a classification system.
Kraepelin played the dominant role in the early development of the biological viewpoint. His textbook, *Lehrbuch der Psychiatrie,* published in 1883, not only emphasized the importance of brain pathology in mental disorders but also made several related contributions that helped establish this viewpoint. The most important of these was his system of classification, which became the forerunner of today's DSM-III (discussed in Chapter 1). Kraepelin noted that certain symptom patterns occurred with sufficient regularity to be regarded as specific types of mental disease. He then proceeded to describe and clarify these types of mental disorders, working out the scheme of classification that is the basis of our present categories. The integration of the clinical material underlying this classification was a herculean task and represented a major contribution to the field of psychopathology.

Kraepelin looked upon each type of mental

Emil Kraepelin (1856–1926), by integrating clinical data, worked out one of the first systematic classification systems, a forerunner of the modern DSM-III.

disorder as separate and distinct from the others, and thought that the course of each was as predetermined and predictable as the course of measles. Such conclusions led to widespread interest in the accurate description and classification of mental disorders, for by this means the outcome of a given type of disorder could presumably be predicted even if it could not yet be controlled.

Advances achieved as a result of early biological views.
Although early biologically based thinking was perhaps too widely adopted before its limitations were recognized, it represented the first great advance of modern science toward the understanding and treatment of mental disorder. Demonology as a causal explanation was finally demolished with the demonstration that natural events could sometimes account for abnormal behavior—with the result that mental patients were now seen as sick rather than morally depraved. In turn, an enormous research effort was undertaken to discover specific causes of disorder that would yield to specific medical treatment. Such efforts necessarily entailed differentiating various forms of abnormality, leading to a promising system for classifying separate disorders. These were substantial accomplishments.

And yet, not all of the consequences of this early thinking were positive. Because the disorders best understood in terms of then-available knowledge were ones in which brain damage or deterioration were a central feature, as in general paresis, there naturally developed an expectation that *all* abnormal behavior would eventually be explained by reference to gross brain pathology of one sort or another. To be sure, "organic mental disorders" do occur and we will describe them in Chapter 13, but the vast majority of abnormal behavior is *not* associated with physical damage to brain tissue. Thus, a conceptual model that is inappropriate to much abnormal behavior, sometimes called the "medical model," became somewhat stubbornly entrenched by these early but limited successes.

It may be noted here that a medical-model orientation is not limited to biological viewpoints on the nature of mental disorder. It has also extended into some more psychosocial theorizing by way of the adoption of a *symptom/underlying-cause* point of view. The assumption is made, in other words, that abnormal behavior is a "symptom" of some sort of underlying, internal pathology (or "illness")—even though that pathology may be seen as psychological in nature. As we shall see later in the chapter, Freud, who was a physician, took this approach in developing the psychoanalytic viewpoint of abnormal behavior.

Modern biological thinking

As we have seen, the earliest disorders recognized to have biological or organic components were those associated with gross destruction of brain tissue. In essence, then, such disorders were *neurological* diseases—to which was added, in many but not all cases, a psychological/behavioral aberration. It is important here to distinguish between neurological disease of the brain (the temporary or permanent disruption of brain functioning by physical or chemical means) and the abnormal mental states (such as delusions) that sometimes accompany neurological disease.

Even in cases of brain damage, thought content that is bizarre by a given culture's standards need not be, and probably never is, the direct result of the brain damage. Rather, the neurologically damaged person will have more challenges to overcome, and these will probably be made all the more difficult because of the person's lack of resources for coping with those challenges. In such instances it would not be unusual for the psychopathological manifestations of the disorder to be psychologically induced,

The effect of chemical processes on behavior is most evident in cases involving the use of intoxicating substances. The youth shown above would probably not exhibit this kind of behavior under conditions of normal sobriety.

especially if the individual were lacking in personal resources at the outset. Moreover, while behavioral *impairment* (e.g., memory loss) is readily accounted for by structural damage to the brain, it is not so readily apparent how such damage could produce the often bizarre *content* of the behavior one frequently observes in these conditions. For example, we can understand by reference to brain damage how loss of neurons in general paresis could lead to difficulties in *executing* behavior; but the fact that the individual claims to be Napoleon is not likely to be the result simply of a loss of neurons. So far as we know, there are no "I am (or am not) Napoleon" neurons in the brain. Such an idea must be the product of some sort of functional integration of many different neural structures, some of which have been "programmed" by past experience.

In addition, many conditions temporarily disrupt the information-processing capabilities of the brain *without* inflicting permanent damage or death to the neural cells involved. In these cases, normal functioning is altered by the context—especially the chemical context—in which they operate. The most routine example here is probably that of alcohol intoxication. In that condition, behavior that would normally be inhibited is sometimes given free rein, only to be regretted the morning after.

The point is that we now realize that many processes short of brain damage can affect the functional capacity of the brain and thus change behavior. This is the basic tenet of the biological perspective today—that biochemical imbalance in the brain can result in abnormal behavior. Some adherents of this view even suggest that psychological stress can bring on such biochemical imbalance.

The most substantial of the sources of a resurgent biological impetus derive from discoveries in two areas: (a) behavior genetics and (b) biophysical therapies. Since we will be examining these processes in depth later, we will deal with them here only briefly.

Behavior genetics.
Genes affect biochemical processes and thereby the structure and physiologic functioning of organisms. Though behavior is never determined exclusively by genes, organisms are genetically "programmed" through biochemical processes to more or less adapt, physically and behaviorally, to their environment. In general, the more complex the organism, the greater its built-in capacity to meet and overcome the challenges of its environment. It requires little imagination to suppose that because of genetic endowment some human organisms have a greater or lesser adaptive capacity than others. This idea is fraught with many unfortunate sociopolitical, racial overtones, and it has occasionally been misused by both scientists and politicians. Nonetheless, there is substantial evidence that some mental disorders may have a hereditary component. Since any intergenerational genetic transmission of "traits" is, by definition, a biological process, the biological viewpoint has received significant support from many recent findings that implicate heredity as an important causal factor in several of the major mental disorders (e.g., Neale & Oltmanns, 1980; Paykel, 1982).

The extent to which genetically determined hormone levels control the behavioral propensities of fetuses and newborns is still far from understood. Knowledge in this area is probably most advanced in the area of gender-related behaviors. Building on the earlier work of Money and Ehrhardt (1972), several investigators have amassed convincing evidence that the brain pathways that determine behavior in males and females differ in certain ways because chromosomal differences cause differences in the hormones produced in each sex (Ehrhardt & Meyer-Bahlburg, 1981; MacLusky & Naftolin, 1981; McEwen, 1981; Rubin, Reinisch, & Haskett, 1981).

It appears probable, too, that many broad, temperamental features of newborns and children are genetically determined. It would not be surprising if such characteristics turned out to be relevant to individuals' later mental health. The idea that temperament affects mental health is a very ancient one, but, in its modern guise, it constitutes an important element in the biological approach to mental disorders.

Biophysical therapies.
Advances in the understanding and treatment of mental disorders, with certain exceptions, essentially languished through the first third of the current century—while discharge rates from mental hospitals were declining and resident populations of such hospitals were rising at an alarming pace. The earlier version of the biological viewpoint had not fulfilled its promise. Then, beginning in the 1930s, new therapies were introduced that seemed to have significant benefits in some cases and, furthermore, seemed to alter the biophysical status of the organism. One of these then-revolutionary therapies, namely electroconvulsive therapy (ECT), is still in wide use today. ECT produces a convulsion by passing an electric current through the brain. In certain instances, this treatment results in the patient's prompt return to normal functioning. How electroconvulsive therapy works is still not fully understood, although some promising work has been done in this area (Abrams & Essman, 1982).

More importantly, since the 1950's, we have witnessed many new and often dramatic developments in the use of drugs to treat mental disorders—in particular the more severe ones. In contrast to the situation with ECT, we also have a variety of rather good hunches as to how these medications produce their beneficial effects. That is, we know to at least some extent what biochemical changes are caused by taking these drugs, and we can correlate those effects with beneficial changes in the patient's behavior. These observations in turn have led to intriguing hypotheses about the chemical imbalances that accompany, and may be causally related to, the disorders that respond favorably to particular drugs.

Impact on our views of psychopathology.
In the modern era, biological discoveries have profoundly affected the way we think about human behavior. We now recognize the important role of biochemical factors and innate characteristics, many of which are genetically determined, in both normal and abnormal behavior.

The host of new drugs that can alter dramatically and quickly the severity and even the course of certain mental disorders has brought renewed attention to the biological viewpoint, not only in scientific circles but also in the popular media. Further advances here are a foregone conclusion. Hopes are high that somewhere within the field of biological research lies the answer to many of our mental problems. The biological treatments seem to have more immediate results than other available therapies; and the hope is that they may in most cases lead to immediate results with seemingly little effort—the "cure-all," we might say.

However, it would be well to remind ourselves that very few, if any, of the mental afflictions we suffer as human beings are independent of what we are as personalities or of the problems we face in trying to live our lives. Viewpoints that emphasize these psychological and sociocultural considerations are examined in the pages that follow. Before proceeding, however, it should be noted that biological and psychosociocultural approaches to abnormal behavior are *not* fundamentally incompatible, as superficial analyses often suggest. The real challenge is to understand how the varying factors interact with one another.

Psychosocial viewpoints

There are many more psychosocial interpretations of abnormal behavior than biological ones, reflecting the greater complexity of humans as persons versus humans as biological organisms. Here we shall examine four explanations of human nature and behavior—psychoanalytic, behavioristic, humanistic, and interpersonal. Although these perspectives represent distinct and sometimes conflicting orientations, they are also, as we shall see, in many ways complementary. All of them emphasize the importance of early experience, and all of them take some cognizance of social influences as well as of psychological processes within the individual—hence the term *psychosocial* as a general descriptive label.

The psychoanalytic perspective

The first systematic steps toward understanding psychological factors in mental disorders came about through the astounding contributions of one man—Sigmund Freud (1856–1939). Freud developed his psychoanalytic perspective over a period of five decades of observing and writing. His major principles were based on the clinical study of individual patients who consulted him for treatment of their problems.

In reviewing the psychoanalytic approach, it is useful to divide our discussion into an examination of (a) the roots of psychoanalysis, (b) Freud and the beginnings of psychoanalysis, (c) the basic principles of psychoanalysis, and (d) the impact of psychoanalysis on our views of human nature and human behavior.

Roots of psychoanalytic thought. We find the early roots of psychoanalysis in a somewhat unexpected place—in the study of hypnosis, especially in its relation to hysteria.

1. *Mesmerism.* Our story starts with one of the most notoroious figures in psychiatry, Anton Mesmer (1734–1815), who further developed Paracelsus' notion of the influence of the planets on the human body (see Chapter 2). Their influence was believed to be caused by a universal magnetic fluid, and it was presumably the distribution of this fluid in the body that determined health or disease. In attempting to find a cure for mental disorders, Mesmer came to the conclusion that all persons possess magnetic forces that can be used to influence the distribution of the magnetic fluid in other persons, thus effecting cures.

Mesmer attempted to put his views into practice in Vienna and in various other towns, but it was not until he came to Paris in 1778 that he obtained a following. Here he opened a clinic in which he treated all kinds of diseases by "animal magnetism." The patients were seated around a tub (a *baquet*) containing various chemicals, from which protruded iron rods that were applied to the affected portions of the body, the room was darkened, appropriate music was played, and Mesmer appeared in a lilac robe, passing from

It took some time before Charcot (1825–1893), the leading neurologist of his time, believed that there might be a causal relationship between self-hypnosis and hysteria. Once convinced, however, he did much through lectures about hypnosis, such as the one shown here, and research to promote interest in the role psychological factors may play in mental disorders.

one patient to another and touching each one with his hands or his wand. By this means Mesmer was apparently able to remove hysterical anesthesias and paralyses and to demonstrate most of the phenomena discovered later by the use of hypnosis.

Eventually branded as a charlatan by his medical colleagues, Mesmer was forced to leave Paris, and he shortly faded into obscurity. However, his methods and results were the center of controversy in scientific circles for many years— in fact, mesmerism in the early part of the nineteenth century was as much a source of heated discussion as psychoanalysis was to be in the early part of the twentieth century. This discussion eventually led to a revival of interest in the hypnotic phenomenon as itself an explanation of the "cures" that took place.

2. *The "Nancy school."* One of the physicians who used hypnosis successfully in his practice was the Frenchman Liébeault (1823–1904), who practiced at Nancy. Also in Nancy at this time was a professor of medicine, Bernheim (1840–1919), who became interested in the relationship between hysteria and hypnosis, primarily as a result of Liébeault's success in curing by hypnosis a patient whom Bernheim had been treating unsuccessfully by more conventional methods for some four years (Selling, 1943). Bernheim and Liébeault worked together on the problem and developed the hypothesis that hypnotism and hysteria were related and that both were due to suggestion (Brown & Menninger, 1940). Their hypothesis was based on two

lines of evidence: (a) phenomena observed in hysteria, such as paralysis of an arm, inability to hear, or anesthetic areas in which the individual could be stuck with a pin without feeling pain— all of which occurred when there was apparently nothing organically wrong—could be produced in normal subjects by means of hypnosis; and (b) symptoms such as these could be removed by means of hypnosis so that the patient could use the formerly paralyzed arm, or hear, or feel in the previously anesthetized areas. Thus it seemed likely that hysteria was a sort of self-hypnosis. The physicians who accepted this view ultimately came to be known as the "Nancy school."

Meanwhile, Jean Charcot (1825–1893), who was head of the Salpétrière Hospital in Paris and the leading neurologist of his time, had been experimentally investigating some of the phenomena described by the old mesmerists. As a result of his research, Charcot disagreed with the findings of Bernheim and Liébeault and insisted that there were degenerative brain changes in hysteria. In this Charcot was eventually proved wrong, but work on the problem by so outstanding a scientist did a great deal to awaken medical and scientific interest in hysteria.

In one of the major medical debates of history, during which many harsh words were spoken on both sides, the adherents of the Nancy school finally triumphed. The recognition of one psychologically caused mental disorder (hysteria) spurred research, and it soon became apparent that psychological factors were involved in anxiety states, phobias, and other psychopathology. Eventually Charcot himself, a man of great scientific honesty, was won over to the new point of view and did much to promote an interest in the study of psychological factors in various mental disorders.

Toward the end of the nineteenth century, then, it was clear to many that there were mental disorders with a psychological basis as well as those with a biological basis. But one major question remained to be answered: How do the psychologically caused mental disorders actually come about?

Freud and the beginnings of psychoanalysis.

The first systematic attempt to answer this question was made by Sigmund Freud (1856–1939). Freud was a brilliant young Viennese physician who at first specialized in neurology and received an appointment as lecturer on nervous diseases at the University of Vienna. In 1885, he went to study under Charcot and later became acquainted with the work of Liébeault and Bernheim at Nancy. He was impressed by their use of hypnosis with hysterical patients and came away convinced that powerful mental processes can remain hidden from consciousness.

On his return to Vienna, Freud worked in collaboration with another physician, Joseph Breuer (1842–1925), who had introduced an interesting innovation in the use of hypnosis with his neurotic patients, chiefly women. Unlike hypnotists before him, he directed the patient under hypnosis to talk freely about her problems and about what bothered her. Under these circumstances the patient usually displayed considerable emotion, and on awakening from the hypnotic state felt considerably relieved. Because of the emotional release involved, this method was called the "cathartic method." This simple innovation in the use of hypnosis proved to be of great significance, for not only did it help the patient discharge her emotional tensions by discussion of her problems, but it revealed the nature of the difficulties that had brought about her neurotic symptoms. The patient saw no relationship between her problems and her hysterical symptoms, but the therapist could usually see it quite readily.

Thus was made the discovery of the "unconscious"—the realization of the important role played by unconscious processes in the determination of behavior. In 1893 Freud and Breuer published their joint paper, *On the Psychical Mechanisms of Hysterical Phenomena*, which constituted one of the great milestones of psychodynamics.[1]

Freud soon discovered, moreover, that he could dispense with the hypnotic state entirely. By encouraging the patient to say freely whatever came into her mind without regard to logic or decency, Freud found that she would eventually overcome inner obstacles to remembering and would discuss her problem freely. The new method was called *free association,* and the term *psychoanalysis* was given to the principles involved in analyzing and interpreting what the patient said and did, and in helping her gain insight and achieve a more adequate adjustment.

Freud devoted the remainder of his long and energetic life to the development and elaboration of psychoanalytic principles. His views were formally introduced to American scientists in 1909, when he delivered a famous series of lectures at Clark University at the invitation of G. Stanley Hall, the eminent American psychologist who was then president of the university. These *Introductory Lectures on Psychoanalysis* led to a great deal of controversy that helped publicize the concepts of psychoanalysis to both scientists and the general public.

Basics of the psychoanalytic perspective.

The psychoanalytic perspective is both highly systematized and complex, and we shall not attempt to deal with it in detail. Its general principles, however, may be sketched as follows:

1. *Id, ego, and superego.* Basically the individual's behavior is assumed to result from the interaction of three key subsystems within the personality: the id, ego, and superego.

The *id* is the source of instinctual drives, which are considered to be of two types: (a) constructive drives, primarily of a sexual nature, which constitute the *libido,* or basic energy of life, and (b) destructive drives which tend toward aggression, destruction, and eventual death. Thus *life,* or constructive, instincts are opposed by *death,* or destructive, instincts. Here it may be noted that Freud used the term *sex* in a broad sense to refer to almost anything pleasurable, from eating to creating a painting. The

---

[1]Psychoanalysis is sometimes referred to as a *psychodynamic* theory because it focuses on the "inner dynamics" of "psychic processes," such as drives and motives, to explain behavior.

id is completely selfish, concerned only with the immediate gratification of instinctual needs without reference to reality or moral considerations. Hence it is said to operate in terms of the *pleasure principle.* While the id can generate mental images and wish-fulfilling fantasies, referred to as the *primary process,* it cannot undertake the realistic action needed to meet instinctual demands.

Consequently a second key subsystem develops—the *ego*—which mediates between the demands of the id and the realities of the external world. The basic purpose of the ego is to meet id demands, but in such a way as to ensure the well-being and survival of the individual. This requires the use of reason and other intellectual resources in dealing with the external world, as well as the exercise of control over id demands. Such adaptive measures of the ego are referred to as the *secondary process,* and the ego is said to operate in terms of the *reality principle.* Freud viewed id demands, especially sexual and aggressive strivings, as inherently in conflict with rules and prohibitions imposed by society.

Since the id-ego relationship is merely one of expediency, Freud introduced a third key subsystem—the *superego*—which is the outgrowth of learning the taboos and moral values of society. The superego is essentially what we refer to as *conscience* and is concerned with right and wrong. As the superego develops, it becomes an additional inner control system that copes with the uninhibited desires of the id. However, the superego also operates through the ego system and strives to compel the ego to inhibit desires that are considered wrong or immoral.

Freud viewed the interplay among these subsystems of id, ego, and superego as of crucial significance in determining behavior. Often inner conflicts arise because the three subsystems are striving for different goals. These conflicts are called *intrapsychic conflicts* and, if unresolved, lead to mental disorder.

2. *Anxiety, defense mechanisms, and the unconscious.* The concept of anxiety is prominent in the psychoanalytic perspective. Freud distinguished among three types of anxiety, or "psychic pain," that people can suffer: (a) *reality* anxiety, arising from dangers or threats in the external world; (b) *neurotic* anxiety, caused by the id's impulses threatening to break through ego controls into behavior that will be punished in some way; and (c) *moral* anxiety, arising from

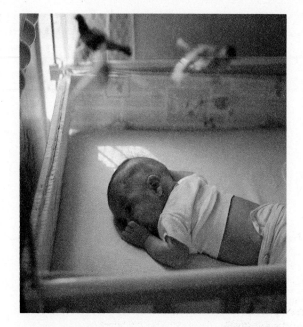

The demands of the id are evident in early childhood; according to Freud, each baby passes through an oral stage, in which thumb-sucking is a dominant pleasure (see page 64).

a real or contemplated action that is in conflict with the individual's superego and thus arouses feelings of guilt.

Anxiety is a warning of impending danger as well as a painful experience, so it forces the individual to undertake corrective action. Often the ego can cope with the anxiety by rational measures; if these do not suffice, however, the ego resorts to irrational protective measures, such as rationalization, which are referred to as *ego-defense mechanisms* and are described in the **HIGHLIGHT** on pages 64–65.

These defense mechanisms alleviate the painful anxiety, but they do so by pushing painful ideas out of consciousness and hence giving the individual a distorted view of reality instead of by dealing directly with the problem. This creates an undesirable schism between actual reality and the individual's perception of it.

A key concept in the psychoanalytic perspective, as we have seen, is that of the *unconscious.* Freud thought that the conscious part of the mind represents a relatively small area while the unconscious part, like the submerged part of an iceberg, is the much larger portion. In the depths of the unconscious are the hurtful memories, forbidden desires, and other experiences

HIGHLIGHT
Summary chart of ego-defense mechanisms

Mechanism	Example
Denial of reality. Protecting self from unpleasant reality by refusal to perceive or face it.	A smoker concludes that the evidence linking cigarette use to health problems is scientifically worthless.
Fantasy. Gratifying frustrated desires by imaginary achievements.	A socially inept and inhibited young man imagines himself chosen by a group of women to provide them with sexual satisfaction.
Repression. Preventing painful or dangerous thoughts from entering conciousness.	A mother's occasional murderous impulses toward her hyperactive two-year-old are denied access to awareness.
Rationalization. Using contrived "explanations" to conceal or disguise unworthy motives for one's behavior.	A fanatical racist uses ambiguous passages from Scripture to justify his hostile actions toward minorities.
Projection. Attributing one's unacceptable motives or characteristics to others.	An expansionist-minded dictator of a totalitarian state is convinced that neighboring countries are planning to invade.
Reaction formation. Preventing the awareness or expression of unacceptable desires by an exaggerated adoption of seemingly opposite behavior.	A man troubled by homosexual urges initiates a zealous community campaign to stamp out gay bars.
Displacement. Discharging pent-up feelings, often of hostility, on objects less dangerous than those arousing the feelings.	A woman harassed by her boss at work initiates an argument with her husband.

that have been *repressed*—that is, pushed out of the conscious. Although the individual is unaware of such unconscious material, it continues to seek expression and may be reflected in fantasies and dreams when ego controls are temporarily lowered. Until such unconscious material is brought to awareness and integrated into the ego structure—for example, via psychoanalysis—it presumably leads to irrational and maladaptive behavior.

3. *Psychosexual development*. Freud viewed personality development as a succession of stages, each characterized by a dominant mode of achieving libidinal (sexual) pleasure. The five stages he outlined follow:

a) *Oral stage.* During the first two years of life, the mouth is the principal erogenous zone; the infant's greatest source of gratification is assumed to be sucking.

b) *Anal stage.* From age 2 to age 3, the membranes of the anal region presumably provide the major source of pleasurable stimulation.

c) *Phallic stage.* From age 3 to age 5 or 6, self-manipulation of the genitals is assumed to provide the major source of pleasurable sensation.

d) *Latency stage.* In the years from 6 to 12, sexual motivations presumably recede in importance as the child becomes preoccupied with developing skills and other activities.

e) *Genital stage.* After puberty the deepest feelings of pleasure presumably come from heterosexual relations.

Freud believed that appropriate gratification during each stage is important if the individual is not to be *fixated* at that level. For example, he held that one who does not receive adequate oral gratification during infancy may be prone to excessive eating or drinking in adult life.

Mechanism	Example
Emotional insulation. Reducing ego involvement by protective withdrawal and passivity.	A child separated from her parents because of illness and lengthy hospitalization becomes emotionally unresponsive and apathetic.
Intellectualization (isolation). Cutting off affective charge from hurtful situations or separating incompatible attitudes by logic-tight compartments.	A prisoner on death row awaiting execution resists appeals on his behalf and coldly insists that the letter of the law be followed.
Undoing. Atoning for or magically trying to dispel unacceptable desires or acts.	A teenager who feels guilty about masturbation ritually touches door knobs a prescribed number of times following each occurrence of the act.
Regression. Retreating to an earlier developmental level involving less mature behavior and responsibility.	A man whose self-esteem has been shattered reverts to child-like "show-off" behavior and exhibits his genitals to young girls.
Identification. Increasing feelings of worth by affiliating oneself with person or institution of illustrious standing.	A youth league football coach becomes excessively demanding of his young players in emulation of an authoritarian pro football coach.
Overcompensation. Covering up felt weakness by emphasizing some desirable characteristic or making up for frustration in one area by overgratification in another.	A dangerously overweight woman goes on eating binges when she feels neglected by her husband.

Based on Anna Freud (1946)

In general, each stage of development places demands on the individual and arouses conflicts that must be resolved. One of the most important conflicts occurs during the phallic stage, when the pleasures of self-stimulation and accompanying fantasies pave the way for the *Oedipus complex.* Oedipus, according to Greek mythology, unknowingly killed his father and married his mother. Each young boy, Freud thought, symbolically relives the Oedipus drama. He has incestuous cravings for his mother and views his father as a hated rival; however, he also dreads the wrath of his dominant male parent and fears especially that his father may harm him by removing his penis. This *castration anxiety* forces the boy to repress his sexual desires for his mother as well as his hostility toward his father. Eventually, if all goes well, the boy identifies with his father and comes to have only harmless tender affection for his mother.

The *Electra complex* is the female counterpart of the Oedipus complex. It is based essentially on the view that the girl experiences penis envy and wants to possess her father and replace her mother. While, as we have seen, the boy renounces his lust out of fear of castration, no such threat can realistically be posed for the girl, who has "nothing to lose." The girl's emergence from the complex is more mild and less complete than the boy's; she essentially settles for a promissory note: one day she will have a man of her own who can give her a baby—a type of penis substitute.

For either sex, resolution of the conflict is considered essential if the young adult is to develop satisfactory heterosexual relationships. However, Freud believed that, because of this

Freud's theories have been discussed, broadened, reinterpreted, and refined by a wide range of scientists, thinkers, and writers—many of whom would not be considered strict "Freudians." At right, in addition to Freud himself, we present a sampling of psychologists whose work has been influenced, in some way, by Freud. Fuller discussions of the contributions of Adler, Horney, and Fromm appear in the section on the interpersonal perspective.

Sigmund Freud, 1856–1939, the founder of psychoanalysis, emphasized the role of unconscious processes and psychosexual stages in the determination of behavior.

Alfred Adler, 1870–1937, broke with Freud over the issue of the importance of social-environmental factors in the development of personality.

difference in the resolution of the complex, the "conscience" is less well developed in women than in men. Lest the reader think this all appears rather one-sided, we should point out that there is discussion today among some psychoanalysts that men may experience *womb envy*, a syndrome in which they are driven to be overachievers in their jobs to compensate for their inability to create a baby (Cantor, 1982).

In short, the psychoanalytic perspective holds that about the best we can hope for is a compromise among our warring inclinations, from which we will realize as much instinctual gratification as possible with minimal punishment and guilt. It thus presents a pessimistic and deterministic view of human behavior that minimizes rationality and freedom for self-determination. On a group level, it interprets violence, war, and related phenomena as the inevitable product of the aggressive and destructive instincts present in human nature.

Newer variants of the psychoanalytic perspective. In seeking to understand his patients, and in the development of his theories, Freud was chiefly concerned with the workings of the id, with the nature of this source of energy and the manner in which it could be channeled or transformed. Later workers, notably including his daughter Anna Freud (1895–1982), were much more concerned with how the ego performed its central functions as the "executive" of personality. It was this second genera-

tion of psychoanalysts, for example, which refined and elaborated on the ego-defense reactions.

For contemporary psychoanalysts, the focus is on neither the nature of the id nor the ego, but rather on the "objects" toward whom the child has directed those impulses and which the child has "introjected" (incorporated) into his or her own personality. "Object" in this context refers to the symbolic representation of another person in the child's environment, most often a parent. The concept of *introjection*, a difficult one for most students, refers to an internalization process wherein the child incorporates symbolically some person viewed with strong emotion. Later this symbol, or object, can influence the way the child experiences events and behaves.

The earliest development of this *object-relations* emphasis in psychoanalysis took place in the 1930s in England under the leadership of Melanie Klein, W. R. D. Fairbairn, and Harry Guntrip. These theorists developed the general notion that internalized objects could have varying conflicting properties—such as exciting or attractive versus hostile, frustrating, or rejecting—and moreover that these objects could become split off from the "central ego" and maintain independent existences, thus giving rise to inner conflict. The individual experiencing such splitting among internalized objects is, so to speak, "the servant of many masters" and cannot therefore lead an integrated, orderly life.

Both Karen Horney, 1885–1952, and Eric Fromm, b. 1900, received training in Freudian psychology but developed their own lines of independent thought. Horney focused on social learning and took issue with Freud concerning the psychology of women. Fromm stressed the importance of the "orientations" people bring to their relationships with one another.

Anna Freud, 1895–1982, elaborated the theory of ego-defense mechanisms and pioneered the psychoanalytic treatment of children.

Margaret Mahler elaborated the objects-relations approach, which many see as the main focus of contemporary psychoanalysis.

The work of Margaret Mahler in the United States has complemented and added additional insights to this approach (see, for example, Mahler et al., 1976). Mahler points out that, for the very young child, objects are not differentiated with respect to self versus other. Only gradually does the child gain an internal representation of self as distinct from representations of other objects. And only gradually is "object constancy" achieved (in which, for instance, the "mother" of yesterday is seen as the same object as the "mother" of today). The process involves a developmental phase of *separation-individuation,* the successful completion of which is said to be essential for the achievement of personal maturity.

Many other American analysts have, in recent years, become advocates of the object-relations point of view. Among the most prolific has been Otto Kernberg (e.g., 1975, 1976), noted especially for his studies of the disorder known as borderline personality (see Chapter 7). Kernberg's view is that the borderline personality, whose chief characteristic is instability (especially in personal relationships), is an individual who is unable to achieve a full and stable personal identity (self) because of an inability to integrate and reconcile pathological internalized objects.

These newer developments in psychoanalysis, which emphasize interpersonal relationships and the manner in which the quality of early relationships affects one's subsequent ability to achieve fulfilling adult interactions, were actually foreshadowed by various defectors from the psychoanalytic ranks, beginning with Alfred Adler (1870–1937), one of the earliest of Freud's disciples. Such ideas have developed largely independently of the psychoanalytic mainstream and have assumed importance in their own right. They will be addressed further in a later section on the interpersonal perspective.

Impact on our views of psychopathology. In historical perspective, psychoanalysis can be seen as the first systematic approach to show how human psychological processes may result in mental disorders. Much as the biological perspective replaced demons and witches with organic pathology as the cause of mental disorders, the psychoanalytic perspective replaced brain pathology with exaggerated ego defenses against anxiety as the cause of at least some mental disorders.

Freud greatly advanced our understanding of both normal and abnormal behavior, and many of the concepts formulated by Freud and his followers have become fundamental to our thinking about human nature and behavior. Two of Freud's contributions stand out as particularly noteworthy:

1. He developed techniques such as free association and dream analysis for becoming acquainted with both the conscious and unconscious aspects of mental life. The data thus obtained led Freud to emphasize (a) the dy-

Ivan Pavlov (1849–1936), a pioneer in showing the part conditioning plays in behavior, is shown here with his staff and some of the apparatus used to condition reflexes in dogs.

namic role of unconscious motives and ego-defense processes, (b) the importance of early childhood experiences in later personality adjustment and maladjustment, and (c) the importance of sexual factors in human behavior and mental disorders. Although, as we have said, Freud used the term *sex* in a much broader sense than it is ordinarily used, the idea caught the popular fancy, and the role of sexual factors in human behavior was finally brought out into the open as an appropriate topic for scientific investigation.

2. He demonstrated that certain abnormal mental phenomena occur as a result of attempts to cope with difficult problems and are simply exaggerations of normal ego-defense mechanisms. With the realization that the same psychological principles apply to both normal and abnormal behavior, much of the mystery and fear surrounding mental disorders was dispelled and mental patients were helped to regain their dignity as human beings.

The psychoanalytic perspective has come under attack from many directions, however—from other perspectives as well as from those within the psychoanalytic tradition. It has been criticized for overemphasis on the sex drive; for undue pessimism about basic human nature; for exaggeration of the role of unconscious pro-

cesses; for its failure to recognize the scientific limits of personal reports of experience; for failure to consider motives toward personal growth and fulfillment; for neglect of cultural differences in shaping behavior; and for a lack of scientific evidence to support many of its assumptions or to evaluate the effectiveness of psychoanalytic therapy. Finally, since psychoanalytic therapy frequently takes months, and even years, it has been criticized for being very expensive.

We have presented psychoanalytic theory in some detail because of its historical importance, not because we necessarily think it has special merit as an explanation of abnormal behavior. Our descriptions of other psychosocial perspectives will be somewhat less detailed.

The behavioristic perspective

While psychoanalysis largely dominated psychological thought about abnormal behavior in the early part of this century, another school—*behaviorism*—was emerging to challenge its supremacy. Behavioristic psychologists believed that the study of subjective experience—via the techniques of free association and dream analysis—did not provide acceptable scientific data, since such observations were not open to verifi-

J. B. Watson, 1878–1958, changed the focus of psychology from the study of inner sensations to the study of outer behavior, an approach he called behaviorism.

B. F. Skinner, b. 1904, formulated the concept of operant conditioning as a kind of conditioning in which reinforcers could be used to make a response more or less probable and frequent.

Albert Bandura, b. 1925, pioneered the study of modeling (see page 72). He clarified and integrated learning principles in his important book, Principles of Behavior Modification, *as well as in later publications.*

cation by other investigators. In their view, only the study of directly observable behavior and the stimuli and reinforcing conditions that "control" it could serve as a basis for formulating scientific principles of human behavior.

The behavioristic perspective is organized around one central theme: the role of learning in human behavior. Although this perspective was initially developed through research in the laboratory rather than through clinical practice with disturbed individuals, its implications for explaining and treating maladaptive behavior soon became evident.

Roots of the behavioristic perspective.
The origins of the behavioristic view of abnormal behavior and its treatment are tied to experimental work on the simple forms of learning, known as *conditioning.* This work began with the discovery of the conditioned reflex by the Russian physiologist Ivan Pavlov (1849–1936). Around the turn of the century, Pavlov demonstrated that a dog would learn to salivate to a nonfood stimulus, such as a bell, after the stimulus had been regularly accompanied by the presentation of food.

Pavlov's discovery excited a young American psychologist, John B. Watson (1878–1958), who was searching for objective ways to study human behavior. Watson reasoned that if psychology were to become a true science, it must abandon the subjectivity of inner sensations and other "mental" events and limit itself to what

could be objectively observed. What better way to do so than to observe systematic changes in behavior brought about simply by rearranging stimulus conditions! Watson thus changed the focus of psychology to the study of outer behavior, an approach he called *behaviorism.*

Watson, a man of great energy and impressive demeanor, saw great possibilities in behaviorism, and he was quick to point them out to his fellow scientists and a curious public. He boasted that, through conditioning, he could take any healthy child and convert him or her into whatever sort of adult one wished the child to become. He also challenged both the psychoanalysts and the more biologically oriented psychologists of his day by suggesting that abnormal behaviors were the product of unfortunate, inadvertent earlier conditioning and could be modified through reconditioning.

By the 1930s, Watson had made an enormous impact on American psychology, one that continues to the present time. As we might expect, Watson's approach placed heavy emphasis on the role of the social environment in "conditioning" personality development and behavior, both normal and abnormal. Modern behavioristically oriented psychologists still accept the basic tenets of Watson's doctrine, although they are now cautious in the claims they make.

While Watson was studying stimulus conditions and their relation to behavioral responses, E. L. Thorndike (1874–1949) and subsequently B. F. Skinner (b. 1904) were exploring the other side of the "conditioning" coin—the fact that, over time, behavior tends to be influenced by the consequences it produces. Behavior that *operates* on the environment is *instrumental* in producing certain outcomes, and those outcomes, in turn, determine the likelihood that the behavior will be repeated on several future similar occasions. Reasonably enough, this type of learning came to be called *instrumental* or *operant conditioning.*

The principles of Pavlovian (also called "classical" or "respondent") and instrumental conditioning had been sufficiently well worked out by 1950 that in that year John Dollard and Neal Miller published a classic work, *Personality and Psychotherapy*, which essentially reinterpreted psychoanalytic theory in favor of the terminology of classical and instrumental conditioning. In essence, they asserted that the ungoverned pleasure-seeking impulses of Freud's id were merely an aspect of the principle of reinforcement (the behavior of all organisms being determined by the maximization of gratification and minimization of pain); that anxiety was merely a conditioned fear response; that "repression" was merely conditioned thought-stoppage; and so on. The groundwork was thus laid for a behavioristic assault on the prevailingly psychoanalytic doctrines of the time. That assault in fact materialized through the 1960s and 1970s, dramatically altering—probably permanently—our ways of viewing abnormal behavior.

Basics of the behavioristic perspective.

As we have noted, *learning* provides the central theme of the behavioristic approach. Since most human behavior is learned, the behaviorists have addressed themselves to the question of how learning occurs. In trying to answer this question, they have focused on the effects of environmental conditions (stimuli) on the acquisition, modification, and possible elimination of various response patterns—both adaptive and maladaptive.

1. *Classical (respondent) and operant conditioning.* Even prior to learning, a specific stimulus may elicit a specific response. For example, food elicits salivation. Food in this case is the *unconditioned* stimulus, and the salivation is the *unconditioned* response. Through conditioning, the same response may come to be elicited by a wide range of other stimuli in the manner dem-

onstrated by Pavlov. This form of conditioning is called *classical conditioning*—its hallmark is that the response is elicited by the stimulus.

Probably the chief importance of classical conditioning in abnormal psychology lies in the fact that many responses of the autonomic nervous system, including those relating to fear or anxiety, can be conditioned. Thus, a fear of the dark can be learned if fear-producing stimuli (e.g., frightening dreams or fantasies) occur regularly during conditions of darkness.

In operant conditioning, the individual learns how to achieve a desired goal. The goal in question may be to obtain something that is rewarding or to avoid something that is unpleasant. Here a response typically precedes the desired stimulus, as when an individual kicks a coffee machine that has failed to function. If the kick causes it to produce coffee, the next time the coffee machine does not work, the person will probably kick it again. As we grow up, operant learning becomes an important mechanism for discriminating between what will prove rewarding and what will prove unrewarding—and for acquiring the competencies essential for achieving our goals and coping with our world.

Unfortunately, however, there is no guarantee that what we learn will be accurate or useful. Thus we may learn to value things that seem attractive but actually will hurt us; we may fail to learn needed competencies for coping, or we may learn coping patterns such as helplessness, bullying, or other irresponsible behavior that is maladaptive rather than adaptive.

2. *Reinforcement.* Essential to both respondent and operant conditioning is *reinforcement*—the strengthening of a new response by its repeated association with some unconditioned stimulus. Such a stimulus is called a *reinforcer* and has traditionally been called either positive (pleasant) or negative (aversive).

In operant conditioning, a behavior is strengthened by being repeatedly associated either with a reward or with an avoidance of some aversive condition. For example, a child may learn a response if the response has in the past produced a reward, such as candy, or avoided a punishment, such as a spanking. We should emphasize here that negative reinforcement and punishment are not one and the same: in the former an aversive situation is avoided; in the latter, the learner simply experiences an un-

Should this woman find that her response provides the desired stimulus—gum—the principles of operant conditioning would suggest that she may use the same tactic in future, similar situations.

pleasant situation. The unpleasantness does not *reinforce* anything; it is the avoidance that the person comes to see as desirable. Technically speaking, then, there is no such thing as *negative* reinforcement; there can be only an actual, positive reward or a "reward" based on avoiding a bad situation.

Initially a high rate of reinforcement may be necessary to establish a response, but lesser rates are usually sufficient to maintain it. In fact, a learned response appears to be especially persistent when reinforcement is intermittent—when the reinforcing stimulus does *not* invariably follow the response—as demonstrated in gambling when occasional wins seem to keep the response going. However, when reinforcement is consistently withheld over time, the conditioned response—whether classical or operant—eventually *extinguishes.* The subject stops making the response.

There is a special problem in extinguishing a response learned through *avoidance conditioning,* in which the subject has been conditioned to anticipate an aversive event and to respond in such a way as to avoid it. For example, a boy who has been bitten by a vicious dog may develop a conditioned avoidance response in which he consistently avoids all dogs. When he sees a dog, he feels anxious; avoiding contact lessens his anxiety and is thus reinforcing. As a result, his avoidance response is highly resistant to extinction. It also prevents him from having experiences with friendly dogs that could bring about reconditioning. We shall examine the sig-

nificance of such conditioned avoidance responses in our later discussions of patterns of abnormal behavior.

3. *Generalization and discrimination.* When a response is conditioned to one stimulus or set of stimulus conditions, it tends to become associated with other stimuli in proportion to the degree of similarity between the original and the new stimuli; this process is called *generalization.* A person who had been beaten as a child by a very authoritarian father might later experience an involuntary fear of authority; this person would be generalizing based on past experience.

A process complementary to generalization is *discrimination,* which occurs when the individual learns to distinguish between similar stimuli and to respond differently to them. The ability to discriminate may be brought about through selective reinforcement. For example, since red strawberries taste good and green ones do not, a conditioned discrimination will occur if the individual has experience with both. According to the behavioristic perspective, complex processes like attending, perceiving, forming concepts, and solving problems are all based on an elaboration of this basic discriminative process.

The concepts of generalization and discrimination have many implications for the development of maladaptive behavior. While generalization enables us to use past experience in sizing up new situations, there is always the possibility of making inappropriate generalizations—as when a delinquent youth fails to develop discriminations between "responsible" and "irresponsible" behavior, or when a child of wealthy parents learns to regard only rich people as worthy of respect. In some instances, a discrimination that is needed may be beyond the individual's capability—as when a bigoted person deals with others as stereotypes rather than as individuals—and may lead to inappropriate and maladaptive behavior.

4. *Modeling, shaping, and learned drives.* Other basic concepts of the behaviorist approach are modeling, shaping, and primary and secondary drives.

Modeling involves precisely what the term implies—demonstration of desired response patterns by parents or others. If the individual is capable of imitating the act modeled and is rewarded for doing so or sees the model being rewarded for such behavior, new performances can be acquired very rapidly. Often, of course, a child spontaneously imitates parental behavior; hence parents are viewed as important models in a child's early development. Unfortunately, a child may imitate maladaptive as well as adaptive behavior.

Often an appropriate response is not available in a person's behavioral repertoire, a matter that presents problems for therapy based on the behaviorist approach, since a response cannot be reinforced until it occurs. In such cases it is often possible to engage in *shaping* the response by reinforcing successive approximations of the desired behavior. Here behavior that is in the right direction—even though it does not represent the final performance to be achieved—is reinforced, while other responses are not reinforced and hence extinguish. For example, in getting a mute schizophrenic person to speak, slight movement of the lips may be reinforced first; later, when the individual starts to make sounds, the sounds are reinforced instead. Thus behavior is gradually shaped until the final goal of coherent speech is achieved.

Behaviorists view motivation as being based on a limited number of primary biological drives, such as hunger and thirst, that are directly related to meeting bodily needs. The many different motives in everyday life are seen as learned extensions of these primary drives. For example, an infant soon learns that parental approval leads to the gratification of bodily needs and thus learns to seek parental approval. With time this seeking may generalize or come to be associated with academic achievement and other behavior valued by the parents. Thus motives for approval, achievement, and so on, are seen as merely extensions of our more basic biological drives and are called *secondary drives.* And as with other learned behavior, motives that lead to maladaptive as well as adaptive behavior may be learned and reinforced.

The cognitive-behavioral revolution.   As we have seen, the behavioristic viewpoint was a reaction to the "subjectivism" of an earlier era in psychology. It sought to banish private mental events from psychological study because they were unobservable and therefore not suitable for scientific research. In its extreme form behaviorism even outlawed such terms as "mind" and "thought." Although there were always some who vigorously rejected behaviorism, it quickly gained wide acceptance among psychologists. As a result, the constraints imposed by the behavioristic point of view inhibited the development of cognitive psychology for some three decades after the 1920s.

Beginning in the 1950s and continuing to the present, psychologists, including the behaviorists, rediscovered the mind *per se:* its workings as an information-processing system became a focus of study for researchers across a broad range of psychological subspecialties.

Developments in clinical psychology, the main focus of our concerns, paralleled this extensive reorientation of the larger field. It may come as something of a surprise to learn that this reorientation in clinical psychology has been led in many instances by individuals who formerly identified with the behavioral tradition. In fact, however, such a development should not be surprising. A hallmark of clinical behavioristic practice has always been the precise identification of specific problem behaviors, followed by the use of techniques directed specifically at those behaviors. This is in contrast to, for example, psychoanalytic practice, wherein diverse problems are assumed to be due to a limited array of intrapsychic conflicts (e.g., an unresolved Oedipus complex), and where treatment techniques tend not to focus directly on the person's particular problems or complaints. In addition, behaviorally oriented therapies, such as *systematic desensitization* (described in Chapter 17), have from the outset relied heavily on having

Behaviorists believe conditioning *can operate in many different situations and can have special impact on the developing child. In the photo at the far left, the child is clearly not feeling threatened by a rather fierce-looking dog. By contrast, the middle photo shows children responding with fear to a strange-looking adult figure—a department store Santa. Presumably, with time these children will come to see Santa Claus as a friendly and likeable figure. At right, a child exhibits one form of* modeling, *in this case imitating the role of parent.*

clients conjure up images in their minds, certainly a process that is cognitive in nature. Cognitive-behavioral clinicians have simply shifted their focus from overt behavior *per se* to the underlying cognitions assumed to be producing that behavior. The issue then becomes one of altering the maladaptive cognitions.

To a large extent, cognitive-behavioral clinicians are concerned with the "self-statements" to which their clients are prone, or in other words with what these persons say to themselves by way of interpreting their experiences. For example, if one is inclined to interpret a large proportion of events in one's life as reflecting negatively on one's personal worth, then depressed feelings are a likely outcome. The cognitive-behavioral clinician would approach this situation with a variety of techniques designed to alter the negative cognitive bias the client harbors (see, for example, Beck et al., 1979; Kendall & Bemis, 1983; Meichenbaum, 1977).

Impact on our views of psychopathology.

By means of a relatively few basic concepts, behaviorism attempts to explain the acquisition, modification, and extinction of all types of behavior. Maladaptive behavior is viewed as essentially the result of (a) a failure to learn necessary adaptive behaviors or competencies, such as how to establish satisfying personal relation-

ships; or (b) the learning of ineffective or maladaptive responses. Maladaptive behavior is thus seen as resulting from learning that has gone awry and is defined in terms of specific, observable undesirable responses.

For the behaviorist, the focus of therapy is accordingly on changing specific behaviors—eliminating undesirable reactions and bringing about the learning of desirable ones. A number of *behavior-modification* techniques have been developed, based on the systematic application of learning principles (see **HIGHLIGHT** on page 74). Many examples of the application of these techniques will be given in later chapters.

The behavioristic approach has been heralded for its preciseness and objectivity, for the wealth of research it has generated, and for its demonstrated effectiveness in changing specific behaviors. The behavior therapist specifies what behavior is to be changed and how it is to be changed. Later, the effectiveness of the therapy can be evaluated objectively by the degree to which the stated goals have been achieved. On the other hand, the behavioristic perspective has been criticized for being concerned only with symptoms, for ignoring the problems of value and meaning that may be important for those seeking help, and for denying the possibility of choice and self-direction.

As we have seen, however, today many be-

HIGHLIGHT

Some behavior-modification techniques based on learning principles

Learning principle	Technique	Example in Treatment
Behavior patterns are developed and established through repeated association with positive reinforcers.	Use of positive reinforcement to establish desired behavior.	Paul and Lentz (1977) successfully rehabilitated a group of chronic mental patients by providing them with tokens contingent on desirable behavior. The tokens could subsequently be used to "purchase" food, pleasant surroundings, etc.
The repeated association of an established behavior pattern with aversive stimuli results in avoidance behavior.	Use of aversive stimuli to eliminate undesirable behavior (aversive conditioning).	Forgione (1976) eliminated pedophiliac behavior in two men by administering painful electric shocks during their viewing of photographs of themselves practicing their deviant behavior upon life-size child mannequins.
When an established behavior pattern is no longer reinforced, it tends to be extinguished.	Withdrawal of reinforcement for undesirable behavior.	Liberman and Raskin (1971) reported improvement in the treatment of depression by instructing family members of depressed person to provide attention for constructive behavior but to ignore depressive behavior.
Avoidance behavior will be inhibited or reduced if the conditions that provoke it are repeatedly paired with positive stimuli.	Desensitization to conditions that elicit unreasonable fear or anxiety.	Rimm and Lefebvre (1981) cited the successful treatment of phobias concerning loud noises and high places in a 45-year-old air force veteran. The treatment, known as systematic desensitization, consisted of having the man repeatedly imagine fearful scenes relating to his phobias while in a state of deep relaxation.
A specified behavior can gradually be established if successive approximations of the behavior are reinforced.	Shaping of desired behavior.	Rekers, Lovaas, and Low (1975) successfully used social reinforcement to develop masculine sex-typed behavior in an 8-year-old boy whose behavior was considered to be inappropriately feminine. They reinforced masculine or neutral behavior with expressions of interest and gave no attention to behavior that was considered feminine. Their treatment was begun in the home, then extended to the school setting in order to maximize generalizability of the treatment. "Masculine" social skills and sports were also taught over a period of several months. A follow-up evaluation when the boy was 12 years old showed that the new behaviors were being maintained.
Reinforcement can operate to modify covert behavior (cognitions) as well as overt behavior.	Cognitive restructuring.	Goldfried, Linehan, and Smith (1978) told highly anxious subjects to imagine being in an anxiety-arousing test situation and then presented them with instructions for reducing their anxiety. Subjects not only learned to react to test situations with less anxiety but responded in other social circumstances with more adaptive attitudes.

havioristically oriented clinicians and researchers have been attempting to incorporate cognitive processes, including imagery and self-awareness, into their picture of psychological functioning. Bandura (1974) has gone so far as to state that human beings do have "a capacity for self-direction" and that recognition of this capacity "represents a substantial departure from exclusive reliance upon environmental control" (pp. 861, 863). The behavioral therapies discussed in Chapter 17 reflect this shift.

Yet, despite this "humanistic" trend, the most ardent behaviorists, like Skinner, have continued to emphasize the potential use of modern science and technology for planning a better future world. In his famous novel, *Walden Two* (1948), and its nonfiction version, *Beyond Freedom and Dignity* (1971), Skinner has depicted the utopian world he thinks would result from the systematic application of learning principles and behavior-modification procedures to our present world problems. Skinner (1974) has stated the matter very succinctly: "In the behavioristic view, man can now control his own destiny because he knows what must be done and how to do it" (p. 258). He does not explain how people who have no choice could choose to exert such control.

Whatever its limitations and paradoxes, the behavioristic perspective has had and continues to have a tremendous impact on our contemporary views of human nature and behavior in general and on psychopathology in particular.

The humanistic perspective

The focus of the humanistic perspective is on people's conscious experiences and perceptions and on freeing them from crippling assumptions and attitudes so that they can develop their potentialities and live fuller lives. Its emphasis is thus on growth and self-actualization rather than on cure of disease or alleviation of disorder, and its practitioners do not typically deal with individuals suffering from serious mental disorders.

The humanistic perspective has been influenced by both the psychoanalytic and the behavioristic perspectives, but it is in significant disagreement with both. The behavioristic perspective, with its focus on the stimulus situation

and observable behavior, is seen as an oversimplification that underrates the importance of the individual's psychological makeup, inner experience, and potential for self-direction. At the same time, humanistic psychologists disagree with the negative and pessimistic picture of human nature portrayed by psychoanalytic theory and its stress on the overwhelming power of irrational, unconscious impulses. Rather, the humanistic perspective views our basic nature as "good," emphasizes present conscious processes—paying less attention to unconscious processes and past events—and places strong emphasis on our inherent capacity for responsible self-direction. In these senses, the humanistic perspective tends to be as much a statement of values—of how we *ought* to view the human condition—as it is an attempt to account for what in fact seems to be the case, at least among persons more or less stifled by personal problems. Humanistic psychologists also tend to emphasize the individual's present purposes and perceptions and to regard prior causes as much less important. Furthermore, they find much of empirical research designed to investigate causal factors too simplistic to uncover the complexities of human behavior.

Some objection has been raised to the use of the term *humanistic* to describe only the more experientially oriented therapies because it seems to imply that other approaches demean the individual or view humans as simply objects with which to tinker. All approaches, of course, aim ultimately at more effective, happier human beings and are "humanistic" in that sense, just as all are interested in changing behavior and thus recognize the importance of learning. Their labels indicate their special focus but do not imply that they exclude all other factors.

Roots of the humanistic approach. The humanistic perspective has been heavily influenced by such outstanding psychologists as William James, Gordon Allport, Abraham Maslow, Gardner Murphy, Carl Rogers, and Fritz Perls. Although some of its roots extend deep into the history of psychology—as well as philosophy, literature, and education—others are of relatively recent origin. It appears to have emerged as a major perspective in psychology in the 1950s and 1960s when many middle-class Americans realized their simultaneous material affluence and spiritual emptiness. (A related modern movement—the existential perspective—is described in the **HIGHLIGHT** on page 77.)

As a "third force" in contemporary psychology, the humanistic approach recognizes the importance of learning and other psychological processes that have traditionally been the focus of research; but as noted above, it focuses, usually optimistically, on the individual's future rather than on the past. This perspective is also concerned with processes about which we have as yet little scientific information—such as love, hope, creativity, values, meaning, personal growth, and self-fulfillment. In essence, humanistic psychologists feel that modern psychology has failed to address itself to many of the problems that are of crucial significance in the lives of all of us. Inevitably, its formulations are less based on empirical observation than those of behaviorism.

Basics of the humanistic perspective.

Though not readily subject to empirical investigation, certain underlying themes and principles of humanistic psychology are discernible and are described below.

1. *Self as a unifying theme.* In the first comprehensive textbook on psychology, published in 1890, William James included a discussion of consciousness of self. This concept was later dropped by the behaviorists because the self could not be observed by an outsider. Though the behaviorists have again incorporated cognitive aspects of human behavior into their perspective, it was the humanists of the fifties and sixties who kept the concept of self as the focus of their perspective.

Among humanistic psychologists, Carl Rogers has developed the most systematic formulation of the self-concept, based largely on his pioneering research into the nature of the psychotherapeutic process. Rogers (1951, 1959) has stated his views in a series of propositions that may be summarized as follows:

a) Each individual exists in a private world of experience of which the I, me, or myself is the center.

b) The most basic striving of the individual is toward the maintenance, enhancement, and actualization of the self.

c) The individual reacts to situations in terms of the way he or she perceives them, in ways

consistent with his or her self-concept and view of the world.

d) Perceived threat to the self is followed by defense—including the narrowing and rigidification of perception and behavior and the introduction of self-defense mechanisms.

e) The individual's inner tendencies are toward health and wholeness; under normal conditions we behave in rational and constructive ways and choose pathways toward personal growth and self-actualization.

In using the concept of self as a unifying theme, humanistic psychologists emphasize the importance of individuality. Because of our great potential for evaluation and learning and the great diversity in our genetic endowments and backgrounds of experience, each one of us is unique. In studying "human nature," psychologists are thus faced with the dual task of describing the uniqueness of each individual and identifying the characteristics that all members of the human race have in common.

2. *Focus on values and personal growth.* Humanistic psychologists place strong emphasis on values and the process of value choices in guiding our behavior and achieving a meaningful and fulfilling way of life. They consider it crucial that each one of us develop values based on our own experience and evaluations rather than blindly accepting values held by people around us; otherwise we deny our own experiences of value and lose touch with our own real feelings.

To evaluate and choose for ourselves requires a clear sense of our own self-identity—the discovery of who we are, of what sort of person we want to become, and why. Only in this way can we actualize our potentialities and achieve responsible self-direction.

According to the humanistic view, psychopathology is essentially the blocking or distortion of personal growth and natural tendencies toward physical and mental health. Such blocking or distortion is generally the result of one or more of these causal factors: (a) the exaggerated use of ego-defense mechanisms so that the individual becomes increasingly out of touch with reality; (b) unfavorable social conditions and faulty learning; and (c) excessive stress.

3. *Positive view of human nature and potential.* In contrast to the psychoanalytic and behavioristic perspectives, the humanistic approach takes a much more positive view of human na-

HIGHLIGHT

The existential perspective

During the middle part of this century, as the humanistic perspective was becoming an influential force in the field of psychology, a related intellectual movement—centered in Europe—was also beginning to have a notable impact among psychologists. This was *existentialism,* a philosophical outlook with roots in the work of such nineteenth-century thinkers as Martin Heidegger and Soren Kierkegaard.

The existential perspective resembles the humanistic in its emphasis on the uniqueness of the individual, the quest for value and meaning, and the existence of freedom for self-direction and self-fulfillment. However, the existential perspective represents a somewhat less optimistic view of human beings and places more emphasis on the irrational tendencies in human nature and the difficulties inherent in self-fulfillment—particularly in our bureaucratic and dehumanizing mass society. In short, the matter of living seems much more a "confrontation" for the existentialists. And the existentialists place considerably less faith in modern science and more in the inner experience of the individual in his or her attempts to understand and deal with the deepest human problems. The following summarizes some of the basic tenets of existentialism.

1. *Existence and essence.* A basic theme of existentialism is that our existence is given, but what we make of it—our essence—is up to us. The adolescent boy who defiantly blurts out, "Well, I didn't ask to be born" is stating a profound truth; but in existential terms, it is completely irrelevant. For whether he asked to be born or not, here he is in the world and answerable for himself—for one human life. What he makes of his essence is up to him. It is his responsibility to shape the kind of person he is to become and to live a meaningful and constructive life.

2. *Choice, freedom, and courage.* Our essence is created by our *choices,* for our choices reflect the values on which we base and order our lives. As Sartre put it: "I am my choices."

In choosing what sort of person to become, we are seen as having absolute *freedom;* even refusing to choose represents a choice. Thus the locus of value is within each individual. We are inescapably the architects of our own lives.

3. *Meaning, value, and obligation.* A central theme in the existential perspective is the will-to-meaning. This is considered a basic human characteristic and is primarily a matter of finding satisfying values and guiding one's life by them. As we have noted, this is a difficult and highly individual matter, for the values that give one life meaning may be quite different from those that provide meaning for another. Each of us must find his or her own pattern of values.

Yet this should not be interpreted as a purely nihilistic or selfish orientation. Existentialism also places strong emphasis on our *obligations* to each other. The most important consideration is not what we can get out of life but what we can contribute to it. Our lives can be fulfilling only if they involve socially constructive values and choices.

4. *Existential anxiety and the encounter with nothingness.* A final existential theme that adds an urgent and painful note to the human situation is that of *nonbeing* or *nothingness.* In ultimate form it is death, which is the inescapable fate of all human beings. It is this awareness of our inevitable death and its implications for our living that can lead to *existential anxiety*—to deep concern over whether we are living a meaningful and fulfilling life.

We can overcome our existential anxiety and deny victory to nothingness by living a life that counts for something. If we are perishable, we can at least perish resisting—living in such a way that nothingness will be an unjust fate.

The implications of this philosophy for students of abnormal psychology are clear. Existential psychologists focus on the importance of establishing values and acquiring a level of spiritual maturity worthy of the freedom and dignity bestowed by the special circumstance of one's humanness. It is the avoidance of and refusal to deal with such central issues that creates corrupted, meaningless, and wasted lives. Much abnormal behavior, therefore, is seen as the product of a failure to deal constructively with existential despair and frustration.

Before the turn of the twentieth century, William James, 1842–1910, (top left) set the stage for the humanistic perspective in a chapter on the concept of the self in his book Principles of Psychology.

A. H. Maslow, 1908–1970, (top right) devoted more than two decades to showing the potentialities of human beings for higher self-development and functioning.

Carl R. Rogers, b. 1902, (bottom left) has contributed significantly to the humanistic perspective with his theoretical formulations and his systematic studies on the therapeutic process and its outcomes.

Fritz Perls, 1893–1970, (bottom right) was influential in the development of therapeutic procedures for enhancing human experiencing and functioning, particularly in the context of confrontation groups.

ture and potential. Despite the myriad instances of violence, war, and cruelty that have occurred from ancient times, humanistically oriented psychologists conclude that under favorable circumstances, human propensities are in the direction of friendly, cooperative, and constructive behavior. They regard selfishness, aggression, and cruelty as pathological behavior resulting from the denial, frustration, or distortion of our basic nature. Similarly, they suggest that although we can be misled by inaccurate information, handicapped by social and economic deprivation, and overwhelmed by the number and complexity of issues we are expected to act upon, we still tend to be rational creatures. We try to find sense and meaning in our experience, to act and think in consistent ways, and to follow standards and principles we believe are good. According to this view, we are not passive automatons but active participants in life with some measure of freedom for shaping both our personal destiny and that of our social group.

Impact on our views of psychopathology. From a broad perspective, the major impact of the humanistic perspective on our views of psychopathology has been its emphasis on our capacity for full functioning as human beings. In a sense, the humanistic perspective has introduced a new dimension to our thinking about abnormal behavior. "Abnormality" is seen as a failure to develop sufficiently our tremendous potentials as human beings—as a blocking or distortion of the individual's natural tendencies toward health and personal growth rather than as abnormality or deviance *per se*. In fact, Maslow (1962, 1969) has even expressed concern about the "psychopathology of the normal"—that is, the disappointing and wasteful failure of so many "normal" people to realize their potentialities as human beings.

Therapy, according to this way of thinking, is not a means of moving the individual from maladjustment to adjustment but of fostering personal growth toward a socially constructive and personally fulfilling way of life. As might be expected, humanistic psychologists are keenly interested in encounter groups, awareness training, and other experiential techniques for fostering personal growth, building more satisfying relationships with others, and finding more effective methods of coping.

The humanistic perspective has been criticized for its diffuseness, for a lack of scientific rigor in its conceptualizations, and for expecting too much from psychology. But while some psychologists would view its goals as "grandiose," others would view them as a useful description of the challenging long-range task that confronts psychology today.

The interpersonal perspective

We are social beings, and much of what we are is a product of our relationships with others, beginning with our first experiences in life. It would be logical to expect that much of psychopathology would reflect that fact—that it would be rooted in unfortunate tendencies we have developed in the course of finding our way around in our interpersonal environment. It is also true that abnormal behavior has its chief impact on our relationships with other people. Hence, it should not be surprising that many theorists have concluded that abnormal behavior is best understood by analyzing the individual's relationships, past and present, with other people (see **HIGHLIGHT** on page 80). This is the focus of the interpersonal perspective.

Roots of the interpersonal perspective.
The roots of the interpersonal perspective lie clearly in the psychoanalytic movement. The defection of Alfred Adler from the psychoanalytic viewpoint of his teacher, Freud, in 1911 grew out of Adler's emphasis on social rather than inherited determinants of behavior. Adler objected to the prominence Freud gave to inherited "instincts" as the basic driving forces of personality. In Adler's view, people were inherently social beings motivated primarily by the desire to belong to and participate in the group.

Over time, a number of other important theorists originally trained in the Freudian mold took issue with psychoanalytic theory for its neglect of crucial social factors. Among the best known of these were Eric Fromm (b. 1900) and

Karen Horney (1885–1952). Fromm focused on the "orientations," or dispositions—exploitive, for example—that people adopt in their interactions with others. He believed that these basic orientations to the social environment contained the roots of much psychopathology. Horney independently developed a similar view, and in particular vigorously rejected the demeaning view of female psychology (e.g., the idea that women experience "penis envy") propounded by Freud. According to Horney, "femininity" was a product of the culturally determined social learning that women nearly always experienced.

Erik Erikson (b. 1902) also extended interpersonal aspects of psychoanalytic theory. He elaborated and broadened Freud's psychosexual stages by describing conflicts that come into focus at eight stages, each of which can be resolved in a healthy or unhealthy way. For example, during the oral stage the child may learn either basic *trust* or basic *mistrust*. Although these conflicts are never fully resolved once and for all, failure to develop toward the appropriate pole of each conflict handicaps an individual for meeting the tasks of the later stages. For example, trust is needed for later competence in many areas of life; a clear sense of identity is a necessary prerequisite for satisfying intimacy with another person; such intimacy, in turn, is an important precondition for becoming a nurturing parent.

As we have seen, contemporary psychoanalytic thought has partially corrected for the challenges leveled at the original version by these more socially oriented theorists. The recent emergence of the object-relations approach within the psychoanalytic tradition has rendered that system much more "interpersonal" in focus than it had been heretofore, so much so that many foresee the possibility of a genuine rapprochement and integration of the psychoanalytic with more distinctly social and interpersonal viewpoints (Fine, 1979). Still, psychoanalytic theory continues to emphasize the primacy of libidinal energies and dark intrapsychic conflicts, an emphasis that many interpersonally oriented theorists find both unnecessary and objectionable.

Currently, the dominant interpersonal theory is that developed by Harry Stack Sullivan (1892–1949), a brilliant American psychiatrist, to whom we now turn.

Sullivan's interpersonal theory. While, as we have seen, the roots of interpersonal theory had long been present in the thinking of many individuals, it remained for Sullivan to offer a comprehensive and systematic theory of personality and its development that was explicitly interpersonal in focus.

Sullivan (1953) maintained that the concept of personality had meaning only when defined in terms of an individual's characteristic forms of relating to others. That is, he argued, personality development proceeds through various stages involving different patterns of interpersonal relationships. At first, for example, interactions are mainly with parents, who begin the socialization of the child. Later, with a gradual emancipation from parents, peer relationships become increasingly important; and in young adulthood, intimate relationships are established, culminating typically in marriage. Failure to progress satisfactorily through these various stages paves the way for later maladaptive behavior.

In this developmental context, Sullivan was concerned with the anxiety-arousing aspects of interpersonal relationships during early development. Since the infant is completely dependent on parents and siblings (called *significant others*) for meeting all physical and psychological needs, lack of love and care lead to an insecure and anxious human being. Sullivan emphasized the role of early childhood relationships in shaping the self-concept, which he saw as constructed largely out of the reflected appraisals of significant others. For example, if a little girl perceives others as rejecting her or treating her as being of little or no worth, she is likely to view herself in a similar light and to develop a negative self-image that almost inevitably leads to maladjustment.

The pressures of the socialization process and the continual appraisal by others lead a child to label some personal tendencies as the "good-me" and others as the "bad-me." It is the "bad-me" that is associated with anxiety. With time, the individual develops a *self-system* that serves to protect him or her from such anxiety through the control of awareness; the individual "selectively inattends" to elements of experience that cause anxiety. If severe anxiety is aroused by some especially frightening aspect of self-experience, the individual perceives it as the "not-me," totally screening it out of consciousness or

HIGHLIGHT
Toward an interpersonal diagnostic system

While acknowledging that the DSM-III diagnostic system is an improvement over its predecessors, Mc-Lemore and Benjamin (1979) argue that it continues to be fundamentally flawed in at least three ways: (a) it still calls on the diagnostician to make impressionistic clinical judgments; (b) it still categorizes human beings by reference to certain broadly defined "illnesses"; and, especially, (c) it almost totally neglects the social context in which maladaptive behavior occurs. They note that abnormality is typically a disturbance in the manner in which a person relates to others: "We submit that rigorous and systematic description of social behavior is uniquely critical to effective definition and treatment of the problems that bring most individuals for psychiatric or psychological consultation" (p. 18).

The solution, according to these authors, is to seek the careful and rigorous development of a diagnostic system organized not around alleged entities of mental disorder but rather around disordered forms of interpersonal functioning. Building on the work of earlier investigators, they suggest that the beginnings of such a system should incorporate dimensions of autonomy-interdependence, friendliness-hostility, and (where the situation is one of high interdependence between the person and others) dominance-submission. Since the most important and central of the behaviors associated with traditional (DSM) psychiatric diagnoses involve precisely these dimensions, they argue, it should be possible to include virtually all DSM-III diagnoses within this more systematic and potentially more meaningful framework. For example, the DSM-III diagnosis of *major depression* might, in interpersonal terms, be described as a "position of appeasement" (hostile-submission) toward another person's stance of accusation and blame (hostile dominance), which leads to internalized self-accusation and blame (hostile domination of self). The *narcissistic personality disorder*, on the other hand, might be viewed as a hostile assertion of autonomy ("Ignore it, pretend it's not there") by becoming preoccupied with oneself and one's own affairs and by reverting to fantasy as a principal means of gratification.

Success in the effort to construct a new system would doubtless enhance both the reliability and validity of psychiatric diagnosis (see Chapter 1). Benjamin (1982) is continuing to develop the model proposed here.

even attributing it to someone else. However, such actions lead to an incongruity between the individual's perceptions and the world as it really is, and may therefore result in maladaptive behavior. Here we can readily see a similarity between Sullivan's views and those of both Freud and Rogers.

The "good-me" and "bad-me" constructs are especially important aspects of a much broader and more profound idea—that is, that *all* of our mental processing concerning ourselves, others, and our relationships with them is influenced by precedents or prototypes established in earlier relationships. These mental prototypes, which Sullivan called "personifications," determine the manner in which we perceive an experience in our current relationships. That is, we each have our own ideas of what characteristics, behaviors, and interactions we expect of "mom," "teacher," "lover," and "friend." Unfortunately, this means that we may distort or misrepresent what is happening in important present relationships. When such distortions are severe, the relationship is apt to become very complicated and confusing. One reason for this is that, since these distortions shape our behavior toward the other person, they will tend to become self-fulfilling. The result is often anxiety and, ultimately, a dissolution of the relationship.

Other features of the interpersonal perspective.

Many subdisciplines of the social sciences and psychiatry have contributed to the interpersonal perspective in recent years. Some of the contributions are described briefly below.

1. *Social exchange, roles, and games.* Three ways of viewing our relationships with other people are helpful in understanding both satisfying and hurtful interactions.

The *social-exchange* view, developed largely by Thibaut and Kelley (1959) and Homans (1961), is based on the premise that we form relationships with each other for the purpose of satisfying our needs. Each person in the relationship wants something from the other, and the exchange that results is essentially a trading or bargaining one. When we feel that we have entered into a bad bargain—that the rewards are not worth the costs—we may attempt to work out some compromise or simply terminate the relationship.

A second way of viewing interpersonal rela-

Specific social roles are assigned to the teacher in this classroom and to her students. If any member of this social group significantly diverges from his or her prescribed role, interpersonal complications are likely to occur.

tionships is in terms of *social roles.* Society prescribes role behavior for teachers, generals, and others occupying given positions. While each individual lends a personal interpretation to the role, there are usually limits to the "script," beyond which a person in a given role is not expected to go. Similarly, in intimate personal relationships, each person holds certain role expectations—in terms of obligations, rights, duties, and so on—that the other person in the relationship is expected to meet. If one spouse fails to live up to the other's role expectations or finds them uncomfortable, or if husband and wife have different conceptions of what a "wife" or "husband" should be or do, serious complications in the relationship are likely to occur.

Another view of interpersonal relationships focuses on the "games people play." Eric Berne (1964, 1972) pointed out that such games are not consciously planned but rather involve a sort of role playing of which the persons are either entirely or partially unaware. For example, a woman who lacks self-confidence may marry a man who is very domineering and then complain that she could do all sorts of outstanding things "if it weren't for you."

Such games presumably serve two useful functions: (a) as substitutes for or defenses against true intimacy in daily life, intimacy for which many people are unprepared; and (b) as stabilizers to help maintain a relationship. But they are likely to prove a poor substitute for a more honest relationship. Though called "games" in the sense of being ploys, they are often deadly serious.

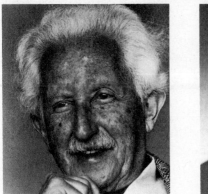

Erik Erikson, b. 1902, (left) saw interpersonal implications in Freud's psychosexual stages. Erikson described eight psychosocial stages, each offering the child an opportunity to work out a conflict in a healthy or unhealthy way.

The interpersonal model is based largely on the work of Harry Stack Sullivan, 1892–1949, (right) who believed personality existed only in interaction with others.

2. *Causal attribution in interpersonal relations.* Another contributor to the interpersonal approach is **attribution theory** (Bem, 1972; Brehm, 1976; Heider, 1958; Jones & Davis, 1965; Weary & Mirels, 1982). All we actually see is a series of events, but we often interpret one event as having been "caused" by some earlier event. Sometimes we attribute these "causes" to something in the environment, such as rewards or punishments; sometimes we assume traits or "dispositions" in other people or in ourselves to account for the behavior that takes place. These dispositions and other causes are not seen but are just assumed to exist, as underlying realities. Assuming them helps us explain consistency in people's behavior and makes it possible to predict what we and others are likely to do in the future.

For example, if a person does something mean, we may assume that he or she has a quality of "meanness" and expect it to cause mean behavior in the future. Or if we do something stupid, we may attribute stupidity to ourselves as a trait in our personality. On the other hand, if we see ourselves as simply conforming to some stupid regulation that has to be followed to get credit for a course, we would view our behavior as caused by the environment and not indicating anything about our own qualities.

According to attribution theorists, the attributions we make are important in our relationships with others because they form the basis for continuing *evaluations* and *expectations*. However inaccurate they may be, they become important parts of our picture of the world and tend to become self-fulfilling prophecies. Also, they tend to make us see other people and ourselves as unchanging and unchangeable, leading us to fall into unnecessary "ruts" in our relationships with one another. Obviously, these ideas are similar to the Sullivanian notion of distorted personifications.

3. *Communication and interpersonal accommodation.* Interpersonal accommodation is the process whereby two persons evolve patterns of communication and interaction that enable them to attain common goals, meet mutual needs, and build a satisfying relationship.

People use many cues, both verbal and nonverbal, to interpret what is really being said to them. Sullivan believed that faulty communication is far more common than most people realize, especially in family interactions on an emotional level.

If individuals in a close relationship have a tangle of unresolved misunderstandings and conflicts, they will probably have trouble communicating clearly and openly with each other. In fact, the final phase of a failing marriage is often marked by almost complete inability of the partners to communicate.

In addition to establishing and maintaining effective communication, interpersonal accommodation involves meeting a number of other adjustive demands, such as establishing mutually satisfying role relationships, resolving disagreements constructively, and dealing adequately with external demands that can markedly affect the relationship. Sullivan thought that interpersonal accommodation is facilitated when the motives of the persons in the relationship are complementary, as when both persons are strongly motivated to give and receive affection. When interpersonal accommodation fails and the relationship does not meet the needs of one or both partners, it is likely to be characterized by conflict and dissension, and eventually to be ended. The principles of interpersonal behavioral accommodation have been analyzed at length by Benjamin (1974, 1977, 1979, 1982), Carson (1969, 1979), Leary (1957), and Wiggins (1982).

Impact on our views of psychopathology.

The interpersonal perspective places strong emphasis on unsatisfactory interpersonal relationships in the past and/or present as the primary causal factors in many forms of maladaptive behavior. Such relationships may extend back to childhood, as when a boy's self-concept was distorted by parents who evaluated him as worthless or by rigid socialization measures that made it difficult to accept and integrate the "bad-me" into his self-concept. Poor interpersonal relationships may also result from self-defeating "games" that individuals learn to play, from uncomfortable roles they are given, from faulty assumptions about the causes of their own or others' behavior, or from unsuccessful attempts to separate one's self from parents and other adults in order to become a fully functioning adult.

In any case, the focus of interpersonal therapy is on the alleviation of current pathogenic, or problem-causing, relationships and on helping the individual achieve more satisfactory relationships. Such therapy is concerned with verbal and nonverbal communication, social roles, processes of accommodation, the client's causal attributions (including those supposedly motivating the behavior of others), and the general current interpersonal context of behavior. The therapy situation itself is used as a vehicle for new learning of interpersonal skills.

Like the humanistic viewpoint, the interpersonal approach is handicapped by incomplete information concerning most aspects of interpersonal relationships. As a result, many of Sullivan's concepts and those of later investigators lack adequate scientific grounding. Despite such limitations, however, the interpersonal perspective has been useful in focusing attention on the quality of the individual's close personal relationships as a key factor in determining whether behavior will be effective or maladaptive.

In reviewing these psychosocial perspectives regarding human behavior—psychoanalytic, behavioristic, humanistic, and interpersonal—we have seen that each contributes to our understanding of psychopathology, but that none alone seems to account for all the complex types of maladaptive behavior exhibited by human beings. Each has a substantial amount of evidence to support it, yet each one also depends on generalizations from limited kinds of events and observations. In attempting to explain a complex disorder such as alcoholism, for example, the psychoanalytic perspective focuses on intrapsychic conflict and anxiety; the behavioristic perspective focuses on faulty learning and environmental conditions that may be exacerbating or maintaining the alcoholism; the humanistic perspective focuses on the ways in which the individual's problems regarding values, meaning, and personal growth may be contributing to the drinking problem; and the interpersonal perspective focuses on difficulties in one's past and present relationships.

Thus it becomes apparent that adopting one perspective or another has important consequences: it influences our perception of maladaptive behavior as well as the types of evidence we look for and how we are likely to interpret the data. In later chapters we shall utilize concepts from all these viewpoints when they seem relevant, and in many instances we shall find it useful to contrast different ways of explaining and treating the same behavior.

Emergence of the sociocultural viewpoint

By the beginning of the twentieth century, sociology and anthropology had emerged as independent scientific disciplines and were making rapid strides toward understanding the role of sociocultural factors in human development and behavior.[2] Soon it became apparent that human beings are almost infinitely malleable and that personality development reflects the larger society—its institutions, norms, values, ideas, and technology—as well as the immediate family and other interpersonal relationships to which individuals are exposed. Eventually, too, it became clear that a relationship exists between sociocultural conditions and mental disorders—for example, between the particular stressors in a society and the frequency and types of mental

---

[2]Prominent early contributors to this field were Ruth Benedict, Ralph Linton, Abram Kardiner, Margaret Mead, and Franz Boas.

Margaret Mead, 1901–1978, the world-famous anthropologist, spent years studying other societies and amassing cross-cultural data. Her Coming of Age in Samoa *(published in 1928) gave a favorable picture of many aspects of life in a "primitive" society and was influential in establishing an attitude of* cultural relativism *among many scientists and thinkers. Here she is shown in native garb with two Samoan adolescents.*

disorders that occur in it. It was also observed that the patterns of both physical and mental disorders in a given society may change over time as sociocultural conditions change. These sociocultural discoveries have added another dimension to modern perspectives concerning abnormal behavior.

Changing interpretations of anthropological findings

The relationships between sociocultural factors such as poverty, discrimination, or illiteracy and maladaptive behavior during childhood or adulthood are complex. It is one thing to observe that an individual who falls victim to psychological disorders has come from harsh environmental circumstances. However, it is quite difficult to show empirically and unequivocally that these circumstances were both *necessary* and *sufficient* conditions for producing the later disorder.

Evidence that sociocultural factors have influenced personality adaptation or resulted in particular abnormal disorders is fairly compelling but difficult to tie down. It is virtually impossible to conduct controlled experiments. Both economic and ethical restraints prevent investigators from rearing children with similar genetic or biological endowments in diverse social or economic environments in order to find out which variables, if any, played a part in the individuals' later adjustment.

However, natural occurrences in human history have provided a laboratory for the re-

searcher. Groups of human beings have in fact been exposed to very different environments, from the Arctic to the tropics to the deserts. Human societies have developed different means for economic subsistence and different types of family structures for propagating and maintaining the species under different and often adverse conditions. Human groups have evolved highly diverse social and political systems. It seems that nature has indeed done the social scientists a great favor by providing such a wide array of human groups for study.

Yet the investigator who attempts to conduct cross-cultural research is plagued by numerous technological and methodological problems, such as (a) different language and thought systems; (b) political and cultural climates that prevent objective inquiry; (c) difficulties in finding appropriately trained local scientists to collaborate in the research and prevent the ethnocentric attitudes or values of "outsiders" from distorting the findings; and (d) high costs of large-scale cross-cultural research.

In the earliest cross-cultural studies, Western-trained anthropologists made observations of the behavior of "natives" and considered those behaviors in the context of Western scientific thought. One of the earliest attempts at applying Western-based concepts in other cultures was the classic study of Malinowski (1927), *Sex and Repression in Savage Society*. In this work he attempted to explain the behavior of "savages" through the use of the then dominant psychoanalytic perspective. But Malinowski found little evidence among the Trobriand Islanders of any Oedipal conflict as described by Freud. He concluded that the sexually based behavior postulated by psychoanalytic theory was not universal but rather was a product of the patriarchal family in Western society.

Shortly thereafter, Ruth Benedict (1934) pointed out that even the Western definition of "abnormality" might not be applicable to behavior in other cultures. Citing various ethnographic reports, she indicated that what is considered abnormal in one society is sometimes considered normal in another. For example, she noted that cataleptic and trancelike states were often valued by "simpler" peoples. Thus she concluded that "normality" is simply a culturally defined concept.

Early research also yielded evidence that some types of abnormal behavior occurred only

Is "abnormality" in the eye of the beholder?

Throughout history, most people's knowledge of human behavior has been limited to the behavior of their own cultural group—past or present—or that of near neighbors. We live in the first age in which people in all parts of the world have access to knowledge about each other. It was only in the last century that Western anthropologists began to bring home pictures and stories of the dress and customs of far-away peoples, and the first reaction of Westerners was to see these people as colorful, outlandish, backward, and often incomprehensible.

It is all too easy to regard one's own ways as "normal"—also moral, rational, and superior—and to see different values and customs as inferior and "abnormal." But what seems strange is in large part a matter of what you happen to be used to. Our ways can seem as strange to others as their ways do to us.

Male beauty contest, Bororo tribe, West Africa

Pie-eating contest, Massachusetts, USA

Arab woman, Morocco

Reunion, USA

*Young girls,
Banbi State, Nigeria*

*B*ehind the diversity of detail in different cultures, many universal values and strivings are expressed, such as the need for meaning and predictability, the search for beauty and self-enhancement, the prizing of love and belonging, the enjoyment of chances to demonstrate skill and competence, and the effort to prepare the young for responsible participation in the society. These needs are met in different ways in different cultures, but if they are not met, individual and social disorientation may result.

Members of all groups strive to express a sense of selfhood through dress and personal adornment. In some cases, this involves the simple human desire to enhance one's appearance; in others, it serves a larger purpose— to identify oneself as belonging to a particular group or social order.

*Father and son,
Edinburgh, Scotland*

*Woman
applying
makeup,
USA*

*Cheerleader clinic,
USA*

Asaro mudmen, New Guinea

*A*ll groups tend to develop ritual behaviors with meaning for the group, from traditional ceremonies to dances and community events. The meanings these rituals express, however, can differ drastically from group to group.

*Children dancing,
Bali*

Family en route to traditional ceremony, Japan

87

in certain cultures (see **HIGHLIGHT** on page 89.) These and other early anthropological findings led many investigators to take a position of *cultural relativism* concerning abnormal behavior. According to this view, as we saw in Chapter 1, there are no universal standards of "normality" or "abnormality" that can be applied to all societies. In fact, there was for a time a tendency to accept the "anthropologist's veto": any general principle could be rejected if a contrary instance somewhere in the world could be demonstrated. For example, schizophrenia would no longer be viewed as abnormal if its symptoms were somewhere accepted as a normal behavior pattern.

The relativistic view of abnormal behavior is no longer widely held (Strauss, 1979). Instead, it is generally recognized that the more severe types of mental disorder delineated in Western society are, in fact, found and considered maladaptive among peoples throughout the world. Research supports the view that many psychological disturbances are "universal," appearing in most cultures studied (Carpenter & Strauss, 1979; Cooper et al., 1972; Murphy, 1976; World Health Organization, 1975).

For example, although the relative incidence and specific symptoms vary, schizophrenia can be found among nearly all peoples, from the most primitive to the most technologically advanced. When individuals become so mentally disordered that they can no longer control their behavior, perform their expected role in the group, or even survive without special care, their behavior is considered abnormal in any society.

However, cultural influences cannot be disregarded. While there appear to be "universals," there is also reason to believe that cultural factors are very influential in what disorder develops, in the form that it takes, and in its course. How the disordered individual is received and treated and what is expected can influence whether the individual recovers or develops a chronic disorder (Murphy & Hall, 1972).

The importance of cultural influences on the way psychological disorders are expressed has been illustrated in a comparison of psychiatric patients from Italy, Switzerland, and the United States carried out by Butcher and Pancheri (1976). Patients grouped according to diagnostic category produced very similar general personality patterns on the Minnesota Multiphasic Personality Inventory (MMPI, see Chapter 15), but

the Italian patients also showed an exaggerated pattern of physical complaints that differentiated them from both the Swiss and American patients, regardless of clinical diagnosis.

This finding was consistent with earlier work by Opler and Singer (1959) and Zola (1966). For example, Zola examined symptom expression in two samples of second-generation American patients (Italian and Irish) at an ear-nose-throat clinic in Boston. When patients were matched on the basis of actual physical disorder, Zola found that the Italian patients made more physical complaints than the Irish. He attributed this difference to a defense mechanism which he called *dramatization,* in which the Italian patients, once identified as ill, tended to exaggerate or dramatize their physical problems to a greater extent than the other patients.

These findings illustrate an important point— the need for greater study of cultural influences on psychopathology. This neglected area of research may yet answer many questions about the origin and course of behavior problems (Draguns, 1979; Marsella, 1980). Marsella, for example, cites evidence indicating that certain features of psychological depression, as we know it, do not occur in some other cultures. Hence these features (e.g., strong guilt feelings) are probably not basic to depression but are rather produced by cultural variables. In a shrinking world, with instant communication and easy transportation, it is crucial for our science and our professional crafts to take a world view.

Sociocultural influences in our own society

As we narrow our focus to our own society, we find a number of early studies dealing with the relation of social class and other subgroup factors to the nature and incidence of mental disorders. For example, in a pioneering 1939 study, Faris and Dunham found that a disproportionate number of the schizophrenics admitted to mental hospitals came from the lower socioeconomic areas of a large city. The rate of admission decreased with distance of residence from these disorganized and deteriorating sections of the city. Studies since then have consistently found a relationship between social class and psychopathology (Dohrenwend & Dohrenwend, 1974).

Early studies concerning social class were gradually augmented by studies dealing with ur-

HIGHLIGHT
Unusual patterns of behavior considered to be culture-bound disorders

Name of disorder	Culture	Description
Amok	Malaya (also observed in Java, Phillippines, Africa, and Tierra del Fuego)	A disorder characterized by sudden, wild outbursts of homicidal aggression in which the afflicted person may kill or injure others. The rage disorder is usually found in males who are rather withdrawn, quiet, and inoffensive prior to the onset of the disorder. Stress, sleep deprivation, extreme heat, and alcohol are among the conditions thought to precipitate the disorder. Several stages have been observed: typically in the first stage the person becomes more withdrawn; then a period of brooding follows in which a loss of reality contact is evident. Ideas of persecution and anger predominate. Finally, a phase of automatism or *Amok* occurs, in which the person jumps up, yells, grabs a knife, and stabs people or objects within reach. Exhaustion and depression usually follow, with amnesia for the rage.
Anorexia nervosa	Western nations (particularly the U.S.)	A disorder occurring most frequently among young women in which a preoccupation with thinness produces a refusal to eat. This condition can result in death (see Chapter 8).
Latah	Malay	A fear reaction often occurring in middle-aged women of low intelligence who are subservient and self-effacing. The disorder is precipitated by the word *snake* or by tickling. It is characterized by *echolalia* (repetition of the words and sentences of others) and *echopraxia* (repetition of the acts of others). The disturbed individual may also react with negativism and the compulsive use of obscene language.
Koro	Southeast Asia (particularly Malay Archipelago)	A fear reaction or anxiety state in which the person fears that his penis will withdraw into his abdomen and he will die. This reaction may appear after sexual overindulgence or excessive masturbation. The anxiety is typically very intense and of sudden onset. The condition is "treated" by having the penis held firmly by the patient or by family members or friends. Often the penis is clamped to a wooden box.
Windigo	Algonquin Indian hunters	A fear reaction in which a hunter becomes anxious and agitated, convinced that he is bewitched. Fears center around his being turned into a cannibal by the power of a monster with an insatiable craving for human flesh.
Kitsunetsuki	Japan	A disorder in which victims believe that they are possessed by foxes and are said to change their facial expressions to resemble foxes. Entire families are often possessed and banned by the community. This reaction occurs in rural areas of Japan where people are superstitious and relatively uneducated.

Based on Kiev (1972), Lehmann (1967), Lebra (1976), and Yap (1951).

ban-rural, ethnic, religious, occupational, and other subgroups in relation to mental disorders. In one of these—an extensive study of mental disorders in Texas—Jaco (1960) found the incidence of psychoses to be three times higher in urban than in rural areas, and higher among the divorced and separated than among the married or widowed. And in a study by Levy and Rowitz (1974), the highest rates of mental disorders were found in the areas of large cities that were undergoing rapid and drastic social change. More recent research tends to confirm these findings (Bloom, Asher, & White, 1978; Dooley & Catalano, 1980). However, it must be emphasized that these are merely correlational findings and hence to not support strong causal inferences.

The study of the incidence and distribution of physical and mental disorders in a population, as in the research just cited, is referred to as *epidemiology.* The epidemiological approach serves to indicate both the social conditions that are correlated with a high incidence of given disorders and the *high-risk* areas and groups— those for whom the risk of pathology is especially high. In our later discussion we shall point out high-risk groups with respect to heart attacks, suicide, drug dependence, and other maladaptive patterns of behavior in our society.

This information provides a basis for formulating prevention and treatment programs; in turn, the effectiveness of these programs can be evaluated by means of further epidemiological studies.

With the gradual recognition of sociocultural influences, the heretofore almost exclusive concern with the individual patient has broadened to include a concern with societal, communal, familial, and other group settings as contributors to mental disorders. It has become apparent that an individual's maladaptive behavior might be caused not by faulty internal processes but by abnormal conditions in the surrounding social environment. As Lennard and Bernstein (1969) put it, "Therapeutic or damaging potentials often inhere in social contexts rather than in individuals . . ." (p. 205).

The sociocultural viewpoint has led to the introduction of programs designed to alleviate social conditions that foster maladaptive behavior and to the provision of community facilities for the early detection, treatment, and long-range prevention of mental disorders. We shall deal

with the clinic facilities and other programs— both governmental and private—that have been established as a result of the community mental health movement in later chapters.

Toward an interdisciplinary approach

As the research engendered by the biological, psychosocial, and sociocultural perspectives gradually led to a better understanding of the role of all these factors in mental disorders, it became increasingly apparent that explanation based on only one of the three levels was likely to be incomplete. Usually, interaction of several causal factors produces the disorders that we see. For example, an individual may have a biological predisposition to severe mood swings but may be getting along satisfactorily until some severe crisis brings on a depressive state.

Even in the mental disorder *paresis,* it was observed that some patients became depressed and others expansive and happy with approximately the same brain pathology. Similarly, in psychoses associated with senile and arteriosclerotic brain damage, researchers found that some patients became severely disordered mentally with only a small amount of brain damage, whereas others showed only mild symptoms despite relatively extensive brain damage.

Gradually investigators came to realize that even where brain damage was present, the patient's psychological reaction to it and to the resulting change in his or her life situation were of vital importance in determining the overall clinical picture. It also became apparent that the emotional support of family members—as well as the kind of situation to which the patient would be returning after discharge from the hospital—were significant factors in determining the *prognosis,* that is, the likelihood that the patient would improve. On the other hand, in certain functional psychoses in which the patient's disorder was apparently the result of psychological rather than organic factors, it was nevertheless found that the use of organic therapies— such as antidepressant drugs or electroconvulsive shock—produced dramatic results. And finally, the symptoms, prognosis, and reaction to a given treatment might all vary somewhat for individuals from different cultural backgrounds.

Such considerations have led to the emergence of the *interdisciplinary approach,* which calls for the integration of biological, psychosocial, and sociocultural factors into a comprehensive clinical picture. In dealing with a particular case, of course, we may be concerned primarily with one set of determinants or another. For example, one case of homicidal behavior may be closely associated with drug intoxication, another with pent-up frustration and hostility, and still another with the learning of criminal values in a faulty environment. Thus the problem becomes one of assessing and dealing with the particular interaction of these three sets of determinants—biological, psychosocial, and sociocultural—in each particular case.

The interdisciplinary approach has led to more integration of research findings from such varied disciplines as genetics, biochemistry, neurophysiology, psychology, sociology, and anthropology in efforts to understand and cope with abnormal behavior. On a practical level, it has led to the meaningful coordination of medical, psychological, and other mental health personnel in the work to assess, treat, and prevent mental disorders. It has become increasingly apparent that maladaptive behavior can be fully understood and effectively dealt with only in this comprehensive way.

Summary

Abnormal psychology, as a relatively immature scientific discipline, has within it many points of view contending for special or exclusive attention in the interpretation and understanding of abnormal behavior.

The early biological viewpoint focused on neurological brain damage as a model for the understanding of abnormality, a model we now see as limited even for the cases to which it most clearly applies. Modern biological thinking in the mental disorders is focused on the biochemistry of brain functioning, and, at least in respect to the more severe disorders, shows much promise for advancing our knowledge of how the mind and the body interact to produce maladaptive behavior.

The psychosocial viewpoints on abnormal behavior are oriented toward much more complex questions than is the biological, and hence there are more individual perspectives within it forming a less cohesive class. The "granddaddy" of these perspectives is Freudian psychoanalysis, for many years preoccupied with questions about libidinal energies and their containment but more recently showing a distinctly social or interpersonal thrust under the guise of "object-relations" theory. A rapprochement with the interpersonal perspectives, notably that of Sullivan, would seem both possible and desirable as we move into the future.

The behavioristic perspective, which claims its roots in attempts to make all of psychology an objective science, was slow in overcoming a dominant psychodynamic bias, but in the last 20 years has established itself as a significant force in the field. It has achieved a reputation for producing excellent results, and its ability to accommodate itself to the current dominance of cognitive thinking in psychology ensures its continued growth and importance.

The humanistic perspective was considered relatively briefly, mainly because it does not chiefly concern itself with the origins and treatment of severe mental disorder. Rather, it tends to focus on the conditions that maximize superior functioning in individuals who are "getting along." As such, it has to do with personal values and personal growth.

The origins of the interpersonal perspective can be traced back to defections from the psychoanalytic ranks of individuals who took exception to the emphasis Freud placed on internal determinants of motivation and behavior. As a group, these theorists have emphasized that the important aspects of human personality have social or interpersonal origins. The most fully articulated and currently important of these views is that of Harry Stack Sullivan.

Finally, any comprehensive approach to the study of human behavior—normal or abnormal—cannot fail to take account of the sociocultural context in which a given form of behavior occurs. Everything considered, it would appear that a multidisciplinary perspective is essential if we are to achieve the goal of a full understanding of a given instance of abnormal behavior.

Causal factors in abnormal behavior

Simone Marye, Personnage, Chien, et Oiseaux (1959–61). Marye (1890–1961) had a successful, if rather conventional, career as a sculptress in the 1920s. Her popularity did not last long, however, and she was dogged by poverty, poor health, and loneliness throughout her last thirty years. She was institutionalized at age 67 with the diagnosis of Alzheimer's disease. Marye drew this strangely proportioned, childlike design while hospitalized; by this time, she was almost totally out of touch with reality, retaining little but a professed devotion to Buddhism.

In most cases, abnormal behavior does not arise suddenly, "out of the blue," in a person with faultless biological and psychological makeup—if any such person ever existed! Rather, we can usually see more or less clearly—although often only in retrospect—the pattern of factors that rendered the individual fragile or vulnerable in respect to the particular circumstances that surrounded the emergence of abnormality. Or, at the very least, we can usually piece together a number of reasonable hypotheses about these background flaws—assuming, of course, that we have a substantial amount of information concerning the person's background.

Of course, all of us harbor *vulnerabilities,* "weak spots," that could under certain circumstances render us susceptible to behaving abnormally. Whether or not we ever do appears to depend not only on the nature, number, and degree of these vulnerabilities but also importantly on the way they combine in any given individual, as well as on the nature and severity of life challenges faced. Commenting on the enormous complexity and widespread individual differences implied here, Meehl (1978) has suggested that severe mental breakdown might as often as not be the consequence of "bad luck." He notes, however, that such a conclusion does not justify abandonment of our search for understanding or our efforts to prevent and treat mental disorder.

In the preceding chapter, we described several theoretical viewpoints concerning abnormal behavior, each of which focuses on different origins, or background events, that contribute to maladaptive behavior. In brief, the biological viewpoint emphasizes various *organic conditions* that can impair brain functioning and lead to psychopathology. Of the psychosocial viewpoints, the psychoanalytical focuses on *intrapsychic conflicts that lead to anxiety;* the behavioristic, on *faulty learning;* the humanistic, on *blocked or distorted personal growth;* and the interpersonal on *unsatisfactory relationships.* Finally, the sociocultural viewpoint focuses on *pathological social conditions.* In this chapter we will look in more detail at these origins of our human vulnerabilities, reviewing available research on the subject. Before proceeding, however, we must give some additional attention to the concept of causation in abnormal behavior.

Perspectives on causation

In attempting to analyze the causal factors in abnormal behavior, it will be helpful to consider briefly (a) the distinctions between primary, predisposing, precipitating, and reinforcing causes; (b) the problem of feedback and circularity in abnormal behavior; and (c) the concept of diathesis-stress as a broad causal model of abnormal behavior.

Primary, predisposing, precipitating, and reinforcing causes

Regardless of one's theoretical perspective, several terms can be used to specify the role a factor plays in the *etiology,* or causal pattern, of abnormal behavior. The *primary cause* is the condition that must exist for the disorder to occur—syphilis of the brain is an example in the case of general paresis. A primary cause is a necessary but not always sufficient factor in abnormality. Many recognized disorders appear not to have primary causes as such. A *predisposing cause* is a condition that comes before and paves the way for a possible later occurrence of disorder under certain conditions; an example on the psychological level would be parental rejection, which would probably predispose a child toward difficulty in handling close personal relationships later. A *precipitating cause* is a condition that proves too much for the individual and "triggers" the disorder; an example might be a crushing disappointment. Often the precipitating cause may seem insignificant and related only tangentially, if at all, to a primary or predisposing cause. In short, it can be the "straw that breaks the camel's back." Leaving the cap off the toothpaste may be a minor annoyance in the basically well-adjusted family, but the same act can precipitate a full-fledged argument in a family already experiencing major difficulties in communicating. Finally, a *reinforcing cause* is a condition that tends to maintain maladaptive behavior that is already occurring. An example would be the extra attention, sympathy, and removal from unwanted responsibility that often come when one is "ill"; these pleasant experiences may contribute to a delay in recovery. Reinforcing causes have received a great deal of emphasis in recent years, especially among behaviorally oriented psychologists.

In a given case, a primary cause may be either absent or unknown, or two or more factors may share primary responsibility (see **HIGHLIGHT** on page 95). Likewise, the exact patterning of primary, predisposing, precipitating, and reinforcing causes may be far from clear; a given factor or event may contribute to disorder in more than one way. For example, should a child lose a parent through death, that loss will be both primary and precipitating in the child's subsequent grief reaction, and it might also *predispose* the child to severe reactions to loss in adulthood.

As in the above example, serious adjustment challenges early in life, whatever their specific nature, may in certain instances predispose a person toward specific difficulties later in life. In other words, all the various types of causal factors discussed above (including primary, precipitating, and reinforcing) may act as predisposing factors, that is, they may play important roles in increasing a person's vulnerability to disorder.

This eight-year-old girl has just learned that her parents and three sisters were killed when their car was struck by a train shortly after they had dropped her off at a friend's home. Traumatic experiences of this nature can have a profound effect on later personality development and adjustment.

HIGHLIGHT

Predisposing causes of depressive reactions to rape

Atkeson et al. (1982) assessed depressive responses to rape in a group of 115 victims of sexual assault, following them up for a period of 12 months after the occurrence of the crime. Most of these women experienced depressive emotion immediately following the assault, but as a group they were not significantly more depressed than a nonvictim control group at the 4-months' follow-up. However, a subgroup of these victims continued to be depressed even at the 12-month follow-up. Demographic variables such as age and socioeconomic variables were found to be related to subsequent depression (older and poorer women being the more affected). Yet, surprisingly, the level of trauma experienced during the rape had no detectable effect on long-term depressive symptomatology.

Adequate support immediately after the rape *did* appear to lessen long-term effects.

The strongest determinants of adjustment in the long-term postrape period were associated with the level of prior functioning of the victim. Less functional individuals were much more vulnerable to depression after having been raped than were their more fortunate sisters. Slower recoveries from the rape experience were experienced by women who already had had psychological problems of one sort or another, including, especially, problems involving depression, anxiety, and obsessive-compulsive behavior. Additionally, problems with sexual relationships generally and with physical health seem to have hampered rapid recovery from the stress of rape.

essarily independent of each other, and they may—and most likely do—occur in varying combinations in given individuals.

Genetic endowment as a determinant

Probably the most unique aspect of our human inheritance is a superior brain. It has been described as the most highly organized apparatus in the universe, consisting of some ten billion nerve cells, or neurons, with countless interconnecting pathways as well as myriad connections with other parts of the body. The human brain provides a fantastic communication and computing network with tremendous capabilities for learning and "storing" experience; for reasoning, imagining, and problem solving; and for integrating the overall functioning of the organism. It is the brain that makes possible the enormous adaptability of the human species to varied and changing conditions of existence, but it often does so at a price—a price being paid by those unfortunate persons who are the subject matter of abnormal psychology. The nervous systems of lower organisms are not nearly so flexibly adaptive, but by the same token they are

much less likely to go awry or lead to behavior that is ultimately self-injurious.

It would appear that the essential characteristics of human inheritance are basically the same for people of all racial and ethnic groups. However, the specific features of this endowment vary widely; except for identical twins, no two human beings have ever begun life with the same genetic endowment. Thus heredity not only provides the potentialities for development and behavior typical of the species but also is an important source of individual differences.

Our inheritance begins at conception, when the egg cell of the female is fertilized by the sperm cell of the male and each embryo receives a *genetic inheritance* that provides potentialities for development and behavior throughout a lifetime. Since our behavior is inevitably influenced by our biological inheritance, it should hardly be surprising that certain vulnerabilities have their source at this very basic level. Some inherited defects cause structural abnormalities that interfere directly with the normal development of the brain. Others are much more subtle, but may still render a person susceptible to even the most severe of the mental disorders. In general, *chromosomal anomalies* (irregularities) are likely to produce abnormalities in the brain. On the other hand, the more subtle influences are usually transmitted in the genetic code itself, manifesting themselves as metabolic or biochemical irregularities; in other words, the individual may inherit *faulty genes.*

Chromosomal anomalies.

Advances in cellular biological research have enabled us to detect chromosomal irregularities rather readily, thus making it possible to study their effect on future development and behavior. The first major breakthrough in this area was the discovery that most normal human cells have 46 chromosomes in which are encoded the hereditary plan—the overall strategy or information for guiding development. When fertilization takes place, the normal inheritance consists of 23 pairs of chromosomes—one of each pair being from the mother and one from the father. Twenty-two of these chromosome pairs are called *autosomes;* they determine general anatomical and physiological characteristics. The remaining pair, the *sex chromosomes,* determine the individual's sex and certain other characteristics. In the female, both of these sex chromosomes—one from each parent—are designated as *X chromosomes.* In the male, the sex chromosome from the mother is an X but that from the father is different and is called a *Y chromosome.*

Research in developmental genetics has shown that abnormalities in the structure or number of the chromosomes are associated with a wide range of malformations and disorders. For example, the presence of an extra chromosome is characteristic of *Down's syndrome,* a type of mental retardation in which there is a *trisomy* (three instead of two) of one autosomal pair, chromosome #21 (see **HIGHLIGHT** on page 100). Here the extra chromosome is the *primary* cause of the disorder, but because the probability of this defect rises sharply with the age of the mother, and less sharply but still significantly with the age of the father (Matsunaga et al., 1978), parental age at conception may be regarded as a possible predisposing cause. Fortunately, it is a cause that manifests itself in Down's syndrome only rarely.

Anomalies may also occur in the sex chromosomes, producing a variety of complications that may predispose the person to the development of abnormal behavior. For example, Klinefelter's syndrome also involves 47 chromosomes, but in this case the pathogenic element

HIGHLIGHT
Death in Guyana

In late November 1978 the news media reported the shocking story of the mass suicide—or murder—of over 900 persons, members of a religious cult, the People's Temple, who had migrated to the Guyanan jungle from the United States only a few years before. The facts of the gruesome event have been fairly well pieced together, but the questions it raised may never be satisfactorily answered.

Following repeated reports that members of the commune were being mistreated and held against their will, Congressman Leo J. Ryan of California and 17 others had gone to Guyana to investigate. They were allowed to talk to members but as their plane prepared to leave, shooting broke out and five of the party, including the congressman, were killed.

Evidently the founder and leader of the People's Temple, the Reverend Jim Jones, had planned the shootings. He called the people together, told them that the Guyanese authorities would arrest and torture them, and said that he could not allow any of his beloved children to suffer such a terrible fate—they must all choose the dignity of "revolutionary suicide" instead. Two huge vats of Kool-Aid laced with cyanide were prepared, and with armed guards ringing the group to prevent escape, the people were exhorted to drink the potion and give it to their children. Nurses helped the reluctant. At some point Jones shot himself or was shot. A handful escaped into the surrounding jungle, but the rest perished.

Who was the Reverend Jim Jones, and how did he achieve such power over his followers?

Jones had founded the People's Temple in the early 1950s in Indianapolis. It was devoted to fundamentalist Christianity and socialism and drew an interracial following. In 1963, convinced that Indianapolis would soon be destroyed in a nuclear holocaust, Jones moved with over 100 of his followers to Ukiah, California, later going to San Francisco, where his following grew rapidly, with the elderly and the underprivileged disproportionately represented.

Jones staged "miracles," such as cancer "cures," and claimed at various times to be a reincarnation of Jesus, Father Divine, Lenin, and even God himself. But behind the scenes, he was delighting in beatings and other public chastenings of his followers, after which they were expected to say "Thank you, father," and he would embrace them, saying, "Father loves you. You're a stronger person now. I can trust you."

Meanwhile, he was developing paranoid fears of assassination by the U.S. government and in 1972 began the commune at Jonestown, Guyana, where he went himself in 1977. At Jonestown many members were stripped, paddled, forced to sign false confessions, and humiliated in other ways. Yet when Jones would ask if they would lay down their and their children's lives for him, they would scream, "I will, father!" Would-be defectors were discouraged by armed guards and by assurances that the CIA would kill them if they returned to the United States.

Jones' physician in the United States was quoted as saying that Jones had a serious illness and was "literally burning his brains with drugs" (Moody & Graham, 1978, p. 10). Did he perhaps know he was dying and did he want to take his loved ones with him? We will probably never know.

Even harder to understand is how such a person could have attracted and held such a devoted following. Yet there have been repeated examples of this kind of blind devotion to charismatic cult leaders and repeated examples of followers being induced to commit acts they had never before thought of committing, including burglary and murder. There have always been cults, but they seem to flourish especially in times of violence, social disorganization, and great uncertainty; for the faithful, they offer security and absolute truth. Often the people who join them are alienated and estranged individuals whose identification with and loyalty to a powerful leader give their lives meaning. There is also an element of idealism: the group stands for noble values. And there is an element of elitism: in this corrupt and evil world, *we* stand for truth and goodness. Once in the group, individuals are subjected to powerful pressures from other group members.

With this grounding, individuals will do whatever they have to do to prove their absolute commitment to the leader. What they must do depends on the values and mental stability of the leader. But the state of mind that followers can reach is shown in these statements (Moody & Graham, 1978, p. 9):

"My husband and I would have been willing to kill for Jones." (Statement by a woman at Ukiah.)

"I was nothing going nowhere. I was bored and unhappy at home. The Joneses made me feel like I was someone. Just the sound of his voice made you feel like you had power." (Statement by a 16-year-old girl who went with the group from Indiana to California.)

So what "caused" the deaths at Guyana? Was it the madness of the leader? The vulnerabilities of the members that had predisposed them to blind followership? The troubled times in which we live? The isolation of Jonestown? All these factors and others would seem to have played a part, highlighting again the need to look for patterns of interacting factors rather than single causes in trying to understand the puzzles of human behavior.

The basic facts of this tragic event are presented in the December 4, 11, and 18, 1978, issues of *Time.*

is an extra X chromosome; these individuals have male body structures (although they are usually infertile) and a predominantly male gender identity. They are far more likely than boys with the usual 46 chromosomes to develop several kinds of psychopathology, such as juvenile delinquency and problems arising from gender identity confusion (Wright, Schaefer, & Solomons, 1979). Such individuals are said to be "at high risk" for these outcomes.

Studies by Sergovich et al. (1969) and Hanerton et al. (1975) indicate that the incidence of observable chromosomal abnormalities in newborns is approximately one half of 1 percent. The exact causes of chromosomal anomalies are not yet fully understood. Some have evidently been passed on from one or both of the parents; some apparently occur in the combining of egg and sperm or from genetic mutations occurring after conception.

A search for chromosomal irregularities in schizophrenia and other psychoses has not proved fruitful, and none of the chromosomal anomalies thus far observed has appeared to be directly related to such disorders. Even in the case of Down's syndrome, where a trisomy has been identified, it has been estimated that 65 percent of the fetuses spontaneously abort (Creasy & Crolla, 1974). The potential effects of extreme chromosomal irregularities are largely unknown because they ordinarily result in the death of the embryo. Nearly 50 percent of stillborn infants have such chromosomal abnormalities (Poland & Lowry, 1974).

One thing appears certain: females are less susceptible to defects from sex-linked genetic disorders because they have two X chromosomes. If one proves faulty, the other member of the pair generally can handle the work of development. Nevertheless, females are sometimes born with a missing or extra sex chromosome (XO, called Turner's syndrome, or XXX), either of which may produce abnormalities. Since males have a single X chromosome paired with a single Y chromosome, a defect in either may mean trouble.

Faulty genes. It is important to distinguish between chromosomal irregularities, which, with modern techniques, can now usually be directly observed—as in the case of too many or too few chromosomes in the cells of the body—

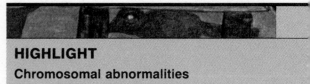

HIGHLIGHT
Chromosomal abnormalities

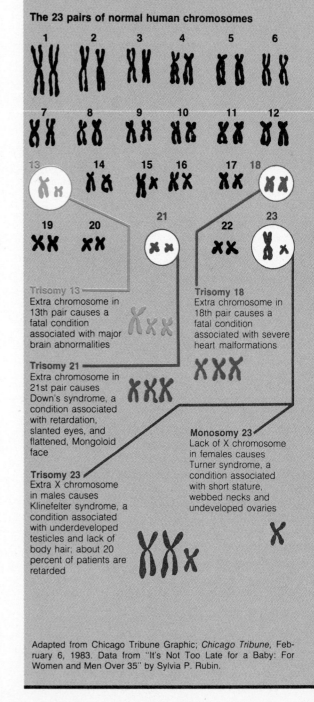

The 23 pairs of normal human chromosomes

Trisomy 13
Extra chromosome in 13th pair causes a fatal condition associated with major brain abnormalities

Trisomy 21
Extra chromosome in 21st pair causes Down's syndrome, a condition associated with retardation, slanted eyes, and flattened, Mongoloid face

Trisomy 23
Extra X chromosome in males causes Klinefelter syndrome, a condition associated with underdeveloped testicles and lack of body hair; about 20 percent of patients are retarded

Trisomy 18
Extra chromosome in 18th pair causes a fatal condition associated with severe heart malformations

Monosomy 23
Lack of X chromosome in females causes Turner syndrome, a condition associated with short stature, webbed necks and undeveloped ovaries

Adapted from Chicago Tribune Graphic; *Chicago Tribune*, February 6, 1983. Data from "It's Not Too Late for a Baby: For Women and Men Over 35" by Sylvia P. Rubin.

and genetic faults (that is, involving specific genes), which can exist in the absence of obvious chromosomal deviations. The *genes* are the long molecules of DNA (deoxyribonucleic acid) that occur at various locations on the chromosome. Individual genes may sometimes contain information that causes bodily processes to malfunction. Unfortunately, we cannot yet predict with any great certainty the occurrence of such malfunctions.

However, through the use of electron microscopes, we can study the internal structure of the genes, and we can gain information concerning the code that regulates the development and functioning of the organism, a code that is carried by the biochemical constituents of the now-familiar spiraling ladder of the DNA molecule—the "double helix." Genes carry the instructions for specific body traits, such as eye color and blood type; they also provide the "assembly instructions" for determining organic development. Thus they are the specific units or bearers of an individual's biological inheritance.

Some genes are called *dominant* genes: their instructions are activated even if the other member of the pair carries contradictory instructions. *Recessive* genes are genes whose instructions are discarded unless the individual has inherited two such genes, one from each parent. In the field of abnormal psychology, however, it is not usual for genetic influences to express themselves in such simple, straightforward ways. This is partly because behavior, unlike physical characteristics such as eye color, is *never* determined exclusively by genetic endowment: it is *always* a product of the interaction of environment with the structural and functional characteristics of the organism. Genes can affect behavior only indirectly, through their influence on the physical and chemical properties of the body, whose development they regulate.

The few instances in the field of abnormal psychology in which relatively straightforward predictions can be made on the basis of known laws of inheritance invariably involve gross neurological impairment; here, abnormal behavior arises, in part, as a consequence of central nervous system malfunction. Examples of such relatively rare disorders include Huntington's chorea (Lynch, Harlan, & Dyhrberg, 1972) and Tay-Sachs disease (Thompson & O'Quinn, 1979). Generally, such disorders occur where there is a

The wedding of "General" Tom Thumb and Miss Lavinia Bump in 1863 united two midgets in marriage. The groom was 38 inches tall, the bride 32 inches. Their small stature was probably caused by the combination of recessive genes inherited from each set of parents.

pairing of two recessive genes, each of which is faulty in some respect.

It appears likely that many of the most interesting (if still largely obscure) genetic influences in abnormal behavior do not usually involve dominant and recessive relationships in one or only a few gene pairs. Rather it is now believed by most experts that pathogenic genetic influences operate *polygenically,* that is, through the action of many genes together in some sort of additive or interactive fashion. A genetically vulnerable individual is one who has inherited a large number of these genes that, in the aggregate, represent faulty heredity. These faulty genes, in turn, may lead to metabolic difficulties or other malfunctioning that predisposes the individual to later difficulty.

Although marked advances have been made in identifying faulty genes, most of the information we have on the role of genetic factors in mental disorders is based not on studies of genes but on studies of families. The family history method requires that the investigator observe a large sample of relatives of each *proband* or *index case* (the subject, or carrier of the trait in question, such as schizophrenia) in order to see whether the incidence increases in proportion to the degree of hereditary relationship. In addition, the incidence of the trait in a normal population is compared with its incidence among the relatives of index cases.

Such research is much more difficult and complicated to carry out than may at first appear, and the history of research in this area, particularly with regard to schizophrenic disorders, is littered with many erroneous conclusions and patently biased reports. For example, many studies have been made of the rates at which schizophrenia in one monozygotic (that is, genetically identical) twin is predictive of schizophrenia in the other. Such rates are called *concordance rates.* Reports from such studies have varied between 6 percent and 86 percent. An accurate figure, we now believe, would be slightly under 50 percent, but this figure is hard to interpret because twins, especially identical twins, almost always share highly similar environments as well as heredity. The main point is that in many instances of this disorder (and very probably in certain other mental disorders) there does seem to be a modest hereditary component—an innate predispositional vulnerability.

As was noted in Chapter 3, evidence of this type constitutes a main prop to the currently resurgent biological viewpoint. Whether an individual with this pathogenic genetic endowment will develop schizophrenia will be determined by many factors that operate after conception. We still lack definitive knowledge about these other factors and how they interact with genetic endowment. We shall take up this matter of genetic influences in schizophrenia in greater detail in Chapter 10.

It should not be surprising that, given a favorable life situation, an individual's inherited vulnerability probably will never result in abnormal behavior. The weight of evidence suggests that in a genetically predisposed person *the most likely outcome is nonoccurrence* of the disorder. The field of physical disease, too, is rife with examples of genetic predispositions that never attain the status of observable disease; these include predispositions for diabetes, hypertension, coronary heart disease, and some forms of cancer (Bergsma, 1974; Kaiser Foundation, 1970).

Constitutional liabilities

The term *constitutional* is used to describe any characteristic that is either innate or acquired so early—often as early as the prenatal environment—and in such strength that it is functionally similar to a genetically determined characteristic. Physique, physical handicaps, and basic reaction tendencies are among the many traits included in this category. Here our focus will be on the role of these constitutional factors in the etiology of maladaptive behavior.

Physique.   Though some early research has sought to establish a direct link between physique and psychopathology—say, for example, between muscular physique and criminal behavior (Glueck & Glueck, 1968; Sheldon, 1954)—most data suggest that the link, if any, is not primarily biological but is rather a product of social learning. The muscular person, for instance, may learn that aggression often pays off.

A look at everyday situations makes it evident that physique and other aspects of physical appearance do play an important role in both personality development and adjustment. Beauty, for example, is highly valued in our society. One need only attend a social gathering, watch television, or note the billions of dollars spent each year on cosmetics to see the influence of beauty on people's behavior and on their feelings about themselves.

It is reasonable to assume that physically attractive persons on the whole have advantages in life not shared by the less attractive, and, indeed, mental disorder has been found to be correlated with judged unattractiveness (Napoleon, Chassin, & Young, 1980). Snyder, Tanke, and Berscheid (1977) have demonstrated that college males who believed they were talking on the telephone to an attractive female behaved quite differently from those who believed they were talking to an unattractive female. Interestingly, the females *assumed* to be attractive responded to the greater interest shown them and were rated by independent judges listening to recordings of the conversations as in fact *being* attractive, a good example of the circularity in causation mentioned earlier. On the other hand, the females assumed to be unattractive responded to their telephone partners' behavior in ways that led the judges to rate them as unattractive. What had been reality only in the minds of the male subjects became "reality" in the behavior of their otherwise unknown female partners. This study suggests that other people's reactions to our real or imagined characteristics may determine our own behavior, often in a way that conforms to their expectations. Further experimental confirmation of this point has recently been provided by Christensen and Rosenthal (1982) in a study in which male and female college students were provided with arbitrary expectations concerning strangers with whom they were asked to interact. The behavior of the strangers did indeed conform to the students' expectations. Interestingly, males tended to *produce* stronger conformation behaviors in their partners, while female partners were more likely to conform to expectations.

Physical handicaps.   Genetic defects or environmental conditions operating before or after birth may result in physical handicaps. A defect that a child is born with is called a *congenital defect.* In this country an estimated 5 out of every 100 babies are born with mental or physical defects (Wright et al., 1979). About a third of these defects are considered to be definitely inherited; another sixth are due to drugs or disease; the rest—about half in all—result from unknown causes, though many of these may yet prove to be hereditary. Some of the aberrations are apparent at birth, while others—such as mental retardation, endocrine disturbances, and heart defects—may not be detected until months or years later. Often such anomalies are minor, but more serious congenital defects constitute one of the five leading causes of death during childhood, accounting for over half a million deaths yearly. It is estimated that nearly half of the deaths occurring in pediatric hospitals are due to disorders with significant genetic components (Wright et al., 1979).

The most common birth difficulty associated with later mental disorders—including mental retardation, hyperactivity, and emotional disturbances—is low birth weight, which is defined as a birth weight of 5½ pounds or less. This is most often a factor in premature births but can also occur in full-term births.

Prenatal conditions that can lead to premature birth and/or to low birth weight include nutritional deficiencies, disease, exposure to radia-

Severe physical disabilities can make dealing with the tasks and challenges of life just that much more stressful. Many individuals (such as those shown here) manage to come to terms with their physical limitations and function as independent members of society; others accept the role of a "cripple" or misfit with its ensuing psychological problems.

tion, drugs, emotional stress, or excessive use of alcohol or tobacco on the part of the mother.

It appears that some of the risk factor associated with low birth weight may be lessened by special treatment of the infant, such as systematic stroking and massage, during the first postnatal month (Rice, 1977); unfortunately, the likelihood that such special treatment will occur is, in most cases, remote since such infants tend to spend their early days in incubators.

Mothers who are subjected to severe emotional stress during pregnancy appear to have a much higher incidence of premature deliveries. Even in the case of full-term babies, severe maternal stress appears to be associated with hyperactivity in the fetus during later pregnancy, and after birth to be reflected in feeding difficulties, sleep problems, irritability, and other difficulties (Blau et al., 1963; Sontag, Steele, & Lewis, 1969). As might be expected, socioeconomic status has been found to be related to fetal and birth difficulties, the incidence being several times greater among mothers on lower socioeconomic levels (Robinson & Robinson, 1976).

It would appear that the fetus is not so well protected as many investigators formerly thought—that a variety of biological and psychological conditions affecting the mother during pregnancy can have profound effects on the child's development and adjustment.

Primary reaction tendencies. Newborns differ in how they react to particular kinds of stimuli. Some are startled by slight sounds or cry if sunlight hits their faces; others are seemingly insensitive to such stimulation. These reactions differ from baby to baby and are examples of *primary reaction tendencies,* characteristic ways of behaving that appear to have been established prior to any extensive interaction with the environment. These behaviors are regarded as constitutional rather than genetic because it seems likely they are due to more than genetic influences alone; that is, prenatal environmental factors may also play a role in their development. They include such things as sensitivity to stimuli, "temperament," and activity level (Rothbart, 1981). It is of note that longitudinal studies have shown that these reaction tendencies are relatively enduring from infancy to young adulthood.

Recent studies suggest that even the different styles of behavior exhibited by most, though by no means all, men and women may be due in part to primary reaction tendencies caused by early hormonal influences on the developing nervous system. Though we know that any such influences may be largely overridden by differential social learning and sex-typing experiences, subtle vestiges of biological determination may yet remain and manifest themselves in gender-related primary reaction tendencies (Ehrhardt & Meyer-Bahlburg, 1981; Money & Ehrhardt, 1972; Pervin, 1978; Rubin, Reinisch, & Haskett, 1981). Sex differences that might fall into this category can occur in the cognitive, affective, and behavioral realms. After a careful review of the available evidence, Pervin (1978) concluded, in part, as follows:

"In cognitive functioning, there is no evidence of overall differences in intelligence but considerable evidence suggesting differences in special abilities. Females tend to perform better than males on tests of verbal ability while males tend to perform better than females on tests of mathematical ability and the manipulation of spatial relationships. . . . The differences between the sexes tend to be small and the overlap between the sexes great.

"[In] the realm of affective functioning . . . enough studies have reported differences in activity level [higher for males], fearfulness [higher for females], and emotional responses to frustration [higher for males] to suggest that basic differences in affective functioning may exist . . . .

"In overt behavioral functioning, the evidence suggests that males are higher in aggression and dominance behavior while females are higher in dependence and nurturance behavior. . . . The evidence for a difference in aggression seems to be most reliable since it comes from a variety of sources—evolutionary, cross-cultural, developmental, and biological-hormonal . . . ." (pp. 176–77)

Primary reaction tendencies also include characteristic ways of reacting to stress. Some infants react to changes in routine or other stress by running a fever; others, by digestive disorders; still others, by sleeping disturbances. Several investigators have attempted to relate such primary reaction vulnerability to stress and maladaptive behavior.

In a classic longitudinal study of infant development, Chess, Thomas, and Birch (1965) found that 7 to 10 percent of all babies are "difficult"—

they evidence irregular patterns of eating, sleeping, and bowel movement; tend to cry a great deal and to show a predominantly negative mood; and are inclined to be irritable and have difficulty in adjusting to change. These researchers concluded that since the mother does not gain the satisfactions she expected from having her baby, the temperamental difficulty becomes overlaid and complicated by an unsatisfactory mother-infant relationship. In recent follow-up work with adopted children, Maurer, Cadoret, and Cain (1980) confirmed the relationship between membership in the "difficult" group and later childhood adjustment difficulties.

Thomas, Chess, and Birch (1968) have made the point that a poor "fit" between the child's temperamental characteristics and the structure and flexibility of environmental demands, particularly those within the home, can lead to "dissonant stress." Such stress in turn may lead to a behavioral disturbance whose form in part reflects the child's temperamental characteristics. The problem is complicated if the child also exhibits developmental deviations of one sort or another, such as mental retardation. Such deviations increase the likelihood of behavior disorder and thus make a "good fit" between temperament and environmental conditions even more crucial if untoward consequences are to be avoided. A number of factors may thus help determine the relationships between constitutionally derived temperamental features and subsequent behavior disorder (Buss & Plomin, 1975; Thomas & Chess, 1977).

Other longitudinal studies have followed children believed to be at high risk by virtue of having abnormal prenatal conditions or having been born to parents with serious problems. As was noted in Chapter 1, such studies have potential advantages in clarifying causal patterns. They start with subjects who have not yet developed a disorder and try to predict which ones will succumb, or, as in the above case, watch what actually happens and try to identify the conditions that seem to push a child in one direction or the other. These studies are difficult and expensive, however, and can encounter many unforeseen difficulties. Thus most of our evidence still comes from research in which individuals who have already developed a disorder are studied, and the researcher tries to reconstruct a picture of the probable causes.

Incomplete though our knowledge is, however, one conclusion we can draw is that childhood disturbance is often followed by adult disturbance, though its specific form is a poor predictor of the particular nature of later adult difficulties (Fish, 1975; Hanson, Gottesman, & Meehl, 1977; Meehl, 1978). To at least some extent, early manifestations of vulnerability seem to be diffuse and nonspecific; what later abnormality will result is hard to predict.

Brain dysfunction

As we saw in Chapter 2, the first real scientific breakthrough in understanding at least some aspects of psychopathology came when researchers proved that the behavior shown in general paresis was related to definite destruction of brain tissue. We now realize that significant damage or loss of brain tissue places a person at risk for psychopathology.

Excepting the some 25 percent of mental retardates who acquire it before birth or during childhood, organic brain pathology is infrequent in younger populations and is therefore not a major factor in contributing to the vulnerability of this age group to psychiatric disorder. The incidence of such damage increases notably among the elderly, owing chiefly to the aging process itself (Alzheimer's disease) or to associated cardiovascular insufficiency (see Chapter 13). It is estimated that at least 17 percent of persons above the age of 65 have significant brain damage (Kolata, 1981a). Brain damage increases vulnerability by rendering a person less competent to cope. At the same time, the disabilities experienced themselves contribute a significant source of stress. Therefore, it should not surprise us that some 5 percent of persons over the age of 60 develop psychiatric symptoms and are diagnosed as having organic mental disorders (Dohrenwend et al., 1980). These elderly patients typically occupy a substantial proportion (overall about 20 percent) of the beds in mental hospitals.

Gross brain pathology, in which there are observable (by special means) defects in brain tissue, may be only a small part of the brain pathology "story." Adequate brain functioning is dependent on the efficiency with which an excited nerve cell, or neuron, can transmit its "message" across a synapse to the next neuron in established pathways in the brain. These "interneuronal" (or "transsynaptic") transmissions are accomplished by special chemicals that are released into the synaptic cleft by the excited presynaptic neuron. If there is an appropriately coded receptor on the postsynaptic neuron, the chemicals will cause either an increased or a decreased likelihood that the latter neuron will "fire." These chemicals are called *biogenic amines* or, increasingly, *neurotransmitters.* Whether or not the neural message is successfully transmitted to the postsynaptic neuron depends on the *concentration* of the substance within the synaptic cleft. This situation can be complicated by the fact that the cleft is normally bathed in various biochemical juices that may or may not have transmitter properties.

Clearly, the normal functioning of the brain is dependent on a delicately balanced biochemical system. Some people, probably in part on a genetic basis, may be prone under stress to experience disruptions in this delicate balance; this, in turn, would render them vulnerable to brain malfunction and therefore to serious psychopathology. Much research is currently under way to correlate specific neurotransmitter anomalies (presumed diatheses) with specific psychopathological outcomes. We shall have much more to say about such matters in subsequent chapters.

Physical deprivation or disruption

Although we do not fully understand the processes involved, it is apparent that digestive, circulatory, and other bodily functions operate in such a way as to maintain the body's physiological equilibrium and integration. In the mechanisms for ensuring normal blood chemistry, for maintaining constant body temperature, and for combating invading microorganisms, we see this continuous endeavor of the body to preserve *steady states*—to maintain physiological variables within a range essential to survival—an endeavor generally referred to as *homeostasis.* Prolonged or severe disruption of steady states—either due to deprivation or to excess of our basic needs—can threaten our survival, and, at the very least, leave us vulnerable to other stresses. In this section we shall cover deprivation of visceral needs; stimulation and activity; and accidents, disease, and chronic pain.

Visceral needs.   The most basic of all human requirements are those for food, oxygen, water, sleep, for the elimination of wastes, and for other conditions and substances necessary for life. In order to survive and meet adjustive demands, the organism must constantly renew itself through rest and by taking in nutrients to replace materials used up in the process of living. Prolonged interference with such renewal weakens the organism's resources for coping with even normal adjustive demands and makes it vulnerable to special stresses. Prisoners have sometimes been "broken" by nothing more persuasive than the systematic prevention of sleep or deprivation of food over a period of several days.

Experimental studies of volunteers who have gone without sleep for periods of 72 to 98 hours show increasing psychological disorganization as the sleep loss progresses—including disorientation for time and place and feelings of depersonalization. As Berger (1970) has summarized it, "One thing is sure . . . we must sleep in order to stay sane" (p. 70).

Studies of dietary deficiencies have pointed to marked changes in psychological functioning, the exact change depending largely on the type and extent of the deficiency. Some of these effects were demonstrated in a pioneering study of semistarvation carried out by Keys (1950) and his associates during World War II.

Thirty-two conscientious objectors served as volunteer subjects. The men were first placed on an adequate diet for three months, then placed on a very low calorie diet characteristic of European famine areas for a period of six months, and then provided with a three-month period of nutritional rehabilitation.

During the six-month period of semistarvation, subjects had an average weight loss of 24 percent. At the same time, subjects also showed dramatic personality and behavioral changes. They became irritable, unsociable, and increasingly unable to concentrate on anything but food. In some instances they resorted to stealing food from one another and lying in attempts to obtain additional food rations. Among other psychological changes were apathy, loss of pride in personal appearance, and feelings of inadequacy. By the close of the experiment, there was a marked reduction or disappearance of their interest in sex, and the predominant mood was one of gloom and depression. Food dominated the men's thought, conversation, and even daydreams. They even pinned up pictures of chocolate cake instead of pretty women. In some cases, they went so far as to replan their lives in the

During the semistarvation period in the Keys et al. (1950) experiment, the hunger drive became the most important factor affecting the subjects' behavior. The men became unsociable, frequently ignoring such amenities as table manners.

light of their newly acquired respect for food. The investigators concluded that by the end of the twenty-fifth week, hunger had become the dominant influence in the behavior of their subjects.

In ordinary life, chronic deprivation may result in lowered resistance to stress. Insufficient rest, inadequate diet, or attempts to carry a full work load under the handicap of a severe cold, fatigue, or emotional strain may deplete a person's adjustive resources and result in increased predisposition to personality disorganization.

Perhaps the most tragic deprivation of all is seen in young children who are malnourished. If they survive, the scars of vulnerability remain for life. Severe malnutrition during infancy not only impairs physical development and lowers resistance to disease, but also stunts brain growth and results in markedly lowered intelligence (Amcoff, 1980; Cravioto & DeLicardie, 1975; Winick, 1976). Peterson (1978) has also noted the importance of deficits of thiamine, niacin, and vitamin B_{12} as potential causes of organic brain syndromes, which we shall discuss in more detail in Chapter 13.

In a postmortem study of infants who had died of malnutrition during their first year of life, Winick (1968) found the total brain cell con-

tent to be 60 percent below that of normal infants. Further research on animals showed the same type of effect in the offspring of malnourished mothers (Winick & Rosso, 1973). In the case of babies who suffer severe malnutrition but survive, the stunting of brain growth is considered irreversible, since the period of fastest growth of the brain is from about five months before until ten months after birth. Even in "affluent" America, in a random sample of areas in ten states where 75 to 80 percent of the resident families were living either in poverty or close to it, a study by the U.S. Public Health Service found that 15 percent of all children studied showed evidence of physical and mental growth retardation associated with malnutrition (reported in Winick, 1976).

Malnutrition because of faulty diet, resulting in a wide range of physical disorders and generally lowered resistance to stress, is found even in lower middle-income families (Reice, 1974). Among adults, Robinson and Winnik (1973) have reported on the higher incidence of psychoses and other mental disturbances among individuals who follow a "crash diet" to achieve rapid weight loss. In some cases, such reactions result from disappointed expectations: weight loss does not solve long-standing psychological and social problems (Knittle et al., 1982). However, changes in mental status can be directly produced by severe nutritional deficiencies (Baker & Lyen, 1982).

The tragic effects of malnourishment can be seen in this picture of a child in a destitute persons camp, Dacca, Bangladesh.

Stimulation and activity. We have known for some time that healthy mental development depends on the child's receiving adequate amounts of stimulation from the environment. Beginning in the 1940s (Spitz, 1945), a number of researchers have described a "hospitalism" syndrome among understimulated, institutionalized infants, a syndrome in which an alarming proportion of the children simply waste away and die. While psychological vulnerabilities induced by such deprivation are probably primary and will be considered in a later section, it is also possible that the physical development of the brain is adversely affected by an insufficiently reactive environment (Shapiro, 1968). Supporting this view are numerous animal studies demonstrating enhanced biological development produced by conditions of special stimulation (Wright et al., 1979), including positive changes in brain chemistry and anatomy (Krech, 1966; Krech, Rosenzweig, & Bennett, 1962; Rosenzweig et al., 1968).

Undoubtedly, however, there are limits to how much stimulation is optimal and beneficial to a developing organism. We know that the functioning of adult humans can be seriously impaired by sensory overload (Gottschalk, Haer, & Bates, 1972), and that excessive "life change" can contribute to the occurrence of physical illness (Rabkin & Struening, 1976; Rahe & Arthur, 1978). It would therefore be somewhat surprising to find infants and children not adversely affected by unstructured and chaotic levels of stimulation and stimulus change. Unfortunately, solid research on this issue is lacking.

In general, there appears to be for each individual an optimal level of stimulation and activity; it varies over time, but it is likely that stimulation must be maintained within these limits for normal psychological functioning. Under excessive pressure, we may strive to reduce the level of input and activity. On the other hand, under some conditions—such as boredom—we may strive to increase the level of stimulation by doing something different or engaging in an "exciting" activity. As we shall see, certain personality types, such as the antisocial personality, have inordinate needs for excitement.

Accidents, disease, and physical pain. At all stages of life, people can be troubled by other kinds of physical problems and disabilities. Accidents and disease exact a high toll in our society. Each year accidents alone take the lives of over 100,000 persons and permanently disable at least a million others; they are by far the leading cause of death among preschoolers. These figures suggest that accidental injuries are the "neglected disease" of modern civilization, often leaving in their wake physical mutilation, disrupted lives, and severe problems of adjustment.

In addition, over 20 million persons suffer from heart conditions or other serious physical impairments that may be both painful and debilitating; many of these victims are young people. The U.S. Department of Health and Human Services estimates that approximately one fifth of this country's under-seventeen age group will, at some time in their lives, suffer from at least one chronic physical condition that adversely affects their resilience. When such conditions involve severe and long-continued pain, they may gradually wear down the individual's adjustive resources and lead to discouragement and despair. Chronic disease may also reduce the individual's expected life span.

Except in the case of defects that seriously restrict one's activities, are severely disabling, or are chronically painful, however, the significance of a physical impairment depends primarily on the way the individual evaluates and adjusts to it. Common and undesirable reactions to physical disabilities are feelings of inferiority, self-pity, and hostility. Another obstacle to good stress management that a disabled person faces is the tendency to accept the role of a "cripple," which society often seems to expect and encourage. This picture is often complicated by family members who either encourage such a sick role or expect performance beyond the individual's capabilities. As a consequence of such obstacles, the individual—whether child, adolescent, or adult—may develop psychological handicaps that are much more disabling than the physical impairment.

All of us, at one time or another, are forced to undergo the experience of physical pain. From early infancy on we tend to withdraw from painful stimuli and try to avoid objects that have brought us pain or discomfort in the past. The threat or experience of pain is acutely unpleasant and highly motivating.

Severe hunger, thirst, and fatigue can be extremely painful, as can most forms of intense stimulation such as heat, cold, and pressure.

The precise influence of physical pain on behavior has never been fully delineated, although experience and observation indicate that it can be very great. Through the centuries, torture and pain have been used to elicit confessions as well as for punishment. When pain is severe and long-continued—as it is in certain types of disease—it may gradually wear down the sufferer's adjustive resources and lead to overwhelming feelings of hopelessness and despair.

Psychosocial factors

In contrast to animals lower on the phylogenetic scale, who have "built-in" patterns of behavior and who mature rapidly, the human infant begins life with few built-in patterns and a far greater capacity to learn from experience. But the price of such a high degree of modifiability is initial helplessness and a long period of immaturity, with the necessity of mastering the "know-how" and "know-why" of living. In our society, such learning is coming to occupy most of the life cycle.

The various influences operating upon us, and the manner in which they contribute to the perspectives we develop, may with good fortune outfit us with resourcefulness and resilience in facing the challenges that will inevitably come our way. Unfortunately, such a happy outcome is by no means guaranteed—not even for people with superb biological and constitutional equipment.

In this section we undertake an examination of psychosocial factors that seem to render persons vulnerable to disorder. It should be noted at the outset, however, that our knowledge in this area is less precise and reliable than in the case of biological predispositions. Even though a host of psychosocially based theoretical orientations, as were summarized in Chapter 3, have been offered for our guidance, few of them have turned out to be very helpful in definitely establishing the background factors contributing to mental disorder. Our discussion will be organized according to the following groupings of causal factors: the self, motivation, early deprivation or trauma, inadequate parenting, and pathogenic family structures. As we shall see,

such factors typically do not operate alone. They contribute to vulnerability in interaction with each other and with other psychosocial factors; with particular genetic and constitutional factors; and with the particular setting or environment in which they operate.

Self as a determinant

As we grow and learn to distinguish between self and nonself, a part of our total perceptual field is gradually defined as "me," "I," or "self." As this self-structure develops, it becomes the integrating core of the personality—the reference point around which we organize our experiences and coping patterns. Problems that arise are perceived, thought about, and acted upon in relation to the self; that is, we come to perceive our self as an active agent in determining our own behavior—as indicated by such statements as "I know," "I want," and "I will."

Fundamental to determining what we know, want, and do are some basic assumptions that we make about ourselves and our world and the relationship between the two. These assumptions make up our frame of reference, or *cognitive map*—our guide, one might say, through the complexities of living. This map includes our views of what we are, what we might become, what's important to us. This is our *self-identity:* what we know and what we believe, what we hold dear and what we revere. It is also the source of many of our vulnerabilities, many of which can predispose us to abnormal behavior.

Parts of our cognitive map may be valid, some invalid; others may be true for us but not for others; still others may be held with varying degrees of conviction; they may be more or less explicit and conscious. Although our daily decisions and behavior are in large part shaped by our frame of reference, we may be quite unaware of the assumptions on which it is based— or even of having made assumptions at all. We think we are simply "seeing things the way they are." It is unthinkable that other pictures of the world might be possible or that other rules for "right" might exist. Thus many of our thoughts, actions, and feelings are based on internalized rules and ways of seeing things that we would be hard pressed to articulate or define.

Many aspects of the self can be seen as principles or rules for processing information, for organizing one's raw experience. As such, they can be to a large extent "invisible." As Vallacher, Wegner, and Hoine (1980) have put it, we look "through" these rules—rarely "at" them. For this reason, the rules, once established, may be hard to identify, and it may be difficult to deliberately change them. New experience tends to be *assimilated* into our existing cognitive framework, even if the new information has to be reinterpreted or distorted to make it fit. We tend to cling to existing assumptions and reject or distort new information that is contradictory to them. *Accommodation*—changing our existing framework to make it possible to incorporate discrepant information—is more difficult and threatening, especially where very important assumptions are challenged.

Because we experience the self as the very core of our existence, we tend to develop a system of ego-defense mechanisms to maintain the picture of our adequacy and worth and to defend ourselves from self-devaluation. Rationalizing our mistakes, blaming others or "bad breaks" for feelings we think we should not have, and avoiding activities in which we think we might not do well are familiar ways in which we protect our self-esteem and avoid anxiety.

Several aspects of our frame of reference merit further mention. For one thing, our assumptions about reality, possibility, and value afford us a sense of self-identity and also a *self-ideal*—a picture of what we could and should be. An unclear self-identity or a marked discrepancy between "real" and "ideal" selves can lead to serious inner conflict. Second, our pattern of assumptions contributes to consistency in perceiving, thinking, feeling, and acting—to the evolution of a characteristic *life-style*, which may or may not make us vulnerable to disorder. Third, our assumptions serve not only as guides to behavior but also as *inner controls.* For example, value assumptions may or may not predispose us to steal or to behave in other unethical ways. Such value assumptions are often referred to as the "superego," or "conscience."

When our inner controls are strong and direct our behavior in accordance with the expectations and norms of our society, we are said to be *socialized.* In some cases, for reasons we shall examine later, these inner controls do not develop to an adequate degree; and under certain conditions—such as alcoholic or drug intoxication—they may give way. However, society does its best to see that such restraints are well developed and maintained, for without them, organized social life would be impossible.

Our developing sense of selfhood becomes an increasingly important force in directing our own behavior, for better or for worse. Although much of our behavior is shaped by external demands and influences, each of us nevertheless typically perceives ourself as an active force in initiating our plans and actions. It is the *I* who is seen as wanting or needing some things while trying to avoid others, and it is the *I* who perceives and responds to new situations in light of personal motives, assumptions, and feelings. In the process, each of us achieves an increasing sense of identity and of *self-direction.*[1] Many, indeed, see the achievement of selfhood as the central task of adolescence (Onyehalu, 1981).

As the above discussion implies, the self is conceived as a set of rules (e.g., for processing information or for selecting behavior alternatives) on the one hand and as the *product* of those rules (e.g., a sense of selfhood, self-identity) on the other (Vallacher et al., 1980). Deficiencies or deviations in either aspect of the development of the self may render a person vulnerable to disorder. For example, if a person's information-processing rules differ in important respects from those of peers, then that person's "reality" will be correspondingly different and may lead to rejection, isolation, despair, and ultimate disorder. Similarly, should an individual's self-identity require propping up by membership in an eccentric cult, seriously maladaptive behavior may be the outcome.

The achievement of a strong, adaptive, adult selfhood is evidently a complicated matter, which is at present only partly understood. Most of what is known can be related to stages in the development of the self or to the basic requirements and needs of the self. Each of these topics is briefly summarized below.

Development of the self.   The growth of the self proceeds along certain identifiable lines under the combined influence of inner and outer determinants. Within limits, growth follows a predictable sequence and proceeds in a characteristic direction toward increasing differentiation, integration, and complexity. However, the

---

[1]Bandura (1978) has presented a systematic analysis of the guiding functions of the self from the perspective of social learning theory.

maintenance of the progression depends on a favorable environment and on the individual's learning essential information and competencies along the way.

The acquisition of appropriate principles or rules in mental organization—in the entity we are here calling the *self*—is neither assured in a given individual's development, nor is it trivial in determining future adaptability/vulnerability. Indeed, as we shall see in Chapter 13, most so-called mentally retarded persons—who as a group are at high risk for mental disorder—are intellectually disabled not by virtue of inadequate brain tissue but rather because such tissue has been insufficiently "programmed" to manage the complexities of modern life. Failure at this level—whether the inadequate programming involves intellectual, personal, or social skills—will result in the person's being less able than the more fortunate to cope effectively with adjustive demands.

1. *Developmental stages and tasks.* Studies of infants and children by Gesell (1953), Piaget (1970), and others have shown that human development tends to follow a definite sequence, not only in physical and motor development but also in intellectual, emotional, and social development. Crawling and sitting up come before walking; early diffuse emotional reactions become differentiated into love, humor, grief, and other patterns; and language behavior progresses from random vocalizations to the words that eventually become vehicles for thinking.

In the present context, it is not necessary to review the stages of human development—prenatal, infancy, childhood, adolescence, adulthood, and old age—or to delineate the details of development in intellectual or other specific areas. But it is important for our purposes to know that at each stage of development, certain tasks or competencies must be mastered if the individual is to maintain a normal schedule of growth. For example, learning to walk and talk are major tasks of infancy; establishing a sense of identity and acquiring the intellectual, emotional, and interpersonal competencies needed for adulthood are key tasks of adolescence.

If developmental tasks are not mastered at the appropriate stage, the individual suffers from immaturities and incompetencies and is placed at a serious disadvantage in adjusting at later developmental levels—that is, the individual becomes increasingly vulnerable through ac-

Exploring the environment is one of the tasks of childhood and helps develop the child's physical and motor skills.

cumulated failures to master psychosocial requirements. A young child who has not learned to walk or talk is at a serious disadvantage in entering nursery school; the adolescent who does not have friends misses a major opportunity for acquiring the skills in interacting with others that will be helpful later for establishing satisfactory adult relationships. The demands of a given developmental period may be relatively easy or difficult to meet, depending on how well the tasks at prior developmental levels have been mastered.

Some developmental tasks are set by the individual's own needs, some by the physical and social environment. Members of different socioeconomic and sociocultural groups face somewhat different developmental tasks, and social and technological changes may create new developmental tasks for all of us.

2. *The crucial roles of maturation and learning.* Built-in maturational processes[2] provide the potentials for the orderly progression of development, but these potentials can be realized only under favorable environmental conditions. During early development, **critical periods** occur during which certain types of stimulation and learning are essential for normal development.

---

[2]***Maturation*** refers to growth following birth that is determined primarily by genetic factors and occurs more or less independently of learning.

We have already noted the likelihood that, in the absence of adequate stimulation, biological development will be stymied. The same can be said for psychosocial development. Some infants appear to be more severely affected than others by early deprivation: mental retardation, inability to form warm interpersonal relationships, and antisocial behavior have all been shown to be associated with extreme emotional, social, and intellectual deprivation during critical periods of infancy.

The effects of parental deprivation and of aversive stimulation on children's psychosocial development will be examined later in this as well as subsequent chapters. Here we may simply point out that if needed stimulation and learning are lacking during early critical periods, the functions expected to develop at these times (a) may not appear; (b) may be slower in making their appearance; or (c) may be only partially adequate. And once the critical period has passed, it may be difficult or impossible to correct the physiological and/or psychological vulnerabilities that have been incurred.

Simple conditioning, as described in Chapter 3, is common in infancy and early childhood, and provides many new response patterns—often without the child's awareness of such learning. However, as their perceptual and cognitive capabilities develop, children become increasingly active agents in pursuing their own interests and shaping their own learning. In fact, by the age of four most children have a fairly clear picture of themselves and their world, and their ability to discriminate, interpret, and evaluate experience makes them less susceptible to simple conditioning.

But while children show similarities in learned abilities, they also show differences. Mischel (1973) has identified five learning-based differences that become apparent early in childhood: (a) Children have acquired different levels of competency in different areas; (b) they have learned different concepts and different strategies for coding and categorizing their experience and thus "process" new information differently in accordance with these strategies and structures; (c) although they have all learned that certain things follow from certain others, what they have learned to expect is quite different, depending on their unique experiences; (d) they have learned to find different situations attrac-

tive or disagreeable and thus to seek very different things; and (e) they have learned different ways of coping with impulses and regulating their behavior; they have long since developed a characteristic "style" of dealing with the exigencies of life. Differences in these general areas will continue through childhood and into the adult years and will keep shaping later learning.

Such learned variations make some children far better prepared than others for further learning and personal growth. The ability to make effective use of new experience depends very much on what is already there—on the degree to which past learning has either prepared the child for assimilating new learning in ways that will be facilitative and productive or left the child psychologically vulnerable. Partly for this reason, most theories of personality development emphasize the importance of early experience in shaping the main directions that an individual's coping style will take.

Requirements and needs of the self. The psychological requirements for healthy human development and functioning are influenced by learning and social requirements to a far greater degree than are biological requirements, and the goals relating to their gratification are capable of greater variation. A position of leadership, for example, highly valued in our society as a means of meeting needs for adequacy and worth, was found by Mead (1949) to be a nuisance and burden to the Arapesh, who avoided leadership roles whenever possible.

Despite wide individual and group differences in human motives, however, there does appear to be a common core of psychological strivings related to maintenance and actualization. Although psychological requirements are less readily identified than requirements for food, water, sleep, and the like, the following basic core of psychological strivings characterize all of us. It is worth noting again that disruptions or blocking of any of them can make us more vulnerable to abnormal behavior.

1. *Understanding, order, and predictability.* Human beings strive to understand and achieve a meaningful picture of their world. Otherwise we would have no basis for evaluating new situations and choosing adjustive actions. Unless we can see order and predictability in our environment, we cannot work out an intelligent response to it. Social customs, rules, and laws are in part a reflection of this need for order and predictability.

People do not like ambiguity, lack of structuring, chaos, or events that seem beyond their understanding and control. Even the most "primitive" people develop explanations for lightning, thunder, death, and other frightening phenomena. Accurate or not, such explanations tend to impose order and meaning on seemingly random events, thereby giving a sense of potential prediction and control. Modern science is simply a more sophisticated attempt in the same direction.

Our striving for understanding, order, and predictability is evidenced in our tendency to maintain the consistency and stability of our frame of reference. When new information contradicts existing assumptions, we experience *cognitive dissonance*—an unpleasant state of tension—and are uncomfortable until the discrepancy can be reconciled. Such reconciliation, as we have seen, may involve assimilation of the new information, perhaps by distorting its meaning, or, more rarely, by accommodating the current belief system to the new input. In fact, Aronson (1973) concluded that cognitive dissonance may result in such acute discomfort that an individual may risk his or her life in an effort to resolve it. In other instances, the individual may *choose* to die rather than have an important belief system challenged.

2. *Adequacy, competence, and security.* Each of us needs to feel capable of dealing with life's problems. Seeing oneself as incapable of coping with a stressful situation is conducive to confusion and disorganization.

Feelings of adequacy are dependent on the development of intellectual, social, and other skills for dealing with life's demands. Several investigators have pointed out that even the early playful and investigatory behavior of children involves a process of "reality testing" that fosters the development of learning, reasoning, and other coping abilities.

The need for security develops with and is closely related to the need for adequacy. We soon learn that failure to meet biological or psychological needs leads to unpleasant results. Consequently we strive to maintain whatever conditions can be counted on to assure present and future need gratification. The need for se-

curity is reflected in the preference for jobs with tenure, in social security legislation, in insurance against disability and other contingencies, and in society's emphasis on law and order. Feelings of insecurity may have widely differing effects on behavior; but pervasive and chronic feelings of insecurity typically lead to fearfulness, apprehension, and failure to participate fully in one's world. The more adequate we feel and the greater our level of competence, the less aware we are of our need for security, the more we may value the exploration of unfamiliar paths and freedom for self-direction, and the less vulnerable we are to demoralization and breakdown.

In this general context, it is interesting to note that one of the key functions of psychotherapy is to help patients achieve a sense of adequacy, competency, and mastery over their lives. Indeed, Bandura (1977a) has argued forcefully that this is the function basic to *all* the varied forms of psychological treatment.

3. *Love, belonging, and approval.* To love and to be loved are crucial to healthy personality development and adjustment. In their extensive study of patterns in child rearing, Sears, Maccoby, and Levin (1957) concluded that the most crucial and pervasive of all the influences toward healthy development of children were the love and warmth imparted by the parents. More recent research has tended to confirm this finding (e.g., Main & Weston, 1981). For the child who feels loved and accepted, many conditions that might otherwise impair development—such as a physical handicap, poverty, or harsh discipline—may be largely neutralized. On the other hand, if a child feels unloved, no lavishing of material benefits on him or her will make up for it: the hurt will distort personal development and perhaps lead to attempts to retaliate, as we shall see in Chapter 14.

Evidence of our needs for love, belonging, and approval is provided in the **HIGHLIGHT** on page 114, which describes the nature and effects of the "silent treatment." The need for close ties to other people continues throughout life and becomes especially important in times of severe stress or crisis. In a study of terminal cancer patients, Bard (1966) concluded that the need for affiliation and human contact is never greater than it is as death approaches. Kubler-Ross (1975) confirms this need in dying patients, but

HIGHLIGHT
The "silent treatment"

Eloquent testimony to our needs for love, belonging, and approval is provided by the experience of small groups of scientists, officers, and enlisted personnel who voluntarily subjected themselves to isolated antarctic living for the better part of a year. During this period troublesome individuals were occasionally given the "silent treatment" in which a man would be ignored by the group as if he did not exist.

This "isolation" procedure resulted in a syndrome called the "long eye," characterized by varying combinations of sleeplessness, outbursts of crying, hallucinations, a deterioration in habits of personal hygiene, and a tendency for the man to move aimlessly about or to lie on his bunk staring into space. These symptoms cleared up when he was again accepted by and permitted to interact with other members of the group.

Based primarily on Rohrer (1961) and on Popkin, Stillner, Osborn, Pierce, and Shurley (1974).

she also notes the tendency of others to withdraw at this critical juncture.

4. *Self-esteem, worth, and identity.* Closely related to the needs for adequacy and social approval is the need to feel good about oneself and worthy of the respect of others.

Self-esteem has its early foundation in parental affirmation of worth and in mastery of early developmental tasks; it receives continual nourishment from the development of new competencies and from achievement in areas deemed important; and eventually it comes to depend heavily on the values and standards of significant others. If we can measure up to those standards—for example, in terms of physical appearance, achievement, or economic status—we can approve of ourselves and feel worthwhile.

Intermeshed with feelings of self-esteem and worth is one's sense of self-identity. This, too, is heavily influenced by significant others and by one's status and role in the group. Here it is interesting to note that despite changes in physical appearance, in status, and in social roles, people tend to maintain continuity in their basic feelings of self-identity. That is, we think of ourselves as the same *I* or *me* today that we were a few years ago and will be tomorrow.

Probably most of us would like to change in certain ways, and many of us work hard at becoming the finer or more capable or more attractive self we would like to be. A few people, as we shall see in Chapter 12, even come to the point of undergoing sex-change surgery to achieve a body consistent with what they feel is their *real* identity. But though we may wish to make such changes in our present self-identity, it is doubtful, in most instances, that we would willingly give it up. When a person's sense of self-identity and continuity becomes disorganized, the experience is usually not only acutely painful; it also weakens the fundamental underpinnings and stability of the personality. This in turn limits the person's resourcefulness in coping with stressful challenges that may occur either because of the consequences of an unstable selfhood (e.g., putting intolerable demands on a partner for self-reconfirmation) or because of unrelated "chance" events.

Sargent (1973) has reported on the loss of self-identity often experienced by convicted prisoners and its consequences in terms of self-esteem, worth, and adequacy.

"The prisoners increasingly depend on authority, become susceptible to suggestion, tend toward magical thinking, and become more anxious and impulsive. In some cases the symptoms reach psychotic propротions." (p. 390)

5. *Values, meaning, and hope.* Surprisingly, there has been little research on the human need for values, meaning, and hope. But we can infer such needs from observations of the typical results when people are unable to find satisfying value patterns, are "planless," or lack hope. Values, meaning, and hope appear to act as catalysts: in their presence energy is mobilized, competencies are developed and used, and satisfactions are achieved. Without them, life seems futile and the individual is bored and enervated.

In extreme cases, hopelessness may lead to apathy and even death. For example, reports from prisoner-of-war camps have told of cases in which prisoners who had lost hope simply pulled their blankets over their heads and waited for death to come (Nardini, 1952; *U.S. News & World Report*, 1973).

Closely related to our needs for values and meaning are our goals and plans, for we live in the future as well as in the past and present. Our goals and plans serve as a focus for both our strivings and our hopes. When we feel uncertain and anxious about the future, personal adjustment and effectiveness are likely to be impaired.

6. *Personal growth and fulfillment.* As already indicated, we strive not only to maintain ourselves and survive but also to express ourselves, to improve, to grow—*to actualize our potentialities.* Huxley (1953) made this point very eloquently:

"Human life is a struggle—against frustration, ignorance, suffering, evil, the maddening inertia of things in general; but it is also a struggle *for* something. . . . And fulfillment seems to describe better than any other single word the positive side of human development and human evolution—the realization of inherent capacities by the individual and of new possibilities by the race; the satisfaction of needs, spiritual as well as material; the emergence of new qualities of experience to be enjoyed; the building of personalities." (pp. 162–63)

The strivings for fulfillment take different forms with different people, depending on their abilities, values, and life situations. In general, however, we appear to share certain strivings as human beings: (a) toward developing and using our potentials in constructive and creative ways, as in art, music, writing, science, athletics, and other pursuits that foster creative self-expression; (b) toward enriching the range and quality of our experiences and satisfactions, as, for example, in travel; (c) toward increasing our relatedness to the world—forming warm and meaningful relationships with others and becoming involved in the "human enterprise"; and (d) toward "becoming a person"—answering the question "Who am I?" and becoming the "self" that we feel we should be. Here it may be noted that the various psychological strivings discussed above may all be considered routes to self-actualization. Many of our deepest satisfactions come through improving our understanding and competence, forming loving relationships with others, and acquiring values that contribute to a meaningful and fulfilling life.

The strivings discussed above appear to represent the basic core of psychological requirements that emerge through normal interaction with the world and that contribute significantly to the direction of behavior. The strength of a given psychological striving and the behaviors for meeting it vary considerably, of course, from one person to another, and from one social

Parents play a critical role in the child's growth toward physical and psychological competence.

group to the next. It is apparent, too, that bio-logical and psychological strivings are closely in-terrelated and that failure to meet a particular one may adversely influence our entire motiva-tional structure as well as physical and psycho-logical well-being.

It is in relation to maintenance and actualiza-tion strivings that we use the terms *adjustment* and *maladjustment,* which refer to outcomes of these strivings. The term *therapy,* too, becomes meaningful only in this context: the goal of ther-apy—whatever its particular orientation—is to help individuals meet their needs in a socially constructive way.

Motivation and behavior

The preceding discussion has dealt with the na-ture of our basic needs and strivings. These do not operate apart from other psychological pro-cesses. In this section we shall consider (a) their role in the mobilization of energy; (b) their influ-ence on other psychological processes; (c) their conscious and unconscious aspects; (d) the priorities among them; and (e) their relation to one's life-style. How our needs and strivings op-erate within each context can contribute not only to our motivational states but also to our predis-positions to behave maladaptively.

Levels of activation.   Motivation accounts for not only the direction but also the activation of behavior—the energy mobilized in pursuit of our goals.

Activation can vary in degree from very low to very high, from deep sleep to intense excite-ment. At any moment a person's level of acti-vation is influenced by a wide range of individ-ual and situational factors. It is affected by the way one perceives the situation and evaluates its potential satisfaction and frustrations; it is af-fected by many inner conditions, including bio-logical drives, emotions, and drugs; it is affected by sudden loud noises and strange or novel stimuli; and it is affected by fatigue, disease, and pain.

Usually, efficient task performance requires a moderate level of activation. With too low a level, the person may fail to expend the energy and effort essential for task achievement, while very high levels tend to result in poorly coordi-

nated functioning and an increase in impaired performance.

Although there are individual differences in personal tempo and sensitivity or excitability, most people learn to respond to familiar situ-ations with appropriate levels of activation. However, an individual is likely to react with an overly high level of activation in the face of an unfamiliar challenge or under stressful condi-tions to which he or she is particularly vulnera-ble. Similarly, conditions such as severe fatigue, intense inner conflict, or faulty assumptions and loss of hope may lead to extreme and inappro-priate fluctuations in activation, as well as to slow recovery from the effects of prior activation and energy output.

Motivation, attending, and perceiving. Needs and motives influence perceiving, reason-ing, learning, and other psychological processes. For example, people are most likely to perceive those aspects of the environment that are related to the gratification of immediate or long-term needs. A person lost in the desert and suffering from intense thirst would likely ignore the vivid colors of the sunset and keep scanning the sur-roundings for some indication of water. This tendency of the organism to single out particular elements considered to be especially relevant to its purposes is called *selective vigilance.*

While motivation may sensitize the individual to particular stimuli, we have already seen that it may also have the opposite effect. People tend to screen out or distort information that is in-compatible with their expectations, assump-tions, and wishes. Proud parents may selec-tively perceive the desirable traits and behaviors of their children while tending not to perceive undesirable ones; people often do the same thing in evaluating themselves. This tendency to avoid perceiving unpleasant stimuli or unde-sired information is sometimes referred to as *perceptual defense.*

Motivation also influences what we learn, as well as how rapidly and how much. And de-spite our attempts to be logical, our motivation may influence our beliefs and subvert our thought processes in helping us justify our as-sumptions and behavior. This is why we cannot usually be objective judges in disputes in which we have a vested interest and why we need um-pires and referees in sports contests.

Conscious and unconscious aspects of motivation.   We noted that the concept of unconscious motivation is basic to the psychoanalytic perspective. Although considerable controversy exists among psychologists concerning the nature and importance of unconscious processes in human behavior, there is abundant evidence that we are often unaware of what our needs and goals really are. Yet to view consciousness and unconsciousness as separate or unrelated can also lead to erroneous and misleading conclusions. There are probably many more motives of which we are "more or less" aware than there are of which we are either wholly conscious *or* wholly unconscious.

Many of our biological needs operate on a relatively unconscious level, and we may become aware of others—for example, via feelings of hunger and thirst—only when they become pressing. Psychological needs, such as those for security, adequacy, social approval, and self-esteem, may also operate on relatively unconscious levels. Thus we may criticize our associates, join exclusive clubs, and even get married for reasons of which we are largely unaware. Of course, we may think of good reasons to justify our behavior, but they may not be the real reasons at all.

Hierarchy of needs.   Maslow (1970, 1971) has suggested that human needs form a hierarchy from the most basic biological requirements to the needs for self-actualization. According to this formulation, the level that commands the individual's attention and effort is ordinarily the lowest one on which there is a seriously unmet need. For example, unless needs for food and safety are reasonably well met, behavior will be dominated by these needs. With their gratification, however, the individual is free to devote time and energy to meeting needs on higher levels.

Maslow used the term *deficiency motivation* to refer to motives aimed at meeting the needs on lower levels, since these motives are activated by deficiencies and force the individual to take action to restore equilibrium. He used the term *growth motivation* to refer to motives aimed at meeting the higher-level needs for self-actualization. Although meeting lower-level needs is clearly necessary for maintenance of the organism, Maslow considered a long-term preoccupation with *only* the maintenance needs to be unhealthy because of the resulting failure to develop the individual's uniquely human potentialities.

Maslow's hierarchy concept tends to be borne out by observations of behavior under extreme conditions. Friedman (1949) reported that: "In all survivors of the Nazi concentration camps, one might say the self-preservation instinct became so dominant that it blotted out all other instincts." Similarly, in the Japanese prisoner-of-war camps in World War II, it was a common pattern for those inmates who had been subjected to prolonged deprivation and torture to obtain food at the expense of their fellow prisoners and in other ways surrender the loyalties and values they had held under more normal conditions (Nardini, 1952, 1962).

Under conditions of extreme deprivation, most people do appear likely to sacrifice their higher-level actualization needs to meet more basic needs for survival. As Maslow acknowledged, however, there are many exceptions, as shown by the countless number of people who have remained faithful to ethical, social, or religious values despite severe deprivation, torture, and even certain death.

Motive patterns and life-style.   Each individual tends to develop a relatively consistent life-style, an essential element of which is a continuing *motive pattern* centered around particular strivings and goals. Some persons are concerned primarily with love and relatedness, others with material possessions and power, and still others with personal growth and self-actualization. Alternatively, certain common motives may be inhibited or blocked by neurotic anxieties, of which more will be said in Chapter 6. An individual's motive pattern is in part a product of past rewards and punishments; in part an outgrowth of reality, possibility, and value assumptions; and in part a reflection of the demands, limitations, and opportunities of the environment.

Well-adjusted people tend to have a reasonably accurate view of themselves in relation to their world and hence to have a fairly realistic *level of aspiration.* Maladjusted and vulnerable people, on the other hand, tend to be unrealistic—to set their goals too high or too low or to pursue unrewarding goals. In many cases, mal-

The motivation toward artistic expression or personal achievement is part of what Maslow called "growth motivation"—the desire to develop oneself beyond the satisfaction of the self's basic needs.

adjusted people seem unable to formulate meaningful life plans and goals and drift through life with little or no sense of direction. Usually such persons experience feelings of dissatisfaction, aimlessness, and being "lost."

Many of our more important motives involve other people. Examples are needs to dominate, to submit, to love, or to aggress against an oppressor. The possibilities that such needs will be satisfied depends very much on the behaviors and motives of the other people in our lives. For example, it is difficult to fulfill a need to dominate in the absence of someone who will "submit." We often find, therefore, that seriously maladaptive expressions of needs occur in situations in which two or more persons are in regular interaction with each other.

Although each of us tends to show a relatively consistent pattern of motives, this pattern undergoes change over time. The key motives of the child are not those of the adolescent, nor are the motives of the adolescent those of the adult or older person. Similarly, changes in one's life situation may lead to the modification of motive patterns. For example, a football player with a serious injury may find it necessary to make changes in his established motive pattern. Broadly speaking, one may develop important new motives, show shifts in the priorities of existing motives, or discard motives that have formerly been of significance. Some of these changes emerge as the products of experience and learning; others seem to result from new requirements at different life stages; and still others are influenced by changed environmental conditions.

Changes in motive patterns are closely related to changes in self-structure, each causing and resulting from changes in the other. As new demands require new behaviors, we strive to maintain consistency between our sense of self and our picture of what we are doing and need to do in our situation. Almost certainly, these changes bring about changes in our predispositions toward or away from abnormal behavior.

Early deprivation or trauma

Parental deprivation refers to an absence of adequate care from and interaction with parents or parent-substitutes during the formative years. It can occur even in intact families where, for one reason or another, parents are unable (e.g., because of mental disorder) or unwilling to provide for the child's needs for close and frequent human contact. Its most severe manifestations, however, are usually seen among abandoned or orphaned children who may either be institutionalized or placed in a succession of psychologically unwholesome foster homes.

The consequences of parental deprivation can be interpreted from several of the psychosocial viewpoints. Such deprivation might result in fixation at the oral stage of psychosexual development (Freud); it might interfere with the development of basic trust (Erikson); it might retard the attainment of needed skills because of a lack of available reinforcements (Skinner); self-actualizing tendencies may be preempted by maintenance and defensive requirements (Rogers, Maslow); or it might stunt the development of the child's capacity for relatively anxiety-free exchanges of tenderness and intimacy with others (Sullivan). Any of these might in a given instance of deprivation be the most productive way of conceptualizing the problems that follow, or some combination of them may be superior to any one in the insight it affords us. The latter point serves as a reminder that these viewpoints are not mutually exclusive; rather, they tend to focus on different aspects of the situation.

These orphans, turned out of the house by an uncle, were found wandering barefoot in subzero temperatures. Two were suffering from frostbite. A family situation of this type can have lasting impact on a child's psychological, as well as physical, development.

From any viewpoint, the effects of parental deprivation can be extremely serious. Faulty development has often been observed in infants experiencing deprivation. Many studies have focused on the role of the mother, but all such studies are essentially concerned with warmth and stimulation, whether it comes from the mother, the father, or institutional staff members.

Institutionalization. In an institution, as compared with an ordinary home, there is likely to be less warmth and physical contact, less intellectual, emotional, and social stimulation, and a lack of encouragement and help in positive learning.

A study by Provence and Lipton (1962) compared behavior of infants living in institutions with that of infants living with families. At one year of age, the institutionalized infants showed a general impairment in their relationship to people, rarely turning to adults for help, comfort, or pleasure and showing no signs of strong attachment to any person. These investigators also noted a marked retardation of speech and language development, emotional apathy, and impoverished and repetitive play activities. In contrast to the babies living in families, the institutionalized infants failed to show the personality differentiation and learning that "can be thought of both as accomplishments of the first year of life and as the foundation upon which later learning is built" (p. 161). With more severe and pervasive deprivation, development may be even more retarded.

The long-range effects of severe early deprivation of parental love and stimulation are suggested by the early findings of Beres and Obers (1950) in their study of 38 adolescents who had been institutionalized between the ages of about three weeks and three years. At the time of the study, sixteen to eighteen years after discharge from the orphanage, 4 were diagnosed as psychotic, 21 as having a character disorder, 4 as mentally retarded, and 2 as neurotic. Only 7 were judged to have achieved a satisfactory personality adjustment. In general, it would appear that "affectionless psychopathy"—characterized by inability to form close interpersonal relationships and often by antisocial behavior—is a syndrome commonly found among children who have been institutionalized at an early age, particularly before the age of one year.

These early findings have received general confirmation in a review of more recent research on child abandonment by Burnstein (1981). Burnstein concludes that abandoned children are at high risk for psychological disturbance and that excessive levels of aggressiveness, rebelliousness, and disobedience are especially likely. Such behaviors are suggestive of interpersonal anxieties that are defended against by the adoption of "antiweak," "antitrust" orientations to the world. In any event, the long-range prognosis for children suffering early and prolonged parental deprivation is considered unfavorable (Rutter, 1972; Tizard & Rees, 1975; Wolkind, 1974).

Although some earlier estimates of the pathological effects of such deprivation were exaggerated, it is now clear that many children deprived of normal parenting in infancy do suffer damage in their personality development. The extent to which early deprivation can be "made up for" by abundant love and attention at a later time is not yet known. It does appear, however, that attachment to some particular adult (typically the mother)—once considered the essential element in healthy development—is not, in fact, the critical factor. Research by Leiderman and Leiderman (1974) comparing "monomatric" with "polymatric" (one mother versus several mothers) households, and by Kagan, Kearsley, and

Zelazo (1976) on the effects of early placement in quality daycare settings, failed to show any substantial deficits in multiple-mothered children. Belsky and Steinberg (1978) reached a similar conclusion concerning quality daycare settings. Whether damage is reversible appears to depend on a number of factors, including the duration of prior deprivation and the quality and time of therapeutic enrichment efforts (see **HIGHLIGHT** on page 121). It does seem clear that restoration becomes increasingly difficult as the child gets older (Freedman, Kaplan, & Sadock, 1976).

Deprivation in the home.   By far the greatest number of infants subjected to parental deprivation are not separated from their parents, but rather suffer from inadequate or distorted care at home. Here the parents typically neglect or devote little attention to the child and are generally rejecting.

The effects of such deprivation may be devastating. The early work of Ribble (1944, 1945), for example, showed that rejecting, indifferent, or punishing mothers may cause tense, unsatisfied, and negative behavior in their infants even at a very early age. In fact, Bullard and his associates (1967) delineated a "failure to thrive" syndrome that "is a serious disorder of growth and development frequently requiring admission to the hospital. In its acute phase it significantly compromises the health and sometimes endangers the life of the child" (p. 689). In a follow-up study conducted eight months to nine years after hospitalization of such children for treatment, Bullard found that almost two thirds of the subjects showed evidence "either of continued growth failure, emotional disorder, mental retardation, or some combination of these" (p. 681).

The effects of deprivation vary considerably from infant to infant; in some societies, practices that we would expect to be permanently damaging turn out not to be. For example, Kagan (1973) compared the development of year-old Guatemalan Indian infants with that of American-raised infants. Due to the custom of the culture, Guatemalan Indian infants spend their first year in a psychologically impoverished environment. Kagan found that they were, by comparison, severely retarded in their development. However, after the first year, the environment of these infants was enriched, and by the age of eleven, they performed as well or better than American children on problem-solving and related intellectual tasks.

Prolonged neglect may have serious long-term effects even where the child shows minimal immediate difficulties. In a recent study involving a follow-up of individuals averaging 43.7 years of age who (a) had had adjustment difficulties as children and (b) had become schizophrenic in young adulthood, Roff and Knight (1981) found childhood maternal neglect to be significantly associated with relatively poor long-term outcomes. The association appears to have been further due to serious family disorganization and disruption, factors which we will discuss later.

Parental rejection of the child is closely related to deprivation and may be shown in various ways—by physical neglect, denial of love and affection, lack of interest in the child's activities and achievements, harsh or inconsistent punishment, failure to spend time with the child, and lack of respect for the child's rights and feelings. In a minority of cases, it also involves cruel and abusive treatment. Parental rejection may be partial or complete, passive or active, and subtly or overtly cruel.

Regardless of its specific nature or intensity, parental rejection has been associated with a more or less specific pattern of development in child victims. These children tend to be overly aggressive and prone to impulsive behavior (Lefkowitz et al., 1973; Patterson, 1979; Pemberton & Benady, 1973; Sears, Maccoby, & Levin, 1957). Pringle (1965) reported that adults who had experienced significant rejection in childhood had serious difficulty in giving and receiving affection, while Yates (1981) has more recently found that severely abused children lacked the capacity to form meaningful relationships, some of them resembling adult narcissistic personalities (see Chapter 14). Other reported behaviors associated with parental rejection include such things as diminished intellectual functioning (Hurley, 1965), excessive fears (Poznansky, 1973), and running away from home (Stierlin, 1973).

A consideration of why parents reject their children would take us too far afield, but it would appear that a large proportion of such parents have themselves been the victims of parental rejection (Kaplun & Reich, 1976; Wright, et al., 1979). In this sense, lack of love has been

HIGHLIGHT

Separation from parents as a traumatic experience

Bowlby (1960, 1973) has summarized the effects on children from two to five years of age of being separated from their parents during prolonged periods of hospitalization. He cited three stages of their separation experience:

1. Initial protest—characterized by increased crying, screaming, and general activity.

2. Despair—which included dejection, stupor, decreased activity, and general withdrawal from the environment.

3. Detachment—following the children's discharge from the hospital and reunion with their mothers—in which the children appeared indifferent and sometimes even hostile toward their mothers.

The effects of long-term or permanent separation from one or both parents are complex. When the separation occurs as early as three months after birth, the infant's emotional upset seems to be primarily a reaction to environmental change and strangeness, and he or she usually adapts readily to a surrogate parent figure. But once attachment behavior has developed, the emotional hurt of separation may be deeper and more sustained, and the child may go through a period of bereavement and have greater difficulty adjusting to the change. It would appear that the age at which the infant is most vulnerable to long-term separation or loss is from about three months to three years. The long-term consequences of such loss appear to depend not only on the time of its occurrence, but also on the child in question, the previous relationship with the parent, and the quality of subsequent parental care.

The magnitude of the problem of separation from parents is indicated by the statistic that well over 10 million children in the United States have had the experience of losing at least one parent through separation, divorce, or death.

referred to as a "communicable disease." And, of course, rejection is not a one-way street; the child may also reject the parents. This pattern sometimes occurs when the parents belong to a low-status minority group of which the child is ashamed. Although the results of such rejection have not been studied systematically, it would appear that children who reject their parents deny themselves needed models, loving relationships, and other essentials for healthy development.

Early trauma. Most of us have had traumatic experiences that temporarily shattered our feelings of security, adequacy, and worth, and were important in influencing our later evaluations of ourselves and our environment. The following illustrates such an incident.

"I believe the most traumatic experience of my entire life happened one April evening when I was eleven. I was not too sure of how I had become a member of the family, although my parents had thought it wise to tell me that I was adopted. That much I knew, but what the term *adopted* meant was something else entirely. One evening after my step-brother and I had retired, he proceeded to explain it to me—with a vehemence I shall never forget. He made it clear that I wasn't a 'real' member of the family, that my parents didn't 'really' love me, and that I wasn't even wanted around the place. That was one night I vividly recall crying myself to sleep. That experience undoubtedly played a major role in making me feel insecure and inferior."

Such traumas are apt to leave psychological wounds that never completely heal. As a result, later stress that reactivates these wounds is apt to be particularly difficult for the individual to handle and often explains why one person has difficulty with a problem that is not especially stressful to another. Psychic traumas[3] in infancy or early childhood are especially damaging for the following reasons:

a) Conditioned responses are readily established in situations that evoke strong emotions; such responses are often highly resistant to extinction. Thus one traumatic experience of being unable to swim and almost drowning in a deep lake may be sufficient to establish a fear of water that endures for years or a lifetime.

b) Conditioned emotional responses stemming from traumatic experiences may generalize to other situations. A child who has learned to fear water may also come to be fearful of riding in boats and other situations associated with even the remotest possibility of drowning.

c) Traumatic situations result in emotional conditioning rather than in cognitive learning. Consequently, exposure to similar situations tends to reactivate an emotional response rather than a rational appraisal of the situation, which would provide more flexibility of response and be more likely to be adaptive.

The aftereffects of early traumatic experiences depend heavily on the support and reassurance given the child by parents or other significant persons. This appears particularly important when the trauma involves an experience that arouses strong feelings of inadequacy and self-devaluation, such as being ridiculed for stuttering or clumsiness.

Many traumatic experiences in childhood, though highly upsetting at the time, are probably of minor significance in their long-term consequences, and some children are less vulnerable than others and show more resilience and recoverability from hurt. Not all children who experience a trauma—for example, a parent's death (Crook & Eliot, 1980)—exhibit discernable long-term effects. However, a child exposed to repeated early traumatic experiences is likely to show a disruption in normal personality development. And even though subsequent experiences may have a mollifying influence, the detrimental effects of such early traumas may never be completely obliterated, partly because experiences that would provide the necessary relearning are thereafter selectively avoided. The child whose capacity for basic trust has been severely curtailed does not venture out toward others far enough to learn that *some* people in the world are trustworthy.

Inadequate parenting

All the psychosocial viewpoints on abnormal behavior focus attention in one way or another on the behavioral tendencies the child acquires in the course of early social interaction with others—chiefly parents or parent-surrogates. While their explanations vary considerably, as we have seen, all the viewpoints accept the general principle that certain deviations in parenting can have profound effects on the child's subsequent ability to cope with life's various challenges.

Before proceeding, it should be noted that a parent-child relationship is always bidirectional. As with any continuing relationship, the behav-

---

[3]The terms *psychic trauma* and *traumatic* are used here to mean any aversive (unpleasant) experience that inflicts serious psychological damage on the individual.

ior of each person affects the behavior of the other. Some children are easier to love than others; some parents are more sensitive than others to an infant's needs. Patterns are established for which it is often hard to say which person was originally the most responsible.

In occasional cases we can now identify characteristics in an infant that have been largely responsible for the unsatisfactory relationship that has developed between parent and child. One example is the "difficult baby," described by Chess and her associates (see pages 104–5), a baby whose irregularities are considered partly responsible for the mutually unsatisfying relationship between mother and child.

Another example is the withdrawn, unresponsive, *autistic* child. It has been observed that the parents of such children often seem cold, emotionally reserved, and "intellectual," and early researchers had blamed this parental coldness and "distance" for the child's autism— thereby adding the burden of guilt to the problems these parents already were facing. Infantile autism is now recognized as usually related to a congenital neurological deficit in the child; evidently the parents restrict their emotional involvement, often unconsciously, as a way of coping with a profoundly unresponsive child (Schopler, 1978). There is also evidence that some of the disturbance commonly found in the parents of schizophrenic patients is a reaction *to* the child's disturbance rather than the other way around.

In most cases, however, the influence of the parent on the child is more important in shaping the child's behavior than vice versa. Several specific patterns of parental influence appear with great regularity in the background of children who show emotional disturbances and other types of faulty development. Six of these patterns will be discussed here.

Overprotection and restrictiveness. Overprotective parents may watch over their children constantly, protect them from the slightest risk, overly clothe and medicate them, and make up their minds for them at every opportunity. In essence, they smother the child's growth.

While fathers have been known to overprotect their children, the problem is probably more common among mothers (Weinraub & Frankel, 1977). Such maternal reactions appear to repre-

sent a compensatory type of behavior in which the mother attempts, through her contact with the child, to gain satisfactions that normally should be obtained in her marriage. It is not uncommon in such cases for the mother to call the male child her "lover" and actually to encourage the child in behaviors somewhat typical of courting. A corollary syndrome also occurs between fathers and daughters.

In a study of the family background of children referred to a child guidance clinic, Jenkins (1968) found that those youngsters characterized as "overanxious" were likely to have an infantilizing, overprotective mother. Similarly, in his study of children with excessive fears, Poznanski (1973) found a dependent relationship upon an overprotective mother to be one key reason for the fears. Roff and Knight (1981), in a longitudinal study (mentioned earlier) of middle-aged men who had experienced schizophrenic episodes, found that maternal overanxiousness and overprotectiveness as well as maternal neglect predicted poor outcomes of their disorders.

In shielding the child from every danger, the overprotective mother fails to provide the opportunities the child needs for reality testing and development of essential competencies. In addition, her overprotection implies that she regards the child as incapable of coping with everyday problems. It is not surprising that such children often reach adolescence and young adulthood feeling inadequate and threatened by a dangerous world. When the time finally comes for such children to be on their own, they usually find themselves unprepared for the challenge (see **HIGHLIGHT** on page 124).

Closely related to overprotection is restrictiveness. Here the parents rigidly enforce restrictive rules and standards and give the child little autonomy or freedom for growing in his or her own way. Whether justified or not, parental restrictiveness is one of the most commonly heard complaints of adolescents. Restrictiveness may foster well-controlled, socialized behavior, but it can also nurture fear, dependency, submission, repressed hostility, and some dulling of intellectual striving (Baumrind, 1971; Becker, 1964). Often, too, extreme behavior on the part of the adolescent is a way of rebelling against severe restrictions. This conflict between rebellion and submission is not infrequently reflected in promiscuous sexual behavior among adolescent girls.

HIGHLIGHT
One case of overprotection

I was a girl who had almost everything: a beautiful home; money for personal pleasure whenever I asked; nice clothes; and parents who coddled me, picked up after me, and chauffeured me wherever I wanted to go. What didn't I have? Well, I didn't have any knowledge of how to sort out laundry or run a washing machine. I didn't know how to discipline myself to use time properly, to make sure I got enough sleep, to feed myself the right food. I didn't have the basics for coping with life on my own.

My parents—undoubtedly out of love, but with a mixture of guilt added—had, for some reason, overcompensated during my childhood. They had done

too much for me. And when the time came for me to be on my own, I struggled for independence from this overprotective nest, stumbled over my newfound physical, moral, and social freedoms, and suffered a crushing fall. But by the time I hit bottom, I had learned one principle that I hope will guide me throughout the rest of my life: I can make it on my own. I learned this the hard way. I only hope that, by sharing my experience, I can help others become independent young adults without the physical and emotional trauma I endured.

Quoted from Traub (1974, p. 41).

Unrealistic demands.   Some parents place excessive pressures on their children to live up to unrealistically "high" standards. For example, a child may be expected to excel in school and other activities. Where the child has the capacity for exceptionally high-level performance, things may work out; but even here the child may be under such sustained pressure that little room is left for spontaneity or development as an independent person.

Typically, however, the child is never quite able to live up to parental expectations and demands. Nothing the child does seems good enough. If a child raises a grade of C to a B, rather than giving praise, the parents may ask why it was not an A. Effort only brings more painful frustration and self-devaluation. Those parents who promote feelings of failure by their excessive demands also tend to discourage further effort on the child's part. Almost invariably such a child eventually comes to feel, "I can't do it, so why try?"

One need only observe a child's eager "Watch me, Mommy," while demonstrating some new achievement, to understand how important the mastery of new competencies and parental recognition for such mastery are to healthy development. And research studies, such as the investigation of the antecedents of self-respect in children carried out by Coopersmith (1967), have shown that high parental expectations are both common and helpful for the child's devel-

opment. Yet such expectations need to be realistic and to take into consideration the capabilities and temperament of each child. The child who is repeatedly rebuffed in his or her efforts to gain approval and self-esteem is very unlikely to develop effective coping techniques, as Sullivan (see Chapter 3) in particular noted.

Often, unrealistic parental demands focus on moral standards—particularly with regard to sex, alcohol, and related matters. For example, the parents may instill in the child the view that masturbation or any other sexual activity is terribly sinful and can lead only to moral and physical degeneration. The child who accepts such parental standards may face many guilt-arousing and self-devaluating conflicts.

In still other instances, parental demands are unrealistically low, and the parents do not care what happens as long as the child stays out of trouble. Coopersmith (1967) found that the children of such parents were significantly lower in both achievement and self-esteem than were children whose parents had high but realistic expectations for them. Thus we can see that unrealistic expectations and demands—either too high, too low, or distorted and rigid—can be important causes of faulty development and maladjustment.

Overpermissiveness and indulgence.   It happens less commonly than is popularly supposed, but sometimes one or both parents will cater to the child's slightest whims and in so doing fail to teach and reward desirable standards of behavior. In essence, the parent surrenders the running of the home to an uninhibited son or daughter.

Pollack (1968), for example, has quoted a permissive father who finally rebelled at the tyranny of his nine-year-old daughter, and in a near tantrum exploded with, "I want one thing clearly understood—I live here, too!" (p. 28). Similarly, one of the authors has observed a three-year-old girl essentially demolish the living room of a neighbor's home in full view of her doting mother. When the mother finally intervened, she was repeatedly struck and kicked by this little tyrant, who was in turn not punished in any way for her behavior.

Overly indulged children are characteristically spoiled, selfish, inconsiderate, and demanding. Sears (1961) found that much permissiveness and little discipline in the home were correlated positively with antisocial, aggressive behavior, particularly during middle and later childhood. Unlike rejected, emotionally deprived children, who often find it difficult to enter into warm interpersonal relationships, indulged children enter readily into such relationships but exploit people for their own purposes in the same way that they have learned to exploit their parents. In dealing with authority, such children are usually rebellious since, for so long, they have had their own way. Overly indulged children also tend to be impatient, to approach problems in an aggressive and demanding manner, and to find it difficult to accept present frustrations in the interests of long-range goals (Baumrind, 1971, 1975).

The fact that their important and pampered status in the home does not transfer automatically to the outside world may come as a great shock to indulged youngsters; confusion and adjustive difficulties may occur when "reality" forces them to reassess their assumptions about themselves and the world. When they fail to do so in an adequate manner, as is often the case, their careers as adults tend to be littered with repeated interpersonal failures and eventual frustration and disillusionment.

Faulty discipline. Parenthood is one of the most important and demanding commitments adults undertake, yet typically their preparation for doing so is woefully inadequate. Despite the

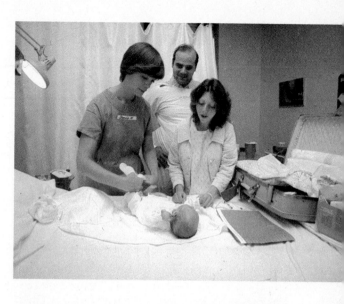

The love parents naturally feel toward their offspring will often express itself in terms of definite hopes and goals for the future. In some instances, this may lead to excessively high or unrealistic expectations, forcing the child too quickly into adult responsibilities or adult roles.

increasing availability of special programs such as "parent effectiveness training" and a variety of sophisticated books on the subject, most parents still rely primarily on what they learned of parenting from their own parents, who may or may not have been ideal models (Wright et al., 1979). The question of disciplining children is a particularly controversial and confusing one for most parents (Baumrind, 1975). Many are tempted to resolve the problem by abdicating the responsibility. In other cases parents have resorted to excessively harsh discipline, convinced that if they "spare the rod" they will spoil the child. And in still other cases parents have seemed to lack general guidelines, punishing children one day and ignoring or even rewarding them the next for doing the same thing.

There is no question that well-placed permissiveness can be good and creative for a child. But overpermissiveness and lack of discipline tend to produce a spoiled, inconsiderate aggressive child—and an insecure one as well. On the other hand, overly severe or harsh discipline may have a variety of harmful effects, including fear and hatred of the punishing person, little initiative or spontaneity, and less friendly feelings toward others. When accompanied by rigid moral standards, overly severe discipline is likely to result in a seriously repressed child who lacks spontaneity and warmth and devotes much effort toward controlling impulses that are, in fact, natural but are assumed to be sinful. Such children often subject themselves to severe self-recrimination and self-punishment for real or imagined mistakes and misdeeds. Overly severe discipline, combined with restrictiveness, also may lead to rebellion and socially deviant behavior as children grow older and are subjected increasingly to outside influences that may be incompatible with parental views and practices.

When severe discipline takes the form of physical punishment for broken rules—as opposed to withdrawal of approval and privileges—the result tends to be increased aggressive behavior on the part of the child (Eron et al., 1974; Faretra, 1981; Patterson, 1979). Apparently physical punishment provides a model of aggressive behavior that the child then tends to emulate.

Similarly, inconsistent discipline makes it difficult for the child to establish stable values for guiding behavior. A child who is punished one time and ignored and rewarded the next for the same behavior is at a loss to know what behavior is appropriate. Deur and Parke (1970) found that children with a history of inconsistent reward and punishment for aggressive behavior were more resistant to punishment and to the extinction of their aggressive behavior than were children who had experienced more consistent discipline. This study supports earlier findings showing a high correlation between inconsistent discipline and later delinquent and criminal behavior.

In the past, discipline was conceived as a method for both punishing undesirable behavior and preventing such behavior in the future. Discipline is now thought of more positively as providing needed structure and guidance for promoting healthy growth on the part of the child. For example, Baumrind (1975) has found that "authoritative" discipline is associated with development in youngsters of a general competence for dealing with others and with one's environment. Where coercion or punishment is deemed necessary, it is considered important that the parent make it clear exactly what behavior is considered inappropriate; it is also considered important that the child know what behavior is expected, and that positive and consistent methods of discipline be worked out for dealing with infractions. In general, it would appear that freedom should be commensurate with the child's level of maturity and with his or her ability to use it constructively.

Inadequate and irrational communication. Parents can discourage a child from asking questions and in other ways fail to foster the "information exchange" essential for helping the child develop a realistic frame of reference and essential competencies. Such limited and inadequate communication patterns have commonly been attributed to socially disadvantaged families, but these patterns are not restricted to any one socioeconomic level.

Such patterns may take a number of forms. Some parents are too busy with their own concerns to listen to their children and try to understand the conflicts and pressures they are facing. As a consequence, these parents often fail to give needed support and assistance during crisis periods. Other parents may have forgotten that the world often looks different to a child or adolescent and that rapid social change can lead to a very real communication gap between generations.

In other instances faulty communication may take more deviant forms in which the messages become completely garbled because the listener distorts, disconfirms, or blocks out the speaker's intended meaning. A good example of such pathological communication is provided by Haley (1959). The setting is a meeting in the hospital involving a schizophrenic young man, his parents, and his therapist. Some time prior to the meeting, the patient had sent his mother a Mother's Day card containing the inscription, "For Someone Who's Been Like a Mother To Me." We pick up the conversation at the point following a confrontation between mother and son concerning the obliquely hostile inscription:

"*Patient:* Well, I meant to sting you just a tiny bit by that outside phrase.
Mother: You see I'm a little bit of a psychiatrist too, Simon, I happen to be —(laughing). So I felt so— when you talked to (the therapist) I brought along that card—I wanted to know what's behind your head. And I wanted to know—or you made it on purposely to hurt me—Well, if you did, I—I . . .
Patient: (interrupting) Not entirely, not entire . . .
Mother: (interrupting and overlapping) I'll take all—Simon, believe me. I'll take all the hurt in the world if it will help you—you see what I mean?
Therapist: How can you . . .
Mother: (continuing) Because I never meant to hurt you—Huh?
Therapist: How can you hurt anybody who is perfectly willing to be hurt? (short pause)
Father: What's that?
Mother: I uh—a mother sacrifices—if you would be— maybe a mother you would know too. Because a mother is just a martyr, she's sacrificing—like even with Jesus with his mother—she sacrificed too. So that's the way it goes on, a mother takes over anything what she can help . . .
Therapist: (interrupting) What mother?
Mother: (continuing) her children.
Patient: (interrupting and overlapping) Well, uh, I'll tell you Ma—listen, Ma, I didn't mean to—to sting you exactly that outside part there.
Therapist: Well, you said so.
Patient: Oh, all right, but it—it wasn't that exactly. No, I'm not giving ground—uh—it's hard to explain this thing. Uh—uh—what was I going to say? Now I forgot what I was going to say. (short pause) I mean I felt that this—this is what I mean, uh—that I felt that you could have been a better mother to me than you were. See there were things.
Mother: Uh . . .

Father: Well you said . . .
Patient: (interrupting) You could have been better than you were. So that's why—that's that—I felt—it was, uh—uh, was all right to send it that way.
Mother: Well, if you meant it that way that's perf— that's what I wanted to know—and that's all I care you see. But I still say, Simon, that if you would take your father and mother just like they're plain people—you just came here and you went through life like anybody else went through—and—and don't keep picking on them and picking them to pieces— but just leave them alone—and go along with them the way they are—and don't change them—you'll be able to get along with everybody, I assure you.
Patient: (interrupting) I mean after all a card is a card— why I'd—it seems to me kind of silly (anguish in his voice and near weeping) to bring that thing in here— they have sold them at the canteen, Ma . . .
Therapist: Are you anxious now . . .
Patient: Why . . .
Therapist: Are you anxious now because she said . . .
Patient: I shouldn't be blamed for a thing like that, it's so small . . .
Mother: (overlapping) I'm not blaming you.
Patient: (continuing) I don't even remember exactly what the thing was.
Mother: (overlapping) Well, that's all I wanted to know (laughs).
Patient: (continuing) I didn't want to—to—to—to blame you or nothing." (Haley, 1959, p. 360)

This conversation continued in similar fashion until the patient conceded that what he had meant by the inscription was that his mother had been a *real* mother to him. This produced a considerable reduction in general tension, but it was, of course, at the expense of reality.

Such deviant forms of intrafamilial communication are often found in the families of schizophrenic individuals. Although other types of pathogenic parent-child relations are also seen in abundance in such cases, many investigators believe that family communication deviance has a special relevance for the schizophrenic type of disorder (Carson, 1983; Liem, 1980). It is still not established, however, that such communication patterns are causal factors; rather, they may be only correlations. That is, it is also possible that the presence of a schizophrenic or preschizophrenic child in the household might cause parents to communicate in strange ways.

In any event, the types of deviance found in the households of schizophrenic individuals are quite varied. They include fragmented ways of communicating, erotic attachments between parent and child, difficulties in maintaining a focus of attention, inability to establish closure about a topic of conversation, and undue amounts of hostile and critical attention focused on the member who is at risk for a schizophrenic episode (Liem, 1980). We shall have more to say about these matters in Chapter 10.

Undesirable parental models. Important in any relationship are the behaviors that one individual shows to the other. This is particularly true in parent-child interactions. Since children tend to observe and imitate the behavior of their parents, parental behavior can have a highly beneficial or detrimental effect on the way a youngster learns to perceive, think, feel, and act. We may consider parents as undesirable models if they have faulty assumptions about reality, possibility, and values, or if they depend excessively on defense mechanisms in coping with their problems—as when they consistently project the blame for their own mistakes onto others, if they lie and cheat, if they refuse to face and deal realistically with problems, or if there is a marked discrepancy between their proclaimed values and the values reflected in their actual behavior.

Undesirable parental models are undoubtedly an important reason why mental disorders, delinquency, crime, and other forms of maladaptive behavior tend to run in families. But it should be pointed out that there is nothing inevitable in the effects of parental pathology on the child's development. The pathology of one parent may be compensated for by the wisdom and concern of the other, or an alcoholic parent may perhaps serve as a "negative model," showing the child what *not* to be like. Kadushin (1967) has cited a number of studies in which children coming from homes with undesirable parental models have grown up to be successful and well-adjusted adults. And Bleuler (1974) found that even the extreme stress of being reared by a psychotic parent did not prevent half to three-quarters of the children he studied from remaining normal.

Although the reasons for such favorable outcomes are not clear, it is useful to emphasize that specific pathogenic parent-child patterns always take place in a broader social context. The context may tend to either minimize or exacerbate the influence of a particular condition. For

The unfortunate effects of modeling can be seen in this youngster, who is clearly patterning his behavior (even down to the stance he assumes in handling the cigarette) after adults he has seen.

These children's attitudes toward race and politics as they grow into adulthood will almost certainly be influenced by the example of their parents.

example, the positive and growth-producing experiences a child might have with grandparents could conceivably neutralize even very negative influences within the immediate family. On the other hand, a seriously disturbed mother or father (or both) may create such a pathological atmosphere that no external agencies, however benign, could prevent serious damage to the development of the child. A summary of faulty parent-child relationships is presented in the **HIGHLIGHT** on page 130.

Pathogenic family structures

The pathogenic parent-child patterns so far described, such as maternal rejection, are rarely found in severe form unless the total familial context is abnormal. Hence, pathogenic family structure can be regarded as an overarching risk factor that increases an individual's vulnerability to particular stressors. Thus, in the Roff and Knight (1981) longitudinal study of persons who became schizophrenic in early adulthood, two types of mothering—neglect and overanxious, overprotective behavior—were found to be common among those individuals who had poor long-term outcomes. But it was also demonstrated that each of these patterns of mothering occurred in a particular type of disordered family structure. This confirmed earlier reports concerning two family patterns that appear especially predictive of a schizophrenic outcome in offspring. Maternal neglect was found to be associated with a *discordant* family pattern, whereas maternal anxiety and overprotectiveness tended to be associated with a *disturbed* one. Each of these family structures is described below, followed by disrupted, inadequate, and antisocial family patterns.

Discordant and disturbed families. In a discordant family one or both of the parents is not gaining satisfaction from the relationship and may express feelings of frustration and disillusionment in hostile ways such as nagging, belittling, and doing things purposely to annoy the other person. A common source of conflict and dissatisfaction is value differences, which may lead to serious disagreements about a variety of topics, including sexual behavior and how money is spent. Whatever the reasons for difficulties, seriously discordant relationships are likely to be frustrating, hurtful, and generally

pathogenic in their effects on both the adults and the children. Children who grow up in discordant families are likely themselves to find it difficult to establish and maintain marital and other intimate relationships.

In a disturbed family, one or both of the parents behave in grossly eccentric or abnormal ways and may keep the home in constant emotional turmoil. Such homes differ greatly, but it is common to find (a) parents who are fighting to maintain their own equilibrium and are unable to give the child needed love and guidance; (b) gross irrationality in communication patterns as well as faulty parental models; and (c) almost inevitably, the enmeshment of the child in the emotional conflicts of the parents.

Earlier, Lidz et al. (1965) had described two similar patterns in the family backgrounds of many schizophrenic patients they studied. They called these patterns (a) *marital schism,* in which both parents are constantly embroiled in deep-seated conflict; and (b) *marital skew,* wherein the healthier marital partner, in the interest of minimizing open disharmony, essentially accepts and supports the frequently bizarre beliefs and behavior of the spouse. Schism and skew are roughly equivalent, respectively, to discordant and disturbed family patterns. In either instance, the children are caught up in an unwholesome and irrational psychological environment.

Disrupted families. A third type of family pattern that may be pathogenic is the *disrupted family.* A disrupted family is incomplete, whether as a result of death, divorce, separation, or some other circumstance. Owing partly to greater cultural acceptance of divorce, more than a million divorces are now occurring yearly in the United States, with a rate of increase averaging about 8 percent each year. Although certain persons contribute disproportionately to such figures through multiple divorces and remarriages, the statistics nevertheless provide a sobering commentary on the strains and difficulties of extended intimate relationships. It is estimated that, at any one time, over 10 percent of the ever-married adult population is currently separated or divorced (Bloom, Asher, & White, 1978). Estimates have indicated that, as of 1980, over three million households were headed by divorced mothers alone, a figure that has doubtless increased since then.

HIGHLIGHT
Summary chart of faulty parent-child relationships

Undesirable condition	Typical effect on child's personality development
Rejection	Feelings of anxiety, insecurity, low self-esteem, negativism, hostility, attention-seeking, loneliness, jealousy, and slowness in conscience development
Overprotection—domination	Submissiveness, lack of self-reliance, dependence in relations with others, low self-evaluation, some dulling of intellectual striving
Overpermissiveness—overindulgence	Selfishness, demanding attitude, inability to tolerate frustration, rebelliousness toward authority, excessive need of attention, lack of responsibility, inconsiderateness, exploitativeness in interpersonal relationships
Perfectionism, with unrealistic demands	Lack of spontaneity, rigid conscience development, severe conflicts, tendency toward guilt and self-condemnation if there is failure to live up to parental demands
Faulty discipline: Lack of discipline	Inconsiderateness, aggressiveness, and antisocial tendencies
Harsh, overly severe discipline	Fear, hatred of parent, little initiative or spontaneity, lack of friendly feelings toward others
Inconsistent discipline	Difficulty in establishing stable values for guiding behavior; tendency toward highly aggressive behavior
Inadequate and irrational communications	As in case of "double bind" communications, the tendency toward confusion, lack of an integrated frame of reference, unclear self-identity, lack of initiative, self-devaluation
Undesirable parental models	The learning of faulty values, formulation of unrealistic goals, development of maladaptive coping patterns

The exact effects of faulty parent-child relationships on later behavior depends on many factors, including the age of the child, the constitutional and personality makeup of the child at the time, the duration and degree of the unhealthy relationship, his or her perception of the relationship, and the total family setting and life context, including the presence or absence of alleviating conditions and whether or not subsequent experiences tend to reinforce or correct early damage. There is no uniform pattern of pathogenic family relationship underlying the development of later psychopathology, but the conditions we have discussed often act as predisposing factors.

Stressful as unhappy marriages are, dissolution of a marital relationship can also be enormously stressful and can produce much disorder, both mental and physical. The divorced and separated are markedly overrepresented among psychiatric patients, although the direction of the causal relationship is not always clear. In their comprehensive review of the effects of marital disruption, Bloom et al. (1978) concluded that such disruption is a major source of psychopathology, physical illness and death, suicide, and homicide.

Divorce can have traumatic effects on a child. Feelings of insecurity and rejection may be aggravated by conflicting loyalties and sometimes, by the spoiling the child receives while staying with one or the other parent—maybe not the one he or she would prefer to be with. However, some children adjust quite well to the divorce of their parents, particularly those who were relatively well-adjusted prior to the breakup (Kurdek et al., 1981).

It has been commonly assumed that the loss of a father is more traumatic for a son than for a daughter, but some doubt has been raised about this assumption. It is now believed that absence of the father has adverse effects on the formation of a secure gender identity for both girls and boys (Hetherington, Cox, & Cox, 1978). For example, Hetherington (1973) found that "the effects of father absence on daughters appear during adolescence and manifest themselves mainly as an inability to interact appropriately with males" (p. 52).

The long-range effects of family disruption on the child may vary greatly, even being favorable in many instances as contrasted to remaining in a home torn by marital conflict and dissension (Hetherington et al., 1978) Detrimental effects may be minimized if a substitute model for the missing parent is available, if the remaining family members are able to compensate for the missing parent and reorganize the family into an effective functioning group, or if a successful remarriage follows that provides an adequate environment for child rearing. Above all, the remaining parent—usually the mother—can help her child work through the crisis period by coping well with both her own emotional upset and that of her child.

Unquestionably, parental separation or divorce involves very real stresses for children; it is hardly surprising that some succumb to these stresses and develop maladaptive responses. Delinquency and other maladaptive behaviors are much more frequent among children and adolescents from disrupted homes than among those from intact ones. We are beginning to learn, however, that we are not always justified in inferring that the disrupted home has caused the maladaptive behavior. Since both broken homes and delinquency are most common among families in lower socioeconomic circumstances, it seems equally likely that both the broken homes and the childhood deviance are in large part caused by the stressors of poverty and exclusion from the mainstream of society.

Inadequate families.   An *inadequate family* is characterized by inability to cope with the ordinary problems of family living. It lacks the resources, physical or psychological, for meeting demands with which most families can satisfactorily cope. Consequently, the inadequate family relies heavily on continued outside assistance and support in resolving everyday problems.

The incompetencies of such a family may stem from immaturity, lack of education, mental retardation, or other shortcomings of the parents. Sometimes, of course, environmental demands are so severe that they overtax the adjustive resources of families that would normally be more adequate.

A family that is floundering against odds too great for its resources, for whatever reason, cannot give its children the feeling of safety and security they need, or adequately guide them in the development of essential competencies. Nor can financial or other outside assistance be counted on to meet the needs of such families, for families, like individuals, need to feel they are self-directing and in control of their own destinies.

Antisocial families.   Here the family espouses values not accepted by the wider community. In some families the parents are overtly or covertly engaged in behavior that violates the standards and interests of society, and they may be chronically in difficulty with the law. Such antisocial values usually handicap relationships within the family, as well as provide undesirable models for the child.

Children in such families may be encouraged in dishonesty, deceit, and other undesirable behavior patterns; or they may simply observe and imitate the undesirable behavior and attitudes of their parents. In some cases, children may develop a high degree of courage, self-discipline, and loyalty to the family group at the expense of identification with society as a whole. More often, the models they see are immature and self-seeking, and the social interactions they observe and take part in are shallow and manipulative—a poor preparation for interacting well with people outside the family.

Pathogenic interpersonal relationships and interactions are by no means confined to the family, but may also involve the peer group and other individuals outside the family. Particularly during adolescence, when young people are becoming progressively independent of parents, their relationships outside the family are likely to be important influences on their further development.

In sum, we know that a large number of psychosocial influences may prevent an individual from developing the resources needed for coping with life challenges. Whether or not the person's vulnerability will ultimately manifest itself in a disorder appears to depend not only on the *level* of stressors experienced by the persons (the subject of the next chapter) but also importantly on certain factors in the sociocultural context. Such factors may operate to lessen or to enhance an individual's overall vulnerability to particular forms of disorder. Since our knowledge in this area is limited, our discussion will be brief.

Sociocultural factors

As we pointed out in Chapter 3, the sociocultural viewpoint grew out of observations of varying value and behavior patterns among different cultural groups. These observations brought an enormously increased appreciation of the power of social and cultural forces in the shaping of behavior and personality. We also noted that a number of cultures and subcultures seem to protect their members from the more serious forms of personal misery and disorganization, as shown by incidence rates for some disorders that are markedly below worldwide averages. In some cultures, of course—that of southern Ireland being a recent example—incidence rates for certain disorders are markedly *above* the average (Torrey, 1980). We can assume that these differences occur because the culture itself in some way either protects its members from or instills within them a measure of vulnerability to disorder.

For reasons of temperament, personal conditioning, and other individual factors, not all individuals adopt the prevailing cultural patterns. These people may escape some of the detrimental influences but may also miss the protection of the more adaptive ones. This is especially common in our Western society, where we are exposed to so many competing values and patterns instead of the more consistent patterns of many simpler societies. The main point to be made in this section is that in our society several social and cultural influences may act to increase the vulnerability of many of us to the development of abnormal behavior. We begin with a general overview of the role of culture in determining an individual's behavior pattern. We

then turn to particular factors in the sociocultural environment that may increase vulnerability: low socioeconomic class, disorder-engendering social roles, prejudice and discrimination, economic and employment problems, and social change and uncertainty.

Sociocultural environment as a determinant

In much the same sense that we receive a genetic inheritance that is the end product of millions of years of biological evolution, we also receive a sociocultural inheritance that is the end product of many thousands of years of social evolution—the significance of which was well pointed up by Huxley (1965):

"The native or genetic capacities of today's bright city child are no better than the native capacities of a bright child born into a family of Upper Paleolithic cave-dwellers. But whereas the contemporary bright baby may grow up to become almost anything—a Presbyterian engineer, for example, a piano-playing Marxist, a professor of biochemistry who is a mystical agnostic and likes to paint in water colours—the paleolithic baby could not possibly have grown into anything except a hunter or food-gatherer, using the crudest of stone tools and thinking about his narrow world of trees and swamps in terms of some hazy system of magic. Ancient and modern, the two babies are indistinguishable. . . . But the adults into whom the babies will grow are profoundly dissimilar; and they are dissimilar because in one of them very few, and in the other a good many, of the baby's inborn potentialities have been actualized." (p. 69)

Because each group fosters its own cultural patterns by systematically teaching its offspring, all its members tend to be somewhat alike—to conform to certain "basic personality types." Individuals reared among headhunters become headhunters; individuals reared in societies that do not sanction violence learn to settle their differences in nonviolent ways. In New Guinea, for example, Mead (1949) found two tribes—of similar racial origin and living in the same general geographical area—whose members developed diametrically opposed characteristics. The Arapesh were a kindly, peaceful, cooperative people, while the Mundugumor were warlike, suspicious, competitive, and vengeful. Such differences appear to be social in origin.

The more uniform and thorough the education of the younger members of a group, the more alike they will become. Thus in a society characterized by a limited and consistent point of view, there are not the wide individual differences typical of a society like ours, where children have contact with many diverse, often conflicting, beliefs. Even in our society, however, there are certain core values that we attempt to perpetuate as essential to our way of life.

Subgroups within a general sociocultural environment—such as family, sex, age, social class, occupational, and religious groups—also foster beliefs and norms of their own, largely by means of *social roles* that their members learn to adopt. Expected role behaviors exist for the student, the teacher, the army officer, the priest, the nurse, for example.

The extent to which role expectations can influence development is well illustrated by "masculine" and "feminine" sex roles in our own society and their effects on personality development and characteristic behavior. While a combination of masculine and feminine traits (*androgyny*) has in recent years often been proclaimed to be psychologically ideal for both men and women, many men and women continue to show evidence of having been strongly affected by assigned masculine and feminine gender roles (Lubinsky et al., 1983). Moreover, there is accumulating evidence that the acceptance of gender-role assignments may have substantial implications for mental health. In general, research studies show that excessive "femininity" is associated with maladaptive behavior and vulnerability to disorder for *either* biological sex. Baucom (1983), for example, has recently shown that high feminine-sex-typed women tend to reject opportunities to be in control in a group problem-solving situation, an effect he likens to "learned helplessness," which has in turn been implicated as a causal factor in depression (Abramson et al., 1978).

The individual, being a member of various subgroups, is subject to various role demands. And, of course, social roles change as group memberships—or position in a given group—change. In fact, the life of the individual can be viewed as consisting of a succession of roles—child, student, worker, husband or wife, parent, and senior citizen. The various groups may allow the individual considerable leeway in role behavior, but there are limits. Conformity to role demands is induced by the use of positive and negative reinforcers—money, prestige, status,

punishment, or loss of membership in the group—as well as through instruction. When social roles are conflicting, unclear, or uncomfortable, or when an individual is unable to achieve a satisfactory role in the group, healthy personality development may be impaired.

Each individual interacts with various other persons and groups, typically beginning with family members and gradually extending to peer group members and other significant persons in his or her world. Much of an individual's personality development reflects experiences with these key people. Relationships in a Boy Scout troop will likely have effects on development quite different from relationships in a delinquent gang. The behavior patterns children learn depend heavily on what models they observe, whose expectations they are trying to meet, and what rewards are forthcoming for their behavior.

Pathogenic societal influences

Since each of us belongs to different subgroups and experiences different interpersonal relationships, we each participate in the sociocultural environment in a unique way. As a consequence of such "differential participation," no two of us grows up in quite the same world. In the situations that follow, different social roles and social experiences can be seen as significant influences in the development of maladaptive behavior.

Low socioeconomic class. An inverse correlation exists between socioeconomic class standing and the prevalence of abnormal behavior—the lower the socioeconomic level, the higher the incidence of abnormal behavior, at least in our society (Eron & Peterson, 1982). The strength of the correlation seems to vary with different types of disorder, however. Some disorders may be related to social class only minimally or perhaps not at all.

We do not understand all the reasons for this relationship. Undoubtedly some inadequate and disturbed persons drift onto the lower rungs of the economic ladder and remain there; these people will often have inadequate and disturbed children. At the same time, affluent persons will be better able to get prompt help or to conceal their problems.

In addition, it is almost certainly true that

Slum environments appear more likely to foster abnormal behavior than other, more privileged environments. Many individuals, however, emerge from low socioeconomic environments with strong, highly adaptive personalities and attitudes.

persons of lower socioeconomic status encounter more, and more severe, stressors in their lives than do the well-to-do and frequently have fewer resources for dealing with them. As Kohn (1973) has pointed out, the conditions under which lower class youngsters are reared tend not to enable them to develop the coping skills needed in our increasingly complex society. Hence, the tendency for abnormal behavior to appear frequently in lower socioeconomic groups may be at least partly due to predispositional coping deficits.

Disorder-engendering social roles. An organized society sometimes calls on its members to perform roles in which the prescribed behaviors are either deviant in and of themselves or may produce maladaptive reactions in persons asked to perform them. The soldier who is called upon by his society to kill and maim other human beings may subsequently develop very serious feelings of guilt. Or he may have latent emotional problems resulting from the horrors commonly experienced under combat conditions, and hence be vulnerable to disorder. As a nation, we are still struggling with the many problems of this type that have emerged among veterans of the Vietnam war, whose rates of abnormality have been well above national averages (Strayer & Ellenhorn, 1975) and who, as a

group, are expected to have continuing problems well into the future (Horowitz & Solomon, 1975).

Militaristic regimes and organizations are especially likely to foster problematic social roles. Military officialdom in Germany during the Nazi holocaust willingly participated in the most heinous and cold-blooded mass murders humankind has ever known. Some of our own street gangs demand extreme cruelty and callousness on the part of their members. And well-organized terrorist groups, feeling that world society is ignoring their just claims, train their members for destruction and murder that threaten the security of all of us.

In an experiment that had to be prematurely terminated because of its disturbing effects on the participating subjects, Zimbardo and his associates (1975) demonstrated the power of the roles of "guard" and "prisoner" to produce extremely maladaptive behavior in otherwise normal persons in just a few days. An unintended consequence of this study was that its subjects would have to "live with" some things about themselves they may have preferred not to learn.

There is, of course, no easy answer to the problems of violence and coercion in the modern world; people will often resort to force when other methods of redress or persuasion

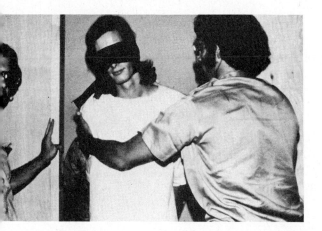 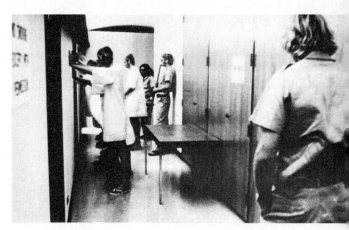

*In the Zimbardo et al. (1975) prison experiment, the subjects were given distinctive roles
and uniforms: the "guards" wore khaki uniforms and dark glasses; "prisoners" wore short,
loosely fitting smocks with identification numbers on front and back. Investigators and
subjects alike were clearly unprepared for the behaviors that resulted. Guards soon became
actively hostile, cruel, and sadistic. Passive hostility in the prisoners gave way to
demeaning obedience. The experiment, though not completed, clearly illustrated the
enormous power that social situations and social roles can have on human behavior.*

fail. As long as such actions occur, large numbers of people will be subjected to conditions of extraordinary stress and will feel compelled to enact difficult and painful social roles. In some cases, the end result will be psychological disorder.

Prejudice and discrimination.

Incalculable numbers of persons in our society have been subjected to attacks on their self-esteem and to demoralizing stereotypes, not to mention overt discrimination in areas such as employment and education. We have made progress in race relations since the 1960s, but the lingering effects of mistrust and discomfort among various cultural groups can be observed with striking clarity on almost any college campus. For the most part, students socialize informally only with members of their own subcultures, despite the attempts of many well-meaning college administrators to "break down the barriers." The tendency of students to avoid crossing the barriers needlessly limits the educational experience for many and probably contributes to continued misinformation and prejudice about the characteristics of outgroup members.

We have also made progress in recent years in recognizing the demeaning and often disabling social roles our society has historically assigned to women. But, again here, much remains to be done. Many more women than men present themselves for treatment for various emotional disorders, notably depression, and many mental health professionals believe this is a consequence both of the vulnerabilities (e. g., passivity, dependence) intrinsic to the traditional roles assigned to women as well as of the special stressors with which many women must cope (e.g., full-time mother *and* full-time homemaker) in attempting to fulfill traditional role requirements.

Economic and employment problems.

Economic difficulties and unemployment have repeatedly been implicated as factors that enhance vulnerability and therefore lead to elevated rates of abnormal behavior (Dooley & Catalano, 1980). Recession and inflation coupled with high unemployment are sources of chronic anxiety for many people. Inflation, for example, has imposed special hardships on people whose finances cannot keep pace with the economic spiral, such as those on fixed retirement incomes. Unemployment has placed a burden on a sizable segment of our population, bringing with it both financial hardships and self-devaluation. In fact, unemployment can be as debilitating psychologically as it is financially (Nelson, 1974).

As an indication of the toll that unemployment exacts, periods of extensive unemployment are typically accompanied by increases in certain types of maladaptive behavior, such as depression, suicide, and crime (Brenner, 1973). Hardest hit by economic and employment problems are those at the bottom of the social ladder who are already handicapped by poorer education, poorer nutrition, more broken or unstable families, overcrowding, inadequate housing, and feelings of helplessness and of rejection by the larger society.

Even for many people who *are* employed, a major source of demoralization is job dissatisfaction. Job dissatisfaction is related to anxiety, tension, and a wide range of psychophysiologic disorders; it has also been related to impaired marital and family relationships.

Whatever the possibilities for job satisfaction in an increasingly computerized and complicated society, the demand for it seems to be increasing (Gartner & Riessman, 1974). People no longer see money alone as an adequate return for their investment of time and energy; they also desire meaningful employment and an integration of education, work, and leisure into a fulfilling life pattern. The difficulties of achieving this adds yet another dimension to the job picture: many people may succeed in realizing their career ambitions and still find themselves unhappy or disillusioned with their work.

Social change and uncertainty. The rate and pervasiveness of change today are different from anything our ancestors ever experienced. All aspects of our lives are affected—our education, our jobs, our family life, our leisure pursuits, our economic security, and our beliefs and values. Constantly trying to keep up with the new adjustments demanded by these changes is a source of considerable stress. In fact, Toffler (1970) proposed the term "future shock" to describe the profound confusion and emotional upset resulting from social change that has become too rapid.

Simultaneously, we confront an inevitable squeeze as the consumable natural resources of the earth dwindle and as our environment becomes increasingly noxious with pollutants—while environmentalists vie with those who feel their jobs will be threatened by tighter controls. No longer are Americans confident that the future will be better than the past or that technol-

ogy will solve all our problems. On the contrary, our attempts to cope with existing problems seem increasingly to create new problems that are as bad or worse. Despair, demoralization, and a sense of helplessness are well-established predisposing conditions for abnormal reactions to stressful events (Dohrenwend et al., 1980; Frank, 1978).

Summary

In most instances, the occurrence of episodes of abnormal or maladaptive behavior may be conceived as the joint product of an individual's vulnerability ("diathesis") to disorder and of the nature and intensity of stressors currently challenging an individual's coping resources. In general, such vulnerabilities are considered *predisposing* causes. Predisposing causal influences are the focus of this chapter, although other types of causes (primary, precipitating, and reinforcing) are discussed. In practice, it is often difficult to make distinctions between these various types of causes.

Predisposing causes of mental disorder may be classified as biological, psychosocial, and sociocultural in origin. While these three classes can interact with each other in complicated ways, certain known predisposing causes are especially related to each.

In examining biologically based vulnerabilities, we must consider genetic endowment (including chromosomal irregularities), constitutional factors, primary reaction tendencies, and varied disruptions of the biological system. All of these essentially physical disturbances may create conditions rendering a person vulnerable to disorder.

In psychosocially determined sources of vulnerability, the situation becomes somewhat more blurred. It is clear, however, that the *self* plays a central role as both an information-processing system and as a collection of attributions and values concerning one's personal identity. Stability and coherence of selfhood appears to be an important bulwark against breakdown. Sources of psychosocially determined vulnerability include early social deprivation, severe emotional trauma, inadequate parenting, and, often relatedly, certain types of pathogenic family organizations or structures.

Sociocultural variables are also important sources of vulnerability to disorder, or, conversely, of resistance to it. The incidence of particular disorders varies widely among different cultures; unfortunately, we know little of the specific factors involved in these variations. In our own culture, certain prescribed roles, such as those relating to gender, appear to be more predisposing to disorder than others. Low socioeconomic status (in our own culture) is associated with greater risk for various disorders, possibly because it is often difficult for economically distressed families to provide their offspring with requisite coping resources. Additionally, certain roles evolved by given cultures may in themselves be maladaptive, and certain large-scale cultural trends, such as rapid technological advance, may render previously effective coping resources obsolete for many members of the rapidly evolving culture. In circumstances such as the latter, which today are not uncommon, we see both an increase in challenge (enhanced stressors) together with lessened effectiveness of previously acquired techniques for minimizing the impact of stressful events.

Part 2

Patterns of abnormal (maladaptive) behavior

5

Stress and adjustment disorders

Miguel Hernandez, Odalisques (1947–48). Hernandez (1893–1957), a Spaniard of working-class background, was interned in a concentration camp in France for fighting on the Republican side during the Spanish Civil War. He drew his first designs during his imprisonment in the camp. After his release, Hernandez began to work in oil, eventually to the exclusion of almost all other activities. He spent the last ten years of his life in Paris under a cloud of loneliness and spiritual exhaustion. This strikingly warm and harmonious painting is all the more remarkable for having been created by one who endured such difficult personal trials.

A ny one of us may break down if the going gets tough enough. When conditions of overwhelming stress occur, even a previously stable individual may develop temporary (transient) psychological problems. That is, the individual may experience a lowering or breakdown of integral, adaptive functioning. This breakdown may be sudden, as in the case of an individual who has gone through a severe accident or fire; or it may be gradual, as in the case of a person who has been subjected to prolonged conditions of tension and loss of self-esteem culminating in a marital breakup. Usually the individual makes a good recovery once the stressful situation is over, although in some cases there may be long-lasting damage to his or her self-concept and an increased vulnerability to certain types of stressors. That is, today's stress can be tomorrow's vulnerability. In the case of the individual who is quite vulnerable to begin with, of course, a stressful situation may precipitate more serious and more lasting psychopathology.

In the preceding chapter, we focused on the "diathesis," or vulnerability, half of the diathesis-stress model of abnormal behavior; we saw that our vulnerabilities can predispose us to abnormal behavior. In this chapter, we shall focus on the role of stress as a precipitating causal factor in abnormal behavior. We shall see that the impact of stress depends not only on its severity but perhaps more importantly on the individual's preexisting vulnerabilities.[1]

We shall first look at stress in terms of what it is, what factors affect it, and how we react to it. Then we shall turn to some specific instances of situations that result in severe stress and examine their effect on adjustment. As you will notice, many of our examples will be drawn from wartime situations. Abhorrent as war is, it has provided a research setting that can perhaps never be duplicated in civilian life: a "laboratory" in which the effects of severe environmental stressors on the personality integration of thousands of men could readily be evaluated.

---

[1]It is important to point up here that there exists a duality in the relationship between diathesis and stress: As we saw in Chapter 4, many of the factors that contribute to diatheses are also sources of stress. This is especially true in the case of psychosocial factors, such as emotional deprivation, inadequate parenting, and the like. The simplest way to distinguish our discussion in this chapter from that in the preceding one is that here our focus will be on the *precipitating* nature of stress; in Chapter 4, we focused on its *predisposing* nature.

Grinker (1969), in referring to efforts to help soldiers who had developed transient reactions to combat during World War II, put it succinctly:

"The entire range of factors from the biological to the sociological were sharply etched in miniature and required only a magnified view for understanding. Likewise time was compressed so that in rapid succession we could view predisposition, precipitation, breakdown, and recovery." (p. 3)

Through these efforts, and those in later wars, marked strides have been made in the understanding and treatment of many forms of psychopathology. These forward strides have led, in turn, to a better understanding of mental disorders on the part of the general public. For the first time, millions of people became aware of the potential effects of extreme stress on personality integration. They learned that stress could seriously impair adaptive behavior or even incapacitate the individual; and they learned that this was not a disgrace—it could happen to anyone.

They also learned that such impairments need not be permanent. In the last part of the chapter we shall look at attempts made by mental health workers to intervene in the stress process—either to prevent stress reactions or to limit their intensity and duration once they've developed.

Adjustive demands and stress

Life would be simple indeed if our needs were automatically gratified. But, as we know, many obstacles, both personal and environmental, prevent this. Such obstacles place adjustive demands on us and can lead to the experience of stress. The term *stress* has typically been used to refer *both* to the adjustive demands placed on an organism and to the organism's internal biophysical responses to such demands. To avoid confusion, we shall refer to adjustive demands as *stressors* and to the effects they create within an organism as *stress.*

All situations, positive and negative, that require adjustment are stressful. Thus, according to Canadian physiologist Hans Selye (1976a), the notion of stress can be broken down further into positive stress, *eustress,* and negative stress, *distress.* (In most cases, a wedding would be eustress; a funeral, distress.) Both types of stress tax the individual's resources and adjustment, though distress typically has the potential to do more damage. Let us look further now into (a) categories of stressors: (b) factors influencing the severity of stress; and (c) the unique and changing stressor patterns that characterize each person's life.

Categories of stressors

Adjustive demands, or stressors, stem from a number of sources. These sources can be conveniently viewed as stemming from three basic categories: frustrations, conflicts, and pressures. Though we shall consider these categories separately, it will be apparent that they are all closely interrelated.

Frustrations. When one's strivings are thwarted, either by obstacles that block progress toward a desired goal or by absence of an appropriate goal, frustration occurs. Frustrations can be particularly difficult for the individual to cope with because they so often lead to self-devaluation, making us feel we have failed in some way or are incompetent.

A wide range of obstacles, both external and internal, can lead to frustration. Inflation, group prejudice and discrimination, unfulfillment in a job, and the death of a loved one are common frustrations stemming from the environment; physical handicaps, lack of needed competencies, loneliness, guilt, and inadequate self-control are sources of frustration that can result from our personal limitations.

Conflicts. In many instances stress results from the simultaneous occurrence of two or more incompatible needs or motives: the requirements of one preclude satisfaction of the other(s). In essence, we have a choice to make, and we experience conflict while trying to make it. On the simplest level, for example, an early marriage may mean foregoing or shortening one's college education; accepting one job may mean turning down another that seems equally desirable.

Selye has distinguished between two types of stress: eustress and distress. Eustress refers to the demands placed on us by positive events; distress is associated with negative events, such as the aftermath of a tornado or the loss and sorrow caused by the death and funeral of a loved one. In general, distress has greater potential for causing difficulties in adjustment.

Although we are dealing with frustration and conflict as if they were distinct sources of stress, this differentiation is largely for convenience, since the key element in conflict is often the frustration that will result from either choice. For example, some young people refrain from premarital sexual intercourse because their moral values make such behavior unacceptable. Such a decision, though resolving their conflict, does not always resolve their frustration!

In addition, the necessity of making a choice commonly involves cognitive and emotional strain: it is often difficult "to make up one's mind," especially when each alternative offers values that the other does not, and the choice is an important one. A major factor in determining the ultimate choice seems to be the attempt to minimize or reduce the amount of stress being experienced.

Conflicts with which everyone has to cope may be conveniently classified as approach-avoidance, double-approach, and double-avoidance types.

1. *Approach-avoidance conflicts* involve strong tendencies both to approach and to avoid the same goal. Perhaps an individual wants to join a high-status group but can do so only by endorsing views contrary to personal values; or a former smoker may want to smoke during a party but realize that doing so may jeopardize his or her desire to quit.

Approach-avoidance conflicts are sometimes referred to as "mixed-blessing" dilemmas, because some negative and some positive features must be accepted regardless of which course of action is chosen.

2. *Double-approach conflicts* involve choosing between two or more desirable goals, such as which of two movies to see on the only free night of the week. To a large extent, such simple "plus-plus" conflicts result from the inevitable limitations in one's time, space, energy, and personal and financial resources; and they are usually handled in stride. In more complex cases, however, as when an individual is torn between two good career opportunities, or between present satisfactions and future ones, decision-making may be very difficult and stressful. And though the experience may be more eustress than distress, the stress is still very real and the choice difficult; in either case, the individual gives up something.

3. *Double-avoidance conflicts* are those in which the choice is between more or less equally *undesirable* alternatives, such as going to a party when you'd rather stay home or being considered impolite if you cancel out at the last moment. Neither choice will bring satisfaction, so the task is to decide which course of action will be least disagreeable—that is, least stressful.

It can be seen that this classification of conflicts is somewhat arbitrary, and that various combinations among the different types are perhaps the rule rather than the exception. Thus a "plus-plus" conflict between alternative careers may also have its "plus-minus" aspects growing out of the responsibilities that either imposes. But regardless of how we categorize conflicts, they represent a major source of stress that can become overwhelming in intensity.

Pressures.   Stress may stem not only from frustrations and conflicts, but also from pressures to achieve specific goals or to behave in particular ways. In general, pressures force a person to speed up, intensify effort, or change the direction of goal-oriented behavior. All of us encounter many different pressures in the course of everyday living, and often we handle them without undue difficulty. In some instances, however, pressures seriously tax our coping resources, and if they become excessive, they may lead to maladaptive behavior.

Pressures may originate from external or internal sources. A student may feel under severe pressure to make good grades because her parents demand it, or she may submit herself to such pressure because she wants to gain admission to graduate school. The long hours of study, the tension of examinations, and the sustained concentration of effort over many years result in considerable stress for many students. Where a student is handicapped by inefficient study habits, inadequate financial resources, personal problems, or other difficulties, the continuing effort for academic achievement may be highly stressful.

Occupational demands can also be highly stressful, and many jobs make severe demands in terms of responsibility, time, and performance. Carruthers (1980) has noted that some occupations, such as coal miner, air flight crew-member or auto racer, apparently place the individual under an unusually high degree of stress which results in a vulnerability to heart

Every student can probably identify to an extent with the frustration of class registration, just one of the stressful demands education can make.

disease. Carruthers has pointed out that "man's stone-age biochemistry and physiology has in several important respects failed to adapt to his present-age situation" (p. 11). In almost any job, if the individual is not really interested in or well suited to the work, occupational demands are likely to be a major source of stress, regardless of the actual demands of the work situation.

For some people, the most intense pressures are self-imposed, due to inner motivations: they may have a high need to achieve along with an unrelenting perfectionism that places great pressures on their adjustment. For example, an ambitious businesswoman may take on project after project until her "spare" time for months ahead has been committed, yet her high standards for excellence mean that each project will demand torturous activity and a great deal of time to complete.

It is apparent that a given situation may involve elements of all three categories of stressors—frustration, conflict, and pressure. For example, a serious financial loss may not only lead to lower living standards but may also confront the individual with evidence of poor judgment. If such evidence is contrary to the individual's self-image as too shrewd to make a poor investment, the resulting cognitive dissonance may add to the complexity of the stressful situation.

An individual's motivation can heighten occupational pressures of responsibility, time, and performance. Doctors may, for example, experience stress due to their life-and-death responsibility for patients, the time required to keep up with professional reading, and the pressure to perform well in both reassuring and curing patients.

Although a particular stressor may predominate in any situation, we rarely deal with an isolated demand but usually with a continuously changing pattern of interrelated and sometimes contradictory demands.

Factors influencing the severity of stress

The severity of stress is gauged by the degree of disruption in functioning that it entails. For example, an individual will experience severe disruption of both physiological and psychological processes if deprived of food for a long time.

The actual degree of disruption that occurs or is threatened depends partly on the characteristics of the stressor and partly on the individual's resources—both personal and situational—and the relationship between the two. On a biological level, for example, the severity of stress created by invading viruses depends both on the strength and number of the invaders and on the organism's ability and available medical resources to resist and destroy them. On a psychological level, the severity of stress depends not only on the nature of the stressor and the individual's resources but also on how the stressor is perceived and evaluated. For example, a divorce may be very stressful for one partner but not for the other.

The nature of the stressor.   The impact of a stressor depends on its importance, duration, cumulative effect, multiplicity, and imminence. Where most stressors can ordinarily be dealt with as a matter of course, stressors that involve important aspects of an individual's life—such as death of a loved one, a divorce, loss of job, or a serious illness—tend to be highly stressful for most people (Grant et al., 1981; Holmes & Rahe, 1967; Rahe & Arthur, 1978; Zilberg, Weiss, & Horowitz, 1982). Furthermore, the longer a stressor operates, the more severe its effects. Prolonged exhaustion imposes a more intense stress than does temporary fatigue. Often, too, stressors appear to have a cumulative effect (Singer, 1980). A married couple may maintain amicable relations through a long series of minor irritations or frustrations only to "explode" and dissolve the relationship in the face of the "last straw," that is, the precipitating stressor.

Encountering a number of stressors at the same time makes a difference too. If a man has a heart attack, loses his job, and receives news that his son has been arrested for drug abuse—all at the same time—the resulting stress will be more severe than if these events occurred separately.

Finally, in most difficult situations, including those involving conflict, the severity of stress increases as the need to deal with the demand approaches. For example, in a now-classic study, Mechanic (1962) found that although graduate students thought about their examinations from time to time and experienced some anxiety during the prior three months, they did not demonstrate intense anxiety until the examinations were nearly upon them. Similar experiences have been reported by sports parachutists as the hour of their next jump approaches (Epstein & Fenz, 1962, 1965). Persons anticipating other stress situations—such as major surgery—have found that the severity of stress increased as the time for the ordeal approached (Janis & Leventhal, 1965).

The individual's stress tolerance and resources.

Most of us are well aware of the fact that one person's stressor is another person's "piece of cake." The differences here can be due to three factors: the individual's perception of threat, stress tolerance, and external resources and supports.

1. *Perception of threat.* If the situation is *seen* as presenting a serious threat, it is highly stressful, especially if resources for dealing with it are believed to be inadequate—whether they really are or not. And if we are generally unsure of our adequacy and worth, we are much more likely to experience threat than if we feel generally confident and secure.

Often new adjustive demands that have not been anticipated and for which no ready-made coping patterns are available will place an individual under severe stress. That is why the training of emergency workers such as police and firefighters normally involves repeated exposure to controlled or contrived stressors until coping patterns have become "second nature." In the same vein, the course of recovery from the stress created by major surgery can be markedly facilitated when adequate attention is given to providing the patient with realistic expectations beforehand (MacDonald & Kuiper, 1983). The same sense of adequacy and control can be achieved when the stress has been chosen voluntarily, rather than having been imposed by others or having come unexpectedly (Averill, 1973). Understanding the nature of a stressful situation, preparing for it, and knowing how long it will last, all lessen the severity of the stress when it does come.

2. *Stress tolerance.* If a person is marginally adjusted, the slightest frustration or pressure may be highly stressful. The term *stress tolerance* or *frustration tolerance* refers to one's ability to withstand stress without having integrated functioning seriously impaired.

Both biologically and psychologically, people vary greatly in overall vulnerability to stressors as well as in the types of stressors to which they are most vulnerable. Emergencies, disappointments, and other problems that one person can take in stride may prove incapacitating to another. As we have seen, early traumatic experiences can leave the individual especially vulnerable to certain kinds of stressors.

3. *External resources and supports.* Lack of external supports—either personal or material—makes a given stressor more potent and weakens an individual's capacity to cope with it. A divorce or the death of one's mate evokes more stress if one is left feeling alone and unloved than if one is still surrounded by people one cares about and feels close to.

Pressures to violate one's principles or beliefs are less stressful and more easily withstood when one has an ally than when one is alone. It is hardly surprising that individuals exposed to highly stressful situations turn to others for support and reassurance.

Environmental supports are a complex matter, however, and behavior by one's family or friends that is intended to provide support may actually increase the stress. In his study of graduate students facing crucial examinations, Mechanic (1962) compared the effects of different types of behavior on the part of the spouses:

"In general, spouses do not provide blind support. They perceive the kinds of support the student wants and they provide it. The [spouse] who becomes worried about examinations also may provide more support than the spouse who says, 'I'm not worried, you will surely pass.' Indeed, since there is a chance that the student will not pass, the person who is supportive in a meaningful sense will not give blind assurance. . . . Often a statement to the effect, 'Do the best you can' is more supportive than, 'I'm sure you are going to do well.' The latter statement adds to the student's burden, for not only must he fear the disappointment of not passing, but also the loss of respect in the eyes of his spouse." (p. 158)

Often the culture provides for specific rituals or other courses of action that give support as the individual attempts to deal with certain types of stress. For example, most religions provide rituals that help the bereaved through their

Stress tolerance may be increased by the environmental support of a prescribed course of action. This may have been the rationale for this 1979 evacuation drill in Tokyo, which helped prepare citizens for a possible earthquake. Such plans might have saved some of the ninety thousand lives claimed by a 1923 earthquake in the same city.

ordeal, and in some faiths, confession and atonement help people deal with stresses related to guilt and self-recrimination.

In sum, the interaction between the nature of the stressor and the individual's resources for dealing with it is important in determining the severity of stress. However great the stressor, it creates little stress if the individual can easily handle it.

Stressor patterns are unique and changing

Each individual faces a unique pattern of adjustive demands. This is true partly because of differences in the way people perceive and interpret similar situations. But objectively, too, no two people are faced with exactly the same pattern of stressors. Each individual's age, sex, occupation, economic status, personality makeup, competencies, and family situation help determine the demands he or she will face. The stressor pattern a child faces will differ in many ways from that of an older person, and the pattern faced by a carpenter will differ from that of a business executive.

Sometimes key stressors in a person's life center around a continuing difficult life situation. These are considered to be *chronic,* or long-lasting. A person may be frustrated in a boring and unrewarding job from which there is seemingly no escape, suffer for years in an unhappy and conflictful marriage, or be severely frus-

trated by a physical handicap or a chronic health problem.

More often than not, stressor patterns change with time—both predictably, as when we enter different life periods, and unpredictably, as when an accident, a death in the family, or a drastic social change makes new demands. Too, the type of stressors—eustress and distress—vary. Some of these changes bring only minor stress, while others place us under severe or excessive stress. But regardless of severity, the stressor pattern we face today is somewhat different from what it was a week ago; and it will be different in the future from what it is now. The total pattern at any time determines the part any one stressor will play and how much difficulty we are likely to have coping with it. And it is the way that we cope with stressors over time that shapes the course of our lives.

From time to time, most of us experience periods of especially *acute* (sudden and intense) stress. The term *crisis* is used to refer to times during which the stress situation approaches or exceeds the adaptive capacities of the individual or group. Crises are often especially stressful because the coping techniques we typically use do not work.

A crisis may center around a traumatic divorce, or an episode of depression in which the person seriously considers suicide, or the aftermath of a serious injury or disease that forces difficult readjustments in one's self-concept and way of life. How often such crises occur in the life of the average person is unknown, though estimates range from about once every ten years to about once every two years. In view of the complex and rapidly changing society in which we live, the latter estimate may be more realistic.

The outcome of such crises has profound significance for the person's subsequent adjustment. An effective new method of coping developed during a period of crisis may be added to the person's previous repertoire of coping behaviors; or inability to deal adequately with the crisis may impair one's ability to cope effectively with similar stressors in the future because of expectation of failure. For this reason "crisis intervention"—providing psychological help in times of severe and special stress—has become an important element in contemporary approaches to treatment and prevention of abnormal behavior. We shall discuss such intervention in more detail in Chapter 18.

It is important to remember that life changes, even some favorable eustress-like ones, place new demands on us and thus may be somewhat stressful. The faster such changes come upon us, the greater the stress. Research efforts to determine the relationship between stress and possible physical and mental disorder have been many; one effort to *quantify* stress is summarized in the **HIGHLIGHT** on page 149.

Reactions to life stress

Evidence suggests that some particularly hardy individuals may be relatively immune to stressors that would impair the functioning of most of us (Kobasa, 1979). But, in general, stress beyond a minimal level threatens the well-being of the organism and engenders automatic, persistent attempts at its resolution. It forces a person, in short, to try to do something about it. What is done depends on many factors. Sometimes inner factors—such as one's frame of reference, motives, competencies, or stress tolerance—play the dominant role in determining one's reactions to stress; at other times, environmental conditions—such as social demands and expectations—are of primary importance. Any stress reaction, of course, reflects the interplay of a combination of inner and outer determinants—

some more influential than others, but all working together to make the individual react in a certain way. In this section, we shall consider some general principles of adjustive behavior and reactions to stress; then we shall examine some characteristic stages that occur during decompensation under excessive stress.

General principles of reactions to stress

In reviewing certain general principles that underlie reactions to stress, we shall find it convenient to conceptualize three interactional levels. On a biological level there are immunological defenses against disease and damage-repair mechanisms; on a psychological and interpersonal level there are learned coping patterns and self-defenses; and on a sociocultural level there are group resources, such as labor unions, religious organizations, and law-enforcement agencies.

The failure of coping efforts on any of these levels may seriously increase an individual's vulnerability on other levels. For example, a breakdown of immunological defenses against disease may impair not only bodily functioning but psychological functioning as well; chronically poor psychological coping patterns may lead to peptic ulcers or other "diseases of adaptation"; and the failure of a group on which one depends may seriously interfere with one's own ability to satisfy basic needs.

Typically, our stress reactions have certain basic characteristics: they are (a) holistic, (b) economical, (c) either automatic or planned, (d) emotional, and (e) task- or defense-oriented.

By *holistic,* we mean that an organism reacts to a stressor as an integrated unit. Since all of an individual's adjustive behavior must use the same bodily equipment—sense organs, nervous system, glands, muscles, and so on—the overall adjustive demands of the moment will determine how it is used. If there are several competing demands, the one that is most important, or is perceived as most important, will commandeer the organism's adjustive resources, and some functions or actions will be inhibited while others are facilitated.

This coordination is well illustrated by emergency emotional reactions—for example, in the moment just prior to a traffic accident. Here,

HIGHLIGHT
Measuring life stress

Holmes and his colleagues (Holmes & Holmes, 1970; Holmes & Rahe, 1967; Rahe & Arthur, 1978) have developed the Social Readjustment Rating Scale (SRRS), an objective method for measuring the cumulative stress to which an individual has been exposed over a period of time. This scale measures life stress in terms of "life change units" (LCU) involving the following events.

Events	Scale of Impact	Events	Scale of Impact
Death of spouse	100	Change in responsibilities at work	29
Divorce	73	Son or daughter leaving home	29
Marital separation	65	Trouble with in-laws	29
Jail term	63	Outstanding personal achievement	28
Death of Close Family Member	63	Wife begins or stops work	26
Personal injury or illness	53	Begin or end school	26
Marriage	50	Change in living conditions	25
Fired at work	47	Revision of personal habits	24
Marital reconciliation	45	Trouble with boss	23
Retirement	45	Change in work hours or conditions	20
Change in health of family member	44	Change in residence	20
Pregnancy	40	Change in schools	20
Sex difficulties	39	Change in recreation	19
Gain of new family member	39	Change in church activities	19
Business readjustment	39	Change in social activities	18
Change in financial state	38	Small mortgage or loan	17
Death of close friend	37	Change in sleeping habits	16
Change to different line of work	36	Change in number of family get-togethers	15
Change in number of arguments with spouse	35	Change in eating habits	15
		Vacation	13
High mortgage	31	Christmas	12
Foreclosure of mortgage or loan	30	Minor violations of the law	11

For persons who had been exposed in recent months to stressful events that added up to an LCU score of 300 or above, these investigators found the risk of developing a major illness within the next two years to be very high, approximating 80 percent.

digestive and other bodily processes not immediately essential for survival are slowed down or stopped (inhibited) while the driver's resources for increased activity and effort are mobilized (excited)—with a heightening of muscle tonus, the release of stored sugar into the bloodstream, and the secretion of *adrenaline,* a key agent in helping the body react with vigor to immediate, urgent stressor conditions.

In general, the processes of excitation and inhibition provide the organism with the flexibility it needs for dealing with stressors. Only under unusual or pathological conditions does the or-

ganism function "segmentally" rather than as an integrated unit. Such segmental action may occur as a consequence of interference with the integrating functions of the higher brain centers by alcohol, drugs, or brain damage; or it may occur as a consequence of excessive psychological stress.

By *economical,* we mean that an organism typically responds in a way that entails a minimum expenditure of resources to deal with a stressor, employing first those defenses that are least expensive. If these are ineffective, then additional and more costly resources are brought into operation. For example, the sleeper who is being dive-bombed by a mosquito might first simply cover her head with a pillow; that failing, she might well interrupt her sleep, get out of bed, and, with newspaper in hand, wait sleepily for "her chance."

Here, too, alcohol, drugs, or brain damage can be disruptive, causing people to overreact and thus waste their resources.

The principle of economy is also relevant in a slightly different context. We tend to maintain our existing patterns of thought and action not only because they provide a basic source of security in dealing with the world but also because it takes less effort to follow established patterns than to modify them or adopt new ones. This tendency to resist change in established ways of perceiving and acting has been referred to as "inertia" on the individual level and as *cultural lag* on the social level. These concepts help explain the tendency of maladaptive behavior patterns to persist when conditions change and even when new, more effective patterns have become available.

Reactions to stressors are typically *automatic,* as in the case of biological immunological defenses activated to fight disease or psychological tension-reducing and repair mechanisms such as crying. Even if the individual is aware of what he or she is doing, such responses are not usually planned or consciously thought out. Seeing what one wants to see, screening out or distorting threatening information, and repressing painful experiences are other examples of automatic and mainly unconscious processes. Automatic functioning on a psychological level also commonly takes the form of habits, in which responses that were once conscious and planned no longer require the individual's attention.

Automatic functioning can be a boon in processing routine stressors, since it frees one's attention for problems that require careful thought, but it can also impair effective adjustment. In all but routine situations, the ability to adapt effectively depends on conscious effort and the flexibility to choose an appropriate response. That is, by *planning* how we will respond to a particular stressor, we can, in essence, make some headway toward preventing or reducing the likelihood that our reaction to the stressor will be severe.

Reactions to stress entail *emotions,* and the type of emotion experienced contributes to the nature of the overall response. The specific emotions that occur are heavily influenced by past learning and by the perceived significance of the stress situation to the individual. Three of the more common emotional states experienced during stressful situations are anger, fear, and anxiety. Anger, if intense, can lead to impulsive behavior of a destructive nature, such as assault or homicide. In a situation that elicits extreme fear, such as a fire, the individual may panic or "freeze" and become unable to function in an organized manner. The emotional state of anxiety seems to bring with it the greatest variety of responses: though the precise nature of the threat is usually unclear to the individual, the anxiety or "psychic pain" demands some sort of protective action. As we shall see, the defenses mustered to cope with anxiety may run almost the entire gamut of abnormal behavior.

Finally, in coping with stress, a person is confronted with two challenges: (a) to meet the requirements of the stressor, and (b) to protect the self from psychological damage and disorganization. A person who feels competent to handle a stressful situation tends to act in a *task-oriented* way—that is, *to direct behavior primarily at dealing with the requirements of the stressor.* Typically, this means the individual objectively appraises the situation, works out alternative solutions and decides on an appropriate course of action, and takes action and evaluates feedback. The steps in a task-oriented reaction—whether the reaction turns out to be effective or ineffective—are generally flexible enough to enable the individual to change course.

Task-oriented reactions may involve making changes in one's self or one's surroundings or both, depending on the situation. The action may be overt—as in showing one's spouse more affection; or it may be covert—as in lowering one's level of aspiration. And the action may involve retreating from the problem, attacking it directly, or trying to find a workable compromise. Any of these types of action will be appropriate under certain circumstances. For instance, if one is faced with a situation of overwhelming physical danger—such as a forest fire—the logical task-oriented response might well be to remove oneself from the area.

When one's feelings of adequacy are seriously threatened by the stressor, reactions will tend to be *defense-oriented*—that is, *directed pri-*

The anger associated with stress can lead to destructive and impulsive behavior that is much different from the individual's usual reactions.

marily at protecting the self from hurt and disorganization, rather than at resolving the stressor situation. Typically, the person using defense-oriented reactions may be thought of as someone who has forsaken more productive task-oriented action in favor of overriding concerns for maintaining the integrity of the self, however ill-advised and self-defeating the effort may prove to be in the long run. Since much maladaptive behavior is the result of defense-oriented behavior patterns, we shall examine them in more detail.

Defense-oriented reaction patterns

Defense-oriented reactions to stress, as we have noted, are aimed chiefly at protecting the self from hurt and disorganization.

Two types of defense-oriented reactions are commonly differentiated. The first consists of responses such as crying, repetitive talking, and mourning that seem to function as psychological damage-repair mechanisms. The second type consists of the so-called ego- or self-defense mechanisms introduced in Chapter 3 (pages 64–65). These mechanisms, including such responses as denial and repression, function to relieve tension and anxiety and to protect the self from hurt and devaluation.

Of these two types of defensive reaction, the second is clearly more important in behavior that is maladaptive. These defense reactions protect the individual from both external threats, such as devaluating failures, and internal threats, such as guilt-arousing desires or actions. They appear to protect the self in one or more of the following ways: (a) by denying, distorting, or restricting the individual's experience; (b) by reducing emotional or self-involvement; and (c) by counteracting threat or damage. Often, of course, a given defense mechanism may offer more than one kind of protection.

These defense mechanisms are ordinarily used in combination rather than singly, and often they are combined with task-oriented behavior. We all use them to some extent for coping with the problems of living. In fact, Gleser and Sacks (1973) have concluded that we tend to be fairly consistent in the particular mechanisms we use.

We shall review here some of the ego-defense mechanisms that seem particularly pertinent to coping during times of stress.

1. *Denial of reality.* Probably the simplest and most primitive of all self-defense mechanisms is denial of reality, in which an attempt is made to "screen out" disagreeable realities by ignoring or refusing to acknowledge them. The tendency toward perceptual defense is part of this inclination to deny or avoid reality. One may turn away from unpleasant sights, refuse to discuss unpleasant topics, faint when confronted with a traumatic situation, deny criticism, or become so preoccupied with work that there is no time to deal with marital, child-rearing, or other personal problems. Under extreme conditions, such as imprisonment, an individual may experience the feeling that "This isn't really happening to me." Here the defensive reaction appears, at least temporarily, to provide insulation from the full impact of the traumatic situation. Similarly, Kubler-Ross (1975) has noted that persons having terminal illnesses go through a stage of denial before being able to come to grips effectively with their situation.

2. *Repression.* This is a defense mechanism by means of which threatening or painful thoughts and desires are excluded from consciousness. Although it has often been referred to as "selective forgetting," it is more in the nature of selective remembering. For although the material that is repressed is denied admission to conscious awareness, it is not really forgotten. The soldier who has seen his best friend's head blown off by shrapnel may find the experience so terribly painful that he excludes it from consciousness and becomes "amnesic" with regard to the battle experience. When brought to an aid station, he may be nervous and trembling, unable to recall his name or what has happened to him, and manifesting other signs of his ordeal. But the intolerable battle experience, screened from consciousness, may be brought into awareness by means of hypnosis or sodium pentothal interviews.

Repression is an extremely important self-defense mechanism in that it affords protection from sudden, traumatic experiences until time has somewhat desensitized the individual to the shock. Repression may also help the individual control dangerous and unacceptable desires and at the same time alleviate anxiety.

Repression, in varying degrees, enters into other defense mechanisms. There is some evidence that it is only when repression fails that stronger, more maladaptive defenses are tried.

3. *Emotional insulation.* Here the individual reduces emotional involvement in disappointing or hurtful situations. Such "emotional anaesthesia" is commonly seen as one phase of a grief reaction following significant loss.

In more extreme cases of long-continued frustration, as in chronic unemployment or prison confinement, many persons lose hope, become resigned and apathetic, and adapt themselves to a restricted way of life. Such "broken" individuals thus protect themselves from the bitter hurt of sustained frustration by becoming passive recipients of whatever life brings them. Similarly, in extreme forms of alienation the individual may become noninvolved and apathetic, feeling isolated, bewildered, and without hope.

Up to a point, emotional insulation is an important means of defense against unnecessary disappointment and stress. But life involves calculated risks, and most people are willing to take a chance on active participation. Emotional insulation provides a protective shell that prevents a repetition of previous pain, but it reduces the individual's healthy, vigorous participation in life.

4. *Intellectualization (isolation).* This defense mechanism is related to emotional insulation. Here the emotional reaction that would normally accompany a painful event is avoided by a rational explanation that divests the event of personal significance and painful feeling. The hurt over a parent's death is reduced by saying that he or she lived a full life and died mercifully without pain. Failures and disappointments are softened by pointing out that "it could have been worse." Cynicism may become a convenient means of reducing guilt feelings over not living up to one's ideals. Even the verbalization of good intentions, as in a glib admission that "I should work harder" or that "I should be less selfish and more interested in the welfare of others," seems to cut down on guilt and relieve one of the necessity of positive action.

Intellectualization may be employed under extremely stressful conditions as well as in dealing with the milder stressors of everyday life. Bluestone and McGahee have found that this defense mechanism was often used by prisoners awaiting execution. They have described the pattern as follows: "So they'll kill me; and that's that'—this said with a shrug of the shoulders suggests that the affect appropriate to the thought has somehow been isolated" (1962, p. 395).

5. *Regression.* Regression is a defense mechanism in which one returns to the use of reaction patterns long since outgrown. When a new addition to the family has seemingly undermined his status, a little boy may revert to bed-wetting and other infantile behavior that once brought him parental attention.

We might expect something akin to regression to occur merely on the basis of the frequent failure of newly learned reactions to bring satisfaction. In looking for other, more successful modes of adjustment, it would be only natural to try out discarded patterns that previously had brought satisfaction.

However, regression is a more generalized reaction than merely trying out older modes of response when new ones have failed. For in regression the individual retreats from reality to a less demanding personal status—one that involves lowered aspirations and more readily accomplished satisfactions. This point is well illustrated by Bettelheim's reference to a general "regression to infantile behavior" seen in nearly all the prisoners at the Nazi concentration camps of Dachau and Buchenwald.

"The prisoners lived, like children, only in the immediate present: . . . they became unable to plan for the future or to give up immediate pleasure satisfactions to gain greater ones in the near future. . . . They were boastful, telling tales about what they had accomplished in their former lives, or how they succeeded in cheating foremen or guards, and how they sabotaged the work. Like children, they felt not at all set back or ashamed when it became known that they had lied about their prowess." (1943, p. 443)

Although we have sampled only five defense mechanisms above, we can draw some conclusions about them all: they are, in the main, learned reactions; they are designed to deal with inner hurt, anxiety, and self-devaluation; and they operate on relatively automatic and habitual levels. And, though defense mechanisms may serve useful protective functions, they usually involve some measure of self-deception and reality distortion and may seriously interfere with the effective resolution of the actual problem. For these reasons, ego-defense mechanisms are considered maladaptive when they become the predominant means of coping with stressors.

Decompensation under excessive stress

As we have seen, stressors create a challenge to the organism's adaptive resources, bringing into play both task- and defense-oriented reactions.

Most of the time, these varied reactions are successful in containing the threat. When stressors are sustained or severe, however, the adaptive capabilities of the organism may be overwhelmed, in which case there is a lowering of integrated functioning and eventually a possible breakdown of the organism. This lowering of integration is referred to as *decompensation.* Whether stress becomes "excessive" depends, as we have seen, not only on the nature of the adjustive demand but also on the individual's tolerance for stress and available resources for coping with it. In this section, we shall deal first with some of the generalized effects of excessive stress. Then we shall move on to specific forms of decompensation on biological, psychological, and sociocultural levels.

Effects of severe stress.   Stress is a fact of life, and our reactions to stress can give us competencies we need and would not develop without being challenged to do so. Stress can be damaging, however, if demands are too severe for our coping resources or if we believe and act as if they were. Severe stress can exact a high cost in terms of lowered efficiency, depletion of adaptive resources, wear and tear on the system, and, in extreme cases, severe personality and physical deterioration, and even death.

1. *Lowering of adaptive efficiency.* On a physiological level, severe stress may result in alterations that can impair the body's ability to fight off invading bacteria and viruses. On a psychological level, perception of threat brings a narrowing of the perceptual field and increased rigidity of cognitive processes so that it becomes difficult or impossible for the individual to see the situation objectively or to perceive the range of alternatives actually available. This process often appears to be operating in suicidal behavior.

Our adaptive efficiency may also be impaired by the intense emotions that commonly accompany severe stress. Acute stage fright may disrupt our performance of a public speech; "examination jitters" may lead us to "blow it" despite adequate preparation. In fact, high levels of fear, anger, or anxiety may lead not only to impaired performance but to disorganization of behavior.

2. *Lowering of resistance to other stressors.* In using its resources to meet one severe stressor, the organism may suffer a lowering of tolerance for other stressors. Selye (1976b) demonstrated

In this stress-education class, children and young teenagers are taught both task- and defense-oriented procedures, including relaxation techniques, which may help them avoid the decompensation associated with severe and accumulated stressors.

the lethal effects of a succession of noxious stimuli on animals. Similarly, soldiers who develop tolerance for the rigors of combat may show a lowering of resistance to other stressors, such as viral infections or bad news from home.

It appears that the coping resources of the system are limited: if they are already mobilized against one stressor, they are not available for coping with others. This helps explain how sustained psychological stress can lower biological resistance to disease, and how sustained bodily disease can lower resistance to psychological stressors. Interestingly, prolonged stress may lead to either pathological over-responsiveness to stressors—as illustrated by the "last straw" response—or to pathological insensitivity to stressors, as in loss of hope and extreme apathy. Sklar and Anisman (1981), in reviewing research on the influence of stress on cancer, have concluded that stress does affect physiological functioning, producing biological changes which may influence the growth of cancer.

In general, it would appear that severe and

sustained stress on any level leads to a serious reduction in the overall adaptive capacity of the organism.

3. *Wear and tear on the organism.* Probably most of us believe that even after a very stressful experience, rest can completely restore us. In his pioneering studies of stress, however, Selye has found evidence to the contrary:

"Experiments on animals have clearly shown that each exposure leaves an indelible scar, in that it uses up reserves of adaptability which cannot be replaced. It is true that immediately after some harassing experience, rest can restore us almost to the original level of fitness by eliminating acute fatigue. But the emphasis is on the word *almost.* Since we constantly go through periods of stress and rest during life, even a minute deficit of adaptation energy every day adds up—it adds up to what we call *aging.*" (1976, p. 429)

Other independent studies have strongly supported Selye's findings and also indicate that, in general, symptom intensity is directly related to the severity of the adjustive demand placed on the organism (Coleman, 1973; Rahe & Arthur, 1978; Uhlenhuth & Paykel, 1973).

When pressure is severe and long continued, physiological mobilization may become chronic and in time lead to irreversible pathology in bodily organs—ranging from peptic ulcers and high blood pressure to heart attacks or strokes. In some individuals sustained or very severe stress appears to lead to chemical changes that interfere with brain functioning and seriously impair the individual's ability to think, feel, and act in an integrated manner.

Biological decompensation. It is difficult to specify the exact biological processes underlying an organism's response to stress. A model that helps explain the course of biological decompensation under excessive stress has been advanced by Selye (1976b) in his formulation of the *general adaptation syndrome.* Selye found that the body's reaction to sustained and excessive stress typically occurs in three major phases: (a) *alarm and mobilization*—representing a general "call to arms" of the body's defensive forces brought about by the activation of the autonomic nervous system; (b) *stage of resistance*—in which biological adaptation is at the maximum level of operation in terms of bodily resources used; and (c) *exhaustion and disintegration*—in which bodily resources are depleted and the organism loses its ability to resist so that further exposure to the stress can lead to disintegration and death (see **HIGHLIGHT** on this page).

Where decompensation does not run its entire course and result in the death of the organism, maintenance mechanisms attempt to repair damage and reorganize normal function. If the stress has resulted in extensive damage, this restorative process is often a matter of reorganizing "remaining parts and resources," but there is a permanent lowering of the previous level of integration and functioning.

Psychological decompensation. Personality decompensation under excessive stress is somewhat easier to delineate. It appears to follow a course resembling that of biological decompensation and may, in fact, involve specific biological responses.

1. *Alarm and mobilization.* At first there is an alerting of the organism and a mobilizing of resources for coping with the stressor. Typically involved at this stage are emotional arousal and increased tension, heightened sensitivity and alertness (vigilance), and determined efforts at self-control. At the same time, the individual undertakes various coping measures—which may be task-oriented or defense-oriented or a combination of the two—in attempts to meet the emergency. During this stage, symptoms of maladjustment may appear, such as continuous anxiety and tension, gastrointestinal upset or other bodily manifestations, and lowered efficiency—indications that the mobilization of adaptive resources is not proving adequate.

2. *Stage of resistance.* If the stress continues, the individual is often able to find some means for dealing with it and thus to resist psychological disintegration. Resistance may be achieved temporarily by concerted task-oriented coping measures; the use of ego-defense mechanisms may also be intensified during this period. Even in the stage of resistance, however, there may be indications of strain, including psychophysiologic symptoms and mild reality distortions. During the late phases of this stage the individual tends to become rigid and to cling to previously developed defenses rather than trying to reevaluate the stressor situation and work out more adaptive coping patterns.

3. *Stage of exhaustion.* In the face of continued excessive stress, the individual's adaptive resources are depleted and the coping patterns

HIGHLIGHT
Selye's general adaptation syndrome (GAS)

The general adaptation syndrome (GAS), shown in the diagram below, graphically illustrates the individual's general response to stress. In the first phase ("alarm reaction") the organism shows an initial lowered resistance to stress or shock. If the stress persists the organism shows a defensive reaction or resistance ("resistance phase") in an attempt to adapt to stress. Following extensive exposure to stress, the energy necessary for adaptation may be exhausted, resulting in the final stage of the GAS—collapse of adaptation ("collapse phase").

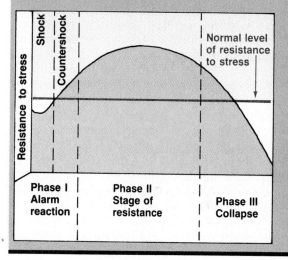

called forth in the stage of resistance begin to fail. Now, as the stage of exhaustion begins, there is a lowering of integration and an introduction of exaggerated and inappropriate defensive measures. The latter reactions may be characterized by psychological disorganization and a "break with reality," involving delusions and hallucinations. These appear to represent increased disorganization in thought and perception along with a desperate effort to salvage some measure of psychological integration and self-integrity by restructuring reality. Metabolic changes that impair normal brain functioning may also be involved in delusional and hallucinatory behavior. Eventually, if the excessive stress continues, the process of decompensation proceeds to a stage of complete psychological

Hans Selye, 1907–1982, the Canadian psychologist whose "general adaptation syndrome" helps explain how individuals react under stress.

disintegration—perhaps involving continuous uncontrolled violence, apathy, or stupor, and eventually death.

As we shall see, relatively severe psychological decompensation may be precipitated by sudden and extreme stress; but more often the decompensation is a gradual and long-range process. Typically, of course, treatment measures are instituted before decompensation runs its course. Such measures may increase the individual's adaptive capabilities or alleviate the stressor situation so that the process of decompensation is reversed to *recompensation.*

Sociocultural decompensation.   Although social science has made only modest inroads into the understanding of group pathology, it would appear that the concept of decompensation is just as applicable here as on biological and psychological levels. In the face of wars, economic problems, and other internal and external stressors that surpass their adjustive capabilities, societies may undergo varying degrees of decompensation, often resorting to extreme measures in their attempts to maintain their organization and resist disintegration. This process has been depicted by the historian Toynbee and other writers in their descriptions of the decline and fall of civilizations throughout history.

In completing our immediate discussion of decompensation, it may be emphasized that the outcome in a given situation—on biological and psychological as well as on sociocultural levels—depends on the extent to which any damage can

be repaired and remaining resources reorganized. In some instances the functional level may be permanently lowered following excessive stress; in other cases the individual or group may attain a higher level of integration and functioning than before the episode.

Psychological disorders and stress

The psychological research literature and the clinical observations on the relationship between stress and psychopathology are so substantial that the role of stressors in symptom development is now formally emphasized in diagnostic formulations. In DSM-III, for example, the diagnostician can specify on Axis IV (shown on p. 19) the specific psychosocial stressor(s) facing the individual. Ratings can range from none to catastrophic and can be used with any Axis I or II diagnosis. The Axis IV scale is particularly useful in relation to two Axis I categories: *adjustment disorder* and *posttraumatic stress disorder* (acute, chronic, or delayed). Both of these disorders involve patterns of psychological and behavioral disturbance that occur in response to identifiable stressors. The key difference between the two disorders lies not only in severity of the disturbance but also in the nature of the stressor and the time frame during which the disorder occurs. In both disorders, the stressor can be identified as a causal factor and can be specified on Axis IV.

In *adjustment disorders,* the stressor is usually one that is a *common* stressor experience (such as divorce) but the individual's response, which occurs within three months of the stressor, is beyond what one would normally expect in terms of impaired social or occupational functioning. Furthermore, the individual's response is not merely one instance of overreaction to stress but rather a continuing pattern that typically lessens or disappears after (a) the stressor has subsided or (b) the individual learns to adapt to the stressor. Predisposition on the part of the individual is not involved.

There are several subclasses of adjustment disorder as defined by the predominant symptoms the individual is experiencing: *adjustment disorder with depressed mood; adjustment disorder with anxious mood; adjustment disorder with mixed emotional features; adjustment disorder with disturbance of conduct; adjustment disorder with mixed disturbance of emotions and conduct; adjustment disorder with work inhibition;* and *adjustment disorder with withdrawal.*

In *posttraumatic stress disorder,* the stressor is *uncommon* (e.g., an extremely traumatic experience such as rape) and the symptoms, which begin immediately or soon after the trauma, are typically dramatic, including (a) a recurring sense that one is reexperiencing the actual traumatic event; (b) a general lack of responsiveness to the present environment; and (c) a variety of psychological disturbances. The time frame is important here: an *acute* posttraumatic disorder begins within six months of the stressor; a *chronic* posttraumatic disorder is long-lasting—that is, it lasts six months or more. Finally, there is even a category for a *delayed* posttraumatic disorder, which is defined as beginning at least six months after the stressor.

Of the posttraumatic stress disorders, the delayed posttraumatic stress disorder is less well defined and more difficult to diagnose than disorders that emerge shortly after the precipitating incident. In fact, some authorities have questioned whether these disorders should be diagnosed as posttraumatic stress disorders at all. Instead, they would use other anxiety-based categories (to be discussed in the next chapter).

We shall now look first at some stressor situations that typically cause adjustment disorders. Then we shall look at three stressor situations that can lead to later posttraumatic stress disorder: catastrophes, combat, and POW/concentration camp detainment.

Adjustment disorders: Reactions to difficult life stressors

For most of us, the chances of experiencing first-hand the terrors of war or confinement in a prisoner-of-war camp are quite remote. Even natural disasters like floods, fires, tornadoes and plane crashes, though more common, still never involve most of us. However, situations do not have to be as severe or generally devastating as combat, imprisonment, or natural calamities to precipitate psychological stress reactions. Most of us face less dramatic but intensely stressful

situations—sometimes over an extended period of time—that require great adjustive effort and can produce long-term psychological problems. These represent adjustment disorders, and situations that cause them may include unemployment, bereavement, divorce or separation, and forced relocation.

Stress from unemployment. Managing the stress associated with unemployment requires great coping strength, especially for people who have previously earned an adequate living and suddenly find themselves destitute, with no way to better their condition. The negative impact of losing one's job and being unable to find suitable employment has seemingly been epidemic in the last decade. The economic decline of the automobile, steel, and mining industries especially has transformed many normally thriving communities into depressed areas and many typically industrious employees into idle individuals who are unable to earn a living wage. Some communities, at the time of this writing, report unemployment rates as high as 50 percent, and the nation as a whole shows an overall unemployment rate of 10.4 percent. In almost any community one can find numerous examples of workers who have been laid off from jobs they have held for many years and who are facing the end of their unemployment compensation. The following case is typical of the problems that unemployment can bring:

David C., a 49-year-old construction foreman who was married and had two children attending college, had worked for a large building construction firm since he graduated from high school. One afternoon in May of 1982 his company, without warning, filed for bankruptcy, closed down its remaining job sites, and began to liquidate its resources.

David was stunned. The unexpected changes in his life were not easy for him to face. Early efforts to find other employment were met only with frustration, since other construction companies were experiencing similar economic problems and layoffs.

After a few weeks his savings were depleted, and he took a step he never dreamed possible: he applied for unemployment compensation. This was a tremendous blow to his self-esteem. He had always been self-sufficient and had taken great pride in being a hard worker and a good provider for his family. He was particularly upset at not being able to pay the tuition and living costs for his two sons in college and he felt a great sense of failure when they remained on their summer jobs rather than returning to school. His wife, who had never worked outside the home since their marriage, took a job in a local department store in order to meet some of the family's living expenses.

After some searching David seemingly gave up on finding a job and began to spend more time in bars. His drinking problems intensified. When he returned home in the evenings he sulked around the house and rebuffed most attempts by other family members to socialize or communicate. During this period family arguments were so frequent that Joel, his eldest son, felt that he couldn't tolerate the tension anymore and enlisted in the army. In February, eight months after he lost his job, David saw a notice in the newspaper indicating that a local company was taking applications for 25 construction jobs the following Monday. He arrived at the company's employment office early in the morning only to find that there were about 3000 other applicants ahead of him—some who had arrived the day before and had stood in line all night in the bitter cold. He left the lot dejected. That same week the bank initiated foreclosure proceedings on his house since he had not made a mortgage payment in seven months. He was forced to sell his house at a great loss and move into an apartment.

At the time of this writing, almost a year later, David remains unemployed with no prospect of finding a job. Consequently, no conclusion of his case can be written. The enormous negative impact his unemployment is having on his psychological adjustment is evident.

The long-range effects of this kind of stressful situation is not certain. Some people can ultimately take setbacks such as David is experiencing in stride and can adapt without suffering long-range adjustment difficulties once the initial stressful situation has ended. For many, however, unemployment can have serious long-term effects. Most of today's college students have parents or grandparents who lived through the severest period of unemployment in our country's history, the Great Depression of the 1930s. For those who went through it, the Depression often left psychological and emotional wounds that never fully healed. The following excerpt from Studs Terkel's book, *Hard Times*, provides a good illustration of the types of stressors brought about by the Depression, the means people used to cope, and the long-range impact of their experiences.

"Ward James *He is seventy-three. He teaches at a fashionable private school for boys, out East. He was born in Wisconsin; attended school there.*

"'BEFORE THE CRASH, I was with a small publishing house in New York. I was in charge of all the produc-

tion and did most of the copy. It was a good job. The company was growing. It looked like a permanent situation. I was feeling rather secure. . . .

"'Until 1935, I had my job with this publishing house. They insisted I take a month vacation without pay and a few other things, but it wasn't really too distressing. It became tougher and tougher.

"'I was fired. No reasons given. . . .

"'I was out of work for six months. I was losing my contacts as well as my energy. I kept going from one publishing house to another. I never got past the telephone operator. It was just wasted time. One of the worst things was occupying your time, sensibly. You'd go to the library. You took a magazine to the room and sat and read. I didn't have a radio. I tried to do some writing and found I couldn't concentrate. The day was long. There was nothing to do evenings. I was going around in circles, it was terrifying. So I just vegetated.

"'With some people I knew, there was a coldness, shunning: I'd rather not see you just now. Maybe *I'll* lose my job next week. On the other hand, I made some very close friends, who were merely acquaintances before. If I needed $5 for room rent or something, it was available.

"'I had a very good friend who cashed in his bonus bonds to pay his rent. I had no bed, so he let me sleep there. (Laughs.) I remember getting down to my last pair of pants, which looked awful. One of my other friends had just got a job and had an extra pair of pants that fit me, so I inherited them. (Laughs.)

"'I went to apply for unemployment insurance, which had just been put into effect. I went three weeks in succession. It still hadn't come through. Then I discovered the catch. At that time, anybody who earned more than $3,000 a year was not paid unemployment insurance unless his employer had O.K.'d it. It could be withheld. My employer exercised his option of not O.K.'ing it. . . .

"'I finally went on relief. It's an experience I don't want anybody to go through. It comes as close to crucifixion as . . . . You sit in an auditorium and are given a number. The interview was utterly ridiculous and mortifying. In the middle of mine, a more dramatic guy than I dived from the second floor stairway, head first, to demonstrate he was gonna get on relief even if he had to go to the hospital to do it.

"'There were questions like: Who are your friends? Where have you been living? Where's your family? I had sent my wife and child to her folks in Ohio, where they could live more simply. Why should anybody give you money? Why should anybody give you a place to sleep? What sort of friends? This went on for half an hour. I got angry and said, "Do you happen to know what a friend is?" He changed his attitude very shortly. I did get certified some time later. I think they paid $9 a month.

"'I came away feeling I didn't have any business

living any more. I was imposing on somebody, a great society or something like that. . . .'

"*Do you recall the sentiments of people during the depths of the Depression?*

"'. . . Everyone was emotionally affected. We developed a fear of the future which was very difficult to overcome. Even though I eventually went into some fairly good jobs, there was still this constant dread: everything would be cut out from under you and you wouldn't know what to do. It would be even harder, because you were older. . . .

"'Before the Depression, one felt he could get a job even if something happened to this one. There were always jobs available. And, of course, there were always those, even during the Depression [who said]: If you wanted to work, you could really get it. Nonsense.

"'I suspect, even now, I'm a little bit nervous about every job I take and wonder how long it's going to last—and what I'm going to do to cause it to disappear.

"'I feel anything can happen. There's a little fear in me that it might happen again. It does distort your outlook and your feeling. Lost time and lost faith. . . .'" (Terkel, 1970, pp. 421–23)

Ward James started his ordeal with self-confidence and demonstrated competence. Many victims of chronic unemployment, however, have no such resources to help them. For some population subgroups—especially young minority males—there is now and always has been an economic depression, more pervasive and just as debilitating as the Great Depression was for the white majority. Indeed, for young black men the rates of unemployment today are over twice those for whites during the 1930s.

The impact of chronic unemployment upon the individual's self-concept, sense of worth, and feeling of belongingness is shattering. To be continuously unemployed and poor in an affluent society is extremely frustrating and self-devaluating. The vulnerability of the lower socioeconomic segment of the population to these difficult conditions helps explain why it contributes a disproportionately higher number of victims to penal institutions and to mental hospitals than to other population classes.

Stress from bereavement. In most societies, death is an unwelcome intruder. Most people think of death as a remote event that will happen at some time in the far distant future—when they will have pretty well completed their lives anyway. In spite of the fact that death is a

certainty for us all and the loss of friends and relatives is inevitable, many of us deny and ignore it—and remain unprepared. When someone close to us dies, we are psychologically upended. Often the first reaction is disbelief. Then, as we begin to realize the significance of what has happened, our feelings of sadness, grief, and despair (even, perhaps, anger at the departed person) frequently overwhelm us.

Grief over the loss of a loved one is a natural process that seems to allow the survivors to mourn their loss and then free themselves for life without the departed person. The following description of the normal grief process ("uncomplicated bereavement" in DSM-III terms) was provided by Janis et al. (1969):

". . . Typically, the normal grief pattern following the loss of a loved one begins with a period of numbness and shock. Upon learning of the death, the person reacts with disbelief. For several days his feelings may be blunted and he may be in a semidazed state, punctuated by episodes of irritability and anger. In some instances the protest reactions take the extreme form of outbursts of impotent rage, as when adult brothers and sisters bitterly blame one another for having failed to do something that might have prolonged the life of their elderly parent. This initial phase usually ends by the time of the funeral, which often can release the tears and feelings of despair that had been bottled up in the grief-stricken person. Thereafter, a very intense grief reaction ensues: The mourner weeps copiously, yearns for the lost person, and wishes he had been more helpful and considerate while the loved one was still alive. . . . Attacks of agitated distress are likely to alternate with periods of more silent despair, during which the sufferer is preoccupied with memories of the dead person.

"For many days and perhaps weeks the mourner remains somewhat depressed and apathetic, expresses a general sense of futility, and becomes socially withdrawn, although he still goes through the motions of carrying out his usual social obligations. During this period of despair, he is likely to suffer from insomnia, psychosomatic [psychologically induced] intestinal disorders, loss of appetite, restlessness, and general irritability. A tendency to deny the fact of the death may persist for many weeks; the mourner continues to think of the dead person at times as still alive and present in the house. There is also a tendency to idealize the dead person in memory and . . . to seek companionship mainly with persons who are willing to limit their conversation to talking about him.

"The mourner is usually able to return to work and resume other daily activities, such as talking with friends and relatives, after about two or three weeks.

But he may continue to withdraw from certain types of social affairs that used to give him pleasure. After a month or two the most acute symptoms begin to subside, but there may still be residual sadness, yearning, and attacks of acute grief during the ensuing months." (pp. 179–80)

Some individuals do not go through the normal process of grieving, perhaps because of their personality makeup or as a consequence of the particular situation: the individual may, for instance, be expected to be stoical about his or her feelings or may have to manage the affairs of the family. Other individuals may develop exaggerated or prolonged depression after the normal grieving process should have run its course, i.e., lasting no longer than one year. Such pathological reactions to the death of another person are more likely to occur in people who have a history of emotional problems and who harbor a great deal of resentment and hostility against the deceased, thus experiencing intense guilt. They are usually profoundly depressed and may, in some instances, be suffering from "major depression"—see Chapter 9.

The following case illustrates an extreme or pathological grief reaction (with, in this instance, a positive outcome):

Nadine, a 66-year-old former high school teacher, lived with Charles, age 67, her husband of 40 years (also a retired teacher). The couple had been nearly inseparable since they met—they even taught at the same schools during most of their teaching careers. They lived in a semirural community where they had taught and had raised their three children, all of whom had married and moved to a large metropolitan area about a hundred miles away. For years they had planned their retirement and had hoped to be able to travel around the country visiting friends. A week before their fortieth anniversary, Charles had a heart attack and after five days in the intensive care unit had a second heart attack and died.

Nadine took Charles's death quite hard. Even though she had a great deal of emotional support from her many friends and her children, she had great difficulty adjusting. Elaine, one of her daughters, came and stayed a few days and encouraged her to come to the city for a while. Nadine declined the persistent invitation even though she had little to do at home. Friends called on her frequently but she seemed almost to resent their presence. In the months following the funeral, Nadine's reclusive behavior persisted. Several well-wishers reported to Elaine that her mother was not doing well and was not even leaving the house to go shopping. They reported that Na-

dine sat alone in a darkened house—not answering the phone and showing reluctance to come to the door. She had apparently lost interest in activities she had once enjoyed.

Greatly worried about her mother's welfare, Elaine organized a "campaign" to get her mother out of the house and back to doing the things she had formerly done. Each of the children and their families took turns at visiting, spending time with her, and taking her places until she finally began to show interest in living again. In time, Nadine agreed to come to each of their homes for visits. This proved to be a very therapeutic step since Nadine had always been very fond of children and took pleasure in the time spent with her eight grandchildren. (She actually extended the visits longer than she had planned.)

Stress from divorce or separation. The deterioration or ending of an intimate relationship is one of the more potent of stressors and one of the more frequent reasons why people seek psychotherapy. Divorce, though more generally accepted today, is still a tragic and usually stressful outcome to a relationship of closeness and trust. We noted in Chapter 4 that marital disruption is a major source of vulnerability to psychopathology: individuals who are recently divorced or separated are markedly overrepresented among people with psychological problems.

Many factors make a divorce or separation unpleasant and stressful for everyone concerned: the acknowledgment of failure in a relationship important to both oneself and the society; the necessity of "explaining" the failure to family and friends; the loss of valuable friendships that frequently accompanies the rupture; the economic uncertainty and hardships that both partners frequently experience; and when children are involved, the problem of custody, living arrangements, and so on.

After the divorce or separation, new problems typically emerge. The readjustment to a single life-style, perhaps after many years of marriage, can be a very difficult experience. Since in many cases it seems that friends as well as assets have to be divided, new friendships need to be made. New opposite-sex relationships may require a great deal of personal change. Even where the separation has been relatively agreeable, new adaptation and coping strength will be needed. Thus it is not surprising that many people seek counseling after the breakup of a significant relationship.

The following case illustrates how the stress

in a marital breakup can adversely affect a quite capable and generally well-functioning person.

Janice was a petite, attractive 33-year-old manager of an office that employed over fifty people. She had always been very competent and got a great deal of satisfaction out of her career. For several months, however, she had been quite upset and depressed about her marital situation and unable to sleep. She had lost 12 pounds because of her poor appetite and was experiencing painful "burning" feelings in her stomach; she was worried about having ulcers.

Janice's second marriage had begun to show signs of trouble almost from the start. Shortly after the wedding, two years before, her husband's drinking had increased. He often stayed out quite late and on two occasions did not come home at all. Usually he lied about his whereabouts, but for the first few months Janice was tolerant of his transgressions, trying to make this second marriage work. Her husband, whom she regarded as a charming person she "couldn't stay mad at" was always forgiven, and they "had a great time making up." In the most recent incident, however, he had returned late at night with "evident traces of another woman." This was the final straw, and Janice moved out.

The intense stress she was experiencing over the breakup of the marriage appeared to be directly related to her sense of failing in life for a second time. Her first marriage had ended in divorce after her hus-

band of seven years developed a severe drinking problem, stayed away from home a great deal, and frequently abused her physically.

Janice's marital problems did not interfere with her performance at work; but, besides depression and physical problems, she began to experience problems with her teenage daughter. As a result, she entered psychotherapy, hoping it would help her know herself better and understand why she had married two "losers."

Janice was seen in therapy for about six months, during which time she gained a great deal of insight into her own motivation for marrying alcoholics: she wished to "save" them from themselves. Janice's father had been an alcoholic and had died when she was a teenager—from chronic drinking. During therapy, Janice was able to "resist" taking her husband back and was able to feel more comfortable about living with her daughter.

Stress from forced relocation. Being uprooted from one's home seems to threaten to cut us off from all we hold dear—the sanctity of hearth and home. Yet that is what happened in recent years at Love Canal and at Times Beach, Missouri. In both cases, families found their homes and themselves exposed to deadly toxins that had contaminated the environment. They were faced with a difficult choice: to stay and possibly risk their health and that of their chil-

The devastating discovery that they were living over a toxic time bomb probably shattered the emotional, physical, and financial security of many residents of Love Canal, whose relocations were hampered by prolonged legal battles over responsibility and compensation.

dren; or to relocate and face the stresses that such uprooting would inevitably bring. As it turned out, for residents of Love Canal and Times Beach there was no choice: the danger was all too real, and families were forced to relocate. Understandably, in circumstances such as these, the accompanying stress can be severe.

Imagine, then, the trauma of refugees who are forced not only to leave their homes but also their homeland and to face the stress of adapting to a new and unfamiliar culture. Such has been the case for refugees throughout history. For those who come to the United States, the "land of opportunity" may appear to be a nightmare rather than a haven. Such was the case for Pham, a 34-year-old Vietnamese refugee who killed his sons and himself:

Pham's ordeal began with a comfortable life in a wealthy Vietnamese family and a good job as a Saigon pharmacist. It ended after six months in the United States in a small two-bedroom apartment in Washington, D.C. The county police called it a "murder-suicide."

Police believe that the refugee, a lab technician in a local community college's work-study program, administered the poison to his own family and then took his own life. Only Pham's wife survived the administration of the poison.

Two seven-page suicide notes, one in Vietnamese and one in English, began, "To whom it may concern. We committed suicide by cyanide. The reason is that I lost my mind. I cannot live here like a normal person. . . ."

Pham, according to relatives, had been depressed over what he considered his financial and social failures in America. He was despondent over having to study five years to become a pharmacist here, and about his difficulties communicating in English.

Pham was a dutiful son who had never been away from home before leaving for Thailand. He was homesick for his native country and for the parents who remained behind.

"He had a lot of expectations about America," said one relative, "he just could not cope." (Adapted from the *Washington Star,* December 8, 1980)

The suffering experienced by Pham is not unique in the world today. It is estimated that there are over 16 million refugees in the world, mostly from third-world or developing countries, with only about 11 percent of them relocating in developed nations like the United States and Canada (Brandel, 1980). Most of the refugees move between third-world countries; for example, there are more than a million Af-

ghan refugees living near the border of Pakistan in makeshift living quarters.

In the United States, recent refugees have come from many countries—Poland, Russia, Africa, Iran, Cuba, Haiti, Laos, Vietnam, and Cambodia. The largest group of refugees entering the United States recently is the Southeast Asians—over a half a million have arrived since 1975. Although many of these individuals were functioning well in their homeland and will, in time, become successful and happy citizens in their new homeland, many have had difficulty adjusting and will require special services for some time to come (Williams, 1984).

Reactions to catastrophic events

Over half of the survivors of the disastrous Cocoanut Grove nightclub fire—which took the lives of 492 people in Boston in 1942—required treatment for severe psychological shock (Adler, 1943). When two commuter trains collided in Chicago in 1972, leaving 44 persons dead and over 300 injured, the tragedy also left scores of persons with feelings of fear, anxiety, and guilt; more than 80 of them attended a voluntary "talk session" arranged by the psychiatric adult outpatient clinic of the University of Chicago (Uhlenhuth, 1973). Psychological evaluation of 8 of the 64 survivors of the collision of two jet planes on Santa Cruz de Tenerife Island in 1977, in which 580 people died, indicated that all the survivors studied suffered from serious emotional problems stemming directly from the accident (Perlberg, 1979).

With few exceptions, people exposed to plane crashes, automobile accidents, explosions, fires, earthquakes, tornadoes, sexual assault, or other terrifying experiences show psychological "shock" reactions—transient personality decompensation. The symptoms may vary greatly, depending on the nature and severity of the terrifying experience, the degree of surprise, and the personality make up of the individual. A "disaster syndrome" has been delineated that appears to characterize the reactions of many victims of such catastrophes. This syndrome may be described in terms of the reactions during the traumatic experience, the initial reactions after it—the acute posttraumatic stress—and the complications that may be long-lasting or arise later—the chronic or delayed posttraumatic stress.

The aftermath of catastrophic events, such as the burning of one's home, may bring about a "disaster syndrome," which includes psychological reactions during the traumatic event, reactions immediately following the event, and complications that may be long-lasting or delayed.

Initial "disaster syndrome" and acute posttraumatic stress. The initial responses to a disaster typically involve the shock stage, the suggestible stage, and the recovery stage. (Similar stages can be identified for victims of rape—see the **HIGHLIGHT** on pages 164–165.) It is in the third stage that *acute posttraumatic stress disorder* may develop.

1. *Shock stage,* in which the victim is stunned, dazed, and apathetic. Frequently unaware of the extent of personal injuries, the victim tends to wander about aimlessly until guided or directed by someone else, and is unable to make more than minimal efforts to help either him or herself or others. In extreme cases the individual may be stuporous, disoriented, and amnesic for the traumatic event.

2. *Suggestible stage,* in which the victim tends to be passive, suggestible, and willing to take directions from rescue workers or others less affected by the disaster. Here the individual often expresses extreme concern over the welfare of others involved in the disaster and attempts to be of assistance; however, his or her behavior tends to be inefficient even in the performance of routine tasks.

3. *Recovery stage,* in which the individual may be tense and apprehensive and show generalized anxiety, but gradually regains psychological equilibrium—often in the process showing a need to repetitively tell about the catastrophic event.

These three stages are well illustrated in the *Andrea Doria* disaster, in which 52 persons died and over 1600 were rescued.

"On July 25, 1956, at 11:05 P.M., the Swedish liner *Stockholm* smashed into the starboard side of the Italian liner *Andrea Doria* a few miles off Nantucket Island, causing one of the worst disasters in maritime history. . . . During the phase of initial shock the survivors acted as if they had been sedated . . . as though nature provided a sedation mechanism which went into operation automatically. [During the phase of suggestibility] the survivors presented themselves for the most part as an amorphous mass of people tending to act passively and compliantly. They displayed psychomotor retardation, flattening of affect, somnolence, and in some instances, amnesia for data of personal identification. They were nonchalant and easily suggestible. [During the stage of recovery, after the initial shock had worn off and the survivors had received aid,] they showed . . . an apparently compulsive need to tell the story again and again, with identical detail and emphasis." (Friedman & Linn, 1957, p. 426)

In some cases the clinical picture may be complicated by intense feelings of grief and depression (see **HIGHLIGHT** on page 166). Where the individual feels that his or her own personal inadequacy contributed to the loss of loved ones in the disaster, the picture may be further complicated by strong feelings of guilt, and the posttraumatic stress may stretch into a period of months. This pattern is well brought out in the following case of a husband who failed to save his wife in the jet crash at Tenerife in 1977.

"Martin's story is quite tragic. He lost his beloved wife of 37 years and blames himself for her death, because he sat stunned and motionless for some 25 seconds after the [other plane] hit. He saw nothing but fire and smoke in the aisles, but he roused himself and

HIGHLIGHT
Aftereffects of rape

Reactions to rape vary greatly among victims, depending on the relationship of the victim to the offender and the life circumstances of the victim, among other factors. Here we shall examine some of these factors and then look at typical coping behavior of rape victims, rape counseling, and possible long-term effects of rape.

Factors affecting reaction to rape

A woman's response to rape may vary depending on her relationship to the offender. In a "stranger" rape—one in which the victim does not know the offender—the victim is very likely to experience strong fear of physical harm and death. In an "acquaintance" rape situation, the reaction is apt to be slightly different (Ellison, 1977). In such a situation, the victim not only may feel fear but also may feel that she has been betrayed by someone she had trusted. She may feel more responsible for what happened and experience greater guilt. She may also be more hesitant to seek help or report the rape to the police out of fear that she will be held partially responsible for it.

The age and life circumstances of the victim may also influence her reaction to rape (Notman & Nadelson, 1976). For a young child who knows nothing about sexual behavior, rape can lead to sexual fears and confusion, particularly if the child is encouraged to forget about the experience without thoroughly talking it over first. For women between the ages of 17 and 24, rape can increase the conflicts over independence and separation that are normal in this age group. In an effort to be helpful, parents of young adult rape victims often encourage various forms of regression, such as moving back to the family home, which may in the long run prevent mastery of this developmental phase. Married rape victims with young children face the task of explaining their experience to their children. Sometimes the feelings of vulnerability that result from rape leave a woman feeling temporarily unable to care for her children.

Husbands and boyfriends can also influence rape victims' reactions by their attitudes and behavior. Rejection, blaming, uncontrolled anger at the offender, or insistence on early resumption of sexual activity can increase the woman's negative feelings.

Coping behavior of rape victims

Several researchers have interviewed rape victims in hospital emergency rooms and rape crisis centers soon after the rape (Burgess & Holmstrom, 1974, 1976; Holmstrom & Burgess, 1975; McCombie, 1976; Sutherland & Scherl, 1970). Although based on small samples and nonstandardized interview formats, their findings are the best data currently available on the typical phases victims go through in coping with rape. The following represents an integration of these data.

1. **Anticipatory phase.** This is the period before the actual rape when the offender "sets up" the victim and the victim begins to perceive that a dangerous situation exists. In the early minutes of the anticipatory phase, victims often use defense mechanisms such as denial to preserve an illusion of invulnerability. Common thoughts are "Rape could never happen to me," and "He doesn't really mean that."

2. **Impact phase.** This phase begins with the victim's recognition that she is actually going to be raped and ends when the rape is over. The victim's first reaction is usually intense fear for her life, a fear much stronger than her fear of the sexual behavior itself. Symonds (1976) has described the paralytic effect of intense fear on victims of crime, showing that it usually leads to varying degrees of disintegration in the victim's functioning and possibly to complete inability to act. When the victim later recalls her behavior during this phase, she may feel guilty about not reacting

led his wife to a jagged hole above and behind his seat. Martin climbed out onto the wing and reached down and took hold of his wife's hand, but 'an explosion from within literally blew her out of my hands and pushed me back and down onto the wing.' He reached the runway, turned to go back after her, but the plane blew up seconds later. . . .

"[Five months later] Martin was depressed and bored, had 'wild dreams,' a short temper and became easily confused and irritated. 'What I saw there will terrify me forever,' he says. He told [the psychologist who interviewed him] that he avoided television and movies, because he couldn't know when a frightening scene would appear." (Perlberg, 1979, pp. 49–50)

In some instances "the guilt of the survivors" seems to center around the view that they may have deserved to survive no more or perhaps even less than others. As one stewardess expressed it after the crash of a Miami-bound jet

more efficiently, and she needs to be reassured that her reaction is a common one. Major physiological reactions such as vomiting sometimes occur during this phase, but a woman who tries to simulate such reactions in order to escape generally discovers that she cannot produce them voluntarily.

3. Posttraumatic recoil phase. This phase begins immediately after the crime. Burgess and Holmstrom (1974, 1976) observed two emotional styles among the rape victims they interviewed in hospital emergency rooms. Some victims exhibited an *expressed style* where feelings of fear and anxiety were shown through crying, sobbing, and restlessness. Others demonstrated a *controlled style* in which feelings appeared to be masked by a calm, controlled, subdued façade. Regardless of style, most of the victims felt guilty about the way they had reacted to the offender and wished that they had reacted faster or fought harder. Feelings of dependency were increased, and victims often had to be encouraged and helped to call friends or parents and make other arrangements. Physical problems such as general tension, nausea, sleeplessness, and trauma directly related to the rape were common.

4. Reconstitution phase. This phase begins as the victim starts to make plans for leaving the emergency room or crisis center and ends, often many months later, when the stress of the rape has been assimilated, the experience shared with significant others, and the victim's self-concept restored. Certain behaviors and symptoms are typical during this phase.

a) Motor activity, such as changing one's telephone number and moving to a new residence, is common. The victim's fear is often well justified at this point since, even if the offender has been arrested and charged with rape, he is often out on bail.

b) Frightening nightmares in which the rape is relived are common. As the victim moves closer toward assimilating the experience, the content of the dreams gradually shifts until the victim successfully fights off the assailant.

c) Phobias—including fear of the indoors or outdoors (depending on where the rape took place), fear of being alone, fear of crowds, fear of having people behind one, and sexual fears—have been observed to develop immediately following rape.

Counseling rape victims

The women's movement has played a crucial role in the establishment of specialized rape counseling services such as rape crisis centers and hotlines. Rape-crisis centers are often staffed by trained paraprofessionals who provide general support for the victim, both individually and in groups. Crisis centers also have victim advocacy services, in which a trained volunteer accompanies the victim to the hospital or police station, helps her understand the procedures, and assists her with "red tape." The victim advocate may also accompany the victim to meetings with the district attorney and to the trial—experiences that tend to temporarily reactivate the trauma of the rape.

Long-term effects

Whether a rape victim will experience serious psychological decompensation depends to a large extent on her past coping skills and level of psychological functioning. The previously well-adjusted woman will regain her prior equilibrium, but rape can precipitate severe pathology in a woman with prior psychological difficulties (Atkeson et al., 1982). Comparisons of women who have been raped with those who have not indicate that, though victims feel that the rape has had and continues to have an impact on them, there are generally no significant differences in overall psychological adjustment between victims and nonvictims (Oros & Koss, 1978).

in the Everglades of Florida which took many lives, "I kept thinking, I'm alive. Thank God. But I wondered why I was spared. I felt, it's not fair . . ." (*Time*, Jan. 15, 1973, p. 53).

Chronic or delayed posttraumatic stress.

Sometimes individuals who undergo terrifying experiences exhibit a reaction pattern that may endure for weeks, months, or even years. As has been noted, clinically the posttraumatic stress reaction would be diagnosed as *chronic* should it continue for longer than six months; should it not begin until six months after the catastrophe, it would be diagnosed as *delayed*.

In either case, posttraumatic stress includes the following symptoms: (a) anxiety, varying from mild apprehension to episodes of acute anxiety commonly associated with situations

HIGHLIGHT
The emotional aftermath of a devastating tornado

"Many saw it coming. At first it looked like a huge, mushroom-shaped black cloud with three narrow stems. Then the stems merged into one devastating funnel, six tenths of a mile wide. Winds in the funnel reached 318 miles an hour, four times the force of a hurricane. . . . The tornado took only 22 minutes to cut a horrifying 16-mile path from the outskirts of Xenia, directly through the main intersection of town. . . . Almost half of the seven-square-mile town [was] destroyed in a tornado that may have been the largest ever observed on earth. . . .

The power of the storm was incredible. . . . Automobiles were wrapped like untidy Band-Aids around the shattered trees. . . . Of 2,757 homes damaged by the storm, 1,095 were totally destroyed. The three-story high school and both junior high schools were demolished. . . . Twenty-five people died quickly; seven others lingered a day or two in hospitals before they expired. About 2,500 were injured, some very seriously. . . ." (Schanche, 1974, pp. 18–19)

The immediate reactions of "direct victims," who had lived through the full impact of the tornado, tended to follow the stages of acute "disaster syndrome"—initial feelings of disbelief and numbness,

followed by repetitive talking about the disaster experience, and gradual progress toward assimilation of the experience and adjustment to it. Where loved ones were lost, the pattern was, of course, much more complicated.

Prominent among the acute posttraumatic stress symptoms two months after the disaster were anxiety reactions relating to fear of another tornado and feelings of depression that had not yet fully cleared up. The most significant posttraumatic stress symptoms were found among the very young, who appeared to develop a "school phobia" characterized by fear of leaving home and refusal to return to school. Often this pattern appeared to be exacerbated by parents who were afraid to let the children leave.

While the "direct survivors" of the disaster were most seriously affected, the "indirect survivors" who had not experienced the major impact of the tornado also evidenced emotional reactions, such as guilt for being spared, difficulty in sleeping, and uncharacteristic conflicts with their husbands or wives. As Schanche expressed it, "Such natural disasters seem invariably to suck an emotional storm in their wake that frequently cuts a wider swath than the disaster itself. In this psychological aftermath, the nonvictims often suffer as much, if not more, than the direct victims of the tragedy" (p. 19).

---

that recall the traumatic experience; (b) chronic tension and irritability, often accompanied by fatigability, insomnia, the inability to tolerate noise, and the complaint that "I just can't seem to relax"; (c) repetitive nightmares reproducing the traumatic incident directly or symbolically; (d) complaints of impaired concentration and memory; and (e) feelings of depression. In some cases the individual may withdraw from social contact and avoid experiences that might increase excitation—commonly manifested in the avoidance of interpersonal involvement, loss of sexual interest, and an attitude of "peace and quiet at any price."

This posttraumatic syndrome may be complicated by a physical mutilation that necessitates changes in one's way of life; it may also be complicated by the psychological effects of disability compensation or damage suits, which tend to prolong posttraumatic symptoms (Okura, 1975).

Causal factors in trauma reactions. The intensity of the trauma reactions seems to be dependent on the suddenness of the disaster and the amount of life threat contained in the situation. The world, which before seemed relatively secure and safe, suddenly becomes a terrifying place.

One survivor of the jet crash in the Everglades remembered reading a book one minute and the next "waking up in a puddle of water with one shoe, my jacket and glasses gone, and an engine lying not far from my head." Adapted from *Time* magazine, January 15, 1973, p. 53).

During the initial reaction to the catastrophe, symptoms of being stunned, dazed, and "numbed" appear to stem in part from psychological decompensation associated with the traumatic event; they also appear in part to be defense mechanisms protecting individuals from the full impact of the catastrophe until they are better prepared to assimilate the trauma into their life experience. The stage of suggestibility apparently results from the individual's temporary inability to deal with the situation alone, plus a tendency to regress to a passive-dependent position in which one feels safer knowing that someone else is in charge.

During the stage of recovery, the recurrent nightmares and the typical need to tell about the disaster again and again with identical detail and emphasis appear to be mechanisms for reducing anxiety and desensitizing the individual to the traumatic experience. The tension, apprehensiveness, and hypersensitivity that often accompany the recovery stage appear to be residual effects of the shock reaction and to reflect the individual's realization that the world can become overwhelmingly dangerous and threatening. As we have seen, feelings of guilt about having failed to protect loved ones who perished may be quite intense, especially in situations where some responsibility can be directly assigned.

Contrary to popular opinion, panic is not common among people in the impact area of a disaster. For example, most victims of floods and hurricanes do not panic. Instead, *panic,* defined as acute fear followed by flight behavior, tends to occur only under fairly specific conditions: (a) when a group of persons is directly threatened, for example, by fire; (b) when the situation is viewed as one in which escape is possible at the moment but maybe only for a few minutes or not for everyone; and (c) when the group is taken by surprise and has no prearranged plan for dealing with such a disaster (McDavid & Harari, 1968).

Under such conditions there may be a complete disorganization or demoralization of the group, with each individual striving for self-preservation; the emotional, panic-stricken behavior of others seems to be contagious, and a person may be overwhelmed by fear. Behavior may be extremely irrational and nonadaptive and can actually result in needless loss of life. For example, in the disastrous Iroquois Theater fire in Chicago in 1903, 500 people were killed in less than eight minutes due to trampling and asphyxiation rather than burns. Similarly, in the catastrophic Cocoanut Grove fire of 1942, no lives need have been lost had people exited in an orderly way. Instead, the exits were jammed

by a rush of panic-stricken people so that many were trampled and those behind them could not get out.

In broader perspective, most people function relatively well in catastrophes, and, in fact, many behave with heroism (Rachman, 1978). It is the precipitating and predisposing factors that may determine who develops traumatic reactions and who does not, and why some recover much more rapidly than others (see **HIGHLIGHT** on pages 168–69). And, of course, what the individual brings to the situation in terms of personal and external resources (discussed earlier on p. 146) plays a major role in influencing the severity of the traumatic reaction.

In all cases of posttraumatic stress, conditioned fear—the fear associated with the traumatic experience—appears to be a key causal factor. Thus prompt psychotherapy following the traumatic experience is considered important in preventing such conditioned fear from "building up" and becoming resistant to change.

Treatment and outcomes.   Mild reassuring therapy and proper rest (induced by sedatives if necessary) usually lead to the rapid alleviation of symptoms in posttraumatic stress. It would also appear that repetitive talking about the experience and repetitive reliving of the experience in fantasy or nightmares may serve as built-in repair mechanisms in helping the individual adjust to the traumatic experience. As Horowitz has concluded from his own experimental findings and an early review of available literature,

"A traumatic perceptual experience remains in some special form of memory storage until it is mastered. Before mastery, vivid sensory images of the experiences tend to intrude into consciousness and may evoke unpleasant emotions. Through such repetitions the images, ideas, and associated affects may be worked through progressively. Thereafter, the images lose their intensity and the tendency toward repetition of the experience loses its motive force." (1969b, p. 552)

In general, the more stable and better integrated the personality and the more favorable the individual's life situation, the more quickly he or she will recover from a severe stress reaction. It would also appear to be important to work through the traumatic experience if posttraumatic symptoms are to be avoided.

For many people who experience a disaster, there is probably some benefit in receiving at least some psychological counseling, no matter how brief, to begin the "working through" process. This observation seems to be borne out in the data. In a survey of available literature on the effects of disasters on individuals and groups, Kinston and Rosser (1974) found that, contrary to what one might expect, only 10 percent of the individuals in a disaster required immediate intervention such as sedative medication, removal from the scene, rest, and psychological counseling. Yet this low statistic may not tell the whole story. It appears that the psychological reaction to a disaster may take some time to develop. For example, Parker (1975) studied victims of a severe cyclone that devastated Darwin, Australia, in 1974. The data here were in sharp contrast to the average 10 percent of individuals needing help immediately after a disaster. Parker found that within a few days after the cyclone, 58 percent of the victims showed some evidence of psychological dysfunction. Ten weeks after the cyclone had struck, 41 percent continued to show problems, and at a follow-up fourteen months later, 22 percent of the victims were still not functioning up to capacity, either psychologically or socially. These percentages for posttraumatic stress reactions appear to be typical. It may be that these could be lower if victims received more psychological help immediately after the disaster.

Traumatic reactions to military combat

During World War I traumatic reactions to combat conditions were called "shell shock," a term coined by a British pathologist Col. Frederick Mott, who regarded such reactions as organic conditions produced by minute hemorrhages of the brain. It was gradually realized, however, that only a very small percentage of such cases represented physical injury from concussion of exploding shells or bombs. Most of these men were suffering instead from the general combat situation with its physical fatigue, ever present threat of death or mutilation, and severe psychological shocks. During World War II, traumatic reactions to the continuing stressor of combat passed through a number of classifications, such as "operational fatigue" and "war neuroses," before finally being termed "combat fatigue" or "combat exhaustion" in the Korean war and the Vietnam war.

Even the latter terms were none too aptly chosen, since they implied that physical exhaustion played a more important role than was usually the case. However, they did serve to distinguish such disorders for purposes of treatment

that it would be appropriate for them to discuss their feelings with professional psychologists; and (d) the counseling was set up outside of the police department's influence, thus assuring anonymity.

The counseling—crisis intervention therapy (see Chapter 18)—focused on providing support and reassurance and allowing individuals to vent their pent-up or unmanageable emotions. For most of the individuals involved, brief crisis intervention was effective in providing symptom relief. But a few individuals required more extensive long-term psychotherapy. The following description is of a 42-year-old police officer who suffered a severe reaction to the stress of the San Diego air crash.

Don had been a model police officer during his 14 years on the force. He was highly evaluated by his superiors, had a masters degree in social work, and had attained the rank of sergeant. While patrolling in a squad car, he heard that there had been an accident, and he quickly drove to the scene to give aid to any survivors. When he arrived he wandered around "in a daze," looking for someone to help—but

there was only destruction. He later remembered the next few days as a bad dream.

He was quite depressed for several days after the cleanup, had no appetite, couldn't sleep, and was impotent. Images and recollections of the accident would come to him "out of nowhere." He reported having a recurring dream in which he would come upon an airplane crash while driving a car or flying a plane. In his dream, he would rush to the wreckage and help some passengers to safety.

Don decided that he needed help and sought counseling. Because of his deteriorating mood and physical condition, he was placed on medical leave from the police force. Eight months after the accident he was still in therapy and had not returned to work. During therapy it became apparent that Don had been experiencing a great deal of personal dissatisfaction and anger prior to the crash. His prolonged psychological disorder was not only a result of his anguish over the air crash but also a vehicle for expressing other problems (Davidson, 1979a).

Based on Davidson, 1979a, 1979b; O'Brien, 1979

from psychological disorders that happened to occur under war conditions but might well have occurred in civilian life—for example, among individuals showing a history of maladaptive behavior that was aggravated by the increased stress of combat service. In most cases, men who became psychological casualties under combat conditions had adjusted satisfactorily to civilian life and to prior military experiences.

It has been estimated that in World War II 10

percent of the American men in combat developed combat exhaustion; however, the actual incidence is not known, since many received supportive therapy at their battalion aid station and were returned to combat within a few hours. Records were kept mainly on men evacuated from the front lines who were considered the more seriously disturbed cases. Of the slightly over 10 million men accepted for military service during World War II, approximately 1,363,000 were given medical discharges, of which approximately 530,000—39 percent—were for neuropsychiatric reasons (including combat exhaustion, psychosis, neurosis, and other personality disorders that made them unsuitable for military life). In fact, combat exhaustion was the disability causing the single greatest loss of manpower during that war (Bloch, 1969). In the Korean war the incidence of combat exhaustion dropped from an initial high of over 6 percent to 3.7 percent; 27 percent of medical discharges were for psychiatric reasons (Bell, 1958). In the Vietnam war the figure dropped to less than 1.5 percent for combat exhaustion, with a negligible number of discharges for psychiatric disorders (Allerton, 1970; Bourne, 1970).

The marked decrease in combat exhaustion cases in the Vietnam war was apparently due to a number of factors, including (a) better frontline medical care; (b) the sporadic nature of the fighting, in which brief intensive encounters were followed by periods of relative calm and safety—as contrasted with weeks and months of prolonged combat that many soldiers went through in World War II and the Korean war; and (c) a policy of rotation after twelve months of service (thirteen months for Marines). Each soldier was given a DEROS (date of expected return from overseas), which indicated a clear time when the exceptional stress would be over for him. This knowledge of a definite end to the stressful situation appears to have made it more bearable at the time (Kormos, 1978). Some, however, argue that the apparent decrease in combat exhaustion among soldiers in Vietnam may have been related to methods of treatment and release and to inadequate follow-up studies of soldiers returned to combat. As Glasser (1971) notes:

"The men [who are given a date of expected return] are not lost to the fight, and the terrifying stupidity of war is not allowed to go on crippling forever. At least, that is the official belief. But there is no medical or

Although reported cases of combat exhaustion appeared to decrease in the Vietnam war (compared to World War II and Korea), the stress of the war clearly took its toll on many American GIs.

psychiatric follow-up on the boys after they've returned to duty. No one knows if they are the ones who die in the very next fire fight, who miss the wire stretched out across the tract, or gun down unarmed civilians. Apparently, the Army doesn't seem to want to find out." (p. 178)

We shall discuss the possible long-range, or residual, effects of combat later in this chapter.

Clinical picture in combat stress problems.   The specific symptoms in combat exhaustion have varied considerably, depending on the branch of the service, the severity and nature of the traumatic experience, and the personality makeup of the individual. Common symptoms among combat troops have been dejection, weariness, hypersensitivity, sleep disturbances, and tremors. In flight crews, after long combat flying, the more typical symptoms have included anxiety—frequently with accompanying dejection and depression—phobias about combat missions, irritability, tension, and *startle reactions* (see case cited below). In addition, where the stress has been cumulative, symptoms have often differed from those brought on by a sudden, intense combat situation since they are more extreme and persistent.

Despite such variations, however, there was surprising uniformity in the general clinical picture for those soldiers who developed combat exhaustion in World War II and later in the Korean war. The first symptoms were a failure to maintain psychological integration, with increasing irritability and sensitivity, disturbances of sleep, and often recurrent nightmares.

"The irritability is manifested externally by snappishness, overreaction to minor irritations, angry reactions to innocuous questions or incidents, flareups with profanity and even tears at relatively slight frustrations. The degree of these reactions may vary from angry looks or a few sharp words to acts of violence.

"Subjectively, the state of irritation is perceived by the soldier as an unpleasant 'hypersensitiveness' and he is made doubly uncomfortable by a concomitant awareness of his diminishing self-control. One patient put this very vividly by saying —'The first thing that brought home to me the fact that I was slipping was this incident: A fellow next to me took some cellophane off a piece of hard candy and crumpled it up, and that crackling noise sounded like a forest fire. It made me so mad I wanted to hit him. Then I was ashamed of being jumpy.'

"In association with this 'hypersensitiveness' to minor external stimuli, the 'startle reaction' becomes manifest (increasingly so as time goes on). This is a sudden leaping, jumping, cringing, jerking or other form of involuntary self-protective motor response to sudden, not necessarily very loud noises, and sometimes also to sudden movement or sudden light.

"The disturbances of sleep, which almost always accompany the symptom of increased irritability, consist mainly in the frustrating experience of not being able to fall asleep even upon those occasions when the military situation would permit. Soldiers have to snatch their rest when they can. . . . Opportunities for sleep become very precious and an inability to use them very distressing. Difficulties were experienced also in staying asleep because of sudden involuntary starting or leaping up, or because of terror dreams, battle dreams, and nightmares of other kinds.

"This triad of increased 'sensitivity,' irritable reactions and sleep disturbances represents the incipient state of 'combat exhaustion.' It usually does not lead to referral [for treatment]. It may exist without much change for days, weeks, or even months. Sooner or later, often upon the occasion of some incident of particularly traumatic significance to the soldier, the marginal and very unstable equilibrium is upset and the soldier becomes a casualty." (Bartemeier et al., 1946, pp. 374–75)

When the combat casualties reached the aid station or the clearing station, they presented a somewhat typical pattern of symptoms, differing only in the degree of personality decompensation. Most cases followed a similar pattern in which the patient felt he was losing control and could no longer face the stress. The patients typically appeared dejected, confused, and extremely tired. Sometimes they cried uncontrollably; at other times, they sat, without speaking, and stared off into space (W. C. Menninger, 1948). In extreme experiences of unusually traumatic combat, a soldier might repress the episode so that he was amnesic for the entire battle experience.

The following diary covers a period of about six weeks of combat in the South Pacific during World War II and illustrates the cumulative effect of combat stresses on an apparently stable personality.

"Aug. 7, 1942, Convoy arrived at Guadalcanal Bay at approximately 4 A.M. in the morning. Ships gave enemy a heavy shelling. At 9 A.M. we stormed the beach and formed an immediate beachhead, a very successful landing, marched all day in the hot sun, and at night took positions and rested. Enemy planes attacked convoy in bay but lost 39 out of 40 planes.

"Aug. 8, 1942. Continued march in the hot sun and in afternoon arrived at airport. Continued on through the Jap village and made camp for the night. During the night Jap navy attacked convoy in battle that lasted until early morning. Enemy had terrific losses and we lost two ships. This night while on sentry duty I mistook a horse for a Jap and killed it.

"Aug. 19, 1942. Enemy cruiser and destroyer came into bay and shelled the beach for about two hours. The cruiser left and the destroyer hung around for the entire morning. We all kept under shelter for the early afternoon a flying fortress flew over, spotting the ship and bombed it, setting it afire we all jumped and shouted with joy. That night trouble again was feared and we again slept in foxholes.

"Aug. 21, 1941. The long awaited landing by the enemy was made during the night 1500 troops in all and a few prisoners were taken and the rest were killed. Bodies were laying all over the beach. In afternoon planes again bombed the Island. [Here the writing begins to be shaky, and less careful than previously.]

"Aug. 28, 1942. The company left this morning in higgins Boats to the end of the Island, landed and started through thick Jungle and hills. It was hot and we had to cut our way through. In afternoon we contacted the japs. our squad was in the assault squad so we moved up the beach to take positions the enemy trapped us with machine gun and rifle fire for about two hours. The lead was really flying. Two of our men were killed, two were hit by a hand greade and my corporal received a piece of shrampnel in back,—was wounded in arm, out of the squad of eight we have five causitry. We withdrew and were taken back to the Hospital.

"Sept. 12, 1942. Large jap squadron again bombed Island out of 35 planes sent over our air force knocked down 24. During the raid a large bomb was dropped just sevety yards from my fox hole.

"Sept. 13, 1942. At one o'clock three destroyers and one cruiser shelled us contumally all night The ships turned surch lights all up and down the beach, and stopped one my foxhole seveal time I'm feeling pritty nervese and scared, afraid I'll be a nervas reack befor long. slept in fox hole all night not much sleep. This morning at 9:00 we had another air raid, the raid consisted of mostly fighter planes. I believe we got several, this afternoon. we had a nother raid, and our planes went out to met them, met them someplace over Tulagi, new came in that the aircraft carrier wasp sent planes out to intersept the bombers. This eving all hell broke lose. Our marines contacted enemy to south of us and keep up constant fire. . . .

"Sept. 14, 1942. This morning firing still going on my company is scaduted to unload ships went half ways up to dock when enemyfire start on docks, were called back to our pososeion allon beach, company called out again to go after japs, hope were lucker than we were last time [part of this illegible]. Went up into hills at 4:00 P.M. found positions, at 7:00 en 8 sea planes fombed and strifed us, 151942 were strifed biy amfibious planes and bombed the concussion of one through me of balance and down a 52 foot hil. I was shaking likd a leaf. Lost my bayanut, and ran out of wathr. I nearves and very jumpy, hop I last out until morning. I hope seveanly machine s guns ore oping up on our left flank there going over our heads.

"Sept. 16. this morning we going in to take up new possissons we march all moring and I am very week and nerves, we marched up a hill and ran in to the affaul place y and z company lost so many men I hardly new what I was doing then I'm going nuts.

"Sept. 17. don't remember much of this day.

"Sept. 18. Today I'm on a ship leaving this awful place, called Green Hell. I'm still nerves and shakey."(Stern, 1947, pp. 583–86)

In the Vietnam war, soldiers were seldom exposed to prolonged periods of shelling and bombardment; combat reactions were typically more sudden and acute as a result of some particular overwhelming combat experience.

In the recorded cases of combat exhaustion among soldiers in all of those wars, the common core was usually overwhelming anxiety. In comparison, it is interesting to note that, in most cases, wounded soldiers have shown less anxiety or other combat exhaustion symptoms—ex-

cept in cases of permanent mutilation. Apparently the wound, in providing an escape from the stressful combat situation, removes the source of the anxiety. A similar finding was reported among Israeli soldiers hospitalized during the Yom Kippur war.[2] Those soldiers hospitalized for physical injuries—even severe ones such as paralysis or loss of limb—showed no appreciable psychological disturbances. In contrast, those hospitalized because of psychiatric problems—such as severe symptoms of depression, thought disorders, and obsessiveness—were quite disturbed about their physical symptoms, even minor ones—more so than the seriously physically injured (Merbaum & Hefez, 1976).

In fact, it has not been unusual for a soldier to admit that he has prayed to be hit or to have something "honorable" happen to remove him from battle. Upon approaching full recovery and the necessity of returning to combat, an injured soldier may sometimes show prolongation of his symptoms or a delayed traumatic reaction of nervousness, insomnia, and other symptoms that were nonexistent when he was first hospitalized.

Causal factors in combat stress problems. In a combat situation, with the continual threat of injury or death and repeated narrow escapes, one's ordinary methods of coping are relatively useless. The adequacy and security feelings the individual has known in a relatively safe and dependable civilian world are completely undermined. As one combat medic in Vietnam expressed it,

"I was always afraid. In fact, I can't remember not being afraid. For one thing, a combat medic doesn't know what's happening. Especially at night, everybody screaming or moaning and calling, 'Medic, medic.' I always saw myself dying, my legs blown off, my brains spattered all about, shivering in shock, and talking madly. This is what I *saw* in reality." (Polner, 1968, p. 18)

However, we must not overlook the fact that in all the wars we have been discussing, 90 percent or more of the soldiers subjected to combat

---

[2]The Yom Kippur war began on October 6, 1973, the Jewish Holy Day of Atonement (Yom Kippur), when the Egyptian and Syrian forces attacked Israel in an effort to regain control of the Sinai Peninsula and the Golan Heights. A ceasefire was agreed to on October 23, and on November 11, a peace agreement calling for talks to resolve differences was signed.

have not become psychiatric casualties, although most of them have evidenced severe fear reactions and other symptoms of personality disorganization that were not serious enough to be incapacitating. In addition, many soldiers have tolerated almost unbelievable stress before they broke, while others became casualties under conditions of relatively slight combat stress.

Consequently, it appears that to understand traumatic reactions to combat, we need to look at the wars we have known and examine other factors such as constitutional predisposition, personal maturity, loyalty to one's unit, and confidence in one's officers—as well as stress.

1. *Biological factors.* Do constitutional differences in sensitivity, vigor, and temperament affect one's resistance to the stress of combat? The probabilities are that they do, but there is a dearth of actual evidence.

Factors about which we have more information are the conditions of battle that tax the soldier's physical stamina. Grinker and Spiegel described this vividly in a World War II study:

"Battle conditions are notoriously destructive to health. Frequently men must go for days without adequate sleep or rest. . . . The purely physiological effects of nearby blasts are also a factor. Many men are repeatedly subjected to minimal doses of blast. They are knocked over by the compression wave, or perhaps blown slightly off the ground, if they are lying prone. In some instances they are temporarily numbed or even stunned. . . . Lastly, the continued auditory irritation of constant explosions, bangs, snaps of machine guns, whines of artillery shells, rustle of mortars . . . wears down resistance."(1945, pp. 68–70)

Add other factors that have often occurred in combat situations—such as severe climatic conditions, malnutrition, and disease—to the strain of continual emotional mobilization, and the result is a general lowering of the individual's physical and psychological resistance to all stressors.

2. *Psychosocial factors.* A number of psychological and interpersonal factors may contribute to the overall stress load experienced by soldiers and predispose them to break down under the increased burden of combat. Such factors include a reduction in personal freedom, frustrations of all sorts, and separation from home and loved ones. Letters from home that create worry or hurt add to the soldier's already difficult ad-

justive burden—particularly since he is far away and helpless to take any action. A soldier who has withstood months of combat may break when he finds that his wife has been unfaithful, or when she stops writing. Central, of course, are the many stresses arising from the combat situation itself. Several of these combat stressors will be considered here.

a) Fear and anxiety. Although not all soldiers experience the same degree of threat and anxiety in combat situations, emergency mobilization of emotional resources continues as long as the crisis exists. With time, increasingly severe feelings of threat and anxiety usually occur as the soldier experiences narrow escapes and sees buddies killed or wounded.

The hypersensitivity shown in the startle reaction follows directly from this continued fear and anxiety. Consequently, the buzz of a fly or the striking of a match may produce marked overreactions. This hypersensitivity is, of course, intensified when the stimulus bears a direct association with some traumatic combat experience. A soldier who has been strafed by attacking planes may be terrified by the sight of approaching aircraft. As continued emotional mobilization and fatigue take their toll of adjustive resources, the common symptom of irritability makes its appearance and adds to the soldier's anxiety by making him aware of his diminishing self-control. In our normal lives, too, prolonged emotional stress and fatigue tend to increase irritability and keep our nerves "on edge."

Difficulties in falling asleep and other sleep disturbances are common accompaniments of fear and sustained emotional arousal, and in combat conditions, soldiers often go for days without adequate sleep (W. C. Menninger, 1948). However, the dynamic significance of the recurrent nightmares is not fully understood. How and why does the traumatic material become reactivated during sleep, when the soldier desperately needs quiet and rest? In some cases the repeated dreams are so terrifying that the soldier is even afraid to go to sleep. It may be, however, that the continual reliving of a traumatic battle experience in dreams gradually serves to discharge the anxiety associated with it and to desensitize the individual to the point where he can assimilate the experience.

Stupor or amnesia in severe combat exhaustion cases is thought to result from temporary repression, enabling the individual to avoid consciousness of the traumatic experience until its emotional intensity has cooled down to the point where he can tolerate memory of it. Here the defensive function of repression is clearly demonstrated, since the repressed material can be brought to consciousness in full detail under the influence of hypnosis or various drugs, such as sodium pentothal.

b) Strangeness, unpredictability, and inability to take action. Strangeness and unpredictability can be a source of severe threat and stress. When the soldier knows what to expect and what to do, the chances are much better of coming through with a minimum of psychological disorganization (Rachman, 1978). But even the best training cannot fully prepare a soldier for all the conditions of actual battle. The factor of unpredictability also partly explains the effectiveness of new "secret weapons" for which enemy soldiers are not prepared.

It appears that having some activity or duty to perform, even though it does not lessen the danger, provides an outlet for tension and thus helps the soldier keep his fear and anxiety within manageable limits. Conditions that necessitate immobilization in the face of acute danger can lower the soldier's stress tolerance.

c) The necessity of killing. Having to kill enemy soldiers and sometimes civilians can also be an important factor in combat reactions. Most of us have strong moral convictions against killing or injuring others, and for some soldiers it is psychologically almost impossible to engage in killing. In extreme cases, such soldiers may even be unable to defend themselves when attacked. In other instances, the soldiers engage in killing but later experience intense feelings of guilt, together with fear of retaliation and punishment.

A good fighter, a machine gunner, one day killed five of the enemy almost simultaneously. "His first reaction was elation—but suddenly he felt that it was wrong to enjoy this and thereupon developed anxiety with some depression, so severe that he was incapacitated." (Saul, 1945, p. 262)

Over time, soldiers may become habituated to killing enemy soldiers and may even take pride in it—perhaps as a job well done, a feeling reinforced by the praise of buddies. In this context, Lifton (1972) has referred to "numbed warfare," in which the enemy is reduced to nonhuman status—to "Huns" or "Gooks"—so the soldier can feel that he is merely getting rid of animals or scum or devils. This attitude was epitomized by the statement of an American officer in Vietnam that the mass slaughter of civilians by American soldiers at My Lai was "no big deal."

On the other hand, the soldier may come to see further combat as the means by which he will inevitably receive dreaded retaliation and punishment for his actions. Thus, anxiety arising out of combat experience may reflect not only a simple fear of death or mutilation but also emotional conflicts and guilt feelings generated by the experience of killing.

d) Length of combat duty. The longer a soldier is in combat, the more vulnerable—and more anxious—he is likely to feel. Although, as Tuohy (1967) found, most soldiers on their arrival in Vietnam had the notion of their invulnerability—that anyone but themselves was likely to get killed—they soon found that Vietnam was a dangerous place and that "war really is hell." This time of realization is when many soldiers show their first signs of anxiety. And after a soldier has been in combat and has seen many of his buddies killed and wounded as well as having had narrow escapes himself, he usually loses whatever feeling of invulnerability he may have had. Often the death of a buddy leads to a serious loss of emotional support as well as to feelings of guilt if the soldier cannot help feeling glad that it was his buddy and not himself who was killed. When a soldier has almost completed the number of missions or duration of duty necessary for rotation, he is particularly apt to feel that his "luck has run out" and that the next bullet will "have his name on it."

e) Personal characteristics. Any personality characteristics that lower the individual's resistance to stress or to particular types of stressors may be important in determining his reactions to combat. Personal immaturity—often stemming from parental overprotection—is commonly cited as making the soldier more vulnerable to combat stress.

In their study of personality characteristics of Israeli soldiers who had broken down in combat in the Yom Kippur war, Merbaum and Hefez (1976) found that over 25 percent had reported psychological treatment prior to the war and another 12 percent had experienced difficulties previously in the six-day Israeli-Arab war of 1967. Thus about 37 percent of these men had clear histories of some instability that may have predisposed them to breakdown under the special stress of war. On the other hand, the others—over 60 percent—had not shown earlier difficulties and would not have been considered to be at risk for such breakdown.

A background of personal maladjustment does not always make an individual a "poor risk" for withstanding the stresses of combat. Some individuals are so accustomed to anxiety that they can cope with it more or less automatically, whereas soldiers who are feeling severe anxiety for the first time may be terrified by the experience, lose their self-confidence, and go to pieces. It has also been observed that sociopaths, though frequently in trouble in the armed services during peacetime for disregarding rules and regulations, have often demonstrated good initiative and effective combat aggression against the enemy. However, the soldiers who function most effectively and are most apt to survive the rigors of combat usually come from backgrounds that fostered self-reliance, ability to function in a group, and ready adjustment to new situations (Bloch, 1969; Borus, 1974; Grinker, 1969; Lifton, 1972).

3. *Sociocultural factors.* General sociocultural factors that play an important part in determining an individual's adjustment to combat include clarity and acceptability of war goals, identification of the soldier with his combat unit, *esprit de corps*, and quality of leadership.

a) Clarity and acceptability of war goals. In general, the more concretely and realistically war goals can be integrated into the values of the individual in terms of "his stake" in the war and the worth and importance of what he is doing, the greater their supportive effect will be on him. The individual who is fighting only because he is forced to, or to "get the damned war over with," is not as effective and does not stand stress as well as the soldier who knows what he is fighting for and is convinced of its importance. Time and again soldiers who have felt strongly about the rightness of their cause and its vital importance to themselves and their loved ones have shown incredible endurance, bravery, and personal sacrifice under combat conditions.

b) Identification with combat unit. The soldier who is unable to identify himself with or take pride in his group lacks the feeling of "we-ness" that is a highly supportive factor in maintaining

Biological, psychosocial, and sociocultural factors—alone or in combination—may cause an individual to break down under the stress of combat.

stress tolerance. Lacking this, he stands alone, psychologically isolated and less able to withstand combat stress. In fact, the stronger the sense of group identification, the less chance that the soldier will crack up in combat.

When a soldier has been removed because of combat exhaustion, he often returns to his unit with feelings of apprehension that his unit will not accept him or have confidence in him in the future (Tuohy, 1968). If the group does accept him, he is likely to make a satisfactory readjustment to further combat; if it does not, he is highly vulnerable to subsequent breakdown.

c) Esprit de corps. Closely related to group identification is *esprit de corps,* the morale of the group as a whole. The spirit of the group seems to be contagious. When the group is generally optimistic and confident prior to battle, the individual is also apt to show good morale. If the unit has a reputation for efficiency in battle, the individual soldier is challenged to exhibit his maximum effort and efficiency.

On the other hand, when the unit is demoralized or has a history of defeats and a high loss of personnel, the individual is likely to succumb more easily to anxiety and panic. This is particularly true if there is also a lack of confidence in leaders or in the importance of immediate combat objectives.

d) Quality of leadership. Confidence in military leaders is of vital importance. When the soldier in a combat situation respects his leaders, has confidence in their judgment and ability, and can accept them as relatively strong father or brother figures, his morale and resistance to stress are bolstered. On the other hand, lack of confidence or dislike of leaders is detrimental to morale and to combat stress tolerance.

Several other supportive factors merit brief mention. The "buddy system," in which the individual is encouraged to develop a close personal relationship with another member of his unit, often provides needed emotional support. The pursuit of short-range military objectives appears, in general, to cause less stress than the pursuit of long-range ones, where there always seems to be another hill or town to take. Finally, hatred of the enemy apparently tends to raise the combat soldier's stress tolerance.

Importance of early intervention. In most cases the decompensation brought on by the acute stress of combat conditions has been quickly reversed when the soldier has been taken out of combat and given brief therapy—usually warm food, sedation to help him get some rest, and supportive psychotherapy.

In World War II, many men were able to return to combat after a night or two of rest. Soldiers whose symptoms proved resistant to such treatment were evacuated to medical facilities behind the lines. It was found, however, that the farther the soldier was removed from the combat area, the less likely he was to be able to return to battle. Removal to a remote area seemed to encourage the maintenance of symptoms and a reluctance to return to his unit. During the first combat engagements of American forces in North Africa, combat exhaustion cases were transported to base hospitals hundreds of miles behind the battle lines; under these conditions less than 10 percent of the soldiers were able to return to duty (W. C. Menninger, 1948). In contrast, approximately 60 percent of those treated immediately within fifteen to twenty miles of the front lines were sent back to combat duty, and apparently the majority readjusted successfully (Ludwig & Ranson, 1947). Such statistics varied, however, ranging from a high of 80 to 90 percent returning to duty where the soldiers were from units with only a month or so of combat, down to 30 to 35 percent for "old" divisions.

Comparable statistics were obtained in the Korean war, with some 65 to 75 percent of the U.S. soldiers treated at the division level or forward being returned to combat duty, and less than 10 percent of those showing up as repeaters (Hausman & Rioch, 1967). Statistics on the effective management of combat-related stress disorders in the Vietnam war are not entirely clear. Early reports of the percentage of soldiers who responded favorably to immediate treatment appeared to show even higher success rates for the soldiers in Vietnam than for the soldiers in Korea (Allerton, 1970; Bloch, 1969). Yet recent evidence suggests that the intervention practices in Vietnam may not have reduced later adjustment problems much better than the methods employed in Korea. Adjustment problems among both groups appear to be comparable (Thienes-Hontos, Watson, & Kucala, 1982).

The lessons learned in World War II were translated in the Korean and Vietnam wars into the principles of *immediacy, proximity,* and *expectancy. Immediacy* refers to the early detection of signs of combat exhaustion, such as sleeplessness, tremulousness, and crying spells, and the removal of the soldier for immediate treatment. *Proximity* refers to the treatment of the soldier as near as possible to his combat unit and the battle zone. *Expectancy* refers to (a) a "duty-expectant" attitude—the attitude that anxiety, fear, and tension are not conditions of sufficient severity to require permanent removal from battle and that every soldier, despite anxieties and traumatic experiences, is expected to perform combat duties; and (b) the removal, insofar as possible, of any gain to the soldier from maintaining these symptoms—for example, reassignment to noncombatant duty when not fully justified—such as apparently occurred in World War II.

This kind of three-pronged approach on the part of treatment personnel—who often were themselves in the forward area under enemy fire—reminded the soldier in Vietnam or Korea that he was a morally responsible person who could hold up as the going got tougher and perform his combat duties despite his fear and tension. In essence, personal responsibility and a "doing role" were stressed rather than a "sick role." The result was that most soldiers found themselves able to bear much more stress than they would have believed possible and that the number of combat exhaustion cases declared unfit for further combat duty was minimized.

Residual effects of severe stress. In some cases, the residual effects of combat exhaustion persist for a sustained period of time (see **HIGHLIGHT** on this page). In other cases, soldiers may develop psychological problems for the first time after they leave the armed forces. For example, some soldiers who have stood up exceptionally well under intensive combat experiences have reportedly developed what might be called "delayed combat reactions"—or delayed posttraumatic stress disorder—upon their return home, often in response to relatively minor stresses in the home situation that they had previously been capable of handling. Evidently these soldiers have suffered some long-term damage to their adaptive capabilities, in some cases complicated by memories of killing enemy soldiers or civilians, tinged with feelings of guilt and anxiety (Haley, 1978; Horowitz & Solomon, 1978; Polner, 1968).

Shatan (1978) found six common responses among Vietnam veterans being treated for posttraumatic stress: (a) guilt feelings and self-punishment; (b) feelings of being scapegoated; (c) rage and other violent impulses against indiscriminate targets; (d) loss of sensitivity and compassion; (e) alienation of their feelings about themselves; and (f) mistrust of and doubts of love toward others. He illustrated the posttraumatic stress disorder among American soldiers who served in Vietnam with the story of Dwight Johnson, who was killed in a robbery attempt in Detroit after winning the Medal of Honor in Vietnam:

"Jon Nordheimer's front-page *New York Times* story [1971] sensitively described Sgt. Dwight Johnson's apathy and alienation, his demoralization by unemployment, and his suspicion that he was being exploited by the army, even when he was in the hospital. His government's highest martial honor weighed heavily around his neck each time he was praised for slaughter—and thereby forced to recall that he was the sole survivor of his tank crew, buddies during eleven months of warfare. While the army used him in recruiting drives, empty promise piled upon empty promise and his cynicism grew.

"Johnson had been placed in restraints and narcotized for 24 hours immediately after his final day of combat—the action for which he received the supreme distinction. Yet, 48 hours later, he was back in the U. S. with a non-psychiatric discharge. His emotional difficulties received no official interest until he became a 'hot property.' His treatment began more than a year after his return home, at the Valley Forge Army

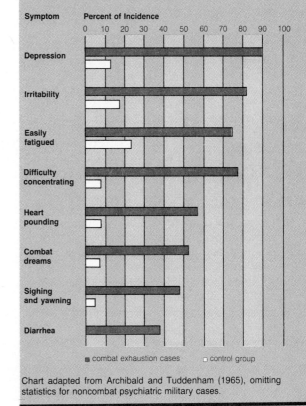

HIGHLIGHT
Residual effects of combat exhaustion among outpatients at a VA clinic

Twenty years after the end of World War II Archibald and Tuddenham (1965) made a follow-up study of residual effects of combat exhaustion in 62 combat exhaustion cases. This chart compares the incidence of several symptoms in this group and in 20 veterans who had not suffered combat exhaustion during the war. In addition to the symptoms listed here, the more severe combat exhaustion cases revealed various other symptoms, including difficulties in work and family relationships, social isolation, and narrowing of interests. Alcoholism was a problem for about 20 percent of both groups.

In many cases, symptoms had appeared to clear up when the stress was over, only to reappear in chronic form later. It seems evident that intense and sustained stress can lead to lasting symptoms even if the victims receive follow-up care. Although the combat exhaustion veterans were receiving assistance at a Veterans Administration outpatient psychiatric clinic, they were not receiving additional disability compensation as a result of prolonged stress reaction.

Chart adapted from Archibald and Tuddenham (1965), omitting statistics for noncombat psychiatric military cases.

Hospital. There he was diagnosed as suffering from 'depression caused by post-Vietnam adjustment problems.'

"On several occasions, he asked his psychiatrist how society would react if he were to respond to the black dilemma in Detroit with the same uncontrolled ferocity that had earned him the highest recognition in battle. He found his ultimate answer, not in a distant jungle but on the floor of a hometown grocery. There he lived out his haunting fantasies and nightmares of being killed at point-blank range." (pp. 46–47)

Similarly, in a follow-up study of ninety-two combat veterans of the Vietnam war, Polner (1968) cited a number of cases in which combat experiences continued to disturb the men after their return to civilian life. In most instances the difficulties appeared to center around guilt feelings over killing. For example, one veteran said, "I can't sleep, I'm a murderer." He continued,

"We were outside Bac Lieu, out on an eight-man patrol along with 15 ARVNs [South Vietnamese soldiers]. Our orders were to move ahead and shoot at anything suspicious. My God, how I remember that damned day! It was hot and sticky. The mosquitoes were driving me crazy. And there was this boy, about 8 or 9. He had his hand behind his back, like he was hiding something. 'Grab him,' someone screamed, 'he's got something!' I made a move for him and his hand moved again. 'Shoot!' I fired. Again and again, until my M-2 was empty. When I looked he was there, all over the ground, cut in two with his guts all around. I vomited. I wasn't told, I wasn't trained for that. It was out-and-out murder. . . .

"You know I killed nine people as an adviser." (p. 12)

Many of the other veterans interviewed by Polner, however, felt that they had simply done their duty in a worthwhile cause.

In another study of Vietnam returnees, Strange and Brown (1970) compared combat and noncombat veterans who were experiencing emotional difficulties. The combat group showed a higher incidence of depression and of difficulties in their close interpersonal relationships. They also showed a higher incidence of aggressive and suicidal threats but did not actually carry them out. In a later study of veterans of Vietnam who were making a satisfactory readjustment to civilian life, DeFazio, Rustin, and Diamond (1975) found that the combat veterans *still* reported certain symptoms twice as often as the noncombat veterans. Based on a

questionnaire checklist obtained from 207 veterans who had been out of the armed forces for over 5 years, DeFazio et al. found the following percentages of combat veterans still reporting symptoms: (a) frequent nightmares—68 percent; (b) considers self a hothead—44 percent; (c) many fears—35 percent; (d) worries about employment—35 percent; (e) difficulties with emotional closeness—35 percent; (f) tires quickly—32 percent.

More recent studies aimed at clarifying the effects of combat stress on postmilitary adjustment tend to support the earlier findings. Penk et al. (1981) studied veterans in treatment at two inpatient alcohol-drug treatment centers; they found that, as a group, the combat veterans were having more difficulties than noncombat veterans in social and intimate relationships, and in their ability to express feelings, trust other people, and control their tempers. Roberts et al. (1982) found these same problems in a group of combat-experienced veterans who had been diagnosed as having posttraumatic stress disorder. Interestingly, in the Penk et al. study, though the combat veterans were obviously having substantial difficulties, they did not show, on personality scales measuring general level of adjustment, significantly more disturbance than noncombat veterans. This suggests that their adjustment problems may reflect more difficulty with personal *relationships* than with their own long-term personality *characteristics*.

Often posttraumatic stress symptoms appear to be exacerbated by stimuli associated with the soldier's combat experiences. For example, two combat veterans reported that each time the temperature in their apartments rose to about 75 to 80 degrees Fahrenheit, they experienced an increase in terrifying nightmares (DeFazio et al., 1975). In some cases, one significant incident may precipitate a chronic reaction, as described in the **HIGHLIGHT** on page 179.

It is not known why some soldiers suffer from posttraumatic stress while others do not. Worthington (1978) found that U.S. soldiers who experienced problems readjusting after their return home from the Vietnam war also tended to have had greater difficulties before and during their military service than soldiers who adjusted readily.

It would appear, too, that returning to an unaccepting social environment can increase a soldier's vulnerability to posttraumatic stress. For

HIGHLIGHT
A case of posttraumatic stress disorder

The posttraumatic stress disorder can occur as a reactivation of previously experienced traumatic events. A recent case reported by Christenson et al. (1981) shows how a recent event may "trigger" past traumas and result in serious adjustment problems.

"Mr. A. a 55-year-old divorced man, was admitted with severe anxiety, multiple somatic complaints, feelings of hopelessness, somatovegetative signs of depression, and suicidal ideations. He had required psychiatric hospitalization for "nerves" shortly after his discharge from the service at the end of World War II. He subsequently had a good adjustment and a stable marriage and work history. Three years before this admission Mr. A abruptly left his job as an emergency room technician and began drinking heavily. Eventually his wife left him, and the actual signing of divorce papers precipitated the symptoms that led to his admission.

"It was only after another patient on the ward began talking of his difficulties during World War II that Mr. A revealed the following history. He had been stationed in the South Pacific and had survived two battles in which his ship had been destroyed and many people around him violently killed. Shortly after these events his unit was instructed that island children were being wired as human bombs, and an order was issued to shoot all children approaching the camp. When Mr. A was on duty, he had been forced to shoot a 10-year-old boy. After this incident Mr. A began having nightmares of exploding shells, violent scenes of people being killed, and scenes of himself killing the boy. These cleared over a period of a few years.

"Mr. A's recent deterioration (3 years ago) came after an episode at work in the emergency room where he was told to clean up a child in one of the rooms. He was unaware that the child (a 9-year-old boy) was already dead when he was brought to the emergency room. When Mr. A discovered that the boy was dead, he was horrified, left work, and never returned. His nightmares resumed, but he felt unable to discuss these war episodes with his wife. At times he would wake up screaming and throw his wife to the floor to "cover" her from exploding shells. It was this unexplained behavior that forced their separation.

"During this hospital stay Mr. A was able to talk about these war episodes for the first time in 35 years. He actively participated in a small therapy group of World War II veterans that focused on the veterans ventilating their feelings about traumatic war experiences. Mr. A was also treated with 150 mg h.s. of doxepin.

"Gradually Mr. A's depression cleared, and he claimed he was less anxious than at any time since the war. He was sleeping through the night without nightmares. Mr. A made appropriate arrangements to resume his most recent job and had an optimistic view of the future. He identified the opportunity to openly discuss his war experiences as the most important factor in his recovery." (p. 984)

example, in a one-year follow-up of Israeli men who had been psychiatric war casualties from the Yom Kippur war, Merbaum (1977) found that they not only continued to show extreme anxiety, depression, and extensive physical complaints, but in many instances they appeared to have become more disturbed over time. Merbaum hypothesized that their psychological deterioration had probably been due to the unaccepting attitudes of the community: in a country so reliant upon the strength of its army for its survival, there is considerable stigma attached to psychological breakdown in combat. Because of the stigma, many of the men were experiencing not only isolation from their com-munity, but also self-recrimination about what they perceived as failure on their own part. These feelings only exacerbated the soldiers' already stressful situation.

The nature and extent of the delayed post-traumatic stress syndrome are somewhat controversial. Reported cases of delayed stress syndrome among Vietnam combat veterans are often difficult to relate explicitly to combat stress since these individuals may also be having other significant adjustment problems as well. Individuals experiencing difficulties in adjustment may erroneously attribute their present problems to specific incidents from their past, i.e., experiences in combat. In recent times, the wide publicity given to the "delayed poststress syndrome" make it easy for patient's and clinicians to "find" a precipitating cause in the patient's background; indeed, the frequency with which this disorder has recently been diagnosed in some settings suggests that its increased usage may, in part, come as much from its plausibility and popularity as from its true incidence.

Reactions of prisoners of war and concentration-camp survivors

One of the best descriptions of reactions to the difficult situation of being a prisoner of war is that of Commander Nardini, an eyewitness and participant, who described the effects of imprisonment and mistreatment of American soldiers following the fall of Bataan and Corregidor during the early part of World War II.

"Our national group experience accustoms us to protection of individual rights and recourse to justice. The members of this group found themselves suddenly deprived of name, rank, identity, justice, and any claim to being treated as human beings. Although physical disease and the shortages of food, water, and medicine were at their highest during this period, emotional shock and reactive depression . . . undoubtedly contributed much to the massive death rate during the first months of imprisonment.

"Conditions of imprisonment varied from time to time in different places and with different groups. In general there was shortage, wearisome sameness, and deficiency of food; much physical misery and disease; squalid living conditions; fear and despair; horrible monotony . . . inadequate clothing and cleansing facilities; temperature extremes; and physical abuse.

". . . Hungry men were constantly reminded of their own nearness to death by observing the steady, relentless march to death of their comrades. . . . Men quibbled over portions of food, were suspicious of those who were in more favored positions than themselves, participated in unethical barter, took advantage of less clever or enterprising fellow prisoners, stole, rummaged in garbage, and even curried the favor of their detested captors. There was a great distortion of previous personality as manifested by increased irritability, unfriendliness, and sullen withdrawal. . . . Hungry, threatened men often found it difficult to expand the horizon of their thinking and feeling beyond the next bowl of rice. . . .

"Disease was abundant . . . fever, chills, malaise, pain, anorexia, abdominal cramps from recurrent malaria (acquired in combat), and dysentery plagued

nearly all and killed thousands. . . . most men experienced bouts of apathy or depression. These ranged from slight to prolonged deep depressions where there was a loss of interest in living and lack of willingness or ability to marshal the powers of will necessary to combat disease. An ever present sign of fatal withdrawal occurred 3 to 4 days before death when the man pulled his covers up over his head and lay passive, quiet, and refusing food.

". . . One of the most distressing features was the highly indefinite period of imprisonment. The future offered only visions of continued hunger, cold, disease, forced labor, and continued subservience in the face of shouting, slappings, and beatings. . . . Strong hostility naturally arose from the extreme frustration. . . . Little could be done with these hostile feelings. . . . It was not possible to demonstrate recognizable signs of hostility to the captors for obvious reasons. Therefore, where there were mixed groups of Allied prisoners, much hostility was turned from group to group and in other instances to individuals within the group. . . . In many cases hostile feelings were obviously turned inward and joined with appropriate feelings of frustration to produce serious waves of depression. . . . Self pity, in which some indulged, was highly dangerous to life. . . ."(Nardini, 1952, pp. 241–44)

A common syndrome manifested by POW's during the Korean war was delineated by Farber, Harlow, and West (1956). They referred to this syndrome as "DDD"—debility, dependency, and dread. *Debility* was induced by semistarvation, disease, and fatigue, and led to a sense of terrible weariness and weakness. *Dependency* was produced by a variety of techniques, including the use of solitary confinement, the removal of leaders and other accustomed sources of support, and occasional and unpredictable respites that reminded the prisoners that they were completely dependent on their captors for what happened to them. *Dread* was described as a stage of chronic fear that their captors attempted to induce—fear of death, of pain, of nonrepatriation, and of permanent deformity or disability due to neglect or inadequate medical treatment. The net effect of these conditions was a well-nigh intolerable state of mental and physical discomfort that rendered the men more amenable to brainwashing.

In the Vietnam war, soldiers were better prepared in terms of what to expect and what to do in the event of capture. Consequently they fared much better, in general, than did the POWs of earlier wars. However, for some, the experience was too much to bear. For example, Kushner

For many former POWs, the bright promise of a happy return to family and home was fulfilled. But others found that joy soon turned to bitterness as they struggled to pick up the threads of their past lives.

(1973)—a medical doctor and fellow prisoner—reported that two of the twenty-two men in a Viet Cong POW camp in which conditions were particularly bad simply gave up and died.

Even men who were well adjusted prior to captivity in Vietnam developed problems of maladjustment as a result of being imprisoned. Ursano, Boydstun, and Wheatley (1981) conducted an extensive evaluation of 325 air force officers upon their repatriation from North Vietnam and subsequently followed up 253 of them for a period of five years after their release. In spite of the fact that these airmen had all been generally well-educated officers who had been previously screened for psychological adjustment, many of them showed psychological adjustment problems after their release. Over 23 percent of them were given psychiatric diagnoses following their extensive psychological evaluation. When their length of captivity was taken into account, those men who had been imprisoned longest (i.e., taken captive before 1969) had the greatest percentage of formal diagnoses (27.1 percent) while only 17.1 percent of those captured after 1969 had received formal diagnoses. Apparently the severity of stress, measured both by the length of imprisonment and the harshness of treatment (men captured before 1969 were treated most cruelly), contributed to the development of psychological problems among the POWs.

Descriptions of prisoners in Nazi concentration camps, who were subjected to even more inhuman and sadistic conditions, emphasize the psychological toll of the experience. (Bettelheim, 1943, 1960; Chodoff, 1970; Eitinger, 1961, 1962, 1969; Frankl, 1963; Friedman, 1948; Hafner, 1968). Inmates of concentration camps also showed greater use of the defense mechanisms of denial and isolation of affect. The feeling that "This isn't really happening to me" was widespread. Chodoff (1970) has cited the case of a young prisoner "who would not see the corpses she was stepping over" and the even more poignant picture "of her fellow inmates who refused to believe that the smoke arising from the crematorium chimneys came from the burning corpses of their mothers" who had been selected—because of age—to be killed first. Isolation of affect apparently reached the degree of almost total emotional anesthesia in the case Chodoff cited of a young female prisoner who stated "I had no feelings whatsover" while being stripped naked and having all her hair shaved off in front of SS troopers (p.83).

Concentration-camp inmates also tended to form hopes of deliverance via miraculous events, possibly because their situation was even more hopeless than that of the POWs, and any hope would have been unrealistic.

The most obvious causal factors in all these reactions to long-continued stressful situations are, of course, the environmental stressors—the conditions in the environment whose demands, over a period of time, are too great for comfortable accommodation. But the unusual stressors are not the whole story. Here, as in the case of other disorders, the individual's reaction depends on the whole pattern of biological, psychosocial, and sociocultural factors.

Some individuals adjust with a minimum of strain to the same situations that are too much for others. Likewise, a supportive group increases the individual's ability to withstand stress. But in any event, the past shows us that the toll is great. About half of the American prisoners in Japanese POW camps during World War II died during their imprisonment; an even higher number of prisoners of Nazi concentration camps died. Among those who survived the ordeal, there was often residual organic as well as psychological damage and a lowering of tolerance to stress of any kind.

Without question, the "reentry problem" has been a difficult one for former POWs and concentration-camp survivors as they have tried to adjust to the sudden and major changes in their world, as well as to social changes that took place during their imprisonment.

The residual damage to survivors of Nazi concentration camps was often extensive and commonly included anxiety, insomnia, headaches, irritability, depression, nightmares, impaired sexual potency, and "functional" diarrhea (that is, diarrhea that occurs in any situation of stress, even relatively mild stress). Such symptoms were attributed not only to the psychological stressors of concentration-camp experiences but also to biological stressors, such as head injuries, prolonged malnutrition, and serious infectious diseases (Eitinger, 1964, 1969, 1973; Sigal et al., 1973; Warnes, 1973).

Among returning POWs, psychological problems were often masked by the feelings of relief and jubilation that accompanied release from confinement. Even when there was little evidence of residual physical pathology, however, survivors of prisoner-of-war camps commonly showed impaired resistance to physical illness, low frustration tolerance, frequent dependence on alcohol and drugs, irritability, and other indications of emotional instability (Chambers, 1952; Goldsmith & Cretekos, 1969; Hunter, 1978; Strange & Brown, 1970; Wilbur, 1973).

Another measure of the toll taken by the prolonged stress of being in a POW or concentration camp was the higher death rate after return to civilian life (see **HIGHLIGHT** on this page). Among returning POWs from the Pacific area af-

HIGHLIGHT
Failure to readjust after captivity: a tragic ending

When the POWs held in North Vietnam were finally released in 1973, most Americans felt relieved that the Asian war was at last over. The prisoners who returned—some after many years of captivity—were welcomed back into society. But a few of the returning prisoners found the United States to be as hostile an environment as the North Vietnamese camp.

One such soldier, Jerry L., returned to the United States to find himself facing charges of collaboration with the enemy and the possibility of a military court martial. His alleged behavior during captivity had received adverse publicity, and Jerry's friends and relatives reacted by treating him with coldness and suspicion. Shortly after his return, Jerry died of self-inflicted gunshot wounds.

Two psychologists were asked by the district attorney's office to construct a "psychological autopsy" to clear up the circumstances surrounding the unexpected death. In conducting their investigation, Selkin and Loya (1979) encountered resistance from Jerry's family and from the military. Jerry's wife and other family members believed that the government had mistreated Jerry and that his death was related to the military's lack of support and medical attention plus the extreme anxiety caused by the charges of collaboration. As a result, the family was at first reluctant to provide information about Jerry's early life, though they later became more cooperative. Meanwhile, military officials initially refused to release Jerry's records—though they, too, finally decided to cooperate.

Selkin and Loya discovered that Jerry had been following what appeared to be a "suicidal life course that had begun long before the war in Vietnam" (p. 89). Jerry had long tended to drink heavily when under stress and had a history of delinquency and other maladjustments. Despite this, the military had provided Jerry with little psychiatric attention after his release. Although he spoke briefly with a "partially trained" psychiatrist, he was not offered psychological help or a psychiatric follow-up after he returned home. It was apparent that "no one in any official capacity made an honest attempt to understand him or take a careful look at his life situation" (p. 90).

This investigation indicates both the relationship of prior psychological problems to adjustment after captivity and the importance of the environment to the successful repatriation of prisoners of war. A few days after the psychological autopsy, the government dropped all charges against other POWs who had been accused of collaborating with the enemy.

ter World War II, Wolff (1960) found that within the first six years, nine times as many died from tuberculosis as would have been expected in civilian life, four times as many from gastrointestinal disorders, over twice as many from cancer, heart disease, and suicide, and three times as many from accidents. Comparable figures have been reported for concentration-camp survivors by Eitinger (1973).

Aware that problems may show up years after release, military psychologists and psychiatrists have been following representative groups of Vietnam war POWs on a long-term basis with checkups every year. These former POWs differ from those in earlier wars in that they were almost all flight crew personnel, which meant they were officers and somewhat older than the rank-and-file combat personnel. In the examination made two years after their return, it was found that the longer the imprisonment, the more predisposed the individual to psychiatric problems (O'Connell, 1976). Other factors that seemed to predispose soldiers to later problems were harshness of POW treatment and isolation (Hunter, 1976). The most frequent problems requiring psychological help were depression and marital difficulties (Hunter, 1978, 1981).

A great deal has been written about the long-term adjustment problems of concentration-camp survivors. Some writers, for example Krystal (1968) and Niederland (1968), who based their views on the survivors of the death camps who later sought psychological treatment, have contended that concentration-camp survivors carry psychological scars with them for the rest of their lives. Other writers have concluded that these emotional scars are so profound that they can be transmitted to the survivors' children (Schneider, 1978; Epstein, 1979).

We must bear in mind, however, that most of the conclusions about the psychopathology in concentration-camp survivors and their children are based upon cases of people who are undergoing or have undergone psychotherapy. While the observations of the writers may have a great deal of validity for particular individuals and may support the idea that some people do not deal effectively with life after experiencing an extremely stressful event, these clinical studies cannot be viewed as representative. The biased nature of the sample (psychotherapy patients) precludes generalization about concentration-camp survivors in general.

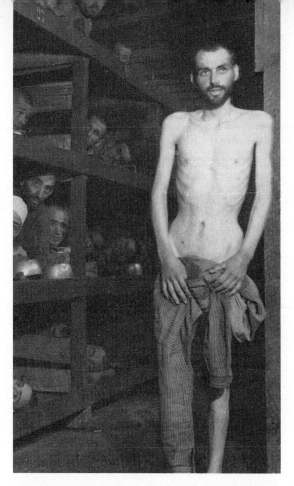

The physical stresses and psychological horrors of life in concentration camps left permanent scars on many of those who survived the ordeal.

Few reports have dealt with the psychological adjustment of subjects who are broadly representative of concentration-camp survivors and have employed an appropriate control group in the study. A recent study by Leon et al. (1981) examined personality characteristics of concentration-camp survivors and their children nearly 35 years after their release from the camps and compared their personality patterns, as measured by the MMPI, with an appropriate control group (European Jews who managed to escape the Holocaust) and their children. Considering the ordeal they experienced, most of the survivors had apparently adapted quite well and showed no general personality adjustment problems when compared with the control group. Similarly, the children of survivors showed no general adjustment problems when compared with children of control subjects. These findings attest to the great strength and resilience of these individuals in adapting to life problems following a most horrifying experience.

Prevention of stress disorders

If we know that extreme or prolonged stress can produce maladaptive psychological reactions that have a predictable course, is it possible to intervene in the situation early in the process to *prevent* the development of emotional disorder? When it is known that an unusually stressful situation is about to occur, is it possible to "inoculate" the individual by providing information about it ahead of time and suggesting some possible ways of coping with it? If preparation for the stressors of battle can help soldiers avoid breakdown, why not prepare people from all walks of life to competently meet anticipated special stressors?

Janis did just this with patients about to undergo dangerous surgery. His findings have provided a substantial base for preventive efforts aimed at reducing emotional problems of patients following their surgery (Janis, 1958; Janis et al., 1969).

Janis (1958) conducted interviews before and after the surgery to determine the relationship between level of preoperative fear and level of adjustment after the surgery. He found that patients with moderate fear did better than those with either high or low fear. Those who greatly worried about suffering pain or being mutilated by the surgery exhibited, after surgery, extreme anxiety, emotional outbursts, and fearfulness about participating in postoperative treatment. Those who showed very little anticipatory fear displayed afterward an acute preoccupation with their vulnerability and were often angry and resentful toward the staff for being "mistreated." Those, on the other hand, who were moderately fearful before surgery were the most cheerful and cooperative in the postoperative treatment.

An important finding in Janis' work is that the individual who is outwardly calm and appears to feel invulnerable to real danger is likely to have more postcrisis problems than individuals who have been "part-time worriers" beforehand.

Janis suggests that the "work of worrying" may involve processes similar to the "work of mourning" following bereavement. In this case,

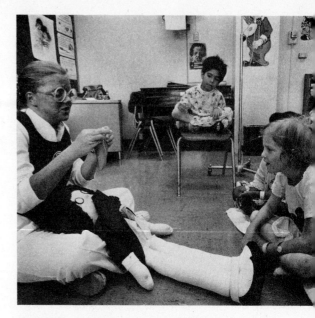

Nurses at the University of Illinois Hospital use Annie Anatomy to explain what happens during surgery. The doll, whose heart, lungs, stomach, bladder, liver, kidneys, intestines, ribs, and arm bones can be removed, helps the children overcome their fear and stress.

however, it is accomplished before the trauma, helping the individual understand and "work through" the dangerous and aversive situation and be emotionally ready to adjust to it when it comes. Later studies, too, have shown that when patients are prepared for the experience of surgery by being given accurate information about the procedures and a warning about the pain and discomfort they will experience, they are less likely to experience a severe emotional reaction following surgery (Egbert et al., 1964).

Work in cognitive-behavioral therapy has also focused on "stress inoculation" training to prepare individuals for difficult events they will be facing (MacDonald & Kuiper, 1983; Meichenbaum & Cameron, 1983; Meichenbaum, Turk, & Burstein, 1975). Here individuals are prepared to tolerate an anticipated threat by changing the things they say to themselves before the crisis.

A three-stage process is employed. The first provides information about the stressful situation and about ways people can deal with such dangers. In the second phase, self-statements that promote effective adaptation—for example, "Don't worry, this little pain is just part of the treatment"—are rehearsed. In the third phase, the individual practices making such self-statements while being exposed to a variety of ego-threatening or pain-threatening stressors, such as unpredictable electric shocks, stress-inducing films, or sudden cold. This last phase allows the person to apply the new coping skills learned earlier. We shall discuss stress-inoculation training and the use of self-statements in greater detail in Chapter 17.

Summary

Many factors influence an individual's response to stressful situations. The impact of stress depends not only on its severity but also on the individual's preexisting vulnerabilities. The individual's response to conflict situations may be viewed differently depending upon whether the conflict is approach-avoidant, double-approach, or double-avoidant. There is a wide variety of psychosocial stressors, and individuals will respond to them in different ways. In attempting to deal with stressful events, for instance, individuals may react with task-oriented or defense-oriented mechanisms. The effects of extreme or prolonged stress on the organism can bring about psychological decompensation.

The DSM-III diagnostic categories for classifying individual problems in response to stressful situations can be found in two different sections of the manual—in a section devoted to adjustment disorders and in a separate section included with the anxiety disorders. In the section on adjustment disorder, several categories are available for classifying psychological adjustment problems of mild severity. More intense psychological disorders in response to trauma or excessive stress—such as imprisonment, military combat, rape, and natural disasters—may be categorized as posttraumatic stress disorders (under the anxiety disorders section of DSM-III). These disorders may involve a variety of symptoms including intense anxiety, denial, repression, apathy, depression, and the lowering of ethical standards. In most cases the symptoms recede as the stress diminishes, especially if the individual is given brief supportive psychotherapy. However, in extreme cases, such as those involving excessive psychological stress, there may be residual damage or the disorder may actually not occur until some time after the trauma. Posttraumatic stress disorders may be described as acute, chronic, or delayed, depending upon the onset and duration of the symptoms.

In personality adjustment problems, several present-day life situations may produce a great deal of stress and psychological maladjustment: prolonged unemployment, loss of a loved one through death, marital separation or divorce, and forced migration.

Reactions to catastrophic life events—such as accidents, fires, and tornadoes—may also cause serious psychological problems, as in the "initial disaster syndrome." Individuals can make use of several mechanisms in their attempts to deal with the psychological effects of major calamities. The clinical picture of personality deterioration under excessive stress is well illustrated by examples from military combat, from traumatic imprisonment such as that which occurred in the Nazi concentration camps during World War II, and from the experience of POWs. Many factors are found to contribute to breakdown under excessive stress, including the intensity or harshness of the stress situation, the length of the traumatic event, the individual's biological makeup and personality adjustment prior to the stressful situation, and the ways his or her problems are managed once the stressful situation is over.

The treatment of stress-related psychological problems is most effective when intervention is applied early. Crisis intervention therapy, a brief problem-focused counseling approach, may aid the victim of a traumatic event in readjusting to life after the stressful situation has ended. In some situations it may be possible to prevent the maladaptive response to stress by preparing the individual in advance to deal with the stress. This approach to stress management has been shown to be effective in cases where the individual is facing a known traumatic event such as major surgery or the pending breakup of a relationship. In these cases, the professional attempts to prepare the individual in advance to better cope with the stressful event through developing more realistic and adaptive attitudes about the problem to be faced.

6

Anxiety-based disorders (neuroses)

The basic nature of the neurotic process

Neurotic anxiety

Neurotic paradox

Neurotic styles

The role of inhibition in neurotic styles

Interpersonal aspects of neurotic styles

Anxiety disorders

Generalized anxiety and panic disorders

Obsessive-compulsive disorder

Phobic disorder

Somatoform disorders

Somatization disorder

Hypochondriasis

Psychogenic pain disorder

Conversion disorder

Dissociative disorders

Psychogenic amnesia and fugue

Multiple personality

Depersonalization disorder

General causal factors, treatment, and outcomes

Development and maintenance of neurotic behaviors

Treatment and outcomes

Heinrich Müller, The Fly-Man and the Snake. *Müller (1865–1930), a Swiss vineyardist and amateur inventor, was institutionalized as a mental patient at the age of 41. In the hospital, he occupied his time by "experimenting" with bizarre, home-made machines and by drawing disturbing, hallucinatory sketches like the one shown here.*

In our discussion of stress and the individual's reaction to it, we dealt primarily with stable people who had been subjected to excessive stressor demands. In this chapter we shall look at disorders in which maladaptive learning, often in early development, has led to persistent feelings of threat and anxiety in facing the everyday problems of living. In these cases, ordinary methods of coping, including the "normal" use of ego-defense mechanisms, have proven inadequate, and the individual has come to rely increasingly on more extreme defensive reactions. While these defenses may help alleviate the acute feelings of threat and anxiety, they exact a high price in self-defeating behavior.

Although neurotic behavior is maladaptive, it does not involve gross distortion of reality or marked personality disorganization, nor is it likely to result in violence to the individual or to others. Rather, we are dealing here with individuals who are typically anxious, ineffective, unhappy, and often guilt-ridden; they do not ordinarily require hospitalization but nevertheless are in need of therapy. Incidence rates are difficult to determine, but it has been estimated that there are at least 20 million individuals in the United States who suffer from one of the many variants of neurotic disorder.

The term ***neurosis*** was coined by the Englishman William Cullen and first used in his *System of Nosology,* published in 1769, to refer to disordered sensations of the nervous system. It reflected the long-held belief that neurological malfunction must be involved in neurotic behavior. This belief endured until the time of Freud, himself a neurologist, who postulated that neurosis stemmed from intrapsychic conflict rather than disordered reactions in the nervous system. Specifically, Freud held that neurosis is the outcome of an inner conflict involving an unbearable wish (approach tendency of the id) and the ego's and superego's prohibitions against its expression (avoidance tendency). *Anxiety* in this formulation is a signal provided by the ego that a dangerous impulse has been activated.

The basic model, therefore, was one of approach-avoidance conflict (see p. 143). This view became widely accepted; significantly, however, it broadened the scope of behaviors considered to be neurotic—that is, any nonpsychotic disorder that might have psychological conflict at its base could be considered neurotic. In more recent years, the role of maladaptive learning to *avoid* anxiety has also been recognized in the origins of neurotic behavior.

Thus, the term "neurotic," though used loosely by the general public to refer to virtually any maladaptive behavior, actually has a quite specific meaning. It refers to those disorders in which inner psychological conflict, the anxiety it produces, and the resulting efforts of the individual to build defenses to "manage" the anxiety are thought to be central in causing the behavioral abnormality. In other words, the concept of neurosis involves a certain specific type of causal pattern and reaction. Yet some have found the concept objectionable as "too theoretical" since it refers to essentially unobservable inner states. In response to such objections, the authors of the DSM-III eliminated "neuroses" as a general category. In its place are the new categories of anxiety, somatoform, and dissociative disorders (to be discussed in this chapter). Our own view—and that of many in the field—is that abandonment of the concept of neurosis may have been premature (e.g., Gossop, 1981; Schumer, 1983). It has robust research and clinical support, and it remains a viable and useful way to conceptualize many of the behaviors to be described in this chapter.

We shall begin by considering the basic nature of the neurotic process. We shall then examine the concept of neurotic style and describe some fairly common neurotic living patterns, patterns that sometimes evolve into the more definitive symptomatic states of anxiety, somatoform, and dissociative disorders. Following a description of these clinical disorders, we shall move to a consideration of more specific causal factors, general methods of treatment, and treatment outcomes.

The basic nature of the neurotic process

The neurotic process can be seen as having a basic core consisting of an unusually severe type of fear response, in the special form of anxiety, together with inadequate and misdirected attempts on the individual's part to manage and control these extremely painful feelings. A typical outcome is that the individual not only fails to reduce the anxiety but actually, through misdirected efforts at resolution, renders it more complicated and self-sustaining. We shall deal with both anxiety and the central paradox of the neurotic process in the sections that follow.

Neurotic anxiety

Freud considered anxiety to be the "central problem" of neurosis, and most theorists since—while often heatedly disagreeing with him on other issues—have adopted essentially the same view (Fischer, 1970; Ryckman, 1978). Anxiety, always unpleasant, is, as it increases in intensity, one of the most painful of the emotions. It is essentially indistinguishable from fear in terms of the feelings experienced. But in fear, as conventionally conceived, we can identify *what* we are afraid of, and we have the reassurance that most other people faced with similar circumstances would be equally frightened. By contrast, the person experiencing anxiety has feelings of dread and apprehension that do *not* make sense to the average person, and often not to the person who is experiencing the anxiety. The anxious person behaves outwardly (and measurements of internal physiological indicators confirm this) as though he or she is terribly frightened, even terrified; yet no obvious external threat can be found that is proportional to the intensity of the reaction. Indeed, if a cause *is* identified by the clinically anxious person (that is, a person formally diagnosed by a clinician as being atypically anxious), it usually turns out to be some aspect of life or of the environment that most of us would regard as minor— for example, the necessity of entering a shopping mall. A fair number of neurotic persons would not be able to negotiate such a simple act because its mere contemplation would fill them with "irrational" terror.

The response of intense fearfulness, in itself, is well understood in terms of the evolution of the species. After all, there are many situations in which fear is adaptive—for example, in facilitating escape from a truly dangerous situation. Unfortunately, it appears that this "built-in" fear response pattern has evolved on a human level into one that is readily learned or acquired as a

People experiencing neurotic anxiety may show the same behaviors and physiological changes associated with fear or terror, reactions that are out of proportion to the actual external threat.

response to stimuli that are not only threatening but also nonthreatening. In other words, humans can easily be conditioned to fear harmless stimuli. This type of fear is called *anxiety.*

Evidently, few of us escape at least some such conditioning; most of us harbor some anxieties we could not readily explain to most of our peers. But, at the same time, most of us have developed ways of avoiding anxiety-producing situations—ways that are probably no more discernable to ourselves than to our associates. For example, the professor who is made anxious by lecturing may demand of his department more time for his research without becoming aware of the connection between this demand and his discomfort over lecturing. Yet most of us "muddle through" despite our irrational and unrecognized fears or anxieties. This chapter is concerned with those who, for one reason or another, do *not* learn to manage their anxieties in a way that permits them to remain fully functional.

Neurotic paradox

As we have seen, neurotic behavior has at its center some sort of inordinate anxiety response. This propensity to experience more or less severe anxiety causes the neurotic person to evaluate many everyday problems as threatening, and to resort in such situations to indirect, defensive maneuvers. These defense-oriented behaviors seriously interfere with effective coping and problem-solving, resulting in a self-defeating life-style that blocks personal growth and self-fulfillment. Usually, neurotic individuals have trouble establishing or maintaining satisfying interpersonal relationships, feel vaguely guilty for trying to avoid rather than cope with reality, and are dissatisfied and unhappy with their way of life.

Because the task of dealing with their anxieties tends to become the overriding concern of their lives, neurotic persons have little enthusiasm or energy for anything else. They become "wrapped up" in themselves and their problems, often confirming others' impressions of them as egocentric and unable to give even slight attention to the needs of others, including members of their own families.

The behavior of the neurotic individual, in fact, presents us with a paradox, one first noted by Freud. Namely, it seems on the surface to defy the basic expectation that all behavior is directed to the maximization of pleasure and the minimization of pain. The behavior of the typical neurotic, in contrast, seems to the external observer to be extremely maladaptive, to ensure that in the long run it can bring only grief to the person enacting it. We can dismiss such a paradox in the case of an individual who is psychotic—irrational over a broad range of behavior—but it is less easily dismissed in the neurotic individual, who in many areas of life may seem very much in touch with reality, and in certain cases even "super-rational," as in the case of many obsessive-compulsive neurotics who may ruminate for hours over trivial decisions.

The seeming paradox is resolved when we recognize that the self-defeating nature of neurotic behavior usually becomes clear only after some time has elapsed. By contrast, the *immediate* effect of the behavior is to reduce anxiety and permit the individual to retain a measure of psychic comfort in the present situation. But, because no long-range solution can be accomplished under these circumstances—and, in fact, since the typical effect of these defensive reactions is to make matters more complicated and less solvable—the neurotic person tends ultimately to get more deeply into trouble. The unfortunate consequences are due in no small measure to the fact that accurate perception of events is made difficult due to conditions of high anxiety and to the complications introduced by the person's neurotic attempts to contain the anxiety.

For example, let us take the case of an insecure young man who is very much in love and engaged to be married. His fiancée, however, abruptly breaks the engagement. He reacts with intense feelings of self-devaluation, anxiety, and depression, coupled with a considerable measure of hostility. Thereafter his behavior follows a new pattern. Whenever a relationship with a woman begins to get serious, he experiences anxiety and breaks it off. He has acquired a conditioned fear of close relationships with members of the opposite sex, and his anxiety and avoidance behavior do not permit him to try out the possibility that he might be more successful the next time. Thus the fear and avoidance behavior are maintained because they are reinforced by reduction of anxiety. Moreover, his defensive behavior, based on the expectation of rejection, tends to ensure that he will in fact be rejected.

Keeping these observations in mind, we now turn to a discussion of general neurotic styles. We will be concerned with the role played by inhibition in neurotic behavior, with certain common patterns of inhibition in neurotic styles, and with the manner in which these styles affect interpersonal relationships.

Neurotic styles

There has never been a precise equivalent to the concept of *"neurotic style"* in the formal DSM categories, nor is there likely to be, since these styles, as general "symptomless" ways of coping with anxiety, do not warrant the status of mental disorders. By "symptomless," we mean that neurotic styles do not entail disabilities that would be obvious to everyone. Rather, they involve general ways of behaving that interfere with the individual's effectiveness and ability to satisfy personal needs. We include them here for two reasons: (a) many individuals who seek the services of mental health practitioners are less troubled by specific clinical symptoms *per se* than by unsatisfactory interpersonal relationships caused by neurotic styles, as in the example given above; and (b) an understanding of neurotic styles should enhance our understanding of the established DSM categories of neurotic symptom disorders, since generalized neurotic behavior patterns often accompany these specific disorders. Concerning this point, Shapiro (1965) has written: "Every reader with clinical experience and, for that matter, every sensitive person will know that [neurotic] symptoms or outstanding pathological traits regularly appear in contexts of attitudes, interests, intellectual inclinations and endowments, and even vocational aptitudes and social affinities with which the given symptom or trait seems to have a certain consistency."(p. 3)

In other words, disabling neurotic symptoms are usually embedded within a broader context of related personal characteristics. As we shall see, many of these related characteristics seem to arise from the same sources as do the symptoms. An example at this point may help clarify.

A 30-year-old man, married and with two children, was referred to a psychologist because of a persistent paralysis of his left arm and hand. Though the paralysis had developed following an auto accident, there was no evidence of organic damage that would account for it. It was diagnosed as a "conversion disorder," to be described below. The history revealed that he had been very dependent on an aunt who had raised him but had subsequently died when he was 15. He responded by making a show of self-sufficiency, but his work history as an adult was marred by a series of dissatisfactions and changes of employment—primarily because he invariably grew to feel that not enough was being done for him by his employers. Prior to the accident, his marital relationship had also become disrupted because his wife, having become more independent, was spending less time at home. The patient had bitterly complained that she was not being a "good mother."

Despite making a somewhat halfhearted attempt to resolve his difficulties in psychotherapy, treatment progress was reported as very slow. The paralysis continued, and the patient appeared to have settled comfortably into the role of helpless victim. (Adapted from Spitzer et al., 1983)

We see here the interplay between the patient's life-style prior to the accident and the particular symptom he developed in response to increased stress and the "opportunity" the accident afforded. Dependency appeared to be the principal theme both before and afterward. As we shall see, neurotic dependency of this sort is usually the product of the *inhibition*, by anxiety, of independent, autonomous behavior (Hine, 1971; Hine et al., 1972, 1983). We turn now to a consideration of how inhibition functions in neurotic styles.

The role of inhibition in neurotic styles

As indicated earlier, a person can be conditioned to respond with anxiety (or fear) to certain nonnoxious stimuli. The person can then respond in the same way to other stimuli having similar properties. Once the anxiety response is established, the individual will learn to avoid the stimuli that provoke it. In the neurotic process, certain of the individual's own *behaviors,* or even the person's thoughts of engaging in them, will evoke the anxiety response. These anxiety-inspiring behaviors are then avoided or inhibited. Should they be important or essential for good adjustment, the affected person may be deprived of the means to function effectively in the world.

Let us suppose, for example, that a child is born to parents who do not tolerate aggressive behavior in any form, so much so that they repeatedly threaten to abandon their child any time she displays normal childhood levels of aggressive conduct. It is possible that such a child will learn to respond with strong anxiety to the more "aggressive" elements of her behavioral repertoire, or to any internal (i.e., motivational impulse) or external demand to act aggressively. In other words, she will have pronounced inhibitions with respect to aggression and perhaps even related behavior, such as normal assertiveness. Here we may introduce the notion of an inhibited behavior *system*—a whole cluster of related behaviors that act as anxiety-eliciting stimuli. Insofar as aggressive or assertive behaviors are in some situations appropriate and adaptive, there will be an important gap in a child's adaptive repertoire as he or she grows into adulthood.

The scenario given here is hypothetical, and we do not mean to suggest that all such anxieties are learned in this or comparable ways. In fact, it is often difficult to determine precisely the sources of a neurotic person's special fears concerning the enactment of certain types of behavior. We certainly cannot rule out a constitutional element as a possibility in some cases, and indeed Shapiro's (1965) discussion of neurotic styles strongly hints at constitutional origins.

In any event, as the above example illustrates, one important characteristic of a person adopting a neurotic style is that of a deficit in behavioral repertoire. That is, certain types of behavior that would seem adaptive and even expected in certain circumstances *do not occur.* They are blocked or inhibited by the anxiety their expression would cause. Two other characteristics often seen accompanying such deficits deserve brief mention, partly because of their importance as diagnostic clues. They are:

(a) A tendency for the person to behave, often with inflexibility and in an exaggerated manner, in ways that are the seeming opposite of the behaviors that are "missing." Evidently, this is a defense employed by the person to further lessen the likelihood of expressing, or perhaps even recognizing the existence of, the behavior system that is inhibited by anxiety. In the case of neurotic inhibition of aggressive behavior, for example, we might be struck by the person's extreme and unfailing agreeableness, even in situations that would seem to call for a vigorous defense of self—for example, in being unjustly humiliated by a bullying superior.

(b) The failure of neurotic defenses to contain fully either the anxiety underlying them or indirect evidence of the inhibited behavior system. Hence, the person who adopts a neurotic style will often show signs of anxiety, such as excessive sweating or muscular tension, while attempting to pursue smoothly the well-practiced defensive stance he or she will typically have developed. Total success in blocking the expression of inhibited behavior systems is rarely, if ever, achieved. The trained observer, or even the especially sensitive layperson, will usually be able to detect in the person a tendency for the inhibited system to reveal itself, but normally only in very indirect ways. The behavior of a client of one of the authors provides an instructive example. The client, a well-educated man who was a victim of severe inhibition of aggression, repeatedly interrupted the therapist's comments with "respectful" requests that the therapist define the meaning of the relatively common words he was using, the client claiming to have a "poor vocabulary." The therapist's own extreme annoyance at these interruptions ultimately provided the clue to understanding. As subsequently confirmed by the client, his constant requests for interpretation of vocabulary items were his way of expressing his "aggressive" feelings that the therapist was acting like a "pompous ass." So much for the self-esteem hazards of the therapist's trade!

Let us now review four inhibition patterns common to neurotic styles that can be seen in our own culture: aggression/assertion, responsibility/independence, compliance/submission, and intimacy/trust. Our illustrations should be considered as mere models or prototypes, much oversimplified for pedagogic reasons. They are based to a considerable extent on the analyses of Hine and colleagues (1971, 1972, 1983).

Aggression/assertion inhibition. The problems associated with this form of neurotic style have been illustrated above. The person is markedly uncomfortable in any situation in which aggressive, self-assertive actions would seem to be reasonable responses. Instead, the person rigidly clings to a typically cooperative, agreeable, and "forgiving" stance, showing little or no hostile response to even extreme provocation. The anger and hostility presumably felt at some levels are largely stifled, though their intensities may build over time in the face of continued provocation. Physical and/or psychological problems (e.g., hypertension or compulsive behavior) are not uncommon long-term results. Fortunately less common is the so-called "overcontrolled hostility syndrome" (Megargee, 1966), in which buried anger and resentment may lead to a sudden outburst of incredibly intense violence. Out of such circumstances are bred tales of, say, the much-admired Eagle scout who one day hacks his mother to death with an axe.

Responsibility/independence inhibition. Some individuals acquire in the course of their development a marked, anxiety-driven aversion to exercising personal independence or legitimate authority over others. Situations or events calling for assertions of independence or authority are, for these people, occasions of painful stress and anxiety. Hence, such persons normally arrange their lives in a manner that minimizes the likelihood they will be called upon for displays of strength and autonomous action. They may, for example, prove to be incompetent at many of the simple tasks of life. Related to and normally accompanying these traits is a notable submissiveness and clinging dependency on others. Few people can tolerate such childlike dependency indefinitely, and therefore such a person's relationships usually turn out to be unsatisfactory and short-lived. The development of symptoms consistent with this "helpless" state, e.g., agoraphobia (fear of open spaces), is a not uncommon complication of this neurotic style.

Compliance/submission inhibition. Individuals who deny their impulses to comply or submit constitute a significant proportion of the

The inability to establish feelings of intimacy and trust with others can result in a series of failed relationships and, ultimately, personal loneliness.

"rebels" within our own and other cultures. They tend to reject both ready-made solutions to personal problems offered by various professional, religious, and media figures, and also "imposed" solutions to world problems on a global scale. Presumably, persons with this form of anxiety have learned that reliance on "established" authority, parental or otherwise, leads to greater disaster than does reliance on the self. Accordingly, they become anxious and rebellious when they are required, or are motivated, to obey or "go along."

Compliant, submissive, and dependent behaviors are highly appropriate to many life circumstances—e.g., when one has a serious physical illness or when a strong but legitimate authority frustrates one's plans—but they are responses that exact an enormous cost in anxiety from the individual who fears submission. Such an individual may display intense, inappropriate "strength" in the form of defiance, noncompliance with legitimate authority, inability to accept help in adversity, dangerous risk-taking, and wariness about anyone else's being in control. Traits of this sort are of course highly valued in American folklore. And it is certainly true that, in moderation, they can be functionally adaptive. When they are based on unrealistic fears of

submission, however, they rarely can be contained within the moderate range. The result is often behavior that is unsatisfying, self-defeating, and on occasion dangerous to health and physical survival. For example, the person who cannot submit, comply, and depend in the treatment period immediately following a heart attack will have a significantly diminished life expectancy.

Intimacy/trust inhibition. People who feel unusually strong anxiety over establishing close personal attachments with others are typically at least as needful as the rest of us for relationships of mutual trust and intimacy, and indeed may spend inordinate amounts of time and energy in seeking them. However, at a crucial point in the relationship—perhaps when it seems to be going especially well or when an enhanced commitment is demanded—the person suddenly becomes wary and retreats. Explicit suspiciousness and cynicism about the sincerity of the other frequently enter the picture at this point, and the often bewildered other is more or less forcefully driven away. In cases of severe intimacy/trust inhibition, this sequence is played out very rapidly, with the result that few if any potential relationships ever really get off the ground. When the problem is this severe, there is often a trend toward the development of even more serious psychopathology. In milder instances, the person can manage an occasional long-term relationship, although in such cases the person usually maintains a certain aloofness and distance.

Interpersonal aspects of neurotic styles

As the above descriptions illustrate, individuals who adopt neurotic styles can create not only frustration and misery for themselves, but also serious problems for persons with whom they interact. Typically, people who behave neurotically do not have large networks of enduring relationships, and they tend to be quite dependent (although not necessarily in any obvious way) upon the few they have. Consequently, most relatively nonneurotic persons sooner or later find it not to their advantage to attempt to deal with the conflicting and unpredictable demands placed upon them by their neurotic partners. For reasonably well-functioning individuals who happen to be drawn to neurotically functioning persons, it is literally a "no-win" situation. For example, a man may find that a woman with compliance/submission inhibition is in many respects an "ideal"partner; she will "take charge" in all situations and will not allow herself or her mate to be taken advantage of or controlled. Yet the man in such a relationship might well find it difficult *never* to have his suggestions taken seriously, *never* to be allowed to take the lead. Hence, the typical experience of the neurotic person is that others fall by the wayside in terms of any permanent relationship, which may be yet another source of anxiety and insecurity.

But it need not turn out that way, particularly if the prospective friend or lover is also neurotic in a complementary way. For example, two persons with aggression/assertion inhibitions may hit it off quite well in a sustained way because both are so frightened of aggression that neither presents a hint of provocation to the other. The relationship is characterized by a level of "understanding" and "niceness" that astounds external observers, although such observers may also be aware of a certain lack of zest and spontaneity in the interactions of the mutually inhibited pair. The actors, in effect, protect each other from their darker sides.

Other sustainable relationship types of a mutually neurotic sort readily come to mind. For example, a person with responsibility/independence inhibition married to a person with compliance/submission inhibition may find that the marriage results in a reasonably stable standoff. Of course, the relationship is apt to be punctuated by stormy episodes because, as we have seen, the inhibited portion of the neurotic individual's behavioral repertoire is unlikely to remain totally and permanently in abeyance. Thus, even in cases of this kind of "perfect match," the upshot can often be a major crisis, sometimes ending in the divorce court.

In the sections that follow, we will consider neurotic processes whose manifestations are more specific, more obvious, and often more dramatic than in the neurotic styles discussed above. While not differing from neurotic styles in their fundamental organization (so far as we can tell), these conditions are far more readily recognized, even by the untrained eye. In essence, neurotic styles *impair* the quality of a person's life; neurotic symptoms are *disabling* in one way or another. Consequently, a great deal more attention has been paid to the neurotic symptom disorders in the historical development of the field of psychopathology. We also have in regard to them more research and precise clinical description on which to rely. It is important to reiterate, however, that neurotic styles and neurotic symptoms can and often do occur together. A typical instance is that of a basically neurotic person who undergoes an abrupt increase in life stressors—resulting in the development of more or less florid neurotic *symptoms*. As noted earlier, DSM-III divides this group of problems into three main classes: anxiety, somatoform, and dissociative disorders. We shall do the same.

Anxiety disorders

As we have seen, anxiety and the individual's efforts to control it are viewed as key factors in the development of neurotic problems. In the *anxiety disorders,* either of these two factors—that is, the anxiety itself or the individual's efforts to resist or defend against it—is the central feature of the clinical picture. The DSM-III recognizes two basic forms of anxiety disorder: *anxiety states* and *phobic disorder*. The anxiety states include *generalized anxiety disorder, panic disorder, obsessive-compulsive disorder,* and *posttraumatic stress disorder* (the last of which was covered in Chapter 5). Anxiety disorders are fairly common, and it is estimated that about 2 to 4 percent of the general population have at some time been diagnosed as having either a phobic disorder or some other anxiety disturbance.[1]

Generalized anxiety and panic disorders

Although anxiety is a central feature of all the neurotic patterns, all but this one include avoidance mechanisms that succeed to some extent in allaying the feelings of threat. Here, however, such mechanisms have not been perfected, and feelings of threat and anxiety are the central feature.

Generalized anxiety disorder is characterized by chronic (at least one months' duration) diffuse anxiety and apprehensiveness, which may be punctuated by recurring episodes of more acute, disabling anxiety. But since neither the chronic anxiety nor the acute anxiety attacks appear to stem from any particular threat, the pervasive anxiety is said to be "free-floating." While there are no data available on the incidence of generalized anxiety disorders *per se*, the experience of acute anxiety attacks is one of the most common patterns of the neurotic disorders.

Individuals suffering from generalized anxiety disorder live in a relatively constant state of tension, worry, and diffuse uneasiness. They are oversensitive in interpersonal relationships, and frequently feel inadequate and depressed. Usually they have difficulty concentrating and making decisions, dreading to make a mistake. The high level of tension they experience is often reflected in strained postural movements, overreaction to sudden or unexpected stimuli, and continual nervous movements. Commonly, they complain of muscular tension, especially in the neck and upper shoulder region, chronic

mild diarrhea, frequent urination, and sleep disturbances that include insomnia and nightmares. They perspire profusely and their palms are often clammy; they may show cardiovascular changes such as elevated blood pressure and increased pulse rate. They may experience breathlessness and heart palpitations for no apparent reason.

No matter how well things seem to be going, individuals with generalized anxiety disorder are apprehensive and anxious. Their vague fears and fantasies—combined with their general sensitivity—keep them continually upset, uneasy, and discouraged. Not only do they have difficulty making decisions, but after decisions have been made they worry excessively over possible errors and unforeseen circumstances that may lead to disaster. The lengths to which they go to find things to worry about are remarkable; as fast as one cause for worry is removed, they find another, until relatives and friends lose patience with them (see **HIGHLIGHT** on page 197).

Even after going to bed, people who suffer from generalized anxiety disorder are not likely to find relief from their worries. Often they review each mistake, real or imagined, recent or remote. When they are not reviewing and regretting the events of the past, they are anticipating all the difficulties that may arise in the future. Then, after they have crossed and recrossed most of their past and future bridges and managed to fall asleep, they frequently have anxiety dreams—dreams of being choked, being shot, falling from high places, or being chased by murderers, with the horrible sensation that their legs will move only in slow motion.

As we have seen, the persistent raised level of anxiety may be punctuated from time to time by acute *anxiety attacks*—recurring periods of acute panic that last anywhere from a few seconds to an hour or more. In the DSM-III system, an anxiety attack is diagnosed as a *panic disorder,* and is given a separate category under the anxiety disorder classification. Typically, these attacks come on suddenly, mount to high intensity, and then subside—all in the absence of any obvious cause, such as a life-threatening situation or physical exertion. Symptoms vary from one person to another, but they can include "palpitations, shortness of breath, profuse sweating, faintness and dizziness, coldness and pallor of the face and extremities, urge to urinate, gastric sensations and an ineffable feeling

---

[1]Incidence statistics relative to the various neurotic patterns are rough estimates based on cases diagnosed in clinics and hospitals. Sources for these estimates include APA (1980), Dohrenwend et al. (1980), Templer and Lester (1974), and Woodruff, Guze, and Clayton (1972).

A

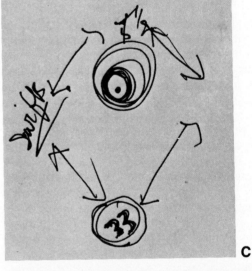

B

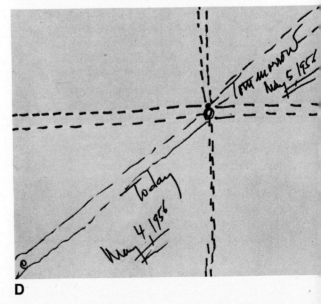

C

D

Drawing is often considered a primitive but effective method of communicating one's inner thoughts and feelings. Of course, the therapist must exercise caution to avoid misinterpretation. The four pictures shown here were drawn by a woman assessed as suffering from an acute anxiety disorder. Although she was a successful businesswoman, having risen progressively through jobs of greater and greater responsibility, she felt herself incapable of achieving further advancement—that she had "reached the end of the line." Subsequently, she experienced feelings of frustration, inadequacy, and anxiety.

Sketch A was drawn hurriedly under great tension. The smoking buildings on the left represent New York City, the woman's place of employment, and the buildings on the right, her desired place of employment. Separating the two is the middle structure, which contains the "aggressive, agitated figures of her male competitors in the business world."

In **Sketch B,** the woman appeared to represent herself in a cage by the boxed-in dot. She then partially blotted out the crude diagram "by rapidly placed crosshatching, as though to deny the admission that she found herself so trapped."

Sketch C appears to represent "the merry-go-round on which she has been moving, from one firm to another, around and around, always seeking advancement, without finding any satisfying fulfillment." Finally, **Sketch D** indicates her anxiety over her present dilemma—"What road today? What road tomorrow?" (Adapted from Brown, 1957, pp. 171–74)

HIGHLIGHT

Fantasies of anticipated harm in anxiety disorders

In a study of 32 anxiety-neurotic individuals, Beck, Laude, and Bohnert (1974) found unrealistic expectations and fantasies of harm associated with these patients' heightened levels of anxiety and with anxiety attacks. The degree of anxiety was related to the severity of, and perceived likelihood of, the anticipated harm.

These expectations and fantasies centered around both physical and psychological dangers—such as being involved in an accident, becoming sick, being violently attacked, failing, and being humiliated or rejected by significant others. In this context, the following examples are instructive.

Patient	Fantasy of anticipated harm	Stimuli triggering anxiety
Physician Male, age 32	Fear of sudden death	Any gastrointestinal symptoms
Teacher Male, age 25	Fear of inability to function as a teacher and of ending up on skid row	Anticipation of giving lecture
Homemaker Female, age 30	Fear of physical catastrophe happening to member of family	Sirens, news of deaths, fires, accidents, etc.
Student Male, age 26	Fear of psychological harm, school failure, rejection by everyone, illness	Schoolwork, confrontation with people, any physical symptom
Laborer Male, age 35	Continuous visual fantasies of accident, fear of imminent death	Any noises that might suggest danger (e.g., traffic noises)
Psychologist Male, age 40	Fear of heart attack, cerebral hemorrhage, fainting in public and subsequent disgrace	Physical sensations in chest or abdomen, back pains, hearing about heart attacks
Artist Female, age 35	Fear of heart attacks	Exertion, anticipation of exertion, reading or hearing about heart attacks
Student Male, age 18	Fear of appearing foolish and subsequent rejection by others	Contact with or anticipated contact with others

Often the fantasies and images reported by a given patient were related to past personal experiences. For example, in the preceding cases, the homemaker had experienced the death of a close friend and the artist's mother had died of a heart attack. These investigators concluded that the expectations and fantasies of anxious patients "not only hold up mirrors to their psychopathology but provide entry points for treating it" (p. 325).

of imminent death'' (Lader & Mathews, 1970, p. 377). The physiological symptoms, together with the sensation of impending death or catastrophe, make an anxiety attack a terrifying experience.

Usually the attack subsides after a few minutes. If it continues, the individual may frantically implore someone to summon a doctor. After medical treatment has been administered, commonly in the form of reassurance and a sedative, the person quiets down. Such attacks vary in frequency from several times a day to once a month or even less often. They may occur during the day, or the person may awaken from a sound sleep with a strong feeling of apprehension that rapidly develops into an attack. Between attacks the individual may appear to be relatively unperturbed, but mild anxiety and tension usually persist.

Many of these individuals show mild depression as well as chronic anxiety (Downing & Rickels, 1974; Prusoff & Klerman, 1974). This finding is not unexpected in view of their generally gloomy outlook on the world. Nor is it surprising that excessive use of tranquilizing drugs, sleeping pills, and alcohol often complicates the clinical picture in generalized anxiety disorder.

It was noted earlier that, where symptoms emerge out of a neurotic style, those symptoms tend to be psychologically consistent with the preexisting neurotic style. As the following two case descriptions illustrate, anxiety disorders often develop from responsibility/independence inhibitions:

Thomas G., a 44-year-old Protestant minister, upon discovery of his wife's infidelity, began to experience chronic anxiety. He was quick to take the blame for the failure of the marriage, sure that his inattentiveness to the needs of his wife and children had driven her away. Yet he was angry at her for creating a public embarrassment for him. He was contemplating a divorce, but such an action would violate his convictions. He was also torn by the feeling that because his marriage had failed he had failed the church, too, and must resign from the ministry. But he loved his work so much that he could not imagine being without it.

During the week before he came for therapy, he had been unable to sleep, lying awake worrying about his problems. He could not eat and complained of a strong burning sensation in his stomach and feelings of being constantly choked up. He was unable to think clearly enough to prepare his sermon for Sunday or to follow through on several commitments he had made previously.

Mr. G.'s present stress only exaggerated problems he had had for many years. He reported that he had always been an insecure and dependent person who found a great deal of emotional support in the church and in his strong, independent wife. She was a "take charge" person who had always handled all their personal matters, including shopping for his clothes. Any thought of an end to either his marriage or his position with the church made him extremely anxious and insecure. But now it seemed that continuing in the marriage and in his current position would be intolerable.

In short, the minister was a man who was able to function when surrounded by familiar supports but who became overwhelmed when he was forced to face the necessity of leading a self-directed life. His reaction was an exacerbation of long-standing neurotic difficulties, not merely an adjustment disorder to a stressful event.

In cases where the individual with responsibility/independence inhibition has achieved a measure of success in containing the anxiety—in building a wall of relative security around it—collapse may occur when impulses threaten to jeopardize that security, as in the following case.

A successful business executive developed acute anxiety attacks about once every two or three months. His wife was eight years older than he, and he was no longer physically attracted to her. He had found himself increasingly interested in younger women and had begun to think how much more enjoyable it would be to have a younger, more companionable wife. During this period he met a woman with whom he was sure he had fallen in love. It was shortly thereafter that the anxiety attacks began to occur. They were preceded by a period of several days of increased tenseness and anxiety, but the attacks came on suddenly and were intense.

The man was at a complete loss to explain his attacks. But the explanation was not difficult to find. He had had a poverty-stricken and insecure childhood and felt basically inferior, insecure, and threatened by a harsh world. These feelings had been intensified when he had failed college courses in his second year, even though the failure had resulted primarily from excessive outside work. He had been able to achieve some security, however, by marrying a strong, older woman who had instilled considerable self-confidence and initiative in him. The relationship had proved very fruitful financially, and the man was living in a style which, as a youth, "I hadn't dared to imagine in my wildest dreams!" His persistent thoughts about divorcing his wife, on whom he felt dependent for his security and style of life, thus represented a severe threat to the moderately successful adjustment he had been able to achieve. The anxiety attacks followed.

While styles of responsibility/independence inhibition may be common antecedents of anxiety disorders, including their phobic varieties (see below), the correspondence is far from perfect. Other types of neurotic style—or even no neurotic style at all—can precede the onset of anxiety. The following case is a rather clear illustration of an anxiety disorder growing out of an aggression/assertion inhibition.

An 18-year-old male student developed severe anxiety attacks just before he went out on dates. In therapy it was revealed that he came from a very insecure home in which he was very much attached to an anxious, frustrated, and insecure mother. Intellectually capable and a good student, he had entered college at 16. But during his two years on campus he had difficulty getting dates, especially with college women of his choice. The student he had been dating recently, for example, would not make any arrangements to go out until after 6:00 P.M. of the same day, after her chances for a more preferable date seemed remote. This had increased his already strong feelings of inferiority and insecurity and had led to the development of intense hostility toward the opposite sex, mostly on an unconscious level.

About two months before coming to the college clinic for assistance, he had experienced the anxiety-arousing fantasy of choking the young woman to death when they were alone together. As he put it, "When we are alone in the car, I can't get my mind off her nice white throat and what it would be like to choke her to death." At first he put these thoughts out of his mind, but they returned on subsequent nights with increasing persistence. Then, to complicate the matter, he experienced his first acute anxiety attack. It occurred in his car on the way over to pick up his date and lasted for only a few minutes, but he was panic-stricken and thought that he was going to die. After that he experienced several additional attacks under the same conditions.

The relationship of the inhibited aggressiveness to the persistent fantasies and anxiety attacks seemed clear in this case. Yet it was not at all apparent to the young man, who was at a complete loss to explain either his fantasies or the anxiety attacks.

Obsessive-compulsive disorder

An *obsession* is a persistent preoccupation with something, typically an idea or a feeling. A *compulsion* is an impulse experienced as irresistible. In *obsessive-compulsive disorder*, individuals feel compelled to think about something that they do not want to think about or to carry out some action against their will. These individuals usually realize that their behavior is irrational but cannot seem to control it.

The incidence of obsessive-compulsive disorders has been variously estimated to be from about 12 to 20 percent of the anxiety disorders. Age and sex differences have not been systematically studied. As Nemiah (1967) has pointed out, obsessive-compulsive behaviors cover a wide range:

"The phenomena may be manifested psychically or behaviorally; they may be experienced as ideas or as impulses; they may refer to events anticipated in the future or actions already completed; they may express

desires and wishes or protective measures against such desires; they may be simple, uncomplicated acts and ideas or elaborate, ritualized patterns of thinking and behavior. . . ."(p. 916)

Most of us have experienced minor obsessional thoughts, such as persistent thoughts about a coming trip or date, or a haunting melody that we cannot seem to get out of our minds. In the case of obsessive reactions, however, the thoughts are much more persistent, appear irrational to the individual, and interfere considerably with everyday behavior.

Neurotic-obsessive thoughts may center around a wide variety of topics, such as concern over bodily functions, committing immoral acts, attempting suicide, or even finding the solution to some seemingly unsolvable problem. Particularly common are obsessive thoughts of committing some immoral act. A wife may be obsessed with the idea of poisoning her husband, a daughter with the thought of pushing her mother down a flight of stairs.

Even though obsessive thoughts are usually not carried out in action, they remain a source of torment to the individual. This pattern is well illustrated in a classic case described by Kraines (1948) of a woman who

"complained of having 'terrible thoughts.' When she thought of her boyfriend she wished he were dead; when her mother went down the stairs, she 'wished she'd fall and break her neck'; when her sister spoke of going to the beach with her infant daughter, the patient 'hoped that they would both drown.' These thoughts 'make me hysterical. I love them; why should I wish such terrible things to happen? It drives me wild, makes me feel I'm crazy and don't belong to society; maybe it's best for me to end it all than to go on thinking such terrible things about those I love.' " (p.183)

As in the case of obsessive thoughts, most of us show some compulsive behavior—stepping over cracks in sidewalks, walking around ladders instead of under them, or turning away when a black cat crosses our path—but without the degree of compulsiveness of the neurotic individual. Most of us also resort to minor obsessive-compulsive patterns under severe pressure or when trying to achieve goals that we consider of critical importance. Many historical figures have shown an "obsessive-compulsive" adherence to their goals despite discouragement and

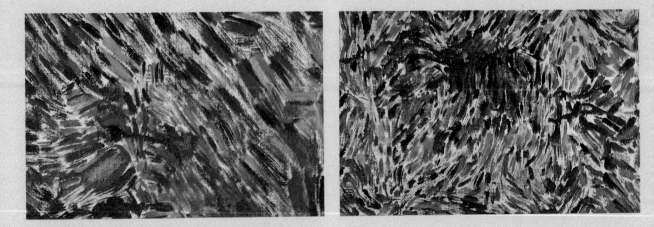

*T*hese paintings, all in different media and all almost exactly the same size, were done by a neurotic patient with obsessive-compulsive tendencies. These tendencies are manifested in the paintings by the rigidity and sameness of the brush strokes, the seeming need to cover the entire canvas, and the obvious attempt at symmetry.

In an effort to break the patient from his rigid mold, the therapist gave him a piece of paper twice as large as the ones on which the previous paintings had been done. The patient, however, folded the paper to the same size as the previous paintings and did the same kind of painting.

T
hese three paintings are part of a series of approximately 20 paintings done over a six-month period by a patient diagnosed as suffering from an anxiety disorder. The first painting (above) indicates great hostility toward women, evidenced by the beetle on the forehead, pointed ears, and bald head. At this stage also the patient, while showing some obvious art ability, had difficulty finishing the painting, especially the background and edges.

The second painting (top right) was done after about three months in therapy. The fragmentation of the image was interpreted as indicating the patient's feelings of ambivalence and confusion at this stage.

The same woman is shown in the third painting (bottom right) but she now has hair, the scarab is gone from her forehead, the pointed ears are modified, and her facial expression is less hostile. The patient, while not completely relieved of his hostility and paranoia toward women, was considered to have reached a point where he could express his feelings in a socially acceptable manner.

HIGHLIGHT

Cognitive and motor behavior patterns in obsessive-compulsive disorder

Symptoms	Examples
Cognitive	
Obsessions. Recurrent, persistent ideas, thoughts, images or impulses involuntarily coming to awareness	Ideas of contamination, dread, guilt; urges to kill, attack, injure, confess, or steal.
Ruminations. Forced preoccupation with thoughts about a particular topic, associated with brooding, doubting, and inconclusive speculation.	Uncontrollable fantasies concerning sexual relations with strangers or distant acquaintances.
Cognitive rituals. Elaborate series of mental acts the patient feels compelled to complete. Termination depends on proper performance.	Prior to retiring for the evening, the patient feels required to recite mentally a long series of prayers learned in childhood.
Motor	
Compulsive motor rituals. Elaborate, often time-consuming activities frequently associated with everyday functions such as eating, toileting, grooming, dressing, and sexual activity.	Handwashing (sometimes reaching 400 or more washes per day), compulsive counting (e.g., of passersby) or "checking," touching of objects.
Compulsive avoidances. Substitute actions performed instead of appropriate behavior that induces anxiety.	A student becomes involved in several distracting activities prior to exams, leaving no time to study.

ridicule: Columbus persisted for 18 years in his efforts to secure financial backing for his expedition to "India," and Darwin assembled evidence for 22 years before he would present his ideas on evolution.

In compulsive disorders, people feel compelled to perform some act which seems strange and absurd to them and which they do not want to perform. Such compulsive acts vary from relatively mild ritual-like behavior, such as making the sign of the cross periodically during the day, to more extreme behavior, such as washing one's hands as often as ten times each hour. They can involve actual physical acts or can be essentially cognitive in nature, i.e., involving feelings and thoughts (see **HIGHLIGHT** on this page). The performance of the compulsive act usually brings a feeling of reduced tension and satisfaction (Carr, 1971; Hodgson & Rachman,

1972). On the other hand, anxiety mounts if the person tries to resist the compulsion.

An obsessive-compulsive disorder is considered maladaptive because it represents irrational and exaggerated behavior in the face of stressors that are not unduly upsetting to most people, and because such patterns reduce the flexibility of behavior and the capability for self-direction. In general, such behavior takes place in the context of a personality characterized by feelings of inadequacy and insecurity, rigid conscience development, a tendency toward feelings of guilt, and high vulnerability to threat.

As in all of the anxiety disorders, certain maladaptive personality characteristics show up at a greater than expected level in the backgrounds of the affected persons. Significantly, a large proportion of obsessive-compulsive individuals are found to have been unusually preoccupied with issues of *control* long before their symptoms appeared. These individuals will often have histories suggesting marked discomfort in any situation in which they felt they did *not* have control. This is reminiscent of what we have earlier called compliance/submission inhibition, and indeed there is often ample evidence of this neurotic style in the past and present of the symptomatic obsessive-compulsive person. The following case is illustrative.

Prior to his hospitalization, this patient had his life ordered in the most minute detail. He arose in the morning precisely at 6:50, took a shower, shaved, and dressed. His wife had breakfast ready precisely at 7:10 and followed a menu that he worked out months in advance. At exactly 7:45 he left for the office where he worked as an accountant. He came home precisely at 5:55, washed, then read the evening paper, and had dinner precisely at 6:30, again as per menu. His schedule was equally well worked out for evenings and weekends, with a movie on Tuesday, reading on Wednesday, rest on Monday and Thursday, and bridge on Friday. Saturday morning he played golf and Sunday morning and evening he attended church. Saturday evening usually involved having guests or visiting others. He was fastidious in his dress. Each shirt had to be clean and unwrinkled, his suit pressed every two days, and so on. His demands, of course, also included his wife, who was inclined to be easy-going and was upset when he "blew up" at the smallest variation from established routine.

By means of his carefully ordered existence the patient had managed to make a reasonably successful adjustment until he became involved in a business deal with a friend and lost a considerable sum of money. This proved too much for him and precipitated a severe anxiety reaction with considerable agitation and depression, necessitating hospitalization.

In this case, we assume that the patient's need to be in utter control of all phases of his life was driven by anxiety over being controlled by something or someone else—i.e., by problems of compliance/submission. When his ritualistically ordered existence in fact failed to protect him from another's exploitation, he fell apart.

Quite often, the extraordinary concern with self-imposed regularity and control in the pre-obsessive-compulsive individual takes the form of exaggerated perfectionism or concerns that one's actions may lead to terrible consequences. The following case is illustrative of this characteristic, and also incidentally indicates how in-

Sometimes anxiety over being controlled by external forces can lead an individual to try to exert control through compulsive behaviors like constantly checking the time.

tractable and persistent this personality organization may become.

A 32-year-old high-school cooking teacher developed marked feelings of guilt and uneasiness, accompanied by obsessive fears of hurting others by touching them or by their handling something she had touched. She dreaded to have anyone eat anything she had prepared, and if students in her cooking class were absent, she was certain they had been poisoned by her cooking. In addition, she developed the obsessive notion that a rash at the base of her scalp was a manifestation of syphilis, which would gnaw at her brain and make a "drooling idiot" of her.

Accompanying the obsessive fears were compulsions consisting primarily of repeated hand-washings and frequent returns to some act already performed to reassure herself that the act had been done right, such as turning off the gas or water.

In treatment the patient was self-centered but highly sensitive and conscientious. She had graduated from college with honors and considered herself highly intelligent. About three years before her present difficulties she had married a noncollege man of whom she had been very much ashamed because of his poor English, table manners, and other characteristics which she thought led to a very poor social showing. As a result, she had rejected him in her thinking and behavior and had treated him in what she now considered a very cruel manner. On one occasion she had also been unfaithful to him, which was directly opposed to her moral training.

Over a period of time, however, she came to realize that he was a fine person and that other people thought highly of him despite his lack of social polish. In addition, she gradually came to the realization that she was very much in love with him. At this point she began to reproach herself for her cruel treatment of him. She felt that he was a truly wonderful husband, and that she was completely unworthy of him. She was sure her past cruelty and unfaithfulness could never be forgiven. "Heaven knows that every word he says is worth fifty words I say. If I were real honest and truthful I would tell my husband to leave me."

In some cases of obsessive-compulsive symptomatology, the preexisting behavior seems to involve aggression/assertion inhibition. Many parents, for instance, have fleeting thoughts and fantasies about committing mayhem on their children. Fortunately, these are rarely expressed in action, and most such parents are able in good-humored fashion to be amused or at least not frightened by these impulses. Not so for parents harboring inhibitions of aggression/assertion, as the following case illustrates.

A farmer developed obsessive thoughts of hitting his three-year-old son over the head with a hammer. The father was completely unable to explain his "horrible thoughts." He stated that he loved his son very much and thought he must be going insane to harbor such thoughts. In the treatment of this case it was revealed that the patient's wife had suffered great pain in childbirth and had since refused sexual relations with him for fear of again becoming pregnant. In addition, she lavished most of her attention on the son, and their previously happy marriage was now torn with quarreling and bickering.

It would appear here that the farmer could not be sufficiently assertive to allow himself to experience his resentment toward his son, resulting in its being deeply buried. His feelings could emerge only in seemingly automatic, alien thoughts.

Phobic disorder

A *phobia* is a persistent fear of some object or situation that presents no actual danger to the person or in which the danger is magnified out of all proportion to its actual seriousness. The following list of the common phobias and their objects will give some hint of the variety of situations and events around which phobias may be centered:

Acrophobia—high places
Agoraphobia—open places
Algophobia—pain
Astraphobia—storms, thunder, and lightning
Claustrophobia—closed places
Hematophobia—blood
Monophobia—being alone
Mysophobia—contamination or germs
Nyctophobia—darkness
Ocholophobia—crowds
Pathophobia—disease
Pyrophobia—fire
Syphilophobia—syphilis
Zoophobia—animals or some particular animal

Some of these phobias involve an exaggerated fear of things that most of us fear to some extent, such as darkness, fires, disease, and snakes. Others, such as phobias of open places or crowds, involve situations that do not elicit fear in most people. In many cases people develop particular phobias that are not part of a neurotic pattern; this is the case with most snake phobias.

Based on a survey of a Vermont community, Agras, Sylvester, and Oliveau (1969) estimated the overall presence of phobic individuals in the general population to be 7.7 percent, though only .2 percent of the population were bothered by severely disabling phobias.

Phobic disorder occurs more commonly among adolescents and young adults than among older people. It is also more frequently diagnosed in females than in males, possibly because strong fears have traditionally been more compatible with female roles than with male roles in our society.

Of course, most of us have minor irrational fears, but in phobic disorders such fears are intense and interfere with everyday activities. For example, phobic individuals may go to great lengths to avoid entering a small room or passageway, even when it is essential for them to do so. People who suffer from phobias usually admit that they have no real cause to be afraid of the object or situation, but say they cannot help themselves. If they attempt to approach

Acrophobia—a persistent, exaggerated fear of high places—may cause some people to feel intensely uncomfortable at almost any height above the ground. These window washers (left), by contrast, must be virtually fearless even at truly dangerous heights. Fear of flying is a common enough phobia to warrant regular classes (right) in which "students" are brought together and are asked to perform various exercises designed to help them combat their fear.

rather than avoid the phobic situation, they are overcome with anxiety, which may vary from mild feelings of uneasiness and distress to a full-fledged anxiety attack.

Phobic individuals usually show a wide range of other symptoms in addition to their phobias, such as tension headaches, back pains, stomach upsets, dizzy spells, and fear of "cracking up." At times of more acute panic, such individuals often complain of feelings of unreality, of strangeness, and of "not being themselves." Feelings of depression frequently accompany phobias, and many patients report serious interpersonal difficulties. In some instances, they also have serious difficulty in making decisions—a condition that Kaufman (1973) somewhat facetiously called *decidophobia*.

The particular phobias that develop are often influenced by cultural factors. For example, a phobia of flying would not likely have become common until we entered the age of commercial air travel. In some cases, phobic reactions may also be obsessive, as when a persistent obsessive fear of contamination dominates the neurotic individual's consciousness. In certain instances

the phobia is a rather transparent displacement; the person substitutes an easily avoided fear-inspiring object for one that is less easy to deal with.

Regardless of how it begins, phobic behavior tends to be reinforced by the reduction in anxiety that occurs each time the individual avoids the feared situation. In addition, phobias may be maintained in part by "secondary gains" (that is, benefits derived from being disabled), such as increased attention, sympathy, and some control over the behavior of others. For example, a phobia of driving may enable a homemaker to escape from responsibilities outside the home, such as shopping or transporting her children to and from school.

The latter example suggests that phobias may sometimes serve the interest of seemingly remote objectives, such as avoidance of adult independence and responsibility, and this indeed appears to be the case. We noted earlier that neurotic styles of responsibility/independence inhibition appear quite often as a background factor in individuals who develop certain phobic symptoms. This seems particularly true where

Claustrophobia, a fear of small, enclosed places, may be reinforced by the reduction in anxiety the person feels each time a "dangerous" situation is avoided.

the individual displays multiple phobias ("panphobia") concerning numerous objectively benign life circumstances. The problem is well illustrated in the following situation.

A married woman in her mid-30s complained of marked fear, bordering on panic, of driving her auto in unfamiliar neighborhoods, riding in elevators, flying, and entering tall buildings and shopping centers. During the initial interview, she revealed that she had had these fears for some 18 years. Over the years she had been in almost continuous treatment. A variety of therapists had employed different modes of intervention, including psychoanalysis and behavior therapy. None of these measures had brought significant relief, and by this point the patient had become so expert at "managing" therapists that she could avoid confronting her problems. Her situation appeared rather unpromising.

The history revealed a long series of dependent relationships, chiefly with males (including male therapists), culminating in marriage to an older, previously married professional man. Initially, the husband had appeared very "strong" although somewhat given to tyrannical outbursts; over time, this strength proved to be to a large extent illusory, the product of what we would call compliance/submission inhibition. As the husband's appearance of strength evaporated, the wife's phobic symptoms increased in severity, driving her back into therapy once again. Of course, with the wife's increase in phobic symptoms, the husband's life became more miserable and hectic, since he had to assume the responsibilities (e.g., driving the chil-

dren to various functions) she allegedly could no longer perform. The marriage deteriorated rapidly under the assault of these conflicting neurotic styles, fortified in the wife's case by the emergence of "disabling" symptoms.

A clear understanding of these dynamic factors, together with a measure of confidence (in light of her history) that conservative treatment would almost certainly fail, enabled the therapist to intervene forcefully and vigorously into this complicated situation. For example, he largely ignored the patient's fears and insisted on concentrating on her relationship with her husband. As was expected, the patient became markedly dependent on the therapist as her condition improved to the extent that she continued to complain of phobias even after her phobic behavior had essentially disappeared. Meanwhile, her marital situation became more stable and secure as she came to accept and even be sympathetic with her husband's insecurities. Rather than contribute to the client's growing dependency on him, the therapist terminated further therapy sessions. He assured the doubtful client that there was no need for further therapy, and that any remaining fears would clear up spontaneously. Several weeks later, the client telephoned to say that, in fact, they had!

While some phobias, once established, remain fairly circumscribed, others tend to "spread" or generalize to additional situations, possibly because of an "incubation" effect that is thought to occur with some types of anxiety (Eysenck, 1976). The following case illustrates this spreading effect to situations only minimally related to the basic trauma.

An 18-year-old woman had been given strict "moral" training concerning the evils of sex, and she associated sexual relations with vivid ideas of sin, guilt, and hell. This basic orientation was reinforced when she was beaten and sexually attacked by a young man on her fifteenth birthday. Nevertheless, when the young man she was dating kissed her and "held her close," it aroused intense sexual desires. These were extremely guilt arousing, however, and led to a chain of avoidance behaviors. First she stopped seeing him in an effort to get rid of her "immoral" thoughts; then she stopped all dating; then she began to feel uncomfortable with any young man she knew; and finally she became fearful of any social situations where men might be present. At this point her life was largely dominated by her phobias and she was so "completely miserable" that she requested professional help.

As a group, the anxiety disorders, while clearly outside the normal range, rarely strike us as utterly strange or exotic, probably because we have all at one time or another experienced relatively strong fears or apprehensions we could not rationally explain. And, as was noted, most of us are not even strangers to mild obsessive and compulsive phenomena. In the following sections we take up neurotic patterns that are more remote from the experience of most people.

Somatoform disorders

"Soma" means *body*, and somatoform disorders involve an anxiety-based neurotic pattern in which the individual complains of bodily symptoms that suggest the presence of a physical problem, but for which *no organic basis can be found*. Such individuals are typically preoccupied with their state of health and with various presumed disorders or diseases of bodily organs. Though no organic basis exists, these individuals sincerely believe their symptoms are real and serious, and they should not be confused with persons who feign physical illness (malingerers) in order to obtain some special treatment.

In our discussion we shall focus on four more or less distinct somatoform patterns: *somatization disorder, hypochondriasis, psychogenic pain disorder*, and *conversion disorder*. While all four involve the neurotic development of physical symptoms, the patterns of causation and the most effective treatment approaches may differ somewhat. A fifth pattern involving complaints of bodily symptoms but not included in the current classification is neurasthenic disorder, described in the **HIGHLIGHT** on page 208–9.

Somatization disorder

This disorder is characterized by multiple complaints of physical ailments over a long period, beginning before age 30, which are inadequately explained by either physical disorder or physical injury. The diagnostician need not be convinced that these claimed illnesses actually existed in the background history of the patient; the mere reporting of them is sufficient. The DSM-III provides a list of 37 symptoms that qualify as possible indicators of *somatization disorder;* somatization disorder is suspected if men claim at least 12 and women at least 14 of them, the gender difference being due to a category of reproductive system complaints seen only in women (see **HIGHLIGHT** on page 210). To qualify, the symptoms must be reported as having been severe enough to require medication, to require consulting a physician, or to cause an alteration in life-style.

The difference between somatization disorder and hypochondriasis, discussed below, is none too clear in the DSM-III diagnostic manual, apparently because the two disorders (if they are in fact distinct) are closely related. The main differences seem to be that hypochondriasis may have its onset after 30, that the abnormal health concerns characteristic of hypochondriasis need not focus on any particular set of symptoms, and that the hypochondriac mostly fears that he or she *might* have a serious disease rather than claims explicit symptoms or physical disabilities. The somatization disorder diagnosis is new to the DSM-III, and so it has not as yet been subjected to extensive clinical and research scrutiny.

Hypochondriasis

One of the most frequently seen somatoform patterns is *hypochondriasis,* which is characterized by the individual's multiplicity of complaints about possible physical illness—complaints that are usually not restricted to any physiologically coherent symptom pattern and that express a preoccupation with health matters and unrealistic fears of disease. Although hypochondriacal individuals repeatedly seek medical advice, their fears are not in the least lessened by their doctors' reassurances; in fact, they are disappointed when no physical problem is found.

Individuals with this disorder may complain of uncomfortable and peculiar sensations in the general area of the stomach, the chest, the head, the genitals, or anywhere else in the body. They usually have trouble giving a precise description of their symptoms, however. They may begin by mentioning pain in the stomach, which on further questioning is not a pain but a gnawing sensation, or perhaps a feeling of heat. Their mental orientation keeps them constantly on the alert for new illness manifestations.

Hypochondriacal patients are likely to be avid readers of popular magazines on medical topics, and are apt to feel certain they are suffering from every new disease they read or hear about. Tuberculosis, cancer, tumors, and numerous other diseases are readily diagnosed by these individuals. Their morbid preoccupation with bodily processes, coupled with their ignorance of medical pathology, often leads to some interesting diagnoses. One patient diagnosed his condition as "ptosis of the transvex colon," and added, "If I am just half as bad off as I think, I am a dead pigeon."

This attitude appears to be typical: such individuals are sure they are seriously ill and cannot recover. Yet—and this is revealing—despite their exaggerated concern over their health, *they do not usually show the fear or anxiety that might be expected of those suffering from such horrible ills.* The fact is that they are usually in good physical condition. Nevertheless, they are not malingering; they are sincere in their conviction that their symptoms represent real illness.

A classic illustration of the shifting symptoms and complaints in a very severe case of hypochondriacal disorder is presented in the following letter that a hospitalized patient wrote to her anxious relatives.

"Dear Mother and Husband:
"I have suffered terrible today with drawing in

HIGHLIGHT
Neurasthenic disorder

In outpatient mental health and medical clinics, a frequent pattern of complaints centers on chronic mental and physical fatigue, various aches and pains, and a general lack of vigor and interest in life. This pattern, referred to as *neurasthenia*, has been considered to be relatively common among young adults, particularly frustrated homemakers. The DSM-III classification no longer includes neurasthenia as a category. However, the frequency with which this disorder has been diagnosed in the past—it is said to be the most commonly diagnosed disorder in the Soviet Union—warrants our giving it separate consideration.

Clinical picture
The principal complaint in neurasthenic disorder is tiredness. Mental concentration is difficult and fatiguing; such individuals are easily distracted and accomplish little. They lack the vigor required to carry activities through to completion. Even minor tasks seem to require herculean effort. They usually spend a good deal of time sleeping in an attempt to counteract fatigue; yet regardless of the amount of sleep they get, they awaken unrefreshed.

Typically, neurasthenic individuals sleep poorly and feel "just rotten" when they drag themselves out of bed in the morning. On the rare occasions when they feel refreshed, they are completely upset by minor emotional setbacks, such as some criticism of their behavior, and their fatigue and listlessness return. Even when things seem to be going relatively well, the fatigue tends to get worse as the day wears on, although by evening they may feel somewhat better and may go to a movie or a party without experi-

throat. My nerves are terrible. My head feels queer. But my stomach hasn't cramped quite so hard. I've been on the verge of a nervous chill all day, but I have been fighting it hard. It's night and bedtime, but, Oh, how I hate to go to bed. Nobody knows or realizes how badly I feel because I fight to stay up and outdoors if possible. . . .

"These long afternoons and nights are awful. There are plenty of patients well enough to visit with but I'm in too much pain.

"The nurses ignore any complaining. They just laugh or scold.

"Eating has been awful hard. They expect me to eat like a harvest hand. Every bite of solid food is agony

encing anything like their usual exhaustion. In fact, one of the most significant things about this fatigue is its selective nature. Such individuals often show relatively good energy and endurance in doing anything that really interests them.

It is important here to note two symptoms that distinguish these individuals from those suffering from severe depression. First, neurasthenic individuals do *not* report being depressed; instead, they report feelings of listlessness and frustration. Second, neurasthenic individuals do not show the deep emotional involvement typical of depressed persons; rather, they are somewhat more apathetic and withdrawn.

Causal factors

Historical attempts to explain the causal factors of neurasthenic reactions centered around the concept of "nerve weakness," which is the literal meaning of the older term *neurasthenia*. Beard (1905), an early American psychiatrist who first applied the term to the fatigue syndrome, attributed the condition to prolonged conflict and overwork, which presumably depleted the nerve cells of essential biochemical elements. This conception later gave rise to the Weir Mitchell method of treatment for "nervous exhaustion," which involved a long period of complete rest and relaxation for the patient.

Neurasthenic patients, however, rarely reveal a history of overwork, nor is rest what they most need. Rather, it appears to be prolonged frustration, discouragement, and hopelessness that reduces motivation and leads to the characteristic listlessness and fatigue. In addition, there are likely to be sustained emotional conflicts centering around hostility toward one's mate and guilt over the abandonment of cherished goals.

Much of the psychological benefit derived from these patterns is due to the individual's obvious sincerity—the complaints are made without awareness of their actual function. The neurasthenic individual often gets credit for putting up a noble battle against heavy odds. Thus, as in other neurotic reactions, neurasthenic symptoms may have important secondary gains. They tend to force others to show sympathy and concern, and may be used aggressively to control the behavior of others.

In understanding the causal factors of neurasthenic patterns, it is important to note that feeling fatigued and unable to cope with the world is common in our high-pressure society, but the normal individual carries on and makes a fairly satisfactory adjustment. Neurasthenic individuals, by contrast, are typically people who lack self-confidence, are overdependent on others, and feel completely inadequate in the face of a situation they perceive as frustrating and hopeless. Their symptoms enable them to escape the necessity of dealing with such a threatening world.

Aspects of treatment

Neurasthenic reactions are frequently very resistant to treatment. Tranquilizing drugs may alleviate some of the underlying anxiety but have not proven very helpful. In general, treatment to date has centered around helping patients gain some understanding of their problems, learn more effective coping techniques, and achieve enough self-confidence and courage to stop feeling sorry for themselves and get back into the "battle of life."

to get down, for my throat aches so and feels so closed up. . . .

"My eyes are bothering me more.

"Come up as soon as you can. My nose runs terrible every time I eat.

"The trains and ducks and water pipes are noisy at night.

Annie"
(Menninger, 1945, pp. 139–40)

Individuals suffering from hypochondriasis often show a morbid preoccupation with digestive and excretory functions. Some keep charts of their bowel movements, and most are able to give detailed information concerning diet, constipation, and related matters. Many use a wide range of self-medications of the type occupying significant proportions of television commercial time. However, they do not show losses or distortions of sensory, motor, and visceral functioning that occur in conversion disorder (to be discussed below); nor do their complaints have the bizarre delusional quality—such as "insides rotting away" or "lungs drying up"—that typically occurs in psychosis.

Most of us as children learn well the lesson that, when sick, special comforts and attention are provided, and furthermore that one is excused from a number of responsibilities, or, at least, is not expected to perform certain tasks. The hypochondriacal adult is someone for whom the lesson has proved exceptionally alluring and persistent. In effect, the complaining hypochondriac is saying (a) "I *deserve* your attention and concern," and (b) "You may *not* legitimately expect me to perform as a well person would." Typically, these messages are conveyed with more than a touch of angry accusation and whining complaint. In short, hypochondriasis may be viewed as a certain type of interpersonal strategy—a neurotic style, if you will—even though it is normally considered a symptom disorder. The central difficulty appears to be similar to what has been described as responsibility/independence inhibition, wherein the hypochondriacal individual inhibits expressions of responsibility and power and claims dependency status, albeit in a manner disguised by the apparent existence of an illness. The manipulation of others to which the hypochondriac is often prone represents perhaps the indirect expression of certain inhibited aims to dominate and control.

Psychogenic pain disorder

Psychogenic pain disorder is characterized by the report of severe and lasting pain. Either no physical basis is apparent, or the reaction is greatly in excess of what would be expected from the physical pathology. Psychogenic pain disorder is believed to be fairly common among psychiatric patients and is more commonly diagnosed among women.

The reported pain may be vaguely located in the area of the heart or other vital organs, or it may center in the lower back or limbs. (Tension headaches and migraines would not be included here, since they involve underlying physiological changes, such as muscle contractions.) People with psychogenic pain disorders flirt with an invalid life-style. They tend to "doctor-shop"—seeking both a physical confirmation of their pain and some medication. This behavior continues in spite of the fact that several visits to doctors have failed to indicate any underlying physical problem. Sadly enough, in many cases psychogenic pain patients actually wind up being disabled—either through addiction to pain medication or through the crippling effects of surgery they have been able to obtain as treatment for their condition.

The extreme preoccupations of people with hypochondriasis may lead them to treat their symptoms with a variety of over-the-counter medications.

Although technically a disorder should be diagnosed as a psychogenic pain disorder only where no adequate organic basis for the pain can be found, some vaguely related injury or physical problem may be found in the medical history of a pain patient. Usually, however, the past incident serves more as perceived "justification" for the patient's physical concern rather than as a predisposing factor to the present pain.

As the following case illustrates, the psychological foundations of psychogenic pain appear to be very similar to those involved in hypochondriasis. This case also illustrates that the removal of "reinforcement" for the neurotic behavior is sometimes quite effective in aiding the patient to find more satisfying ways of relating to the social environment.

Mrs. X., a 50-year-old obese homemaker and mother of four children was admitted to a pain treatment program. At the time of her admission, she complained of pain in her back, legs, neck, and knee. She had been unable to stoop or bend for the past seven years. She had difficulty in sleeping, walking, or sitting, and had weakness in her legs. She reported that it hurt her to wear clothes, and even to breathe, and that she was depressed and unable to do housework other than prepare light meals and change pillowcases. She

reported "funny noises" in the back of her skull, sweating at night, and pain "in all muscle groups of the body." She was taking 16 to 20 pain pills a day, including aspirin, Darvon, Valium, and Librium.

Mrs. X. reported that her childhood health had been relatively normal, except that she had had asthma. Her first complaints of back pain began with her first pregnancy at age 16. Since that time she had had numerous operations (e.g., an appendectomy, a vaginal repair, a urethral hernia repair, a hysterectomy, and surgery for varicose veins).

Her first admission to the hospital because of chronic pain had been at age 40. At that time, no organic cause for the pain was found. There followed in the next ten years multiple admissions to the hospital for back pain, whiplash, and acute gastric distress (due to the large number of medications she was taking); in addition, she sought numerous outpatient evaluations by neurology, neurosurgery, arthritis, and physical medicine and rehabilitation clinics. She also received psychological consultations, and on three occasions she was treated with psychotherapy. Additional records revealed innumerable visits to general practitioners and specialists. None of the treatments she received was successful.

At the time of her admission to the pain treatment program, Mrs. X. lived with her husband and youngest daughter. Her husband, a skilled blue-collar worker, had himself had back pain for 17 years. Mr. and Mrs. X. had little in common except their need for constant medical attention—he for his back pain and she for her many medical complaints. Mrs. X. reported that she was fearful of following her own vocational plans (she had previous experience as a librarian and shop clerk) because of her husband's "rigidity." She was quite angry with her husband, and it appeared that she tried to punish him as well as communicate with him through her many pain behaviors.

Mrs. X's therapy involved an 8-week behavior modification program for chronic pain, designed to extinguish all nonverbal and verbal behaviors that communicated to others that she had pain and to reinforce responses, such as exercise and work, incompatible with her pain behavior. Medications were placed in a "pain cocktail," which was a concoction of all of the medications she was taking in a single liquid that disguised the form and taste of the medications. These medications were administered on a time-contingent basis six times a day, rather than a pain-contingent basis. The medications in the liquid were reduced each week until there were no active ingredients in the "cocktail." Mrs. X. was informed that the reduction in medication was taking place.

During the program, all the staff avoided any reinforcement of Mrs. X.'s pain complaints. About the fourth week, Mrs. X. was assigned a "job," which required increasing work during the remainder of her hospitalization. During the 8-week period, her husband was seen weekly to teach him to stop reinforcing his wife's pain behaviors and to reinforce activity and work.

During the early part of her hospitalization, Mrs. X. was angry, complained, and had spells of crying. She was unable to walk from her bed to the dining room without receiving pain medication. About a month later she began to exhibit exceedingly inappropriate behavior, such as talking to herself in a mirror, lying on the hall floor and kicking, and making sexual advances toward younger female patients. These behaviors were interpreted as substitutes for Mrs. X.'s now-unreinforced pain behaviors, and the staff was instructed to ignore them. With time, Mrs. X.'s work and activity levels increased and her inappropriate behaviors subsided.

At the time of her discharge from the program, Mrs. X. was functioning at a physical and activity level considered normal for her age and sex, and she was using no pain medications. Six months following the program she became somewhat depressed but she required no formal treatment other than the support of her social worker.

In the ten years since she took part in the pain treatment program, Mrs. X. has been leading a normal life and has been employed as a librarian and shop clerk.

Conversion disorder

Conversion disorder, earlier called *hysteria,* involves a neurotic pattern in which symptoms of some physical malfunction or loss of control appear without any underlying organic pathology. The case of paralysis presented on page 191 was of this nature. It is one of the most intriguing and baffling patterns in psychopathology, and we still have much to learn about it.

As we mentioned in Chapter 2, the term *hysteria* was derived from the Greek word meaning "uterus." It was thought by Hippocrates and other ancient Greeks that this disorder was restricted to women and that it was caused by sexual difficulties, particularly by the wandering of a frustrated uterus to various parts of the body because of sexual desires and a yearning for children. Thus the uterus might lodge in the throat and cause choking sensations, or in the spleen, resulting in temper tantrums. Hippocrates considered marriage the best remedy for the affliction.

This concept of the relationship between sexual difficulties and unfounded body ailments was later advanced in modified form by Freud. He used the term *conversion hysteria* because he believed that the symptoms were an expression of repressed sexual energy—that is, the psychosexual conflict was seen as *converted* into a bodily disturbance. For example, a sexual conflict over masturbation might be "solved" by developing a paralyzed hand. This was not done consciously, of course, and the person was not aware of the origin or meaning of the physical symptom.

In contemporary psychopathology, reactions of this type are no longer interpreted in Freudian terms as the "conversion" of sexual conflicts or other psychological problems into physical symptoms. Rather, the physical symptoms are now usually seen as serving a defensive function, enabling the individual to escape or avoid a stressful situation without having to acknowledge responsibility for doing so.

Conversion disorders were once relatively common in civilian and especially in military life. In World War I conversion disorder was the most frequently diagnosed psychiatric syndrome among soldiers; it was also relatively common during World War II. Conversion disorder typi-

During World War I, conversion disorders allowed soldiers a way of escaping from the stress of war, the severity of which is evident on the face of this infantry corporal in the Argonne Forest.

cally occurred under highly stressful combat conditions and involved men who would ordinarily be considered stable. Here, conversion symptoms—such as being paralyzed in the legs—enabled the soldier to avoid the anxiety-arousing combat situation without being labeled a coward or being subjected to court-martial.

Today, conversion disorders constitute only 5 percent of all neurotic disorders treated. Interestingly enough, their decreasing incidence seems to be closely related to our growing sophistication about medical and psychological disorders: a conversion disorder apparently loses its defensive function if it can be readily shown to lack an organic basis. In an age that no longer believes in such phenomena as being "struck" blind or suddenly afflicted with an unusual and dramatic paralysis with no organic basis, the cases that occur increasingly simulate

more exotic physical diseases that are harder to diagnose, such as mononucleosis or convulsive seizures.

Even psychologically sophisticated people have been known to develop conversion symptoms under stress, however.

A 29-year-old physician in the first year of a psychiatric residency was experiencing a great deal of stress from problems in both his personal life and his hospital work. His marriage was deteriorating and he was being heavily criticized by the rather authoritarian chief of psychiatry for allegedly mismanaging some treatment cases. Shortly before he was to discuss his work in an important hospital-wide conference being conducted by the chief psychiatrist, he had an "attack" in which he developed difficulty in speaking and severe pains in his chest. He thought his condition was probably related to a viral infection, but physical findings were negative.

Here we see with particular clarity how a conversion symptom may serve the function of escape from unwanted responsibility.

The range of symptoms in conversion disorder is practically as diverse as for physically based ailments. In describing the clinical picture in conversion disorder, it is useful to think in terms of three categories of symptoms: sensory, motor, and visceral.

Sensory symptoms. Any of the senses may be involved in sensory conversion reactions. The most common forms are as follows:

Anesthesia—loss of sensitivity
Hypesthesia—partial loss of sensitivity
Hyperesthesia—excessive sensitivity
Analgesia—loss of sensitivity to pain
Paresthesia—exceptional sensations, such as tingling

Some idea of the range of sensory symptoms that may occur in conversion disorders can be gleaned from Ironside and Batchelor's (1945) study of hysterical visual symptoms among airmen in World War II. They found blurred vision, photophobia (extreme sensitivity to light), double vision, night blindness, a combination of intermittent visual failure and amnesia, deficient stereopsis (the tendency to look past an object during attempts to focus on it), restriction in the visual field, intermittent loss of vision in one

HIGHLIGHT
Conversion reactions in student naval aviators

Mucha and Reinhardt (1970) reported on a study of 56 student aviators with conversion reactions who were assessed at the U.S. Naval Aerospace Medical Institute in Pensacola, Florida. In the group, representing 16 percent of a total population of 343 patients at the Institute, four types of symptoms were found. These were, in order of frequency: visual symptoms (most common), auditory symptoms, paralysis or paresthesias (prickling sensations) of extremities, and paresthesia of the tongue.

Generally, the 56 students came from middle-class achievement-oriented families. The fathers of 80 percent of them were either high-school or college graduates and were either professional men or white-collar workers. Interestingly enough, 89 percent of the cases had won letters in one or more sports in high school or college; all were college graduates and presently were flight students, officer candidates, or officers.

Commenting on the relatively high incidence of conversion reactions among the patients at the Institute, Mucha and Reinhardt emphasized three conditions which they considered of etiological significance:

1. Unacceptability of quitting. In the students' previous athletic training, physical illness had been an acceptable means of avoiding difficult situations, whereas quitting was not. Moreover, the present training environment tended to perpetuate this adaptation, since the military is also achievement-oriented, and does not tolerate quitting as a means of coping with stress situations.

2. Parental models and past experience. Seventy percent of the parents of these students had had significant illnesses affecting the organ system utilized in the students' disorders; and a majority of the students had had multiple physical symptoms prior to enlistment—often as a result of athletic injuries.

3. Sensitization to the use of somatic complaints. As a result of their previous experience, the students were sensitized to the use of somatic complaints as a face-saving means of coping with stressful situations.

"When faced with the real stress of the flight training program and with frequent life-or-death incidents, they resorted to this unconscious mechanism to relieve the stress and to avoid admitting failure. To admit failure would be totally unacceptable to the rigid demands of their superegos." (p.494)

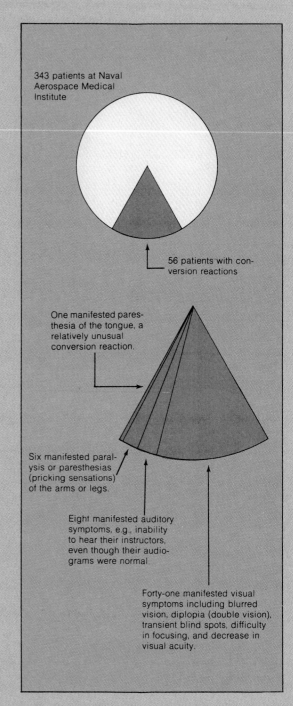

343 patients at Naval Aerospace Medical Institute

56 patients with conversion reactions

One manifested paresthesia of the tongue, a relatively unusual conversion reaction.

Six manifested paralysis or paresthesias (pricking sensations) of the arms or legs.

Eight manifested auditory symptoms, e.g., inability to hear their instructors, even though their audiograms were normal.

Forty-one manifested visual symptoms including blurred vision, diplopia (double vision), transient blind spots, difficulty in focusing, and decrease in visual acuity.

eye, color blindness, jumbling of print during attempts to read, and failing day vision. They also found that the symptoms of each airman were closely related to his performance duties. Night fliers, for example, were more subject to night blindness, while day fliers more often developed failing day vision. Results of a later study of student military aviators who developed conversion disorders are reported in the **HIGHLIGHT** on page 214.

The other senses may also be subject to a wide range of disorders; a puzzling and unsolved question in hysterical blindness and deafness is whether the individual actually cannot see or hear, or whether the sensory information is received but screened from consciousness (Theodor & Mandelcorn, 1973). In general, the evidence supports the latter hypothesis, that the sensory input is screened from consciousness.

Motor symptoms.

Motor conversion reactions also cover a wide range of symptoms, but only the most common need be mentioned here.

Paralysis conversion reactions are usually confined to a single limb, such as an arm or a leg, and the loss of function is usually selective. For example, in "writer's cramp" the person cannot write but may be able to use the same muscles in shuffling a deck of cards or playing the piano. Tremors (muscular shaking or trembling) and tics (localized muscular twitches) are common. Occasionally there are contractures that usually involve flexing of the fingers and toes, or there is rigidity of the larger joints, such as the elbows and knees. Paralyses and contractures frequently lead to walking disturbances. A man with a rigid knee joint may be forced to throw his leg out in a sort of arc as he walks. Another walking disturbance worthy of mention is *astasia-abasia,* in which the individual can usually control leg movements when sitting or lying down, but can hardly stand and has a very grotesque, disorganized walk, with both legs wobbling about in every direction.

The most common conversion disturbances of speech are *aphonia,* in which the individual is able to talk only in a whisper, and *mutism,* in which he or she cannot speak at all. Interestingly enough, a person who can talk only in a whisper can usually cough in a normal manner. In true laryngeal paralysis both the cough and the voice are affected. Aphonia is a relatively common conversion reaction and usually occurs after some emotional shock, whereas mutism is relatively rare. Occasionally, symptoms may involve convulsions, similar to those in epilepsy. However, such individuals show few of the usual characteristics of true epilepsy—they rarely, if ever, injure themselves, their pupillary reflex to light remains unaffected, they are still able to control excretory functions, and they do not have attacks when others are not present.

Visceral symptoms.

Visceral conversion reactions also cover a wide range, including headache, "lump in the throat" and choking sensations, coughing spells, difficulty in breathing, cold and clammy extremities, belching, nausea, and so on. Occasionally, persistent hiccoughing or sneezing occurs.

Actual organic symptoms may be simulated to an almost unbelievable degree. In a pseudoattack of acute appendicitis, the person not only may evidence pain in the lower abdominal region and other typical symptoms of acute appendicitis, but also may have a temperature far above normal. Cases of conversion reactions of malaria and tuberculosis have also been cited in the literature. In the latter, for example, the individual may show all the usual symptoms—coughing, loss of weight, recurrent fever, and night sweats—without actual organic disease. Even cases of pseudo-pregnancy have been cited, in which the menstrual cycle ceases, there is an enlargement of the abdominal area, and the woman experiences morning sickness.

Since the symptoms in conversion disorder can simulate almost every known disease, accurate diagnosis can be a problem. However, in addition to specialized medical techniques, several criteria are commonly used for distinguishing between conversion disorders and organic disturbances:

a) A certain *belle indifference,* in which the patient describes what is wrong in a rather matter-of-fact way, with little of the anxiety and fear that would be expected in a person with a paralyzed arm or loss of sight. Mucha and Reinhardt (1970) reported that all of the 56 student fliers in their study (p. 214) showed this pattern, seeming to be unconcerned about long-range effects of their disabilities.

b) The frequent failure of the dysfunction to conform clearly to the symptoms of the particular disease or disorder. For example, little or no wasting away or atrophy of the "paralyzed" limb occurs in paralyses that are conversion reactions, except in rare and long-standing cases.

c) The selective nature of the dysfunction. For example, in conversion blindness the individual does not usually bump into people or objects; "paralyzed" muscles can be used for some activities but not others; and uncontrolled contractures usually disappear during sleep.

d) The interesting fact that under hypnosis or narcosis the symptoms can usually be removed, shifted, or reinduced by the suggestion of the therapist. Similarly, if the individual is suddenly awakened from a sound sleep, he or she may be tricked into using a "paralyzed" limb.

Where conversion symptoms are superimposed on an actual organic disorder, the difficulty in making a diagnosis may be increased. However, it is usually fairly easy to distinguish between a conversion reaction and *malingering.* Malingerers are consciously perpetrating a fraud by faking the symptoms of a disease, and this fact is reflected in their demeanor. Individuals with a conversion disorder are usually dramatic and apparently naive; they are concerned mainly with the symptoms and willingly discuss them. If inconsistencies in their behaviors are pointed out, they are usually unperturbed. To the contrary, malingerers are inclined to be defensive, evasive, and suspicious; they are apt to be reluctant to be examined and slow to talk about their symptoms, lest the pretense be discovered. Should inconsistencies in their behaviors be pointed out, malingerers immediately become more defensive. Thus conversion disorder and malingering are considered distinct patterns, although sometimes they overlap.

The phenomenon of *mass hysteria,* as typified by outbreaks of St. Vitus's dance and biting manias during the Middle Ages, is a form of conversion disorder that has become a rarity in modern times. However, as we saw in Chapter 2, some outbreaks do still occur (for some recent examples, see pages 39–40). In all such cases, suggestibility clearly plays a major role, in which a conversion reaction in one individual rapidly spreads to others.

In the development of a conversion disorder, the following chain of events typically occurs:

(a) a desire to escape from some unpleasant situation; (b) a fleeting wish to be sick in order to avoid the situation (this wish, however, is suppressed as unfeasible or unworthy); and (c) under additional or continued stress, the appearance of the symptoms of some physical ailment. The individual sees no relation between the symptoms and the stress situation. The particular symptoms that occur are usually those of a previous illness or are copied from other sources such as illness symptoms observed among relatives or on television or read about in magazines. However, they may also be superimposed on an existing organic ailment, be associated with anticipated secondary gains, or be symbolically related to the conflict situation.

As in the case of the other somatoform disorders described above, the stressor situation that leads to conversion symptoms most often is one that requires responsible or independent actions on the part of the "victim," whose performance of these actions is inhibited by anxiety. Indeed, the persons most susceptible to conversion disorders are those who generally avoid responsibility, either to escape unpleasant realities or to achieve ends that they themselves regard as less than laudable.

Aggression/assertion inhibition also occurs with some regularity as a background feature in conversion disorder. Abse (1959) has cited the case of a middle-aged male patient who suffered total paralysis of his legs after his wife left him for another man. During the course of treatment it became apparent that he had a strong wish to pursue his wife and kill her and her lover. Although the wish had been repressed, it was quite intense, and the paralysis apparently represented a massive—and quite effective—defense against the possibility that this wish might be carried out. This appears to be an instance in which "appropriate" levels of anger or retaliation have been blocked, leading to a build-up of murderous impulses.

Sometimes, conversion disorders seem to stem from feelings of guilt and the necessity for self-punishment. In one case, for example, a female patient developed a marked tremor and partial paralysis of the right arm and hand after she had physically attacked her father. During this incident she had clutched at and torn open his shirt with her right hand, and apparently the subsequent paralysis represented a sort of symbolic punishment of the "guilty party," while preventing a recurrence of her hostile and forbidden behavior.

Not uncommonly, conversion symptoms develop following some accident or injury as a result of which the individual hopes to receive monetary compensation. These reactions usually occur after accidents in which the individual might have been seriously injured but is actually only shaken up or slightly injured. Later, in discussions with family or friends, it may be agreed that the individual would have had a strong legal case if there had been an injury. "Are you sure you are all right? Could you possibly have injured your back? Perhaps there *is* something wrong with it." With the aid of a sympathetic lawyer, the individual may proceed to file suit for compensation for alleged injuries.

Here it is especially hard to distinguish between the malingerer's deliberate simulation of injury and the unconscious deception of an individual suffering from conversion disorder (Lewis, 1974). Apparently in many conversion reaction cases there is a combination of the two, in which conscious acting is superimposed on unconscious acting or role playing. In these cases the patient shows an amazingly rapid recovery once there has been proper compensation for the "injuries."

Whatever specific causal factors may be involved, however, the basic motivational pattern underlying conversion disorder seems to be to avoid or reduce anxiety-arousing stress by getting sick—thus converting an intolerable emotional problem into a face-saving physical one. Once the response is learned, it is maintained because it is repeatedly reinforced—both by anxiety reduction and by the interpersonal gains (in terms of sympathy and support) that result from being sick.

Dissociative disorders

Like somatoform disorders, *dissociative disorders* are ways of avoiding stress while gratifying needs—in a manner permitting the person to deny personal responsibility for his or her unacceptable behavior. In the case of dissociative

disorders, however, the person avoids the stress by, in essence, escaping—dissociating—from his or her core personality. Dissociative patterns include psychogenic amnesia and fugue states, multiple personality, and depersonalization. These patterns are quite rare; hence, our coverage of them will be relatively brief.

Psychogenic amnesia and fugue

Amnesia is partial or total inability to recall or identify past experience. It may occur in neurotic and psychotic disorders and in brain pathology, including brain injury and diseases of the nervous system. If the amnesia is caused by brain pathology, it usually involves an actual failure of retention. That is, either the information is not registered and does not enter memory storage, or, if stored, it cannot be retrieved; it is truly lost (Hirst, 1982).

Psychogenic amnesia, on the other hand, is usually limited to a *failure to recall.* The "forgotten" material is still there beneath the level of consciousness, as becomes apparent under hypnosis or narcosis (a sleeplike state induced by drugs) interviews, and in cases where the amnesia spontaneously clears up. Four types of psychogenic amnesia are recognized: *localized* (the person remembers nothing that happened during a specific period—usually the first few hours following some traumatic event); *selective* (the person forgets some but not all of what happened during a given period); *generalized* (the person forgets his or her entire life history); and *continuous* (the person remembers nothing beyond a certain point in the past). The latter two types occur only very rarely.

As we have noted, psychogenic amnesia is fairly common in initial reactions to intolerably traumatic experiences, such as those occurring during combat conditions and immediately after catastrophic events. However, some neurotically functioning individuals develop such amnesias in the face of stressful life situations with which most people deal more effectively.

In typical psychogenic amnesic reactions, individuals cannot remember their names, do not know how old they are or where they reside, and do not recognize their parents, relatives, or friends. Yet their basic habit patterns—such as their ability to read, talk, and so on—remain in-

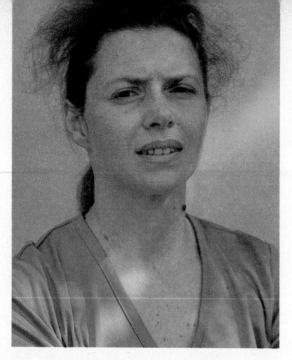

This woman, dubbed "Jane Doe," was emaciated, incoherent, partially clothed, covered by insect and animal bites, and near death when discovered by a Florida park ranger in September 1980. Her recovery was further complicated by a rare form of psychogenic amnesia, generalized amnesia, in which she had lost the memory of her name, her past, and her ability to read and write. Judging from her accent, linguistic experts said the woman was probably from Illinois. Although interviews conducted under the effect of drugs revealed that the woman had apparently had a Catholic education, her few childhood memories were so common that they were meaningless. In a dramatic attempt to recover her past, Jane Doe and her doctor appeared on the "Good Morning America" television program and appealed to relatives to step forward. The response was overwhelming and authorities came to believe that Jane Doe was the daughter of a couple from Roselle, Illinois, whose daughter had gone to the Ft. Lauderdale area to open a boutique. Their last contact with their daughter had been a phone call in 1976. Despite the couple's certainty, Jane Doe was never able to remember her past.

tact, and they seem quite normal aside from the amnesia.

In this amnesic state a person may retreat still further from real-life problems by going away in what is called a *fugue* state. A fugue reaction is a defense by actual flight—the individual is not only amnesic but also wanders away from home, often assuming a partially or completely new identity. Days, weeks, or sometimes even years later such individuals may suddenly find themselves in a strange place, not knowing how they got there and with complete amnesia for the period of the fugue. Their activities during the fugue may vary from merely going on a

round of motion pictures to traveling across the country, entering a new occupation, and starting a new way of life.

The pattern in psychogenic amnesia is essentially the same as in conversion disorder, except that instead of avoiding some unpleasant situation by getting sick, the person does it by avoiding thoughts about it. Apparently, virtually any type of inner conflict involving wishes that are unacceptable to the person and are therefore anxiety-arousing may serve as the basis of the amnesic reaction and its elaboration into fugue. The threatening information becomes inaccessible, owing either to some sort of automatic cognitive blockage or to deliberate suppression. In patterns involving suppression, individuals apparently tell themselves that they will not remember some traumatic event or situation; subsequently they try to believe and behave as though they actually were amnesic. For example, in a study of 98 amnesia cases, primarily among military personnel, Kiersch (1962) found 41 to be of this "feigned" ("factitious" in DSM-III terminology) type.

People experiencing psychogenic amnesia are typically egocentric, immature, highly suggestible individuals who are faced with an extremely unpleasant situation from which they see no escape. Often, they previously experienced a conscious impulse to "forget" and run away from it all but were too cowardly to accept the solution at the time. Eventually, however, the stress became so intolerable that they suppressed large segments of their personality and all memory for the stressful situation, thus allowing more congenial patterns to carry on. As O'Neill and Kempler (1969) have pointed out, psychogenic amnesia is highly selective and involves only material that is basically intolerable or threatening to the self.

During such dissociative reactions the individual appears normal and is able to engage in complex activities. Not uncommonly, the activities chosen reflect in a rather transparent manner parts of the person's previously inhibited desires and motives. This is well illustrated in an interesting case described by Masserman (1961).

"Bernice L., a 42-year-old housewife, was brought to the Clinics by her family, who stated that the patient had disappeared from her home four years previously, and had recently been identified and returned from R _____, a small town over a thousand miles away. On rejoining her parents, husband and child she had at first appeared highly perturbed, anxious, and indecisive. Soon, however, she had begun to insist that she really had never seen them before, that her name was not Bernice L. but Rose P. and that it was all a case of mistaken identity; further, she threatened that if she were not returned to her home in R _____ immediately, she would sue the hospital for conspiracy and illegal detainment. Under treatment, however, the patient slowly formed an adequate working rapport with the psychiatrist, consented to various ancillary anamnestic procedures such as amytal interviews and hypnosis, and eventually dissipated her amnesia sufficiently to furnish the following history:

"The patient was raised by fanatically religious parents, who despite their Evangelical church work and moralistic pretenses, accused each other of infidelity so frequently that the patient often questioned her own legitimacy. However, instead of divorcing each other, the parents had merely vented their mutual hostility upon the patient in a tyrannically prohibitive upbringing. In the troubled loneliness of her early years the patient became deeply attached to her older sister, and together they found some security and comfort; unfortunately, this sister died when the patient was seventeen and left her depressed and unconsolable for over a year. After this, at her parents' edict, the patient entered the University of A _____ and studied assiduously to prepare herself for missionary work. However, during her second semester at the University, she was assigned to room with an attractive, warm-hearted and gifted girl, Rose P., who gradually guided the patient to new interests, introduced her to various friendships, and encouraged her to develop her neglected talent as a pianist. The patient became as devoted to her companion as she had formerly been to her sister, and was for a time relatively happy. In her junior year, however, Rose P. became engaged to a young dentist, and the couple would frequently take the patient with them on trips when a chaperone was necessary. Unfortunately, the patient, too, fell 'madly in love' with her friend's fiancé, and spent days of doubt and remorse over her incompatible loves and jealousies. The young man, however, paid little attention to his fiancée's shy, awkward, and emotionally intense friend, married Rose P. and took her to live with him in Canada. The patient reacted with a severe depression, the cause of which she refused to explain to her family, but at their insistence, she returned to the University, took her degree, and entered a final preparatory school for foreign missionaries.

"On completion of her work she entered into a loveless marriage with a man designated by her parents and spent six unhappy years in missionary out-posts in Burma and China. The couple, with their two children, then returned to the United States and settled in the parsonage of a small midwest town. Her life as a minister's wife, however, gradually became less and less bearable as her husband became increasingly preoccupied with the affairs of his church, and as the many prohibitions of the village (e.g., against movies, recreations, liberal opinions and even against secular music) began to stifle her with greater weight from year to year. During this time the patient became increasingly prone to quiet, hazy reminiscences about the only relatively happy period she had known—her first two years in college with her friend, Rose P.—and these years, in her daydreaming, gradually came to represent all possible contentment. Finally, when the patient was thirty-seven, the culmination of her disappointments came with the sickness and death of her younger and favorite child. The next day the patient disappeared from home without explanation or trace, and her whereabouts, despite frantic search, remained unknown to her family for the next four years.

"Under treatment in the Clinics, the patient recollected that, after a dimly remembered journey by a devious route, she finally reached A _____, the college town of her youth. However, she had lost all conscious knowledge of her true identity and previous life, except that she thought her name was Rose P. Under this name she had begun to earn a living playing and teaching the piano, and was so rapidly successful that within two years she was the assistant director of a conservatory of music. Intuitively, she chose friends who would not be curious about her past, which to her remained a mysterious blank, and thereby eventually established a new social identity which soon removed the need for introspections and ruminations. Thus the patient lived for four years as though she were another person until the almost inevitable happened. She was finally identified by a girlhood acquaintance who had known both her and the true Rose P. in their college years. The patient at first sincerely and vigorously denied this identification, resisted her removal to Chicago, where her husband was now assigned, and failed to recognize either him or her family until her treatment in the Clinics penetrated her amnesia. Fortunately, her husband proved unexpectedly understanding and cooperative, and the patient eventually readjusted to a fuller and more acceptable life under happily changed circumstances." (pp. 35–37)

Multiple personality

Dual and multiple personalities have received a great deal of attention and publicity in fiction, television, and motion pictures. Actually, however, they are rare in clinical practice. Only slightly more than a hundred cases can be found in psychological and psychiatric records.

Multiple personality is a dissociative reaction, usually due to stress, in which the patient manifests two or more complete systems of personality. Each system has distinct, well-developed emotional and thought processes and represents a unique and relatively stable personality. The individual may change from one personality to another at periods varying from a few minutes to several years, though the former is the more common time frame. The personalities are usually dramatically different; one may be gay, carefree, and fun-loving, and another quiet, studious, and serious. Needs and behaviors inhibited in the main or basic personality are usually liberally displayed by the others.

Various types of relationships may exist between the different personalities. Usually the individual alternates from one personality to the other, and cannot remember in one what happened in the other. Occasionally, however, while one personality is dominant and functions consciously, the other continues to function subconsciously and is referred to as a *co-conscious* personality. In these cases the co-conscious personality is usually intimately aware of the thoughts of the conscious personality and of things going on in the world, but indicates its awareness through automatic writing (in which the individual writes a message without full awareness or conscious control) or in some other way. The conscious personality usually knows nothing of the co-conscious personality.

Relationships may become highly complicated when there are more than two personalities, as in the case described in the **HIGHLIGHT** on this and the facing page. Some of the personalities may be mutually amnesic while others are only one-way amnesic.

In a sense, we are all multiple personalities, in that we have many conflicting and warring tendencies and frequently do things that surprise both ourselves and others. This is illustrated by many common sayings, such as "I don't know why I did it" or "I didn't think he had it in him." It is also illustrated by the changed behavior many persons indulge in at conventions when they are away from their families and associates and "cut loose." In pathological cases, there is evidently such a deep-seated conflict between contradictory impulses and be-

HIGHLIGHT
The three faces of Evelyn

Most of us are familiar with the classic case of multiple personality reported by Thigpen and Cleckley (1954), which was widely publicized and made into the movie *The Three Faces of Eve*. From psychological studies of the patient undertaken independently and using the Semantic Differential Technique, Osgood and Luria (1954) concluded that the three "personalities" indeed had very different affective meaning systems, but they were anxious to analyze another multiple personality in order to further substantiate their findings.

A recent opportunity to conduct a detailed objective study of another case of multiple personality was presented when the late psychiatrist, R. F. Jeans, referred his patient, Gina, a single, 31-year-old woman of Italian descent, to Osgood, Luria, Jeans, and Smith for independent study using objective psychological evaluation procedures (Osgood et al., 1976).

Gina was the youngest of nine children of immigrant parents. Her parents were fairly old when Gina was born. Gina considered her mother to be a domineering woman, while she saw her father as a passive and ineffectual man. The mother believed that Gina had a great deal of ability and pushed her to achieve and get ahead in life. Gina had high educational aspirations and had earned a master's degree. At the time she sought psychological help she was employed as an editor and test developer for a large publishing firm.

Gina was referred to therapy by a group of her friends who were concerned about her somnambulism (sleepwalking), episodic amnesia, and unusual and inefficient behavior. Gina said she often was awakened during the night by the sound of her mother's name, but her roommate reported that it was Gina herself who screamed out the mother's name. Gina was a rather masculine woman in appearance and interests. She had not had much experience with men and seldom dated. When she was 28 years old she had a

liefs that a resolution is achieved through separating the conflicting parts from each other and elaborating each into a more-or-less autonomous personality system. In this way the individual is able to carry out incompatible systems of behavior without the stress, conflict, and guilt that would otherwise occur.

The pattern of conflict between personalities is well brought out in Lipton's comprehensive

brief "platonic" affair with a former priest. A short time later she became quite involved with a married man (T.C.) who promised to get a divorce but failed to do so. She reportedly had not dated other men since because she wanted to remain faithful to T. C.

In the beginning of therapy, Gina's sexual identification problems were prominent. She had repressed her feminine identification, although the content of her reported dreams revealed that a feminine identification was still "quite lively and increasingly unwilling to remain shut out of consciousness." At this point, one of Gina's other personalities who called herself "Mary Sunshine" began to emerge. She was quite the opposite of Gina—in sexual identification, attitudes, and mannerisms. Mary Sunshine was a vivacious, bubbling, seductive personality whom Jeans viewed as a warmer, nicer, and more accepting person than Gina.

Interestingly, Gina became aware of Mary Sunshine through several puzzling events. Neither she nor her roommate liked hot chocolate although empty cups that had had chocolate in them kept showing up near Gina's bed. Also, in spite of her high income and her generally frugal existence, Gina found her bank account depleted at the end of each month. She once found herself on the phone ordering a sewing machine even though she knew nothing about sewing. Gina also became surprised at having certain emotions that she had never before experienced. Once, while watching a movie, for example, she began to experience tender emotions which were not in keeping with Gina's usual tough self. The new personality, Mary Sunshine, alternated with Gina for some time.

After a period of therapy a third personality, Evelyn, appeared—an apparent balance of the personalities of Gina and Mary. Therapeutic improvement came rapidly after Evelyn emerged and began to accumulate information about Gina and Mary. Evelyn learned to live without the extreme defenses of either Gina or Mary. She began to date and eventually mar-

ried. Nine years after the termination of therapy she was reportedly happily married with no recurrence of her previous problems.

Late in therapy, a double form of the Semantic Differential was administered by the therapist and given a blind analysis by Osgood, Luria, and Smith. They were told only that there were three accessible personalities who communicated by "inner conversations"; that the patient was 32 years old, white, childless, single, and worked as an editor; and that the patient had eight older siblings (two brothers). The ten scales used were as follows: Valuable—Worthless; Clean—Dirty;   Tasty—Tasteless;   Large—Small; Strong—Weak;   Deep—Shallow;   Fast—Slow;   Active—Passive; Hot—Cold; Relaxed—Tense.

The descriptions generated by blind interpretations of the three personalities clearly validated Jeans' clinical descriptions (Osgood et al., 1976)

Gina was described as a moralistic, straightlaced person. She was seen as tense, inhibited, and quite self-critical, as well as disturbed and full of hatred. She also was considered to derive gratification from her disorder.

Mary was described as an ebullient person, more relaxed and "much more full of love of people." She was also viewed as a rather childish and playful person who placed no value on her job. She seemed to accept fraudulence as a way of life. Mary had a more active interest in males and sex than either Gina or Evelyn.

Evelyn represented a balance between Gina and Mary. She seemed more mature than the "childish" Mary and more relaxed than Gina. She placed more emphasis on reality and a job and task orientation. The blind interpretation suggested that the personality represented by Evelyn was probably the product of the preceding therapy.

and excellent analysis of the case of Sara and Maud K., excerpts of which are given below.

". . . in general demeanor, Maud was quite different from Sara. She walked with a swinging, bouncing gait contrasted to Sara's sedate one. While Sara was depressed, Maud was ebullient and happy.

". . . in so far as she could Maud dressed differently from Sara. Sara had two pairs of slippers. One was a worn pair of plain gray mules; the other,

gaudy, striped, high-heeled, open-toed sandals. Sara always wore the mules. Maud would throw them aside in disgust and don the sandals. Sara used no make-up. Maud used a lot of rouge and lipstick, [and] painted her fingernails and toenails deep red. . . . She liked red and was quickly attracted by anything of that color. Sara's favorite color was blue.

"Sara was a mature, intelligent individual. Her mental age was 19.2 years, IQ, 128. A psychometric done on Maud showed a mental age of 6.6, IQ, 43. Sara's vocabulary was larger than Maud's, and she took an intelligent interest in words new to her. When Maud heard a new word, she would laugh and mispronounce it, or say, 'That was a twenty-five cent one.' In sharp contrast to Sara, Maud's grammar was atrocious. A typical statement was, 'I didn't do nuttin'.' Sara's handwriting was more mature than Maud's.

"Sara did not smoke and was very awkward when she attempted it. Maud had a compulsion to smoke. At times she insisted she 'had to' and would become agitated and even violent if cigarettes were denied her. She would smoke chain fashion as many cigarettes as were permitted but two would satisfy her for a while. . . .

"Maud had no conscience, no sense of right and wrong. She saw no reason for not always doing as she pleased. She felt no guilt over her incestuous and promiscuous sexual relationships. Sara on the other hand had marked guilt feelings over her previous immoral sexual behavior.

"It seemed that Sara changed to Maud at the point when Sara's feeling of guilt was greatest." (1943, pp. 41–44)

Judging from the previous history of this patient, it would appear that the development of a dissociated personality in the form of Maud had, among other things, enabled Sara to gratify her sexual desires by engaging in promiscuous sexual relations without conscious knowledge and hence without guilt feelings. Apparently Sara reverted to Maud when her guilt feelings over her own previous promiscuous sexual behavior became too intense and self-devaluating.

Further light is cast on Sara's background by the report of two of her previous high-school friends that "she was 'boy crazy' and was always chasing after some boy, often being rude to her girlfriends, that she dyed her hair red, and that she smoked and used Listerine to deceive her mother about smoking. Sara denied all this but Maud readily recalled it" (Lipton, 1943, p. 47). It is interesting to note that this patient later became psychotic, apparently as a result of the failure of the dissociative reaction to solve her inner stress satisfactorily.

Because multiple personalities can be induced experimentally, the question has been raised as to whether the cases reported by therapists are in fact artificial creations produced inadvertently by suggestions of the therapist. Regarding this problem, Berman (1975) has pointed out:

"Certainly there are good reasons for doubting the tales of split personalities: The therapists' intense involvement with their patients; their own belief in the reality of splitting; the use of hypnosis and other methods of suggestion. While some cases may be fictitious, and while in others a therapist's expectations may have unconsciously encouraged the birth of the personalities detected, I believe that true cases of multiple personality do occur. One way to detect these genuine cases is to learn if the split appeared before therapy began, or if the reported personalities led separate lives outside the consulting room." (p. 78)

Depersonalization disorder

A relatively more frequent dissociative disorder that occurs predominantly in adolescents and young adults is *depersonalization,* in which there is a loss of the sense of self. Such individuals feel that they are, all of a sudden, different—for example, that they are someone else or that their body has become drastically changed and has become, perhaps, quite grotesque. Frequently the altered state is reported as an "out of body experience" in which individuals feel that they are, for a time, floating above their physical bodies and observing what is going on below. Mild forms of the experience are extremely common and are no cause for alarm. Reports of "out of body experiences" have included perceptions that the person has visited other planets or a relative who is in another city. The disorder is often precipitated by acute stress resulting from a toxic illness, an accident, or some other traumatic event, as in the following case.

Charlotte D., a recently separated 19-year-old woman, was referred to an outpatient mental health service by her physician because she had experienced several "spells" in which her mind left her body and went to a strange place in another state. The first instance had occurred two months earlier, a few days after her husband had left her without explanation. Since then, she had had four episodes of "traveling" that had occurred during her waking state and had lasted for about 15 to 20 minutes. She described her experiences as a dreamy feeling in which her arms and legs were not attached to her body and other people around her were perceived as zombie-like. Typically she felt dizzy and had pains in her stomach for hours after each spell.

Individuals who experience depersonalized states are usually able to function between episodes, at least marginally, but they often experience a great deal of anxiety associated with the episode and with fears of losing control. These characteristics distinguish neurotic depersonalization disorders from the feelings of depersonalization that sometimes occur with the personality deterioration and severe regression of psychosis, as we shall see in Chapter 10.

General causal factors, treatment, and outcomes

In our preceding discussion we described the basic nature of neurotic disorders, noting that they may be manifested in general behavioral styles, in certain characteristic symptoms, or both. We presented a variety of specific neurotic patterns. Now let us focus more closely on relevant causal factors and give some attention to treatment considerations and to the outcomes that may be expected.

Development and maintenance of neurotic behaviors

As we have seen, Freud considered anxiety to be the central problem in neurosis, a conclusion echoed over the years by many writers of widely differing theoretical persuasions. It is also basically the approach we have taken in seeking to conceptualize the varied behavioral phenomena traditionally grouped together as "neurotic." To understand these disorders, then, we need to understand the origins of relatively severe anxiety and of the inefficient and self-defeating modes often used to cope with it. We approach these questions from biological, psychosocial, and sociocultural perspectives.

Biological factors. The precise role of genetic and constitutional factors in neurotic behavior has not been delineated. Ample evidence from army records and civilian studies indicates that the incidence of neurotic patterns is much higher in the family histories of neurotic individuals than in the general population, but the extent to which such findings reflect the effect of heredity is not known. Other explanations for these correlations are readily available, such as the likelihood that modeling of symptoms occurs among family members. For example, in

the "panphobia" case described earlier (page 206), the client's mother had also suffered lifelong phobic reactions and had sought actively to transmit her fears to her daughter.

In a study of concordance rates of neurotic disorder in identical and fraternal twins in the military, Pollin et al. (1969) found that among identical twins the rate was only one and a half times as high as it was among fraternal twins. Since the environmental background of identical twins is likely to be more similar than that of fraternal twins, these investigators concluded that heredity plays a minimal role in the development of neurotic behaviors. After evaluating the evidence, Cohen (1974) came to a similar conclusion: "the concept of a genetically based disease or defect cannot provide a satisfactory explanation for the diversity and variability of most neurotic phenomena" (p. 473).

Sex, age, glandular functioning, and other physiological factors have also been investigated without illuminating the causal picture. It is known, of course, that stress tolerance is lowered by loss of sleep, poor appetite, and increased irritability associated with prolonged emotional tension—but such conditions are by no means exclusive to the neurotic disorders. A more promising possibility centers around constitutional differences in ease of conditioning. For example, extreme sensitivity and autonomic lability (instability) may predispose the individual to a "surplus" of conditioned fears and hence to avoidance behavior. On the other hand, certain innate features of temperament might predispose an individual to develop particular ways of managing whatever anxiety is present. But as yet the evidence is inconclusive; a great deal more research is needed to clarify the possible role of constitutional and other biological factors in the development of neurotic disorders.

Psychosocial factors. The psychological and interpersonal causal factors in maladaptive behavior that we reviewed in Chapter 4 as predisposing an individual to develop specific problems are especially applicable to neurotic behaviors. Relevant here are early psychic trauma, pathogenic parent-child and family patterns, and disturbed interpersonal relationships.

Each of the psychosocial viewpoints summarized in Chapter 3 has posed a hypothesis about psychological causes of neurotic behaviors.

1. *Anxiety-defense.* Traditionally, neurotic disorders have been explained within the framework of anxiety-defense, as originally proposed by Freud and elaborated by later investigators. According to this view, threats stemming from internal or external sources elicit intense anxiety; this anxiety, in turn, leads to the exaggerated use of various ego-defense mechanisms and to maladaptive behavior. Although today other causal factors are also taken into account, this view still has broad generality and explanatory power, as illustrated in earlier sections of this chapter. As we have already indicated, however, it is now thought that virtually any human propensity—not just primitive sexual and aggressive impulses—may become blocked or inhibited by anxiety, leading to essentially defensive—and ultimately maladaptive—behaviors. This view does not address the *sources* of such maladaptive anxiety, but it seems likely that most of them relate to faulty conditioning and learning, to which we now turn.

2. *Faulty learning.* In recent years faulty learning, a major focus of the behavioral perspective, has become the most widely used explanation for both the development and the maintenance of neurotic behaviors. Faulty learning is seen in the acquisition of maladaptive approaches to stressful situations, as well as in the typical failure of neurotic individuals to learn the competencies and attitudes needed for coping with normal life problems. For an individual who feels basically inadequate and insecure in a competitive and hostile world, making the effort to become competent is especially difficult; relying on a defensive and avoidant life-style is less threatening and brings enough short-term alleviation of anxiety to be repeatedly reinforced.

The principles of simple learning—that is, conditioning—may in certain instances account for the *acquisition* of irrational fears and anxieties in the first place. As noted earlier, the physiological arousal pattern associated with fear has been shown in countless experiments to be readily conditioned to previously neutral stimuli. Furthermore, through *generalization,* the newly acquired fear may spread to other, similar stimuli, including internal ones such as motives to engage in certain actions. The generalization process seems especially pertinent to certain phobias in which occurs a "displacement" of anxiety from one situation to another having similar elements or characteristics.

The powerful role of learning in the development of neurotic behaviors was supported in a recent survey by Öst and Hugdahl (1981). These investigators administered questionnaires to 106 adult phobic patients concerning, among other things, the purported origins of their fears. In describing the situations they considered as sources of their phobias, 58 percent cited conditioning experiences, and another 17 percent described situations that were based on indirect or "vicarious" learning.

An important point to consider in any discussion of acquired or learned fears (anxieties) is that, almost certainly, some stimuli more readily come to elicit fear than do others. This is an aspect of a far more general principle that we have come to appreciate only in recent years; that is, what can be learned is to a considerable extent species-specific. The term "preparedness" has been used to refer to the likelihood that humans are *biologically* predisposed to develop certain types of fears (Seligman & Hager, 1972). For example, we seem much more likely to acquire a fear of snakes than a fear of grapefruits. Thus, any listing of commonly observed types of phobias, while it is apt to be extensive, is also finite.

Conditioning is by no means the only way in which people can learn irrational fears. Abundant evidence exists that much human learning, including the learning of fears, is *observational* in nature. Frightening events in which the subject in no way participates may nevertheless become the occasion for marked and persistent fear arousal. How many people have had their enjoyment of the beach marred by having seen the movie *Jaws?* Similarly, as noted above, fears can be transmitted from one person to another by a *modeling* process: merely observing the fear of another in a given situation may cause that situation to become a fearful one for the observer. For example, if a child's parents prove to be more or less uniformly anxious in situations calling for assertive behavior, that child might well grow up with a similar maladaptive anxiety. Of course, the same result might be accomplished via a conditioning process if the parents routinely punish the child for any show of assertiveness.

3. *Blocked personal growth.* We have noted the emphasis placed by the humanistic perspective on values, meaning, personal growth, and self-fulfillment; we have also seen how stressful one's life situation can become when it is devoid

The fear associated with a stimulus such as a large black dog may, through generalization, be associated with other similar stimuli, leading to a phobia of all dogs.

of meaning and hope, as depicted by reports of former inmates of concentration and POW camps. In any case, lack of meaning and blocked personal growth often appear to stem from a lack of needed competencies and resources or a feeling that duty requires one to remain in a self-stifling role. As a result, the individual's main efforts are devoted to simply trying to meet basic needs, rather than to personal growth. According to the humanistic perspective, such a life-style can ultimately bring feelings of anxiety, hostility, and futility—feelings that may inspire neurotic behaviors.

4. *Pathogenic interpersonal relationships.* As we have seen, certain interactions within families and other early relationships can set the stage for children to develop a neurotic life-style in later life. For example, parents who overprotect or indulge their children may prevent them from developing the independent, effective coping techniques required in their adult years. Or insecure parents may instill their own excessive concern with ailments in their children. Much of what a person becomes in later life—attitudes, values, and often even particular symptoms—can be traced to interactions within the family during the formative years.

It is apparent that the preceding views of psychosocial causation are interrelated and may apply in varying degrees to a given case. This is an important point to remember. Though we may have focused at times on one or another feature of a person's behavior, in most cases all of the concepts discussed above are helpful in understanding the development of neurotic behavior.

Sociocultural factors. Reliable data on the incidence of neurotic disorders in other societies is meager. Kidson and Jones (1968) failed to find classical neurotic patterns among the aborigines of the Australian western desert; but they did note that as these groups were increasingly exposed to contemporary civilization, hypochondriacal concerns and other somatic complaints occurred. In general, however, it would appear that conversion disorder is more common among the people of underdeveloped countries, while anxiety and obsessive-compulsive disorders are more common in technologically advanced societies.

In our own society, neurotic disorders are found among all segments of the population. There appear to be significant differences, however, in the incidence and types of patterns manifested by particular subgroups. In general, neurotic individuals from the lower educational and socioeconomic levels appear to show a higher than average incidence not only of conversion disorder but also of aches, pains, and other somatic symptoms. Neurotic individuals from the middle and upper classes, on the other hand, seem especially prone to anxiety and obsessive-compulsive disorders—with such subjective symptoms as "unhappiness" and general feelings of dissatisfaction with life.

Although there has been little systematic research on the effects of specific sociocultural variables in the development of neurotic disorders, it seems clear that the social environment influences both the individual's likelihood of adopting a neurotic reaction and the particular form that reaction is most likely to take. Thus, as social conditions continue to change in our own society and elsewhere, we can expect that there will be corresponding changes in both the incidence and prevailing types of neurotic behavior.

Treatment and outcomes

The treatment of neurotic disorders may involve a wide range of goals and procedures. Treatment may be aimed at alleviating distressing symptoms, changing the individual's basic defensive and avoidant life-style, or both; it may include drug therapy or psychotherapy, or some combination of these approaches. Anxiety, phobic, and conversion disorders usually respond more readily to treatment than do other neurotic patterns, but the outlook here is, in general, favorable. Andrews and Harvey (1981) have reanalyzed the data on overall outcomes of psychosocial therapy specifically as these data relate to neurotic disorders. They have used a technique known as "meta-analysis"[2] (Smith, Glass, & Miller, 1980). Results from 81 controlled studies involving the treatment of neurotic individuals indicated that the average client who had received treatment was more functional than nearly 80 percent of comparably disordered, untreated control clients evaluated at the same time. Also, the relapse rate for treated clients during two years following therapy was insignificant.

For present purposes, we shall keep our discussion brief and focused on the aspects of treatment that are particularly relevant to neurotic behavior. These therapies will be more thoroughly examined in Chapters 16 and 17.

Drug therapy and other biological approaches. "Psychopharmacological agents are the most widely prescribed, widely misprescribed, most frequently abused, and probably the most advertised of all the pharmaceuticals available to the practicing clinician. They clearly occupy a role at or near the center of medical practice" (Levenson, 1981, p. xi)

As the above statement attests, a large proportion of the patients seen by medical practitioners are neurotic individuals seeking relief from their various aches and pains. Most often minor tranquilizing drugs such as Valium or Librium are prescribed. These drugs are used—and misused—for relief of tension and for relaxation; they may also reduce anxiety and stabilize emotional reactivity. Neurotic individuals frequently attempt to control their anxiety or other symptoms by self-medication with nonprescription drugs, including alcohol.

Available statistics indicate that some 70 percent or more of neurotic patients show some alleviation of symptoms following drug therapy, and most of them are able to function more effectively (Bassuk & Schoonover, 1977; Covi et al., 1974; Engelhardt, 1974; Prusoff & Klerman, 1974). But these drugs can have undesirable effects—such as drowsiness—and in some cases the patient develops an increasing tolerance for and dependence on the drug. In addition, many persons expect too much of a treatment that is merely palliative, and the masking of their symptoms may prevent them from seeking needed psychotherapy.

Other biological treatment procedures have been used to reduce neurotic behavior with mixed results. Electrosleep—a relaxed state of sleep induced by means of the application of low-intensity electric current to the brain—has led to mixed results with individuals suffering from anxiety disorders (Hearst et al., 1974; Rosenthal & Wulfsohn, 1970). Similarly, biofeedback-induced muscle relaxation has produced mixed findings in the treatment of chronic anxiety and related tension-induced disorders (Bird, Cataldo, & Parker, 1981; Blanchard & Epstein, 1978; Blanchard & Young, 1974; Coates & Thoreson, 1981).

Psychological approaches. Individual psychotherapies, behavior therapy, family therapy, and multimodal therapy have been utilized in the treatment of neurotic disorders.

1. *Individual psychotherapies.* These therapies are oriented toward helping individuals achieve greater knowledge and understanding of themselves and their problems, healthier attitudes, and better coping skills. The various types of therapy included in this general category differ somewhat in their specific goals and procedures—each reflecting the particular psychosocial perspective on which it is based—but all stress the need for self-understanding, a realistic frame of reference, a satisfying pattern of values, and the development of effective techniques for coping with adjustive demands.

These objectives sound deceptively easy to achieve; actually they share a number of stumbling blocks. First is the problem of creating a therapeutic situation in which neurotic individuals feel safe enough to lower their defenses, explore their innermost feelings, thoughts, and assumptions, and begin to recognize the possi-

---

[2]As utilized here, *meta-analysis* is a systematic method of arriving at a general statement of results by examining many controlled studies published in the pertinent literature. This technique of evaluating the outcome of therapy has recently been the subject of a special section of the *Journal of Consulting and Clinical Psychology* (1983), *51* (1).

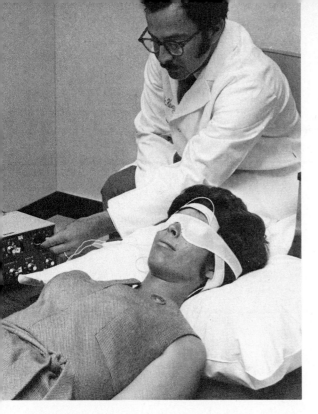

Electrosleep, produced when low levels of electric current are applied to the brain, is among the biological treatments of neurotic behavior that have had mixed results.

chiefly in interpersonal difficulties. Interpersonal therapies tend to be very active and confrontative in focusing on an alteration of maladaptive interpersonal behavior. Hence, they tend to be efficient and relatively brief (Anchin & Kiesler, 1982).

2. *Behavior therapy.* As we have seen, behavior therapy focuses on (a) removing specific symptoms or maladaptive behaviors; (b) developing needed competencies and adaptive behaviors; and (c) modifying environmental conditions that may be reinforcing and maintaining the maladaptive behaviors. In this last context, Bandura (1969) has stated, "A treatment that fails to alter the major controlling conditions of the deviant behavior will most certainly prove ineffective." (p. 50)

The behavior therapy method most commonly used in the treatment of neurotic behaviors is systematic desensitization (see **HIGHLIGHT** on pages 228–29). Here clients are placed—symbolically or actually—in situations that are increasingly closer to the situation they find most threatening, and an attempt is made to associate the fear-producing situations with states that are antagonistic to anxiety, such as relaxation. Other forms of "guided exposure" to fear-producing stimuli also continue to show much promise (Biran & Wilson, 1981).

As we saw in our discussion of specific types of neurotic disorders, some maladaptive behaviors—such as conversion paralyses—may be extinguished by removing reinforcements that have been maintaining the behavior while simultaneously providing reinforcements for more responsible coping patterns. Other maladaptive behaviors—such as obsessive thoughts and compulsions—can often be removed by mild aversive conditioning (Bandura, 1969, 1973; Stern, Lipsedge, & Marks, 1973). Here, too, the conditioning works best when combined with reinforcement of more adaptive alternative behaviors (Sturgis & Meyer, 1981).

As noted in Chapter 3, many behaviorists in recent years have been using behavior therapy to change cognitive behavior (Mahoney, 1978; Meichenbaum, 1977). Individuals who are experiencing neurotic problems, such as anxiety attacks, may be viewed as behaving anxiously in response to internal thoughts and beliefs (cognitions). Here the therapist attempts to change the behavior by changing the individual's inner thoughts and beliefs that may be causing, or

bility of other options. Second is the problem of providing opportunities for neurotic individuals to learn new ways of perceiving themselves and their world, and new ways of coping. Third is the problem of helping them transfer what they have learned in the therapy situation to real life; even when they understand the nature and causes of their self-defeating behavior and have learned that more effective coping techniques are available, they may still be "unable to risk the initial venture into the heretofore out-of-bounds area of living" (Salzman, 1968, p. 465). Fourth is the problem of changing conditions in their life situation that may be reinforcing and thus maintaining the neurotic life-style. For example, a domineering and egocentric husband who will not participate in the therapy program may tend to block his wife's efforts toward self-direction and make it more difficult for her, to give up her insecure, neurotic behavior; he may even manage to sabotage the entire treatment program.

The behavior patterns we have called neurotic styles would seem especially amenable to treatments emphasizing an interpersonal approach, since these conditions are manifested

HIGHLIGHT

Treatment of a patient with multiple phobias by a desensitization technique using imagery

Frankel (1970) has reported on the treatment of a 26-year-old married woman who suffered from disabling fears of sexual relations, earthquakes, and enclosed places. The background of the case, the treatment procedure, and the outcome are summarized below.

Symptoms

1. The sexual fear. The woman reported that she had been able to have sexual relations with her husband only about 10 times in their 3 years of marriage. Her sexual phobia appeared to have a learned basis. She had been molested by an older male at age 5, had been raped by a gang of juvenile delinquents when she was 15, had been "pawed" by intoxicated male visitors of her divorced mother, and had had sexual relations with 3 men prior to her marriage—each of whom had professed love for her but stopped seeing her after the sexual contact. In an effort to "hold her husband" she had had sexual relations with him a few times, but she always had a "cold feeling, like I'm going to suffocate—like I can't breathe" during sexual relations. In the third month of marriage, the couple conceived a son, after whose birth they had sexual relations only twice.

2. The earthquake fear. The woman stated that several times a day her thoughts were occupied by an uncontrollable fear of being in an earthquake. Her sequence of thoughts was always the same. First she would imagine that the ground was shaking and the house rocking, and that she rushed to pick up the baby. She would next imagine herself standing in a doorway, with the house collapsing around her. At this point the anxiety would become "unbearable." The recurrent thoughts about being in an earthquake were especially prominent when she tried to go to sleep,

with the result that she was physically tired, irritable, and anxious during the day. Although a physician had prescribed tranquilizers, she reported that they did not help. On several occasions, she had arisen during the night, picked up her son, and rushed to a doorway. Interestingly enough, she had never been in an earthquake, nor did she personally know anyone who had.

3. Fear of closed places. The woman reported that she had always been fearful of elevators, small rooms, and even being surrounded by people. However, she did not recall ever being locked up in a small enclosure, and did not know anyone who had. She would climb many flights of stairs rather than take an elevator. Just prior to seeking therapy, she had been caught up in a large crowd greeting a visiting dignitary. She reported feeling anxiety, panic, and fear of suffocation. She screamed and pushed people out of the way until she was able to flee.

Treatment

Since the woman's most disabling fear was that of earthquakes, it was decided to treat that fear first, then the fear of sexual relations, and finally the fear of enclosed places. The treatment procedure employed was a variation of implosive therapy, in which the woman was instructed to proceed through sequences of thoughts and images of herself in the fear-producing situation.

"The implosive technique raises the client's anxiety level and maintains it until it passes a peak and begins to decline. This reduction in anxiety is seen as the beginning of extinction of the fear response, but it also may be seen as providing the occasion for reinforcement for the toleration of a high degree of anxiety. That is, the ability to proceed through an imag-

reinforcing, the neurotic behavior. This is called *cognitive mediation.* We will discuss this cognitive-behavioral therapy in more detail in Chapter 17.

Although behavior therapy is usually directed toward changing specific "target behaviors"—such as removing phobias—it often seems to have more far-reaching positive results (Marks, 1978). A client who overcomes a specific phobia gains confidence in his or her ability to over-

come other problems. Ultimately the individual learns that coping effectively with adjustive demands is more rewarding than trying to avoid them. Thus while cognitive-behavioral therapies usually focus more on modifying the internal cognitions of the patient and behavior therapy focuses more on the removal of specific target behaviors, the outcomes of these two forms of therapy are often comparable (Sloane et al., 1975; Smith et al., 1980).

ery sequence which elicits high anxiety is itself reinforced first by success in sustaining anxiety and then by mastery implied by its reduction." (p. 497)

Thus, whenever the woman became "too upset to go on"—a point at which she had previously put the imagery "out of her mind"—she was encouraged to continue with the description of her imagery and her feelings toward it. For example, in the earthquake sequence where she imagined that the house was collapsing around her as she stood in the doorway with her son, she was asked such questions as "What's happening now?" "What's happening next?"

"The content produced by the client involved the house collapsing on her, her son trapped under her as large beams fell on her, the earthquake finally ending, her being pinned under beams and being unable to move, screaming for help for several hours with no one coming to her aid, and finally being able to move a beam, stand up, walk away from the rubble, and breathe a sigh of relief at being alive and unharmed." (p.498)

The imagery sequences lasted from 15 to 30 minutes, and the remainder of each 50-minute therapy session centered on the discussion of the vividness of the imagery sequences and the feelings they elicited. Since the woman could come in only once a week for therapy, she was instructed to proceed along the entire imagery sequence on her own whenever the fear of earthquakes entered her thoughts. She was instructed not to put the thoughts "out of her mind" under any circumstances. This treatment was continued until the fear of earthquakes no longer troubled her. A similar procedure was used in dealing with her sexual fear and her fear of enclosed places.

Outcome

The entire treatment procedure lasted five months, but the fear of earthquakes was reduced from the highest to the lowest rating (on a 10-point scale) in four sessions. The woman reported that she thought less and less about earthquakes and had no difficulty sleeping. Even though a mild earthquake did occur about six weeks after treatment began, she stated that she was "not bothered in the slightest by its occurrence." Six months after the treatment ended, she showed no recurrence of the fear or evidence of substitution of other fears.

With respect to the sexual phobia, treatment enabled the woman to resume sexual relations with her husband. At first she did not enjoy the sex act; six months after treatment ended she felt increasing pleasure and confidence but was still unable to have an orgasm; and at the end of a year she reported that she was able to gain a great deal of pleasure in sex and to have an orgasm about once in every three or four sexual experiences. Her overall relationship with her husband improved also.

The fear of enclosed places decreased from a fairly high rating to zero after seven sessions. During the fifth session of treatment, the woman remembered that she had accidentally been trapped in an airtight cabinet at about age 6 and would have suffocated if her mother had not found her in time. Memory of the event came after she successfully rode down three floors in an elevator. Thus it would appear that behavior change can be followed by "insight."

Frankel reported that none of the fears reappeared after the conclusion of treatment and that no substitute symptoms appeared. He also emphasized that the treatment was largely self-administered, a marked advantage over more typical therapy approaches.

3. *Family therapy.* Often there are pathogenic family interactions that are keeping the neurotic individual in a continually "sick situation." As Melville (1973) has expressed it, "In a family there is no such thing as one person in trouble" (p. 17). As a consequence of such findings, increasing emphasis has been placed on treating the family system rather than focusing primarily on the individual (Fox, 1976; Gurman & Kniskern, 1978).

4. *Multimodal therapy.* As this term, coined by Lazarus (1981), implies, a *combination* of varied approaches may be used in the treatment of a given individual for neurotic behaviors. In fact, there is increasing evidence (see, for example, Goldfried, 1980) that professional therapists are lessening their former strong allegiances to particular therapies, and are increasingly willing to learn and to employ techniques they formerly criticized. For example, one could think of using

Systematic desensitization is frequently used to help people overcome simple phobias such as the fear of snakes. In this type of therapy, patients are placed in a series of situations, each closer to the situation that would provoke the most anxiety, while they practice relaxation techniques to counter their anxiety. Here a number of patients have progressed from handling rubber snakes (upper left) and peering at snakes through glass (center top) to actually handling living but harmless snakes. Note that some patients first handle the snake while wearing rubber gloves.

an interpersonal therapeutic strategy to defeat the neurotic style of a client while simultaneously employing behavior therapy techniques to eradicate particular symptoms. In our judgment, this "ecumenical" trend in psychosocial treatment represents a maturing of the field, and we strongly applaud it.

No matter what therapeutic techniques are employed, it often requires a great deal of courage and persistence on the part of the neurotic individual to face problems realistically and give up the defensive and avoidant life-style that has helped alleviate feelings of inadequacy and anxiety. For some, this seems too great a task, and they present themselves in such a way as to put the whole responsibility for their well-being and happiness on the therapist.

As Weiss and English so succinctly described it nearly forty years ago, it sometimes seems as if the neurotic person is saying:

"There's my story, doctor (after taking plenty of time to tell it in detail). Now you pat me . . . and take my pains away . . . and give me inspiration and happiness and tell me how to be successful, and while you are about it, get my mother-in-law out of the house and I'll pay you when I get a job." (1943, p. 119)

Despite the difficulties involved, however,

powerful forces are aligned on the side of psychotherapy. For one thing, neurotic individuals who seek help are usually experiencing considerable inner distress, so that they are motivated to change. When helped, in a supportive environment, to understand their problems and learn more effective and satisfying ways of coping with them, they usually find the courage to "see it through." Although outcomes vary considerably, it appears that from 70 to 90 percent of the people who receive appropriate kinds of help for their neurotic behavior benefit from it (Bergin & Lambert, 1978).

In concluding our discussion of neurotic disorders, several additional points may be mentioned. Fear of committing suicide is a common neurotic symptom, but the actual incidence of suicide among neurotic individuals does not appear to be higher than for the general population. Nor does the life span of these individuals appear to be adversely affected by their chronic tension and somatic disturbances, unless these disturbances result in pathologic organ changes (to be discussed in the following chapter). The question has also been raised as to whether neurotic behavior is likely to develop into psychotic behavior; the answer seems to be a definitive *no*. In only 5 percent or fewer of the cases of neurotic behavior does excessive stress lead to se-

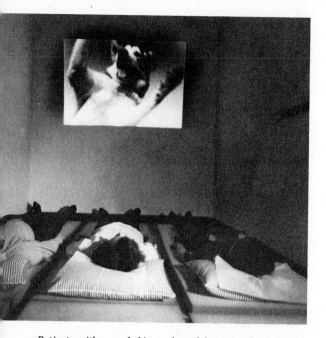

Patients with cynophobia, or fear of dogs, watch a series of slides of dogs, beginning with small, cuddly ones and progressing to lunging, hostile ones, like the snarling German shepherd shown here. Eventually the phobia sufferers should be able to overcome their fear and touch live animals.

vere personality decompensation and psychotic patterns.

Finally, the question has been raised as to how a neurotic style affects creativity and productiveness. Many authors have described neurotic individuals as "pleasantly different" and more likely than the "normal" person to be innovative and productive. In general, however, the evidence indicates that by relying on defensive strategies, neurotic individuals reduce their potential for positive accomplishment as well as their enjoyment of life.

Summary

This chapter is concerned with maladaptive behavior patterns that appear to have *anxiety* at their core or base. Sometimes the patterns, while not involving disabling symptoms as such, do act to inhibit behavior that would be appropriate, effective, and adaptive in certain situations. We have termed these conditions *neurotic styles*. In other cases, anxiety, or defenses against it, gives rise to disabling symptoms. Formerly, these symptom disorders were officially called *neuroses*, but the DSM-III has largely abandoned that term. We have chosen to retain the term *neurotic* for its pedagogic and descriptive advantages. Neurotic symptom disorders, on careful assessment, often turn out to be related to preexisting neurotic styles.

Four relatively common neurotic styles are those involving inhibition of aggression/assertion, responsibility/independence, compliance/submission, and intimacy/trust behaviors. Of the neurotic symptom disorders, the generalized anxiety disorders are those in which, for some reason, the person has been unable to develop means of controlling and containing relatively severe anxiety, with the result that it surfaces in overt, fearful behavior. In somatoform disorders, the individual "somatizes" anxiety (i.e., diverts it to the body), causing psychologically based disabilities, preoccupations with disability, or both. In dissociative disorders, anxiety causes aspects of the individual's personality to "split off" and function to a greater or lesser extent independent of the core self. To a large extent, somatoform and dissociative symptoms represent defenses against experiencing the full impact of anxiety.

The experience of anxiety in neurotic disorders is indistinguishable from strong fear; however, it does not have an identifiable source that is rational or realistic. Most such anxieties are believed to be acquired through conditioning or other learning mechanisms, although some persons may be constitutionally predisposed to acquire such responses.

Many neurotic persons are treated by physicians, often with drugs designed to allay anxiety. Such treatment is essentially palliative in nature, and it is not without dangers. There are a number of alternative means of achieving anxiety reduction. In general, psychosocial treatments, which typically aim at solving the person's problems, have a reasonably good record with the neurotic disorders. However, some neurotic persons fail to achieve satisfactory benefits from any form of treatment.

Personality disorders and crime

Vojislav Jakíc, Les Descendants du Dessin—Dessin Insolite *(1973). Jakíc (b. 1932) the son of a Montenegrin priest, was raised in a small town in Serbia. Ostracized as a boy by his peers because of his ethnic background, he developed an introverted personality. While at school Jakíc became aware of his artistic ability. He began art studies in Belgrade at the age of 20. Thereafter, his life was marked by chronic illness, poverty, and lack of recognition, as well as by increasing paranoia.*

It is probably meaningless to speak of an end-product in the developmental process; people continue to change throughout their lives. Healthy adjustment through the life cycle is, after all, chiefly a matter of flexibly adapting to changing demands, opportunities, and limitations associated with different life stages. Nevertheless, certain broad traits, coping styles, and ways of interacting in the social environment that are more or less characteristic of a given person emerge during development. These are normally crystallized into established patterns by the end of the adolescent years. These represent the individual's *personality,* the unique pattern of traits and behaviors that characterize the individual.

For most of us, our adult personality is attuned to the demands of society. In other words, we readily comply with societal expectations and demands. In contrast, there is a certain group of individuals who, although not necessarily displaying obvious symptoms of disorder, nevertheless seem in one way or another to be ill-equipped to become fully functioning members of society—*any* society. For these individuals, personality formation has been so warped that they are unable to perform adequately the varied roles expected of them by the societies in which they live. These are the people who might be diagnosed as having *personality disorder,* or *character disorder.*

Personality disorders typically stem not from reactions to stress, as in adjustment disorders or posttraumatic stress disorders; nor from deenses against anxiety, as in the neurotic disorders. Rather the disorders to be examined here stem from immature and distorted personality development, resulting in individuals with persistent maladaptive ways of perceiving, thinking, and relating to the world around them. These maladaptive approaches to the world usually cause significant impairment of functioning and in some cases cause subjective distress. Essentially individuals with personality disorders are "acting out" patterns of behavior rather than experiencing intrapsychic disturbances. That is, the individual behaves in ways that are contrary to the prevailing social attitudes or expectations of others rather than stifling such behavior and experiencing inner anxiety. Often these patterns of personality and behavior are recognizable by adolescence and continue into adult life.

The category of personality disorders is a broad one, with behavior problems that differ greatly in form and severity. On the mildest end of the spectrum we find individuals who generally function adequately but would be described by their relatives or associates as troublesome or eccentric. They have characteristic ways of approaching situations and other people that make them difficult to get along with, yet they are often quite capable or even gifted in their careers. At the other end of the spectrum are individuals whose more extreme and in many cases unethical "acting out" against society makes them less able to function in a normal setting; many are incarcerated in prisons or maximum security hospitals, although their ability to manipulate others may keep them from getting caught.

The prevalence of personality disorders is unknown, since many of these individuals never come in contact with mental health or legal agencies. Many such individuals, however, do become identified through the correctional system or through court-ordered psychological evaluations stemming from family problems such as family abuse. Others eventually show up in the statistics of alcohol treatment programs. Although we have no accurate estimates as to what percentage of incarcerated individuals would be classified as having personality disorders, it is believed that the figure would be quite high.

In this chapter, we shall consider several types of disordered personality that have been identified, then examine one of them—antisocial personality—in greater detail, and finally look at criminal behavior, in which these disorders often—but not always—play a role.

Personality disorders are also often a factor in several disorders that will be considered in other chapters, such as alcoholism and pathological gambling (Chapter 11), sexual deviations (Chapter 12), and delinquency (Chapter 14). Although "juvenile delinquency" does in fact sometimes represent the early stages of a lifelong process of personality disorder, it often does not: much of the acting-out behavior of adolescence, including much delinquency, is limited to the adolescent years. This is why delinquency will be discussed with the other special disorders of childhood and adolescence. Finally, the behavior patterns associated with personality disorders can be similar to those determined primarily by the residual effects of head injuries or other brain pathology. In such cases, the behavior is evidence of organic brain disorder, which we consider in Chapter 13. Qualifications aside, let us move on to an examination of personality disorders.

Personality disorders

The behaviors characteristic of personality disorders are chiefly, although not exclusively, problems where the individual typically causes at least as much difficulty in the lives of others as in his or her own life. These people live aberrant lives that others find confusing, exasperating, unpredictable, and, in varying degrees, unacceptable—although rarely as bizarre or out of contact with reality as those persons with psychotic disorders (to be discussed in Chapters 9 and 10). By and large, persons with personality disorders do not have obvious mental disorders, nor do they suffer unduly from anxiety or depression. Their persistent behavioral deviations apparently are *not* the product of pathological processes but rather seem to be intrinsic to their personalities; for one reason or another they developed in an aberrant manner and never learned to take part in mutually respectful and satisfying social relationships. In the past these disorders were thought to center around personality characteristics referred to as *temperament* or *character traits*, suggesting the possibility of hereditary or "constitutional" influence, as well as longstanding learned habit patterns.

The formal definition of personality disorders in DSM-III is as follows:

"Personality *traits* are enduring patterns of perceiving, relating to, and thinking about the environment and oneself, and are exhibited in a wide range of important social and personal contexts. It is only when *personality traits* are inflexible and maladaptive and cause either significant impairment in social or occupational functioning or subjective distress that they constitute *personality disorders*. The manifestations of personality disorders are generally recognizable by adolescence or earlier and continue throughout most of adult life, though they often become less obvious in middle or old age. . . .

Delinquency can sometimes be a prelude to the development of a personality disorder in adulthood. In many cases, however, delinquent behavior ends with adolescence.

"The diagnosis of a "personality disorder" should be made only when the characteristic features are typical of the individual's long-term functioning and are not limited to discrete episodes of illness."(APA, 1980, p. 305)

The behavior patterns of personality disorders are rather new to clinical texts and diagnostic manuals: they were not clearly described until the publication of the American Psychiatric Association's first *Diagnostic and Statistical Manual* (DSM-I) in 1952. Before that, they were regarded as "disorders of character" found in people who were otherwise essentially normal—problems "without psychosis" (Murray, 1938).

In the DSM-III, the personality disorders are regarded as different enough from the standard psychiatric syndromes (which are coded on Axis I) to warrant being coded on a separate Axis II. This axis represents longstanding personality traits that are inflexible and maladaptive and that cause social or occupational adjustment problems or personal distress; included here are reaction patterns so deeply embedded in the personality structure (for whatever reason) that they are extremely resistant to modification. Though an individual might be diagnosed on Axis II only, he or she might be diagnosed on both Axes I and II, which would reflect the existence of both a currently active "mental" disorder and a more chronic, underlying "personality" disorder.

A special caution is in order regarding the personality disorders. Perhaps more misdiagnoses occur here than in other categories. There are four special problems. One is the comparative paucity of research on these disorders; they are not as sharply defined as other diagnostic categories, nor do we have as clear a set of criteria for them. For example, although Small and Small (1971) found a number of common characteristics in a group of individuals classified as passive-aggressive personalities, their subjects were limited to hospitalized cases and may not have been representative of all passive-aggressive personalities.

A second problem is that the diagnostic categories are not mutually exclusive–often an individual will show characteristics of more than one type of personality disorder, which makes diagnosis difficult. For example, an individual might show the suspiciousness, mistrust, avoidance of blame, and guardedness of paranoid personality disorder along with the withdrawal, absence of friends, and aloofness that are characteristic traits of schizoid personality disorder. Furthermore, in many cases, the personality disorder is part of a larger pattern of pathology. For example, an individual who is addicted to drugs might also be characterized as having a dependent personality. In this case, the long-continuing personality disorder might well have been a causal factor in the development of the addiction. Here the drug problem would be recorded on Axis I and the dependent personality disorder on Axis II.

A third problem is that the personality characteristics that are features of the personality disorders are dimensional in nature—that is, they range from normal expressions to pathological exaggerations and can be found, on a smaller scale and less intensely expressed, in many normal individuals (Frances, 1980). For example, liking one's work and being conscientious about the details of one's job does not make one a "compulsive personality" nor does being economically dependent automatically make a spouse a dependent personality. Applying diagnostic labels to people who are functioning well enough to be outside a hospital setting is always risky; it is especially so where diagnosis involves judgment about characteristics that are also typical of normal individuals.

A fourth problem is that personality disorders are defined by inferred traits rather than by clearly observed behaviors. There are objective behavioral criteria for drug intoxication or somatization disorder but not for dependent or compulsive personality patterns. Traits are inferred from consistencies in behavior but can never be seen directly. For this reason, some researchers have questioned the whole concept of traits (e.g., Mischel, 1968), urging instead that predictions always be based on observable behavior.

Any one of these problems can lead to unreliability of diagnoses and often does (Mellsop et al., 1982). Some day a more objective scheme for the personality disorders may be devised that accounts for the problems described here. In the meantime, however, the trait-based categories will continue to be used, with the recognition that they are more dependent on the observer's judgment than one might wish.

Millon (1981), in a scholarly, comprehensive text devoted to the personality disorders, has tried to make some headway in dealing with the problems inherent in categorizing personality disorders. Not only does he provide a theoretical analysis of each of the disorders but also he presents his views on the remaining controversies surrounding some of the diagnoses. He acknowledges the very substantial gaps in knowledge that continue to exist in this area of psychopathology and finds very little agreement, even on such basic matters as the trait dimensions that best describe this vast realm of socially problematic behavior. He is critical of the DSM-III subcategories (to be discussed) and proposes instead that personality disorders be categorized according to individual differences in learned coping patterns:

"Learned coping patterns may be viewed as complex forms of instrumental behavior, that is, ways of achieving positive reinforcements and avoiding negative reinforcements. These strategies reflect what kinds of reinforcements individuals have learned to seek or avoid (pleasure-pain), where individuals look to obtain them (self-others), and how individuals have learned to behave in order to elicit or escape them (active-passive). Eight basic coping patterns and three severe variants were derived by combining the *nature* (positive or pleasure versus negative or pain), the *source* (self versus others), and the *instrumental behaviors* (active versus passive) engaged in to achieve various reinforcements." (Millon, 1981, p. 59)

Millon's approach to the personality disorders is still at the conceptual stage and is as yet unsubstantiated by empirical evidence; nonetheless, it represents potentially useful directions for research.

With these cautions, we shall look now at those elusive and often exasperating clinical features of the personality disorders.

Clinical features of personality disorders

The several special types of personality disorder are classified according to the particular characteristic (dependence, avoidance, etc.) that is most prominent, although, as we have seen, in given cases the dividing lines are often unclear. This characteristic, in turn, is predictive of what kind of disordered relationships can be expected. Although we shall look individually at the several types of personality disorder that have been delineated according to the particular distorted trait pattern that is prominent, let us look first at a number of features they all seem to have in common:

a) Perhaps most characteristic in all of them is the pattern of disrupted personal relationships. Whether they are narcissistic or dependent or passive-aggressive, they usually leave a trail of disturbed personal relationships marked by difficulties they have caused others.

b) Their problems are generally long-standing and marked by behavior that is considered troublesome to others. There is not usually an "episode" of pathological behavior that can be identified but rather a persistent pattern of recurring problems.

c) Whatever the particular trait pattern they have developed (obstinacy, covert hostility, or suspiciousness, for example), it colors each new situation they meet and leads to a repetition of the same maladaptive patterns of behavior. For example, the dependent person "wears out" a relationship with someone, such as a spouse, by incessant and extraordinary demands; after that partner leaves, the person immediately goes into another dependent relationship and repeats the behavior. Thus personality disorders are marked by considerable consistency over time, with no apparent learning from previous troubles.

d) It follows from the preceding that these disorders are in a sense disorders of reputation: they are marked by the imprint the behavior has on others rather than by the pain felt by the individual. Typically these individuals are known not by what they have reported to the clinician but by the report of others. They rarely take the initiative in seeking therapy and when referred for therapy by others have little or no motivation to profit from it. Instead, they are likely to disrupt or sabotage it—or to leave it if possible.

e) Finally, the patterns of behavior reflected in personality disorders are highly resistant to change. These individuals typically neither seek to change nor to accommodate much to demands other people place upon them to alter their behavior.

All these characteristics lead to the fractured and deteriorated relationships that are the hallmark of the personality disorders.

Types of personality disorders

The DSM-III personality disorders are grouped into three clusters on the basis of similarities among the disorders.

Cluster I includes *paranoid, schizoid,* and *schizotypal* personality disorders. Individuals with these disorders often seem odd or eccentric, although their unusual behavior takes quite different forms.

Cluster II includes *histrionic, narcissistic, antisocial,* and *borderline* personality disorders. Individuals with these disorders have in common a tendency to be dramatic, emotional, and erratic. Their impulsive behavior, often involving antisocial activities, is more colorful, more forceful, and more likely to get them into contact with mental health or legal authorities than is true of disorders in the first cluster.

Cluster III includes *avoidant, dependent, compulsive,* and *passive-aggressive* personality disorders. In this cluster of disorders, unlike the others, there is often anxiety and fearfulness, making it difficult in some cases to distinguish them from anxiety-based disorders. Because of this anxiety, individuals suffering from these disorders are more likely than the others to seek help.

Paranoid personality disorder.   Individuals with this disorder typically are suspicious, hypersensitive, rigid, envious, and argumentative. They tend to see themselves as blameless, instead finding fault for their own mistakes and failures in others—even to the point of ascribing evil motives to others. Such individuals are constantly expecting trickery and looking for clues to validate their expectations, while disregarding all evidence to the contrary. They are keenly aware of power and rank, envious of those in high places, and disdainful of those who seem weak or soft. The following case demonstrates well the behaviors characteristic of this disorder:

"A 40-year-old construction worker believes that his co-workers do not like him and fears that someone might let his scaffolding slip in order to cause him injury on the job. This concern followed a recent disagreement on the lunch line when the patient felt that a co-worker was sneaking ahead and complained to him. He began noticing his new "enemy" laughing with the other men and often wondered if he were the butt of their mockery. He thought of confronting them, but decided that the whole issue might just be in his own mind, and that he might get himself into more trouble by taking any action.

"The patient offers little spontaneous information, sits tensely in the chair, is wide-eyed and carefully tracks all movements in the room. He reads between the lines of the interviewer's questions, feels criticized, and imagines that the interviewer is siding with his co-workers. He makes it clear that he would not have come to the personnel clinic at all except for his need for sleep medication.

"He was a loner as a boy and felt that other children would form cliques and be mean to him. He did poorly in school, but blamed his teachers—he claimed that they preferred girls or boys who were 'sissies.' He dropped out of school, and has since been a hard and effective worker; but he feels he never gets the breaks. He believes that he has been discriminated against because of his Catholicism, but can offer little convincing evidence. He gets on poorly with bosses and co-workers, is unable to appreciate joking around, and does best in situations where he can work and have lunch alone. He has switched jobs many times because he felt he was being mistreated.

"The patient is distant and demanding with his family. His children call him 'Sir' and know that it is wise to be 'seen but not heard' when he is around. At home he can never comfortably sit still and is always

Many of the traits associated with personality disorders are seen in less extreme form in the general population. A social psychologist's experiment on vandalism highlights the pervasiveness of these characteristics and the difficulties in setting the point at which they should be considered abnormal. An automobile was "abandoned" on a New York city street and photographers hidden to record the action. In the first picture, a white middle-class family strips the car of its most valuable components; in the second, a man takes the best tires. Finally, after the car had been completely stripped, wanton destruction began; passersby broke windows and bashed in the metal until only a useless hulk remained. Should the behavior of these individuals be considered pathological? (Based on Zimbardo, 1973.)

busy at some chore or another. He prefers not to have people visit his house and becomes restless when his wife is away visiting others."(Spitzer et al., 1981, p. 37)

The cardinal features of pervasive suspiciousness and mistrust of other people leave the paranoid personality prone to numerous difficulties and hurts in interpersonal relationships. This, typically, leads to an individual who is continually "on guard" for perceived attacks by others.

Schizoid personality disorder.
Individuals with this disorder typically show an inability to form social relationships and a lack of interest in doing so. Such individuals are unable to express their feelings and are seen by others as cold and distant; they often lack social skills and can be classified as "loners," with solitary interests and occupations.

The following case of a schizoid personality illustrates a fairly severe personality problem in a man who was functioning adequately as judged both by occupational criteria and by his own standards of "happiness." When he sought help, it was at the encouragement of his supervisor and his physician.

Bill D., a highly intelligent but quite introverted and withdrawn 33-year-old computer analyst, was referred for psychological evaluation by his physician, who was concerned that Bill might be depressed and unhappy. At the suggestion of his supervisor, Bill had recently gone to the physician for rather vague physical complaints and because of his gloomy outlook on life. Bill had virtually no contact with other people. He lived alone in his apartment, worked in a small office by himself, and usually saw no one at work except for the occasional visit of his supervisor to give him new work and pick up completed projects. He ate lunch by himself and about once a week, on nice days, went to the zoo for his lunch break.

Bill was a lifelong loner: as a child he had very few friends and always preferred solitary activities over family outings (he was the oldest of five children). In high school he had never dated and in college had gone out with a woman only once—and that was with a group of students after a game. He had been active in sports, however, and had played varsity football in both high school and college. In college he had spent a lot of time with one relatively close friend—mostly drinking. However, this friend now lived in another city.

Bill reported rather matter-of-factly that he has a hard time making friends; he never knows what to say in a conversation. On a number of occasions he has thought of becoming friends with other people but simply can't think of the right words, so "the conversation just dies." He reported that he has given some thought lately to changing his life in an attempt to be more "positive," but it never seems worth the trouble. It is easier for him not to make the effort because he becomes embarrassed when someone tries to talk with him. He is happiest when he is alone.

In short, the central problem of the schizoid personality is an inability to form *attachments* to other people. It is as though the needs for love, belonging, and approval fail to develop in these individuals, or—if they do—are somehow obliterated at an early stage. The result is a profound barrennesss of interpersonal experience.

Schizotypal personality disorder.
Individuals with this disorder are seclusive, oversensitive, and eccentric in their communication and behavior. They tend to be egocentric and frequently see chance events as related to themselves. Though both schizotypal and schizoid personality are characterized by behavior patterns of isolation and withdrawal, the two can be distinguished in that schizotypal personality—but not schizoid personality—also involves oddities of thought, perception, or speech. Though reality contact is usually maintained, highly personalized and superstitious thinking are characteristic of individuals with schizotypal personality. Their oddities in thinking, talking, and other behavior are similar to those often seen in more severe form in schizophrenic patients; in fact, they might formerly have been diagnosed as exhibiting simple or latent schizophrenia. A genetic association with schizophrenia is widely suspected, but evidence for it is not yet conclusive (Neale & Oltmanns, 1980).

The following case is fairly typical.

"A 41-year-old male was referred to a community mental health center's activities program for help in improving his social skills. He had a lifelong pattern of social isolation, and spent hours worrying that his angry thoughts about his older brother would cause his brother harm. He had previously worked as a clerk in civil service, but had lost his job because of poor attendance and low productivity.

"On interview the patient was distant and somewhat distrustful. He described in elaborate and often irrelevant detail his rather uneventful and routine daily life. He told the interviewer that he had spent an hour and a half in a pet store deciding which of two brands of fish food to buy, and explained their relative merits. For two days he had studied the washing instructions on a new pair of jeans—Did 'Wash before wearing' mean that the jeans were to be washed before wearing the first time, or did they need, for some reason, to be washed each time before they were worn? He did not regard concerns such as these as senseless, though he acknowledged that the amount of time spent thinking about them might be excessive. When asked about his finances, he could recite from memory his most recent monthly bank statement, including the amount of every check and the running balance as each check was written. He knew his balance on any particular day, but sometimes got anxious if he considered whether a certain check or deposit had actually cleared. He was very sensitive to questions put by the interviewer, reading in criticism where none was intended." (Spitzer et al., 1981, p. 234)

The distinguishing feature of the schizotypal person is peculiar thought patterns, which are in turn associated with a loosening—although not a complete rupture—of ties to reality. The individual appears to lack some key integrative competence of the sort that enables most of us to "keep it all together" and more or less on track. As a result, many basic abilities, such as being able to communicate clearly, are never fully mastered, and the individual tends to drift aimlessly and unproductively through the adult years.

Histrionic personality disorder.
Individuals with this disorder typically show behavior patterns of immaturity, excitability, emotional instability, a craving for excitement, and self-dramatization (an attention-seeking device that is often seductive in nature). Sexual adjustment is usually poor and interpersonal relationships are stormy. These individuals often show dependence and helplessness and are quite gullible. Usually they are self-centered, vain, and overconcerned about approval from others, who see them as overly reactive, shallow, and insincere.

The following case illustrates the histrionic personality pattern:

Pam, a 22-year-old secretary, was causing numerous problems for her supervisor and coworkers. According to her supervisor, Pam was unable to carry out her

Attention-seeking behavior is characteristic of the histrionic personality disorder. Here a young person breaks into an impromptu dance while waiting for a commuter train.

duties without constant guidance. Seemingly helpless and dependent, Pam would overreact to minor events and job pressures with irritability and occasional temper tantrums. If others placed unwanted demands on her, she would complain of physical problems, such as nausea or headaches; furthermore, she frequently missed work altogether. To top it off, Pam was flirtatious and often demandingly seductive toward the men in the office.

As a result of her frequent absenteeism from work and her disruptive behavior in the office, Pam's supervisor and the personnel manager recommended that she be given a psychological evaluation and counseling in the Employee Assistance Program. She went to the first appointment with the psychologist but failed to show up for follow-up visits. She was finally given a discharge notice after several incidents of temper outbursts at work.

Both Pam's physical complaints and her seductive behavior are examples of attention-seeking tactics commonly found in the histrionic personality pattern. When these tactics fail to bring about the desired result, irritability and temper outbursts typically follow.

Narcissistic personality disorder. Individuals with this disorder show an exaggerated sense of self-importance and a preoccupation with receiving attention. These persons are grandiose and expect and demand special treatment from others. Yet the fragility of their self-esteem is revealed by their preoccupation with how others are regarding them. They typically disregard the rights and feelings of others, especially if it helps serve their own goals. Their sense of entitlement is frequently a source of astonishment to others, although they themselves regard their lavish expectations as merely their just dues. By and large, they do not permit others to be genuinely close to or to become dependent on them.

A central element in the narcissistic personality pattern is an inability to take the perspective of another, to see things other than "through their own eyes." In more general terms, they lack the capacity for *empathy*, which is an essential ingredient for mature relationships. In this sense, all children begin life as narcissists and only gradually acquire a perspective-taking ability. For reasons that are far from entirely understood—although one suspects that parental "spoiling" may have something to do with it—some children do not show normal progress in this area, and indeed, in extreme cases, show little or none. The latter grow up to become adult narcissistic personalities.

The following case is illustrative.

"A 25-year-old, single, graduate student complains to his psychoanalyst of difficulty completing his Ph. D. in English Literature and expresses concerns about his relationships with women. He believes that his thesis topic may profoundly increase the level of understanding in his discipline and make him famous, but so far he has not been able to get past the third chapter. His mentor does not seem sufficiently impressed with his ideas, and the patient is furious at him, but also self-doubting and ashamed. He blames his mentor for his lack of progress, and thinks that he deserves more help with his grand idea, that his mentor should help with some of the research. The patient brags about his creativity and complains that other people are 'jealous' of his insight. He is very envious of students who are moving along faster than he and regards them as 'dull drones and ass-kissers.' He prides himself on the brilliance of his class participation and imagines someday becoming a great professor.

"He becomes rapidly infatuated with women and has powerful and persistent fantasies about each new woman he meets, but after several experiences of sexual intercourse feels disappointed and finds them dumb, clinging, and physically repugnant. He has many 'friends,' but they turn over quickly, and no one relationship lasts very long. People get tired of his continual self-promotion and lack of consideration of them. For example, he was lonely at Christmas and insisted that his best friend stay in town rather than visit his family. The friend refused, criticizing the patient's self-centeredness; and the patient, enraged, decided never to see this friend again." (Spitzer et al., 1981, pp. 52–53)

Individuals with narcissistic personality patterns typically do not seek psychological treatment since they view themselves as nearly perfect and in no need of personal change. Those who do enter treatment often do so at the insistence of another person, such as a husband or wife, and tend to terminate therapy prematurely—particularly if the therapist is confrontational and questions the patient's self-serving behavior.

Antisocial personality disorder. Individuals with this disorder continually violate the rights of others through aggressive, antisocial behavior, without remorse or loyalty to anyone. Some antisocial personalities have enough intelligence and social charm to devise and carry out elaborate schemes for conning large numbers of people. Imposters fit in this category. Because this pattern has been studied more fully than the others, it will be examined in some detail later in this chapter.

A brief clinical description should suffice here.

Mark, a 22-year-old, came to a psychology clinic on court order. He was awaiting trial for car theft and armed robbery. His case records revealed that he had a long history of arrests beginning at age nine, when he was picked up for vandalism. He had been expelled from high school for truancy and disruptive behavior. On a number of occasions he had run away from home for days or weeks at a time—always returning in a disheveled and "rundown" condition. To date, he has not held a job for more than a few days at a time, even though his generally charming manner enables him to readily obtain jobs. He is described as a loner, with very few friends. Though initially charming, Mark usually soon antagonizes those he meets with his aggressive, self-oriented behavior.

Mark was generally affable and complimentary during the therapy session. At the end of it, he enthusiastically told the therapist how much he'd benefited from the counseling and looked forward to future sessions.

Mark's first session was his last. Shortly after it, he skipped bail and presumably left town in order to avoid his trial.

Borderline personality disorder. Individuals with this disorder show a pattern of behavior that resembles features of both the personality disorders and some of the more severe psychological disorders, particularly the affective disorders (to be discussed in Chapter 9). Thus, the designation of "borderline" personality. The behavior pattern of these individuals is one of instability, reflected in drastic mood shifts and behavior problems. Often they display intense anger outbursts with little provocation, and they may show a disturbance in basic identity which preoccupies them and produces a basically negative outlook. Such individuals are frequently described as impulsive and unpredictable, angry, empty, and periodically unstable. They may have short episodes in which they appear to be out of contact with reality. A low frustration tolerance is common. Also common in the history of these individuals is a series of intense but stormy relationships, typically involving an overidealization of a friend or lover that later ends in bitter disillusionment and disappointment. Self-mutilation and suicide attempts, often flagrantly manipulative, are frequently part of the clinical picture, as the following case illustrates.

"A 26-year-old unemployed woman was referred for admission to a hospital by her therapist because of intense suicidal preoccupation and urges to mutilate herself by cutting herself with a razor.

"The patient was apparently well until her junior year in high school, when she became preoccupied with religion and philosophy, avoided friends, and was filled with doubt about who she was. Academically she did well, but later, during college, her performance declined. In college she began to use a variety of drugs, abandoned the religion of her family, and seemed to be searching for a charismatic religious figure with whom to identify. At times massive anxiety swept over her and she found it would suddenly vanish if she cut her forearm with a razor blade. Three years ago she began psychotherapy, and initially rapidly idealized her therapist as being incredibly intuitive and empathic. Later she became hostile and demanding of him, requiring more and more sessions, sometimes two in one day. Her life centered on her therapist, by this time to the exclusion of everyone else. Although her hostility toward her therapist was obvious, she could neither see it nor control it. Her difficulties with her therapist culminated in many episodes of her forearm cutting and suicidal threats, which led to the referral for admission." (Spitzer et al., 1981, pp. 111–12)

Clinical observation of persons whose behavior meets the criteria of borderline personality disorder points strongly to a problem of achieving a coherent sense of self as a key predisposing causal factor in this type of disorder. These persons somehow fail to complete the process of achieving an articulated self-identity and hence do not really become individuals in their own right. This lack of individuation leads to complications in interpersonal relationships.

Avoidant personality disorder. Individuals with this disorder are hypersensitive to rejection and apprehensive of any sign of social derogation; such individuals readily see ridicule or disparagement where none was intended. There is a lifelong pattern of limited social relationships and reluctance to enter into social interaction. These individuals are too fearful of criticism and rebuff to seek out other people, yet they desire affection and are often lonely and bored. Unlike the schizoid personality, they do not enjoy their aloneness: their inability to relate comfortably to other people is a source of acute distress and low self-esteem, as shown by the following case.

Sally, a 35-year-old librarian, lived a relatively isolated life and had few acquaintances and no close personal friends. From childhood on, she had been very shy and had withdrawn from close ties with others to keep from being hurt or criticized. Two years before she entered therapy, she had a date to go to a party with an acquaintance she had met at the library. The moment they arrived at the party, Sally felt extremely uncomfortable because she was "not dressed properly." She left in a hurry and refused to see her acquaintance again. It was because of her continuing concern over this incident that—two years later!—Sally decided to go into therapy, even though she dreaded the possibility that the psychologist would be critical of her.

In the early treatment sessions, she sat silently much of the time, finding it too difficult to talk about herself. After several sessions, she grew to trust the therapist, and she related numerous incidents in her early years in which she had been "devastated" by her alcoholic father's obnoxious behavior in public. Though she tried to keep her school friends from knowing about her family problems, when this became impossible she instead limited her friendships, thus protecting herself from possible embarrassment or criticism.

When Sally first began therapy, she avoided meeting people unless she could be assured that they would "like her." With therapy that focused on enhancing her assertiveness and social skills, she made some progress in her ability to approach and talk with people.

Sally's extreme need to avoid situations in which she might be embarrassed is the keynote of the avoidant personality. Life is full of risks; it is as though these individuals cannot face even the slightest risk of embarrassment or criticism. They want guarantees of success before they'll participate—and if they can't have them, they just won't play the game.

Dependent personality disorder. Individuals with this disorder show extreme dependence on other people and acute discomfort—even panic—at having to be alone. These individuals usually build their lives around other persons and subordinate their own needs to keep the other person involved with them. They lack self-confidence and feel helpless even when they have actually developed good work skills or other competencies. They function well as long as they are not required to be on their own. The following case is one in which a woman with a dependent personality experienced such distress following desertion by her husband that she sought help.

Sarah D., a 32-year-old mother of two and a part-time tax accountant, came to a crisis center late one evening after Michael, her husband of a year and a half, abused her physically and then left home. Although he never physically harmed the children, he frequently threatened to do so when he was drunk. Sarah appeared acutely anxious and worried about the future and "needed to be told what to do." She wanted her husband to come back and seemed rather unconcerned about his regular pattern of physical abuse. At the time, Michael was an unemployed resident in a day treatment program at a halfway house for paroled drug abusers that taught abstinence from all addictive substances through harassment and group cohesiveness. He was almost always in a surly mood and "ready to explode."

Although Sarah had a well-paying job, she voiced great concern about being able to make it on her own. She realized that it was foolish to be "dependent"

Persons who suffer from avoidant personality disorder often feel extremely uncomfortable in social situations, especially those in which one is called upon to "perform" in front of others. Parties or social dinners are among the events that may cause acute stress in such individuals.

upon her husband, whom she referred to as a "real loser." (She had had a similar relationship with her first husband, who had left her and her oldest child when she was 18.) Several times in the past few months Sarah had made up her mind to get out of the marriage but couldn't bring herself to break away. She would threaten to leave, but when the time came to do so, she would "freeze in the door" with a numbness in her body and a sinking feeling in her stomach at the thought of "not being with Michael."

As a result of their lack of confidence, dependent personalities passively allow other people to take over the major decisions in their lives—such as where they will live and work, what friends they will have, and even how they will spend their time. These individuals typically appear "selfless" and bland, since they usually feel they have no right to express even mild individuality.

Compulsive personality disorder. Individuals with this disorder show excessive concern for rules, order, efficiency, and work, coupled with an insistence that everyone do things their way and an inability to express warm feelings. Such individuals tend to be overinhibited, overconscientious, overdutiful, and rigid, and to have difficulty relaxing or doing anything just

for fun. There is usually a preoccupation with trivial details and poor allocation of time.

The behavior patterns of this disorder are somewhat similar to those of neurotic compulsive disorders. In obsessive-compulsive disorder, however, the individual suffers from the persistent intrusion of particular undesired thoughts (obsessions) or actions (compulsions) that are a source of extreme anxiety because the individual recognizes that they are irrational but cannot seem to control them. Obsessive personalities, on the other hand, have a whole life-style characterized by obstinacy and compulsive orderliness. Although they may be anxious about getting all their work done in keeping with their exacting standards, they are not anxious about their compulsiveness itself (Pollak, 1979). An example of compulsive personality is reflected in the following case.

Alan appeared to be well suited to his work as a train dispatcher. He was quite conscientious, perfectionistic, and attended to minute details. However, he was not close to his coworkers and, reportedly, they thought him "odd." He would get quite upset if even minor variations to his daily routine occurred. For example, he would become tense and irritable if coworkers did not follow exactly his elaborately constructed schedules and plans. If he became tied up in traffic, he would beat the steering wheel and swear at other drivers for holding him up.

In short, Alan got very little pleasure out of life and worried constantly about minor problems. His rigid routines were impossible to maintain, and he often developed tension headaches or stomachaches when he couldn't keep his complicated plans in order. His physician, noting the frequency of his physical complaints and his generally perfectionistic approach to life, referred him for a psychological evaluation. Psychotherapy was recommended to him, although the prognosis for significant behavioral change was considered questionable. He did not follow up on the treatment recommendations because he felt that he could not afford the time away from work.

Other people tend to view compulsive personalities as rigid, stiff, cold, and *even* disorganized—in spite of their frequent and extensive preoccupation with the details in their lives.

Passive-aggressive personality disorder.
Individuals with this disorder typically express hostility in indirect and nonviolent ways, such as procrastinating, pouting, "forgetting," or being obstructionistic, stubborn, or intentionally inefficient. Passive-aggressive individuals resent and manage not to comply with demands others make on them; the behavior is most apparent in their work situations but also occurs in their social relationships. Resentment against authority figures, coupled with a lack of assertiveness, is typical.

The passive-aggressive personality pattern is clearly shown in the following case that was referred for marital therapy. Though the marital problems were the major focus of the initial sessions, Wanda's adjustment difficulties required additional attention.

David and Wanda met through a singles travel club and were initially attracted to each other because of their mutual interest in travel and dancing. After a brief courtship, they married. Since then, two successive pregnancies had left them with two lovely children but little time or money to pursue their early interests in travel and dance.

In the early sessions, David, a 29-year-old sales representative, complained that Wanda, a 28-year-old homemaker, is a "great procrastinator" and that she keeps the house a "shambles." Apparently Wanda also "forgets" to cook, sometimes because she becomes preoccupied with a book or a puzzle. She is

often unaware of the time and feeds the children late; too, she often does not have dinner ready when David comes home. On the other hand, after some prodding, Wanda revealed that she finds herself in an intolerable situation. She is unhappy with her marriage; she sees her husband as a selfish, picky person who is obsessive about the cleanliness of the house and the preparation of the meals, as well as unaware of the difficulties of caring for two young children. It was clear from these early sessions that David and Wanda were frustrated in their marriage and each harbored great resentments toward the other.

In subsequent therapy sessions it became apparent that Wanda's problems were consistent with a lifelong pattern and not just the result of her present situation. She is a rather passive and nonassertive person who has difficulty making her objections known to others. She had great difficulty making her feelings known to David about her disappointments in the marriage. Instead, she dealt with her frustration through indirect means—intentional inefficiency. She related several incidents in her life in which she had periods of ineffective functioning or, as she called it, stubbornness. Inevitably, these periods had occurred during times of frustration. For example, her parents had hoped she would pursue a career in music, as they had; rather than tell them she had no desire to be a musician, she instead could "just never seem to complete" her university assignments and eventually flunked out of school.

In addition to the marital therapy sessions, it was recommended that Wanda also be seen in individual psychotherapy to explore further her personal adjustment problems. As for the maintenance of the house, it was recommended that, for the time being at least, they hire outside help.

In sum, we can see in the passive-aggressive personality a pattern of never confronting a problem situation directly. This characteristic way of reacting to problems is really no solution at all. It is frustrating for others, who must deal with the inefficient behavior typically without knowing the real reason for it; and it is frustrating for the individual, because it typically does not productively resolve the problem.

Causal factors in personality disorders

Establishing the causal factors in personality disorders has not progressed very far, partly because such disorders were not even included in the official diagnostic classifications before 1952 and partly because they are less amenable to thorough study. Many individuals with these disorders are never seen by clinical personnel. Typically, those who do come to the attention of clinicians or legal authorities have already developed the "full-blown disorder," so that only *retrospective* study is possible—that is, going back through what records may exist in an effort to reconstruct the chain of events that may have led to the disorder. As we have seen, researchers have more confidence in *prospective* studies, in which groups of individuals are observed before a disorder appears and followed over a period of time to see which individuals develop problems and what causal factors have in fact been present.

Research on causal factors in disordered personality is also made difficult by the fact that, for the most part, general traits of personality rather than specific behavior patterns are being studied in the personality disorders. It is hard to identify the point at which "great attention to detail" ceases to be within the normal range and becomes characteristic of compulsive personality.

Of possible biological factors, it has been suggested that the constitutional reaction tendencies that infants display (high or low vitality, special sensitivity, and so on) may predispose them to the development of particular personality disorders. And though some research suggests that genetic factors may be important for the development of paranoid personality (Kendler & Gruenberg, 1982) and borderline personality (Loranger et al., 1982), the constitutional basis for the personality disorders remains largely hypothetical, with the possible exception of antisocial personality, to be discussed later.

Among psychological factors, early learning is usually assumed to contribute the most in predisposing the individual to develop a personality disorder, yet, quite honestly, the "data" in support of this belief are based only on speculation and inference. Again, except to some extent for antisocial personality, research has simply not yet established particular antecedents for these disorders.

Sociocultural factors contributing to personality disorder are even less well defined. We do know that the incidence and form of psychopathology in general vary somewhat with time and place, and some clinicians believe that personality disorders have increased in this society

in recent years (Smith, 1978). If this is true, we can expect to find the increase related to changes in the assumptions, priorities, and activities in our culture generally. Is our present high value on impulse gratification, instant solutions, and pain-free benefits leading more people to develop the self-centered, manipulative, and irresponsible life-style that we see in more extreme form in the personality disorders? Only further research can clarify this picture.

Treatment and outcomes

Personality disorders are usually considered to be especially resistant to therapy. For example, speaking of antisocial personalities, Ellis (1977) pointed out that

"[they] are exceptionally difficult to treat with psychotherapy. They only rarely come for treatment on a voluntary basis; and when they are treated involuntarily, they tend to be resistant, surly, and in search of a "cure" that will involve no real effort on their part. Even when they come for private treatment, they are usually looking for magical, effortless "cures," and they tend to stay in treatment only for a short period of time and to make relatively little improvement." (p. 259)

In many cases people with personality disorders who are seen clinically are there as part of another person's treatment—as, for example, in couple counseling, where the partner identified as the "patient" has a spouse with a personality disorder. Or a child referred to a child guidance center may have a parent with a personality disorder. In these cases, of course, the problems of the so-called patient may be due in no small measure to the great strain that the family member with severe personality disorder is causing to other family members. The narcissistic father, who is so self-centered and demanding of attention from others that family relationships are constantly strained, leaves little room for small children to grow into self-respecting adults. Likewise, a mother whose typical manner of responding to others is through passive-aggressive maneuvers such as procrastination, obstruction, and pouting may create an unhealthy family atmosphere that cripples the child's development.

A child subjected to such extreme, inescap-

Family counseling is one way of approaching the problem of family influence in the development of personality disorder.

able, and often quite irrational behavior on the part of one or both parents may become the "weak link" that breaks, bringing the family into therapy. Many a child or family therapist has quickly concluded after seeing a child in the family context that psychological attention, if it is to be effective at all, must be focused upon the parental relationships. The following case clearly illustrates the problem:

Mrs. A. brought her 7-year-old son, Christopher, to a mental health center for treatment because he was fearful of going out and recently had been having bad nightmares. Mrs. A. sought help at the recommendation of the school social worker after Chris refused to return to school. She voiced a great deal of concern for Chris and agreed to cooperate in the treatment by attending parent effectiveness training sessions. However, she seemed quite reluctant to talk about getting her husband involved in the treatment. After much encouragement, she agreed to try to bring him to the next session. He adamantly refused to participate, however. Mrs. A. described him as a "very proud and strong-willed man" who was quite suspicious of other people. She felt that he might be afraid people would blame him for Chris's problems. She reported that he had been having a lot of problems lately—he had seemed quite bitter and resentful over some local political issues and tended to blame others (particularly

minority group people) for his problems. He refused to come to the clinic because he "doesn't like social workers."

After several sessions of therapy, Mrs. A. confessed to her therapist that her husband's rigid and suspicious behavior was disrupting the family. He would often come home from work and accuse her of, for example, "talking with Jewish men." He was a very domineering person who set strict house rules and enforced them with loud threats and intimidation. Both Mrs. A. and Chris were fearful of his tyrannical demands, but his suspicious nature made it difficult for them to explain anything to him. Mrs. A. also felt a great deal of sympathy for her husband because she felt that deep down inside he was very frightened; she reported that he kept numerous guns around the house and several locks on the doors for protection against outsiders, whom he feared.

Because they usually enter treatment only at someone else's insistence and do not believe that there is any need for them to change, individuals with personality disorders typically put the responsibility for treatment on others and are adept at avoiding the focus of therapy themselves. In addition, the difficulty they have in forming and maintaining good relationships generally tends to make the therapeutic relationship a stormy one at best. The pattern of acting out, typical in their other relationships, is carried into the therapy situation, and instead of dealing with their problem at the verbal level, they may become angry at the therapist and loudly disrupt the sessions. Or they may behave in socially inappropriate ways outside the session to show the therapist that the therapy is not working.

When questioned about such behavior, these individuals often drop out of treatment or become even more entrenched in their defensiveness. In some cases, however, confrontation can be quite effective. For individuals who become identified with a therapy group, or who are sufficiently "hooked" into couple therapy not to flee the session when their behavior comes under scrutiny, the intense feedback from peers or spouse often is more acceptable than confrontation by a therapist in individual treatment (Gurman & Kniskern, 1978; Lubin, 1976).

In some situations, therapeutic techniques must be modified. For example, recognizing that traditional individual psychotherapy tended to encourage dependency in persons already too dependent, Leeman and Mulvey (1973) developed a treatment strategy in individual outpatient therapy for altering the dependent individual's basic life-style instead of fostering it. First, they would inform a patient at the outset that the therapy would be brief. Next, they made it clear that they "would not assume responsibility for managing the patient's life" (p. 36) and that they expected strength on the part of the patient "both to tolerate feelings and to behave in more adaptive and self-satisfying ways" (p.36). Therapy sessions were then kept focused on relationships outside of therapy rather than on the treatment relationship, and demands were made on the patient to *change* his or her behavior—not just to understand it. Several highly dependent patients, including one "veteran" of ten years of individual psychotherapy, responded favorably to this treatment, and most reported that they were doing much better two and a half years later.

In general, therapy for individuals with personality disorders is much more likely to be effective in situations like prisons, where acting-out behavior can be constrained and the individual cannot leave the situation (Vaillant, 1975). Outpatient treatment is not promising in most cases. The tenacity of these disorders and the failure of the individuals either to profit from or-

dinary therapy or to learn from their life experiences is shown in the following case of an individual diagnosed as a passive-aggressive personality:

Charles, age 29, appeared to be a highly successful salesman in a large retail shoe store. He was a handsome, friendly, and outgoing person who quickly impressed customers and gained ready admirers. His relationships with coworkers and employers, however, were an entirely different matter. He was a very disorganized person who couldn't keep the bookkeeping and stock in order. He was a procrastinator who promised everything but delivered nothing. He responded to criticism by his employers with smiles and promises but was never able to get organized. He never expressed anger toward his supervisor or disgruntled customers but seldom fulfilled their demands.

One evening, after he had been criticized for his sloppiness, he was directed to straighten out his "mess" and lock up the store after everyone else had left. He failed to comply and actually left the store open with the lights on. This was the last straw for his employer, and Charles was fired.

Over the years, his stubborn and passive-aggressive actions had lost him several other jobs. In each situation he had been able to secure a sales position quite readily but in short order his behavior had angered his employers and the ensuing criticisms had made him even more intractable.

Finally, he entered therapy at his wife's insistence because of marital problems they were experiencing. His behavior toward his wife was similar to his behavior in other personal relationships: he was obstinate and unyielding even though he always smiled and never lost his temper. After only two weeks in therapy he began to miss sessions until after a month he stopped coming altogether because "he had to look for work."

Antisocial (psychopathic) personality

Antisocial personality, as we have seen, is a personality disorder in which the outstanding characteristics are a marked lack of ethical or moral development and an apparent inability of the individual to follow approved models of behavior. Basically, these individuals are unsocialized and seemingly incapable of significant loyalty to other persons, groups, or social values. These characteristics often bring them into repeated conflict with society. The terms *psychopathic personality* and *sociopathic personality* are also commonly used in referring to this disorder.

The category called *antisocial personality* includes a mixed group of individuals: unprincipled business people, shyster lawyers, quack doctors, high-pressure evangelists, crooked politicians, imposters, drug pushers, a sizeable number of prostitutes, and assorted delinquents and criminals. Few of these individuals find their way into community clinics or mental hospitals. A much larger number are confined in penal institutions, but a history of repeated legal or social offenses is not sufficient justification for assuming that an individual is psychopathic. In point of fact, the great majority of psychopaths manage to stay out of corrective institutions, although they tend to be in constant conflict with authority (see **HIGHLIGHT** on page 249).

The worldwide incidence of psychopathic personality is not known. In the United States, however, incidence is estimated to be about 3 percent of American males and about 1 percent of American females (APA, 1980). Onset is in early childhood for males but typically not until the onset of puberty for females.

Clinical picture in antisocial personality

Typically intelligent, spontaneous, and usually very likeable on first acquaintance, antisocial personalities are deceitful and manipulative, callously using others to achieve their own ends. Often they seem to live in a series of present moments, without consideration for the past or future. The following example is illustrative.

Two 18-year-old youths went to visit a teenager at her home. Finding no one there, they broke into the house, damaged a number of valuable paintings and other furnishings, and stole a quantity of liquor and a television set. They sold the TV to a mutual friend for a small sum of money. Upon their apprehension by the police, they at first denied the entire venture and then later insisted that it was all a "practical joke." They did not consider their behavior particularly inappropriate, nor did they think any sort of restitution for damage was called for.

Also included in the general category of antisocial individuals are "hostile psychopaths," who are prone to acting out the impulses in remorseless and often senseless violence. In other cases antisocial individuals are capable of assuming responsibility and pursuing long-range goals, but they do so in unethical ways with a complete lack of consideration for the rights and well-being of others.

Only individuals 18 or over are diagnosed as antisocial personalities. According to the DSM-III classification, this diagnosis is made if the following criteria are met: (a) if there have been at least three instances of deviant behavior such as theft, vandalism, or unusually aggressive behavior before age 15; (b) if there have been at least four behavior problems such as financial irresponsibility, illegal occupation, ineffective functioning as a parent, or poor work history since age 15 and no period longer than five years without such a problem; (c) if the antisocial behavior endures, with no "remission" lasting longer than five years (unless the person is incapacitated or imprisoned); (d) if the antisocial behavior is not a symptom of another mental disorder.

To fill in the clinical picture, let us begin by summarizing characteristics that antisocial personalities tend to share; then we shall describe three quite different cases which illustrate the wide range of behavior patterns that may be involved.

Common characteristics.   While all the following characteristics are not usually found in a particular case, they are typical of antisocial personalities in general.

1. *Inadequate conscience development and lack of anxiety and guilt.* Antisocial personalities are unable to understand and accept ethical values except on a verbal level. They make glib verbalizations and claims of adherence to high standards of morality that have no apparent connection with their behavior. In short, though their intellectual development is typically normal or above, their conscience development is severely retarded, or nonexistent.

Antisocial personalities tend to "act out" tensions and problems rather than worry them out. Their apparent lack of anxiety and guilt, combined with the appearance of sincerity and candor, may enable them to avoid suspicion and

HIGHLIGHT
Wanted: Everyday psychopaths

Most antisocial individuals who have been studied have been cases who were institutionalized, leaving us in ignorance about the far larger number who never get caught. Widom (1977) tried an ingenious approach for reaching this larger group. She ran advertisements in the local newspapers which read:

"Are you adventurous? Psychologist studying adventurous, carefree people who've led exciting, impulsive lives. If you're the kind of person who'd do almost anything for a dare and want to participate in a paid experiment, send name, address, phone, and short biography proving how interesting you are to . . . ." (p. 675)

Widom had hoped to attract psychopathic individuals and apparently did just that. When given a battery of tests, those who responded turned out to be similar in personality makeup to institutionalized psychopathic individuals. Although she did not go further than this in studying these individuals, her method suggests a way of making contact with samples of uninstitutionalized psychopathic personalities.

detection for stealing and other illegal activities. They often show contempt for those they are able to take advantage of—the "marks."

2. *Irresponsible and impulsive behavior; low frustration tolerance.* Antisocial individuals generally have a callous disregard for the rights, needs, and well-being of others. They have learned to take rather than earn what they want. Prone to thrill-seeking and deviant and unconventional behavior, they often break the law impulsively and without regard for the consequences. They seldom forego immediate pleasure for future gains and long-range goals. They live in the present, without realistically considering either past or future. External reality is used for immediate personal gratification. Unable to endure routine or to shoulder responsibility, they frequently change jobs.

3. *Ability to put up "a good front" to impress and exploit others, projecting blame onto others for their own socially disapproved behavior.* Often antisocial individuals are charming and likeable, with a disarming manner that easily wins friends. Typically, they have a good sense of humor and an optimistic outlook. Though frequent liars, they usually will seem sincerely sorry if caught in a lie and promise to make amends—but not do so. They seem to have good insight into other people's needs and weaknesses and are very adept at exploiting them. For example, many psychopaths engage in unethical sales schemes in which they use their charm and the confidence they inspire in others to make "easy money." They readily find excuses and rationalizations for their antisocial conduct, typically projecting the blame onto someone else. Thus they are often able to convince other people—as well as themselves—that they are free of fault.

4. *Rejection of authority and inability to profit from experience.* Antisocial individuals behave as if social regulations do not apply to them: they do not play by the rules of the game. Frequently they have a history of difficulties with educational and law-enforcement authorities. Yet, although they often drift into criminal activities, they are not typically calculating professional criminals. Despite the difficulties they get into and the punishment they may receive, they go on behaving as if they will be immune from the consequences of their actions.

5. *Inability to maintain good interpersonal relationships.* Although initially able to win the liking and friendship of other people, antisocial personalities are seldom able to keep close friends. Irresponsible and egocentric, they are usually cynical, unsympathetic, ungrateful, and remorseless in their dealings. They seemingly cannot understand love in others or give it in return. As Horton, Louy, and Coppolillo (1974) have expressed it, the psychopathic personality "continues to move through the world wrapped in his separateness as though in an insulator, touched rarely and never moved by his fellow man" (p. 622).

Antisocial personalities pose a menace not only to chance acquaintances but also to family and friends. Manipulative and exploitive in sexual relationships, they are irresponsible and unfaithful mates. Although they often promise to change, they rarely do so for any considerable length of time.

Many of the preceding characteristics may be found in varying degrees in neurotic individuals, in those dependent on drugs, and in those showing other maladaptive behavior patterns. In the case of the antisocial personality, however, these characteristics are extremely pronounced and occur apart from other "symptoms" of psychopathology. Whereas most neurotic individuals, for example, are beset by worry and anxiety and have a tendency to avoid difficult situations, antisocial personalities act on their impulses fearlessly, with little or no thought for the difficulties they may be incurring.

Patterns of behavior. Some well-known cases from recent history can be used to illustrate the range and variability of behavior that may be found among individuals labeled as psychopathic personalities.

The most dangerous psychopathic personalities from the standpoint of society as a whole are those who are not only intelligent and completely unscrupulous but also show sufficient self-control and purposefulness of behavior to achieve high political office. This point is well illustrated by the case of Nazi Field Marshal Hermann Goering.

"Goering had a better family background than most of his Nazi associates. His father had been Governor of German Southwest Africa and Resident Minister at Haiti. Hermann attended several boarding schools but he was bored and restless till he got to the Military Academy, where he settled down to his studies. He entered the army as an infantryman but he took flying lessons surreptitiously and got himself transferred to the Air Force against the wishes of his superior officers. He was a courageous and impetuous flyer and after the death of Richthofen he took charge of The Flying Circus.

"At the close of the First World War Goering went to Sweden where he worked as a mechanic and as a civil aviator. He married a wealthy woman and was able to return to Germany and enroll at the University of Munich. In Munich he met Hitler and joined the Nazi movement. . . .

"Goering's manner of living is described as 'Byzantine splendor' and as 'piratical splendor.' He built a pretentious country home near Berlin and furnished it magnificently with tapestries and paintings and antiques. He had a private zoo. He required his servants to address his wife as Hohe Frau, thus giving her the distinction of nobility. He felt that the Germans liked his display of luxury—that it gave food for their imagination and gave the people something to think about. Goering was given to exhibitionism and he had a passion for uniforms, gold braid, medals, and decorations. . . .

"Goering was coarse and gross. He was a Gargantuan eater and drinker. He was ribald in jest. He laughed uproariously when his pet lion urinated on a lady's dress. He once horrified his men and women guests at his country estate by having a bull and a cow mate before them. Personally he enjoyed the spectacle and declared that it was an old Teutonic custom.

"'Our Hermann' was popular with the masses and they smiled good-naturedly at his antics and self-display. He demanded that they make sacrifices in order to win victory and exhorted them to choose guns instead of butter. He patted his fat belly and said that he had lost forty pounds in the service of his country. The Germans appreciated his sense of humor. . . .

"Goering was unscrupulous in his exercise of authority. . . . When he was made Chief of the Prussian Police he told his men to shoot first and inquire afterward. 'If you make a mistake, don't talk about it.' 'The faults which my officials commit are my faults; the bullets they fire are my bullets.' Goering regarded his bullets as an effective form of propaganda. He introduced the concentration camp and declared that it was not his duty to exercise justice, but to annihilate and exterminate. He reintroduced decapitation as an honest old German punishment. Goering is given credit for plotting the Reichstag Fire and for the planning and direction of the Blood Purge. Goering admitted that he had no conscience; his conscience was Adolf Hitler." (Bluemel, 1948, pp. 78–82)

One of the most interesting types of persons found in the category of antisocial personality is the impostor, whose abilities are often outstanding and might seemingly have been channeled in socially approved ways. This is well brought out in the following unusual case.

One of the boldest imposters of recent times was Ferdinand Waldo Demara, Jr. As an adolescent, he ran away from a rather tragic family situation and after unsuccessful attempts first to become a Trappist monk and then to teach school, he joined the army. Soon thereafter he went AWOL, joined the navy, and was assigned to duty on a destroyer during World War II.

Goering's love of dramatic display and magnificence is evident in this 1943 photograph.

Here, by a ruse, he got hold of some navy stationery with which he managed to obtain the transcript of college grades of an officer who was on leave. He then "doctored" this transcript by substituting his own name and adding some courses; when photostated, it looked so impressive that he used it to apply for a commission. While waiting for his commission to come through, he amused himself by obtaining other records, including the full credentials of a Dr. French, who had received a Ph.D. degree in psychology from Harvard. Informed during a visit to Norfolk that he could expect his commission as soon as a routine security check was completed, he realized that such a check would surely expose him. Under cover of darkness, he left his navy clothes on the end of a pier with a note that "this was the only way out."

Now that Demara was "dead"—drowned in the oily waters off Norfolk—he became Dr. French. He obtained an appointment as Dean of Philosophy in a small Canadian college and taught courses in general, industrial, and abnormal psychology. Eventually, however, he had a disagreement with his superior and reluctantly left.

During this period he had become friends with a physician by the name of Joseph Cyr and had learned a considerable amount about the practice of medicine from him during the cold winter months when neither man had much to occupy his time. Interested in the possibility of getting a license to practice in the States, the trusting doctor had given Demara a complete packet including his baptism and confirmation certificates, school records, and his license to practice medicine in Canada.

Using these credentials, without Dr. Cyr's knowledge, Demara now obtained a commission for himself as lieutenant in the Royal Canadian Navy. His first assignment was to take sick call each morning at the base. To help solve his problem of lack of knowledge in the field, he went to his superior officer and stated that he had been asked to work up a rule-of-thumb guide for people in lumber camps, most of whom did not have physicians readily available. His senior officer, delighted with the project, prepared a manual covering the most serious medical situations, which served as a basic guide for amateur diagnosticians. Demara then used this manual faithfully as his own. He also studied medical books and evidently picked up considerable additional knowledge.

Assigned to duty on the aircraft carrier HMCS *Magnificent*, Demara was criticized by his senior medical officer for his lack of training in medicine and surgery, especially for his deficiency in diagnosing medical problems. Learning of the report, Demara took characteristic bold action. He commandeered several seamen's compartments in the lower area of the ship, posted them with quarantine signs, and sent there for observation the patients whom he was having trouble diagnosing—in the meantime giving them penicillin. The chief medical officer knew nothing of this plan— Demara had confided only in a bosun's mate—and the reports of Demara's performance, based only on cases that Demara reviewed with his superior officer, became more favorable.

Perhaps the climax of Demara's incredible career came during the Korean War when—still as Lieutenant Cyr—he was assigned as the ship's doctor to the Canadian destroyer *Cayuga*. As the *Cayuga* proceeded to the combat zone, Demara studied medical books and hoped that his skill would never be put to test. But fate decreed otherwise. One afternoon the destroyer spotted a small Korean junk littered with wounded men who had been caught in an ambush. "Dr. Cyr" was summoned and knew that there was no escape for him.

"Nineteen suffering men were lifted tenderly from the junk. Three were so gravely wounded that only emergency surgery could save them. Demara had read books on surgery, but had never seen an operation performed.

"The self-taught 'M.D.' cleaned and sutured the 16 less seriously wounded men, while gathering his courage for the great ordeal. Then he commandeered the captain's cabin as an emergency operating room. Working hour after hour with slow, unskilled hands, but drawing on all the resources of his great memory and natural genius, Demara performed miracles, while the ship's officers and dozens of enlisted men helped and watched.

"From one wounded man he removed a bullet that had lodged near the heart; from the second, a piece of shrapnel in the groin. For the third man, Demara collapsed a lung which had been perforated by a bullet. . . .

When his ship was sent to Japan for refitting, an eager young press officer seized on "Dr. Cyr's" exploits and wrote them up in full. His story was released to the civilian press, and the "miracle doctor" became world famous. This publicity proved to be Demara's temporary undoing, for it led to queries from the real Dr. Joseph Cyr as to whether the physician mentioned in the press releases was a relative, and when Dr. Cyr saw the newspaper picture, he was shocked to find it was that of an old friend.

Dropped from the Canadian navy without fanfare—largely because he had managed to get a license to practice medicine in England and was now a licensed physician—Demara went through a difficult period. Wherever he went, he was soon recognized, and he lost job after job. He managed to work for a year at a state school for retarded children and did so well that he received a promotional transfer to a state hospital for the criminally insane. Here he found that the patients seemed to like him and that he was able to communicate with them. The experience began to bother him and he started to drink heavily and eventually resigned.

One morning after a prolonged drinking bout, he woke up in a southern city and realized his drinking was getting out of hand. He joined the local chapter of Alcoholics Anonymous as Ben W. Jones, whose credentials he had acquired along the way. With the help of sympathetic friends in Alcoholics Anonymous and a few fraudulent references obtained by ingenious methods, he was hired as a guard in a state penitentiary. Here he did a remarkable job, instituting a number of badly needed reforms in the maximum security block. Again he found himself able to communicate with the men, and he was promoted to assistant warden of maximum security. Ironically, one of his reform measures was to ask the townspeople to contribute old magazines, and before long one of the prisoners read the issue of *Life* that contained his picture and case history and recognized the new assistant warden.

Trying to get away lest he wind up as a prisoner in the same penitentiary, Demara was jailed in a nearby state and given considerable publicity but eventually released. Some time later he telephoned Dr. Crichton, from whose report most of this material has been adapted, to say "I'm on the biggest caper of them all. Oh, I wish I could tell you." (Summarized from Crichton, 1959; quoted passages from Smith, 1968.)

By way of postscript, it may be mentioned that in early 1970 there was a newspaper report of Demara functioning successfully as a minister in a small northwestern community, this time

During the 1960s Ferdinand Waldo Demara, the "great impostor," turned to the religious life and took up residence in an interfaith monastery in central Missouri.

with the congregation's full knowledge of his past.

As we shall see, many persons diagnosed as "antisocial personalities" do eventually settle down to responsible positions in the community. Furthermore, Brantley and Sutker (in press), in reviewing the literature on psychopaths, point out that—although much of the literature has focused on the generally negative aspects of antisocial personalities—these individuals also have positive qualities: as a group they seem to be

"robust, socially facile and ingenious in many situations. . . . In fact, there are . . . data on which to build a case for their capacity to respond with appropriate emotional expression in most interpersonal situations. Certainly, the extreme cases among groups in which individuals are diagnosed as antisocial personality or sociopathic may represent the epitome of distaste for authority as well as disregard for the wishes of significant others in their lives. Among their ranks, however, are daring, adventuresome, resourceful persons who may have capabilities to outperform so-called normals when the going gets rough."

Causal factors in antisocial personality

As is the case with all the personality disorders discussed here, the causal factors in antisocial personality are still not fully understood. Our perspective is complicated by the fact that the causal factors involved appear to differ from case to case, as well as from one socioeconomic level to another. However, more research has been conducted on the antisocial personality than on any of the other personalities, so we do, at least, have a broader basis of data upon which to draw. Contemporary research in this area has variously stressed constitutional deficiencies, the early learning of antisocial behavior as a coping style, and the influence of particular family and community patterns.

Constitutional factors. Because the antisocial individual's impulsiveness, acting out, and intolerance of discipline tend to appear early in life, several investigators have focused on the role of constitutional deficiencies as causative factors in antisocial personality disturbances.

1. *Malfunction of inhibitory mechanisms in the central nervous system.* In a review and interpretation of studies indicating a relatively high incidence of EEG abnormalities among psychopathic personalities, particularly involving slow-wave activity in the temporal lobe of the brain, Hare (1970) concluded that such abnormalities reflect the malfunction of inhibitory mechanisms in the central nervous system, and that "this malfunction makes it difficult to learn to inhibit behavior that is likely to lead to punishment" (pp. 33–34).

It may be emphasized, however, that most psychopathic personalities do not show abnormal EEGs, and when they do, there is no conclusive evidence that the EEG patterns are directly related to the development of their behavior. In addition, many individuals who show similar EEG patterns are not psychopathic. So when brain anomalies do occur in psychopathic individuals, they are probably predisposing factors rather than primary determinants of the maladaptive behavior.

2. *Deficient emotional arousal.* Research evidence indicates that a primary reaction tendency typically found in psychopathic individuals is a deficient emotional arousal; this presumably renders them less prone to fear and anxiety in stressful situations and less prone to normal conscience development and socialization.

In an early study, for example, Lykken (1957) concluded that psychopathic individuals have fewer inhibitions about committing antisocial acts because they suffer little anxiety. Similarly, Eysenck (1960) concluded that psychopathic individuals are less sensitive to noxious stimuli and have a slower rate of conditioning than normal individuals. As a result, psychopathic individuals presumably fail to aquire many of the conditioned reactions essential to normal avoidance behavior, conscience development, and socialization. Support for this viewpoint is found in the findings of Chesno and Kilmann (1975) who concluded that sociopathic individuals, as contrasted with normal persons, "were relatively unsuccessful in acquiring active avoidance responses" (p. 150).

Hare (1970) and other later investigators have reported comparable findings with respect to the psychopathic individual's lack of normal fear and anxiety reactions and failure to learn readily from punishment. However, the latter point merits qualification. Schmauk (1970) confirmed earlier observations that such individuals were less adept than nonpsychopathic individuals in learning to avoid physical and social punishments, but found them to be more adept than normal persons in learning to avoid the loss of money—a type of punishment that was apparently *meaningful* to them. These findings are more understandable when it is added that the individuals observed in the experiment were inmates of a penal institution where physical and social punishments were relatively mild for most forms of misbehavior, whereas money was both hard to come by and very valuable for obtaining niceties beyond the grim prison fare.

In addition, it may be noted that while the lack of normal emotional arousal may be based on constitutional deficiencies, it may also be based partially on learning. Often in the past psychopathic individuals have managed to avoid the full consequences of their antisocial behavior by such devices as lies and plausible excuses, dramatic shows of remorse, and empty but convincing promises of "good" behavior in the future. In fact, the absence of anxiety attributed to these individuals has been questioned by Vaillant (1975), who believes that they have simply learned to handle their anxiety differently. In Vaillant's view, rather than succumb to anxiety like neurotic individuals, they conceal it and in most cases find ways to escape from it. When they cannot flee, they may experience the anxiety, but they hide their feelings. Vaillant believes that this concealment of anxiety was learned because anxiety was intolerable to the parents. He points out that escaping from anxiety-arousing situations is an immature defense, like those found in adolescence.

3. *Stimulation seeking.* In his study of criminally psychopathic individuals, Hare (1968) reported that these individuals operate at a low level of arousal and are deficient in autonomic variability. He considered these characteristics—together with their lack of normal conditioning to noxious and painful stimuli—indicative of a "relative immunity" to stimulation, which in turn would likely prompt psychopathic individuals to seek stimulation and thrills as ends in themselves. In a study comparing psychopathic and normal individuals, Fenz (1971) also found that the former seemed to have an insatiable need for stimulation. Several other investigators, using Zuckerman's Sensation-Seeking Scale (Zuckerman, 1972, 1978), have noted that individuals involved in a variety of antisocial behaviors—such as prison escapes (Farley & Farley, 1972), drug use (Kilpatrick et al., 1976), and chronicity of arrests among skid-row alcoholics (Malatesta, Sutker, & Treiber, 1981)—have higher sensation-seeking scores and a low tolerance for boredom.

Such findings support the earlier view of Quay (1965), who concluded that psychopathic behavior is, in essence, an extreme form of stimulation-seeking behavior:

"The psychopath is almost universally characterized as highly impulsive, relatively refractory to the effects of experience in modifying his socially troublesome behavior, and lacking in the ability to delay gratification. His penchant for creating excitement for the moment without regard for later consequences seems almost unlimited. He is unable to tolerate routine boredom. While he may engage in antisocial, even vicious, behavior, his outbursts frequently appear to be motivated by little more than a need for thrills and excitement. . . . It is the impulsivity and the lack of even minimal tolerance for sameness which appear to be the primary and distinctive features of the disorder." (p. 180)

What such extreme stimulation-seeking might

mean in the total context of a personality also characterized as impulsive, lacking in judgment, deficient in inner reality and moral controls, and seemingly unable to learn from punishment and experience can hardly bode well. Though further investigation is needed, it seems plausible that stimulation-seeking "unchecked by conditioned fear response is a two-edged sword for antisocial behavior" (Borkovec, 1970, p. 222).

Family relationships. Perhaps the most popular generalization about the development of the antisocial personality is the assumption of some form of early disturbance in family relationships.

1. *Early parental loss and emotional deprivation.* A number of early studies reported that an unusually high number of antisocial individuals had experienced the trauma of losing a parent at an early age—usually through the separation or divorce of their parents. For example, Greer (1964) found that 60 percent of one group of antisocial individuals he studied had lost a parent during childhood, as contrasted with 28 percent for a control group of neurotic individuals and 27 percent for a control group of normal subjects.

Since many normal people have experienced the loss of a parent at an early age, it would seem to require considerably more than parental loss to produce a psychopathic personality. In reviewing the available evidence, Hare (1970) suggested that the factor of key significance was not the parental loss *per se,* but rather the emotional disturbances in the family relationships created before the departure of a parent.

This point is supported by the findings of Wolkind (1974) who found a high incidence of "affectionless psychopathy" in a group of 92 institutionalized children. In many of these cases the antisocial disorder seemed to have been caused by pathogenic family situations prior to the children's being placed in an institution.

2. *Parental rejection and inconsistency.* A number of studies have attempted to relate parental rejection and inconsistent discipline to inadequate socialization and antisocial personality. After an extensive review of the available literature, McCord and McCord (1964) concluded that severe parental rejection and lack of parental affection were the primary causes of psychopathic personality.

Thrill-seeking is one hallmark of the antisocial personality.

Another aspect of this picture has been pointed out by Buss (1966), who concluded that two types of parental behavior foster psychopathy. In the first, parents are cold and distant toward the child and allow no warm or close relationship to develop. A child who imitates this parental model will become cold and distant in later relationships; although the child learns the formal attributes and amenities of social situations, he or she does not develop empathy for others or become emotionally involved with them.

The second type of parental behavior involves inconsistency, in which parents are capricious in supplying affection, rewards, and punishments. Usually they are inconsistent in their own role enactments as well, so that the child lacks stable models to imitate and fails to develop a clear-cut sense of self-identity. Often the parents reward not only "superficial conformity" but "underhanded nonconformity"—that is, nonconformity that goes undetected by outsiders. Thus, they reinforce behaviors that lead to psychopathic behavior. Similarly, when the parents are both arbitrary and inconsistent in punishing the child, avoiding punishment becomes more important than receiving rewards. Instead of learning to see behavior in terms of right and wrong, the child learns how to avoid blame and

punishment by lying or other manipulative means.

In Chapter 4 we noted that among the damaging effects of parental rejection and inconsistent discipline are slow conscience development and aggression on the part of the child. We also noted that children subjected to inconsistent reward and punishment for aggressive behavior were more resistant to efforts to extinguish the behavior than were children who experienced more consistent discipline. However, it seems desirable to exercise caution in using parental rejection and inconsistency as basic explanations of psychopathic personalities. In the first place, these same conditions have been implicated in a wide range of later maladaptive behaviors. In addition, many children coming from such family backgrounds do not become antisocial personalities or evidence other serious psychopathology. Thus further explanation is needed.

3. *Faulty parental models and family interactions.* In an early study of 40 male antisocial personalities, Heaver (1943) emphasized the influence exerted by faulty parental models—typically a mother who overindulged her son and a father who was highly successful, driving, critical, and distant.

Greenacre (1945) added a number of details that have been supported by later studies of an-

Parents who exhibit adaptive, caring behavior are unlikely to foster personality disorders in their children.

tisocial individuals from middle-class families. The father is a successful and respected member of the community and is distant and fear-inspiring to his children. The mother, on the other hand, is indulgent, pleasure-loving, frivolous, and often tacitly contemptuous of her husband's importance. When such families are heavily dependent on the approval and admiration of their communities—as in the case of some clergy and politicians—it is crucial that they maintain the illusion of a happy family by concealing and denying any evidence of bickering or scandal. Thus the children learn that appearances are more important than reality, and they, too, become part of the show-window display, where a premium is put on charm and impressing others rather than on competence and integrity. This need to please and to win social approval for their parents' sake seems to bring out a precocious but superficial charm in some of these children, together with great adroitness in handling people for purely selfish ends.

The son in such a family cannot hope to emulate his successful and awe-inspiring father, but, aware of the extension to himself of the high evaluation that is placed on his father, he develops a feeling of importance and of being exempt from the consequences of his actions. Frequently the prominence of the father does, in fact, protect the child from the ordinary conse-

quences of antisocial behavior. If we add one additional factor—the contradictory influence of a father who tells his son of the necessity for responsibility, honesty, and respect for others, but who himself is deceitful and manipulative—we appear to have a family background capable of producing a middle-class psychopathic personality.

Supporting this explanation is Hare's (1970) finding of a high incidence of psychopathic personalities—particularly fathers—in the families of children who later manifest such behavior themselves. In this context, Hare concluded that "at least part of a psychopath's behavior results from modeling another individual's psychopathic behavior" (p. 107).

The intermittent reinforcement of short-term gains and success in avoiding punishment also make the psychopathic life-style especially resistant to change. With relative freedom from anxiety, guilt, and remorse, there is little motivation to learn different patterns.

Sociocultural factors. Antisocial personality is thought to be more common in lower socioeconomic groups. Although we have emphasized the part played by constitutional and family factors in the formation of psychopathic personalities, it would appear that social condi-

are serious crimes such as murder and robbery for which there are severe legal penalties, including later restriction of citizen rights to vote and hold office. Misdemeanors, as the name implies, are minor offenses such as disorderly conduct and vagrancy. Whether a particular behavior is classified as a felony or a misdemeanor varies considerably from state to state—illustrating once again the importance of social definitions in the labeling of behavior as "abnormal."

Incidence

Official figures compiled by the Federal Bureau of Investigation indicate that the crime rate is higher in the United States than in most other countries, and that the rate for most crimes, though showing a slight decline in 1982 and 1983, continues at a high level.[1] For 1982 the FBI reported the commission of over 12.5 million serious crimes, including homicide, forcible rape, robbery, aggravated assault, burglary, larceny, and auto theft. This represents an overall decline of 4 percent from 1981 to 1982. Of the violent crimes, murder and robbery each declined 7 percent, and forcible rape declined 5 percent. Only aggravated assault increased—by 1 percent.

Though these statistics certainly raise hopes that we are finally seeing some progress in the battle against crime, some experts caution that these decreases might be normal, cyclical variations and should not be taken as a trend toward more law-abiding behavior. Others have pointed out that some of the reduction in crimes probably results from the fact that many courts are imposing more and longer prison sentences than they were in previous years. In actual fact, the problem of crime in the U. S. is even more serious, since it has been estimated that from one third to one half of all serious crimes are not reported to the police.

Some investigators have pointed out that the figure for serious crime is not as ominous as it seems, since over a million of the cases are auto thefts, which many people feel should not be included in this classification. But there would appear to be little room for complacency when it is realized that in the decade from 1972 to 1981,

violent crimes—homicide, rape, robbery, and assault—increased 58 percent! And the 1982 figures are hardly modest: some 21,000 homicides, 77,000 forcible rapes, 540,000 robberies, and 650,000 aggravated assaults (see the **HIGHLIGHT** on page 260).

Among lower-income groups, blacks are almost twice as likely as whites to be victims of crimes of violence and slightly more likely than whites to be victims of crimes against property. Middle- and upper-income groups, whether black or white, are about equally exposed to crime, but much more often to crimes against property than to crimes against the person. By and large, whites tend to victimize whites and blacks to victimize blacks. Criminals most often strike in the vicinity in which they live, and often they know their victims personally.

Crime rates vary considerably from one region of the country to another, from city to city, and from metropolitan to suburban and rural areas. They are much higher in the West than in the Northwest or South, higher in New York City and Los Angeles than in Philadelphia, and much higher in metropolitan centers than in smaller cities and rural areas. However, the crime rate is increasing more rapidly in the latter than in metropolitan centers.

Over 10 million Americans are arrested each year for having committed, or for suspicion of having committed, a serious crime. Among these, the lower-income groups are overrepresented (Gunn et al., 1978), as is the black population (Owens, 1980). Approximately 80 percent of both juvenile and adult offenders are male; and the great majority of violent crimes are committed by males. However, American females are apparently committing more murders, armed robberies, assaults, and other serious crimes. Their rates for violent crimes increased by 65 percent from 1970 to 1975 and since then to 1981 these rates decreased only 12 percent (Burquist, 1981). About 10 percent of all murders were committed by persons under 18 years of age, and 43 percent by persons under 25. As a consequence of apprehension and conviction for such crimes, over 400,000 individuals, including over 80,000 women and 74,000 juveniles, are in federal, state, and local prisons (U. S. Department of Justice Survey, 1982). In addition, more than a million others, both male and female, are on probation.

---

[1]Many of the statistics in this section are based on *Uniform Crime Reports* for 1981 and 1982.

The cost of crime in the United States each year is estimated at over $85 billion, an incredible and wasteful financial toll; and this says nothing of the toll in human resources and human suffering (see **HIGHLIGHT** on page 262–263).

Causal factors in criminal behavior

In our discussion of the personality disorders, we noted the importance of pervasive personal pathology, pathogenic family and peer patterns, and general sociocultural factors that foster antisocial behavior. These same factors have also been examined in relation to adult criminal behavior.

Biological factors. A number of early investigators attributed criminal behavior to heredity. Prominent among these investigators were Lombroso and his followers, who became known as the "Italian School of Criminology" (Lombroso-Ferrero, 1911). According to Lombroso, the criminal was a "born type" with "stigmatizing" features—such as low forehead, an unusually shaped head and jaw, eyebrows growing together above the bridge of the nose, and protruding ears. Supposedly such features clearly distinguished the criminal from normal people. These stigmata were considered to be a throwback to the "savage" and thus to signal an individual predisposed to criminal behavior.

Although Lombroso's view has long since been discarded, a number of recent investigators have dealt with the possibility that an extra Y chromosome—a genetic anomaly that can occur in males—is associated with much criminal behavior. Although there are many exceptions, men of the XYY chromosomal type are characterized by unusual height, borderline intelligence, and a tendency to show episodes of extremely aggressive behavior.

The earliest study in this area was that of Jacobs and her colleagues (1965) who published their findings of 197 mentally abnormal inmates of a special security institution in Scotland. All were considered to have violent and dangerous criminal tendencies. Seven—3.5 percent—were of the XYY chromosomal type.

In an intensive review of later research findings, Jarvik, Klodin, and Matsuyama (1973) re-

HIGHLIGHT
Crime clocks, 1980

In an average 24-hour period in 1980 in the United States, a violent crime took place once every 24 seconds. The rates for various categories of violent and property crimes were as follows:

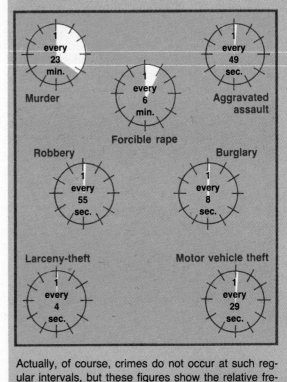

Actually, of course, crimes do not occur at such regular intervals, but these figures show the relative frequency of the crimes in the different categories.

Based on Uniform Crime Reports, 1981.

ported that the total frequency of XYY males in the criminal population approximated 2 percent. This frequency is about 15 times that found for the male population in general.

Presumably the extra Y chromosome stimulates excessive production of testosterone, the male hormone that has been linked by some investigators to aggression. However, this hypothesis is not as simple as it first seems. For one thing, not all XYY males are aggressive. In addition, their crimes are more often against property than persons.

More recently, Witkin et al. (1976) have questioned the hypothesis that the extra Y chromosome predisposes the individual to violence. At the present time there is simply no convincing evidence that the XYY male has a genetic predisposition to criminal behavior.

Tendencies toward violent behavior have been related to several other biological variables, including brain damage, mental retardation, psychomotor epilepsy, nutritional deficits, and degenerative brain changes associated with old age. An estimated 10 to 20 million Americans have some form of minor brain damage, and a number of investigators are exploring the possi-

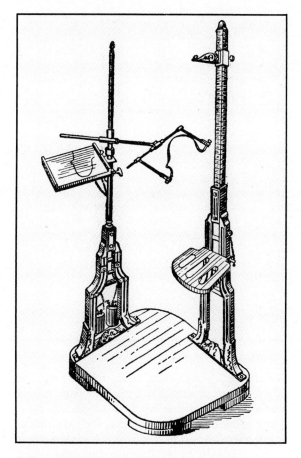

Italian criminologist Cesare Lombroso believed that criminals could be identified by specific physical characteristics, including the shape of the head. By measuring the skulls of known criminals with devices like this "craniograph," he compiled a classification of "criminal types."

bility of a link between such conditions and criminal behavior, particularly in conjunction with other factors such as severe stress or the use of alcohol or other drugs (Kiester, 1974).

Although a disproportionately high incidence of abnormal EEGs has been reported for both male and female prisoners, there is no conclusive evidence of the relation of brain lesions to serious crime except in a distinct minority of cases (Climent et al., 1973; Small, 1966).

Personal and family pathology. As we have pointed out, although crime is a legal term and not a psychiatric one, Gunn et al. (1978) have found that about a third of sentenced prisoners could be regarded, on the basis of psychiatric examination, to be psychiatric cases. Even among criminals who show no biological pathology related to their criminal behavior, psychopathology is common. Antisocial personality, alcoholism, and drug dependence appear to be associated with individuals who commit serious crimes. One can also find a disproportionately high number of borderline and actual psychotic individuals in this group. (Guze, Goodwin, & Crane, 1969; Sutker & Moan, 1973). Severe life stress, particularly in conjunction with personal pathology, also appears to be an important factor in triggering impulsive acts of violence and other antisocial behavior.

Many criminals who show psychological problems come from homes torn by conflict and dissension, often resulting in parental separation or divorce; also frequently found in their family backgrounds are parental rejection and inconsistent and severe punishment. These characteristics appear to be particularly common in—but not exclusive to—prison inmates who have committed crimes of violence (Climent et al., 1973; Sutker & Moan, 1973). Again, however, it is risky to draw causal inferences, since many persons who come from backgrounds similar to those just described do not evidence psychopathology and do not engage in criminal behavior. (The life history of one young killer is outlined in the **HIGHLIGHT** on page 264.)

Sociocultural influences. The social values and attitudes to which individuals are exposed have an enormous impact on their behavior. As we saw in Chapter 4, environmental factors can

HIGHLIGHT
Facts about homicide

Homicides are classified, in terms of intent, into: (1) first-degree murder, characterized by premeditation and planning, or committed during a felony, such as rape or robbery; (2) second degree murder, in which there is no premeditation or planning, e.g., as when the homicide is committed "in the heat of passion"; and (3) manslaughter, committed without malice or intention, as when a driver accidentally kills a pedestrian in a crosswalk. Relevant to these three categories are the following data concerning homicide in the United States.

Incidence	For reasons that are unclear, the homicide rate gradually increased from 1972 until 1975, when a decline occurred. The rate again moved upward and continued rising through 1981, when again the overall rate slowed following a general decrease in violent crimes. In 1981, 10 people in the United States for every 100,000 were murdered—a total of 22,516. Murders made up 2 percent of all violent crimes. For each actual murder, many more attempts are unsuccessful and the victim lives (80 percent of gunshot victims and 90 percent of stab victims). Thus, homicidal *acts* are far more common in our society than the statistics on homicide would indicate.
Who kills whom?	Ten percent of all homicides are committed by youths under 18 years of age and 43 percent by persons under 25. Fifty-five percent of all homicides are committed by relatives or acquaintances of the victim and about 73 percent of the murderers are identified. About 17 percent of the homicides are committed within the family relationship and about half of these involve spouse killing spouse. The victims of homicide are predominantly male (77 percent); 54 percent are white and 44 percent are black.

have a powerful influence on development—factors such as low social class or low socioeconomic level, for example, may be associated with the development of many psychological problems. Similarly, research has identified social and economic factors as possible causes of criminality (Reiss, 1976), although this hypothesis has by no means gone unchallenged (Tittle et al., 1978). Recently, McGarvey et al. (1981) conducted a large-scale study with a well-documented sample of 3421 Danish subjects to determine if social class was related to the development of criminal behavior. They found that social class of the family of origin was indirectly related to later criminality, with education as the mediating experience: low education was strongly related to adult criminality, and social class was directly related to educational attainment.

Other environmental or social factors may influence the development of criminal behavior. Viewing violence on television may cause some

Methods or weapons used	By far the greatest number of homicides result from shooting (63 percent) with handguns being the weapon of choice in half of all homicides. The high incidence of murders committed by firearms is not surprising in view of the widespread possession of guns by civilians in the U.S. Nineteen percent of the homicides are committed with knives or other cutting instruments and 13 percent involve other weapons such as blunt instruments, poison, or explosives. Six percent of the homicides are committed with personal weapons such as fists or feet.
Motives	As we have noted in listing the three categories of homicide, motives may be diverse, or the homicide may even be accidental. However, aside from murders committed for calculated monetary gains by individuals associated with organized crime, homicide is typically considered a "crime of passion." It often results from quarrels combined with a lowering of inner reality and ethical restraints; for example, intoxicants complicate the motivational picture in about half of all homicide cases. In some instances the victim—for whatever reason—seems to invite being killed, as by striking the first blow; and, as we shall see, homicide may be associated with such mental disorders as schizophrenia and paranoia. Felony-related motives accounted for 17.1 percent of homicides while arguments over such issues as love triangles (2.5 percent), alcohol or narcotics (4.1 percent), property or money (3.0 percent), accounted for 42.2 percent.
Psychosocial factors	Although diverse personality types may commit homicide, offenders tend to come from homes or neighborhoods in which violence is an aspect of daily life. Often they have a history of violent tendencies and behavior. In ghetto slums, homicide rates are disproportionately high. Homicide rates also show marked cross-cultural differences—with Iceland and Colombia, South America, representing extremes in rates of incidence among the major countries. Iceland's rate is zero, while that for Colombia is five times that of the United States. In general, it would appear that an increase in homicidal acts tends to accompany technological and social change.

Uniform Crime Reports, 1981.

children, particularly those with a predisposition to aggressive behavior, to engage in violent behavior (Comstock et al., 1978). Television may have an impact on other kinds of crime as well. Hennigan et al. (1982) found that television advertising, in which the American family is depicted as upper or middle class and where happy people are consuming expensive products, may contribute to the commission of crimes of larceny, for example. Rather than teaching the viewer how to commit larceny, it seems that television may motivate the deprived and frustrated viewer to thievery by exposing him or her to goods that are out of reach.

The violent crime of rape may be encouraged, in part, by the sociocultural environment. One hypothesis holds that rapists differ from other men not in the type of attitudes they hold but in the degree to which they hold certain attitudes that are prevalent in our culture having to do with sex, men, women, and violence. For example, there is a myth, *not* upheld by research

HIGHLIGHT
The "kid nobody wanted"

Exploding into the headlines in the early 1950s was the story of Billy Cook, "hard-luck" killer from Joplin, Missouri, whose days were ended in the gas chamber at San Quentin. He was captured by a Mexican posse in Lower California after a murderous rampage which extended across several states from Missouri to California. Cook's life motto was "Hard Luck," which he had tattooed on the knuckles of his left hand.

"Hard luck" was an appropriate motto for the youth: his mother died when he was five years old, and his father thereupon abandoned him, with his brothers and sisters, in a mine cave. In addition, he was handicapped with a deformed right eyelid. Nobody wanted Billy when he was offered for adoption, resentful and squint-eyed, and it was only a matter of time until his tantrums became too much for the county-appointed guardians to control. Billy quit school at the age of 12, and when brought before the court he was sent to the reformatory at his own request. From then on, almost all of his life was spent behind bars, first in the reformatory and then in the state penitentiary, to which he was "graduated" at 18.

Released from prison, Cook looked up his father and announced his intention to "live by the gun and roam." He got a job washing dishes, bought a gun, and was on his way—stealing his first car from a Texas mechanic with whom he hitched a ride. Robbed and locked in the trunk, the mechanic escaped to freedom by prying open the lid, but the next kidnap victims—an Illinois farmer, his wife, and three small children who picked Cook up near Oklahoma City when the first stolen car broke down—were not so lucky. Not daring to set them free, Cook forced them to drive back and forth through four states while he decided what to do with them. It was a three-day nightmare which included a foiled escape attempt; it finally ended in Joplin where Cook shot them and threw their bodies down a mine shaft.

A horrible pattern of kidnapping and murder had been set in motion, and as the hunted Cook desperately attempted to elude the law, he hitched three more rides and took the cars' occupants as captives. He spared the life of one kidnap victim, a Blythe, California, deputy officer whom he left tied up in the desert; but he shot and killed a Seattle businessman—the crime for which he eventually received the death penalty. The big interstate manhunt that was on for

Cook spread into Mexico when he was reported seen there with two companions—California prospectors who picked him up below the border and were his prisoners for eight days. When Cook was apprehended, less than a month had gone by since he had hitched the ride with the Texas mechanic. But though the time was brief, the toll was high: nine people kidnapped, six killed.

As if in explanation of his deeds, Billy Cook said when arrested, "I hate everybody's guts, and everybody hates mine."

Both before and after the Billy Cook case, a number of gruesome homicide cases have been reported. Among these are the cases of Jack the Ripper, the Boston Strangler, Richard Speck, the Manson family, and the finding of the bodies of over 30 teenage boys interred beneath the home of a "model citizen" in a Chicago suburb. In the case of Billy Cook, however, there seems to be an almost classic portrayal of the extent to which extreme parental and societal rejection, undesirable peer group models, and a life spent mainly as an inmate of penal institutions combined to produce a psychopathic killer.

Based on *Life* (1951) and *Time* (1951, 1952).

evidence (Kirkpatrick & Kanin, 1957), that women really enjoy being roughed up during sex. Other examples of beliefs in our culture that can be viewed as supportive of rape are the belief that women have an unconscious wish to be raped—a belief held by 71 percent of a group of Minnesota residents; nearly as many also believed that rape victims were mostly women of ill repute (Hotchkiss, 1978). Such beliefs would be likely to encourage false perceptions of a rape situation on the part of both the men and women.

So far, research to test this hypothesis has led to conflicting results. One study found no difference between rapists, normal men, and police officers in degree of acceptance of rape-supportive beliefs (Feild, 1978). Another study found rapists extremely aroused by tape recordings of erotic situations involving force, whereas non-rapist men were only slightly aroused by these situations but much more aroused by erotic situations not involving force (Abel et al., 1978). More research on why men rape is urgently needed if effective preventive programs are to be developed.

Often personal pathology appears to stem primarily from social pathology, as evidenced by the unusually high incidence of both juvenile and adult offenses in the slums of our large cities. These areas are characterized by severe social disorganization that leads to a very different form of socialization. The values of the larger society are often held in low repute or rejected altogether, and widespread feelings of helplessness and hopelessness combined with hostility toward established authority are characteristic. Under such conditions, aggressive and illegal behavior may become the norm for an entire subgroup.

1. *Crime as a profession.* The concept of *differential association*, first developed by Sutherland in the late 1930s, has provided a framework for understanding the importance of subcultural influences in the "training" of professional criminals—people such as hired killers, burglars, and forgers. As Sutherland and Cressey (1966) noted, the basic process of socialization is much the same for everyone: the individual comes to accept the values and behavioral standards emphasized by those with whom he or she associates on a repeated and intimate basis—most notably, parents and peers.

In the case of a young person growing up in a subculture where criminal behavior is the norm, the values and standards internalized—and the skills learned—are likely to be quite different from those emphasized in conventional society. Thus, individuals who become professional criminals usually acquire their training in much the same way that legitimate professionals do: by responding to the learning opportunities, values, and reinforcements that their environment has provided. Unlike the antisocial personality, they are "socialized"—but in a deviant way.

Typically, professional criminals specialize in a particular type of crime, such as forgery or burglary, and develop a particular style of operation. Their goal is to make money in the quickest and safest way possible. In general, they attempt to avoid violence, since it would greatly increase the risk of detection and imprisonment. Often they are highly skilled. Their crimes are usually well planned and may even be rehearsed. Possible arrest and imprisonment are hazards of their profession for which they are prepared; if they are imprisoned, they try to adapt to prison life and do "easy time."

By and large, professional criminals do not appear to show significant psychopathology aside from their adherence to the values and codes of their own group.

2. *Organized crime.* It is difficult to assess or discuss the nature and incidence of organized crime, since it has not been defined legally in the same sense as individual criminal *acts* like forcible rape and homicide. In addition, organized crime actively maintains a low level of social visibility. In general, however, the "organized criminal" is an individual who commits criminal acts while occupying a position in an organization specifically set up for perpetrating specific criminal activities.

The largest criminal organization in the United States, by all accounts, is La Cosa Nostra, also known as "the mafia," "the syndicate," and "the mob." Originally, organized crime families focused on illegal activities such as the production and sale of alcohol (during Prohibition), gambling, prostitution, and drug dealing. In more recent years, these families have added legitimate businesses to their enterprises. Estimates indicate that from 15 to 50 thousand business operations—including many loan com-

The role that television plays in inducing criminal or violent behavior has long been a subject of controversy. Recent studies seem to indicate that TV may contribute to aggressive and antisocial behavior by routinely presenting violent action and by making viewers aware of a host of consumer products that may be beyond their means.

panies, hotels, gambling casinos, race tracks, and restaurants—are currently funded by more than 20 billion dollars of mafia money (Kaplan & Kessler, 1976); even many labor unions and government agencies have been infiltrated by organized crime (Block & Chambliss, 1981). Operating in most, if not all, of the big cities and many smaller ones, the syndicate represents a powerful and pervasive force.

3. *Trends in criminal behavior.* During the early 1960s a number of investigators noted the growing prevalence of individuals who committed criminal acts primarily for ego-satisfaction and "kicks." A thrill is derived from performing some taboo act—usually a senseless act of violence—which serves to intensify the present moment, clearly differentiating it from the routine of daily life. Whereas professional criminals carefully calculate their acts, usually with an eye on material gain with minimum risk, this new criminal type commits violent acts on impulse, simply because it "makes me feel good." As one youth told Yablonsky (1962) after a gang killing,

"If I would of got the knife, I would have stabbed him. That would of gave me more of a build-up. People would have respected me for what I've done and things like that. They would say, 'There goes a cold killer.'"

Typically, the illegal acts of such criminals are spontaneous and unpremeditated; in most cases there is no evidence that they have even had prior contact with their victims. Even when they participate in planned criminal acts, they are still interested primarily in kicks. Unlike most other criminals, they seek no gain other than the pleasure to be derived from the criminal act itself.

More recently still, another group of criminals has emerged, who now constitute a large segment of today's prison population. As Alexander (1974) has described them,

"They are mostly losers, mostly poor and black. Their chief crime, in Huey Newton's memorable phrase, is being 'illegitimate capitalists,' unemployables whose only hope of enjoying the good things of life is in ripping off the system." (p. 35)

The poor, the powerless, and the undereducated are much more likely to be caught, prosecuted, punished, or even held in jails for months before being tried. And if found guilty, their sentence is likely to be more severe.

While the affluent have probably always fared somewhat better, there is evidence of a widening "class gap" in the organization and administration of our legal system. As Doleschal and Klapmuts (1974) have pointed out, the rich, powerful, and intelligent members of our society are rarely caught, prosecuted, or punished. This gap increases the resentment of those at the bottom and heightens their feelings of not being part of the broader society, thus also increasing their feelings of justification in simply taking what they want.

Admittedly the causes of violence and other forms of crime in the United States are both complex and varied. But as a former United States Attorney General pointed out,

"Much crime develops from poverty and deprivation. Most victims of crime are the poor themselves. There will be no marked crime reduction until we understand that—but more importantly, until we act upon it." (Saxbe, 1974, p. 12)

Approaches to dealing with criminals

We have yet to find what might be considered the ideal method for dealing with individuals convicted of crime. Early forms of punishment centered on revenge or retribution, and involved such tactics as confinement in stocks, public physical abuse, and execution. Early in the nineteenth century, imprisonment gained popularity; and in the twentieth century efforts to rehabilitate and resocialize the criminal have grown as we have sought to "understand" and "correct" patterns of criminal behavior.

The trends in dealing with criminal behavior have in many ways paralleled those used for psychopathology in general—that is, a movement from incarceration to correction, and to some extent, deinstitutionalization. It is obvious that many of the same procedures are needed for successful treatment, such as early detection and correction of unhealthy personality trends, correction of undesirable social conditions, and provision of adequate treatment personnel and facilities. But since crime represents a vast range of individuals and behaviors, it is also apparent that no simple formula or single generalization can either explain it or suggest an easy solution to it. Because its complex social, economic, and psychological bases are not fully understood, its eradication must be considered a long-range, rather than an immediately achievable, goal. And, as such, we can see that the parallel paths of mental hospitals and penal institutions has diverged substantially in the twentieth century, with far more community placements available for the mentally ill than for former criminals (Felton & Shinn, 1981).

For present purposes let us briefly examine three aspects of the treatment of criminal offenders: (a) the traditional reliance on punishment, (b) attempts at rehabilitation, and (c) some correctional trends and prospects.

Traditional reliance on punishment. In 1843, Jeremy Bentham concluded that if punishment were certain, swift, and severe, many a person would avoid criminal behavior. The view is still widely held that punishment is the most effective way of making offenders realize the error of their ways and curing them of their criminal tendencies. Such punishment has actually been thought to serve three purposes: (a) revenge by society—"giving the criminal his or her due"; (b) protection of society; and (c) deterrence from future crimes—both for the offenders who are punished and for others, through example.

Emphasis on revenge and retaliation against criminals is based on the premise that the guilty, who have brought distress to others, have a debt to pay and ought to suffer. Imprisonment becomes a means not only to exact revenge on the criminal but also to protect the rest of society. But imprisonment is usually only for a limited time, and unfortunately it may simply serve to expose the offender to prison codes of behavior, to reinforce criminal values, to permit learning of new criminal skills or refining of old ones, and to augment the individual's degradation and feeling of separateness from society. In fact, prisons have been called "universities of crime."

So though prisons do provide protection for society while the offender is incarcerated, most prisons seem to do little to impart the third goal of deterrence. The failure of our present system to do this is shown by high crime rates and the fact that the rate of recidivism (rearrest for new crimes following release from prison) is over 66 percent nationwide and as high as 90 percent in some areas of the country (Goldfarb, 1974; Lamb & Grant, 1982; Murphy, 1970). In fact, 80 percent of all felonies committed in the U.S. are by people who have been imprisoned at least once before (Gottfredson, Hindelang, & Parisi, 1978).

Several factors limit the deterrent effect of punishment. One is the uncertainty and delay that often surround the punishment. Many offenders are never caught; of those arrested, many are never convicted. In addition, the long delay that commonly separates sentencing from the offense lessens the impact of punishment as a deterrent force. Spiraling caseloads have strained our judicial system to the point where there are often delays of several months or longer between arrest and trial.

Another factor limiting the deterrent effect of punishment is the lack of guilt feelings among many of those who are punished. Many prisoners, for example, see themselves as victims of society rather than as perpetrators of crimes. Similarly, many imprisoned offenders see their problem as one of having gotten caught—as "bad luck" rather than "bad character."

Logically, it might seem that the more severe the punishment allotted, the greater its deterrent effect would be, but for certain crimes at least—including homicide and rape—this has not been the case (Melville, 1973; Schwartz, 1968). For example, states that have used the death penalty have had homicide rates as high or higher than those that have not. For other types of crimes, the deterrent effect of increasingly severe and certain punishment may be different, but no conclusive evidence is presently available. In addition, severe penalties may lead to the takeover of some criminal activities—such as drug peddling—by organized crime if the profits are considered worth the risk. In any event, punishment does nothing to change the personal or social reasons why individuals commit crimes; thus it is hardly surprising that using punishment to deter crime has not been notably successful.

Rehabilitation. Many people believe that imprisonment without rehabilitation and socialization is neither a clear deterrent to criminal behavior nor a proper form of treatment. Yet less than 4 percent of the employees in penal institutions are treatment staff—the rest are guards, administrators, and other personnel. Less than 13 percent of state and local correctional personnel handle all the probations and parolees, although the latter constitute more than two thirds of the nation's criminal offender population. In view of these figures, both treatment facilities in penal institutions and supervision facilities for parolees appear to be sadly inadequate, which helps explain the high recidivism rate.

Concern for rehabilitation rather than punishment of criminal offenders led, some years ago, to a greater use of indeterminate sentences and parole to shorten the time in prison, as well as to a variety of innovative attempts to encourage behavior change during imprisonment.

1. *Indeterminate sentences and paroles.* The indeterminate sentence was intended to (a) enable qualified rehabilitation personnel to determine—within broad limits—when an offender should be released; (b) introduce flexibility into the widely disparate ideas of different judges about the appropriate sentences for convicted offenders; and (c) facilitate return to the community of prisoners who could meet qualifications for parole.

Unfortunately, the indeterminate sentence also makes the fate of prisoners more subject to the whim of those in power, particularly when it is capriciously applied. Prisoners may be kept longer instead of released earlier. And putting in time is no longer enough. Prisoners must conform in ways that may seem alien or impossible or even wrong to them. Many inmates would prefer a clear penalty to an indeterminate sentence in which they have to please the authorities in order to get out. In addition, this whole structure is based on the questionable assumption that law-enforcement personnel can predict the behavior of paroled offenders.

In recent years, the indeterminate sentence has come under increased criticism and there are numerous efforts being made to require mandatory prison sentences for some crimes. The current feeling is that long-term imprisonment of some offenders is necessary for the protection of society.

2. *Innovative approaches to treatment.* A number of innovative approaches to dealing with criminal offenders have also been suggested, and some have been tried out on a limited basis. Among these have been study and work furloughs and restitution programs, in which the individual is given a job and works to pay the victim for property damaged or stolen instead of serving time in prison. Many states now have such restitution programs; they are most often used for juveniles.

There has also been a limited attempt at sexual integration of prisons, conjugal visits, and integration of family and institutional treatment programs. Although imprisonment means different things to different people, it tends in general to be degrading, as well as to create serious sexual problems that may lead to homosexual behavior—particularly since about half of the prisoners are under 25 years of age. And where the prisoner is married and has a family, imprisonment places a tremendous burden on the spouse and children. To help counteract this problem, prisons in Mexico, Sweden, India, and a number of other countries allow conjugal visits. In the United States the first prison to allow conjugal visits was the Mississippi State Penitentiary. This practice, including overnight visits by friends of unmarried prisoners, seems to be gaining support in the United States.

Other innovative approaches to rehabilitation range from transcendental meditation through

Some rehabilitation programs seek to encourage personal growth and enrichment by making large libraries and study programs available to the inmates. Others attempt to prepare offenders for the outside world by teaching them vocational skills. In recent years, the concept of rehabilitation has come under attack from some social critics and penologists.

behavior therapy techniques to the use of drugs and other medical measures for prisoners who have brain abnormalities that apparently make them prone to anger and impulsive violence. However, the involuntary "treatment" of offenders by medical and psychological procedures has become a matter of considerable controversy centered around the issue of the offender's rights.

In England an entire prison was organized as a therapeutic environment. Enhanced personal adjustment for the individuals was possible in this setting, as indicated, for example, by fewer fights among inmates than is typical in traditional prison settings. However, long-term success was disappointing, as measured by the number of prisoners staying out of prison following release: about the same percent as usual (70 percent) had been reconvicted after two years (Gunn et al., 1978).

While some people feel that rehabilitation has not been given a fair chance, the high rate of recidivism has led to general disillusionment with this approach. As Schwartz (1975) has expressed it, " 'Rehabilitation' in prison is at best a myth and at worst a fraud" (p. 5). In any event, there is a strong trend at the present time away

from the goal of rehabilitation and back toward imprisonment as punishment.

Even this concept of the punitive nature of imprisonment, however, has been called into question. There is evidence that some prisoners are not adversely affected by imprisonment. Bukstel and Kilmann (1980) reviewed 90 studies that evaluated the effects of imprisonment on performance, personality, and attitudinal factors and found that, while some individuals showed personality deterioration with confinement, others actually improved in adjustment and others showed no appreciable change.

Some correctional trends and prospects.

While serious efforts are being made to improve law-enforcement and correctional procedures, there is a good deal of disagreement among governmental agencies, law-enforcement officials, criminologists, and other social scientists concerning the most effective measures to take. There appears, however, to be increasing agreement on the following points:[2]

a) At the present time, no methods of reha-

---

[2]Based in part on Fersch (1980), Holden (1975), and Schwartz (1975).

bilitation have been found that are both predictably effective and socially acceptable. Therefore, some people must be imprisoned to protect society.

b) Such criminal offenders should be given a flat maximum sentence to "fit the crime," but with provision for time off for good behavior—for example, for each day the individual abides by prison rules.

c) Rehabilitation programs, though no longer viewed as a panacea, should be available in prison for those who want them, but participation in such programs should not be made a condition of parole, at least until they have been proven effective.

d) Overcrowded facilities should be eliminated and inmates confined to smaller, more flexible, and less dehumanizing prisons.

e) Treatment of prisoners should not vary with respect to sex, race, or social class. Standards for correctional personnel should be established and maintained, and adequate facilities for helping paroled prisoners make the transition to society should be available.

Implicit in the above measures is the realization that prison is not presently a good place to send people for rehabilitation—especially those who have not committed violent or serious crimes. As Guthrie (1975) quoted one former state prison official as saying, "If you had a friend who was having some adjustment problems unrelated to crime, you wouldn't think of sending him to San Quentin for a couple of months to get rehabilitated" (p. 5). Probation or early parole for such offenders and a concentrated effort to integrate institutional, family, and community facilities into a broadly based correctional program would be expected to have better results.

At almost the opposite extreme from those who maintain a firm belief in rehabilitation are people who hold that some criminals simply can't be rehabilitated. They point specifically to those criminals who are responsible for a disproportionate number of the crimes annually committed in the United States. Increasingly seen as hard-core, violent offenders—and called "violent predators" by many—these criminals are the subjects of research efforts to pull together a psychological profile that can define them, perhaps even before they have engaged in a significant number of criminal acts (Chaiken & Chaiken, 1982). Some of the many characteristics of the violent predator seem to be the following: they tend to be young, repeat offenders; to have a history of hard-drug use; and to engage in violent offenses.

What use may ultimately be made of such a psychological profile remains in question. There are those who advocate lengthy imprisonment of identified violent predators—even *before* they have committed many serious crimes. The potential for violation of individual constitutional rights are enormous here, and because of this, such "preventive imprisonment" will be unlikely to take hold. However, the very fact that many people are considering this as a possible option surely points up the pervasive frustration with our lack of success to date in dealing with violent criminals.

Ultimately, of course, any effective approach to crime must elicit citizen and community involvement. Only with such involvement might it be possible to incorporate ex-offenders into the community in responsible ways and deal adequately with both the causes of crime and the injustices in our legal system.

Summary

Personality disorders, in general, appear to be extreme or exaggerated patterns of personality traits that predispose the individual to troublesome behavior—often of an interpersonal nature. A number of personality disorders have been delineated in which there are persistent maladaptive patterns of perceiving, thinking, and relating to the environment. Three general "clusters" of personality disorder have been described. Paranoid, schizoid, and schizotypal personality disorders are disorders in which the individual seems odd or eccentric; histrionic, narcissistic, antisocial, and borderline personality disorders are disorders which share a common tendency to be dramatic, emotional, and erratic; avoidant, dependent, compulsive, and passive-aggressive personality disorders, unlike the previous disorders, may actually appear more like anxiety-based disorders in that these individuals may show fearfulness or tension. All of these disorders reflect a common core of immaturity, self-centeredness, lack of feeling for others, manipulativeness, and a tendency to "act out" and to project blame for problems and frustrations onto others.

For most of the personality disorders, little research into causality has been conducted.

One of the most notable of the personality disorders is the antisocial, or psychopathic, personality. In this disorder, the individual is callous and unethical, without loyalty or close relationships but often with superficial charm and intelligence. Both constitutional and learning factors seem to be important in causing the disorder. There is some evidence to suggest that genetic factors may predispose the individual to the development of this disorder. Unlike the anxiety-based disorders described in the previous chapter, the antisocial personality does not appear to experience anxiety. The disorder often begins and is recognized in childhood or adolescence but only individuals who are 18 or over are given the diagnosis of antisocial personality.

Treatment of these individuals is fraught with difficulties, because they rarely see any need for self-change and tend to blame other people for the difficulties they get into. Traditional psychotherapy is typically ineffective, but where control is possible, as in institutional settings, newer methods incorporating meaningful reinforcement and behavior modification have had some success.

Antisocial personalities may engage in criminal behavior, but many individuals who are incarcerated for crimes are not antisocial personalities. A great number of crimes are committed by "professional" criminals rather than antisocial personalities. In fact, in many cases the personality patterns, particularly the immaturity, impulsivity, and inability to learn from experience of antisocial persons make them unsuitable for "organized" criminal activities.

The incidence of crime is higher in the United States than in most other countries; however, there has been a leveling off since the early 1980s. In exploring the causes of criminal behavior, we can say that biological factors do not appear to account for criminal behavior as well as do such factors as family pathology and social conditions.

Society's approach to dealing with individuals who engage in criminal behavior appears to be changing. The indeterminate sentence and generous use of parole and other rehabilitative approaches appear to be giving way to more restrictive approaches. This tendency to rely less on rehabilitation and more on keeping some individuals locked up "to protect society," particularly in cases involving people who are believed to be prone to acts of violence, appears to be based on the fact that, to date, rehabilitation of criminals has not proven very effective. Yet the traditional methods of punishment for criminal acts have also been questioned. It is apparent that we are still searching for the answer to how we might best deal with criminals.

Psychological factors and physical illness

Gaston Duf, Pâûlîhinêle gânsthêrs vitrês-he (1949). As a child, Duf (b. 1920) was frequently terrorized by his father, often seeking the protection of his mother. When his parents finally married, Duf, then 18, reacted violently. After two suicide attempts, he was institutionalized in 1940. He began his artistic career while in the asylum, painting strange, powerful animals, as well as comically proportioned, motley human figures like this one.

Traditionally, the medical profession has concentrated research efforts on understanding and controlling the organic factors in disease. In psychopathology, on the other hand, interest has centered primarily on uncovering psychological factors that may lead to the development of mental disorders. Today we realize that both these approaches are limited: although an illness may be primarily physical or primarily psychological, it is always a disorder of the whole person—not just of the lungs or the psyche.

Fatigue or a bad cold may lower tolerance for psychological stress; an emotional upset may lower resistance to physical disease; maladaptive behavior, such as excessive alcohol use, may contribute to the impairment of various organs, like the brain and liver. Furthermore, the overall life situation of an individual has much to do with the onset of a disorder, its form, duration, and prognosis.

Recovery is apt to be more rapid for the patient eager to get back to work than for the one who will be returning to a frustrating job or an unpleasant home. In short, the individual is a biopsychosocial unit.

There seems little doubt, too, that sociocultural influences affect the types and incidence of disorders found in different groups. The ailments to which people are most vulnerable—whether physical, psychological, or both—are determined in no small part by when, where, and how they live.

The interdisciplinary approach to treatment of physical disorders thought to have psychological factors as a major aspect of their causal patterns is broadly known as *behavioral medicine.* The field includes professionals from many disciplines—including medicine, psychology, and sociology—who seek to incorporate biological, psychological, and sociocultural factors into the total picture. Its emphasis, however, is essentially on the role psychological factors play in the occurrence, maintenance, and prevention of physical illness.

Since we are dealing here with *psychogenic*—that is, psychologically induced—disorders, it is only natural that psychologists have found this an area of major interest. *Health psychology* is emerging as the subspecialty within the behavioral-medicine approach that deals specifically with psychology's contributions to diagnosis, treatment, and prevention of these psychogenic physical illnesses (Bradley & Prokop, 1981; Weiss, Herd, & Fox, 1981).

A behavioral-medicine approach is now reflected not only in treatment of physical illnesses brought on primarily by emotional tension, but also in cases where only physical causes are obvious. We might, for example, ask whether emotional factors may have lowered the resistance of a tuberculosis patient and hence contributed to the onset of the disease. We might also ask how the individual will react to the changes in life situations brought about by the disease. Some patients apparently give up when medically the chances seem good that they will recover. Others with more serious organic pathology recover or survive for long periods of time. Dunbar, a pioneer in the field, concluded that it is often "more important to know what kind of patient has the disease than what kind of disease the patient has" (1943, p. 23).

Since this is a text about abnormal psychology, we will not go deeper into primarily physical diseases like tuberculosis, in which the primary cause is the tubercle bacillus, however important psychological and sociological factors may be in the outcome of the disease. We are mainly concerned in this chapter with the *psychophysiologic disorders* (formerly called *psychosomatic disorders*)—physical disorders in which psychological factors play a major causative role.

In the DSM-III classification, the category of psychophysiologic disorder has been dropped. As we have seen, all patients are now rated separately on different axes for psychiatric symptoms, developmental personality factors, and accompanying physical disorders. Thus there is no place on the first two axes for the classic psychophysiologic disorders, which are physical illnesses even though psychologically induced. To permit some sort of psychiatric coding for these disorders, Axis I provides a category called *"psychological factors affecting physical condition,"* to be used when a physical disorder, coded on Axis III, involves psychological factors that have either *definitely* or *probably* played a primary role in the initiation or exacerbation of the disorder.

In the present chapter, after a broader consideration of the role of psychological factors in both health and illness, we shall look at five classic psychophysiologic patterns in some detail. Then we shall examine possible causal factors, and, finally, highlight several treatment approaches in this rapidly developing area.

Psychological factors in health and disease

Research has repeatedly yielded evidence that mental and emotional processes are implicated in some way both in good health and in the majority of the physical diseases that afflict humankind. But definitive proof of such relationships, and a beginning understanding of what is happening in the body, are relatively recent accomplishments. The boundaries of this field seem virtually limitless. In this section we shall summarize some of the evidence of the close relationship between psychological and physical processes. Then we shall introduce briefly two of the physiological mechanisms that may be involved when physical illness follows psychological stress or chronic negative emotions. Finally, we shall look briefly at the added factor of lifestyle and its possible affect on our physical well-being.

Emotions and health

The sometimes devastating effects of attitudes of hopelessness and helplessness on organic functioning have long been known, partly through anthropological research on "voodoo death" and similar phenomena. Today, many surgeons will not undertake a major operation until they are convinced that the patient is reasonably optimistic about the outcome. In the literature there are numerous reports of "apathy deaths" in situations such as concentration and prisoner-of-war camps; and every year in our cities there are reports of "unexplained" deaths among persons who believed themselves to be in hopeless circumstances—for example, after having ingested dosages of poisonous substances that were actually too small to be lethal.[1]

Less dramatically, but in many ways of equal or greater importance, the effects of multiple life changes on a variety of illnesses have been amply documented in the research on significant

---

[1]Such phenomena have been extensively reviewed by both Seligman (1975) and Jones (1977).

life changes and subsequent health status, as outlined in Chapter 5. To cite only two examples, Rahe (1974) noted a study on the health status of physicians that demonstrates a marked correspondence between health problems experienced and amount of change-related stress undergone in an immediately preceding period. Similarly, in a study of 192 men between the ages of 30 and 60, Payne (1975) found that longstanding physical *and* psychological health problems were related to larger degrees of life change, even when the changes had been favorable. Evidently the amount of adjustment required overtaxed the individuals' resources.

Often it appears that any severe stress serves to pave the way for, precipitate, or aggravate a physical disorder in a person already predisposed to it (G. W. Brown, 1972). This is in keeping with the *diathesis-stress model* we discussed in Chapter 4. A person who is allergic to a particular protein may find resistance further lowered by emotional tension; similarly, where an invading virus has already entered the body —as is thought to be the case in multiple sclerosis—emotional stress may interfere with the body's normal defensive forces or immunological system.

In like manner, any stress may tend to aggravate and maintain certain specific disorders, such as rheumatoid arthritis (Robinson et al., 1972). Day (1951), another pioneer in psychophysiologic disorders, once pointed out, "To develop chronic active pulmonary tuberculosis a person needs some bacilli, some moderately inflammable lungs . . . and some internal or external factor which lowers the resistance to the disease." He noted further that unhappiness was among the stressors that could lower resistance. Here we can see the potential role of stress in the development of physical disorders, including those labeled "psychophysiologic" as well as many that are not.

The relationship between psychological factors and good health has also been well documented (e.g., Jones, 1977); that is, positive emotions seem often to produce a certain immunity to physical disease or to be associated with speedy and uncomplicated recoveries when disease does strike. In fact, this is so much the case that it complicates efforts to determine the true effectiveness of new treatment techniques, such as new drugs. The patient who *believes* the treatment is going to be effective has a much better

There is evidence that voodoo spells sometimes actually result in death for the unfortunate victim of the curse. It is not known how such curses work, but it is thought that the feelings of hopelessness, fear, and abandonment inspired by the curse may act as key factors in bringing about the individual's death.

chance of showing improvement than does the patient who is neutral or pessimistic—even when the treatment is subsequently shown to have no direct or relevant physiological effects. This has become known as the *placebo* effect, and it accounts in part for the controversies that arise periodically between the scientific community and the general public regarding the efficacy of certain drugs or other treatments—Laetrile in the treatment of cancer being a well-known example. It has even been suggested that, had it not been for the placebo effect, the profession of medicine as we know it would not have survived to the present century, because until this century the profession in fact had very little else to offer sufferers of disease. Perhaps its survival and prosperity from ancient times is in part a tribute to the power of "faith" in healing (Shapiro & Morris, 1978).

The fundamental unity of mind and body is perhaps nowhere better documented than in health and illness. The development of psychophysiologic disorder, as described later in this chapter, is only one example of this enormous influence of mental factors on bodily functioning.

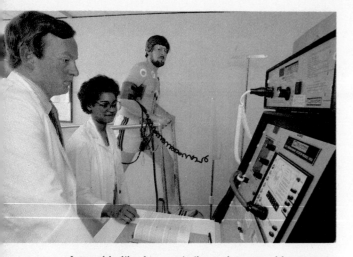

Internal bodily changes similar to those caused by stress can be induced by carefully monitored physical activity. Business executives sometimes undergo detailed physical examinations to determine how well their bodies will respond to the stressful demands of their daily lives.

Autonomic excess and "classic" psychophysiologic illness

The classic notion of psychophysiologic disorder, proceeding from the early work of Dunbar (1943) and F. Alexander (1950), was predicated on the idea that strong emotions in themselves, whether consciously recognized or not, would over time produce pathologic anatomical and physiological changes in certain organ systems. As is well known, strong emotions are accompanied by various internal bodily changes—such as elevated heart rate, dumping of stored sugar into the bloodstream, and secretion of hormones from the inner core of the adrenal glands. Many of these inner bodily changes are readily perceived by the aroused person. These often very intrusive bodily changes are a product chiefly of autonomic nervous system arousal. It was but a short step for early researchers to infer that internal stressors, such as psychological conflicts, could bring about the observed breakdown in certain organ systems through aberrant or excessive autonomic nervous system activity. To a large extent, they appear to have been right, although—as so often happens—many of their early conceptions were frequently oversimplified.

The predisposing psychological processes in the classic psychophysiologic disorders, such as peptic ulcer, are seen as similar in many ways to those found in the development of the anxiety-based disorders described in Chapter 6. That is, the person typically has acquired unrealistic fears or anxieties that severely limit both effective coping behaviors and the likelihood of need gratification. Instead, defensive and ultimately self-defeating strategies are repeatedly invoked, leading to frustration and continued high arousal. Under these conditions, some persons—for reasons that remain unclear but undoubtedly have to do with individual differences in vulnerability—develop psychophysiologic disorders more readily than anxiety disorders, although development of one reaction by no means precludes development of the other.

Selye and the stress-response system

While the classic psychophysiologic disorders involve excesses and aberrations of autonomic nervous system activity, this is only one of the pathways by means of which the mental and emotional life of the individual may adversely affect biological functioning. Selye's (1976) general adaptation syndrome, mentioned in Chapter 5, depicts three stages of response to any continuing serious stressor: alarm and mobilization, resistance, and exhaustion. The autonomic nervous system is implicated most significantly in the first of these stages. As severely stressful circumstances continue to impinge upon the organism, the second stage, resistance, comes into play, followed finally, if the stress continues, by the depletion of adaptive resources and significant damage or death to the organism.

In the second and third stages, it seems to be the endocrine (hormonal) system that is mainly involved, although interaction with the autonomic nervous system is maintained at many levels. That is, when severe stress becomes chronic and constant, we are obliged to shift our attention somewhat away from the autonomic system per se (where the adrenal gland's central core or *medulla* plays a prime role) to certain influences of the adrenal *cortex* (the covering mantle of the adrenal gland). Under the influence of the anterior pituitary—which is in turn influenced by hypothalamic (emotional) stimulation—

the adrenal cortex releases into the bloodstream certain hormonal substances that have profound effects on physiological functioning. One group of these substances, the *glucocorticoids* (including hydrocortisone, corticosterone, and cortisone) are involved in sugar metabolism and are especially important in this context.

As part of a stress-response mechanism, the glucocorticoids have paradoxical effects. They promote an increase in available blood sugar for energy mobilization and facilitate blood redistribution, but they also hamper processes by which the body controls tissue damage, and they reduce resistance to infection and possibly other pathological processes. Their specific effects include the following: (a) delay of growth of new tissue around a wound, including surgically acquired ones; (b) inhibition of the formation of disease-fighting antibodies and general impairment of the immunological surveillance system; (c) decrease in the number of circulating white blood cells, which are also critical in fighting infections; and (d) depression of thyroid activity with a resulting inhibition of bodily growth and decreased production of the sexual and reproductive hormones.

Small wonder, then, that the endocrine stress-response system has been implicated as a significant factor in diseases and dysfunctions ranging from cancer to infertility. It is also seen as the probable mediating factor in the increased incidence of illness and death following bereavement (Engel, 1961; Klerman & Izen, 1977). And it would be surprising if this system were not responsible, at least in part, for the relationship between illness and recent life changes (Coyne & Holroyd, 1982; Holmes & Masuda, 1974; Rahe, 1974; Rahe & Arthur, 1978).

While efforts to relate specific stressors to specific psychophysiologic disorders have not generally been successful, stress is a key underlying theme in these disorders. Stress may serve as a predisposing, precipitating, or reinforcing factor in the causal pattern, or it may merely aggravate a condition that might have occurred anyway. Often stress appears to speed up the onset, increase the severity of the disorder, and/or interfere with the body's immunological defenses and other homeostatic functions. Presuming we all have at least one vulnerable organ somewhere in our bodies, a high chronic level of stress puts us at risk for a psychogenic disorder sooner or later.

Life-style as an added factor in health maintenance

Today a great deal of attention is being paid to the role of life-style in the development or maintenance of many health problems. Numerous aspects of the way we live are now considered influential in the development of some severe physical health problems: diet—particularly overeating and consuming too many high-cholesterol foods; lack of exercise; smoking cigarettes; excessive alcohol use; constantly facing high-stress situations; and just ineffective ways of dealing with day-to-day problems are but a few of the many life-style related patterns that are viewed as contributing causes.

This growing awareness of the role individual factors play in susceptibility to disease, its impact and course, has resulted in more attention to life-style by both physicians and psychologists working in health-care settings (Engel, 1977; Weiner, 1977). Particularly in this area of life-style factors, *health psychology*—which focuses heavily on prevention and health maintenance—is growing rapidly. New efforts are being made to determine more precisely what role personality or life-style factors play in the genesis and course of disease. Finding the answers becomes all the more important when we realize that life-style factors—habits or behavior patterns presumably under our own control—are believed to play a major role in three of the leading causes of death in this country: coronary heart disease, automobile accidents, and alcohol-related deaths (National Center for Health Statistics, 1982).

We cannot help but be struck by the rather sobering observation of Knowles (1977), who takes the position that most people are born healthy and suffer *premature* death and disability only as a result of personal misbehavior and environmental conditions. He believes that most health problems could be drastically reduced if only:

"no one smoked cigarettes or consumed alcohol and everyone exercised regularly, maintained optimal weight on a low-fat, low-refined carbohydrate, high-fiber content diet, reduced stress by simplifying their lives, obtained adequate rest and recreation, . . . drank fluoridated water, followed the doctor's orders for medication and self-care once disease was detected, and used available health resources." (p. 1104)

It is generally acknowledged that personal life-style influences psychophysiologic well-being.

Before anyone rushes to alter radically his or her life-style according to the severe regimen outlined by Knowles, it should be pointed out that the connection between many life-style habits or patterns and physical illness awaits conclusive proof. In many cases the connection, though seemingly strong, is still one of correlation, with the proof based more on common sense than definitive data. For example, the extent to which rates of physical diseases, such as coronary heart disease, can be controlled or reduced through such means as reducing serum cholesterol levels has not been sufficiently established.

Nonetheless, even in cases where proof of causation exists, it is very difficult for most individuals to alter significantly their life-styles toward more "healthy" directions to reduce their risk for disease—even if they want to! Some of the most serious risk factors, such as cigarette smoking, are not easy habits to alter, even when the connection between the habit and the disease is direct and seemingly evident. After having two heart attacks and surgery to remove one cancerous lung, one man continued to smoke two and a half packs of cigarettes a day even though he frequently said, "I know these things are killing me a little at a time . . . but they have become so much a part of my life I can't live without them!"

The remainder of this chapter will focus on the possible connections between emotions, life-style, and psychophysiologic disorders.

Classic psycho-physiologic disorders

The clinical picture in classic psychophysiologic disorders tends to be *phasic:* typically there is an upsurgence of symptoms followed by their waning or disappearance. The sequence of their appearance and disappearance appears to be directly related to the amount of stress the individual is experiencing. For example, an assembly-line worker's ulcers may be quiescent during a three-week vacation. However, there are many exceptions to this general trend. It is also of interest to note that there are often marked differences between the sexes in the incidence of specific disorders; some are much more common among men and others more common among women.

Even in the case of the more or less "standard" psychophysiologic diseases, however, the same diseases sometimes occur without any significant psychological components. For example, not all ulcers are due primarily to psychological factors. And a further caveat is appropriate at the outset. As with disorders manifested exclusively by mental or behavioral phenomena, psychophysiologic ailments do not seem to appear from nowhere in an individual who is not in some sense physiologically predisposed toward the particular condition in question. Many misconceptions about psychophysiologic disorders—not all of them by laypersons—may be traced to a failure to recognize the importance of underlying predispositional factors in virtually any disorder that is alleged to have a psychophysiologic component.

The complexities to be taken into account are well illustrated in what is perhaps the foremost of the classic psychophysiologic illnesses—peptic ulcer—which we shall discuss next. Then we shall follow with a discussion of other psychophysiologic disorders, including anorexia nervosa, migraine, and tension headaches, hypertension, and coronary heart disease.

Peptic ulcers

Peptic ulcers were first observed in our Western culture during the early part of the nineteenth century. In the beginning they were found primarily in young women, but in the second half of the nineteenth century there was a shift, and today the incidence of ulcers is some two or three times higher among men than women. Contemporary Western civilization apparently is conducive to the chronic emotional reactions that lead to peptic ulcers, and it is estimated that about one in every ten Americans now living will at some time develop one; furthermore, approximately 10,000 Americans die every year from peptic ulcer (Whitehead et al., 1982).

The ulcer itself results from an excessive flow of the stomach's acid-containing digestive juices, which eat away the lining of the stomach or duodenum (the first part of the small intestine), leaving a crater-like wound. Although dietary factors, disease, and other organic conditions may also lead to ulcers, it is now recognized that worry, repressed anger, resentment, anxiety, dependency, and other negative emotional states may stimulate the flow of stomach acids beyond what is needed for digestion. The result is that the stomach begins to digest itself, which is the specific precondition for ulcer formation.

It has long been believed that conflicts centering on dependency needs are especially likely to be found in individuals who develop ulcers. In support of this belief we have available to us something of a landmark study, the scope of which has not since been equaled (Weiner et al., 1957).

Relying on prior evidence of a high rate of gastric secretion in ulcer-prone individuals, as indicated in part by a high level of pepsinogen in the blood serum, Weiner and his colleagues tested a population of 2073 army draftees and chose for study those men found to be maximum and minimum gastric secreters. These were groups of men, in other words, who should be at maximum and minimum risk for ulcer formation by virtue of constitutional predisposition.

Membership in one or the other group did in fact predict the incidence of ulcer formation during the stress of basic training. Of perhaps even greater importance, however, is the fact that a battery of psychological tests also correctly predicted the group in which pepsinogen-level recruits would fall, and even correctly identified at an above-chance level which high-pepsinogen recruits would develop ulcers. These test results showed evidence of major unresolved dependency (in Freudian terms "oral") conflicts, with resultant frustration and suppressed hostility.

The important point established by this study was that *neither* a high pepsinogen level *nor* dependency conflicts was alone responsible for the development of peptic ulcer. Taken together, however, they constituted a pathogenic predisposition that, on exposure to a special stressor (basic training), could be expected to challenge the equilibrium of a dependent individual, thus producing an abnormally high risk of ulcer formation.

The dependency of the ulcer-prone individual is not always obvious at the behavioral level. In fact, such an individual may seem to be quite independent or autonomous. The dependency, however, may be revealed by a personality test.

The relationship between ulcer-related gastric distress and psychic dependency is illustrated in the following case report.

George P., a single, white, 50-year-old male, was admitted to the hospital for the fifth time in six years with complaints of severe stomach pain, "heartburn," and generalized weakness and malaise. He vomited persistently following the ingestion of any solid food. He anticipated that he would be treated with medication and possibly stomach surgery, as he had been in the past, and he resolutely denied any possible connection between his ailment and emotional factors.

George had left his parents' home early in his youth after a dispute with his father. With the nation in the midst of the depression of the 1930s, George had spent most of his time traveling around the country, taking on temporary jobs when he could find them. When he was 21, he had returned home because his father was dying of stomach cancer. After his father's death, George essentially took up the role of his mother's chief friend and confidant, a relationship that lasted for some 20 years until his mother's death. During this period, George engaged in various unprofitable business ventures. He showed little, if any, interest in women other than his mother, and his sexual experience was confined to occasional visits to prostitutes. He described this period in his life in idyllic terms.

The 20-year period with his mother was interrupted only by a four-year tour in the navy during World War II. George had apparently adjusted reasonably well to his period of military service, during which he was a cook and was not exposed to combat action. It was shortly after his departure from military service that George had had his first bout with stomach distress and had been admitted to the hospital. His second serious attack occurred some 10 years later, shortly after his mother's death. This second attack was diagnosed as peptic ulcer. George had stomach surgery the following year, followed by three additional hospital admissions for peptic ulcer within a 4-year period.

George's behavior on the hospital ward on these visits was significant. He was very demanding of attention from the staff, although diagnostic studies confirmed that he was not in any gross physical danger. He appeared to make himself at home in the hospital, ordering staff members about in an imperious manner. It was plain that he had no interest in an early discharge, notwithstanding the stabilization of his physical condition. Staff members were in agreement that George would be very unlikely to accept formal psychological treatment for his problems. He was referred for outpatient care, including medication and informal counseling. (Adapted from Goldstein & Palmer, 1975, pp. 177–87)

With George P.'s case at hand, we can make some reasonable conclusions. First, we can assume that George was biologically predisposed to develop this particular malady, especially so when we consider his father's death from stomach cancer. Second, it seems fairly obvious that George had problems with dependency, particularly on his mother.

Typically, the psychological aspects of peptic ulcers do not seem as clear-cut as they are in George's case; yet we probably know more about peptic ulcers than we do about any other psychophysiologic illness. Examining peptic ulcer, therefore, provides a good opening to the field. However, the reader is cautioned not to be overly optimistic about the ease of identifying specific causal factors in these disorders.

Anorexia nervosa

Anorexia nervosa is a disorder in which the individual, by refusing food or by vomiting shortly after eating, loses so much weight that he or she risks dying from starvation. Sufferers of this disorder typically see themselves as "fat," no matter how emaciated they might really be. Some consider anorexia nervosa to be related to conversion disorder. However, given its widespread and very serious effects on various organ systems, it seems fitting to include it within the psychophysiologic category. In DSM-III, "an-

Singer Karen Carpenter died in 1983 at the age of 32 following a longtime battle with anorexia nervosa. Though the official cause of death was listed as cardiac arrest, her anorexia was considered to be a strong contributing factor.

orexia nervosa" is classified as one of several "eating disorders."

Once apparently quite rare, the incidence rates have increased alarmingly in recent years, for reasons that remain obscure. It is estimated that some 1 percent of women between the ages of 12 and 25—approximately 260,000 women—suffer from anorexia nervosa (*U.S. News & World Report*, August 30, 1982). Anorexia nervosa is much more common in females than in males, on the order of 20 to 1 (Crisp, 1977). This difference suggests that an underlying sex difference may play a causal role. In a survey of studies, estimates of the death rate ranged from 0 to 19 percent, with about one half of the studies reporting a death rate below 5 percent (Hsu, 1980). Since it can be fatal, anorexia nervosa must always be regarded as a clinical emergency requiring prompt therapeutic intervention.

Criteria for diagnosing anorexia nervosa are as follows (based on Feighner et al., 1972):

a) Onset before age 25;

b) Anorexia with accompanying weight loss of at least 25 percent of original body weight;

c) A distorted, implacable attitude toward eating, food, and weight that overrides hunger, admonitions, reassurance, and threats;

d) No known medical illness that could account for the anorexia and weight loss;

e) No other known psychiatric disorder;

f) At least two of the following manifestations:
  —cessation of menstruation,
  —soft, downy hair over body surface,
  —persistent resting pulse of 60 beats per minute or less,
  —periods of overactivity,
  —binges of compulsive eating,
  —vomiting, which may be self-induced.

Several psychosocial characteristics have been noted among anorexic patients. They are usually reported as being from the upper socioeconomic levels. (Crisp et al., 1976). Onset of the disorder is confined largely to the adolescent or young adult years. A history of unusual or bizarre eating habits, including uncontrolled eating binges, is common. A distorted bodily image, particularly an overestimation of one's physical dimensions, is almost universal. In terms of personality characteristics, these patients are usually described as sensitive, dependent, introverted, anxious, perfectionistic, selfish, and unusually stubborn. They almost invariably report little or no interest in sex. Typically, they have been extremely conscientious in regard to conventional "duties" such as school work (Bemis, 1978; Bruch, 1978; Palazzoli, 1978).

Anorexic girls usually describe their mothers in very unflattering terms: excessively dominant, intrusive, overbearing, and markedly ambivalent. We must register caution here, however, in light of the possibility that mothers respond in these ways to the self-starvation of their children. By contrast, anorexic girls usually describe their fathers as "emotional absentees."

Anorexia often begins when life changes are requiring new or unfamiliar skills concerning which the person feels inadequate, such as occurs in going off to college, getting married, or even reaching puberty. The characteristic conflict activated by such events seems to be, on the one hand, a desire to achieve autonomy and, on the other, a pronounced fear of attaining the status of an independent adult (Bruch, 1978; Palazzoli, 1978). Food then becomes the phobic and obsessional context in which this drama is played out.

Not infrequently, the disorder begins as an extension of the ritual of normal dieting, which is common among young women. What distinguishes the normal dieter from the one who converts it into a dangerous flirtation with disaster remains a mystery. In any event, there seems to be increasing acknowledgment that the syndrome of anorexia may be the extreme end of a continuum. We may thus speak meaningfully of a *pre-anorexic state*, in which individuals have extreme but not yet self-injurious aversions to food.

The case of Mary S., including her marked activity in the face of dwindling energy resources and her unfailing denial of the growing seriousness of her condition, is in most respects fairly typical of the anorexic syndrome:

"Mary S., aged sixteen and one-half years, grew disgusted with a close friend who began to put on weight by eating candy. The two girls agreed to go on a reducing diet, although Mary weighed only 114 pounds. A year later she graduated from high school and obtained a job as a stenographer. She began to lead a very busy life, working every day and going dancing at night with a young man who paid her attention. As her activities increased, her weight loss became more apparent, and soon her menses disappeared. Up to this time her dieting had been a voluntary control of eating, but now her appetite failed. Some months later one of the patient's sisters lured her boyfriend from her; Mary began to feel tired, and had to force herself to keep active. The onset of dizzy spells caused her to consult a doctor, who suggested a tonsillectomy. After the operation she refused to eat, but continued her active pace, including dancing every night. She now weighed 71 pounds. Two months later she became so dizzy and weak that she could no longer walk, and was finally brought to the hospital weighing 63 pounds. In three days, two and a half years after beginning her diet, Mary S. was dead of bronchopneumonia." (Nemiah, 1961, p. 10)

Anorexia nervosa, then, is a very puzzling and paradoxical psychophysiologic entity. Quite literally, its victims, apparently without "intention," engage in a protracted program of self-destruction, refusing others' urgent efforts to rescue them. It seems likely that the etiology of anorexia nervosa involves a substantial psychological component, although its features and mode of operation remain, to a large extent, a matter of speculation. Then, at some point in the process of withdrawal from eating, biological factors seem to develop their own demands, taking the behavior beyond conscious control and making it exceedingly difficult to reverse, as we shall see later in the chapter in our discussion of treatment measures. The best current guess is that such biological alteration is localized in the

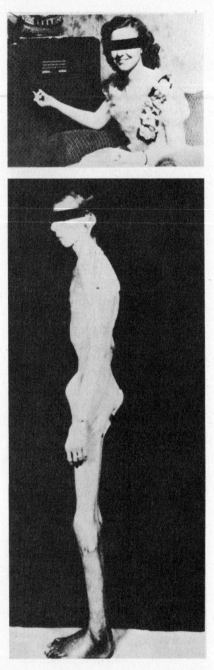

The woman in these pictures was diagnosed as suffering from a severe case of anorexia nervosa. At age 18 (top), she weighed 120 pounds—within the normal range for her height of 5½ feet. She lost weight over a period of some 19 years, during which time she was married and divorced; at the age of 37, she was admitted to the hospital weighing 47 pounds (bottom). About a year and a half of therapy in and out of the hospital, her weight had risen to 88 pounds (Bachrach, Erwin, & Mohr, 1965). At the time of a 16-year follow-up, she weighed 55 pounds, only 8 more than she had weighed at the outset of therapy (Erwin, 1977).

region of the hypothalamus, a richly interconnected structure in the brain involved in the regulation of motives and emotions (Bemis, 1978; Walsh, 1980).

Migraine and tension headaches

Although headaches can result from a wide range of organic conditions, the majority of them—about 9 out of 10—seem to be related to emotional tension. More than 50 million Americans suffer from tension or migraine headaches, with the overall incidence apparently being higher among women than men. In a recent survey, Andrasik, Holroyd and Abell (1979) found that 52 percent of a large group of college students reported headaches at least once or twice a week.

Research in this area has focused primarily on migraine, an intensely painful headache that recurs periodically. Although typically involving only one side of the head, migraine is sometimes more generalized; it may also shift from side to side.

Migraine was described extensively by medical writers of antiquity, but the cause of the pain remained a mystery until the 1940's, when interest was focused on the pain-sensitive arteries of the head. By dilating these arteries with an injection of histamine, researchers found it possible to reproduce the pain of migraine. Turning to actual cases of migraine, they discovered that the onset of the headaches was accompanied by progressive dilation of these cranial arteries. In addition, persons with headaches on one side of the head (*unilateral headaches*) showed dilation of the cranial arteries only on the side where the pain occurred. As the attack subsided, either spontaneously or following the administration of drugs, the pain diminished and the arteries returned to their normal size.

It has also been shown that a variety of experimentally induced stressors—frustrations, excessive demands for performance, and threatening interviews—cause vascular dilation among migraine sufferers but not among other persons. The **HIGHLIGHT** on page 283 traces the course of a headache induced during a discussion that evoked feelings of hostility in the subject—a migraine sufferer.

The vast majority of headaches are so-called

HIGHLIGHT
Migraine Headaches

The side-view drawing of the head at left below shows the location of pain-sensitive cranial arteries, with the dotted lines marking the areas where the headache is felt as various parts of the arteries dilate.

The graph traces the course of a headache induced during a discussion which evoked feelings of hostility in a subject. Both the changes in the amplitude of the artery pulsations and the corresponding increase and diminution in the intensity of the pain reported are shown. The headache was completely relieved by means of an injection which the subject believed would end the suffering but which actually could have had no physical effect.

From *Wolff's headache and other head pain*, Fourth Edition, by Donald J. Dalessio. Copyright © 1980 by Oxford University Press, Inc. Reprinted by permission.

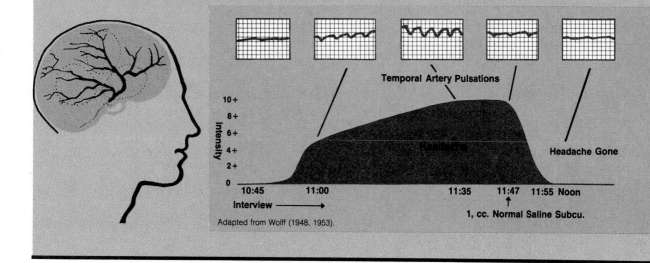

Adapted from Wolff (1948, 1953).

"simple" tension headaches. These, too, involve stress and vascular changes, but the changes are thought to be different from those in migraine headaches. Here, emotional stress seems to lead to contraction of the muscles surrounding the skull; these contractions, in turn, result in vascular constrictions, which cause headache pain. However, we should note here that, with the more precise measurement techniques now available, the evidence for the physiological differences between migraine and tension headaches is being drawn into question (Blanchard & Andrasik, 1982). Though further studies will be needed, it may be that the physiological processes are similar for the two types of headaches and that the difference is rather one of degree.

Both tension and migraine headaches usually appear during adolescence and recur periodi-

cally during periods of stress. The pain can often be relieved with analgesics, with muscle-relaxant drugs, or with certain relaxation-inducing psychological procedures, including biofeedback. Of the two types, migraine headaches are usually more painful and slower to respond to treatment than simple tension headaches.

The presumed psychological predispositions for psychogenic headaches are less clear than in the case of peptic ulcer. However, there seems to be a growing consensus among clinicians that it is important to the typical headache-prone person to feel in *control* of events impinging on him or her. Such individuals are usually described as highly organized and perfectionistic (Williams, 1977). In one instance, a highly skilled nurse, who specialized in the demanding field of cardiac emergencies and who was subject to excruciatingly severe migraine attacks, went to a clinic for therapy but was so bent on maintaining control of virtually every aspect of the therapeutic relationship that she managed to sabotage it with a regularity astonishing to both herself and her therapist.

In a recent study by Andrasik et al. (1982), the traditionally held belief that migraine sufferers show higher levels of depression, passivity, nonassertiveness, hostility and high-achievement strivings was not supported. Psychological tests of migraine sufferers revealed psychologically normal profiles. Instead, it was the tension headache sufferers who showed the greatest psychopathology. This finding suggests that tension headaches might be more indicative of psychological problems than migraine headaches.

Hypertension

During states of calm, the beat of the heart is regular, the pulse is even, blood pressure is relatively low, and the visceral organs are well supplied with blood. With stress, however, the vessels of the visceral organs constrict, and blood flows in greater quantity to the muscles of the trunk and limbs—changes that help put the body on an emergency footing for maximum physical exertion. With the tightening or restricting of the tiny vessels supplying the visceral organs, the heart must work harder. As it beats faster and with greater force, the pulse quickens and blood pressure mounts. Usually, when the crisis passes, the body resumes normal functioning and the blood pressure returns to normal. But under continuing emotional strain, high blood pressure may become chronic.

About 12 percent of Americans suffer from chronically high blood pressure, or *hypertension*. Although Wing and Manton (1983) reported a reduced incidence of death due to hypertension, it nevertheless is the primary cause of more than 60,000 deaths each year, and a major predisposing factor in another million or more deaths a year from strokes and cardiovascular disease. Not only is it a major risk factor in cardiovascular diseases (Coates et al., 1981); it is also a risk factor in kidney failure, blindness, and a number of other physical ailments. For reasons that are not entirely clear but apparently relate in part to diet, the incidence of hyperten-

sion is about twice as high among blacks as among whites (Edwards, 1973; Mays, 1974).

Unlike the other psychophysiologic disorders we have dealt with, there are usually no symptoms to signal high blood pressure. The individual experiences no personal distress. In severe cases, some people complain of headaches, tiredness, insomnia, or occasional dizzy spells—symptoms often easy to ignore—but most persons suffering from hypertension receive no warning symptoms. In fact, Nelson (1973) reported on one survey encompassing three middle-class neighborhoods in Los Angeles which revealed that a third of the adults tested had high blood pressure; only half of them had been aware of it. As Mays (1974) has described the situation,

"In most instances . . . the disease comes as silently as a serpent stalking its prey. Someone with high blood pressure may be unaware of his affliction for many years and then, out of the blue, develop blindness or be stricken by a stroke, cardiac arrest or kidney failure." (p. 7)

Since there is no such thing as "benign hypertension," high blood pressure is considered an insidious and dangerous disorder. Ironically, high blood pressure is both simple and painless to detect by means of a medical examination.

In some cases a physical cause of hypertension can be identified. For example, it may be attributable to a narrowing of the aorta or one of its arteries, to the excessive use of certain drugs, or to dietary factors. The normal regulation of blood pressure, however, is so complex that when it goes awry in a particular case, identifying the causal factors is extremely difficult. Kidney dysfunction, for example may be a cause or an effect of dangerously elevated pressures—or both.

Obvious preexisting organic factors can be ruled out in 90 to 95 percent of hypertension cases (Byassee, 1977); thus the condition is often called *essential* hypertension (*essential* being a term used to denote an absence of known physical causes). Recently, obesity, long suspected as an etiological factor, has emerged as a possible underlying factor in several other known correlates of hypertension, such as poor diet and lack of exercise (Ostfeld & D'Atri, 1977). Obesity, of course, can be a factor contributing to the current level of experienced stress.

A number of investigators have shown that

chronic hypertension may be triggered by emotional stress. For example, a highly stressful job markedly increases the risk of high blood pressure (Edwards, 1973), and the stresses of ghetto life—as well as dietary factors—have been identified as playing a key role in the high incidence of hypertension among black people (Mays, 1974).

The classical psychoanalytic interpretation of hypertension is that affected persons suffer from suppressed rage, but there is only scattered evidence to support his hypothesis. Although there is high incidence of hypertension in the black ghetto population, among whom suppressed rage might be expected to run high (Harburgh et al., 1973), the suppressed-rage hypothesis concerning the etiology of essential hypertension cannot be said to be firmly established in respect to all, or even necessarily a majority, of affected persons.

More recently, a variant of suppressed-rage hypothesis has been proposed by McClelland (1979). According to this view, the individual is driven not so much by rage and the need to supress it as by power motives and the need to inhibit their expression. Unexpressed anger is then a frequent accompaniment. In a well-conceived study designed to test these ideas, McClelland found that personality measures of "need for power" and "activity inhibition" were indeed jointly associated with elevated blood pressures. Moreover, he demonstrated that this inhibited power motive syndrome in men in their 30s accurately predicted elevated pressure and signs of hypertensive disease in these same men twenty years later.

As the following case illustrates, hypertensive reactions may appear even in young people.

Mark _____, a senior in law school, evidenced episodes of extreme hypertension whenever he was subjected to stress. He became aware of these episodes when he failed to pass his physical examination for induction into the armed forces because of exceptionally high blood pressure. In a later check at a medical clinic, under nonstressful conditions, his blood pressure was normal; however, under simulated stress conditions, his blood pressure showed extreme elevation, and it happened again when he returned for another physical examination at the induction center.

Of course, the severity of Mark's hypertension at an early age might suggest that his is a case where biological vulnerabilities are playing a major role. Although most people show temporary alterations in blood pressure under stress, it would appear that under severe and sustained stress, persons like Mark run a high risk of developing chronic hypertension.

Coronary heart disease

Deaths from coronary heart disease declined by about 20 percent between 1968 and 1976 (Stern, 1979). This decline has been attributed to change in diet, (including foods with less cholesterol), a lowered consumption of cigarettes, and an increase in physical exercise. Despite these hopeful statistics, coronary heart disease is often referred to as "the twentieth-century epidemic." More people in the United States die from coronary heart disease than from any other cause, to say nothing of the many additional thousands who survive but suffer crippling effects.[2]

For unknown reasons women are rarely victims of coronary heart disease before menopause; afterward, however, their rate is the same as that for men. An as yet unexplained and seemingly contradictory finding comes from Phillips et al. (1983): in a study of 61 men suffering from heart disease, they found that the men who had a high level of the female sex hormone estradiol—an estrogen-related hormone—were more likely to have heart disease than those who did not. Obviously, more research is needed to uncover the causes of this deadly disease. We can say for certain, however, that a very frequent antecedent to coronary heart disease is hypertension—itself a leading psychophysiologic disorder, as we have seen.

In a study of sudden cardiac death, Rahe and Lind (1971) gathered life-change data on 39 subjects over the last three years prior to their deaths. (The chart developed by researchers to estimate stressfulness of various life-change units is shown on page 149). Both for those with prior histories of coronary heart disease and for those without, there was a threefold increase in the number and intensity of life-change units during the final six months of their lives as com-

---

[2]***Coronary heart disease*** is a broad term used to refer to a variety of heart disorders, such as *cardiac arrest, coronary insufficiency, coronary thrombosis, myocardial infarction, angina pectoris,* and, of course, *heart attack.* The term can be used to refer to either a continuing condition, such as angina pectoris, or a sudden episode, such as cardiac arrest or heart attack.

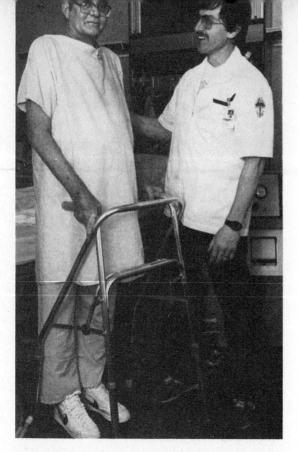

In late 1982, retired dentist Barney Clark, 61, underwent the first artificial heart transplant as treatment for cardiomyopathy, a degenerative disease of the heart. Despite his positive spirit and enthusiastic attitude, Clark died after 112 days.

pared to the rest of the three years prior to death.

Similarly, in a study of 50 patients, aged 40 to 60, admitted consecutively to a hospital following their first heart attack—as contrasted with 50 healthy controls—Thiel, Parker, and Bruce (1973) found significant differences between the two groups with respect to the incidence of divorce, loneliness, excessive working hours, sleep disturbances, nervousness, anxiety, and depression. While leaving room for exceptions resulting primarily from biological factors, these investigators, as well as Rahe and Lind, concluded that their findings point to a direct relationship between life stressors and heart attacks.

In a study of 229 men from three countries (Finland, Sweden, and the United States) who had recently survived a myocardial infarction (one type of heart attack), it was found that common background factors included heavy work responsibility, time urgency coupled with hostility when slowed by others, and dissatisfaction with the achievement of life goals (Romo et al., 1974). Again it would appear that severe stress and heart attacks tend to be causally related.

Stress is not, of course, exclusively a product of the environment, unrelated to one's personal idiosyncrasies. Some individuals seem to carry their stress around with them, so to speak, and manage to convert the most ordinary of life circumstances into a struggle for dominance, power, and control. This is the all-too-familiar Type A person, originally described by Friedman and Rosenman (1959). The Type A pattern has been described in terms of an eagerness to compete, frequent engagement with self-imposed deadlines, intense desire for recognition, mental and physical alertness and quickness, and strong drives toward self-selected but poorly defined goals (Chesney, Eagleston, & Rosenman, 1981; Hurd et al., 1980; Matthews, 1982).

Type A males in the 39- to 49-year age range are said to run a risk of coronary heart disease that is six times greater than that of Type B men—men who are less impatient and exhibit traits that are otherwise opposite to those of Type A (Suinn, 1977). In a study of 156 patients, Blumenthal et al. (1978) found that the Type A behavior pattern was significantly reported among patients with moderate to severe coronary disease as compared to patients with mild coronary disease.

In spite of the obvious biological factors involved in coronary heart disease, it still seems quite clear that the course of this lethal and disabling type of disease is in part influenced by personal proclivities that are unrelated to the other risk factors in coronary disease, such as hypertension, extreme obesity, smoking, and diet. The implication is that a change of life-style may be quite as important as, say, a change of diet in preventing coronary disease. Unfortunately, there is no real assurance that the one is any more easy to change than the other.

Other specific symptom patterns

We have now sampled some major psychophysiologic disorders. In our discussion of peptic ulcers, anorexia nervosa, psychogenic headache, hypertension, and coronary heart disease, most of the principal dimensions of psychophysiologic illness have been introduced, at least in passing.

A large number of other physical diseases have also been considered at various times—and often with less justification—to be predominantly psychophysiologic. A good example here is *asthma*, a disorder in which breathing becomes difficult because of bronchiolar constriction. Not so very long ago, this bronchiolar constriction was assumed to be caused by emotional problems, sometimes even a specific type of emotional conflict. Further research, however, has cast doubt on this idea (Alexander, 1981). Current thinking emphasizes not only the role of psychological factors but also the importance of predisposing physical factors: in many—perhaps most—cases of asthma there may be some type of innate vulnerability to interference with the autonomic regulation of breathing. Support for this position is provided by the fact that asthma attacks sometimes occur at times when the individual is not under stress; here, apparently, the triggering factors are biological.

On the other hand it is clear that emotional upheaval may trigger an attack in a predisposed person. It is also clear that some asthmatics learn to use their symptoms—or the threat of their emergence—to control the people around them.

A similar situation exists with respect to several other disorders that had often been assumed to be psychologically caused. It is now recognized that *either* biological or psychological factors may play the triggering role in given cases of skin eruptions, allergies, ulcerative colitis, chronic diarrhea, rheumatoid arthritis, varied menstrual disorders, Raynaud's disease (a serious circulatory disorder), chronic disturbances of the sleep cycle, enuresis, insatiable hunger and obesity, excessive sweating, hiccoughs, and varied endocrine disturbances.

General causes of psychophysiologic disorders

In this section we shall be concerned both with the general causes of psychophysiologic disorders and with the problem of organ specificity—

Life stress is an underlying causal factor in all of the psychophysiologic disorders.

of why, under stress, one individual develops peptic ulcers, another hypertension, and still another migraine headaches.

Much remains to be learned about the interacting roles of biological, psychosocial, and sociocultural variables in predisposing an individual to psychophysiologic disorders as well as in precipitating and maintaining them. However, the primary causal factor that underlies all of these disorders is a psychological one, *life stress*. In essence, chronic emotional tension elicited by life situations perceived as threatening can cause profound changes in the physiological functioning of the human body; these changes, in turn, can trigger the development of the various disorders we refer to as psychophysiologic.

In general, the development of psychophysiologic disorders appears to involve the following sequence of events: (a) the arousal of negative emotions in response to long-term stressful situations—the degree of arousal depending not only on the nature of the stressful situation, but also on the individual's perception of the situation and stress tolerance for it; (b) the failure to deal adequately with these emotions—either through appropriate expression or through a changed frame of reference or improved competence—with the result that the emotional arousal continues on a chronic basis; and (c) the responses of various organ systems to the emotional arousal, involving either damage to specific organs or more generalized changes that weaken the body's immune system. In the discussion that follows, we shall be concerned with the possible significance of particular biological, psychosocial, and sociocultural variables in contributing to this chain of events.

Biological factors

A number of biological factors have been implicated in psychophysiologic disorders, directly or indirectly. These include genetic factors, differences in autonomic reactivity, somatic weakness, and failures in the immunologic processes.

Genetic factors.   Research by Gregory and Rosen (1965) has demonstrated that the brothers of ulcer patients are about twice as likely to have ulcers as comparable members of the general population. Increased frequencies of hypertension, migraine, and other reactions have also been reported for close relatives of individuals with these disorders.

Although we now know that learning could be a factor in such family resemblances, further research evidence is needed, and genetic factors should not be ruled out. In fact, it would probably be difficult to discover any disease of humankind in which genetic factors could be ruled out entirely.

The implicated *interaction* of genetic and psychological influences is illustrated in the findings of Liljefors and Rahe (1970), who studied the role of life stress in coronary heart disease among twins. The subjects consisted of 32 pairs of identical male twins, between 42 and 67 years of age, in which only one twin in each pair suffered from coronary heart disease. These investigators found that the twins suffering from heart disease were more work oriented, took less leisure time, had more home problems, and, in general, experienced greater dissatisfactions in their lives.

Differences in autonomic reactivity and somatic weakness.   In our earlier discussion of vulnerability and causal factors in Chapter 4, we noted that individuals vary significantly in "primary reaction tendencies." Even very young infants reveal marked differences in their sensitivity to aversive stimuli; some infants react to such stressors by developing a fever, others by digestive upset, and still others by disturbances

in sleeping. Such differences in reactivity continue into adult life, and presumably help account for individual differences in susceptibility to psychophysiologic disorders, as well as for the type of disorder a given individual is most likely to develop.

In connection with the latter point, Wolff (1950) suggested that people can be classified as "stomach reactors," "pulse reactors," "nose reactors," and so on, depending on what kinds of physical changes stress characteristically triggers in them. For example, a person who has an inherited tendency to respond to stressors with increased cardiac output and vasoconstriction may be at risk for the development of chronic hypertension (Friedman & Iwai, 1976), whereas one who reacts with increased secretion of stomach acids will be more likely to develop peptic ulcers.

Sometimes a particular organ is especially vulnerable because of heredity, illness, or prior trauma. The person who has inherited or developed a "weak" stomach presumably will be prone to gastrointestinal upsets during anger or anxiety.

Presumably, the weakest link in the chain of visceral organs will be the organ affected. However, caution must be exercised to avoid *ex post facto* reasoning, since it would not be safe to conclude when a particular organ system is affected that it must have been weak to begin with. Also, as we shall see, conditioning may play a key role in determining which organ system is involved.

Disruption of corticovisceral control mechanisms.   Other biological explanations have focused on the role of cortical control mechanisms in regulating autonomic functioning (see **HIGHLIGHT** on page 289). According to one hypothesis, the corticovisceral control mechanisms of the brain may fail in their homeostatic functions, so that the individual's emotional response is exaggerated in intensity and physiological equilibrium is not regained within normal time limits (Halberstam, 1972; Lebedev, 1967). Such control failures might well be central to deficient hypothalamic regulation of *both* the autonomic nervous system and the adrenocortical hormones of the endocrine system, which control the body's immunity to disease.

In the face of continued stress, it appears that the body's control mechanisms are disrupted,

HIGHLIGHT

Biological clocks

The 24-hour rhythmic fluctuations observable in the activity and metabolic processes of plants and animals—indeed, all living creatures on earth—are referred to as *circadian* cycles, from the Latin words meaning "about a day." Thus, normal functioning for each system or individual appears to follow a biological clock; and an upset in this cycle, caused by changes in schedule or other factors, may cause malfunctioning in the form of physical or psychophysiologic complaints.

Thousands of experiments with lower animals have established the relationship between biological clocks and normal functioning. And humans—although found to be somewhat more adaptable to environmental changes than lower animals—have revealed similar cyclic fluctuations in activity and sleep, body temperature, chemical constituents of the blood, and so on. Interestingly enough, these cycles have remained essentially the same even for human subjects who have lived in caves, cut off from all means of knowing whether it was day or night for periods as long as several months.

In studies of disturbances in circadian cycles in humans—e.g., a sudden reversal of sleep schedules from night to daytime—subjects have demonstrated various degrees of adaptability. And in experiments that simulated manned space flights, some subjects reacted well to unusual schedules of work and rest—e.g., working for four hours, then resting for four hours—while others were unable to adapt to them.

A report prepared for the National Institute of Mental Health by Weitzman and Luce (1970) has noted the potential adverse effects of technological change—including abrupt time changes associated with jet travel—on "the invisible circadian cycle that may govern our susceptibility to disease or shock, our emotions, our performance, our alertness or stupefaction" (p. 279).

thereby affecting the immunologic processes and predisposing the individual to psychophysiologic disorders (Cohen, 1981; Stein, 1981). In essence, the immune response involves the production of lymphocytes (antibodies) to fight off foreign substances such as bacteria or viruses. Hill, Greer, and Felsenfield (1967) found that frightening or noxious stimulation is associated with a decrease in lymphocyte production. More recent studies have demonstrated that decreased immune function occurs among individuals during the period of bereavement following the death of their spouse (Bartrop, Lazarus, & Luckhurst, 1977; Schleiffer et al., 1980.)

In assessing the role of biological factors in psychophysiologic disorders, most investigators would take into consideration each of the factors we have described. Perhaps the greatest emphasis at present would be placed on the characteristic autonomic activity of given individuals, the vulnerability of affected organ systems, and possible alterations in cortical control mechanisms of the brain that normally regulate autonomic and endocrinologic functioning.

Psychosocial factors

Though the role of psychological factors is considered to be prominent in the causality picture of psychophysiologic disorders, it is still not altogether clear. Factors that have been emphasized include personality characteristics, including failure to learn adequate coping patterns, interpersonal relationships, and learning in the autonomic nervous system.

Personality characteristics and inadequate coping patterns. The work of Dunbar (1943, 1954) and a number of other early investigators raised the hope of identifying specific personality factors associated with particular psychophysiologic disorders—for example, rigidity, high sensitivity to threat, and chronic underlying hostility among those who suffer from hypertension. The ability to delineate ulcer types, hypertensive characters, and so on, would, of course, be of great value in understanding, assessing, and treating psychophysiologic disorders—and perhaps even in preventing them.

Later research evidence suggests that such an approach is oversimplified. For example, although Kidson (1973) found hypertensive patients as a group to be significantly more insecure, anxious, sensitive, and angry than a nonhypertensive control group, a sizable number of the control-group members also showed these characteristics. Similarly, Jenkins (1974), using Friedman and Rosenman's Type A formulation described earlier (p. 286), gave test questionnaires to 2700 men who had not had heart attacks up to that time and then followed them over a four-year period. The men who had scored high on Type A behavior had twice as many heart attacks during this follow-up period as those who had scored low. Nevertheless, the majority of high scorers did not have heart attacks, and some of the low scorers did.

So even though personality makeup seems to play an important role, we still do not know why some individuals with similar personality characteristics do *not* develop psychophysiologic disorders; nor can we account adequately for the wide range of personality makeup among the individuals who suffer from psychophysiologic disorders. Usually we can at best conclude only that particular personality factors are weakly but significantly correlated with the occurrence of a psychophysiologic disorder.

Many individuals suffering from psychophysiologic disorders appear unable to express their emotions adequately by verbal means, nor have they effectively learned to use various ego-defense mechanisms—such as rationalization, fantasy, and intellectualization—to alleviate their emotional tension. As a consequence, they rely primarily on repression, which does screen their feelings from conscious awareness. However, the physiological components of the emotion continue and may finally lead to structural damage.

Normally, when individuals are subjected experimentally to frustrating experiences, blood pressure rises and the heart beats more rapidly. If, then, they are given an opportunity to express physical or verbal aggression against the frustrator, there is a rapid return to normal blood pressure and heart rate. If they are permitted only fantasy aggression or no aggression at all, however, there is a much slower return to normal physiological functioning (Hokanson & Burgess, 1962). Thus besides looking at people's ability to cope with the stress of frustration or

conflict or whatever, it seems necessary to consider their ability to deal adequately with the accompanying emotional tensions.

In general, it appears that attitudes, coping patterns, and personality makeup are important psychological factors in the overall causal pattern of psychophysiologic disorders. Without doubt, they merit further exploration.

Interpersonal relationships. In our previous discussions, we have repeatedly noted the destructive effects that stressful interpersonal patterns—including marital unhappiness and divorce—may have on personality adjustment. Such patterns may also influence physiological functioning. In fact, death rates from varied causes, including physical disease, are markedly higher in persons who have recently undergone marital problems or divorce than in the general population (Bloom, Asher, & White, 1978).

Loss of a spouse through death also puts the survivor at risk. In an extensive review of the literature, Stroebe and Stroebe (1983) concluded that men are slightly more adversely affected by the death of their wives than women are by the death of their husbands. For example, in an earlier study of widowers, Parkes, Benjamin, and Fitzgerald (1969) reported that during the six-month period following the death of their wives, the widowers' death rate was 40 percent above the expected rate. In fact, the incidence of cardiac deaths among them was so high that the investigators referred to this pattern as "the broken-heart syndrome."

Lynch (1977), in a book entitled *The Broken Heart,* argues convincingly that the relatively high incidence of heart disease in industrialized communities stems in part from the absence of positive human relationships. He notes that heart disease and other illnesses are more prevalent among individuals lacking human companionship and for whom loneliness is common. This includes not only those individuals who have recently lost a spouse through death but also single or divorced individuals.

Other studies have focused on the role of pathogenic family patterns. For example, studies of some asthmatic patients have found that the mothers of such patients have in many cases felt ambivalent toward their children and tended to reject them, while at the same time being overprotective and unduly restrictive of the children's activities (Lipton, Steinschneider, & Richmond, 1966; Olds, 1970). Since individuals coming out of such family backgrounds tend to be overdependent and insecure, it would hardly be surprising if they should react with chronic emotional mobilization to problems that do not seem threatening to most people. On the other hand, as we have seen, a strictly psychophysiologic interpretation of asthma is questionable. Severe asthma is a terrifying and life-threatening disorder. It would not be surprising on this basis alone to discover that asthmatic children are overdependent and insecure, or that their mothers tend to become ambivalent, protective, and restrictive after the asthma appears.

Learning in the autonomic nervous system.

Although Pavlov and other investigators have demonstrated that autonomic responses can be conditioned—as in the case of salivation—it was long assumed that an individual could not learn to control such responses voluntarily. We now know that this assumption was wrong. Not only can autonomic reactivity be conditioned involuntarily via the classical Pavlovian model, but operant learning in the autonomic nervous system can apparently also take place.

Thus the hypothesis has developed that psychophysiologic disorders may arise through accidental reinforcement of such symptom and behavioral patterns. "A child who is repeatedly allowed to stay home from school when he has an upset stomach may be learning the visceral responses of chronic indigestion" (Lang, 1970, p. 86). Similarly, an adolescent girl may get little or no attention from being "good," but the reactions that follow her starving herself to the point of severe weight loss may make her the center of attention. If this pattern is continued, she might learn to avoid weight gain at all costs and correspondingly learn a profound aversion to food. The increasing alarm of her parents and others would presumably serve as a potent reinforcement for her to continue in her dietetically errant ways.

Although causal factors other than conditioning are now thought to play a role in most cases of psychophysiologic disorders, it seems clear that regardless of how a psychophysiologic response may have developed, it may be elicited by suggestion and maintained by the reinforcement provided by *secondary gains,* an indirect benefit derived from the response. The role of suggestion was demonstrated by a study in which 19 of 40 volunteer asthmatic subjects developed asthma symptoms after breathing the mist of a salt solution that they were told contained allergens, such as dust or pollen. In fact, 12 of the subjects had full-fledged asthma attacks. When the subjects then took what they thought was a drug to combat asthma (actually the same salt mist), their symptoms disappeared immediately (Bleeker, 1968). Here we see the effect of suggestion on an autonomically mediated response. Why the other 21 subjects remained unaffected is not clear.

In short, it would appear that some psychophysiologic disorders may be acquired or maintained or both in much the same way as other behavior patterns. Indeed, this is a basic tenet of the currently growing field of behavioral medicine, one aspect of which examines the applications of various behavior modification and psychotherapeutic techniques to alter overt and/or covert organismic reactions related to physical disease processes (Bradley & Prokop, 1982; Williams & Gentry, 1977).

Sociocultural factors

The incidence of specific disorders, both physical and mental, varies in different societies, in different strata of the same society, and over time, as we have seen. In general, psychophysiologic disorders, including ulcers, hypertension, anorexia nervosa, tension headaches, and coronary heart disease, do not occur among nonindustrialized societies like the aborigines of the Australian Western Desert (Kidson & Jones, 1968) and among the Navajo Indians of Arizona and certain isolated groups in South America (Stein, 1970). As these societies are exposed to social change, however, gastrointestinal, cardiovascular, and other psychophysiologic disorders begin to make their appearance. There is evidence of change in the nature and incidence of psychophysiologic disorders in Japan paralleling the tremendous social changes that have taken place there since World War II (Ikemi et al., 1974). For example, the incidence of hypertension and coronary heart disease has increased markedly with the post-war westernization of Japanese culture.

After an extensive review of the literature within our society, Senay and Redlich (1968) found that psychophysiologic disorders were no respectors of social class or other major sociocultural variables. Similarly, Kahn (1969) found that only a small number of executives develop peptic ulcers; in fact, blue-collar workers who are dissatisfied with their jobs are more likely to develop ulcers than successful business executives who are moving up on the occupational ladder. And while black people in our society show a higher incidence of hypertension than whites, this finding is confounded by different dietary habits, including the excessive use of salt by many black citizens (Mays, 1974).

This statement is not meant to minimize the importance of ghetto life stressors, but to point out that stress is common in other communities as well. For example, we noted that one survey found a third of the adults in three middle-class neighborhoods in Los Angeles to be suffering from hypertension. Although a higher stress level probably contributes to the higher incidence of hypertension among blacks than among whites, it apparently does not provide the entire explanation.

In general, it would appear that any sociocultural conditions that markedly increase the stressfulness of living tend to play havoc with the human organism and lead to an increase in psychophysiologic disorders as well as other physical and mental problems.

Treatment and outcomes

As we saw earlier in the chapter, the distinction between the classic psychophysiologic disorders and other illnesses that have psychogenic components has become blurred; thus the treatment program for almost any physical illness may include not only the physical procedures appropriate to the particular illness but also an attempt to lessen the stressfulness of the individual's situation and to encourage an optimistic attitude. There are, however, more specific forms of intervention in the case of the classic psychophysiologic disorders.

Though a particular environmental stressor may have been a key causal factor in the development of a psychophysiologic illness, removal of this stressor, even combined with development of more effective coping techniques, may be insufficient for recovery if organic changes

have taken place. Furthermore, such changes may have become irreversible.

Treatment, therefore, begins with an assessment of the nature and severity of the organic pathology currently involved as well as the roles of psychosocial and organic factors in the total causal pattern. In hypertension, for example, the role of dietary factors may far outweigh that of current psychosocial conditions in causation. Dietary patterns, however, reflect cultural patterns and attitudes—that all-important lifestyle—which also may have to be reckoned with. Thus a thorough assessment involving the past and present roles of biological, psychosocial, and sociocultural factors seems to be essential to the development of an effective treatment program.

Except for psychophysiologic disorders involving serious organic pathology, treatment is similar to that for anxiety-based disorders; the outcomes of treatment are likewise reasonably favorable. Instead of going into detail concerning the methods of treatment and outcomes for each type of disorder, we shall briefly summarize the general treatment measures that are used. More detailed discussion of these therapies can be found in Chapters 16 and 17.

Biological measures

Aside from immediate and long-range medical measures, such as emergency treatment for bleeding ulcers or long-range treatment for coronary heart disease, biological treatment can involve the use of mild tranquilizers aimed at reducing emotional tension. Such drugs, of course, do not deal with the stressful situation or the coping reactions involved. But by alleviating emotional tension and distress symptoms, they may provide the individual with a "breathing spell," during which to "regroup" his or her coping resources. Of course, there is always the need to guard against too readily prescribing tranquilizers to insulate patients against everyday stress that they might be better off facing. Too, some patients may come to rely too much on their prescription for a "cure," and this can be a deterrent in effectively treating psychophysiologic disorders.

Other drugs, such as those used to control high blood pressure, are prescribed on a more specific basis. A change of diet may be indicated

WOLCOTT'S INSTANT PAIN ANNIHILATOR.

The search for biological "cure-alls" for common ailments such as headaches and nervous tension has had a long— and sometimes bizarre—history. This advertisement for an "instant pain annihilator" promised immediate relief from assorted physiological and psychological complaints.

in certain psychophysiologic reactions, including peptic ulcers, migraine headaches, and hypertension. Acupuncture as a method of treatment is still undergoing research; although it does appear useful in alleviating certain types of symptoms, such as the pain of tension and migraine headaches, a notable problem here has been that of disentangling acupuncture effects and placebo effects (Berk, Moore, & Resnick, 1977; Chaves & Barber, 1973; Gaw, Chang, & Shaw, 1975). Electrosleep—cerebral electrotherapy—has produced mixed results in the treatment of psychophysiologic disorders as it has in the anxiety-based disorders. Preliminary findings appear promising in the use of this method for insomnia, but more research is needed (Hearst et al., 1974; Miller, 1974; Rosenthal, 1972).

An interesting method of treatment that progresses from biological measures to psychotherapy is *Morita therapy*, which has been reported as being effective with a number of psychophy-

siologic as well as anxiety-based disorders (Gibson, 1974; Kora & Ohara, 1973; Murase & Johnson, 1974). Morita therapy is not widely used in the United States, but it is very popular in Japan. In this therapy, the patient is initially subjected to absolute bed rest for a period of four to seven days with no reading, writing, visitors, or other such external stimuli permitted. By the end of this period, the patient usually finds positive reinforcement in responding to external stimuli. Then begins a graded series of tasks, starting with light work and proceeding through heavy manual labor to a focus on interpersonal relationships and finally the establishment of purposive, goal-directed behavior designed to eliminate any maladaptive life-style behaviors and reorient the individual's life pattern.

Psychosocial measures

In the treatment of psychophysiologic disorders, one-on-one verbally oriented psychotherapies—aimed at helping patients understand their problems and achieve more effective coping techniques—have been relatively ineffective. On the other hand, family therapy has shown some promising results, particularly in the case of anorexia nervosa (Minuchin, 1974). Rather than singling out the individual, in family therapy the whole family structure and patterns of communication are examined; those that are thought to be preventing the individual from developing positive relationships within the family (resulting in personal maladjustment) are then targeted for change.

It is interesting to note here that, while classical psychoanalytic theory is the only viewpoint to attempt to explain how the emotions can affect bodily organs, it has had very little impact on treatment of psychophysiologic disorders (Agras, 1982). That is, psychoanalytic approaches have not derived treatment methods that can reverse or prevent the process in predictable ways. Instead, the most promising psychological measures appear to lie in the direction of behavior therapy and biofeedback.

Behavior therapy. Behavior-modification techniques are based on the assumption that since autonomic responses can be learned, they can also be unlearned via extinction and differential reinforcement. In one case, the patient, June C., was a 17-year-old girl who had been sneezing every few seconds of her waking day for a period of 5 months. Medical experts had been unable to help her, and Kushner, a psychologist, volunteered to attempt treatment by behavior therapy.

"Dr. Kushner used a relatively simple, low power electric-shock device, activated by sound—the sound of June's sneezes. Electrodes were attached to her forearm for 30 minutes, and every time she sneezed she got a mild electric shock. After a ten-minute break, the electrodes were put on the other arm. In little more than four hours, June's sneezes, which had been reverberating every 40 seconds, stopped. Since then, she has had only a few ordinary sneezes, none of the dry, racking kind that had been draining her strength for so long. 'We hope the absence of sneezes will last,' said Dr. Kushner cautiously. 'So do I,' snapped June. 'I never want to see that machine again.'"(*Time*, 1966, p. 72)

In a follow-up report, Kushner (1968) stated that a program of maintenance therapy had been instituted, and at the end of 16 months the intractable sneezing had not recurred.

Wolpe (1969a) reported a strategy involving deconditioning of anxiety reactions to particular stresses through relaxation and desensitization training. Using these techniques, he was successful in treating peptic ulcers, migraine, neurodermatitis (a skin eruption that involves severe itching and is believed to be psychogenic), and many other psychophysiologic disorders.

Since Wolpe's early work, a large number of studies have been done on the effects of various behavioral-relaxation techniques in selected psychophysiologic disorder. Results obtained have been variable, though generally encouraging. For example, simple tension headaches have proven quite amenable to general relaxation treatment procedures (Cox, Freudlich, & Meyer, 1975; Tasto & Hinkle, 1973); the same kinds of procedures have not been quite as effective when used in the treatment of essential hypertension (Blanchard et al., 1979; Schwartz, 1978; Surwit, Shapiro, & Good, 1978).

The potential of behavior therapy alone in treating psychophysiologic disorders remains to be established. A great deal of work is continuing in this area, and it looks promising. Taking a broad view, it may turn out that the greatest contribution of behavioral approaches to health maintenance will be in the area of altering self-injurious "habits," such as smoking and excessive alcohol use, in systematic programs that teach "self-control" (Blanchard & Andrasik, 1982; Goldfried & Merbaum, 1973; Weisenberg, 1977).

Biofeedback. In bowling or serving a tennis ball, we receive immediate feedback and can correct our behavior accordingly, but such feedback is usually not available with respect to autonomic functions, such as heart rate and brain waves. Biofeedback devices are designed to provide such feedback: they monitor these functions and convert the information into signals like lights or sounds that the individual can readily perceive.

In an early study involving the control of heart rate, for example, Lang, Stroufe, and Hastings (1967) provided subjects with equipment that measured heart rate. The subjects received visual feedback on the dial and were instructed to maintain their heart rates within prescribed limits. Although the subjects could not explain how they did it, they gradually became able to do so: somehow, mental set and exposure to feedback information enabled them to achieve the desired result.

More recent studies have dealt with control of a wide range of psychophysiologic and other disorders, including hypertension, headache, backache, muscular spasms, teeth grinding, epilepsy, and irregular heartbeat. However, the actual magnitude and duration of results is a matter of some controversy. For example, Davis et al., (1973) used relaxation training facilitated by biofeedback training in the treatment of bronchial asthma in children. Asthma symptoms were reduced in nonsevere cases but not in cases considered severe. Similarly, as in the case of general relaxation training, biofeedback treatment of hypertension has yielded somewhat equivocal results (Surwit et al., 1978).

On the other hand, a number of researchers have pointed to the success of biofeedback in treating migraine and tension headaches (Blanchard et al., 1983; Budzynski, 1974; Friar & Beatty, 1976). Budzynski, for example, reported that 81 percent of his patients with migraine headaches were helped to a significant extent by biofeedback.

As in the case of behavior therapy for psychophysiologic disorders, biofeedback training has been undergoing enormous expansion and development into virtually all areas of psychophy-

Relaxation techniques can be used in a variety of settings. Here a college football team is being taken through various relaxation exercises in order to limit the chance of injury during a hard physical workout.

siologic medicine (Fuller, 1978). In fact, some investigators caution that the field may be developing faster than is warranted by sound research data (Katkin & Obrist, 1978). One of the questions at hand here seems to be what, exactly, is the nature of biofeedback? It begins to appear that it may represent simply a more complex approach to teaching people to relax. A recent study by Blanchard et al. (1980) may add some credence to this hypothesis: these researchers found that biofeedback and relaxation training were equally effective in treating headaches. Though more research will undoubtedly be done in this area, it may be that the more complicated and expensive task of teaching biofeedback skills may give way to the simpler teaching of basic relaxation skills—especially so if both continue to be equally effective treatments.

Cognitive-behavioral treatment. The treatment of psychophysiologic disorders has also been attempted with cognitive-behavioral techniques. In one study, these techniques were shown to be effective at reducing maladaptive behaviors—such as rushing, impatience, and hostility—characteristic of Type-A personalities (Jenni & Wollersheim, 1979). In two studies de-

signed to teach patients how to cope better with life stresses that precipitated headaches, researchers show that decreases in the frequency of headaches could be obtained with stress-management techniques (Holroyd & Andrasik, 1978; Holroyd, Andrasik, & Westbrook, 1977). Though we shall look at these techniques in more detail in Chapter 17, they basically involve teaching individuals to use more effective coping skills to lower their experience of stress and thus reduce headaches.

Combined treatment measures

To be treated successfully, psychophysiologic disorders usually require prompt medical attention for the physical conditions combined with psychological therapy to alter or reduce the maladaptive behavioral factors underlying the disorder. The treatment for anorexia nervosa clearly illustrates the need for combined medical and psychological measures. If the anorexic individual's condition becomes life-threatening, extreme measures must be taken to get her to eat. Typically, hospitalization is necessary. The patient may initially be fed intravenously, but since the disorder is apparently under voluntary control, therapy must ultimately focus not only on weight gain but also on the psychological factors underlying the patient's refusal to eat.

Several treatment approaches have been successful in promoting weight gain among anorexics. One includes making the patient stay in isolation, earning privileges—such as time for socializing—only as she gains weight. Leon (1983) reports the scenario:

"Given the compliant, perfectionistic behavioral characteristics of many anorexics, it might not be surprising that once the youngster has made the decision to eat in order to gain relief from isolation or to gain a variety of social and other reinforcers, she compliantly follows the daily weight gain criteria set up for her and systematically gains weight. It has been my experience, however, in viewing charts of the weight histories of many treated anorexics that their weight precipitously plummets once they are released from the hospital. Thus, compliance with the treatment regimen has brought relief from the aversiveness of the hospital situation and has also affected hospital discharge." (Leon, 1983)

That is, Leon reports that, in many cases, there is no significant long-term normalization in eating patterns. This is a major drawback if therapy focuses single-mindedly on just the immediate need to gain weight. Leon goes on to say,

"The crucial issue of the regulation of food intake as one of several treatment goals is underscored by the fact that some anorexics after release from the hospital continue eating until the point of obesity or develop bulimia-vomiting patterns to control their weight. Thus, treatment should also address the personal concerns about self-control over one's body and one's environment, and other difficulties related to family interactions that the anorexic might be attempting to cope with through self-starvation."

This seems related to an earlier finding by Halmi, Falk, & Schwartz (1981), in which data suggested that the choice of treatment did not seem to be a factor in successful weight gain for hospitalized patients: they typically gained weight regardless of the treatment condition employed! Though the obvious goal with the anorexic patient is to get her to gain weight, therapy for her psychological adjustment may be far more important and more elusive in terms of long-term success.

Lucas, Duncan, and Piens (1981) reported on an interesting therapeutic setting developed at the Mayo Clinic and designed to deal with both the physiological and psychological needs of the anorexic patient. Their approach was a combined medical-psychiatric effort, with a coordinated team of professionals who focused on the problems of malnutrition as well as the psychological family problems in each case. The first step in their treatment efforts was to remove the anorexic person from the home situation. The individual was placed in an inpatient ward where the nutritional problems were dealt with by staff members who monitored the food intake. The patient was given social rewards— such as time with peers—for appropriate consumption of food. Group psychological treatment with a supportive orientation was provided, in which the patient was allowed the opportunity to express her thoughts, concerns, and fears. While the inpatient treatment program was in progress, the staff also worked with the family in an effort to resolve the family behaviors that might be encouraging the patient's anorexic behavior. This approach combined medical efforts with individual and family therapy.

Sociocultural measures

Sociocultural treatment measures are targeted more toward preventive efforts and are typically applied to selected populations or subcultural groups thought to be at risk for developing disorders. Within these groups, efforts are made to alter certain life-style behaviors in order to reduce the overall level of susceptibility to a disorder. For example, cigarette smoking is associated with increased risk for heart disease; in order to reduce the general risk of heart disease, efforts might be made to reduce or prevent cigarette smoking in groups that are vulnerable to the smoking habit—for example, adolescents. Similarly, some correlation appears to exist between high cholesterol diet and coronary heart disease; at high risk here are middle-aged men, and efforts might be made to alter their dietary practices in order to reduce the rate of coronary heart disease in the total population.

An excellent example of a community-based prevention-oriented program aimed at reducing the incidence of atherosclerotic disease (a predisposing factor in coronary heart disease) comes from Finland. The North Karelia Project (named after the province in which it was conducted) was a large-scale effort that included 60,000 "subjects" (the province residents) and involved several types of community intervention efforts.

The overall goal was to promote greater public awareness of the high-risk factors—especially cigarette smoking and high serum cholesterol caused by eating high-fat foods—in atherosclerotic disease; then the effort was made to get individuals to reduce these factors by smoking less and eating low-fat foods.

Project staff (a) provided information through the mass media—such as a seven-session TV course aimed at reducing smoking—and public meetings; (b) organized existing health-care services and initiated new ones to focus on eliminating high-risk factors through the formation of self-help groups; (c) trained community leaders, such as teachers, to work on the program; (d) promoted the distribution and sale of healthy low-fat foods; and (e) devised a method by which they could measure the effects of the program (McAlister et al., 1980; Puska, 1983; Puska et al., 1979).

Early results were encouraging. The intervention program was shown to lower effectively the coronary heart disease risk in the population:

death from heart disease fell 27 percent for men and 42 percent for women. The self-report survey on smoking behavior indicated that there was a reduction of cigarette consumption among participants; significant reductions were also found in serum cholesterol levels in the blood.

As we learn more about the role of biological, psychosocial, and sociocultural factors in the etiology of psychophysiologic disorders, it becomes increasingly possible to delineate "high-risk" individuals and groups—such as the heart attack-prone Type-A personalities and groups living in a precarious and rapidly changing life situation. This, in turn, enables treatment efforts to focus on early intervention and prevention. In this context, counseling programs—aimed at fostering changes in maladaptive life-styles of individuals and families and remedying pathological social conditions—seem eminently worthwhile.

Summary

Research has clearly established that emotional factors influence the development of many physical disorders and play an important role in the course of the disease process. Psychological factors may be instrumental in the development of some physical disorders, referred to as psychophysiologic disorders. The specific mechanisms by which emotional states result in physical disorders has not been clearly delineated. However, the general psychophysiologic pattern is mediated through the autonomic nervous and endocrine systems as conceptualized in Selye's general adaptation syndrome. General life-style patterns are also seen as important contributors to physical disorders.

In the DSM-III, psychophysiologic disorders are diagnosed as Axis I under the category of "psychological factors affecting physical condition"; the specific physical disorder is noted on Axis III.

Physical disorders that have been determined to have important emotional causes cover a wide range of bodily systems and organs. One of the most widely studied psychophysiologic disor-ders is peptic ulcer, an erosion of the stomach lining that results from excessive secretion of stomach acid. Another psychophysiologic disorder, anorexia nervosa, involves refusal of food to the extent that the individual's health is endangered, and occurs predominantly among young women. Migraine and tension headaches are also included in the psychophysiologic disorders. Although these conditions are less life threatening than other disorders covered in this chapter, they nonetheless can result in a great deal of suffering. Two other important, and potentially life-threatening disorders were described in this chapter—hypertension and coronary heart disease.

Although specific causal processes underlying the psychophysiologic disorders have not been clearly isolated, there are a number of factors that may be involved. There is strong evidence that genetic factors play a role in predisposing some individuals to develop certain physical disorders. Psychosocial factors such as learning history, development of maladaptive coping skills, and difficult interpersonal relationships may result in the individual's being unable to manage stress well. The development of physical problems occurs as a result of the individual's inadequate coping response. Sociocultural factors play an important but less clearly defined role in the development of psychophysiologic disorders. It is generally believed among physicians and medical psychologists that life-style factors, including diet, smoking, excessive alcohol use, may be important causal factors in the psychophysiologic disorders.

In the treatment of psychophysiologic disorders it is important to account both for the physical manifestations of the problems as well as the emotional factors that underly the problem. Psychoanalytic theory and psychoanalytic therapy, upon which most early work in the psychophysiologic disorders was based, has not proven to be an effective treatment approach. In recent years, learning-based treatments, particularly behavior modification of life-style patterns, relaxation therapy, and biofeedback therapy have been recognized as generally more effective approaches to treating the psychophysiologic disorders.

9

Affective disorders and suicide

Guillaume Pujolle, Les Aigles—La Plume d'Oie *(1940). Pujolle (b. 1893) was born in the Haute-Garonne area in France. A joiner by trade, he was torn by emotional conflicts and was eventually admitted to a hospital in Toulouse. He began to draw in 1935. His pictures (such as the one at left) have a dream-like, fluid appearance, composed as they are of a mosaic of broad, undulating strips of color.*

An *affective disorder* is a disturbance of mood sufficiently intense to warrant professional attention. Of course, we are all subject to mood changes, ranging from mild depression or "the blues" to states in which things seem to be going unusually well and we experience high energy and optimism. For some, however, the endpoints on this continuum become abnormally extended—most often on the depression side—leading to extremes of mood that are clearly maladaptive. Consider the following:

A nationally prominent businesswoman, noted for her energy and productivity, was unexpectedly deserted by her husband for a younger woman. Following her initial shock and rage, she began to have uncontrollable weeping spells and serious doubts about her business acumen. Decision-making, in particular, became an enormous ordeal. Her spirits worsened over a relatively brief period of time, and she began to spend more and more of her time in bed, refusing to deal with anyone. Simultaneously, her consumption of alcohol increased to the point that she was rarely entirely sober. Within a period of weeks, serious financial losses were incurred owing to her inability, or refusal, to keep her affairs in order. She felt she was a "total failure." Finally, having become alarmed, members of her family essentially forced her to accept an appointment with a clinical psychologist.

How was the psychologist to deal with such a person? Was something "wrong" with her, or was she merely experiencing normal human emotion consequent to her husband's departure? The psychologist concluded that the woman was suffering from a mental disorder of the type to be discussed in this chapter, and treatment was initiated. The diagnosis, based on the severity of the symptoms and the degree of impairment, was "major depression."

When a "mood change," because of its extent, brings about behavior that seriously endangers the welfare of the person undergoing it, psychologists and other mental health professionals conclude that the person is disordered. Such mood disorders are extremely heterogeneous, as is suggested by the many types of depression recognized in the DSM-III (**HIGHLIGHT** on page 300). It is extremely likely that *within* each of the affective disorder diagnoses, such as that of major depression, more than one type of disordered process is represented. With the intensive research now occurring in relation to these disorders, we hope to be able to achieve

HIGHLIGHT
Varieties of depression according to DSM-III

The DSM-III distinguishes among a number of different types of depressive disorder. These diagnoses are listed below together with their main differentiating features.

Diagnosis	Main features
Organic affective syndrome, depressed Primary degenerative dementia with depression Multi-infarct dementia with depression Hallucinogen affective disorder, depressed	Notably depressed mood, including symptoms associated with major depression, whose primary cause is considered to be interference with normal brain functioning by some organic process. Where the organic process is known (e.g., multi-infarct dementia), it is specified in the diagnosis on Axis I or III.
Major depression	Person has one or more major depressive episodes in the absence of any manic episode. Prominent and persistent depressed mood, accompanied by symptoms such as poor appetite, insomnia, psychomotor retardation, decreased sex drive, fatigue, feelings of worthlessness or guilt, inability to concentrate, and thoughts of death or suicide.
Bipolar disorder, depressed	Person experiences a major depressive episode (as above) and has had one or more manic episodes.
Dysthymic disorder	For the past two years, person has been bothered all or most of the time by a depressed mood, but not of sufficient severity to meet the criteria for major depression.
Cyclothymic disorder, depressed	At present or during the past two years, person has experienced episodes resembling dysthymic disorder (as above), but also has had one or more periods of hypomania—characterized by elevated, expansive, or irritable mood not of psychotic proportions.
Adjustment disorder with depressed mood	The person reacts with a maladaptively depressed mood to some identifiable stressor occurring within the past three months. "Uncomplicated bereavement" does not qualify. It is assumed the reaction is temporary.

in the reasonably near future much finer discriminations among them at biological, psychosocial, and sociocultural levels. But the millennium has not yet arrived, and so, for the most part, our discussion will be organized around the DSM-III categories.

Affective disorders are so named because they involve changes in **affect,** a term that is roughly equivalent to *emotion* or, as we have pointed out, to *mood.* In all such disorders extremes of affect—extreme elation or deep depression—dominate the clinical picture. By contrast, the schizophrenic and paranoid disorders to be discussed in the next chapter are predominantly disturbances of *thought,* although often they have some distortion of affect, too. In severe cases, disturbances of both thought and affect may involve a loss of contact with reality and a total involvement of the personality; in these cases, the traditional terms *psychosis* or *psychotic* have been applied.

A disorder of the thought processes is not usually a notable feature in affective disorders, except perhaps where the disorder reaches extreme intensity; even here, the disturbed thinking often seems in some sense "appropriate" to the extremes of emotion that the person is experiencing. For example, the delusional idea that one's internal organs have totally deteriorated—an idea not uncommonly held by severely depressed persons—ties in with the person's whole mood of despondency. This type of disordered thinking is termed *mood-congruent* (that is, consistent with the predominant mood) and is considered clinically less significant than bizarre ideas not fitting in with the person's apparent emotional state.

Affective disorders are not new in the history of humankind. Descriptions of affective disorders are found among the early writings of the Egyptians, Greeks, Hebrews, and Chinese; similar descriptions are found in the literary works of Shakespeare, Dostoevski, Poe, and Hemingway. The list of historical figures who suffered from recurrent depression is a long and celebrated one, including Moses, Rousseau, Dostoevski, Queen Victoria, Lincoln, Tchaikovsky, and Freud. Here it is apparent that we are again dealing with mental disorders that appear to be common to the human race, both crossculturally and historically.

Depressions of mild intensity are so much a part of the fabric of our lives that incidence and prevalence figures for them would be difficult to estimate and would probably not be very meaningful in any event. Of the two types of major affective disorders, *major depression* (a "unipolar" form of disorder in which only depressive episodes occur) is much more frequent and has increased in recent years, while *bipolar disorder* (in which both manic and depressive episodes occur) has decreased.[1] In fact, it has been estimated that some 8 to 10 persons in 100—about

25 million Americans—will experience a severe depressive episode at some time in their lives (Brown, 1974). Over 2 million of these will suffer profound depressions (President's Commission on Mental Health, 1978). The great majority of cases occur between the ages of 25 and 65, although such reactions may occur anytime from early childhood to old age. Poznanski and Zrull (1970) have described depressive reactions among children ranging from 3 to 12 years of age, and cases have been observed even after age 85. As we shall see, in the affective disorders, females are considerably more at risk than males.

Fortunate indeed (and very likely nonexistent!) is the adult person who has never experienced at least mild depression from time to time. As we shall see, there is reason to conceive of such mild affective disturbance as being *on the same continuum* as the more severe disorders on which we shall be concentrating; the difference seems chiefly to be one of degree, not of kind. At some point along this continuum, however, as we encounter the more extreme or psychotic phenomena, subtle biological factors very likely become implicated, rendering the person less amenable to psychological treatment approaches.

Our discussion will start with the milder disturbances usually regarded as normal. From there, we will move to disorders of affect in which the individual's functioning is clearly impaired but in which there is little or no evidence of pervasive personality breakdown or loss of contact with reality.[2] Finally, we will deal with the so-called "major" affective disorders, a group of conditions currently undergoing intensive scientific investigation. Throughout, we will focus primarily on depression, which is much more common than its seeming psychological opposite, mania.

Suicide is a distressingly frequent and virtually always possible outcome of relatively significant depressive episodes. In fact, such epi-

---

[1]*Mania* is characterized by intense and unrealistic feelings of excitement and euphoria; in this sense it can be seen as the opposite of *depression*, which involves feelings of extraordinary sadness and dejection. Full discussions of "major depression" and "bipolar disorder" appear on pages 308–9 and 309–13 of this chapter, respectively.

[2]Traditionally, this level of affective disturbance has been termed neurotic, and the term *depressive neurosis* is still used by many clinicians to designate depressions of this level of severity. As used in this context, *neurosis* refers to a disorder with an intermediate *level* of severity. Elsewhere in this text, we used the term and its derivatives to refer to a particular *type* of disorder—one chiefly characterized by anxiety, internal conflict, and defense, as described in Chapter 6; as it happens, a disorder of this type is also usually of intermediate severity. Some depressive behavior appears to be a product of neurotic disorder as we use the term.

sodes are undoubtedly the most common of the predisposing causes leading to physical self-destruction. The latter part of the chapter includes a discussion of the varieties, causes, and prevention of suicidal behavior.

Affective disturbances and disorders

Sadness, discouragement, pessimism, and a sense of hopelessness about being able to improve matters are familiar themes to most people. Most of us are prone to repeated cycles in and out of this state throughout our lives. Depression is unpleasant, even noxious, when we are in it, but it usually does not last very long; sometimes, it seems almost to be self-limiting. As we come out of it, we often experience it as having been in some sense useful: we were "stuck," and now we can move on; the former situation was easier to get out of than we thought it could be, and our newer perspective encompasses all sorts of possibilities.

This familiar scenario contains certain hints that may be significant to depression generally, including its more severe forms. The more important of these are that (a) depression, in its mild form, may actually be adaptive; (b) much of the "work" of depression seems to involve self-exposure to images, thoughts, and feelings that would normally be avoided; and (c) depression may, at least under some circumstances, be self-limiting. All of these considerations suggest that the capacity to experience depression may be a normal—even a desirable—state of affairs, provided of course that it is maintained within certain limits of time and extent. They also suggest the idea of *normal* depressions—depressions we would expect to occur in anyone undergoing certain traumatic but rather common life events, such as significant personal or economic losses.

Normal depression

While the distinction between "normal" and "abnormal" is especially fuzzy here, any reasonable estimate would suggest that normal depres-

sions far surpass abnormal ones in terms of the numbers of persons affected at a given time. Most people suffering from normal depression will not seek or need the specialized services of a mental health professional—although, in doubtful cases, it is certainly better to err on the conservative side and seek such assistance.

Normal depressions are almost always the result of more or less obvious recent stress. In fact, as noted in the **HIGHLIGHT** on page 300, some depressions are considered "adjustment disorders" (in response to stressors) rather than "affective disorders." We discuss such reactions here as well as in Chapter 5 because we doubt such sharp demarcations are justified by the facts. We shall consider some of these kinds of depressions below, although it should be noted that "uncomplicated bereavement" is not considered a disorder at all within the DSM-III framework.

Grief and the grieving process. We usually think of grief as the psychological process one goes through following the death of a loved one. While this may be the most common and intense form of grieving, many other types of loss will give rise to a similar state in the affected person. Loss of a favored status or position (including one occasioned by "promotion" out of it), separation or divorce, financial loss, the breakup of a romantic affair, retirement from a valued occupation, separation from an important friend, absence from home for the first time, or even the disappearance or death of a cherished pet may all give rise to the symptoms of acute grief.

Whatever the source, the condition has certain characteristic qualities. The grieving person will normally "turn off" on events that would normally provoke a strong response; figuratively, he or she seems to roll up in a ball, fending off any and all possibilities of additional involvement and hurt by the simple expedient of losing interest in nearly all external happenings. At the same time, the griever often becomes very actively involved in fantasies that poignantly depict the now unavailable former situation of satisfaction and gratification. Initially very painful, these fantasies, if only by sheer repetition, gradually lose their capacity to evoke pain—a process of erasure (Sullivan, 1956).

In the typical instance, the capability for response to the external world is gradually re-

Grief for the loss of a loved one is considered a form of "normal" depression.

gained, sadness abates, zest returns, and the person moves out again into a more productive engagement with the fluctuations of life. This is the normal pattern; some people, however, become stuck somewhere in the middle of the sequence, in which case they enter into a more serious psychological status to be described in a later section. Clayton (1982) estimates that the process of grieving following bereavement is normally completed within one year, during which time the grieving person may experience the "full depressive syndrome" (i.e., major depression, to be examined below). If depressive symptoms persist beyond the first year after loss, therapeutic intervention may be called for.

Ignoring for the moment such potential complications, it is easy to see grief as having an adaptive function. In fact, the lack of grief under conditions in which it would seem warranted would generally be of concern to a mental health professional. On the other hand, as we have seen in Chapter 8, a prolonged sense of hopelessness may endanger physical health.

Other normal mood variations. Many situations in life other than obvious loss can provoke depressive feelings, and some people seem especially prone to develop depressive responses. It is a commonplace observation, for example, that doctoral candidates in various fields, including those in clinical psychology, frequently undergo pronounced depressive reactions soon after completion of their final oral exams. A seemingly similar phenomenon is the so-called postpartum depressive reaction of some new mothers (and sometimes fathers) on the birth of a child. Pitt (1982) indicates that as many as 50 percent of women experience at least an attack of "the blues" following childbirth, 10 percent of them having reactions of moderately severe depression. Possibly this reflects a feeling of "let down" after sustained effort and anticipation, or perhaps the reality never quite matches the expectation, leading to feelings of depression.

A large number of college students experience greater or lesser bouts of depression during their college years of supposed freedom and personal growth. Normal depressions among college students were studied by Blatt, D'Afflitti, and Quinlan (1976) in an effort to determine the basic dimensions of the experience. In brief, they found that the depression was similar for males and females, and that it involved chiefly three main psychological variables: (a) dependency, the sense that one is in need of help and support from others; (b) self-criticism, the tendency to exaggerate one's faults and engage in self-devaluation; and (c) inefficacy, the sense that events in the world are independent of—not contingent upon—one's own actions or efforts. In subsequent work, Blatt and colleagues (1982) focused on the first two of these dimensions and were able to replicate earlier results. It should be noted that themes of the sort identified by Blatt et al. (dependency, self-criticism, etc.) also tend to dominate the thinking of more severely depressed persons. This supports the notion of a continuum from normal to abnormal depression.

Mild to moderate affective disorders

The point on the severity continuum at which affective *disturbance* becomes affective *disorder* is, in the final analysis, a matter of clinical judgment. Unfortunately, while criteria exist for exercising this judgment, they are not precise enough to guarantee consensus among different clinicians. Although the more severe forms of affective disorder are obviously abnormal to even the casual observer, there is a gray area where distinction between normal and abnormal is difficult to establish.

It is customary to differentiate the affective disorders along three principal dimensions: (a) *severity*—the number of dysfunctions experienced in various areas of living and the relative degree of impairment evidenced in each area (e.g., sexual performance and satisfaction); (b) *type*—the question of whether depressive, manic, or mixed symptoms predominate; and (c) *duration*—the question of whether the disorder is acute, chronic, or intermittent, with periods of relatively normal functioning between the episodes of disorder. The following discussion reflects these customary divisions, as do the DSM-III categories on which we will partially depend. There are three main DSM-III categories for affective disorders of mild to moderate severity: *cyclothymic disorder, dysthymic disorder,* and *adjustment disorder with depressed mood.* Each of these is considered below.

Cyclothymic disorder.

It has long been recognized that certain persons are subject to cyclical mood alterations with relative excesses of elation ("hypomania") and depression that, while substantial, are not disabling. In the predecessors to DSM-III (DSM-I and -II) this pattern was included under the personality disorders; it was not related to the affective disorders *per se*. That judgment has now been altered; indeed, some clinicians feel that *cyclothymic disorder* is but a mild form of major bipolar disorder (see page 309). Evidence for this latter view is equivocal. Von Zerssen (1982) and colleagues have found little evidence for a connection between cyclothymic disorder and major bipolar disorder or, for that matter, any other affective syndrome. On the other hand, Depue et al. (1981) have made an impressive case for a "subsyndromal" cyclothymic personality type that is at high risk for bipolar disorder.

Regardless of how this controversy is eventually resolved, the DSM-III definition of cyclothymic disorder does indeed make it sound like a junior-grade version of major bipolar disorder *minus* psychotic features such as delusions. In the depressed phase of cyclothymic disorder, the person's mood is dejected and there is a distinct loss of interest or pleasure in usual activi-

ties and pastimes. In addition, the individual may exhibit sleep irregularity (too much or too little): low energy level; feelings of inadequacy; decreased efficiency, productivity, talkativeness, and cognitive sharpness; social withdrawal; restriction of pleasurable activities, including a relative disinterest in sex; a pessimistic and brooding attitude; and tearfulness. The counterpart hypomanic phase consists essentially of the opposites of these characteristics, except that the sleep disturbance is invariably one of an apparent decreased need for sleep. As in the case of bipolar disorder, there may be lengthy periods between episodes, in which the person functions in a relatively adaptive manner. However, in cyclothymic disorder, the overall time frame necessitates at least a two-year span of disturbance for adults and one year for children.

The following case is illustrative.

"A 29-year-old car salesman was referred by his current girl friend, a psychiatric nurse, who suspected he had an Affective Disorder, even though the patient was reluctant to admit that he might be a 'moody' person. According to him, since the age of 14 he has experienced repeated alternating cycles that he terms 'good times and bad times.' During a 'bad' period, usually lasting four to seven days, he oversleeps 10–14 hours daily, lacks energy, confidence, and motivation—'just vegetating,' as he puts it. Often he abruptly shifts, characteristically upon waking up in the morning, to a three-to-four-day stretch of overconfidence, heightened social awareness, promiscuity, and sharpened thinking—'things would flash in my mind.' At such times he indulges in alcohol to enhance the experience, but also to help him sleep. Occasionally the 'good' periods last seven to ten days, but culminate in irritable and hostile outbursts, which often herald the transition back to another period of 'bad' days. He admits to frequent use of marijuana, which he claims helps him 'adjust' to daily routines.

In school, A's and B's alternated with C's and D's, with the result that the patient was considered a bright student whose performance was mediocre overall because of 'unstable motivation.' As a car salesman his performance has also been uneven, with 'good days' canceling out the 'bad days'; yet even during his 'good days' he is sometimes perilously argumentative with customers and loses sales that appeared sure. Although considered a charming man in many social circles, he alienates friends when he is hostile and irritable. He typically accumulates social obligations during the 'bad' days and takes care of them all at once on the first day of a 'good' period." (Spitzer et al., 1981, pp. 31–32)

In short, cyclothymic disorder consists of mood swings that, at either extreme, are of maladaptive but nonpsychotic intensity.

Dysthymic disorder. The symptoms of *dysthymic disorder* are essentially identical to those indicated for the depressed phase of cyclothymic disorder. The main difference is that dysthymically disordered persons evidence no tendency toward hypomanic episodes in their life histories. Rather, they exhibit moderate, nonpsychotic levels of depression over a chronic period—that is, at least two years of more or less uninterrupted duration. Normal moods may briefly intercede, but they last at most from a few days to a few weeks. As in the case of cyclothymic disorder, no identifiable precipitating circumstance need necessarily be present, though such circumstances are frequently observed for depressions of this general type. Indeed, the depressed person tends to call forth reactions from the social environment that will bring about "bad" feelings on a continuous basis. This touches on the issue of the alleged "endogenous" (i.e., caused from within) nature of certain affective disorders, an issue to which we will return in a later section.

The following case, which includes self-sustaining features, is reasonably typical.

"A 28-year-old junior executive was referred by a senior psychoanalyst for 'supportive' treatment. She had obtained a master's degree in business administration and moved to California a year and a half earlier to begin work in a large firm. She complained of being 'depressed' about everything: her job, her husband, and her prospects for the future.

She had had extensive psychotherapy previously. She had seen an 'analyst' twice a week for three years while in college, and a 'behaviorist' for a year and a half while in graduate school. Her complaints were of persistent feelings of depressed mood, inferiority, and pessimism, which she claims to have had since she was 16 or 17 years old. Although she did reasonably well in college, she consistently ruminated about those students who were 'genuinely intelligent.' She dated during college and graduate school, but claimed that she would never go after a guy she thought was 'special,' always feeling inferior and intimidated. Whenever she saw or met such a man, she acted stiff and aloof, or actually walked away as quickly as possible, only to berate herself afterward and then fantasize about him for many months. She claimed that her therapy had helped, although she still could not re-

Depressive symptoms include a loss of interest or pleasure in one's usual activities, low energy level, social withdrawal, and an attitude of dejection or pessimism.

member a time when she didn't feel somewhat depressed.

Just after graduation, she married the man she was going out with at the time. She thought of him as reasonably desirable, though not 'special,' and married him primarily because she felt she 'needed a husband' for companionship. Shortly after their marriage, the couple started to bicker. She was very critical of his clothes, his job, and his parents; and he, in turn, found her rejecting, controlling, and moody. She began to feel that she had made a mistake in marrying him.

Recently she has also been having difficulties at work. She is assigned the most menial tasks at the firm and is never given an assignment of importance or responsibility. She admits that she frequently does a 'slipshod' job of what is given her, never does more than is required, and never demonstrates any assertiveness or initiative to her supervisors. She views her boss as self-centered, unconcerned, and unfair, but nevertheless admires his success. She feels that she will never go very far in her profession because she does not have the right 'connections' and neither does her husband, yet she dreams of money, status, and power.

Her social life with her husband involves several other couples. The man in these couples is usually a friend of her husband's. She is sure that the women find her uninteresting and unimpressive, and that the people who seem to like her are probably no better off than she.

Under the burden of her dissatisfaction with her marriage, her job, and her social life, feeling tired and uninterested in 'life,' she now enters treatment for the third time." (Spitzer et al., 1981, pp. 10–11)

Adjustment disorder with depressed mood.

Basically, *adjustment disorder with depressed mood* is behaviorally indistinguishable from dysthymic disorder or the depressed phase of cyclothymic disorder. It differs from the latter two conditions in that it requires the existence of an identifiable (presumably precipitating) psychosocial stressor in the client's life within three months prior to the onset of depression. The justification for rendering a clinical diagnosis is that the client is experiencing impaired social or occupational functioning or the observed stressor would not normally be considered severe enough to account for the client's reaction. There is a difficulty here, of course, since assessing stressor severity is a highly subjective matter. Also, the diagnosis assumes that the person's problems will remit when the stressor ceases or when a new level of adjustment is achieved. This causes further difficulties, since it calls for the diagnostician to predict a benign future course; if enhanced adjustment does not occur, we must assume a continuation of the stressor or a failure of the client to make the "new" adjustment. Presumably, chronic cases of this sort would, in most instances, need to be rediagnosed as dysthymic disorder.

Despite evident problems with this particular set of formal diagnostic criteria, there are doubtless many cases of relatively brief but moderately severe depression (involving definitely maladaptive behavior) that occur in reaction to circumstances generally regarded by most as stressful. ("Uncomplicated bereavement," by the way, would not be included under this diagnosis.) The following excerpt from a clinical interview is illustrative of an adjustment disorder with depressed mood.

Pt.: Well, you see, doctor, I just don't concentrate good, I mean, I can't play cards or even care to talk on the phone, I just feel so upset and miserable, it's just sorta as if I don't care any more about anything.

Dr.: You feel that your condition is primarily due to your divorce proceedings?

Pt.: Well, doctor, the thing that upset me so, we had accumulated a little bit through my efforts—bonds and money—and he (sigh) wanted one half of it. He said he was going to San Francisco and get a

job and send me enough money for support. So (sigh) I gave him a bond, and he went and turned around and went to an attorney and sued me for a divorce. Well, somehow, I had withstood all the humiliation of his drinking and not coming home at night and not knowing where he was, but *he* turned and divorced me and this is something that I just can't take. I mean, he has broken my health and broken everything, and I've been nothing but good to him. I just can't take it, doctor. There are just certain things that people—I don't know—just can't accept. I just can't accept that he would turn on me that way.

It should be noted that few, if any, depressions—including milder ones—occur in the absence of significant anxiety. The depressed person will normally also be notably fearful and anxious. Yet the relationship between depression and anxiety is far from clear. Perhaps the person becomes frightened as a consequence of observing the physically paralyzing effects of his or her own developing depression. Alternatively, perhaps there is a more intrinsic relationship between anxiety and depression, even at the neurophysiological or neurochemical level (Roth & Mountjoy, 1982). Some investigators, such as Seligman (1975) and Brown and Harris (1978), believe that depression may be a naturally occurring consequence of anxiety, particularly under conditions interpreted as hopeless. In any event, because of the close association the treatment of depression often includes specific treatment for anxiety as well.

In the range of mild to moderate affective disorders, there are no recognized manic or hypomanic counterparts to dysthymic disorder or adjustment disorder with depressed mood. The implicit assumption appears to be that all mania-like behaviors must be manifestations of a cyclothymic or bipolar process, or perhaps must exist along a continuum on which these two conditions fall. Considering behavior alone, however, any such assumption is readily challenged. Most clinicians are familiar with a type of person who is chronically overactive, dominating, counterdependent, deficient in self-criticism, and perhaps excessively optimistic concerning the outcome of various plans and schemes; such persons are by no means a rare breed. It would be unfortunate, however, to confuse this person's behavior with that of the classic manic syndrome. Such persons are almost invariably found to have underlying anxiety which they are attempting to manage by overactivity in the standard fashion of neurotic defense, and their problems are perhaps best considered manifestations of what we have called compliance/submission inhibition (see pages 192–93).

Incidentally, these individuals are unlikely to present themselves for treatment at a psychological or psychiatric clinic. The more common pattern is for them to show up in medical clinics with beginning psychophysiologic disease—perhaps as Type A patients with coronary problems (see Chapter 8).

Moderate to severe affective disorders

We have noted that affective disorders seem to array themselves along an unbroken continuum of severity; there are no discernable gaps in this continuum by means of which we might distinguish different basic types of disorder. We must now add a qualification to this general proposition; the continuum does not quite tell the whole story. Affective disorders differ, as we have seen, along the dimensions of severity, type, and duration. Yet both *severity* and *type* are often hard to pin down: the *profile*, or pattern, of symptoms (e.g., sleep disturbance, psychomotor retardation/agitation) may vary greatly from individual to individual and may exist at least partially independently of severity. An obvious distinction, for example, can be drawn between manic- and depressive-symptom profiles, but different profiles of symptoms—at varying levels of intensity—may occur *within* different instances of either mania or depression. So far researchers have devoted little attention to different profiles of symptoms within mania; on the other hand, a great deal of attention has been given to identifying and describing qualitatively different types of depression. For example, in a recent study employing cluster analysis, Andreasen and Grove (1982) confirmed that depressed patients' symptoms varied both in terms of severity and type.[3] Moreover, the types they identified show a reasonable correspondence with DSM-III-defined subtypes of depression.

Severe depressive symptoms nearly always indicate the presence of a major affective disorder.

Considerations such as these assume increased importance as we move from milder forms of affective disorder into the *major affective disorders.* Contrary to what one might expect, a major affective disorder is not necessarily a disorder of marked severity. DSM-III coding provides for diagnosing a major affective disorder where severe (i.e., psychotic) features are not present and even—by use of the qualifying phrase "in remission"—where there are currently no notable symptoms at all! It is plain, therefore, that the diagnostic term refers not to something necessarily observable in the current behavior of the person but to some inferred behavior potential that the person is presumed to possess. In current practice, in fact, use of the term normally implies a biological defect or aberration that renders the person *liable* to episodes of more or less severe affective disorder. It is therefore possible to have a major affective disorder with only mild current symptoms. By contrast, severe symptoms—either manic or de-

---

[3]Cluster analysis basically employs correlational techniques (see p. 25) to establish which symptoms covary with others among a representative group of patients. When groups of symptoms show strong covariation, they fall into the same "cluster" and are therefore assumed to identify a subtype of the disorder in question.

pressed—are almost never considered other than outward manifestations of a major disorder.

Major depression.

To a large extent, the diagnostic criteria for major depression involve merely more intense forms of the symptoms for the depressive phase of cyclothymic disorder. There can be marked sadness of mood, fatigue, insomnia or hypersomnia (i.e., too little or too much sleep), loss of interest in pleasurable activities, diminished cognitive capacity, and self-denunciation to the point of claiming worthlessness and/or guilt out of proportion to any past indiscretions. In addition there is often decreased appetite and significant weight loss (or, much more rarely, their opposites), a slowdown—or, more rarely, agitation—of mental and physical activity, and preoccupation with death and suicide. Psychotic features, such as delusions, hallucinations, or depressive stupor (the patient is mute and unresponsive) may or may not accompany the foregoing. Normally, any delusions or hallucinations are mood-congruent, that is, they involve themes of personal inadequacy, guilt, deserved punishment, death, disease, and so forth.

The following conversation between a therapist and a patient illustrates a major depression of moderate severity.

Th.: Good morning, how are you today?
Pt.: (Pause) Well, okay I guess, doctor. . . . I don't know, I just feel sort of discouraged.
Th.: Is there anything in particular that worries you?
Pt.: I don't know, doctor . . . everything seems to be futile . . . nothing seems worthwhile any more. It seems as if all that was beautiful has lost its beauty. I guess I expected more than life has given. It just doesn't seem worthwhile going on. I can't seem to make up my mind about anything. I guess I have what you would call the "blues."
Th.: Can you tell me more about your feelings?
Pt.: Well . . . my family expected great things of me. I am supposed to be the outstanding member of the family . . . they think because I went through college everything should begin to pop and there's nothing to pop. I . . . really don't expect anything from anyone. Those whom I have trusted proved themselves less than friends should be.
Th.: Oh?
Pt.: Yes, I once had a very good girlfriend with whom I spent a good deal of time. She was very important to me . . . I thought she was my friend but

now she treats me like a casual acquaintance (tears).
Th.: Can you think of any reason for this?
Pt.: Yes, it's all my fault. I can't blame them—anybody that is . . . I am not worthy of them. I have sinned against nature. I am worthless . . . nobody can love me. I don't deserve friends or success. . . .
Th.: You sinned against nature?
Pt.: Well . . . I am just no good. I am a failure. I was envious of other people. I didn't want them to have more than I had and when something bad happened to them I was glad. Now I am being repaid for my sins. All my flaws stand out and I am repugnant to everyone. (Sighs) I am a miserable failure. . . . There is no hope for me.

For this patient, the most prominent clinical feature—aside from the general mood depression—is self-denunciation.

The most severe form of major depression is the depressive stupor, and is illustrated in the following.

The patient lay in bed, immobile, with a dull, depressed expression on his face. His eyes were sunken and downcast. Even when spoken to, he would not raise his eyes to look at the speaker. Usually he did not respond at all to questions, but sometimes, after apparently great effort, he would mumble something about the "Scourge of God." He appeared somewhat emaciated, his breath was foul, and he had to be given enemas to maintain elimination. Occasionally, with great effort, he made the sign of the cross with his right hand. The overall picture was one of extreme vegetativelike immobility and depression.

There are basically two subcategories of major depression: (a) single episode (the person has not had a previous episode of the disorder), and (b) recurrent (the patient *has* had one or more previous episodes). (A further subtype of major depression is discussed in the **HIGHLIGHT** on page 309.) The diagnosis of major depression cannot be made if the patient has ever experienced a manic episode; in that case, the current depression is viewed as a depressive episode of bipolar disorder. Accordingly, major depression is also known as *unipolar disorder.*

The proportion of cases exhibiting a recurrent form of the disorder is difficult to estimate reliably because of wide variations in the results of different studies. Coryell and Winokur (1982) have recently tabulated data from the available work in this area and have reported recurrence

HIGHLIGHT
The melancholia subsyndrome

Hippocrates, in the third century B.C., ascribed depression to an excess of "black bile" and named it *melancholia*—the literal rendering of the words. The name has persisted, although the concept to which it refers has since undergone considerable revision. Both of DSM-III's predecessors included the diagnosis *involutional melancholia*, referring to a supposedly distinct type of depression having its first onset in the "involutional" years—that is in the late middle to late periods of life. Current opinion is that serious depressions making a first appearance in this phase of life are in fact *not* distinctive in any other way and hence do not warrant separate diagnostic status.

However, the DSM-III retains the term *melancholia* in referring to a subset of major depression ("major depression with melancholia"). This diagnosis is ap-

propriate when the person, in addition to showing a marked inability to experience pleasure, has at least three of the following characteristics of mood or behavior: (a) a quality of depressed mood that is experienced by the person as distinctly different from normal grieving; (b) depression that is regularly worse in the morning; (c) awakening that occurs at least two hours earlier than usual in the morning; (d) marked psychomotor retardation or agitation; (e) significant loss of appetite or weight loss; (f) excessive or inappropriate guilt.

Many clinicians believe that depressions having melancholic features (as defined here) are unlikely to have been precipitated by identifiable preceding stressors and are deeply rooted in the biology of the organism.

figures ranging from 39 to 95 percent of cases, averaging about 63 percent. Despite the variable results from different studies, it is clear that the risk of having additional episodes is considerable for the individual experiencing a first one. The duration of a given episode is estimated, on average, to be about four months (Perris, 1982). The traditional view has been that between episodes the person suffering from a recurrent major affective disorder is essentially normal. That view has been increasingly called into question as more and better research data have become available (Coryell & Winokur, 1982). Indeed, given the frequently devastating effects such episodes have on the life circumstances of a person, it would be surprising to find no lasting compromises in personal adjustment. And, presumably, such compromises increase with successive episodes.

The prospects for "complete recovery" (i.e., no recurrence of an episode for a period of five years) from major depression are not particularly encouraging, being somewhere on the order of 40 percent (Coryell & Winokur, 1982). However, as we learn more about managing depression, there appear to be definite possibilities for limiting both the severity and the dura-

tion of attacks, and increasingly for preventing recurrences (Klerman, 1982).

Bipolar disorder.   As we have seen, depression and mania—despite their seeming opposition—are sometimes closely related. Cyclothymic disorder, described earlier, is a case in point, but a far more dramatic one is bipolar disorder. The sixth-century physician Alexander Trallianus was probably the first to recognize recurrent cycles of mania and melancholia in the same person, thus anticipating by several hundred years Bonet's (1684) "folie maniaco-mélancolique" and Falret's (1854) "folie circulaire." It remained for Kraepelin, however, in 1899, to introduce the term *manic-depressive psychosis* and to clarify the clinical picture. Kraepelin described the disorder as a series of attacks of elation and depression, with periods of relative normality in between and a generally favorable prognosis.

Bipolar affective disorder is distinguished by at least one episode of mania. Bipolar disorders are classified as depressive, manic, or mixed, according to their predominant pattern. Even though a patient is exhibiting only manic features, it is assumed that there is in fact a bipolar disorder. Substantial manic or mixed patterns are much less common than the depressive pattern.

The features of the depressive form of bipolar disorder are clinically (that is, by observation alone) indistinguishable from those of major depression (Perris, 1982), and we will therefore not describe them in detail here. The essential difference is that these depressive episodes alternate with manic ones, either closely or separated by an interval of relatively normal functioning.

As in the case of the relationship between depressive symptoms of cyclothymic disorder and those of major depression, manic symptoms in bipolar disorder tend to be extreme forms of symptoms associated with the hypomanic phase of cyclothymic disorder. The person who experiences a manic episode has a markedly elevated, euphoric, and expansive mood, often interrupted by occasional outbursts of irritability—particularly when others refuse to "go along with" the manic person's antics and schemes. There is a notable increase in activity, which may appear as an unrelievable restlessness. Mental activity, too, speeds up, so that the individual may evidence a "flight of ideas" and may experience thoughts that "race" through the brain. High levels of verbal output in speech or in writing are common features. Inflated self-esteem is a constant element and at the severe level becomes frankly delusional, so that the person harbors feelings of enormous grandeur and power. The person sleeps only briefly, and in extreme cases rarely or hardly at all. Typically, personal and cultural inhibitions are let go, and the individual may indulge in foolish ventures, ignore personal hygiene, make crude and inappropriate sexual advances, or otherwise indicate some form of contempt for conventional restraints.

The following conversation illustrates a manic episode of moderate severity. The patient is a 46-year-old woman.

Dr.: Hello, how are you today?

Pt.: Fine, fine, and how are you, Doc? You're looking pretty good. I never felt better in my life. Could I go for a schnapps now? Say, you're new around here, I never saw you before—and not bad! How's about you and me stepping out tonight if I can get that sour old battleship of a nurse to give me back my dress. It's low cut and it'll wow 'em. Even in this old rag, all

the doctors give me the eye. You know I'm a model. Yep, I was No. 1—used to dazzle them in New York, London and Paris. Hollywood has been angling with me for a contract.

Dr.: Is that what you did before you came here?

Pt.: I was a society queen . . . entertainer of kings and presidents. I've got five grown sons and I wore out three husbands getting them . . . about ready for a couple of more now. There's no woman like me, smart, brainy, beautiful, and sexy. You can see I don't believe in playing myself down. If you are good and know you're good you have to speak out, and I know what I've got.

Dr.: Why are you in this hospital?

Pt.: That's just the trouble. My husbands never could understand me. I was too far above them. I need someone like me with savoir faire you know, somebody that can get around, intelligent, lots on the ball. Say, where can I get a schnapps around here—always like one before dinner. Someday I'll cook you a meal. I've got special recipes like you never ate before . . . sauces, wines, desserts. Boy, it's making me hungry. Say, have you got anything for me to do around here? I've been showing these slowpokes how to make up beds but I want something more in line with my talents.

Dr.: What would you like to do?

Pt.: Well, I'm thinking of organizing a show, singing, dancing, jokes. I can do it all myself but I want to know what you think about it. I'll bet there's some schnapps in the kitchen. I'll look around later. You know what we need here . . . a dance at night. I could play the piano, and teach them the latest steps. Wherever I go I'm the life of the party.

This case is particularly illustrative of the inflated self-esteem characteristic of the manic individual.

The following case description is interesting in its simultaneous and interactive portrayal of *two* manic patients, one severely disturbed and the other less so. The former, in particular, provides an illustration of the extreme excitement that can occur during a manic reaction. The scene is the courtyard of a public mental hospital in the days prior to the advent of effective antimanic medication.

A manic patient had climbed upon the small platform in the middle of the yard and was delivering an impassioned lecture to a number of patients sitting on benches surrounding the platform. Most of the audience were depressed patients who were hallucinating and muttering to themselves and not paying a bit of attention to the speaker. However, the speaker had an "assistant" in the form of another manic patient who would move rapidly around the circle of benches shaking the occupants and exhorting them to pay attention. If anyone started to leave, the assistant would plump him back in his seat in no uncertain terms. In the background were a number of apparently schizophrenic patients who were pacing a given number of steps back and forth, and beyond was a high wire fencing surrounding the yard.

The speaker herself was in a state of delirious mania. She had torn her clothing to shreds and was singing and shouting at the top of her voice. So rapidly did her thoughts move from one topic to another that her "speech" was almost a complete word hash, although occasional sentences such as "You goddam bitches" and "God loves everybody, do you hear?" could be made out. These points were illustrated by wild gestures, screaming, and outbursts of song. In the delivery of her talk, she moved restlessly back and forth on the platform, occasionally falling off the platform in her wild excitement. Her ankles and legs were bleeding from rubbing the edge of the platform during these falls, but she was completely oblivious of her injuries.

Fortunately, the degree of excitement in manic reactions can now be markedly reduced by means of various drugs, and scenes such as this need no longer occur. The typical stages in a manic reaction are summarized in the **HIGH-LIGHT** on page 312.

Bipolar disorder, like major depression, is typically an intermittent or episodic phenomenon, although with both forms of disorder a relatively small number of patients who otherwise meet diagnostic criteria remain disturbed over long periods of time, even years. It is not known whether or not these unremitting cases represent fundamentally different psychopathological entities. The diagnostic subcategories for bipolar disorder—mixed, manic, and depressed—are intended to refer to particular, present episodes. The latter two of these are self-explanatory; the "mixed" is something of an anomaly. "Mixed" cases are those in which the "full symptomatic picture" of both manic and (major) depressive episodes occur, either intermixed or alternating every few days. Such cases do indeed occur, although they are rare.

As we have seen, a person who appears to be depressed cannot be diagnosed as bipolar unless he or she has exhibited at least one manic episode in the past. This means that many bipolars whose initial episode(s) is (are) depressive in na-

ture will be misdiagnosed, at least at the outset and possibly (if no manic episodes are observed) throughout their lives. On the other hand, misdiagnosis is automatically prevented if the person presents distinctly manic symptoms: by definition, this would be a bipolar disorder, even though researchers have acknowledged the existence of a unipolar type of manic disorder (Andreasen, 1982; Nurnberger et al., 1979). The sometimes arbitrary nature of the DSM-III diagnostic system is perhaps nowhere clearer than in this instance. Nevertheless, we will here follow DSM-III in assuming that bipolar disorder is a distinct entity and that all cases of mania not accounted for on other grounds (e.g., brain damage, toxicity) are instances of bipolar disorder.

Persons affected with a bipolar disorder seem in many ways to be even more unfortunate than those who suffer from major depression. On average, they have their first episode at a younger age (25–30 versus 40–45); they suffer from more episodes in the course of their lifetimes (although these episodes tend to be about a month shorter in duration); and they have a substantially higher mortality rate from suicide and other causes (Perris, 1982). The long-term outcomes for the two forms of disorder, however, do not appear to differ greatly, and the probabilities of "full recovery" (i.e., symptom-free for a period of five years) are about equally discouraging—about 40 percent (Coryell & Winokur, 1982).

In contrast to the gender neutrality of most types of maladaptive behavior, affective disorders at all levels of severity are more prevalent among women than among men, at a ratio approaching two-to-one overall. While this gender discrepancy is quite marked in the case of major depression, it is lessened but still discernable for bipolar disorder (Boyd & Weissman, 1982). The diminishing magnitude of the discrepancy in bipolar disorder may be related to an apparent tendency for specifically manic episodes to occur more frequently in males (Angst, 1980). In any event, the finding of a sex differential may have considerable theoretical importance. At least with respect to major depression, the discrepancy appears to be neither artifactual nor a product of differential psychosocial advantage for men versus women. For some reason, women seem to be much more prone than men to repeated depressive attacks (Amenson & Lewin-

HIGHLIGHT

Stages of a manic episode based on daily behavior ratings of a hospitalized patient

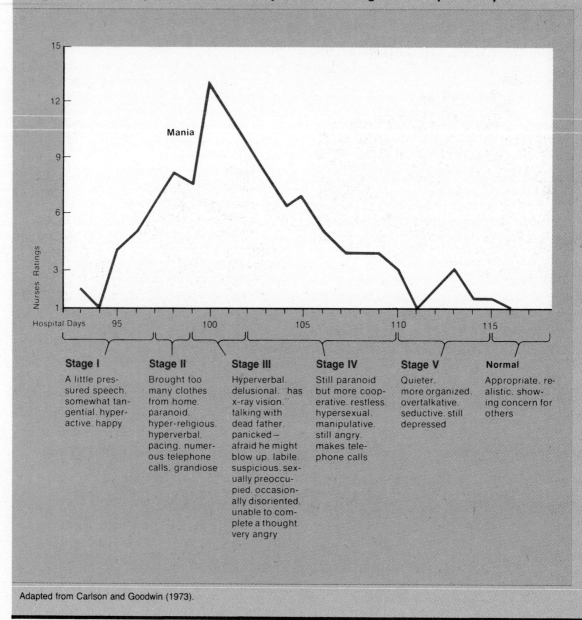

Stage I

A little pressured speech. somewhat tangential. hyperactive. happy

Stage II

Brought too many clothes from home. paranoid. hyper-religious. hyperverbal, pacing. numerous telephone calls. grandiose

Stage III

Hyperverbal. delusional. "has x-ray vision." talking with dead father. panicked— afraid he might blow up. labile. suspicious. sexually preoccupied. occasionally disoriented. unable to complete a thought. very angry

Stage IV

Still paranoid but more cooperative. restless. hypersexual. manipulative. still angry. makes telephone calls

Stage V

Quieter. more organized. overtalkative. seductive. still depressed

Normal

Appropriate. realistic. showing concern for others

Adapted from Carlson and Goodwin (1973).

On occasion, affective disorders can become severe enough to warrant hospitalization.

sohn, 1981). We cannot rule out a biological explanation at this time, nor can we confirm it.

Schizoaffective disorder. Occasionally, clinicians are confronted with a patient whose disorder of mood is the equal of anything seen in the major affective disorders but whose mental and cognitive processes are so deranged as to suggest the presence of a *schizophrenic* psychosis (see Chapter 10). Such cases are quite likely to be diagnosed as schizoaffective disorder (listed in DSM-III under *Psychotic disorders not elsewhere classified*). It is a controversial diagnosis. Some clinicians believe these individuals are *basically* schizophrenic; others believe they are suffering primarily from affective psychoses; and still others consider it a distinct entity unto itself. The suggestion that a person might be *both* schizophrenic and affectively disordered is not generally accepted, although we find this a reasonable suggestion.

The often very severe disturbances of thought seen in these conditions, such as mood-incongruent delusions and hallucinations, are indeed reminiscent of schizophrenic phenomena. Unlike schizophrenia, however, the schizoaffective pattern tends to be very episodic, with a good prognosis for individual attacks, with lucid periods between episodes, and with a relatively good prognosis for recovery using the five-year criterion (Angst, 1980)—all characteristics of affective disorders.

The following case illustrates the mixed picture one sees in this type of disorder.

"A 44-year-old mother of three teenagers is hospitalized for treatment of depression. She gives the following history: One year previously, after a terminal argument with her lover, she became acutely psychotic. She was frightened that people were going to kill her and heard voices of friends and strangers talking about killing her, sometimes talking to each other. She heard her own thoughts broadcast aloud and was afraid that others could also hear what she was thinking. Over a three-week period she stayed in her apartment, had new locks put on the doors, kept the shades down, and avoided everyone but her immediate family. She was unable to sleep at night because the voices kept her awake, and unable to eat because of a constant "lump" in her throat. In retrospect, she cannot say whether she was depressed, denies being elated or overactive, and remembers only that she was terrified of what would happen to her. The family persuaded her to enter a hospital, where, after six weeks of treatment with Thorazine, the voices stopped. She remembers feeling "back to normal" for a week or two, but then she seemed to lose her energy and motivation to do anything. She became increasingly depressed, lost her appetite, and woke at 4:00 or 5:00 every morning and was unable to get back to sleep. She could no longer read a newspaper or watch TV because she couldn't concentrate.

"The patient's condition has persisted for nine months. She has done very little except sit in her apartment, staring at the walls. Her children have managed most of the cooking, shopping, bill-paying, etc. She has continued in outpatient treatment, and was maintained on Thorazine until four months before this admission. There has been no recurrence of the psychotic symptoms since the medication was discontinued; but her depression, with all the accompanying symptoms, has persisted.

"In discussing her past history, the patient is rather guarded. There is, however, no evidence of a diagnosable illness before last year. She apparently is a shy, emotionally constricted person who 'has never broken any rules.' She has been separated from her husband for ten years, but in that time has had two enduring relationships with boyfriends. In addition to rearing three apparently healthy and very likable children, she cared for a succession of foster children full time in the four years before her illness. She enjoyed this, and was highly valued by the agency she worked for. She has maintained close relationships with a few girl friends and with her extended family." (Spitzer et al., 1981, pp. 235–36)

Causes of affective disorders

In considering the development of major affective disorders, we again find it useful to examine the possible roles of biological, psychosocial, and sociocultural factors.[4]

---

[4]Overviews of research on depression and the delineation of causal models may be found in Blaney (1977), Carson & Carson (1984), and Paykel (1982).

Biological factors. A biological basis for severe manic and depressive reactions is suggested by the fact that once the reaction is underway, it becomes relatively "autonomous" until it runs its course or is interrupted by drugs or other intervention. Attempts to establish a biological basis for these disorders have run the familiar gamut from genetic and constitutional factors through neurophysiological and biochemical alterations; even various related considerations, such as sleep disturbances, have been implicated.

1. *Hereditary predisposition.* The incidence of affective disorders is considerably higher among the relatives of individuals with clinically diagnosed affective disorders than in the population at large. In an early study, Slater (1944) found that approximately 15 percent of the brothers, sisters, parents, and children of "manic-depressive" patients had developed the same disorder, as compared with an expectancy of about 0.5 percent for the general population.

Kallmann (1958) found the concordance rate for these disorders to be much higher for identical than for fraternal twins. Other studies have supported these earlier findings (Perris, 1979).

Twin studies such as those cited above have proven useful in many areas of psychological research. However, various difficulties with the twin method (see, for instance, page 363) led a number of years ago to the invention of the adoption method. This method involves the psychiatric evaluation of persons who were adopted out of their biological families at an early age, and the comparison of their disorders with those of their biological and adoptive family members. If a predisposition to develop a given disorder is inheritable, it should show up (so the logic goes) more often among biological, as opposed to adoptive, relatives of the affected adoptees. Application of the adoption method is much more advanced in relation to schizophrenia than the affective disorders, but the results of two such studies on affective disorders, those of Cadoret (1978) and Mendlewicz and Rainer (1977), have been published as of this writing. Both indicate a genetic influence in the affective disorders, but, unfortunately, neither is methodologically beyond criticism (Carson & Carson, 1984).

Despite these problems, and if one adopts a "weight of evidence" standard, it must be acknowledged that the case for *some* hereditary influence in the affective disorders is quite strong (Nurnberger & Gershon, 1982). The risk for relatives of people with bipolar disorders (including an enhanced risk for *unipolar* disorder) appears to be greater than for relatives of people who suffer from unipolar disorders, but this may merely reflect the likelihood that unipolar disorder is a more diffuse and heterogeneous category (Carson & Carson, 1984).

It should be noted that the disproportionately high number of female cases of affective disorder has been tied to the evidence for genetic transmission of predisposition. On the basis of findings indicating higher concordance among female than male members of families, Winokur, Clayton, and Reich (1969) proposed that the gene or genes in question may be located on the X chromosome. If this were totally true, then there would be *no* evidence of father-to-son transmission, since the X chromosome in males can only be inherited from the mother. The investigators in this early study found precisely this anomaly. Since then, however, numerous cases of apparent father-to-son transmission have been unearthed. The overall picture, recently reviewed by Nurnberger and Gershon (1982), has thus become somewhat murky—and includes at least one confirmation of the Winokur et al. father-son anomaly (Mendlewicz, 1980). Nonetheless, research continues on the X-linkage hypothesis, particularly into its possible predisposing role in bipolar disorders.

2. *Neurophysiological factors.* Following the early lead of Pavlov, a great deal of interest has been expressed in the possibility that imbalances in excitatory and inhibitory processes may predispose some people toward extreme mood swings. That is, manic disorders might result from excessive excitation and weakened inhibition, and depressive disorders from excessive inhibition.

To support this viewpoint, several investigators have pointed out that in monkeys—highly excitable and unequilibrated animals—the processes of excitation do in fact predominate over the processes of inhibition. In many other species, including humans, there is a greater equilibrium of excitatory and inhibitory processes, but within any species there are wide individual differences, probably stemming from both genetic and environmental influences. Presumably

such neurophysiological differences could predispose some individuals to affective disorders under stress.

In considering the possible role of neurophysiological factors in manic and depressive reactions, it is relevant to note Engel's (1962) conclusion that the central nervous system is apparently "organized to mediate two opposite patterns of response to a mounting need." The first is an active, goal-oriented pattern directed toward achieving the gratification of needs from external sources; the second, in contrast, is a defensive pattern aimed at reducing activity, heightening the barrier against stimulation, and conserving the energy and resources of the organism. The latter, as we have seen, is closely related to phenomena observed even in mild depressive states. Manic reactions appear to be an exaggerated form of the first response pattern.

But the inhibition/excitation view appears to be oversimplified as an explanation of manic and depressive disorders. It does not explain, for example, how the two extremes can sometimes be observed to exist simultaneously in the same patient. In any event, a great deal more research is needed before we can arrive at definitive conclusions concerning the role of neurophysiological factors in the severe affective disorders.

3. *Biochemical factors.* Kraepelin considered manic-depressive psychoses to be toxic, and a good deal of research effort has been directed toward finding possible metabolic alterations and brain pathology in individuals with these disorders. Increasingly prominent since the 1960s has been the view that depression and mania both may arise from disruptions in the delicate balance of the functioning levels of biogenic amines in the brain.

Biogenic amines serve as neural transmitters or modulators that regulate the movement of nerve impulses across the synapse from one neuron to the next. A growing body of evidence suggests that various biological therapies often used to treat severe affective disorders—such as electroconvulsive therapy, potent antidepressant drugs, and lithium carbonate—may affect the functioning of certain biogenic amines in the brain. This, in turn, would affect the transmission of nerve impulses within the brain, which would, of course, have widespread effects at the behavioral level. Two such amines, *norepine-*

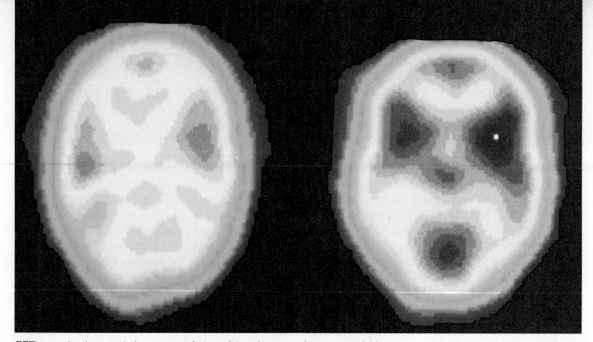

PET scans (positron emission tomography) can be used to trace the rates at which glucose is consumed in the brain. Here, green and yellow indicate low to moderate rates of consumption; red indicates relatively higher rates. The normal brain at left shows intermediate levels of activity. The brain at right, that of a person diagnosed as bipolar, suggests increased glucose consumption. Researchers cannot yet make a causal connection between varying levels of brain activity and specific disorders; however, differences such as those shown here are creating great interest among members of the scientific community.

phrine and *5-hydroxytryptamine* (also known as *serotonin*), have been implicated in the affective disorders. It has been found, for example, that drugs known to have potent antidepressant properties have the biochemical effect of increasing the concentrations of one or the other (or both) of these transmitters at the synaptic juncture. Such evidence is only correlational, but it nonetheless constitutes an important lead in the search for causes. Studies of this sort—that is, administering certain drugs and taking note of both their biochemical and their behavioral effects—have been increasingly employed in attempts to identify subtypes of affective disorder (Akiskal, 1979). By now, however, it is quite clear that simple answers are unlikely to be forthcoming in the biogenic amine area (Zis & Goodwin, 1982).

Although we have not yet pinpointed the underlying biochemical mechanisms involved, the evidence that such mechanisms play a causal role, especially in the maintenance of these disorders, is becoming quite compelling. This case rests essentially on three facts that are beyond reasonable dispute: (a) a predisposition to this type of disorder may be genetically transmitted; (b) the behavioral symptoms of the disorder of-

ten abate promptly with certain biological interventions; and (c) certain profound alterations of bodily function, such as changes in the sleep cycle, often accompany the affective symptoms.

Psychosocial factors. Growing awareness of biological factors in the etiology of affective disorders does not, of course, imply that psychosocial factors are irrelevant. In Chapter 4 we outlined various ways in which biological influences may interact with life experience to produce an observed behavior. In the present case, evidence for an important psychological element in most of these types of disorder is at least as strong as evidence for biological factors. Most likely, then, we are dealing with a complex interaction between the two.

1. *Stress as a precipitating factor.* In Chapter 8, we learned something of the ways in which psychosocial stressors may lead to altered bodily functioning. We are now in a position to suggest that such stressors may also affect the biochemical balances in the brain, at least in predisposed persons.

Barchas and his colleagues (1978), in a summary of research in this area, suggest that psychosocial stressors may cause long-term changes

Life events that trigger overwhelming feelings of loss and pain can act as precipitating factors in the development of affective disorders. This photo vividly captures the intense response of a native Frenchman to the occupation of his country by German troops during World War II.

in the manner in which impulses are transmitted from one brain neuron to another, and that these changes may play a role in the development of affective disorders. Essentially the same point has been made by other leading researchers in the field, notably Akiskal (1979).

There is no basic incompatibility between biochemical and psychosocial approaches to understanding the affective disorders. In fact, evidence of interactions between biological and psychosocial factors of the kind described here represent a breakthrough of enormous importance in our understanding of the major affective disorders. At the same time, this evidence should not be allowed to blind us to the probability that in some affective disturbances—certainly the milder ones—the contribution of an abnormal biological factor will turn out to be minimal or nonexistent. We have already seen that the milder depressions almost always have clear stressor antecedents; the occurrence of depressive affect following "losses," for instance, would seem understandable on psychological grounds alone—not requiring the postulation of extraordinary biochemical changes.

In the case of psychotic affective disorders, too, most investigators have been impressed with the high incidence of aversive life events that apparently have served as precipitating factors. Beck (1967) has provided a broad classification of the most frequently encountered precipitating circumstances: (a) situations that tend to lower self-esteem; (b) thwarting of important goals or the posing of an insoluble dilemma; (c) physical disease or abnormality that activates ideas of deterioration or death; (d) single stressors of overwhelming magnitude; (e) several stressors occurring in a series; and (f) insidious stressors unrecognized as such by the affected person. Paykel (1982) has comprehensively reviewed the literature on "life events" occurring before episodes of affective disorder and has arrived at conclusions generally in agreement with Beck's earlier listing. In particular, and perhaps not surprisingly, separations from people important in one's life (through death, for example) are strongly associated with the emergence of depressive states, although such losses also tend to precede other types of disorder as well. Research data on life events preceding specifically *manic* attacks are contradictory and inconclusive (Dunner & Hall, 1980). The **HIGHLIGHT** on this page summarizes the stressors that had most often preceded severe depression in one study.

An interesting example of the apparent role of aversive life events as precipitating causes of psychotic affective disorders has been described by Hartmann (1968).

A patient had six severe manic episodes between the ages of 44 and 59, all of which required hospitalization. The patient also had a number of depressive episodes, two of which required hospitalization. Typically this patient tended to be overactive in his general functioning, but during the early autumn he usually either ran for a political office himself or took an active role in someone else's campaign. In the process, he would become increasingly manic; when the ventures led to defeat—which they almost invariably did—he would become depressed in November or December.

Other descriptions of major affective disorders somewhat subtly convey the notion that these disorders often occur *de novo*—out of the blue, so to speak—in the absence of either notable personal distress or significant psychosocial antecedents. This implies that such episodes must be *endogenous*—caused from within—rather than precipitated by life events. Since the issue is an important one, we shall take a closer look at the evidence.

Estimates of the proportion of affective disorders preceded by precipitating stressors vary from almost none (Winokur & Pitts, 1964) to almost all (Leff et al., 1970; Paykel, 1973; Travis, 1933). In general, studies that adhere most closely to precise research methodology tend to produce the highest estimates of antecedent stress. Partly as a result of such data, there is currently considerable doubt as to the validity of sharply distinguishing an endogenous subset of affective disorders (Andreasen, 1982; Prange, 1973; Stainbrook, 1977; Thompson & Hendrie, 1972; White, Davis, & Cantrell, 1977). The "spontaneous" occurrence of affective disorders seems to be at best an infrequent phenomenon, and even where that seems to be the case we may have overlooked a stressor that was not obvious.

If we take the position—and the data seem to justify doing so—that some people *are* more prone than others to develop affective disorders, then it would seem reasonable to suppose that

HIGHLIGHT
Stressors preceding severe depression

In an intensive study of 40 depressed patients, Leff, Roatch, and Bunney (1970) found that each patient had been subjected to multiple stressful events prior to early symptoms and to a clustering of such events during the month preceding the actual breakdown in functioning. The chart shows the ten types of stressors most frequently involved.

Stressful event	Patients affected (From total of 40)
	0 10 20 30 40
Sexual (personal) identity threat. e.g., failure to meet perceived male or female role demands	30
Changes in marital relationship	19
A move, often involving changes in work	18
Being made to face denied reality	13
Physical illness	12
Failure in job performance	11
Failure of children to meet parents' goal	10
Increased responsibility	10
Damage to social status	7
Death of important person	7

Strikingly similar to the findings of Leff and her associates are those of Paykel (1973). In that study, which involved 185 depressed patients, it was found that comparable stressful events preceded the onset of the depressive breakdown. In order of significance, these events were categorized as (a) marital difficulties, (b) work moves or changes in work conditions, (c) serious personal illness, and (d) death or serious illness of an immediate family member. More recent reports have supported these findings (Brown, 1972; Brown, 1974; Paykel, 1982).

these high-risk individuals would react more intensely to subtle, easily overlooked stressors than would individuals less at risk for this type of disorder. And if there is a threshold above which biological factors that increase symptom intensity play an important role with progressive mood deviation, then these high-risk, low-stress cases would exhibit relatively severe symptoms. Unfortunately, the available evidence does not permit us to evaluate this hypothesis directly.

2. *Predisposing personality characteristics.* Beck (1967) argues convincingly that psychosocial stressors provoke severe depressive psychoses only in persons who already have a negative cognitive set, consisting of negative views of the self, negative views of the world, and negative views of the future. According to this hypothesis, the stressor merely serves to activate negative cognitions that have heretofore been dormant. The result is an abnormally extreme negative affect. Obviously, Beck's "negative cognitive set" is in the nature of a *psychological* predisposing variable.

It might also be expected that exaggerated mood swings in the child would be fostered by observations of similar emotional patterns in the parents, and would then persist as learned maladaptive response patterns. The high incidence of affective disorders in the families of manic and depressive patients would have provided greater than average opportunity for such learning. In their study of 14 depressed children, Poznanski and Zrull (1970) reported that five of the parents were depressed at the time of the child's referral; one father had commited suicide, apparently during an episode of depression. These investigators concluded:

". . . in those cases where parental depression was known, one source of the child's depression could be based on identification with the parent, particularly the parent's affective reaction to stress and difficulties within his own life." (p. 14)

Attempts to delineate a typical personality pattern for adults who later suffer serious affective episodes have met with limited success. In general, however, manic patients—whatever their childhood backgrounds may have been—are described as ambitious, outgoing, energetic, sociable, and often highly successful, both prior

to their breakdown and after remission. As contrasted with members of control groups, they tend to place a higher conscious value on achievement, are very conventional in their beliefs, and are deeply concerned about what others think of them. Depressive patients share these characteristics, but they appear to be more obsessive, anxious, and self-deprecatory. They also tend to show an unusually rigid conscience development, which prevents the overt expression of hostile feelings and makes them particularly prone to feelings of guilt and self-blame when things go wrong.[5] The definitely bipolar types—those destined to experience affective swings between mania and depression—might be expected to share the personality characteristics of both groups, perhaps in alternating phases. Depue et al. (1981) present strong evidence suggesting that this is the case. It must be noted, however, that all such findings are subject to numerous qualifications. Many persons who exhibit the traits described will never have a serious affective disorder, and many who do not *will* have such a disorder.

3. *Feelings of helplessness and loss of hope.* Feelings of helplessness and hopelessness have been emphasized as basic to depressive reactions by investigators of differing theoretical orientations. Bibring (1953), a psychoanalyst, held that the basic mechanism of depression is "the ego's shocking awareness of its helplessness in regard to its aspirations . . . such that the depressed person . . . has lost his incentives and gives up, not the goals, but pursuing them, since this proves to be useless" (p. 39). In later studies, other investigators have referred to "learned helplessness" in severe depression; presumably the individual, perceiving no way of coping with the stress, eventually stops fighting and gives up (Hiroto & Seligman, 1975; Seligman, 1973, 1975; Weiss, 1974).

Laboratory experiments have identified conditions that can lead to "learned helplessness," but attempts to relate such conditions directly to clinical depression have not fared very well. Animals with experimentally induced "helpless-

---

[5]The description of characteristics that are commonly ascribed to the personality makeup of manic and depressive patients is based on the following references: Akiskal and McKinney (1975), APA (1980), Bagley (1973), Beck (1971), Becker (1977), Becker and Altrocchi (1968), Chodoff (1972), Ferster (1973), Lewinsohn and Graf (1973), Libet and Lewinsohn (1973), Peto (1972), and Von Zerssen (1982).

ness" do not respond to opportunities to avoid aversive stimulation. However, it is apparent that humans in general do not behave like laboratory animals when subjected to conditions that supposedly induce helplessness (see the special issue of the *Journal of Abnormal Psychology*, February 1978). It also appears that efforts to salvage the learned helplessness model of depression by substantially revising it (Abramson et al., 1978) have not significantly improved its power (Carson & Carson, 1984).

Feelings of helplessness and hopelessness and their behavioral consequences have been dealt with from a behavioristic viewpoint by several investigators. Lazarus (1968) has concluded that "depression may be regarded as a function of inadequate or insufficient reinforcers . . . some significant reinforcer has been withdrawn" (pp. 84–85). Similarly, Lewinsohn (1974) has concluded that feelings of depression—along with other symptoms of this clinical picture—can be elicited when the individual's behavior no longer results in accustomed reinforcement or gratification. The failure to receive "response-contingent positive reinforcement" (RCPR), in turn, leads to a reduction in effort and activity, thus resulting in even less chance of coping with aversive conditions and achieving need gratification. The question here, however, is not whether depressed persons have low rates of RCPR—they certainly do, almost by definition—but rather whether this is a cause or an effect of the depressed state. The evidence suggests that it is an *effect*, thus illustrating once again the hazards of confusing cause with correlation.

Various additional aspects of the behavioristic approach to depression are discussed at length by Blaney (1977), Carson and Carson (1984), and Eastman (1976). As these discussions are somewhat technical, their contents will not be reviewed here. Suffice it to say that much work is continuing in this area, and that various kinds of "reinforcement" approaches to the analysis of depression are showing promise, albeit in some unanticipated ways. We will get to some of this work in considering the interpersonal aspects of depression, below.

While the behavioristic perspective seems potentially helpful in understanding depressive reactions, it would seem at first glance less applicable to manic reactions. However, one might speculate that the latter represent attempts to obtain needed reinforcers via an indiscriminate increase in activity level. As in the case of depressive reactions, however, such reinforcers are not forthcoming. Here the conclusion of Ferster (1973) seems directly applicable: "It seems likely . . . that any factor which causes a temporary or long-term reduction in positively reinforced ways of acting . . . will also produce bizarre or irrational behavior as a by-product" (p. 859). Not adequately accounted for in this explanation, however, are the feelings of euphoria that characterize manic reactions.

4. *Extreme defenses against stress.* Manic and depressive psychoses may be viewed as two different but related defense-oriented strategies for dealing with severe stress.

In the case of mania, individuals try to escape their difficulties by a "flight into reality." In less severe form, this type of reaction to stress is shown by the person who goes on a round of parties to try to forget a broken love affair, or tries to escape from a threatening life situation by restless activity, occupying every moment with work, athletics, sexual affairs, and countless other crowded activities—all performed with professed gusto but with little true enjoyment.

In mania this pattern is exaggerated. With a tremendous expenditure of energy, the manic individual tries to deny feelings of helplessness and hopelessness and to play a role of competence. Once this mode of coping with difficulties is adopted, it is maintained until it has spent itself in emotional exhaustion, for the only other alternative is an admission of defeat and inevitable depression. This is well brought out in the following case of a moderately disturbed manic patient.

"He neglected his meals and rest hours, and was highly irregular, impulsive, and distractible in his adaptations to ward routine. Without apparent intent to be annoying or disturbing he sang, whistled, told pointless off-color stories, visited indiscriminately, and flirted crudely with the nurses and female patients. Superficially he appeared to be in high spirits, and yet one day when he was being gently chided over some particular irresponsible act he suddenly slumped in a chair, covered his face with his hands, began sobbing, and cried, 'For Pete's sake, doc, let me be. Can't you see that I've just got to act happy?' " (Masserman, 1961, pp. 66–67)

Unfortunately, as manic disorders proceed, any defensive value they may have had is negated, for thought processes are speeded up to a point where the individual can no longer "process" incoming information with any degree of efficiency. In a manner of speaking, "the programmer loses control of the computer," resulting in severe personality decompensation.

In the case of depression, the person apparently gains some relief from the intolerable stress situation by admitting defeat and withdrawing psychologically from the fight. Also, the slowing down of thought processes may serve to decrease suffering by reducing the sheer quantity of painful thoughts. However, these feelings of relief are gained at the expense of a sense of adequacy and self-esteem, and thus are accompanied by marked guilt and self-accusation. Like the soldier who panics and flees from combat, the individual may feel relieved to be out of an intolerable situation but may also feel guilty and devalued.

Since depressive patients tend to blame themselves for their difficulties, they often go over the past with a microscope, picking out any possible sins of omission or commission and exaggerating their importance in relation to the present difficulties. They may even accuse themselves of selfishness, unfaithfulness, or hostile acts that did not occur. These self-accusations seem to be attempts to explain and find some meaning in their predicament and at the same time achieve some measure of expiation and atonement. The entire process has a certain paradoxical quality: on the one hand, the depressive individual appears to feel entirely lacking in any capacity to determine events that might occur and on the other hand tends to accept personal responsibility for all negative events that *do* occur. Clearly, this requires a degree of cognitive distortion, even in relatively mild cases.

It may be that the remission of depressive disorders even without treatment occurs because the effort at expiation and atonement has been successful. In such cases, there may be a gradual working through of feelings of unworthiness and guilt, in which the individual pays the price for past failures by self-punishment and is thereby cleansed and ready for another go at life.

In bipolar reactions, the shift from mania to depression may tend to occur when the defensive function of the manic reaction breaks down. Similarly, the shift from depression to mania may tend to occur when the individual, devalued and guilt-ridden by inactivity and an inability to cope, finally feels compelled to attempt some countermeasure, however desperate.

While the view of manic and depressive psychoses as extreme defenses seems plausible up to a certain level of severity of disorder, it is becoming very difficult, as we have seen, to account satisfactorily for the more extreme versions of these states without acknowledging the importance of contributory biological causation. It seems that certain biological mechanisms become involved at some point and thereafter tend to maintain the disorder. The effectiveness of biological treatment in alleviating severe episodes lends support to this hypothesis. And yet there remain questions in this area, if only because the *impact* of manic and depressive behavior on others is so notable and may contribute to the maintenance.

5. *Interpersonal effects of affective disorders.* The manic individual apparently feels that wishing to rely on others or to be taken care of is threatening and unacceptable. Instead, such an individual maintains self-esteem and feelings of adequacy and strength by establishing a social role in which control of other people is possible (Janowsky, El-Yousef, & Davis, 1974). The **HIGH-LIGHT** on page 322 describes several techniques by which such control may be achieved.

On the other hand, the depressed individual tends to adopt a role that attempts to place others in the position of providing support and care—and thus reinforcement (Ferster, 1973; Janowsky et al., 1970). Positive reinforcement does not necessarily follow, however. Depressive behavior can, and frequently does, elicit negative feelings and rejection in other persons (Coyne, 1976; Hammen & Peters, 1977, 1978; Howes & Hokanson, 1979). Coyne (1976) has suggested that the presence or absence of support may depend on whether the depressed individual is skillful enough to circumvent and turn to advantage the negative affect he or she tends to create in the other person. Especially if the other person is prone to guilt feelings, the skillful depressive patient may be able to extract considerable sympathy and support, at least over the short term.

HIGHLIGHT

Playing the manic game

Janowsky and his associates (1970, 1974), noting the extent to which manic patients intentionally induce discomfort in other people, pointed to the following techniques that are used in "playing the manic game."

1. Manipulating the self-esteem of others—either lowering or raising it—as a means of exerting leverage over them.

2. Discovering areas of sensitivity and vulnerability in others for purposes of exploitation.

3. Projecting responsibility in such a way that other people become responsible for the manic's own actions.

4. Progressively testing limits by challenging them or finding loopholes in them.

5. Creating interpersonal distance between themselves and others by deliberately evoking the anger of and alienating staff members.

Although the reasons for the use of these techniques are not clear, these investigators suggest that the manic's feeling of being threatened by and unable to rely on others may be a contributing factor. In any event, these interpersonal maneuvers appeared typical of the clinical picture in mania and disappeared when the manic episode remitted.

Observations such as these raise questions about the extent to which depressive symptoms function as a sort of inept and defeated attempt to exert power over other people. We do not as yet have reliable answers to such questions, although the casual experience of most of us in interacting with depressed people is that of feeling "under pressure." We do know that depressed persons can be quite sensitive about power cues and that they are not averse to the use of power (Hokanson et al., 1980).

These and other considerations discussed earlier in the chapter may mean that we should look more closely at issues of power in depression—and conceivably in mania as well. Arieti (1982; Arieti & Bemporad, 1980) has suggested the existence of two types of depression, one involving submission to a dominant personality (and the consequent failure to thrive as a person), the other concerned with failure to achieve unattainable goals. Blatt et al. (1982) present data supporting such a dichotomy, identifying dependent and self-criticizing depressive modes that correspond to the Arieti subtypes. Coyne, Aldwin, and Lazarus (1981), in an imaginative survey on coping with stress, amply document the dependency element in their depressed subjects but report surprisingly little evidence of self-criticism. Since self-criticism is normally considered a central element in depression, this is a somewhat puzzling finding. These authors are probably correct in asserting that more attention needs to be paid to the role of interpersonal relationships in depressive disorders.

Other investigators have seen depressive reactions as an attempt to communicate a particular message. As Hill (1968) has expressed it,

"Symptoms, then, whether they be verbal expressions, deviant behavior, or simple motor postures or movements, are forms of communication. They are postures in the sense that they communicate the internal need state of the patient, his distress, his fear and anger, his remorse, his humble view of himself, his demands, and his dependency." (p. 456)

Depressive reactions can often be seen as attempts of the individual to communicate feelings of discouragement and despair—to say, in effect, "I have needs that you are failing to meet." Too often, however, this communication goes unheeded. Thus in failing marriages, which are commonly associated with depressive reactions, we may see one partner trying to communicate his or her unmet expectations, distress, and dependency—and then becoming increasingly depressed and disturbed when the other partner fails to make the hoped-for response.

General sociocultural factors. The incidence of affective disorders seems to vary considerably among different societies: in some, manic episodes are more frequent, while in others, depressive episodes are more common.

In early studies, Carothers (1947, 1951, 1959) found manic disorders fairly common among the East Africans he studied, but depressive disorders relatively rare—the exact opposite of their incidence in the United States. He attributed the low incidence of depressive disorders to the fact that in traditional African cultures the individual has not usually been held personally responsible for failures and misfortunes. The culture of the Kenya Africans Carothers observed may be taken as fairly typical in this respect:

Their behavior in all its major aspects is group-determined. Even religion is a matter of offerings and invocations in a group; it is not practiced individually and does not demand any particular attitude on the part of the individual. Similarly, grief over the death of a loved one is not borne in isolation, but appropriate rites are performed amid great public grieving. In these rites, widowed persons express their grief dramatically in ways prescribed by custom, and then resume the tenor of their life as if no bereavement had occurred.

Psychologically speaking, Kenyans receive security because they are part of a larger organism and are not confronted with the problems of individual self-sufficiency, choice, and responsibility that play such a large part in our culture. They do not set themselves unrealistic goals, and they have no need to repress or feel guilty about "dangerous" desires. Their culture actively discourages individual achievement of success, does not consider sexual behavior as evil, and is tolerant of occasional outbursts of aggressive hostility.

In addition, Kenyans feel a great humbleness toward their natural environment, which is often harsh in the extreme. They always expect the worst, and hence can accept misfortunes with equanimity. Here too, responsibility and blame are automatically placed on forces outside themselves. Although they attempt to counteract misfortune and assure success in their ventures by performing appropriate rituals, the outcome is in the hands of the gods. They are not personally responsible and hence do not ordinarily experience self-devaluation or the need for ego-defensive measures. When excessive stress and decompensation do occur, there tends to be a complete disorganization of personality—as in the hebephrenic type of schizophrenia, which is the most common type of psychotic reaction. (Adapted from Carothers, 1947, 1951, 1953)

Needless to say, much has changed in Africa since Carothers made these observations, and more recent data suggest a quite different picture. In general, it appears that as societies develop toward the more "advanced" forms of Western culture, their members become more prone to the development of what might be called Western-style affective disorders (Marsella, 1980).

Even in those nonindustrialized countries where depressive disorders are relatively common, they seem less closely associated with feelings of guilt and self-recrimination than in the developed countries (Kidson & Jones, 1968; Lorr & Klett, 1968; Zung, 1969). In fact, among several groups of Australian aborigines, Kidson and Jones (1968) found not only an absence of guilt and self-recrimination in depressive reactions but also no incidence of attempted or actual suicide. In connection with the latter finding, they stated:

"The absence of suicide can perhaps be explained as a consequence of strong fears of death and also because of the tendency to act out and project hostile impulses." (p. 415)

These conclusions are generally supported in Marsella's (1980) comprehensive review of the cross-cultural literature concerning depression. While various methodological problems make it inadvisable at this time to say with certainty that depression occurs less frequently in cultures other than our own, there is little doubt that it generally takes a different form from that customarily seen here. For example, in some non-Western cultures, symptoms of depression lack substantial psychological components, being limited to the so-called vegetative manifestations, such as sleep disturbance, loss of appetite, weight loss, and loss of sexual interest. Interestingly, in some such cultures there is not even a *concept* of depression that would be reasonably comparable to our own.

In our own society, the role of sociocultural factors in affective disorders remains unclear, but it would appear that conditions that increase life stress lead to a higher incidence of these as well as other disorders. For example, Jaco (1960) found that while psychotic affective disorders were distributed more evenly in the population than schizophrenia, the incidence was significantly higher among the divorced than among the married and about three times higher in urban than in rural areas. Bloom, Asher, and White (1978) have confirmed that divorce is a frequent precipitant of serious depression. There is also some evidence that the incidence of psychotic depression is higher in the upper socioeconomic classes (Bagley, 1973), though this effect appears limited to bipolar disorder (Boyd & Weissman, 1982). Why this should be the case is open to speculation, but the frequency of depression among people of high educational and occupational status has been confirmed in a carefully controlled study (Monnelly, Woodruff, & Robins, 1974). Finally, it should be mentioned that the relatively high percentage of women who suffer from affective disorders may not be found in non-Western cultures (Rao, 1970).

Treatment and outcomes

Antidepressant, tranquilizing, and antianxiety drugs are all used with the more severely disturbed manic and depressive patients. The role of medication in the mild and moderate forms of affective disturbance remains somewhat equivocal at this time, and most such patients are likely to do as well with only psychological forms of therapy (Klerman, 1982; Segal, Yager, & Sullivan, 1976).

Lithium carbonate, a simple mineral salt, was first tried for the treatment of affective disorders in the 1940s by Cade of Australia but was found to have adverse side effects. Thanks to a series of refinements since then, however, lithium therapy has become highly effective in the treatment of manic psychoses and, more recently, in the treatment of some depressive psychoses as well (Coppen, Metcalfe, & Wood, 1982; Davis, 1976; Depue & Monroe, 1978; Segal et al., 1976). It is believed by some that lithium is effective in depression only where the underlying disorder is bipolar in nature. Lithium therapy is often effective in preventing the cycling between manic and depressive episodes.

For most psychotic depressive patients, the drug treatment of choice will be one of the antidepressants such as imipramine, or amitriptyline. These drugs are often effective in prevention as well as treatment for patients subject to recurrent episodes (Davis, 1976; Hollon & Beck, 1978; Mindham, 1982).

Since an estimated 60 percent or more of depressed patients are also anxious, tranquilizing and antianxiety drugs are commonly used in combination with antidepressants (Cole, 1974; Raskin, 1974). Here it is useful to note the reminder of Lehmann (1968) that

"Depression and anxiety are two symptoms which very often co-exist in the same patient. They are nevertheless different symptoms and they may vary independently in their intensity. Of the two symptoms, anxiety is by far the more conspicuous and depression the more dangerous." (p. 18)

Unfortunately, antidepressant drugs usually require a few days before their effects are manifested. Thus electroconvulsive therapy (ECT) is often used with patients who present an immediate and serious suicidal risk (Brown, 1974; T. D. Hurwitz, 1974). There is a complete remission of symptoms in severely depressed patients after about four to six convulsive treatments in some 70 percent of the cases (Kiloh, 1982). Maintenance dosages of antidepressant and antianxiety drugs ordinarily are then used to maintain the treatment gains achieved until the depression has run its course. If necessitated as a last resort, electroconvulsive therapy should be used very sparingly, however, because of its distressing side effects, including temporary memory loss and disorientation. Furthermore, there is compelling evidence that, in at least some cases, ECT produces brain damage (Breggin, 1979).

Treatment is not ordinarily confined to drugs or drugs plus electroconvulsive therapy, but usually is combined with individual and/or group psychotherapy directed at helping the patient develop a more stable long-range adjustment. Studies on the efficacy of the drugs/psychotherapy combination have recently been reviewed by Klerman and Schechter (1982), whose conclusions are encouraging; apparently, the two therapies make independent but complementary contributions when combined.

A number of techniques of psychotherapy have been developed particularly for the treatment of depression. The following case of a 37-year-old homemaker who had been depressed since the recent death of her mother will serve as an example. The treatment program was directed toward reinforcing behavior incompatible with depression and relieving feelings of helplessness and hopelessness. The therapist began by observing the patient in her home.

"The therapist recorded each instance of 'depressive-like' behavior, such as crying, complaining about somatic symptoms, pacing, and withdrawal. He also noted the consequences of these behaviors. Initially, she had a high rate of depressive behaviors and it was noted that members of her family frequently responded to them with sympathy, concern, and helpfulness. During this time, her rate of adaptive actions as a housewife and mother were very low, but she did make occasional efforts to cook, clean house, and attend to the children's needs. . . .

"The therapist, in family sessions, instructed her husband and children to pay instant and frequent attention to her coping behavior and to gradually ignore her depressed behavior. They were taught to acknowledge her positive actions with interest, encouragement, and approval. Overall, they were not to decrease the amount of attention focused on the patient but rather switch the contingencies of their attention from 'sick woman' to 'housewife and mother.' Within one week, her depressed behavior decreased sharply and her 'healthy' behavior increased.

"A clinical experiment was then performed to prove the causal link between her behavior and the responses generated in her family. After the 14th day, the therapist instructed the family members to return to providing the patient with attention and solicitude for her complaints. Within three days, she was once again showing a high level of depressive behavior, albeit not as high as initially. When the focus of the family's attentiveness was finally moved back to her coping skills and away from her miserableness, she quickly improved. One year after termination, she was continuing to function well without depressive symptoms." (Liberman & Raskin, 1971, p. 521)

There are many such behavioral approaches to the psychosocial treatment of depression, as described and catalogued by T. Carson and Adams (1981). While the efficacy of many of these has not yet been adequately established, preliminary results have been generally quite encouraging.

A promising therapeutic innovation has been developed by Beck and his colleagues, whose cognitively oriented views on depression were discussed earlier in the section on predisposing personality characteristics. Their approach involves a highly structured systematic effort at correcting the aberrant cognitions that are presumed to underlie the depressed state. Preliminary work comparing the outcomes of this type of therapy with those of antidepressant medication suggests that specific cognitive therapy may be at least as effective as drugs in alleviating depression (Beck et al., 1979; Rush et al., 1977). Other cognitive and cognitive-behavioral therapies for depressive disorders have been developed at a high rate in recent years and are showing considerable promise (Hollon, 1979). A specific, interpersonally based therapy has been recently developed and appears quite promising; clinical comparisons of this method with methods involving drug treatment are under way (Weissman et al., 1982).

Of course, in any overall treatment program, it is important to deal with unusual stressors in the patient's life, since an unfavorable life situation may lead to a recurrence of the depression and may necessitate longer treatment.

Even without formal therapy, as we have noted, the great majority of manic and depressive patients recover from a given episode within less than a year. And with modern methods of treatment, the general outlook has become increasingly favorable—so much so that most hospitalized patients can now be discharged within 60 days. While relapses may occur in some instances, these can now often be prevented by maintenance therapy.

At the same time, the mortality rate for depressive patients appears to be about twice as high as that for the general population because of the higher incidence of suicide (Leonard, 1974; Zung & Green, 1974). Manic patients also have a high risk of death, due to such things as accidents (with or without alcohol as a contributing factor), neglect of proper precautions to safeguard health, or physical exhaustion (Coryell & Winokur, 1982). Thus while the development of effective drugs and other new approaches to therapy have brought greatly improved outcomes for patients with affective disorders, the need clearly remains for still more effective treatment methods, both immediate and long term. Also, there appears to be a strong need for additional studies of factors that put people at high risk for depressive disorders, and the application of relevant findings to early intervention and prevention.

Suicide

The risk of suicide is a significant factor in depressive disorders—*all* depressive disorders. While it is obvious that people on occasion commit suicide for other reasons, the vast majority of those who complete the act do so during or following a depressive episode. Paradoxically, the act often occurs at a point when the individual appears to be emerging from the deepest phase of the depressive attack. The risk of suicide is about 1 percent during the year in which a depressive episode occurs, and it rises to 15 percent over the lifetime of an individual who has recurrent episodes (Klerman, 1982). When compared to rates for other possible causes of death—especially in younger age groups—these are *very* substantial figures.

References to the taking of one's own life are found throughout written history (Farberow, 1975). Dido, the founder and queen of Carthage, stabbed herself on a funeral pyre in grief and rage when Aeneas deserted her and led the Trojans onward toward their destiny; Zeno, founder of stoic philosophy, reportedly hanged himself at the age of 98 owing to disgust at stubbing his toe. More recently, we have had the examples of Ernest Hemingway, Marilyn Monroe, Sylvia Plath, Jimi Hendrix, and Freddie Prinze—all superbly talented people enjoying lives of success and public acclaim. And, among the less successful, we have witnessed the horror of large-scale self-massacre by members of the People's Temple in Jonestown, Guyana. How shall we account for such dramatic reversals of the fundamental will to live? The main purpose of the present section is to provide a partial answer to this disturbing and age-old question.

At the present time, suicide ranks among the first ten causes of death in most Western countries. In the United States, estimates show that over 200,000 persons attempt suicide each year, and that over 5 million living Americans have made suicide attempts at some time in their lives. Official figures show that some 26,000 successful suicides occur each year, meaning that about every 20 minutes someone in the United States commits suicide. Indeed, the problem may be much more serious than these figures suggest, since many self-inflicted deaths are certified in official records as being attributable to other "more respectable" causes than suicide. Most experts agree that the number of actual suicides is at least twice—and possibly several times—as high as the number officially reported (Wekstein, 1979).

Statistics, however accurate, cannot begin to convey the tragedy of suicide in human terms. As we shall see, probably the great majority of persons who commit suicide are actually quite ambivalent about taking their own lives. The irreversible choice is made when they are alone and in a state of severe psychological stress, unable to see their problems objectively or to evaluate alternative courses of action. Thus a basic humanitarian problem in suicide is the seemingly senseless loss of life by an individual who may be ambivalent about living, or who does not really want to die. A second tragic concern arises from the long-lasting distress among those left behind that may result from such action. As Shneidman (1969) has put it, "The person who commits suicide puts his psychological skeleton in the survivor's emotional closet . . ." (p. 22).

In our present discussion, we shall focus in turn on some additional aspects of the incidence and clinical picture in suicide, on factors that appear to be of causal significance, on degrees of intent and ways of communicating it, and on issues of treatment and prevention.

Clinical picture and causal pattern

Since the clinical picture and etiology of suicide are so closely interrelated, it is useful to consider these topics under one general heading. This will lead us to a consideration of the following questions: Who commits suicide? What are the motives for taking one's own life? What general sociocultural variables appear to be relevant to an understanding of suicide?

Who commits suicide? In the United States, the peak age for suicide attempts is between 24 and 44. Three times as many men as women *commit* suicide, but more women make suicide *attempts*. Most attempts occur in the context of

Ernest Hemingway and Marilyn Monroe are among the many celebrated and successful people who are known or are thought to have committed suicide.

interpersonal discord or other severe life stress. For females, the most commonly used method is drug ingestion, usually barbiturates; males tend to use methods more likely to be lethal, particularly firearms, which is probably the reason that successful suicides are higher among men. However, there is evidence that this long-established pattern may be changing; data from various Western countries, including the United States, indicate that the incidence of completed suicide has been increasing at a faster rate for women than for men in recent years. Also, more widows than widowers complete the act (Suter, 1976), although this seems due mainly to the disproportionate incidence of widowhood. The reasons for these trends are unknown but are probably related to the changes that are occurring in sex roles. Another perplexing trend is that rates of completed suicide among teenagers and even children seem to be increasing at an alarming pace (Klagsbrun, 1976; Pfeffer, 1981; Wells & Stuart, 1981). The trend is by no means limited to youngsters from deprived or problem-

atic backgrounds, although they do account for a sizable percentage of the statistics (Miller, Chiles, & Barnes, 1982); suicide rates for children from very affluent circumstances also are on the increase (*Time*, September 1, 1980).

Thus, while the overall national rate has increased slightly but consistently in recent years, disproportionate increases have occurred among females and among younger members of the population. The greatest increase has been among 15- to 24-year-olds; the rate for this age group has almost doubled in a decade and a half. An estimated 80,000 young people will attempt suicide in the next 12 months, and some 4000 will succeed. In fact, suicide now ranks as the second most common cause of death for 15- to 24-year-olds (the first is auto accidents). Most of us feel that there is something especially tragic when a young person—physically healthy and having seemingly unlimited horizons—undertakes an irreversible self-destructive action.

Many college students seem peculiarly vulnerable to the development of suicidal motivations, perhaps especially those attending the larger, more prestigious colleges. The rate seems to be higher in large universities than in community colleges and small liberal arts colleges (Peck & Schrut, 1971). The combined stressors of academic demands, problems of social interaction, and career choice—in interaction perhaps with challenges to their basic values—evidently make it impossible for such students to continue making the adjustive compromises their life situations demand (see **HIGHLIGHT** on page 329). Some 10,000 college students in the United States attempt suicide each year, and over 1000 of them succeed.

The greatest incidence of suicidal behavior among college students occurs at the beginning and the end of the school quarter or semester. Approximately three times as many female as male students attempt suicide, but more males than females succeed. More than half of those who attempt suicide take pills, about one third cut themselves, and the remainder—mostly males—use other methods, such as hanging or gunshot (Klagsbrun, 1976; Ryle, 1969).

Other high-risk groups include depressed persons, the elderly (white), alcoholics, the separated or divorced, individuals living alone, migrants, people from socially disorganized areas, members of some Native American tribes, and certain professionals such as physicians, dentists, lawyers, and psychologists (Wekstein, 1979). Both female physicians and female psychologists commit suicide at a rate about three times that of women in the general population; male physicians have a suicide rate about twice that of men in the general population (Ross, 1974; Schaar, 1974; Wekstein, 1979). The **HIGHLIGHT** on page 338 provides more information on people at high risk for suicidal behavior. Summing up, Seiden (1974) has called suicide "the number one cause of unnecessary, premature, and stigmatizing death" in the United States.

Factors associated with suicide. Events, circumstances, and mental states found to be related to the onset of depression are also generally linked to suicidal behavior. Thus we find that current stressors (Slater & Depue, 1981), depressed *and* angry feelings (Weissman, Fox, & Klerman, 1973), interpersonal crises of various sorts (Paykel, Prusoff, & Myers, 1975), failure and consequent self-devaluation (Wekstein,

1979), inner conflict (Menninger, 1938), and the loss of a sense of meaning and hope (Farberow, Shneidman, & Leonard, 1963) all can produce, independently or in combination, a mental state that looks to suicide as a possible way out. Should a person also happen to be drinking excessively at the time (or using drugs with similar effects), the danger of successful suicide is markedly increased.

The following, a composite profile of the "average" physician suicide, shows how a number of the above factors can lead a person to suicide.

"Statistically, he is a 48-year-old doctor graduated at or near the top of his high prestige medical school class, now practicing a peripheral specialty associated with chronic problems, where satisfactions are difficult and laggard. Because he is active, aggressive, ambitious, competitive, compulsive, enthusiastic and individualistic, he is apt to be frustrated easily in his need for achievement and recognition, and in meeting his goals. Unable to tolerate delay in gratification, he may prescribe large amounts of anesthetics or psychoactive drugs in his practice. Add a nonlethal annoying physical illness, mood swings, personal problems with drugs and alcohol—itself a reflection of suicide proneness—in one who may feel a lack of restraints by society, and one who has a likely enough combination to induce significant anxiety and depression, symptoms which not only may require psychiatric treatment, but which also often hamper a worthwhile relationship with a psychiatrist. Self-seeking and self-indulgent, versatile and resourceful, lacking control, he may often resort to hasty, impulsive or immature behavior—possibly suicide." (Ross, 1975, pp. 16–17)

The specific factors leading a person to suicide may take many forms. For example, one middle-aged man developed profound feelings of guilt after being promoted to the presidency of the bank for which he worked; shortly after his promotion, he fatally slit his throat. Similarly, suicide may be associated with severe financial reverses, loss of social status, imprisonment, or other difficult situations.

General sociocultural factors. Suicide rates vary considerably from one society to another. Hungary, with an annual incidence of 33.1 per 100,000, has the world's highest rate.[6] Other Western countries with high rates—20 per

---

[6]Incidence rate is calculated in terms of the number of completed suicides per 100,000 of the population per year. The figures given are those reported in Wekstein, 1979.

HIGHLIGHT
Warning signs for student suicide

A change in a student's mood and behavior is a significant warning of possible suicide. Characteristically, the student becomes depressed and withdrawn, undergoes a marked decline in self-esteem, and shows deterioration in habits of personal hygiene. This is accompanied by a profound loss of interest in studies. Often he or she stops attending classes and stays at home most of the day. Usually the student's distress is communicated to at least one other person, often in the form of a veiled suicide warning. A significant number of students who attempt suicide leave suicide notes.

When college students attempt suicide, one of the first explanations to occur to those around them is that they may have been doing poorly in school. As a group, however, they are superior students, and while they tend to expect a great deal of themselves in terms of academic achievement and to exhibit scholastic anxieties, grades, academic competition and pressure over examinations are not regarded as significant precipitating stressors. Also, while many lose interest in their studies prior to the onset of suicidal behavior and their grades get lower, the loss of interest appears to be associated with depression and withdrawal caused by other problems. Moreover, when academic failure does appear to trigger suicidal behavior—in a minority of cases—the actual cause of the behavior is generally considered to be loss of self-esteem and failure to live up to parental expectations, rather than the academic failure itself.

For most suicidal students, both male and female, the major precipitating stressor appears to be either the failure to establish, or the loss of, a close interpersonal relationship. Often the breakup of a romance is the key precipitating factor. It has also been noted that there are significantly more suicide attempts and suicides by students from families where there has been separation, divorce, or the death of a parent. A particularly important precipitating factor among college males appears to be the existence of a close emotional involvement with a parent that is threatened when the student becomes involved with another person in college and tries to break this "parental knot."

Although most colleges and universities have mental health facilities to assist distressed students, few suicidal students seek professional help. Thus, it is of vital importance for those around a suicidal student to notice the warning signs and try to obtain assistance.

Sources drawn on for this description include Hendin (1975), Miller (1975), Murray (1973), Nelson (1971), Pausnau and Russell (1975), Peck and Schrut (1971), Shneidman, Parker, and Funkhouser (1970), and Stanley and Barter (1970).

100,000 or higher—include Czechoslovakia, Finland, Austria, Sweden, Denmark, and the Federal Republic of Germany. The United States has a rate of 12.6 per 100,000, which is roughly comparable to that of Canada. Countries with low rates (less than 9 per 100,000) include Greece, Italy, Israel, the Netherlands, Norway, and Portugal. Among certain groups, such as the aborigines of the Australian, western desert, the suicide rate drops to zero—possibly as a result of a strong fear of death (Kidson & Jones, 1968).

Religious taboos concerning suicide as well as the attitudes of a society toward death are apparently important determinants of suicide rates. Both Catholicism and Mohammedanism strongly condemn suicide, and suicide rates in Catholic and Arab countries are correspondingly low. In fact, most societies have developed strong sanctions against suicide, and many still regard it as a crime as well as a sin.

Japan is one of the very few major societies in which suicide has been socially approved under certain circumstances—for example, in response to conditions that bring disgrace to the individual or the group. During World War II, large numbers of Japanese villagers were reported to have committed mass suicide when faced with imminent capture by Allied forces. There were also reported instances of group suicide by Japanese military personnel under threat of defeat. In the case of the *Kamikaze*, Japanese pilots who deliberately crashed their planes into American warships during the final stages of hostilities, self-destruction was a way of demonstrating complete personal commitment to the national purpose. It is estimated that approxi-

As a form of public protest in Vietnam, this Buddhist monk in 1963 turned himself into a burning torch as spectators solemnly looked on.

mately a thousand young Japanese males destroyed themselves in this exercise of patriotic zeal.

Societal norms cannot wholly explain differences in suicide rates, however, for the incidence of suicide often varies significantly among societies with similar cultures and also among different subgroups *within* given societies. For example, it is difficult to account for marked differences in suicide rates between Sweden and the United States, and we have noted differences in our own society with respect to sex, occupation, and age. In fact, the Scandinavian countries in general, sharing as they do a relatively common ethnic background and cultural pattern and overall high rates of suicide, pose a puzzling problem because the rate in Norway has remained stable and relatively low by world standards for the past century (Retterstøl, 1975)—thus exploding the myth that the high level of social welfare programs in Scandinavia is responsible for encouraging suicide by removing the challenge, and hope, of "making one's own way."

In a pioneering study of sociocultural factors in suicide, the French sociologist Émile Durkheim (1897) attempted to relate differences in suicide rates to differences in group cohesiveness. Analyzing records of suicides in different countries and for different historical periods, Durkheim concluded that the greatest deterrent to committing suicide in times of personal stress is a sense of involvement and identity with other people. More recent studies, including an exceptionally well-designed one by Slater and Depue (1981), tend to confirm this venerable idea.

Durkheim's views also appear relevant to understanding the higher incidence of suicide among subgroups in our society who are subjected to conditions of uncertainty and social disorganization in the absence of strong group ties. In a study sponsored by the National Institute of Mental Health, Hall et al. (1970) found that low-income persons from large urban areas have an especially high rate of suicidal gestures and attempts. Similarly, suicide rates have been found to be higher than average among people who are "downwardly mobile" (or who fear they may become so) and among groups undergoing severe social pressures. For example, in 1932 at the height of the Great Depression in the United States the suicide rate increased from less than 10 to 17.4 per 100,000; and during the early years of severe recession of the mid- and late 1970s, the suicide rate increased to above 12 per 100,000 (NIMH, 1976; Wekstein, 1979). Following the same trend of thought, we could point to the environmental pressures that appear to contribute to the high rate of suicide among black youth in our society or to the marked increase in suicide among Eskimo teenagers in Alaska, who appear to find themselves trapped in a sort of "no-man's-land" between their past culture and assimilation into the "white world." (Parkin, 1974).

A number of investigators, including Havighurst (1969) and Binstock (1974), have suggested that there is an inverse relationship between homicide and suicide in most cultures and ethnic groups. Where homicides are high, the suicide rate tends to be lower, and vice versa. Presumably, where homicide rates are high, frustration and hostility are turned outward against others rather than inward against oneself.

Suicidal ambivalence

From the standpoint of intent or motivation, suicide appears to be one method of obtaining relief from an aversive life situation. However, since most people undergoing severe stress do not commit suicide—for example, only a small number of patients who develop terminal cancer take their own lives—the question arises as to why an individual uses this method of coping rather than another. This is not an easy question to answer; it involves consideration not only of stress but also of other aspects of the individual's psychological state at the time of the suicide attempt.

Degree of intent.   The ambivalence that typically accompanies thoughts of suicide finds classic expression in Hamlet's famous soliloquy:

To be, or not to be: that is the question:
Whether 'tis nobler in the mind to suffer
The slings and arrows of outrageous fortune,
Or to take arms against a sea of troubles,
And by opposing end them? To die: to sleep;
No more; and by a sleep to say we end
The heart-ache and the thousand natural shocks
That flesh is heir to, 'tis a consummation
Devoutly to be wish'd. To die, to sleep;
To sleep: perchance to dream: ay, there's the rub;
For in that sleep of death what dreams may come
When we have shuffled off this mortal coil,
Must give us pause. . . .

(*Hamlet*, Act III, Scene i)

Recognizing that the vast majority of people who contemplate suicide do not in fact kill themselves, some investigators have focused on analyzing the degree of intent associated with suicidal behavior. Thus Farberow and Litman (1970)—echoing Hamlet—have classified suicidal behavior into three categories: "To be," "Not to be," and "To be or not to be."

The "To be" group involves individuals who do not really wish to die, but rather wish to communicate a dramatic message to others concerning their distress and contemplation of suicide. Their suicide attempts involve minimal drug ingestion, minor wrist-slashing, and similar nonlethal methods. They usually arrange matters so that intervention by others is almost inevitable, although sometimes things do go awry. This group is estimated to make up about two thirds of the total suicidal population. As we have seen, a large—although decreasing—proportion of those who make unsuccessful attempts are women. It seems probable that traditional sex-role socialization of females predisposes many women to feel helpless and to fantasize being rescued—and thus to communicate in this mode (Suter, 1976).

In contrast, the "Not to be" group includes persons who seemingly are intent on dying. They give little or no warning of their intent to kill themselves, and they usually arrange the suicidal situation so that intervention is not possible. Although these persons use a variety of different methods for killing themselves, they generally rely on the more violent and certain means, such as shooting themselves or jumping from high places. It has been estimated that this group makes up only about 3 to 5 percent of the suicidal population. Successful preventive intervention with this group is at best a doubtful goal, even when the person is protectively incarcerated. In an interesting experiment, a pseudo-suicidal "patient" (actually one of the investigators) gained admission to a mental hospital ward on "suicidal status." Though he was supposedly being carefully watched, he discovered multiple opportunities to do himself in (Reynolds & Farberow, 1976).

The "To be or not to be" group constitutes about 30 percent of the suicidal population. It is comprised of persons who are ambivalent about dying and tend to leave the question of death to chance, or, as they commonly view it, to fate.

Degree of suicidal intent is known to vary widely from individual to individual. In this case, the efforts of police and others to avert this young man's death were unsuccessful. Not long after this photo was taken, the man, 26 years old, jumped from the Julien Dubuque Bridge into the Mississippi River.

Although loss of a love object, strained interpersonal relationships, financial problems, or feelings of meaninglessness may be present, the individual still entertains some hope of working things out. The methods used for the suicide attempt are often dangerous but moderately slow acting, such as fairly high drug ingestion, or cutting oneself severely in nonvital parts of the body, thus allowing for the possibility of intervention. The feeling can be summed up as, "If I die the conflict is settled, but if I am rescued that is what is meant to be." Often the persons in this group lead stormy, stress-filled lives and make repeated suicide attempts. After an unsuccessful attempt, there is usually a marked reduction in emotional turmoil. This reduction is not stable, however, and in a subsequent trial by fate, the verdict may well be death. In a follow-up study of 886 persons who had made suicidal attempts, Rosen (1970) classified them as serious (21 percent) or nonserious (79 percent). During the year following the attempts, the rate of suc-

cessful suicide was twice as high among the group whose earlier attempts had been classified as serious.

Farberow and Litman's classification is largely descriptive and has little practical value in terms of predicting suicidal behavior. As we indicated, however, it does seem possible to infer the degree of intent from the lethality of the method used—a conclusion strongly supported by the more recent findings of Beck, Beck, and Kovacs (1975). The concept of intent is also a very useful reminder that most people who contemplate suicide retain at least some urge to live. Their hold on life, however tenuous, provides the key to successful suicide prevention programs.

Communication of suicidal intent. Research has clearly demonstrated the tragic fallacy of the belief that those who threaten to take their lives seldom do so. In fact, such people represent a very high-risk group in comparison with the general population. In a cross-cultural study, Rudestam (1971) conducted extensive interviews with close friends or relatives of 50 consecutive suicides in Stockholm and Los Angeles and found that at least 60 percent of the victims in both cities had made "direct" verbal threats of their intent. An additional 20 percent had made "indirect" threats.

In a similar study involving suicide deaths in Vienna and Los Angeles, Farberow and Simon (1975) found substantial differences between the two cities. In Los Angeles, 72 percent had made direct references to intent, versus only 27 percent in Vienna; the corresponding figures for indirect references were 25 percent and 2 percent. It would thus appear that cultural factors determine to some extent the likelihood that suicidal intent will be "signaled" to others.

Indirect threats typically include references to being better off dead, discussions of methods of committing suicide and burial, statements such as "If I see you again . . . ," and dire predictions about the future.

Whether direct or indirect, communication of suicidal intent usually represents "a cry for help." The person is trying to express distress and ambivalence about suicide; the statements are both warnings and calls for help. Unfortunately, the message is often not received or is received with skepticism and denial. The latter pattern is particularly apt to occur when the sui-

HIGHLIGHT

Types of suicide notes

The Tuckman et al. (1959) study classified suicide notes according to types of emotional content. A sampling of these various types appears below.

Positive emotional content

"Please forgive me and please forget me. I'll always love you. All I have was yours. No one ever did more for me than you, oh please pray for me please." (Tuckman et al., 1959, p. 60)

Negative (hostile) emotional content

"I hate you and all of your family and I hope you never have a piece of mind. I hope I haunt this house as long as you live here and I wish you all the bad luck in the world." (Tuckman et al., 1959, p. 60)

Neutral emotional content

"To Whom It May Concern,

"I, Mary Smith, being of sound mind, do this day, make my last will as follows—I bequeath my rings,

Diamond and Black Opal to my daughter-in-law, Doris Jones and any other of my personal belongings she might wish. What money I have in my savings account and my checking account goes to my dear father, as he won't have me to help him. To my husband, Ed Smith, I leave my furniture and car.

"I would like to be buried as close to the grave of John Jones as possible." (Darbonne, 1969, p. 50)

Mixed emotional content

Dear Daddy:

Please don't grieve for me or feel that you did something wrong, you didn't. I'll leave this life loving you and remembering the world's greatest father.

I'm sorry to cause you more heartache but the reason I can't live anymore is because I'm afraid. Afraid of facing my life alone without love. No one ever knew how alone I am. No one ever stood by me when I needed help. No one brushed away the tears I cried for "help" and no one heard. I love you Daddy, Jeannie

---

cidal person has given repeated warnings but has not made an actual suicide attempt. As a consequence, the recipients of the message may state that they did not think it would happen; or that they thought it might happen but only if the person became much more depressed. In this area, "crying wolf" needs to be taken seriously.

As several investigators have pointed out, many people who are contemplating suicide feel that living may be preferable if they can obtain the understanding and support of their family and friends. Failing to receive it, they go on to actual suicide.

Suicide notes.   A number of investigators have analyzed the content of suicide notes in an effort to better understand the motives and feelings of persons who take their own lives. In a pioneering study of 742 suicides, Tuckman, Kleiner, and Lavell (1959) found that 24 percent left notes, usually addressed to relatives or friends. The notes were either mailed or found on the

person of the deceased or near the suicide scene. With few exceptions, the notes were coherent and legible. In terms of emotional content, the suicide notes were categorized into those showing positive, negative, neutral and mixed affect. Of course, some notes showed combinations of these affective components. The **HIGHLIGHT** on this page provides examples of notes showing differing types of emotional content.

Shneidman and Farberow (1957), in another pioneering study, approached the question of the content of suicide notes by comparing 33 notes written by actual suicides with 33 composed by matched subjects who were asked to simulate a presuicidal state. The principal difference between the actual and the fictitious notes was that the actual ones had a greater number of thought units of a "neutral" quality. Evidently only the genuine writer tends to deal concretely with the idea of actually being gone; therefore he or she incorporates much more material of an instructional and admonishing sort to survivors.

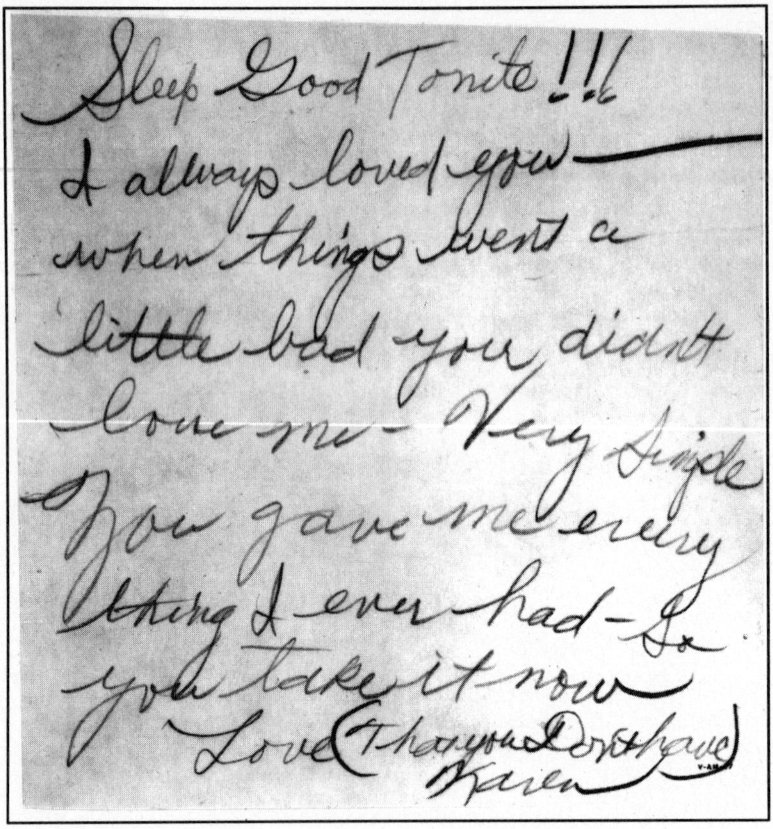

Sleep Good Tonite !!!
I always loved you —
when things went a
little bad you didn't
love me — Very Simple
You gave me every
thing I ever had — So
you take it now —
Love (Thank you Don't have)
Karen

Suicide notes may have mixed
emotional contents, including
both positive and negative
feelings.

The genuine writers, however, also expressed more intense feelings of self-blame, hatred, demand, and vengeance.

In a more recent study, Cohen and Fiedler (1974) compared 220 cases of completed suicides who left notes with 813 cases of nonnote writers. In contrast to the findings of Tuckman et al.—who reported no differences with respect to such variables as sex, race, and marital status—these investigators found that 26 percent of female suicides left notes as contrasted with 19 percent of males. They also found that 40 percent of the separated or divorced females in their sample left notes as contrasted with approximately 31 percent of single females, 25 percent of married females, and 16 percent of widows. Whites left notes almost three times as often as nonwhites. In terms of content, the use of emotional categories corresponded to those reported by Tuckman and his associates—with positive, neutral, mixed, and negative being used in that order of frequency. In the study by

Farberow and Simon (1975) noted earlier, 46 percent of the residents of Los Angeles who committed suicide had left notes, but only 18 percent of the Viennese had done so. It would appear that the wish to communicate with survivors "after the fact" varies considerably with a host of demographic and cultural variables.

An understanding of the reasons for or motives underlying note-writing (or its absence) could possibly help make the bases of the variations clearer. On this point, Cohen and Fiedler (1974) concluded,

"Many note writers seem to be motivated to influence the responses of survivors. The desire to be remembered positively by a survivor may account for the large number of statements expressing positive affect. By statements of love and concern, a note writer may try to reassure both the survivor and himself of the worth of their relationship and his own worth as a person." (pp. 93–94)

However, these investigators, as well as Shneidman (1973), expressed disappointment that suicide notes—written by persons on the brink of life's greatest mystery—failed to contain any "great insights" or "special messages" for the rest of us. As Cohen and Fiedler (1974) express it,

"the large quantity of references to the concrete, mundane features of everyday life is not congruent with the romantic conception of suicide as a grand, dramatic gesture preceded and accompanied by a corresponding state of the psyche into which the suicide note should serve as a kind of window. Perhaps all the drama takes place before the action is decided or it is anticipated in the act itself. Whatever role the dramatic elements may play, the large number of references to the commonplace squares best with the conception of suicide notes as communications tailored to the needs of both the suicide and his survivors as these are perceived by the suicide under the existing circumstances." (pp. 94–95)

Suicide prevention

The prevention of suicide is an extremely difficult problem. One complicating factor is that most persons who are depressed and contemplating suicide do not realize that their thinking is restricted and irrational and that they are in need of assistance. Less than one third voluntarily seek psychological help; others are brought to the attention of mental health personnel by family members or friends who are concerned because the person appears depressed and/or has made suicide threats. The majority, however, do not receive the assistance they so desperately need. Yet, as we have seen, most persons who attempt suicide do not really want to die and give prior warning of their intentions; if the individual's "cry for help" can be heard in time, it is often possible to intervene successfully.

Currently the main thrust of preventive efforts is on crisis intervention. Efforts are gradually being extended, however, to the broader tasks of alleviating longer-term stressful conditions known to be associated with suicidal behavior and trying to better understand and cope with the suicide problem in "high-risk" groups.

Crisis intervention.   The primary objective of crisis intervention is to help the individual cope with an immediate life crisis. If a serious suicide attempt has been made, the first step involves emergency medical treatment. Typically such treatment is given through the usual channels for handling medical emergencies—the emergency rooms of general hospitals or clinics. It would appear, however, that only about 10 percent of suicide attempts are considered of sufficient severity to warrant intensive medical care; the great majority of attempters, after initial treatment, are referred to inpatient or outpatient mental health facilities (Kirstein et al., 1975; Paykel et al., 1974).

When persons contemplating suicide are willing to discuss their problems with someone at a suicide prevention center, it is often possible to avert an actual suicide attempt. Here the primary objective is to help these individuals regain their ability to cope with their immediate problems—and to do so as quickly as possible. Emphasis is usually placed on (a) maintaining contact with the person over a short period of time—usually one to six contacts; (b) helping the person realize that acute distress is impairing his or her ability to assess the situation accurately and to choose among possible alternatives; (c) helping the person see that there are other ways of dealing with the problem that are preferable to suicide; (d) taking a highly directive as well as supportive role—for example, fostering a dependent relationship and giving specific suggestions to the person about what to do and what not to do; and (e) helping the person see that the present distress and emotional turmoil will not be endless (see **HIGHLIGHT** on page 336). When feasible, the understanding and emotional support of family members or friends may be elicited; and, of course, frequent use may be made of relevant community agencies. Admittedly, however, these are "stopgap" measures and do not constitute complete therapy.

In terms of long-range outcomes, people who have made previous suicide attempts are more likely to kill themselves than those who have not, although only about 10 percent of people who unsuccessfully attempt suicide kill themselves at a later time (Seiden, 1974; Wekstein, 1979; WHO, 1974). As Seiden has expressed it, the suicidal crisis "is not a lifetime characteristic of most suicide attempters. It is rather an acute situation, often a matter of only minutes or hours at the most" (p. 2). Since the suicide rate

HIGHLIGHT

How a suicide prevention center answers calls for help

The first of the currently more than 200 professionally organized and operated suicide prevention centers in the United States was established in Los Angeles in 1958. Its founders, Norman L. Farberow and Edwin S. Shneidman, realized the great need for the services such a center could provide while collecting data for a study on suicide on the wards of their local county hospital. Patients who attempted suicide received adequate treatment for their physical injuries, but little attention was given to their psychological distress. On discharge they often returned to the same environmental stressors which had produced their self-destructive conflicts.

Initially the Suicide Prevention Center searched the medical wards for persons who had attempted suicide and then, on the basis of interview and other assessment data, it helped them find a mental health resource in the community for the kind of treatment they needed. As the SPC became better known, people telephoned for help, and it soon became apparent that the SPC could best serve as a crisis facility. To do so, it has to be accessible and the staff has to be trained in certain basic meanings of suicidal behavior as well as in therapy procedures.

Taking calls for help centers on five steps, which may or may not occur concomitantly. Farberow has enunciated them as follows:

1. Establish a relationship, maintain contact, and obtain information. The worker has to be able to listen nonjudgmentally and to assure the caller of interest, concern, and availability of help.

2. Identify and clarify the focal problem. Often the caller is so disorganized and confused that he or she is overwhelmed with all problems, both major and mi-

nor, having seemingly lost the ability to determine which is most important.

3. Evaluate the suicide potential. The staff person must determine quickly how close the caller is to acting on self-destructive impulses, if he or she has not already done so. The staff person does this by evaluating the information obtained from the caller against a schedule of crucial items, such as age and sex, suicide plan, and so on, as shown in the Highlight on page 338.

4. Assess the individual's strengths and resources. A crisis often presents an opportunity for constructive change. The staff worker attempts to determine the caller's strengths, capabilities, and other resources as he or she works out a therapeutic plan.

5. Formulate a constructive plan and mobilize the individual's own and other resources. The staff person, together with the caller or significant others, determines the most appropriate course of action for the caller. This may range from involvement of family and friends to referral to a clinic or a social agency or to recommendation of immediate hospitalization.

The emphasis is on crisis intervention and referral, not on long-term therapy, although in recent years therapy groups and other long-range treatment measures have been introduced.

In its organization and operation, the Los Angeles Suicide Prevention Center has provided a prototype for the other suicide prevention centers that have been established throughout the United States.

Based on information supplied by the Los Angeles Suicide Prevention Center.

for previous attempters is so much higher than that for the population in general, however, it is apparent that suicide attempters remain a relatively high-risk group.

Farberow (1974) has pointed out that it is important to distinguish between (a) individuals who have demonstrated relatively stable adjustment but have been overwhelmed by some acute stress—about 35 to 40 percent of persons

coming to the attention of hospitals and suicide prevention centers; and (b) individuals who have been tenuously adjusted for some time and in whom the current suicidal crisis represents an intensification of ongoing problems—about 60 to 65 percent of suicidal cases. For individuals in the first group, crisis intervention is usually sufficient to help them cope with the immediate stress and regain their equilibrium. For individuals in the second group, crisis intervention may also be sufficient to help them deal with the present problem situation, but with their life-style of "staggering from one crisis to another," they are likely to require more comprehensive therapy.

During recent years the availability of competent assistance at times of suicidal crisis has been expanded through the establishment of suicide prevention centers. At present, there are over 200 such centers in the United States. These centers are geared primarily toward crisis intervention—usually via 24-hour-a-day availability of telephone contact. Some centers, however, offer long-term therapy programs, and they can arrange for the referral of suicidal persons to other community agencies and organizations for special types of assistance. Such suicide prevention centers are staffed by a variety of personnel: psychologists, psychiatrists, social workers, clergy, and trained volunteers. Although there was initially some doubt about the wisdom of using nonprofessionals in the important first-contact role, experience has shown that the empathetic concern and peer-type relationships provided by volunteer workers can be highly effective in helping an individual through a suicidal crisis. For a guide to suicide prevention center personnel in gauging the seriousness of suicide threats, see the **HIGHLIGHT** on page 338.

It is difficult to evaluate the long-range impact of emergency aid provided by suicide prevention centers, but such facilities seem to have the potential, at least, for significantly reducing suicide rates. The Suicide Prevention Center of Los Angeles (Farberow & Litman, 1970) has reported that in comparison with an estimated suicide rate of 6 percent among persons judged to be high risks for suicide, the rate has been slightly less than 2 percent among approximately 8000 high-risk persons who used their services.

One difficult problem with which suicide prevention centers have to deal is that the majority of persons who are seen do not follow up their initial contact by seeking additional help from the center or other treatment agency. In a follow-up of 53 persons who committed suicide after contact with the Cleveland Suicide Prevention Center, Sawyer, Sudak, and Hall (1972) reported that none had recontacted the center just prior to death. They also found that "the in-terval between the time of last contact with the Center and the time of death ranged from 30 minutes to 32 months with a median interval of 4 months" (p. 232). Since this report was issued, systematic attempts have been made to expand the services of suicide prevention centers to help them better meet the needs of clients. Thus many centers have introduced long-range after-care or maintenance-therapy programs.

Focus on high-risk groups and other measures. Many investigators have emphasized the need for broadly based preventive programs aimed at alleviating the life problems of people who, on the basis of statistics, fall into high-risk groups with respect to suicide. Few such programs have actually been initiated, but one approach has been to involve older males— a very high-risk group—in social and interpersonal roles that contribute to others as a means of lessening their frequent feelings of isolation and meaninglessness. Among this group, such feelings often stem from forced retirement, financial problems, the death of loved ones, impaired physical health, and feeling unwanted.

Another innovative approach to dealing with persons who are contemplating suicide—and who in this sense represent a very high-risk group—was originated by a group of volunteers called the Samaritans, begun in England in 1953 by Reverend Chad Varah. The service extended by the Samaritans is simply that of "befriending." Befrienders offer support to the suicidal person with no strings attached. They are available to listen and help in whatever way needed, expecting nothing in return—not even gratitude. Since their founding, the Samaritans have spread throughout the British Commonwealth and to many other parts of the world as well, and preliminary findings concerning their effectiveness in suicide prevention seem most promising (Farberow, 1974, 1975; Wekstein, 1979).

Other measures to broaden the scope of suicide prevention programs include (a) the use of "psychological autopsies" (psychological profiles of individuals who have committed suicide); (b) assessment of the environments of high-risk groups, often including their work environments; and (c) training of clergy, nurses, police, teachers, and other professional personnel who come in contact with large numbers of people in the community. An important aspect of such

HIGHLIGHT

"Lethality scale" for assessment of suicide potentiality

In assessing "suicide potentiality," or the probability that a person might carry out a threat of suicide, the Los Angeles Suicide Prevention Center uses a "lethality scale" consisting of ten categories:

1. Age and sex. The potentiality is greater if the individual is male rather than female, and is over 50 years of age. (The probability of suicide is also increasing for young adults aged 15 to 24.)

2. Symptoms. The potentiality is greater if the individual manifests such symptoms as sleep disturbances, depression, feelings of hopelessness, or alcoholism.

3. Stress. The potentiality is greater if the individual is under stress from the loss of a loved one through death or divorce, the loss of employment, increased responsibilities, or serious illness.

4. Acute vs. chronic aspects. The immediate potentiality is greater when there is a sudden onset of specific symptoms, such as those mentioned above. The long-term potentiality is greater when there is a recurrent outbreak of similar symptoms, or a recent increase in long-standing maladaptive traits.

5. Suicidal plan. The potentiality is greater in proportion to the lethality of the proposed method and the organizational clarity and detail of the plan.

6. Resources. The potentiality is greater if the person has no family or friends, or if they are unwilling to help.

7. Prior suicidal behavior. The potentiality is greater if the individual has made one or more prior attempts or has a history of repeated threats and depression.

8. Medical status. The potentiality is greater when there is chronic, debilitating illness or the individual has had many unsuccessful experiences with physicians.

9. Communication aspects. The potentiality is greater if communication between the individual and his or her relatives has been broken off and they reject efforts by the individual or others to reestablish communication.

10. Reaction of significant others. Potentiality is greater if a significant other, such as the husband or wife, evidences a defensive, rejecting, punishing attitude and denies that the individual needs help.

The final suicide potentiality rating is a composite score based on a weighing of each of the ten individual items.

Another interesting approach to the assessment of suicide potentiality involves the use of computers and actuarial methods to predict the risk not only of suicide but also of assaultive and other dangerous behaviors (Greist et al., 1974). Clinicians find this information helpful in making decisions regarding the amount of control needed or the amount of freedom that can safely be allowed. In a test of the system comparing computer accuracy with that of unaided judgments of clinicians, the computer predicted 90 percent of actual suicide attempts, versus only 30 percent for clinicians (*Time*, July 24, 1978).

Material concerning the lethality scale based on information supplied by the Los Angeles Suicide Prevention Center.

---

training is to be alert for suicidal communications. For example, a parishioner might clasp the hand of a minister after church services and intensely say, "Pray for me." Since such a request is quite normal, the minister who is not alert to suicidal "cries for help" might reply with a simple, "Yes, I will" and turn to the next person in line—only to receive the news a few days later that the parishioner has committed suicide.

Ethical issues in suicide prevention.
Most of us respect the preservation and fulfillment of human life as a worthwhile value. Thus suicide is generally considered not only tragic but "wrong." However, efforts to prevent suicide also involve problems of ethics. If individuals wish to take their own lives, what obligation—or right—do others have to interfere? This question has been taken seriously by Thomas

Do people have a "right to die?" Recent controversies over this question have given rise to organized advocate groups such as the one shown above; this particular group asserts that individuals do, in fact, have such a right.

Szasz (1976), whose view of the problem is captured in the following:

"In regarding the desire to live as a legitimate human aspiration, but not the desire to die, the suicidologist stands Patrick Henry's famous exclamation . . . on its head. In effect, he says, 'Give *him* commitment, give *him* electroshock, give *him* lobotomy, give *him* life-long slavery, but *do not let him choose* death!' By so radically illegitimizing another person's (not his own!) wish to die, the suicide-preventor redefines the aspiration of the other as not an aspiration at all." (p. 177)

Needless to say, Szasz's ideas are controversial.

Certainly a persuasive case can be made for the right of persons afflicted with a terminal illness, who suffer chronic and debilitating pain,

to shorten their agony (see **HIGHLIGHT** on page 340). But what about the rights of persons who are not terminally ill and who have dependent children, parents, a spouse, or other loved ones who care about them and will be hurt by their death? Here the person's "right to suicide" becomes considerably less apparent, particularly in the case of those who are ambivalent about taking their lives, where intervention may help them regain their perspective and see alternative ways of dealing with their distress.

Here we may reemphasize that the great majority of persons who attempt suicide either do not really want to die or are ambivalent about taking their lives; and even for the minority who do wish to die, the desire is often a transient

HIGHLIGHT
A "right" to suicide?

Every year millions of persons find out that they are suffering from a fatal disease, that they have no reasonable hope of living much longer, and that the near future will bring either agonizing pain or drug-induced clouding of consciousness, or both. What is a rational response to this awareness, and on what philosophical and moral grounds does one make it? What are the responsibilities of loved ones and professional caretakers in confronting the dilemma of the doomed person? Should nature simply be allowed to take its course? Should one submit passively to this apparent indication of "God's will"? Or should the individual take his or her own life before the pain becomes too agonizing and/or the medication too incapacitating?

There are, of course, no final, universal answers to such questions. But many people believe that, in such circumstances, suicide is an inviolable right and is in fact the most reasonable choice available. Some even take the position that healthy individuals have a moral obligation to help the stricken person take his or her life.

In our society, sanctions against helping a person commit suicide have been stronger than those against taking one's own life. Indeed, in most jurisdictions in the United States, aiding and abetting another person's suicide is a felony carrying rather severe penalties. Nevertheless, such assistance is rendered from time to time, and occasionally accounts of the circumstances are made public. Such was the case in the planned suicide of Carmen, whose sister, novelist Jessamyn West (1976) wrote poignantly of her active participation in Carmen's suicide.

Carmen was diagnosed as suffering from terminal cancer, and indications were strong that it would be a painful and prolonged death. She decided to commit suicide. At first she planned on doing it alone, but she subsequently decided that she wanted Jessamyn to be with her through it all. Jessamyn traveled to Carmen's home, and the sisters initiated a conspiracy to ensure that nothing would interfere with their plans. They knew that if they were discovered, others would try to intercede and prevent what each had decided was the only acceptable outcome. Though their extensive preparations were not accomplished joyously, neither were they characterized by inordinate gloom. Carmen and Jessamyn wanted, above all, to be certain that the method chosen would in fact be fatal. Finally, at the appointed time, Carmen died peacefully in the arms of her sister.

Was this a wrongful death?

one. With improvement in the person's life situation and lifting of depression, the suicidal crisis is likely to pass and not recur. As Murphy (1973) has expressed it, "The 'right' to suicide is a 'right' desired only temporarily" (p. 472). Certainly in such cases intervention seems justified.

The dilemma becomes more intense, however, when prevention requires that the individual be hospitalized involuntarily; when personal items, such as belts and sharp objects, are taken away; and when calming medication is forcibly administered. Sometimes considerable restriction is needed to calm the individual. And even then the efforts may be fruitless. For example, in a study of hospitalized persons who were persistently suicidal, Watkins, Gilbert, and Bass (1969) reported that "almost one third used methods from which we cannot isolate them—seven head ramming, two asphyxia by aspira-

tion of paper, one asphyxia by food, and three by exsanguination by tearing their blood vessels with their fingers" (p. 1593). Here again, however, as in the case of terminal illness and suffering, we are talking about a distinct minority of suicide cases.

Admittedly the preceding considerations do not resolve the issue of a person's "basic right to suicide." As in the case of most complex ethical issues, there does not seem to be any simple answer. But unless and until there is sufficient evidence to confirm this alleged right—and agreement on the conditions under which it may be appropriately exercised—it seems the wiser course to encourage existing suicide prevention programs and to foster research into suicidal behavior with the hope of reducing the toll in human life and misery taken each year by suicide in our society.

Summary

Affective disorders are those in which extreme variations in mood—either "low" or "high"—are the predominant feature. We all experience such variations at mild to moderate levels in the natural course of life. In some instances, however, the extremity of the person's mood in either direction is causally related to behavior that most would consider maladaptive. This chapter describes the official categories of disorder associated with such maladaptive mood variations.

The large majority of these disorders involve some type of mental depression, in which the individual experiences, at the mildest levels, self-depreciation, excessive dependency, and a sense that outcomes are independent of one's coping efforts. As these problems deepen into disorder, all of these characteristics are intensified, and the person may become preoccupied with feelings of guilt and worthlessness. Often in such cases basic biological functioning seems to be altered—for example, the sleep pattern may be dramatically altered or the person may become uninterested in food or eating. In the hypomanic or manic variants (i.e., in cyclothymic or bipolar disorders in which the current episode is one of being excessively "high"), essentially the opposite pattern obtains. However, depressive syndromes are much more common than manic ones, and they appear to be much more diffuse and heterogeneous in nature than those in which manic or hypomanic episodes appear in the person's history. In the latter instance, the person is normally considered to have a (bipolar) predisposition to react in both depressive and manic ways.

Except for certain syndromes that seem secondary to organic brain impairment, the affective disorders are divided into major and nonmajor categories. The major affective disorders are those of major depression and bipolar disorder. Far more common are a variety of depressive (or, less often, hypomanic) conditions that are typically less severe in intensity, including dysthymic disorder, cyclothymic disorder, and adjustment disorder with depressed mood. In general, the efficacy of biologically based treatments, such as drugs or ECT, is limited to the more severe or major disorders. In the milder forms of affective disorder, psychosocial treatments, of which there are an increasing variety, seem equally or more effective.

Suicide is a constant danger with depressive syndromes of whatever type or severity. Accordingly, an assessment of suicide risk is essential in the proper management of depressive disorders. A small minority of suicides appears unavoidable—chiefly those of the deliberate "not to be" type. A substantial amount of suicidal behavior (e.g., taking slow-acting drugs where there is a high likelihood of discovery) is motivated more by considerations of indirect interpersonal communication than of a wish to die. Somewhere between these extremes is a large group of persons who are desperately ambivalent about killing themselves and who initiate dangerous courses of action that they may or may not carry to completion, depending on momentary events and impulses. Suicide prevention efforts are normally and properly focused mostly on this ambivalent group. Of course, a reasonable and ethical argument can be made that, in certain circumstances, efforts to deter suicide are philosophically questionable.

Schizophrenic disorders and paranoia

Le Voyageur Français, Le Pays des Météores *(1902–1905). The Voyageur's real name, and most of the details of his life, remain undiscovered. He is thought to have been a professional artist or decorator who was institutionalized at Villejuif, France, for schizophrenia. He painted rather conventional scenes, and then "signed" them in the corner with an intricate pattern composed of abstract masses of color. The painting at left shows the extremely bizarre effect resulting from the clash of painting and "signature."*

A s we saw in Chapter 9, the psychotic affective disorders involve chiefly a disturbance of mood; to the extent that disruptions of perceptual, cognitive, and information-processing mechanisms (e.g., delusions and hallucinations) occur in the psychotic affective disorders, they seem secondary to the more primary mood dysfunction. By and large, the opposite is true in schizophrenic and paranoid disorders, where there is often no obvious relationship between mood and thinking. However, this observation does not provide a reliable basis for distinguishing these supposedly separate psychopathological processes. As we have already noted in connection with so-called schizoaffective disorders, many cases fall between the cracks (Mellor, 1970).

With the schizophrenias and the possibly related paranoid syndromes, we move into a realm of behavioral disorder that represents in many ways the ultimate in psychological breakdown. The symptoms of these disorders include the most extreme to be found in human behavior, and they include virtually all of the pathological processes encountered thus far in our survey plus something more. What that "something more" may be, as we shall see, is not readily grasped or defined, but it is clearly within the psychotic range: the schizophrenic individual's whole personality is pervasively involved, and there is a more or less sharp break with reality as most of us conceive it.

In addition to a temporary worsening of schizophrenic symptoms under stress, many schizophrenic persons also display characteristics seen in different types of behavioral disorders. There is evidence of a genetically transmitted diathesis. Even after allowing for the appearance of similar symptoms among persons allegedly suffering from different disorders, it is remarkable how often schizophrenic individuals exhibit aspects of *all* of the psychopathological processes considered in earlier chapters. Usually, people diagnosed as schizophrenic engage in relatively transparent neurotic defense reactions; often they are bothered with psychophysiologic ailments of one sort or another, particularly in the early or acute phases of the disorder; often they show pronounced personality or character deviations prior to breakdown; finally, they are capable of extremes in mood that are easily the equal of anything seen in the psychotic affective disorders. In short, the schizophrenic disorders may truly be said to be the arena in which all the major problems of the mental health disciplines come together.

Paranoia and paranoid conditions have traditionally been seen as merely particular manifestations of schizophrenic processes, mostly because of the not uncommon co-occurrence of schizophrenic and paranoid symptoms in the same person. Consequently, researchers have identified a paranoid *subtype* of schizophrenia (e.g., the DSM-III diagnosis: *schizophrenic disorder, paranoid type*). Reconceptualizations (Magaro, 1981; Meissner, 1981) have called this traditional view into question, however, suggesting that schizophrenic and paranoid processes are quite distinct, although a given individual may be affected with both in varying degrees. Specific paranoid processes will be discussed in the latter part of the chapter.

The schizophrenias

The *schizophrenias* are a group of psychotic disorders characterized by gross distortions of reality; withdrawal from social interaction; and disorganization and fragmentation of perception, thought, and emotion. We will focus here on the adult forms of such mental derangements. Similar childhood syndromes will be discussed in Chapter 14. While the clinical picture may differ in schizophrenic reactions, the disorganization of experience that typifies acute schizophrenic episodes is well illustrated in the following description:

"Suspicious and frightened, the victim fears he can trust neither his own senses, nor the motives of other people . . . his skin prickles, his head seems to hum, and 'voices' annoy him. Unpleasant odors choke him, his food may have no taste. Bright and colorful visions ranging from brilliant butterflies to dismembered bodies pass before his eyes. Ice clinking in a nearby pitcher seems to be a diabolic device bent on his destruction.

"When someone talks to him, he hears only disconnected words. These words may touch off an old memory or a strange dream. His attention wanders from his inner thoughts to the grotesque way the speaker's mouth moves, or the loud scrape his chair makes against the floor. He cannot understand what the person is trying to tell him, nor why.

"When he tries to speak, his own words sound foreign to him. Broken phrases tumble out over and over again, and somewhat fail to express how frightened and worried he is." (Yolles, 1967, p. 42)

Schizophrenic disorders were at one time attributed to a type of "mental deterioration" beginning early in life. In 1860 the Belgian psychiatrist Morel described the case of a 13-year-old boy who had formerly been the most brilliant pupil in his school but who, over a period of time, lost interest in his studies, became increasingly withdrawn, seclusive, and taciturn, and appeared to have forgotten everything he had learned. He talked frequently of killing his father, and evidenced a kind of inactivity that bordered on stupidity. Morel thought the boy's intellectual, moral, and physical functions had deteriorated as a result of hereditary causes and hence were irrecoverable. He used the term *démence précoce* (mental deterioration at an early age) to describe the condition and to distinguish it from disorders of old age.

The Latin form of this term—**dementia praecox**—was subsequently adopted by the German psychiatrist Kraepelin to refer to a group of rather dissimilar conditions that all seemed to have the feature of mental deterioration beginning early in life. Actually, however, the term was rather misleading, since the problems usually become apparent not during childhood but during adulthood, and there is no conclusive evidence of permanent mental deterioration in most cases.

It remained for a Swiss psychiatrist, Bleuler, to introduce in 1911 a more acceptable descriptive term for this disorder. He used *schizophrenia* (split mind) because he thought the disorder was characterized primarily by disorganization of thought processes, a lack of coherence between thought and emotion, and an inward orientation away from reality. The "splitting" thus does not imply multiple personalities but a splitting within the intellect and between the intellect and emotion.

It is by no means clear that schizophrenia is a unitary process, however. The existence of a single diagnostic label—in this case, *schizophrenia*—does not by itself establish similarity of underlying organization in each case of schizophrenia, any more than does a medical diagnosis of high blood pressure, which can be due to many different underlying conditions. Thus many clinicians today believe that there may be several schizophrenias, with different causal patterns and dynamics (Bellak, 1980).

Schizophrenic disorders occur in all societies, from the aborigines of the Australian western desert and the remote interior jungles of Malaysia to the most technologically advanced societies. In the United States the estimated incidence of schizophrenia is about 1 percent of the population, a figure that has been quite stable over time. There are approximately one million *actively* schizophrenic persons in the United States at the present time (Berger, 1978) and probably 10 to 15 times more than that who are subject to schizophrenic episodes (Dohrenwend et al., 1980). But only about 600,000 are treated in a typical year. About one fourth of the patients admitted each year to mental hospitals and clinics are diagnosed as being schizophrenic, and since schizophrenic individuals often require prolonged or repeated hospitalization, they usually constitute about half the patient population for all available mental hospital beds (President's Commission on Mental Health, 1978).

Although schizophrenic disorders sometimes occur during childhood or old age, about three fourths of all first admissions are between the ages of 15 and 45, with a median age of just over 30. The incidence rate is about the same for males and females. Because of their complexity, their high rate of incidence, especially during the most productive years of life, and their tendency to recur and/or become chronic, the schizophrenias are considered the most serious of all psychotic disorders, as well as among the most baffling.

A case study

We depart somewhat from our usual format in discussing the clinical syndromes in order to present a unique and uniquely well-documented case study involving the schizophrenic syndrome. It involves a family of six—two biological parents and their four, monozygotic, quadruplet daughters—in which all four daughters became schizophrenic prior to age 25. Some appreciation of just how remarkable this circumstance is can

The Genain quadruplets as infants.

be derived from the combined improbability of viable quadruplicate births, identical heredity, and perfect concordance for schizophrenia: a fairly liberal estimate is that it would occur once in every one and one-half *billion* births! We are indebted for the thorough knowledge we have of this family to David Rosenthal (1963) and his colleagues, working under the auspices of the National Institute of Mental Health. For obvious reasons, certain specific data, such as names and dates, have been omitted or falsified in the report, and we shall honor that consideration in our synopsis. Should the reader be prepared to jump to the conclusion that these are obviously cases of genetically determined disorder, we counsel keeping an open mind on this point.

Background and early years. Some time in the early 1930s, quadruplet girls were born to Mr. and Mrs. Henry Genain, the product of a marriage occasioned by Mr. Genain's threatening to kill the reluctant Mrs. Genain unless she consented to it. Except for their low birth weights, ranging from Nora's 4 lb., 8 oz., to Hester's 3 lb., the girls appeared to be reasonably normal babies, albeit premature. Hester had to be fitted with a truss (an abdominal compression device) because of a bilateral hernia but was nevertheless discharged from the hospital with her sisters as basically healthy some six weeks after the birth. These were the only children the Genains ever had, partly because of pronounced difficulties in their sexual relationship.

The most pervasive, if not necessarily the most formative, feature of the girls' early life was their fame. From birth they received a great deal of attention from the media and the public. Early on, in fact, their parents started charging admission (25 cents) to members of the public to visit the home and view the babies, a scheme that terminated when the parents became concerned about the possibility of kidnaping or the transmission of some disease to the children. In subsequent years the children were encouraged in dancing and singing as a team, and they performed often at various functions and at school assemblies. Their fame as performers was apparently limited by a decided lack of talent, although there was once a suggestion that a Hollywood motion-picture firm might be interested in them; nothing came of this. Partly as a result of their "celebrity" status, the girls tended to stick very closely together for mutual protection; they rebuffed intrusions even from children their own age, with the result that they became social isolates. They were encouraged in this social isolation by their parents, who shared certain peculiar but very strong anxieties about the dangers of "the outside world." Possibly because of irritation from her truss, Hester began to masturbate regularly by the age of three, a habit she continued for many years to the considerable consternation of her parents.

Notwithstanding their genetic identity and physical similarity, the girls were sharply differentiated by their parents virtually from birth. In fact, they were treated as though they were two sets of twins—a superior and talented set consisting of Nora and Myra, and an inferior, problematic set consisting of Iris and Hester—the latter being the "runt of the litter," so to speak, and the one regarded from an early age as "oversexed." Complying with these parental attributions, the girls did in fact pair up for purposes of mutual support and intimacy-exchange; when threatened from the outside, however, they became a true foursome.

Mr. Genain's derived fame resulted in his being elected (and reelected for more than 20 years) to a minor political office, having been pushed into running by his ambitious wife. His job was not very demanding, and he spent most of his time drinking and hounding the members of his family concerning his various fears and obsessions. Prominent among these were that there would be break-ins at the home unless he patrolled the premises constantly with a loaded gun, and, especially as the girls developed into adolescence, that unless he watched over them with total dedication they would get into sexual trouble or be raped.

In fact, he imposed almost unbelievable restrictions and surveillance on the girls until the point of their breakdowns. By contrast, he was himself sexually promiscuous and is reported to have sexually molested at least two of his daughters; quite possibly Myra, who distanced herself from him with singular persistence, was the only one of the girls to escape his attentions. Beginning at an early age, and persisting through early adulthood, Mr. Genain insisted on being present when his daughters dressed and undressed. He also insisted on watching them change their sanitary pads during menstruation. In general, this weak, ineffectual, alcoholic man imposed his will on the remainder of the family through the institution of terror, aided and abetted by his fairly constant drunkenness.

Mr. Genain's preoccupation with sexuality, while extreme and almost preemptive of anything else, was at least matched by that of his wife. Mrs. Genain managed to see sexuality and sexual threats in the most innocuous of circumstances, and yet was curiously impervious to certain real sexual phenomena occurring before her eyes. When the girls complained to her about Mr. Genain's sexual attentions, she dismissed these happenings with the rationale that Mr. Genain was merely testing their virtue; if they objected to his advances, then clearly all was well! Not that she saw Mr. Genain as a paragon of virtue; on the contrary, she recited his many faults of breeding and grossness to anyone who would listen. Nevertheless, she stuck by him to the end (a typically alcoholic end), and by and large confirmed and supported his bizarre constructions of reality. Hester, the chronic masturbator, was a particular thorn in her side—all the more so when she discovered that, at about age 12, Hester had apparently seduced Iris into the practice of mutual masturbation, which Iris professed to like very much. Apparently unable to think of any more appropriate response to this dilemma, the parents—on the advice of an obviously unqualified physician—forced the two girls to submit to clitoral circumcisions, a measure whose drastic quality was exceeded only by its lack of success in altering the offending behavior. In general, however, Mrs. Genain enjoyed the status accorded her as the mother of quadruplets, and she remained unfailingly involved in the girls' lives in an overwhelming and intrusive way. Most of her affection, such as it was, was reserved for the "good" quads, Nora and Myra.

Adolescence, young adulthood, and breakdown. Except for their extreme social isolation, the girls had a relatively uneventful junior high school experience. They were regarded by their teachers as conforming, hard-working and "nice," except for some competition among them in respect to grades and adult approval. Hester clearly lagged behind the others, and Iris could not quite keep up with the remaining two in academic performance. Essentially the same pattern continued into high school. In the summer preceding the girls' senior year, Hester, whose behavior had become somewhat peculiar and who was apparently suffering from some type of psychophysiologic gastrointestinal distress, finally became disturbed to the point that her parents could hardly manage her. She was very temperamental, often did not seem to know what she was doing, was destructive of household furnishings, would tear both her own and her sisters' clothing, and on one occasion struck Nora with such force as to render her unconscious. Hester had just turned 18; she never thereafter regained a full measure of effective mental functioning.

The other three girls completed their senior year of high school, engaging in a kind of conspiracy of silence regarding the missing Hester, who remained at home. Outwardly, they appeared to be normal adolescents, although they were not permitted to have boyfriends and they continued to have various physical difficulties, including menstrual irregularities and persistent enuresis (bed-wetting). Following their graduations, they obtained modest employment as office workers. However, they continued to be constantly hounded and spied upon by their suspicious father, lest they become involved in sexual liaisons. They were not permitted to date. Of the three, Myra maintained the most independence, essentially defying her father's edict that she not go out at night to meetings and the like.

None of the three young women was comfortable in the world of work, feeling inadequate to the responsibilities heaped upon them by allegedly insensitive bosses. Nora was the first to evidence unusual "nervousness," and at age 20 began to have a series of vague physical complaints. She eventually quit her job and took to her bed at home, gradually becoming more disturbed. She would stand on her knees and elbows until they became irritated and bled, began to walk and talk in her sleep, and moaned and groaned a great deal, especially at mealtime. Her behavior continued to deteriorate until, at age 22, she underwent her first of several hospital admissions with the diagnosis of schizophrenia.

In the meantime, Iris had likewise become increasingly disturbed, also resigning from her job. She was troubled by "spastic colon," vomiting, insomnia, and the belief that people were paying her undue attention. In fact, Mr. Genain was at the time paying her a great deal of attention, which disturbed her greatly. Within several months after Nora's first admission, Iris "just went to pieces." She screamed, was markedly agitated, complained of hearing voices and of people fighting, and drooled at meals, being unable to swallow anything but liquids. She, too, was hospitalized for the first of many admissions toward the end of her twenty-second year. The diagnosis was schizophrenia.

Myra did not break down until age 24. Onset was similar to that of her sisters: vomiting, panic, insomnia, and waking up at night screaming. Myra resisted hospitalization at this time, and in fact was not hospitalized until the entire family was shortly thereafter moved to the Clinical Center of the National Institute of Mental Health (NIMH), where, as a unit, they underwent the lengthy and detailed study of which this history is one product. On arrival at the Center, Myra was found to be autistic, disordered in thought, and markedly impaired in judgment and reality testing. She was diagnosed as schizophrenic.

It may be significant that in each of the cases of Nora, Iris, and Myra, deterioration began shortly following an incident in which a man had made rather insistent "improper advances." In paradoxical but characteristic fashion, both parents had minimized the significance of these incidents when the girls complained.

Course and outcome. By the time of their arrival at the Clinical Center at age 24, Nora had undergone three separate hospital admissions and Iris five. Hester had somehow escaped this fate, although she was often bizarre and psychotic at home. With all four of the daughters simultaneously disturbed in varying degrees, the home atmosphere had become truly chaotic.

Once at the NIMH, the sisters were offered varied forms of treatment and care, including the new antipsychotic medications that had recently become available. They remained at NIMH for three years. At that time, Myra was the only one capable of attaining a sustainable discharge. The other three sisters had to be transferred to a state hospital at the end of their NIMH stay. Mr. Genain had died of liver disease in the interim.

It is important to note that, while the earliest symptoms of the quads were similar in certain respects, the courses and outcomes of their disorders differed markedly and to some extent in ways that could have been predicted. The most serious and "regressed" of the types of schizophrenia is *hebephrenic*. In the various diagnoses accorded to them in the course of their hospitalizations, Nora and Myra were never so diagnosed, although Nora was sometimes regarded as having "hebephrenic features." By contrast, Iris and Hester moved through the "milder" catatonic and undifferentiated phases of disorganization into full hebephrenic disorganization. The quads' outcomes show a corresponding pattern. At the time of Rosenthal's 1963 report, Myra was working steadily, married, and doing well. Nora was making a marginal adjustment outside of the hospital. Iris was still fluctuating between periods of severe disturbance and periods of relative lucidity in which she could manage brief stays outside of the hospital. Hester remained continuously hospitalized in a condition of severe hebephrenic psychosis and was considered essentially a "hopeless case."

It is a tribute to the scientific diligence of the NIMH staff, and to David Rosenthal, who has maintained both a humane and a scientific interest in this unfortunate family, that we have a follow-up report after some 20 years (Sargent, 1982a). In general, the relative adjustment of the sisters, now in their 50s, remains as it was in the 1960s. Myra continues to do well and has had two children in the interim. The other three women now live at home with their mother, with Nora continuing to show a higher level of functioning than Iris or Hester. All of the quads are on continuous medication, and even the beleaguered Hester appears to have overcome to an extent her originally dismal prognosis. It is of considerable interest that newer techniques of neurological assessment show Nora has impairments of the central nervous system similar to Hester, and yet her outcome seems far better than Hester or even Iris. It is possible that the original pairing of Iris with Hester was inappropriate (at least in the limited sense implied here) and quite destructive of Iris' psychosocial development. In any event, we see that the quads, despite their identical heredity, array themselves along a very considerable range of possible outcomes associated with schizophrenic breakdown.

Interpretive comment. We have here, then, four genetically identical women, all of whom have experienced schizophrenic disorders. The disorders, however, have been very different in severity, chronicity, and eventual outcome. Quite obviously, these differences must be ascribed to differences in the environments the quads experienced, including their intrauterine environments, which presumably contributed to their modest variations detectable at birth. Clearly Hester, in relative parental disfavor from the beginning, faced the harshest environmental conditions, followed closely by her "twin," Iris. The outcome for these women has been extremely grim. Myra was the most favored youngster and clearly the one who experienced the least objectionable parental attention. Nora was a close second in this respect but had the misfortune of being her incestuous father's "favorite"; in recent tests, she also proved to have a compromised central nervous system (specifically, an imbalance of metabolic rates in different brain areas) comparable to that of Hester. And though Nora has not done as well as Myra, she has emerged as clearly superior in functioning to the other two sisters. We see here the enormous power of environmental forces in determining personal destiny.

But let us look again. The fact is that we have four genetically identical individuals, all of whom became schizophrenic within a period of six years—three of them within a period of some two years. Is this not a compelling case for genetic determination? Indeed it is, and an independent family history suggests that the father of the quads harbored some very pathogenic

In 1981, the Genains performed a rendition of "Alice Blue Gown" at a 51st birthday party held in their honor at the National Institute of Mental Health.

genes, which of course could have been passed on to his daughters. On the other hand, we must ask what would have happened to these girls even if *no* pathogenic genes had been involved. As Rosenthal (1963) points out, these parents failed spectacularly in the most elementary tasks of parenthood. Can we imagine that the Genain sisters would have been reasonably well-adjusted had they possessed no defective genes? That seems very unlikely.

In the final analysis, it makes sense to conclude that *both* heredity and environment, operating in some complex interaction, contributed to the Genain sisters' vulnerabilities. In this instance, unfortunately, it is difficult to make even an estimate of the relative magnitude of the two types of influence. In some other instances of schizophrenic disorder, one can make a shrewd guess—based on genetic history, developmental experience, and the like—about the relative contribution from each of these two broad sources of behavioral variation. As we have seen, however, and as we shall see again in this chapter, the central fact always is the interaction between the two.

We shall have occasion to refer to the Genains from time to time in the pages that follow.

Clinical picture in schizophrenia

Sometimes schizophrenic disorders develop slowly and insidiously. Here the early clinical picture may be dominated by seclusiveness, gradual lack of interest in the surrounding world, excessive daydreaming, blunting of affect, and mildly inappropriate responses. This pattern is referred to as *process schizophrenia*—that is, it develops gradually over a period of time and tends to be long-lasting. The outcome for process schizophrenia is considered generally unfavorable, partly because the need for treatment is usually not recognized until the behavior pattern has become firmly entrenched. *Poor premorbid* or *chronic schizophrenia* are alternative terms referring to this pattern and are approximately equivalent in meaning to "process."

In other instances, the onset of schizophrenic symptoms is quite sudden and dramatic and is marked by intense emotional turmoil and a nightmarish sense of confusion. This pattern, which usually is associated with identifiable precipitating stressors, is referred to as *reactive schizophrenia* (alternatively, *good premorbid* or *acute schizophrenia*). Here the symptoms usually clear up in a matter of weeks, though in some cases an acute episode is the prelude to a more chronic pattern.

This process-reactive distinction, however, should be viewed not as a dichotomy but rather as a continuum. The distribution of schizophrenic individuals can be envisioned in the familiar bell-shaped curve, with relatively few falling at either the process or reactive extremes and most falling somewhere in the middle. Of the Genain quadruplets, Hester—who never seemed quite as well off mentally as her sisters and who seemed to move in imperceptible steps toward increasing deterioration—would be considered a relatively pure *process* type. By contrast, Myra, the least disturbed before her breakdown, the last to succumb, and the only one to regain effective control of her life, would be considered a relatively more *reactive* case.

Another distinction, which has gained increased prominence in recent years, is that between *paranoid* and *nonparanoid* symptom patterns among persons diagnosed as schizophrenic. In the paranoid pattern, delusions, particularly persecutory or grandiose ones, are a

HIGHLIGHT
Regression to "primary" thought processes in schizophrenia

Some investigators, particularly those adhering to the psychoanalytic perspective, have emphasized regression to more primitive levels of thinking as a primary feature of schizophrenia. In essence, more highly differentiated and reality-oriented "secondary" thought processes, which follow the rules of logic and take external reality into consideration, are replaced by "primary" thought processes, which involve illogical ideas, fantasy, and magical thinking. Presumably, such primary thought processes characterize the thinking of children. They live in a world that is partly fantasy and partly real, and they develop all manners of fantastic notions about things and events around them. They talk to imaginary playmates, personify inanimate objects, and attribute various powers to these figments of their imagination. Not uncommonly, they feel that they are the center of the world and develop ideas of omnipotence.

The regressed schizophrenic individual does not, however, perceive, think, and feel in ways precisely like those of a child. For example, children, unlike schizophrenic individuals, can usually distinguish between their fantasies and the world of reality, and most children, despite their fantasies, imperfect logic, and lack of perspective, clearly do not qualify as schizophrenic. Thus it would appear that regression in schizophrenia does not represent a wholesale return to childhood, but rather a defensive pattern that enables the schizophrenic individual to assume a position of dependency and hence avoid problems and responsibilities that he or she perceives to be overwhelming.

---

dominant feature; in the nonparanoid forms, such delusions, if present at all, tend to be rare and fleeting. Evidence is building that important differences exist between those who exhibit a predominant paranoid symptom pattern and those who exhibit few, or no, or inconsistent paranoid symptoms. In general, paranoid schizophrenic individuals tend to be more "reactive" than "process" in type and to have a more benign course and outcome (Ritzler, 1981); they may also be genetically less vulnerable to schizophrenia than nonparanoid types (Kendler & Davis, 1981). It has been found, however, that a substantial number of people originally diagnosed as having paranoid schizophrenic symptoms are later diagnosed as having nonparanoid ones (Kendler & Tsuang, 1981). It is of interest to note that all of the Genain sisters exhibited exclusively *nonparanoid* symptomatology during the active phases of their disorders.

Whether process, reactive, paranoid, or nonparanoid in the general sense of these terms, schizophrenia encompasses many specific symptoms that vary greatly over a period of time in an individual's life and from one individual to another. The basic experience in schizophrenia, however, seems to be one of disorganization in perception, thought, and emotion. The DSM-III specifies in rather concrete terms a list of criteria for the diagnosis. What follows is an extended description of those criteria.

Disorganization of a previous level of functioning. This is perhaps the accepted cardinal sign of schizophrenic breakdown; it distinguishes the schizophrenias from various developmental anomalies, such as infantile autism, in which the person has never attained a suitable degree of integrated behavioral functioning. The impairment always occurs in areas of routine daily functioning, such as work, social relations, and self-care, such that observers note that the person is not him- or herself any more. (See **HIGHLIGHT** on this page.)

Disturbance of language and communication. Often referred to as "formal thought disorder," this, too, is conventionally considered a prime indicator of the presence of a schizophrenic disorder. Basically, there is a failure to conform to the semantic and syntactic rules governing verbal communication in the individual's known language—*not* attributable to low intelligence, poor education, or cultural deprivation. Meehl (1962) aptly referred to the process as one of "cognitive slippage"; others have referred to it as "derailment of associations." However labeled, the phenomenon is readily recognized by experienced clinicians: the patient seems to be using words in combinations that sound communicative, but in the final analysis the listener becomes aware of understanding little or nothing of what has been said. Meehl cited as an example the statement, "I'm growing my father's hair" (see **HIGHLIGHT** on page 352).

Content of thought. Disturbances in the content of thought involve certain rather standard types of delusion. Prominent among these are the false beliefs that one's thoughts, feelings, or actions are being controlled by external agents, that one's private thoughts are being broadcast indiscriminately to others, that thoughts are being inserted involuntarily by alien forces, or that some mysterious agency has robbed one of one's thoughts. Other absurd delusions of varied content are also commonly observed, including delusions of grotesque bodily changes.

Perception. Major perceptual disruption often accompanies the manifestations already indicated. A breakdown in perceptual filtering is frequently observed, wherein the patient seems unable to sort out and properly dispose of the great mass of sensory information to which all of us are exposed in most waking moments. As a result, everything "gets through," overwhelming the meager resources the person has for appropriate information-processing. This point is well illustrated in the following excerpts from statements of schizophrenic persons:

"I feel like I'm too alert . . . everything seems to come pouring in at once . . . I can't seem to keep anything out . . . ."

"My nerves seem supersensitive . . . objects seem brighter . . . noises are louder . . . my feelings are so intense . . . things seem so vivid and they come at me like a flood from a broken dam."

"It seems like nothing ever stops. Thoughts just keep coming in and racing round in my head . . . and getting broken up . . . sort of into pieces of thoughts and images . . . like tearing up a picture. And everything is out of control . . . I can't seem to stop it."

It is estimated that approximately 50 percent of patients diagnosed as schizophrenic experience this breakdown of perceptual selectivity during the onset of their disorders (Freedman & Chapman, 1973). Other even more dramatic perceptual phenomena include hallucinations—perceptions for which there are no discernable external stimuli. Hallucinations in the schizophrenias are normally in the auditory mode, although they can also be visual and even olfactory. The typical hallucination is one in which a voice or voices keep up a running commentary on the individual's behaviors or thoughts.

Affect. The schizophrenic syndromes are often said to include an element of clearly inappropriate emotion, or affect. In the more severe or chronic cases, the picture is one of apparent *anhedonia* (inability to experience joy or pleasure), emotional shallowness, or "blunting": on casual observation, the person appears virtually not to have emotions, so that even the most compelling and dramatic events produce at most an intellectual recognition of what is happening. In other instances, particularly in the acute phases, the person may show very strong affect, but the type of emotion is discordant with the situation or with the content of his or her thoughts. For example, such a person may laugh uproariously upon receipt of the news of a parent's death.

Sense of self. The person often is perplexed about his or her identity, including gender identity, and, in addition, frequently is confused about the boundaries separating the self from the rest of the world. The latter confusion is often associated with frightening "cosmic" or "oceanic" feelings of being somehow intimately tied up with universal powers, and appears to be related to ideas of external control and similar delusions.

Volition. Almost universally in these cases, goal-directed activity initiated by the individual is disrupted, whether due to individual intent or to inability to carry through a course of action. For example, the person may be quite unable to marshal sufficient resources to maintain minimum standards of personal hygiene.

Relationship to the external world. Ties to the external world of reality are almost by definition loosened in the schizophrenic disorders, and in extreme instances the withdrawal may be

HIGHLIGHT
Schizophrenic writings

The personality decompensation in psychotic reactions is frequently manifested in the content and form of patients' letters and other spontaneous writings. These examples clearly reveal the "loosening" and deviations of thought, the distortion of affect, and the lowered contact with reality so common among schizophrenic individuals. The postcard is a reproduction of a card sent by a paranoid schizophrenic man.

> To: The football department and its members present and future
> The University of New Mexico, Albuquerque, N. M.
>
> I depend on correct, honest supplementation of this card by telepathy as a thing which will make clear the meaning of this card. There exists a Playing of The Great Things, the correct, the constructive, world or universe politics, out-in-the-open telepathy, etc. According to the Great Things this playing is the most feasible thing of all; but it is held from newspaper advertising and correct, honest public world recognition, its next step, by telepathic forces (it seems), physical dangers, and lack of money. Over 10,000 cards and letters on this subject have been sent to prominent groups and persons all over the world. Correct, honest contact with the honest, out-in-the-open world. This line of thought, talk, etc. rule. The plain and frank, etc. Strangers. The Great Things and opposites idea. References: In the telepathic world the correct playings. Please save this card for a history record since it is rare and important for history.

The handwritten excerpts are from a letter written by an 18-year-old woman, also diagnosed as paranoid schizophrenic. As is apparent from the first and last parts of the letter, shown here, the handwriting is of two quite different types, suggestive of the writer's emotional conflict and personality disorganization. Lewinson (1940) included this letter in her study of handwriting characteristics of different types of psychotic patients. Among such patients generally, she found that handwriting typically showed abnormal rhythmic disturbances, with rigidity or extreme irregularity in height, breadth, or depth.

> "Dear Dad 15.) — oct 9
> ...... Please come to see me immediately It's very urgent that I see you as quickly as possible
>   Just now my insides are rotting with each meal & have to eat with very disagreeable old hag
>
> * * * * * * *
>
> But it's a matter of life or death & if I don't get any response from you as yet haven't I swear by that Bible I jump in front of a car that now in need of fun & am Goddam it come up as soon as possible Here are the Fatal Day & the one Red Letter day is the one that see do it on when released last chance! Danger Oct 9, 10, 11, 12, 1314 15 16 be a corpse on 16th of the month when I'm out Goodbye forever Helen R

nearly total. This detachment is usually accompanied by the elaboration of an inner world in which the person develops illogical and fantastic ideational constructions having little or no relationship to reality as perceived by others. Since the days of Bleuler, this process has generally been referred to as *autism*.

Motor behavior. Various peculiarities of movement are sometimes observed in the schizophrenias; indeed, this is the chief and defining characteristic of the catatonic subtype of schizophrenia, of which more will be said later. These motor disturbances range from an excited sort of hyperactivity to a marked decrease in all movement or an apparent motor clumsiness. Also included here are various forms of rigid posturing, ritualistic mannerisms, and bizarre grimacing.

Problems in defining schizophrenic behavior

In an effort to provide for a clear-cut diagnosis of schizophrenia and to sharply distinguish it from affective or other disorders, DSM-III criteria contain a number of exclusionary phrases. For example, auditory hallucinations do not "count" in a diagnosis of schizophrenia unless their content is inconsistent with a depressed or elated mood, or else appear as part of a marked communication disturbance. But such an approach is justified only if one assumes that affective disorders and schizophrenia cannot occur together; the data suggest this may be a questionable assumption (see p. 313).

There are other problems with the DSM-III diagnostic criteria for schizophrenia. For one thing, the criteria are a curious mixture of an older set of concepts originally proposed by Bleuler (1911, 1950) and a newer set, chiefly those of Schneider (1959), which appear to have only an obscure and unspecified relationship to each other. In consequence, we cannot be sure that persons on whom much of our research knowledge depends—those who were diagnosed as schizophrenics under, say, DSM-II—can be grouped with persons described as schizophrenic under DSM-III. In one study peripherally concerned with this dilemma, a group of 68 DSM-II-defined schizophrenic patients was reduced to 35 when DSM-III criteria were applied, a reduction of 51 percent! Where did all the schizophrenics go? They went—perhaps not surprisingly—into the ranks of the affectively disordered (Winters, Weintraub, & Neale, 1981). Despite the questions it raises, the Winters et al. study does demonstrate that DSM criteria for schizophrenia have become more stringent, which should produce advantages in the long run by making the group more homogeneous and therefore more amenable to effective research investigation.

The most radical approach to the problem of defining schizophrenia has been articulately advanced by Sarbin and Mancuso (1980), who suggest that there is, in fact, no such thing as schizophrenia—that the idea is a mythical construction not differing in logical substance from the concept of the unicorn. These authors consider "schizophrenia" to be essentially a "moral verdict" concerning certain forms of unacceptable or unintelligible behavior rather than a legitimate medical diagnosis. Their argument in the authors' judgment, cannot be summarily dismissed.

Not even Sarbin and Mancuso, however, deny the existence of the *behaviors* under consideration here, nor do they deny that certain of these behaviors, although not obviously interrelated, tend to occur together just as "syndromes" of symptoms seem to occur together in various physical (medical) disorders whose underlying causes are not completely understood—as, for instance, in kidney dysfunctions of undetermined origin. This is precisely the way in which Bellak (1979) approaches the perplexing problem of defining schizophrenia. He sees the behaviors that we conventionally associate with "schizophrenia" as the "final common pathway" of severe adaptive breakdown—whatever the source of that breakdown. While acknowledging that such issues are far from settled, we believe the preponderance of evidence to be on Bellak's side, and hence adopt his position in what follows. We also adopt the position that DSM-II- and DSM-III-defined diagnoses of schizophrenia share a common core of psychopathology despite the fact that it is now, by DSM-III standards, more narrowly defined.

In any case, it will be clear that the clinical picture in what is called schizophrenia often includes bizarre elements that may be unintelligible to either the individual or observers. An individual may show peculiarities of movement, gesture, and expression; act out inappropriate sexual and other fantasies; or simply sit apathetically staring into space. We shall elaborate on these and other behavioral anomalies in describing the various types of schizophrenia.

On the other hand, not all the symptoms occur in every case. There is, in fact, no constant, single, universally accepted "sign" of the presence of schizophrenia. Thus the symptom picture may differ markedly from one schizophrenic person to another. Also, the symptom picture may change greatly over time, sometimes even as a result of the individual's being labeled as a schizophrenic and given a "sick" role to which he or she then conforms. Most schizophrenic people "fade in and out of reality" as a function of their own inner state and the environmental situation. They might be in "good contact" one day and evidence delusions and hallucinations the next. Likewise, an acute schizophrenic reaction may clear up fairly rapidly or may progress to a chronic condition.

One consequence of the fact that a large array of peculiarities or deficiencies of behavior may be taken as evidence of the presence of schizophrenia is that virtually anyone can deliberately perform in such a way as to be diagnosed as schizophrenic. This was one of the truly unassailable points made in a controversial study by Rosenhan (1973), in which eight normal people gained admission to twelve mental hospitals by reporting that they had hallucinations and some anxiety about them. All but one received a diagnosis of schizophrenia, and although they then started acting as "normal" as they could, it was fifty-two days before the last one gained release. Although the study has been criticized, it demonstrated that schizophrenia can be feigned and misdiagnosed.[1] Though few people would be inclined to take advantage of this opportunity, we will note in a later section that some, in fact, do.

Types of schizophrenia

The American Psychiatric Association's DSM-III classification lists five formal subtypes of schizophrenia, which are summarized in the **HIGHLIGHT** on page 355. We shall focus on four of these in

our present discussion: *undifferentiated, catatonic, disorganized (hebephrenic),* and *paranoid.* Of these, the undifferentiated and paranoid types are the most common.

Undifferentiated type. As the term implies, this is something of a "wastebasket" category. The individual so diagnosed meets the usual criteria for being schizophrenic—including (in varying combinations) delusions, hallucinations, thought disorder, and bizarre behavior—but does not clearly fit into one of the other subtypes because of a mixed symptom picture. People in the acute, early phases of a schizophrenic breakdown frequently exhibit undifferentiated symptoms, as do those who are in transitional phases from one to another of the standard subtypes, which in fact happens rather often. Each of the Genain sisters was given an undifferentiated diagnosis at least once, and all but Myra received such a diagnosis on several different occasions.

The case of David F. illustrates the onset of an undifferentiated schizophrenic episode (Bowers, 1965). David felt great apprehension about his future as he approached the end of his undergraduate days. He also felt inadequate in his relationship with his girlfriend, Laura—a relationship characterized by emotionally charged separations and reconciliations, as well as by sexual experimentation, in which David frequently doubted his sexual adequacy. When Laura dated another boy and refused to tell David the details, David thought the date had involved intercourse, and he wrote a vindictive poem in which he called Laura a whore. After mailing the poem he felt guilty, and he was quite disturbed to find that his best friend sided with Laura. David began to stay in his room more, attending only a few classes.

These excerpts from David's diary were written shortly before his hospitalization.

". . . and there's old Hawthorne's [American writer Nathaniel Hawthorne] bosom serpent for you eating away hissing all night I lie there and I lie there and think and think and think all the time trying not to think I think anyway or reminisce rather (delightful pastime) until pow I feel like the top of my head blows off and I smash my fist into something and begin all over again like a one cycle engine." (p. 348)

"Tuesday, March 10, 10 P.M. I can't cope, I can't come to grips . . . it's Hawthorne's disease blazing away, red guilt or little stringy black warts (they're

HIGHLIGHT
Types of schizophrenia

Undifferentiated type	A pattern of symptoms in which there is a rapidly changing mixture of all or most of the primary indicators of schizophrenia. Commonly observed are indications of perplexity, confusion, emotional turmoil, delusions of reference, excitement, dreamlike autism, depression, and fear. Most often, this picture is seen in patients who are in the process of breaking down and becoming schizophrenic. However, it is also seen when major changes are occurring in the adjustive demands impinging on a person with an already-established schizophrenic psychosis. In such cases it frequently foreshadows an impending change to another primary schizophrenic subtype.
Paranoid type	A symptom picture dominated by absurd, illogical, and changeable delusions, frequently accompanied by vivid hallucinations, with a resulting impairment of critical judgment and erratic, unpredictable, and occasionally dangerous behavior. In chronic cases, there is usually less disorganization of behavior than in other types of schizophrenia, and less extreme withdrawal from social interaction.
Catatonic type	Often characterized by alternating periods of extreme withdrawal and extreme excitement, although in some cases one or the other reaction predominates. In the withdrawal reaction there is a sudden loss of all animation and a tendency to remain motionless for hours or even days in a single position. The clinical picture may undergo an abrupt change, with excitement coming on suddenly, wherein the individual may talk or shout incoherently, pace rapidly, and engage in uninhibited, impulsive, and frenzied behavior. In this state, the individual may be dangerous.
Disorganized (hebephrenic) type	Usually occurs at an earlier age than most other types of schizophrenia, and represents a more severe disintegration of the personality. Emotional distortion and blunting typically are manifested in inappropriate laughter and silliness, peculiar mannerisms, and bizarre, often obscene, behavior.
Residual type	Mild indications of schizophrenia shown by individuals in remission following a schizophrenic episode.

growing with a virulence I swear I never noticed before) . . . music helps a bit and I've conducted the Eroica all over the room three times already today, waving my arms and occasionally hitting things . . . all very dramatic . . . to think I worried myself about sleeping too much last fall! I've given the jargon a once over; it stems from incest drives, castration fears, masturbation complexes, homosexual doubts, oedipal fixations bullshit bullshit it was around before the jargon and its got me . . . already at table I've been making curious unconscious slips as if the synapses suddenly rot away and I come disconnected its all right its all right I'm going to be a lawyer and make lots of money and grow up to be as weak as my father as torn as my mother look ahead!!" (p. 349)

"Midnight Tuesday. . . . Boy, that Nathan and Laura business really pulled the cork I'm bad or mad or just dull? Down on my knees before the crescent moon I got my pants dirty. This is undoubtedly one of the most prolix records of a scarringover process (I'm sealing like one of those puncture proof tires, but in slow motion) I should be back to my habitual state of callousness in a couple of days with no apparent damage, maybe I can even go on staving off like this ("a poem is a momentary stay against confusion" Frost . . . this is quite a poem) till I die." (p. 351)

"Thursday, March 12, 11 A.M. I'm out! I'm through . . . boomed out of the tunnel sometime last night and it's raining stars . . . whooey . . . its nice out there's time for everything . . . I can do it I did it and if it happens again I'll do it again twice as hard I got a dexamyl high going and I'm not on dexamyl and

I've been up for forty eight or more hours and I'm giddygiddygiddy and I took a test this morning and it was on Voltaire and I kicked him a couple of good ones for being down on Pascal that poor bastard with his shrivelled body and bottomless abysess they're not bottomless!! You get down far enough and it gets thick enough and black enough and then you claw claw claw your way out and pretty soon you're on top again. And I licked it by myself, all alone. No pandering psychiatrists or priests or friends by myself. Now, I must admit I'm a little leery; I dashed back to the typewriter to give it form to write it down and sew it in my vest like Pascal so if the Thing hits me again I'll have this in my vest and I'll kick it in the teeth again but Pascal saw God and yet still it hit him again. . . will it hit me again? Who cares . . . I just sat in on one of those weddings of the soul and I tooted tooted . . . I don't care I can use it I can run on it it will be my psychic gasoline now I don't have to sleep sleep all the time to get away with it . . . but if I lose my typewriter?" (p. 351)

"Saturday, March 14, 11 A.M. . . . Falling asleep last night a thousand million thoughts bubbled then the number the age 18 what happened when I was 18? (my stomach hurts . . . it really physically does . . . that blue bear has all kinds of tricks . . . I'm going out for coffee) Well I DO have to go out to get some money but I MUST be merciless with the blue bear. He has no quarter for me. . . . and not scare myself with eery consequences . . . the newspaper odds are AGAINST automobile deaths, that was the resistance mechanism trying to stop me again I'm hot on your tail blue bear that doesn't mean anything what does that mean it means that I'm feeling the denied homosexual instincts, feeling the woman in me and getting over her that's it that's what Faulkner's bear was a woman I have the quotes up on my wall I wrote them down a week ago. . . . woman is a bear you must kill the bear to be a man no that isn't what I've got on my wall the quotes go 'Anyone could be upset by his first lion.'" (p. 356)

David was hospitalized four days after writing this. His experiences illustrate well the massive breakdown of filtering, the panic at loss of control, and the desperate attempts to understand what is going on that are typical in early undifferentiated schizophrenia.

Fortunately, most patients "work through" their problems and recover from such acute undifferentiated episodes within a period of weeks or months. Such was the case for David. However, recurrent episodes are not uncommon in this type of disorder, especially in the absence of vigorous follow-up treatment. Myra Genain's breakdown was similar to David's, but she required several years of psychotherapy to ensure a lasting recovery. In some few instances, treatment efforts are unsuccessful, and the mixed symptoms of the early undifferentiated disorder slide into a more chronic phase, typically developing into the more specific symptoms of other subtypes.

Catatonic type. Though catatonic reactions often appear with dramatic suddenness, usually the patient has shown a background of eccentric behavior, often accompanied by some degree of withdrawal from reality. Though at one time very common in Europe and North America, catatonic reactions have seemingly become less frequent in recent years.

The central feature of catatonic is the pronounced motor symptoms, either of an excited or a stuporous type, which sometimes make for difficulty in differentiating this condition from a psychotic affective disorder. As in the case of the Genains, all of whom had early diagnoses of catatonia, the clinical picture is often an early manifestation of a disorder that will become chronic and intractable unless the underlying process is somehow arrested.

Some catatonic patients alternate between periods of extreme stupor and extreme excitement, sometimes quite violent, but in most cases one reaction or the other is predominant. In a study of 250 people diagnosed as suffering from catatonic schizophrenia, Morrison (1973) found that 110 were predominantly withdrawn, 67 were predominantly excited, and 73 were considered "mixed." No significant differences were found between these groups with regard to age, sex, or education.

During a catatonic stupor, the person loses all animation and tends to remain motionless in a rigid, unchanging position—mute and staring into space—sometimes maintaining the same position for hours or even days, until the hands and feet become blue and swollen because of the immobility. One patient felt that he had to hold his hand out flat because the forces of "good" and "evil" were waging a "war of the worlds" on his hand, and if he moved it, he might tilt the precarious balance in favor of the forces of evil. Surprisingly, despite their seeming withdrawal and apparent lack of attention to their surroundings while in this condition, catatonic individuals may later relate in detail events that were going on around them.

Some of these patients are highly suggestible

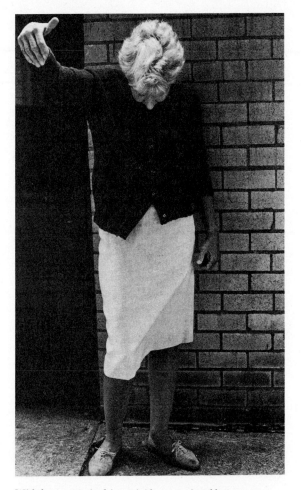

With her arm raised in a rigid, uncomfortable pose, a woman diagnosed as catatonic schizophrenic stands silent and motionless, apparently oblivious to her surroundings. Catatonic schizophrenic patients may alternate between periods of extreme withdrawal and extreme excitement, but in most cases one reaction or the other predominates.

and will automatically obey commands or imitate the actions of others *(echopraxia)* or mimic their phrases *(echolalia).* If the patient's arm is raised to an awkward and uncomfortable position, he or she may keep it in that position for minutes or even hours. Ordinarily, patients in a catatonic stupor resist stubbornly any effort to change their position and may become mute, resist all attempts at feeding, and refuse to comply with even the slightest request. They pay no attention to bowel or bladder control, and may drool saliva. Their facial expression is typically vacant, and their skin appears waxy. Threats and painful stimuli have no effect, and they

have to be dressed and washed and have their eliminative processes taken care of.

Suddenly and without warning, catatonic patients may pass from states of extreme stupor to great excitement, during which they seem to be under great "pressure of activity" and may become violent. They may talk or shout excitedly and incoherently, pace rapidly back and forth, openly indulge in sexual activities such as masturbation, attempt self-mutilation or even suicide, or impulsively attack and try to kill others. The suddenness and the extreme frenzy of these attacks make such patients very dangerous to both themselves and others. These excited states may last a few hours, days, or even weeks.

The following case illustrates some of the symptoms typical of catatonic reactions.

"Todd Phillips, a 16-year-old high school student, was referred to a psychiatric hospital by his family physician. His family had been very upset by his increasingly strange behavior over the preceding eight months. They had consulted their family physician, who treated him with small doses of antipsychotic medication, without any improvement.

"Although Todd has had many problems since he was a small child, there was a distinct change about eight months ago. He began spending more and more time in his room and seemed uninterested in doing many of his usual activities. His grades dropped. He started stuttering. He used to weigh about 215 pounds, but began to eat less, and lost 35 pounds. For no reason, he started drinking large quantities of water.

"More recently, there was a change for the worse. A few months ago he began taking Tai Chi lessons and often stood for long periods in karatelike positions, oblivious to what was going on around him. He stopped doing his homework. He took an inordinately long time to get dressed, eat his meals, or bathe. Before getting dressed in the morning he would go through an elaborate ritual of arranging his clothes on the bed before putting them on. When his parents asked him a question, he repeated the question over and over and did not seem to hear or understand what was said.

"At school he received demerits for the first time for being late to class. His family began to lose patience with him when he eventually refused to go to school. When his father tried to get him out of bed in the morning, he lay motionless, sometimes having wet the bed during the night. It was at this point that his parents, in desperation, consulted their family physician.

"When first seen in the hospital, Todd was a disheveled looking, somewhat obese adolescent, standing motionless in the center of the room with his head flexed forward and his hands at his sides. He appeared perplexed, but was correctly oriented to time and place. He was able to do simple calculations, and his recent and remote memory were intact. He answered questions slowly and in a peculiar manner. An example of his speech follows:

Q: Why did you come to the hospital?
A: Why did I come? Why did I come to the hospital? I came to the hospital because of crazy things with my hands. Sometimes my hands jump up like that . . . wait a minute . . . I guess it's happening . . . Well, yes, see it's been happening (making robotlike gestures with his hands).
Q: What thoughts go through your head?
A: What thoughts go through my head? What thoughts go through my head? Well, I think about things . . . like . . . yes, well . . . I think thoughts . . . I have thoughts. I think thoughts.
Q: What thoughts?
A: What thoughts? What kinds of thoughts? I think thoughts.
Q: Do you hear voices?
A: Do I hear voices? I hear voices. People talk. Do I hear voices? No . . . people talk. I hear voices. I hear voices when people talk.
Q: Are you sick?
A: Am I sick? No I'm not sick . . these fidgeting habits, these fidgeting habits. I have habits. I have fidgeting habits.
Throughout the examination he made repetitive chewing and biting motions. Occasionally, when questioned, he would smile enigmatically. He seemed unresponsive to much of what was going on around him. His infrequent movements were slow and jerky, and he often assumed the karatelike postures that his parents described, in which he would remain frozen. If the examiner placed the patient's hands in an awkward position the patient remained frozen in that position for several minutes. "(Spitzer et al., 1983, pp. 139–40)

Although the matter is far from settled, some clinicians interpret the catatonic patient's immobility as a way of coping with the reduced filtering ability and increased vulnerability to stimulation: it seems to provide a feeling of some control over external sources of stimulation though not necessarily over inner ones. Freeman has cited the explanation advanced by one patient: "I did not want to move, because if I did everything changed around me and upset me horribly so I remained still to hold onto a sense of permanence" (1960, p. 932).

Disorganized (hebephrenic) type. Disorganized or hebephrenic disorders usually occur at an earlier age and represent a more severe disintegration of the personality than in the other types of schizophrenia. Fortunately, they are considerably less common than the other forms.

Typically the individual has a history of oddness, overscrupulousness about trivial things, and preoccupation with religious and philosophical issues. Frequently, he or she is brooding over the dire results of masturbation or minor infractions of social conventions. While schoolmates are enjoying normal play and social activities, this person is gradually becoming more seclusive and more preoccupied with fantasies.

As the disorder progresses, the individual becomes emotionally indifferent and infantile. A silly smile and inappropriate, shallow laughter after little or no provocation are common symptoms. If asked the reason for their laughter, patients may state that they do not know or may volunteer some wholly irrelevant and unsatisfactory explanation. Speech becomes incoherent and may include considerable baby talk, childish giggling, a repetitive use of similar-sounding words, and a derailing of thought along the lines of associated meanings that may give a punlike quality to speech. In some instances speech becomes completely incoherent.

Hallucinations, particularly auditory ones, are common. The voices heard by hebephrenic patients may accuse them of immoral practices, "pour filth" into their minds, and call them vile names. Delusions are usually of a sexual, religious, hypochondriacal, or persecutory nature and are changeable and fantastic. For example, one woman insisted not only that she was being followed by enemies but that she had already been killed a number of times. Another claimed that a long tube extended from the Kremlin direct to her uterus, through which she was being invaded by Russians.

In occasional cases, individuals become hostile and aggressive. They may exhibit peculiar mannerisms and other bizarre forms of behavior. These may take the form of word salad (meaningless repetition of words or sentences), facial grimaces, talking and gesturing to themselves, sudden inexplicable laughter and weeping, and in some cases an abnormal interest in urine and feces, which they may smear on walls and even on themselves. Obscene behavior and absence of any modesty or sense of shame are characteristic. Although they may exhibit outbursts of anger and temper tantrums in connection with fantasies, they are indifferent to real-life situations, no matter how horrifying or gruesome they may be.

The clinical picture in disorganized schizophrenia is shown in the following interview:

The patient was a divorcée, 32 years of age, who had come to the hospital with bizarre delusions, hallucinations, and severe personality disintegration and with a record of alcoholism, promiscuity, and possible incestuous relations with a brother. The following conversation shows typical hebephrenic responses to questioning.

Dr.: How do you feel today?
Pt.: Fine.
Dr.: When did you come here?
Pt.: 1416, you remember, doctor (silly giggle).
Dr.: Do you know why you are here?
Pt.: Well, in 1951 I changed into two men. President Truman was judge at my trial. I was convicted and hung (silly giggle). My brother and I were given back our normal bodies 5 years ago. I am a policewoman. I keep a dictaphone concealed on my person.
Dr.: Can you tell me the name of this place?
Pt.: I have not been a drinker for 16 years. I am taking a mental rest after a "carter" assignment or "quill." You know, a "penwrap." I had contracts with Warner Brothers Studios and Eugene broke phonograph records but Mike protested. I have been with the police department for 35 years. I am made of flesh and blood—see doctor (pulling up her dress).
Dr.: Are you married?
Pt.: No. I am not attracted to men (silly giggle). I have a companionship arrangement with my brother. I am a "looner" . . . a bachelor.

The prognosis is poor if a schizophrenic person becomes hebephrenic. As we have seen, Iris and Hester, the two least functional of the Genain sisters, were also the only two of the sisters to have been definitely hebephrenic during the course of their disorders. To at least some extent, the disorganized, hebephrenic variety of schizophrenia may be regarded as the "last stop" on a downward-coursing path of "process" schizophrenic psychosis. At this point, no form of treatment intervention yet discovered has a marked likelihood of effecting more than a very modest "recovery."

This drawing depicts a "tree man" holding a bleeding human head. The young woman who drew it, diagnosed as disorganized or hebephrenic schizophrenic, described her creation as a "comical print." Preoccupation with bizarre fantasies is considered characteristic of hebephrenic schizophrenic patients.

Paranoid type. Formerly about one half of all schizophrenic first admissions to mental hospitals and clinics were of the paranoid type. In recent years, however, the incidence of the paranoid type has shown a substantial decrease, while the undifferentiated type has shown a marked increase.

Frequently paranoid-type persons show a history of growing suspiciousness and of severe difficulties in interpersonal relationships. The eventual symptom picture is dominated by absurd, illogical, and changeable delusions. Persecutory delusions are the most frequent and may involve a wide range of ideas and all sorts of plots. The individual may become highly suspicious of relatives or associates and may complain of being watched, followed, poisoned, talked about, or influenced by electrical devices rigged up by "enemies."

In addition to persecutory themes, themes of grandeur are also common in the delusions of the paranoid type. Such individuals may, for example, claim to be the world's greatest economist or philosopher, or some prominent person of the past, such as Napoleon, the Virgin Mary, or even Christ. These delusions are frequently accompanied by vivid auditory, visual, and other hallucinations. Patients may hear singing, or God speaking, or the voices of their enemies, or they may see angels or feel electric rays piercing their bodies at various points.

The individual's thinking and behavior become centered around the themes of persecution and/or grandeur in a pathological "paranoid construction" that—for all its distortion of reality—provides a sense of identity not otherwise attainable. There thus tends to be a higher level of adaptive coping and of preservation of cognitive integrative skills in the paranoid-type schizophrenic person than in other schizophrenic persons, which is undoubtedly one of the important bases for the paranoid-nonparanoid distinction noted earlier and increasingly employed by both clinicians and researchers (see **HIGHLIGHT** on page 361).

Despite this seeming "advantage" the paranoid-type schizophrenic enjoys, such persons are far from easy to deal with. The weaving of delusions and hallucinations into the paranoid construction results in loss of critical judgment and in erratic, unpredictable behavior. In response to a command from a "voice," such an individual may break furniture or commit other violent acts. Occasionally paranoid schizophrenic patients can be dangerous, as when they attack people they are convinced have been persecuting them. In general, they show less extreme withdrawal from the outside world than individuals with most other types of schizophrenia.

The following conversation between a doctor and a man diagnosed as chronic paranoid schizophrenic illustrates well the illogical, delusional picture, together with continued attention to external data that are misinterpreted, which these individuals experience.

> **Dr.:** What's your name?
> **Pt.:** Who are you?
> **Dr.:** I'm a doctor. Who are you?
> **Pt.:** I can't tell you who I am.
> **Dr.:** Why can't you tell me?
> **Pt.:** You wouldn't believe me.
> **Dr.:** What are you doing here?
> **Pt.:** Well, I've been sent here to thwart the Rus-

sians. I'm the only one in the world who knows how to deal with them. They got their spies all around here though to get me, but I'm smarter than any of them.
> **Dr.:** What are you going to do to thwart the Russians?
> **Pt.:** I'm organizing.
> **Dr.:** Whom are you going to organize?
> **Pt.:** Everybody. I'm the only man in the world who can do that, but they're trying to get me. But I'm going to use my atomic bomb media to blow them up.
> **Dr.:** You must be a terribly important person then.
> **Pt.:** Well, of course.
> **Dr.:** What do you call yourself?
> **Pt.:** You used to know me as Franklin D. Roosevelt.
> **Dr.:** Isn't he dead?
> **Pt.:** Sure he's dead, but I'm alive.
> **Dr.:** But you're Franklin D. Roosevelt?
> **Pt.:** His spirit. He, God, and I figured this out. And now I'm going to make a race of healthy people. My agents are lining them up. Say, who are you?
> **Dr.:** I'm a doctor here.
> **Pt.:** You don't look like a doctor. You look like a Russian to me.
> **Dr.:** How can you tell a Russian from one of your agents?
> **Pt.:** I read eyes. I get all my signs from eyes. I look into your eyes and get all my signs from them.
> **Dr.:** Do you sometimes hear voices telling you someone is a Russian?
> **Pt.:** No, I just look into eyes. I got a mirror here to look into my own eyes. I know everything that's going on. I can tell by the color, by the way it's shaped.
> **Dr.:** Did you have any trouble with people before you came here?
> **Pt.:** Well, only the Russians. They were trying to surround me in my neighborhood. One day they tried to drop a bomb on me from the fire escape.
> **Dr.:** How could you tell it was a bomb?
> **Pt.:** I just knew.

While it is true, as we have seen, that many paranoid schizophrenic individuals have histories of gradual onset and long-lasting difficulties in interpersonal relationships and productive functioning, it is also true that very few of them show the true "process" pattern of schizophrenia (Ritzler, 1981). Sometimes, indeed, onset is quite rapid and occurs in individuals with entirely adequate, even distinguished, pasts. In fact, one of the most famous cases of paranoid schizophrenia involved a very high ranking German judge, Dr. Daniel Paul Schreber, who described his disorder at length in memoirs published after his partial recovery. Freud used

HIGHLIGHT

An assassin diagnosed as chronic paranoid schizophrenic

Sirhan B. Sirhan, the convicted assassin of Senator Robert F. Kennedy, was diagnosed as chronic paranoid schizophrenic by expert witnesses—psychologists and psychiatrists—appointed by the court.

Although proud of his deed and believing himself to have been a great patriot who acted on behalf of the Arab people (Kennedy had proposed a short time previously that the United States send 50 military aircraft to Israel), Sirhan seemed to have no recollection of the actual assassination. Diamond (1969), who examined Sirhan, suspected that the amnesia covered a psychotic break. He hypnotized Sirhan and was able to observe an entirely different individual, one who vividly remembered killing Kennedy and who was intensely emotional when asked any question about the Arab-Israeli conflict. For example, when asked about a terrifying experience of his boyhood, the bombing of Jerusalem by the Israelis in 1948, Sirhan "suddenly crumpled in agony like a child, sobbing and shivering in terror. The tears poured down his face" (p. 54).

According to Diamond, Sirhan planned the killing under self-hypnosis and lacked conscious awareness of it. An example of a "truly split" personality, whose arrogance and "cool front" provided a "simulation of sanity," Sirhan apparently preferred to think of himself as a sane patriot and be convicted of the assassination—rather than face his psychotic behavior and the possibility of being declared criminally insane.

Pages from Sirhan's "trance" notebooks were introduced in evidence at his trial for Robert F. Kennedy's murder. Commenting on them, Diamond (1969) said: "Sirhan's trances obviously took his mind into a voodoo world. He thought he saw Kennedy's face come before him in the mirror, blotting out his own image, and he began to write kill-Kennedy orders to himself . . . 'RFK must die,' he wrote, 'Robert F. Kennedy must be assassinated before June 5, 1968.' . . . Actually his self-hypnosis worked better than he knew. Without real knowledge or awareness of what was happening in the trances, he rigorously programmed himself for the assassination exactly the way a computer is programmed by magnetic tape. In his unconscious mind there existed a plan for the fulfillment of his sick, paranoid hatred of Kennedy and all who might want to help the Jews. In his conscious mind there was no awareness of such a plan or that he, Sirhan, was to be the instrument of assassination" (p. 50). While interesting and persuasive, it may be pointed out that other professionals such as clinical psychologists or psychiatrists might place a different interpretation on these comments from Sirhan's notebook.

Sirhan has requested that he be paroled, having served the minimum "time" for the crime for which he was incarcerated. His plea has been turned down twice by the parole board.

these memoirs in developing his now largely discredited theory that paranoid thinking is due to repressed homosexuality.

Schreber's disorder began with the idea that he was to be transformed into a woman by some sort of conspiracy, and, once the transformation was accomplished, he was to be delivered over to a certain man for the purpose of sexual abuse. During the course of the disorder, the idea of conspiracy came gradually to be replaced by the idea that his "emasculation" and subsequent impregnation were inspired by a divine plan involving world redemption. In fact, he would be impregnated by divine rays so that a new race of humans might be created.

Schreber also felt that he was being persecuted by certain people, including his former physician, and he heaped verbal abuse upon these enemies. In turn, he heard voices that mocked him and jeered at him. At various times, he became convinced that he was dying of strange illnesses, such as "softening of the brain" and "the plague." At another point he believed he was dead and his body, which was being handled by others in all sorts of revolting ways, was decomposing. He was tormented so much by such thoughts that he in fact attempted suicide on several occasions and demanded of the hospital staff that they provide him with the cyanide he was sure they were intending for him anyway. He felt he was "the plaything of the devils." As his thoughts turned more toward religion in the later phases of the disorder, he claimed to see "miraculous apparitions" and to hear "holy music." (Adapted from Spitzer et al., 1981)

In this case, we see clearly the deterioration from a previous level of functioning, the bizarre ideas, and the hallucinatory experiences so characteristic of schizophrenia generally. The paranoid subtype diagnosis is appropriate because of the prominent delusions of both persecution (he is being conspired against) and grandiosity (he has been selected by God to be impregnated and start a new race). Dr. Schreber regained sufficient control to secure his release from the hospital some nine years after the onset of his disorder; at the time, however, he was still considered delusional.

Other schizophrenic patterns. The remaining subcategories of schizophrenia contained in the DSM-III classification deserve brief mention, though we shall not discuss them in detail. The *residual* type is a category used for persons regarded as having recovered from schizophrenia but as still manifesting some signs of their past disorder.

As was noted in the preceding chapter, *schizoaffective disorder* (manic or depressive or mixed) is applied to individuals who show features of both schizophrenia and severe affective disorder. In the DSM-III classification, this disorder is not listed as a formal category of schizophrenic disorder but rather under *Psychotic disorders not elsewhere classified*.

Also included in the category of *Psychotic disorders not elsewhere classified* is **schizophreniform disorder,** a category reserved for schizophrenic psychoses of less than six months' duration. It may include any of the symptoms described above, but is probably most often seen in an undifferentiated form. At the present time, all new cases of schizophrenia would first receive a diagnosis of schizophreniform disorder. Because of the possibility of an early and lasting remission in a first episode of schizophrenic breakdown, prognosis for the disorder is better than for established forms of schizophrenia, and it would appear likely that by keeping it out of the formal category of schizophrenic disorder, the potentially harmful effects of labeling may be minimized.[2]

Biological factors in schizophrenia

Despite extensive research on schizophrenia, the etiology of this disorder is still unclear. Primary responsibility for its development has been attributed variously to (a) biological factors, including heredity and various biochemical and neurophysiological processes; (b) psychosocial factors, including early psychic trauma, pathogenic interpersonal and family patterns, faulty learning, difficulties in social roles, and decompensation under excessive stress; and (c) sociocultural factors, especially as influences on the types and incidence of schizophrenic reactions. These three sets of factors are not mutually exclusive, of course, and it seems likely that all are involved.

---

[2]There is currently considerable controversy over whether two of the personality types, *borderline personality disorder* and *schizotypal personality disorder* (see pages 239 and 241–242) may in fact be related generically and perhaps genetically to schizophrenia. An entire issue of the authoritative government publication *Schizophrenia Bulletin* (1979, Vol. 5) was devoted to papers taking different positions on this controversy.

Heredity. In view of the disproportionate incidence of schizophrenia in the family backgrounds of schizophrenic patients, a number of investigators have concluded that genetic factors must play an important causal role. While the evidence seems persuasive, it remains circumstantial, based on demonstrations of high concordance rates among close relatives of schizophrenics.

1. *Twin studies.* Twin studies, which we discussed briefly in Chapter 4, are designed to find out whether the concordance rate is greater for *identical* (monozygotic) twins, who develop from a single fertilized egg and share the same genetic inheritance, than it is for *fraternal* twins, whose genetic inheritance is comparable to that of other siblings.

While the incidence of schizophrenia among twins is no greater than for the general population, early studies—which tended to be methodologically naive by modern standards—found very high concordance rates for schizophrenia among monozygotic, or identical, twins relative to fraternal twins or ordinary siblings. More recent studies using refinements in methodology have reported substantially lower concordance rates for both kinds of twins.

In a major study in Norway, Kringlen (1967) found a 38 percent concordance rate for identical twins, as contrasted with 10 percent for fraternal twins; Cohen et al. (1972), studying a large sample of twin pairs who were veterans of the American armed forces, found a concordance rate of 23.5 percent for identical and 5.3 percent for fraternal twins.[3] Similarly, Gottesman and Shields (1972) found a concordance rate of 42 percent for identical and 9 percent for fraternal twins. They also found that the concordance was much higher for identical twins with severe schizophrenic disorders than for those with mild schizophrenic symptoms. In severe cases, when one identical twin became schizophrenic, it was usually just a question of time before the other did also. The lowest concordance rate thus far reported is 6 percent, but this was obtained in a study in which no "age-correction" factor was employed and in which a very narrow definition of concordance was applied (Tienari, 1968). In

other words, no adjustment, or correction, was made in the 6 percent figure for the nonschizophrenic co-twins who were not yet beyond the age of risk for schizophrenia (about age 45) and who might later become schizophrenic, and "concordance" was accepted only when the co-twin showed a definite schizophrenic psychosis rather than some other form of severe disorder. This study illustrates the extent to which the concordance rate that is found can depend on the definitions and methods of the researcher. In fact, by 1976 the concordance rate for these twins had risen to 16 percent (Gottesman & Shields, 1976).

If schizophrenia were exclusively a genetic disorder, the concordance rate for identical twins would, of course, be 100 percent. In fact, however, there appear to be more *discordant* than *concordant* pairs, notwithstanding the remarkable example of the Genain sisters. On the other hand, there is clearly *some* concordance. What this means is that a twin may have an enhanced risk of schizophrenia if the co-twin is schizophrenic. In other words, the twin studies show us that *predisposition* for the disorder is associated with genetic variables. It does not prove a *genetic* transmission of predisposition, however, because environmental factors cannot be ruled out: the environments, both prenatal and postnatal, of identical twins must inevitably be more similar than the environments of individuals sharing any other type of relationship, including fraternal twinship. Moreover, since somewhat over half of the identical co-twins of schizophrenic patients do not develop the disorder, it means that there is a good chance the environment will be sufficiently benign to protect even the individual with a substantial predisposition, whatever the source.

2. *Children reared apart from their schizophrenic parents.* Several studies have attempted to overcome the shortcomings of the twin method in achieving a true and unassailable separation of hereditary from environmental influences by using what is called the *adoption strategy.* Here, concordance rates are established for the biological and the adoptive relatives of individuals who have been adopted out of their biological families at an early age (preferably at birth) and have subsequently become schizophrenic. If concordance is greater among the subjects' biological than adoptive relatives, a hereditary influence is strongly suggested; the

[3]The lower concordance rates in the Cohen et al. study may be partially explained by the fact that the veteran sample was not representative of the general twin population, since it consisted entirely of men who had been considered fit for military service.

Art by
schizophrenic
individuals

Although schizophrenia typically involves severely disorganized thinking and disturbances of communicative abilities, quite often schizophrenic individuals exhibit a remarkable artistic facility, particularly in the areas of painting and drawing. Not infrequently, the work of these artists also reflects movement through stages of the disorder or stages of therapy. On these pages and at various points throughout the rest of this chapter, we will present instances of notable art created by people who have suffered schizophrenic breakdowns.

L ouis Wain (1860–1939) was a well-known and popular artist who painted pictures of cats in human situations, such as wearing glasses and having tea parties. In the mid-1920s he suffered a schizophrenic breakdown and thereafter was confined to mental institutions, where he continued to paint. These paintings show his transition from realistic and recognizable portraits to representations that became increasingly stylized and ornamental—and in the end unrecognizable. Wain's paintings are remarkable for the clues they provide to his mental state and the distortions of perception that are characteristically schizophrenic.

reverse pattern would indicate environmental causation.

Heston (1966) was among the first to use one of several variants of this basic method. In a follow-up study of 47 persons who had been born to schizophrenic mothers in a state mental hospital and placed with relatives or in foster homes shortly after birth, Heston found that 16.6 percent of these subjects were later diagnosed as schizophrenic. In contrast, none of the 50 control subjects selected from among residents of the same foster homes—whose mothers were not schizophrenic—later became schizophrenic. In addition to the greater probability of being labeled schizophrenic, Heston found that the offspring of schizophrenic mothers were more likely to be diagnosed as mentally retarded, neurotic, and psychopathic. They also had been involved more frequently in criminal activities, and had spent more time in penal institutions. Thus Heston concluded that children born to schizophrenic mothers, even when reared without contact with them, were more likely not only to become schizophrenic but also to suffer a wide spectrum of other disorders. Heston's findings have been confirmed by other investigators.

These findings could mean that the genes involved in schizophrenia are very diffuse in their effects, but other quite tenable hypotheses present themselves. For example, some researchers (e.g., Mednick, 1978) have noted a pronounced tendency for schizophrenic women to mate with psychopathic and criminally disposed men, who may therefore also have made an abnormal genetic contribution to these offspring of schizophrenic mothers.

Other studies of children who have schizophrenic mothers and/or fathers but were adopted at an early age and reared by presumably normal parents have found from 20 to 31.6 percent developing disorders in the "schizophrenic spectrum" (Rosenthal, 1970; Rosenthal et al., 1971; Wender, 1972; Wender et al., 1974). In general, these adoption studies have provided the strongest evidence yet obtained for the genetic transmission of a vulnerability to schizophrenia, and evidence from this type of study continues to build in an impressive manner (Kety et al., 1978; Kinney & Jacobsen, 1978).

Nonetheless, the adoption work so far completed has not gone unchallenged. Benjamin (1976a) discovered that, when proper statistical analysis was applied to one of the more important samples in the adoption study series, the schizophrenic adoptee/biological relative concordance turned out to be most in evidence among half-siblings (i.e., siblings sharing only one parent in common) of schizophrenic adoptees—not parents or full siblings, who were also studied. Benjamin (1976a, 1976b) admits that this is a peculiar finding and makes the point that it violates a basic assumption implicit in such studies, namely, that genetic effects should be lesser, not greater, with a lesser biological relationship.

Another challenge to the available adoption studies has been leveled by Sarbin and Mancuso (1980), who note that the data as reported contain a fair number of confusing anomalies, including the fact that the adopted children studied have exceptionally low rates of schizophrenic breakdown, while their relatives (especially the biological ones) have exceptionally high rates. They also note that many youngsters are adopted in the first place because social agencies find them mistreated in their biological families; we would expect to find a high proportion of seriously disturbed people among such families. Hence what appears to be a genetic transmission of schizophrenia may have more to do with, for instance, the long-range effects of child-battering or other traumatic experience. The fact that comparatively few of the adopted children in these studies became schizophrenic is attributed by Sarbin and Mancuso to the excellent work of adoption agencies, particularly adoption agencies located in Denmark, which has been the host country for most of this work.

3. *Family studies.* Another line of research has studied the incidence of schizophrenia among children reared by their schizophrenic parents. Rieder (1973) found a wide spectrum of psychopathology reported among the adult offspring of schizophrenic parents, ranging from schizophrenia to psychopathic personality disorders. The offspring of schizophrenic parents also showed a high incidence of psychological maladjustment as children—estimated at 20 percent—with two types being prominent: a withdrawn schizoid type and a hyperactive, antisocial, delinquent type. Thus Rieder concluded that the offspring of schizophrenic parents differ from the offspring of nonschizophrenic parents.

In the same vein, Kringlen (1978) showed that 28 percent of children born to parents who had both become schizophrenic at some point in their adult lives were classifiable as psychotic or borderline psychotic; 20 percent of these children of schizophrenic parents had developed clinical schizophrenia. But—and this observation deserves special note—28 percent of the children of such unions were diagnosed as entirely normal. That is, nearly one third of these children escaped any form of psychopathology despite what must have been a very heavy genetic risk *and* the environmental hazards of association with two psychotic parents! Evidently having two schizophrenic parents increases the risks of poor mental health—but it need not always have ill effects.

4. *Studies of high-risk children.* The research strategy of monitoring over time children known to be at high risk for schizophrenia by virtue of having been born to a schizophrenic parent is basically one intended to identify the environmental factors that cause breakdown (or resistance to it) in predisposed persons. As we have seen in Chapter 4, this strategy, pioneered by Mednick and Schulsinger (1968) and followed up by numerous additional research projects (see, for example, Garmezy, 1978a, 1978c; Neale & Oltmanns, 1980; Rieder, 1979), has thus far not paid off very well in terms of isolating specific environmental factors. What it *has* done is show abundantly once again that having a schizophrenic parent is a very good predictor of psychological disorder, including schizophrenia. It seems likely that much of this predictability comes about as a result of the genetic transmission of vulnerability. One problem with such studies is that the child exposed to a psychotic parent, or one whose parent is frequently missing because of required hospitalizations (Mednick et al., 1978), is not quite comparable in environmental terms to the otherwise matched youngster whose parents are psychologically well-adjusted.

What shall we make, then, of the case for genetic transmission determining predisposition to schizophrenia? Taking the strictest of stands, we are forced to the Scottish verdict: *not proved.* It remains a judgment call, and ours is that there is probably some genetic influence that renders certain individuals vulnerable to schizophrenia. Too many independent sources of information—though some of them admittedly imperfect and incomplete on an individual basis—when taken together point to a relatively convincing case for

genetic contribution. We believe, too, that the classic methods of investigation in this field have been exhausted, and that nothing definitive is likely to be confirmed by further use of these essentially genealogical techniques. Rather, the next major advances will likely come from the use of techniques that can somehow pinpoint biochemical "markers" (e.g., levels of certain chemicals in the body) that are both specific for particular forms of schizophrenia *and* are readily tracked from one generation to the next. No such technique is yet available, but—given the incredible speed of advances in this and related areas—we would not be surprised if some were available soon. We turn now to a consideration of the biochemistry of the schizophrenias.

Biochemical factors.   Research into the possibility of biochemical abnormalities in schizophrenic patients was given a boost in the 1950s when a connection was made between schizophrenic symptoms and the long-established fact that the presence of some chemical agents in the bloodstream, even in minute amounts, can produce profound mental changes (Huxley, 1954). Lysergic acid (LSD) and mescaline, for example, can lead to a temporary disorganization of thought processes and a variety of psychotic-like symptoms that have been referred to as "model psychoses." Such findings encouraged investigators to look for an *endogenous hallucinogen*—a chemical synthesized within the body under stressful conditions that might account for the hallucinations and disorganization of thought and affect in schizophrenia and other psychotic disorders. A direct descendant of this line of thinking is the so-called *transmethylation hypothesis* of schizophrenia (see Carson, 1984). According to this view, chemically methylated versions of the biogenic amines or their metabolites accumulate in the brain, creating biochemical conditions similar to those following the ingestion of a hallucinogen. While the hypothesis cannot yet be wholly dismissed, partly because there are large numbers of methylated compounds in the body that have not yet been evaluated, it is not considered a very likely explanation (Meltzer, 1979).

The idea that schizophrenia may be caused by autointoxication from errant chemicals manufactured within the patient's own body is by no means new. It has a very long but undistinguished history, and it has been the source of numerous specific hypotheses that have enjoyed a transitory fame, only to be discarded and forgotten as later research disproves them. The riddle of schizophrenia is unlikely to be solved so simply.

If schizophrenia turns out to be in part biochemically caused—a hypothesis entirely consistent with the genetic evidence—it seems more likely that it will turn out to be due to some form of deficit in the *regulation* of chemicals that occur naturally in the nervous systems of all of us. At present, as in the case of the psychotic affective disorders, the best hypothesis is that there is aberrant biochemistry relating to the biogenic amines that control transmission of nervous impulses across synapses in the brain. Among the more attractive of the current ideas in this area is the so-called "dopamine hypothesis" of schizophrenia (Sachar et al., 1978; Snyder, 1978). Dopamine is a catecholamine like norepinephrine, of which it is in fact a chemical forerunner. Dopamine is the transmitter substance involved in certain important brain pathways.

According to the simplest form of the dopamine hypothesis, schizophrenia is the product of a functional excess of dopamine at certain synaptic sites. Variants of this view include hypotheses that the schizophrenic person has too many postsynaptic dopamine receptors or that these receptors have for some reason become "supersensitive." The most important—albeit indirect—evidence for the general hypothesis is that the clinical effectiveness of the various antipsychotic drugs is highly correlated with the extent to which they block dopamine action at the receptor. Correlation does not, of course, establish a causal relationship, and in recent times the dopamine hypothesis has proven less than satisfactory. Dopamine-blocking drugs, for instance, are therapeutically *nonspecific* for schizophrenia (that is, they are also used effectively to treat many organic mental disorders and some manias), and the receptor blocking effect is accomplished too quickly (within hours) to be consistent with the clinical picture of a gradual improvement (usually over several weeks) following initiation of drug therapy. In light of these and other observations, Davis (1978) has suggested that some other (unspecified) factor *causes* schizophrenia, the symptoms of which are then magnified by neural transmission accomplished by dopamine. Subsequent research has provided no serious challenge to this view (Carson, 1984).

The near demise of the dopamine hypothesis in its etiologic aspect has been a serious disappointment, particularly for those researchers and clinicians sincerely believing that the answer to the schizophrenia puzzle must lie in the domain of biochemistry. To date, no other biochemical theory of schizophrenia has garnered support equal to that of the dopamine theory. We should note, however, that there seems to be a growing interest in the possibility that the brain's natural opiates, the enkephalins and endorphins, may be implicated in schizophrenia (Volavka, Davis, & Ehrlich, 1979). This idea is too new at present to permit adequate evaluation. Ultimately, it seems likely that a complete understanding of the biochemistry of schizophrenic disorders will have to include a sense of how psychological factors interact with biochemical balances in the brain.

Neurophysiological factors. A good deal of research has focused on the role of neurophysiological disturbances in schizophrenia. These disturbances are thought to include an imbalance in excitatory and inhibitory processes and inappropriate arousal. Such processes would be expected to disrupt the normal attentional and information-processing capabilities of the organism, and there seems to be a growing consensus that such disturbances underlie and are basic to the cognitive and perceptual distortions characteristic of individuals diagnosed as schizophrenic (Neale & Oltmanns, 1980).

Consistently, schizophrenic persons are found to be deficient in their ability to track visually a moving target, a deficiency attributed to a disorder of "nonvoluntary attention." There is even some evidence that the close relatives of schizophrenics share this deficit (Kuechenmeister et al., 1977). Earlier work in this area has been well reviewed by Neale and Oltmanns (1980), and follow-up studies (Iacono, Tuason, & Johnson, 1981; Latham et al., 1981) continue to establish the reliability of the phenomenon.

A set of related findings indicate that schizophrenic individuals sometimes experience difficulties in maintaining attention and deficiencies in autonomic arousal prior to schizophrenic breakdown; that is, these problems are often

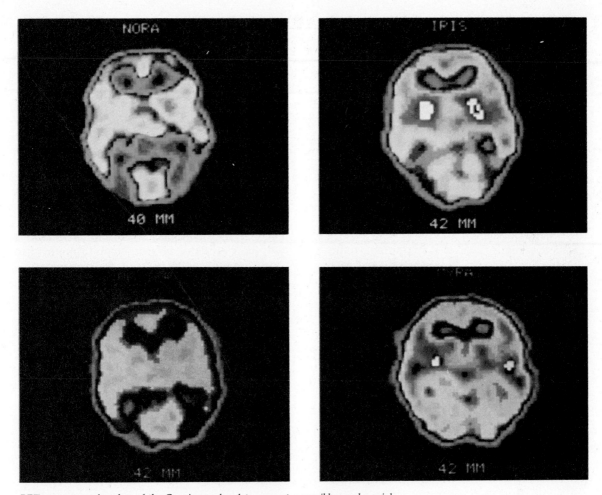

PET scans recently taken of the Genain quadruplets suggest a possible psychosocial impact resulting from the early matching of two pairs of co-twins. The scans indicate comparatively more severe brain impairment for Hester and Nora. The large areas of blue and yellow show that their brains consume lower levels of glucose, one indicator of lessened brain activity. The orange spots on the scans of Iris and Myra suggest more normal energy usage. Yet it is Iris, originally "matched" with Hester, who has had the poorer clinical outcome than either Nora or Myra.

present in individuals who are merely "at risk" for schizophrenia (Buchsbaum et al., 1978; Er-lenmeyer-Kimling & Cornblatt, 1978; Mednick, 1978; Spring & Zubin, 1978). As yet, however, the role of these neurophysiological divergences in the development of schizophrenia is not clear.

Considerable evidence, reviewed by Magaro (1980, 1981), suggests that schizophrenic persons process information in a way that is both abnormal and relatively specific to schizophrenic disorders. Briefly, these persons seem to be unable to match the sensory data they receive with the preexisting schematic patterns most of us

use to interpret or decode such data; the schizophrenic person, according to this view, accomplishes the task "automatically," unguided by preestablished cognitive processes. Applying this general approach, Magaro has been able to integrate and make sense of a multitude of findings which show that schizophrenic persons perform deficiently on cognitive tasks. Whether or not Magaro is right remains to be seen. Deficient performance on cognitive tasks among schizophrenics is well-documented (Rabin, Doneson, & Jentons, 1979), but, as has been pointed out by Sarbin and Mancuso (1980), such findings are virtually guaranteed in advance by the process of labeling certain people as schizophrenic.

Findings of abnormal neurophysiological processes in schizophrenia do not necessarily imply that such abnormalities are genetic in origin. Many could be the product of faulty early conditioning or of biological deviations caused by other factors. For example, problems of this sort could as likely arise from mechanical difficulties in the birth process as from genetic predestination. In fact, the frequency of obstetrical complications in the histories of persons who later become schizophrenic is markedly above that of the general population (McNeil & Kaij, 1978). In addition, recently developed computerized techniques of neurological assessment have established that some cases of schizophrenia, particularly chronic schizophrenia, are associated with organic brain degeneration in the form of enlargement of the ventricles (hollow areas filled with cerebrospinal fluid) lying deep within the brain structure (Andreasen et al., 1982a, 1982b; Golden et al., 1982).

The finding of an organic element associated with *some* cases of schizophrenia, particularly those in the "process" and "chronic" ranges, is of enormous significance for at least these types of schizophrenia. It fits in with growing evidence that a schizotypal personality pattern precedes many cases of outright schizophrenic pathology (Chapman & Chapman, 1980; Kendler, Gruenberg, & Strauss, 1981), and it suggests the possibility of estimating risk for these types of schizophrenia well in advance of the development of obvious symptoms (Grove, 1982).

Finally, in this connection, we must look at the most curious finding yet reported in relation to schizophrenia: the unusual distribution of dates of birth for persons who as adults become schizophrenic. In the northern hemisphere, the birth dates of persons who later become schizophrenic tend to occur in the late winter and early spring months, at a rate approximating a 10 percent deviation from the norm (Shur & Hare, 1983; Watson et al., 1982). Many fanciful explanations might be put forth to explain this bizarre and unexpected phenomenon. One of them suggests that the presence of cold weather during the prenatal or early postnatal period brings with it an increased risk of schizophrenia. This, in turn, suggests the existence of a pathogen whose activity is seasonally controlled—

most likely a living pathogen. The possibility that some schizophrenias are due to a toxic, slow-acting organism, say an unknown virus, is consistent with these curious findings (Meltzer, 1979). It is also consistent with the demonstrable fact that some cases are associated with the degeneration of brain tissue. Finally, to return momentarily to the Genains, we note again that recent assessments show at least two of the quads to be probably brain-impaired (Sargent, 1982a).

At this point, it is likely that the student-reader will be either committed to a biological interpretation of schizophrenia or will be uncertain of what to think. We have treated this section in some detail because of our observation that many students tend to come to premature conclusions on either side of the biogenic-psychogenic controversy. We hope we have demonstrated that biological considerations in the etiology of schizophrenia cannot reasonably be dismissed. Yet comparable conclusions exist relating to psychosocial and sociocultural factors. When we have a complete theory of the origins of schizophrenic breakdown, it will of necessity encompass biological as well as psychosocial and sociocultural factors. In the meantime, it is reasonable to take the view that *anything* that reduces the adaptive capacity of the organism, including varied biological factors, may result in an increased probability of schizophrenic breakdown at some point in the life cycle.

Psychosocial factors in schizophrenia

Many behavioral scientists hold views that contrast sharply with that in which schizophrenia is held to be caused by biological factors. Here schizophrenic individuals are seen as persons who escape from an unbearable world and seemingly unsolvable conflicts by altering their inner representations of reality. Although biological factors may complicate the clinical picture, the origins of the disorder are held to be primarily psychosocial.

In this section we shall deal with the psychosocial patterns that appear particularly relevant to the development of schizophrenia: (a) early psychic trauma and increased vulnerability; (b) pathogenic parent-child and family interactions; (c) faulty learning and coping; (d) social role problems; and (e) excessive stress and decompensation.

Early psychic trauma and increased vulnerability.

A number of investigators have placed strong emphasis on the early traumatic experiences of children who later become schizophrenic.

In a pioneering study of the psychoses of children and adolescents, Yerbury and Newell emphasized the total lack of security in human relationships, the severely disturbed home life, and the brutal treatment that many of these children had experienced. Of 56 psychotic cases,

"Ten of them had been shocked by the deaths of parents. . . . Four were so disoriented upon learning of their adoption that they could not reconcile themselves to the true situation. Four children had lived with mentally ill mothers who were finally hospitalized. Sex traumas were reported in 14 cases of children who were overwhelmed with guilt and fear. . . . Three children were horrified by incest in the home, and three girls had become pregnant. . . . Six children had been tormented, beaten, tied, and confined by their companions so that they were terrified in the company of children, and felt safe only with adults." (1943, p. 605)

Similarly, Bettelheim (1955) cited the poignant case of a boy who was rejected by his mother and placed in an orphanage. Here he never learned the names of any of the other boys but referred to them as "big guys" and "little guys"; he lived in a terrifying world of shadowy figures who had the power to beat him up and hurt him without reason.

Karl Menninger has provided a vivid picture of the defenses—and special vulnerabilities—of adolescents and young adults who have suffered deep hurts and have come to view the world as a dangerous and hostile place:

"Children injured in this way are apt to develop certain defenses. They cover up, as the slang expression puts it. They deny the injury which they have experienced or the pain which they are suffering. They erect a façade or front, 'All's well with me,' they seem to say. 'I am one of the fellows; I am just like everybody else. I am a normal person.' And indeed they act like normal persons, as much as they can. . . . Often they are noticeable only for a certain reticence, shyness, perhaps slight eccentricity. Just as often, they are not conspicuous at all. . . .

"What is underneath that front? . . . There is in-

tense conflict and tension and anxiety and strong feelings of bitterness, resentment and hate toward those very people with whom the external relationships may be so perfectly normal. 'I hate them! They don't treat me right. They will never love me and I will never love them. I hate them and I could kill them all! But I must not let them know all this. I must cover it up, because they might read my thoughts and then they wouldn't like me and wouldn't be nice to me.'

"All this is covered up as long as possible. . . . For the chief problem in the person who is going to develop what we call schizophrenia is, 'How can I control the bitterness and hatred I feel because of the unendurable sorrow and disappointment that life has brought to me?' . . .

". . . the regimen under which they live has much to do with their successful adaptation. Given certain new stresses, the façade may break down and the underlying bitterness and conflict may break through. . . ." (1948, pp. 101–4)

Instead of withdrawing, children who have been traumatized may try to relate aggressively to other people. Such children are highly vulnerable to hurt, however, and their existence is usually an anxious one. Often their lives are a series of crises, precipitated by minor setbacks and hurts that they magnify out of all proportion (Arieti, 1974). In other instances, the individual manifests a pattern of somewhat disorganized paranoid thinking, often coupled with rebellious behavior involving pathological lying, episodes of unbridled aggression, and various types of delinquent behavior.

Although most children who undergo early psychic trauma show residual effects in later life, most do not become schizophrenic. Conversely, not all schizophrenic patients have undergone such traumatic childhood experiences. Thus early psychic trauma appears to be only one among many interactional factors that may contribute to schizophrenia. Anthony (1978) has even suggested that early traumatic experiences may be less important than the overall continuing context in which they occur:

"The 'headline' experiences—the attacks, the paranoid accusations, the incestuous approaches, the brutalities—seem easier for the child to endure than the constant confusions, mystifications, inconsistencies, and other seemingly minor problems of everyday living. It is not abnormality itself that proves so disturbing but the oscillations between normality and abnormality, and the wider these are, the more difficult it is for the child to sustain." (p. 481)

Richard Saholt (1924–) was a shy, fearful child with a belittling, abusive father. Naturally left-handed, he was forced to change handedness, back and forth, several times and developed a severe speech impediment. While serving in World War II, he survived many weeks of fighting at subzero temperatures in the Italian Alps, where he patrolled behind enemy lines and witnessed explosions that mutilated or killed many of his buddies. Ninety percent of his outfit died.

Home from the war, he had nervous twitches, was jumpy and scared, and suffered from depression, stomach trouble, and blackouts. In five years he started and quit 15 schools and lost 30 jobs. Each year for 29 years he sought disability compensation but was turned down. Twice, he attempted suicide.

Unable to express his torment verbally, he began to collect words and pictures to create dozens of montages such as those shown here—montages of war, insanity, terror, and violence. It was these montages that helped him gain a total disability pension in 1974, with a diagnosis of chronic undifferentiated schizophrenia.

Somewhat ironically, the montages have brought him recognition and appreciation as an artist, and the validation of his claim by the Veterans Administration has given him feelings of exoneration and—at last— sanity. He says, "For myself, I can accept that my cries and tries went unheeded for so long. What I don't accept is that other people have to still endure such pain. I hope, by these works, to increase the awareness of the physical, mental, and social ills of today."

Walter Anderson believed that his role in life was to live in close contact with Nature and help bring the natural world to life through his painting. From 1947—following treatment for schizophrenia—to the time of his death in 1965, Anderson lived as a recluse in Ocean Springs, Mississippi. On nearby Horn Island, he swam, crawled, and waded with the creatures of the ponds and woods, and he meticulously recorded the joys of the natural world in notebooks and in thousands of paintings. Only after his death did outsiders see for the first time the extraordinary mural of nature that covered the walls of his home.

The absence of solid evidence pinpointing specific types of psychic insult or trauma differentiating the backgrounds of schizophrenic from nonschizophrenic persons has prompted Meehl (1978) to suggest that emotionally significant events do not themselves launch a person on the path to schizophrenia; rather the particular patterns and sequences in which the events occur help bring on the disorder. The person who is to become schizophrenic has the "bad luck" to experience emotionally charged events in a temporal network that is, for the particular individual, pathogenic. If Meehl is right, the research task of discovering particular early life events that increase vulnerability to schizophrenia becomes formidable indeed, and perhaps even impossible.

The situation looks considerably more hopeful when, as Anthony (1978) recommends, we look at overall contextual features of the individual's development, as we do in the following section.

Pathogenic parent-child and family interactions. Studies of interactions in schizophrenic families have focused on such factors as (a) "schizophrenogenic" parents; (b) destructive marital interactions; (c) pseudo-mutuality and role inflexibility; (d) faulty communication; and (e) the undermining of personal authenticity. Here it may be noted that the focus of research has shifted in recent years from parent-child to total family interactions.[4]

1. *"Schizophrenogenic" mothers and fathers.* Many studies have been made of the parents of individuals who have developed schizophrenia—particularly the mothers of male patients. Typically, these mothers have been characterized as rejecting, domineering, cold, overprotective, and impervious to the feelings and needs of others. While verbally such a mother may seem accepting, basically she rejects the child. At the same time, she depends on the child rather than the father for her emotional satisfactions and feelings of completeness as a woman. Perhaps for this reason she tends to dominate, possessively overprotect, and smother the child—encouraging dependence on her.

These descriptions of *schizophrenogenic*

----

[4]A comprehensive review of family interaction in disturbed and normal families may be found in Jacob (1975). Neale and Oltmanns (1980) also review the area.

mothers originally derived from the observations of clinicians whose impressions could have been biased to an unknown degree. However, they have recently received confirmation in a well-designed longitudinal study that eliminated the possibility of bias affecting the results; the study shows that a mothering style involving the above characteristics does show up as a significant factor in the backgrounds of adult schizophrenics experiencing unfavorable outcomes (Roff & Knight, 1981). While these are impressive findings, they are also correlational in nature and so do not permit unqualified inferences about the *etiologic* significance of the schizophrenogenic mothering style. Still, we can say that the causal hypothesis remains very attractive.

Often combined with this mothering pattern, observers have noted, are rigid, moralistic attitudes toward sex that cause the mother to react with horror to any evidence of sexual impulses on the child's part. In many instances the mother is overtly seductive in physical contacts with her son, thus augmenting his sexual conflicts. In general, the mother-son relationship in schizophrenia appears to foster immaturity and anxiety in the youth—depriving him of a clear-cut sense of his own identity, distorting his views of himself and his world, and causing him to suffer from pervasive feelings of inadequacy and helplessness.

Nor are the daughters of such mothers likely to fare very well. In this connection, we refer the reader's attention to the description of Mrs. Genain given at the beginning of this chapter.

While mothers have been singled out for most of the attention in this area, fathers have not gone entirely unscathed. Roff and Knight (1981) have found that the mother-son relationship described above can be especially damaging if the father is passive and uninvolved in his relationship to his son. This is consistent with what has already been observed and reported about fathers and schizophrenia. Available studies have typically described a somewhat inadequate, indifferent, or passive father who appears detached and humorless—a father who rivals the mother in his insensitivity to others' feelings and needs. Often, too, he appears to be rejecting toward his son and seductive toward his daughter. At the same time, he is often highly contemptuous and derogatory toward his wife, thus making it clear that his daughter is more important to him. This treatment of the wife tends to force her into competition with her daughter, and it devalues her as a model for her daughter's development as a woman. In fact, the daughter may come to despise herself for any resemblance to her mother. Against this background, the daughter often moves into adolescence feeling an incestuous attachment to her father, which creates severe inner conflict and may eventually prove terrifying to her. The problems of the Genain sisters in attempting to cope with their seriously disturbed father are relevant here.

As might be expected, studies have shown a high incidence of emotional disturbance on the part of both mothers and fathers of schizophrenics. Kaufman et al. (1960) reported that both the mothers and fathers of 80 schizophrenic children and adolescents studied were emotionally disturbed: the mothers almost uniformly used psychotic-like defense patterns, and the fathers used seriously maladaptive coping patterns. Other studies concerned with the mental health status of the parents of schizophrenics, reviewed by Hirsch and Leff (1975), come to basically similar conclusions.

Meissner (1981) makes the interesting suggestion that the themes of persecution and grandeur that preoccupy paranoid sufferers derive from a common source, namely a disturbance in the parental personalities the person has internalized or "introjected" (see page 66). These introjects exist as polar opposites and tend to prevent the resolution and integration of the person's own identity. There are two groups of polarities: one group having to do with aggression, the other with narcissism. The aggressive polarities move between extreme feelings of aggression and victimization; the narcissistic polarities between feelings of superiority and inferiority. In Meissner's words:

"In terms of the victim introject [the individual] sees himself as weak, ineffectual, inadequate, helpless, vulnerable, and victimized. In terms of the aggressor introject he seems himself as strong, powerful, domineering, controlling, hostile, and destructive. In terms of the superior introject, in narcissistic terms, he sees himself as superior, special, privileged, perfect, entitled, and even grandiose. In terms of the inferior introject, which provides the opposite pole to the narcissistic superior introject, he sees himself as inferior, worthless, valueless, shameful, and humiliated. Typically in the paranoid patient the victim introject tends to predominate in the patient's internal subjectively available sphere, while the aggressive aspects are projected to the outside in the form of hostile and destructive persecutors." (p. 625)

As was indicated in Chapter 4, however, we cannot reasonably assume that disturbance always passes from parent to offspring: it can work in the other direction as well. And quite aside from the original source of psychopathology, it would appear that once it begins, the members of a family may stimulate each other to increased displays of pathological behavior. For example, studies by Mishler and Waxler (1968) and Liem (1974) both contain quite unequivocal evidence that parents' attempts to deal with the disturbed behavior of schizophrenic sons and daughters had pathological effects on their own behavior and communication patterns. In fact, the bidirectionality of effects may be the single most important thing we have learned from studying the families of schizophrenic persons (Carson, 1984).

2. *Destructive marital interactions.* Of particular interest here is the work of Lidz and his associates, which continued over some two decades. In an initial study of 14 families with schizophrenic offspring, Lidz et al. (1965) failed to find a single family that was reasonably well integrated. Eight of the 14 couples lived in a state of severe chronic discord in which continuation of the marriage was constantly threatened—a condition the investigators called *marital schism*. A particularly malignant feature was the chronic undermining of the worth of one marital partner by the other, which made it clear to the children that the parents did not respect or value each other. Each parent expressed fear that the child would resemble the other parent; a child's resemblance to one parent was a source of concern and rejection by the other parent.

The other 6 couples in this study had achieved a state of equilibrium in which the continuation of the marriage was not constantly threatened but in which the relationship was maintained at the expense of a basic distortion in family relationships; in these cases, family members entered into a "collusion" in which the maladaptive behavior of one or more family members was accepted as normal. This pattern was referred to as *marital skew*. The Genain family, for example, would be considered severely skewed since it was organized chiefly around the bizarre actions and ideas of Mr. Genain. Lidz (1978) believes that a major effect of such severe family disturbance is the encouragement of "egocentric cognitive regression" in youngsters subjected to it, giving rise eventually to the distinctive cognitive derangements characteristic of the schizophrenic state. In these and other cases regarding parental influences, of course, both biological and psychological influences are likely to be involved. It is of considerable interest and importance that the Roff and Knight (1981) study found both types of marital interaction patterns described by Lidz and his colleagues to be predictive of later poor outcomes for schizophrenic offspring. An especially strong effect showed up for loss of a parent before age seven, and, as might be expected, many such "losses" were due to parental separation or divorce occasioned by marital disharmony.

3. *Pseudo-mutuality and role inflexibility.* Wynne et al. (1958) found that schizophrenic family relationships often had the appearance of being mutual, understanding, and open, but in fact were not—a condition they termed **pseudo-mutuality.** These investigators also found considerable rigidity in the family role structure, which tended to depersonalize the children and block their growth toward maturity and self-direction.

Similarly, Bowen (1959, 1960), studying the backgrounds of 12 schizophrenic patients, found "striking emotional distance" between the parents typical. He referred to the emotional barrier as having the characteristics of an "emotional divorce." Although the parents in such families often maintained a façade of love—for example, making a big drama out of giving each other presents at Christmas—there was an underlying withdrawal accompanied by severe disappointment and often hostility. The patient's function had often been that of an unsuccessful mediator between the parents. In the case of the male patients, however, the most common pattern was an intense association between mother and son that excluded the father. Bowen also noted that, as the years passed, the son was threatened by signs of the mother's aging or by other characteristics that might prevent her from being the strong person upon whom he was dependent, while the mother was threatened by any signs

of personality growth that might prevent the son from remaining "her baby."

Pseudo-mutuality seems related to a variety of role distortions in schizophrenic families. Stabenau et al. (1965) found that such families were characterized by the assignment of inflexible and simplified roles to each member. Brodey has expressed this as an analogy, using a model based on the theater:

"The family drama is unlike the modern theatre. It is more like the morality play of medieval times. Actors take allegorical role positions that are stereotyped and confined—one is Good; another, Evil; a third, Temptation." (1959, p. 382)

In general, it would appear that the rigid and inflexible roles played by the family members permit a façade of continuing relatedness with each other and with the world, and make the business of living seemingly understandable and controllable. But basically the role provided for the child is destructive to personal growth.

4. *Faulty communication.* Bateson (1959, 1960) was one of the first investigators to emphasize the conflicting and confusing nature of communications among members of schizophrenic families. He used the term **double-bind** to describe the effect of one such pattern. Here the parent presents to the child ideas, feelings, and demands that are mutually incompatible. For example, the mother may be verbally loving and accepting but emotionally anxious and rejecting; or she may complain about her son's lack of affection but freeze up or punish him when he approaches her affectionately. The mother subtly but effectively prohibits comment on such paradoxes, and the father is too weak and ineffectual to intervene. In essence, such a son is continually placed in situations where he cannot win. He becomes increasingly anxious; presumably, such disorganized and contradictory communications in the family come to be reflected in his own thinking.

Singer and Wynne (1963, 1965a, 1965b) have linked the thought disorders in schizophrenia to two styles of thinking and communication in the family—*amorphous* and *fragmented*. The amorphous pattern is characterized by failure in differentiation; here, attention toward feelings, objects, or persons is loosely organized, vague, and drifting. Fragmented thinking involves greater differentiation but lowered integration,

*T*hese paintings were made by a male patient diagnosed as suffering from undifferentiated schizophrenia. Over a period of about nine years, he did hundreds of paintings in which the tops of the heads of males were always missing, though the females were complete. He was unable to communicate verbally, and when asked about his life would often draw a "comic strip" that told a story, such as the one shown here.

In an attempt to maneuver the patient into a position to complete a man's head, the therapist made the outline of a suit of clothes on a canvas, low enough so that a head would logically fit in the picture, and urged the patient to finish the drawing. The patient, however, painted only a suit.

with erratic and disruptive shifts in communication. Feinsilver (1970) found supporting evidence for such amorphous and fragmented thinking in the impaired ability of members of schizophrenic families to describe essential attributes of common household objects to each other. And Bannister (1971) found that schizophrenic thinking tends to be even more "loose" and disordered when the individual is dealing with persons and interpersonal relationships than when dealing with objects.

In their recent work, Singer and Wynne (Singer, Wynne, & Toohey, 1978; Wynne, Toohey, & Doane, 1979) refer generally to "communication deviance" (or "transactional style deviance") as being at the heart of the purported negative effects parents have on their preschizophrenic children. Following up on this work, Goldstein and colleagues (Doane et al., 1981; Goldstein et al., 1978; Lewis et al., 1981), in a longitudinal study employing the "high risk" strategy (see page 27), have found that high communication deviance in parents does indeed increase the likelihood of schizophrenic spectrum disorders among offspring. Even if interpreted cautiously, such findings show great promise in enhancing our understanding of the origins of schizophrenia.

5. *Undermining personal authenticity.* The philosopher Martin Buber (1957) pointed out that a confirmation of authenticity is essential to normal interpersonal relationships.

"In human society at all its levels, persons confirm one another in a practical way, to some extent or other, in their personal qualities and capacities, and a society may be termed human in the measure to which its members confirm one another. . . ." (p. 101)

Such confirmation apparently is often denied the person who later becomes schizophrenic. Several investigators have noted that the members of schizophrenic families consistently disqualify one or more members' statements and actions. In one family, for example, the father strongly approved of whatever the younger son did while he was equally disproving of the behavior of the older son. Thus the brothers might make similar statements about some matter, and the father would agree with one and find some basis for disqualifying or discrediting the statement of the other. Similarly, at Christmas time, the younger son's present to his father was praised and appreciated, while that of the older son was criticized and found disappointing by the father. The mother and younger sister went along with this differential treatment. Later, at the age of 27, the older son was hospitalized and diagnosed as a paranoid schizophrenic.

Such contradictory and disconfirming communications subtly and persistently mutilate the self-concepts of one or more of the family members, usually that of a particular child, as in the preceding example. The ultimate of this mutilation process occurs when

". . . no matter how [a person] feels or how he acts, no matter what meaning he gives his situation, his feelings are denuded of validity, his acts are stripped of their motives, intentions, and consequences, the situation is robbed of its meaning for him, so that he is totally mystified and alienated." (Laing & Esterson, 1964, pp. 135–36)

In the general context of faulty parent-child and family interactions, we may note that Lidz (1968, 1973) has characterized the parents of schizophrenics as "deficient tutors": they create a family milieu inappropriate for training a child in the cognitive abilities essential for categorizing experience, thinking coherently, and communicating meaningfully. Coupled with feelings of inadequacy and other damage to the child's emerging self-concept, this may help explain the later cognitive distortions, communication failures, difficulties in interpersonal relationships, and identity confusion that commonly occur in schizophrenia.

Yet most of the children from families with pathogenic characteristics do not become schizophrenic. Thus pathogenic family interactions that undermine personal authenticity cannot be the sole cause in those that do.

Faulty learning and coping. It appears that faulty learning typically plays a key role in schizophrenia, as it does in most other forms of maladaptive behavior. From early traumatic experiences—both within the family setting and in the outer world—the child may learn conditioned fears and vulnerabilities that lead to perception of the world as a dangerous and hostile place. Perhaps of even greater importance is faulty learning on a cognitive level, resulting from irrationalities in social interaction, attempts to meet inappropriate or impossible expectations and demands, and observation of pathological models.

1. *Deficient self-structure.* Such faulty learning is typically reflected in (a) grossly inaccurate assumptions concerning reality, possibility, and value; (b) a confused sense of self-identity coupled with basic feelings of inadequacy, insecurity, and self-devaluation; (c) personal immaturity, often reflected in overdependence on others and overemphasis on being a "good boy" or a "good girl"; and (d) a lack of needed competencies coupled with ineffective coping patterns. These characteristics appear capable of paving the way for schizophrenic and other seriously maladaptive behaviors. If we consider the developmental problems of the Genain sisters in this light, we can see how very difficult it must have been for them, as members of a tightly knit and socially isolated foursome, to gain the understandings and skills they needed.

The results of such faulty learning are often seen in such individuals' attempts to deal with inner impulses and establish satisfying interpersonal relationships. In the sexual sphere, schizophrenic individuals' problems are often complicated by rigidly moralistic attitudes toward sexual behavior. At the same time, they usually have had few, if any, meaningful sexual relationships. As a consequence, their sexual fantasies—like those of the early adolescent—may be somewhat chaotic and encompass a wide range of sexual objects and behaviors. Such fantasies often lead to severe inner conflicts and to self-devaluation. Similarly, the hostility they may feel toward people important to them is apt to be particularly difficult for such "good" individuals to handle: they tend to view such hostility as both immoral and dangerous and do not know how to express it in socially acceptable ways. At the same time, they may be completely upset at being the object of hostility from those on whom they feel dependent.

Lack of competencies in dealing with sexual and hostile fantasies and impulses, combined with a general deficiency in social skills, usually leads to disappointment, hurt, and devaluation in intimate interpersonal relationships. As we shall see, the stresses which commonly precipitate schizophrenic episodes typically center

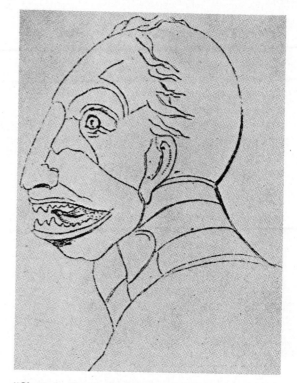

"Ghost of a Flea," a drawing of one of his own hallucinations by William Blake (1757–1827), the English poet and painter. According to Blake, the flea was in his room and told him that fleas contained the damned souls of bloodthirsty men. In both his poetry and his visual art, Blake gave many evidences of schizophrenic ideation (Born, 1946).

around the difficulties in such relationships. The inability of such individuals to establish and maintain satisfying interpersonal relationships does not void their needs for acceptance, approval, and love; it only reduces their chances for meeting these needs.

2. *Exaggerated use of ego-defense mechanisms.* Feeling inadequate and devalued and lacking an adequate frame of reference and needed competencies, such individuals, not surprisingly, learn to rely excessively on ego-defense mechanisms rather than on task-oriented coping patterns. These defense mechanisms often include psychophysiologic elements that have substantial secondary gain by "excusing" the person's withdrawal and nonperformance, particularly in early stages of the disorder. This was apparently the case with the Genain sisters, though somatic symptoms conceivably may also express an underlying biological defect. In any case, the development of a schizophrenic process does not preclude the use of neurotic forms of coping.

The exaggerated use of many ego-defense mechanisms is common. Emotional insulation protects these individuals from the hurt of disappointment and frustration. Regression enables them to lower their level of aspiration and accept a position of dependence. Projection helps them maintain feelings of adequacy and worth by placing the blame for their failures on others and attributing their own unacceptable desires to someone else. Wish-fulfilling fantasies give them some measure of compensation for feelings of frustration and self-devaluation.

The exaggerated use of such defense mechanisms as projection and fantasy appears particularly likely to predispose an individual to delusions and hallucinations, which not only represent the breakdown of organized perception and thought processes, but also—as part of schizophrenic reorganization of reality—may have marked defensive value. Delusions of grandeur and persecution enable these individuals to project the blame for their own inadmissible thoughts and behaviors; hallucinations—such as voices that "pour filth into their minds" or keep them informed of what their "enemies" are up to—may serve a comparable defensive purpose. Delusions of grandeur and omnipotence may grow out of simple wishful thinking and enable them to counteract feelings of inferiority and inadequacy. Hallucinations, such as conversations in which they hear the voice of God confer great power upon them and assign them the mission of saving the world, may likewise have comparable defensive value.

In acute schizophrenic episodes the initial picture is somewhat different, as we have seen, and is dominated by massive disorganization of thought, with panic at the loss of control over thoughts and feelings and desperate attempts to understand the terrifying experience. As yet the individual has not developed defenses to cope with the situation, but no one can continue indefinitely in this state of panic and confusion. Either the acute schizophrenic episode clears up eventually, or various extreme defenses, such as the ones mentioned above, are likely to develop.

Although extreme ego-defense mechanisms are commonly observed in schizophrenic patients, it is often unclear to what extent they are a causal factor, as opposed to a reaction to the frightening experience of disorganization. Here it may be emphasized that a schizophrenic breakdown often appears to represent a total defensive strategy. In essence, the individual seems to withdraw from the real world and evolve a defensive strategy that makes it possible to distort and "reshape" aversive experiences so that they can be assimilated without further self-devaluation. Even though this defensive system may be illogical and far from satisfactory, it relieves much of the inner tension and anxiety and protects the individual from complete psychological disintegration.

Social role problems. Social role behavior has been tied into the development and course of schizophrenic reactions in several different ways. A factor emphasized by Cameron and Margaret (1949, 1951) in their intensive studies of schizophrenic patients was the failure of such individuals to learn appropriate role-taking behavior. Inflexible in their own role behavior and uncomprehending of the role behavior of others, they do not know how to interact appropriately with other people.

Laing (1967, 1969, 1971) has carried this view of role behavior a step further, to the schizophrenic's creation of his or her own social role as protection from destructive social expectations and demands. Describing the so-called normal world as a place where all of us are "bemused and crazed creatures, strangers to our true selves, to one another, and to the spiritual and material world" (1967, p. 56), Laing maintains that a split arises between the false outer self and the true inner self. When the split reaches a point where it can no longer be tolerated, the result is a psychotic breakdown which usually takes the form of schizophrenia. In this view the "madness" labeled schizophrenia represents the individual's attempts to recover a sense of wholeness as a human being.

In essence, according to Laing, the individual dons the "mask of insanity" as a social role and a barricade. Behind this "false self" and often turbulent façade, however, the real person—the "true inner self"—remains. In this hidden inner world, despite the outward role of madness, the schizophrenic individual's hopes and aspirations may remain very much intact. Accordingly, Laing thinks treatment should focus less on removing "symptoms" than on finding a path to this remote and often inaccessible sanctuary and assisting the individual to regain wholeness as a person.

Laing thus suggests that at least some schizophrenic phenomena may represent partially voluntary enactments on the part of the patient. On reflection, it is not wholly incredible—given the miserable possibilities available to many persons for basic need gratification—that some should opt for the schizophrenic way of life. Though it may entail a certain amount of self-stigmatization and renunciation of personal liberties, these might be mild penalties to pay for escape from constant failure, contempt, rejection, and often brutality. For many, life in a modern mental hospital is distinctly more pleasant in many dimensions than would be life "outside"—in, let us say, an urban ghetto. Given our society's commitment to care for those who appear to be unable to care for themselves, and given the frequency of personal situations of hopelessness and despair, it may be that we should expect this form of "dropping out"—that an *absence* of it would be the occasion for surprise (Carson, 1971).

In any event, we do know that the occurrence of schizophrenic symptoms depends to a remarkable extent on the context in which the individual is being observed (Levy, 1976; Ritchie, 1975; Shimkunas, 1972). Such symptoms may come and go or be otherwise modified, depending on what demands are currently being placed on the patient. For example, a demand for intimate exchange appears to exacerbate schizophrenic symptoms. We also know that a certain subset of mental patients diagnosed as schizophrenic are quite skillful in controlling both the diagnoses they receive and the likelihood of their discharge from the hospital (Braginsky, Braginsky, & Ring, 1969; Drake & Wallach, 1979). In some ways, these are deeply disconcerting findings that mock much of the research reported. They will require careful consideration by future investigators—if only to weed out from studies those who are feigning their symptoms.

A related issue here is the use of the "insanity defense" by persons accused of serious crimes. While infrequently employed, it tends to arise in dramatic cases in which the felonious act seems "senseless," that is, unintelligible to the average person. We can never be ultimately certain that such a plea is valid, or even that it has a viable meaning (Szasz, 1963). This is a problem with which our society will eventually have to come to grips.

Excessive stress and decompensation. Brown (1972) found a marked increase in the severity of life stress during the ten-week period prior to an actual schizophrenic breakdown. Problems typically centered around difficulties in intimate personal relationships. Similarly, Schwartz, and Myers (1977) found interpersonal stressors to be significantly more common among schizophrenics than among members of a matched control group. As yet, however, we have not come up with a truly adequate classification of the types of stressors that are likely to precipitate a schizophrenic episode (Dohrenwend & Egri, 1981). We do know that relapse into schizophrenia following recovery is often associated with a certain type of negative communication directed at the patient by family members (Vaughn & Leff, 1976; 1981). Forgus and DeWolfe (1974) found that schizophrenic patients seemed to have been defeated by their whole life situation as well as by difficulties in close personal relationships.

As we noted, the course of decompensation (disorganization of thought and personality) in reactive schizophrenia tends to be sudden, while that in process schizophrenia tends to be gradual. The actual degree of decompensation may vary markedly, depending on the severity of stress and the makeup of the individual. And the course of recovery or recompensation may also be relatively rapid or slow. Similarly, the degree of recovery may be complete, leading to a better integrated person than before; it may be partial but sufficient for adequate adjustment; or the individual's defenses may be stabilized on a psychotic level, eventuating in chronic schizophrenia.

General sociocultural factors in schizophrenia

While disorders of thought and emotion are common to schizophrenia the world over, cultural factors may influence the type, the symptom content, and even the incidence of schizophrenic disorders in different societies. For example, one of the more puzzling findings is that first admission rates for schizophrenia are

A

A patient diagnosed as schizophrenic, paranoid type, was unable to respond at all when asked by the therpist to make an original drawing. Therefore, with the therapist's help, a picture (A) was selected from a magazine for the patient to copy. One of his first attempts was picture B, a pencil drawing on manila paper showing great visual distortion, as well as an inability to use colors and difficulty in using letters of the alphabet.

B

C

D

*T*he evident visual distortion was a diagnostic aid for the therapist, who was able
to learn from it that the patient, who was extremely fearful, saw things in this distorted
way, aggravating his fear. In picture C the patient has shown obvious improvement,
although it was not until a year after therapy began that he was able to execute a
painting with the realism of picture D.

very high in the Republic of Ireland (southern Ireland), but not among Irish Catholics residing elsewhere, including Northern Ireland (Murphy, 1978). One possibility is that different diagnostic criteria are employed in the Irish Republic. This does not seem to be a wholly satisfactory explanation, however, because there are many areas around the world in which the incidence of schizophrenia has been clearly shown to be exceptionally high or exceptionally low when compared to the overall incidence rate of about 1 percent. It appears that certain cultures, like certain mothers and fathers, are schizophrenogenic; conversely, others seem to protect their members from the ravages of the disorder, at least to a degree.

Systematic differences in the content and form of a schizophrenic disorder between cultures and even subcultures were documented by Carothers (1953, 1959) in his studies of different African groups. Carothers found the hebephrenic type of schizophrenia to be most common among African tribal groups in remote areas. He attributed this finding to a lack of well-developed ego-defense mechanisms among the members of these groups, thus making a complete disorganization of personality more likely when schizophrenia did occur. Similarly, Field (1960) described the initial schizophrenic breakdown among natives in rural Ghana as typically involving a state of panic. Here it was observed that when individuals were brought quickly to a shrine for treatment, they usually calmed down and in a few days appeared recovered. But when there was considerable delay before reaching the shrine, the individual often developed a classic hebephrenic disorder.

In another study of schizophrenia among the aborigines of West Malaysia, Kinzie and Bolton (1973) found the acute type to be by far the most common manifestation; they also noted that symptom content often "had an obvious cultural overlay, for example, seeing a 'river ghost' or 'men-like spirits' or talking to one's 'soul' " (p. 773). However, the clinical picture seems to be changing as rural Africans and other people from developing nations are increasingly exposed to modern technology and social change (Copeland, 1968; Kinzie & Bolton, 1973; Torrey, 1973, 1979).

An important consideration in crosscultural studies is that opinions concerning what is "normal" by professionals from another culture may not always correspond with the opinions held by members of the community in question. For example, in describing the schizophrenic disorders of members of the Hawaii-Japanese community, professional observers emphasized seclusiveness and shallow, blunted emotionality. Community members, on the other hand, were impressed by evidence of uncontrolled emotionality and distrust, behaviors that are strongly counter to the values of that community (Katz et al., 1978).

Focusing on sociocultural factors within our own society, Murphy (1968) summarized the picture as follows:

"There is a truly remarkable volume of research literature demonstrating an especially high rate of schizophrenia . . . in the lowest social class or classes . . . of moderately large to large cities throughout much of the Western world. It is not altogether clear what is the direction of causality in this relationship—whether the conditions of life of the lowest social classes are conducive to the development of schizophrenia, or schizophrenia leads to a decline in social class position—but present evidence would make it seem probable that some substantial part of the phenomenon results from lower class conditions of life being conducive to schizophrenia." (p. 152)

Unfortunately, the data are not quite as clear as Murphy indicates (Sanua, 1969), but his conclusion would probably be accepted by most investigators. Interestingly, there seems to be a reverse effect in India; there, the upper classes (castes) experience higher rates of schizophrenia than the lower classes (Torrey, 1979).

In a sophisticated review of the evidence relating social class and the incidence of schizophrenia, Kohn (1973) suggested that the conditions of lower-class existence impair the individual's ability to deal resourcefully with varied life stressors. The correlation is decidedly imperfect, however, for we know that some lower-class persons emerge from their backgrounds with superabundant resourcefulness. Here it may also be emphasized that alleged ethnic differences in the incidence and clinical pictures of schizophrenia—for example, between blacks, chicanos, and Anglo-Americans—disappear when social class, education, and related socioeconomic conditions are equated.

In concluding our review of causal factors in schizophrenia, it may be pointed out that research on the causation of human behavior is, as Shakow (1969) expressed it, "fiendishly complex," even with normal subjects.

"Research with disturbed human beings is even more so, particularly with those with whom it is difficult to communicate, among them schizophrenics. The marked range of schizophrenia, the marked variance within the range and within the individual, the variety of shapes that the psychosis takes, and both the excessive and compensatory behaviors that characterize it, all reflect this special complexity. Recent years have seen the complication further enhanced by the use of a great variety of therapeutic devices, such as drugs, that alter both the physiological and psychological nature of the organism. Research with schizophrenics, therefore, calls for awareness not only of the factors creating variance in normal human beings, but also of the many additional sources of variance this form of psychosis introduces." (Shakow, 1969, p. 618)

Or as Bannister (1971) has pointed out, "We will eventually have to develop a theory of what makes all people march before we can say very much about why some people march to a different drummer" (p. 84).

In general, however, it appears that there is no one clinical entity or causal sequence in schizophrenia. Rather we seem to be dealing with several types of maladaptive behavior resulting from an interaction of biological, psychosocial, and sociocultural factors; the role of these factors undoubtedly varies according to the given case and clinical picture. Often the interaction appears to involve a vicious spiral, in which life stress triggers metabolic changes that impair brain functioning, the latter, in turn, intensifying anxiety and panic as the individual realizes he or she is losing control. And so the spiral continues until more permanent defensive patterns are established, treatment is undertaken, or the disorder "has run its course." In severe instances, the "course" may be as long as 40 years. It is important to note that although full recovery is rare after such a lengthy period of disorder, it does sometimes occur (M. Bleuler, 1978).

Treatment and outcomes

Until recent times, the prognosis for schizophrenia was generally unfavorable. Under the routine custodial treatment in large mental hospital settings, the rate of discharge approximated only 30 percent.

For most schizophrenic individuals, the outlook today is not nearly so bleak. Improvement in this situation came with dramatic suddenness when the phenothiazines—major tranquilizing drugs—were introduced in the 1950s. Chemotherapy, together with other modern treatment methods, permits the majority of cases to be treated in outpatient clinics; a schizophrenic individual who enters a mental hospital or clinic as an inpatient for the first time has an 80- to 90-percent chance of being discharged within a matter of weeks or, at most, months. However, the rate of readmission is still extremely high, with 45 percent of all discharged patients being readmitted during the first year after release.

Overall, about one third of schizophrenic patients recover, which means technically that they remain symptom-free for five years; only some 10 percent now show the classical pattern of inexorable deterioration and permanent disability. The remainder of persons experiencing a first schizophrenic episode—some 60 percent of the total—show varying degrees of personality impoverishment and episodic psychotic behavior. Obviously, this is the group on whom our major efforts at solution should be concentrated. Outcome ratios appear less favorable where the onset of symptoms occurs at an early point in the life cycle (Bender, 1973; Gross & Huber, 1973; Morrison, 1974; Roff, 1974). For an overview of conditions that would suggest a favorable prognosis in schizophrenia, see the **HIGH-LIGHT** on page 386.

As we have done with respect to other disorders, we shall postpone until later chapters a detailed discussion of the various kinds of treatment employed for schizophrenia. Here we note merely that, contrary to widespread belief, such treatment is by no means limited to biological forms of intervention. Indeed, a breakthrough in the fashioning of a demonstrably powerful form of psychosocial intervention in schizophrenia is the most hopeful development to appear in the past quarter century (Paul & Lentz, 1977). Briefly, this treatment involves the use of a token economy program for hospitalized schizophrenic patients; we shall say more of this remarkable advance in later chapters. In addition, psychodynamic therapy, considered by many to be irrelevant to the treatment of the schizophrenias, has produced significant gains, particularly in cases in which the therapist is experienced in dealing with the difficult therapeutic

HIGHLIGHT

Conditions associated with favorable outcomes in the treatment of schizophrenia

1. Reactive rather than process schizophrenia, in which the time from onset of full-blown symptoms is 6 months or less.

2. Clear-cut precipitating stressors.

3. Adequate heterosexual adjustment prior to schizophrenic episode.

4. Good social and work adjustment prior to schizophrenic episode.

5. Minimal incidence of schizophrenia and other pathological conditions in family background.

6. Involvement of depression or other schizoaffective pattern.

7. Favorable life situation to return to and adequate aftercare in the community.

In general, the opposite of the preceding conditions—including poor premorbid adjustment, slow on-

set, and relatives with schizophrenia—are indicative of an unfavorable prognosis.

Here it may be noted that in a 5-year follow-up study of 61 schizophrenic individuals in the United States, Hawk, Carpenter, and Strauss (1975) failed to find any differences in long-range outcomes between acute and other subtypes of schizophrenia. (Data could be obtained on only 61 out of the original sample of 131 cases.) This study was part of an International Pilot Study of Schizophrenia (IPSS) designed to include transcultural data on over 1200 patients in 9 countries—Colombia, Czechoslovakia, Denmark, India, Nigeria, Taiwan, U.S.S.R., the United Kingdom, and the United States.

Based on Caffey, Galbrecht, and Klett (1971); Fenz and Velner (1970); Hawk, Carpenter, and Strauss (1975); Morrison (1974); Roff (1974); Stephens, Astrup, and Mangrum (1966); Turner, Dopkeen, and Labreche (1970); and Yarden (1974).

problems these individuals present (Karon & Vandenbos, 1981). Overall, psychosocial approaches to the treatment of schizophrenia have compiled a very respectable record (Smith, Glass, & Miller, 1980).

It seems fitting to end our consideration of the schizophrenic syndromes with some conclusions reached at a major international conference on schizophrenia held at the University of Rochester. The following conclusions were cited by Joseph Zubin (1978), a leading researcher in the area:

"1. First, schizophrenia today is much less disabling than in the first half of this century.

2. The course of the disorder, even when little or no therapeutic or custodial intervention takes place, is rather varied.

3. The assumption that psychosocial therapeutic approaches are of limited value is no longer tenable.

4. Close relationships with family or important others in itself is not disabling to the schizophrenic, but close involvement with hostile environments is.

5. Social impoverishment leads to clinical impov-

erishment, whereas social enrichment leads to clinical improvement.

6. The vulnerability concept is regarded as useful by all participants." (p. 641)

Paranoia

The term *paranoia* has been in use a long time. The ancient Greeks and Romans used it to refer more or less indiscriminately to any mental disorder. Our present, more limited use of the term stems from the work of Kraepelin, who reserved it for cases showing delusions and impaired contact with reality but without the severe personality disorganization characteristic of schizophrenia.[5]

Currently three main types of psychoses are

---

[5]There is a marked dearth of recent research on paranoia, and in this section we have been forced to draw on a number of earlier but seemingly definitive studies.

included under the general heading of paranoid disorders: paranoia, acute paranoid disorder, and a third type—shared paranoid disorder (also known as folie à deux), which is described briefly in the **HIGHLIGHT** on page 388.

a) *Paranoia,* with a delusional system that develops slowly, becomes intricate, logical, and systemized and centers around delusions of persecution and/or grandeur. Aside from the delusions, the patient's personality remains relatively intact, with no evidence of serious disorganization and no hallucinations (unlike paranoid schizophrenia, discussed earlier in the chapter).

b) *Acute paranoid disorder,* with transient and changeable paranoid delusions, lacks either the logical and systematic features of paranoia or the bizarre fragmentation and deterioration often found in paranoid schizophrenia. Usually the condition is related to some evident stress and is a transient phenomenon. Paranoid states often color the clinical picture in other types of psychopathological reactions.[6]

Our primary focus in this section is on paranoia. Paranoia is rare in clinic and mental hospital populations, but this provides a somewhat misleading picture of its actual occurrence.

Many exploited inventors; persecuted teachers, business executives, or other professionals; fanatical reformers; morbidly jealous spouses; and self-styled prophets fall in this category. Unless they become a serious nuisance, these individuals are usually able to maintain themselves in the community and do not recognize their paranoid condition nor seek help to alleviate it.

In some instances, however, they are potentially dangerous, and in virtually all instances they are inveterate "injustice-detectors," very inclined to institute legal actions of one sort or another.

Clinical picture in paranoia

In paranoia the individual feels singled out and taken advantage of, mistreated, plotted against, stolen from, spied upon, ignored, or otherwise mistreated by "enemies." The delusional system usually centers around one major theme, such as financial matters, a job, an invention, an unfaithful spouse, or other life affairs.[7] For example, a woman who is failing on the job may insist that her fellow workers and superiors have it in for her because they are jealous of her great ability and efficiency. As a result, she may quit her job and go to work elsewhere, only to find friction developing again and her new job in jeopardy. Now she may become convinced that the first company has written to her present employer and has turned everyone here against her so that she has not been given a fair chance. With time, more and more of the environment is integrated into her delusional system as each additional experience is misconstrued and interpreted in the light of her delusional ideas. (See **HIGHLIGHT** on page 389.)

Although the evidence that paranoid persons advance to justify their claims may be extremely tenuous and inconclusive, they are unwilling to accept any other possible explanation and are impervious to reason. A husband may be convinced of his spouse's unfaithfulness because on two separate occasions when he answered the phone the party at the other end hung up. Argument and logic are futile. In fact, any questioning of his delusions only convinces him that his interrogator has sold out to his enemies.

Milner cited the case of a paranoid man, aged 33, who murdered his wife by battering her head with a hammer. Prior to the murder, he had become convinced that his wife was suffering from some strange disease and that she had purposely infected him because she wished him to die. He believed that this disease was due to a "cancer-consumption" germ. He attributed his conclusion in part to his wife's alleged sexual perversion and also gave the following reasons for his belief:

"1. His wife had insured him for a small sum immediately after marriage.

2. A young man who had been friendly with his wife before their marriage died suddenly.

3. A child who had lived in the same house as his wife's parents suffered from fits. (He also believed that his wife's parents were suffering from the same disease.)

---

[6]Comprehensive reviews of early studies of paranoid states may be found in Tanna (1974) and in Meissner (1978).

[7]At one time it was customary to distinguish several types of paranoid disorders in accordance with the delusional ideas manifested—whether persecutory, grandiose, erotic, jealous, or litigious. But a classification in terms of delusional content has been found not to be very helpful.

HIGHLIGHT
Folie à deux

A relatively neglected phenomenon in the functional psychoses is that of *folie à deux,* or shared paranoid disorder,—a form of psychological "contagion" in which one person copies and incorporates into his own personality structure the delusions and other psychotic patterns of another person. Familial relationships between individuals in 103 cases studied by Gralnick (1942) fell within one of the following four categories:

sister ⇄ sister	40 cases
husband ⇄ wife	28 cases
mother ⇄ child	24 cases
brother ⇄ brother	11 cases

Among the explanatory factors—all environmental—emphasized by Gralnick were the following: (a) length of association, (b) dominance-submission, (c) type of familial relationship, and (d) prepsychotic personality. The high incidence in the husband-wife category is particularly striking, since common heredity would play no part as an etiological factor in these cases.

In another study, Soni and Rockley (1974) reported on 8 cases of *folie à deux* seen at a European hospital. Their findings supported those of Gralnick and emphasized the role of pathological prepsychotic characteristics, such as increased suggestibility and submissive roles, as well as the type of relationship, in explaining why these patients acquired the delusions of their partners.

4. For several months before the crime his food had had a queer taste, and for a few weeks before the crime he had suffered from a pain in the chest and an unpleasant taste in the mouth." (1949, p. 130)

Although ideas of persecution predominate, many paranoid individuals develop delusions of grandeur in which they endow themselves with superior or unique ability. Such "exalted" ideas usually center around messianic missions, political or social reforms, or remarkable inventions. Paranoid persons who are religious may consider themselves appointed by God to save the world and may spend most of their time "preaching" and "crusading." Threats of fire and brimstone, burning in hell, and similar persuasive devices are liberally employed. Many paranoid persons become attached to extremist political movements and are tireless and fanatical crusaders, although they often do their cause more harm than good by their self-righteousness and their condemnation of others.

Some paranoid individuals develop remarkable inventions that they have endless trouble in patenting or selling. Gradually they become convinced that there is a plot afoot to steal their invention, or that enemies of the United States are working against them to prevent the country from receiving the benefits of their remarkable talents. Hoffman cited the case of an individual who went to Washington to get presidential assistance in obtaining a patent for a flame thrower that, he claimed, could destroy all the enemies of the United States. He would patiently explain who he was. "There's God who is Number 1, and Jesus Christ who is Number 2, and me, I am Number 3." (1943, p. 574)

Aside from the delusional system, such an individual may appear perfectly normal in conversation, emotionality, and conduct. Hallucinations and the other obvious signs of psychopathology are rarely found. This normal appearance, together with the logical and coherent way in which the delusional ideas are presented, may make the individual most convincing.

In one case an engineer developed detailed plans for eliminating the fog in San Francisco and other large cities by means of a system of reflectors which would heat the air by solar radiation and cause the fog to lift. The company for whom he worked examined the plans and found them unsound. This upset him greatly and he resigned his position, stating that the other engineers in the company were not qualified to pass judgment on any really complex and advanced

HIGHLIGHT

Sequence of events in paranoid mode of thinking

A number of investigators have concluded that the most useful perspective from which to view paranoia is in terms of a *mode of thinking*. The sequence of events that appears to characterize this mode of thinking may be summarized as follows:

1. Suspiciousness—the individual mistrusts the motives of others, fears he or she will be taken advantage of, is constantly on the alert.

2. Protective thinking—selectively perceives the actions of others to confirm suspicions, now blames others for own failures.

3. Hostility—responds to alleged injustices and mistreatment with anger and hostility, becomes increasingly suspicious.

4. Paranoid illumination—the moment when everything "falls into place"; the individual finally understands the strange feelings and events being experienced.

5. Delusions—of influence and persecution that may be based on "some grain of truth," presented in a very logical and convincing way; often later development of delusions of grandeur.

Over time, the paranoid individual may incorporate additional life areas, people, and events into the delusional system, creating a "pseudo-community" whose purpose is to carry out some action against him or her. Paranoid individuals who respond in this manner may come to feel that all the attention they are receiving from others is indicative of their unique abilities and importance, thus paving the way for delusions of grandeur.

Based in part on Swanson, Bohnert, and Smith (1970).

engineering projects like his. Instead of attempting to obtain other employment, he then devoted full time trying to find some other engineering firm that would have the vision and technical proficiency to see the great potentialities of his idea. He would present his plans convincingly but become highly suspicious and hostile when questions concerning their feasibility were raised. Eventually, he became convinced that there was a conspiracy among a large number of engineering firms to steal his plans and use them for their own profit. He reported his suspicions to the police, threatening to do something about the situation himself unless they took action. As a consequence of his threats, he was hospitalized for psychiatric observation and diagnosed as suffering from paranoia.

The delusional system is apt to be particularly convincing if one accepts the basic premise or premises upon which it is based. For example, where the delusional system develops around some actual injustice, it may be difficult to distinguish between fact and fancy. As a result, the individual's family and friends, as well as well-meaning public officials, may be convinced of the truth of the claims. However, the individual's inability to see the facts in any other light,

typical lack of evidence for far-reaching conclusions, and hostile, suspicious, and uncommunicative attitude when the delusional ideas are questioned usually provide clues that something is wrong.

The following case history is a rather classic description of a mild paranoia; it reveals the development of a logically patterned delusional system and the pertinent selection of environmental evidence that involves more and more individuals in the supposed conspiracy. Despite this woman's delusional system, however, she was not severely out of touch with reality; there are many nonhospitalized cases in the community who reveal similar symptomatology to a more serious degree.

The patient was a 31-year-old nurse who was commissioned a second lieutenant in the Army Nurse Corps shortly after the beginning of World War II. From the start she found it difficult to adjust to fellow nurses and to enlisted men under her supervision, the difficulty apparently arising from her overzealousness in carrying out ward regulations in the minutest detail. In any event, "No one could get along with her." After some two years of service, she was transferred to a new assignment.

". . . Initially she made an excellent impression, but soon showed herself to be a perfectionist, a hypercritical and domineering personality who insisted on the immediate, precise, exact and detailed execution of orders. Within a 14-week period she was transferred on three separate occasions from post to post, and at each new post her manner and her attitude, despite her precise and meticulous efficiency, constituted a virtual demand that nurses, wardmen, patients, and medical officers conform to her exceedingly rigid ideas about the management of ward and even departmental routines. . . .

"During the course of her last assignment, she received every possible help. She requested additional responsibility and was, therefore, assigned, as charge nurse, to the Eye, Ear, Nose, and Throat Clinic. Within a week she lodged a complaint with the commanding officer of the hospital, accusing the enlisted men of conspiring against her, the nurses of lying about her, and the officer in charge of lack of co-operation. She was, therefore, transferred to one of the wards, where she expected wardmen, nurses and patients to execute her orders on the instant, in minute and exact detail, and where she violently berated them because of their inability to do so. A week later, the responsible medical officer requested that she be relieved from duty there. Instead, she discussed the problem with the chief nurse and promised to correct her attitude. Within four days, the patients as a group requested her removal. Two weeks later, the ward officer repeated his request. She was, therefore, given a five-day leave, and during her absence all ward personnel were contacted in an attempt to help her adjust when she returned to duty.

"During this period she became convinced that she was being persecuted. She grew tense and despondent, kept rigidly to herself, was unable to sleep in a room with a ticking clock, and frequently burst into tears. As she herself said, 'Some of the nurses deliberately went out of their way to annoy and criticize me. They wanted to make me trouble. That's why I was so upset.' On three separate occasions, she requested the appointment of a Board of Officers to investigate these alleged discriminatory acts. Finally she demanded that a Board of Officers be convened to determine her efficiency as a nurse. Instead, she was ordered to report to our hospital for psychiatric observation.

"On admission, few details of her military history were known. She seemed alert and co-operative, was well oriented in all three spheres [time, place, person], and was thought to be in complete contact. Extreme care, however, was necessary when addressing her. Even fellow patients would warn newcomers to the ward. 'Be careful what you say when she's around. She won't mean it, but she'll twist your state-ments without changing your words, and give them some meaning you never intended.' In addition, she was bitter about the unfair treatment she had received in the Army, wished to reform the Medical Department and the Army Nursing Corps, and indignantly repudiated the existence of any condition that could justify placing her under NP [neuropsychiatric] observation. . . .

"The diagnosis of 'paranoia, true type' was made, and she was returned to the United States, one month after admission to the hospital, a rigid and overzealous individual whose inelasticity had antagonized her associates and aroused severe emotional strain within herself, firmly convinced that she was being persecuted because of the necessary and badly needed work which she had much too efficiently performed. . . . She was received in the States as a patient in the very hospital to whose psychiatric section she had previously, for so brief a period of time, been assigned as ward nurse." (Rosen & Kiene, 1946, pp. 330–33)

Paranoid individuals are not always as dangerous as we have been led to believe by popular fiction and drama, but there is always the chance that they will decide to take matters into their own hands and deal with their enemies in the only way that seems effective. In one instance, a paranoid school principal became convinced that the school board was discriminating against him and shot and killed most of the members of the board. In another case a paranoid man shot and killed a group of seven persons he thought had been following him. The number of husbands and wives who have been killed or injured by suspicious paranoid mates is undoubtedly large. As Swanson, Bohnert, and Smith (1970) have pointed out, such murderous violence is commonly associated with jealousy and the loss of self-esteem; the spouse feels that he or she has been deceived, taken advantage of, and humiliated. Paranoid persons may also get involved in violent and destructive subversive activities as well as in political assassinations.

Causal factors in paranoia

Most of us on various occasions may wonder if we are not "jinxed," when it seems as if everything we do goes wrong and the cards seem to be "stacked against us." If we are generally somewhat suspicious and disposed to blame others for our difficulties, we may feel that most people are selfish and ruthless and that honest

In August 1977, David Berkowitz of New York City was arrested in connection with the ''Son of Sam'' murders. Although two court-appointed psychiatrists declared Berkowitz ''paranoid,'' he was judged fit to stand trial. Berkowitz was sentenced to a minimum of 30 years in prison. He later claimed to have fabricated his paranoid symptoms ''so as to find . . . justification for my criminal acts against society.''

people, no matter what their ability, do not have a fair chance. As a result, we may feel abused and become somewhat bitter and cynical. Many people go through life feeling underrated and frustrated and brooding over fancied and real injustices. Meissner (1978) regards such attitudes as a normal and essential phase of personality development, a necessary component in the achievement of personal identity and autonomy. Most people, according to this view, are able to grow beyond this phase in development, where a central feature is the ''need for an enemy.'' Some few are not, however, in which case they chronically entertain paranoid explanations of their problems.

As we have seen, recent thinking in this area has tended to view schizophrenic and paranoid processes as quite independent of one another, although sometimes occurring together in the same individual, in which case paranoid schizophrenia is the outcome (Magaro, 1980, 1981; Meissner, 1981). According to Magaro, schizophrenic and paranoid cognitions are of a different order and are related to two different stages of information-processing. Whereas schizophrenia is seen as a disorder of *perception,* paranoia is regarded as a disorder of *conception.* The paranoid individual, in fact, is said to *overconceptualize* his experience at the expense of relative inattention to the actual data that are perceived. For example, the (nonparanoid)

schizophrenic individual might perceive his thoughts as inspired by external sources; the paranoid individual might carry this one step farther and conclude that this experience is due to a systematic plot by his ''enemies'' to harass and punish him. As a result, meanings may be imposed on incoming information that have no or at most a minimal relationship to what has happened, at least as far as issues of great personal significance are concerned.

We have already noted that individuals with paranoid schizophrenia tend not to show the extensive cognitive disorganization seen in other forms of schizophrenia. It should also be noted that biological factors have rarely been implicated in the paranoid disorders, as they have been in schizophrenia—although it must be acknowledged that very little work has been done in this area. Most observers believe that psychosocial factors are sufficient to account for the development of most of the paranoid forms of thought.

It may also be noted that the maintenance of a severely paranoid ''fix'' on the world does indeed require drastic derangements of the organism's basic cognitive equipment, although it does not require that such equipment be subject to virtual functional annihilation. If the individual were unable to function on a day-by-day basis, paranoia would be impossible as an effective coping strategy.

Faulty learning and development. Most individuals who later become paranoid seem as children to have been aloof, suspicious, seclusive, stubborn, and resentful of punishment. When crossed, they became sullen and morose. Rarely did they show a history of normal play with other children or good socialization in terms of warm, affectionate relationships (Sarvis, 1962; Schwartz, 1963; Swanson et al., 1970).

Often the family background appears to have been authoritarian and excessively dominating, suppressive, and critical; frequently, some family members have practiced "mind reading" the thoughts of other family members. Such a family has often been permeated with an air of superiority that was a cover-up for an underlying lack of self-acceptance and feelings of inferiority, creating for the child, in turn, the necessity of proving superiority. Inevitably the family background of such individuals colors their feelings about people in general and their way of reacting to others. Inadequate socialization is likely to keep them from understanding the motives and points of view of others and lead them to suspicious misinterpretation of unintentional slights. Also they tend to enter into social relationships with a hostile, dominating attitude that drives others away. Their inevitable social failures then further undermine their self-esteem and lead to deeper social isolation and mistrust.

In later personality development these early trends merge into a picture of self-important, rigid, arrogant individuals who long to dominate others and readily maintain their unrealistic self-picture by projecting the blame for difficulties onto others and seeing in others the weaknesses they cannot acknowledge in themselves. They are highly suspicious of the motives of other people and quick to sense insult or mistreatment. Such individuals lack a sense of humor—which is not surprising, since they view life as a deadly serious struggle—and are incapable of seeing things from any viewpoint but their own. Typically, they categorize people and ideas into "good" and "bad" and have difficulty in conceiving of something as having both good and bad qualities or shades of gray. Their goals and expectations are unrealistically high, and they refuse to make concessions in meeting life's problems by accepting more moderate goals. They expect to be praised and appreciated for even minor achievements, and when such praise is not forthcoming, they sulk and withdraw from normal contacts.

As was suggested in our discussion of "introjected" parental personalities in paranoid schizophrenia (see page 374), many problems of paranoid individuals can be seen as problems of selfhood. The person may seem unable to achieve distance from or objectification of deeply internalized struggles involving issues of aggression, victimization, power, weakness, and humiliation. Although such individuals may have broad interests and appear normal in general behavior, they are usually unable to relate closely to other persons; they appear inaccessible, are overly aggressive, and maintain a somewhat superior air. Meissner (1978) views these personality traits as in large measure manifestations of a desperate attempt to maintain autonomy and a related fear of submission to the will of others, as though submission would constitute nothing less than total personality disintegration.

Failure and inferiority. The lives of paranoid individuals are replete with failures in critical life situations—social, occupational, and marital—stemming from their rigidity, their unrealistic goals, and their inability to get along with other people. Such failures jeopardize their view of themselves as being adequate, significant, and important and expose their easily wounded pride to what they interpret as the rejection, scorn, and ridicule of others.

Their failures are made more difficult to cope with by their utter inability to understand the causes. Why should their efforts to improve the efficiency of the company—which people approve in principle—lead to such negative reactions from others? Why should people dislike them when they are striving so hard to do the best possible job down to the very last detail? Unable to see themselves or the situation objectively, they simply cannot understand how they tend to alienate others and why they are rebuffed and rejected.

Although their feelings of inferiority are masked behind their air of superiority and self-importance, many aspects of their behavior give them away. Clues in profusion are found in their continual craving for praise and recognition, their hypersensitivity to criticism, their exact and formal adherence to socially approved

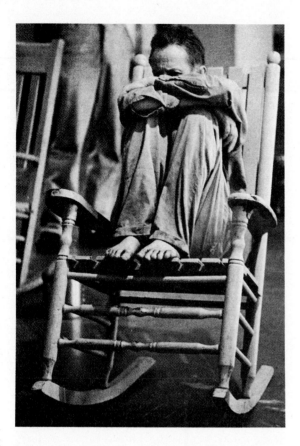

In paranoia a person feels singled out and taken advantage of, mistreated, plotted against, stolen from, spied upon, ignored, or otherwise mistreated by "enemies."

behavior, and their conscientious and overzealous performance of the most minute occupational tasks.

In essence, then, the paranoid individual is confronted with experiences of failure that in effect say, "People don't like you," "Something is wrong with you," "You are inferior." But he or she is incapable of dealing with the problem in a task-oriented way, instead tending to intensify the existing defenses, becoming more rigid, opinionated, and prone to blame others. This defensive pattern is a protection against having to face unbearable feelings of inferiority and worthlessness. In this connection, Meissner (1978) reports the case of a young man who was sexually seduced by his drunken mother. He lived in terror that his "sin" would be discovered, and in the process developed an elaborate paranoid system of thought.

Elaboration of defenses and the "pseudo-community."   A rigid, self-important, humorless, and suspicious individual such as we have described becomes understandably unpopular with other people—in effect, an aversive stimulus. Thus, as Lemert (1962) has noted, the paranoid person frequently becomes in fact a target of actual discrimination and mistreatment. Ever alert to injustices, both imagined and real, such an individual easily finds "proof" of persecution.

In this context, Grunebaum and Perlman (1973) have pointed to the naivete of the preparanoid person in assessing the interpersonal world—in terms of who can be trusted and who cannot—as a fertile source of hurtful interactions. As they express it, "The ability to trust others realistically requires that the individual be able to tolerate minor and major violations of trust that are part of normal human relationships" (p. 32). But the preparanoid individual is unprepared for the "facts of life," tending to both trust and mistrust inappropriately and to overreact when others are perceived, accurately or not, as betraying the trust.

Some persons do not go beyond this stage, simply continuing as paranoid personalities, continually expecting—and inducing—rejection and rebuff.

Where paranoia develops, it usually does so gradually, as mounting failures and seeming betrayals force these individuals to an elaboration of their defensive structures. To avoid self-devaluation, they search for "logical" reasons for their lack of success. Why were they denied a much-deserved promotion? Why was it given to someone less experienced and obviously far less qualified? They become more vigilant, begin to scrutinize the environment, search for hidden meanings, and ask leading questions. They ponder like a detective over the "clues" they pick up, trying to fit them into some sort of meaningful picture.

Gradually the picture begins to crystallize—a process commonly referred to as "paranoid illumination." It becomes apparent that they are being singled out for some obscure reason, that other people are working against them, that they are being interfered with. In essence, they protect themselves against the intolerable assumption "There is something wrong with me" with the projective defense "They are doing something to me." Now they have failed not because of any inferiority or lack on their part but because others are working against them. They are on the side of good and the progress of humankind while their enemies are allied with the forces of evil. With this as their fundamental defensive premise, they proceed to distort and falsify the facts to fit it and gradually develop a logic-tight, fixed, delusional system.

Cameron (1959) has referred to this process as the building up of a paranoid "pseudo-community" in which the individual organizes surrounding people (both real and imaginary) into a structured group whose purpose is to carry out some action against him or her. Now the most trivial events may take on an ominous meaning. If a new employee is hired, the person was obviously planted as a spy. If a subordinate makes a mistake, it is done to discredit his or her competence as a supervisor. Even the most casual conversation of others may have a hidden and sinister meaning. This pseudo-community is not all-inclusive, however, but remains limited in scope to those stressor areas—such as occupational failure—that present the greatest threat to the individual's feelings of adequacy and worth. In other life areas not directly involved with the paranoid system, the individual may be quite rational and may function adequately. Over a period of time, of course, additional life areas and experiences may be incorporated into the delusional system.

The role of highly selective information processing in the development of these delusional systems should be emphasized. Once these individuals begin to suspect that others are working against them, they start carefully noting the slightest signs pointing in the direction of their suspicions and ignore all evidence to the contrary. As Swanson et al. (1970) have pointed out,

"Suspicious thinking is remarkably rigid thinking. The suspicious person has something on his mind constantly. He looks at the world with a definite expectation. Suspiciousness requires intense attention. The paranoid reads more between the lines than he sees in the lines themselves, thus overlooking the obvious." (P. 14)

With this frame of reference, it is quite easy, in our highly competitive, somewhat ruthless world, to find ample evidence that others are working against us. The attitude itself of paranoid individuals leads to a vicious circle, for their suspiciousness, distrust, and criticism of others drive their friends and well-wishers away and keep them in continual friction with other people, generating new incidents for them to grasp hold of and magnify. Often people do in fact have to conspire behind their backs in order to keep peace and cope with their eccentricities.

One additional factor often mentioned in connection with the development of paranoia is that of sexual maladjustment. Like schizophrenic patients, most paranoid individuals reveal sexual difficulties, not infrequently centering around homosexual conflicts. As we have seen, the factor of homosexuality was, in fact, strongly emphasized by Freud, who concluded that paranoia represents the individual's attempt to deal with homosexual tendencies that the ego is not prepared to acknowledge. Most contemporary investigators, however, believe that the critical factors in paranoia are the individual's serious difficulties in interpersonal relationships generally, compounded by overwhelming feelings of inadequacy and inferiority. While underlying sexual conflicts, both heterosexual and homosexual, may be involved in the clinical picture, they do not appear to be of primary significance.

Many early schizophrenic and paranoid patients make allusions to being "queer" or "gay," or to the thought that other people think they are. On investigation, it turns out that they typically have never engaged in homosexual behavior and show no indication of wishing to do so. Here it may be that they have finally hit upon an "explanation" for the feeling of being so different from others, and for the slights and contempt they believe are emanating from others. An explanation of this sort may be better than no explanation at all as far as the troubled person is concerned.

Treatment and outcomes

In the early stages of paranoia, treatment with individual and/or group psychotherapy may prove effective, particularly if an individual voluntarily seeks professional assistance. Here, behavior therapy appears to show particular promise; for example, the paranoid thinking may be altered by a combination of aversive conditioning, removal of factors in the person's life situation that are reinforcing the maladaptive behavior, and development of more effective coping patterns.

Once the delusional system is well established, however, treatment is extremely difficult. It is usually impossible to communicate with such individuals in a rational way concerning their problems. In addition, they are not prone to seek treatment, but are more likely to be seeking justice for all the wrong done to them. Nor is hospitalization likely to help, for they are likely to see it as a form of punishment. They are apt to regard themselves as superior to other patients and will often complain that their families and the hospital staff have had them "put away" for no valid reason; seeing nothing wrong with themselves, they refuse to cooperate or participate in treatment.

Eventually, however, they may realize that their failure to curb their actions and ideas will result in prolonged hospitalization. As a result, they may make a pretext of renouncing their delusions, admitting that they did hold such ideas but claiming that they now realize the ideas are absurd and have given them up. After their release, they are often more reserved in expressing their ideas and in annoying other people, but they are far from recovered. Thus the prognosis for complete recovery from paranoia has traditionally been unfavorable.

Summary

The schizophrenic disorders, especially, and the paranoid disorders often associated with them represent the major challenge facing the mental health professions—partly because virtually all of the psychopathological processes previously described come together in these classes of disorders.

One extraordinary case—that of the Genain quadruplets—sheds light on the sources and the complexity of schizophrenic disorders. All four of the Genain sisters became schizophrenic prior to the age of 25. After carefully tracking the progress of the Genains through the years, researchers have concluded that both biological and psychosocial factors contributed to the quads' vulnerability to schizophrenia.

The schizophrenias are characterized by a loss in level of previous functioning, disturbances of communication, bizarre delusions and hallucinations, aberrations of perception and affect, and, in some instances, peculiarities of motor behavior. The last is associated with the catatonic subtype of the disorder.

Other subtypes of schizophrenia include undifferentiated (mixed symptoms not fitting into other categories or moving rapidly among them), disorganized or hebephrenic (incoherent, silly, or inappropiate affect), and paranoid (persistent ideas or hallucinations regarding persecution or grandiosity). Given these variations, as well as other anomalies, some have questioned whether such a "thing" as schizophrenia exists.

Hardly anybody questions the existence of a cluster of behaviors, called schizophrenic, that constitutes the behaviors that are the most unintelligible to the average person. Such behaviors have been correlated with biological, psychosocial, and sociocultural variables. As yet, however, none of these broad sources of behavioral variation has been definitely established as an etiologic factor in schizophrenia. Several leads in each area are quite promising. The evidence suggests that the traditional pessimism with respect to understanding the sources of schizophrenic behavior is to a large extent unjustified.

The paranoid disorders, in which schizophrenic disorganization seems *not* to be a significant factor, form a subgroup of psychoses that are even less well understood than the others. Here, the person harbors ideas of persecution (e.g., injustice is being perpetrated against one), grandiosity (e.g., one has a special mission beyond the pale of ordinary citizens), or both. But, the person is entirely functional—including, often, highly organized cognitive functioning—in areas that do not impinge on the delusional thought-structure (the paranoid construction) in which the person is centrally involved. These people can often function at a marginal level in society. Treatment of them is currently difficult, at best.

Substance-use and other addictive disorders

Aloïs Wey, Maisons *(1977). Wey (b. 1894) attended for a short time a primary school where he developed an interest in art and drawing. At the age of 14, Wey quit school and entered upon a difficult life complicated by bouts with alcoholism and by exacting toil, first as a helper in his father's roofing business, later as a master roofer, a factory worker, an electrician, a miner, a cook. At the age of 80, in retirement and living in a rest home, Wey resumed drawing. Many of his works take as their subjects exotic architectural structures, quite often resembling the architecture of foreign countries (though Wey's travels in other lands have, in fact, been quite limited).*

Addictive behavior, whether involving the abuse of substances such as alcohol or cocaine or the excessive ingestion of high-caloric food resulting in extreme obesity, is one of the most pervasive and intransigent mental health problems facing society today. Addictive disorders represent disorders of self-control and can be seen all around us: in extremely high rates of alcoholism, in tragic exposés of cocaine abuse among star athletes and entertainers, and in reports of the "epidemic" proportions of eating disorders in the United States.

The DSM-III classification of addictive or substance-related disorders is divided into two major categories. First, *substance-induced organic disorders* are included within the organic mental disorders. These disorders refer to organic impairment resulting from such factors as *toxicity*, the poisonous nature of the substance (for example, amphetamine delusional disorder, alcoholic intoxication, or cannabis delusional disorder) or physiologic changes in the brain due to vitamin deficiency (for example, alcohol amnestic disorder, also known as Korsakoff's syndrome). Second, a number of addictive disorders are covered in a separate category that focuses on what are known as *substance-use disorders.* These disorders can be distinguished from the organic disorders described above in that they refer to maladaptive behaviors resulting from regular and consistent use of the substance involved.

The substance-use disorders are further subdivided into two general groups: *substance abuse* and *substance dependence.* Substance-abuse disorders generally involve a pathological use of a substance resulting in self-injurious behavior or in the person's inability to limit his or her use of the substance. Substance-abuse disorders also usually involve an impairment in work or social relations and use of the substance for at least one month. Substance-dependence disorders are more severe forms of substance-use disorder and involve a physiological dependence on the substance. Dependence on the substance in these disorders means that the individual will show either *tolerance* for the drug or *withdrawal symptoms* when the drug is unavailable. ("Tolerance" refers to the need for increased amounts of the substance in order for the individual to achieve the desired effects; "withdrawal symptoms" are physical symptoms such as sweating, tremors, and tension that accompany abstinence from the drug.)

The most commonly used problem drugs are the *psychoactive*—that is, drugs affecting mental functioning: alcohol, barbiturates, minor tranquilizers, amphetamines, heroin, and marijuana. Some of these drugs, such as alcohol, can be purchased legally by adults; others, such as the barbiturates, can be used legally under medical supervision; still others, such as heroin, are illegal. Currently, drug legislation, particularly in relation to marijuana, is a controversial matter.

The increasing problem of substance abuse and dependence in our society has caused both public and scientific attention to be focused on it. In the past, abuse and dependence, particularly involving alcohol and heroin, were considered to be evidence of "moral weakness." But public outcry and treatment approaches—such as imprisonment—based on this concept have proven ineffective. Thus, until recently, little progress was made toward the identification of causal factors or the development of effective methods of treatment. Although our present knowledge concerning alcohol or drug abuse and dependence is far from complete, investigating them as maladaptive patterns of adjustment to life's demands rather than as moral deficiencies is leading to clear progress in understanding and treatment. Such an approach, of course, does not mean that the individual bears no personal responsibility in the development of the problem; the widespread notion that drug dependence and abuse can be viewed as forms of "disease" has, as we shall see later, clouded the issue in an unfortunate way.

In addition to the abuse and dependence disorders that involve a particular substance, there are disorders that have all the features of an addictive condition but do not involve substances with chemically addicting properties. Two of these disorders, pathological gambling and the overeating that leads to extreme obesity, are discussed in this chapter because the maladaptive behavior involved and the treatment approaches shown to be effective with them suggest that they are quite similar in many ways to the various drug-use and drug-induced disorders.

Alcohol abuse and dependence

As we noted in Chapter 1, Cambyses, King of Persia in the sixth century B.C., had the dubious distinction of being one of the first alcoholics on record. People of many other early cultures, including the Egyptian, Greek, and Roman, made extensive and often excessive use of alcohol. Beer was first made in Egypt around 3000 B.C. The oldest surviving winemaking formulas were recorded by Marcus Cato in Italy almost a century and a half before the birth of Christ. About 800 A.D. the process of distillation was developed by an Arabian alchemist, thus making possible an increase in both the range and the potency of alcoholic beverages.

Incidence and effects of problem drinking

The terms *alcoholic* and *alcoholism* have been subject to some controversy and are used differently by different groups. The World Health Organization, for instance, uses the term *alcoholic* to refer to any person with life problems related to alcohol. The National Council on Alcoholism, on the other hand, uses a more restrictive definition: certain diagnostic signs delineating extent and severity of abuse must be present for an individual to be classified as an alcoholic. Some behaviorists are recommending a still more restrictive definition: they prefer to use the term *problem drinkers* for most alcohol abusers, conceptualizing "problem drinking" as a continuum, with "alcoholics" constituting a small subgroup at the extreme end (Miller, 1979; Miller & Caddy, 1977). In this chapter we will use the definition of The President's Commission on Mental Health (1978), which uses the term *alcoholic* to refer to individuals with serious drinking problems, whose drinking impairs their life adjustment in terms of health, personal relationships, and/or occupational functioning.

However defined, alcoholism is a major problem in the United States. A recent survey of needed services for small communities found alcoholism to be one of the problems most frequently cited (NIMH, 1978). An estimated 10 to 15 million adult Americans experience frequent episodes of abusive use of alcohol. Yet only about 1 million of these individuals currently receive treatment for their drinking problems.

The potentially detrimental effects of excessive alcohol—for the individual, his or her loved ones, and society—are legion. Bengelsdorf (1970a) has pointed out that

". . . its abuse has killed more people, sent more victims to hospitals, generated more police arrests, broken up more marriages and homes, and cost industry more money than has the abuse of heroin, amphetamines, barbiturates, and marijuana combined." (p. 7)

In addition to the serious problems they create for themselves, excessive drinkers pose serious difficulties for, on the average, some four to six other persons, including mates, children, friends, employers, and even total strangers, as in cases where they are involved in automobile accidents while under the influence of alcohol. The National Institute on Alcohol Abuse and Alcoholism and other national agencies agree that alcohol abuse is by far the most devastating drug problem in the United States today.

Alcohol has been associated with over half the deaths and major injuries suffered in automobile accidents each year, and with about 50 percent of all murders, 40 percent of all assaults, 35 percent or more of all rapes, and 30 percent of all suicides. About one out of every three arrests in the United States results from the abuse of alcohol. The financial drain imposed on the economy by alcoholism is estimated to be over $25 billion a year, in large part comprised of losses to industry from absenteeism, lowered work efficiency, and accidents, as well as the costs involved in the treatment of alcoholics. The life span of the average alcoholic is about 12 years shorter than that of the average nonalcoholic, and alcohol now ranks as the third major cause of death in the United States, behind coronary heart disease and cancer. In a recent follow-up study of alcoholics, Polich, Armor, and Braiker (1981) found that 14.5 percent of their sample of alcoholic subjects had died during the 4½-year period since the study began. These deaths were attributed to alcohol-related conditions such as cirrhosis, suicide, gastrointestinal hemorrhage, and automobile accidents.

Alcoholism in the United States cuts across all age, educational, occupational, and socioeconomic boundaries. It is considered a serious problem in industry, in the professions, and in the military; it is found among such seemingly unlikely candidates as airline pilots, politicians, surgeons, law-enforcement officers, and teenagers. The once popular image of the alcoholic as an unkempt resident of Skid Row is inaccurate. In fact, the latter group constitutes less than 5 percent of all alcoholics; it is even estimated that half or more of the people on Skid Row—such as the Bowery in New York—are either moderate drinkers or nondrinkers. (Further myths about alcoholism are noted in the **HIGHLIGHT** on page 400).

Problem drinking may develop during any life period from early childhood through old age. However, the great majority of problem drinkers are men and women who are married and living with their families, who hold jobs—often important ones—and who are accepted members of their communities. And although alcoholism has traditionally been considered to be more common among males than females, recently authorities have become aware of a growing problem of alcohol abuse among women. Since many women do not work outside the home, it is often easier for them to conceal their alcoholism.

The commonly used incidence figure of 5 males to 1 female is considered a conservative estimate (Efron, Keller, & Gurioli, 1974). A survey by Celentano and McQueen (1978) showed that of 81 percent of the men who drank alcohol, 26 percent considered themselves heavy drinkers; of 68 percent of the women who drank, 8 percent considered themselves heavy drinkers.

Clinical picture of alcohol abuse and dependence

The Roman poet Horace, in the first century B.C., wrote lyrically about the effects of wine:

It discloses secrets; ratifies and confirms our hopes; thrusts the coward forth to battle; eases the anxious mind of its burthen; instructs in arts. Whom has not

HIGHLIGHT
Some common misconceptions about alcohol and alcoholism

1. Alcohol is a stimulant.

2. Alcohol is essential to the treatment of certain diseases.

3. You can always detect alcohol on the breath of a person who has been drinking.

4. One ounce of 86 proof liquor contains more alcohol than a 12-ounce can of beer.

5. Drinking several cups of coffee can counteract the effects of alcohol and enable the drinker to "sober up."

6. Alcohol can help a person sleep more soundly.

7. Impaired judgment does not occur before there are obvious signs of intoxication.

8. The individual will get more intoxicated by "mixing" liquors than by taking comparable amounts of one kind—e.g., bourbon, Scotch, or vodka.

9. Exercise or a cold shower helps speed up the metabolism of alcohol.

10. People with "strong wills" need not be concerned about becoming alcoholics.

11. Alcohol cannot produce a true addiction in the same sense that heroin does.

12. One cannot become an alcoholic by drinking just beer.

13. Alcohol is far less dangerous than marijuana.

14. In a heavy drinker, damage to the liver shows up long before brain damage appears.

15. The physiological withdrawal reaction from heroin is considered more dangerous than is withdrawal from alcohol.

a cheerful glass made eloquent! Whom not quite free and easy from pinching poverty!

Unfortunately, the effects of alcohol are not always so benign or beneficial. According to the Japanese proverb, "First the man takes a drink, then the drink takes a drink, and then the drink takes the man."

General effects of alcoholic intoxication.
Alcohol is a depressant which affects the higher brain centers, impairing judgment and other rational processes and lowering self-control. As behavioral restraints decline, the drinker may indulge in the satisfaction of impulses ordinarily held in check. In fact, alcohol has been called a "catalyst" for violence, including homicide, assault, and rape.

Some degree of motor incoordination soon becomes apparent, and the drinker's sense of discrimination and perception of cold, pain, and other discomforts are dulled. Typically the drinker experiences a sense of warmth, expansiveness, and well-being. In such a mood, unpleasant realities are screened out and the drink-

er's feelings of self-esteem and adequacy rise. Casual acquaintances become the best and most understanding of friends, and the drinker enters a generally pleasant world of unreality in which worries are temporarily left behind.

When the alcohol content of the bloodstream reaches 0.1 percent, the individual is considered to be intoxicated (see **HIGHLIGHT** on page 401). Muscular coordination, speech, and vision are impaired, and thought processes are confused. Even before this level of intoxication is reached, however, judgment becomes impaired to such an extent that the person misjudges his or her condition. For example, drinkers are certain of their ability to drive safely long after their driving has in fact become quite unsafe.

When the blood alcohol reaches approximately 0.5 percent, the entire neural balance is upset and the individual "passes out." Here unconsciousness apparently acts as a safety device, since concentrations above 0.55 percent are usually lethal.

In general, it is the amount of alcohol actually concentrated in the bodily fluids, not the amount consumed, that determines intoxication.

HIGHLIGHT

Alcohol levels in the blood after drinks taken on an empty stomach by a 150-pound male drinking for one hour*

Effects	Time for all alcohol to leave the body—hours	Alcohol concentration in blood—percent	Amount of beverage
Gross intoxication	10	0.15	5 highballs (1½ oz. whiskey each) or 5 cocktails (1½ oz. whiskey ea.) or 27½ oz. ordinary wine or ½ pint whiskey
Clumsiness—unsteadiness in standing or walking	6	0.12	4 highballs or 4 cocktails or 22 oz. ordinary wine or 6 bottles beer (12 oz. ea.)
Exaggerated emotion and behavior—talkative, noisy, or morose	4	0.09	3 highballs or 3 cocktails or 16½ oz. ordinary wine or 4 bottles beer
Feeling of warmth, mental relaxation	2	0.06	2 highballs or 2 cocktails or 11 oz. ordinary wine or 2 bottles beer
Slight changes in feeling	1	0.03	1 highball or 1 cocktail or 5½ oz. ordinary wine or 1 bottle beer

Calories

5½ oz. wine	115
12 oz. beer	170
1½ oz. whiskey	120

*Blood alcohol level following given intake differs according to the person's weight, the length of the drinking time, and the sex of the drinker. (*Time*, April 22, 1974, p. 77)

However, the effects of alcohol vary for different drinkers, depending on personality, physical condition, amount of food in the stomach, and duration of the drinking. In addition, the user of alcohol may gradually build up a tolerance for the drug so that ever increasing amounts may be needed to produce the desired effects. The attitude of the drinker is important, too: although actual motor and intellectual abilities decline in direct ratio to the blood concentration of alcohol, many persons who consciously try to do so can maintain apparent control over their behavior, showing few outward signs of being intoxicated even after drinking relatively large amounts of alcohol.

Exactly how alcohol works on the brain is not

yet fully understood, but several physiological effects are common. One is a tendency toward increased sexual stimulation but, simultaneously, lowered sexual performance. As Shakespeare wrote in *Macbeth,* alcohol "provokes the desire, but it takes away the performance."

Second, an appreciable number of problem drinkers also experience "blackouts"—lapses of memory. At first these occur at high blood alcohol levels, and the individual may carry on a rational conversation and engage in other relatively complex activities but have no trace of recall the next day. For heavy drinkers even moderate drinking can elicit a memory lapse.

A third curious phenomenon associated with alcoholic intoxication is the "hangover," which many drinkers experience at one time or another. Some observers consider the hangover to be a mild form of withdrawal. As yet, no one has come up with a satisfactory explanation or remedy for the symptoms of headache, nausea, and fatigue characteristic of hangovers.

Chronic alcohol use and dependence.

Although many investigators have maintained that alcohol is a dangerous systemic poison even in very small amounts, newer studies indicate that in moderate amounts—up to about three shots of whiskey, half a bottle of wine, or four glasses of beer per day—alcohol is not harmful to most people and may actually be beneficial to reduce the tension of everyday life stress (HEW, 1974). For pregnant women, however, these amounts are believed to be dangerous; in fact, no safe level has been established (see **HIGHLIGHT** on page 403).

For individuals who drink immoderately, the picture is highly unfavorable. For one thing, the alcohol that is taken in must be assimilated by the body, except for about 5 to 10 percent which is eliminated through breath, urine, and perspiration. The work of assimilation is done by the liver, but when large amounts of alcohol are ingested, the liver may be seriously overworked and eventually suffer irreversible damage. In fact, over time the excessive drinker has a 1-in-10 chance of developing cirrhosis of the liver, a pathological condition in which liver cells are irreparably damaged and replaced by fibrous scar tissue.

For another thing, alcohol is a high-calorie drug. A pint of whiskey—enough to make about 8 to 10 ordinary cocktails—provides about 1200 calories, which is approximately half the ordinary, caloric requirement for a day. Thus, consumption of alcohol reduces the drinker's appetite for other food. Since alcohol has no nutritional value, the excessive drinker often suffers from malnutrition. Furthermore, heavy drinking impairs the body's ability to utilize nutrients, so the nutritional deficiency cannot be made up by popping vitamins. The excessive intake of alcohol also impairs the activity of the white blood cells in fighting disease and is associated with a greatly increased risk of cancer (HEW, 1974). And in addition to the other problems, the excessive drinker usually suffers from chronic fatigue, oversensitivity, and depression.

Initially alcohol may seem to provide a useful crutch for dealing with the stresses of life, especially during periods of acute stress, by helping screen out intolerable reality and enhancing the drinker's feelings of adequacy and worth. Eventually, however, the excessive use of alcohol becomes counterproductive, resulting in lowered feelings of adequacy and worth, impaired reasoning and judgment, and gradual personality deterioration. Behavior typically becomes coarse and inappropriate, and the drinker assumes increasingly less responsibility, loses pride in personal appearance, neglects spouse and family, and becomes generally touchy, irritable, and unwilling to discuss the problem. As judgment becomes impaired, the excessive drinker may be unable to hold a job and generally becomes unqualified to cope with new demands that arise. General personality disorganization and deterioration may be reflected in loss of employment and/or marital breakup. By this time, the drinker's general health is likely to have deteriorated, and brain and liver damage may have occurred. For example, Golden et al. (1981) found significant structural changes in the left hemisphere of the brains of chronic alcoholics. In another study, alcoholics over age 40 failed to recover from visual-spatial brain dysfunction as readily as did younger alcoholics, and they were less able to compensate for impairments (Goldman, Williams, & Klisz, 1983).

The development of alcohol dependence.

Excessive drinking can be viewed as progressing insidiously from early- to middle- to late-stage alcoholism. (The **HIGHLIGHT** on page 404 presents

HIGHLIGHT

"Fetal alcohol syndrome": How much drinking is too much?

Research indicates that heavy drinking by an expectant mother can affect the health of the unborn baby. Newborn infants whose mothers drank heavily during pregnancy have been found to have frequent physical and behavioral abnormalities. For example, such infants are lighter and smaller than average and sometimes show facial and limb irregularities (Jones & Smith, 1975; NIMH, 1978a; Smith, Jones, & Hanson, 1976; Streissguth, 1976; and Ulleland, 1972). In fact, *The Third Report on Alcohol and Health* (HEW, 1978) reports that alcohol abuse in pregnant women is the third leading cause of birth defects (the first two being *Down's syndrome* and *spina bifida*, the latter referring to the incomplete formation and fusion of the spinal canal).

How much drinking endangers the newborn's health? The HEW report warns against drinking more than one ounce of alcohol per day or the equivalent (two 12-ounce cans of beer or two 5-ounce glasses of wine, for example). The actual amount of alcohol that can safely be ingested during pregnancy is not known, but it is clear that existing evidence for fetal alcohol syndrome is strongest when applied to heavy alcohol users rather than light to moderate users (Kolata, 1981b). Nonetheless, the American Medical Association (1982) recently approved a report recommending that pregnant women abstain from using alcohol as the "safest course" until safe amounts of alcohol consumption can be determined. Moreover, the National Institute of Alcohol Abuse and Alcoholism (NIAAA) has sponsored a campaign to warn against drinking any alcohol during pregnancy. Their campaign slogan is "For baby's sake . . . and yours, don't drink during pregnancy." This slogan has been criticized by some writers on alcoholism, such as Kolata (1981b), who report that the evidence for damaging effects among women who are light drinkers is minimal.

some of the common "early warning signs" of excessive drinking.) Alcohol dependence is reached when symptoms of alcohol tolerance or alcohol withdrawal can be identified. Some investigators view alcohol dependence as recognizable through a number of related symptoms of alcohol use. In their extensive study of the "natural course of alcoholism," Polich et al. (1981) evaluated the presence of alcohol-dependence symptoms among drinkers in their sample of identified alcoholics. They concluded that several secondary symptoms of dependence—including blackouts, missing meals, and continuous drinking—could be viewed not as isolated events but as related problems (see **HIGHLIGHT** on page 405).

In an extensive study of over 2000 drinkers who had progressed to late-stage physiological and psychological dependence, Jellinek (1952, 1971) proposed that the following stages are common in the development of dependence on alcohol.

1. *The prealcoholic symptomatic phase:* Drinkers who later lose control start out drinking in conventional social situations but soon find that it brings a rewarding relief from tension. Initially they drink to relieve tension only occasionally; gradually, however, they resort to alcohol almost daily.

2. *The prodromal phase:* The second phase is marked by sudden onset of blackouts; the drinker shows few, if any, signs of intoxication and might be able to carry on a reasonable conversation or go through quite elaborate activities but with no memory of these events the next day.

3. *The crucial phase:* The third stage is characterized by the loss of control over drinking; any consumption of alcohol—which now typically begins in the afternoon—seems to trigger a chain reaction that continues until the drinker is either too intoxicated or too sick to drink any more.

4. *The chronic phase:* As alcohol becomes increasingly dominant in the drinker's life, the person finds him- or herself intoxicated during the daytime on a weekday and might continue in this state for several days until entirely incapacitated.

Though Jellinek's stages are useful in attempting to understand the persistence of drinking motivation in individuals with drinking problems, most investigators today do not fully subscribe to them. Rather, they see alcohol use

HIGHLIGHT
Early warning signs of drinking problems

1. Frequent desire—increase in desire, often evidenced by eager anticipation of drinking after work and careful attention to maintaining supply.

2. Increased consumption—an increase that seems gradual but is marked from month to month. The individual may begin to worry about it at this point and lie about the amount consumed.

3. Extreme behavior—the commission of various acts that leave the individual feeling guilty and embarrassed the next day.

4. "Pulling blanks"—inability to remember what happened during an alcoholic bout.

5. Morning drinking—either as a means of reducing a hangover or as a "bracer" to help start the day.

A person who exhibits this pattern is well on the road to loss of control. The progression is likely to be facilitated if there is environmental support for heavy or excessive drinking from the spouse or the individual's job situation or sociocultural setting.

and abuse problems as being multiformed and not reducible to a common unitary process. For example, some drinkers who become alcoholics follow the stages, while others do not. There are so-called "spree" drinkers who remain sober and handle responsible positions for long periods of time, but then in the face of some stressful situation will lose control completely—usually winding up in a hospital or jail. It has also been shown that blackouts may not be experienced or may occur in later stages of alcoholism. And in some instances, individuals appear to skip even the social drinker phase, becoming what has been referred to as "instant alcoholics." Finally a new trend has become apparent in our society, involving "multiple addictions," in which dependence on alcohol is complicated by the concurrent use of barbiturates, amphetamines, tranquilizers, and/or other psychoactive drugs. This is apparently particularly common among young alcoholics and, of course, may markedly change the nature and course of the clinical picture.

Psychoses associated with alcoholism.

Several acute psychotic reactions fit the DSM-III classification of substance-induced disorders. These reactions may develop in individuals who have been drinking excessively over long periods of time or who have a reduced tolerance for alcohol for other reasons—for example, because of brain lesions. Such acute reactions usually last only a short time and generally consist of confusion, excitement, and delirium. They are often called *alcoholic psychoses* because they are marked by a temporary loss of contact with reality. There are four commonly recognized subtypes of such reactions.

1. *Pathological intoxication* is an acute reaction that occurs in persons whose tolerance to alcohol is chronically very low (such as epileptics or those of an unstable personality makeup) or in normal persons whose tolerance to alcohol is temporarily lessened by exhaustion, emotional stress, or other conditions. Following the consumption of even moderate amounts of alcohol, these individuals may suddenly become disoriented and may even commit violent crimes. This confused, disoriented state is usually followed by a period of deep sleep, with complete amnesia afterward. The following case history illustrates this pattern.

The patient was hospitalized following an altercation in a bar in which he attacked and injured a woman and her date. On admission to the hospital he seemed very friendly and cooperative—in fact, almost servile in his desire to please those in authority. His personal history revealed that he had been involved in five such incidents during the previous two years. His family background was torn with bickering and dissension. Both parents were stern disciplinarians and severely punished him for the most minor disapproved behavior. He was taught to feel that sex was very evil.

In his previous altercations he had been arrested twice for disturbing the peace. In each case these incidents took place in bars where, after a few drinks, he would become aggressive, loud, and abusive, daring any and all to do anything about it. His latest escapade and arrest involved an attack on a woman; this had apparently been provoked by her kissing her date and making what the patient interpreted as sexual overtures in public. He approached the woman in a threatening manner, slapped her, knocked her date out when he attempted to intervene, and then hit her several times with his fists before he was forcibly restrained by other customers. He was amnesic for the entire episode, apparently "coming to" on his way to the hospital.

It was felt in this case that the woman's behavior aroused unacceptable and therefore threatening sexual desires in the patient, against which he defended himself by becoming hostile and attacking her. The alcohol apparently served to lower his normal behavioral restraints, permitting his hostility to be expressed in overt antisocial behavior.

2. *Delirium tremens* is probably the best known of the various alcoholic psychotic reactions. A fairly common occurrence among those who drink excessively for a long time, this reaction may occur during a prolonged drinking spree or upon the withdrawal of alcohol after prolonged drinking.

The delirium usually is preceded by a period of restlessness and insomnia during which the person may feel generally uneasy and apprehensive. Slight noises or sudden moving objects may cause considerable excitement and agitation. The full-blown symptoms include (a) disorientation for time and place in which, for example, a person may mistake the hospital for a church or jail, or no longer recognize friends, or identify hospital attendants as old acquaintances; (b) vivid hallucinations, particularly of small, fast-moving animals like snakes, rats, and roaches, which are clearly localized in space; (c) acute fear, in which these animals may change in form, size, or color in terrifying ways; (d) extreme suggestibility, in which a person can be made to see almost any form of animal if its presence is merely suggested; (e) marked tremors of the hands, tongue, and lips—as implied by the name of this disorder; and (f) other symptoms, including perspiration, fever, a rapid and weak heartbeat, a coated tongue, and a foul breath.

The delirium typically lasts from three to six days and is generally followed by a deep sleep. When the person awakens, there are few symptoms—aside from possible slight remorse—but frequently the individual will have been rather

HIGHLIGHT

Alcoholics reporting symptoms of alcohol dependence

Symptom	Percent reporting any occurrence in 30-day period
Tremors (had the "shakes")	31
Morning drinking (had a drink as soon as they woke up)	41
Loss of control (tried to stop drinking but couldn't)	32
Blackouts (memory lapses)	29
Missing meals (missed a meal because of drinking)	42
Continuous drinking (12 hours or more)	37
One or more of the above symptoms	64

Adapted from Polich et al., (1981).

badly scared, and may not resume drinking for several weeks or months. Usually, however, there is eventual resumption, followed by a return to the hospital with a new attack. The death rate from delirium tremens as a result of convulsions, heart failure, and other complications once approximated 10 percent (Tavel, 1962). With such newer drugs as chlordiazepoxide, however, the current death rate during delirium tremens and acute alcoholic withdrawal has been markedly reduced.

The following is a brief description of a 43-year-old male delirium tremens patient.

The subject was brought forcibly to the psychiatric ward of a general hospital when he fired his shotgun at 3:30 A.M. while "trying to repel an invasion of cockroaches." On admission he was confused and disoriented and had terrifying hallucinations involving "millions and millions" of invading cockroaches. He

Alcoholism in the United States cuts across all age, educational, occupational, and socioeconomic boundaries, and embraces a wide range of "types" of drinkers.

leaped from his bed and cowered in terror against the wall, screaming for help and kicking and hitting frantically at his imaginary assailants. When an attendant came to his aid, he screamed for him to get back out of danger or he would be killed too. Before the attendant could reach him he dived headlong on his head, apparently trying to kill himself.

The subject's delirium lasted for 3½ days, after which he returned to a state of apparent normality, apologized profusely for the trouble he had caused everyone, stated he would never touch another drop, and was discharged. However, on his way home he stopped at a bar, had too much to drink, and on emerging from the bar collapsed on the street. This time he sobered up in jail, again apologized for the trouble he had caused, was extremely remorseful, and was released with a small fine. His subsequent career is unknown.

3. In *acute alcoholic hallucinosis,* the main symptoms are auditory hallucinations. At first the individual usually hears a voice making certain simple statements. With time, however, the hallucinations usually extend to the voices of several people, all of them critical and reproachful. The individual's innermost private weaknesses, particularly sexual ones, may be itemized and discussed, and various horrible punishments then proposed. The clanking of chains, the sharpening of knives, the sound of pistol shots, or footsteps approaching in a threatening manner may be heard. Terror-stricken, the individual may scream for help or attempt suicide.

This condition may continue for several days or even weeks, during which time the person is depressed but fairly well oriented and coherent, apart from the hallucinations. After recovery, he or she usually shows considerable remorse as well as some insight into what has happened.

Investigators are less inclined than formerly to attribute this psychotic reaction solely to the effects of alcohol. Generally, it seems to be related to a broad pattern of maladaptive behavior, as in the following case:

The subject was hospitalized after a suicide attempt in which he slashed his wrists. He had been hospitalized once before after a similar incident in which he tried to hang himself with a bath towel. He was unmarried and lived alone.

The patient had been drinking excessively for a three-year period. He was not in the least particular about what he drank as long as it contained alcohol. For several days prior to his last suicide attempt he had heard voices that accused him of all manner of "filthy sex acts." He was particularly outraged when they accused him of having committed homosexual acts with his mouth and of having had relations with animals. He complained of a terrible taste in his mouth and imagined that his food had been poisoned as a means of punishing him for his sins. He was generally fearful and apprehensive and slept poorly.

After a stay of two weeks in the hospital, the patient made a good recovery and was discharged. At this time he seemed to have some insight into his difficulties, stating that he felt that his sexual problems had something to do with his suicide attempt.

The psychotic symptoms of this individual were apparently triggered by alcohol, but it seems probable that they could have been similarly brought on by other drugs, illness, exhaustion, or other types of stress.

4. *Korsakoff's psychosis* was first described by the Russian psychiatrist Korsakoff in 1887. The outstanding symptom is a memory defect (particularly with regard to recent events) which is concealed by falsification. Individuals may not recognize pictures, faces, rooms, and other objects that they have just seen, although they may feel that these people or objects are familiar. Such persons increasingly tend to fill in gaps with reminiscences and fanciful tales that lead to unconnected and distorted associations. These individuals may appear to be delirious, hallucinated, and disoriented for time and place, but ordinarily their confusion and disordered conduct are closely related to their attempts to fill in memory gaps. The memory disturbance itself seems related to an inability to form new associations in a manner that renders them readily retrievable. Such a reaction usually occurs in older alcoholics, after many years of excessive drinking.

The symptoms of this disorder are now considered to be due to vitamin B deficiency and other dietary inadequacies. A diet rich in vitamins and minerals generally restores the patient to more normal physical and mental health. However, some personality deterioration usually remains in the form of memory impairment, blunting of intellectual capacity, and lowering of moral and ethical standards.

Causes of alcohol abuse and dependence

In trying to identify the causes of problem drinking, some researchers have stressed the role of genetic and biochemical factors; others have viewed it as a maladaptive pattern of adjustment to the stress of life; still others have emphasized sociocultural factors, such as the availability of alcohol and social approval of excessive drinking. As with most other forms of maladaptive behavior, it would appear that there may be several types of alcohol dependence in which there are somewhat different patterns of biological, psychosocial, and sociocultural causal factors.

Biological factors. In the alcohol-dependent person, cell metabolism has adapted itself to the presence of alcohol in the bloodstream and now demands it for stability. When the alcohol in the bloodstream falls below a certain level, there are withdrawal symptoms. These may be relatively mild—involving a craving for alcohol, tremors, perspiration, and weakness— or more severe, with nausea, vomiting, fever, tachycardia (rapid heartbeat), convulsions, and hallucinations. The shortcut to ending them is to take another drink. Once this point is reached, each drink serves to reinforce alcohol-seeking behavior because it reduces the unpleasantness.

Some observers have asked whether certain individuals start out with a physiological predisposition to alcoholism—perhaps leading to an unusual craving for alcohol once it has been experienced, and hence a greater-than-average tendency toward loss of control. Presumably such a craving could result from some genetic vulnerability. There is some evidence to suggest that there may be biochemical mechanisms related to individual differences in alcohol tolerance (Schuckit, 1980; Schuckit & Rayses, 1979).

Research studies over the past three decades have shown that alcohol dependence does tend to run in families (Goodwin, 1976, 1979). In a study of 259 hospitalized alcoholics, for example, Winokur et al. (1970) found that slightly over 40 percent had had an alcoholic parent— usually the father. Whether this familial incidence results from shared genes or a shared alcoholic environment is a matter of some controversy. In an early study, Roe, Burks, and Mittelmann (1945) followed the case histories of 36 children who had been taken from severely alcoholic parents and placed in foster homes. The likelihood of their becoming alcoholic turned out to be no greater than that of a control group of 25 children of nonalcoholic parents. Some years later, in a review of a number of available studies, Rose and Burks (1968) reported comparable results, thus casting doubt on the genetic hypothesis.

More recent studies however, have supported the genetic viewpoint. For example, Goodwin et al. (1973) found that children of alcoholic parents who had been adopted by nonalcoholic foster parents still had nearly twice the number of alcohol problems by their late twenties as did a control group of adopted children whose real parents did not have a history of alcoholism. In another study, Goodwin and his colleagues (1974) compared the sons of alcoholic parents who were adopted in infancy by nonalcoholic parents with those raised by their alcoholic parents. Both adopted and nonadopted sons later evidenced high rates of alcoholism—25 percent and 17 percent respectively. These investigators concluded that it was being born to an alcoholic parent rather than being raised by one that increased the risk of the son's becoming an alcoholic.

On the other hand, the great majority of children who have alcoholic parents do not themselves become alcoholics—whether or not they are raised by their real parents. The successful adjustment outcomes have not been sufficiently studied (Heller, Sher, & Benson, 1982). Thus we do not know the precise role of genetic factors in the etiology of alcoholism though available evidence suggests that they might be important as predisposing causes. Of course, constitutional predisposition to alcoholism could be acquired as well as inherited. But it is not known whether there are acquired conditions, such as endocrine or enzyme imbalances, that increase an individual's vulnerability to alcoholism.

Some research has suggested that certain ethnic groups, particularly orientals and native Americans, have abnormal physiological reactions to alcohol. Fenna et al. (1971) and Wolff (1972) found that oriental and Eskimo subjects showed a hypersensitive reaction, including flushing of the skin, a drop in blood pressure, and nausea following the ingestion of alcohol. The relatively lower rates of alcoholism among oriental groups are tentatively considered to be related to a faster metabolism rate. Schaefer (1977), however, has questioned these and other metabolism studies as a basis for interpreting cultural differences in alcoholism rates and, using more explicit criteria of metabolism rate,

found no differences in alcohol metabolism between a group of Reddis Indians and Northern European subjects (Schaefer, 1978). He concluded that further research into metabolism rate differences and sensitivity to alcohol needs to be integrated with studies focusing upon relative stress in various cultures.

Psychosocial factors. Not only do alcoholics become physiologically dependent on alcohol; they develop a powerful psychological dependence as well. Since excessive drinking is so destructive of an individual's total life adjustment, the question arises as to why psychological dependence is learned. A number of psychosocial factors have been advanced as possible answers.

1. *Psychological vulnerability.* Is there an "alcoholic personality"—a type of character organization that predisposes a given individual to turn to the use of alcohol rather than to some other defensive pattern of coping with stress?

In efforts to answer this question, investigators have reported that potential alcoholics tend to be emotionally immature, to expect a great deal of the world, to require an inordinate amount of praise and appreciation, to react to failure with marked feelings of hurt and inferiority, to have low frustration tolerance, and to feel inadequate and unsure of their ability to play expected male or female roles. With respect to the last characteristic, for example, Winokur et al. (1970), Pratt (1972), and McClelland et al. (1972) have viewed heavy drinking by some young men as an attempt to prove their masculinity and achieve feelings of adequacy and competency. Similarly, Wilsnack (1973a, 1973b) concluded that the potential female alcoholic places strong value on the traditional female role, while at the same time her sense of adequacy as a female is highly fragile:

"She may manage to cope with her fragile sense of feminine adequacy for a number of years, but when some new threat severely exacerbates her self-doubts she turns to alcohol in an attempt to gain artificial feelings of womanliness. Her excessive drinking may then begin a vicious circle that culminates in the alcoholic's characteristic loss of control over her drinking." (1973a, p. 96)

Beckman (1978) found that female alcoholics have lower self-esteem than either male alcoholics or women who have no history of alcohol abuse. Antisocial personality and depression are two clinical syndromes that have also been commonly associated with later excessive drinking (Jones, 1968, 1971; Seixas & Cadoret, 1974; Weissman et al., 1977; Woodruff et al., 1973).

While such findings provide promising leads, it is difficult to assess the role of specific personality characteristics in the development of alcoholism. Certainly there are many persons with similar personality characteristics who do not become alcoholics, and others with dissimilar ones who do. The only characteristic that appears common to the backgrounds of most problem drinkers is personal maladjustment, yet most maladjusted people do not become alcoholics. The personality of alcoholics may be as much a result as a cause of their dependence on alcohol—for example, the excessive use of alcohol may lead to depression or a depressed person may turn to the excessive use of alcohol, or both.

It is apparent that longitudinal studies are needed to determine whether or not there are personality characteristics that predispose one to the loss of control. One prospective analysis has in fact found evidence of such factors. Loper, Kammeier, & Hoffman (1973) compared the performance of male alcoholics on psychological tests taken several years before, while they were in college, with that of a sample of their classmates who did not later develop problems with alcohol. During college, the alcoholics had differed from their nonalcoholic classmates in being more immature, impulsive, and antisocial.

Although the significance of prealcoholic personality factors remains unclear, alcoholics do tend to show a distinct cluster of personality traits once their drinking pattern has been established. Included here are low stress tolerance, a negative self-image, and feelings of inadequacy, isolation, and depression. By the time the alcoholic comes to the attention of a clinic or hospital, he or she also tends to manifest a lack of responsibility, impaired impulse control, and a decided tendency toward deceitfulness, characteristics that have apparently resulted from environmental stressors such as marital breakup or unemployment, and the exaggerated use of ego-defense mechanisms—particularly denial, rationalization, and projection. In this context, Wikler (1973) has pointed out that during the

later stages of alcoholism, there tends to be a "curious twist in the alcoholic's thinking" (p. 10). For example, instead of blaming herself for drinking excessively and letting the dinner burn, a wife may excuse herself and project the blame onto her husband, who is now perceived as a "nag." And as the alcoholic's life situation continues to deteriorate and stress increases, there is a tendency to rely increasingly on such ego-defense mechanisms.

2. *Stress, tension reduction, and reinforcement.* A number of investigators have pointed out that the typical alcoholic is discontented with his or her life situation and is unable or unwilling to tolerate tension and stress (AMA Committee on Alcoholism and Drug Dependency, 1969). In fact, Schaefer (1971) has concluded that alcoholism is a conditioned response to anxiety. The individual presumably finds in alcohol a means of relieving anxiety, resentment, depression, or other unpleasant feelings. Each drink relieves tension; thus the behavior is reinforced. Eventually, drinking becomes the habitual pattern for coping with stress.

Some investigators hold that anyone who finds alcohol to be tension-reducing is in danger of becoming an alcoholic, even without an especially stressful life situation. However, if this were true, we would expect alcoholism to be fare more common than it is, since alcohol tends to reduce tensions for most persons who use it. In addition, this model does not explain why some excessive drinkers are able to maintain control over their drinking and continue to function in society while others are not.

At the opposite end of the spectrum are investigators who reject the view that alcoholism is a learned maladaptive response, reinforced and maintained by tension reduction. They point out that the long-range consequences of excessive drinking are too devastating, far outweighing its temporary relief value. However, as Bandura (1969) has pointed out,

"This argument overlooks the fact that behavior is more powerfully controlled by its immediate, rather than delayed, consequences, and it is precisely for this reason that persons may persistently engage in immediately reinforcing, but potentially self-destructive behavior. . ." (p. 530)

There is increasing support in the literature that alcohol reduces the magnitude of the individual's response to stressful situations, thereby reinforcing the drinking of alcohol. Levenson et al. (1980) found that alcohol had a dampening effect on the individual's feeling of stress. It seems that alcoholics drink to feel better at the moment, even though they know they will feel worse later.

3. *Marital and other intimate relationships.* As we have noted, alcoholism tends to run in families. But while genetic factors may be an influence, it is clear that an alcoholic parent also constitutes a highly undesirable model for the child. Thus children of alcoholics may have special problems in learning who they are, what is expected of them, and what to esteem in others. Further, their range of coping techniques is likely to be more limited than that of the average child.

Of course, in some cases they may learn to perceive the parent as a negative model—as someone *not* to emulate or model their behavior after. Here it would appear that an alcoholic parent creates so many problems for the family that the child comes to see the alcoholic behavior as highly undesirable. This learning process is well illustrated in the case of a 26-year-old Miami divorcée:

"After attending a Dade County alcohol rehabilitation center for the past three months, Barbara is sober and plans to remain that way. She fears, however, that her drinking may have permanently hurt her children. 'They remember my wine-drinking days when I'd throw up in their wastebasket. Now if they see me drinking a Coke, my older girl will come over and taste it and then reassure the younger one: "It's O.K." ' " (*Time*, April 22, 1974, p. 81).

Excessive drinking often begins during crisis periods in marital or other intimate personal relationships, particularly crises which lead to hurt and self-devaluation. For example, in a study of a hundred middle- and upper-class women who were receiving help at an alcoholism treatment center, Curlee (1969) found that the trauma which appeared to trigger the alcoholism was related to a change or challenge in the subject's role as wife or mother, such as divorce, menopause, or children leaving home (the so-called empty-nest syndrome). Many women appear to begin their immoderate drinking during their late thirties and early forties when such life situation changes are common.

After a review of available literature, Siegler, Osmond, and Newell (1968) described a more extreme pattern of family interaction in alcoholism, in which one person is assigned the role of "alcoholic" while the others play complementary roles, such as martyred wife, neglected children, disgraced parents, and so forth. Since in this conceptualization alcoholism represents a long drawn-out family game which is circular and self-reinforcing, it appears relatively useless to ask how it all began.[1]

A husband who lives with an alcoholic wife is often unaware of the fact that, gradually and inevitably, many of the decisions he makes every day are based on the expectation that his wife will be drinking. In a case such as this, the husband is becoming "drinking-wife-oriented." These expectations, in turn, may make the drinking behavior more likely. Eventually the entire marriage may center around the drinking of the alcoholic spouse. And in some instances, the husband or wife may also begin to drink excessively, possibly through the reinforcement of such behavior by the drinking mate, or to blank out the disillusionment, frustration, and resentment that are often elicited by an alcoholic spouse. Of course, such relationships are not restricted to marital partners but may also occur in those involved in love affairs or close friendships (Al-Anon, 1971).

Excessive use of alcohol is the third most frequent cause of divorce in the United States (and often a hidden factor in the two most common causes—financial and sexual problems). Persons who abuse alcohol are about seven times more likely to be divorced or separated than nonabusers (Levitt, 1974). The deterioration in their intimate interpersonal relationships, of course, further augments the stress and disorganization in their life situations.

Sociocultural factors.   In a general sense, our culture has become dependent on alcohol as a social lubricant and a means of reducing tension. Thus numerous investigators have pointed to the role of sociocultural as well as physiological and psychological factors in the high rate of alcohol abuse and alcohol dependence among Americans.

Here it is of interest to note the conclusions

---

[1] An informative discussion of the games alcoholics play may be found in Steiner (1977).

of Pliner and Cappell (1974) concerning the reinforcing effects of social drinking in our society, in which liquor has come to play an almost ritualistic role in promoting gaiety and pleasant social interaction.

"According to the present results, if it is the case that much of the early drinking experience of . . . individuals takes place in such convivial social settings, drinking will be likely to become associated with positive affective experiences. This reinforcing consequence may in turn make drinking more probable in the future. Thus, to the extent that a social context can enhance the attraction of alcohol, for some individuals it may play a crucial role in the etiology of pathological patterns of alcohol consumption." (p. 425).

Bales (1946) outlined three cultural factors that appear to play a part in determining the incidence of alcoholism in a given society: (a) the degree of stress and inner tension produced by the culture; (b) the attitudes toward drinking fostered by the culture; and (c) the degree to which the culture provides substitute means of satisfaction and other ways of coping with tension and anxiety. This has been borne out by cross-cultural studies.

The importance of the level of stress in a given culture is shown in studies of preliterate societies. In a pioneering study of 56 preliterate societies, Horton (1943) found that the greater the insecurity level of the culture, the greater the amount of alcohol consumption—due allowance having been made for the availability and acceptability of alcohol. And in a study of 57 tribal societies, Schaefer (1974) reported that people tended to drink to excess in societies in which the spirits of dead ancestors were believed to be unpredictable, malicious, and capricious. On the other hand, people in societies in which the families were dominated by father-son interaction tended to abstain from excessive drinking.

Rapid social change and social disintegration also seem to foster excessive drinking. For example, the U.S. Public Health Service's Alaska Native Medical Center has reported excessive drinking to be a major problem among Eskimos in many places in rural Alaska (*Time*, April 22, 1974). This problem is attributed primarily to rapid change in traditional values and way of life, in some cases approaching social disintegration. It is perhaps also relevant to note that alcoholism is a major problem in the world's two

Research studies have shown that alcohol dependence tends to run in families. However, the great majority of children who have alcoholic parents do not themselves become alcoholics. Thus the role genetic factors play in the development of alcoholism remains unclear.

superpowers—the United States and The Soviet Union.

The effect of cultural attitudes toward drinking is well illustrated by Muslims and Mormons, whose religious values prohibit the use of alcohol, and by orthodox Jews, who have traditionally limited their use largely to religious rituals. The incidence of alcoholism among these groups is minimal. On the other hand, the incidence of alcoholism is high among Europeans, who comprise less than 15 percent of the world's population yet consume about half the alcohol (Sulkunen, 1976). Interestingly, Europe and six countries that have been influenced by European culture—Argentina, Canada, Chile, Japan, the United States and New Zealand—make up less than 20 percent of the world's population yet consume 80 percent of the alcohol (Barry, 1982). The French appear to have the highest rate of alcoholism in the world, approximating 15 percent of the population. France has both the highest per capita alcohol consumption and the highest death rate from cirrhosis of the liver, a disease related to alcoholism (Noble, 1979). Thus it appears that religious sanctions and social custom can determine whether alcohol is one of the modes of coping commonly used in a given group or society.

But while there are many reasons why people drink—as well as many conditions that can predispose them to do so and reinforce drinking behavior—the combination of factors that result in a person's becoming an alcoholic are still unknown.

Treatment and outcomes

A multidisciplinary approach to treatment of drinking problems appears to be most effective because the problems are often complex, thus requiring flexibility and individualization of treatment procedures. Also, the needs of the alcoholic change as treatment progresses.

Formerly it was considered essential for the treatment of a problem drinker to take place in an institutional setting, which removes the individual from what may well be an aversive life situation and which makes possible more control over his or her behavior. However, an increasing number of problem drinkers are now being treated in community clinics, especially drinkers who do not require hospitalization for withdrawal treatment. Outpatient treatment for alcoholism appears to be as effective as inpatient treatment (Polich, et al., 1981). When hospitalization is required, the length of the hospital stay is often rather short— an average of roughly 28 days. (In some treatment programs, stays are now being limited to 7 to 14 days.) Halfway houses are also being used increasingly to bridge the gap between institutionalization and return to the community and to add to the flexibility of treatment programs.

The objective of a treatment program includes physical rehabilitation, control over the alcohol-abuse behavior, and development of a realization on the part of the individual that he or she can cope with the problems of living and lead a much more rewarding life without alcohol. Although traditional treatment programs usually include the goal of abstinence from alcohol, many current programs are attempting to promote controlled drinking as a treatment goal for some problem drinkers. More will be said of this development later in the chapter.

Biological measures. Included here are a variety of treatment measures ranging from detoxification procedures to use of medication.

In acute intoxication, the initial focus is on detoxification, or elimination of alcoholic substances from the individual's body, on treatment of withdrawal symptoms, and on a medical regimen for physical rehabilitation. These can best be handled in a hospital or clinic, where drugs, such as chlordiazepoxide, have largely revolutionized the treatment of withdrawal symptoms. Such drugs function to overcome motor excitement, nausea, and vomiting, prevent delirium tremens and convulsions, and help alleviate the tension and anxiety associated with withdrawal. There is a growing concern, however, that the use of tranquilizers at this stage does not promote long-term recovery. Accordingly, some detoxification clinics are exploring alternative approaches, including a gradual weaning from the alcohol instead of a sudden cutoff.

Detoxification is optimally followed by psychosocial measures, including family counseling and the use of community resources relating to employment and other aspects of the individual's social readjustment. Maintenance doses of mild tranquilizers are also used at times to reduce anxiety and help the individual sleep. Such use of tranquilizers may be less effective than no treatment at all, however. Usually patients must learn to abstain from tranquilizers as well as from alcohol, since they tend to misuse the one as well as the other. And under the influence of tranquilizers, they may even return to the use of alcohol.

Disulfiram (Antabuse), a drug that creates extremely uncomfortable effects when followed by alcohol, may be administered to prevent an immediate return to drinking. However, such deterrent therapy is seldom advocated as the sole approach, since pharmacological methods alone have not proven effective in treating alcoholism. For example, an alcoholic may simply discontinue the use of Antabuse when he or she is released from the hospital or clinic and begin to drink again. In fact, the primary value of drugs of this type appears to lie in their interruption of the alcoholic cycle for a period of time, during which therapy may be undertaken.

Psychosocial measures.   Although individual psychotherapy is sometimes effective, the focus of psychosocial measures in the treatment of alcoholism more often involves group therapy, environmental intervention, behavior therapy, and the approach of Alcoholics Anonymous.

   1. *Group therapy.* In the rugged give-and-take of group therapy, alcoholics are sometimes forced to face their problem and recognize its possible disastrous consequences, but also to begin to see new possibilities for coping with it. Often, but by no means always, this double recognition paves the way for learning more effective methods of coping and other positive steps toward dealing with their drinking problem.

   In some instances the spouses of alcoholics and even their children may be invited to join in group therapy meetings. In other situations, family treatment is itself the central focus of therapeutic effort. In the latter case, the alcoholic individual is seen as a member of a disturbed family in which all the members have a reponsibility for cooperating in treatment. Since family members are frequently the persons most victimized by the alcoholic's addiction, they often tend to be judgmental and punitive, and the alcoholic, who has already passed harsh judgment on himself or herself, tolerates this further source of devaluation very poorly. In other instances, members of a family may unwittingly encourage an alcoholic to remain addicted, as, for example, when a wife with a need to dominate her husband finds that a continually drunken and remorseful spouse best meets her need.

   2. *Environmental intervention.* As with other serious maladaptive behaviors, the total treatment program in alcoholism usually requires measures to alleviate the patient's aversive life situation. As a result of their drinking, alcoholics often become estranged from family and friends, and their jobs are lost or jeopardized. Typically the reaction of those around them is not as understanding or supportive as it would have been if they had a physical illness of comparable magnitude. Simply helping them learn more effective coping techniques may not be enough if the social environment remains hostile and theatening. For alcoholics who have been hospitalized, halfway houses—designed to assist them in their return to family and community—are often an important adjunct to the total treatment program.

   Relapses and continued deterioration are generally associated with a lack of close relationships with family or friends, or with living in a high-risk environment. In a study of black male alcoholics, for example, King et al. (1969) have pointed to the ghetto cycle of broken homes, delinquency, underemployment, alcoholism, and, once again, broken homes. In general, it would appear unlikely that an alcoholic will remain abstinent after treatment unless the negative psychosocial factors that operated in the past are dealt with.

   As a consequence, the concept of a "community reinforcement approach" has been developed. This approach focuses on helping problem drinkers achieve more satisfactory adjustments in key areas of their lives, such as marriage, work, and social relations. Unfortunately, it is not always possible to make these needed changes. But this approach seems to offer a promising conceptual basis for the direction of future treatment programs.

   3. *Behavior therapy.* One of the most rapidly developing forms of treatment for alcohol abuse disorders is behavior therapy, of which several types exist. One is aversive conditioning, involving a wide range of noxious stimuli. The Romans used this technique by placing a live eel in a cup of wine; forced to drink this unsavory cocktail, the alcoholic presumably would feel disgusted and from then on be repelled by wine.

   Today a variety of pharmacological and other deterrent measures can be employed after detoxification. One approach involves the intramuscular injection of emetine hydrochloride, an emetic. Before experiencing the nausea that results from the injection, the patient is given alcohol, so that the sight, smell, and taste of the beverage become associated with severe retching and vomiting. With repetition, this classic conditioning procedure acts as a strong deterrent to further drinking—probably in part because it adds an immediate and unpleasant physiological consequence to the more general socially aversive consequences of excessive drinking.

   Among other aversive methods has been the use of mild electrical stimulation, which presumably enables the therapist to maintain more exact control of the aversive stimulus, reduces possible negative side effects and medical complications, and can even be administered by means of a portable apparatus that can be used by the patient for self-reinforcement. Using a procedure which paired electrical stimulation with stimuli associated with drinking, Claeson and Malm (1973) reported successful results—no relapses after twelve months—in 24 percent of a patient group consisting mostly of advanced-stage alcoholics.

Another approach, called *covert sensitization*, involves extinguishing the drinking behavior by associating it with noxious mental images rather than chemical or electrical stimuli (Cautela, 1967). Positive results have been reported, with reduction of drinking for a time. However, the long-term effects of covert sensitization generally have not been impressive. To expect such stimuli as images (which are under the control of the individual) to change a deeply ingrained life pattern is perhaps unrealistic. Covert sensitization procedures might be effectively used as an early step, with other treatment procedures then employed while the person remains abstinent. The most important effect of any type of aversion therapy with alcoholics seems to be this temporary extinction of drinking behavior, making it possible for other psychosocial methods to be used effectively (Davidson, 1974).

Other behavioral techniques have also received a great deal of attention in recent years, partly because they are based on the hypothesis that some problem drinkers need not give up drinking altogether but can learn to drink moderately (Gottheil, et al., 1982; Miller, 1978; Nathan, 1977; Sobell & Sobell, 1978). In an early study, Sobell and Sobell (1973) described the range of procedures used in what they term "individualized behavior therapy" for alcoholics. This treatment included both individual and group procedures but attempted to tailor the treatment to meet the needs of each particular patient.

"Procedures included subjects being videotaped while intoxicated under experimental conditions, providing subjects when sober with videotape self-confrontation of their own drunken behaviors, shaping of appropriate controlled drinking or nondrinking behaviors respective to treatment goal, the availability of alcoholic beverages throughout treatment, and behavior change training sessions. 'Behavior change training sessions' is a summary phrase to describe sessions which concentrated upon determining setting events for each subject's drinking, training the subject to generate a series of possible alternative responses to those situations, to evaluate each of the delineated alternatives for potential short- and long-term consequences, and then to exercise the response which could be expected to incur the fewest self-destructive long-term consequences. Behavior change training sessions consisted of discussion, role playing, assertiveness training, role reversal or other appropriate behavioral techniques, respective to the topics under consideration during a given session." (p. 601).

Pendery, Maltzman, and West (1982) followed up on the subjects of the original Sobell study who reportedly had attained the ability to drink socially without losing control. They found that only 1 out of 20 subjects was still successful in controlling drinking. Nearly all of the subjects previously reported to be successful had had to be rehospitalized within a year of treatment. These findings stirred some controversy over the research findings reported by the Sobells, but review committees have since cleared the Sobells of any possible falsification of their data (Dickens et al., 1982; Jensen, 1983). Probably no longitudinal study is free of methodological shortcomings, especially when working with people who suffer from alcohol addiction. Clearly, additional research will be needed to determine the success or failure of controlled drinking as a treatment approach.

Other investigators (Lovibond & Caddy, 1970) have conducted blood alcohol discrimination training sessions, which are aimed at getting the alcoholic to control drinking by becoming aware of intoxicating levels of alcohol in the blood. Miller and Muñoz (1976) and Miller (1978) used *behavioral self-control training* to teach alcoholics to monitor and reduce their alcohol intake. Patients kept records of their drinking behavior and the therapy sessions focused upon determining blood alcohol concentration based upon their intake. Strategies for increasing future intake control were discussed along with identifying alternatives to alcohol consumption.

Self-control training techniques, in which the goal of therapy is to get the alcoholic to reduce alcohol intake without necessarily abstaining altogether, has a great deal of appeal for drinkers. It is difficult, of course, for individuals who are extremely dependent upon the effects of alcohol to abstain totally from drinking. Thus, many alcoholics fail to complete traditional treatment programs. The idea that they might be able to

These paintings were done by W_____, a 40-year-old male with a history of alcoholism, repeated loss of employment, and hospitalization for treatment. His interest in painting, which gradually became the key aspect of his treatment program at an alcoholism treatment center, also led to a new way of life following his discharge. In the first painting (top), W_____ depicted alcoholism as a magnet-like vise that drew and crushed his consciousness. He symbolized his feelings in sober periods between drinking sprees as the chained tree, and the nebulous higher power to which he looked for help as a descending dove. The egg and the eye, a motif W_____ used in earlier work to depict his unrealistic view of alcohol, are merged into a straining muscular arm reaching back to the more placid

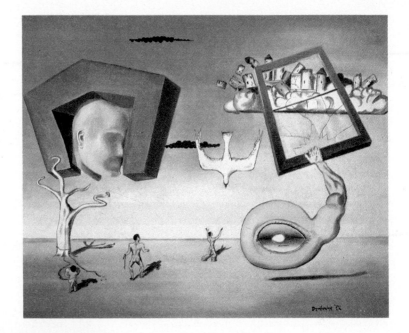

past and unattainable dream castles, that is, futile quests with which W_____ associated his past abuses of alcohol. In the second painting, the overriding concept is of constructive action. Three portals are depicted, (left) one leading to a world "blown to hell"; another (right) with two entrances, one leading downward to an abyss, the other to barrenness; and finally a third portal (middle) in the shape of a cross; symbolic of hope, that leads upward to a pleasant landscape, representing goal or purpose.

learn to control their alcohol intake and at the same time enjoy the continued use of alcohol might serve as a motivating element.

Several approaches to learning controlled drinking have been attempted (Lloyd & Salzberg, 1975), and some recent work has suggested that some alcoholics can learn to control their alcohol intake (Miller, 1978; Miller & Caddy, 1977). Whether the alcoholic who has learned to recognize intoxicating levels of alcohol and to limit intake to lower levels will maintain these skills over long periods of time has not been sufficiently demonstrated.

Most workers in the field still assume that total abstinence should be the goal for all problem drinkers. Some groups, such as Alcoholics

Anonymous, are rather adamant in their opposition to programs aimed at controlled drinking for alcohol-dependent individuals. This controversy is not likely to be resolved in the near future since the controlled drinking research has not produced unequivocal results, nor has it been persuasive enough to win a large number of followers.

4. *Alcoholics Anonymous.* A practical approach to the problem of alcoholism which has reportedly met with considerable success is that of Alcoholics Anonymous (AA). This organization was started in 1935 by two individuals, Dr. Bob and Bill W. in Akron, Ohio. Bill W. recovered from alcoholism through a "fundamental spiritual change," and immediately sought out Dr. Bob, who, with Bill's assistance, achieved recovery. Both in turn began to help other alcoholics. Since that time AA has grown to over 10,000 groups with over a million members. In addition, AA groups have been established in many other countries of the world.

Alcoholics Anonymous operates primarily as a nonprofessional counseling program in which both person-to-person and group relationships are emphasized. AA accepts both teenagers and adults with drinking problems, has no dues or fees, does not keep records or case histories, does not participate in political causes, and is not affiliated with any religious sect, although spiritual development is a key aspect of its treatment approach. To ensure the anonymity of the alcoholic, only first names are used. Meetings are devoted partly to social activities, but consist mainly of discussions of the participants' problems with alcohol, often with testimonials from those who have recovered from alcoholism. Here, recovered members usually contrast their lives before they broke their alcohol dependence with the lives they now live without alcohol.[2]

An important aspect of AA's rehabilitation program is that it lifts the burden of personal responsibility by helping alcoholics accept that alcoholism, like many other problems, is bigger than they are. Henceforth, they can see themselves not as weak-willed or lacking in moral strength, but rather simply as having an afflic-

tion—they cannot drink—just as other people may not be able to tolerate certain types of medication. By mutual help and reassurance through participation in a group composed of others who have shared similar experiences, many an alcoholic acquires insight into his or her problems, a new sense of purpose, greater ego strength, and more effective coping techniques. And, of course, continued participation in the group helps prevent the crisis of a relapse.

Affiliated movements, such as Al-Anon Family Groups and Ala-teen, are designed to bring family members together to share common experiences and problems, to gain understanding of the nature of alcoholism, and to learn techniques for helping the alcoholic individual deal with the problem of alcoholism.

The generally acknowledged success of Alcoholics Anonymous is based primarily upon anecdotal information rather than objective study of treatment outcomes. One recent study, Brandsma et al. (1980), however, included an AA treatment in their extensive comparative study of treatments of alcoholics. The success of this treatment method with severe alcoholics was quite limited. One important finding was that the AA method had very high dropout rates compared to other therapies. Apparently many alcoholics are unable to accept the "quasi-religious" quality of the sessions and the group testimonial format that is so much a part of the AA program. The individuals who were assigned to the AA group subsequently encountered more life difficulties and drank more than the other treatment groups.

Results of treatment.   Statistics on the long-range outcomes of treatment for alcoholism vary considerably, depending on the population studied and on the treatment facilities and procedures employed. They range from low rates of success for hardcore alcoholics to recoveries of 70 to 90 percent where modern treatment and aftercare procedures are used.

In their extensive four-year follow-up of a large group of treated alcoholics, Polich et al. (1981) found that the course of alcoholism after treatment was variable:

"There is no single pattern, and no definite path, characterizing the 4-year history of alcoholics in this

---

[2]The term *alcoholic* is used by AA and its affiliates to refer either to individuals who currently are drinking excessively or to persons who have recovered from such a problem but must continue to abstain from alcohol consumption in the future.

study. Instead, we find remission, frequent relapse, and diverse forms of behavior among alcoholics. Our conclusions about the course of alcoholism depend upon recognizing these multidimensional and highly diverse features of alcoholic behavior." (p 201)

In some respects the findings of this study were not encouraging and seemed to point to the treatment intransigence of alcoholics. Only 7 percent of the total sample (922 males) abstained from alcohol use throughout the four-year period, and 54 percent continued to show alcohol-related problems. (Thirty-six percent of the sample demonstrated alcohol-dependency symptoms, and another 18 percent showed adverse consequences—e.g., arrests—from drinking.)

On the positive side, however, the Polich et al. study can be viewed as demonstrating a clear beneficial effect of treatment for some individuals. Although 54 percent showed drinking problems at follow-up, over 90 percent of the subjects had had serious drinking problems at the beginning of treatment—a significant reduction. Interestingly, although only 7 percent of the alcoholics had been able to abstain from drinking for the full four-year period, others had abstained for shorter periods. For example, 21 percent had abstained for one year or more; an additional 7 percent had abstained for six months. An impressive finding, and one that will fuel the controlled-drinking versus total-abstinence controversy, was that 18 percent of the alcoholics had been able to drink without problems during the six-month period before follow-up.

The outcome of treatment is most likely to be favorable when the drinking problem is discovered early, when the individual realizes that he or she needs help, when adequate treatment facilities are available, and when alcohol-use reduction is an acceptable treatment goal (as opposed to strict abstinence). However, Fontana and Dowds (1975) reported a "honeymoon effect" following treatment of severe alcohol abuse. They found a frequent pattern of decreased alcohol consumption with a return to initial drinking levels at a six-month follow-up.

Over the past few years, great progress has been made in the treatment of alcoholism by the introduction of employee programs in both government and industry. Such programs have proven highly effective in detecting drinking problems early, in referring drinkers for treatment, and in ensuring the effectiveness of aftercare procedures. When it is realized that an estimated 5 percent of the nation's work force are alcoholics and an additional 5 percent are considered alcohol abusers, it is apparent that such programs can make a major impact in coping with the alcohol problem in our society (Alander & Campbell, 1975). (See **HIGHLIGHT**, p. 419.) Unfortunately, many alcoholics refuse to admit they have an alcohol problem or to seek assistance before they "hit bottom"—which, in many cases, is the grave.

In their study of various treatments of chronic, severe alcohol problems, Brandsma et al. (1980) found that direct treatment—whether professional or paraprofessional, insight-oriented or rational behavior therapy—was more effective than an untreated control condition. The investigators randomly assigned chronic alcoholics to treatment groups—insight-oriented, rational behavior therapy, Alcoholics Anonymous, self-help (paraprofessional) therapy, or a nontreatment control group. One important finding was that professional treatment was more effective than nonprofessional treatment, although either of the two major therapeutic orientations (insight-oriented versus rational-behavior therapy) was equally effective. As noted above, Alcoholics Anonymous was the least effective, partly due to a high dropout rate.

There is clearly no miracle cure for alcoholism. Nevertheless, it would appear that for the great majority of alcoholics there is a treatment program that can be tailored to their needs and provide a good chance for recovery.

Relapse prevention. One of the greatest problems in the treatment of addictive disorders, such as alcoholism or any of the behaviors described in this chapter, is the problem of maintaining abstinence or self-control once the behavioral excesses have been checked. Most alcohol treatment programs show high success rates in "curing" the addictive problems, but many programs show lessening rates of abstinence or controlled drinking at various periods of follow-up. The problems with many treatment programs is that they do not pay sufficient attention to the important element of maintaining the behavior and preventing relapse into previous maladaptive patterns.

In recent years, some researchers have been focusing on the problem of relapse prevention by examining the thought processes that lead the abstinent individual back into the self-indulgent patterns that got him or her in trouble in the first place. The cognitive-behavioral approach to relapse prevention by Marlatt and his colleagues (Cummings, Gordon, & Marlatt, 1980; Marlatt & Gordon, 1980) shows great promise in this area.

The cognitive-behavioral view holds that the definition of relapse behavior should be broadened beyond the previously held notion that people resume drinking because of a "craving" based on vaguely understood physiological needs. Instead, the behaviors underlying relapse are "indulgent behaviors" and are based on the individual's learning history. When an individual is abstinent or has the addiction under control, he or she gains a sense of *personal control* over the indulgent behavior. The longer the person is able to maintain this control, the greater the sense of achievement—the *self-efficacy* or confidence—and the greater the chance that he or she will be able to cope with the addiction and maintain control.

However, according to Marlatt, the individual may violate this rule of abstinence through a gradual, perhaps unconscious, process rather than through the sudden "falling off the wagon" that constitutes the traditional view of craving and relapse. In the cognitive-behavioral view, the individual may inadvertently make a series of "mini-decisions," even while maintaining abstinence, that begin a chain of behaviors making relapse inevitable. For example, the abstinent alcoholic who buys a quart of bourbon just in case his friends drop by or the dieting obese woman who changes her route to work to include a pass by the bakery are both unconsciously preparing the way for relapse. Marlatt refers to these minidecisions which place the individual at risk as "apparently irrelevant decisions." These decisions are easy for the individual to make, since they do not appear to be related to the abstinent behavior; however, they lead the individual into a situation in which some form of relapse is likely to occur.

Another type of relapse behavior involves the "abstinence violation effect," in which even minor transgressions are seen to have drastic significance by the abstainers. The effect works this way. The abstinent individual may hold that he or she should not, under any circumstance, transgress or give in to the old habit. Abstinence-oriented treatment programs are particularly guided by this prohibitive rule. What happens, then, when an abstinent man becomes somewhat self-indulgent and takes a drink offered by an old friend? He may lose some of the sense of self-efficacy, the confidence needed to control his drinking. Since the vow of abstinence has been violated, he may feel guilty about giving in to the temptation and rationalize that he "has blown it and become a drunk again, so why not go all the way?"

Marlatt and his colleagues recommend a cognitive-behavioral treatment program for preventing relapse. Clients are taught to recognize the apparently irrelevant decisions that serve as "early warning signals" of the possibility of relapse. High-risk situations are targeted, and the individuals learn to assess their own vulnerability to relapse. Clients are also trained to be prepared for the abstinence violation effect, and, if they do relapse, not to become so discouraged that they lose their confidence. Some cognitive-behavioral therapists have actually employed a "planned relapse" phase in the treatment to supervise the individual's cognitive behavior and to help the client through this important problem area.

Drug abuse and dependence

Aside from alcohol, the psychoactive drugs most commonly associated with abuse and dependence in our society appear to be (a) narcotics, such as opium and its derivatives; (b) sedatives, such as barbiturates; (c) stimulants, such as cocaine and amphetamines; (d) antianxiety drugs, such as meprobamates; and (e) hallucinogens, such as LSD and PCP (see **HIGHLIGHT** on pages

HIGHLIGHT

Alcoholism treatment programs in business and industry

Many business and industrial organizations have recognized the extent of alcohol-abuse problems among their own employees and have developed programs to help them recover from alcoholism and lead more productive lives. One company, the Control Data Corporation of Minneapolis, has been providing an alcoholism rehabilitation program for its employees for more than ten years. This program has been so successful that it has served as the basis for a more comprehensive employee assistance program (which we shall examine in Chapter 18) devoted to an even broader scope of problems. Since its inception, the alcohol rehabilitation program has provided support and assistance for hundreds of employees during their recovery from alcoholism and their return to work. About 13 percent of the personal problems dealt with in the employee assistance program are alcohol-related difficulties.

In establishing the alcoholism rehabilitation program, Control Data management attempted to ensure "that an individual suffering from alcoholism receives the same type of assurances of job security and benefits as individuals suffering from other types of medical problems" (Shields, Emerson, & Mount, 1979, p. 1). The Control Data program offers a number of services related to alcohol abuse, including substance-abuse evaluation, counseling services, referral to inpatient treatment, follow-up, and postrecovery job placement.

The Personnel Research Department and the Employee Advisory Resource Department recently conducted a study to determine if the alcoholism rehabilitation program had been successfully performing the services it was designed to provide. The staff surveyed 102 alcoholics who had returned to work after treatment and a control group of 106 individuals who had been out on some other type of medical leave. The staff attempted to determine (a) whether corporate policies relating to the treatment of alcoholics were being carried out as intended, and (b) whether the training programs aimed at sensitizing managers to deal with alcohol-related problems had been effective. The alcoholic subjects were mostly male (90 percent); had attained a relatively higher level of education; tended to be professionals (engineers, technicians, and executives); and had been with the company somewhat longer than the individuals comprising the medical patient control group (Shields et al., 1979).

The results of the study indicated that leaves of absence for the treatment of alcoholism had not negatively influenced the individuals' working relationships. No overall difference between alcoholics and medical patients appeared in terms of job satisfaction upon their return to work. In fact, the alcoholics reported a greater degree of happiness than the medical patients. Both groups reported satisfaction with the way they were treated and both indicated that they felt secure in their jobs. The most negative finding was that alcoholics reported less confidence in their chances for promotion than the medical patients.

What kinds of corporations would benefit from this type of alcohol rehabilitation program? Especially for companies with a stable work force and a low turnover rate, this type of program would be cost effective. Rehabilitated employees have several years of productive service in which to "repay" the cost of the treatment.

422–23). Caffeine and nicotine are also drugs of dependence, and disorders associated with tobacco withdrawal and caffeine intoxication are included for the first time in DSM-III classification, but we shall not deal with them in our present discussion.

Drug abuse and dependence may occur at any age but seem to be most common during adolescence and young adulthood. Clinical pictures vary markedly, depending on the type, amount, and duration of drug usage, the physiological and psychological makeup of the individual, and, in some instances, the social setting in which the drug experience occurs. Thus it appears most useful to deal separately with some of the drugs that are more commonly associated with abuse and dependence in contemporary society.[3]

Opium and its derivatives (narcotics)

People have used opium and its derivatives for over 5000 years. Galen (A.D. 130–201) considered theriaca, whose principal ingredient was opium, to be a veritable panacea:

"It resists poison and venomous bites, cures inveterate headache, vertigo, deafness, epilepsy, apoplexy, dimness of sight, loss of voice, asthma, coughs of all kinds, spitting of blood, tightness of breath, colic, the iliac poisons, jaundice, hardness of the spleen, stone, urinary complaints, fevers, dropsies, leprosies, the trouble to which women are subject, melancholy and all pestilences."

Even today, opium derivatives are still used for some of the conditions Galen mentioned.

Opium is a mixture of about eighteen nitrogen-containing agents known as *alkaloids*. In 1805 it was found that the alkaloid present in the largest amount (10 to 15 percent) was a bitter-tasting powder that proved to be a powerful sedative and pain reliever; it was thus named *morphine* (after Morpheus, god of sleep in Greek mythology). After introduction of the hypodermic needle in America about 1856, morphine was widely administered to soldiers during the Civil War, not only to those wounded in battle but also to those suffering from dysentery. As a consequence, large numbers of Civil War veterans returned to civilian life addicted to the drug, a condition euphemistically referred to as "soldier's illness."

Scientists concerned with the addictive properties of morphine hypothesized that one part of the morphine molecule might be responsible for its analgesic properties[4] and another for its addictiveness. Thus, at about the turn of the century it was discovered that if morphine were treated by an inexpensive and readily available chemical called *acetic anhydride*, it could be converted into another powerful analgesic called *heroin*. Heroin was hailed with enthusiasm by its discoverer, Heinrich Dreser (Boehm, 1968). Leading scientists of his time agreed with Dreser on the merits of heroin, and the drug came to be widely prescribed in place of morphine for pain relief and related medicinal purposes. However, heroin turned out to be a cruel disappointment, for it proved to be an even more dangerous drug than morphine, acting more rapidly and more intensely and being equally if not more addictive. Eventually heroin was removed from use in medical practice.

As it became apparent that opium and its derivatives—including codeine, which is used in some cough syrups—were perilously addictive, the United States Congress enacted the Harrison Act in 1914. Under this and later acts, the unauthorized sale and dispensation of certain drugs became a federal offense; physicians and pharmacists were held accountable for each dose they dispensed. Thus, overnight, the role of a narcotic user changed from that of addict—which was considered a vice, but tolerated—to that of criminal. Unable to obtain drugs through legal sources, many turned to illegal ones, and eventually to other criminal acts as a means of maintaining their suddenly expensive drug supply. The number of addicts declined, however, and stayed near 40,000 for several decades.

During the 1960s there was a rapid increase in the use of heroin. There were an estimated 150,000 or more addicts in New York City alone, and some 300,000 in the country as a whole—and public attention was focused on the "heroin epidemic" (Bazell, 1973; Greene & Dupont, 1974). Recent surveys show that heroin use continues at a high rate. Johnston, Bachman, and O'Malley (1979) reported that 1.1 percent of the high-school seniors they surveyed had tried heroin. Fishburne, Abelson, and Cisin (1980), using results from a nationwide survey, reported that .5 percent of youths between 12 and 17, 3.5 percent of young adults between 18 and 25, and 1.0 percent of adults reported using heroin at least once. If we apply these percentages to current population figures, then the number of individuals who have tried heroin is astounding: 117,095 youths; 1,119,475 young adults; and 1,239,540 adults.

---

[3]It may be noted that the most common action of all drugs—even those which are medically prescribed—is their alteration of cell metabolism. Typically, this change in cellular action is a temporary one designed to help combat the patient's problem. Nevertheless, the changes that drugs bring about in "target cells" are in a direction *away from normal functioning*. Thus, medication does not result in cells performing "better than ever." Of course, some drugs—such as hormones—do replace or supplement substances which are normally present in the body, and in this sense, they may improve the normal functioning of various organs and cells; but in general, drugs tend to block some important functions of cells. Hence, the general rule of thumb is the fewer drugs the better.

[4]An *analgesic* is a drug that alleviates pain without inducing unconsciousness.

The number of heroin addicts in the United States has been estimated at anywhere from 380,000 (Dogoloff, 1980) and 400,000 (Seidler, 1980) to 450,000 (Strategy Council on Drug Abuse, 1979). Yet according to a report from the National Institute on Drug Abuse (NIDA, 1981), heroin-related hospital admissions have decreased in recent years from 47 percent of total drug-related admissions to 37 percent.

Effects of morphine and heroin. Morphine and heroin are commonly introduced into the body by smoking, "snorting" (inhaling the bitter powder), eating, "skin popping," or "mainlining," the last two being methods of introducing the drug via hypodermic injection. Skin popping refers to injecting the liquefied drug just beneath the skin, and mainlining to injecting the drug directly into the bloodstream. In the United States, the young addict usually moves from snorting to mainlining.

Among the immediate effects of heroin is a euphoric spasm (the *rush*) lasting 60 seconds or so, which many addicts compare to a sexual orgasm. This is followed by a "high," during which the addict typically is in a lethargic, withdrawn state in which bodily needs, including needs for food and sex, are markedly diminished; pleasant feelings of relaxation, euphoria, and reverie tend to dominate. These effects last from 4 to 6 hours and are followed—in addicts—by a negative phase which produces a desire for more of the drug.

The use of opium derivatives over a period of time usually results in a physiological craving for the drug. The time required to establish the drug habit varies, but it has been estimated that continual usage over a period of 30 days is sufficient. Users will then find that they have become physiologically dependent upon the drug in the sense that they will feel physically ill when they do not take it. In addition, users of opium derivatives gradually build up a tolerance to the drug so that even larger amounts are needed to achieve the desired effects (see **HIGH-LIGHT** on page 425).

When persons addicted to opiates do not get a dose of the drug within approximately 8 hours, they start to experience *withdrawal symptoms.* The character and severity of the reaction depend on many factors, including the amount of the narcotic habitually used, the intervals between doses, the duration of the addiction, and especially the addict's health and personality.

Contrary to popular opinion, withdrawal from heroin is not always dangerous or even very painful. Many addicted persons withdraw without assistance. However, in some instances withdrawal is both agonizing and perilous.

Initial symptoms usually include a running nose, tearing eyes, perspiration, restlessness, increased respiration rate, and an intensified desire for the drug. As time passes, the symptoms become more severe, usually reaching a peak in about 40 hours. Typically there is chilliness alternating with vasomotor disturbances of flushing and excessive sweating, vomiting, diarrhea, abdominal cramps, pains in the back and extremities, severe headache, marked tremors, and varying degrees of insomnia. Beset by these discomforts, the individual refuses food and water, and this, coupled with the vomiting, sweating, and diarrhea, results in dehydration and weight losses of as much as 5 to 15 pounds in a day. Occasionally there may be delirium, hallucinations, and manic activity. Cardiovascular collapse may also occur, and may result in death. If morphine is administered, the subjective distress experienced by the addict ends, and physiological equanimity is restored in about 5 to 30 minutes.

If the addict stops taking the drug, the withdrawal symptoms will usually be on the decline by the third or fourth day, and by the seventh or eighth day will have disappeared. As the symptoms subside, the individual resumes normal eating and drinking, and rapidly regains lost weight. An additional hazard now exists in that after withdrawal symptoms have ceased, the individual's former tolerance for the drug also will have disappeared, and death may result from taking the former large dosage.

Recently, several investigators have reported a stable pattern of controlled use of heroin (Harding et al., 1980; Zinberg, 1980). These researchers have found that some users tend to both limit and control their heroin use.

In some cases individuals may have enough self-control to use opiates without allowing them to interfere with their work and ruin their lives. But the danger in the use of such drugs— especially heroin—is very great. Kirsh (1974) noted that occasional, not hardcore, narcotics

HIGHLIGHT
Psychoactive drugs commonly involved in drug abuse

Classification	Drugs	Usage
Sedatives	Alcohol (ethanol)	Reduce tension Facilitate social interaction "Blot out"
	Barbiturates 　Nembutal (pentobarbital) 　Seconal (secobarbital) 　Veronal (barbital) 　Tuinal (secobarbital) 　　and amobarbital)	Reduce tension Induce relaxation and sleep
Stimulants	Amphetamines 　Benzedrine (amphetamine) 　Dexedrine (dextroamphetamine) 　Methedrine (methamphetamine) Cocaine (coca)	Increase feelings of alertness and confidence Decrease feelings of fatigue Stay awake for long periods Decrease feelings of fatigue Increase endurance Stimulate sex drive
Narcotics	Opium and its derivatives 　Opium 　Morphine 　Codeine 　Heroin Methadone (synthetic narcotic)	Alleviate physical pain Induce relaxation and pleasant reverie Alleviate anxiety and tension Treatment of heroin dependence
Psychedelics and hallucinogens	Cannabis 　Marijuana 　Hashish Mescaline (peyote) Psilocybin 　(psychotogenic mushrooms) LSD (lysergic acid diethylamide-25) PCP (phencyclidine)	Induce changes in mood, thought, and 　behavior "Mind expansion" Induce stupor
Antianxiety drugs (minor tranquilizers)	Librium (chlordiazepoxide) Miltown (meprobamate) Valium (diazepam) Others, e.g., 　Compōz (scopolamine)	Alleviate tension and anxiety Induce relaxation and sleep

In reviewing this list, it is important to note that it is by no means complete; for example, it does not include new drugs, such as Ritalin, which are designed to produce multiple effects; it does not include the less commonly used volatile hydrocarbons, such as glue, paint thinner, gasoline, cleaning fluid, and nail-polish remover, which are highly dangerous when sniffed for their psychoactive effects; and it does not include the antipsychotic and antidepressant

Medical usage	Tolerance	Physiological dependence	Psychological dependence
No	Yes (reverse tolerance later)	Yes	Yes
Yes	Yes	Yes	Yes
Yes	Yes	No	Yes
No	No (minimal)	No	Yes
Yes, except heroin	Yes	Yes	Yes
Yes	Yes	Yes	Yes
No, except in research	No—possible reverse tolerance (marijuana)	No	Yes
No	No	No	Yes
Yes	Yes	Yes	Yes

drugs, which are abused, but relatively rarely. We shall deal with these as well as the antianxiety drugs in our discussion of therapy with drugs in Chapter 16. It also should be emphasized that abuses of various kinds can occur with both prescriptive and nonprescriptive drugs, and with both legal and illegal drugs. In all cases, drugs should be used with great care.

users were overrepresented to a great degree among heroin overdose cases treated in the emergency room of a New York hospital. In general, tolerance builds up so rapidly that larger and more expensive amounts of the drug are soon required, and withdrawal treatments are likely to do little to end the problem. Most addicted individuals—even after withdrawal—find it extremely difficult to break their dependence. Biochemical alterations appear to be at least partly reponsible for the individual's continued craving for the narcotic drug even after completion of the withdrawal treatment.

Typically the life of a narcotic addict becomes increasingly centered around obtaining and using drugs, so the addiction usually leads to socially maladaptive behavior as the individual is eventually forced to lie, steal, and associate with undesirable companions in order to maintain a supply of the drug. Contrary to the common picture of a "dope fiend," however, most narcotic addicts are not hardened criminals. Many addicts resort to petty theft to support their habit but very few commit crimes of violence. Some female addicts turn to prostitution as a means of financing their addiction.

It should be noted that narcotic drugs introduced during pregnancy can have seriously damaging effects on the development of infants after birth. Householder et al. (1982) reviewed the effects of narcotics addiction in mothers and the subsequent problems of their offspring. They concluded that in later childhood these infants show increasingly frequent disturbances of activity levels, attention span, sleep patterns, and socialization.

Along with the lowering of ethical and moral restraints, addiction has adverse physical effects on the well-being of the individual. Lack of an adequate diet may lead to ill health and increased susceptibility to a variety of physical ailments. The use of unsterile equipment may also lead to a variety of ailments, including liver damage from hepatitis. In addition, the use of such a potent drug as heroin without medical supervision and government controls to assure its strength and purity can result in fatal overdosage. Injection of too much heroin can cause coma and death. Between May 1979 and April 1980 there were more than 894 deaths associated with heroin usage in the United States (Project DAWN, 1980).

Usually, however, addiction to opiates leads

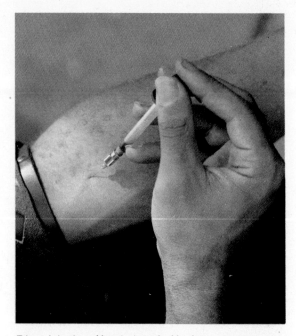

Direct injection of heroin into the bloodstream presents risks of infection, overdose, and destruction of the blood vessels.

to a gradual deterioration of well-being. The ill health and general personality deterioration often found in opium addiction do not result directly from the pharmacological effects of the drug, but are generally the product of the sacrifice of money, proper diet, social position, and self-respect, as the addict becomes more desperate to procure the required daily dosage. For example, Westermeyer (1982), in a book detailing his experiences treating opium addicts in Southeast Asia in the 1960s, concludes that long-term opium use has very clear dangers in terms of one's health and the social and economic deprivation it can bring to the entire family of the user. On the other hand, narcotic addicts with financial means to maintain both a balanced diet and an adequate supply of the drug without resorting to criminal behavior may maintain their drug dependence over many years without the usual symptoms of physical or mental disorder.

Causal factors in opiate abuse and dependence. There is no single causal pattern that fits all addiction to narcotic drugs. A recent study by Fulmer and Lapidus (1980) concluded that the three most frequently cited reasons for beginning to use heroin were pleasure, curios-

HIGHLIGHT
Tolerance in drug usage

Tolerance to a drug develops in an individual when the same dosage produces decreased effects after repeated use. Drugs that produce tolerance include alcohol, heroin, and barbiturates. As an individual's tolerance to a drug increases, he or she tends to increase the dose taken. The degree of tolerance and the rate at which it is acquired depend on the specific drug, the person using it, and the frequency and magnitude of its use.

The mechanisms by which physiological tolerance is acquired are not fully understood. There is some evidence that the central nervous system develops some degree of tolerance for various drugs; but, in addition, learning may play an important role in changing an individual's attitude toward a drug and response to it after repeated use. Thus with some drugs, such as marijuana, the individual may learn to control some effects and maintain relatively normal functioning.

Two aspects of drug tolerance that merit brief mention are "cross-tolerance" and "reverse tolerance." "Cross-tolerance" may occur when the individual who develops tolerance to one drug also shows tolerance to drugs whose effects are similar. A heavy drinker, for example, may show tolerance not only to alcohol but also to barbiturates, tranquilizers, and anesthetics. "Reverse tolerance" may occur in the use of some drugs, such as the hallucinogens; here, with experience, the desired effects may be achieved through the use of smaller doses. Both physiological and psychological (learning) factors appear to play a significant part in this process.

Based on Commission of Inquiry into the Non-Medical Use of Drugs (1970).

---

ity, and peer pressure. Pleasure was the single most widespread reason—given by 81 percent of addicts. Other reasons such as life stress, personal maladjustment, and sociocultural conditions also play a part (Bry, McKeon, & Pandina, 1982).

Recently, Alexander and Hadaway (1982) argued convincingly that opiate addiction could be more sufficiently explained by an "adaptive" orientation than by the traditional view that people become addicted by being "exposed" to opiates. They cited evidence that simply using heroin or other opiates for a period of time is not sufficient. cause for continued, addictive use of the substance—many people have not, even after prolonged use, been compelled to continue usage. Alexander and Hadaway conclude that "opiate users are at risk of addiction only under special circumstances, namely, when faced with severe distress and with no more salubrious way of coping than by habitual use" (p. 367).

Although the following categorization of causal factors is somewhat artificial, it does provide a convenient means of ordering our discussion.[5]

---

[5]The interested reader may find a monograph published by the National Institute on Drug Abuse (Lettieri, Sayers, & Pearson, 1980) particularly informative. These authors discuss the views of 43 researchers on drug abuse.

1. *Neural bases for physiological addiction.* Research teams have isolated and studied receptor sites for narcotic drugs in the brain (Goldstein, et al., 1974; Pert & Snyder, 1973). Such receptor sites are specific nerve cells into which given psychoactive drugs fit like keys into the proper lock. This interaction of drug and brain cell apparently results in the action of the drug, and in the case of narcotic drugs leads to addiction. Preliminary findings indicate that there are two or more receptor sites which produce the effects of these drugs; apparently one site produces pleasurable euphoria and another the painkilling action.

Recently it has been learned that the human body produces its own opium-like substances, called *endorphins,* in the brain and pituitary gland. These substances are produced in response to stimulation and are believed to play a role in the organism's reaction to pain (Akil, et al., 1978, Bolles & Fanselow, 1982). Some investigators suspect that the endorphins may play a role in drug addiction, speculating that chronic underproduction of the endorphins may lead to a craving for narcotic drugs. Hollt et al. (1975) experimented on animals to determine whether drugs like heroin or methadone influence the production of endorphins by causing actual changes in the receptor sites; they found only transient changes and no modification of the underlying receptor mechanisms. Research has not been extensive at this point. However, some indication that endorphins may be a factor in addiction was suggested in a study by Su et al. (1978). These researchers attempted to block methadone withdrawal by administering endorphins and found that endorphins were moderately effective in reducing withdrawal symptoms.

Research on the role of endorphins in drug addiction has generally been inconclusive and disappointing. According to Watson and Akil (1979), before the anatomical and physiological bases of addiction and drug tolerance can be understood, many complex problems of measurement must be resolved.

2. Addiction associated with the relief of pain. Many patients are given narcotic drugs, such as morphine, to relieve pain during illness or following surgery or serious injury. The vast majority of such patients never develop an addiction, and when their medication is discontinued, they do not again resort to the use of morphine. Those narcotic addicts who blame their addiction on the fact they they used drugs during an illness usually show personality deficiencies which predisposed them to the use of drugs— such as immaturity, low frustration tolerance, and the ability to distort and evade reality by way of a flight into drug-induced fantasy.

3. Addiction associated with psychopathology. During the 1960s, studies placed strong emphasis on the high incidence of psychopathic personalities among heroin addicts. In a comparison between a group of 45 young institutionalized male addicts and a control group of nonaddicts, Gilbert and Lombardi (1967) found that distinguishing features were "the addict's psychopathic traits, his depression, tension, insecurity, and feelings of inadequacy, and his difficulty in forming warm and lasting interpersonal relationships" (p. 536). Similarly, in a study of 112 drug abusers admitted to Bellevue Psychiatric Hospital in New York, Hekimian and Gershon (1968) found that heroin users usually showed psychopathic personality characteristics. Meyer and Mirin (1979) found that opiate addicts were highly impulsive and showed an inability to delay gratification.

Recent research supports the finding that narcotics dependence tends to develop in association with psychopathic personality and other psychopathology (Sutker & Archer, in press). As in the case of alcoholism, however, it seems essential to exercise caution in distinguishing between personality traits before and after addiction, for the high incidence of psychopathology among narcotics addicts may in part result from, rather than precede, the long-term effects of addiction.

4. Addiction associated with sociocultural factors. In our society there are so-called narcotics subcultures, in which addicts can obtain drugs and protect themselves against the sanctions of society. Apparently the majority of narcotics addicts do participate in the drug culture. The decision to join this culture has important implications for the future life of addicts, for from that point on they will center their activities around their role of drug user. In short, their addiction becomes their way of life.

With time, most young addicts who join the drug culture become increasingly withdrawn, indifferent to their friends (except those in the drug group), and apathetic about sexual activity. They are likely to abandon scholastic and athletic endeavors, and to show a marked reduction in competitive and achievement strivings. Most of these addicts appear to lack good sex-role identification, and to experience feelings of inadequacy when confronted with the demands of adulthood. While feeling progressively isolated from the broader culture, they experience a bolstering of their feelings of group belongingness by continued association with the addict milieu; at the same time, they come to view drugs both as a means of revolt against constituted authority and conventional values and as a device for alleviating personal anxieties and tensions.

Treatment and outcomes.   Treatment for heroin addiction is initially similar to that for alcoholism, in that it involves building up the addict both physically and psychologically and providing help through the withdrawal period. Addicts often dread the discomfort of withdrawal, but in a hospital setting it is not abrupt and usually involves the administration of a synthetic drug that eases the distress.

After withdrawal has been completed, treatment focuses on helping the former addict make an adequate adjustment to his or her community and abstain from the further use of narcotics.

Traditionally, however, the prognosis has been unfavorable. Despite the use of counseling, group therapy, and other measures, only about 13 percent of persons discharged from government rehabilitation programs in England did not become readdicted (Stephens & Cottrell, 1972). These and comparable findings from studies in the United States led to the hypothesis that withdrawal does not remove the craving for heroin and that a key target in treatment must be the alleviation of this craving.

An approach to dealing with the problem of physiological craving for heroin was pioneered by a research team at the Rockefeller University in New York. Their approach involved the use of the drug methadone in conjunction with a rehabilitation program (counseling, group therapy, and other procedures) directed toward the "total resocialization" of the addict (Dole & Nyswander, 1967; Dole, Nyswander, & Warner, 1968). Methadone hydrochloride is a synthetic narcotic which is related to heroin and is equally addictive physiologically. Its usefulness in treatment lies in the fact that it satisfies the addict's craving for heroin without producing serious psychological impairment.

As a result of impressive preliminary findings, the federal government in 1972 agreed to a licensing program for physicians and clinics utilizing methadone in the treatment of narcotics addicts. But as methadone treatment became more widely employed, it became apparent that methadone alone is not sufficient to rehabilitate narcotics addicts. Although some former addicts do make good adjustments with little ancillary treatment, most require vocational training and other supportive measures if the overall treatment program is to prove effective. It would also appear essential that methadone treatment be monitored very carefully, since there are a limited but rising number of reports of liver damage and other undesirable side effects following the long-term use of methadone (Thornton & Thornton, 1974). In addition, it is important to prevent the illicit use of methadone, since there are serious dangers—including overdosage—when it is not used in a well-organized heroin treatment program (Greene, Brown, & Dupont, 1975).

There is also the ethical problem of weaning the addict from heroin only to addict him or her to another narcotic drug that may be required for life. A response might be that addicts on methadone can function normally and hold jobs—not possible for most heroin addicts. In addition, methadone is available legally, and its quality is controlled by government standards. Nor is it necessary to increase the dosage every time. In fact some patients can eventually be taken off methadone without danger of relapse to heroin addiction. Many heroin addicts can also be treated without undergoing initial hospitalization, and during treatment are able to hold jobs and function in their family and community settings (Newman & Cates, 1977).

Barbiturates (sedatives)

In the 1850s, new chemical compounds known as *bromides* were introduced. They immediately became popular as sedatives and were taken by millions of people. But with use came abuse; and the excessive consumption of bromides resulted in toxic psychoses—involving delusions, hallucinations, and a variety of neurological disturbances—which for a time became a leading cause of admissions to mental hospitals (Jarvik, 1967).

In the 1930s powerful sedatives called *barbiturates* were introduced. While the barbiturates have their legitimate medical uses, they are extremely dangerous drugs commonly associated with both physiological and psychological dependence as well as with lethal overdoses. Literally billions of barbiturate pills, including pills with fixed combinations of barbiturates and amphetamines, are manufactured each year in the United States. Between May 1979 and April 1980, 33 percent of female and 22 percent of male drug-related deaths involved barbiturate usage (Project DAWN, 1980).

Effects of barbiturates. The barbiturates are widely used by physicians to calm patients and/or induce sleep. They act as depressants—somewhat like alcohol—to slow down the action of the central nervous system. Shortly after taking the drug, the individual experiences a feeling of relaxation in which tensions seem to disappear, followed by a physical and intellectual lassitude and a tendency toward drowsiness and sleep—the intensity of such feelings depending on the type and amount of the barbiturate taken. Strong doses produce sleep almost immediately; excessive doses are lethal because they result in paralysis of the respiratory centers of the brain.

Excessive use of barbiturates leads to increased tolerance as well as to physiological and psychological dependence. The barbiturates most often involved in such abuse are the short-acting ones such as Seconal ("red devils") and tuinal ("rainbows"); long-acting barbiturates, such as phenobarbital, are not so subject to abuse because of their failure to produce quick results.

In addition, excessive use of barbiturates leads to a variety of undesirable side effects, including sluggishness, slow speech, impaired comprehension and memory, extreme and sudden mood shifts, motor incoordination, and depression. Problem solving and decision-making require great effort, and the individual usually is aware that his or her thinking is "fuzzy." Prolonged excessive use of this class of drugs leads to brain damage and personality deterioration. And, whereas with opiates tolerance increases the amount needed to cause death, this is not true for the barbiturates, which means that users can easily ingest a fatal overdose, either intentionally or accidentally. Indeed, barbiturates are associated with more suicides than any other drug.

Causal factors in barbiturate abuse and dependence.

Though many young people experiment with barbiturates, or "downers," most do not become dependent. In fact, the individuals who do become dependent on barbiturates tend to be middle-aged and older persons who often rely on them as "sleeping pills" and who do not commonly rely on other classes of drugs except, possibly, alcohol and the minor tranquilizers. Often these persons are referred to as "silent abusers" since they take the drugs in the privacy of their homes and ordinarily do not become public nuisances. Barbiturate dependence seems to occur in the emotionally maladjusted person who seeks relief from feelings of anxiety, tension, inadequacy, and the stresses of life.

An exception to the above picture has occurred in recent years with the introduction of "new, improved" diet pills. Previous diet pills had usually been amphetamines alone, but the new pills are fixed-ratio combinations of amphetamines and barbiturates—the latter being added to reduce the "jitteriness" often caused by the amphetamines. Unfortunately, both of these drugs are highly addictive, either separately or in combination, and since the addition of barbiturates may make the amphetamines more tolerable, "addiction prone" persons may rapidly increase their pill intake, thus increasing the possibility of addiction to both drugs (Kunnes, 1973).

In addition to being used with amphetamines, barbiturates are also commonly used with alcohol. Some teenagers claim they can achieve an intense high—a kind of controlled hypersensitivity—by combining barbiturates, amphetamines, and alcohol. However, one possible effect of combining barbiturates and alcohol is death, since each drug *potentiates* (increases the action of) the other (see **HIGHLIGHT** on page 429).

Treatment and outcomes.

As with many other drugs, it is often essential in treatment to distinguish between barbiturate intoxication, which results from the toxic effects of overdosage, and the symptoms associated with drug withdrawal. We are concerned primarily with the latter. Here the symptoms are more dangerous, severe, and long-lasting than in opiate withdrawal. The patient becomes anxious and apprehensive and manifests coarse tremors of the hands and face; additional symptoms commonly include insomnia, weakness, nausea, vomiting, abdominal cramps, rapid heart rate, elevated blood pressure, and loss of weight. Between the sixteenth hour and the fifth day convulsions may occur. An acute delirious psychosis often develops, which may include symptoms similar to those found in delirium tremens.

For individuals used to taking large dosages, the withdrawal symptoms may last for as long as a month, but usually they tend to abate by the end of the first week. Fortunately, the withdrawal symptoms in barbiturate addiction can be minimized by the administration of increasingly smaller doses of the barbiturate itself, or by another drug producing pharmacologically similar effects. The withdrawal program is still a dangerous one, however, especially if barbiturate addiction is complicated by alcoholism or dependence on other drugs.

Judi A. was a young attractive girl from a middle-class family who apparently was seeking something that eluded her. She died of an overdose of barbiturates. The newspaper account of her death began with a statement from the autopsy report:

"The unembalmed body for examination is that of a well-developed, well-nourished Caucasian female measuring 173 cm. (68 inches), weighing 100–110 pounds, with dark blonde hair, blue eyes, and consistent in appearance with the stated age of . . . .

"Judi A. had lived only 17 years, 5 months and 27 days before her nude body was found on a grimy bed which had been made up on the floor of a run-down apartment in Newport Beach [California].

"The inside of her mouth and her tongue were a bright red. The fingers of both hands were stained with the same color . . . A small pill was found on the bed near the body, another was discovered on the floor.

"Judi's death was classified as an accident because there was no evidence that she intended to take her own life. Actually it was about as accidental as if she'd killed herself while playing Russian roulette.

"Judi didn't intentionally take too many reds. She was familiar with them, had taken them before, knew what to expect. She'd even had an earlier scare from a nonfatal overdose.

"But her mind, clouded by the first few pills, lost count and she ingested a lethal number. She was dying before she swallowed the last pill. . . ." (Hazlett, 1971, p. 1)

A complete investigation was ordered, in which it came to light that Judi took drugs when she was unhappy at home, apparently often feeling unloved and unwanted. Following her parents' divorce, she lived with her grandparents—who seemed to have been unaware of her drug problem and hence had not attempted to help her with it.

Judi escalated the odds against herself by combining barbiturates with alcohol. Her friends said she was not particularly different from the other girls they knew, most of whom also took pills in combination with beer or wine. In Judi's case, however, the combination was lethal. She was never able to find the something that eluded her, but she did ultimately find death.

Amphetamines and cocaine (stimulants)

In contrast to the barbiturates, which depress or slow down the action of the central nervous system, the amphetamines and cocaine have chemical effects that stimulate or speed it up.

Amphetamines. The earliest *amphetamine* to be introduced—Benzedrine, or amphetamine sulfate—was first synthesized in 1927 and became available in drugstores in the early 1930s as an inhalant to relieve stuffy noses. However, the manufacturers soon learned that some customers were chewing the wicks in the inhalers for "kicks." Thus, the stimulating effects of amphetamine sulfate were discovered by the public before the drug was formally prescribed as a stimulant by physicians. In the late 1930s two newer amphetamines were introduced—Dexedrine (dextroamphetamine) and Methedrine (methamphetamine hydrochloride). The latter preparation is a far more potent stimulant of the central nervous system than either Benzedrine or Dexedrine, and hence is considered more dangerous. In fact, its abuse is lethal in an appreciable number of cases.

Initially these preparations were considered to be "wonder pills" that helped people stay alert and awake and function temporarily at a level beyond normal. During World War II military interest was aroused in the stimulating effects of these drugs, and they were used by both allied and German soldiers to ward off fatigue

(Jarvik, 1967). Similarly, among civilians, amphetamines came to be widely used by night workers, long-distance truck drivers, students cramming for exams, and athletes striving to improve their performances. It was also discovered that the amphetamines tend to suppress appetite, and they became popular among persons trying to lose weight. In addition, they were often used to counteract the effects of barbiturates or other sleeping pills that had been taken the night before. As a result of their many uses, the amphetamines were widely prescribed by doctors.

Since the passage of the Controlled Substance Act of 1970 (DEA, 1979), the amphetamines have been classified as "schedule II" substances—that is, drugs with high abuse potential that require a prescription for each purchase. As a result, medical use of the amphetamines has declined in recent years, and they are more difficult to obtain legally. Nevertheless, it is apparently easy to find illegal "street" sources of the amphetamines, which thus remain among the most widely abused drugs.

Today the amphetamines, or "pep pills," are used medically for curbing the appetite when weight reduction is desirable; for treating individuals suffering from narcolepsy—a disorder in which people cannot prevent themselves from continually falling asleep during the day; and for treating hyperactive children. Curiously enough, the amphetamines have a calming rather than a stimulating effect on many of these youngsters. Amphetamines are still also sometimes prescribed for alleviating mild feelings of depression and relieving fatigue and maintaining alertness for sustained periods of time.

1. *Causes and effects of amphetamine abuse.* Despite their legitimate medical uses, amphetamines are not a magical source of extra mental or physical energy, but rather serve to push users toward a greater expenditure of their own resources—often to a point of hazardous fatigue. In fact, athletes have damaged their careers by using "speed" to try to improve their stamina and performance (Furlong, 1971). It has also been suggested that amphetamines are much too freely prescribed for weight reduction, in view of their short-term effectiveness and possible dangers.

As with other drugs, the effects of amphetamines vary with the type, the dosage, the length of time they are taken, and the physical and psychological state of the individual user. Although amphetamines are not considered to be physiologically addictive, the body does build up tolerance to them very rapidly. Thus, habituated users may consume pills by the mouthful several times a day whereas such amounts would be lethal to nonusers. In some instances, users inject the drug to get faster and more intense results. To get "high" on amphetamines, persons may give themselves from 6 to 200 times the daily medical dosage usually prescribed for dieters. If lesser amphetamines do not provide a sufficient reaction, they may use Methedrine, or "speed," to produce the desired high. In some instances, amphetamine abusers go on "sprees" lasting several days.

For the person who exceeds prescribed dosages, consumption of amphetamines results in heightened blood pressure, enlarged pupils, unclear or rapid speech, profuse sweating, tremors, excitability, loss of appetite, confusion, and sleeplessness. In some instances, the jolt to body physiology from "shooting" Methedrine can raise blood pressure enough to cause immediate death. In addition, the chronic abuse of amphetamines can result in brain damage as well as a wide range of psychopathology, including a disorder known as *amphetamine psychosis*, which investigators consider to be very similar to paranoid schizophrenia.

Suicide, homicide, assault, and various other acts of violence are associated with amphetamine abuse. In the United States, Ellinwood (1971) studied 13 persons who committed homicide under amphetamine intoxication and found that, in most cases, "the events leading to the homicidal act were directly related to amphetamine-induced paranoid thinking, panic, emotional lability [instability], or lowered impulse control" (p. 90). And a study of 100 hospital admissions for amphetamine intoxication revealed that 25 of the subjects had attempted suicide while under the influence of the drug (Nelson, 1969).

2. *Treatment and outcomes.* Withdrawal from the amphetamines is usually painless physically, since physiological addiction is absent or minimal. In some instances, however, withdrawal on a "cold turkey" basis from the chronic excessive use of amphetamines can result in cramping, nausea, diarrhea, and even convulsions (AMA, 1968a; Kunnes, 1973).

But psychological dependence is another matter, and abrupt abstinence commonly results in feelings of weariness and depression. The depression usually reaches its peak in 48 to 72 hours, often remains intense for a day or two, and then tends to lessen gradually over a period of several days. However, mild feelings of depression and lassitude may persist for weeks or even months after the last dose. Where brain damage has occurred, residual effects may also include impaired ability to concentrate, learn, and remember, with resulting social, economic, and personality deterioration.

Cocaine.

Like opium, *cocaine* is a plant product discovered and used in ancient times. It was widely used in the pre-Columbian world of Mexico and Peru (Guerra, 1971). And it has been endorsed by such diverse figures as Sigmund Freud and the legendary Sherlock Holmes. Its use has increased significantly in the United States, especially among middle- and upper-income groups who can afford the high cost of the drug (see **HIGHLIGHT** on page 432). Hospital admissions for cocaine abuse nearly doubled between 1978 and 1981 (NIDA, 1981).

Like opium, cocaine may be ingested by sniffing, swallowing, or injecting. And like the opiates, it precipitates a euphoric state of four to six hours' duration, during which the user experiences feelings of peace and contentment. However, this blissful state may be preceded by headache, dizziness, and restlessness. When cocaine is chronically abused, acute toxic psychotic symptoms may occur similar to those in acute schizophrenia in which the user encounters frightening visual, auditory, and tactual hallucinations, such as the "cocaine bug" (Post, 1975). In rare cases cocaine use is fatal (Wetli & Wright, 1979); a recent study showed that 8.5 percent of males who died of drug-related causes had been using cocaine (Project DAWN, 1980).

Because of its anesthetic qualities, cocaine is sometimes used as a substitute for morphine. Unlike the opiates, however, cocaine stimulates the cortex of the brain, inducing sleeplessness and excitement, as well as stimulating and accentuating sexual processes. Consequently, some individuals have been known to administer it as an aid to seduction. Dependence on cocaine also differs from that on opiates, in that tolerance is not increased appreciably with its use, nor is there any physiological dependence.

However, psychological dependence on cocaine, like addiction to opiates, often leads to a centering of behavior around its procurement, concurrent with a loss of social approval and self-respect. The following case illustrates this pattern:

The subject was a strikingly pretty, intelligent woman of 19 who had divorced her husband two years previously. She had married at the age of 16 and stated that she was terribly in love with her husband but he turned out to be cruel and brutal.

The woman was too ashamed of her marital failure (her parents had violently opposed the marriage and she had left home against their will) to return to her home. She moved away from her husband and got a job as a cocktail waitress in the same bar where her husband had been accustomed to taking her. She was severely depressed, and several of his friends insisted on buying her drinks to cheer her up. This process continued for almost a year, during which she drank excessively but managed to hold her job.

Following this, she met a man in the bar where she worked who introduced her to cocaine, assuring her that it would cheer her up and get rid of her blues. She states that it both "hopped me up and gave me a feeling of peace and contentment." For a period of several months she purchased her supplies of cocaine from this same man until she became ill with appendicitis and was unable to pay the stiff price he asked. Following an appendectomy, she was induced to share his apartment as a means of defraying her expenses and ensuring the supply of cocaine which she had now become heavily dependent on psychologically. She stated that she felt she could not work without it. During this period she had sexual relations with the man although she considered it immoral and had severe guilt feelings about it.

This pattern continued for several months until her "roommate" upped his prices on the cocaine, on the excuse that it was getting more difficult to obtain, and suggested that she might be able to earn enough money to pay for it if she were not so prudish about whom she slept with. At this time the full significance of where her behavior was leading seems to have dawned on her and she came voluntarily to a community clinic for assistance.

Treatment for psychological dependence on cocaine does not differ appreciably from that for other drugs which involve no physiological dependence. Aversion therapy, group techniques, and related procedures may all be used. However, as in the case with other such drugs, feelings of tension and depression may have to be dealt with during the immediate withdrawal period.

HIGHLIGHT
Cocaine: a drug for the affluent

Cocaine or "coke," though usually costing more than $100 an ounce, has recently become one of the most widely abused of the illegal drugs. The white powdery derivative of the coca plant, grown usually in the Andes countries of Bolivia or Peru and processed in Colombia, cocaine is prized for the "high" it produces along with the presumed low risk of physical or addictive problems. From early pre-Columbian civilizations to the present, the coca plant has provided pleasure in the form of an intense, vivid feeling of euphoria that lasts for about a half hour. Many cocaine users also believe that the drug has aphrodisiac properties and enhances sexual experience.

In recent times, perhaps because of its exorbitant price, cocaine has become known as the "high" for the affluent. Many celebrities—actors, musicians, professional athletes—have become involved in cocaine use. The popularity of the drug is reflected in the frequent allusions to it in comedy skits and in movies and the reported availability of the drug at popular celebrity hangouts. Some entertainers have even claimed that the use of cocaine has been instrumental in releasing the "creative potential" in their work.

Tragically, the activities of many of these individuals have led to drug-related problems and drug abuse. Some celebrities have faced legal difficulties as a result of cocaine use; Louise Lasser (of the TV show "Mary Hartman, Mary Hartman") and comedian Flip Wilson were charged with cocaine-related offenses. MacKenzie Phillips of television's "One Day at a Time" developed serious personal problems and had to seek psychological treatment for cocaine abuse. Comedian Richard Pryor narrowly escaped death when he accidentally set himself afire while using cocaine. Professional athletes, such as baseball player Ferguson Jenkins and football player Thomas "Hollywood" Henderson, had their athletic careers adversely affected by cocaine use. Football players Randy Crowder, Donald Reese, and "Mercury" Morris received jail sentences for attempting to sell cocaine to undercover police agents. Recently, another outstanding football player, Carl Eller, disclosed his extensive cocaine abuse throughout his career in an effort to draw attention to the widespread problem in the National Football League and to encourage efforts to help other players avoid the perils of cocaine.

LSD and related drugs (hallucinogens)

The *hallucinogens* are drugs whose properties are thought to induce hallucinations. In fact, however, these preparations do not so often "create" sensory images as distort them, so that the individual sees or hears things in different and unusual ways.

The major drugs in this category are *LSD* (lysergic acid diethylamide), *mescaline,* and *psilocybin.* Not long ago, *PCP,* or "angel dust," became popular as well. Our present discussion will be restricted largely to LSD because of its unusual hallucinogenic properties.

LSD.   The most potent of the hallucinogens, the odorless, colorless, and tasteless drug LSD can produce intoxication with an amount smaller than a grain of salt. It is a chemically synthesized substance first discovered by the Swiss chemist Hoffman in 1938.

1. *Effects of LSD.* Hoffman was not aware of the potent hallucinatory qualities of LSD until some five years after his discovery, when he swallowed a small amount. This is his report of the experience:

"Last Friday, April 16, 1943, I was forced to stop my work in the laboratory in the middle of the afternoon and to go home, as I was seized by a peculiar restlessness associated with a sensation of mild dizziness. On arriving home, I lay down and sank into a kind of drunkenness which was not unpleasant and which was characterized by extreme activity of imagination. As I lay in a dazed condition with my eyes closed (I experienced daylight as disagreeably bright) there surged upon me an uninterrupted stream of fantastic images of extraordinary plasticity and vividness and accompanied by an intense kaleidoscope-like play of colours. This condition gradually passed off after about two hours." (Hoffman, 1971, p. 23)

Hoffman followed up this experience with a series of planned self-observations with LSD, some of which he described as "harrowing." Researchers thought LSD might be useful for the induction and study of hallucinogenic states or "model psychoses," which were thought to be related to schizophrenia. About 1950, LSD was introduced into the United States for purposes of such research as well as to ascertain whether it might have medical or therapeutic uses. Despite considerable research, however, LSD has not proven therapeutically useful.

After taking LSD, a person typically goes through about eight hours of changes in sensory perception, lability of emotional experiences, and feelings of depersonalization and detachment. The peak of physiological and psychological effects usually occurs between the second and fourth hours. Physiological effects include increased heart rate, elevation of blood pressure, and faster and more variable breathing.

As LSD takes effect, the most important psychic manifestation is a tremendous intensification of sensory perception. Objects seem to become clearer, sharper, brighter, and endowed with dimensions not perceived before. One young woman lost herself in contemplation of a flower, seeing in it colors she had never seen before, hearing the movements of its petals, and feeling that at last she understood its essential nature. Another phenomenon associated with the drug is "humanity identification"—a sensation in which one feels in empathic concert with all humankind in experiencing such universal emotions as love, loneliness, or grief.

In addition to the intensity of the basic perceptual and affective reactions that occur in the early stages of the LSD experience, Katz, Waskow, and Olsson (1968) have pointed to certain contradictory aspects of that experience. These include the following:

"1. Very strong but opposing emotions occuring approximately at the same time, emotions which may not have a cognitive counterpart;
2. A feeling of being out of control of one's emotions and thoughts;
3. A feeling of detachment from the real world;
4. A feeling of perceptual sharpness, but at the

Fear shows in the eyes of this young woman, who is undergoing a terrifying drug "trip."

same time perceptions of the outer world as having an unreal quality;
5. The perception of the world and others as 'friendly' but 'suspicious.'" (p. 13)

The LSD "trip" is not always pleasant. It can be extremely harrowing and traumatic, and the distorted objects and sounds, the illusory colors, and the new thoughts can be menacing and terrifying. For example, Rorvik (1970) has cited the case of a young British law student who tried to "continue time" by using a dental drill to bore a hole in his head while under the influence of LSD. In other instances, persons undergoing "bad trips" have set themselves aflame, jumped from high places, and taken other drugs which proved a lethal combination. Of 114 subjects admitted to the Bellevue Hospital in New York City with acute psychoses induced by LSD, 13 percent showed overwhelming fear and another

12 percent experienced uncontrollably violent urges; suicide or homicide had been attempted by approximately 9 percent (Rorvik, 1970). In a study of chronic users of LSD, Blacker and his associates (1968) found that the "bad trip" usually began in a context of ire. For example, one of their subjects reported that he had taken LSD when he was angry with his mother. Initially his trip had been beautiful; then it exploded. He suddenly became very fearful, thought he could hear monsters coming up the stairs, and was convinced that they would come through the door to his room and eat him.

The setting in which LSD is taken appears to be influential in determining its effect, but a favorable milieu alone is no guarantee against adverse reactions. Even a single dose can trigger serious psychological complications. For example, in a study of 52 persons admitted to a New York hospital with LSD-induced psychoses, it was found that 26 had taken the drug only one time, and only 12 of the subjects had shown evidence of serious maladjustment prior to their LSD psychosis (AMA, 1968b). On the other hand, the same individual may be affected differently by the drug at different times. In fact, the preceding investigators cited cases of persons who had used LSD 100 or more times without apparent difficulty and then suddenly had developed severe, adverse reactions.

An interesting and unusual phenomenon that may occur following the use of LSD is the *flashback,* an involuntary recurrence of perceptual distortions or hallucinations weeks or even months after taking the drug. These experiences appear to be relatively rare among individuals who have taken LSD only once—although they do sometimes occur. On the other hand, it has been conservatively estimated that about 1 in 20 consistent users experiences such flashbacks (Horowitz, 1969a). Some persons react with fear to these recurrent images, which "seem to have a will of their own"; extreme anxiety and even psychotic reactions may result. It has been estimated that about 3 percent of persons who use LSD under illegal conditions experience such psychotic reactions.

Some studies have indicated that LSD may cause chromosomal damage and a lowering of immunological defenses to disease, but others have challenged these reports. In any event, users of LSD do not develop physiological dependence; however, some chronic users have developed psychological dependence, in the sense that they focus their life around this type of drug experience.

2. *Use of LSD for self-improvement.* Despite the possibility of adverse reactions through use of the drug, LSD was widely publicized during the 1960s, and a number of relatively well-known people experimented with it and gave glowing accounts of their "trips." In fact, during this period an "LSD movement" was under way, based on the conviction that the drug could "expand the mind" and enable one to use talents and realize potentials previously undetected. As a result, a considerable number of people attempted to use LSD as a vehicle for achieving greater personal insight, increased sensitivity, mystic experiences, and better understanding of their place in the universe. This category included a sizable number of painters, writers, and composers, who attempted to use the drug not only for personal growth but also a means of creating more original and meaningful works of art.

There is no evidence that LSD enhances creative activity: no recognized works of art have apparently been produced under the influence of the drug or as a consequence of a psychedelic experience. And although several artists have claimed improved creativity stemming from their LSD experiences, objective observers recognize few, if any, improvements in the work of these artists (AMA, 1968b). In fact, under the direct influence of LSD, the drawings of one well-known American painter showed progressive deterioration; later, when asked if he felt his LSD experience had improved his creativity, he replied in the negative (Rinkel, 1966).

3. *Treatment and outcomes.* For acute psychoses induced by LSD intoxication, treatment requires hospitalization and is primarily a medical matter. Often the outcome in such cases depends heavily on the personal stability of the individual prior to taking the drug; in some cases prolonged hospitalization may be required.

Fortunately, brief psychotherapy is usually effective in treating psychological dependence on LSD as well as in preventing the recurrence of flashbacks which may still haunt the individual as a result of a bad trip. As in the case of trauma experienced in combat or civilian disasters, therapy is aimed at helping the individual work through the painful experience and integrate it into his or her self-structure.

Mescaline and psilocybin.
Two other well-known hallucinogens are mescaline and psilocybin. Mescaline is derived from the small, disclike growths ("mescal buttons") at the top of the peyote cactus; psilocybin is a drug obtained from a variety of "sacred" Mexican mushrooms known as *psilocybe mexicana.*

These drugs have been used for centuries in the ceremonial rites of Indian peoples living in Mexico, the American Southwest, and Central and South America. In fact, they were used by the Aztecs for such purposes long before the Spanish invasion. Both drugs have mind-altering and hallucinogenic properties, but their principal effect appears to be enabling the individual to see, hear, and otherwise, experience events in unaccustomed ways—transporting him into a realm of "nonordinary reality."

As with LSD, there is no definite evidence that mescaline and psilocybin actually "expand consciousness" or create new ideas; rather, they seem primarily to alter or distort experience.

Marijuana is most often smoked in the form of a rolled cigarette, or "joint."

Marijuana

Although *marijuana* may be classified as a mild hallucinogen, there are significant differences in the nature, intensity, and duration of its effects as compared with those induced by LSD, mescaline, and other major hallucinogens.

Marijuana comes from the leaves and flowering tops of the hemp plant, *cannabis sativa.* The plant grows in mild climates throughout the world including parts of India, Africa, Mexico, and the United States. In its prepared state, marijuana consists chiefly of the dried green leaves—hence the colloquial name "grass." It is ordinarily smoked in the form of cigarettes ("reefers" or "joints") or in pipes, but it can also be baked into cookies and other foods. In some cultures the leaves are steeped in hot water and the liquid is drunk, much as one might drink tea. Marijuana is related to the stronger drug, hashish, which is derived from the resin exuded by the cannabis plant and made into a gummy powder. *Hashish,* like marijuana, may be smoked, chewed, or drunk.

Both marijuana and hashish can be traced far back into the history of drug usage. Cannabis was apparently known in ancient China (Blum, 1969; Culliton, 1970), and was listed in the herbal compendiums of the Chinese emperor Shen Nung, written about 2737 B.C.

Until the late 1960s marijuana use in the United States was confined largely to members of lower socioeconomic minority groups and to people in entertainment and related fields. In the late 1960s, however, there was a dramatic increase in its use among youth in our society, and during the early 1970s it was estimated that over half the teenagers and young adults had experimented with marijuana in social situations, with about 10 percent presumably going from occasional to habitual use. In 1981, an estimated 30 percent of people in the United States had used marijuana and over 13 percent were reportedly current users (HHS, 1980; NIDA, 1981).

Effects of marijuana.
The specific effects of marijuana vary greatly, depending on the quality and dosage of the drug, the personality and

mood of the user, the user's past experience with the drug, the social setting, and the user's expectations. However, there is considerable consensus among regular users that when marijuana is smoked and inhaled, the individual gets "high." This state is one of mild euphoria distinguished by increased feelings of well-being, heightened perceptual acuity, and pleasant relaxation, often accompanied by a sensation of drifting or floating away. Sensory inputs are enhanced: music sounds fuller, colors look brighter, smells seem richer, and food tastes better. Somehow the world seems to become more meaningful, and even minor events may take on extraordinary profundity. Often there is a stretching out or distortion of the individual's sense of time, so that an event lasting but a few seconds may seem to cover a much longer span. Short-term memory may also be affected, as when one notices a bite taken out of a sandwich but does not remember having taken it. For most users, pleasurable experiences, including sexual intercourse, seem to be greatly enhanced. When smoked, marijuana is rapidly absorbed and its effects appear within seconds to minutes but seldom last more than 2 to 3 hours. The effects of THC (a synthetically produced drug that appears to be the active ingredient in cannabis) are slower in making their appearance, requiring 30 minutes to over 2 hours following oral ingestion.

Marijuana may lead to unpleasant as well as pleasant experiences. For example, if an individual takes the drug while in an unhappy, angry, suspicious, or frightened mood, unsavory events may be magnified. And with high dosages, as well as with certain unstable or susceptible individuals, marijuana can produce extreme euphoria, hilarity, and overtalkativeness; it can also produce intense anxiety and depression as well as delusions, hallucinations, and other psychotic-seeming behavior.

It is of interest to note, however, that in a study reported by Nelson (1969), only three hospital admissions for marijuana abuse or intoxication were reported out of 90,733 consecutive admissions, while thousands of admissions and hundreds of deaths were associated with the abuse of alcohol, barbiturates, and amphetamines. The U.S. Drug Enforcement Agency's report on drug-related deaths between May 1976 and April 1977 found that only one death out of 3,809 was induced by marijuana (Project DAWN 1977).

The short-range physiological effects of marijuana include a moderate increase in heart rate, a slowing of reaction time, a slight contraction of pupil size, bloodshot and itchy eyes, a dry mouth, and an increased appetite. Furthermore, Braff et al. (1981) reported that marijuana induces a slowing of information processing and memory dysfunction. Continued use of high dosages over time tends to produce lethargy and passivity. Here marijuana appears to have a depressant as well as a hallucinogenic effect. However, the effects of long-term and habitual use of the drug are still under investigation, although a number of possible adverse side effects have been related to the prolonged heavy use of marijuana.

Marijuana has often been compared to heroin, but the two drugs have little in common with respect either to tolerance or to physiological dependence. Although studies conducted in Eastern countries have found evidence of tolerance to marijuana at high dosage levels over long periods of time, studies in the U.S.—which have involved lower dosages for shorter time periods—have failed to find evidence of tolerance (HEW, 1971). In fact, habitual users often show "reverse tolerance." This may be due in part to the users' having learned the proper method of smoking and to the suggestive influence of anticipated effects. In any event, habitual users rarely feel it necessary to increase their doses to maintain desired effects. In addition, many habitual users of marijuana claim the ability to "turn off" its effects or "come down" from a marijuana "high" if conditions in the situation require it, and a limited amount of research evidence tends to support their claim (Cappell & Pliner, 1973). Nor does marijuana lead to physiological dependence, as heroin does, so discontinuance of the drug is not accompanied by withdrawal symptoms. Marijuana can, however, lead to psychological dependence, in which the individual experiences a strong need for it whenever he or she feels anxious and tense.

Marijuana use and controversies.   Aside from alcohol, no drug has triggered so much debate and confusion in our society as marijuana. Many persons, including members of the drug subculture, see no dangers in its use and even consider it a boon to humanity; other persons see serious dangers in its use and feel that the possession or use of marijuana should be subject to severe legal sanctions.

What are the facts about marijuana? Unfortunately, despite an increasing amount of research, we still do not have adequate answers to a number of pertinent questions.

1. *What are the reasons for using marijuana?* In the late 1960s and 1970s, the reasons for using marijuana appeared to run the gamut: (a) curiosity, thrill-seeking, and easy euphoria; (b) peer pressure for doing the "in thing" with a given group; (c) desire for self-improvement through gaining new insights and help in realizing one's potential; and (d) the urge to diminish stressful conflicts, insecurities, and anxieties. The last reason was often associated with the discouragement of slum life as well as with the disillusionment of many youth during the 1960s, including teenage runaways, who "dropped out" of the mainstream of society and joined drug subcultures.

2. *Is there a specific personality pattern associated with marijuana use?* A number of psychological studies have been directed toward this question but results are far from conclusive. Several studies (Graham & Cross, 1975; Hogan, et al., 1970) have found important personality differences between chronic users and nonusers. Users showed more spontaneity, adventuresomeness, and novelty seeking, while nonusers appeared well socialized, conforming, and respectful of authority; they strove for traditional values and rarely acted on impulse. However, most of the published research has examined personality differences only after the marijuana use has begun.

One recent study reported observations of three groups of college students: (a) nonusers of marijuana, (b) continuous users of marijuana, and (c) students who switched to marijuana during the period of the study. Kay et al. (1978) tested a large group of college students on several occasions with the California Psychological Inventory (CPI), the Adjective Check List (ACL), and a drug questionnaire. Replicating Hogan et al. (1970), they found personality differences between users and nonusers; they also found that marijuana users of the 1970s were similar to those of the 1960s in personality correlates.

The nonusers who later switched to marijuana use provided an interesting comparison. Most of them had switched to marijuana use within their first year at college. In terms of their measured personality characteristics they appeared to fall between the users and nonusers, showing some characteristics of both other groups. Their original CPI scores also suggested more flexibility than the nonuser group. Over time, they came to resemble the user group in their self-descriptions on the Adjective Check List. The authors concluded that individuals with certain personality characteristics such as flexibility are more likely to use marijuana than conforming, conservative individuals.

3. *Does the use of marijuana have harmful effects?* In the fourth of a series of reports on the use of marijuana, the National Institute of Drug Abuse (NIDA, 1976) summarized findings from research projects that had been funded by this agency. The essential thrust of the report was that marijuana poses serious threats to highway safety in ways similar to alcohol intoxication.

With regard to the harmfulness of marijuana to the physical health of habitual or heavy users, the findings were inconclusive—though suggestive. For example, there was some evidence of (a) adverse effects on cardiac functioning, (b) irritation of the lungs resulting from deep inhalation, (c) weakening of the body's immune mechanisms, (d) a decrease of male sex hormones, and (e) brain damage. Until more definitive research findings become available, it seems probable that the controversy concerning the possible hazards of marijuana use is likely to continue.

Marijuana has been found to be beneficial in some medical treatments, particularly in relieving the pain of glaucoma and the painful side effects of chemotherapy for cancer. Specifically, marijuana suppresses the vomiting reaction produced by chemotherapy. In New Mexico, a court has ruled in favor of permitting a patient to use marijuana to relieve pain, but has provided no legal means by which the patient could obtain the drug.

4. *Does the use of marijuana enhance creativity?* Most investigators have given a definite *no* to this question (Braden, Stillman, & Wyatt, 1974; Yolles, 1969). Although marijuana may induce fantasies that seem creative, at least to the person experiencing them, what actually is produced in terms of writing, painting, or other creative pursuits is usually evaluated as no better —and often worse—than what might be otherwise produced. As with the use of LSD and other hallucinogens, individuals may think they have found "the key to the universe"; when they come down, however, it is not there.

5. *Should marijuana be legalized?* Defenders of marijuana have long argued that the drug is no more dangerous than alcohol—and possibly less so, since it is not appreciably related to violence or crime in the United States and is not physiologically addictive. They have pointed out that legalization would provide freer access to a source of pleasure and tension reduction; would ensure a safer product since the federal government could supervise its production, distribution, and sale; and would provide an added source of revenue through taxation. In addition, they consider it illogical to sanction the use of drugs known to be dangerous, such as alcohol and nicotine-containing tobacco, while outlawing marijuana.

The crime of possessing small amounts of marijuana—but not "pushing"—has been reduced from a felony to a misdemeanor by the federal government and most state governments. Opponents of legalization have taken a variety of stands against possession and sale, one being that use of marijuana leads to use of hard drugs. But though a high proportion of heroin addicts have also used marijuana, this is not proof of a causal relationship; it is likely that an even larger proportion of heroin users have used alcohol and other drugs. The vast majority of marijuana users have never become involved with heroin. A second line of argument against legalizing marijuana contends that frequent use of the drug produces an "a-motivational syndrome," that is, the long-term user becomes lethargic and does not take responsibility for his or her actions (Rae-Grant, 1981). A third argument sees the removal of governmental restrictions as inevitably leading to a marked increase in marijuana use, a result that apparently has not occurred thus far. Perhaps the most convincing argument against legalization is that it is ill-advised to legalize *any* drug before we have definitive evidence concerning its long-range effects.

Other addictive disorders: Extreme obesity and pathological gambling

Not all addictive disorders involve the use of substances with chemical properties that induce dependency. People can develop "addictions" to certain activities that can be just as life-threatening as severe alcoholism and just as damaging, psychologically and socially, as drug abuse. We are including two such disorders in this chapter. They are similar to other addictions in their behavioral manifestations, their etiologies and their resistance to treatment.

Extreme obesity

To get an idea of how extensive the problem of obesity is just look around at almost any social event or public place and count the number of individuals who are seriously overweight. Jeffrey and Katz (1977) estimate that from 40 to 80 million Americans fall in this category. Obesity is a serious but often overlooked health problem in the United States today. Stewart and Brook (1983) found, in a survey of 5,817 Americans, aged 14 to 61, that 10 percent were moderately overweight and 12 percent severely overweight.

In this discussion we are concerned with *hyperobesity*—extreme obesity in which the individual is 100 pounds or more above ideal body weight. Such obesity is not simply an unattractive characteristic. It can be a dangerous, life-threatening disorder, resulting in such conditions as diabetes, musculoskeletal problems, high blood pressure, and other cardiovascular diseases that can place the individual at high risk for heart attacks. Although some cases of extreme obesity result from metabolic or hormonal disorders, most individuals who are obese become so simply through taking in more calories than they burn off.

Obesity, as a disorder, may be placed in several diagnostic categories, depending on which characteristics are being emphasized. If we focus on the physical changes, for example, we may view obesity as a psycho-physiologic disturbance, since psychological factors lead to the physical changes. Many clinicians, however, view the central problem not as the excessive weight itself but as the long-standing habit pattern of overeating. Thus obesity resulting from gross, habitual overeating is considered to be more like the problems found in the personality disorders—especially those involving loss of control over an appetite of some kind (Kurland, 1967; Leon et al., 1978).

Causes of persistent overeating. What prompts people to overeat to the point of obesity, despite an awareness of the detrimental effects on their health and a consciousness of the strong social prejudice in favor of the "body beautiful"? Several potential causal factors have been explored; although results are not conclusive, biological and learning factors seem to be of importance.

1. *Biological factors.* Some people seem to be able to eat high-calorie foods without significant weight gain, while others become overweight easily and engage in a constant struggle *not* to gain weight. Most people gain weight with advancing age, but this could be related to reduced activity as well as to the fact that older people are likely to continue their earlier eating habits even though they need fewer calories. As already indicated, some individuals have metabolic or endocrine anomalies that can produce obesity at any age, though these cases seem to be relatively rare.

Obesity in adults is related to the number and size of the *adipose cells* (fat cells) in the body (Hirsch, 1972). Individuals who are obese have markedly more adipose cells than people of normal weight. When weight is lost, the size of the cells is reduced but not their number. There is some evidence that the total number of adipose cells stays the same from childhood on (Crisp et al., 1970). It is possible that overfeeding infants

and young children may cause them to develop more adipose cells and may thus predispose them to overweight or obesity in adulthood.

2. *Psychosocial factors.* In many cases the key determinants of excessive eating and obesity appear to be family behavior patterns. In some families the customary diet or an overemphasis on food consumption may produce obesity in many or all family members. In such a family the fat baby may be seen as the healthy baby, and there may be great pressure on infants and children to eat more than they want. In other families eating (or overeating) becomes a habitual means of alleviating emotional distress.

There are currently three quite different psychological views concerning the causes of gross habitual overeating.

a) According to the *psychodynamic* view, obese individuals are fixated at the oral stage of psychosexual development (Bychowski, 1950). They are believed to eat to excess and orient their lives around oral gratification because their libidinal energies and psychological growth have not advanced to a more mature level.

This view has been elaborated by Bruch (1973), who distinguishes between *developmental* obesity and *reactive* obesity. She sees developmental obesity as developing in childhood as a response to parental rejection or other severe disturbance in the parent-child relationship. Supposedly, the parents overcompensate for their emotional rejection by overfeeding and overprotecting the child. Such children never learn to distinguish different internal signals because the mother responds to all signs of distress by giving them food. Bruch sees this pattern as leading to a distorted perception of internal states—that is, a lack of awareness of satiation when enough food has been ingested.

Reactive obesity is defined by Bruch as obesity that occurs in adults as a reaction to trauma or stress. Here individuals are thought to use the defense mechanism of overfeeding themselves to lessen their feelings of distress or depression. Though this may be depicted as "truth" in countless cartoons and sitcoms, the research findings are inconclusive.

b) According to the *externality* hypothesis, eating is under the control of external cues instead of the individual's internal state. Whereas hunger and its satisfaction dictate the eating

Family eating patterns are often key causal factors in extreme obesity.

patterns of persons of normal weight, obese persons are seen as being at the mercy of environmental inducements. Regardless of how recently or amply they have eaten, they may be prompted to eat again simply by the sight or smell of food.

This reliance upon external cues is pointedly illustrated in the complaint of an obese 29-year-old patient:

I crave food . . . everywhere I go, whatever I do, I am reminded of food. Today after breakfast, I rode to work on the bus. The advertisements made me so hungry that I had to stop at the coffee shop for rolls before I went into the office. When I watch TV I find myself constantly eating—I want everything. I can't stop. My big downfall is "munchies"—peanuts, potato chips, brownies. Going to the grocery store, I lose control and before you know it I have to get another grocery cart—and the first one is just full of junk. I

can sit down in the evening to write a letter and before I know it the jar of peanuts is completely gone!

Other investigators, however, reject the externality hypothesis. Rodin (1974) found obese persons no more sensitive to external cues than persons of normal weight. Leon and Roth (1977), too, in a review of research on this hypothesis, found the evidence highly equivocal.

c) The simplest explanation—and therefore the easiest to accept—seems to be found in the *behavioral* view. Both the weight gain and the tendency to maintain excessive weight can be explained quite simply in terms of learning principles (Jordan & Levitz, 1975; Leon & Chamberlain, 1973; Stuart, 1971b).

For all of us, eating behavior is determined in part by conditioned responses to a wide range of environmental stimuli. For example, people are encouraged to eat at parties and movies, while watching TV, and even at work. Eating is reinforced in all these situations, and it is difficult to avoid the many inducements to eat. Thus there is a wide assortment of seemingly unavoidable reinforcers and conditioned stimuli in the lives of most Americans.

Obese persons, however, have been shown to be conditioned to more cues—both internal and external—than persons of normal weight. Anxiety, anger, boredom, and social inducements all may lead to overeating. Eating in response to such cues is then reinforced because the taste of good food is pleasurable and the individual's emotional tension is reduced. All this increases the probability that overeating will continue at an even higher level.

But with such frequent overfeeding, obese persons may then learn not to be responsive to satiety cues, no longer feeling full when they have had enough. Meanwhile, physical activity, because its short-term effects are often aversive rather than pleasant, tends *not* to be reinforced, especially as pounds accumulate. Thus the obese individual may become less and less active.

3. *Sociocultural factors.* Different cultures have very different concepts of human beauty. Some value slimness, others, a rounded contour. In some cultures, obesity is even valued as a sign of social influence and power.

Within our own society, obesity seems to be related to social class, occurring six times as often in lower-class adults and nine times more often in lower-class youngsters. (Stunkard et al., 1972). Here, however, obesity may be related to a high carbohydrate diet in lower-class families.

Treatment of extreme obesity. Losing weight is a preoccupation of many Americans and the sale of dietary aids and weight-loss programs is big business. Jeffrey and Katz (1977) estimated that over $16,000 is spent every minute—a total of $8 billion a year—on diet pills, diet aids, diet books, diet programs, and so on. Diet plans abound, with new programs emerging as often as clothing fads.

Treatment of extreme obesity has included a variety of approaches including dietary programs, group self-help programs, medical measures ranging from appetite-suppressing drugs to intestinal bypass surgery, and behavioral management techniques.

In actuality, the success rate of most of these devices and programs is quite low. In fact, the average outcome from diets has been reported to be a regaining of 105 percent of the weight lost (Stuart, 1967). Cyclic loss and regaining can even be dangerous because it may do serious damage to the cardiovascular system, further compounding the problem.

Most obese patients who seek professional help have failed on many diets in the past. Some of the most successful dietary programs are the self-control behavioral management programs, conducted in groups and including the use of follow-up booster sessions (Kingsley & Wilson, 1977).

There are also a number of weight-loss group programs conducted by commercial organizations like TOPS (Take Off Pounds Sensibly) and Weight Watchers (Bumbalo & Young, 1973). These programs provide strong group pressures to reduce weight by public praise of weight loss and public disapproval and "punishments" for failures. Thus they provide both community support and encouragement to maintain better eating habits. Individuals who remain with these group programs lose about 14 pounds on the average (Garb & Stunkard, 1974); however, less than a third of those who begin the programs stay for 24 months.

Fasting or starvation diets under medically controlled conditions generally produce weight loss in hyperobese patients—with some studies reporting losses of over 100 pounds (Leon, 1976). However, this method of rapid weight loss may involve several dangerous potential complications such as hypertension, gout, and kidney failure (Munro & Duncan, 1972; Runcie & Thompson, 1970).

Psychological distress may also accompany such starvation, with severe personality deterioration and psychosis occurring in some cases (Swanson & Dinello, 1970). And maintaining the lower weight level remains a problem: patients tend to regain the lost weight rapidly. After reviewing the research on therapeutic fasting, Leon (1976) concluded that "the equivocal weight maintenance results and the number of serious physical complications associated with prolonged starvation suggests that this technique should be used only in extreme situations." (p. 572)

Another questionable medical treatment of

the hyperobese patient has centered on the use of *anorexigenic drugs* to reduce the patient's appetite. Diet pills, such as the amphetamines, suppress the desire for food and, as a result, have been extensively used. Again, however, maintenance of weight loss once the diet pills are gone often becomes a problem.

Moreover, diet pills often present a problem in their own right. As we have seen, the amphetamines are addicting substances and are particularly dangerous when used in combination with other substances such as alcohol. The general ineffectiveness of amphetamines for long-term weight control and their high abuse potential has made these drugs of doubtful value in weight-reduction programs.

Another experimental medical treatment for extreme obesity has been the *jejunoileal bypass operation.* This surgical procedure involves disconnecting and bypassing a large portion of the small intestine. The operation results in a reduction of the food-absorptive capacity of the intestine, thus producing a drastic weight loss—typically over 100 pounds in less than a year (Payne, Dewind & Commons, 1963). However, severe postoperative side effects have been reported, including diarrhea, hair loss, and death in as high as 6 percent of the cases. The dangers and the undesirable side effects of this surgical procedure make it a last ditch effort in cases of extreme obesity.

The most effective psychological treatment procedures for the extremely obese patient are behavioral management methods, which teach the individual to take off weight gradually through reduced food intake and exercise (Jeffery, Wing, & Stunkard, 1978). A number of methods using positive reinforcement, self-monitoring, and self-reward can produce moderate weight loss over time. In general, these procedures, based upon positive reinforcement, are more effective than classic conditioning procedures such as aversive conditioning in which shock or unpleasant thoughts may be paired with eating behavior (Leon, 1976).

The treatment of extremely obese patients is often a difficult and frustrating task for all concerned. Even with the most effective treatment procedures, such as behavioral management training, treatment failures abound, partly due to the necessity of self-motivation in treatment.

In one case involving a 15-year-old high-school student named Beth, a variety of treatment and counseling approaches were used, including a token reward system for eating balanced meals with smaller portions. Though she reportedly complied with the point system and earned rewards for the first three weeks she nevertheless lost little weight. She reported that she had cut down on high-calorie snacks but was still eating large portions at mealtimes. The treatment sessions focused upon problems occurring in her school and with her family that were related to her eating problem. Ways of maintaining her diet were also explored, as were issues concerning the decision to eat and her commitment to change. The primary emphasis was on self-control and self-management techniques. She was also taught a system of self-monitoring of her food intake.

After 16 treatment sessions over a period of 5 months, Beth had only decreased her weight from an original 208½ pounds to 207¼ pounds. The therapist confronted her with her apparent lack of commitment and pointed up the difference between wanting to lose weight and wanting to change her eating style.

Two weeks later, Beth came to the final session having decided that her independence in eating what she wanted was more important to her at this point in her life than changing her eating patterns.

The poor outcome in this example illustrates the tenacity of the problem of extreme obesity. As in Beth's case, many patients lose interest in the remote goal and choose to remain obese rather than make the difficult and persistent effort required to lose weight and keep it off.

Pathological gambling

Although the behavior pattern known as ***pathological*** or ***compulsive gambling*** does not involve a chemically addictive substance, it can be considered an addictive disorder because of the personality attributes that tend to characterize the individuals and the similar treatment problems involved. It also involves behavior maintained by short-term gains despite long-term disruption of the individual's life.

Gambling is usually defined as wagering on games or events in which chance largely determines the outcome. In modern societies money is typically the item of exchange; in other societies, seashell currency, beads, jewelry, and food are often used. The ancient Chinese frequently wagered hairs of their head—and sometimes even fingers, toes, and limbs—on games of chance (Cohen & Hansel, 1956). But regardless of the item of exchange, gambling seems to be an enduring human proclivity. Judging from written history and the studies of anthropologists, gambling has occurred and continues to occur almost universally and among all social strata.

Clinical picture in pathological gambling.

Gambling in our society takes many forms, from casino gambling to betting on horse races (legally or otherwise), to numbers games, lotteries, dice, bingo, and cards. The exact sums that change hands in legal and illegal gambling are unknown, but it has been estimated that habitual gamblers in the United States lose more than 20 billion dollars each year.[6]

If one were to define gambling in its broadest sense, even playing the stock market might be considered a game of chance. Sherrod (1968) has humorously pointed to the need for a clearer definition of terms:

"If you bet on a horse, that's gambling. If you bet you can make three spades, that's entertainment. If you bet cotton will go up three points, that's business. See the difference?" (p. 619)

In any event, gambling appears to be one of our major national pastimes, with some 50 percent of the population gambling at one time or another on anything from Saturday-night poker games to the outcome of sporting events such as the World Series and the Super Bowl. Usually, such gambling is a harmless form of social entertainment; the individual places a bet and waits for the result. Win or lose, that is that. But while most people can take it or leave it, an estimated 6 to 10 million Americans get "hooked" on gambling.

These pathological gamblers[7] are habitual losers who are practically always out of luck, usually in debt, and sometimes in jail. Despite their

---

[6]Statistics in this section are based on Solomon (1972), Strine (1971), and Livingston (1974).

[7]Although these individuals have traditionally been called *compulsive gamblers*, they more closely resemble psychopathic personalities or addictive individuals than obsessive-compulsive personalities (Bolen, Caldwell, & Boyd, 1975; Moran, 1970). In DSM-III pathological gamblers are classified under a separate heading: "Disorders of impulse control not elsewhere classified."

difficulties, however, they tend to be of average intelligence or above, and many have completed one or more years of college. They are usually married and often have responsible managerial or professional positions that provide a reasonably good income (see **HIGHLIGHT** on page 444). Whatever the individual gambler's situation, a recent survey confirmed that the activities of the compulsive gambler significantly affect the social, psychological, and economic well-being of his or her family (Lorenz & Shuttlesworth, 1983).

Causal factors in pathological gambling.

Although a few psychologists and psychiatrists have dealt with the topic of pathological gambling, very little systematic research has been done and the causal factors are not yet well understood. It seems to be a learned pattern that is highly resistant to extinction. Often the person who becomes a pathological gambler has won a substantial sum of money the first time he or she gambled; chance alone would dictate that a certain percentage of individuals would have such "beginner's luck." Bolen and Boyd (1968) consider it likely that the reinforcement an individual receives during this introductory phase is a significant factor in later pathological gambling. And since anyone is likely to win from time to time, the principles of intermittent reinforcement could explain the addict's continued gambling despite excessive losses. Bolen and Boyd were struck particularly by the similarity between slot-machine players and Skinner's laboratory pigeons; the latter, placed on a variable reinforcement schedule, "repetitively and incessantly pecked to the point of exhaustion and eventual demise while waiting the uncertain appearance of their jackpot of bird seed" (1968, p. 629).

Despite their awareness that the odds are against them, and despite the fact that they rarely or never repeat their early success, compulsive gamblers continue to gamble avidly. To "stake" their gambling they often dissipate their savings, neglect their families, default on bills, and borrow money from friends and loan companies. Eventually they may resort to writing bad checks, embezzlement, or other illegal means of obtaining money, feeling sure that their luck will change and that they will be able

HIGHLIGHT

A case of pathological gambling

John _____ was a 40-year-old rather handsome man with slightly graying hair who managed an automobile dealership for his father. For the previous two years, he had increasingly neglected his job and was deep in debt as a result of his gambling activities. He had gambled heavily since he was about 27 years old. His gambling had occasioned frequent quarrels in his first marriage and finally a divorce. He married his second wife without telling her of his problem, but it eventually came to light and created such difficulty that she took their two children and returned to her parents' home in another state.

John joined an encounter group in the stated hope that he might receive some assistance with his problems. In the course of the early group sessions, he proved to be an intelligent, well-educated man who seemed to have a good understanding of his gambling problem and its self-defeating nature. He stated that he had started gambling after winning some money at the horse races. This experience convinced him that he could supplement his income by gambling judiciously. However, his subsequent gambling—which frequently involved all-night poker games, trips to Las Vegas, and betting on the races—almost always resulted in heavy losses.

In the group John talked about his gambling freely and coherently—candidly admitting that he enjoyed the stimulation and excitement of gambling more than sexual relations with his wife. He was actually rather glad his family had left since it relieved him of certain responsibilities toward them as well as feelings of guilt for neglecting them. He readily acknowledged that his feelings and behavior were inappropriate and self-defeating, but stated that he was "sick" and that he desperately needed help.

It soon became apparent that while John was willing to talk about his problem, he was not prepared to take constructive steps in dealing with it. He wanted the group to accept him in the "sick role" of being a "pathological gambler" who could not be expected to "cure" himself. At the group's suggestion he attended a couple of meetings of Gamblers Anonymous but found them "irrelevant." It was also suggested that he try aversive therapy, but he felt this would not help him.

While attending the group sessions, John apparently continued to gamble and continued to lose. After the eighth encounter group session, he did not return. Through inquiry by one of the members, it was learned that he had been arrested for embezzling funds from his father's business, but that his father had somehow managed to have the charges dropped. John reportedly then left for another state and his subsequent history is unknown.

---

to repay what they have taken. Whereas others view their gambling as unethical and disruptive, they are likely to see themselves as taking "calculated risks" to build a lucrative business. Often they feel alone and resentful that others do not understand their activities.

In a pioneering and well-controlled study of former pathological gamblers, Rosten (1961) found that as a group they tended to be rebellious, unconventional individuals who did not seem to fully understand the ethical norms of society. Half of the group described themselves as "hating regulations." Of 30 men studied, 12 had served time in jail for embezzlement and other crimes directly connected with their gambling.

Rosten also found that these men were un-

realistic in their thinking and prone to seek highly stimulating situations. In the subjects' own words they "loved excitement" and "needed action." Although the men admitted that they had known objectively the all-but-impossible odds they faced while gambling, they had felt that these odds did not apply to them. Often they had the unshakable feeling that "tonight is my night"; typically they had also followed the so-called Monte Carlo fallacy—that after so many losses, their turn was coming up and they would hit it big. Many of the men discussed the extent to which they had "fooled" themselves by elaborate rationalizations. For example, one gambler described his previous rationalizations as covering all contingencies: "When I was ahead, I could gamble because I was playing with others' money. When I was behind, I had to get even. When I was even, I hadn't lost any money" (Rosten, 1961, p. 67).

It is of interest to note that within a few months after the study, 13 of Rosten's 30 subjects either had returned to heavy gambling, had started to drink excessively, or had not been heard from and were presumed to be gambling again.

Later studies strongly support the earlier findings of Rosten. They describe pathological gamblers as typically immature, rebellious, thrill-seeking, superstitious, and basically psychopathic (Bolen & Boyd, 1968; Bolen, Caldwell, & Boyd, 1975; Custer, 1982; and Graham, 1978a).

The most comprehensive study is that of Livingston (1974), who observed, interviewed, and tested 55 mostly working-class men who had joined Gamblers Anonymous to try to stop gambling. Livingston found that these men often referred to their "past immaturity" in explaining their habitual gambling. They also described themselves as having a "big ego" and acknowledged a strong need for recognition and adulation from others.

Although these men had usually been able to cover their losses early in their gambling careers, the course was downhill, leading to financial, marital, job, and often legal problems. Eventually things got so bad that it seemed the only way out of their difficulties was the way they got in—by gambling.

A more recent study by Graham (1978) compared the psychological test performance of pathological gamblers with that of alcoholics and heroin addicts. The three groups of addicts showed many similar characteristics. The individuals in each group were self-centered, narcissistic, tense, nervous, and anxious; they overreacted to stress and were pessimistic and brooding. They were characterized by acting-out, impulsive behavior; they had periodic outbursts of anger, were frustrated with their own lack of achievement, were reluctant to open up emotionally for fear of being hurt, often showed superficial remorse, and were passive-dependent and manipulative. They stated a desire to "turn over a new leaf" but showed a poor prognosis for behavior change in traditional therapy. These similarities suggest that common personality characteristics may be involved as predisposing factors in the three disorders.

Treatment and outcomes. Treatment of pathological gamblers is still a relatively unexplored area. However, Boyd and Bolen (1970) have reported on a study in which eight pathological gamblers and their spouses were treated together through group psychotherapy—an approach based on the finding that the pathological gambler's marital relationship is generally chaotic and turbulent, with the spouse frequently showing seriously maladaptive behavior patterns also. There was a complete cessation of gambling in three of these cases and a near cessation in the other five. The extent to which changes in the gamblers' marital relationships influenced the outcome of treatment can only be surmised—six of the eight couples showed a significant improvement. Other treatment approaches, including aversion therapy and covert sensitization (Cotler, 1971) and cognitive-behavioral therapy (Bannister, 1975) have been tried with individual cases, but further studies are needed before we can evaluate the potential effectiveness of psychotherapy in the treatment of this disorder.

Some pathological gamblers who want to change find help through membership in Gamblers Anonymous. This organization was founded in 1957 in Los Angeles by two pathological gamblers who found that they could help each other control their gambling by talking about their experiences. Since then, groups have been formed in most of the major cities in the United States. The groups are modeled after Alcoholics Anonymous, and they view those who gamble as personally responsible for their own actions. The only requirement for membership is an expressed desire to stop gambling. In group discussions, members share experiences and try to gain insight into the irrationality of their gambling and to realize its inevitable consequences. As with Alcoholics Anonymous, members try to help each other maintain control and prevent relapses. Unfortunately, only a small fraction of pathological gamblers find their way into Gamblers Anonymous. Of those who do, only about 1 in 10 manages to overcome the addiction to gambling (Strine, 1971).

A novel inpatient treatment program for pathological gamblers has been developed at the Brecksville, Ohio, Veterans' Administration Medical Center (1981). This program, initiated in 1972, has helped many individuals and has served as a model program for a number of other hospitals.

The Brecksville program for treatment of pathological gamblers, which lasts for a minimum of 28 days, is integrated into the Alcohol Treatment Program. Five inpatient beds in the 55-bed unit are set aside for pathological gamblers. Alcoholics and gamblers are housed together and share many common program elements because their problems are viewed as quite similar.

It may seem that inpatient hospital treatment for a "social" problem such as pathological gambling is an overly drastic and unwarranted measure. However, in a number of circumstances such measures seem necessary. For example, the gambler might be quite depressed or be experiencing severe panic or desperation and may present a possible suicide risk; or the individual may have allowed his or her health to deteriorate; or the individual's legal situation might require confinement; or in some areas of the country the individual may not have access to outpatient attention for his or her gambling behavior (e.g., there may not be a local chapter of Gamblers Anonymous).

The treatment goals for these pathological gamblers include abstinence from gambling, major life-style changes, participation in the programs of Gamblers Anonymous, and, since gambling behavior is viewed as "trivial" and of no social value, the acquirement of more adaptive forms of recreation.

A variety of treatment approaches are used during the individual's hospital stay: (a) the ward is managed according to strict rules of discipline, and any deviation from the rules may result in discharge from the hospital; (b) group therapy is provided; (c) workshops devoted to helping the resident learn more adaptive living skills are offered; (d) educational lectures related to the problems of gambling are given; (e) attendance at AA and Gamblers Anonymous meetings is required; and (f) the individual is expected to get involved in planned recreational activities.

Pathological gambling, as an addictive disorder, is on the increase in the United States. Furthermore, several state legislatures have recently passed liberalized gambling legislation to permit state-operated lotteries, horse racing, and gambling casinos in an effort to increase state tax

Gambling behaviors are encouraged in certain settings, such as this Las Vegas casino.

revenues. In the context of this apparent environmental support and "official" sanction for gambling, it is likely that pathological gambling will increase substantially as more and more individuals "try their luck." Given that pathological gamblers are resistant to treatment, it is likely, too, that our future efforts toward developing more effective preventive and treatment approaches will need to be increased as this problem continues to grow.

Summary

Addictive disorders—such as alcohol or drug abuse, extreme overeating, and pathological gambling—are among the most widespread and intransigent of mental health problems facing us today.

Alcohol and drug abuse problems can be viewed in the DSM-III system as substance-induced organic disorders or as substance-use disorders. Many problems of alcohol or drug use involve difficulties that stem solely from the intoxicating effects of the substances. Dependence occurs when an individual develops a tolerance for the substance or exhibits withdrawal symptoms when the substance is removed or is not available. Several psychoses related to alcoholism have been identified: pathological intoxication, delirium tremens, acute alcoholic hallucinosis, and Korsakoff's psychosis.

Drug abuse disorders may involve physiological dependence on substances such as the opiates—particularly heroin—or the barbiturates; however, psychological dependence may occur with any of the popular drugs that are commonly used today—for example, marijuana or cocaine.

A number of factors have been considered important in the etiology of alcoholism. Although the data are not conclusive, it appears that genetic factors may play some role in causing susceptibility, as may other biological factors such as metabolic rates and sensitivity toward alcoholism. Psychological factors such as psychological vulnerability, stress and the desire for tension reduction, and marital and other relationships are also seen as important elements in the etiology of alcohol-use disorders. However, the existence of an "alcoholic personality type" has been the subject of some controversy. Finally, sociocultural factors may predispose an individual to turn toward alcoholism.

Possible causal factors in drug abuse include the influence of peer groups, the existence of a so-called drug subculture, and the availability of drugs as tension reducers or as pain relievers. Some recent work on a possible physiological basis for drug abuse has been explored. The discovery of endorphins, morphine-like substances produced by the body, has raised speculation that there may be a biochemical basis to drug addiction.

Treatment of individuals who abuse alcohol or drugs is generally difficult and often has a poor outcome. Many reasons can be found for the poor prognosis: the problem situation may reflect a long history of psychological difficulties; interpersonal and marital distress may be involved; financial and legal problems may be present—and all such problems may be operating on an individual who denies that problems exist and is not motivated to work on them.

A number of approaches to the treatment of chronic alcoholism or drug abuse have been developed. Frequently the situation requires biological or medical measures—for example, medication to deal with problems of withdrawal and delerium tremens, or dietary evaluation and treatment for malnutrition. Psychological therapies such as group therapy and behavioral interventions may be effective with some alcoholic or drug-abusing individuals. Another source of help for alcoholics is widely available through the lay organization Alcoholics Anonymous; however, the extent of successful outcomes with this program has not been sufficiently studied.

Most treatment programs show high success rates in "curing" addictive problems but show lowered success rates at follow-up. Recent work in the area of relapse prevention has contributed new insights into the problem of maintenance of self-control once the addictive behaviors have been checked. Part of this approach involves making the individual aware of factors that can lead to relapse and preparing him or her to deal with this phenomenon.

Not all addictive disorders involve the use of substances such as alcohol or drugs. Some individuals eat to excess to the point of endangering their health or gamble to such an extent that they wreck their lives and damage or destroy their family relationships. These disorders, extreme obesity and pathological gambling, involve many of the same psychological mechanisms that seem to underly chronic alcoholism or drug addiction. Treatment approaches found to be effective for alcoholism and drug abuse appear to work about the same with obese clients and with pathological gamblers. Many of the same difficulties concerning response to treatment and relapse also plague treatment of obese individuals and compulsive gamblers.

Psychosexual disorders and variants

Aloïse, Le Manteau du Matador *(1948–50). Aloïse (1886–1964) was born in Lausanne to a family marked by mental disorder. As she grew to adulthood, she retreated more and more into a dream world of religious fanaticism and sexual fantasy, and showed signs of neglecting her personal appearance. At the age of 32, Aloïse was admitted to a psychiatric clinic, where she lapsed into a dull, autistic state. Her drawings characteristically exhibit strongly erotic content, often depicting full-bodied, desirable women and handsome young men (such as the "matador" at the center of this picture).*

At lower levels on the phylogenetic scale of animal life, reproductive processes are not sexual and seem to be essentially preprogrammed and more or less "automatic." The individuals of a species show very little individuality or variation in their reproductive functioning.

As we move up the scale, reproduction becomes sexual in nature, thus becoming more complicated in requiring the cooperation and mutual participation of two or more organisms having differentiated roles in the procreative process. By the time we reach the level of the higher animals, we see the reproductive process richly infused with elements of behavioral distinctiveness: individuals differ considerably in their sexual behavior and show selectivity in choosing mates. Sexual functioning also incorporates other behavioral characteristics, such as aggressiveness in the case of males.

This expansion of the repertoire of reproductive behavior continues up to the human level, but the gap between humankind and even the highest of the other animals is a huge one. It is paralleled only in the advantage humans enjoy in intellectual power by virtue of their possession of conceptual language.

Several dimensions of variation underlie this phylogenetic progression in reproductive behavior. The most important of these, for our concerns, is the increasing freedom from rigidly programmed, instinctual, stereotyped forms of sexual behavior as we move up the scale. The freedom of the human female from recurrent, biologically based cycles of "heat" and nonreceptivity is but one example of this enhanced flexibility and independence from controlling neurobiological mechanisms. Of perhaps even greater importance is the enormously increased adaptability in human sexual needs themselves, as a result of their partial disengagement from their primary biological base. With a loosened connection between sex and procreation at the human level, sexual behavior is no longer simply the expression of instinct but has become at least as much a matter of *learned* patterns of attraction, activity, and consummation. To put it another way, human sexuality has to a large extent come under the control of "higher" neural processes.

These gains in flexibility and adaptability of the sexual functions have come at some cost. Nature is almost necessarily wise, at least in the

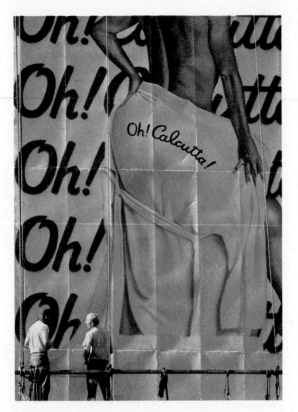

Our society constantly surrounds us with blatantly sexual images and messages, but gives us uncertain or contradictory guidance in defining appropriate sexual behavior.

long run; human cultures may or may not be. The varieties of human sexuality do indeed encompass an enormous range when compared with what is found for any species at a lower level, and much of the variation adds zest and richness to our lives, enhances our happiness, and intensifies our loves. But sexuality at the human level is also much more likely to go awry, causing profound misery for the individuals involved and for those close to them. This chapter is concerned with such "abnormalities" of human sexuality. They fall naturally into two distinct classes. The psychosexual dysfunctions involve inhibitions in sexual desire or problems with psychophysiological functioning in the sexual response cycle; premature ejaculation would be an example. The psychosexual variants or deviations include those forms of sexual behavior that fall outside the range of generally accepted heterosexual activity, such as exhibitionism. In our discussion, we make a further distinction

between *victimless* sexual variants and variants that involve *force* or *nonconsent*. It should be noted that not all forms of sexual "abnormality," especially those in which no one is victimized, are considered disorders requiring treatment or are seen as inevitably causing difficulties in one's personal life.

Human societies have generally exhibited a kind of "double vision" regarding sexual behavior: on the one hand, there is typically a rather elaborate code limiting sexual behavior and directing that sexual acts shall encompass only certain narrowly defined "proprieties," while on the other there is an informal expectation, mostly followed in practice, that these limits will be regularly and routinely exceeded by at least the more venturesome of the society's members. It is only in recent times, thanks in large part to the pioneering work of Kinsey and his associates (1948, 1953), that we have come to understand how widespread and extreme are the personal problems with sexuality and the deviations from formal propriety within our own culture.

Psychosexual dysfunctions

The term *psychosexual dysfunction* refers to impairment either in the desire for sexual gratification or in the ability to achieve it. With but few exceptions, such impairments occur in the absence of anatomical or physiological pathology and are based on faulty psychosexual adjustment and learning. They vary markedly in degree and, regardless of which partner is alleged to be dysfunctional, the enjoyment of sex by both parties in the relationship is typically adversely affected.

Like sexuality in general, sexual dysfunctions of one sort or another were until recently either ignored entirely by polite society or—if discussed at all—were the subject of turgid medical treatises written by authors who were usually as ill-informed and prejudiced as their readers. Then, with the popularization of Freud, there came an era in which all such difficulties in sexual functioning (and some that were not even "difficulties" in the normally accepted sense) were ascribed to unconscious conflicts of childhood origin—requiring years of psychoanalytic treatment for their resolution. We now know, thanks again to courageous work—chiefly by Masters and Johnson (1966, 1970, 1975)—that the common sexual dysfunctions are both more numerous and considerably less complex and mysterious than had once been believed. We shall first describe several of the most common ones and then discuss issues of causation and treatment.

Dysfunctions affecting the male

Here we shall briefly discuss several dysfunctions that may affect the male: erectile insufficiency, premature ejaculation, retarded ejaculation, and ejaculatory incompetence.

Erectile insufficiency.   Inability to achieve or maintain an erection sufficient for successful sexual intercourse—formerly known as *impotence*—is known clinically as *erectile insufficiency*. In *primary insufficiency*, the male has *never* been able to sustain an erection long enough to accomplish a satisfactory duration of penetration—usually defined as including intravaginal ejaculation. In *secondary insufficiency*, the male has had a history of at least one successful attempt at coitus but is presently unable to produce or maintain the required level of penile rigidity. Primary insufficiency is a relatively rare disorder, but it has been estimated that half or more of the male population has experienced the secondary variety on at least a temporary basis, especially in the early years of sexual exploration.

Prolonged or permanent erectile insufficiency before the age of 60 is relatively rare and is often due to psychological factors. In fact, according to the findings of Kinsey and his associates, only about one fourth of males become impotent by the age of 70 and even here many cases are due to psychological factors. More recent studies have indicated that men and women in their 80s and 90s are quite capable of enjoying sex (Burros, 1974; Kaplan, 1975; Masters & Johnson, 1975). To the degree that men do experience difficulties in their later years, it appears that in some cases they may simply be complying with the societal expectation of declining performance (Tollison & Adams, 1979).

Of course, some cases of erectile insufficiency, estimated to be on the order of 15 percent (Kaplan, 1975), *are* caused by organic or medical conditions. These can be quite varied and can include certain types of vascular disease, diabetes, neurological disorders, kidney failure, hormonal irregularities, and excess blood levels of certain drugs, including alcohol (Wagner & Green, 1981). Distinguishing between psychogenic and organically caused insufficiency for diagnostic purposes is at best a complicated process. The normal male has several erections per night, associated with periods of REM ("rapid eye movement") sleep. It has been suggested that organically based insufficiency can be distinguished from psychogenic on the basis of an absence of these nocturnal erections. However, it now appears that many other factors must also be evaluated in order to establish a proper diagnosis (Wagner, 1981).

Premature ejaculation.   Often psychologically related to erectile insufficiency, premature ejaculation refers to an unsatisfactorily brief period between the commencement of sexual stimulation and the occurrence of ejaculation, the most serious result being the failure of the female partner to achieve satisfaction. Exact definition of prematurity is not possible, however, because of pronounced variations in both the likelihood and the latency of female orgasm in sexual intercourse. LoPiccolo (1978) suggests that an inability to tolerate as much as four minutes of stimulation without ejaculation is a reasonable indicator that the male may be in need of sex therapy. This suggested guideline is subject to numerous qualifications, however, including the age of the client—the alleged "quick trigger" of the younger male being more than a mere myth.

Retarded ejaculation or ejaculatory incompetence.   It is of some interest that, while problems of female orgasmic dysfunction have received wide attention in the popular press, one rarely hears public mention of the corollary problem in males. It is as though there were a conspiracy of silence concerning the matter. As a result many males suffering from late ejaculation or inability to ejaculate during intercourse are condemned to worry needlessly about their supposedly unique defect, a type of worry likely to worsen the problem. In fact, relatively few cases of ejaculatory retardation or incompetence are seen by sex therapists, but our own clinical experience suggests that the problem is much more widespread than this observation would seem to indicate, a conclusion shared by Kaplan (1974). It appears that many men are too embarrassed by the problem even to contemplate therapy for it. It is of interest that many men having difficulty ejaculating intravaginally can nevertheless achieve orgasm by other means of stimulation (Tollison & Adams, 1979).

Dysfunctions affecting the female

Somewhat paralleling the male sexual dysfunctions are arousal insufficiency, orgasmic dysfunction, vaginismus, and dyspareunia in women.

Arousal insufficiency. This dysfunction, formerly and somewhat pejoratively referred to as *frigidity,* is in many ways the female counterpart of erectile insufficiency (the DSM-III lists both as "Inhibited sexual excitement"). Not uncommonly, it is accompanied by complaints of an absence of sexual feelings and of being unresponsive to most or all forms of erotic stimulation. Its chief physical manifestation is a failure to produce the characteristic lubrication of the vulva and vaginal tissues during sexual stimulation, a condition that may make intercourse quite uncomfortable.

Orgasmic dysfunction. Many women who are readily sexually excitable and who otherwise enjoy sexual activity nevertheless experience greater or lesser difficulty in achieving orgasm. Of these women, many do not routinely experience orgasm during sexual intercourse without direct stimulation of the clitoris; indeed this pattern is so common that it can hardly be considered dysfunctional. A small proportion of women are able to achieve orgasm *only* through direct mechanical stimulation of the clitoris. Even fewer are unable to have the experience under any known conditions of stimulation; the latter condition is called *primary orgasmic dysfunction,* analogous to primary erectile insuffi-

ciency in the male. The diagnosis of orgasmic dysfunction is complicated by the fact that the subjective quality of orgasm varies widely among females and within the same female from time to time, making precise evaluations of occurrence and quality difficult (Singer & Singer, 1978).

Vaginismus. An involuntary spasm of the muscles at the entrance to the vagina that prevents penetration and sexual intercourse is called *vaginismus.* In some cases, women who suffer from vaginismus also have arousal insufficiency, possibly as a result of conditioned fears associated with a traumatic rape experience; in other cases, however, they are sexually responsive, but are still afflicted with this disorder. This form of sexual dysfunction is relatively rare, but, when it occurs, it is likely to be extremely distressing for both the affected woman and her partner (Tollison & Adams, 1979).

Dyspareunia. *Dyspareunia* means *painful coitus;* it can occur in the male but is far more common in the female. This is the form of sexual dysfunction most likely to have an organic basis—for example, in association with infections or structural pathology of the sex organs. However, it often has a psychological basis, as in the case of women who have an aversion to sexual intercourse. Understandably, it is often associated with vaginismus. This form of sexual dysfunction is also rare.

Inhibited sexual desire. Inhibited sexual desire, as distinguished from inhibited sexual excitement (male erectile insufficiency or female arousal insufficiency), is a dysfunction in which either a man or a woman shows little or no sexual drive or interest. As the term implies, it is assumed that the biological basis of the sex drive remains unimpaired, but that for some reason sexual motivation is blocked. These people usually come to the attention of clinicians only at the behest of their partners, who typically complain of an insufficient frequency of sexual interaction. The latter fact exposes one problem with this diagnosis, because it is known that preferences for frequency of sexual contact vary widely among otherwise "normal" individuals of both sexes. Who is to decide what is "not enough?"

Nevertheless, there do appear to be some people who are almost totally lacking in an interest in sex. In extreme cases, sex actually becomes psychologically aversive. Formerly considered rare and largely limited to females, inhibited sexual desire has in recent years become a fairly common diagnosis and is applied relatively frequently to males. Doubtless this change is due at least in part to changing role expectations, of which more will be said below.

Causal factors in sexual dysfunctions

Both sexual desire and genital functioning may be affected by a wide range of organic conditions including injuries to the genitals, disease, fatigue, excessive alcohol consumption, and abuse of certain drugs, including tranquilizers. Most cases of sexual dysfunction, however, seem traceable to psychosocial rather than physical causes. Although specific causal factors vary considerably from one type of sexual dysfunction to another, the following psychosocial factors are commonly found.

Early experiences may shape our ideas and expectations about sex, perhaps determining patterns of later sexual behavior.

Faulty learning. In some nonindustrialized societies, older members of the group instruct younger members in sexual techniques before marriage. But in our society, though we recognize that sexual behavior is an important aspect of marriage, the learning of sexual techniques and attitudes is too often left to chance. The result is that many young people start out with faulty expectations and a lack of needed information or harmful misinformation that can impair their sexual adequacy. In fact, Kaplan (1974) has concluded that couples with sexual problems are typically practicing insensitive, incompetent, and ineffective sexual techniques; this conclusion would be readily endorsed by most investigators in the field (LoPiccolo & LoPiccolo, 1978; Tollison & Adams, 1979).

In our society many people, but perhaps especially females, have been subjected to early training that depicted sexual relations as lustful, dirty, and evil. The attitudes and inhibitions thus established can lead to a great deal of anxiety, conflict, and guilt about sexual relations, whether in or out of marriage. Faulty early conditioning may also have taken the form of indoc-

trination in the idea that the woman has a primary responsibility to satisfy the man sexually— and therefore to suppress her own needs and feelings. Masters and Johnson (1970) consider such faulty learning to be the primary cause of orgasmic dysfunction in females. In vaginismus a somewhat different conditioning patterning has occurred, leading the female to associate vaginal penetration with pain—either physical, psychological, or both. This defensive reflex comes into operation when penetration is attempted by the sexual partner (Kaplan, 1975).

Although males may also be subjected to early training emphasizing the evils of sex, such training apparently is a far less important factor for them. However, another type of faulty early conditioning was found by Masters and Johnson (1970) to be a key factor in premature ejaculation in males: a first sex experience with a prostitute or in a lovers' lane parking place or some other situation in which hurried ejaculation was necessary. Apparently, once this pattern was established, the individual has been unable to break the conditioned response. In other instances, initial difficulties in sexual functioning have led to conditioned anxieties which in turn have impaired subsequent performance. We shall elaborate on this point in the section that follows.

Feelings of fear, anxiety, and inadequacy. In a study of 49 adult males with an erectile disorder, Cooper (1969) found anxiety to be a contributing factor in 94 percent of the cases and the primary problem for those whose erectile problems had started early. Similarly, Kaplan (1974) has concluded from her studies that "a man who suffers from impotence is often almost unbearably anxious, frustrated, and humiliated by his inability to produce or maintain an erection" (p. 80). Males who suffer from premature ejaculation may also experience acute feelings of inadequacy—and often feelings of guilt as well—stemming from their lack of control and inability to satisfy their sexual partner via intercourse.

Females may also feel fearful and inadequate in sexual relations. A woman may be uncertain whether her partner finds her sexually attractive, and this may lead to anxiety and tension that interfere with her sexual enjoyment. Or she may feel inadequate because she is unable to have an orgasm or does so infrequently. Sometimes a woman who is not climaxing will pretend to have orgasms in order to make her sexual partner feel that his performance is fully adequate. The longer a woman maintains such a pretense, however, the more likely she is to become confused and frustrated; in addition, she is likely to feel resentful toward her partner for being so insensitive to her real feelings and needs. This, in turn, only adds to her sexual problems.

From a more general viewpoint, Masters and Johnson (1975) have concluded that most sexual dysfunctions are due to crippling fears, attitudes, and inhibitions concerning sexual behavior, often based on faulty early learning and then exacerbated by later aversive experiences. All this may lead to the adoption of a "spectator role" in sexual relations, rendering wholehearted participation impossible.

Interpersonal problems. Interpersonal problems may cause a number of psychosexual dysfunctions. Lack of emotional closeness can lead to erectile or orgasmic problems. The individual may be in love with someone else, may find his or her sexual partner physically or psychologically repulsive, or may have hostile and antagonistic feelings as a result of prior misunderstandings, quarrels, and conflicts. A one-sided interpersonal relationship—in which one partner does most of the giving and the other most of the receiving—can lead to feelings of insecurity and resentment with resulting impairment in sexual performance (Friedman, 1974; Lobitz & Lobitz, 1978; Simon, 1975).

For the female, lack of emotional closeness often appears to result from intercourse with a partner who is a "sexual moron"—rough, unduly hasty, and concerned only with his own gratification. As Kaplan (1974) has pointed out,

"Some persons have as much difficulty giving pleasure as others do in receiving it. These individuals don't provide their partners with enough sexual stimulation because they lack either the knowledge and sensitivity to know what to do, or they are anxious about doing it." (p. 78)

In other instances the individual may be hostile toward and not want to please his or her sexual partner. This seems to occur rather frequently in unhappy and failing marital or other intimate relationships in which channels of communication have largely broken down and sexual relations continue as a sort of habit or duty or simply to gratify one's own sexual needs.

Many investigators feel that an individual should be able to experience pleasure and orgasm with any personally acceptable partner, providing, of course, that the individual has no emotional commitment to some other person. However, Switzer (1974) has aptly pointed to a generally agreed-on conclusion: "Orgasm has especially delightful overtones when you're with a person whom you love and when you can abandon yourself" (p.36).

Changing male-female roles and relationships. There was an increase in erectile problems during the 1970s which a number of investigators have related to two phenomena during that period: (a) the increasing changes being achieved by the women's movement in our society, and (b) the growing awareness of female sexuality (Burros, 1974). These trends have led women to want and expect more from their lives, including their sexual relationships. Women are no longer accepting the older concept of being the passive partner in sex, and many are taking a more aggressive and active role in sexual relations.

This new role appears to threaten the image many men have of themselves as the supposedly "dominant" partner who takes the initiative in sexual relations (Steinmann & Fox, 1974). In fact, some men appear to regard sexually assertive women who play an active role in sex as "castrating females" (Kaplan, 1974). In addition, the greater assertiveness and expectancy of women makes many men feel that they are under pressure to perform. As Ginsberg, Frosch, and Shapiro (1972) have expressed it,

"This challenge to manhood is most apparent in a sexually liberated society where women are not merely available but are perceived as demanding satisfaction from masculine performance." (p 219).

The result may be not only impaired male performance but even erectile failure.

Changing male-female roles in sexual relationships also place greater demands on the female. The expectation of taking an active rather than a passive role may cause the female to make unrealistic demands on her own sexual responsiveness—such as expecting to have a highly pleasurable orgasm each time she engages in sexual relations. Such demands are likely to lead to some degree of unfulfilled aspirations, confusion, and self-devaluation, which in turn impair her actual sexual performance. This seems especially true when the female assumes a "spectator's role" and almost literally monitors her own sexual performance—thus depriving it of spontaneity and naturalness.

Treatment and outcomes

The treatment of sexual dysfunctions has undergone nothing less than a revolution during only the past few years. Once regarded as very difficult and intractable therapeutic challenges, most instances of sexual dysfunction now yield quite readily to programs of treatment involving new techniques that are still being developed and improved (Anderson, 1983; Leiblum & Pervin, 1980; LoPiccolo & LoPiccolo, 1978; Tollison & Adams, 1979). As a result, success rates approaching 90 percent or more for many dysfunctions have become quite routine.

The turning point is uniformly considered to be the publication in 1970 of Masters and Johnson's *Human Sexual Inadequacy*, the product of an eleven-year search to develop truly effective treatment procedures for the common dysfunctions, both male and female. The success rates claimed by this team of dedicated clinical researchers astonished the professional community and rapidly led to the widespread adoption of their general approach, which combines elements of traditional and behavioral therapy in a framework emphasizing direct intervention aimed at the dysfunction itself (see **HIGHLIGHT** on page 456).

While the early confidence inspired by Masters and Johnson's reported results has waned somewhat in the interim (Leiblum & Pervin, 1980; Vandereycken, 1982; Zilbergeld & Evans, 1980), their work has unquestionably unleashed a groundswell of new therapeutic techniques. Despite differences in emphasis and methods in different treatment programs, there seems to be general agreement on the importance of removing crippling misconceptions, inhibitions, and fears, and fostering attitudes toward and participation in sexual behavior as a pleasurable, natural, and meaningful experience.

Because of the manner in which sexual dysfunctions are presented and described by those suffering from them, it is easy to lose sight of a crucial issue emphasized by Masters and Johnson and by virtually all those who have followed in their footsteps. That is, sexual dysfunctions are *not* normally disorders of individuals, but rather of relationships between individuals. Thus, the new treatments for sexual dysfunction typically involve *both* parties to the relationship in which the disorder manifests itself, confirming in part the old adage that there are no "frigid" women apart from inept or clumsy men. J. LoPiccolo (1978) puts it this way:

"It must be stressed that all sexual dysfunctions are *shared disorders*; that is, the husband of an inorgasmic woman is partially responsible for creating or maintaining her dysfunction, and he is also a patient in need of help. Regardless of the cause of the dysfunction, both partners are responsible for future change and the solution of their problems." (p.3)

With competent treatment, success rates vary between 60 and 100 percent, depending in part on the individual or couple and on the nature of

HIGHLIGHT

Treatment of sexual dysfunction

Masters and Johnson, widely known for their studies of sexual response and their therapeutic approach to problems of sexual dysfunction, are pictured counseling a couple at their clinic in St. Louis—the Reproductive Biology Research Foundation. These investigators have concluded from their research efforts (1970) that some 50 percent of American marriages suffer from sexual dysfunction, a factor they consider largely responsible for our high divorce rate. In their view, sexual dysfunction is a form of faulty communication which probably extends to other areas of a couple's relationships as well; consequently, their treatment program is oriented toward improving communication in a marriage and preventing it from being wrecked by ignorance and faulty attitudes about sex.

Stressing the concept that sex is an experience that both partners must enter into without reservation or shame, Masters and Johnson insist that fears or anxieties that either partner may have concerning intercourse—pressures that can turn it into a dreaded "command performance"—must be eliminated. In addition, they treat the married couple as a unit rather than as separate individuals.

Generally, the following steps appear to be basic to the treatment program of Masters and Johnson as well as to that of other prominent sex clinicians: (a) a thorough medical examination to rule out the possibility of organic causes of the sexual dysfunction;

(b) *sensate focus*—learning to experience pleasure in caressing each other's bodies and genitals while temporarily abstaining from intercourse; and (c) prescribed sexual experiences and therapy sessions. Beyond these basic principles, the formats employed by various major sex clinics vary considerably.

For the majority of couples participating in Masters and Johnson's treatment program, it appears that a change is effected in attitudes, feelings, and communication, and that sexual relations become an intimate, normal, and desirable experience. Five-year follow-up studies of 510 married couples and 57 unmarried men and women revealed that the program's rate of failure varied markedly with the type of sexual inadequacy—from zero for cases of vaginismus and 2.2 percent for cases of premature ejaculation to 40.6 percent for cases of primary ejaculatory insufficiency. Overall, the failure rate in treatment was only 20 percent.

Some researchers (e.g., Zilbergeld & Evans, 1980) have questioned the high rates of success reported by Masters and Johnson, and these rates have been, in fact, difficult to replicate (Leiblum & Pervin, 1980). It may be, however, that sex clinicians are now seeing more intractable types of dysfunctions. Widespread self-help efforts, supported by a host of readily available popular publications, are probably having some success with difficulties in the milder ranges.

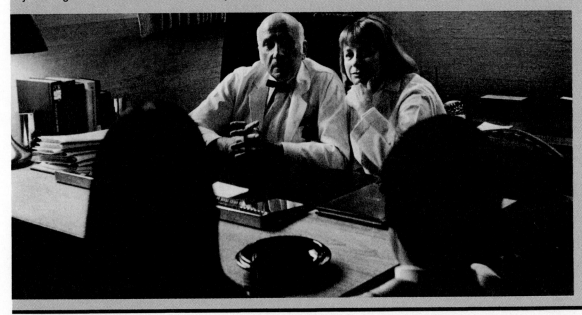

the problem. For example, Masters and Johnson (1970) and Kaplan (1975) have reported success rates approaching 100 percent in the treatment of premature ejaculation and vaginismus, but considerably lower rates in the treatment of male erectile and female organismic dysfunctions. Even in this latter area, however, there have been signs of success; a recent review by Anderson (1983) indicates that the overall outlook on treatment of primary orgasmic dysfunction in women is quite encouraging. The term "competent treatment" should be stressed here, since there are several thousand sex clinics in the United States, and the quality of treatment may range from sophisticated psychotherapy to sheer charlatanism. Indications are strong, in fact, that unqualified practitioners have entered this field in abundance in recent years, often charging astronomical fees for their inexpert services.

Psychosexual variants and deviations

Our view of ourselves as male or female, the social demands made upon us for playing our expected sexual role, our concept of what sexual behavior is appropriate, and our anticipation of what will be exciting and pleasurable—all these are for the most part learned, and they help determine the sexual practices we develop as adults. And through conditioning, almost any object or situation can become sexually stimulating—particularly among preadolescents and adolescents—including erotic literature, sex scenes in plays and films, pictures of nude or partially nude individuals, and underclothing or other objects intimately associated with members of the opposite sex. Sexual arousal may also accompany strong emotional reactions—such as fear and excitement—especially if associated with the performance of some forbidden act.

Given the many channels that human sexual interest may take, especially when for some reason the usual patterning has become blocked, it is hardly surprising that many persons find their principal sexual satisfactions in practices outside the range of what is considered acceptable in the

given culture. The sexual drive is normally sufficiently powerful to override all but the most severe social sanctions; thus we see variant sexual needs frequently erupting into variant sexual behavior.

Variant sexual behavior is behavior in which satisfaction is dependent primarily on something other than a mutually desired sexual engagement with a sexually mature member of the opposite gender. So defined, the domain encompasses a vast array of preference patterns in which the psychosexual development of the affected individual has for some reason deviated from the standard, to-be-expected adult heterosexual course.

The specter of these *psychosexual variants* seems peculiarly threatening to many people in our society, and expressions of tolerance for such behavior as homosexuality, for example, can arouse intense emotion. It is certainly true that some forms of sexual variation, such as rape and child molestation, are contrary to the welfare of society and its members. Other forms, however, are generally victimless and thus constitute no obvious, rationally based threat to the public order. For this reason, we make a distinction between *victimless* sexual variants—in which the acts involved do not seriously infringe on the rights of noninvolved others and/or are engaged in by mutually consenting adults and are nonharmful to the partners—and sexual deviations that involve nonconsent or assault. In the former category we would place gender identity disorders, uncomplicated male and female homosexuality, most cases of fetishism, and transvestism. The more problematic of the sexual variants, from the standpoint of the welfare of society, include voyeurism, exhibitionism, sexual sadism and masochism, pedophelia, incest, and rape. In most jurisdictions, laws against acts in the latter category not only exist but are actively enforced, and rightly so.

A key point—one particularly emphasized by Adams and Chiodo (1983) and by Barlow (1974)—deserves mention at the outset. In considering these behaviors, we tend to focus our attention on the variant arousal patterns themselves to the exclusion of other, perhaps equally important factors that may help cause or maintain the variant behavior. Other factors that must often be given equal weight in most forms of variant sexuality are (a) the absence of a normal level of arousal to adults of the opposite sex; (b) significant deficits in the social skills normally needed for successful adult heterosexual relationships; and (c) failure to establish a firm psychological gender identity.

A good illustration of the importance of this broadened view for both understanding and therapy is provided in findings of several studies on therapy for homosexual individuals who wanted to change their arousal pattern. Adams and Sturgis (1977), reviewing the evidence, concluded that multiple-target treatment procedures aimed at the three factors mentioned above plus the variant arousal pattern greatly enhanced the likelihood of success of sexual reorientation therapy, as compared with approaches focused only on suppression of the variant sexual arousal pattern.

Gender identity: problems and disorder

As has just been noted, a frequent characteristic among individuals manifesting sexually variant behavior is a degree of confusion, uncertainty, or amorphousness in their concepts of themselves as male or female. This is seen most obviously in cases of *gender identity disorder (transsexualism)* and in some cases of transvestism (dressing in the clothes of the opposite sex) and homosexuality. But even where outward behavior appears to conform to societal norms, many persons will prove on careful assessment to have unclear or unstable gender identities and/or to lack an appropriate repertoire of gender-role behaviors (Adams & Chiodo, 1984).

Formation of gender identity.   The formation of gender identity and the acquisition of culturally prescribed gender-role behaviors are obviously matters of great complexity, and our understanding of the processes involved is limited. Research by Money and colleagues (1980; Money & Ehrhardt, 1972), among others, has established that outcomes in this area are powerfully determined by learning—that is, by adaptation to a host of psychosocial forces that are normally quite effective in "shaping up" the person to be psychosocially male or female. But of course differing social environments will on occasion produce blends or blurrings of the cultural concepts of maleness and femaleness, and

the impact of these environments on the developing child will likely be very strong. Many of the most functional men and women in our society seem to have highly developed masculine *and* feminine traits. Conversely, many of the least functional lack a strong identification with *either* side of this traditional behavioral dichotomy and appear confused or "amorphous" with respect to psychosocial gender (Spence & Helmreich, 1978). It seems reasonable to assume that both of these groups contribute disproportionately to the incidence of sexually variant behavior. By the same token, we might assume that those few individuals who become transsexual have strongly masculine or feminine orientations that are discrepant with their anatomical sex. Unfortunately, research data on these issues is largely lacking.

While psychosocial influences seem paramount in determining gender identity and role, there is mounting evidence from both human and animal studies that biological factors are also importantly involved, both generally and in respect to specific preferences for differing forms of sexual expression and satisfaction (Bell, Weinberg, & Hammersmith, 1981; Ehrhardt & Meyer-Bahlburg, 1981; MacLusky & Naftolin, 1981; Money, 1980; Rubin, Reinisch, & Haskett, 1981). Considering the incidence of sexually variant behavior such as transsexualism or homosexuality in the light of a historically strong societal rejection of it, such findings afford us a potentially valuable insight into why some individuals remain strongly driven to adopt the variant behavior despite the vigorous condemnation it often inspires. It may in fact be that they have little choice in the matter. (see the **HIGHLIGHT** on page 459).

This apparent absence of choice seems especially true of gender identity disorders, as defined in the DSM-III, which recognizes separate adult and childhood forms of a profound rejection of one's anatomical sex. In virtually all instances, individuals with this disorder feel themselves to be the victims of some grotesque error of fate in being forced to occupy a body that is alien to their gender-related sense of self. Very often, this anatomically discrepant gender identity is accompanied by role behaviors and dress that affirm the desired identity, and, in sexually active adults, by a "homosexual" orientation and partner choice. Many of these individuals feel

HIGHLIGHT

Transsexualism and a tangled relationship

After a lengthy courtship, Bob and Mae Sylvester married in 1972, Mae having concluded that Bob had overcome, through therapy, his wish to dress in women's clothing. Bob knew better, but was so attached to Mae that he tried to tell himself he was "cured" of his transvestism. After a brief period, the urge to cross-dress became so strong that Bob told Mae he wished occasionally to wear women's clothing at home. Mae responded by telling him it made her "physically sick" to see him dress in that manner. Nevertheless, on the advice of a second therapist, Bob resumed regular cross-dressing—but never in Mae's presence. At about this time, Bob successfully ran for election to the St. Paul, Minnesota, city council. During a term of four years as a member of this body, Bob distinguished himself as an effective and dynamic leader.

Meanwhile, Bob and Mae tried, with essentially no success, to establish a satisfactory sexual relationship. Both agree that their sex life was a disaster. Their relationship was strained further with the emergence of Bob's second identity, an adolescent girl named Susan. Susan was petulant and demanding, and Mae resented the maternal role into which she was now cast. As Susan developed, she wanted more and more "time" and resisted being Bob for an evening at home. Susan demanded, and got, an adolescent girl's bedroom, decorated in pink and mauve with birds, flowers, ribbons, and a pink canopy over the bed. This was apparently the last straw for Mae, and shortly thereafter, in 1981, the couple separated. Bob could not bear to lose the bedroom, so Mae moved out.

Bob had been aware since childhood of his wish to be female. A life-threatening event in February 1982 brought home to him forcefully his wish "just once" to make love as a woman. The next week he initiated procedures to undergo a sex change. On March 28, Bob legally became Susan Elizabeth Kimberly. Surgery to provide her with female genitalia is scheduled for 1984. Ms. Kimberly has transformed her social identity exclusively to that of a woman.

Mae Sylvester's initial reaction to these events was similar to grieving—indeed, for her, her husband Bob *has* died. Nevertheless, she now maintains an active friendship with Susan Kimberly. The two continue to see each other and to share the activities both had enjoyed before the divorce and Susan's reversal of gender identity. Mae says that Susan has retained many of the qualities she had found attractive in Bob.

Based on *Minneapolis Tribune*, May 1, 1983, pp. 1A, 4A–6A.

driven to seek and submit to surgical and endocrinological interventions that hold some promise of bringing them anatomically closer to their gender identity—a venture that is much more likely to have a satisfactory outcome if the desired conversion is male-to-female rather than the opposite. In children, the disorder may be accompanied by stubborn, irrational beliefs that their anatomy will undergo future changes in the desired direction.

Gender identity disorder is quite rare. Its incidence in males is estimated to be somewhat less than 3 per 100,000 and in females just under 1 per 100,000 (Walinder, 1968). These figures do not include children, who typically manifest the disorder before the age of four, and many of whom yield to pressures and adopt sex-appropriate behavior; the few who do not become adult transsexuals (Adams & Chiodo, 1984).

While the hypothesis of biological causation seems plausible to us, it is also possible that reverse-gender identity and behavior could be learned. Green (1974) has noted certain psychosocial factors that appear to be common in the backgrounds of transsexual boys, among them parental indifference to or encouragement of feminine behavior during the first year, maternal overprotection and domination, dressing of the child in female clothes by a female family member, and a lack of male friends in the early years. Obviously, some of these factors could be secondary to the child's displaying effeminate behavior from an early age and hence are not inconsistent with a biological hypothesis.

Gender identity changes. Efforts to alter gender identity by means of behavior therapy and other psychotherapeutic procedures have generally proven unsuccessful. As a consequence, transsexuals who feel a complete inability to accept their sex identity have requested surgical sex change in increasing numbers during recent years.

The first transsexual operation is said to have been performed by F. Z. Abraham in the 1930s. While occasional reports of similar operations were forthcoming for the next two decades, it was not until 1953, when Hamburger reported the case of Christine Jorgensen, that surgical sex change became well known. Johns Hopkins Hospital and the University of Minnesota Hospital were among the first in this country to give official support to sex-change surgery; each has since received thousands of requests from individuals for evaluation and management of their cases.

In males, modern surgical procedures accomplish sex conversion through removal of male organs and their replacement with an artfully designed vagina that apparently works satisfactorily in many cases, even enabling the individual, now a woman, to achieve coital orgasm. Weekly injections of sex hormones stimulate breast development, give more feminine texture to the skin, and also lessen beard growth, though electrolysis is usually needed to remove excess hair. Surgery for female transsexuals generally has been less successful, for although surgeons can remove the breasts, ovaries, vagina, and uterus, and can insert a penis constructed from rib cartilage or plastic, the penis does not function normally. Transplants of reproductive organs are not yet possible in either males or females, and the individual will be sterile after surgery.

Various evaluative studies of the outcome of such operations have been reported. One of the best known early studies is that of Benjamin (1966). This investigator questioned 50 transsexuals who had crossed the sex line from male to female. Their ages at the time of surgery ranged from 19 to 58, with an average age of 32. Of these subjects, 44 reported contentment sexually and socially with their new roles as women; 5 complained either about their ability to perform sexually or about their appearance; and 1 was totally dissatisfied with the results. In another study, Pauly (1968) reviewed the postoperative course of 121 male transsexuals who had received sex-reassignment surgery, and found that satisfactory outcomes outnumbered unsatisfactory ones at a ratio of 10 to 1. He also reported previous unsuccessful attempts by psychotherapy to help these patients achieve male-gender identity. Comparable results have been reported in later studies (Green, 1974).

There has been considerable controversy about sex-conversion surgery, however, and many physicians, as well as other professional persons, remain opposed to the operation. Newman and Stoller (1974) have pointed out that occasionally schizophrenics and other mentally disturbed individuals seek sexual reassignment, but that their desire is only transitory. For this and related reasons, it is recommended that those considering sex-reassignment surgery undergo a trial period first during which they receive hormone therapy and live in the new role to get a clearer understanding of the many psychological and social adjustments that will be required. In general, it would appear that stricter criteria are needed for selecting surgical reassignees (Lothstein, 1982).

The paraphilias

The *paraphilias* are a group of persistent sexual arousal patterns in which unusual objects, rituals, or situations are required for full sexual satisfaction to occur. While mild forms of these activities probably have occurred in the lives of many otherwise normal persons, the paraphiliac is distinguished by the insistence and relative exclusivity with which his or her sexuality focuses on the acts in question—without which orgasm is often not possible. Paraphiliac individuals may or may not have a persistent desire to change their sexual orientations. The DSM-III recognizes nine paraphilias: transvestism, fetishism, voyeurism, exhibitionism, sexual sadism, sexual masochism, pedophilia, zoophilia (sexual attraction to animals), and (of course) atypical paraphilia. Of these, we will discuss all but zoophilia (a relatively rare disorder) and the atypical varieties.

Transvestism. *Transvestism* involves the achievement of sexual excitation by "cross-dress-

Transsexual James Morris, an English writer and mountain climber, resolved the conflict between biological and perceived sex through a sex-change operation. Now Jan Morris, she has written a book entitled Conundrum *describing the transformation.*

ing," that is, dressing as a member of the opposite sex. It is an uncommon condition in which the individual, usually a male, enjoys excursions into the social role of the other sex. Although a male transvestite, for example, regards himself as a man when dressed as a man, he may have feelings of being a woman when dressed in women's clothing. A medical researcher and transvestite himself for 35 years expressed it this way: "The transvestite finds that he is both a 'he' and a 'she' together—at the same time or alternating from one to the other when opportunity permits or desire compels" (*Los Angeles Times*, September 30, 1973). Since transvestism does not directly involve anyone but the cross-dressing individual, it can be considered a victimless sexual variant.

Very little is known about transvestism. Most reports are based on studies of single cases, and most of those studied have been in therapy, which may make them an unrepresentative group. However, Buckner (1970) has formulated a description of the "ordinary" male transvestite from a survey of 262 transvestites conducted by the magazine *Transvestia.*

"He is probably married (about two thirds are); if he is married he probably has children (about two thirds do). Almost all of these transvestites said they were exclusively heterosexual—in fact, the rate of 'homosexuality' was less than the average for the entire population. The transvestic behavior generally consists of privately dressing in the clothes of a woman, at home, in secret. . . . The transvestite generally does not run into trouble with the law. His cross-dressing causes difficulties for very few people besides himself and his wife." (p. 381).

The most extensive studies to date of the personalities of male transvestites are those of Bentler and Prince (1969, 1970) and Bentler, Shearman, and Prince (1970). These investigators obtained replies to a standardized psychological inventory from a large sample of transvestites through the cooperation of a national transvestite organization. The transvestites, compared to matched control groups, showed no gross differences on neurotic or psychotic scales. However, they did present themselves as being more controlled in impulse expression, less involved with other individuals, more inhibited in interpersonal relationships, and more dependent.

Interestingly, it appears that cross-dressing may reduce the strength of some of these tendencies. Gosslin and Eysenck (1980) asked male transvestites to take a personality test while functioning in regular male clothing and while cross-dressed. "Neuroticism" and "introversion" both declined in the cross-dressed condition. This finding was consistent with subjects' reports of less anxiety and shyness when in their female roles.

It would appear that much transvestism can be explained in terms of a simple conditioning model. A male child may receive attention from females in the family who think it is cute for him to dress in feminine attire and hence reinforce this behavior with attention and praise. Such a conditioning process is well portrayed in the case of an adult transvestite studied by Stoller (1974):

"I have pictures of myself dressed as a little girl when I was a small child. My mother thought it was cute. She was right. I was a pretty little girl.

"The highlights of my life as a girl came when I was between the ages of 10 and 17. I had an aunt who was childless and wanted to take me through the steps from childhood to young womanhood. She knew of my desires to be a girl. I would spend every summer at her ranch. The first thing she would do was to give me a pixie haircut, which always turned out pretty good since I would avoid getting a haircut for two months before I went to her ranch. She then would take me into the bedroom and show me all my pretty new things she had bought me. The next day, dressed as a girl, I would accompany her to town and we would shop for a new dress for me. To everyone she met, she would introduce me as her 'niece.'

"This went on every year until I was 13 years old. Then she decided I should start my womanhood. I will never forget that summer. When I arrived I got the same pixie haircut as usual but when we went into the bedroom there laid out on the bed was a girdle, a garter belt and bra, size 32AA, and my first pair of nylons. She then took me over to the new dressing table she had bought me and slid back the top to reveal my very own makeup kit. I was thrilled to death. She said she wanted her 'niece' to start off right and it was about time I started to develop a bust.

"The next morning I was up early to ready myself for the usual shopping trip to town, only this time it was for a pair of high heels and a new dress. I remember I stuffed my bra with cotton, put on my garter belt, and slipped on my nylons with no effort. After all, I became an expert from practice the night before. My aunt applied my lipstick because I was so excited

For many transvestites the switching of sex roles is a private matter; for others it is part of a more flamboyant life-style.

I couldn't get it on straight. Then off to town we went, aunt and 'niece.' What a wonderful day. I shall never forget it." (pp. 209–10)

The adult transvestite who marries faces problems that are well brought out in another case reported by Stoller (1974):

" 'We fell in love and as soon as I felt we could we were married. We have been as happy as two people can be and the best part of it is that she knows all about me and not only accepts me as I am but assists in my transformation and then admires me. . . .'

"This is the way the relationship looks at first, when the wife is pleased to see her husband's femininity. She does not know yet that as he becomes a more successful transvestite her enthusiasm will wane. Then he will be hurt that she is no longer interested in his dressing up, his sexual needs, his work. The fighting will start, neither will understand what has happened, and they will divorce." (p. 212)

Fetishism. *Fetishism* is a victimless sexual variant because, although it sometimes involves crimes such as thievery, its basic nature does not normally interfere with the rights of others except in an "incidental" way. In fetishism there is typically a centering of sexual interest on some body part or on an inanimate object, such as an article of clothing. Males are most commonly involved in cases of fetishism—reported cases of female fetishists are extremely rare. The range of fetishistic objects includes hair, ears, hands, underclothing, shoes, perfume, and similar objects associated with the opposite sex. The mode of using these objects for the achievement of sexual excitation and gratification varies considerably, but it commonly involves kissing, fondling, tasting, or smelling the object.

In order to obtain the required object, the fetishist may commit burglary, theft, or even assault. Probably the articles most commonly stolen by fetishists are women's underthings. One young boy was found to have accumulated over a hundred pairs of panties from a lingerie shop when he was apprehended. In such cases, the excitement and suspense of the criminal act itself typically reinforce the sexual stimulation, and in some cases actually constitute the fetish—the article stolen being of little importance. For example, one youth admitted entering a large number of homes in which the entering itself usually sufficed to induce an orgasm. When it did not, he was able to achieve sexual satisfaction by taking some "token," such as money or jewelry.

Not infrequently, fetishistic behavior consists of masturbation in association with the fetishistic object. Here, of course, it is difficult to draw a line between fetishistic activity and the effort to increase the sexual excitation and satisfaction of masturbation through the use of pictures and other articles associated with the desired sexual object. Utilization of such articles in masturbation is a common practice and not usually considered pathological. However, where antisocial behavior such as breaking and entering is involved, the practice is commonly referred to as fetishistic. For example, Marshall (1974) reported a rather unusual case of a young university student who had a "trouser fetish"; he would steal the trousers of teenagers and then use them in physical contact during masturbation.

A somewhat different, but not atypical pattern of fetishism is illustrated by the case of a man whose fetish was women's shoes and legs.

The fetishist in this case was arrested several times for loitering in public places, such as railroad stations and libraries, watching women's legs. Finally he chanced on a novel solution to his problem. Posing as an agent for a hosiery firm, he hired a large room, advertised for models, and took motion pictures of a number of girls walking and seated with their legs displayed to best advantage. He then used these pictures to achieve sexual satisfaction and found that they continued adequate for the purpose (Adapted from Grant, 1953).

Another type of fetishism involves setting fires. While people who set fires are a mixed group, a sizable number of fires—including some involving loss of life—are set by fetishists who have come to experience relief of sexual tension from setting and watching a fire burn. Such fires include brush and forest fires, as well as fires in buildings.

In approaching the causal factors in fetishism, we may again note that many stimuli can come to be associated with sexual excitation and gratification. Probably most people are stimulated to some degree by intimate articles of clothing and by perfumes and odors associated with the opposite sex. Thus the first prerequisite in fetishism seems to be a conditioning experience. In some instances this original conditioning may be quite accidental, as when sexual arousal and orgasm—which are reflexive responses—are elicited by a strong emotional experience involving some particular object or part of the body. More commonly, probably, the conditioning occurs during masturbatory fantasies.

In some instances, however, the associations involved in fetishism are not easy to explain. Bergler (1947) cited an unusual case in which a man's sex life was almost completely absorbed by a fetishistic fascination for exhaust pipes of automobiles. Nor would just any exhaust pipe do; it had to be in perfect shape, that is to say, undented and undamaged, and it had to emit softly blowing gases. This became far more attractive to him than sexual behavior with women.

Fetishistic patterns of sexual gratification usually become the preferred patterns only when they are part of a larger picture of maladjustment; such a picture typically involves doubts about one's masculinity and potency and fear of rejection and humiliation by members of the opposite sex. By his fetishistic practices and mastery over the inanimate object—which comes to symbolize for him the desired sexual object—the individual apparently safeguards himself and also compensates somewhat for his feelings of inadequacy.

As we have indicated, fetishism, like transvestism, rarely causes direct harm to other people. Unfortunately, this is not always the case with the other paraphilias, many of which do contain a definite element of injury or significant risk of injury—physical or psychological—to one or more of the parties involved in a sexual encounter. Typically—and rightly—these practices have strong legal sanctions against them. We shall consider only the most common forms of these paraphilias: voyeurism, exhibitionism, sadism, masochism, and pedophilia.

Voyeurism.   *Voyeurism, scotophilia,* and *inspectionalism* are synonymous terms referring to the achievement of sexual pleasure through clandestine peeping. Although children often engage in such behavior, it occurs as a sexual offense primarily among young males. These "peeping Toms," as they are commonly called, usually concentrate on females who are undressing, or on couples engaging in sexual relations. Frequently they masturbate during their peeping activity.

How do people develop this pattern? In the first place, viewing the body of an attractive female seems to be quite stimulating sexually for many males. The saying "He feasted his eyes upon her" attests to the appetitive quality of merely "looking" under certain conditions. In addition, the privacy and mystery that have traditionally surrounded sexual activities have tended to increase curiosity about them.

If a youth with such curiosity feels shy and inadequate in his relations with the other sex, it is not too surprising for him to accept the substitute of peeping. In this way he satisfies his curiosity and to some extent meets his sexual needs without the trauma of actually approaching a female, and thus without the failure and lowered self-status that such an approach might bring. As a matter of fact, peeping activities often provide important compensatory feelings of power and superiority over the one being looked at, which may contribute materially to the maintenance of this pattern. Also, of course, the suspense and danger associated with conditions of peeping may lead to emotional excitement and a reinforcement of the sexual stimulation. The peeper does not normally seek sexual activity with those he observes.

If a peeper is married, he is rarely well adjusted sexually in his marriage.

A young married college student had an attic apartment which was extremely hot during the summer months. To enable him to attend school, his wife worked; she came home at night tired and irritable and not in the mood for sexual relations. In addition, "the damned springs in the bed squeaked." In order "to obtain some sexual gratification" the youth would peer through his binoculars at the room next door and occasionally saw the young couple there engaged in erotic scenes. This stimulated him greatly, and he thereupon decided to extend his activities to a sorority house. However, during his second venture he was reported and apprehended by the police. This offender was quite immature for his age, rather puritanical in his attitude toward masturbation, and prone to indulge in rich but immature sexual fantasies.

While more permissive laws concerning "adult" movies and magazines have probably removed much of the secrecy from sexual behavior and also provided an alternative source of gratification for would-be peepers, their actual effect on the incidence of voyeurism is a matter of speculation. For many voyeurs these movies and magazines probably do not provide an adequate substitute for secretly watching the "real life" sexual behavior of an unsuspecting couple.

Although a voyeur may become somewhat reckless in his observation of courting couples and thus may be detected and assaulted by his subjects, peeping does not ordinarily have any serious criminal or antisocial aspects. In fact, many people probably have rather strong inclinations in the same direction, which are well checked by practical considerations such as the possibility of being caught and moral attitudes concerning the right to privacy.

Exhibitionism.   *Exhibitionism* ("indecent exposure") is the most common sexual offense reported to the police in the United States, Canada, and Europe, accounting for about one third of all sexual offenses (Rooth, 1974). Curiously enough, it is rare in most other countries. For example, in Argentina only 24 persons were convicted of exhibitionism during a five-year period; in Japan, only about 60 men are convicted of this offense each year. In still other countries, such as Burma and India, it is practically unheard of.

Exhibitionism involves the intentional exposure of the genitals to members of the opposite sex under inappropriate conditions. The exposure may take place in some secluded location, such as a park, or in a more public place, such as a department store, church, theater, or bus. In cities, the exhibitionist often drives by schools or bus stops, exhibits himself while in the car, and then drives rapidly away. In many instances, the exposure is repeated under fairly constant conditions, such as only in churches or buses, or in the same general vicinity and at the same time of day. In one case a youth exhibited himself only at the top of an escalator in a large department store. The kind of sex object too is usually fairly consistent for the individual exhibitionist. For the male offender this ordinarily involves a young or middle-aged female who is not known to the offender.

In some instances exposure of the genitals is accompanied by suggestive gestures or masturbatory activity, but more commonly there is only exposure. Although it is considered relatively rare, a hostile exposer may accompany exhibitionism with aggressive acts and may knock down or otherwise attack his victim.

In fact, some recent research indicates there is a subclass of exhibitionists who may best be considered antisocial personalities, as described in Chapter 7 (Forgac & Michaels, 1982). Despite the rarity of assaultive behavior in these cases, and the fact that most exhibitionists are anything but the aggressive and dangerous criminals they are often made out to be in newspaper stories, the exhibitionistic act nevertheless takes place without the viewer's consent and also may upset the viewer; thus, society considers exhibitionism to be a criminal offense.

Exhibitionism is most common during the warm spring and summer months, and most offenders are young adult males. Practically all occupational groups are represented. Among women, the exhibition of the genitals is relatively rare, and when it occurs it is less likely to be reported to the police.[1]

Usually exhibitionism by males in public or semipublic places is reported. Occasionally, however, such individuals are encouraged in their activity.

A rather handsome 17-year-old boy had been seating himself beside girls and women in darkened theaters and then exhibiting himself and masturbating. He had been repeatedly successful in obtaining approving collaboration from the "victims" before he finally made the mistake of exposing himself to a police woman. Out of an estimated 25 to 30 exposures, he was reported on only 3 occasions.

In general, cases of exhibitionism appear to fall into one of three categories:

1. *Exhibitionism associated with personal immaturity.* Witzig (1968) found that about 60 percent of the cases of exhibitionism referred by courts for treatment fall into this category. Here the exhibitionism seems to be based on inadequate information, feelings of shyness and inferiority in approaching the opposite sex, and puritanical attitudes toward masturbation. Commonly, there are strong bonds to an overly possessive mother. Often the exhibitionist states that he struggled against the impulse to expose himself in much the same way that the adolescent may struggle against the impulse to masturbate, but that, as sexual or other tensions increased, he felt compelled to carry out his exhibitionistic activities. Often he feels guilty and remorseful afterward, particularly if he has achieved ejaculation.

Although over half of all exhibitionists are married, they usually fail to achieve satisfactory sexual and personal relationships with their wives. Witzig (1968) has pointed out that

"These men almost never like to discuss sexual matters with their wives and frequently avoid undressing before them. The idea of living in a nudist colony is a repulsive thought to most exhibitionists, although they are periodically willing to show off their genitals in quite public places." (p.78).

Many of these offenders state that they married only because of family pressure, and many married at a late age. Thus we are dealing here with an individual who is essentially immature in his sex-role development, even though he may be well educated and competent in other life areas.

Closely related to the exhibitionist's personal immaturity appears to be a second factor: doubts and fears about his masculinity, combined with a strong need to demonstrate masculinity and potency. Apfelberg, Sugar, and Pfeffer (1944),

---

[1]In certain instances, of course, as in some bars and discos, women—and less frequently, men—are paid wages to exhibit their sexual parts.

for example, cited the case of an exhibitionist who achieved sexual satisfaction only when he accompanied the exposure of his genitals with a question to his victim as to whether she had ever seen such a large penis. On one occasion the woman, instead of evidencing shock and embarrassment, scornfully assured him that she had. On this occasion, the defendant stated, he received no sexual gratification.

It is worth noting that exhibitionism rarely takes place in a setting conducive to having sexual relations. The exhibitionist attemps to elicit a reaction that confirms his masculinity without entailing the risk of having to perform adequately in sexual intercourse. Some exhibitionists, on the other hand, fantasize that the victim will "take the first step" and approach them for sexual services (Adams & Chiodo, 1984).

In reviewing the role of personal immaturity and sexual ignorance in exhibitionism, it is interesting to note the conclusion of Rooth (1974) that the "sexual revolution" during the last decade in the Western world may have made matters worse for the exhibitionist: the growing assertiveness of women may make him even more insecure while at the same time he is being bombarded by sexually suggestive material from the "emancipated" mass media, thus increasing his frustration.

2. *Interpersonal stress and acting out.* Another causal factor is suggested by the high incidence of precipitating stress (Blair & Lanyon, 1981). Often the married exhibitionist appears to be reacting to some conflict or stress situation in his marriage, and his behavior is in the nature of a regression to adolescent masturbatory activity. In such instances, an exhibitionist may state that exhibiting himself during masturbation is more exciting and tension-reducing than utilizing pictures of nude women.

An interesting example of stress-induced exhibitionism was published several years ago in the autobiography of a prominent player in the National Football League. Intellectually and physically talented, attractive, wealthy, famous, and married to one of the most beautiful women in the entertainment field, this individual was nevertheless arrested on two occasions for exhibiting himself to preadolescent girls. By his own account, these incidents occurred only during periods of intense pressure, when he felt he was failing in those aspects of his life he most

valued—his athletic career and his marriage (Rentzel, 1972).

Exhibitionism without genital arousal may take place following a period of intense conflict over some problem—often involving authority figures—with which the individual feels inadequate to cope.

"For example, a Marine who wanted to make a career of the service was having an experience with a superior that made it impossible for him to reenlist. He could not admit to himself that he could be hostile to either the corps or the superior. For the first time in his life, he exposed himself to a girl on the beach. Arrested, he was merely reprimanded and returned to the scene of conflict. A short time later he displayed his genitals to a girl in a parking lot. This time he was placed on probation with the stipulation that he seek treatment, and his enlistment was allowed to terminate in natural sequence. He never repeated the act. He was happily married and seemed to be acting out in this instance a vulgar expression of contempt." (Witzig, 1968, p. 77)

3. *Association with other psychopathology.* Exhibitionism may occur in association with a variety of more pervasive forms of psychopathology. Severely mentally retarded youths—both male and female—may exhibit themselves, being apparently unaware or only partially aware of the socially disapproved nature of their behavior. Some exhibitionists come from the ranks of older men with senile brain deterioration who evidence a lowering of inner reality and ethical controls.

In other cases, as we have seen, exhibitionism is associated with psychopathic personality disorders. Here individuals usually have a history of poor school adjustment and erratic work records; often they have had difficulties with authorities as a consequence of other antisocial acts. Their exhibitionism appears to be just one more form of antisocial behavior, in connection with which they may or may not achieve sexual excitation and gratification. In some instances, exhibitionism is associated with manic or schizophrenic reactions. For example, the only woman in a group of offenders studied by Witzig (1968) typically exposed herself prior to the onset of a full-blown psychotic episode.

Sadism. The term *sadism* is derived from the name of the Marquis de Sade (1740–1814), who for sexual purposes inflicted such cruelty on his victims that he was eventually committed as insane. Although the term's meaning has broadened to denote cruelty in general, we shall use it in its restricted sense to denote achievement of sexual stimulation and gratification through the infliction of physical or psychic pain or humiliation on a sexual partner. The pain may be inflicted by such means as whipping, biting, or pinching; the act may vary in intensity, from fantasy to severe mutilation and in extreme cases even murder. Mild degrees of sadism (and masochism) are involved in the sexual foreplay customs of many cultures, and some couples in our own society regularly engage in such practices. Males are ordinarily the aggressors, although Krafft-Ebing (1950) has reported a number of cases in which sadists were women. In one unusual case, the wife required her husband to cut himself on the arm before approaching her sexually. She would then suck the wound and become extremely aroused.

In some cases sadistic activities lead up to or terminate in actual sexual relations; in others, full sexual gratification is obtained from the sadistic practice alone. A sadist may slash a woman with a razor or stick her with a needle, experiencing an orgasm in the process. Showing the peculiar and extreme associations that may occur is the case of a young man who entered a strange woman's apartment, held a chloroformed rag to her face until she lost consciousness, and branded her on the thigh with a hot iron. She was not molested in any other way.

Sometimes sadistic activities are associated with animals or with fetishistic objects instead of other human beings. East (1946) cited the case of a man who stole women's shoes, which he then slashed savagely with a knife. When he was in prison, he was found mutilating photographs that other prisoners kept in their cells by cutting the throats of the women in them. He admitted that he derived full sexual gratification from this procedure.

In other instances, gratification is achieved only if mutilation is performed directly on the victim's person. Chesser (1971) refers to such offenders as *pathological sadists* and notes that they are often extremely dangerous. The following is such a case:

The offender, Peter Kursten, was 47 years old at the time of his apprehension in Düsseldorf, Germany, for

The paraphernalia in this shop window is sold to some sadists and masochists for their sexual needs.

a series of lust murders. He was a skilled laborer, well groomed, modest, and had done nothing that annoyed his fellow workers.

Peter came from a disturbed family background, his father having been an alcoholic who had been sent to prison for having intercourse with Peter's older sister. Peter's own earliest sexual experiences were with animals. When he was about 13 years old, he attempted to have intercourse with a sheep, but the animal would not hold still and he took out a knife and stabbed her. At that moment he had an ejaculation.

After this experience, Peter found the sight of

gushing blood sexually exciting, and he turned from animals to human females. Often he first choked his victim, but if he did not achieve an orgasm he then stabbed her. Initially he used scissors and a dagger, but later he took to using a hammer or an axe. After he achieved ejaculation, he lost interest in his victim, except for taking measures to cover up his crime.

The offender's sexual crimes extended over a period of some 30 years and involved over 40 victims. Finally apprehended . . . he expressed a sense of injustice at not being like other people who were raised in normal families (Adapted from Berg, 1954).

The news media have reported more recent cases in which the victims have been mutilated and killed in association with sadistic sexual practices. In the early 1970s, a "horror story" broke concerning the sadistic homosexual murders of 27 teenage boys in Texas. More recently, the San Francisco city coroner found it advisable to meet with leaders of the local homosexual community to discuss means of curbing serious injuries and deaths due to sado-masochistic practices within that group (*Time,* May 4, 1981). However, there is a lack of available case material on which to base definitive conclusions concerning the actual clinical picture or the causal factors involved in cases of sadism reported by the media.

The causal factors in sadism appear roughly comparable to those in fetishism.

1. *Experiences in which sexual excitation and possibly orgasm have been associated with the infliction of pain.* Such conditioned associations may occur under a variety of conditions. In their sexual fantasies many children visualize a violent attack by a man on a woman, and such ideas may be strengthened by newspaper articles of sadistic assaults on females. Perhaps more directly relevant are experiences in which an individual's infliction of pain on an animal or another person has given rise to strong emotions and, unintentionally, to sexual excitement. We have noted elsewhere the connection between strong emotional stimulation and sexual stimulation, especially during the adolescent period. Just as in fetishism—where simple conditioning seems to make it possible for almost any object or action to become sexually exciting—conditioning can also be an important factor in the development of sadistic tendencies.

2. *Negative attitudes toward sex and/or fears of impotence.* Sadistic activities may protect individuals with negative attitudes toward sex from the full sexual implications of their behavior, and at the same time may help them express their contempt and punishment of the other person for engaging in sexual relations. Several early investigators have described male sadists as timid, feminine, undersexed individuals, and sadistic behavior as apparently designed to arouse strong emotions in the sex object which, in turn, arouses the sadist and makes orgasm possible. The sadist apparently receives little or no satisfaction if the victim remains passive and unresponsive to the painful stimuli. In fact, the sadist usually wants the victim to find the pain exciting, and may even insist that the victim act pleasurably aroused when being stuck with pins, bitten, or otherwise hurt.

For many sexually inadequate and insecure individuals, the infliction of pain is apparently a "safe" means of achieving sexual stimulation. Strong feelings of power and superiority over the victim may for the time shut out underlying feelings of inadequacy and anxiety.

3. *Association with other psychopathology.* In schizophrenia and other severe forms of psychopathology, sadistic sexual behavior and sadistic rituals may result from the lowering of inner controls and the deviation of symbolic processes. Wertham (1949) cited an extreme case in which a schizophrenic individual with puritanical attitudes toward sex achieved full sexual gratification by castrating young boys and killing and mutilating young girls. He rationalized his actions as being the only way to save them from later immoral behavior.

Masochism.   The term *masochism* is derived from the name of the Austrian novelist Leopold V. Sacher-Masoch (1836–1895), whose fictional characters dwelt lovingly on the sexual pleasure of pain. As in the case of the term *sadism,* the meaning of *masochism* has been broadened beyond sexual connotations, so that it includes the deriving of pleasure from self-denial, from expiatory physical suffering such as that of the religious flagellants, and from hardship and suffering in general. In keeping with DSM-III, we shall restrict our present discussion to the sexual aspects of masochistic behavior.

The clinical picture of masochism is similar to that in sadistic practices, except that now pain is inflicted on the self instead of on others (Sack &

Miller, 1975). For example, East (1946) cited the case of a young woman who frequently cut herself on the arms, legs, and breasts, and inserted pins and needles under her skin. She experienced sexual pleasure from the pain and from seeing the blood from the incisions.

Patterns of masochistic behavior usually come about through conditioned learning: as a result of early experiences, an individual comes to associate pain with sexual pleasure. For example, Gebhard (1965) cited the case of an adolescent boy who was having the fractured bones in his arm hurriedly set without an anesthetic. To comfort the boy, the physician's attractive nurse carressed him and held his head against her breast. As a consequence, he experienced a "powerful and curious combination of pain and sexual arousal," which led to masochistic—as well as sadistic—tendencies in his later heterosexual relations.

Such sayings as "being crushed in his arms" or "smothered with kisses" reveal the association commonly made between erotic arousal and pain or discomfort. Thus it is not surprising that many individuals resort to mild sadomasochistic acts such as biting in an attempt to increase the emotional excitement of the sexual act. For most people, however, such behavior does not result in serious physical injury, nor does it serve as a substitute for normal sexual relations. In actual masochism, by contrast, the individual experiences sexual stimulation and gratification from the experience of pain under certain conditions.

In the case of both sadism and masochism, it should be noted that gratification in many instances requires a shared, complementary interpersonal relationship—one sadist and one masochist or, in milder forms, one superior "disciplinarian" and one obedient "slave." Nor are such arrangements limited to heterosexual couples. On the contrary, as suggested earlier, they seem to be very popular in homosexual encounters (Tripp, 1975). One of the authors has treated a promiscuous male homosexual whose singular desire was to be penetrated anally in order to relive an exquisitely painful experience in which, as a boy, his father had administered an enema to him, by far the "closest" experience he'd ever had with his father.

Pedophilia. In *pedophilia* the sex object is a child; the intimacy usually involves manipula-

tion of the child's genitals. Occasionally the child is induced to manipulate the sex organ of the pedophiliac or to engage in mouth-genital contacts. Attempted sexual intercourse is apparently rare (Adams & Chiodo, 1984).

Offenders are diverse in terms of the act committed, the intentionality of and general circumstances surrounding the act, and age, education, and developmental history. Most pedophiliacs are men, but women occasionally engage in such practices. The average age of these offenders is about 40 years. Many offenders are or have been married, and many have children of their own. Indeed, some choose their own children as victims. In an early study of 836 pedophiliac offenders in New Jersey, Revitch and Weiss (1962) found that the older offenders tended to seek out immature children, while younger offenders preferred adolescent girls between 12 and 15. Girls outnumbered boys as victims in the ratio of more than 2 to 1.

In most cases of pedophilia the victim is known to the offender, and the sexual behavior may continue over a sustained period of time; usually there is no physical coercion. Although in some cases the offenders may be encouraged or even seduced by their victims, Swanson (1968) found provocation or active participation by the victim in only 3 of the 25 cases he studied.

Whether or not there is an element of provocation by the victim, the onus is always on the offender. Since pedophiliacs may subject children to highly traumatic emotional experiences as well as physical injury, society's norms relating to pedophilia are explicit and uncompromising. An alleged offender is sometimes considered guilty until proven innocent, in fact, and a number of men have served time in penal institutions because children or their parents interpreted simple affection as attempted intimacy or rape. On the other hand, many cases of sexual assault on children undoubtedly go unreported to spare the child a further ordeal (Sgroi, 1977).

The following causal categories are based on (a) an intensive study of 38 pedophiliac offenders living in a segregated treatment center (Cohen, Seghorn, & Calmas, 1969), and (b) indepth interviews with many pedophiliacs, some of whom had managed to avoid arrest and some of whom had been arrested and had served time (Rossman, 1973).

1. *The personally immature offender.* This is a person who has never been able to establish or maintain satisfactory interpersonal relationships with male or female peers during his adolescent, young adult, or adult life. This was by far the most common type. He is sexually comfortable only with children, and in most cases knows the victim. Usually the act is not impulsive but begins with a type of disarming courtship which eventually leads to sexual play. Either male or female children may be the victims. Groth and Birnbaum (1978) refer to this type of pedophile as being "fixated" at an early stage of development.

2. *The regressed offender.* These are people who during adolescence have shown apparently normal development, with good peer relationships and some dating behavior and heterosexual experiences. Cohen et al. (1969) describe this type of person in the following way:

"Throughout the adolescent period there exists increasing feelings of masculine inadequacy in sexual and nonsexual activities. And, as he enters adulthood, his social, occupational, and marital adjustment is quite tenuous and marginal. There is frequently a history of an inability to deal with the normal stresses of adult life and alcoholic episodes become increasingly more frequent and result in the breakdown of a relatively stable marital, social, and work adjustment. In almost all instances the pedophilic acts are precipitated by some direct confrontation of his sexual adequacy by an adult female or some threat to his masculine image by a male peer." (p. 251)

The most frequent precipitating event is the offender's discovery that his wife or girlfriend is having an affair with another man. In most of these cases the victim selected is a female child, suggesting elements of both retaliation and affirmation of "manhood."

In contrast to the personally immature offender, the regressed offender is not acquainted with his victim, and the act is characteristically impulsive. For example, the offender may be driving a car, see a child, and become overwhelmed by sexual excitation. Groth and Birnbaum (1978), while confirming most of this picture, state that the victim typically *is* known to the offender.

3. *The "conditioned" offender.* Included here are individuals who have had their definitive sexual experiences with young boys, often in reformatories; this conditioned behavior continues into adulthood in terms of sexual preference. These individuals are usually callous and exploitative in their sexual behavior, and tend to cruise cheap motion picture theaters and other areas in search of vulnerable children. In many instances, they pick up young hustlers who are available in most large cities. Some of these men are careful about avoiding detection, while others are not and have a history of one or more arrests for such offenses.

4. *The psychopathic offender.* The individuals included here are psychopathic personalities who prey on children in search of new sexual thrills. In some instances, such individuals patronize child prostitutes who are usually available in large cities as well as in some foreign countries.

This category also includes aggressive psychopaths whose behavior is motivated by both aggressive and sexual components:

"The primary aim is aggression, and is expressed in cruel and vicious assaults on the genitalia or by introducing the penis or elongated objects into the victim orally or anally. The sexual excitement increases as an apparent function of the aggression, but the orgasm itself either does not occur or must be reached through masturbation." (Cohen, et al., 1969, p. 251)

In a case known to one of the authors, for example, the offender's gratification centered on the screams of his young male victim as the penis was roughly thrust into the boy's anus.

Such offenders usually have a history of antisocial behavior and, in general, could be described as hostile, aggressive psychopaths. Ordinarily they select a boy as the object of their aggression. Psychopathic individuals—particularly those who use coercion—are prone to deny their offenses or place the blame on their victims.

A number of investigators have also pointed to other severe psychopathology in pedophiliac offenders. Some are alcoholic or schizophrenic. Many are older individuals in whom brain deterioration has led to a weakening of normal inhibitory controls. In fact, pedophilia and exhibitionism are the most common sexual offenses committed by individuals suffering senile and arteriosclerotic brain damage and displaying organic personality syndromes (Chapter 13).

Other psychosexual deviations

In certain respects, the DSM-III is a quite conservative document, while in others it may exceed proper boundaries (e.g., in the Axis II diagnosis of "developmental arithmetic disorder" in children, which would seem to describe more an educational than a psychiatric problem). Certain sexual deviations, such as incest and rape, are unaccountably (in the authors' judgment) missing from the DSM-III classification; this seems *too* conservative. Accordingly, these two "disorders" are included in what follows even though they are not a part of the official psychiatric nomenclature.

Incest.   Culturally prohibited sexual relations, up to and including coitus, between family members, such as a brother and sister or a parent and child, are known as *incest*. Although a few societies have approved incestuous relationships—at one time it was the established practice for Egyptian pharaohs to marry their sisters to prevent the royal blood from being "contaminated"—the incest taboo is virtually universal among human societies.[2]

An indication of the very real risks involved in such inbreeding has been provided by Adams and Neel (1967), who compared the offspring of 18 nuclear incest marriages—12 brother-sister and 6 father-daughter—with those of a control group matched for age, intelligence, socioeconomic status, and other relevant characteristics. At the end of six months, 5 of the infants of the incestuous marriages had died, 2 were severely mentally retarded and had been institutionalized, 3 showed evidence of borderline intelligence, and 1 had a cleft palate. Only 7 of the 18 infants were considered normal. In contrast, only 2 of the control-group infants were not considered normal—one showing indications of borderline intelligence and the other manifesting a physical defect. Lindzey (1967) concluded that

". . . the consequences of inbreeding are sufficiently strong and deleterious to make it unlikely that a hu-

---

[2]Extensive reviews of the literature on incest which document its near-universality and cite the various reasons given for its taboo may be found in Devroye (1973) and Schwartzman (1974). Interestingly, the degree of relationship for which the taboo is invoked varies widely, in many instances extending beyond "blood relatives."

The drawings shown here are all the work of incest victims. Top: A seven-year-old girl engulfed by a maelstrom. Middle: A teenage girl threatened by a snake. Bottom: A nine-year-old boy caught in a trap in the middle of a country landscape.

man society would survive over long periods of time if it permitted, or encouraged, a high incidence of incest. In this sense, then, one may say that the incest taboo (whatever other purposes it may serve) is biologically guaranteed." (p. 1055)

A number of investigators have also maintained that the incest taboo serves to produce greater variability among offspring, and hence to increase the flexibility and long-term adaptability of the population (Schwartzman, 1974).

In our own society incestuous behavior does occur, but its actual incidence is unknown since it mostly takes place in a family setting (Peters, 1976) and comes to light only when reported to law enforcement or other agencies. It may well be more common than is generally believed, partly because many of the victims do not consider themselves victimized (de Young, 1982; Maisch, 1972). Meiselman (1978) estimates the incidence at 1 or 2 per every 100 persons. Kinsey et al. (1948, 1953) reported an incidence of 5 cases per 1000 persons in a sample of 12,000 subjects, and Gebhard et al. (1965) found 30 cases per 1000 subjects in a group of 3500 imprisoned sex offenders. In both these latter studies brother-sister incest was reported as being 5 times more common than the next most common pattern—father-daughter incest.[3] Mother-son incest is thought to be relatively rare. In a study of 78 cases of incest, which excluded brother-sister incest, Maisch (1972) found that the father-daughter and stepfather-stepdaughter varieties accounted for fully 85 percent of the sample; mother-son incest accounted for only 4 percent. Summit and Kryso (1978) estimate that some 36,000 cases of father-daughter incest occur each year in the United States. This estimate may seriously underestimate the actual occurrence (Herman, 1981). In occasional cases, there may be multiple patterns of incest within the same family.

For an understanding of incestuous behavior, it may be noted that incestuous fantasies and desires are common during the adolescent period, and it is not uncommon for fathers to have such feelings toward their daughters. However, social mores and prohibitions are usually so deeply ingrained that the desires are not often

---

[3]Authorities are more likely to deal with cases of father-daughter incest than with cases of brother-sister incest, since the latter are less likely to be reported.

acted out. Bagley (1969) has suggested that several different causal patterns may be involved where incestuous behavior occurs. The following list represents a slight modification of his schema.

1. *Situational incest.* When brothers and sisters share the same bedroom during the preadolescent or adolescent period (which is not uncommon among poorer families), they may tend to engage in sexual exploration and experimentation. In some cases older brothers seduce their younger sisters without any apparent understanding of the social prohibitions or possible consequences.

2. *Incest associated with severe psychopathology.* In the case of psychopathic fathers, the incest may simply be part of an indiscriminate pattern of sexual promiscuity; in other individuals, such as alcoholics and psychotics, the incestuous relations may be associated with the lowering of inner controls.

3. *Incest associated with pedophilia.* Here a father has an intense sexual craving for young children, including his own. It is evident, however, that pedophilic motivation is not a primary cause of incest, in that most victims are beyond puberty. (A discussion of disturbing exceptions appears in the **HIGHLIGHT** on page 473).

4. *Incest associated with a faulty paternal model.* A father may set an undesirable example for his son by engaging in incestuous relations with his daughter or daughters and may encourage his son to do so as well—either at the time with his sisters, or later in life with his own daughters.

5. *Incest associated with family pathology and disturbed marital relations.* In some instances a rejecting wife may actually foster father-daughter incest. Most (but not all) cases of father-daughter incest, in fact, occur in a setting of marked family disorganization.

In general, incestuous fathers who come to the attention of authorities do not have a history of sexual offenses or other criminal behavior, nor do they show a disproportionate incidence of prior hospitalization for mental disorders (Cavillin, 1966). In fact, such fathers tend to restrict their sexual activity to family members, not seeking or engaging in extramarital sexual relations. For example, in his intensive study of 12 fathers convicted of incestuous relations with their daughters, Cavillin (1966) reported that

HIGHLIGHT
Sexual molestation of young children

While most incestuous contacts between parents and their children occur after the child has attained puberty, very young children—even infants—have been subjected to sexual molestation and abuse by parents or other adults. According to Sgroi (1977), these cases, like those involving adolescents, are markedly underreported. Even in the face of overwhelming evidence, this researcher claims, physicians are extremely reluctant to conclude that a child has been sexually attacked. Apparently it is considered "in bad taste" professionally to draw such a conclusion.

The cases Sgroi uses to illustrate the magnitude of the problem are truly disconcerting. She writes of one city's youngest known rape victim, a child 2 months old; of a 2½-year-old boy and his 4-year-old sister, both of whom acquired acute gonorrhea from their father; of a 17-month-old girl with a torn anus, dead of asphyxiation, with semen in her mouth and throat. In

the face of such horror, one can only applaud Sgroi's attempt to break through the secrecy and "discretion" too often associated with this "last frontier" of child abuse.

Because many cases remain unreported, the actual incidence of child abuse of all types—and especially of sexual abuse—is unknown. In Connecticut, during fiscal years 1973 and 1974, approximately 10 percent of all cases of reported abuse were suspected to involve sexual assault or impropriety—a total of 248 separate incidents. The suspected perpetrator was most often the father or a male relative or boyfriend. This corroborates the earlier findings of De Francis (1969). Assuming Connecticut to be representative of the United States as a whole, many thousands of young children are sexually assaulted or abused each year, and all too often the damage is inflicted by their own parents.

only 2 of the 12 had resorted to extramarital relations, despite feeling they were unloved and rejected by their wives.

Cavillin further reported that the youngest father in the group was 20 and the oldest 56, with an average age of 39. The average age of the daughters was 13, the youngest being 3 and the oldest 18. Five of the 12 fathers had had a relationship with more than 1 daughter, usually beginning with the oldest; in 11 of the cases the relationships had gone on for some time—from 3 months to 3 years—before being reported by the daughters. In all cases, too, the father felt rejected and threatened by his wife. Cavillin's findings are generally confirmed by Maisch (1972), who studied 78 cases of incest coming to the attention of officials in the Federal Republic of Germany, and by Dixen and Jenkins (1981) in a recent literature review.

Most of us feel a profound repugnance when we hear of fathers seducing, or in rare instances *being* seduced by, their daughters. Our disgust is certainly appropriate, especially when we consider the future adjustment difficulties many of these girls must face in trying to come to terms with their experience. However, Offit (1981) of-

fers us a different, more compassionate view of the father's situation in describing her work with a depressed and lonely man who feels grief for the loss of his now-married daughter, a daughter who had been the center of his life and his love for 15 years. Like many incestuous fathers, the man described by Offit does not seem, apart from his "perversion," to be an evil man. Such descriptions remind us that in our haste to condemn—rightly—incestuous relationships, we should not assume that all such relationships are tawdry or utterly lacking in genuine feeling or affection.

The psychological effect of the incestuous relationship on the daughter appears to depend on her age at the time of the relationship and on how much anxiety and guilt she experiences. Most girls studied who were still adolescent expressed feelings of guilt and depression over the incestuous behavior. Some girls in this situation turn to promiscuity; others run away from home to escape the stressful situation. Later difficulties in adult heterosexual adjustment are common. In some instances, no apparent long-range ill effects can be detected (Dixen & Jenkins, 1981). Interestingly, in a case treated by one of the authors in which there had been long-standing sexual molestation by the young woman's father during her childhood and adolescence, she resolutely refused all further sexual contact with him after he provoked her first orgasm. Up to that time, as is often the case, she had assumed a passive, "blameless" position.

Rape. In rape, sexual behavior is usually directed toward a culturally acceptable sex object but under antisocial conditions.[4] Almost exclusively in reported cases, the male is the offender. Depending on the victim's age, such offenses are defined legally as (a) *statutory rape,* which involves the seduction of a minor; and (b) *forcible rape,* in which the unwilling partner is over 18. It is with the latter type that we are concerned in this section.

Rape has increased more rapidly in the last decade than any other type of violent crime, although part of the apparent rise may simply reflect better reporting. In any case, the FBI reported some 77,000 cases of forcible rape in 1982, up from 55,000 in 1974. The actual incidence is considered to be as much as four times higher, because many women wish to avoid the unfortunate consequences that in the past have often followed a complaint of having been raped. These include social stigmatization and, regrettably, crude and insensitive treatment by police. There is hope that the gap between actual and reported incidents of rape has been narrowed in recent years as women have banded together to call attention to these injustices.

Based on information gathered about arrested and convicted rapists, rape, relatively speaking, is a young man's crime. Fifty-six percent of all arrests are of persons under 25 years of age, and a third of these are under 20; the greatest concentration is in the 16-to-24 age group. Of the rapists who get into police records, about half are married and living with their wives at the time of the crime. As a group, they come from the low end of the socioeconomic ladder. Typically they are unskilled workers with low intelligence, low education, and low income. How representative they are of rapists as a whole we do not know.

Rape tends to be a repetitive activity rather than an isolated act, and most rapes are planned events. About 80 percent of rapists commit the act in the neighborhood in which they reside; most rapes take place in an urban setting at night. However, the specific scene of the rape varies greatly. The act may occur on a lonely street after dark, in an automobile in the parking lot of a large shopping center, in the elevator or hallway of a building, and in other situations where the victim has little chance of assistance. Rapists have also entered apartments or homes by pretending to be deliverymen or repairmen. In fact, rapes most often occur in the woman's home.

About a third or more of all rapes involve more than one offender, and often they are accompanied by beatings. The remainder are single-offender rapes in which the victim and the offender may know each other; the closer the relationship, the more brutally the victim may be beaten. When the victim struggles against her attacker, she is also likely to receive more severe injuries or in occasional cases to be killed. On the other hand, one study found that when the victim was able to cry out and run away, she was more likely to be successful in avoiding the rape (Selkin, 1974).

In addition to the physical trauma inflicted on the victim, the psychological trauma may be severe (see **HIGHLIGHT** on pages 164–65). One especially unfortunate factor in rape is the possibility of pregnancy; another is a sexually transmitted disease. Such an incident may also affect the victim's marriage or other intimate relationships. The situation is likely to be particularly upsetting to the husband or boyfriend if he has been forced to watch the rape, as is occasionally the case when a victim is raped by the members of a juvenile gang.

The concept of "victim-precipitated" rape, a favorite of defense attorneys and of some police and court jurisdictions, turns out on close examination to be a myth. According to this view, the victim, though often bruised both psychologically and physically—if not worse—is regarded as the *cause* of the crime, often on such flimsy grounds as the alleged provocativeness of her attire or her past sexual behavior. The attacker, on the other hand, is treated as a decerebrate organism, unable to quell his lust in the face of such "outrageous" provocation—and therefore incapable of a criminal act!

---

[4]Here we are referring to heterosexual rape. Statistics on homosexual rapes, particularly among males, are not available, although scattered reports indicate that such incidents do occur, particularly in prisons.

Women who are repeated victims of rape are especially likely to be suspected of provoking the attacks. In fact, such women tend to be significantly dysfunctional in many areas of their lives and tend also to be victimized in areas other than rape. Far from being the seductresses of popular folklore, they are often more like chronic "losers" with insufficient personal resources to fend off those who would exploit them (Ellis, Atkeson, & Calhoun, 1982). It should be pointed out in this context that *most* college women report having experienced strong unwanted advances from men; such encounters do not imply a special vulnerability to rape (Koss & Oros, 1982).

A number of typologies of rape incidents and of rapists have been proposed, most of them based on inadequate data of questionable representativeness. The system proposed by Groth, Burgess, and Holmstrom (1977) is the most adequately documented one to appear thus far, and it has the additional virtue of appearing to subsume the types identified in earlier work. It is based on the accounts of 133 convicted rapists and 92 victims of rapes occurring during a limited time period in Massachusetts.

Groth et al. noted that rape attacks combine psychological elements of power and anger as well as sexuality, and their strategy was to rank these elements in terms of their apparent salience for each of the 225 separate accounts of rape available to them. In doing so, they discovered *no case* in which sexual satisfaction appeared to be the dominant motive of the rapist; that is, all the rapes were characterized as involving either power motives or anger expression more than sexuality on the part of the rapists. The authors also noted that predominantly power- or anger-inspired rapes could each in turn be divided into two subtypes. These subdivisions form the basis of their classification scheme, as described below.

1. *Power-assertive type.* The essence of a rape in which power motives predominate is that of establishing control over the victim through intimidation; the mode of intimidation employed may involve use of a weapon, physical force not involving severe injury, or simply threats of harm. The achievement of penetration is regarded as a "conquest." The rape is frequently preceded by fantasies that the victim, once overpowered, will willingly participate with wild abandon. Because reality never matches the fantasy, the rapist is frustrated and is likely to repeat the act compulsively on another occasion. The power-assertive rapist tends to have a history of "hypermasculinity," striving always to assert power and domination over those with whom he comes in contact. We may surmise, of course, that such persons in fact have very serious questions about their manhood. In Groth et al.'s sample, 44 percent of the rapes were of the power-assertive variety.

2. *Power-reassurance type.* Like his power-assertive counterpart, the power-reassurance rapist seeks to intimidate and conquer his victim. In this case, however, the underlying sense of weakness, inadequacy, and indistinct gender identity is much more obvious. As in some cases of exhibitionism, the act not uncommonly takes place following some blow to the rapist's fragile ego; the rape is an attempt to "repair the damage." Rapes of the power-reassurance type accounted for 21 percent of Groth et al.'s sample.

3. *Anger-retaliation type.* In comparison with power-oriented rapists, who rarely inflict severe physical damage on their victims, predominantly anger-driven rapists are exceedingly dangerous—sometimes to the point of murdering the women they attack. Here, rage, contempt, and hatred dominate the assault, which is usually brutal and violent. Sexual satisfaction, if it occurs at all, is minimal. In fact, many anger-dominated rapists view normal sex with revulsion and disgust. Here the rape is an expression of hate and rage toward women in general, and the predominant motive is one of revenge for real or imagined slights suffered at the hands of females. Derogation and humiliation are prominent features of this type of attack. Of the rapes studied by Groth et al., 30 percent were of the anger-retaliation type.

4. *Anger-excitation type.* More than any other, this type of rapist fits the category of *pathological sadist.* His attack is one of eroticized aggression; he derives sexual pleasure, thrills, and excitement not from the sexual elements of his assault but from the suffering of his victim. The anger-excitation type accounted for only 5 percent of Groth et al.'s sample.

It might seem from the above descriptions of actual rape occurrences that rapists as a group are a very disturbed segment of the population, and that potential rapists should therefore be easy to recognize. This would be an erroneous and possibly dangerous conclusion, however.

While it is true that a certain proportion of rapists are obviously abnormal on a chronic basis—some even being blatantly psychotic—the literature in this area abounds with instances of rape in which, prior to the attack, the rapist had given no hint whatever of being a dangerous person (Gager & Schurr, 1976; Medea & Thompson, 1974). Whatever the prevention of rape involves, it is not a matter of informal psychodiagnostic predictions.

Conviction rates for rape are low, and most men who have raped are free in the community. Yet one study of rapists who were in the community found that the men had raped anywhere from 5 to 100 times (Abel et al., 1978). Rape is an ugly, intrusive violation of another person's integrity and selfhood that deserves to be viewed with more gravity—and its victims with more sensitivity—than is customarily the case (Gager & Schurr, 1976; Medea & Thompson, 1974).

In recent years new rape laws have been adopted by a majority of states, about a third of them based on the "Michigan model," which describes four degrees of criminal sexual conduct, with different levels of punishment for different degrees of seriousness. In calling the offense *criminal sexual conduct* rather than *rape*, the Michigan law also appropriately places the emphasis on the offender rather than the victim.

Treatment and outcomes

Research concerning effective treatment of variant sexual behavior has not progressed as far or as rapidly as in the case of the dysfunctions, but there are encouraging signs of progress. As was noted at the outset of this discussion, we now know that most sexually variant acts cannot adequately be conceptualized simply as aberrations of sexual arousal. In most instances we also need to look at the individual's level of response to adult heterosexual stimuli, overall degree of social skill with members of the other sex, and gender identity development. Only by taking all these factors into account is it possible to assess a given client's difficulties adequately and fashion treatment procedures for intervening on a broad enough front.

To date, unfortunately, such a broad-front intervention has been the exception rather than the rule in therapeutic attempts to change var-

iant sexuality, and most treatment efforts still focus on the sexual arousal aspects. We are beginning to learn how to suppress a variant arousal pattern, as with aversive conditioning procedures. Similarly, we know something of how to develop or strengthen arousability to appropriate sexual stimuli (Barlow & Abel, 1976). Surely, we will be able to find ways to teach appropriate social skills where they are lacking. In fact, encouraging preliminary reports have emanated from a number of research centers concerned with the problem (Hersen & Eisler, 1976). There is the remaining obstacle of learning how to strengthen an adult client's gender identity, not necessarily in an exclusively "masculine" or "feminine" direction but rather more in terms of overcoming amorphousness and immaturity in the individual's sense of being a man or a woman—an adult person. This promises to be a difficult challenge for clinical research. Having delineated the problem, however, we are in a much better position now than we were even a few short years ago.

A good example of the successful application of broadly based intervention is provided in the treatment by Barlow and his associates of a 17-year-old transsexual male (Barlow & Abel, 1976; Barlow, Reynolds, & Agras, 1973).

This young man had wished to be female for as long as he could recall. He had spontaneously begun cross-dressing before the age of 5; and when he appeared for therapy, his general behavior was markedly effeminate. At this time he was depressed and withdrawn, partly because people ridiculed his appearance and manner. Though he wanted to change his sex, he agreed to try therapy aimed at changing his gender identity.

The first part of the treatment involved the attempt to modify the young man's feminine gender role by teaching him masculine styles of sitting, walking, and standing. "Correct" behavior was modeled by a male therapist; errors in the client's attempts to reproduce this behavior were noted, and he was given abundant praise for his successes. For example, he was taught to cross his legs when sitting so that one ankle rested on the other knee instead of placing one knee atop the other. As his performance improved, the staring and ridicule of others diminished substantially, and the young man began to enjoy his new "masculine" image.

Attempts to improve the client's social skills, which were notably lacking even in his interactions with other males, also utilized behavioral rehearsal techniques and immediate feedback. Since he had affected a high-pitched, effeminate voice, he was also given voice retraining, which proved quite effective. By the end of this phase of the treatment program, the client was reporting much increased confidence and success in his relations with his peers, both male and female.

These gains were consolidated by a fantasy-retraining phase, in which the young man was taught to adopt a masculine role in his sexual and other fantasies. Continuing assessment of his response to erotic stimuli, however, showed that he was still not aroused by heterosexually oriented materials and was still strongly attracted to males. In other words, at this point he was psychologically a male homosexual.

The next step, then, involved increasing the client's responsiveness to heterosexual stimuli and decreasing the variant arousal pattern. Enhancement of arousal to heterosexual stimuli was accomplished by a classical conditioning procedure that systematically paired arousal and orgasm with heterosexual stimuli. This procedure was successful in establishing heterosexual arousal; and at this stage in the treatment, the client was bisexual in terms of his erotic responsiveness. There remained only the therapeutic task of suppressing the homosexual arousal component, which was accomplished by a combination of electric shock and covert sensitization (having the client imagine repugnant scenes). At a follow-up two years later, the young man was attending college and was regularly dating young women.

The successful outcome of this case should not be taken as a routine occurrence. As we have mentioned before, many sexual variants—transsexualism in particular—are normally not amenable to therapeutic reversal. It should also be noted that Barlow and his associates encountered some procedural difficulties in this case, recommending refinements in techniques as a result (Barlow & Abel, 1976; Barlow & Agras, 1973). Furthermore, the techniques used to suppress variant arousal patterns—electric shock and covert sensitization—are highly controversial. However, such use of aversive stimuli is often the most successful method of eradicating unwanted desires.

In addition to the need to improve treatment for the various sexual problems, there is also a need for better treatment of the victims of sexually variant persons. Except in the case of rape, little attention has been given to this serious matter, and even in the case of rape much remains to be done.

Male and female homosexuality

On December 14, 1973, by vote of the trustees of the American Psychiatric Association, *homosexuality* was expunged from the list of officially recognized mental disorders, thus producing an "instant cure" for the millions of gay men and women in our society. Whatever the motives behind this action—and they appear to have been principled and ethical ones—the voting of a disorder out of existence raises questions concerning the fundamental value of applying a medical perspective to personal and sociobehavioral issues. What is the likelihood, for example, that pneumonia or cancer will one day be declared by vote to be no longer diseases? We are not here supporting the position that homosexuality *should* be considered a psychiatric disorder—quite the contrary; we are rather pointing up a certain capriciousness sometimes involved in the "diagnosis" of behavior.

The logical difficulty becomes even more evident when we consider that the APA's intended removal of psychiatric stigma from homosexuality was incomplete. The DSM-III continues to list *ego-dystonic homosexuality* as a mental disorder. This category refers to a situation in which the homosexual orientation is persistently unwanted by the person who has it. The inclusion of subjective distress *about* one's condition as the defining characteristic of a disorder probably renders this diagnosis unique in the annals of medicine. As Adams and Chiodo (1984) point out, discrepancies between values and behaviors are not at all unusual in persons, but we do not ordinarily think of such discrepancies as deciding, or even raising, questions of abnormality. As these authors bluntly put it, "homosexuality is either abnormal or it is not." While this states the question in a straightforward way, it does not supply us with an answer.

In deciding to include a discussion of homosexuality in this text, the present authors have been guided by the definition of abnormality adopted at the outset. The question thus becomes, Is homosexuality maladaptive? For many homosexual persons it clearly is not; for others,

More and more homosexuals are openly proclaiming their sexual preferences and demanding an end to discrimination and harassment.

however, the orientation contributes to notable life problems. For example, in a large-scale Indiana University study of practicing homosexuals in the San Francisco Bay region, Bell and Weinberg (1978) discovered substantial subgroupings of individuals who were clearly miserable and functioning maladaptively as compared with the control heterosexuals. Not all of the problems of the maladaptive subgroups could be attributed to societal hostility toward homosexuals, which in any case is relatively minimal in the region sampled. Rather, it appears that a large proportion of these individuals were persistently unhappy with, and rejecting of, their own homosexuality; that is, their homosexuality was, in DSM-III terms, ego-dystonic. While we have criticized the logical status of the ego-dystonic diagnosis, it does have the virtue of providing access to treatment (and a means of paying for treatment through insur-

ance companies) for those individuals whose distress is strong enough to lead them to attempt reorientation therapy. The existence of this subgroup is the basis for our including a discussion of homosexuality in this text. (The question of whether homosexuality should be treated at all is discussed in the **HIGHLIGHT** on page 479).

Homosexuality has existed throughout recorded history and among some people has been tacitly accepted. The ancient Greek, Roman, Persian, and Moslem civilizations all condoned a measure of homosexuality, and the practice increased as these civilizations declined. In later Greece and Rome, for example, homosexual prostitution existed openly. In fact, it was quite popular for Roman matrons to engage in lesbian activities with their slaves. There is no evidence, however, that homosexuality was an important factor in the decline of these civilization, as some have charged (NAMH, 1971).

In Elizabethan England, an attitude of permissiveness was taken toward homosexuality without apparent harmful effects; in contemporary England, legislation has been passed making it legal for two consenting adults to engage privately in homosexual acts. Most cultures, however, have condemned homosexuality as socially undesirable. In the Netherlands and Denmark, for example, there are no laws against homosexuality, but it is strongly disapproved of (Weinberg & Williams, 1974).

In our own society, homosexual persons—particularly males—are still sometimes arrested and imprisoned under "crimes against nature" statutes as well as being subject to various forms of social disapproval and discrimination. Nevertheless, homosexuals may be otherwise well adjusted, well educated, and highly successful in their occupations. Many have made outstanding contributions in music, drama, and other fields. Not a few of the notable figures of history—including Alexander the Great, Sappho, Michelangelo, Oscar Wilde, Peter Tchaikovsky, Gertrude Stein, and Virginia Woolf—are thought to have been homosexuals.

Continuum of sexual behavior

Contrary to popular opinion, it is not possible to divide people into two clear-cut groups—homosexual and heterosexual. Rather, these two la-

HIGHLIGHT
Should homosexuality be "treated"?

The question of whether homosexual persons should receive therapy to change their sexual orientation has been one of the key issues in the intense controversy over whether homosexuality is a personality disorder or only a normal sexual variant. In recent years a number of therapy programs have been developed in which the explicit purpose is that of "reorienting" the sexual needs of homosexual individuals; many of these programs employ aversive conditioning techniques to suppress or eradicate the homosexual arousal pattern. Since the existence of treatment strongly implies that the condition being treated is undesirable, if not pathological, many supporters of the gay liberation movement object to treatment programs for homosexuality.

This issue has been forcefully brought to the attention of psychologists and other mental health professionals by Davison (1976, 1978), a leading researcher in the development of the new therapies for sexual difficulties. Davison argues that the very existence of sexual reorientation treatment programs strengthens prejudices against homosexual individuals and increases their self-hatred and embarrassment. Therefore, he concludes, the only ethical course is to stop offering this type of treatment—even to those individuals who voluntarily seek it.

Sturgis and Adams (1978) have taken the opposing position, arguing that the question of whether homosexuality is abnormal is entirely irrelevant to the question of whether an individual seeking treatment should have access to it. Sturgis and Adams charge that Davison's position will cause therapists to impose their own values—in this case, the belief that homosexuals should not receive treatment—on clients who may not share these values. For Sturgis and Adams, then, the primary issue is that of the "right to treatment" of those homosexual individuals who desire reorientation therapy. Davison (1978) acknowledges that his position is value-based, but he contends that values are the central consideration in the controversy. He also states that therapists have no absolute responsibility to provide what clients may request.

It seems likely that sexual reorientation programs will continue to be offered to those who request such treatment. In the meantime, the spirited exchange between researchers has sharpened the issues and has provoked a wide-ranging reexamination of attitudes within the professional community.

---

bels signify extreme poles on a continuum; in between, we find individuals whose orientations combine heterosexual and homosexual components. Kinsey et al. (1948), in one of the first extensive studies of male homosexuality, found that of their white male subjects,

13 percent had reacted erotically to other males without having overt homosexual experiences after the onset of adolescence.

37 percent had had a homosexual experience to the point of orgasm after the onset of adolescence.

50 percent of those who remained unmarried to the age of 35 had had an overt homosexual experience to the point of orgasm since the onset of adolescence.

18 percent revealed as much of the homosexual as the heterosexual in their histories.

8 percent engaged exclusively in homosexual activities for at least three years between the ages of 16 and 55.

4 percent were exclusively homosexual from adolescence on.

Since the men in this study had volunteered to be interviewed, these figures may have been somewhat higher than for the general population. Homosexual relationships were found to be far less common among women and, of those reporting homosexual responses, only about a third had proceeded to the point of orgasm (Kinsey et al., 1953). For the Masters and Johnson perspective on homosexuality, see the **HIGHLIGHT** on page 480.

Recent investigators have concluded, however, that lesbianism is more common than previous data would indicate, and that homosexuality is on the increase among both males and females. However, the apparent increase may simply reflect our national climate of greater openness toward sex. As Hoover (1973) has pointed out, "No one is sure whether more women are becoming lesbians now or whether they are just more visible" (p. 9). A possibly re-

HIGHLIGHT
The Masters and Johnson perspective on homosexuality

In recent years, Masters and Johnson (1979) provided new information on homosexuality and offered new hope to individuals who wish to alter their sexual orientation. The publication of this book was awaited impatiently not only because Masters and Johnson are the acknowledged contemporary leaders in research into sexuality and its problems, but also because it promised to bring to the study of homosexuality the same objectivity based on precise physiological and behavioral measurement that characterized their earlier studies of heterosexual individuals.

Most of the data for this book were collected prior to 1968 from a sample of 176 "committed homosexuals"—94 men and 82 women—ranging in age from 21 to 54. The sexual performances of these individuals were compared with those of 681 heterosexual partners. Masters and Johnson acknowledge that their findings may be unrepresentative in two ways: (1) their volunteer samples may not be a true cross-section of people in general; and (2) in ways that are not discernible, sex in the laboratory may differ from sex in more accustomed surroundings. Nevertheless, their data are probably the best that can currently be obtained. Their study focused on the bodily processes in homosexual relations and they have little to say about causal factors except to emphasize the importance of learning in the development of this preference. Their major findings may be summarized as follows:

1. Among persons selected for "sexual efficiency," homosexuals and heterosexuals have about the same low rate of failure to achieve orgasm: 3 per 100 opportunities.

2. Heterosexual sex fantasies are common among homosexual lovemakers, and many heterosexual persons occasionally indulge in homosexual fantasies.

3. Homosexual lovers generally communicate better than their heterosexual counterparts concerning sexual needs and sources of satisfaction; they are less preoccupied with achieving orgasm and more aware of the partner's level of arousal. In lesbian lovemaking particularly, a large amount of time is devoted to foreplay, and breast stimulation does not enter into the lovemaking sequence until much later than is common in heterosexual lovemaking.

4. While the data on sexual fantasies are limited to only 132 cases and may thus be especially lacking in generalizability, certain interesting trends emerge. The theme of forced sex was a more popular fantasy for the homosexuals than for the heterosexuals and tended to be fantasized about in more violent terms. When heterosexual women fantasized about forced sex, which has been found by many researchers to be quite common, they tended to imagine being treated gently and admiringly—although without choice—by their attackers. Among lesbians, on the other hand, fantasies tended to involve revenge upon some other woman, in which attackers humiliated the woman while the person experiencing the fantasy looked on in enjoyment.

5. In a separate (and later) series of 54 homosexual men and 13 lesbians who wished to undergo reorientation therapy, the known failure rate for the treatment devised by Masters and Johnson stood at 35 percent; and it is not expected to exceed 45 percent when the five-year follow-ups have been completed. This finding is of considerable theoretical importance and, of course, offers hope to those who desire reorientation therapy.

lated phenomenon has been an increase in certain kinds of physical disease among members of the gay community (see **HIGHLIGHT** on page 482).

While most people appear capable of engaging in and enjoying homosexual activity at some point in their lives, it would probably not be proper to conclude, as has sometimes been done, that everyone is fundamentally "bisexual." The large majority of persons, given a choice, prefer heterosexual forms of satisfaction. Among true bisexuals—those who are consistently active in both heterosexual and homosexual relationships—there is some question about which arousal pattern is the more fundamental. Laboratory studies of the arousal patterns of self-proclaimed bisexuals have shown that they in fact respond more strongly to homosexual than to heterosexual stimuli, a finding that holds for both men (Tollison, Adams, & Tollison, 1979) and women (Lamson, 1980).

If we can assume that the number of homosexuals has not changed drastically since Kinsey's studies were made, something in excess of 2.6 million men and 1.4 million women in the United States are exclusively homosexual. If we add those who are exclusively homosexual during a period of several years in their lives or who consistently engage in homosexual acts even though they are not exclusively homosexual, the overall figure for men and women would probably exceed some 20 million persons.

The question of causal factors

As noted, some homosexuals would prefer to be heterosexual; others find their orientation troubling and maladaptive, at least at times (though the homosexual life-style can be full and positive—see **HIGHLIGHT** on page 484). In addition, many heterosexuals who experience transitory homosexual episodes or feelings are confused and uncertain about the sources of these "alien" tendencies. What *does* cause sexual desires to become focused on members of one's own sex? Researchers have identified several possible causal factors.

In the first place, it seems increasingly likely that both biological and psychosocial factors are implicated in establishing a homosexual orientation. In this context, Money and Ehrhardt (1972) have described sexual differentiation as somewhat like a relay race—except instead of trying to beat other teams, the race is designed to complete a program.

Initially the XX or XY chromosomes pass the baton to the undifferentiated gonad to determine its destiny as ovary or testis. The gonad then differentiates and passes the baton to the hormonal secretion of its cells, and the process of fetal differentiation into the anatomy of a male or female continues. By birth, the first part of the program is completed. After birth, the baton is passed to environmental variables that play a determining role in shaping the individual's gender identity—usually, but not always, in accordance with his genetic sex.

Thus the initial part of the program is filled in by prenatal events, and the final part of the program by postnatal environmental ones, focusing primarily on learning. However, it is quite possible for the prenatal part of the program to markedly influence postnatal sexual differentiation. In any event, translated into actual sexual behavior, the total program may lead to heterosexual, bisexual, or homosexual patterns or life-styles (Adapted from Money & Ehrhardt, 1972).

1. *Genetic and hormonal factors.* Although Kallmann (1952) reported a 100 percent concordance rate for homosexuality in identical twins as contrasted with only 15 percent for fraternal twins, more recent investigators have not been able to corroborate the view that homosexual tendencies are inherited (Rosenthal, 1970).

It is interesting to note, however, the extensive work of Money and his associates (1969, 1972, 1974, 1980) in this area. These researchers provide a convincing demonstration of the effects of too little or too much male hormone during critical stages of fetal development on later sexual differentiation. For example, they cite examples of genetic females exposed to excessive androgen during fetal development. Although raised as girls, their behavior was "masculinized" in various ways as contrasted to the behavior of a control group of girls not exposed to excessive androgens. Presumably if the significant adults in the early postnatal environment of these androgenized girls were to provide unclear models or communicate unclear messages with respect to male and female sex identity, these girls *might* be more likely than girls in general to become homosexual. Similarly, genetic males exposed to insufficient prenatal androgen and subjected to an ambivalent postnatal environment concerning sexual identity *might* be more likely than males in general to become homosexual.

One of the basic hypotheses underlying the work of Money and his associates is that prenatal or early postnatal hormonal influences may actually affect the formation of brain pathways, leading to propensities toward a relatively masculine or feminine behavioral orientation. Evidence of such influences would not necessarily show up in hormonal imbalances at a later time. Their data are sufficiently strong that one would be ill-advised to dismiss this somewhat exotic conception out of hand. Should it prove to hold up under further scrutiny, it may provide a key

HIGHLIGHT

AIDS: The gay plague

Since 1979 when the first cases were noted, acquired immune deficiency syndrome (AIDS) has imposed an increasing burden of fear on homosexual communities. Concentrated (as of this writing) in the gay community of New York City, this disease destroys the immunological defenses of its victims, rendering them highly vulnerable to sundry lethal diseases, including cancer. As of the second half of 1979 six known cases had been identified, with no resulting deaths. For the six-month period comprising the second half of 1982, 462 new cases were identified; 102 of these persons had died by mid-March of 1983. Clearly, AIDS has become an epidemic of frightening proportions. It imposes on members of the gay community a cruel choice: renounce casual sexual relations or face the risk of permanent disablement or death.

The disease is apparently transmitted for the most part by intimate (sexual) contact. It has also shown up among a group of Haitian immigrants, although its independence from homosexuality in that group is not certain. Also affected are intravenous drug abusers and people requiring frequent blood transfusions. It is likely that AIDS can be transmitted by *heterosexual* intimacy, and there is fear that the disease will invade in force the much larger heterosexual community.

Strenuous efforts, strongly supported by the gay community, are presently under way to discover the cause of AIDS and to develop an effective means of combatting it. Gay leaders, however, point out that these efforts have been slow in getting started, charging prejudice in governmental, medical, and research communities. As of May 1983, no effective remedy was in sight (CBS *Sunday Morning* telecast, May 29, 1983; *Time,* March 28, 1983, pp. 53–55).

to understanding some aspects of the development not only of homosexuality but also of other gender-role variants as well, such as transsexualism.

A great deal of research has also been done on supposed differences in the levels of plasma testosterone in homosexual and nonhomosexual males (Brodie et al., 1974; Kolodny et al., 1971). One research group has even claimed to be able to identify homosexuality in males with 100 percent accuracy by measuring urine hormone levels (Margolese & Janigen, 1973). However, studies have produced widely varying results as to these alleged differences, and no agreement has been reached on the possible reasons for these discrepant findings.

1. *Homosexual experiences, and their positive reinforcement.* The development of homosexuality is frequently associated with pleasant homosexual experiences during adolescence or early adulthood. In an early study of 79 male homosexuals, East (1946) found early homosexual experiences to be the most common environmental factor. More recent studies have tended to support this finding. In a study of 65 lesbians, for example, Hedblom (1973) found that two thirds engaged in their first homosexual contact before the age of 20 and had been willing and cooperative partners. Forty percent of the total group achieved orgasm at the time of their first homosexual experience. In the Indiana University study of San Francisco homosexuals cited earlier, large majorities of both men and women in the sample reported having experienced arousal by a person of the same sex prior to the age of 19. Of those reporting a homosexual encounter before age 19, 62 percent of the men and 73 percent of the women reported enjoying their first such experience (Bell et al., 1981).

In spite of these findings, it seems doubtful that early homosexual experiences lead to later homosexual life-styles except where they are reinforced by pleasurable repetition and/or meet the individual's emotional needs. This kind of emotional support is described in the following excerpt from the case of an adolescent girl who first entered into homosexual behavior in a correctional institution for delinquent girls.

"I have a girl, a simply wonderful girl. . . . I need her. . . . I feel better toward all people. I feel satisfied. Now I have somebody to care for. Now I have

somebody I want to make happy and somebody I will work hard for. . . ." (Konopka, 1964, p. 23)

Bell et al., (1981) made the important point that homosexual *feelings* usually preceded any homosexual encounter in their large sample of gay men and women, and in fact many of these individuals had exhibited gender-role nonconformity well in advance of puberty. In short, many gay men and women report histories of having been "sissies" and "tomboys," respectively, during their developmental years (Adams & Chiodo, 1984).

3. *Negative conditioning of heterosexual behavior.* A variety of circumstances may lead to conditioning in which heterosexual behavior becomes an aversive stimulus. For example, where a boy or girl is ridiculed, rebuffed, and humiliated in an early effort to approach members of the opposite sex, homosexuality may seem a safer source of affection and sexual outlet. If parents catch their son "playing with" a little girl and punish him for being "bad," they may be subtly telling him that heterosexual behavior is evil. Early sexual relations under unfortunate conditions may have a comparable effect. Konopka (1964) concluded: "Girls who have been raped by their fathers (and they are not rare among delinquent girls) find relationships with men either threatening or disgusting and often turn to other girls for the fulfillment of their emotional need for love" (p. 23).

Similarly, findings in the study of homosexuals by the Institute for Sex Research showed that some lesbians had shifted from heterosexual to homosexual behavior after disillusionment with their heterosexual partners; conversely, some lesbians shifted to heterosexuality after disillusionment with the gay life (Bell & Weinberg, 1978). It was also noted that more than a third of the gay females and 20 percent of the gay males had been married. In fact, the great majority of the subjects in this study had had heterosexual relationships prior to adopting a gay life-style.

4. *Family patterns.* A great deal of research attention has been given to the role of family relationships in the development of homosexuality. In a study of 106 male homosexuals who were undergoing psychoanalysis, Bieber et al. (1962) found a common family pattern involving a dominant, seductive mother and a weak or ab-

HIGHLIGHT
Aspects of life in the gay community

In our society, heterosexuality has been regarded as the "appropriate" mode of sexual behavior, while homosexuality has traditionally been seen as a mental disorder. Homosexuals have been regarded as "sick" persons in need of treatment.

However, this traditional view is changing in response to the entreaties of the gay liberation movement and to the accumulating research evidence showing that a homosexual orientation is by no means synonymous with ineffective functioning or personality disorder (Bell, 1974; Bell & Weinberg, 1978; Freedman, 1975; Hooker, 1957; Thompson, McCandless, & Strickland, 1971; Weinberg & Williams, 1974). As we have seen, some homosexual individuals appear unable to manage their orientation adaptively, but this is true of some heterosexuals as well; in most respects, homosexual men and women are indistinguishable from the majority of persons who prefer heterosexual partnerships. In particular, most homosexuals do not evidence overt gender identity problems of the type described in this chapter; their "difference" usually involves relative disinterest in heterosexual activity and a homosexual arousal pattern.

Even adjusted homosexuals, however, must face the special stresses that are associated with the gay life-style. For many, association with the supportive and protective institutions of the gay community appears to be an important factor in such coping.

Broadly speaking, the gay community may be described as a geographical area in which the homosexual subculture and its institutions are located. Thus the apartment buildings on certain streets may be rented exclusively to homosexuals; most of the homes in certain areas may be owned by homosexuals; clothing stores, bookstores, theaters, and other business establishments may cater primarily to homosexual clientele; and a variety of recreational facilities and groups, including ski and travel clubs may be exclusively homosexual in their membership. In addition, there are churches, welfare organizations, service centers, and so on, for homosexuals. In essence, the homosexual community constitutes a subculture with unique customs, value systems, communication techniques, and supportive and protective institutions.

The cornerstone of the gay community, however, is the "gay bar"; it is also the most visible section of the homosexual community in the sense that any person may enter. In major cities, such as Los Angeles, New York, and San Francisco, there are relatively large numbers of such bars; for example, the Los An-

geles area has more than 200 gay bars, the majority of which are for male homosexuals. In these bars friends meet, news and gossip are exchanged, invitations to parties are issued, and warnings about current police activities are circulated. However, the crucial function of the bars, as is often the case with those that cater to heterosexual clientele, is to facilitate making sexual contacts. Typically, these contacts are between strangers, who agree to meet at a certain time and place for sexual purposes. Their relationship is usually transitory, and subsequently each is likely to find a new partner. A central feature of such relationships is the assumption that sexual gratification can be had without obligation or a long-term commitment. When asked what it means to be "gay", one man answered, "To be gay is to go to the bar, to make the scene, to look, and look, and look, to have a one night stand, to never really love or be loved, and to really know this, and to do this night after night, and year after year." (Hooker, 1962, p. 9) This viewpoint may not be characteristic of the majority of homosexuals, but rather of those who find sexual variety of primary importance in their homosexual life-style.

In a more general sense, the homosexual community is characterized by overlapping social networks of varying degrees of cohesiveness. There are, for example, loosely knit friendship groups and tightly knit cliques formed of homosexually married couples or of individuals who often are heterosexually married. In addition, there are organizations concerned with establishing and protecting the rights of homosexuals; of these, the best known are probably the Mattachine societies for male homosexuals, the first having been founded in Los Angeles in 1950 and named after sixteenth-century Spanish court jesters who wore masks. On the female side are the equally well-known Daughters of Bilitis, whose name is taken from *The Songs of Bilitis,* nineteenth-century lyrics that glorify lesbian love. There are also a number of other organizations and facilities, such as the Gay Community Service Centers, oriented primarily toward helping homosexuals deal with the practical problems associated with the gay life-style. Such organizations have been critically important in coping with the current AIDS crisis described in the **HIGHLIGHT** on page 482.

In general, homosexuals who are affiliated with the gay subculture—as well as most who are not—view homosexuality as an alternative sexual pattern or life-style and feel entitled to the same rights and protections as any minority group in society.

sent father. Typically the mother, frustrated by an unhappy marital relationship, established a relationship with the son that became seductive and romantic but stopped just short of physical contact. The son, overstimulated sexually, felt anxious and guilty over his incestuous feelings, and the mother, aware of his feelings and fearful of exposing her own incestuous impulses, discouraged overt signs of masculinity. The father, resenting the son as a rival, also made it clear that the son's developing masculinity was offensive. Often the father showed a preference for a daughter, and the son, in envy, wished he were a girl. Bieber et al. described the end result as follows:

"By the time the H-son has reached the preadolescent period, he has suffered a diffuse personality disorder. Maternal overanxiety about health and injury, restriction of activities normative for the son's age and potential interference with assertive behavior, demasculinizing attitudes and interference with sexuality—interpenetrating with paternal rejection, hostility, and lack of support—produce an excessively fearful child, pathologically dependent upon his mother and beset by feelings of inadequacy, impotence, and self-contempt. He is reluctant to participate in boyhood activities thought to be potentially physically injurious—usually grossly overestimated. His peer group responds with humiliating name-calling and often with physical attack which timidity tends to invite among children. His fear and shame of self, made worse by the derisive reactions of other boys, only drive him further away. . . .

"Failure in the peer group, and anxieties about a masculine, heterosexual presentation of self, pave the way for the prehomosexual's initiation into the less threatening atmosphere of homosexual society, its values, and way of life." (pp. 316–17)

Considerable doubt has been cast on the findings of Bieber et al. Since the subjects studied were patients in psychoanalysis, the retrospective nature of many of the questions required the subjects to think back over several years for answers, and a high degree of inference was used in interpreting the data. On the other hand, the findings of several later investigators have generally supported the findings of Bieber and his associates (Evans, 1969; Snortum et al., 1969; Stephan, 1973; Thompson et al., 1973). Typically the mothers were close-binding, controlling, and affectionate; the fathers were detached, rejecting, and often hostile. Neither parent fostered a masculine self-image or identity.

As children, the male homosexuals in these studies tended to describe themselves as shy, fearful of physical injury, and loners who seldom entered into "rough" competitive sports such as baseball, basketball, or football. A more recent study has shown that the attributed family pattern tends to show up only among individuals who have, at some point in their lives, sought counseling or psychotherapy (Bell et al., 1981).

In contrast, Siegelman (1974) examined the family constellation described by the preceding investigators among gay and nongay males and found that it did not distinguish among them; rather it was indicative of neuroticism or other psychopathology in both groups. Similarly, the well-designed Institute for Sex Research study has failed to turn up any consistent differences in the family backgrounds of homosexuals as compared with heterosexuals (Bell, 1974; Bell & Weinberg, 1978).

Although family patterns may create a wide range of adjustment problems and even severe maladjustment, there are insufficient research data to justify the conclusion that the family background of homosexuals as a group is significantly different from that of heterosexuals.

5. *General sociocultural factors.* It would appear that a variety of sociocultural factors, including the specificity of expected role behavior and the severity of social sanctions for deviations, may markedly influence the incidence of homosexual and other unconventional sexual life-styles. For example, Davenport (1965) has described the sexual mores of the Melanesians in the Southwest Pacific. Premarital intercourse is forbidden among them, and both males and females are encouraged to masturbate. In addition, all unmarried males engage in homosexual relations with the full knowledge of the community, but after marriage they are expected to assume a heterosexual pattern—a transition they appear to have little difficulty in making.

It would also appear that among certain nonindustrialized groups living in areas with limited resources, homosexuality has actually been encouraged at one time or another to help control the population of the group; in other instances it has been encouraged among soldiers—as at one time in Greece and in the French Foreign Legion—because it was thought they would fight more fiercely to protect their lovers

Studies of male homosexuals have failed to show conclusively that family backgrounds of homosexuals differ significantly from those of heterosexuals.

(Churchill, 1967). In any event, it seems clear that social inhibitions and reinforcements can influence the incidence of homosexuality.

Homosexuality and society

Since the general adjustment problems of homosexuals result in part from the self-devaluation fostered by society, the discrimination directed toward them, and the severe sanctions society often imposes on them, many investigators have urged the legalization of homosexual acts between consenting adults in private. For example, a task force of the National Institute of Mental Health concluded their report as follows:

"We believe that most professionals working in this area—on the basis of their collective research and clinical experience and the present overall knowledge of the subject—are strongly convinced that the extreme opprobrium our society has attached to homosexual behavior, by way of criminal statutes and restricted employment practices, has done more social harm than good and goes beyond what is necessary for the maintenance of public order and human decency." (Livingood, 1972, pp. 5–6).

As noted earlier, the centuries-old laws against homosexuality in England were repealed by Parliament in 1967, making homosexual acts between consenting adults in private none of

the law's business. In the United States, Illinois in 1961 was the first state to repeal existing statutes against homosexual acts between consenting adults in private. Many other states have since followed suit.

While the long-range effects of such changes on society remain to be ascertained, there is no evidence to date that they have led to a significant increase in homosexuality or have proven detrimental to the general welfare. And, in general, heterosexual interests seem to remain alive and well through it all, so we need have little fear that our species will be decimated by rampant homoeroticism.

Summary

In contrast to lower animals, the sexuality of humans is remarkably free of biological constraints and is, therefore, highly plastic and subject to acquired inhibitions and acquired appetites. The inhibitions are associated chiefly with psychosexual dysfunctions—varied inabilities to achieve satisfaction or to provide it for one's partner. The sexual appetites may involve psychosexual variants or deviations, in which the individual's preferred modes of arousal and gratification are different from conventionally accepted heterosexual patterns and, in some instances, are thought to threaten the welfare of the group. Some such variants, however, are victimless and cause no great harm either to individuals or to society in general.

Some psychosexual dysfunctions involve inhibited sexual desire in either sex. Other dysfunctions are more gender-specific: for males, erectile insufficiency, premature ejaculation, and ejaculatory retardation or incompetence; for females, arousal insufficiency (analogous to erectile insufficiency in the male), orgasmic dysfunction, vaginismus, and dyspareunia. Great strides have been made in recent years in the treatment of psychosexual dysfunctions in both sexes. Contrary to the situation of less than two decades ago, most people experiencing dysfunctions can now be reassured that, in all likelihood, they will be able to overcome their difficulties with competent professional help.

Of the sexual variants, one of the least understood is gender identity disorder, in which the person feels trapped in a body of the wrong gender, often leading to efforts to have the body altered so as to conform to the person's internal sense of maleness or femaleness. Neither the male nor female pattern is well understood at this time, but it seems likely that both biological and psychosocial factors are implicated in the majority of cases.

The paraphilias are a group of disorders in which sexual satisfaction becomes persistently focused on some unusual object, ritual, or situation. We distinguish between victimless varieties, such as transvestism, and those deviations involving assault or nonconsent, such as exhibitionism. Other paraphilias include fetishism, voyeurism, pedophilia, and sexual sadism and masochism. Little is known about the development of these deviant practices, but it is strongly suspected that, for the most part, they are due to faulty learning.

Discussions of incest (especially of the father-daughter type) and rape are also included here, even though neither of these is recognized in the DSM-III. The chief importance of incest, from an abnormal psychology standpoint, is that the child-victim often suffers serious adjustment difficulties in adolescence and adulthood. Contrary to most public opinion, sexual gratification is *not* the dominant motive in the overwhelming majority of rapes. Motives of power and aggression against women are far more likely to instigate incidents of rape.

Therapy for the sexual dysfunctions has developed at an impressive pace since the beginning of the last decade. The prognosis for the sexual variants and deviations is, in general, far less optimistic—although, even here, treatment successes *do* occur, especially where a comprehensive treatment approach is planned and effected.

The DSM-III recognizes one type of disorder involving homosexuality—"ego-dystonic" homosexuality—in which the individual persistently wishes to change his or her sexual orientation. Homosexuality itself is a complex phenomenon. Both homosexual and heterosexual components exist in varying degrees in everyone, but it cannot be said that everyone is fundamentally "bisexual." Rather, people can be seen as fitting along a sexual continuum, with the labels "homosexual" and "heterosexual" at the extreme poles.

It appears likely that both biological and psychosocial factors contribute to a homosexual orientation. Sociocultural factors—such as social inhibitions and reinforcements—are also thought to influence the incidence of homosexuality.

13

Organic mental disorders and mental retardation

Raymond Oui, Monsieur Oui Oui *(1948?). Having always suffered from severe psychological impairment, Raymond Oui (b. 1915?) was admitted to a psychiatric institution in Lot-et-Garonne, France, in about 1948. During ordinary conversation, Oui continually interjects the word* oui. *He also includes the word repeatedly in his artwork.*

In contrast to most kinds of abnormal behavior, certain problems arise partly as a consequence of gross structural defects in the brain tissue. Such defects impair the normal physiological functioning of those parts of the brain affected—thus, in turn, producing deficits in the mediation of effective thought, feeling, and action.

When such gross structural defects in the brain occur before birth or at a very early age, the typical result is mental retardation, the severity depending on the defect. In mental retardation, the individual fails to develop an optimal level of the various skills that underlie adequate and independent coping with environmental demands. Most mentally retarded persons do not suffer from gross brain damage, but virtually all those individuals who can be described as *severely* retarded have some form of demonstrable organic pathology.

Sometimes the intact brain sustains damage after it has completed all or most of its biological development. A wide variety of injuries, diseases, and toxic chemicals may result in the functional impairment or death of neural cells and, in turn, lead to obviously inadequate psychological functioning and perhaps psychotic behavior.

The person who sustains serious brain damage after he or she has mastered the basic tasks of life is in a very different situation from the person who starts life with a deficit. When brain injury occurs in an older child or adult, there is a *loss* in established functioning. In contrast, the person who began life with severe mental retardation never had these functions to begin with. The difference is an extremely important one psychologically.

In this chapter we shall discuss both situations. The first and largest part of the chapter will be devoted to the organic mental disorders—mental disorders that occur when there has been damage to the normal brain. Then, in the latter part of the chapter, we shall look at mental retardation, in which the individual fails to develop a normal level of intellectual functioning. In both cases, we shall see that the physical deficit in the brain is only one among many causes of the individual's behavior. In fact, in the case of individuals with mild retardation, there may be absolutely no physical deficit at all.

Organic mental disorders

Organic mental disorders that have resulted from interference with the functioning of a normal brain may involve only limited behavioral deficits or a wide range of psychopathology, depending on (a) the location and extent of neural damage, (b) the premorbid (predisorder) personality of the individual, and (c) the nature of the individual's life situation. In many cases involving severe brain damage, mental change is astonishingly slight, whereas in other cases, mild brain damage leads to a psychotic reaction.

In general, we suspect that organic pathology may underlie a psychosis when (a) the psychotic symptoms are especially severe, (b) they are accompanied by notable memory or other intellectual impairment, and (c) few other grounds exist for explaining the symptoms (Strayhorn, 1982). Regarding the first point, Hall and colleagues (1980) found contributory organic disease in 46 percent of a sample of acutely disturbed psychiatric inpatients, whereas signs of organic disease were much less common—about 9 percent—among less disturbed psychiatric outpatients (Hall et al., 1978).

Important to reiterate here is the distinction, introduced in Chapter 3, between neurological disease or impairment and the aberrant mental and behavioral processes that constitute psychiatric symptoms. Neurological disorder impairs the *execution* of behavior—as, for example, in sensorimotor functioning or the performance of complex intellectual tasks. Most neurologically impaired individuals *do not* develop psychiatric symptoms, such as delusions. In similar fashion, Fabrega (1981) distinguishes between "neuropsychiatric disease," which always involves physical change, and "neuropsychiatric illness," which is a psychological and social disturbance. Fabrega points out that a person can have either of these types of disorder without having the other. This chapter is concerned with persons who have both.

The varying effects of significant neurological impairment on individuals are explained by the fact that the individual is a functional unit and reacts as such to all stressors, whether they are organic or psychological. A well-integrated person can withstand brain damage or any other stress better than a rigid, immature, or otherwise psychologically handicapped person. Similarly, the individual who has a favorable life situation is likely to have a better prognosis than one who does not. Since the nervous system is the center for integration of behavior, however, there are limits to the amount of brain damage an individual can tolerate or compensate for without exhibiting impaired functioning (see **HIGHLIGHT** on page 491).

The regenerative capacities of the central nervous system are limited, too. Cell bodies and neural pathways in the brain do not have the power of regeneration, which means that their destruction is permanent. However, the central nervous system abounds in back-up apparatus. If a given circuit is knocked out, others may take over, and functions lost as a result of brain damage may often be relearned. The degree of recovery from disabilities following an irreversible brain lesion may be relatively complete or limited, and recovery may proceed rapidly or slowly. Since there are limits to both the plasticity and the relearning ability of the brain, however, extensive brain damage may lead to a permanent loss of function and result in a wide range of physical and psychological symptoms. In general, especially with severe damage, the greater the amount of tissue damage, the greater the impairment of function.

Location of damage may also be of great significance. The parts of the human brain are to a considerable extent specialized in their function. Thus, the two hemispheres, while interacting on many levels, are involved in quite different types of mental activity. For example, language and related functions are for the most part localized in the left hemisphere for nearly everyone, while appreciation of spatial relations and "intuitive" thought are right-side functions. Even within hemispheres, the various lobes and even various areas within lobes perform somewhat specialized functions.

While none of these relationships between brain location and behavior can be considered constant or universal, it is possible to make certain broad generalizations about the likely effects of damage to particular parts of the brain. Damage to the frontal areas, for example, is associated with either of two contrasting clinical pictures: (a) passivity, apathy, and an inability to "give up" a given stream of associations (per-

HIGHLIGHT

Implications of brain damage

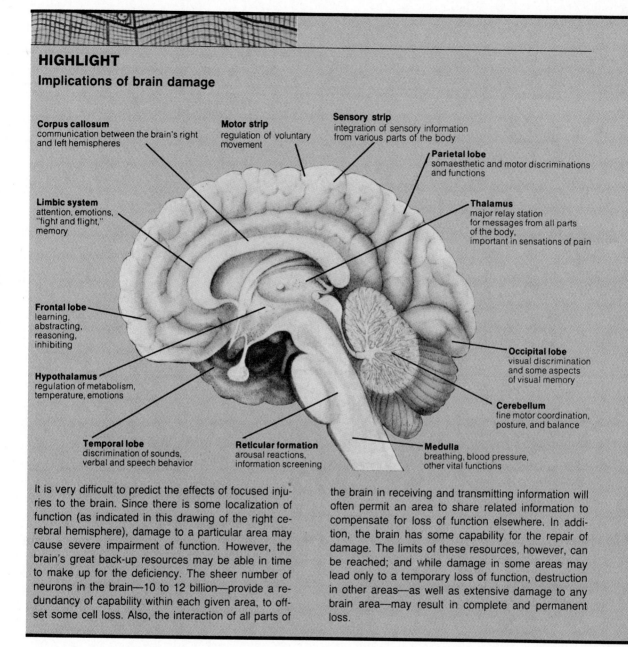

Corpus callosum
communication between the brain's right and left hemispheres

Motor strip
regulation of voluntary movement

Sensory strip
integration of sensory information from various parts of the body

Parietal lobe
somaesthetic and motor discriminations and functions

Limbic system
attention, emotions, "fight and flight," memory

Thalamus
major relay station for messages from all parts of the body, important in sensations of pain

Frontal lobe
learning, abstracting, reasoning, inhibiting

Occipital lobe
visual discrimination and some aspects of visual memory

Hypothalamus
regulation of metabolism, temperature, emotions

Cerebellum
fine motor coordination, posture, and balance

Temporal lobe
discrimination of sounds, verbal and speech behavior

Reticular formation
arousal reactions, information screening

Medulla
breathing, blood pressure, other vital functions

It is very difficult to predict the effects of focused injuries to the brain. Since there is some localization of function (as indicated in this drawing of the right cerebral hemisphere), damage to a particular area may cause severe impairment of function. However, the brain's great back-up resources may be able in time to make up for the deficiency. The sheer number of neurons in the brain—10 to 12 billion—provide a redundancy of capability within each given area, to offset some cell loss. Also, the interaction of all parts of the brain in receiving and transmitting information will often permit an area to share related information to compensate for loss of function elsewhere. In addition, the brain has some capability for the repair of damage. The limits of these resources, however, can be reached; and while damage in some areas may lead only to a temporary loss of function, destruction in other areas—as well as extensive damage to any brain area—may result in complete and permanent loss.

severative thought); or (b) impulsiveness, distractibility, and insufficient ethical restraint (Crockett, Clark, & Klonoff, 1981). Damage to the right parietal lobe often produces distortions of body image, while language function is impaired as a result of significant damage to the left parietal. Temporal lobe damage disrupts attention and memory; extensive bilateral temporal damage can produce a bizarre syndrome in which the individual's remote memory remains intact but nothing *new* can be effectively stored for later retrieval. Temporal damage is also associated with disturbances of eating, sexuality, and the emotions, probably by way of disrupting the functioning of the adjacent limbic lobe, a deeper center mediating these "primitive" functions. Occipital damage produces a variety of visual impairments as well as visual-association deficits; for example, the person may be unable to recognize familiar faces or to correctly visualize and understand symbolic stimuli (Filskov, Grimm, & Lewis, 1981). The **HIGHLIGHT** on page 493 provides additional information on localization derived from neuropsychological tests.

Brain disorders can also be classified as *acute* or *chronic*, the primary consideration being whether the brain pathology is reversible. An acute disorder is likely to be temporary and reversible, whereas a chronic disorder is usually irreversible because of permanent damage to the nervous system. This classification is not a hard and fast one, because an acute condition may leave some residual damage after the major symptoms have cleared up, while a chronic condition may show some alleviation of symptoms over time. However, a general picture can be given of the two types.

1. *Acute brain disorders.* Acute brain disorders are caused by diffuse impairment of brain function. Such impairment may result from a variety of conditions, including high fevers, nutritional deficiencies, and drug intoxication. Symptoms range from mild mood changes to acute delirium. The latter may be complicated by hallucinations, delusions, and other personality disturbances.

The prognosis in acute brain disorders is good; such conditions usually clear up over a short period of time. In some cases, however, the lowering of cortical controls may precipitate a latent psychosis that persists after the immediate brain pathology has cleared up.

2. *Chronic brain disorders.* Chronic brain disorders result from injuries, disease, drugs, and a variety of other conditions. The permanent destruction of brain tissue is reflected in some degree of impairment of higher integrative functions. Where the damage is severe, such symptoms typically include the following:

a) Impairment of orientation—especially for time but often also for place and person;

b) Impairment of memory—notably for recent events and less for events of the remote past, with a tendency to confabulate, that is, to "invent" memories to fill in gaps;

c) Impairment of learning, comprehension, and judgment—with ideation tending to be concrete and impoverished and with inability to think on higher conceptual levels and to plan;

d) Emotional impairment—with emotional over-reactivity and easy arousal to laughter or tears or with a blunting of affect;

e) Impairment of inner reality and ethical controls—with lowering of behavioral standards and carelessness in personal hygiene and appearance.

These symptoms may also occur in acute brain disorders; however, in such cases delirium and hallucinations or stupor are more likely to dominate the clinical picture. In either acute or chronic disorders, the clinical picture may be referred to as *mild, moderate,* or *severe,* depending on the severity of symptoms.

Traditionally the organic mental disorders have been classified by disease entity or recognizable disorder, such as Huntington's chorea, general paresis, and so on. But these are basically physical disorders with various kinds of related psychopathology. In the DSM-III, physical disorders are coded on Axis III, and psychiatric categories are derived from Axes I and II (psychiatric and personality conditions). Thus, with the exception of the senile and presenile dementias, the traditional organic mental disorders no longer appear as psychiatric categories. Instead, only particular clusters of symptoms based on brain damage and often seen in the various organically based psychoses are listed on Axis I. In our discussion, we shall first describe these clusters of symptoms and then go on to describe the clinical picture, causal factors, and treatment approaches for five of the most common mental disorders associated with brain damage.

Organic symptom syndromes

Syndromes are groups of symptoms that tend to cluster together. The organic symptom syndromes include many symptoms similar to those that occur in the schizophrenias and the affective psychoses; but in this case, the symptoms reflect underlying brain pathology. The specific brain pathology may vary from some type of brain disease to the results of withdrawal of a chemical substance on which the person has become physiologically dependent. For our purposes, we shall group these symptom syndromes into four categories: (a) delirium and dementia, (b) amnestic syndrome and hallucinosis, (c) organic delusional syndrome and organic affective syndrome, and (d) organic personality syndrome.

HIGHLIGHT

Behavioral deficits associated with damage to eight brain areas

The Luria-Nebraska neuropsychological battery of tests has been used to identify the effects of brain damage in eight brain areas—i.e., four major brain areas in each hemisphere of the brain. The drawing shows a side view of the left hemisphere of the brain. The table below summarizes the types of behavior that can be affected by damage to each of the eight areas.

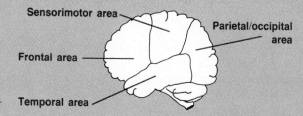

	Frontal area	Temporal area	Sensorimotor area[1]	Parietal/ occipital area
Right Hemisphere	Motor Rhythm Math	Motor Rhythm Tactile Receptive[2]	Motor	Motor Tactile[2]
Left Hemisphere	Receptive Expressive[2] Math	Receptive Expressive Math Memory Intelligence	Expressive Math Intelligence	Expressive Writing Math

[1]The "sensorimotor area" is a strip of tissue extending from each side of the prominent central fissure (the fissure of Rolando); it comprises the posterior portion of the frontal and the anterior parts of the parietal lobes.

[2]*Receptive* and *expressive* refer, respectively, to the ability to understand verbal communications and the ability to formulate or articulate verbal communications. The term *tactile* refers to the sense of touch.

Adapted from Golden, Moses, et al., 1981.

It should be noted that more than one syndrome may be present at one time in a given patient and that syndromes and patterns of syndromes may change over the course of development of a particular disorder. At the behavioral level, they often mimic the types of disorders we have been discussing in previous chapters, sometimes causing serious diagnostic errors to be made (Geschwind, 1975; Malamud, 1975).

Delirium and dementia.   *Delirium* is characterized by a relatively rapid onset of widespread disorganization of the higher mental processes; it is caused by a generalized disturbance in brain metabolism. Information-processing capacities are more or less severely impaired, af-

fecting such basic processes as attention, perception, memory, and thinking. Frequently, there is abnormal psychomotor activity and disturbance of the sleep cycle. In terms of the functional integrity of the brain, delirium is only one step above coma and, in fact, may lead to coma. The delirious person is essentially unable to carry out purposeful mental activity of any kind; current experience appears to make no contact with the individual's previously acquired store of knowlege.

Delirious states rarely last more than a week, terminating in recovery or, less often, in death. They tend, therefore, to be associated with acute rather than chronic brain disturbances. They may result from head injury, toxic or metabolic disturbances, oxygen deprivation, insufficient delivery of blood to brain tissues, or alcohol or other drugs in an addicted person.

Dementia has as its essential feature a noteworthy decrement, or deterioration, in intellectual functioning occurring after the completion of brain maturation (after, that is, about 15 years of age). The individual is otherwise alert and attuned to events in the environment. Memory functioning is invariably affected, and there is usually also marked indication of deficit in abstract thinking, acquisition of new knowledge or skills, problem solving, and judgment.

Normally, dementia is also accompanied by an impairment in emotional control and in moral and ethical sensibilities. It may be progressive or static; occasionally it is even reversible. Its course depends to a large extent on the nature of the etiology.

Etiologic factors in dementia are many and varied. They include degenerative processes that affect some individuals—usually older people, but not always. Repeated cerebrovascular accidents (strokes), certain infectious diseases such as syphilis and meningitis, intracranial tumors and abscesses, certain dietary deficiencies, head injury, anoxia, and the ingestion or inhalation of toxic substances have all been implicated in the production of dementias. As the **HIGHLIGHT** on page 495 makes clear, the most common cause of dementia is degenerative brain disease, particularly of the variety typified by Alzheimer's disease.

Amnestic syndrome and hallucinosis.

The essential feature of the *amnestic syndrome* is a striking deficit in the ability to remember ongoing events more than a few minutes after they have taken place. Immediate memory and memory for events that occurred before the development of the disorder are largely unimpaired, as is memory for words and concepts. An amnestic individual, then, is constrained to live for the most part only in the present or the remote past; the recent past is for most practical purposes unavailable.[1]

_____
[1]Whether the recent past is unavailable in some absolute sense is a question subject to differing interpretations. There is some evidence that these patients may recognize or even recollect events of the recent past if given sufficient cues, which suggests that the information *has* been stored. Thus, the difficulty may be in the *retrieval* mechanism (Hirst, 1982; Warrington & Weiskrantz, 1973).

In contrast to the dementia syndrome, overall cognitive functioning in the amnestic syndrome remains more or less intact. Theoretically, the disorder simply affects the relationships between the short-term and long-term memory systems; the contents of the former are not stored in the latter in a way that permits ready accessibility or retrieval (Hirst, 1982). A common reaction in the amnestic syndrome is for the individual to resist acknowledging the difficulty and to "fill in the gaps" with fanciful details, a process known as *confabulation.*

In the most common forms of amnestic syndrome, those due to alcohol or barbiturate addiction, the disorder is normally irreversible. A wide range of other pathogenic factors may produce the amnestic syndrome. In these cases, depending on the nature and extent of damage to the affected neural structures and on the treatment undertaken, the syndrome may in time abate wholly, in part, or not at all.

The syndrome of *hallucinosis* has as its essential feature the persistent occurrence of hallucinations in the presence of known or suspected brain involvement; the term is not used where hallucinations are part of a more pervasive mental disorder such as schizophrenia. These "false perceptions" arise in a state of full wakefulness, when the person is alert and otherwise well oriented. The hallucinations most often involve the sense of hearing but may affect any sense; for example, visual hallucinations typically accompany psychedelic drug intoxication.

The course of the syndrome varies with the underlying pathology but rarely exceeds one month, assuming discontinuance of the causative agent. As in the case of the amnestic syndrome, the most common etiologic factor is severe or long-standing alcohol dependency.

Organic delusional syndrome and organic affective syndrome.

In the *organic delusional syndrome,* false beliefs or belief systems arise in a setting of known or suspected brain damage and are the chief clinical manifestation of this damage. These delusions vary in content depending to some extent on the particular organic etiology. For example, a distinctly paranoid delusional system is commonly seen with long-standing abuse of amphetamine drugs, whereas grandiose and expansive delu-

HIGHLIGHT

Dementia in 417 patients fully evaluated for dementia

Diagnosis	Number	Percent
Alzheimer's disease or dementia of unknown cause	199	47.7
Alcoholic dementia—Korsakoff's syndrome	42	10.0
Multi-infarct dementia	39	9.4
Normal pressure hydrocephalus	25	6.0
Intracranial masses [tumors]	20	4.8
Huntington's chorea	12	2.9
Drug toxicity	10	2.4
Posttraumatic	7	1.7
Other identified dementing diseases[1]	28	6.7
Pseudodementias[2]	28	6.7
Dementia uncertain	7	1.7

[1]Including epilepsy, subarachnoid hemorrhage, encephalitis, amyotropic lateral sclerosis, Parkinson's disease, hyperthyroidism, syphilis, liver disease, and cerebral anoxic episode, all less than 1 percent incidence.

[2]Including depression (16), schizophrenia (5), mania (2), "hysteria" (1), and not demented (4).

Based on Wells, 1979.

sions are more characteristic of advanced syphilis (general paresis). In addition to infectious processes and the abuse of certain drugs, etiological factors in the organic delusional syndrome include head injury and intracranial tumors.

The *organic affective syndrome,* as the term implies, refers to manic or depressive states caused by impairment of cerebral function. While the organic delusional syndrome may clinically mimic some forms of schizophrenic disorder, the organic affective syndrome closely resembles the symptoms seen in either depressive or manic affective disorders. The reaction may be minimal or severe, and the course of the disorder varies widely, depending on the nature of the organic pathology. Etiological factors include head injury, withdrawal of certain drugs, intracranial tumors or tumors of the hormone-secreting organs, and excessive use of steroids (adrenocortical hormones) or certain other medications.

Organic personality syndrome. The essential feature of the *organic personality syndrome* is a change in the individual's general personality style or traits following brain damage. Normally the change is in a distinctly negative direction; it may include impaired social judgment, lessened control of emotions and impulses, diminished concern about the consequences of one's behavior, and inability to sustain goal-directed activity.

There are multiple etiologies associated with the organic personality syndrome, and the course of the disorder depends on its etiology. Occasionally, as when it is induced by medication, it may be transitory. Very often, however, it is the first sign of an impending deterioration, as when a kindly and gentle old man makes sexual advances toward a child or when a conservative businessman suddenly begins to engage in unwise financial dealings. Some evidence indicates that a common feature in the organic personality syndrome may be damage to the frontal lobes (Blumer & Benson, 1975; Crockett, Clark, & Klonoff, 1981; Hecaen & Albert, 1975; Sherwin & Geschwind, 1978).

All of the organic symptom syndromes may appear singly or in combination in the various types of mental disorders associated with brain pathology. In general, disorders involving the syndromes of delirium, dementia, amnesis, hallucinosis, or delusional thinking may be regarded as roughly equivalent to a psychotic level of functioning. Delirium is nearly always acute and short-lived, whereas disorders that have prominent elements of dementia, amnestic syndrome, or organic personality syndrome usually prove to have a chronic course—that is, they normally involve irreversible changes in the brain tissue.

The DSM-III classification lists about 50 different forms of mental disorder in which organic disturbance is present; many of these are related to drug usage and involve only temporary physiological disruption (see Chapter 10). The disorders we will be discussing in the rest of this section are longer-term disorders in which there is major, often permanent, brain pathology but in which the individual's emotional, motivational, and behavioral reactions to the loss of function also play an important role. Indeed, it is often impossible to distinguish between maladaptive behavior which is directly caused by neurological dysfunction and that which is basically part of the individual's psychological defensive or compensatory reaction to the deficits and disabilities experienced (Fabrega, 1981; Geschwind, 1975).

The five organic mental disorders we will discuss in the next sections are general paresis, disorders involving brain tumors, disorders involving head injury, and the two "old-age psychoses"—senile and presenile dementia and disorders associated with cerebral arteriosclerosis.

General paresis

General paresis is one of several forms of invasion of the central nervous system by the organism responsible for syphilitic infection, the spirochete *treponema pallidum*. As we saw in Chapter 3, it occupies a very important place in the history of the mental health disciplines. Despite the availability of medical resources for cure in the early stages, syphilis is still a significant medical problem. Unless properly treated, it eventually disables and then kills its victims.

The general paretic form of advanced syphilis typically begins with an organic personality syndrome. From there, it advances to stages involving the amnestic syndrome and usually the or-

ganic affective and delusional syndromes. The final stage is profound dementia, deteriorating into delirium and death.

The syphilitic infection itself advances in definable stages; only in the fourth, or last, state do we find the full-blown general paretic disorders. The first obvious symptom of syphilis is a sore, or *chancre*, appearing at the site where the spirochetes have gained entrance to the body, typically the mucous membranes of the genitals. Even if untreated, the sore disappears within four to six weeks, to be followed in another three to six weeks by the appearance of the second stage—a more or less generalized skin rash, once called the *Great Pox*. Disappearance of the rash and other associated symptoms initiates the third stage of syphilis, in which the disease appears to become latent. In fact, during this time the spirochetes continue to multiply and are carried by the bloodstream to various bodily organs, where they proceed to destroy tissue. They seem to have a particular affinity for nervous tissue. In the fourth stage, the accumulated damage produced during the supposed latent period manifests itself in a wide range of disabilities, including general paresis in some instances.

Clinical picture in general paresis. General paresis has also been variously called *general paralysis of the insane, dementia paralytica*, and *paresis*. Approximately 5 to 10 percent of untreated syphilitics eventually develop general paresis. The first symptoms usually appear about 10 to 15 years after the primary infection, although the incubation period may be as short as 2 years or as long as 40. Unless the person receives treatment, the outcome is always fatal, death usually occurring within 2 to 3 years after the initial symptoms appear.

General paresis is associated with a wide range of behavioral and psychological symptoms. During the early phase of this disorder, the individual typically becomes careless and inattentive and makes mistakes at work. At first the person may notice these mistakes but attribute them to fatigue; later, they go unnoticed. Personal habits may show some deterioration, and the once-neat person may become slovenly. Comprehension and judgment suffer, and the individual may show a tendency to evade important problems or may react to them with smug indifference. Accompanying these symptoms is a blunting of affect, so that the individual ceases to share in the joys, sorrows, or anxieties of loved ones. Such individuals seem unable to realize the seriousness of their behavior and may become irritable or resort to ready rationalizations if their behavior is questioned. Overly sentimental behavior is typical, and this phase may involve promiscuous sexual patterns.

As the disorder progresses, a number of well-delineated physical symptoms make their appearance. The pupils are irregular in size, and the pupillary reflex to light is either sluggish or entirely absent. Typically, speech functions become badly disturbed, with considerable stuttering and slurring of words. A phrase that routinely gives trouble and is of diagnostic significance is "Methodist Episcopal." This may be mispronounced in a number of ways, such as "Meodist Epispal" or "Methdist Pispal." Writing is similarly disturbed, with tremulous lines and the omission or transposition of syllables. Frequently, the individual has a rather vacant, dissipated look, with a silly grin.

Paralleling these physical symptoms is a progressive personality deterioration. Paretic individuals tend to be unmannerly, tactless, unconcerned with their appearance, and unethical in their behavior. Memory defects, which may have been noticeable in the early phases of the illness, become more obvious. Afflicted individuals may be unable to remember what they did just a short time before—for example, they may ask when dinner will be served only a few minutes after they have finished eating it. This memory impairment extends to less immediate events, and memory losses are made up for by various fabrications. As their intellectual processes are increasingly impaired, paretic individuals become unable to comprehend the simplest problems and may optimistically squander their money on harebrained schemes or become involved in a variety of antisocial acts.

This entire picture of personality deterioration is usually colored by emotional reactions in the form of either marked euphoria, depression, or apathy. Thus, three categories are commonly used to distinguish clinical types of paretic individuals—*expansive, depressed,* and *demented*—although these types are by no means always distinct, and depressed individuals frequently change categories by becoming euphoric. As the

disease enters the terminal period, the extensive brain damage leads to a similar picture for all three types: the individual leads a vegetative life, expresses little interest in anything, becomes inarticulate in speech, and can no longer manage personal care. Convulsive seizures usually become common. Finally, a terminal infection or breakdown of body functioning leads to death.

The following is a classic example of the expansive type of paresis and well illustrates the euphoria, poorly systematized delusions of grandeur, and ludicrous nature of the plans these individuals make.[2]

"C. W. flew planes from the United States to North Africa. His route began in Florida, passed through Natal, Ascension Island, and terminated in Dakar. His earlier health record was excellent, save for some 'difficulty' in his early twenties. Now, at 38, he was strong, well liked, and an expert pilot in the ferry command. He had completed a dozen or more trips.

"As he flew his plane eastward on his last journey, C. W. was unusually gay, 'It's a great world,' he sang. 'My rich aunt in Oklahoma is going to leave me $30,000,000.'

"During the periods of relief by his co-pilot, he talked loudly and became chummy with other members of the crew. As a matter of fact, he offered to loan the navigator $50,000. Landing safely in Dakar, his high spirits continued. Then his friends found him buying several 'diamonds' from an Arab street merchant, spending most of his cash for this purpose.

" 'Boy,' he exclaimed, 'I got a swell bargain! Six diamonds for $100 cash now and $100 more on my next trip! I sure fooled that Arab; he's never going to collect the rest from me.'

" 'How do you know the diamonds are genuine?' he was asked.

" 'I tested them,' he boasted, 'I struck one with a hammer and it proved hard; diamonds are hard.'

"Upon the return journey, C. W. continued the story of his expected wealth and the sum grew with the distance of travel.

" 'It's $40,000,000 I am getting and I expect to share some of it with you guys,' he announced. When his co-pilot received this astounding information with doubt and anxiety, C. W. could not understand it. When the co-pilot asked him to rest, he assured him that his body was perfect, that he didn't need rest. Then he added that he could fly the plane without gas, which he tried to prove by doing some fancy maneuvers in the sky.

[2]From Fetterman, J. L., *Practical Lessons in Psychiatry*, 1949. Courtesy of Charles C. Thomas, Publisher, Springfield, Illinois.

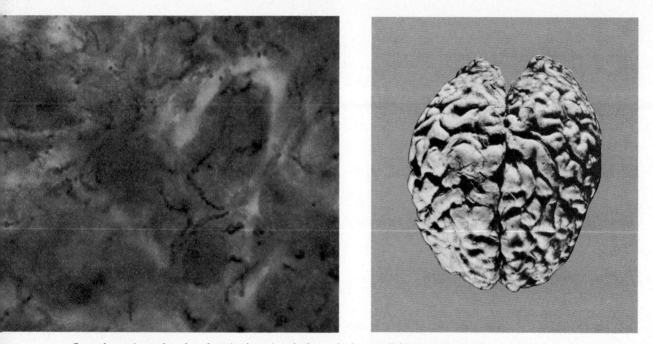

General paresis results when the spirochetes invade the cerebral cortex (left). A postmortem examination typically reveals thickening of the meninges surrounding the brain and atrophy of the convolutions, especially in the frontal and temporal lobes (right).

" 'Funny,' he said later, 'no one seemed to believe me. Even when I offered them a million each they weren't happy, but looked at each other in such a puzzled way. It made me laugh, how they begged me to rest and how worried they looked when I refused. I was the boss and I showed them.'

"When the plane landed in Brazil by a miracle, C. W. was examined by a physician, forced into another plane and brought to Florida. Upon examination he was talkative, eyes gleaming, exuberant with statements of wealth and power. 'I am now one of the richest men in the world,' he said. "I'll give you $5,000,000 to start a hospital. My eyes are jewels, diamonds, emeralds,' . . ."(Fetterman, 1949, pp. 267–68).

Although much is now known about general paresis, a number of questions still puzzle investigators. Why do only some 5 to 10 percent of untreated syphilitics develop general paresis? Why do a higher percentage of whites than blacks develop general paresis after syphilitic infection? Why do far more male than female syphilitics develop general paresis? Some investigators hold that the syphilis-producing spirochetes attack the most vulnerable organs of the body and that general paresis develops in persons whose brain tissue has an especially low resistance to syphilis. Other investigators have suggested that different strains of spirochetes may account for many of the differences. But the final answers to these questions are not yet available.

Treatment and outcomes.   After penicillin had been developed and found effective in the treatment of syphilis, there was a spectacular drop in the number of cases. Thus, during the late 1950s the problem of syphilis was considered solved.

During the period from 1960 to 1970, however, the number of reported cases of syphilis doubled. The increase continued into the 1970s; well over 100,000 new cases were reported each year, and probably an equal or greater number of cases went unreported. It was estimated a decade ago that there might be as many as a half million cases of undetected and untreated syphilis in the United States as a whole (Krugman & Ward, 1973). There is no reason to believe the situation has improved significantly since.

According to statistics gathered from 102 cities in 1969, the sources of infection in syphilis were, in order of frequency, (a) friend of the opposite sex, 47 percent; (b) stranger of the opposite sex, including prostitutes and casual pickups, 20 percent; (c) homosexual contact, 17 percent; and (d) marital partner, 16 percent (Strage, 1971). Contrary to a widely held misconception, it is currently estimated that 5 percent or less of syphilis is spread by prostitutes.

The specific outcomes in cases of paresis receiving medical treatment depend to a large extent on the amount of cerebral damage that has taken place before treatment was started. If the damage is not extensive, the adaptive capacities of the individual—both neurological and psychological—may leave only a small impairment of brain function. Unfortunately, in many cases treatment is not undertaken until the disease has produced extensive and irreparable brain damage. Here, about all that can be hoped for is to prevent further inroads of the deadly spirochete. In such cases, the intellectual picture may show considerable improvement, but the patient's previous level of ability is never regained. For treated paretics as a group, the following rough estimates of outcome may be made:

a) Some 20 to 30 percent show good recovery and can resume their former occupation and activities.

b) Another 30 to 40 percent show some improvement but usually require a transfer to less complex occupational duties as a consequence of residual intellectual or personality impairment.

c) Some 15 to 25 percent show no improvement.

d) About 10 percent die during the course of treatment (or within a 10-year period following the instigation of treatment).

As with other mental disorders, psychotherapy may be an essential aspect of the total treatment program.

The only fully adequate approach to cerebral syphilis is the prevention of syphilitic infection, or early detection and treatment where infection has taken place. In the United States, facilities are provided for the free diagnosis and treatment of syphilis; most states require examinations before marriage, and public education has been vigorously supported by governmental, educational, and religious agencies. It is also mandatory in all states for physicians to report cases of syphilis to local health authorities, though some doctors probably succumb to pressure not to report cases they treat. Unfortunately, many people do not seek diagnosis and treatment, because they have inadequate information or because of the stigma attached to sexually transmitted diseases.

In efforts directed toward finding and treating all infected cases, it has become common practice for patients with infectious syphilis to be interviewed about their sex contacts. Every effort is then made to locate these individuals and screen them for possible syphilitic infection. For example, a successful search was conducted in a case involving a Sacramento, California, prostitute named as a contact by an infected male; she, in turn, produced a list of 310 male contacts. Although they were chiefly interstate truck drivers scattered over 34 states, Canada, and Mexico, authorities were able to locate them and ask for blood tests (*Los Angeles Times*, 1970). In another case, cited by Strage (1971), an infected homosexual male was able to produce a file of nearly 1000 male contacts together with the details of their sexual acts and preferences.

To improve the efficiency of case-finding, investigators have extended interviews to include not only sex contacts of patients but also patients' friends and acquaintances, whose sexual behavior is assumed to be similar to theirs. This is called *cluster testing*.

Although we now have the medical means to eradicate syphilis, it remains a major health problem in our society, because its roots are social as well as medical. However, with the cooperation of international and national agencies, better education, and more adequate facilities for diagnosis and treatment, there is every reason to believe that syphilis can eventually be controlled or even eliminated as a public health problem.

Disorders involving brain tumors

In the writings of Felix Plater (1536–1614), we find the following rather remarkable account of "A Case of Stupor due to a Tumour in the Brain, Circular like a Gland":

"Caspar Bone Curtius, a noble knight, began to show signs of 'mental alienation' which continued through a period of two years until at last he became quite stupefied, did not act rationally, did not take food unless forced to do so, nor did he go to bed unless compelled, at table he just lay on his arms and went to sleep, he did not speak when questioned even when admonished, and if he did it was useless. Pituita dropped from his nose copiously and frequently: this condition continued for about six months, and finally he died. . . . At the post mortem when the skull was opened and the lobes of the brain separated, a remarkable globular tumor was found on the upper surface of the Corpus Callosum, resembling a gland fleshly, hard and funguslike, about the size of a medium sized apple, invested with its own membranes and having its own veins, lying free and without any connection with the brain itself. . . . This tumour, by its mass, produced pressure on the brain and its vessels, which caused stupor, torpor, and finally death. Some doctors who had seen this case earlier attributed it to sorcery, others just to the humors, but by opening the skull we made clear the abstruse and hidden cause." (1664)

A tumor is a new growth involving an abnormal enlargement of body tissue. Such growths are most apt to occur in the breast, the uterus, the prostate, the lungs, or the intestinal tract, although they are sometimes found in the central nervous system. In adults, brain tumors occur with the greatest frequency between the ages of 40 and 60.

Some brain tumors are malignant; they destroy the brain tissue in which they arise. Others are benign; they are not destructive except by reason of the pressure they exert. Since the skull is a bony, unyielding container, a relatively small tumor in the brain may cause marked pressure and thus interfere seriously with normal brain functioning. Unlike their benign counterparts, malignant brain tumors usually originate in malignancies in other organs, typically the lungs; the cancer cells are transported to the brain by a process known as *metastasis*.

Clinical picture in disorders involving brain tumors. The clinical picture that develops in cases of brain tumor is extremely varied and is determined largely by (a) the location, size, and rapidity of growth of the tumor, and (b) the personality and stress tolerance of the individual. Brain tumors may lead to any or all of the recognized organic symptom syndromes discussed earlier.

The brain tumor itself may result in both localized and general symptoms. Damage to a particular part of the brain may result in localized disturbances of sensory or motor functions.

General symptoms appear when the tumor becomes large enough to result in greatly increased intracranial pressure. Common early symptoms are persistent headache, vomiting, memory impairment, listlessness, depression, and "choked disc"—a retinal anomaly characterized by swelling of the optic nerve caused when cerebrospinal fluid is forced into it by intracranial pressure.

As the tumor progresses and the intracranial pressure increases, there may be clouding of consciousness, disorientation for time and place, carelessness in personal habits, irritability, convulsive seizures, vomiting, sensorimotor losses, hallucinations, apathy, and a general impairment of intellectual functions. Terminal stages are usually similar to other types of severe brain damage; the patient is reduced to a vegetative stupor and eventually dies.

Some idea of the relative frequency of symptoms in brain tumor cases may be gleaned from an early study by Levin (1949), who intensively analyzed 22 cases admitted to the Boston Psychopathic Hospital. These patients ranged in age from 22 to 65 years, the majority falling between the ages of 40 and 60 years. There were 11 males and 11 females. Prior to hospitalization the range of symptoms shown by these patients included the following:

Memory impairment or confusion—	13 cases
Depression—	9 cases
Seizures—	8 cases
Headaches—	8 cases
Complaints of visual impairment—	6 cases
Drowsiness—	6 cases
Irritability—	6 cases
Indifference—	5 cases
Restlessness—	4 cases
Complaint of generalized weakness—	4 cases
Loss of sense of responsibility—	3 cases
Paranoid ideas—	2 cases
Tendency to be combative—	2 cases
Euphoria—	2 cases
Aphasia—	2 cases

The interval between the onset of the symptoms and hospitalization varied from 1 week to 6 years, with an average interval of 17 months. In most cases, symptoms were evident 6 months or more prior to admission to the hospital. In this connection, however, it has been pointed out

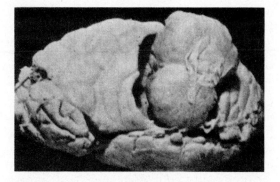

Brain tumors can cause a variety of personality alterations. Above is a picture of a meningioma—a tumor of one of the meninges, or coverings of the brain.

that minor personality changes and depression often serve to mask the more definitive symptoms of a brain tumor—with the result that accurate diagnosis and appropriate treatment are often delayed (Schwab, 1970).

Patients' emotional reactions to the organic damage and to the resulting intellectual impairment vary. Initially, they may be overly irritable, drowsy, and mildly depressed. As the disorder progresses, however, they may have some insight into the seriousness of their condition and become severely depressed, anxious, and apprehensive. Patients who have less insight into their condition usually react to the brain damage and their failing functions by becoming expansive and euphoric. Such patients seem unconcerned about their illness and may joke and laugh in a most unrestrained and hilarious manner. Such reactions are apparently compensatory and are especially frequent in advanced stages when there is considerable brain damage or pressure.

Serious tumors, especially those with psychological complications, are most common in the frontal, temporal, and parietal lobes. Frontal-lobe tumors often produce subtle peculiarities such as inability to concentrate, personal carelessness, loss of inhibitions, and absentmindedness that later becomes a memory defect. Often, too, the individual becomes silly and prone to punning and general jocularity. In an analysis of 90 patients with frontal-lobe tumors, Dobrokhotova (1968) found three common forms of emotional disorder: (a) the absence of spontaneity; (b) disinhibition and lability of affect—often

with euphoria; and (c) forced emotions, which were abruptly expressed and terminated.

Tumors involving the special sensory areas in the brain may result in hallucinations of sight, hearing, taste, and smell. It has been estimated that about half of the patients with brain tumors evidence hallucinations sometime during the course of their illness. Visual hallucinations predominate and may involve dazzling, vividly colored flashes of light, as well as various kinds and sizes of animals and other objects. People with temporal-lobe tumors sometimes experience "Lilliputian hallucinations," in which they see small figures that they usually know are not real. Such hallucinations apparently result from irritation of the visual pathways passing through the temporal lobe. Similarly, irritation of the olfactory pathways may result in the perception of peculiar odors, such as burning rubber. Auditory hallucinations may include buzzing, ringing, roaring, and occasionally voices and conversations.

Although personality change is so common in brain-tumor cases that it has in the past been attributed directly to the tumor, we now realize that such symptoms are neither inevitable nor solely the result of the tumor. As we have noted, adjustive reactions are typically a function of both the stress situation (including biological, psychosocial, and sociocultural stressors) and the personal maturity, stability, and level of stress tolerance of the individual.

A most dramatic example of the importance of the patient's pre-illness personality in determining the psychological effects of brain pathology is provided in John Gunther's (1949) moving account of his son Johnny's struggle against a malignant brain tumor. Johnny was 16 and in his junior year at preparatory school when the tumor was discovered. During the 14 months that preceded his death, he was subjected to two major operations and a variety of other treatment procedures.

Throughout his ordeal, Johnny never lost his courage, his ambition, his sense of humor, or his mental alertness. Although his strength and general physical condition deteriorated steadily and he suffered increasing visual impairment, he fought to carry on a normal pattern of activity and to keep up with his studies by being tutored at home. Through tireless and determined effort, he managed to take and pass college entrance examinations—a six-hour ordeal that followed an hour of standing in line—and to graduate with his class. By this time his physical impairment had become so great that it was a struggle simply to tie his shoelaces or even fasten his belt. At graduation late in May, he could only walk very slowly down the long aisle and grasp his diploma with his weak left hand. Less than a month later, Johnny died.

Treatment and outcomes. Treatment of brain-tumor cases is primarily a medical matter and thus is outside the scope of our present discussion. However, it may be noted that the degree of recovery of the patient in such cases depends both on the size and location of the growth and on the amount of brain tissue that must be removed with the tumor. In some cases there seems to be full recovery, while in others there may be a residue of symptoms, such as partial paralysis and a reduction in intellectual level. Where tumors are well advanced and require extensive surgery, the mortality rate is high. German (1959) found that about 40 percent of all brain tumors were potentially curable, about 20 percent were capable of being arrested for periods of 5 years or more, and the remainder were fatal within a short period of time. Since then, newer methods of detecting and pinpointing brain tumors and improved treatment procedures have resulted in a marked improvement in outcomes (Peterson, 1978).

Disorders involving head injury

Since ancient times, brain injuries have provided a rich source of material for speculation about mental functions. Hippocrates pointed out that injuries to the head could cause sensory and motor disorders, and Galen included head injuries among the major causes of mental disorders.

Head injuries occur frequently, particularly as a result of falls, blows, and accidents. It has been estimated that well over a million persons suffer head injuries each year in automobile and industrial accidents; and a sizable number of cases are the result of bullets' or other objects' actually penetrating the cranium. Yet relatively few persons with head injuries find their way into mental hospitals, since many head injuries do not involve appreciable damage to the brain. Even when a head injury results in a temporary loss of consciousness, the damage to the brain is usually minor.

Most of us have received a blow on the head at one time or other, and in giving the case history of a mental patient, relatives often remember some such incident to which they attribute the observed difficulties. Patients, too, are apt to search their own childhood for evidence of having fallen on their heads or having been hit on the head. Apparently, blaming a head injury is a convenient method of escaping the "disgrace" of a functional mental disorder and at the same time avoiding any hereditary stigma to the family. Consequently, it should be emphasized that only with severe brain injury is there apt to be any residual handicap.

Clinical picture in disorders with head injuries. Head injuries usually give rise to immediate acute reactions, the severity of which depends on the degree and type of injury. These acute reactions may then clear up entirely or develop into chronic disorders.

Perhaps the most famous historical case is the celebrated American crowbar case reported by Dr. J. M. Harlow in 1868. Since it is of both historical and descriptive significance, it merits our including a few details:

"The accident occurred in Cavendish, Vt., on the line of the Rutland and Burlington Railroad, at that time being built, on the 13th of September, 1848, and was occasioned by the premature explosions of a blast, when this iron, known to blasters as a tamping iron, and which I now show you, was shot through the face and head.

"The subject of it was Phineas P. Gage, a perfectly healthy, strong and active young man, twenty-five years of age . . . Gage was foreman of a gang of men employed in excavating rock, for the road way. . . .

"The missile entered by its pointed end, the left side of the face, immediately anterior to the angle of the lower jaw, and passing obliquely upwards, and obliquely backwards, emerged in the median line, at the back part of the frontal bone, near the coronal suture. . . . The iron which thus traversed the head, is round and rendered comparatively smooth by use, and is three feet seven inches in length, one and one fourth inches in its largest diameter, and weighs thirteen and one fourth pounds. . . .

"The patient was thrown upon his back by the explosion, and gave a few convulsive motions of the extremities, but spoke in a few minutes. His men (with whom he was a great favorite) took him in their arms and carried him to the road, only a few rods distant, and put him into an ox cart, in which he rode, supported in a sitting posture, fully three quarters of a mile to his hotel. He got out of the cart himself, with a little assistance from his men, and an hour afterwards (with what I could aid him by taking hold of his left arm) walked up a long flight of stairs, and got upon the bed in the room where he was dressed. He seemed perfectly conscious, but was becoming exhausted from the hemorrhage, which by this time, was quite profuse, the blood pouring from the lacerated sinus in the top of his head, and also finding its way into the stomach, which ejected it as often as every fifteen or twenty minutes. He bore his sufferings with firmness, and directed my attention to the hole in his cheek, saying, 'the iron entered there and passed through my head.' " (1868, pp. 330–32)

Sometime later Dr. Harlow made the following report.

"His physical health is good, and I am inclined to say that he has recovered. Has no pain in head, but says it has a queer feeling which he is not able to describe. Applied for his situation as foreman, but is undecided whether to work or travel. His contractors, who regarded him as the most efficient and capable foreman in their employ previous to his injury considered the change in his mind so marked that they could not give him his place again. The equilibrium or balance, so to speak, between his intellectual faculties and animal propensities, seems to have been destroyed. He is fitful, irreverent, indulging at times in the grossest profanity (which was not previously his custom), manifesting but little deference for his fellows, impatient of restraint or advice when it conflicts with his desires, at times pertinaciously obstinate, yet capricious and vacillating, devising many plans of future operations, which are no sooner arranged than they are abandoned in turn for others . . . his mind is radically changed, so decidedly that his friends and acquaintances said he was 'no longer Gage.' " (1868, pp. 339–40)

It is evident from the above account that Gage acquired an organic personality syndrome from his encounter with the errant crowbar. This relatively dramatic syndrome, however, is not common as a sequel to head injury.

Fortunately, the brain is an extraordinarily well-protected organ; but even so, a hard blow on the head may result in a skull fracture in which portions of bone press upon or are driven into the brain tissue. Even without a fracture, the force of the blow may result in small, pin-

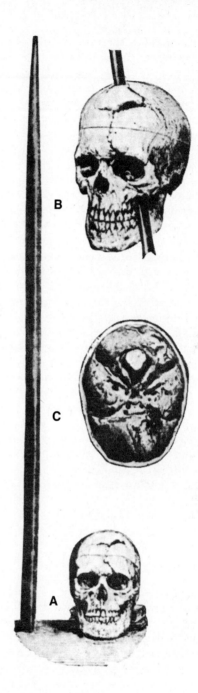

Harlow illustrated his famous crowbar case by these drawings, showing (A) the comparative sizes of the tamping iron and the cranium through which it passed; (B) a view of the cranium showing just where the iron passed through, and also a large section of the skull which was entirely torn away and later replaced; and (C) an upward view from inside the skull, giving the position and relative size of the hole that was made and showing a deposit of new bone partially closing it over.

point hemorrhages throughout the brain or in the rupturing of larger blood vessels in the brain.

The person rendered unconscious by a head injury usually passes through stages of stupor and confusion on the way to recovering clear consciousness. This recovery of consciousness may be complete in the course of minutes, or it may take hours or days. In rare cases an individual may live for extended periods of time without regaining consciousness. In such cases, the prognosis for full recovery is poor.

The specific symptoms, of course, depend largely on the nature of the injury. Normally, if a head injury is sufficiently severe to result in unconsciousness, the person experiences *retrograde amnesia,* or inability to recall events immediately preceding the injury. Apparently, such trauma interferes with the brain's capacity to consolidate into long-term storage the events that were being mentally processed at the time of the trauma.

During the coma that follows severe cerebral injury, pulse, temperature, and blood pressure are all affected, and survival may be uncertain. The duration of the coma is determined primarily by the extent of the injury. If the patient survives, the coma is usually followed by delirium, in which acute excitement may be manifested, with disorientation, hallucinations, and generally anxious, restless, and noisy activity. Often the patient talks incessantly in a disconnected fashion, with no insight into the disturbed condition. Gradually the confusion clears up and the individual regains contact with reality. Again, the severity and duration of residual symptoms depends primarily on the nature and extent of the cerebral damage, the premorbid personality of the patient, and the life situation to which he or she will return.

As mentioned earlier, some degree of bleeding, or *intracerebral hemorrhage,* occurs in most cases of head injury. In severe head injuries there is usually gross bleeding or hemorrhaging at the site of the damage. When the hemorrhaging involves small spots of bleeding—often microscopic sleeves of red cells encircling tiny blood vessels—the condition is referred to as *petechial hemorrhages.* There is some evidence of petechial hemorrhages in most brain injuries, but in fatal cases they are usually multiple or generalized throughout the brain.

Professional boxers are likely to suffer such petechial hemorrhaging from repeated blows to the head; they may develop a form of encephalopathy (area or areas of permanently damaged brain tissue) from the accumulated damage of such injuries. Consequently, some former boxers suffer from impaired memory, slurred speech, inability to concentrate, involuntary movements, and other symptoms—a condition popularly referred to as being "punch-drunk." Johnson (1969) found abnormal EEGs in 10 of 17 retired boxers; and Earl (1966) noted that two former welterweight champions suffered so much brain damage in their professional fights that confinement in mental institutions ended their careers before they reached the age of 30.

With one-time head injuries, resulting syndromes are usually limited to delirium and perhaps some features of the dementia, amnestic, and hallucinosis syndromes—all on a temporary basis. Where the trauma results in the permanent loss of neural tissue, however, all these syndromes may occur in their full-blown and irreversible forms; the person may also experience personality disturbance, affective and delusional syndromes, and a variety of physical impairments and disabilities.

Treatment and outcomes. Immediate treatment for brain damage due to head injury is primarily a medical matter and need not concern us here except for the notation that prompt treatment may prevent further injury or damage—for example, when blood clots must be removed from the brain. In severe cases, immediate medical treatment may have to be supplemented by a long-range program of reeducation and rehabilitation.

Although many patients make a remarkably good recovery, even after severe brain injury, others show various residual symptoms. Common aftereffects of moderate brain injury are chronic headaches, anxiety, irritability, dizziness, easy fatigability, and impaired memory and concentration. Where the brain damage is extensive, the patient's general intellectual level may be markedly reduced, especially where there have been severe temporal or parietal lobe lesions. In addition, various specific neurological and psychological defects may follow localized brain damage, as we have seen. Some 2 to 4 percent of head-injury cases develop posttraumatic epilepsy, usually within two years of the head injury but sometimes much later. In general, the longer the period between the injury and the first convulsive seizure, the more likely seizures are to persist.

In a minority of brain-injury cases—some 2 to 3 percent—there are personality changes, such as those described in the historic case of Phineas Gage. Among older people and individuals who have suffered extensive damage to the temporal lobes, the symptom picture may be complicated by markedly impaired memory for recent events and by confabulation.

The great majority of people suffering from mild concussion recover within a short time. With moderate brain injuries, a sizable number of patients recover promptly, a somewhat larger number suffer from headaches and other symptoms for prolonged periods, and a few develop chronic incapacitating symptoms. In general, an estimated 50 percent of patients with moderate brain injuries show symptoms after 6 months, and about 40 percent show symptoms after 18 months.

In severe brain-injury cases, the prognosis is less favorable (Jennett et al., 1976). Some patients have to adjust to lower levels of occupational and social functioning, while others are so impaired intellectually that they can never adjust to conditions outside an institution. Often, however—even in cases where considerable amounts of brain tissue have been destroyed—patients with previously stable, well-integrated personalities are able to make a satisfactory adjustment. And in many cases there is improvement with time, due largely to reeducation and to the taking over of new functions by intact brain areas.

In general, the following factors indicate a favorable prognosis in cases of head injury: (a) a short period of unconsciousness or posttraumatic amnesia, (b) nonstrategic location of the brain lesion, (c) a well-integrated pre-injury personality, (d) motivation to recover or make the most of residual capacities, (e) a favorable life situation to which to return, and (f) an appropriate program of retraining (Brooks, 1974; Diller & Gordon, 1981).

Various other factors may also have a direct bearing on the outcome of brain injuries. As we mentioned earlier, the results of brain damage in infancy differ from those in adolescence and adulthood, although in both instances the results may range from death to any number of neurological disorders, including epilepsy and mental retardation. Moreover, the outlook for individuals who are also victims of alcoholism, drug dependence, arteriosclerosis, or other organic conditions may be unfavorable. Alcoholics, in particular, are prone to head injuries and other accidents and do not have good recovery records. Severe emotional conflicts sometimes appear to predispose an individual to accidents and also may delay recovery. Although malingering is thought to be rare in brain-injury cases, the hope of receiving monetary compensation—for example, from an insurance settlement—may influence individuals to exaggerate and maintain symptoms.

Senile and presenile dementias

It is a commonplace observation that the organs of the body deteriorate with aging, a process, biologists tell us, that begins virtually at birth. The cause or causes of this deterioration, however, remain largely obscure: science has not yet solved the riddle of aging. Of course, the brain—truly the master organ—is not spared in the generalized aging process. As time goes on, it too "wears out," or degenerates. Mental disorders that sometimes accompany this brain degeneration and occur in old age are called *senile dementias.* Unfortunately, there are a number of rare conditions that result in degenerative changes in brain tissue earlier in life. Disorders associated with such earlier degeneration of the brain are known as *presenile dementias.*

Not only is the age of onset different in the presenile dementias; they are also distinguished from the senile dementias by their different behavioral manifestations and tissue alterations (see **HIGHLIGHT** on page 506). One very important exception is *Alzheimer's disease,* which is the typical and common senile disorder but which can, in certain individuals, occur well before old age. Alzheimer's disease, tragically, sometimes occurs in persons in their 40s and 50s, at the height of their powers and attainment of career success. In these cases, the progress of the disease is normally rapid.

At whatever age it strikes, Alzheimer's disease is associated with degenerative changes in

HIGHLIGHT
Presenile dementias

In addition to early-occurring Alzheimer's disease, two other forms of presenile dementia occur with sufficient frequency to deserve mention: Pick's disease and Huntington's chorea.

Pick's disease
Even rarer than Alzheimer's disease, Pick's disease (first described by Arnold Pick of Prague in papers published in 1892) is a degenerative disorder of the nervous system of unknown cause, usually having its onset in persons between 45 and 50. Women are apparently more subject to Pick's disease then men, at a ratio of about three to two. Onset is slow and insidious, involving difficulty in thinking, slight memory defects, easy fatigability, and, often, character changes with a lowering of ethical inhibitions. At first there is a rather circumscribed atrophy of the frontal and temporal lobes; as the atrophy becomes more severe, the mental deterioration becomes progressively greater and includes apathy and disorientation as well as impairment of judgment and other intellectual functions.

The disease usually runs a fatal course within two to seven years.

Huntington's chorea
Huntington's chorea is a genetically determined degenerative disorder of the central nervous system. It was first described by the American neurologist George Huntington in 1872. With an incidence rate of about 5 cases per 100,000 persons, the disease usually occurs in individuals between 30 and 50. Behavior deterioration often becomes apparent several years before there are any detectable neurological manifestations (Lyle & Gottesman, 1977). The disease itself is characterized by a chronic, progressive chorea (involuntary, irregular, twitching, jerking movements) with mental deterioration leading to dementia and death within 10 to 20 years. Although Huntington's chorea cannot be cured or even arrested at the present time, it can be prevented, at least in theory, by genetic counseling, since its occurrence is a function of known genetic laws.

---

neurons, consisting chiefly of the appearance of senile *plaques* (dark areas of cellular "garbage") and *neurofibrillary tangles* (derangement of the normally regular pattern of fibrous tissue) within the nerve cells (Kolata, 1981a). These changes, in turn, are accompanied by a gross loss of neurons (more than 75 percent) in the basal forebrain. This area of the brain is importantly involved in the production of the neurotransmitter acetylcholine. Current theory, therefore, emphasizes acetylcholine depletion as the most likely primary cause of Alzheimer's disease (Kolata, 1981a; Whitehouse et al., 1982).

The magnitude of the problem of Alzheimer's disease, which accounts for some 50 percent of all cases of dementia, is usually seriously underestimated. One of every six persons in the United States over age 65 is clinically demented; that translates to about 1.5 million people, some 750 thousand of them suffering from Alzheimer's. This figure includes about 30 to 40 percent of all nursing home residents (Kolata, 1981a).

The onset of Alzheimer's disease in older people is usually gradual, involving slow physical and mental letdown. In some cases a physical ailment or some other stressful event is a dividing point, but usually the individual passes into a psychotic state almost imperceptibly, so that it is impossible to date the onset of the disorder precisely. The clinical picture may vary markedly from one person to another, depending on the nature and extent of brain degeneration, the premorbid personality of the individual, and the particular stressors that have been in operation.

Symptoms often begin with the individual's gradual withdrawal from active engagement with life. There is a narrowing of social and other interests, a lessening of mental alertness and adaptability, and a lowering of tolerance to new ideas and changes in routine. Often there is a self-centering of thoughts and activities and a preoccupation with the bodily functions of eating, digestion, and excretion. As these various changes—typical in lesser degree of many older people—become more severe, additional symptoms, such as impairment of memory for recent events, untidiness, impaired judgment, agitation, and periods of confusion, make their appearance. Specific symptoms may vary considerably from day to day; thus, the clinical picture is by no means uniform until the terminal stages, when the patient is reduced to a vegetative level. There is also, of course, individual variation in the rapidity of progression of the disorder; and in rare instances there may be a reversal of psychotic symptoms and a partial recovery.

Alzheimer's disease may take any of the following five forms. However, there is generally a considerable overlapping of symptoms from one form to another.

1. *Simple deterioration.* Simple deterioration, as the name suggests, is a relatively uncomplicated exaggeration of the "normal" changes characteristic of old age. The person gradually loses contact with the environment and develops the typical symptoms of poor memory, tendency to reminisce, intolerance of change, disorientation, restlessness, insomnia, and failure of judgment. This is the most common of the psychotic reactions accompanying Alzheimer's disease, constituting about 50 percent of the entire group.

The following case—involving an engineer who had retired some seven years prior to his hospitalization—is typical of simple deterioration resulting from Alzheimer's disease.

During the past five years, he had shown a progressive loss of interest in his surroundings and during the last year had become increasingly "childish." His wife and eldest son had brought him to the hospital because they felt they could no longer care for him in their home, particularly because of the grandchildren. They stated that he had become careless in his eating and other personal habits and was restless and prone to wandering about at night. He could not seem to remember anything that had happened during the day but was garrulous concerning events of his childhood and middle years.

After admission to the hospital, the patient seemed to deteriorate rapidly. He could rarely remember what had happened a few minutes before, although his memory for remote events of his childhood remained good. When he was visited by his wife and children, he mistook them for old friends, nor could he recall anything about the visit a few minutes after they had departed. The following brief conversation with the patient, which took place after he had been in the hospital for nine months, and about three months prior

to his death, shows his disorientation for time and person:

> **Dr.:** How are you today, Mr. _____?
> **Pt.:** Oh . . . hello (looks at doctor in rather puzzled way as if trying to make out who he is).
> **Dr.:** Do you know where you are now?
> **Pt.:** Why yes . . . I am at home. I must paint the house this summer. It has needed painting for a long time but it seems like I just keep putting it off.
> **Dr.:** Can you tell me the day today?
> **Pt.:** Isn't today Sunday . . . why, yes, the children are coming over for dinner today. We always have dinner for the whole family on Sunday. My wife was here just a minute ago but I guess she has gone back into the kitchen.

2. *The paranoid type.* In the paranoid type of Alzheimer's disease, the memory loss and other manifestations of degeneration are usually not so pronounced as in other types. Confusion and other disturbances of consciousness are not common, and often the individual remains oriented for time, place, and person. In other words, the dementia and amnestic syndromes are not prominent features of this reaction type, at least not in its early phases. Rather, the person develops a pronounced delusional syndrome chiefly involving ideas of persecution. Common among such delusions is the stubbornly held idea, in the absence of any evidence, that the spouse has become sexually unfaithful. Alternatively, such individuals may develop the notion that relatives have turned against them and are trying to rob and kill them. Their suspicions are confirmed by the noxious gases they smell in their room or by the poison they taste in their food. Fortunately, such delusions are poorly systematized and rarely lead to overt physical attacks on alleged persecutors. Approximately 30 percent of psychoses associated with brain deterioration from Alzheimer's disease take a paranoid form.

The following case is fairly typical of this reaction type, except for the prominent amnestic features.

A woman of 74 had been referred to a hospital after the death of her husband because she became uncooperative and was convinced that her relatives were trying to steal the insurance money her husband had left her. In the hospital she complained that the other patients had joined together against her and were trying to steal her belongings. She frequently refused to eat, on the grounds that the food tasted funny and had probably been poisoned. She grew increasingly irritable and disoriented for time and person. She avidly scanned magazines in the ward reading room but could not remember anything she had looked at. The following conversation reveals some of her symptoms:

Dr.: Do you find that magazine interesting?

Pt.: Why do you care? Can't you see I'm busy?

Dr.: Would you mind telling me something about what you are reading?

Pt.: It's none of your business . . . I am reading about my relatives. They want me to die so that they can steal my money.

Dr.: Do you have any evidence of this?

Pt.: Yes, plenty. They poison my food and they have turned the other women against me. They are all out to get my money. They even stole my sweater.

Dr.: Can you tell me what you had for breakfast?

Pt.: . . . (Pause) I didn't eat breakfast . . . it was poisoned and I refused to eat it. They are all against me.

Paranoid disorders of this type tend to develop in individuals who have been sensitive and suspicious. Existing personality tendencies are apparently intensified by degenerative brain changes and the stress accompanying advancing age.

3. *The presbyophrenic type.* The presbyophrenic type of Alzheimer's psychosis is characterized by fabrication, a jovial, amiable mood, and marked amnesia. Persons with this disorder may appear superficially alert and may talk volubly in a rambling, confused manner, filling gaps in present memory with events that occurred 20 or 30 years before. They usually show a peculiar restlessness or excitability and engage in continual aimless activity; for example, an individual may fold and unfold pieces of cloth as if ironing or may collect various discarded objects with a great show of importance. This type of disorder appears to occur most frequently in individuals who have been lively, assertive, and extroverted in their younger days; it accounts for less than 10 percent of all Alzheimer's psychoses.

4. *Depressed and agitated types.* Some people with Alzheimer's disease become severely depressed and agitated and usually suffer from hypochondriacal and nihilistic delusions, often expressing morbid ideas about cancer, syphilis, and other diseases. Delusions of poverty are also common, and such individuals may feel that they are headed for the poorhouse, that nobody wants them, and that they are a senseless burden on their children and just generally "in the way." In some cases, these persons become self-accusatory and develop delusions of great sin. In many respects the symptoms resemble those in psychotic depressions, for which the early phases of the disorder are very often mistaken; and the possibility of suicide must be guarded against. This type constitutes less than 10 percent of Alzheimer's dementia.

5. *Delirious and confused types.* In some cases there is severe mental clouding that causes patients to become extremely restless, combative, resistive, and incoherent. They recognize no one and are completely disoriented for time and place. Such delirious states are often precipitated by acute illness or by traumas, such as a broken leg or hip. Although transient delirious episodes often occur in Alzheimer's dementia, chronic confusion and delirium are uncommon except in terminal states; they account for less than 10 percent of cases.

With appropriate treatment, many persons with Alzheimer's dementia show some alleviation of symptoms. In general, however, deterioration continues its downward course over a period of months or years. Eventually patients become oblivious of their surroundings, bedridden, and reduced to a vegetative existence. Resistance to disease is lowered, and death usually results from pneumonia or some other infection.

On the other hand, important as is the brain degeneration in the Alzheimer's dementias, the causal picture in the behavior we see is much broader. Since the same additional causal factors are often found in the disorders associated with brain deterioration due to cerebral arteriosclerosis, and since similar treatment methods are often effective for both types of disorder, we will present the clinical picture of this other old-age psychotic disorder and then take up the causal factors and treatment approaches for both.

Disorders involving cerebral arteriosclerosis

Disorders with cerebral arteriosclerosis are similar to Alzheimer's dementias, but there are certain differences in both anatomical changes and behavioral symptoms.[3] The typical vascular pa-

---

[3]The term *arteriosclerosis* includes a number of diseases of the blood vessels, of which atherosclerosis is by far the most common and important. Atherosclerosis involves an arterial lesion characterized by a thickening of the arterial wall and a reduction in blood flow.

HIGHLIGHT
Three cases of cerebrovascular pathology

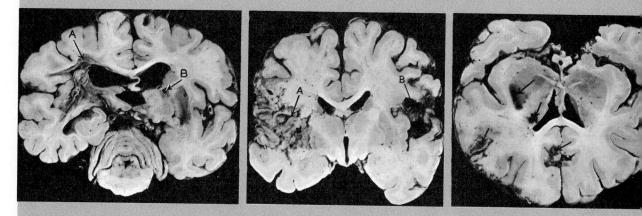

These pictures show cross sections of the brains of persons who suffered from cerebral arteriosclerosis. At the left is a section from the brain of a man who died at 43 after suffering from hypertension and two strokes that had resulted in some paralysis on both sides, emotional lability, and convulsions. The arrows indicate the areas where the cerebrovascular accidents and the specific brain damage occurred.

The center picture shows a section through the frontal lobes of a man who likewise suffered from two strokes; his strokes, however, were separated by an interval of 17 years. The arrow A points to a softening correlated with a recent stroke, which was associated with two months of paralysis on one side; the arrow B points to a cavity resulting from the earlier stroke, which had been associated with aphasia.

Arrows in the picture at right point to scattered emboli in another patient's brain, resulting in the existence of many tiny hemorrhages and widespread local damage.

thology in cerebral arteriosclerosis involves a "hardening" of the arteries of the brain. Large patches of fatty and calcified material accumulate at particular points on the inside lining of the blood vessels and gradually clog the arterial channel. Circulation becomes sluggish and may eventually be blocked altogether.

This blocking, in turn, may result in *cerebrovascular insufficiency* due to impaired circulation in the brain areas supplied by the vessel; or it may result in *intracerebral hemorrhage,* involving a rupture of the vessel with intracranial bleeding. Of course, damage to a large vessel will do more harm than damage to a small one. When the narrowing or eventual blockage is gradual and involves small blood vessels, cerebral nutrition is impaired and there are areas of softening as the brain tissue degenerates. Such areas of softening are found in some 90 percent of patients suffering from arteriosclerotic brain dis-

ease. The **HIGHLIGHT** on this page shows the damage to the brain caused by cerebral arteriosclerosis.

A sudden blocking or rupture in a small vessel is referred to as a *small stroke* and may result in a variety of transient psychological and physical symptoms, ranging from mental confusion and emotional lability to acute indigestion, changes in handwriting, and unsteadiness in gait. Frequently, individuals suffer a succession of small strokes resulting in cumulative brain damage and in the gradual personality change described earlier as organic personality syndrome. The dementia associated with this pattern is called *multiple-infarct dementia.*

When the blockage or rupture involves a large vessel, the individual suffers a major stroke (*cerebrovascular accident*—CVA). Here there is both focal and generalized impairment of brain function, resulting in coma or a state of acute confusion. If the individual survives, the acute symptoms may largely clear up; but typically there will be some degree of residual brain damage.

Cerebrovascular accidents kill more than 200,000 Americans each year; about 3 million persons in the United States are handicapped or incapacitated by cerebral arteriosclerosis. The incidence and severity of psychopathology in the latter cases is not known, but it would appear from recent research that the relationship between disturbed behavior and the occurrence of cerebral arteriosclerosis in the elderly is much weaker than was formerly believed. Some disturbed oldsters show little sign of arteriosclerotic disease, and many with the disease do not develop disturbed behavior (Ernst et al., 1977; Goldfarb, 1974).

Although cerebral arteriosclerosis may occur in young adulthood or middle age, it usually has its onset after age 55, with the sex ratio being about equal (Holvey & Talbott, 1972). This disorder appears to be most common among persons on lower socioeconomic levels, but it occurs in all economic groups. The average age of first admission for persons manifesting psychoses associated with cerebral arteriosclerosis is between 70 and 75.

Clinical picture in disorders with cerebral arteriosclerosis. In about half the cases of disorders with cerebral arteriosclerosis, symptoms appear suddenly. Here individuals are usually admitted to a medical facility in an acutely confused state resulting from a cerebrovascular accident. Such persons show marked clouding of consciousness; disorientation for time, place, and person; incoherence; and often hemiplegia (paralysis of one side of the body). Convulsive seizures are also relatively common and may precede the acute attack, occur at the same time, or appear at a later point in the illness. In severe cases the patient may die without a clearing of the confused state.

Acutely delirious or demented states may last for days, weeks, or even months, with an eventual remission of the acute symptoms. In these cases, there may be varying degrees of residual brain damage and impairment in physical and mental functions. Often the individual is able to compensate for the brain damage, particularly with the help of special rehabilitative measures designed to alleviate physical handicaps and clear up possible aphasic (deficient verbal communication) conditions. Sometimes, however, there is a progressive loss of mental efficiency, accompanied by other psychological symptoms such as emotional lability, irritability, and hypochondriacal concern over bodily functions. In many cases, an accentuation of earlier maladaptive traits appears to follow severe cerebrovascular accidents.

When the onset of the disorder is gradual, early symptoms may include complaints of weakness, fatigue, dizziness, headache, depression, memory defect, periods of confusion, and lowered efficiency in work. Often there is a slowing up of activity and a loss of zest in living. There may be a considerable delay between the appearance of such symptoms and the hospitalization of the individual.

By the time of hospitalization, the clinical picture is usually similar to that in Alzheimer's disease. The memory defect has now increased, although it may be somewhat uneven—for example, it may be more severe when the patient is tired or under emotional stress. Emotional lability becomes pronounced, and the individual may be easily moved to tears or highly irritable, with a tendency to "flare up" at the slightest provocation. Usually the flare-up is brief and ends with tears and repentance. Increased irritability may be accompanied by suspiciousness and poorly organized delusions of persecution.

By this time, there is also a more pronounced impairment of concentration and general intellectual functioning. Interest in the outside world and in others is markedly reduced, as are the individual's initiative and work capacity. Judgment is impaired, and in some instances ethical controls are lowered. Frequently there are feelings of depression associated with some insight into failing physical and mental powers. As in cases with an acute onset, there may be marked fluctuations in the clinical picture, but the usual course of the disease is in the direction of increasing deterioration and death.

Comparison with the clinical picture in Alzheimer's disease. The clinical aspects of Alzheimer's dementia and psychosis with cerebral arteriosclerosis are so much alike that a differential diagnosis is frequently very difficult to make. In some cases, there is a mixture of the two disorders—an Alzheimer's degeneration may be superimposed on an arteriosclerotic condition or vice versa. However, mixed reactions are not nearly so common as might be expected, and usually one condition or the other predominates.

Among the clinically distinguishing features of these two disorders are the following: (a) Alzheimer's dementia is usually gradual and progressive and lasts longer, while psychosis with cerebral arteriosclerosis is more apt to be brought on by a cerebrovascular accident and to run a brief and stormy course ending in death; (b) Alzheimer's dementia usually involves more pronounced intellectual impairment, and paranoid patterns are more common; (c) symptoms common in the arteriosclerotic group but less often seen in Alzheimer's dementia are headaches, dizziness, convulsive seizures, depression, and strong emotional outbursts; and finally (d) the symptoms in cerebral arteriosclerotic disorders typically show more pronounced fluctuations. But although these differences are observable in early and intermediate states, all patients who suffer advanced brain destruction become very much alike.

Causal factors in the psychoses of old age

Early investigators seized on brain damage as the only important factor in the causation of both Alzheimer's dementia and disorders with cerebral arteriosclerosis. But in recent years, with the increased interest and attention devoted to mental disorders of old age, those early beliefs have undergone considerable revision.

Although cerebral damage alone, when sufficiently extensive, may produce marked mental symptoms, it has become evident that with most patients the organic changes are only one part of a set of interactive factors. In the total clinical picture, the prior personality organization of the individual and the stressfulness of the life situation are also of key importance. And since specific brain pathology, personality makeup, and stress factors vary from person to person, we find a somewhat different causal pattern in each case.

Biological factors.   A number of early studies showed a high incidence of Alzheimer's and arteriosclerotic brain disease in the family back-

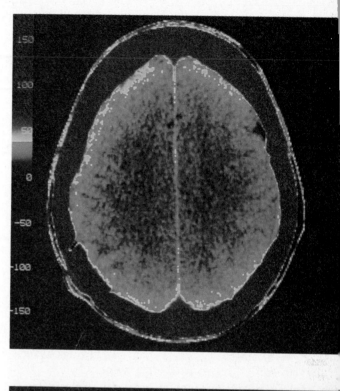

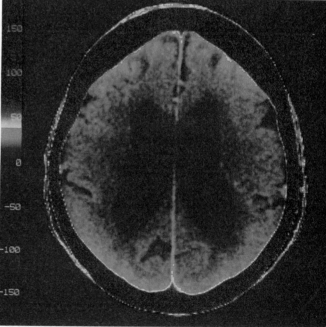

Dramatic differences show up in CAT scans of a normal brain (top) and the brain of a person afflicted with senile dementia (bottom). The dark blue areas in both hemispheres of the diseased brain indicate an enlargement of the ventricles (the large, hollow spaces deep within the brain) due to the degeneration of the brain tissue.

grounds of elderly psychotics (Mayer-Gross, 1944; Post, 1944). However, more recent findings, including observations of aging in twins (Kallman, 1961), indicate that it is unrealistic to consider genetic or constitutional factors as *primary* causal agents in all cases of these mental disorders. This view, of course, does not exclude a role for such factors in the rapidity of physiological aging.

In fact, in the case of Alzheimer's disease, recent research has strongly implicated genetic factors in the early establishment of the characteristic brain degeneration. Nee (reported in Sargent, 1982b) has traced the disease back eight generations in one family that immigrated to this continent in 1837. Of 531 members of the family, 53 have to date been identified as suffering from the disease, even though those who lived to 65 without symptoms were considered free of it. Collateral findings of this NIMH project were that the mean interval between onset of symptoms and death was 6 years (although in one case it was 24) and that the age at onset ranged between 44 and 64 years.

Regardless of the particular cause involved, the organic mental disorders are by definition associated with physical malfunctions of the brain. Some of these malfunctions, such as Alzheimer's disease and multiple-infarct dementia, are relatively well understood. However, we still have little well-established understanding of the precise factors that, for some people, convert brain impairment into psychotic behavior. As suggested earlier, we do know that the extent of brain pathology does not in itself ordinarily account for the psychotic disorders of old age, a point dramatically demonstrated by Gal (1959), who did a postmortem study of 104 patients ranging in age from 65 to 94 and found a lack of correlation between brain damage and behavior. Extensive cerebral damage was found in some patients who had manifested only mild mental symptoms, while minimal cerebral damage was found in others who had shown severe psychopathology.

With progressive cerebral impairment, of course, the degree of residual brain capacity shapes the response in greater measure. This point was well brought out by Ullmann and Gruen in summarizing their findings with 84 patients who had suffered strokes and had shown mild, moderate, or severe degrees of cerebral deficit.

"Patients who have experienced mild strokes with little or no residual mental impairment react to the stress in their own idiosyncratic fashion. Some will integrate the experience successfully; others will become enmeshed in psychopathological maneuvers of varying severity. In patients with moderate or severe brain damage, the situation is quite different. Here the unique features of the stroke are highlighted, the chief of these being that the very organ governing the adaptation to stress is itself impaired. The resulting clinical picture has to be evaluated now, not only in terms of what the experience means to the patient, but also in terms of the capacity the patient has for evaluating the situation." (1961, p. 1009)

Psychosocial factors.   It has been said that next to dying, the recognition that we are aging may be the most profound shock we experience in our lifetime. How older individuals react to their changed status and to the difficult stressors of this age period depends heavily on their personality makeup as well as on the challenges, rewards, and frustrations of their life situation. As important as actual brain changes are, the majority of old-age psychoses relate largely— and often primarily—to psychosocial and sociocultural factors.

1. *The role of the prepsychotic personality.* A number of studies have shown that individuals who are handicapped psychologically by undesirable personality traits are especially vulnerable to psychoses and other mental disorders in old age. Obsessive-compulsive trends, rigidity, suspiciousness, seclusiveness, social inadequacy, and poor adaptability to change are some of the traits that have been emphasized in the background of such individuals. Even negative attitudes toward growing old, which lead to self-devaluation and a negative self-image, can be serious adjustment handicaps during this period of life.

2. *Stressors characteristic in old age.* An older person faces numerous real problems and insecurities that are not characteristic of earlier life periods. In fact, the unfavorable environmental circumstances of older people are often more hazardous to mental health than are organic brain changes. Even well-integrated personalities may break down under the combined assault of cerebral changes and a stressful life situation.

a) *Retirement and reduced income.* Retirement is often the brand that marks a person as a member of the "old-age" group. It can be quite demoralizing if it is forced upon the individual. Repeated studies have shown that most older persons are productive workers and that many would prefer to keep on working when they reach retirement age (Offir, 1974).

Many people depend greatly on their work for status, for self-identity, for satisfying interpersonal relationships, and for meaning in their lives. Retirement often does not allow them to meet these needs, and they may react with the feeling that their usefulness and worth are at an end—a reaction conducive to rapid physical and mental deterioration.

Retirement usually leads also to a severe reduction in income, which further adds to the older person's burden. Most older Americans depend on social security benefits, pensions, and/or savings; for many this means trying to get along on less money than when they were working. Too, the widely publicized instability of the social security system in recent years has caused much anxiety to those for whom the system is the chief means of support.

b) *Fear of invalidism and death.* The gradual physical deterioration of one's body and the increased possibility of falling prey to some chronic and debilitating disease tend to make one more preoccupied with bodily functions and with the possibility of failing health, symptoms common among older people. Such concern is increased when the individual has a history of medical difficulties that are likely to be aggravated by the aging process. Whereas a young person usually expects to make a complete recovery from sickness, many illnesses among older people become chronic, and the individual has to adjust to living with them. When chronic illness and failing health lead to pain, invalidism, and dependence on others, the individual faces a difficult life situation.

With aging and physical deterioration, such individuals are also confronted with the inescapable fact of their own impending death. Some older people react with equanimity, often stemming from deep religious faith in the meaningfulness of human existence and in the certainty of a life hereafter. Others die as they have lived, with little concern for life or human existence. In fact, they may welcome death as a solution to unsolvable problems and a meaningless life. This is sometimes true also of older people who have lost their friends and loved ones and who feel that they have "outlived their time." How-

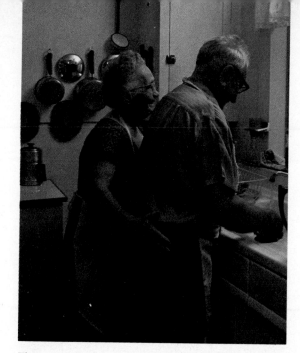

The impact of the stressors of aging can be notably lessened by companionship and shared activity.

ever, for many older people the realization that life is drawing to a close is a highly stressful experience.

c) *Isolation and loneliness.* As the individual grows older, he or she is faced with the inevitable loss of loved ones, friends, and contemporaries. The death of a mate with whom one may have shared many years of close companionship often poses a particularly difficult adjustment problem. This is especially true for women, who in the United States outlive their spouses by an average of at least seven years.

Other factors, too, may contribute to social isolation. Children grow up, marry, and move away; impairment of vision or hearing and various chronic ailments may make social interaction difficult; an attitude of self-pity or an inward centering of interest may alienate family and friends alike. In many instances, the older person also becomes increasingly rigid and intolerant and is unable to make effective use of the opportunities for meaningful social interaction that still remain.

Of course, retirement, lowered income, impaired health, and loneliness are not just matters of inability to maintain a particular lifestyle or to interact with loved ones. In a larger view, they involve the inability to contribute productively and to feel oneself a vital and needed part of the human enterprise. In essence, they progressively destroy the older person's links with the world and feelings of living a meaningful existence.

General sociocultural conditions.

The sociocultural context provides the "climate" in which aging takes place. The importance of this context is suggested by the fact that in the United States, the urban rate of first admissions to mental hospitals and related facilities for both Alzheimer's disease and psychosis with cerebral arteriosclerosis is approximately twice as high as the rural rate. But we do not know how much this indicates that urban living, with its faster pace, noise, crowds, and other stressors, is more conducive to the development of these disorders and how much it indicates that more persons with old-age psychoses are cared for at home in rural areas. The picture is also complicated by the fact that in rural areas the older person enjoys higher social status and is generally able to work productively for a longer period.

In our urban industrial society, the problems of old age have caught us largely unprepared. We have not provided ample conditions for utilizing the experience and wisdom of older people; nor have we provided conditions essential for them to live in reasonable comfort and dignity. In fact, the term "role obsolescence" has been used to describe society's attitude toward older persons as having outlived their usefulness. In our youth-oriented culture, many older people come to perceive themselves as obsolete and worthless—and tend to behave accordingly.

Not infrequently, children assume a patronizing and protective attitude toward their aging parents and in other ways tend to deprive them of dignity, responsibility, and a feeling of importance. Many parents are treated as unwanted burdens, and their children may secretly wish that they would die to relieve them of financial and other responsibilities. In a study of older people in France, De Beauvoir (1970) has pointed out that when the French go away for vacations, they sometimes deposit their aged parents in rest homes. Then, on their return home, they "forget" to pick them up, abandoning them like dogs in a kennel. In the United States, too, many older people are "deposited" in rest homes to die, even though they may be in good health. The effects of being cast aside simply for "being old" may be devastating and, in documented cases, even lethal.

Treatment and outcomes for the old-age psychoses

Whether or not to hospitalize the aged person who is mentally disordered (or indeed the younger one) is often a problem. Individuals manifesting such symptoms as confusion, violent and noisy behavior, depression, antisocial behavior, and disorientation for time, place, and person usually require institutionalization. However, many investigators regard hospitalization as a last resort, feeling that the sudden change in environment and manner of living is especially stressful for the older person and may lead to a feeling of complete hopelessness. In any event, effective treatment of the mental disorders of later life requires a comprehensive use of medical, psychological, and sociological procedures, as indicated by the needs of the individual.

Medical treatment includes both accurate diagnosis and a wide range of procedures, including surgery, drugs, and dietary changes, designed to ameliorate specific physical disorders and to improve the overall health and well-being of the patient. Antipsychotic and antianxiety drugs have proven very valuable in controlling psychotic symptoms and alleviating anxiety and tension, but they are generally not effective in reversing the mental deterioration found in advanced cases of Alzheimer's and arteriosclerotic brain disorders.

There have been favorable reports on the use of group psychotherapy in treating mental disorders associated with old age, but additional research is needed for delineating the most effective psychological treatment procedures. In many hospital settings, "token economies" have proven helpful: desired behavior is rewarded by tokens that patients can exchange for things they want. A key aspect of the best of such reinforcement procedures is that they parallel the organization of outside society and help counteract tendencies toward progressive institutional dependence and chronicity.

Therapy with older patients is also directed toward creating an environment in which the person can function successfully. In a hospital setting or nursing home this includes the provision of comfortable surroundings, together with stimulating activities that encourage the use of whatever capacities remain. Such therapy also includes working with family members in an attempt to help them understand the nature of the patient's disorder and to encourage them to be supportive and show that they care. Where the patient is convalescing at home, follow-up visits by the social worker may be of great value in helping both the patient and the family to adjust.

Even seemingly minor innovations in treatment have shown promising results. In one interesting study, for example, Volpe and Kastenbaum (1967) worked with a group of older men who were so physically and psychologically incapacitated that they required around-the-clock nursing care. These men could perform no services for themselves, were agitated and incontinent, and had a record of striking at each other and tearing off their clothes. Some simple amenities were provided on the ward—games, cards, a record player, and a decorated bulletin board; the men were dressed in white shirts and ties; and at 2 P.M. each day they were served beer in 12-ounce bottles with crackers and cheese. Within a month there was a noticeable change in the group's behavior. The amount of medication they needed dropped sharply, incontinent and agitated behavior decreased significantly, and social responsiveness—as indicated by requests for and participation in parties and dances—markedly increased. The improvement of these men was attributed to their being treated with dignity as responsible individuals and to consequent *"expectancies of mutual gratification* on the part of patients and staff members." In essence, the expectation and demand characteristics of the ward had been changed to those of a social situation instead of a medical one; and the men were cared for in much the same way as in the era of moral treatment, described in Chapter 2.

The extent to which meaningful social roles and expectations may help older people cope with the emotional problems of this life period is illustrated by the following rather unusual case. It involves a professional man who was admitted to a mental hospital for treatment as a result of severe anxiety, indecision, and depression.

The patient's disorder was apparently precipitated by his retirement from the firm for which he had worked for over 40 years. In the course of his hospitalization, the patient showed little improvement until the hospital received a letter from his firm inquiring about his condition. The firm was experiencing difficulty with-

out him and needed his help. Upon receipt of the news the patient showed marked improvement. He was given a leave of absence and returned to his old job. A follow-up study a year later revealed that he was handling his responsibilities with unimpaired judgment, appeared younger, showed good stamina, and reported regularly to work. At this time, he was 80 years old.

It seems clear that the expectation and reinforcement of "normal" social behaviors can often bring about marked behavioral changes in a relatively short time. Kahana and Kahana (1970) found that even such a simple measure as moving young and old people into the same ward appeared to be beneficial for both. The younger ones often tried to help the elderly, which provided them with a sense of purpose; their active interest, in turn, increased the elderly individuals' sense of importance. More recently, Rodin and Langer (1977) have demonstrated the mentally and physically beneficial effects of enhancing a sense of control and independence among the institutionalized aged.

Thus, the psychological prognosis in the psychoses of old age is far from hopeless. Even without complete recovery, many patients can return to their homes, and many others can remain in their homes while being treated in community clinics.[4]

Although the outcome in cases of Alzheimer's and arteriosclerotic brain disorders has traditionally been considered unfavorable because of the irreversibility of the brain damage, recent evidence indicates that behavioral recovery or improvement is possible in about half of the cases when appropriate treatment is provided. Blau (1970) has pointed out that at the Boston State Hospital, which has an active treatment program for elderly patients and fosters aftercare in the community, almost half of the patients over 60 years of age are discharged within 6 months of their admission.

Interestingly, both the greatest number of deaths and the greatest number of improvements among hospitalized elderly psychotic patients occur during the first year after admission. For patients who require continued care in the hospital, about 75 percent die within the first 5 years. In general, the following are considered

---

[4]A summary of recent developments in the rehabilitation and treatment of organically impaired older persons through community resources may be found in Skigen and Solomon (1978).

favorable indicators with respect to outcome: (a) a well-integrated prepsychotic personality; (b) mild, rather than severe, cerebral pathology; (c) absence of such conditions as severe overweight, hypertension, and alcoholism; (d) average or above-average intelligence, education, and technical competence; and (e) a favorable life situation to which to return.

Increasingly aware of the problems confronting senior citizens, federal, state, and local groups are focusing on all aspects of growing old. Scientists in many areas of the biological and social sciences are investigating the pathological and normal aspects of aging and are exploring—in their respective fields—ways to minimize the hazards of the aging process. Senior citizen centers and other community centers and clinics for assisting older people with retirement and other problems are increasing. Specifically designed housing developments also are being built for the elderly, and a number of older people are experimenting with "communal living."

Elderly people are also trying to help one another avoid the special stressors that increase their vulnerability to mental disorders. An encouraging trend here is the growth of such organizations as the American Association of Retired Persons, which numbers over 5 million members. It provides an impressive array of services for its members and fosters legislation to protect the rights and the welfare of older people in our society (Offir, 1974). However, as Neugarten (1974) has pointed out, it seems important that senior citizens not form too strong an age-group identification, which only strengthens the attitudes toward age that tend to divide our society into age-conscious groups. The broader perspective Neugarten advocates is embodied in the Gray Panthers. This group was started by elderly citizens but now includes all age groups and works toward better health services and greater social justice in the society as a whole.

We all need to prepare ourselves for the problems typical of this life period, in the hope that so doing will help us avoid the mental and behavioral deterioration often associated with it. We need to plan ahead for an active and useful life that will take full advantage of the opportunities open to us. Of course, many of the adjustments of old age are highly specific to the situation of the individual and hence cannot be fully

anticipated; but at any age it is important to maintain mental alertness, flexibility, and adaptability while continuing to grow and fulfill one's potential. In short, old age does pose special problems, but it is by no means incompatible with a meaningful and fulfilling life, nor is it necessarily accompanied by gross mental deterioration.

Mental retardation

The American Association on Mental Deficiency (AAMD) has defined *mental retardation* as "significantly subaverage general intellectual functioning existing concurrently with deficits in adaptive behavior, and manifested during the developmental period" (AAMD, 1973, p. 11). Mental retardation is thus defined in terms of *level of behavioral performance*; the definition says nothing about causal factors—which may be primarily biological, psychosocial, or sociocultural or a combination of these.

The American Psychiatric Association has adopted the same definitional approach for its latest classification, DSM-III, listing mental retardation as a disorder beginning before the age of 18. By definition, any functional equivalent of mental retardation that has its onset after age 17 must be considered a dementia rather than mental retardation. The distinction is an important one, because, as has been pointed out, the psychological situation of the individual who acquires a pronounced impairment of intellectual functioning after attaining maturity is vastly different from that of the individual whose intellectual resources were subnormal throughout all or most of his or her development. Some of the more important differences will become apparent in what follows.

Mental retardation is considered to be a specific disorder, but it may occur in combination with other disorders. In fact, other psychiatric disorders occur at a markedly higher rate among retarded individuals than in the general population.

Mental retardation occurs among children throughout the world; in its most severe forms it is a source of great hardship to parents as well as an economic and social burden on the community. The incidence of mental retardation in the United States is estimated to be about 6.8 million persons (see **HIGHLIGHT** on this page). This figure is based on a cutoff point of about IQ 70, which is the cutoff point used by the AAMD. Most states have laws providing that individuals with IQs below 70 who evidence socially incompetent or disapproved behavior can be classified as mentally retarded and committed to an institution.

The incidence of mental retardation seems to increase markedly at ages 5 to 6, to peak at age 15, and to drop off sharply after that. For the most part, these changes in incidence reflect changes in life demands. During early childhood, individuals with only a mild degree of intellectual impairment, who constitute the vast majority of the mentally retarded, often appear to be relatively normal. Their subaverage intellectual functioning becomes apparent only when difficulties with schoolwork lead to a diagnostic evaluation. When adequate facilities are available for their education, children in this group can usually master essential school skills and achieve a satisfactory level of socially adaptive behavior (see **HIGHLIGHT** on page 518). Following the school years, they usually make an acceptable adjustment in the community and thus lose the identity of mentally retarded.

Levels of mental retardation

It is important to remind ourselves once again that any classification system in the behavioral field will have strong features of both arbitrariness and pragmatism. In mental retardation, attempts to define varying levels of impairment have tended to rely increasingly on measurement—largely measurement by means of IQ tests (Robinson & Robinson, 1976). In the above-quoted AAMD definition, for example, the phrase "significantly subnormal general intellectual functioning" translates directly and officially into an IQ test score that is more than two standard deviations below the population mean. This cutoff represents a percentile of about 2.5—that is, a point below which only some 2 to 3 percent of the population score. That means an IQ of approximately 70, according to the most widely used tests of IQ.

It is not improper to define mental retarda-

HIGHLIGHT

Incidence of mental retardation in the United States

Level of retardation	Approximate incidence
Mild (IQ 50–70)	6,332,100
Moderate and severe (IQ 20–49)	420,000
Profound (IQ 0–19)	105,000

Adapted from Robinson and Robinson (1976), p. 37.

tion this way, provided we keep in mind the implications of the definition. The original IQ tests were devised for the explicit purpose of predicting academic achievement among schoolchildren. Other IQ tests developed later were validated largely on the basis of how well they could predict scores on the original ones. Generally, then, what IQ tests measure is an individual's likely level of success in dealing with conventional academic materials, and in fact they do this very well when properly utilized.[5] Thus, when we speak of varying *levels of mental retardation*, we are to a great extent speaking of levels of capacity to succeed in schoolwork.

Of course, this reliance on IQ scores is tempered somewhat by the other main part of the definition—the presence of concurrent "deficits in adaptive behavior." That is, the diagnosis of mental retardation is reserved for individuals who achieve low IQ test scores *and* demonstrate adaptational deficiencies, particularly in the areas of personal independence and social re-

---

[5]In the view of the present authors, it is most unfortunate that "general intelligence" has come to be thought of almost exclusively as a matter of IQ and therefore as facility in handling school tasks. There is surely more to the popular notion of "intelligence" than the talent for getting good grades in school. We would hold, too, that academic talent, which is mostly what IQ tests measure, is but a limited aspect of intellectual fitness. In this context, it is worth noting that the frequent charge of cultural bias on the part of IQ tests is unavoidably accurate: the educational system is the main depository of the dominant culture's products, and facility to deal with it will inevitably come easier to those trained from infancy in its concepts and values.

HIGHLIGHT

Difficulties of mentally retarded people in learning basic academic skills

The basic learning processes of most mentally retarded children—aside from a minority with serious neurological defects—are not essentially different from those of normal children. However, retarded children learn at a slower rate than normal children and are less capable of mastering abstractions and complex concepts. These limitations are especially apparent in learning language and other symbolic skills requiring a high level of abstract ability.

Problems that retarded children typically encounter in learning basic academic skills may be summarized as follows:

1. Difficulty in focusing attention. Studies have shown that such children's poor learning is often due to the fact that their attention is focused on irrelevant aspects of learning situations. Once they know what stimulus dimensions are important—for example, attending to form when the shape of the letters is important in learning the alphabet—they may quickly master appropriate discrimination skills and show marked improvement in performance and learning.

2. Deficiency in past learning. Most formal learning requires prior learning. For example, a child who has not learned basic verbal, conceptual, and problem-solving skills will fall farther behind when he or she begins schooling. Thus, a number of programs have been established to help disadvantaged children of preschool age develop basic skills requisite for learning in school.

3. Expectancy of failure—a self-fulfilling prophecy. Because of having experienced more failure in learning attempts than other children, the mentally retarded child tends to begin tasks with a greater expectancy of failure and to engage in avoidance behavior as well. Often such children feel that forces beyond their control determine the outcome of their actions. Thus, if they succeed in a task, they may not perceive their success as due to their own efforts or ability. They become passive, lose their initiative, and begin to rely too much on others. To counteract this tendency, learning experiences must be programmed into manageable components that can yield continuing experiences of success.

Special education classes should thus be directed at helping the mentally retarded discriminate relevant from irrelevant stimuli in learning and problem-solving situations; they should associate new learning with the children's present information, needs, and life situations; and they should structure learning tasks in a sequence of steps that can be readily mastered by the retarded and so provide experiences of success. Such measures, of course, are useful in all educational settings, but are particularly important in training mentally retarded children.

Based on Bijou (1966), Hagen and Huntsman (1971), Hyatt and Rolnick (1974), Karnes et al. (1970), MacMillan and Keogh (1971), Tarver and Hallahan (1974), and Robinson and Robinson (1976).

---

sponsibility. The same dual criteria are involved in the officially recognized "levels" of retardation, although the IQ score often tends in practice to be the dominant consideration. This is appropriate at the lower end of the scale, since an individual with an IQ of 50 or below will inevitably exhibit gross deficiencies in adaptive behavior as well. At the higher ranges of "retarded" IQ scores, however, behavioral adaptiveness and IQ score seem to be at least partially independent of each other.

Both the American Association on Mental Deficiency and the American Psychiatric Association classifications recognize four levels of retarded mental development, as follows:

a) *Mild mental retardation (IQ 52–67).* As shown in the **HIGHLIGHT** on page 517, this group constitutes by far the largest number of those labeled mentally retarded. Persons in this group are considered "educable," and their intellectual levels as adults are comparable with those of average 8- to 11-year-old children. Their social adjustment often approximates that of the adolescent, although they tend to lack the normal adolescent's imagination, inventiveness, and judgment. Ordinarily they do not show signs of brain pathology or other physical anomalies, but often they require some measure of supervision because of their limited ability to foresee the consequences of their actions. With early diagnosis, parental assistance, and special educational programs, the great majority can adjust socially, master simple academic and occupational skills, and become self-supporting citizens. (Schalock, Harper, & Carver, 1981).

b) *Moderate mental retardation (IQ 36–51).* Individuals in this group are likely to fall in the educational category of "trainable." In adult life, individuals classified as moderately retarded attain intellectual levels similar to those of average 4- to 7-year-old children. While some of the brighter ones can be taught to read and write a little, and some manage to achieve a fair command of spoken language, their rate of learning is relatively slow, and their level of conceptualizing extremely limited. Physically, they usually appear clumsy and ungainly, and they suffer from bodily deformities and poor motor coordination. A distinct minority of these children are hostile and aggressive; more typically they present an affable and somewhat vacuous personality picture.

In general, with early diagnosis, parental help, and adequate opportunities for training, most of the moderately retarded can achieve partial independence in daily self-care, acceptable behavior, and economic usefulness in a family or other sheltered environment. Whether they require institutionalization usually depends on their general level of adaptive behavior and the nature of their home situation.

c) *Severe mental retardation (IQ 20–35).* Individuals in this group are sometimes referred to as "dependent retarded." Among these individuals, motor and speech development are severely retarded, and sensory defects and motor handicaps are common. They can develop limited levels of personal hygiene and self-help skills, which somewhat lessen their dependence; but they are always dependent on others for care. However, many profit to some extent from training and can perform simple occupational tasks under supervision.

d) *Profound mental retardation (IQ under 20).* The term *life support retarded* is sometimes used to refer to individuals in this category. Most of these persons are severely deficient in adaptive behavior and unable to master any but the simplest tasks. Useful speech, if it develops at all, is rudimentary. Severe physical deformities, central nervous system pathology, and retarded growth are typical; convulsive seizures, mutism, deafness, and other physical anomalies are also common. These individuals must remain in custodial care all their lives. However, they tend to

have poor health and low resistance to disease and thus a short life expectancy.

Severe and profound cases of mental retardation can usually be quite readily diagnosed in infancy because of the presence of physical malformations, grossly delayed habit training, and other obvious symptoms of abnormality. But although these individuals show a marked impairment of overall intellectual functioning, they may have considerably more ability in some areas than in others. Indeed, in very occasional cases, seriously retarded persons may show a high level of skill in some specific aspect of behavior that does not depend on abstract reasoning. Thus, one seriously retarded individual was able to remember the serial number on every dollar bill he was shown or had ever seen; another was able to tell the day of the week of a given date in any year, without resorting to paper and pencil or even to making other numerical calculations. In other exceptional cases, a retarded person may show considerable talent in art or music. Viscott (1970) provided a detailed case study of a "musical idiot savant"; Hill (1975) cited the case of a mildly retarded individual with a diagnosed IQ of 54 who could play 11 different musical instruments by ear and possessed outstanding skill in calculating dates. Similarly, Morishima (1975) cited the case of a famous Japanese painter whose assessed IQ was 47. However, such unusual abilities among the retarded are rare.

Contrary to common understanding, the distribution of IQ scores in the United States does not precisely fit "normal curve" expectations, especially at the lower IQ ranges. These ranges tend to show a frequency bulge, with nearly 200,000 more cases than would be expected (Robinson & Robinson, 1976). This finding suggests the operation of an intruding factor that tends to inflate the numbers of cases at lower IQ ranges—probably the presence of major genetic abnormalities and/or brain injuries that are not characteristic of mild retardation.

Mental retardation and organic brain dysfunction

Some instances of mental retardation—something on the order of 25 percent of the cases—occur with known organic pathology. In these cases retardation is virtually always at least moderate, and it is often severe. Profound retardation is fortunately rare; it does not occur in the absence of obvious organic impairment. Organically caused retardation is in essential respects similar to dementia as previously described, except for a different history of prior functioning. In fact, in times past, the young person with organically caused retardation was referred to as *amented*, as distinct from the *demented* person.

In this section we shall consider five biological conditions that may lead to mental retardation, noting some of the possible interrelations between them. Then we shall review some of the major clinical types of mental retardation associated with these organic causes.

1. *Genetic-chromosomal factors.* Mental retardation tends to run in families. This is particularly true of mild retardation. However, poverty and sociocultural deprivation also tend to run in families, and with early and continued exposure to such conditions, even the inheritance of average intellectual potential may not prevent subaverage intellectual functioning.

As we noted in Chapter 4, genetic and chromosomal factors play a much clearer role in the etiology of relatively rare types of mental retardation such as Down's syndrome. Here, specific chromosomal defects are responsible for metabolic alterations that adversely affect development of the brain. Genetic defects leading to metabolic alterations may, of course, involve many other developmental anomalies besides mental retardation. In general, the mental retardation most often associated with known genetic-chromosomal defects is moderate to severe in degree.

2. *Infections and toxic agents.* Mental retardation may be associated with a wide range of conditions due to infection. If a pregnant woman has syphilis or gets German measles, her child may suffer brain damage. Brain damage may also result from infections occurring after birth, such as viral encephalitis.

A number of toxic agents, such as carbon monoxide and lead, may cause brain damage during fetal development or after birth. In some instances, immunological agents, such as anti-tetanus serum or typhoid vaccine, may lead to brain damage. Similarly, certain drugs taken by the mother during pregnancy may lead to congenital malformations; an overdose of drugs administered to the infant may result in toxicity

and brain damage. In rare cases, brain damage results from incompatibility in blood types between mother and fetus—conditions known as Rh, or ABO, system incompatibility. Fortunately, early diagnosis and blood transfusions can now minimize the effects of such incompatibility.

3. *Prematurity and trauma (physical injury).* Follow-up studies of children born prematurely and weighing less than about five pounds at birth have revealed a high incidence of neurological disorders and often mental retardation. In fact, very small premature babies are many times more likely to be mentally retarded than normal infants (MacDonald, 1964).

Physical injury at birth can also result in retardation. Isaacson (1970) has estimated that in 1 birth out of 1000 there is a brain damage that will prevent the child from reaching the intelligence level of a 12-year-old. Although normally the fetus is well protected by its fluid-filled bag during gestation, and its skull appears designed to resist delivery stressors, accidents do happen during delivery as well as after birth. Difficulties in labor due to malposition of the fetus or other complications may irreparably damage the infant's brain. Bleeding within the brain is probably the most common result of such birth trauma. *Anoxia*—lack of sufficient oxygen to the brain stemming from delayed breathing or other causes—is another type of birth trauma that may damage the brain. Anoxia may also occur after birth as a result of cardiac arrest associated with operations, heart attacks, near drownings, or severe electrical shocks.

4. *Ionizing radiation.* In recent years a good deal of scientific attention has been focused on the damaging effects of ionizing radiation on sex cells and other bodily cells and tissues. Radiation may act directly on the fertilized ovum or may produce gene mutations in the sex cells of either or both parents, which, in turn, may lead to defective offspring.

Sources of harmful radiation were once limited primarily to high-energy X rays used for diagnosis and therapy, but the list has grown to include leakages at nuclear power plants and nuclear weapons testing, among others.

5. *Malnutrition and other biological factors.* As we noted in Chapter 4, deficiencies in protein and other essential nutrients during early development can result in irreversible physical and mental damage. Protein deficiencies in the

HIGHLIGHT
Other disorders sometimes associated with mental retardation

Clinical type	Symptoms	Causes
No. 18 trisomy syndrome	Peculiar pattern of multiple congenital anomalies, the most common being low-set malformed ears, flexion of fingers, small jaw, and heart defects	Autosomal anomaly of chromosome 18
Tay-Sach's disease	Hypertonicity, listlessness, blindness, progressive spastic paralysis, and convulsions (death by the third year)	Disorder of lipoid metabolism, carried by a single recessive gene
Turner's syndrome	In females only; webbing of the neck, increased carrying angle of forearm, and sexual infantilism	Sex chromosome anomaly (XO). Mental retardation may occur but is infrequent
Klinefelter's syndrome	In males only; features vary from case to case, the only constant finding being the presence of small testes after puberty	Sex chromosome anomaly (XXY)
Niemann-Pick's disease	Onset usually in infancy, with loss of weight, dehydration, and progressive paralysis	Disorder of lipoid metabolism
Bilirubin encephalopathy	Abnormal levels of bilirubin (a toxic substance released by red cell destruction) in the blood; motor incoordination frequent	Often, Rh (ABO) blood group incompatibility between mother and fetus
Rubella, congenital	Visual difficulties most common, with cataracts and retinal problems often occurring together and with deafness and anomalies in the valves and septa of the heart	The mother's contraction of rubella (German measles) during the first few months of her pregnancy

Based on American Psychiatric Association (1968, 1972), Christodorescu et al. (1970), Donoghue, Abbas, and Gal (1970), Holvey and Talbott (1972), Johnson et al. (1970), Nielsen et al. (1970), Robinson and Robinson (1976).

mother's diet during pregnancy, as well as in the baby's diet after birth, have been pinpointed as particularly potent causes of lowered intelligence.

A limited number of cases of mental retardation are also associated with other biological agents, such as brain tumors that either damage the brain tissue directly or lead to increased cranial pressure and concomitant brain damage. In some instances of mental retardation—particularly of the severe and profound types—the causes are uncertain or unknown, although extensive brain pathology is evident.

Mental retardation stemming primarily from biological causes can be classified into several recognizable clinical types, of which four will be discussed here. The **HIGHLIGHT** on this page presents information on several other well-known forms.

Down's syndrome. *Down's syndrome*, first described by Langdon Down in 1886, is the most common of the clinical conditions associated with moderate and severe mental retardation. About 1 in every 600 babies born in the United States is diagnosed as having Down's syndrome, a condition that "has lifelong implications for physical appearance, intellectual achievement and general functioning" (Golden & Davis, 1974, p. 7).

A number of physical features are often found among children with Down's syndrome, but very few of these children have all of the characteristics commonly thought of as typifying this group. The eyes appear almond-shaped, the skin of the eyelids tends to be abnormally thick; the face and nose are often flat and broad, as is the back of the head; and the tongue, which seems too large for the mouth, may show deep fissures. The iris of the eye is frequently speckled. The neck is often short and broad, as are the hands, which tend to have creases across the palms. The fingers are stubby, and the little finger is often more noticeably curved than the other fingers.

Well over 50 percent of persons with Down's syndrome have cataracts, which are not congenital but tend to make their appearance when the child is about 7 or 8 (Falls, 1970). These cataracts aid in diagnosis, but fortunately they rarely become serious enough to warrant surgery. Interestingly, there appears to be little, if any, correlation between the number of physical symptoms of Down's syndrome and the degree of mental retardation.

Death rates for children with Down's syndrome have decreased dramatically in the past half century. In 1929 the life expectancy at birth for such children was about 9 years; most of the deaths were due to gross physical anomalies, and a large proportion occurred in the first year. Today, thanks to antibiotics, surgical correction of lethal anatomical defects, and better general medical care, many more of these children are living to adulthood (Smith & Berg, 1976). In fact, overall, the mortality rate for this group is only 6 percent higher than that for the general population, though it is still higher than that in the early years and for those who live beyond 40 (Forssman & Akesson, 1965). At present, the average life expectancy for live-born Down's syndrome children at birth is about 16 years; by age 1, it increases to about 22 years (Smith & Berg, 1976).

The terms *mongolism* or *mongoloid* were widely used in the past because the almond-shaped eyes were thought to give Down's syndrome children facial features similar to those of the Mongolian race. At times, the term *mongolian idiot* was also used. These terms are no longer acceptable, however, because they contain negative racial connotations. In addition, the term "idiot" is inappropriate because most of the afflicted children show only moderate mental retardation.

Despite their limitations, children suffering from Down's syndrome are usually able to learn self-help skills, acceptable social behavior, and routine manual skills that enable them to be of assistance in a family or institutional setting. The traditional view has been that the Down's syndrome youngster is unusually placid and affectionate. Recent research questions the validity of that generalization. These children may indeed be very tractable, but probably in no greater proportion than normal youngsters; they may also be equally (or more) difficult in various areas (Bridges & Cicchetti, 1982).

Recent research has also suggested that the intellectual defect in Down's syndrome may not be consistent across various abilities. Down's syndrome children tend to remain relatively unimpaired in their appreciation of spatial relationships and in visual-motor coordination; they show their greatest deficits in verbal and language-related skills (Mahoney, Glover, & Finger, 1981; Silverstein et al., 1982). Inasmuch as spatial functions are known to be partially localized in the right cerebral hemisphere, and language-related functions in the left cerebral hemisphere, one might speculate that the syndrome is especially crippling to the left hemisphere.

Traditionally, the cause of Down's syndrome was assumed to be faulty heredity. A number of early studies demonstrated, however, that more than a single case of Down's syndrome in a family was very infrequent, occurring in less than 1 family in 100. As a consequence of this finding, investigators turned to the study of metabolic factors and concluded that Down's syndrome was probably due to some sort of glandular imbalance. Then, in 1959, the French scientists Lejeune, Turpin, and Gauthier found 47 chromosomes, instead of the usual 46, in several Down's syndrome cases. A trisomy of chromosome 21 has now been identified as a characteristic of Down's syndrome children (see the **HIGH-LIGHT** on p. 100).

Researchers have long believed that the "extra" chromosome in Down's syndrome is in some way contributed by the mother. But in 1973 it was learned that in certain instances it is in fact contributed by the father (Sasaki & Hara, 1973; Uchida, 1973). The reason for the trisomy of chromosome 21 is not clear, but the anomaly seems definitely related to parental age at conception.

It has been known for many years that the incidence of Down's syndrome increases in regular fashion with the age of the mother. A woman in her 20s has about 1 chance in 2000 of having a Down's syndrome baby, whereas the risk for a woman in her 40s is 1 in 50 (Holvey & Talbot, 1972).[6] Evidence of this type led naturally to the speculation that the capacity of the older woman to produce a chromosomally normal fetus was somehow impaired by the aging process.

Recent research, however, strongly suggests that age of fathers at conception is also implicated, particularly at the higher ranges of paternal age (Hook, 1980; Stene et al., 1981). In one study involving 1,279 cases of Down's syndrome in Japan, Matsunaga and associates (1978) demonstrated an overall increase in incidence of the syndrome with advancing paternal age when maternal age was controlled. The risk for fathers aged 55 years and over was more than twice that for fathers in their early 20s. Curiously, these investigators noted that, in their sample, fathers in their early 40s had a lower risk factor than somewhat younger or older men.

Thus, it seems that advancing age in either parent increases the risk of the trisomy 21 anomaly. As yet we do not understand how aging produces this effect. A reasonable guess is that aging is related to cumulative exposure to varied environmental hazards, such as radiation, that might have adverse effects on the processes involved in zygote formation or development.

But whatever the cause of the chromosomal anomaly, the end result is the distortion in the growth process characteristic of this clinical syndrome. There is no known effective treatment. When parents have had a child with Down's syndrome, they are usually quite concerned about having further children. In such cases genetic counseling may provide some indication of the risk—which may be quite small—of abnormality in additional children. In recent years,

the technique known as *amniocentesis* has made it possible to diagnose most cases of Down's syndrome *in utero*, thus permitting parents to make a rational choice concerning termination of the pregnancy if the fetus is abnormal.

Phenylketonuria (PKU). *Phenylketonuria* is a rare metabolic disorder, occurring in about 1 in 20,000 births; retarded individuals in institutions who suffer from PKU number about 1 in 100 (Holmes et al., 1972; Schild, 1972).

In PKU the baby appears normal at birth but lacks an enzyme needed to break down phenylalanine, an amino acid found in many foods. The genetic error manifests itself in pathology only when phenylalanine is ingested, something that is virtually certain to occur if the child's condition remains undiagnosed. In any event, if the condition is undetected, the amount of phenylalanine in the blood increases and eventually produces brain damage.

The disorder usually becomes apparent between 6 and 12 months after birth, although such symptoms as vomiting, a peculiar odor, infantile eczema, and seizures may occur during the early weeks of life. Often the first symptoms noticed are signs of mental retardation, which may be moderate to severe depending on the degree to which the disease has progressed. Motor incoordination and other neurological manifestations relating to the severity of brain damage are also common, and often the eyes, skin, and hair of untreated PKU patients are very pale.

PKU was identified in 1934 when a Norwegian mother sought to learn the reason for her child's mental retardation and peculiar musty odor. She consulted with many physicians to no avail until Dr. Asbjorn Folling found phenylpyruvic acid in the urine and concluded that the child had a disorder of phenylalanine metabolism (Centerwall & Centerwall, 1961).

Most older PKU patients show severe to profound mental retardation, with the median IQ of untreated adult phenylketonurics being about 20. Curiously, however, a number of PKU individuals have PKU relatives with less severely affected intelligence. And Perry (1970) has reported the cases of two untreated PKU patients with superior intelligence. These findings have made PKU something of an enigma. It results from a liver enzyme deficiency involving one or

---

[6]It should be noted that, as in the case of all birth defects, the risk of having a Down's syndrome baby is very high for young teenagers.

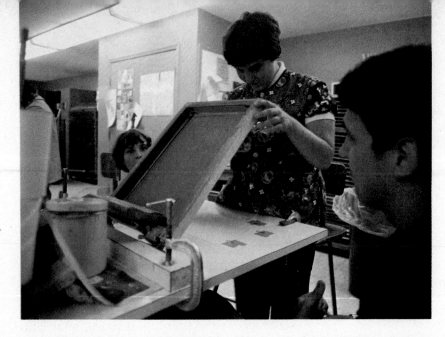

Types of mental retardation vary greatly in severity and in how readily they respond to treatment. Useful and productive activity is an important element in most therapy approaches.

more recessive genes, and 1 person in 70 is thought to be a carrier. However, there may be varying degrees of PKU, or another genetic factor may lessen the destructive potential of the enzyme defect (Burns, 1972).

Methods for the early detection of PKU have been developed, and dietary and related treatment procedures are now used. With early detection and treatment—preferably before an infant is 6 months old—the deterioration process can usually be arrested so that levels of intellectual functioning may range from borderline to normal. However, a few children suffer mental retardation despite restricted phenylalanine intake and other treatment measures.

For a baby to inherit PKU, it appears that both parents must carry the recessive genes. Thus, when one child in a family is discovered to have PKU, it is important that other children in the family be screened as well.

Cretinism (thyroid deficiency). *Cretinism*
provides a dramatic illustration of mental retardation resulting from endocrine imbalance. In this condition, the thyroid either has failed to develop properly or has undergone degeneration or injury; in either case, the infant suffers from a deficiency in thyroid secretion. Brain damage resulting from this insufficiency is most marked when the deficiency occurs during the prenatal and early postnatal periods of rapid growth.

In the valleys of central Switzerland and in other geographical areas where iodine is deficient in the soil, and therefore in the food grown

in it, cretinism was once a common affliction. In such areas infants often were born with defective thyroid glands that remained undeveloped or atrophied later. Because cretinism was observed to run in families in such areas, it was thought to be invariably a hereditary disorder. In 1891, however, Dr. George Murray published his discovery that the injection of thyroid gland extract was beneficial in cases of *myxedema*—a disorder resulting from thyroid deficiency in adult life and characterized by mental dullness. This discovery, in turn, led to the treatment of cretinism with thyroid gland extract and to the realization that this condition, too, was the result of thyroid deficiency.

Although most cases of cretinism result from lack of iodine in the diet, thyroid deficiency may also occur as a result of birth injuries (involving bleeding into the thyroid) or of infectious diseases such as measles, whooping cough, or diphtheria. Less frequently, it may be a result of a genetically determined enzyme defect. The resulting clinical picture will depend on the age at which the thyroid deficiency occurs, as well as on the degree and duration of the deficiency.

Typical descriptions of individuals with cretinism involve cases in which there has been severe thyroid deficiency from an early age, often even before birth. Such an individual has a dwarflike, thick-set body and short, stubby extremities. Height is usually just a little over three feet, the shortness accentuated by slightly bent legs and a curvature of the spine. The individual walks with a shuffling gait that is easily recognizable and has a large head with abundant black, wiry hair. Thick eyelids give the person a sleepy appearance, and the skin is dry and thickened and cold to the touch. Other pronounced physical symptoms include a broad, flat nose, large and flappy ears, a protruding abdomen, and failure to mature sexually. The sufferer reveals a bland personality and sluggish thought processes. Most individuals with cretinism fall within the moderate and severe categories of mental retardation, depending on the extent of brain damage. In cases with less pronounced physical signs of cretinism, the degree of mental retardation is usually less severe.

Early treatment of cretinism with thyroid gland extract is considered essential; infants not treated until after the first year of life may have permanently impaired intelligence. In long-standing cases, thyroid treatment may have some ameliorating effects, but the damage to the individual's nervous system and general physical development is beyond repair.

As a result of public health measures on both national and international levels with respect to the use of iodized salt and the early detection and correction of thyroid deficiency, severe cases of cretinism have become practically nonexistent in the United States and in most, but not all, other countries.

Cranial anomalies. Mental retardation is associated with a number of conditions in which there are relatively gross alterations in head size and shape and for which the causal factors have not been definitely established (Wortis, 1973). In *macrocephaly* ("large-headedness"), for example, there is an increase in the size and weight of the brain, an enlargement of the skull, and visual impairment, convulsions, and other neurological symptoms resulting from the abnormal growth of glia cells that form the supporting structure for brain tissue. Other cranial anomalies include *microcephaly* and *hydrocephalus*, which we shall discuss in more detail.

1. *Microcephaly.* The term *microcephaly* means "small-headedness." It refers to a type of mental retardation resulting from impaired development of the brain and a consequent failure of the cranium to attain normal size. In an early study of postmortem examinations of brains of microcephalic individuals, Greenfield and Wolfson (1935) reported that practically all cases examined showed development to have been ar-

rested at the fourth or fifth month of fetal life. Fortunately, this condition is extremely rare.

The most obvious characteristic of microcephaly is the small head, the circumference of which rarely exceeds 17 inches, as compared with the normal size of approximately 22 inches. Penrose (1963) also described microcephalic youngsters as being invariably short in stature but having relatively normal musculature and sex organs. Beyond these characteristics, they differ considerably from one another in appearance, although there is a tendency for the skull to be cone-shaped, with a receding chin and forehead. Microcephalic children fall within the moderate, severe, and profound categories of mental retardation, but the majority show little language development and are extremely limited in mental capacity.

Microcephaly may result from a wide range of factors that impair brain development, including intrauterine infections and pelvic irradiation of the mother during the early months of pregnancy (Koch, 1967). Miller (1970) noted a number of cases of microcephaly in Hiroshima and Nagasaki that apparently resulted from the atomic bomb explosions during World War II. The role of genetic factors is not as yet clear. Treatment is ineffective once faulty development has occurred; and at present, preventive measures focus on the avoidance of infection and radiation during pregnancy.

2. *Hydrocephalus.* **Hydrocephalus** is a relatively rare condition in which the accumulation of an abnormal amount of cerebrospinal fluid within the cranium causes damage to the brain tissues and enlargement of the cranium.

In congenital cases of hydrocephalus, the head is either already enlarged at birth or begins to enlarge soon thereafter, presumably as a result of a disturbance in the formation, absorption, or circulation of the cerebrospinal fluid (Wortis, 1973). The disorder can also develop in infancy or early childhood following the development of a brain tumor, subdural hematoma, meningitis, or other such conditions. Here the condition appears to result from a blockage of the cerebrospinal pathways and an accumulation of fluid in certain brain areas.

The clinical picture in hydrocephalus depends on the extent of neural damage, which, in turn, depends on the age at onset and the duration and severity of the disorder. In chronic cases the chief symptom is the gradual enlargement of the upper part of the head out of all proportion to the face and the rest of the body. While the expansion of the skull helps minimize destructive pressure on the brain, serious brain damage occurs nonetheless, leading to intellectual impairment and such other effects as convulsions and impairment or loss of sight and hearing. The degree of intellectual impairment varies, being severe or profound in advanced cases.

A good deal of attention has been directed to the surgical treatment of hydrocephalus, and with early diagnosis and treatment this condition can usually be arrested before severe brain damage has occurred (Geisz & Steinhausen, 1974).

Mental retardation and sociocultural deprivation

It was formerly believed that all mental retardation was the result of faulty genes or of other causes of brain pathology. In recent years, however, it has become apparent that adverse sociocultural conditions, particularly those involving a deprivation of normal stimulation, may play a primary role in the etiology of mental retardation.[7]

Two subtypes of mental retardation fall in this general category: (a) mental retardation associated with extreme sensory and social deprivation, such as prolonged isolation during the developmental years, as may have happened in the case of the wild boy of Aveyron, discussed in the **HIGHLIGHT** on page 527; and (b) *cultural-familial retardation,* in which the child is not subjected to extreme isolation but rather suffers from an inferior quality of interaction with the cultural environment and with other people. Since such sociocultural impoverishment may be associated with genetic deficiency in some cases, the child born to a family in such circumstances may be doubly jeopardized. In any event, it has proven all but impossible to assess adequately the differential influences of nature and nurture

in these cases. The field is rife with controversy and, regrettably, has involved one publicized case in which a researcher allegedly manipulated his statistics to prove that mental ability is hereditary (Dorfman, 1978).

Since the great majority of all retarded individuals are of the cultural-familial type, our discussion will focus on this form of retardation.

Cultural-familial mental retardation. Children who fall in this category are usually mildly retarded; they make up the majority of persons labeled as mentally retarded. These children show no identifiable brain pathology and are usually not diagnosed as mentally retarded until they enter school and have serious difficulties in their studies. As a number of investigators have pointed out, however, most of these children come from poverty-stricken, unstable, and often disrupted family backgrounds characterized by a lack of intellectual stimulation, an inferior quality of interaction with others, and general environmental deprivation (Birns & Bridger, 1977; Braginsky & Braginsky, 1974; Feuerstein, 1977).

"They are raised in homes with absent fathers and with physically or emotionally unavailable mothers. During infancy they are not exposed to the same quality and quantity of tactile and kinesthetic stimulations as other children. Often they are left unattended in a crib or on the floor of the dwelling. Although there are noises, odors, and colors in the environment, the stimuli are not as organized as those found in middle-class and upper-class environments. For example, the number of words they hear is limited, with sentences brief and most commands carrying a negative connotation." (Tarjan & Eisenberg, 1972, p. 16)

In fact, three fourths of the nation's mentally retarded come from homes that are socially, economically, and culturally disadvantaged.

Since a child's current level of intellectual functioning is based largely on previous learning—and since schoolwork requires complex skills such as being able to control one's attention, follow instructions, and recognize the meaning of a considerable range of words—these children are at a disadvantage from the beginning because they have not had an opportunity to learn requisite background skills or be motivated toward learning. Thus, with each succeeding year, unless remedial measures are un-

---

[7]American behavioral scientists have used the terms *psychosocial deprivation, psychosocial disadvantage, cultural-familial retardation,* and *sociocultural deprivation* somewhat interchangeably. We shall use the latter term as a more general category in ordering our present discussion.

HIGHLIGHT

The "wild boy of Aveyron"

In 1800, long before the development of psychotherapy, Jean-Marc Itard attempted to inculcate normal human abilities in a "wild boy" who had been captured by peasants in the forests of Aveyron, France. The boy, who appeared to be between 10 and 12 years old, had been exhibited in a cage for about a year by his captors when Itard rescued him. By examining scars on the boy's body, as well as the observation of his personal habits, Itard concluded that he had been abandoned at the age of two or three.

At first Victor (As Itard named the boy) seemed more animal than human. He was oblivious to other human beings, could not talk, and howled and ate off the ground on all fours like an animal. He evidenced unusual sensory reactions; for example, he did not react if a pistol was fired next to his ear, but he could hear the crack of a nut or the crackling of underbrush at a great distance. No adverse reaction seemed to result from his going unclothed even in freezing weather. In fact, Victor had a fine velvety skin, despite his years of exposure.

Victor exhibited animal-like behavior in many ways. He had an obstinate habit of smelling any object that was given to him—even objects we consider void of smell. He knew nothing of love and perceived other human beings only as obstacles—in other words, like the wild animals he had known in the forest. He was typically indifferent and uncomplaining but, very occasionally, he showed a kind of frantic rage and became dangerous to those around him. If he had any sense of self-identity, it was apparently more that of an animal than a human.

Philippe Pinel, Itard's teacher, diagnosed Victor's condition as congenital idiocy—concluding that the boy was incapable of profiting from training. But Itard, although only 25 years old and inexperienced in comparison with Pinel, disagreed; in his view, Victor's savage behavior was the result of early and lengthy isolation from other humans. He believed that human contact and intensive training would enable the boy to become a normal person, and, ignoring Pinel's advice, he began his attempt to civilize "the wild boy of Aveyron."

No procedures had yet been formulated that Itard could use in treating Victor; thus he developed a program based on principles that included the following: (a) without contact with its own kind, a human infant—unlike a lower animal—cannot develop normally; (b) the instinct to imitate is the learning force by which our senses are educated, and this instinct is strongest in early childhood and decreases with age; and (c) in all human beings, from the most isolated savage to the most educated individual, a constant relationship exists between needs and ideas—the greater the needs, the greater the development of mental capacities to meet them.

In attempting to train Victor, Itard developed methods that have had considerable impact on the subsequent treatment of children with serious learning disabilities. Instructional materials were provided to broaden Victor's discrimination skills in touch, smell, and other sensory modalities, appropriate to his environment; language training was begun through the association of words with the objects Victor wanted; and modeling and imitation were used to reinforce Victor's learning of desired social behaviors.

Initial results were indeed promising. Victor learned to speak a number of words and could write in chalk to express his wants. He also developed affectionate feelings toward his governess.

In June 1801, Itard reported to the Academy of Science in Paris on the rapid progress in the first nine months of training. But in November 1806, he could only report that despite significant advances in several areas, Victor had not been made "normal" in the sense of becoming a self-directing and socially adjusted person. Being brought into the proximity of girls, for example, only upset the boy, leaving him restless and depressed, and Itard had to abandon his hope for a normal sexual response as a means of fostering Victor's motivation and socialization.

After devoting five and a half years to the task, Itard gave up the attempt to train "the wild boy of Aveyron." As for Victor, he lived to be 40, but never progressed appreciably beyond the achievements of that first year.

The story of Victor is of absorbing interest to both laymen and scientists. A motion picture that portrays Itard's work with Victor—The Wild Child—was produced by François Truffaut. In scientific circles, the lack of conclusive answers will keep psychologists and others puzzling over the question of whether Victor was a congenital mental retardate, a brain-damaged child, a psychotic, or simply a child who had been so deprived of human contact during early critical periods of development that the damage he had sustained could never be completely remedied.

Based on Itard (1799; tr. Humphrey & Humphrey, 1932) and Silberstein and Irwin (1962).

dertaken, they tend to fall farther behind in school performance. They also fall farther behind in relative ratings on intelligence tests, which, as we have seen, are measures of ability for schoolwork.

A report by the American Psychological Association (1970) noted the following:

"Mental retardation is primarily a psychosocial and psychoeducational problem—a deficit in adaptation to the demands and expectations of society evidenced by the individual's relative difficulty in learning, problem solving, adapting to new situations, and abstract thinking." (p. 267)

This statement was not intended to minimize the possible role of adverse biological factors, including genetic deficiencies, in the total causal pattern. Certainly many of these children reveal histories of prematurity, inadequate diets, and little or no medical care. But in the great majority of cases of cultural-familial mental retardation, no neurological or physical dysfunction has been demonstrated. Thus, efforts to understand mild mental retardation have focused increasingly on the role of environmental factors in impeding intellectual growth.

The problem of assessment. Since mental retardation is defined in terms of both intellectual (academic) and social competence, it is essential to assess both of these characteristics before labeling a person as mentally retarded.

Unfortunately, neither of the preceding tasks is an easy one. Errors in the assessment of IQ can stem from a variety of sources, including (a) errors in administering tests; (b) personal characteristics of the child, such as a language problem or lack of motivation to do well on tests; and (c) limitations in the tests themselves. The latter point has been succinctly stated by Wortis (1972):

"An IQ score, at best, can indicate where an individual stands in intellectual performance compared to others. What others? His nation? His social class? His ethnic group? No intelligence test that has ever been devised can surmount all of these complicating considerations and claim universal validity." (p. 22)

Wortis's point has been widely accepted and echoed by other observers.

While the assessment of social competence

may seem less complicated, especially if it is based on clinical observations and ratings, it is subject to many of the same errors as the measurement of intelligence. Of particular importance are the criteria used by the person or persons doing the assessing. For example, if children are well adapted socially to life in an urban ghetto but not to the demands of a formal school setting, should they be evaluated as evidencing a high, intermediate, or low level of social competence? Competence for what? Again the conclusions of Wortis concerning the assessment of intelligence would appear to apply.[8]

To label a child as mentally retarded—as significantly subaverage in intellectual and adaptive capability—is an act likely to have profound effects on both the child's self-concept and the reactions of others, and thus on his or her entire future life. Most immediately, it may lead to institutionalization. And over the long term, it may be a self-fulfilling prophecy fueled by the tendency to behave in ways consistent with one's self-concept as well as with others' expectations. Obviously it is a label that has profound ethical and social implications.

Treatment, outcomes, and prevention

A number of recent programs have demonstrated that significant changes in adaptive capacity are possible through special education and other rehabilitative measures. The degree of change that can be expected is related, of course, to the individual's situation and level of mental retardation.

Treatment facilities and methods. One problem that often inflicts great anxiety on parents of a mentally retarded child is whether or not to put their child in an institution. In general, the children who are institutionalized fall into two groups: (a) those who, in infancy and childhood, manifest severe mental retardation and associated physical impairment, and who enter the institution at an early age, and (b) those who have no physical impairments but show mild mental retardation and failure to ad-

---

[8]Comprehensive discussions of the problems in assessing and labeling the mentally retarded may be found in Mittler (1977) and Robinson and Robinson (1976).

just socially in adolescence, eventually being institutionalized chiefly because of delinquency or other problem behavior. Here social incompetence is the main factor in the decision. The families of those in the first group come from all socioeconomic levels, whereas a significantly higher percentage of the families of those in the second group come from lower educational and occupational strata.

Studies suggest that, in general, mentally retarded children are likely to show better emotional and mental development in a reasonably favorable home situation than in an institution (Golden & Davis, 1974). Thus, institutionalization is not recommended where the child makes a satisfactory adjustment at home and in school.

The effect of being institutionalized in adolescence depends heavily, of course, on the institution's facilities as well as on the individual. For the many retarded teenagers who do not have families in a position to take care of them, community-oriented residential care seems particularly promising (Landesman-Dwyer, 1981; Seidl, 1974; Thacher, 1978).

Fortunately, as we have seen, most retarded individuals do not need to be institutionalized. For those who do, however, state institutions for the mentally retarded are often desperately overcrowded and in many instances woefully inadequate in terms of the quality of treatment programs offered (Robinson & Robinson, 1976; Tarjan et al., 1973). In 1970, the President's Committee on Mental Retardation reported that in many instances such facilities were no better than prisoner-of-war camps. Since then, some facilities have been greatly improved; but most lack the necessary funds and personnel to provide high-quality rehabilitative programs. Moreover, most private facilities—which are often but not always superior to public ones—are beyond the means of the average family.

For the mentally retarded who do not require institutionalization, educational and training facilities have also been inadequate. In 1970 an estimated 2 million mentally retarded persons who could have used job training and become self-supporting members of their communities were not getting this training (President's Committee on Mental Retardation, 1970). Although conditions may have improved somewhat, it would still appear that the majority of mentally retarded persons in the United States are never reached by services appropriate to their specific needs.

This neglect is especially tragic in view of what we now know about helping these individuals. For example, classes for the mildly retarded, which usually emphasize reading and other basic school subjects, budgeting and money matters, and the development of occupational skills, have succeeded in helping many people become independent, productive members of the community.

Classes for the moderately and severely retarded usually have more limited objectives, but they emphasize development of self-care and other skills that will enable individuals to function adequately and to be of assistance in either a family or institutional setting. Just mastering toilet training and learning to feed and dress themselves may mean the difference between remaining at home and having to be placed elsewhere.

In many more cases than had formerly been thought possible, institutionalized individuals have been found able to get along in the community with adequate preparation and help. For example, Clark, Kivitz, and Rosen (1969) reported on a special project undertaken at the Elwyn Institute in Pennsylvania.

"The goal of this program was the successful discharge to independent living in the community of the institutionalized mentally retarded. The entire staff was oriented toward rehabilitation; emphasis was placed on the development of practical vocational skills; special programs provided remedial teaching and the learning of socialization skills; and counseling and assessment assured the individualization of training to meet each person's needs. As a result of this program, many mentally retarded persons who had been institutionalized for from 2 to 49 years were discharged and obtained skilled or semiskilled jobs in the community while coping successfully with everyday problems. Some married and had families; none had to be readmitted to the institutions." (p. 82)

Today about 70 percent of the approximately 150,000 individuals still in institutions for the retarded are severely or profoundly retarded, and even many individuals with this level of handicap are being helped to be partly self-supporting in community programs (Brown, 1977; Landesman-Dwyer, 1981; Robinson & Robinson, 1976; Rodman & Collins, 1974; Sullivan & Batareh,

HIGHLIGHT
Two innovative deinstitutionalization approaches

In the late 1960s, a University of Illinois psychologist, Marc Gold, reported that even a severely retarded person could, with patience, be taught to assemble a 15-part bicycle brake. Motivated in part by this discovery, professionals and parents of retarded youngsters in many communities began a serious reassessment of long-term biases about the supposed limits of rehabilitation for the retarded. The major result was a proliferation of programs intended to be alternatives to the typical, forbidding public institution. Two such programs were those developed by the Macomb-Oakland Regional Center (MORC) near Detroit and the Eastern Nebraska Community Office of Mental Retardation (ENCOR) in Omaha. These two programs have essentially the same goals—rehabilitation of the retarded toward the achievement of self-esteem, limited competencies, and economic independence—but they differ substantially in their mode of approach.

The MORC program emphasizes placement of children in "community training homes," of which there are over a hundred in operation. These are the private homes of foster parents who have been specially trained in techniques such as behavior modification, speech therapy, and so on. In addition to the foster homes, MORC runs 12 duplexes called "developmental training homes" for children and adults with special, restricting problems. The duplexes are patterned after standard suburban housing developments. Less disabled retarded adults live in groups of seven or eight in residences distributed throughout the community; they learn self-care and social skills in these residences, and, during the day, attend sheltered workshops and other vocational training programs.

One measure of the success of MORC's approach is that a group of seriously disabled adult charges was awarded a subcontract by a private manufacturing firm to cut and drill aluminum components for solar-heating panels, work that would have been completely beyond their capacity a short time before. In fact, individuals with their level of retardation usually would not even have been allowed to work with such tools.

The basic approach of ENCOR, on the other hand, is to rent houses or apartments in the community to be shared by two or three retarded persons; thereafter, the residents are closely supervised by professional staffers to ensure the maintenance of an adequate living arrangement and continued progress toward economic independence. Roommates are selected on the basis of possession of complementary skills, insofar as possible. For example, a nonreader who can cook might be placed with someone who can read but is helpless in the kitchen. Over time, it is hoped, the skills that each possesses separately will become shared ones. A number of living units sponsored by ENCOR have become almost entirely self-sufficient—again a development that could not possibly have occurred had these patients continued to live under the old institutional regimen (Thacher, 1978).

1973; Thacher, 1978; Zucker & Altman, 1973). These developments reflect both the new optimism that has come to prevail and also, in many instances, judicial decisions favorable to the rights of retarded individuals and their families.

During the 1970s, there was a rapid proliferation of alternate forms of care for the mentally retarded. These include, but are not limited to, the use of decentralized regional facilities for short-term evaluation and training, small private hospitals specializing in rehabilitative techniques, group homes or "halfway houses" integrated into the local community, nursing homes for the elderly retarded, placement of severely retarded children in more "enriched" foster-home environments, and varied forms of support to the family for own-home care (see **HIGHLIGHT** on this page).

These varied programs are still too new to permit comprehensive evaluation of their effectiveness in dealing with different groups of retardates and differing levels of retardation. At the least, however, it is clear that they provide a much expanded flexibility in considering the needs of any given retarded individual at any particular point in his or her development and rehabilitation (Robinson & Robinson, 1976).

Although much remains to be learned about the most effective educational and training procedures to use with the mentally retarded—particularly the moderate and severe types—new techniques, materials, and specially trained teachers have produced encouraging results. For example, computer-assisted instruction has been introduced in Canadian programs for the retarded and has been found to be more efficient as well as less expensive than traditional tutor-guided instruction (Brebner et al., 1977; Hallworth, 1977). Operant conditioning methods are being used increasingly to teach a wide variety of skills. Specifically targeted independence training in various essential everyday functions may have great promise (Matson, 1981).

Typically, educational and training procedures involve mapping out target areas of improvement, such as personal grooming, social behavior, basic academic skills, and simple occupational skills. Within each area, specific skills are divided into simple components that can be learned and reinforced before more complex behaviors are required. Target areas are not selected arbitrarily, of course, but realistically reflect the requirements of the individual's life situation. Training that builds on step-by-step progression and is guided by such realistic considerations can bring retarded individuals repeated experiences of success and lead to substantial progress even by those previously regarded as uneducable.

For more mildly retarded youngsters, the question of what schooling is best is likely to be a vexing one for both parents and school officials. For many years, organized parents' groups have fought an uphill battle to ensure the availability of special education classes for retarded children in the public schools, having learned that isolation from age-peers tends to compound the problems of these children. Too often, however, success in getting a retarded child into a public school has meant that the child is treated as very special indeed and—along with other retarded students—becomes isolated *within* the school.

We have begun to learn that this type of "special" education may have very serious limitations in terms of the social and educational development of the child and that many such children fare better by attending regular classes for at least much of the day. Of course, programs of this type—called *mainstreaming*—do require careful planning and a high level of teacher skill (Birns & Bridger, 1977; Borg & Ascione, 1982; Budoff, 1977).

Indeed, a great deal of research in recent years has led to the conclusion that mainstreaming is not the hoped-for panacea (Gottlieb, 1981). In terms of their administration, such programs are difficult to launch and to maintain (Lieberman, 1982); and their success (or lack of it) seems to a large extent to depend on such influences as teacher attitudes and overall classroom climate (Haywood, Meyers, & Switzky, 1982). Moreover, any educational gains realized may come at the expense of deficits in self-esteem suffered by handicapped children as they interact intensively with more advantaged peers (Haywood, Meyers, & Switzky, 1982). Gresham (1982) argues that such dangers may be decreased or eliminated if the retarded children are given social skills training prior to their entry into the mainstream classroom. A reasonable conclusion at this time appears to be that school systems should not attempt mainstreaming without a great deal of advance planning and preparation.

New frontiers in prevention. The problem of preventing mental retardation involves the question of genetic factors as well as the need to control a wide range of biochemical, neurophysiological, and sociocultural conditions. Inevitably, it is a problem concerned with human development in general.

Until rather recently the most hopeful approach to the prevention of mental retardation has been through routine health measures for pregnant women and the use of diagnostic measures to ensure the early detection and, if possible, correction of pathology. In recent years, however, two new frontiers have opened up in the field of prevention. The first involves work in genetics that has revealed the role of certain genetic defects in faulty development, as in Tay-Sachs disease. Tests have been devised to identify parents who have these faulty genes, thus making it possible to provide them with genetic counseling. There are now over 200 clinics in the United States where such counseling is available.

The second frontier in prevention involves the alleviation of sociocultural conditions that deprive children of the stimulation, motivation, and opportunity necessary for normal learning and development. In this connection, Keniston (1977) has said, "It is time to match the strong American tradition of healing individual parents and children with equal efforts to change the factors that make those parents and children need healing. To put it another way, it is time for Americans to start holding the social and economic institutions of our society just as accountable for their influence on family life as we traditionally have held parents" (p. 6). And Birns and Bridger (1977) have emphasized that social reforms will need to include a revamping of the educational system to serve better the varying needs of all children. This "new horizon" was well delineated by the late President John F. Kennedy:

"Studies have demonstrated that large numbers of children in urban and rural slums, including preschool children, lack the stimulus necessary for proper development in their intelligence. Even when there is no organic impairment, prolonged neglect and a lack of stimulus and opportunity for learning can result in the failure of young minds to develop. Other studies have shown that, if proper opportunities for learning are provided early enough, many of these deprived children can and will learn and achieve as much as children from more favored neighborhoods. The self-perpetuating intellectual blight should not be allowed to continue." (1963, p. 286)

President Kennedy's report directed the attention of the nation to the tragic and costly problem of mental retardation. It was not until 1970, however, when the President's Committee on Mental Retardation, the American Psychological Association, and other concerned organizations stressed the necessity for a "broad spectrum" approach, that real impetus was given to implementing essential measures for the prevention of mental retardation. This broad spectrum approach focused on three ways of providing a more supportive sociocultural setting or preventing children from being harmed by adverse environmental conditions:

1. *Application of existing knowledge.* The first phase of this approach involved the provision of more adequate medical and general health care for mother and baby prior to and during pregnancy and after birth of the baby—particularly for the socially disadvantaged and other high-risk groups.

2. *Community services.* Next, the approach focused on the provision of community-centered facilities that would provide a coordinated range of diagnostic, health, education, employment,

rehabilitation, and related services. This phase of the program included the training of needed personnel.

A particularly important development in this area has involved efforts to reach high-risk children early with the intensive cognitive stimulation believed to underlie sound development of mental ability. Project Head Start is a well-known example operating at the local community level. And at the national level, a similar intention is manifested in specialized television programming for children, such as *Sesame Street* and *The Electric Company.* Rigorous assessment of the effectiveness of such efforts is not yet complete, but they do appear to have positive effects on many children. Somewhat ironically, the children who seem to benefit most from these efforts are the children least in need of them—the children of relatively affluent families in which education is strongly valued and in which the parents are likely to encourage their children's exposure to such enriching experiences. Also somewhat sobering is the possibility that Head Start children's performance increases primarily because of enhanced motivation rather than higher rates of cognitive development (Zigler et al., 1982). Where the environment continues to be debilitative over time, much of the gain may be lost (Gray & Ramsey, 1982). Obviously, much remains to be learned and done in the area of early intervention.

3. *Research.* Finally, emphasis was placed on the facilitation and acceleration of research on all phases of the problem: causality, educational procedures, social effects on the family, psychological effects on the individual, and the changing role and functions of state and community agencies.

It is unfortunate that the initiatives begun by the Kennedy administration have eroded in recent years as demands on the federal budget for programs seen as having greater national importance have increased and as the funds committed for helping the retarded have suffered devaluation through inflation. Beginning with the Nixon administration, there were serious cutbacks in training and research in all of the mental health disciplines, and the trend has since become worse. As a result, we have not been able to capitalize fully on our increased understanding of how to reverse or prevent the deficits experienced by mentally retarded youngsters.

Summary

The organic mental disorders are those in which psychiatric symptoms (such as delusions and hallucinations) appear as a result of interference with the functioning of the normal brain, typically involving the destruction of brain tissue. Many of the organic disorders are in some primary sense physical diseases and are accordingly coded on Axis III of DSM-III. Exceptions are the senile and presenile dementias (such as Alzheimer's disease); these disorders are accorded Axis I status, as are the "substance-induced" organic mental disorders (such as dementia associated with alcoholism). The DSM-III recognizes certain "organic brain syndromes" that form a basis for an Axis I psychiatric diagnosis; they are delirium, dementia, amnestic syndrome, hallucinosis, delusional syndrome, affective syndrome, and personality syndrome. These syndromes are in fact the primary behavioral indicators for organic brain disease. Some of them mimic disorders in which no gross brain pathology can be demonstrated.

Organic mental disorders may be acute and transitory; in this case, brain functioning is only temporarily compromised. Chronic organic mental disorders, on which we have focused, involve the permanent loss of neural cells. Psychosocial interventions are often helpful in minimizing psychotic reactions in the chronically disordered, although these people will remain neurologically disabled.

The primary causes of the destruction of brain tissue are many and varied: common ones include certain infectious diseases (such as syphilis), brain tumors, physical trauma, degenerative processes (as in Alzheimer's disease), and cerebrovascular arteriosclerosis. However, the correlation between neurologic brain impairment and psychiatric disorder is not a strong one: some persons having severe damage develop no psychotic symptoms, while others with slight damage have extreme psychotic reactions. While such inconsistencies are not completely understood, it appears that the individual's premorbid personality and life situation are very important in determining his or her reactions to brain damage.

Elderly persons are at particular risk for the development of chronic organic mental disorders, especially those related to brain degeneration caused by Alzheimer's disease. As at younger ages, the reaction to brain damage is determined by many nonbiological factors.

Certain cases of mental retardation, approximately 25 percent of the total incidence, are also related to gross structural defects in the brain. They are distinguished from organic brain syndromes by age-related criteria; that is, the structural defects are either congenital or are acquired before the brain has completed its development. The affected individual is prevented from acquiring certain forms of knowledge and cognitive skills and hence is considered *amented* as opposed to *demented*, the latter term denoting the *loss* of previously acquired abilities. In these cases, retardation is likely to be severe or profound and to be accompanied by obvious physical anomalies of one sort or another. Down's syndrome and phenylketonuria are examples of this type of disorder.

The large majority—some 75 percent—of cases of mental retardation are unrelated to obvious physical defects and are considered cultural-familial in origin, a term that acknowledges our inability to disentangle genetic and environmental influences in the disorder. Caution is warranted in applying the label "mentally retarded" in these cases, because of our heavy reliance on IQ test scores in its definition. The IQ is—and has always been—a measure of *academic* skill, not of ability to survive and perhaps even prosper in other areas of life.

A variety of evidence points to the conclusion that cultural-familial retardation may be treatable and even preventable. While some effects of institutionalization have been undesirable, community-based interventions have compiled an impressive record of accomplishment. We have as yet not found, as a society, completely reliable means of *preventing* cultural-familial retardation, but the future would look considerably brighter if we merely applied more effectively and comprehensively what we already know in this area.

14

Behavior disorders of childhood and adolescence

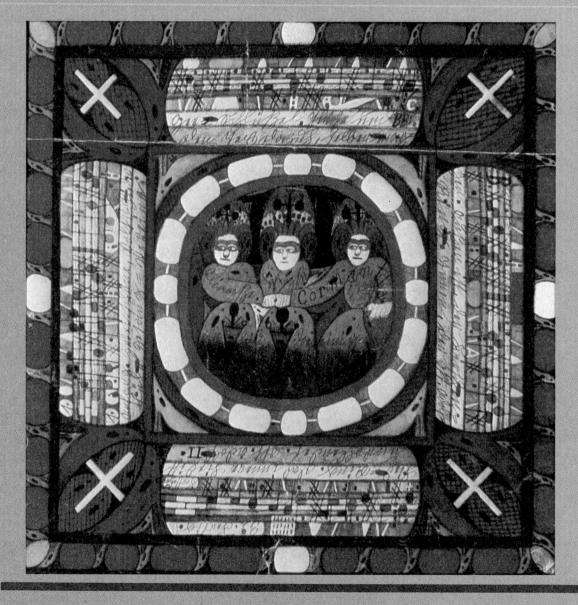

Adolf Wölfli, La Sainte Trinité dans la Ville Géant de Chant-Saint-Adolf. *Wölfli (1864–1930), born in Berne, Switzerland, was abandoned by his father in early childhood and at the age of eight was removed from the care of his mother— occurrences marking the beginning of violent, erratic behaviors that finally culminated in schizophrenic breakdown. In his paintings and drawings, Wölfli typically returns to an idealized childhood, in which as "Saint Adolf," a child divinity, he journeys through the universe, often accompanied by assorted gods and goddesses.*

"We love our own children and take as good care of them as we can, but as a society we tolerate a great deal of unnecessary damage and pain among children. Do Americans love children? Yes, when the children are their own; not nearly as well, when the children are other people's.

"People who think about children's policy know the results of that split view all too well. Of all age groups in America, children are the most likely to be poor. Overall, the [Carnegie] Council estimates that fully a quarter to a third of all American children are born into families with financial strains so great that their children will suffer basic deprivations. In this rich, powerful, and productive land, we prefer not to notice the children who risk freezing to death for lack of heat in tarpaper shacks without plumbing in rural Maine. We discount the slum children who have never slept in a bed of their own or seen a doctor" (Keniston, 1977, p. 274).

Only in this century have childhood behavior disorders become the focus of significant special study. During the nineteenth century, little account was taken of the special characteristics of psychopathology in children; and maladaptive patterns that are considered relatively specific to childhood, such as autism and hyperactivity, received virtually no attention at all.

Since the turn of the twentieth century, with the advent of the mental health movement and the availability of child guidance facilities, marked strides have been made in understanding, assessing, and treating the maladaptive behavior patterns of children and youth. This progress has, however, lagged behind efforts to deal with adult psychopathology. In fact, as we shall see, early efforts at classifying problems of childhood were simply extensions of adult-oriented diagnostic systems. These early conceptualizations seemed to reflect a prevailing view of children as "miniature adults" and failed to take into account special problems, such as those associated with the developmental changes that normally take place in the child or adolescent. Only recently have we come to realize that we cannot fully understand the disorders of childhood without taking into account these developmental processes. Today, even though great progress has been made in providing treatment for disturbed children, our facilities are woefully inadequate in relation to the magnitude of the task, and the majority of problem children do not receive psychological atten-

535

tion. (For a sense of how formidable the task is, see the **HIGHLIGHT** on this page.)

In the first section of this chapter we shall note some general characteristics of maladaptive behavior in children as compared with disorders in adults. Next, we shall examine, in some detail, the issues surrounding the diagnostic classification of children's disorders. Then we shall look at some of the disorders that are relatively specific to the period of childhood and adolescence, giving special attention to the problem of juvenile delinquency. In the final section, we shall give detailed consideration to some of the special factors involved in both treatment and prevention of children's problems.

Maladaptive behavior in different life periods

Since personality differentiation, developmental tasks, and typical stressors differ for childhood, adolescence, and adulthood, we would expect to find some differences in maladaptive behavior patterns in these different life periods. Two special characteristics of childhood disorders have been noted:[1]

1. *Differences in clinical picture.* The clinical picture in childhood disorders is somewhat different from that at other ages, both because some disorders, such as autism, are primarily problems of childhood and because even the disorders that occur at all life periods reflect the developmental level of the individual experiencing them. For example, the suicidal impulses commonly found in adolescent and adult depression are fairly rare in childhood depression (Kovacs & Beck, 1977). And in childhood schizophrenia, although there is the characteristic schizophrenic withdrawal and inability to relate to others, delusions and hallucinations are less common; when they do occur, they are more transient and less well systematized (Elkind & Weiner, 1978). In fact, most of the emotional disturbances of childhood tend to be

HIGHLIGHT

How prevalent are psychological disorders among children?

Estimates of the extent of psychological disorders in children vary depending on populations sampled and methods employed—for example, whether the investigators used teacher reports or parent reports. In a methodologically sophisticated evaluation of data on the prevalence of childhood disorders, Wunsch-Hitzig, Gould, and Dohrenwend (1980) corrected for method variance and obtained more realistic estimates. They found estimates of maladjustment among children to be quite similar for the United States (11.8 percent) and Great Britain (13.2 percent). In both countries, maladjustment among boys significantly exceeded that among girls. There is some tendency for studies to report an increase in maladjustment for adolescent populations.

relatively short-lived, undifferentiated, and changeable, compared with those of later life periods.

2. *Special vulnerability resulting from limited perspective and dependency on adults.* Since personality differentiation in childhood is not as advanced as in adolescence or adulthood, children do not have as clear-cut a view of themselves and their world as they will have at a later age. They have less self-understanding and have not yet developed a stable sense of identity and an adequate frame of reference regarding reality, possibility, and value. The threats of the immediate moment are less tempered by considerations of the past or future and thus tend to be seen as disproportionately important. As a result, children often have more difficulty in coping with stressful events than they will have when they are older.

Children's limited perspective, as might be expected, leads them to use childlike concepts to explain what is happening. For example, in the comparatively rare case of child suicide, the child may be trying to rejoin a dead parent or sibling or pet. For the very young, suicide—or violence against another person—may be undertaken without any real understanding that death is final.

---

[1]At times in this chapter the term childhood disorder is used to refer to both child and adolescent problems.

Children also are more dependent on other people than are adults. Though in some ways this dependency serves as a buffer against outer dangers, it also makes them highly vulnerable to experiences of rejection, disappointment, and failure.

On the other hand, although their inexperience and lack of self-sufficiency make them easily upset by problems that seem minor to the average adult, children typically recover more quickly from their hurts.

Despite these somewhat distinctive characteristics of disturbances in childhood, there is no sharp line of demarcation between the maladaptive behavior patterns of childhood and those of adolescence, nor between those of adolescence and those of adulthood. Thus, although our focus in this chapter will be on the behavior disorders of children and adolescents, we will find some inevitable overlapping with those of later life periods. In this context, it is useful to emphasize the basic continuity of an individual's behavior over the years as he or she attempts to cope with the problems of living.

Classification of childhood and adolescent disorders

Diagnosis of the psychological disorders of childhood has traditionally been a rather confused practice, and until recent times no formal, specific system has been available for classifying the emotional problems of children and adolescents. Kraepelin's (1883) classic textbook on classification of mental disorders did not include childhood disorders. Not until 1952, when the first formal psychiatric nomenclature (DSM-I) was published, was a classification system for childhood disorders made available. The DSM-I system, however, was quite limited and included only two childhood emotional disorders: *childhood schizophrenia* and *adjustment reaction of childhood.* Although several additional categories were added to the 1968 revision (DSM-II), there remained a growing concern, both among clinicians attempting to diagnose and treat problems

of childhood and among researchers attempting to broaden our understanding of childhood psychopathology, that the ways of viewing psychological disorders in children and adolescents were inappropriate and inaccurate.

Several reasons can be found for the early inadequacies of childhood diagnostic systems: First, the greatest problem came from the fact that the same classification system that had been developed for adults' problems was used for children's. No allowance was made for special considerations that enter into childhood conditions, such as the often mixed symptom pattern. Second, in childhood disorders, environmental factors play an important part in the expression of symptoms; that is, symptom manifestations are highly influenced by the family's acceptance or rejection of the behavior (for example, either extreme tolerance of deviant behavior or total rejection and neglect of the child could lead the child to accept his or her extreme behavior as "normal"). Third, normal developmental changes or lags in development might make a given child's behavior stand out as extreme or "abnormal," when the behavior is actually appropriate to the child's age and transitory. In other words, the behaviors of concern might simply be behaviors the child will grow out of in time.

Discontent with the classification system for childhood behavior problems has led in recent years to considerable rethinking, discussion, and empirical investigation of the issues of diagnosis of children and adolescents. Two general solutions to the problem of classification of childhood behavior disorders have become clearly demarcated. The first approach, the *clinical-nosological strategy,* has evolved from previous diagnostic classification systems and is represented in the most recent diagnostic and statistical manual of the American Psychiatric Association, DSM-III. In the clinical-nosological strategy, the clinician—or, in the case of DSM-III, a group of clinicians—arrives at a descriptive class or category by examining, through clinical study, the behaviors that appear to define that class. For example, the similar behaviors that appear in children who are judged to fit the diagnostic class "attention deficit disorder" are employed as the defining criteria of that class.

The second approach, which is favored by many empirical researchers in childhood psychopathology, is the ***multivariate strategy.*** This approach involves the application of sophisticated statistical methods to provide clear behavior clusters or "dimensions" for the widely observed symptoms manifested by children. The researcher gathers his or her observations through teachers', parents', or clinicians' ratings or through presenting symptoms[2] and allows the statistical method—for example, factor analysis—to determine the classification.

Both systems are based upon observation of the individual's behavior, and both result in classifying the person according to the presence or absence of symptoms. Yet there are marked differences between the systems. The clinical-nosological approach, since it derives from the clinical description of cases, generally requires the presence of relatively few symptoms. The multivariate approach, on the other hand, usually requires the presence of a number of related symptoms in order for the case to be included on a dimension. As a result, a clinical-nosological system will tend to have many categories defined by few, possibly quite rare, behaviors, while multivariate approaches typically involve a small number of general classes covering numerous related behaviors.

We shall now turn to a brief description of these two major approaches to the classification of childhood behavior problems.

Clinical-nosological strategy: DSM-III

The revision of diagnostic nomenclature for the childhood disorders was undertaken with several goals in mind. First, there was a great deal of interest in making the DSM-III classification system more comprehensive than previous classification systems. Thus, the range of categories was considerably broadened. A second goal involved the desire to clear up the ambiguity that had existed in previous diagnostic systems, to make diagnosis more reliable. Toward this end, more explicit operational criteria were used to define each category. A third goal was to allow for the consideration of special developmental problems separate from the symptomatic classi-

fication on Axis I. To achieve this goal, Axis II allows for the subclassification of developmental problems such as language or reading deficits. Elements of the DSM-III system are as follows:

1. *Axis I.* Axis I of DSM-III includes a broad range of symptomatic disorders covered under seven general categories: mental retardation; attention deficit disorder; conduct disorder; anxious disorder of childhood and adolescence; eating disorders; stereotyped movement disorders; and pervasive developmental disorders. Disorders similar in form in adults and children, such as schizophrenia and affective disorders, have no specific category in the childhood disorders section of DSM-III. The conditions are diagnosed according to adult diagnostic criteria.

2. *Axis II.* As mentioned earlier, developmental lags can be specified on Axis II. These disorders refer to specific problems with maturation, whether biological or psychological in origin. The inclusion of developmental problems in DSM-III is somewhat controversial, since these conditions are normally dealt with in educational settings rather than mental health facilities. Some criticism has charged that DSM-III has broadened its coverage to include problems that are not psychiatric (Garmezy, 1978b). However, the DSM-III development committee considered these developmental difficulties to be within its broadened concept of mental disorder and to be important to the diagnostic understanding of the emotional problems of childhood and adolescence.

The specific developmental disorders included on Axis II include two disorders that may initially be recognized within the first three years of life, when speech normally develops. These are developmental language disorder and developmental articulation disorder. Two other developmental disorders—developmental reading disorder and developmental arithmetic disorder—are first recognized during the early school years.

How has DSM-III fared thus far in the realms of clinical practice and psychopathology research? Early studies of the appropriateness of DSM-III for children have been reported. It is still too early to determine if the rather extensive changes in diagnostic classification for children and adolescents have substantially eliminated classification problems, and it will take an extended period of trial to determine if DSM-III is

---

[2]*Presenting symptoms* refer to the clinical picture at the time the client is first seen by professional personnel. *Presenting complaint* and *referral problem* are synonymous terms.

acceptable or whether an additional revision is required. It is clear that the DSM-III still contains some rough spots in the categorization of childhood disorders; for example, some concern has been expressed over mental retardation's being classified on Axis I along with emotional disorders. (In this text we have veered slightly from DSM-III's course and considered problems of mental retardation in the chapter on organic disorders.) There is some early indication, however, that use of DSM-III has resulted in both a more reliable classification and more general acceptance among clinicians than DSM-II (Cantwell et al., 1979).

Multivariate strategy

Researchers in childhood psychopathology have long been dissatisfied with existing typological classes for grouping childhood behavior problems. Efforts to develop more empirical classification systems date back to the 1940s, when Hewitt and Jenkins (1946) analyzed case histories of problem children and developed one of the first rating systems for behavior disorders. Examining case records of 500 problem children for the presence or absence of problem behaviors, they organized symptoms into clusters of similar problems. The cluster types were: *unsocialized-aggressive, socialized aggressive,* and *overinhibited.* These three types, as we shall see, show a great deal of consistency and have appeared in subsequent studies, although the rating methods and data analysis procedures used have varied.

Using a somewhat different approach, Peterson (1961) derived a checklist from clinical case material and had teachers evaluate children in their classes by filling it out. This process resulted in two clearly defined clusters—conduct problems and personality problems. Other investigators have created clusters using somewhat different data bases, such as parents' reports (Dreger et al., 1964) and children's psychiatric symptoms (Achenbach, 1966, 1978). Quay (1979), reviewing the multivariate classification studies, concluded that their findings could be categorized under four major headings: *conduct disorder, anxiety-withdrawal, immaturity,* and *socialized-aggressive disorder.* These four problem clusters are believed to account for

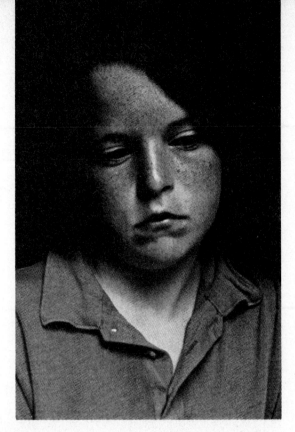

The classification of childhood disorders has always proven to be a difficult enterprise. Nonetheless, researchers have been able to identify clusters of behavior that seem to represent adequately the most common forms of problem behavior in children.

most problem behavior of children, excluding psychosis.

1. *Conduct disorder.* Conduct disorder, a class that emerged from most studies, involves aggressive behavior such as fighting, temper tantrums, defiance, disobedience, destruction of property, uncooperative and resistive behavior, irritability, attention-seeking, inattentiveness, distractibility, and others.

2. *Anxiety-withdrawal.* The second major pattern of problem behavior emerging from the multivariate studies involves anxiety and withdrawal. The symptoms, besides anxiety and withdrawal, include such behaviors as tenseness, shyness, seclusiveness, lack of friends, depression, feelings of inferiority, low self-confidence, and hypersensitivity.

3. *Immaturity.* The third pattern of problem behavior—immaturity—has not been as consistently or frequently obtained as the others. Immaturity suggests a general lack of adaptive skills and is reflected in such behavior as attention deficits, daydreaming, clumsy and uncoordinated behavior, absentmindedness, passivity, low initiative, lack of interest, inability to complete tasks, and so on.

4. *Socialized-aggressive disorder.* The behavior underlying the socialized-aggressive pattern, first identified by Hewitt and Jenkins (1946), involves social maladaptation: having "bad" companions, stealing in the company of others, belonging to a gang, showing loyalty to delinquent friends, keeping late hours, and being truant from home or school.

Comparison of clinical-nosological and multivariate approaches

How does the multivariate approach compare with the present clinical diagnostic classification system of DSM-III? It is not possible, in this text, to give a full, detailed comparative evaluation of the two approaches. Moreover, it would perhaps be premature to do so, since *both* approaches are in their infancy and will, no doubt, enjoy "developmental spurts" over the coming years. However, there are clearly distinct elements in each that will affect, if not determine, its future developments. The divergent goals of the two approaches and the very different methods they employ to reach them make it quite unlikely that they ever will totally agree in their classification of children, although there will, no doubt, be overlap. Which one is the correct view? Neither. They are like photographs of the same scenery taken from different vantage points. While it is possible to recognize that the same terrain is covered by both, each offers a different perspective.

It is possible to see both benefits and problems in both approaches to classification of childhood disorders. Several points of comparison are worth considering:

a) The clinical-nosological approach uses somewhat arbitrary classes or types as the basis for symptom classification. The groupings of actual symptoms used in the multivariate-statistical approach are, perhaps, more true to life. Because of these general strategic differences, the approaches are committed to different classification criteria. For example, the clinical-nosological approach looks for the presence or absence

of certain behavioral clues to determine whether a person fits in a particular class. The multivariate-statistical approach, on the other hand, uses numerical scores based on symptoms to place the individual somewhere on a continuum or dimension. (In this approach, everyone is placed somewhere on the dimension.)

b) The two approaches differ in terms of the coverage of disorders. The clinical-nosological system focuses on *breadth* of coverage. In order to provide a broad, comprehensive classification of disorders, the DSM-III has included conditions—some of them found quite infrequently—for which very little descriptive information is available. In fact, Quay (1979) pointed out that multivariate studies do not support the "multitude of subdivisions" presented in the DSM-III system. The multivariate approach, on the other hand, focuses on *common* elements of symptom groups. Rare behaviors or symptoms, such as one would find with infrequent "syndromes," would not carry much statistical weight in a multivariate study and would be deemphasized in the classification structure. Thus, the multivariate approach emphasizes *depth*, rather than breadth, of coverage.

c) In order to obtain broad coverage, the DSM-III sacrifices some of the diagnostic clarity possible with the multivariate strategy. Because this textbook focuses on the clinical manifestation of disorders, we shall, for practical purposes, follow the DSM-III classification system of childhood and adolescent disorders. Keep in mind, however, that the approach taken here is only one possible way of viewing disorders.

Disorders of childhood and adolescence

In this section, we shall discuss several disorders of childhood and adolescence with a focus on describing the clinical picture of the syndrome, surveying the possible causal factors, and outlining treatment approaches that have been shown to be effective. A broader discussion of treatment methods can be found in Chapters 16 and 17. The disorders that will be covered are: (a) attention deficit disorder; (b) conduct disorder (including an extended discussion of juvenile delinquency); (c) anxiety disorders of childhood and adolescence; (d) pervasive developmental disorder, also known as infantile autism; and (e) several other special symptom disorders. With the exception of autism, these disorders are less stable than most of the abnormal behavior patterns discussed in earlier chapters, and also more amenable to treatment. If treatment is not received, however, the developmental problems of childhood sometimes merge almost imperceptibly into more serious and chronic disorders as the child passes into adulthood.

Attention deficit disorder

Attention deficit disorder is defined by maladaptive behavior that interferes with effective task-oriented behavior in children—particularly impulsivity, excessive motor activity, and an inability to attend. In the past, this disorder has been referred to as *hyperactive syndrome* or the *hyperkinetic reaction of childhood*. The presenting symptoms in attention deficit disorder are relatively common among children seen at child guidance centers. In fact, hyperactivity is the most frequent psychological referral to mental health and pediatric facilities, and it is estimated that between 3 and 5 percent of elementary-school-aged children manifest the symptoms (Ross & Pelham, 1981). The disorder occurs with the greatest frequency before age eight and tends to become less frequent and of shorter duration thereafter. Some residual effects, such as difficulties in attention, may persist into adolescence or adult years. Two major subgroups of attention deficit disorder have been identified: *attention deficit disorder with hyperactivity* and *attention deficit disorder without hyperactivity*. Since most of the research and theoretical discussion has centered around hyperactive behavior, our discussion will focus more upon this subtype.

Clinical picture of attention deficit disorder with hyperactivity.
As the term implies, hyperactive children show excessive or exaggerated muscular activity—for example, aimless or haphazard running or fidgeting. Difficulty in sustaining attention is another central feature of the disorder. Such children are highly

Hyperactive children typically engage in excessive physical activity such as aimless running or fidgeting. They often behave impulsively and do not respond to instructions or demands placed upon them. Such behaviors may be especially problematic in the school setting.

distractible and do not follow instructions or respond to demands placed on them. Impulsive behavior and a low frustration tolerance are also characteristic.

Hyperactive children do not typically show deficits in intelligence, but they tend to talk incessantly and to be socially uninhibited and immature. Barkley and Cunningham (1979) report that hyperactive children usually have great difficulties in getting along with their parents, usually because they do not obey rules. King and Young (1981) found that hyperactive children were viewed more negatively by their peers. In general, however, hyperactive children do not appear to be anxious, although their overactivity, restlessness, and distractibility are often interpreted as indications of anxiety. Usually they do poorly in school, commonly showing specific learning disabilities, such as difficulty in learning to read or in learning other basic school subjects. Hyperactive children also pose behavior problems in the elementary grades.

The following case, involving an eight-year-old girl, reveals a somewhat typical clinical picture:

The subject was referred to a community clinic because of overactive, inattentive, and disruptive behavior. She was a problem to her teacher and to other students because of her hyperactivity and uninhibited behavior. She would impulsively hit other children, knock things off their desks, erase material on the blackboard, and damage books and other school property. She seemed to be in perpetual motion—talking, moving about, and darting from one area of the classroom to another. She demanded an inordinate amount of attention from her parents and her teacher, and she was intensely jealous of other children, including her own brother and sister. Despite her hyperactive behavior, inferior school performance, and other problems, she was considerably above average in intelligence. Nevertheless, she felt "stupid" and had a seriously devaluated self-image. Neurological tests revealed nothing significant.

In spite of the frequency with which the diagnosis is made, there is some disagreement about whether a "hyperactive syndrome" really exists. Quay (1979) argued that the research data on objective symptom classification did not support the existence of the hyperactive disorder separate from conduct disorder. This view has received some recent support from the research literature. In one study, Prinz, Connor, and Wilson (1981) found that hyperactive and aggressive behaviors were often confused with one another, and were in fact highly related rather than being distinct disorders. In another study, Sanson (1980) found that there was virtually no difference between hyperactivity and conduct disorders and concluded that hyperactivity, as a diagnostic category, appeared to have little meaning with respect to etiology or treatment.

Ross and Pelham (1981) concluded that before substantial progress could be made in the understanding of hyperactivity as a diagnostic category, the criteria for defining the disorder would need to be refined. This process would need to include the development of clear normative data on children's behavior, which would make it possible to determine where the hyperactive child actually deviates from normal development. Meanwhile, the symptoms described earlier remain the usual basis for a diagnosis of hyperactivity.

Causal factors in attention deficit disorder with hyperactivity. The lack of clarity in diagnosing hyperactivity and the rather mixed group of individuals classified as having attention deficit disorder with hyperactivity make it difficult for researchers to evaluate the possibility that underlying biological conditions might cause the disorder. Rapoport and Ferguson (1981) recently reviewed the biological evidence for the hyperactivity syndrome and found that the correlations between biological data and hyperactivity were weak and that there was no compelling evidence for a biological basis of the syndrome.

One viewpoint (Feingold, 1977) that has received a great deal of public attention in recent years is that hyperactivity in children may be produced by dietary factors—particularly food coloring. Feingold has proposed a dietary treatment for hyperactive children; however, research to date has not supported the food-additive theory of hyperactivity (Mattes & Gittelman, 1981; Stare, Whelan, & Sheridan, 1980).

The search for a psychological cause of hyperactivity has had similarly inconclusive results; there are no clearly established psychological causes for the disorder. Some evidence suggests that the home environment is quite influential in the development of the disorder (Paternite & Loney, 1980). One recent study suggested that family pathology, particularly parental personality problems, leads to hyperactivity in children. Morrison (1980) found that many parents of hyperactive children had clinical diagnoses of personality disorder or hysteria.

As mentioned, hyperactivity typically is manifested very early in life. Where it develops in later childhood, special stressors leading to anxiety and emotional upset are likely to be key factors. Actually, hyperactivity is a relatively nonspecific pattern in children, and it may occur in anxious, depressed, schizophrenic, or autistic children, as well as in those who clearly evidence brain damage or some kind of brain dysfunction. (The controversy surrounding the concept of minimal brain damage as an explanation for hyperactivity is discussed in the **HIGHLIGHT** on page 543.)

Currently, the hyperactive syndrome is considered to have multiple causes and multiple effects. Thus, labeling a child as "hyperactive" may not indicate much in the way of etiology or appropriate treatment procedures; in addition, such a label may devalue the child in the eyes of the parents and play havoc with the child's self-image if he or she is told about it (Arnold, 1973).

In general, then, it would appear that a thor-

HIGHLIGHT
Minimal brain dysfunction (MBD)

In a three-part study sponsored by the U.S. Department of Health, Education, and Welfare (Chalfant & Scheffelin, 1969; Clements, 1966; Paine, 1969), children with *minimal brain dysfunction* (MBD) have been described as

"... of near average, average, or above average general intelligence with certain learning and/or behavioral disabilities ranging from mild to severe, which are associated with deviations of function of the central nervous system. These deviations may manifest themselves by various combinations of impairment in perception, conceptualization, language, memory, and control of attention, impulse, or motor function. These aberrations may arise from genetic variations, biochemical irregularities, perinatal brain insults or other illnesses or injuries sustained during the years which are critical for the development and maturation of the central nervous system, or from other unknown organic causes" (Paine, 1969, p. 53).

The ten outstanding characteristics of children with MBD are considered, in order of frequency, to be: (1) hyperactivity, (2) perceptual-motor impairments, (3) emotional lability, (4) general coordination deficits, (5) disorders of attention (short attention span, distractibility, perseveration), (6) impulsivity, (7) disorders of memory and thinking, (8) disorders of speech and hearing, (9) specific learning disabilities (reading, writing, spelling, and arithmetic), and (10) neurological signs, including EEG irregularities.

Although the concept of MBD is widely used, it remains controversial. Criticism has been directed especially at the practice of inferring that children have MBD simply because they display "typical symptoms" (such as poor perceptual-motor coordination, difficulty in learning to read, attention problems, and hyperactivity) without conducting tests to determine if they ac-

tually have a neurological defect. It has also been pointed out that the intellectual, emotional, and behavioral manifestations of minimal brain dysfunction may vary greatly from child to child. For example, children with MBD do not necessarily have reading difficulties, nor are they necessarily hyperactive; in fact, they sometimes evidence a low level of motor activity. In their study on the relationship between MBD and school performance, Edwards, Alley, and Snider (1971) found "no evidence that a diagnosis of MBD, based on a pediatric neurological evaluation . . . is a useful predictor of academic achievement" (p. 134).

On the other hand, the specific "symptoms" of young children with serious learning problems are often so remarkably similar that the concept of a neurological learning disability syndrome can hardly be ruled out. In effect, the "computers" of some children seem to function atypically in the processing of auditory and visual information; and it seems likely in such cases that neurological evaluation would reveal brain dysfunction—or even actual brain damage.

Even a clear diagnosis of brain dysfunction or damage may not be particularly useful, of course, unless the precise nature of the disorder can be determined, as well as its significance for behavior, treatment, and outcome. Thus, while the concept of minimal brain dysfunction may be a useful one, there is a strong trend away from using such a vague label (Mayer & Scheffelin, 1975; McGlannan, 1975; Trotter, 1975). Labeling a child as suffering from "minimal brain dysfunction" often provides little specific information, is devaluating to the child, and, in general, "hurts more than it helps."

Based on Bryan (1974), Chalfant and Scheffelin (1969), Clements (1966), Edwards, Alley, and Snider (1971), Lievens (1974), Mayer and Scheffelin (1975), McGlannan (1975), Paine (1969), Trotter (1975), and Tymchuk, Knights, and Hinton (1970).

ough and a more refined assessment of hyperactivity is essential for understanding the causes in any particular case (Loney, Langhorne, & Paternite, 1978; O'Leary & Steen, 1981).

Treatment and outcomes. Although the hyperactive syndrome was first described more than a hundred years ago, there is some dis-

agreement over the most effective methods of treatment, especially regarding the use of drugs to calm the hyperactive child. Here, as with other problem behaviors, variations in treatment procedures may be required to meet the needs of individual children.

Interestingly, cerebral stimulants such as the amphetamines often have a quieting effect on hyperactive children—just the opposite of what we would expect from their effect on adults (Green & Warshauer, 1981). Recent research has shown that amphetamines have similar calming effects on normal children (Zahn, Rapoport, & Thompson, 1980). Such medication decreases the children's overactivity and distractibility and at the same time increases their attention and ability to concentrate. As a result, they are often able to function much better at school (Whalen, Henker, & Dotemoto, 1981). In fact, many hyperactive children who have not been acceptable in regular classes can function and progress in a relatively normal manner when they use such drugs. The medication does not appear to affect their intelligence, but rather seems to help them use their basic capacities more effectively (NIMH, 1971). Although the drugs do not "cure" hyperactivity, they have been found beneficial in about half to two thirds of the cases in which medication appears warranted.

While the short-term pharmacologic effect of stimulants on the symptoms of hyperactive children is apparently well established, their long-term effects are not well known (Weiss, 1981). Some concern has been expressed about the effects of the drugs, particularly when used in heavy dosage over time. Safer and Allen (1973) concluded from a longitudinal study of 63 hyperactive children—49 of whom were on medication and 14 of whom were used as controls—that Dexedrine and Ritalin, two of the most commonly used drugs, can suppress normal growth in height and weight. However, in a carefully controlled study, Beck and colleagues (1975) failed to find such effects. Nevertheless, the use of the drugs should be carefully monitored in order that harmful side effects and addiction can be avoided. Some questions that have been raised concerning the use of these drugs are discussed in the **HIGHLIGHT** on page 545. The use of drug therapy with children will be taken up again in Chapter 16.

Another effective approach to treating hyperactive children involves behavior therapy techniques featuring positive reinforcement and the programming of learning materials and tasks in a way that minimizes error and maximizes immediate feedback and success. The use of behavioral treatment methods (see Chapter 17) for hyperactivity has reportedly been quite successful, at least for short-term gains. Robinson, Newby, and Ganzell (1981), using a token econ-

omy system, were able to increase the number of completed school tasks for hyperactive children up to the average number of tasks completed by other children in the school. (Token reinforcement programs are described in the **HIGHLIGHT** on page 547.) In another approach, Dunn and Howell (1982) successfully used relaxation training to reduce hyperactivity in a group of boys.

Several investigators have reported that impulsive behavior in children can be successfully modified by the use of cognitive-behavioral techniques in which rewards for desired behavior are combined with training in the use of verbal self-instructions (Kendall, 1981; Kendall & Finch, 1978; Meichenbaum, 1977; Meichenbaum & Goodman, 1971). The focus of cognitive-behavioral treatment is to help hyperactive children learn to shift attention less frequently and to behave reflectively rather than impulsively.

In a case reported by Kendall and Finch (1976), a nine-year-old boy was referred to a psychiatric facility for children because of problems at school. The teacher had described him as hyperactive, impulsive, and oversensitive to criticism. After only a month in fourth grade, he had been demoted to third grade because of his inability to adjust.

During the initial interview, the child was constantly moving about. He climbed into and out of chairs, talked rapidly about many topics, and changed the direction and purpose of his behavior without apparent reason. Test data also suggested overactivity and impulsivity to be the central problems.

Therapy sessions started with the therapist's working on a maze and talking aloud as he thought through each step he was performing—defining the problem, indicating the focus of his attention and the approach he was using, and including coping statements such as (after an error made intentionally), "I should have gone slower and thought and been more careful." After the therapist finished the maze, the boy worked it, instructing himself aloud in the same way.

Several other mazes were solved in this way, except that the self-instructions were whispered. Then, the use of self-instructions for target behaviors was rehearsed. For example, to learn not to switch topics during a conversation, the boy practiced the following self-instructions: "What should I remember? I'm to finish talking about what I start to talk about. O.K. I should think before I talk and remember not to switch. If I complete what I'm talking about before I start another topic, I get to keep my dimes. I can look at this card [cue] to remind me" (p. 854).

The boy was given several coins, one of which was

HIGHLIGHT
Drug therapy with children

A number of important questions have been raised concerning the increasing use of drugs in the treatment of certain behavior disorders of children. The principal questions include:

1. Who is being selected for treatment? Few investigators would question the usefulness of amphetamines or related drugs for treating many cases of hyperactivity, but many question the adequacy of assessment procedures used in identifying children who actually need medication. For example, a clear-cut distinction is not always made between the child who appears to need chemotherapy because of minimal brain dysfunction (MBD) and the child whose inattention and restlessness may be the result of hunger, crowded classrooms, irrelevant curriculum content, or anxiety and depression stemming from a pathogenic home situation.

2. Are drugs sometimes being used simply to "keep peace in the classroom"? Those who raise this question point to the possibility that children who manifest bewilderment, anger, restlessness, or lethargy at school may only be showing a normal reaction to educational procedures that fail to spark their interest or meet their needs. To label such children as "sick"—as evidencing hyperactivity or some other behavior disorder—and to treat them through medication, these investigators maintain, is to sidestep the difficult and expensive alternative of providing better educational programs. Possibly such an approach also reinforces the notion—all too prevalent in our culture—that if things are not going well, all the individual has to do is take some type of drug.

3. Do the drugs have harmful side effects? Even in the small dosages usually prescribed for children,

drugs sometimes have undesirable side effects. Such symptoms as decreased appetite, dizziness, headache, and insomnia have been reported in some cases to accompany the use of stimulants, such as methylphenidate-hydrochloride (Ritalin); and recently these drugs have been implicated in suspected growth retardation. Minor tranquilizers also may have adverse side effects, including lethargy. And even with drugs that seem to produce minimal side effects, the possibility of adverse long-range effects resulting from sustained usage during early growth and development is still being assessed.

The consensus among investigators seems to be that drug therapy for children should be used with extreme caution, and only with those children for whom other alternatives simply do not work, such as the hyperactive child who shows definite indications of MBD and cannot control his or her behavior without drug therapy. It is also considered important that drug therapy be undertaken only with the informed consent of the parent, as well as the child if he or she is old enough, and that the child not be given the sole responsibility for taking the medication—a procedure that can lead to drug abuse. At the same time, there is a need to avoid exaggerated public attitudes against the use of drug therapy for children who genuinely need it. Finally, children who do benefit from drug therapy may also need other therapeutic measures for dealing with coexisting problems, such as learning deficiencies and psychological, interpersonal, and family difficulties.

Based on Beck et al. (1975), Cole (1975), Eisenberg (1971), Hayes, Panitch, and Barker (1975), Martin and Zaug (1975), Whalen and Henker (1976), and Winsberg et al. (1975).

---

subject to forfeit each time he switched to some other topic in the middle of what he was saying. Whatever he had left at the end of the session he could keep. It was hoped that this verbal rehearsal and reinforcement for success would help the boy develop control over his own behavior.

The child's in-therapy behavior became less hyperactive, his test performance improved, and the teacher noted improvements in the classroom. Apparently, one of the ways to deal with the problems associated with hyperactivity is to teach children to "stop and think" before undertaking a behavior so that they can

then guide their own performance by deliberate self-instructions.

The continued use of psychological therapy with medication in a total treatment program has reportedly shown good success. Pelham and associates (1980) found that the combination of behavioral intervention and psychostimulant medication was more effective than either treatment alone in modifying the behavior of hyperactive children. Satterfield, Satterfield, and

Cantwell (1981) reported that individualized treatment of various types in conjunction with the use of medication resulted in favorable treatment outcomes in a three-year follow-up.

It should be kept in mind, however, that even though behavioral interventions and medication have reportedly enjoyed short-term successes, there has been insufficient critical evaluation of the long-term effects of either treatment method (O'Leary, 1980). One recent follow-up study of drug treatment of 75 children over a 10- to 12-year period reported that young adults who had been hyperactive children had less education than control subjects and had a history of more auto accidents and more geographical moves. However, the authors found that only a minority continued their antisocial behavior into adulthood or had severe psychopathology (Weiss et al., 1979). Glow (1981) has cautioned against drug treatment for hyperactivity on grounds that, while it may curb the symptoms, it does not cure the disorder. Similarly, Glow has claimed that behavior interventions require a great deal of effort, are not free from hazard, and have not been demonstrated to have long-range effects.

It is clear from an evaluation of the literature on treatment of hyperactivity that not only is there general disagreement about the nature of hyperactivity, but there also is an equal degree of controversy about the most effective treatment approach.

Even without treatment, hyperactive disturbances tend to clear up in the middle teens. The reason for this change is not clear. However, many hyperactive children who show signs of minimal brain dysfunction have a poor prognosis if left untreated. Even though the excessive and exaggerated activity may diminish over time, these individuals may continue to have many serious problems into their teens and even adult years. Hechtman, Weiss, and Perlman (1980) found that hyperactives had significantly more problems than control subjects when they reached young adulthood. The hyperactives showed such problems as low social skills and low self-esteem as young adults. This group may have a higher-than-average incidence of delinquency and other maladaptive behavior during adolescence and beyond (Solomon, 1972). Dvoredsky and Stewart (1981) recently reported two cases in which hyperactive children developed affective disorders as adults.

Attention deficit disorder without hyperactivity. The features of attention deficit disorder can be present in the child without hyperactivity. Here, the child shows evidence of both impulsivity and inattentiveness, which result in some forms of social or task-oriented impairment.

In general, the same concerns over defining the disorder exist for this subcategory as for the attention deficit disorder with hyperactivity. Maurer and Stewart (1980) found that 17 percent of children seen in a child psychiatry service had symptoms that could be classified as attention deficits without hyperactivity. However, they found that 80 percent of these cases also had symptoms of other psychological disorders, mostly *undersocialized conduct disorder, aggressive disorder,* or *learning disability.* They concluded that attention deficit disorder without hyperactivity, as described in DSM-III, is not a clearly defined syndrome.

It will, no doubt, take extended experience with the DSM-III in the clinical setting and in research studies to determine whether the present ways of viewing attention deficit behavior represent the most fruitful approach to understanding and classifying the accompanying problems, which apparently have important implications for the academic and social adjustment of many children.

A perspective on conduct disorders

In the sections on conduct disorders in children and delinquent behavior, we shall turn our attention to several disorders that emphasize the child's or adolescent's relationship to social norms and rules of conduct. In these disorders the child's or adolescent's conduct—specifically, persistent acts of aggressive or antisocial behavior—is the focus. It is important, in the conduct disorders, to distinguish between persistent antisocial acts in which the rights of others are violated and the less serious pranks often carried out by "normal" children and adolescents. We should point out here that the terms *delinquency* and *juvenile delinquency* are legal concepts referring to misdeeds involving violations of the law committed by minors. *Conduct disorders* involve misdeeds which may or may not be against the law.

Token reinforcement programs in the classroom

During the last two decades there has been a systematic attempt to use token reinforcement programs in the classroom as a form of therapy—for example, in modifying the behaviors of hyperactive children who are interfering with their own learning and that of other children.

The essentials of such a token reinforcement program typically involve (a) instructions to the class concerning behaviors that will be reinforced; (b) a method of making a potentially reinforcing stimulus—a token—contingent upon given behavior; and (c) rules governing the exchange of tokens for back-up reinforcers, such as low-calorie candy or the privilege of listening to music through earphones. These essentials must be adapted, of course, to the particular classroom setting, the children, the teacher, and the parents.

Usually there is a "fading" later on in the actual use of tokens and tangible back-up reinforcers; for when more positive and constructive behaviors have been established, they may usually be maintained by praise and related intangible reinforcement that would not have been effective in the earlier portions of the program.

In general, token reinforcement programs have been found to be effective in achieving such stated objectives as (a) reducing hyperactive and disruptive behaviors; (b) increasing attention, study behavior, and academic achievement; and (c) improving interpersonal and other competencies. Often such programs also yield some secondary gains in the form of improved school attendance as well as notably more positive self-concepts on the part of several of the children involved.

The behavior to be described in the following sections may appear to be quite similar to the early stages in the development of personality disorders, discussed in Chapter 5. Indeed, the personality characteristics and causal considerations are quite similar. It is difficult, if not impossible, to distinguish among a conduct disorder in a child, a "predelinquent" pattern of behavior, and the early stages in the ultimate development of an antisocial personality. Behaviorally, the patterns are quite similar and may simply represent three ways of describing or accounting for the same behavior. Many adult antisocial personalities, as children, showed the aggressive behavior and rule violations that often are labeled conduct disorders, and many came into contact with the authorities as a result of this delinquent behavior.

Fortunately, not all children who are described as having disorders of conduct or who engage in delinquent behavior grow up to become antisocial personalities or commit themselves to lives of crime. As we shall see, although these disorders of conduct are quite serious and rather complex to treat, there are effective ways of working with the disordered individuals to help them become accepted and productive members of society.

Conduct disorders in children

The essential symptomatic behavior in the conduct disorders involves the persistent, repetitive violation of rules and a disregard for the rights of others. Stewart and associates (1980) found conduct-disordered children to be characterized by fighting, disobedience, destructiveness, meanness, and, in the case of girls, precocious sexual behavior. Behar and Stewart (1982) found that conduct disorder began at a much earlier age than other disorders of childhood (excluding autism and organic syndromes). The following case is typical of children with conduct disorder and illustrates many of the symptoms commonly found:

Craig, an eight-year-old boy, had already established himself as a social outcast by the time he entered first grade. He had been expelled from kindergarten two times in two years for being unmanageable. His mother brought him to a mental health center at the insistence of the school when she attempted to enroll him in the first grade. Within the first week of school, Craig's quarrelsome and defiant behavior had tried the special education teacher, who was reputedly "excellent" with problem children like him, to the point where she recommended his suspension from school. His classmates likewise were completely unsympa-

Conduct disorders involve a persistent violation of established rules and a disregard for others' rights. When repeated rule-breaking extends to violations of the law, the behavior may then be considered delinquent.

thetic to Craig, whom they viewed as a bully. At even the slightest sign of movement on his part the other children would tell the teacher that Craig was "being bad again."

At home, Craig was uncontrollable. His mother and six other children lived with his domineering grandmother. Craig's mother was ineffective at disciplining or managing her children. She worked long hours as a domestic maid and "did not feel like hassling with those kids" when she got home. Her present husband, the father of the three youngest children (including Craig), had deserted the family.

In general, children who are seen as conduct disordered manifest such characteristics as overt or covert hostility, disobedience, physical and verbal aggressiveness, quarrelsomeness, vengefulness, and destructiveness. Lying, solitary stealing, and temper tantrums are common. Such children tend to be sexually uninhibited and inclined toward sexual aggressiveness. Some may engage in fire-setting, vandalism, and even homicidal acts.

In DSM-III, the broad category "conduct disorder" contains four subtypes. These subtypes are based on two factors : (a) whether the individual shows adequate social bonds, and (b) whether the individual engages in aggressive antisocial behavior. Accordingly, the subtypes are called undersocialized, aggressive; undersocialized, nonaggressive; socialized, aggressive; and socialized, nonaggressive.

Causal factors in conduct disorders in children. Investigators seem generally to agree that the family setting of the conduct-disordered child is typically characterized by rejection, harsh and inconsistent discipline, and general frustration. Frequently the parents have an unstable marital relationship, are emotionally disturbed or sociopathic, and do not provide the child with consistent guidance, acceptance, or affection. In a disproportionate number of cases, the child lives in a home broken by divorce or separation and may have a stepparent or have had a series of stepparents. But whether the home is broken or not, the child feels overtly rejected.

Wolkind (1974) found that the behavior typical of conduct disorder was common among children who had been institutionalized at an early age. This was true even in relatively good institutional settings. He used the term *affectionless psychopathy* in connection with such children and concluded that their antisocial behavior had been heavily influenced by their early family life prior to entering the institution. Evidently the trauma of institutionalization had worsened antisocial trends that had started very early in an inadequate home.

Treatment and outcomes. Therapy for the conduct-disordered child is likely to be ineffective unless some means can be found for modifying the child's environment. This is difficult when the parents are maladjusted and in conflict with each other. And often an overburdened parent who is separated or divorced and working simply does not have the time or inclination to learn and practice a more adequate parental role. In some cases the circumstances may call for the child to be removed from the home and placed in a foster home or institution, with the expectation of a later return to the home if intervening therapy with the parents appears to justify it.

Unfortunately, children who are removed to a new environment often interpret this as further rejection—not only by their parents but by society as well. And unless the changed environment offers a warm, kindly, and accepting—yet consistent and firm—setting, they are likely to make little progress. Even then, treatment may have only a temporary effect. Faretra (1981) followed up 66 aggressive and disturbed adolescents who had been admitted to an inpatient unit. She found that antisocial and criminal behavior persisted into adulthood with a lessening of psychiatric involvement. The most antisocial children were from homes with a history of antisocial problems, one-parent homes, and minority or deprived environments.

By and large, society tends to take a punitive, rather than rehabilitative, attitude toward the antisocial aggressive youth. Thus, the emphasis is on punishment and on "teaching the child a lesson." Such "treatment," however, appears to intensify rather than correct the behavior. Where treatment is unsuccessful, the end product is likely to be a psychopathic personality with a long future of antisocial aggressive behavior. In a longitudinal study of antisocial aggressive behavior in childhood, Robins (1970) found that such behavior is highly predictive of sociopathic behavior in later adolescence and adulthood; similar findings have been reported by Wolkind (1974).

The advent of behavior therapy techniques has, however, made the outlook much brighter for children who manifest conduct disorders. Particularly important is training of the parents in control techniques, so that they function as therapists in reinforcing desirable behavior and modifying the environmental conditions that have been reinforcing the maladaptive behavior. The changes brought about when they consis-

tently accept and reward the child's positive behavior and stop focusing attention on the negative behavior may finally change their perception of and feelings toward the child, leading to the basic acceptance that the child has so badly needed.

Though effective techniques for behavioral management can be taught to parents (Fleischman, 1981), often they have difficulty carrying out treatment plans. If this is the case, other techniques may have to be employed to ensure that the parent or person responsible for the child's discipline is sufficiently assertive to follow through on the program. Shoemaker and Paulson (1976) described a program of assertiveness training for mothers, in which women who had children with aggressive behavior problems were taught more effective skills in self-expression and verbal discipline. Ratings of the children's behavior showed improvement following the assertiveness training.

Delinquent behavior

One of the most troublesome and extensive problems in childhood and adolescence is delinquent behavior, such as destruction of property, violence against other people, and other behavior contrary to the needs and rights of others and in violation of the society's laws. As noted earlier, the term *delinquency* is a legal one; it refers to acts committed by individuals under the age of 16, 17, or 18 (depending on state law). Delinquency is generally regarded as calling for some punishment or corrective action.[3]

The actual incidence of juvenile delinquency is difficult to determine, since many delinquent acts are not reported. In addition, the states differ somewhat in their definitions of delinquent behavior—particularly regarding minor offenses—so that what is considered delinquent behavior in Texas may not be so considered in California or New York. Of the two million young people who go through the juvenile courts each year in the United States, about half are there for actions that would not be considered crimes at all in the case of an adult, such as running away (see **HIGHLIGHT** on pages 550–51).

---

[3]It may be noted here that children under 8 who commit such acts are not considered delinquents, because it is assumed that they are too immature to understand the significance and consequences of their actions.

HIGHLIGHT

Problems that lead children to run away

Of serious concern in the United States is the problem of youngsters who run away from home—an estimated million or more each year. While the average age is about 15, an increasing number are in the 11- to 14-year-old age bracket. Many of these runaways are from the suburbs, and at least half are girls. The following case illustrates this problem.

Joan, an attractive girl who looked older than her 12 years, came to the attention of juvenile authorities when her parents reported her as a runaway. Twice before she had run away from home, but no report had been filed. In the first instance she had gone to the home of a girlfriend and returned two days later; in the second she had hitchhiked to another city with an older boy and returned home about a week later.

Investigation revealed that the girl was having difficulty in school and was living in a family situation torn by bickering and dissension. In explaining why she ran away from home, she stated simply that she "just couldn't take it anymore—all that quarreling and criticism, and no one really cared anyway."

Why do children and adolescents run away? English (1973) concluded that reasons for running away

Incidence of delinquency. Between 1972 and 1981, arrests of persons under 18 years of age for eight serious crimes increased more than 231 percent.[4] In 1981, juveniles accounted for over 1 out of every 3 arrests for robbery, 1 out of 3 arrests for crimes against property, 1 out of 6 arrests for rape, and 1 out of 11 arrests for murder. Although most of the "juvenile crime" was committed by males, the rate has risen sharply for females. In 1981, about 1 teenager out of every 15 in the nation was arrested.

Although delinquency rates are alarmingly high, there appears to be a moderating trend for violent youth crime in recent indicators. A 17-year survey of police records of violent youth

crimes shows that arrests of young people between the ages of 13 and 20 for homicide, robbery, and aggravated assault increased greatly in the 1960s (as much as 84 percent in the case of homicide), then increased much more slowly from 1970 to 1975, and actually declined slightly from 1975 to 1977. Rape arrests increased 17 percent during the 1960s, increased only 1 percent between 1970 and 1975, and then stayed the same during the next two years (Zimring, 1979). Between 1980 and 1981, five major crime-rate categories—robbery, aggravated assault, burglary, larceny-theft, and motor vehicle theft—actually showed slight decreases (Uniform Crime Reports, 1981).

Well over half of the juveniles who are arrested each year have prior police records. Female delinquents are commonly apprehended

---

[4]Statistics in this section are based mainly on Uniform Crime Reports (1981).

from home tend to fall into three categories: (a) getting out of a destructive family situation, as in the case of the girl who runs away to avoid sexual advances by her father or stepfather; (b) running away in an effort to better the family situation; and (c) having a secret, unsharable problem, such as, for girls, being pregnant.

In a study of runaway girls, Homer (1974) distinguished between "run from's," who had usually fought with their parents and run away because they were unable to resolve the situation or their anger, and "run to's," who were seeking something outside the home. The "run to's" were typically seekers of pleasure—sex, drugs, liquor, escape from school, and a peer group with similar interests. Usually they stayed with friends or at other "peer-established" facilities. The "run from's" usually ran away from home only once, while the "run to's" were more likely to be repetitive runaways.

An increasing number of children are "run froms" who are trying to get away from an intolerable home situation. In many instances, for economic or other reasons, they are actually encouraged to leave—and their parents do not want them back. These children have been referred to as the "throwaways" (*U.S. News & World Report*, May 12, 1975, pp. 49–50).

Most do not feel that they can return to their parents but very much want a foster home where they will be treated well and respected.

The majority of runaways are not reported. Of those who are, about 90 percent or more are located by law enforcement officers and, where feasible, returned home. Beginning in late 1974, a toll-free "hot line" was established that informs runaways where the nearest temporary shelter is located and enables them to send messages to their parents if they wish.[1]

Treatment for the child runaway is similar to that for individuals who manifest other emotional problems in this life period. Often family therapy is an essential part of the treatment program. In some instances—as in those involving parental abuse, unconcern, or lack of cooperation—juvenile authorities may place the child in a foster home. However, parents are by no means always the primary reason for their child's running away; and a "what-have-we-done-wrong" attitude may lead to unnecessary feelings of guilt.

---

[1]Two of the toll-free numbers are 1-800-621-4000 and (Illinois only) 1-800-972-6004. These hotlines do not operate from either Alaska or Hawaii.

---

for drug usage, sexual offenses, running away from home, and "incorrigibility," but crimes against property, such as stealing, have markedly increased among them. Male delinquents are commonly arrested for drug usage and crimes against property; to a lesser extent, they are arrested for armed robbery, aggravated assault, and other crimes against the person. However, crimes by juveniles are increasing in our large metropolitan centers to such an extent that the streets are considered unsafe after dark.

Fear of violent juvenile crime has created in many people the idea that juvenile criminals as a class are uncontrollable and psychopathic. However, the extent of dangerous and violent behavior among delinquents has been questioned. Dinitz and Conrad (1980) reported that, of a sample of 811 juveniles arrested for violent

crimes, only about 2 percent had been involved in repeated aggressive or violent acts; and even the acts of this 2 percent were mostly "clumsy and inadvertent" (p. 145).

In general, it has been assumed that both the incidence and the severity of delinquent behavior are disproportionately high for slum and lower-class youth. This view has been supported by findings of the President's Commission on Law Enforcement and Administration of Justice (1967) as well as by later reports (Zimring, 1979). Other investigators, however, have found no evidence that delinquency is predominately a lower-class phenomenon. In a study of 433 teenagers who had committed almost 2500 delinquent acts, Haney and Gold (1973) found "no strong relationship between social status and delinquent behavior" (p. 52). Similar findings have recently been reported by Krohn et al. (1980). It may also be noted that the delinquency rate for socially disadvantaged youth appears about equal for whites and nonwhites.

Causal factors in delinquency.

Various conditions, singly and in combination, may be involved in the development of delinquent behavior. In general, however, there appear to be several key variables: personal pathology, pathogenic family patterns, undesirable peer relationships, general sociocultural factors, and special stress.

1. *Personal pathology.* A number of investigators have attempted to "type" delinquents in terms of pervasive patterns and sources of personal pathology.

a) *Genetic determinants.* Although the research on genetic determinants of antisocial behavior is far from conclusive there has been some evidence reported on possible hereditary contributions to criminality. Schulsinger (1980) identified 57 psychopathic adoptees from psychiatric and police files in Denmark and matched them with 57 nonpsychopathic control adoptees on the basis of age, sex, social class, geographic region, and age at adoption. He found that natural parents of the adopted psychopaths, particularly fathers, were more likely to have psychopathic characteristics than the natural parents of the controls. Since these natural parents had little contact with the offspring, reducing the possibility of environmental influence, the results are interpreted as reflecting the possibility of some genetic transmission of antisocial behavior.

b) *Brain damage and mental retardation.* In a distinct minority of cases of delinquency—an estimated 1 percent or less—brain pathology results in lowered inhibitory controls and a tendency toward episodes of violent behavior (Caputo & Mandell, 1970; Kiester, 1974). Such youths are often hyperactive, impulsive, emotionally unstable, and unable to inhibit themselves when strongly stimulated. Fortunately, their inner controls appear to improve during later adolescence and young adulthood.

Low intelligence appears to be of causal significance in delinquency (Moffitt et al., 1980). Individuals of low intelligence may be unable to foresee the probable consequences of their actions or understand the significance of what

they are doing. This is particularly true of mentally retarded, sexually delinquent girls; but it also applies to retarded delinquent males, who typically commit impulsive offenses, such as petty thievery and minor acts of aggression. Frequently, retarded delinquents fall prey to brighter psychopaths or delinquent gangs, who dominate and exploit them.

c) *Neuroses and psychoses.* A small percentage of delinquent acts appear to be directly associated with neurotic or psychotic disorders. In some cases, the delinquent acts take the form of a behavior such as "peeping" or stealing things that are not needed. This behavior often seems related to deviant sexual gratification in overinhibited adolescents who have been indoctrinated in the belief that masturbation and other overt forms of sexual release are evil and sinful. Often such individuals fight their inner impulses before committing the delinquent act and then feel guilty afterward.

Delinquent acts associated with psychotic behavior often involve a pattern of prolonged emotional hurt and turmoil, culminating after long frustration in an outburst of violent behavior (Bandura, 1973). In the case of both neurotic and psychotic delinquents, the delinquent act is a byproduct of severe personality maladjustment rather than a reflection of antisocial attitudes.

d) *Psychopathic traits.* A sizable number of habitual delinquents appear to share the traits typical of the psychopathic personality—they are impulsive, defiant, resentful, devoid of feelings of remorse or guilt, incapable of establishing and maintaining close interpersonal ties, and seemingly unable to profit from experience. Because they lack needed reality and ethical controls, they often engage in seemingly "senseless" acts that are not planned but occur on the "spur of the moment." They may steal a small sum of money they do not need, or they may steal a car, drive it a few blocks, and abandon it. In some instances they engage in impulsive acts of violence that are not committed for personal gain but rather reflect underlying resentment and hostility toward their world. In essence, these individuals are "unsocialized."

Kendall, Deardorff, and Finch (1977) found that nonoffenders, first offenders, and repeat offenders differed on a measure of socialization, with the repeaters being the most poorly socialized. Ganzer and Sarason (1973) found that both male and female delinquents with multiple arrests were more frequently regarded as sociopathic than were nonrecidivists (those arrested only once).

Although research has focused primarily on male delinquents, several investigators have also emphasized the high incidence of psychopathic personalities among females in state correctional institutions (Cloninger & Guze, 1970; Konopka, 1964, 1967).

e) *Drug abuse.* A sizable number of delinquent acts—particularly theft, prostitution, and assault—are directly associated with drug problems. Most adolescents who are addicted to hard drugs, such as heroin, are forced to steal in an attempt to maintain their habit, which can be very expensive. In the case of female addicts, theft may be combined with or replaced by prostitution as a means of obtaining money.

2. *Pathogenic family patterns.* Of the various pathogenic family patterns that have been emphasized in the research on juvenile delinquency, the following appear to be the most important.

a) *Broken homes.* A number of investigators have pointed to the high incidence of broken homes and multiple or missing parental figures in the background of delinquent youths (Lefkowitz et al., 1977). In general, delinquency appears to be much more common among youths coming from homes broken by parental separation or divorce than from homes broken by the death of a parent.

As we have seen, however, the effects of broken homes vary greatly. Even when the disruption is due to parental separation or divorce, the effects on the children may be more favorable than when they are raised in a home torn by parental conflict and dissension.

b) *Parental rejection and faulty discipline.* In many cases, one or both parents reject the child. When the father is the rejecting parent, it is difficult for a boy to identify with him and use him as a model for his own development. In an early study of 26 aggressively delinquent boys, Bandura and Walters (1963) delineated a pattern in which rejection by the father was combined with inconsistent handling of the boy by both parents. To complicate the pathogenic picture, the father typically used physically punitive methods of discipline, thus modeling aggressive behavior as well as augmenting the hostility the boy already felt toward him. The end result of such a pattern was a hostile, defiant, inadequately socialized youth who lacked normal inner controls and tended to act out his aggressive impulses in antisocial behavior.

The detrimental effects of parental rejection and inconsistent discipline are by no means attributable only to the father. Researchers have found that such behavior by either parent is associated with aggression, lying, stealing, running away from home, and a wide range of other difficulties (Langner et al., 1974; Lefkowitz et al., 1977; Pemberton & Benady, 1973). Often, too, inconsistent discipline may involve more complex family interactions, as when a mother imposes severe restrictions on a youth's behavior and then leaves "policing" to a timid or uncaring father who fails to follow through.

c) *Psychopathic parental models.* Several investigators have found a high incidence of psychopathic traits in the parents of delinquents—particularly but not exclusively in the father (Bandura, 1973; Glueck & Glueck, 1969; Ulmar, 1971). These included alcoholism, brutality, antisocial attitudes, failure to provide, frequent unnecessary absences from home, and other characteristics that made the father an inadequate and unacceptable model. Elkind (1967), for example, cited the case of a "father who encouraged his 17-year-old son to drink, frequent prostitutes, and generally 'raise hell.' This particular father was awakened late one night by the police who had caught his son in a raid on a so-called 'massage' parlor. The father's reaction was, 'Why aren't you guys out catching crooks?' This same father would boast to his co-workers that his son was 'all boy' and a 'chip off the old block' " (p. 313).

Psychopathic fathers—and mothers—may contribute in various ways to delinquent behavior of girls as well. Covert encouragement of sexual promiscuity is fairly common, and in some instances there is actual incest with the daughter. In a study of 30 delinquent girls, Scharfman and Clark (1967) found evidence of serious psychopathology in one or both parents of 22 of the girls, including three cases of incest and many other types of early sexual experience. These investigators also reported a high incidence of broken homes (only 11 of the 30 girls lived with both parents) and harsh, irrational, and inconsistent discipline:

"Any form of consistent discipline or rational setting of limits was unknown to the girls in their homes. Rather, there was an almost regular pattern of indifference to the activities or whereabouts of these girls, often with the mother overtly or indirectly suggesting delinquent behavior by her own actions. This would alternate with unpredictable, irrational, and violent punishment" (p. 443).

Scharfman and Clark concluded that the key factors in the girls' delinquent behavior were (a) broken homes, combined with emotional deprivation; (b) irrational, harsh, and inconsistent parental discipline; and (c) patterns of early sexual and aggressive behavior modeled by psychopathic parents. Here we can readily see the interaction of several pathogenic family conditions in the etiology of delinquent behavior.

In evaluating the role of pathogenic family patterns in delinquency, it should be emphasized that a given pattern is only one of many interacting factors. For example, the term "broken home" is a catchall term to describe the absence of one or both parents because of a variety of conditions, including desertion, separation, death, or imprisonment. A home may be "broken" at different times and under varying circumstances; and broken homes may have differing influences, depending on the individual involved and the total life situation. Consequently, the effects of a given family pattern can be assessed adequately only in relation to the total situation.

d) *Parental relationships outside the family.* Recent research suggests that the parents' interpersonal relationships outside the family may contribute to the child's behavior problems (Griest & Wells, 1983). Wahler (1980) found that the children's oppositional behavior was inversely related to the amount of friendly contacts that parents had outside the home. Wahler et al. (1981) reported that mothers who are isolated or who have negative community interactions are less likely to "track" or control their child's behavior in the community than parents who have friendly relationships outside the family.

3. *Undesirable peer relationships.* Delinquency tends to be a shared experience. In their study

of delinquents in the Flint, Michigan, area, Haney and Gold (1973) found that about two thirds of delinquent acts were committed in association with one or two other persons, and most of the remainder involved three or four other persons. Usually the offender and the companion or companions were of the same sex. Interestingly, girls were more likely than boys to have a constant friend or companion in delinquency. The role of gang membership in delinquency is discussed in the next section.

4. *General sociocultural factors.* Broad social conditions may also tend to produce or support delinquency. (See **HIGHLIGHT** on page 555 for a discussion of the possible influence of television on violent behavior.) Interrelated factors that appear to be of key importance include alienation and rebellion, social rejection, and the psychological support afforded by membership in a delinquent gang.

a) *Alienation and rebellion.* Feelings of alienation and rebellion are common to many teenagers from all socioeconomic levels. Alienated teenagers may outwardly submit passively to their elders' demands, or they may openly disobey parental and other adult authority and create no end of problems for themselves and their families. In either event, alienation from family and from the broader society exposes them to becoming "captives of their peers," to whom they may turn for guidance and approval. Thus, they are vulnerable to pressures to identify with and join peer groups that engage in the use of illegal drugs or other behavior considered delinquent.

In some instances these alienated youths may rebel, leave home, and drift into groups in which delinquent behavior is the way of life, as in the case of runaway teenage girls who become affiliated with organized prostitution. The alienated and rebellious behavior of economically disadvantaged youth may lead to the same pattern, although its onset is much more likely to be directly associated with poverty, deprivation, and discrimination.

b) *The "social rejects."* Our society has become increasingly aware of young people who lack the motivation or ability to do well in school and who "drop out" as soon as they can. With increasing automation and the demand for occupational skills—whether in the trades or in managerial or professional fields—there are few jobs

HIGHLIGHT
Television and violence

Just how much the violence on television serves as a model for violent and criminal behavior has been widely argued. In 1977 the controversy entered the courtroom when a 15-year-old confessed killer was defended by an attorney who claimed that the youth had been brainwashed by TV. The attorney argued that the boy was living in a fantasy world which had been created by television programs that had given him a distorted sense of appropriate behavior. The defense alleged that the youth was intoxicated by television and "pulling the trigger became as common to him as killing a fly" (*Time*, October 10, 1977). The court did not accept the insanity plea but found the youth guilty of murder. In another case, in California, a lawyer argued (unsuccessfully) that the rape of his client, a young girl, had been a reenactment by a group of children of a scene from the TV movie *Born Innocent,* shown shortly before. And in Boston, after the showing of the TV movie *Fuzz,* a woman was set on fire in an apparent imitation of a scene from that film.

A direct causal link between media violence and increased aggressiveness on the part of the viewer is difficult to prove. But the evidence of a relationship between TV violence and later aggressiveness is quite strong. Early laboratory studies in the modeling of aggression showed that children who observed a display of aggression on film later demonstrated similar kicking and punching behavior themselves. Subsequent studies by the same investigator showed that when children viewed films depicting aggression, they showed more aggressive behavior later on (Bandura, 1973).

Other research has focused on the effects of TV on long-term attitudes and perceptions that might predispose a child toward later violent behavior. One such study found that violence on TV desensitized children so that they subsequently had less emotional arousal to violent scenes (Cline et al., 1973). Thus, continued exposure to violence on TV might result in less fear of—or revulsion to—actual violence.

Well-controlled studies by Lefkowitz et al. (1977) demonstrated that children's preference for violent television at age 8 was highly associated with—and thus predictive of—aggressiveness in their behavior toward others: those who preferred violence on TV were more aggressive in their own behavior. Moreover, this relationship was still found to be significant in a 10-year follow-up when the children were young adults.

Even here, however, the direction of causation is not proven: it may have been the more aggressive children who preferred the violent TV in the beginning. But when, as has often happened, crimes occur that follow in detail a particular sequence that the individual has watched on TV or in a movie, it is hard to believe that the portrayed scene had no causal part in the tragedy. The researchers' conclusions in the Lefkowitz study were that in most cases the TV violence was probably only a precipitating cause of aggressive behavior in the case of children already predisposed toward it.

---

for which they can qualify. Augmenting this group of youngsters are students who graduate from high school but whose training does not qualify them for available occupational opportunities.

Whether they come from upper-, middle-, or lower-class homes, and whether they drop out or continue through high school, they have one crucial problem in common—they discover they are not needed in our society. They are victims of "social progress"—"social rejects." While some are able to obtain training in specific job areas, others appear unable to find or hold jobs, and still others drift aimlessly from one unsatisfactory job to another.

c) *Delinquent gang cultures.* With gangs, we are dealing not so much with personal psychopathology as with organized group pathology involving rebellion against the norms of society. As Jenkins (1969) has expressed it:

"The socialized delinquent represents not a failure of socialization but a limitation of loyalty to a more or less predatory peer group. The basic capacity for social relations has been achieved. What is lacking is an effective integration with the larger society as a contributing member" (p. 73).

While the problem of delinquent gangs is most prevalent in lower socioeconomic areas, it is by no means restricted to them. Further, delinquent gangs are not a male province—in recent years, female delinquent gangs have also been formed. Nor does the problem of juvenile delinquent gangs occur only in particular racial, ethnic, or social groups. It is pervasive, most particularly in inner city areas. While there are many reasons for joining delinquent gangs—including fear of personal injury from gang members if one does not join—most members of delinquent gangs appear to feel inadequate in and rejected by the larger society.

Gang membership gives them a sense of belonging and a means of gaining some measure of status and approval. It may also represent a means of committing robberies and other illegal acts for financial gain—acts that the individual could not successfully perform alone (Feldman & Weisfeld, 1973).

It should be emphasized that the majority of delinquents do not belong to delinquent gangs, nor do the majority of juvenile gangs fall in the delinquent category. Many are organized for recreational and other constructive purposes. And not all delinquent gangs are highly organized, cohesive groups. Recently, however, there appears to be an increase in both the organization and cohesiveness of delinquent gangs and in the violence of their activities.

5. *Unusual stress and other factors.* We have noted that many delinquent acts reflect momentary impulses or are part of the regular activities of a delinquent gang. Delinquent behavior may also be precipitated by some relatively minor event, as when a riot is triggered by a fight between two youths. And, of course, it may sometimes be inadvertent, resulting from innocent pranks that backfire.

In some instances, traumatic experiences in the life of a boy or girl appear to act as precipitating events (Coleman, 1973). In an early study of 500 delinquent boys, Clarke (1961) found that in about a third of the cases it was possible to isolate especially stressful events that had preceded the delinquency, such as death of parents, disruption of family life, or discovery that they had been adopted. These events had proved highly disorganizing and often had led to poor school performance, truancy, brooding, and—eventually—delinquent behavior.

Burks and Harrison (1962) also emphasized

the importance of stress as a precipitating factor in some cases of aggressive antisocial behavior, pointing out that the stress functioned to undermine the youths' feelings of adequacy and worth. In an analysis of four case histories—involving arson, murder, and breaking and entering—Finkelstein (1968) found an "accumulation of emotional tensions [leading] at times to temporary disintegration, or at least to a state in which the person in full awareness of what he is doing loses his ego control" (p. 310).

Dealing with delinquency. If they have adequate facilities and personnel, juvenile institutions and training schools can be of great help to youths who need to be removed from aversive environments and given a chance to learn about themselves and their world, to further their education and develop needed skills, and to find purpose and meaning in their lives. In such settings the youths may have the opportunity to receive psychological counseling and group therapy. Here it is of key importance that peer-group pressures be channeled in the direction of resocialization, rather than toward repetitive delinquent behavior. Behavior therapy techniques—based on the assumption that delinquent behavior is learned, maintained, and changed according to the same principles as other learned behavior—have shown marked promise in the rehabilitation of juvenile offenders who require institutionalization.[5] Counseling with parents and related environmental changes are generally of vital importance in the total rehabilitation program.

Probation is widely used with juvenile offenders and may be granted either in lieu of or after a period of institutionalization. In keeping with the trend toward helping troubled persons in their own environments, the California Youth Authority conducted the Community Treatment Project, a 5-year experiment in which delinquents—other than those involved in such crimes as murder, rape, or arson—were granted immediate probation and supervised and assisted in their own communities. The 270 youths treated in this project showed a rehabilitation success rate of 72 percent during a 15-month fol-

---

[5]A review of studies dealing with the application of behavior therapy to juvenile delinquency can be found in Davidson and Seidman (1974).

Professional counseling and therapy can be helpful in dealing with delinquent behavior. However, the support of peer-group members and parents may also be vital in the process of resocialization.

low-up period. In contrast, a comparable group of 357 delinquents who underwent institutional treatment and then were released on probation showed a rehabilitation success rate of only 48 percent (Blake, 1967). Since 90 percent of the girls and 73 percent of the boys committed to the California Youth Authority by juvenile courts were found eligible for community treatment, it would appear that many delinquents can be guided into constructive behavior without being removed from their family or community. It may be noted, however, that a key factor in the success of this pioneering research project was a marked reduction in the case load of supervising probation officers.

The recidivism rate for delinquents—the most commonly used measure for assessing rehabilitation programs—depends heavily on the type of offenders being dealt with as well as on the particular facility or procedures used (Roberts et al., 1974). The overall recidivism rate for delinquents sent to training schools has been estimated to be as high as 80 percent (*Time,* June 30, 1975). And since many crimes are committed by juveniles who have been recently released from custody or who were not incarcerated after being arrested, a number of state legal officials have become advocates of stiffer penalties for some types of juvenile crime. Individuals who commit crimes of senseless violence or armed assault or who have a long history of arrests are more often being given harsher penalties than they once would have been (Fersch, 1980).

Institutionalization seems particularly questionable in the case of "juvenile status offenders," youths whose offenses involve acts that would not be considered criminal if committed by an adult, such as running away from home or engaging in sexual relations. In such instances, institutionalization may aggravate behavioral problems rather than correct them. Mixing status offenders with delinquents or adults who have committeed violent and antisocial offenses may simply provide them with unfortunate learning experiences in how to become more seriously delinquent.

On the other hand, failure to institutionalize delinquents who have committed serious offenses such as robbery, assault, and murder may be a disservice to both the delinquents and the public. In essence, it seems essential to correct the "bizarre lumping" of major felonies, minor misdemeanors, and trivial violations of social norms under the general label of "juvenile delinquency." This would enable many delinquencies to be dealt with by educational and social-work agencies rather than by the justice system. It would also make it possible for treatment programs to meet the needs of individual young people, and society's need for protection would be better met in the long run.

One key task in dealing with troubled youth is opening lines of communication with them. The behavior of even some of the most "hardcore" delinquent gangs has shown marked improvement when social workers or police officers have managed to win their confidence and respect. Often such personnel can help channel the youths' activities into automobile or motorcycle rallies and other programs that provide both recreational and learning opportunities. Too often, however, as in the case of institutional and probation programs, lack of trained personnel and other resources prevent such programs.

The great need, of course, is not only for more effective rehabilitation programs, but also for long-range programs aimed at the prevention of delinquency. This would mean alleviating slum conditions, providing adequate educational and recreational opportunities for disadvantaged youth, educating parents, and delineating a more meaningful societal role for adolescents—tasks for the whole society.

Anxiety disorders of childhood and adolescence

In modern society, no one is totally insulated from anxiety-producing events or situations. All children and adolescents are vulnerable to fears and uncertainties as part of growing up, and most children encounter many normal developmental steps and environmental demands that challenge their adaptation skills.

In this section, we shall describe several related disorders that center around the experience of anxiety and the attempts on the part of some youngsters to deal with these intense feelings through withdrawal, or avoidance of social contact. Anxiety and withdrawal symptoms have a great deal in common. Jenkins (1968) classified 287 of the 1500 disturbed children he studied as suffering from problems of anxiety and withdrawal. Both symptom clusters are more common among boys than among girls. (A possibly related disorder of emotion—childhood depression—is discussed in the **HIGHLIGHT** on page 559). Children with anxiety and withdrawal disorders appear to share the following characteristics: (a) oversensitivity, (b) unrealistic fears, (c) shyness and timidity, (d) pervasive feelings of inadequacy, (e) sleep disturbances, and (f) fear of school. However, the children diagnosed as suffering from an anxiety disorder typically attempt to cope with their fears by becoming overdependent on others for support and help, whereas those who manifest withdrawal, or avoidant, symptoms apparently attempt to minimize their anxiety by turning away from the frightening outer world and withdrawing into themselves.

In the DSM-III, anxiety disorders are covered in three subclassifications: *separation anxiety disorder, avoidant disorder of childhood or adolescence,*

and *overanxious disorder*. We shall briefly describe the clinical picture of each of these syndromes, then deal with causal factors and treatment considerations in later sections.

Separation anxiety disorder. *Separation anxiety disorder* is characterized by unrealistic fears, oversensitivity, self-consciousness, nightmares, and chronic anxiety. The child lacks self-confidence, is apprehensive in new situations, and tends to be immature for his or her age. Such children often are described by their parents as shy, sensitive, nervous, submissive, easily discouraged, worried, and frequently moved to tears. Typically they are overdependent, particularly on their parents. The essential feature of the clinical picture in separation anxiety disorder involves excessive anxiety about separation from major attachment figures, such as mother, and from familiar home surroundings. In most cases there is a clear psychosocial stressor, such as death of a relative or a pet. The following case illustrates the clinical picture in this disorder.

Johnny was a highly sensitive six-year-old boy who suffered from numerous fears, nightmares, and chronic anxiety. He was terrified of being separated from his mother, even for a brief period. When his mother tried to enroll him in kindergarten, he became so upset when she left the room that the principal arranged for her to remain in the classroom. But after two weeks this had to be discontinued, and Johnny had to be withdrawn from kindergarten, since his mother could not leave him even for a few minutes.

Later, when his mother attempted to enroll him in the first grade, Johnny manifested the same intense anxiety and unwillingness to be separated from her. At the suggestion of the school counselor, Johnny's mother brought him to a community clinic for assistance with the problem. The therapist who initially saw Johnny and his mother was wearing a white clinic jacket, and this led to a severe panic reaction on Johnny's part. His mother had to hold him to keep him from running away, and he did not settle down until the therapist removed his jacket. Johnny's mother explained that "He is terrified of doctors, and it is almost impossible to get him to a physician even when he is sick."

When children with separation anxiety disorder are separated from their significant others, they typically become preoccupied with morbid fears, such as the worry that their parents are going to

HIGHLIGHT

Does childhood depression exist as a clinical syndrome?

Clinicians working in child psychiatry and child psychology have long recognized a pattern of symptoms that seemed indicative of depression. Spitz (1946) first described the problem, which he called *anaclitic depression,* as a pattern similar to adult depression that occurred in children experiencing prolonged separation from the mother. This syndrome included developmental retardation and such symptomatic behavior as weepiness, sadness, immobility, and apathy.

Childhood depression has been recognized as a diagnostic problem by a number of recent investigators (Herzog & Rathbun, 1982; Kashani et al., 1981b; and Toolan, 1981). It includes behaviors such as withdrawal, crying, avoidance of eye contact, physical complaints, poor appetite, and even aggressive behavior. The "reality" of childhood depression is accepted so strongly that some investigators (Ossofsky,

1974) even believe that it can be diagnosed in infancy and successfully treated with imipramine, an antidepressant medication. Estimates of the frequency of depressive symptoms in children have ranged from 13 percent (Kashani, et al., 1982) to 23 percent (Kashani, Venzke, & Millar, 1981).

However, many investigators doubt the existence of such a syndrome (Lefkowitz & Burton, 1978; Schulterbrandt & Raskin, 1977). For one thing the symptoms listed are common in many normal children (MacFarlane, Allen & Honzik, 1954; Werry & Quay, 1971). For another, cross-cultural studies of depression do not support the idea of a childhood depression syndrome (Marsella, 1980). One investigator, Makita (1973), noted that out of 3000 cases of disturbed children in Japan, not one was diagnosed as childhood depression.

become ill or die. They cling helplessly to attachment figures, have difficulty sleeping, and become intensely demanding.

Avoidant disorder of childhood or adolescence.

In the *avoidant disorder of childhood or adolescence,* as already indicated, children apparently attempt to minimize their anxiety by turning inward—in effect, detaching themselves from a seemingly dangerous world. The results of this defensive strategy have been described by Jenkins (1969):

"In turning away from objective reality, these children turn away from the normal practice of constantly checking their expectations against experience. With such turning away, their capacity to distinguish fact from fancy tends to deteriorate. They function inefficiently and fail to develop effective patterns of behavior" (p. 70).

Children manifesting an avoidant disorder tend to be seclusive, timid, and unable to form close interpersonal relationships. Often they appear listless and apathetic and are prone to daydreaming and unrealistic fantasies. They tend to cling helplessly to caretakers and become tearful if any demands are placed on them. The following case is fairly typical:

Tommy was a small, slender, seven-year-old boy from a middle-class family. He was enrolled in the second grade at school but failed to function adequately in the classroom. In referring him to the school counselor, the teacher described him as withdrawn, shy, oversensitive, and unable to make friends or to participate in classroom activities. During recess he preferred to remain in the classroom and appeared preoccupied with his thoughts and fantasies. He was seriously retarded in reading achievement and other basic school subjects. Psychological assessment showed that he was superior in intelligence but suffered from extreme feelings of inadequacy and a pervasive attitude of "I can't do it."

Overanxious disorder.

The *overanxious disorder* is characterized by excessive worry and persistent fear; however, the fears are usually not specific and are not due to a recent stressful event. The child appears generally anxious and may worry a great deal about future events. He or she is preoccupied with trivial problems. His or her anxiety may also be expressed in somatic ways—stomach distress, shortness of breath, dizziness, headaches, and the like. Sleeping problems, particularly difficulty in falling asleep, are common. Many children showing problems of overanxious disorder appear to have personality characteristics such as perfectionistic ideas and obsessional self-doubt. The disorder is illustrated in the following case:

Cindy, an overweight eleven-year-old girl, was taken to the emergency room of a hospital following an "attack" of dizziness, faintness, and shortness of breath. She believed she was having a heart attack because of the discomfort she was experiencing in her chest. Cindy had a long history of health problems and concerns and was a frequent visitor to doctors. She had missed, on the average, three days of school a week since school had begun four months before.

Cindy was viewed by her mother as a "very good girl" but "sickly." Cindy was very good about helping around the house and with her two younger sisters. She seemed very conscientious and concerned about doing things right but seemed to lack self-confidence. She always checked out things with her mother, sometimes several times. She was particularly concerned about safety and would, for example, ask her mother frequently if the kitchen stove was turned off right.

Cindy would become extremely fearful at times, often for no external reason. For example, on one clear summer day a few months before, she had become panicked over the possibility that a tornado might strike and had insisted that her family take shelter for several hours in the basement.

Causal factors in anxiety and avoidant disorders. A number of causal factors have been emphasized in explanations of the anxiety and avoidant disorders. The more important of them appear to be the following:

a) Unusual constitutional sensitivity, easy conditionability by aversive stimuli, and the buildup and generalization of "surplus fear reactions."

b) Undermining of feelings of adequacy and security by early illnesses, accidents, or losses that involved pain and discomfort. The traumatic effect of such experiences is often due partly to such children's finding themselves in unfamiliar situations, as during hospitalization. The traumatic nature of certain life changes, such as moving away from friends and into a new situation, can have an intensely negative effect on a child's adjustment. Kashani and associates (1981a) found that the most common recent life event for children being seen in a psychiatric setting was moving to a new school district.

c) The "modeling" effect of an overanxious and protective parent who sensitizes the child to the dangers and threats of the outside world. Often the parent's overprotectiveness communicates a lack of confidence in the child's ability to cope, thus reinforcing the child's feelings of inadequacy.

d) The failure of an indifferent or detached parent to provide adequate guidance for the child's development. Although the child is not necessarily rejected, neither is he or she adequately supported in mastering essential competencies and in gaining a positive self-concept. Repeated experiences of failure, stemming from poor learning skills, may lead to subsequent patterns of anxiety or withdrawal in the face of "threatening" situations.

Sometimes children are made to feel that they must earn their parents' love and respect through outstanding achievement, especially in school. Such children tend to be overcritical of themselves and to feel intensely anxious and devaluated when they perceive themselves as failing. These children are perfectionists who may actually do well but are left with a feeling of failure because they are sure they should have done better.

e) Inadequate interpersonal patterns, which typically extend beyond the family. The withdrawal or avoidant disorder, in particular, "occurs in children who have found human contact more frustrating than rewarding" (Jenkins, 1970, p. 141). For the overanxious child, interpersonal relationships may be somewhat less aversive than for the withdrawn child; nevertheless, they are probably not actually satisfactory.

The various causal factors we have been discussing in relation to the anxiety and withdrawal disorders of childhood can obviously occur in differing degrees and combinations. All of them, however, are consistent with the view that these disorders essentially result from maladaptive learning.

Treatment and outcomes. The anxiety and withdrawal disorders of childhood may continue into adolescence and young adulthood—the first leading to neurotic avoidance behavior and the latter to increasingly idiosyncratic thinking and behavior. Typically, however, this is not the case. As such children grow and have wider interactions in school and peer-group activities, they are likely to benefit from such corrective experiences as making friends and succeeding at given tasks. Teachers have become more and more aware of the needs of both overanxious and shy, withdrawn children—and of ways of

HIGHLIGHT
Behavioral treatment of an acquired anxiety

The following case of functional dysphagia (fear of swallowing) as described by Carstens (1982) illustrates both the rapid acquisition of an anxiety and the effective use of behavioral treatment methods in bringing about anxiety reduction and reeducation.

"A 12-year-old boy whose family belonged to a large Health Maintenance Organization (HMO) choked severely on a bite of pizza, which was removed through use of the Heimlich maneuver. Later he reported that he felt as though he were going to die at the time he choked. In the days that followed he developed a feeling that something was stuck in his throat, and he began to avoid solid foods that needed to be chewed, especially pizza. He came to the emergency room with a complaint of something stuck in his throat. No object was found, and he was subsequently referred to a number of physicians in various specialties, none of whom found a physical explanation for the disorder. . . . The consensus diagnosis was functional dysphagia.

The patient was referred to the psychosocial services department of the HMO four months after the onset of symptoms. At that time his weight was 104 lb, a loss of 27 lb from his documented weight at first report of symptoms. He was eating only soft or ground foods, and avoided all hard or chewy foods because he was afraid they would stick in his throat. The dysphagia appeared to be clearly related to the anxiety experienced during the choking incident, which appeared to have generalized from pizza to all solid food. It was hypothesized that his stress led to a pharyngeal spasm during or after the esophageal phase of swallowing, which further reinforced his anxiety and avoidance. It was further hypothesized that reeducation in correct chewing and swallowing, combined with an overcorrection procedure using relaxation and correct swallowing as competing behavior, would resolve the problem.

In a single 90-minute treatment session, the boy's only direct contact with the author, he was taught the following regimen:

1. He was to relax while eating, leaning forward in his chair and relaxing his shoulders.
2. Before he ate, and whenever he felt tension in his shoulders or throat while eating, he was to take a series of four deep breaths, exhaling slowly, and saying the word "heavy" silently to himself as he breathed, relaxing his shoulders and throat as he did.
3. He was to chew each bite of solid food 20 times before swallowing.
4. When the "stuck" feeling occurred, he was to relax and take ten "correct" swallows of water, in order to practice swallowing without tension. He was then to resume eating solid food.
5. He was to serve himself a full meal three times each day and finish the entire helping of all foods.
6. He was to eat no sweets until completing his meal.
7. He was to seek out and correctly eat previously avoided foods.

At the end of the session, the boy carefully consumed an entire sandwich (from a vending machine) with no "stuck" feeling or anxiety reported. He was given a written copy of instructions to follow.

The patient was asked to call in every day to report his progress, but he failed to do so. When contacted five days after the session, his father reported that he was eating "at will" and had eaten previously avoided foods such as ham, fried chicken, hamburger, and even pizza since beginning the program. The patient said, "I'm eating everything and it feels good, too!" Two days later, telephone follow-up indicated good compliance with the program, and a weight of 108 lb, a 4-lb gain. He continued to "eat everything." Follow-up at six months after treatment indicated a weight of 120 lb, with no resumption of the difficulties. The boy was eating all solid foods, with no discomfort or anxiety." (pp. 195–96)

helping them—and often are able to ensure success experiences for such children and to foster constructive interpersonal relationships. Behavior therapy procedures, employed in structured group experiences within educational settings, can often help speed up and ensure favorable outcomes. Such procedures include assertiveness training, help with mastering essential competencies, and desensitization (see **HIGHLIGHT** on this page.)

This last procedure may be limited in its application to young children, however, for a number of reasons, including the inability of younger children to relax while imagining emotionally charged stimuli (Hatzenbuehler & Schroeder, 1978). With children, desensitization procedures must be explicitly tailored to the particular problem, and *in vivo* methods (using graded real-life situations) may be more effective than use of imagined situations. For example, Montenegro (1968) described the successful treatment of a six-year-old boy, Romeo, who showed pathological anxiety when he was separated from his mother. The treatment included the following procedures.

> a) Exposure of the child to a graded series of situations involving the actual fear-arousing stimulus—that is, separation from the mother for increasingly longer intervals.
> b) Use of food during these separations as an anxiety inhibitor—which might involve taking the child to the hospital cafeteria for something to eat.
> c) Instruction of the parents on how to reduce the child's excessive dependence on the mother—for example, through letting him learn to do things for himself.

After ten consecutive sessions, Romeo's separation anxiety was reduced to the point that he could stay home with a competent babysitter for an hour, and then for increasingly longer periods. During the summer he was enrolled in a vacation church school, which he enjoyed; and when the new semester began at public school, he entered the first grade and made an adequate adjustment. It should be emphasized that the cooperation of the parents—particularly the mother—was a key factor in the treatment.

Pervasive developmental disorders

The DSM-III category involving pervasive developmental disorders includes several severe psychological disorders marked by serious distortions in psychological functioning. These problems cover a wide range of behaviors, including deficits in language, perceptual, and motor development; defective reality testing; and inability to function in social situations. The term *pervasive developmental disorder* is new with DSM-III, although the disorders included under this category have a long history under the names symbiotic psychosis in children and

early infantile autism. The term *pervasive developmental disorders* was chosen over other possibilities because it focuses on the severe and extensive developmental deficits present in children with the disorders.

The problems considered pervasive developmental disorders are Axis I disorders and should not be confused with the specific developmental disorders included in Axis II of DSM-III. The latter consist of developmental delays—for example, in language acquisition—that have an impact on the treatment of the disorder but do not constitute *symptoms* that can be entered on Axis I.

We shall focus here on the pervasive developmental disorder that has received the greatest amount of attention from researchers—*infantile autism.*

Infantile autism. The following illustrates the typical behavior of an autistic child:

The boy is five years old. When spoken to, he turns his head away. Sometimes he mumbles unintelligibly. He is neither toilet trained nor able to feed himself. He actively resists being touched. He dislikes sounds. He cannot relate to others and avoids looking anyone in the eye. He often engages in routine manipulative activities, such as dropping an object, picking it up, and dropping it again. While seated, he often rocks back and forth in a rhythmic motion for hours. Any change in routine is highly upsetting to him. He is in a school for severely psychotic children at UCLA. His diagnosis is childhood autism.

Autism in infancy and childhood was first described by Kanner (1943). It afflicts some 80,000 American children—about 1 child in 2500—and occurs about four or five times more frequently among boys than girls (Schreibman & Koegel, 1975; Werry, 1979). It is identified before the child is 30 months of age (Rutter, 1978) and often is apparent in the early weeks of life. Autistic children come from all socioeconomic levels, ethnic backgrounds, and family patterns. It was once believed that autism was more prevalent among families in upper socioeconomic levels; however, this finding has recently been explained by the particular sampling methods employed in earlier studies (Wing, 1980).

Clinical picture in autism. In autism, the child seems apart or aloof from others, even in the earliest stages of life; consequently, this disorder is often referred to as early infantile autism. Mothers remember such babies as never being "cuddly," never reaching out when being picked up, never smiling or looking at them while being fed, and never appearing to notice the comings and goings of other persons. In fact, autistic children do not evidence any need for affection or contact with anyone, usually not even seeming to know or care who their parents are.

Absence or severely restricted use of speech is characteristic of autistic children. If speech is present, it is almost never used to communicate except in the most rudimentary fashion, as by saying "yes" in answer to a question or by the echolalic (parrotlike) repetition of a few words. Recently, research has focused on trying to understand if echolalia in autistic children is functional. Echolalic verbalizations, previously believed to be meaningless, have been subjected to extensive analysis according to tone, latency, and other speech characteristics (Prizant & Duchan, 1981). The researchers concluded that, far from being meaningless, these verbalizations could aid the clinician or researcher in understanding the communicative and cognitive functioning of autistic children.

Often autistic children show an active aversion to auditory stimuli, crying even at the sound of a parent's voice. However, the pattern is not always consistent: autistic children "may at one moment be severely agitated or panicked by a very soft sound and at another time be totally oblivious to loud noise" (Ritvo & Ornitz, 1970, p. 6).

Self-stimulation is characteristic of these children, usually taking the form of such repetitive movements as head banging, spinning, and rocking, which may continue by the hour. Other bizarre as well as repetitive behavior is typical. This is well described by Gajzago and Prior (1974) in the case of a young autistic boy:

"A was described as a screaming, severely disturbed child who ran around in circles making high-pitched sounds for hours. He also liked to sit in boxes, under mats, and [under] blankets. He habitually piled up all furniture and bedding in the center of the room. At times he was thought deaf though he also showed extreme fear of loud noises. He refused all food except in a bottle, refused to wear clothes, chewed stones and paper, whirled himself, and spun objects. . . . He played repetitively with the same toys for months, lining things in rows, collected objects such as bottle tops, and insisted on having two of everything, one

The autistic child characteristically shows little need for affection or personal contact of any kind.

in each hand. He became extremely upset if interrupted and if the order or arrangement of things were altered" (p. 264).

In contrast to the behavior just described, some autistic children are skilled at fitting objects together. Thus, their performance on puzzles or form boards may be average or above. However, even in the manipulation of objects, difficulty with meaning is apparent. For example, when pictures are to be arranged in an order that tells a story, the autistic child shows a marked deficiency in performance.[6]

When compared with other groups of children on cognitive or intellectual tasks, autistic children often show impairment (James & Barry, 1981). Boucher (1981) found autistic children significantly impaired on memory tasks when compared with both normal and retarded children.

Many autistic children become preoccupied with and form strong attachments to unusual objects such as rocks, light switches, film nega-

---

[6]Although some have regarded autistic children as potentially of normal intelligence, this view has been challenged by a number of investigators who consider many if not most of these children to be mentally retarded (Goodman, 1972). Some autistic children, however, show markedly discrepant abilities. In this context, Goodman described the case of an "autistic-savant" who showed unusual ability at an early age in calendar calculating (rapidly determining the day of any calendar date in history) as well as in other areas, such as naming the capitals of most states and countries. Yet his language development was severely retarded, and he showed the indifference to others and related symptoms characteristic of autistic children.

tives, or keys. In some instances, the object is so large or bizarre that merely carrying it around interferes with other activities. When their preoccupation with the object is disturbed—for example, by its removal or by attempts to substitute something in its place—or when anything familiar in their environment is altered even slightly, they may have a violent temper tantrum or a crying spell that continues until the familiar situation is restored. Thus, autistic children are often said to be "obsessed with the maintenance of sameness."

Finally, and of key importance, autistic children seem to have a blurred and undifferentiated concept of self. Apparently they do not perceive themselves as the center of their world and lack a central reference point for "anchoring" or integrating perceptions. Bettelheim (1967, 1974) has referred to this condition as "the absence of I" or "the empty fortress."

In summary, autistic children typically show difficulties in relationships to other people, in perceptual-cognitive functioning, in language development, and in development of a sense of identity (L. K. Wing, 1976). They also engage in bizarre and repetitive activities and demonstrate a fascination with unusual objects and an obsessive need to maintain the sameness of the environment. This is indeed a heavy set of handicaps.

Because the clinical picture in autism tends to blend almost imperceptibly with that in childhood schizophrenia, a differential diagnosis is often difficult to make. The chief distinguishing feature appears to be the age of onset, with autism becoming evident very early and schizophrenia appearing more gradually and much later, after several years of apparently normal development (see **HIGHLIGHT** on this page). As Bettelheim (1969) has put it, "While the schizophrenic child withdraws from the world, the autistic child fails to ever enter it" (p. 21).

Causal factors in autism.

No brain pathology has been delineated in infant or childhood autism; and since it does not run in families, it cannot be attributed directly to a hereditary defect. In their review of genetic factors in autism and childhood schizophrenia, Hanson and Gottesman (1976) found no evidence for a genetic basis of autism. The possibility remains, however, that defective genes or damage from

HIGHLIGHT
Childhood schizophrenia

Schizophrenia in childhood is found less frequently than autism. The symptomatic behavior in childhood schizophrenia is similar to that in autism, but the onset is gradual and occurs later—usually after the age of 10 or in adolescence. Typically, schizophrenic children have undergone a period of seemingly normal development before beginning to show withdrawal, thought disturbances, and inappropriate emotional behavior. Brodie (1981) concluded that even though genetic factors are influential in childhood schizophrenia, environmental influences appear necessary for the disorder to become manifest.

The long-range prognosis in childhood schizophrenia appears only slightly more favorable than in autism (Bender, 1973; Roff, 1974). The major tranquilizing drugs so helpful in the treatment of adult schizophrenic patients have not proved effective with either autistic or schizophrenic children, although they do have a calming effect.

A more detailed comparison of autism and childhood psychoses may be found in Rutter and Schopler (1978), Rutter (1977), and L. K. Wing (1976).

radiation or other conditions during prenatal development may play a key role in the etiological pattern. Thus, while Judd and Mandell (1968) failed to find significant chromosomal abnormalities in a carefully selected group of 11 autistic children, subtler constitutional defects cannot be ruled out. In fact, most investigators believe that autism begins with some type of inborn defect that impairs the infant's perceptual-cognitive functioning—the ability to process incoming stimulation and to relate to the world.

In his early studies of childhood autism, Kanner (1943) concluded that an innate disorder in the child is exacerbated by a cold and unresponsive mother, the first factor resulting in social withdrawal and the second tending to maintain the isolation syndrome. However, most investigators have failed to find the parents of autistic children to be "emotional refrigerators" (Schreibman & Koegel, 1975; Wolff & Morris, 1971). In a well-controlled study, McAdoo and De Myer (1978) found that the personality characteristics of parents of autistic children were not significantly different from those of parents of other types of disturbed children. He also discovered that the mothers of both autistic and disturbed children had significantly fewer psychological problems than did mothers who were themselves receiving treatment.

As Harlow (1969) has somewhat wryly pointed out, it is often extremely difficult to pinpoint cause and effect in studying relationships between mother and child:

"Possibly . . . some children are rendered autistic by maternal neglect and insufficiency, but it is even more likely that many more mothers are rendered autistic because of an inborn inability of their infants to respond affectionately to them in any semblance of an adequate manner" (p. 29).

On the basis of their intensive study of 53 autistic children, Clancy and McBride (1969) suggested that the usual picture of the autistic child as lacking in language ability and being wholly withdrawn is probably oversimplified. They found that at least some autistic children *do* comprehend language, even though they may not use it to express themselves. These investigators also pointed to the occasional normal commencement of language development, followed by its disappearance as the autistic process becomes manifest. Perhaps even more significantly, they found evidence that the autistic children they studied were very much aware of—and actively involved with—their environment:

"Autistic children actively seek to arrange the environment on their terms, and so as to exclude certain elements, e.g., intervention from other people and variety in any aspect of routine. They show a high degree of skill in manipulating people for their ends, and again this skill is usually obvious in the first year of life. In a socially inverted manner the children are as active and resourceful as normal children" (p. 243).

Tinbergen (1974) came to a somewhat similar conclusion, viewing autism as the result of an approach-avoidance conflict in which the child's natural tendency to explore and relate to the world has been overbalanced by aversive experiences and fear. According to this view, instead of venturing forth into the world, such children withdraw into a world they create for themselves. However, withdrawal is not as haphaz-

ard or disorderly as it may seem; rather, it involves systematic avoidance of many stimuli and events in the real world, including people.

Clearly, much remains to be learned about the etiology of childhood autism. It would appear, however, that this disorder begins with an inborn defect or defects in brain functioning, regardless of what other causal factors may subsequently become involved (Demyer, Hingtgen, & Jackson, 1981).

Treatment and outcomes.   A variety of procedures have been used to treat autistic children. Bettelheim (1967, 1969, 1974), at the Orthogenic School of the University of Chicago, has reported some success in treating autistic children with a program of warm, loving acceptance accompanied by reinforcement procedures (see **HIGHLIGHT** beginning on page 568). Similarly, Marchant and her associates (1974) in England have reported improvement using a method for introducing "graded change" into the environment of autistic children, thus tending to shift their behavior gradually from self-defeating to growth-oriented activities.

Another approach to treating autistic children is called *structural therapy.* Here the environment is structured to provide spontaneous physical and verbal stimulation to the children in a playful and game-like manner. The goal of this approach is to increase the amount and variety of stimuli for these children, gradually making them more aware of themselves and their environment and more related to it. The results of structural therapy have been encouraging, with 12 of 21 cases considered improved enough to be able to return home after the three-year treatment program (Ward, 1978).

In an extensive study of autistic children who were mentally retarded, socially unresponsive, and behaviorally disturbed, Bartak and his colleagues at the Maudsley Hospital in England obtained significant results with educational procedures. Children who were assigned to a structured treatment unit focusing on formal schooling showed greater progress than those placed in units stressing play therapy, either free or structured (Bartak & Rutter, 1973; Russell, 1975). As a result of this work, Bartak (1978) suggests a "qualified optimism" for the educational progress of autistic children.

Behavior therapy in an institutional setting

Nadia, an autistic girl from Britain, drew the sketch shown at top left when she was only four years old. Her drawings—done in ballpoint pen—show a remarkably precocious understanding of the principles of perspective, foreshortening, and movement. At the age of seven and a half, Nadia entered a school for autistic children, where her learning skills improved while her artistic abilities suffered a decline. The man on the horse (top right) was drawn when Nadia was five (before her enrollment in the school). The drawing shown at left, done when Nadia was about eight, is a cruder treatment of the same subject.

has been used successfully in the elimination of self-injurious behavior, the mastery of the fundamentals of social behavior, and the development of some language skills (Lovaas, 1977; Lovaas, Schaeffer, & Simmons, 1974; Williams, Koegel, & Egel, 1981). One interesting finding of studies on the effectiveness of behavior therapy with institutionalized children is that children who were discharged to their parents continued to improve, whereas those who remained in the institution tended to lose much of what they had gained (Lovaas, 1977; Schreibman & Koegel, 1975).

Some of the most impressive results with autistic children have been obtained in projects that involve the parents in the treatment program. Treatment "contracts" with parents specify the desired behavior changes in the child and spell out the explicit techniques for bringing out these changes. Such contracting acknowledges the value of the parent as a potential change agent—in contrast with the previously held belief that the parents were somehow to blame for the child's disorder (Schopler, 1978).

Perhaps the most favorable results are those of Schreibman and Koegel (1975), who reported successful outcomes in the treatment of 10 of 16 autistic children. These investigators relied heavily on the use of parents as therapists in reinforcing normal behavior on the part of their children, and concluded that autism is potentially a "defeatable horror."

It is too early to evaluate the long-term effectiveness of these newer treatment methods or the degree of improvement they actually bring about. Prognosis for autistic children, particularly for children showing the symptoms before the age of two, is poor (Hoshino et al., 1980). Traditionally, the long-term results of the treatment of autism have been unfavorable. Even with intensive long-term care in a clinical facility, where gratifying improvements may be brought about in specific behaviors, the child is a long way from becoming "normal." Gillberg and Schauman (1981) have noted that some autistic children make substantial improvement during childhood, only to deteriorate, showing symptom aggravation, at the onset of puberty. Less than one fourth of the autistic children who receive treatment appear to attain even marginal adjustment in later life.

Other symptom disorders

The behavior disorders we shall deal with here—enuresis, encopresis, sleepwalking, nail-biting, and tics—typically involve a single outstanding symptom rather than a pervasive maladaptive pattern.

Enuresis.   The term *enuresis* refers to the habitual involuntary discharge of urine after the age of three. It may occur during the day but is most common at night (bed-wetting). Among older children, enuresis often occurs in conjunction with dreams in which they imagine that they are urinating in a toilet, only to awaken and discover that they have wet the bed. Enuresis may vary in frequency, from nightly occurrence to occasional instances when the individual is under considerable stress or is unduly tired. Commonly, enuresis occurs from two to five times a week. The actual incidence of enuresis is unknown, but it has been estimated that some 4 to 5 million children and adolescents in the United States suffer from the inconvenience and embarrassment of this disorder (Turner & Taylor, 1974). A survey of children four years of age or older who were patients in nine medical centers found that 25 percent were enuretic (Hague et al., 1981).

Although enuresis may result from a variety of organic conditions, such as disturbed cerebral control of the bladder (Kaada & Retvedt, 1981), most investigators have pointed to a number of other possible causal factors: (a) faulty learning, resulting in the failure to acquire a needed adaptive response—that is, inhibition of reflex bladder emptying; (b) personal immaturity, associated with or stemming from emotional problems; and (c) disturbed family interactions, particularly those that lead to sustained anxiety and/or hostility. In some instances, a child may regress to bed-wetting when a new baby enters the family and becomes the center of attention. Children also may resort to bed-wetting when they feel hostile toward their parents and want to get even, realizing that such behavior is annoying and upsetting to adults. In adolescence and adulthood, enuresis is often associated with other psychological problems. Research evidence supports a multiplicity of possible causes for enuresis, with many cases being explained by either environmental factors or maturational lags (Christie, 1981).

Conditioning procedures have proven effective in the treatment of enuresis (Doleys, 1979). For example, a child may sleep on an electrified mattress that rings an alarm at the first few drops of urine, thus awakening the child and eliciting a reflex inhibition of urination. Fortunately, with or without treatment the incidence of enuresis tends to decrease significantly with age. Among 7-year-olds, an estimated 21.9 percent of boys and 15.5 percent of girls are enuretic, compared with only 3 percent of boys and 1.7 percent of girls at age 14 (Rutter, Yule, & Graham, 1973) and only 1 percent or less of young adults (Murphy et al., 1971). Nevertheless, many experts believe that enuresis should be treated in childhood, since there is currently no way of identifying which children will remain enuretic into adulthood.

HIGHLIGHT

Joey: a "mechanical boy"

These four pictures were drawn by Joey, an autistic boy who entered the Sonia Shankman Orthogenic School of the University of Chicago at the age of 9. His unusual case history has been reported by Bettelheim (1959).

Joey presumably denied his own emotions because they were unbearably painful. Apparently not daring to be human in a world which he felt had rejected him, Joey withdrew into a world of fantasy and perceived himself as a machine that "functioned as if by remote control." This idea is brought out in the drawing at right—a self-portrait in which Joey depicts himself as an electrical robot. Bettelheim interpreted this portrait as symbolizing Joey's rejection of human feelings.

So elaborately constructed and acted out was Joey's mechanical character that "entering the dining room, for example, he would string an imaginary wire from his 'energy source'—an imaginary electric outlet—to the table. There he 'insulated' himself with paper napkins and finally plugged himself in. Only then could Joey eat, for he firmly believed that the 'current' ran his ingestive apparatus" (p.117).

Joey's performance was convincing—so much so that others found themselves responding to him as a mechanical boy rather than as a human being: " . . . one had to look twice to be sure there was neither wire nor outlet nor plug. Children and members of our staff . . . avoided stepping on the 'wires' for fear of interrupting what seemed the source of his very life." When his machinery was idle, Joey "would sit so quietly that he would disappear from the focus of the most conscientious observation. Yet in the next moment he might be 'working' and the center of our captivated attention" (p.117).

In his report on Joey, Bettelheim alluded to the painfully slow process by which Joey was eventually able to establish true relations with other human beings. Three of the drawings (on facing page) depict part of the process. In the earliest of the three (top left) Joey portrays himself "as an electrical 'papoose,' completely enclosed, suspended in empty space and operated by wireless signals." In the next one (bottom left) he apparently demonstrates increasing self-esteem, for although he is still operated by wireless signals, he is much larger in stature. In the final drawing, Joey depicts "the machine which controls him," but in this one, unlike the previous drawings, "he has acquired hands with which he can manipulate his immediate environment" (p.119).

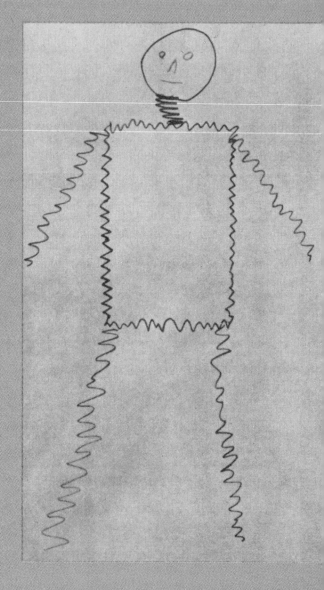

When Joey was 12—three years after he had entered the school—". . . he made a float for our Memorial Day parade. It carried the slogan: 'Feelings are more important than anything under the sun.' Feelings, Joey had learned, are what make for humanity; their absence, for a mechanical existence. With this knowledge Joey entered the human condition" (p. 127).

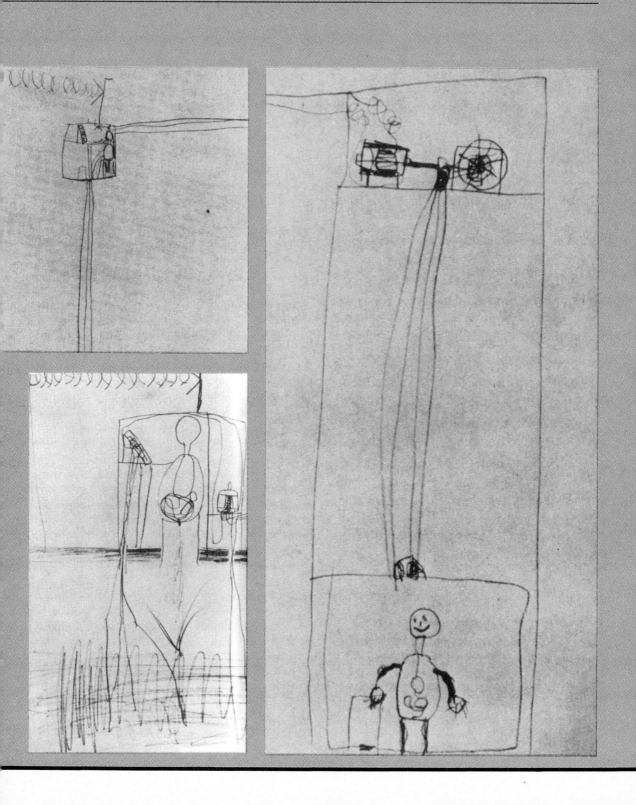

Encopresis. Children who regularly have bowel movements in their clothing after age 3 are referred to as *encopretic.* This condition is less common than enuresis. However, about 2.3 percent of 8-year-old boys and 0.7 percent of 8-year-old girls are encopretic (Bellman, 1966). The list of following characteristics of encopretics was provided by Levine (1976) from a study of 102 cases of encopretic children:

a) The average age was 7, with a range from ages 4 to 13.

b) About one-third of encopretic children were also enuretic.

c) A large sex difference was found, with about six times more boys than girls in the sample.

d) Many of the children soiled their clothing when they were under stress. A common time was in the late afternoon after school. Very few children actually had this problem at school.

e) Most of the children reported that they did not know when they needed to have a bowel movement.

Many encopretic children suffer from constipation; thus an important element in the diagnosis of the disorder involves a physical examination to determine whether there are physiological factors contributing to the disorder. Treatment of encopresis usually involves both medical and psychological aspects. Levine and Bakow (1975) found that of the encopretic children they studied who were treated by medical and behavioral procedures, more than half were cured—that is, no additional incidents occurred within six months following treatment—and an additional 25 percent were improved.

Sleepwalking (somnambulism). Statistics are meager, but it would appear that some 5 percent of children experience regular or periodic sleepwalking episodes. Children subject to this problem usually go to sleep in a normal manner but arise during the second or third hour thereafter and walk in their sleep. They may walk to another room of the house or even outside and may engage in rather complex activities. Finally they return to bed, and in the morning remember nothing that has taken place.

During the sleepwalking, their eyes are partially or fully open; and they avoid obstacles, hear when spoken to, and ordinarily respond to commands, such as to return to bed. Shaking sleepwalkers will usually awaken them, and they will be surprised and perplexed at finding themselves in an unexpected place. Such sleepwalking episodes usually last from 15 minutes to a half-hour.

The risk of injury during sleepwalking episodes is illustrated by the following case study.

". . . 14-year-old Donald Elliot got up from his bunk in his sleep, looked in the refrigerator, then, still asleep, walked out the back door. It would have been just another sleepwalking episode except that Donald was in a camper-pickup truck traveling 50 miles an hour on the San Diego Freeway. Miraculously, he escaped with cuts and bruises. But his experience, and that of many other sleepwalkers, disproves one of the myths about somnambulism: that people who walk in their sleep don't hurt themselves." (Taves, 1969, p. 41)

The causes of sleepwalking are not fully understood. Kales et al. (1966) have shown that sleepwalking takes place during NREM (non–rapid eye movement) sleep, but its relationship to dreaming remains unclear. In general, it would appear that sleepwalking is related to some anxiety-arousing situation that has just occurred or is expected to occur in the near future.

Very little attention has been given to the treatment of sleepwalking. However, Clement (1970) has reported on the treatment of a seven-year-old boy through behavior therapy, as described in the **HIGHLIGHT** on page 571. And Nagaraja (1974) has reported the successful treatment of an eight-year-old boy and a nine-year-old girl with a combination of tranquilizers and psychotherapy. But a good deal of additional research is needed before we can determine the most effective treatment procedures for sleepwalking.

Nail-biting. Probably about a fifth of all children bite their fingernails at one time or another. The incidence appears to be highest among stutterers, children reared in institutions, and children confronted with stressful demands. Although about as many girls as boys bite their nails at early ages, males outnumber females in later age groups.

Nail-biting typically occurs in situations associated with anxiety and/or hostility and appears to be a method of tension reduction that pro-

HIGHLIGHT

Treatment of sleepwalking utilizing conditioning procedures

Bobby, a seven-year-old boy, walked in his sleep on an average of four times a week. His mother kept a record indicating that Bobby's sleepwalking episodes were associated with nightmares, perspiring, and talking in his sleep. During the actual sleepwalking Bobby usually was glassy-eyed and unsteady on his feet. On one occasion he started out the front door. The sleepwalking had commenced about six weeks before the boy was brought for therapy, and usually an episode would begin about 45 to 90 minutes after he had gone to bed.

During treatment the therapist learned that just before each sleepwalking episode Bobby usually had a nightmare about being chased by "a big black bug." In his dream Bobby thought "the bug would eat off his legs if it caught him" (Clement, 1970, p. 23). Bobby's sleepwalking episodes usually showed the following sequence: after his nightmare began, he perspired freely, moaned and talked in his sleep, tossed and turned, and finally got up and walked through the house. He was amnesic for the sleepwalking episode when he awoke the next morning.

Assessment data revealed no neurological or other medical problems and indicated that Bobby was of normal intelligence. However, he was found to be "a very anxious, guilt-ridden little boy who avoided performing assertive and aggressive behaviors appropriate to his age and sex" (p. 23). Assertiveness training and related measures were used but were not effective. The therapist then focused treatment on having Bobby's mother awaken the boy each time he showed signs of an impending episode. Washing Bobby's face with cold water and making sure he was fully awake, the mother would return him to bed, where he was "to hit and tear up a picture of the big black bug." At the start of the treatment program, Bobby had made up several of these drawings.

Eventually, the nightmare was associated with awakening, and Bobby learned to wake up on most occasions when he was having a bad dream. Clement considered the basic behavior therapy model in this case to follow that used in the conditioning treatment for enuresis, where a waking response is elicited by an intense stimulus just as urination is beginning and becomes associated with and eventually prevents nocturnal bed-wetting.

---

vides the individual with "something to do" (thumb-sucking is probably similarly motivated). It represents a learned maladaptive habit that is reinforced and maintained by its tension-reducing properties.

Little attention has been devoted to the treatment of nail-biting. While mild tranquilizers may prove helpful, it is generally agreed that restraint and bitter-tasting applications have yielded poor results. Behavior therapy appears to be more effective. Of course, initial development of this habit in a child may be checked if the child is helped to feel more adequate and secure, especially if he or she is going through some particularly difficult stress period.

Tics.   A tic is a persistent, intermittent muscle twitch or spasm, usually limited to a localized muscle group. The term *tic* is used rather broadly to include blinking the eye, twitching the mouth, licking the lips, shrugging the shoulders, twisting the neck, clearing the throat, blowing through the nostrils, and grimacing, among other actions. In some instances, as in clearing the throat, the individual may be aware of the tic when it occurs; but usually he or she performs the act habitually and does not notice it. In fact, many individuals do not even realize they have a tic unless someone brings it to their attention. Tics occur most frequently between the ages of 6 and 14 (Schowalter, 1980).

The psychological impact tics can have on an adolescent is exemplified in the following case:

An adolescent who had wanted very much to be a teacher told the school counselor that he was thinking of giving up his plans. When asked the reason, he explained that several friends told him he had a persistent twitching of the mouth muscles when he answered questions in class. He had been unaware of this muscle twitch and even after being told about it could not tell when it took place. However, he became acutely self-conscious, and was reluctant to answer questions or enter into class discussions. As a result, his general level of tension increased, and so did the frequency of the tic—which now became apparent even when he was talking to his friends. Thus, a vicious circle had been established. Fortunately, it proved amenable to treatment by conditioning and assertiveness training.

Although some tics may have an organic basis, the great majority are psychological in origin—usually stemming from self-consciousness or tension in social situations. As in the case just described, the individual's awareness of the tic often increases the tension—and the tic. Tics have been successfully treated by means of drugs, psychotherapy, and conditioning techniques. Recently, Ollendick (1981) reported success with tics by using behavioral techniques of self-monitoring and overcorrection.

Planning better programs to help children and youth

In our discussion of several problems of childhood and adolescence, we have noted the wide range of treatment procedures that may be used as well as marked differences in outcomes. In concluding the chapter, let us note (a) certain special factors associated with the treatment of children, and (b) the new emphasis on "child advocacy" and the "rights of children," which involves a social commitment to provide conditions conducive to their optimal development.

Special factors associated with treatment for children

A number of special factors must be considered in relation to treatment for children.

1. *The child's inability to seek assistance.* The great majority of emotionally disturbed children who need assistance are not in a position to ask for it themselves or to transport themselves to and from child guidance clinics. Thus, unlike the adult or the adolescent, who usually can seek help during crisis periods, the child is dependent, primarily on his or her parents. Adults should realize when a child needs professional help and take the initiative in obtaining it. However, sometimes adults neglect this responsibility. Plotkin (1981) recently pointed out:

"Parents have traditionally had the right to consent to health services for their children. In situations where the interest of the parents and children differ the rule has had unfortunate consequences and has left treatment professionals in a quandary" (p. 121).

The legal literature identifies four areas in which the law permits treatment without parental consent—in the case of mature minors, in the case of emancipated minors, in emergency situations, and in situations in which a court orders treatment.[7] Many children, of course, come to the attention of treatment agencies as a consequence of school referrals, delinquent acts, or parental abuse.

2. *"Double deprivation" of children from pathogenic homes.* Many families provide an undesirable environment for their growing children. In fact, studies have shown that up to a fourth of our children may be living in inadequate homes (Joint Commission on the Mental Health of Children, 1968; Rutter, 1977). Yet the care of the child is traditionally the responsibility of the parents, and local and state agencies intervene only in extreme cases—usually those involving physical abuse. This means that children growing up in pathogenic homes are at a double disadvantage. Not only are they deprived from the standpoint of environmental influence on their personality development, but they also lack parents who will perceive their need for help and actively seek and participate in treatment programs.

3. *The need for treatment of the parents as well as the child.* Since most of the behavior disorders specific to childhood appear to grow out of pathogenic family interactions, it is usually essential for the parents, as well as the child, to receive treatment. In some instances, in fact, the treatment program may focus on the parents entirely (see **HIGHLIGHT** beginning on page 574).

---

[7]*Mature* minors are those considered to be capable of making decisions about themselves; *emancipated* minors are those children living independently—away from their parents.

Increasingly, then, the treatment of children has come to mean family therapy, in which one or both parents as well as the child and siblings may participate in all phases of the program. For working parents, however, and for parents who basically reject the child, such treatment may be difficult to arrange, especially in the case of poorer families, who lack transportation as well as money. Thus, both parental and economic factors help determine which emotionally disturbed children will receive assistance.

4. *The possibility of using parents as "change agents."* A recent trend, as we have seen, has been to teach the parents to be change agents. In essence, the parents are trained in techniques that enable them to help their child. Typically such training focuses on helping the parents understand the child's behavior disorder and learn to reinforce adaptive behavior while withholding reinforcement for undesirable behavior. Encouraging results have been obtained with parents who care about their children and want to help (Arnold, 1978; Atkeson & Forehand, 1978; Forehand et al., 1981; Johnson & Katz, 1973; Lexow & Aronson, 1975; Mash et al., 1976; O'Dell, 1974).

5. *The problem of placing the child outside the family.* Most communities have juvenile facilities that, day or night, will provide protective care and custody for child victims of unfit homes, abandonment, abuse, neglect, and related conditions. Depending on the home situation and the special needs of the child, he or she will later either be returned to the parents or placed elsewhere. In the latter instance, four types of facilities are commonly relied on: (a) a foster home; (b) a private institution for the care of children; (c) a county or state institution; or (d) the home of relatives. At any one time, about half a million children are living in foster-care facilities.

The quality of the child's new home, of course, is a crucial determinant of whether the child's problems will be alleviated or made worse by the placement. Although efforts are made to screen the placement facilities and maintain contact with the situation through follow-up visits, there have been too many reported cases of mistreatment of children placed in foster homes and institutions. Perhaps the most dramatic example of unintended harm from placement of children in foster homes was the large number of children who perished in the Jonestown murder-suicide in Guyana in 1978. These youngsters had been placed in the care of Reverend James Jones, who had received large amounts of money for their care.

In cases of child abuse or child abandonment or serious behavior problems of children that the parents cannot control, it has often been assumed that the only feasible action was to take the child out of the home and find a temporary substitute. With the children's own homes so obviously inadequate, the hope has been that a more stable outside placement would be better. But when children are taken from their own homes and placed in an impersonal institution that promptly tries to change them or in a series of foster homes where they obviously do not really belong, they are likely to feel rejected by their own parents, unwanted by their new caretakers or anyone else, rootless, constantly insecure—and lonely and bitter.

Accordingly, the trend today is toward **permanent planning.** First, every effort is made to hold the family together and give the parents the support and guidance they need to be adequate for childrearing. If this is impossible, then efforts are made to free the child legally for adoption and to find an adoptive home as soon as possible. This, of course, means that the public agencies need specially trained staffs with reasonable caseloads and access to resources the families they work with may need.

It was demonstrated in Oregon that when these conditions were met, 90 percent of a group of children in foster care could be either returned to their homes or placed for adoption (see **HIGHLIGHT** on page 576); and as a result the Children's Bureau of Health and Human Services is encouraging the agencies in the various states to move in this direction. Currently it is funding projects in several states to provide intensive support services to "families at risk" in order to prevent the need for outside placement by improving the quality of children's lives in their homes. It is hoped that these projects will both provide training for the staffs of various state agencies in the special skills needed for this kind of help and increase acceptance of the principle of permanent planning.

6. *The importance of intervening early before problems become acute.* Over the last 20 years, a primary concern of many researchers and clinicians has been to identify and provide early help

HIGHLIGHT
The problem of child abuse in contemporary society

There is a growing concern about child abuse in the United States. Over 200,000 cases are reported each year, and undoubtedly many more cases go unreported (Kempe & Kempe, 1979; President's Commission on Mental Health, 1978).

Of the reported cases, 20 to 40 percent of the children have been seriously injured. Although children and adolescents of all ages are physically abused, the most frequent cases involve children under three years of age. There is some evidence that boys are more often abused than girls. It is usually clear that children brought to the attention of legal agencies for abuse have been abused before.

In a recent survey of family violence, Gelles (1978) reported that violence well beyond ordinary physical punishment is a widespread phenomenon in parent-child relationships. Milder forms of punishment, Gelles found, were common among respondents; for example, 71 percent of parents reported having slapped or spanked their children, 46 percent reported pushing and shoving incidents, and around 10 percent reported having thrown something at their children. Gelles extrapolated estimates of serious violence from his survey to the general population and concluded that 46 percent of children had suffered serious abuse, such as being kicked, bitten, or punched by parents.

The seriousness of the problem of child abuse in our society was not realized until the 1960s, when researchers began to report case after case like the following two:

The mother of a 29-month-old boy claimed he was a behavior problem, beat him with a stick and screwdriver handle, dropped him on the floor, beat his head on the wall or threw him against it, choked him to force his mouth open to eat, and burned him on the face and hands. After she had severely beaten him, the mother found the child dead.

Because her 2½-year-old daughter did not respond readily enough to toilet training, the mother became indignant and in a fit of temper over the child's inability to control a bowel movement gave her an enema with near scalding water. To save the child's life a doctor was forced to perform a colostomy (Earl, 1965).

Abused children show impaired cognitive ability and memory when compared with controls (Friedrich, Einbender, & Luecke, 1983). Abused children are also likely to show problems in social development. Barahal, Waterman, and Martin (1981) found that abused children are particularly likely to feel that the outcomes of events are determined by external factors and are beyond their own control. In addition, abused children are dramatically less likely to assume personal responsibility and show less interpersonal sensitivity than control children. Abused children also tend to show more self-destructive behavior than non-abused control subjects (Green, 1978).

Since the 1960s a great deal of research has been aimed at finding out which parents abuse their children and why, in the hope that ultimately these parents can be stopped, or better yet prevented, from abusing their children. We now know that parents who physically abuse their children tend to be young, with the majority under 30. In the majority of the reported cases, they come from the lower socioeconomic levels, although this may only reflect the fact that these parents are more likely to be reported to legal authorities than middle-class parents. An important common

for children who are at special risk. Rather than wait until these children develop acute psychological problems that may require therapy or major changes in living arrangements, psychologists are attempting to identify conditions in such children's lives that seem likely to bring about or maintain behavior problems and, where such conditions exist, to intervene before the child's development has been seriously dis-

torted. An example of this approach is provided in the work of Wallerstein and Kelly (1979):

These researchers identified children who were at risk for psychological disturbance as a result of the fact that their parents were going through a divorce. Each of the 66 participating families was seen by a clinician, and the children were seen separately for several sessions. The goals of the counseling sessions were to provide the children with a means of expressing their

factor among families with abusing parents is a higher-than-average degree of frustration; many stressors are present in their lives, including marital discord, high unemployment, and alcohol abuse (Egeland, Cicchetti, & Taraldson, 1976). Many incidents of physical abuse occur as parental reactions to the child's misbehavior in areas such as fighting, sexual behavior, aggression, and so on (Herrenkohl, Herrenkohl, & Egolf, 1983). Although no clear and consistent personality pattern emerges as typical of child-abusing parents, they seem to show a higher-than-average rate of psychological disturbance (Serrano et al., 1979). There is some evidence from personality testing to show that they tend to be aggressive, nonconforming, selfish, and lacking in appropriate impulse control (Lund, 1975).

Knowledge about causal factors in child abuse is limited and incomplete, since most studies have involved retrospective analysis of cases identified through legal agencies. However, in a study currently in progress, 275 families in a population generally at risk for child abuse were identified before the birth of the child. From this group, the investigators then identified the 25 mothers at highest risk for child abuse and the 25 mothers most likely *not* to be child abusers.

These two groups have now been followed over several years. Eight of the highest-risk group have actually abused their children; none of the other group has done so. There are many striking differences between the two groups. The mothers in the group identified as at lowest risk tend to be older, to show more understanding of the psychological complexity of their children, to have better caretaking skills, and to show more positive feeling for their children. The other mothers, in general, live a more chaotic life. Over

twice as many are single (74 percent as compared with 32 percent). They are also more involved in disrupted relationships, physical fights, and heavy drinking in the immediate family. Continuing analysis of how the quality of care, the nature of the mother-child interaction, and personality characteristics of family members relate to child abuse in this group is planned (Egeland & Brunnquell, 1979).

Several kinds of efforts are being made to reduce the incidence of child abuse:

1. Community education to increase public awareness of the problem. Television advertisements have been especially effective here.

2. Organization of child protection teams by many state and county welfare departments to investigate and intervene in reported cases of child abuse.

3. Teams of mental health specialists in many community mental health centers to evaluate and provide psychological treatment for both abused children and their parents.

4. Parent support groups, often made up of former child abusers, who can offer abusing parents or those at risk for child abuse alternative ways of behaving toward their children.

5. A legal requirement, in many communities, for physicians and other professionals to report cases of child abuse that come to their attention.

Through such efforts on many levels it is hoped that children will be spared abuse and that abusing or potentially abusing parents will be helped to be more adequate and nurturant.

---

worries and frustrations and to strengthen their resources for dealing with them.

In addition to the counseling sessions, there were several follow-up sessions after the divorce to examine the psychological changes in the children and the changes in the family structure over time. The interventions were judged to be successful in lowering the tension levels in the family situations and in enhancing the children's adjustment to their new living arrangements.

Such early intervention has the double goal of reducing the stressors in the child's life and strengthening the child's coping mechanisms. If successful, it can effectively reduce the number and intensity of later problems, thus averting much grief for both the individuals concerned and the broader society.

It is apparent that children's needs can be met only if there are adequate preventive and

HIGHLIGHT
Freeing children for permanent placement

Placement in a foster home, intended as a temporary expedient, too often is the beginning of a period of drifting from one foster home to another, denying the continuity in human relationships that the child acutely needs. In Oregon, staff members at the Regional Research Institute for Human Services carried out a pilot project to see whether it would be possible to reduce the numbers of children in foster care and give them permanent homes—either with their own parents or through adoption.

The project involved 509 children who at the start were in foster placement and were considered unlikely to return home. These cases were turned over to specially trained caseworkers, who made intensive efforts to locate the parent or parents and encourage their taking the child back, offering help to enable them to do so. Each case required a great deal of effort on the part of the caseworker: counseling, legal aid, and so on. Every means of encouragement was exhausted before the caseworker gave up and recommended that the child be placed for adoption.

Many of these parents developed new motivation for taking reponsibility for their children as a result of the help and support offered by the caseworkers, and three years after the project started, 131 of the children had been returned to their parents. An additional 184 had been adopted, with another 15 in the homes of relatives and 37 in contractual foster care. And 92 other children were moving toward one of these options, leaving only a probable 50 of the original 509 children for whom no permanent home seemed likely. This means a success rate of 90 percent.

Besides the immeasurable benefit to the children of at last being in permanent homes, the financial saving to the welfare system was also considerable. It was estimated that 4000 hours of foster care—at a cost of more than $1 million—had been saved. This suggests that some of the money now committed for foster care could be better spent in enabling staff members to work toward permanent planning for these children.

Interestingly, the new approach was also reflected in the fact that, in the state as a whole, fewer children were being placed in foster homes. Although foster care placement will remain an important option in some cases, it is encouraging to know that with concentrated effort by skilled staff, many children can be saved from "foster home drifting."

Based on Regional Research Institute for Human Services (1978).

treatment facilities for children and if it can be ensured that the children who need assistance will receive it. In our final section, we shall look at the leadership government agencies have been providing in spotlighting the special needs of children and youth, and we shall also discuss the responsibility of the society to meet those needs.

Child advocacy programs

Today there are nearly 75 million children and young people under 18 in the United States. This would indicate that a massive social commitment is needed not only to provide adequate treatment facilities for children with problems but also to provide the physical and social conditions that will foster the optimal development of all children.

Unfortunately, however, both treatment and preventive programs in our society have been—and remain—inadequate. In 1970 the National Institute of Mental Health pointed out that fewer than 1 percent of the disturbed children in our society were receiving any kind of treatment, and less than half of those were getting adequate help. In the same year, in its final report, *Crisis in Child Mental Health: Challenge for the 1970s*, the Joint Commission on the Mental Health of Children (1970) referred to our lack of commitment to our children and youth as a "national tragedy." The commission's report concluded:

"Either we permit a fifth of the nation's children to go down the drain—with all that this implies for public disorder and intolerable inhumanity—or we decide, once and for all, that the needs of children have first priority on the nation's resources" (p. 408).

Community centers are one means by which localities have sought to serve the needs of children. Cutbacks in funding for government and social-service agencies, however, have made survival more difficult for all child-oriented advocacy and service programs.

Unfortunately, eight years later, the President's Commission on Mental Health (1978) was still calling attention to the fact that children and adolescents were not receiving mental health services commensurate with their need. The commission's report recommended again that greater efforts and financial resources be expended to serve the mental health needs of children and youth. It appears, however, that the needed financial support and redirected program focuses have not materialized in the years since the report was issued.

There are stirrings, however. A new approach to meeting mental health needs, known as **advocacy**, has been developing in recent years. Advocacy attempts to help children or others receive services that they need but often are unable to obtain for themselves. For example, advocacy might involve representing a retarded or mentally ill individual at a commitment hearing. In some cases, advocacy seeks to better conditions for underserved populations by changing the system (Biklen, 1976).

Twice in recent years the federal government has established a National Center for Child Advocacy to coordinate the many kinds of work for children's welfare that had been going on in different government agencies. Both times the new agency proved ineffective and was given up after a year or so. Currently the physical welfare of children is the responsibility of the Children's Bureau of the Labor Department, and the mental health needs of children are the responsibility of the Alcoholism, Drug Abuse, and Mental Health Administration of the Public Health Service. Delinquents are dealt with by the Justice Department. This fragmentation in services for children means that different agencies serve different needs of children; there is no government agency charged with considering the whole child and planning comprehensively for children who need help.

Outside the federal government, until recently, advocacy efforts for children have been supported largely by legal and special-interest citizens' groups, such as the Children's Defense Fund, a public interest child advocacy organization based in Washington, D.C. Mental health professionals have typically not been involved. Today, however, there is greater interdisciplinary involvement in attempts to provide effective programs of advocacy for children.

In the state of New Jersey, for example, a Division of Mental Health Advocacy has been formed especially to provide advocacy services for disturbed and mentally handicapped children in the state. The staff consists of 15 lawyers and 16 mental health professionals. The aim of the agency is to provide two kinds of advocacy service: *individual case advocacy*, which provides help for individual clients in obtaining specific services or treatment, and *class advocacy*, in which the focus is on problems common to many children. An example of class advocacy would be establishing the right to treatment for a retarded child who is a ward of the state, in order to obtain better treatment programs for retarded children generally (Siggers, 1979). The improvement in the delivery of mental health services for children in New Jersey since this program was established argues persuasively for the involvement of mental health professionals in such advocacy efforts.

Unfortunately, although such programs have made important local gains toward bettering conditions for mentally disabled children, there is still a great deal of confusion, inconsistency, and uncertainty in the advocacy movement as a whole (Biklen, 1976). And the present mood at both federal and state levels seems to be to cut back on funds for social services.

In her presidential address to the Society of Pediatric Psychology, Magrab (1982) warned that the recent economic cutbacks in child-oriented programs and the fragmented nature of existing programs represent a challenge "to the very survival" of psychological services to children. She encouraged mental health and health-care professionals working in child advocacy not to become disheartened with the recent and continuing erosion of services but to exert a unified commitment to broadening advocacy programs by using community resources and by working with parents. Clearly, there is a great threat to existing programs for children and the coming years will require substantial effort on the part of professionals, parent groups, and enlightened elected officials to maintain past gains in services to children and to expand services to other needed areas.

Clearly, the challenge issued by the Joint Commission on the Mental Health of Children in 1970 has not been adequately answered over the subsequent period. However, some important beginning steps have been taken in the work toward child advocacy, the new efforts to identify and help high-risk children, and the present push toward permanent planning for children formerly sent to institutions or foster homes. If the direction and momentum of these efforts can be maintained and if sufficient financial support for them can be procured, the present decade could show substantially more gain in improving the psychological environment for children.

Summary

Traditionally, diagnosing behavior problems of children and adolescents has been a rather confused practice, in part because children have sometimes been viewed as "miniature" adults. It was not until the second half of the twentieth century that a diagnostic classification system focused clearly on the special problems of children.

Two broad approaches to the classification of childhood and adolescent behavior problems have been undertaken: the clinical-nosological approach, reflected most extensively in the DSM-III, and the multivariate approach. Both approaches to classification involve organized classes of symptoms that are based upon observations of behavior. In the clinical-nosological approach, symptoms of behavior problems are grouped together as syndromes based on clinical observations. In the multivariate approach, a broad range of symptoms and observations on cases are submitted to multivariate statistical techniques; the symptoms that group together make up the diagnostic classes referred to as "dimensions."

In this chapter the DSM-III classification system is followed in order to provide clinical descriptions of a wide range of child and adolescent behavior problems. Attention deficit disorder, or the hyperactive syndrome, is one of the more frequent behavior problems of childhood. In this disorder the child shows impulsive, overactive behavior that interferes with his or her ability to accomplish tasks. There is some controversy over the explicit criteria used to distinguish hyperactive children from "normal" children or from children who exhibit other behavior disorders such as conduct disorders. This lack of clarity in defining hyperactivity increases the difficulty of determining causal factors for the disorder. The major approaches to treating hyperactive children have been through medication and through behavior therapy. Using medications, such as amphetamines, with children is somewhat controversial. Behavior therapy, particularly cognitive-behavioral methods, has shown a great deal of promise in modifying the behavior of the hyperactive child.

Another common behavior problem among children and adolescents is that of conduct disorder. In this disorder, the child engages in persistent aggressive or antisocial acts. In cases where the child's misdeeds involve illegal activities, the terms "delinquent" or "juvenile delinquent" may be applied. A number of potential causes of conduct disorder or delinquent behavior have been determined, ranging from biological factors to personal pathology to social conditions. Treatment of conduct disorders and delinquent behavior is often frustrating and difficult; treatment is likely to be ineffective unless some means can be found for modifying the child's environment.

Another group of disorders, the anxiety disorders of childhood and adolescence, are quite different from the conduct disorders. Children and adolescents who suffer from these disorders typically do not cause difficulty for others through their aggressive conduct. Rather they are fearful, shy, withdrawn, insecure, and have difficulty adapting to outside demands. The anxiety disorders may be characterized by extreme anxiety, withdrawal, or avoidance behavior. Likely causes for these disorders are early family relationships that generate anxiety and prevent the child from developing more adaptive coping skills. Behavior therapy approaches—such as assertiveness training and desensitization—may be helpful in treating this kind of disorder.

Some of the most severe and inexplicable childhood disorders are the pervasive developmental disorders, the most prominent example of which is infantile autism. In these disorders, extreme maladaptive behavior occurs during the early years and prevents the affected children from developing psychologically. Autistic children, for example, seem to remain aloof from others, never responding or seemingly not caring about what goes on around them. Many never learn to speak. These disorders more than likely have a strong biological basis. Neither medical nor psychological treatment has been notably successful in helping children with pervasive developmental disorders.

Several other disorders of childhood involve behavior problems centering around a single outstanding symptom rather than pervasive maladaptive patterns. The symptoms may involve enuresis, encopresis, sleepwalking, nailbiting, or tics. In these disorders, treatment is generally more successful than in the other disorders described above.

There are special problems, and special opportunities, involved in treating the disorders of childhood and adolescence. The need for preventive and treatment programs for children is always growing, and in recent years the concept of "child advocacy" has become a reality in some states. Unfortunately, financial and other resources necessary for such services are not always readily available, and the future of programs for improving psychological environments for children remains uncertain.

Part 3

Assessment, treatment, and prevention

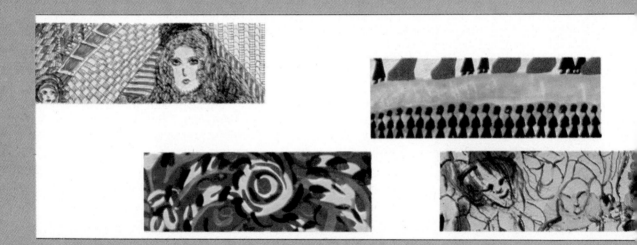

15

Clinical assessment

Gaston Teuscher, Dessin (1976). The son of a soldier in the Swiss army and a midwife of French ancestry, Teuscher (b. 1903) at an early age developed an ambivalent attitude toward women, an attitude that he traces back to his parents' strong desire to have a girl. He has never married, and has devoted much of his life to esoteric mathematical and philosophical pursuits. Teuscher began producing sketches and drawings in 1974, a practice that he continues to this day. He works at a prodigious rate on bits of crumpled paper, stained tablemats—i.e., on whatever materials come immediately to hand.

Clinical assessment is a complex task, yet it is one of the most important activities in clinical work. The thoroughness and accuracy of assessment can determine the extent to which an individual's problems are understood and how well his or her needs are met through therapy.

The goal of assessment is to identify and understand the individual's symptoms within the context of his or her overall level of functioning and environment. This includes determining the nature and severity of any maladaptive behavior and understanding the conditions that may have caused and/or be maintaining it. To do this, the clinician must gather, weigh, and synthesize as much information as possible about the client—usually within a brief period of time and often with limited information. The individual may manifest a perplexing array of psychological problems, and his or her medical and social history may be unknown. In addition, there may be seemingly unsolvable problems in the individual's life situation. Equally important to evaluate are the individual's strengths and resources, including such personal factors as motivation for treatment, capacity for change, ability to participate in the treatment program, and available support from family and others. With all this information in hand, the clinician must then arrive at a working formulation concerning what can be done to promote the individual's well-being. It is an awesome but necessary task.

Depending on the setting, the severity of the problem, and practical considerations, the assessment process may be relatively comprehensive or more selective and problem-oriented, limited to identifying the key problems and the specific conditions that are maintaining or exacerbating them. In either case, it then provides a basis for making decisions concerning the best treatment program, be it hospitalization, the use of medication and/or psychotherapy, the modification of family patterns, or some other approach.

The initial clinical assessment also provides a "baseline" for comparison later with other measures obtained *during* and *following* treatment. This is an important but sometimes forgotten aspect of assessment. It makes it possible to check on the effectiveness of an ongoing treatment program to see if modifications may be needed; it also allows for comparison of the relative effectiveness among different therapeutic and preventive approaches. This is important not only in treating the individual but also in conducting the research that can advance our understanding of the disorders themselves, as well as the development of new and more effective assessment and treatment techniques. All of which, ultimately, will enhance the prognosis for individuals suffering from psychological disorders. Furthermore, the importance of assessment has increased dramatically as the demand for accountability in therapy has grown. In short, assessment is not a one-time venture: it is an ongoing process.

In this chapter, we shall review some of the more commonly used assessment procedures—physical and psychological—and show how the data obtained may be integrated into a coherent clinical picture for use in making decisions about referral and treatment. Our survey will include a discussion of neuropsychological assessment, the clinical interview, behavioral observation, and personality assessment through the use of projective and objective psychological tests. We shall then examine in some detail an illustrative case in which the individual being assessed underwent both neurological and psychological testing. Finally, we shall examine the use of computers in clinical assessment.

But first, let us look at what, exactly, the clinician is trying to find out from assessment.

The information sought in assessment

What does the clinician need to know? First, of course, the problem must be identified. Is it a situational problem, produced by an environmental stressor, or is it a more pervasive and long-term disorder? How is the individual dealing with the problem? Are there indications of self-defeating behavior and personality deterioration, or is the individual using available personal and environmental resources to cope? Does the individual's symptomatic behavior fit any of the diagnostic patterns in DSM-III?

As we have seen, there has been a trend against overdependence on labeling because of the potential damage labels can do in setting up self-fulfilling prophecies for the individual and in blinding members of the therapeutic staff to other relevant behavior on the part of the individual. On the other hand, it is important to have an accurate classification for a number of reasons. In many cases, a formal diagnosis is necessary before insurance claims can be filed. Clinically, knowledge of an individual's type of disorder can help in planning and managing the most appropriate treatment procedures. Administratively, it is essential to know the range of diagnostic problems that are represented among the patient or client population and for which treatment facilities need to be available. If the majority of patients at a facility have been diagnosed as schizophrenic, for example, then the staffing, physical environment, and treatment facilities should be arranged accordingly. Thus, as clear a diagnosis as possible is needed, including a categorization if appropriate.

However, for many clinical purposes, a formal diagnostic classification per se is much less important than having a basic understanding of the individual's history, intellectual functioning, personality characteristics, and environmental pressures and resources. As such, adequate assessment includes much more than the diagnostic label. For example, it should include an objective description of the individual's behavior. How does the individual characteristically respond to other people? Are there *excesses* in behavior, such as eating or drinking too much? Are there notable *deficits*, as, for example, in social skills? How *appropriate* is the individual's behavior? Is the individual manifesting behavior that would be acceptable in some contexts where it is displayed? Excesses, deficits, and appropriateness are key dimensions to be noted if the clinician is to understand the particular disorder that has brought the individual to the clinic or hospital.

In addition, assessment needs to include a description of any long-term personality characteristics that are relevant. Has the individual typically responded in certain deviant ways? Do there seem to be personality traits or behavior patterns that predispose the individual to behave in maladaptive ways?

It is also important to analyze the social context in which the individual operates. What kinds of environmental demands are typically placed on the individual, and what supports or special stressors exist in the individual's life situation? As we have seen, DSM-III classification includes guidelines for rating both the severity of the stressors in the individual's current environment and the level of the individual's overall adjustment during the preceding year (see pages 19–20).

The diverse and often conflicting bits of information about the individual's personality traits, behavior patterns, environmental demands, and so on must then be integrated into a consistent and meaningful picture. Some clinicians refer to this picture as a *dynamic formulation,* because it not only describes the current situation but includes hypotheses about why the person is behaving in maladaptive ways. At this point in the assessment the clinician should have a plausible explanation, for example, for why a normally passive and mild-mannered man suddenly flew into a rage and started breaking up furniture.

The formulation should allow the clinician to develop hypotheses about the patient's future behavior as well. What is the likelihood of improvement or deterioration if the individual's problems are left untreated? Which behaviors should be the focus of change and what treatment methods are most likely to be successful? How much change might reasonably be expected from a particular type of treatment?

Where feasible, decisions about treatment are made with the consent and cooperation of the individual. In cases of severe disorder, however, they may have to be made without the patient's participation. As has already been indicated, important here is a knowledge of the strengths and resources of the patient; in short, what qualities does the patient bring to the treatment program that can enhance the prognosis? (See **HIGHLIGHT** on this page.)

Interdisciplinary sources of assessment data

Since a wide range of factors may play important roles in causing and maintaining maladaptive behavior, assessment may involve the coordinated use of physical, psychological, and environmental assessment procedures. As we have indicated, however, the nature and comprehensiveness of clinical assessments vary de-

HIGHLIGHT

Important questions for clinical assessment

What are the presenting problems? Has the individual had these problems before? Are they of recent onset?

Were there important precipitating events—a recent trauma such as a death in the family or a severe economic loss?

Are there unusually difficult environmental circumstances such as chronic unemployment, traumatic family disturbance?

Does the individual or any family member have a history of psychological problems?

Is there a significant medical history—a precipitating physical disease, medication, or chemical abuse?

What is the patient's present mental and emotional status? Is he or she anxious, depressed? Are the thought processes disturbed? Is the person's affect appropriate? Is there a long-standing personality problem?

What are the individual's strengths? How has he or she successfully handled problems in the past?

Is the individual motivated for treatment? Can he or she be relied upon to take an active part in treatment—for example, to try alternative behaviors? Are there personality problems that may undermine treatment?

Are environmental resources available? Are there supportive friends or family members who might aid in the person's treatment or otherwise influence it positively?

pending on the problem and the facilities of the treatment agency. Assessment by phone in a suicide prevention center, for example, is quite different from assessment aimed at determining whether a particular hospitalized patient is intelligent and verbal enough to profit from individual psychotherapy.

Furthermore, exactly how a clinician goes about the assessment process often depends on his or her basic orientation. For example, the biologically oriented clinician, typically a psychiatrist or neuropsychologist, will likely focus on biological assessment methods aimed at determining any underlying organic malfunctioning that may be causing the maladaptive behavior; the psychoanalytically oriented clinician will likely use unstructured personality assessment techniques, such as the Rorschach, to uncover intrapsychic conflicts; the behaviorally oriented clinician, in an effort to determine the functional relationships between the environmental reinforcements and the abnormal behavior, will rely on such techniques as behavioral observation and self-report to identify maladaptive learned patterns; the humanistically oriented clinician might use interview techniques to uncover blocked or distorted personal growth; and the interpersonally oriented clinician will use such techniques as personal confrontations to pinpoint difficulties in interpersonal relationships. This in no way is meant to imply that clinicians of a particular orientation limit themselves to a particular assessment method or that each assessment technique is limited to a particular theoretical orientation. Rather, as we shall see, it should point up that certain types of assessments are more conducive than others to uncovering particular causal factors or for eliciting information about symptomatic behavior central to understanding and treating the disorder.

In this section we will provide a perspective about the way data are collected, with emphasis on psychosocial assessment procedures. Since there are a number of specific terms used in the assessment process, some of the more commonly used ones are listed with their definitions in the **HIGHLIGHT** on page 587.

Physical evaluation

In some situations or with certain psychological problems, a medical examination is necessary to rule out physical abnormalities or to determine the extent to which physical problems are involved. The medical evaluation may include both general physical and special neurological examinations.

General physical examination.   The physical examination consists of the kinds of procedures most of us have experienced in getting a "medical checkup." Typically, a medical history is obtained and the major systems of the body are checked. This part of the assessment procedure is of obvious import for disorders that focus on physical problems, such as psychophysiologic, somatoform, addictive, and organic disorders.

Neurological examination.   Since brain pathology is involved in some mental disorders, a specialized neurological examination is frequently given in addition to the general medical examination. This may involve getting an *electroencephalogram* (an *EEG*) to assess general brain-wave patterns. An EEG is a graphic record of the electrical activity of the brain. It is obtained by placing electrodes on the scalp and recording the minute brain-wave impulses, through amplification, on an oscillograph. The pattern of these impulses can indirectly reflect brain abnormalities, such as brain lesions. Where EEG's reveal general *dysrythmias*—abnormal brain-wave patterns—other specialized techniques may then be used in an attempt to arrive at a precise diagnosis of the nature and extent of the problem.

Radiological technology such as *computerized axial tomography,* known in brief as the *CAT scan,* is one of these specialized new techniques. Through the use of X rays, the CAT scan reveals images of parts of the brain that might be diseased. This procedure has revolutionized neurological study in recent years by providing the clinician with rapid access without surgery to accurate information about the localization and extent of organic damage. The procedure involves the use of computer analysis applied to X-ray beams across sections of the patient's brain to produce images that the neurologist can then interpret.

An even newer scanning technique is *positron emission tomography,* the *PET scan.* Though the CAT scan is limited to distinguishing anatomical features, such as the shape of an organ, the PET scan allows for an appraisal of *how* the organ is functioning by measuring metabolic processes. The PET scan provides "metabolic portraits" through tracking natural compounds like glucose as they are metabolized by the brain or other organs. Through revealing areas of metabolic activity, the PET scan enables the physician to obtain more clear-cut diagnoses of brain pathology by, for example, pinpointing sights responsible for epileptic seizures, trauma from head damage or stroke, and brain cancer. It is hoped that the PET scan will be able to reveal problems that may not be immediately apparent anatomically. Moreover, the use of PET scans in research on brain pathology occurring in abnormal conditions such as schizophrenia, depression, and alcoholism may lead to impor-

HIGHLIGHT

Terms commonly used in clinical assessment

Actuarial interpretation   Application of interpretations developed from a reference group with test scores similar to those of the subject to evaluate the subject's test performance.

Behavior observation   Direct observation of a subject's behavior in a clinical or real-life situation, often aided by the use of rating scales.

Behavior sample   Assessment data that presumably provide an accurate reflection of the subject's typical behavior.

Halo effect   Tendency when rating a specific trait to be influenced by another trait, such as appearance, or by one's overall impression of the subject.

Intelligence test   Test used for establishing a subject's level of intellectual capacity.

Neuropsychological assessment   The use of psychological tests that measure a subject's cognitive, perceptual, and motor performance to determine extent and locus of brain damage.

Performance test   Test in which perceptual-motor rather than verbal responses are emphasized.

Personality profile   A graphic summary of data from several tests or from subtests of the same test battery or scales that shows the personality configuration of an individual or a group of individuals.

Projective test   Technique using neutral or ambiguous stimuli that subject is encouraged to interpret, and from which the subject's personality characteristics can be analyzed.

Rating scale   Device for recording the rater's judgment of himself or herself or others on defined traits.

Self-monitoring   Self-observation and recording of behavior that is, typically, targeted for change.

Self-report inventory   Procedure in which subject is asked to respond to statements in terms of their applicability to him or her.

Test reliability   Consistency with which a test measures a given trait on repeated administrations of the test to given subjects.

Test validity   Degree to which a test actually measures what it was designed to measure.

Verbal test   Test in which the subect's ability to understand and use words and concepts is important in making the required responses.

---

tant discoveries about the organic processes underlying these disorders and provide clues to more effective treatment.

In many instances, a clinical neuropsychologist will administer a *neuropsychological test battery* to a patient with known or suspected organic brain damage. The purpose of such testing is to describe the behavioral functioning of the individual in terms of brain-behavior relationships. By means of a battery of tests, the individual's performance on perceptual-motor tasks can give valuable clues about that person's cognitive and intellectual impairment following brain damage (Boll, 1978; Filskov & Locklear, 1982; Heaton & Pendleton, 1981). Such testing can even provide clues as to the probable location of the brain damage, though PET scans and other physical tests are still more effective in determining the exact location of the injury.

The Halstead-Reitan battery is one of the most highly regarded of the neuropsychological tests, and its components are described in the **HIGHLIGHT** on page 589. Typically taking about six hours to administer, the Halstead-Reitan can be a problem in some clinical settings where time and funding is limited. In recent years, the Luria-Nebraska battery (Golden, 1978), which takes only two and a half hours to administer, has been receiving attention as an alternative to the Halstead-Reitan. Both these batteries provide their information without the risk of injury or death that can accompany more direct neurological examinations (Filskov & Goldstein, 1974). Still, however, the Halstead-Reitan battery continues to grow in use because it yields a great deal of useful information—more than the Luria-Nebraska—about the individual's cognitive and motor processes (Boll, 1980; Filskov & Locklear, 1982).

In summary, the medical and neuropsycho-

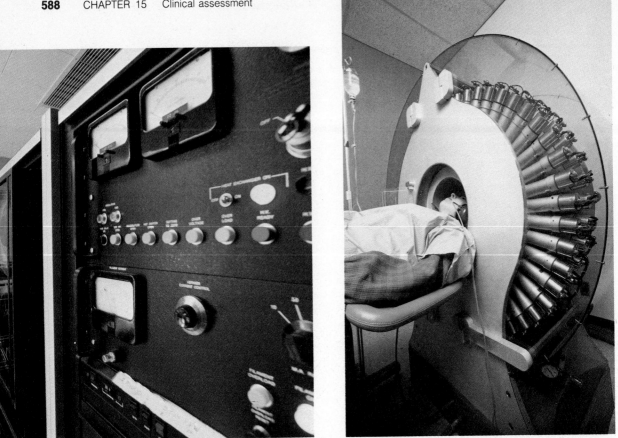

Two new techniques for examining neurological patterns are CAT scan and PET scan. Left: CAT-scanning equipment in operation at a Chicago-area hospital. Right: A woman is placed in a PET-scanning apparatus. For examples of actual PET and CAT scans, see photos on pages 316 and 511.

logical sciences are developing many new procedures to assess brain functioning and behavioral manifestations of organic disorder. Medical procedures to assess organic brain damage include EEG, CAT scan, and PET scan. The new technology, particularly PET scans, hold a great deal of promise for detecting and evaluating organic brain dysfunction and for providing increased understanding of brain functioning through "metabolic maps" of the brain. Neuropsychological testing provides the clinician with important behavioral information on how organic brain damage is affecting the individual's present functioning.

Psychosocial assessment

Psychosocial assessment attempts to provide a realistic picture of the individual in interaction with the environment. This picture includes rel-

evant information concerning the individual's personality makeup and present level of functioning, as well as information about the stressors and resources in his or her life situation. For example, early in the process, clinicians may act like puzzle solvers, absorbing as much information about the client as possible—present feelings, attitudes, memories, demographic facts, etc.—and trying to fit the pieces together into a meaningful pattern. They typically formulate hypotheses and discard or confirm them as they proceed. Starting usually with a global technique, such as the clinical interview, clinicians may later select more specific assessment tasks or tests. The following are some of the psychosocial procedures that may be used.

Assessment interviews. The assessment interview usually involves a face-to-face conversation conducted in such a way that the clinician

HIGHLIGHT

Neuropsychological examination: Determining brain-behavior relationships

The *Halstead-Reitan battery* is a neuropsychological examination composed of several tests and variables from which an "index of impairment" can be computed (Boll, 1978, 1980). In addition, it provides specific information about the subject's functioning in several skill areas. Though it typically takes four to six hours to complete and requires substantial administrative time, it is being used increasingly in neurological evaluations because it yields a great deal of useful information about the individual's cognitive and motor processes (Filskov & Goldstein, 1974; Filskov & Locklear, 1982). Moreover, the Halstead-Reitan battery provides valid information without the risk of injury or death that is so great with more direct, surgical neurological examinations.

The Halstead-Reitan battery for adults is made up of the following tests:

The *Halstead Category Test* measures the subject's ability to learn and remember material, and can provide clues as to his or her judgment and impulsivity. The subject is presented with a stimulus (on a screen) which suggests a number between one and four. The subject presses a button indicating which number is "correct." A correct choice is followed by the sound of a pleasant doorbell and an incorrect choice by a loud buzzer. The person is required to determine from the pattern of buzzers and bells what the underlying principle of the correct choice is.

The *Tactual Performance Test* measures the subject's motor speed, response to the unfamiliar, and learning and use of tactile and kinesthetic cues. The

test consists of a board that has spaces for 10 blocks of varied shapes. The subject is blindfolded (and never actually sees the board) and asked to place the blocks into the correct grooves in the board. Later, the subject is asked to draw the blocks and the board from tactile memory.

The *Rhythm Test* is an auditory perception task used to measure attention and sustained concentration. It is a subtest of Seashore's Test of musical talent and includes 30 pairs of rhythmic beats that are presented on a tape recorder. On this test, the subject is required to determine if the pairs are the same or different.

The *Speech Sounds Perception Test* is a test to determine if the individual can identify spoken words. Nonsense words are presented on a tape recorder, and the subject is asked to identify the presented word from a list of four printed words. This task measures the subject's concentration, attention, and comprehension.

The *Finger Oscillation Task* measures the speed at which the individual can, with the index finger, depress a lever. Several trials are given with each hand.

In addition to the Halstead-Reitan battery, other tests, referred to as *allied procedures*, may be used in a neuropsychology laboratory. For example, Boll (1980) recommends the use of the modified Halstead-Wepman Aphasia Screening Test for obtaining information about a subject's language abilities, and abilities to identify numbers and body parts, to follow directions, to spell, and to pantomime simple actions.

obtains information about various aspects of the patient's situation, behavior, and personality makeup. The interview may vary from a simple set of questions to a more formal format.

In order to minimize sources of error, an assessment interview is often carefully structured in terms of goals, content to be explored, and the type of relationship the interviewer attempts to establish with the subject. Here, the use of rating scales may help focus and score the interview data. For example, the subject may be rated on a three-point scale with respect to self-esteem, anxiety, and various other characteristics. Such a structured interview is particularly effective in giving an overall impression of the

subject and his or her life situation and in revealing specific problems or crises—such as marital difficulties, drug dependence, or suicidal fantasies—that may require immediate therapeutic intervention (Matarazzo, 1983).

Clinical interviews have been criticized as an unreliable source of information on which to base important clinical decisions. Evidence of this unreliability lies in the fact that on the basis of interview data for a particular patient, different clinicians have often arrived at different diagnoses. For this reason, several investigators have attempted to improve the reliability of assessment interviews by specifying observable criteria for diagnosis and providing very specific guidelines for making judgments (Feighner et al., 1972). In these interviews, the questions are specified to elicit quite specific behavioral descriptions and typically take about an hour. For example, the questions are of the "what" variety, such as "What did you do when you became irritated?" They cover a wide range of topics in a fixed sequence, although the interviewer may phrase the questions in his or her own words. High agreement has been found for most diagnostic judgments among interviewers using this standardized, or *structured*, interview format (Helzer et al., 1977).

One of the rating scales most widely used for recording observations in clinical practice and in psychiatric research is the Brief Psychiatric Rating Scale (BPRS). The BPRS provides a structured and quantifiable format for rating clinical symptoms such as somatic concern, anxiety, emotional withdrawal, guilt feelings, hostility, suspiciousness, and unusual thought patterns. It contains 18 scales which are scored from ratings made by the clinician following an interview with the patient. The distinct patterns of behavior reflected in the BPRS ratings enable clinicians to make a standardized comparison of their patients' symptoms with the behavior of other psychiatric patients (Overall & Hollister, 1982). The BPRS has been found to be an extremely useful instrument in clinical research, especially for the purpose of assigning patients to treatment groups on the basis of similarity in symptoms.

A type of assessment that is related to the interview is the *self-report*, in essence, similar to a "self-interview." This approach recognizes that individuals are an excellent source of information about themselves. Assuming that the right questions are asked and that people are willing to disclose information about themselves, the results can be quite valuable. One of the most efficient instruments for obtaining specific information about an individual's problem area is the *self-report schedule* or *problem checklist*. Such checklists may include items that measure fears, problems, moods, and conditions that may be operating as reinforcements in the person's life. Thus they can provide useful information for structuring a behavioral treatment plan.

Clinical observation of behavior. Direct observation of the individual's characteristic behavior has long been considered important for adequate psychosocial assessment. The main purpose of direct observation is to find out more about the person's psychological makeup and level of functioning; though such observations would ideally occur within the individual's natural environment, they are typically confined to clinic or hospital settings. For example, a brief description is usually made of the subject's behavior on hospital admission, and more detailed observations are made periodically on the ward. These descriptions include concise notations of relevant information about the subject's personal hygiene, emotional behavior, delusions or hallucinations, anxiety, sexual behavior, aggressive or suicidal tendencies, and so on.

As in the case of interviews, the use of rating scales in clinical observation helps not only to organize information but also to encourage reliability and objectivity. That is, the formal structure of the scale is likely to keep unwarranted observer inferences to a minimum.

Rating scales commonly used are those that enable the observer to indicate not only the presence or absence of a trait or behavior but also its prominence. The following is an example of such a rating-scale item; the observer would check the most appropriate alternative.

Sexual behavior:
_____ 1. Sexually assaultive: aggressively approaches males or females with sexual intent.
_____ 2. Sexually soliciting: exposes genitals with sexual intent, makes overt sexual advances to other patients or staff, masturbates openly.
_____ 3. No overt sexual behavior: not preoccupied with discussion of sexual matters.
_____ 4. Avoids sex topics: made uneasy by discussion of sex, becomes disturbed if approached sexually by others.
_____ 5. Excessive prudishness about sex: considers sex filthy, condemns sexual behavior in others, becomes panic-stricken if approached sexually.

Observation of the subject's behavior may be made not only to fill in the original picture but also to check on the course or outcome of treatment procedures.

Observations made in clinical settings by trained observers can provide useful behavioral data. Paul and his colleagues (Lichy, 1982; Mariotto, 1979; Paul, 1982; Paul & Lentz, 1977), for example, have developed a comprehensive behavioral assessment program that they have implemented experimentally in a number of hospitals. The program includes evaluating the behavior of chronic patients and monitoring the activities of staff members working with them. Through the use of observational rating systems, they have been able to measure staff behavior in the daily management of patients and ongoing patient behavior on the ward. The behavioral ratings, which provide a careful detailing of day-to-day behavior of both patients and staff, can be used to pinpoint specific behaviors to be changed (either the patient's or the staff's). This observational system provides a wealth of specific behaviors that are analyzed and fed back to patients and staff. There is no question that the chronic patients treated in this program improve under this regimen of careful and continuous assessment of behavior; however, it requires a great deal of staff time to implement, and collecting extensive behavioral assessment data is beyond the means of most clinical settings. As such, Paul (1982) and his colleagues are currently attempting to develop "transportable" behavioral assessment systems that can be used more easily in routine clinical practice.

Recently, a good deal of attention has focused on observing the subject's behavior in his or her natural surroundings. For example, children who have been showing behavior problems may be observed at school, in their peer groups, and in their homes. Here the purpose is to obtain a sampling of their behavior in ordinary situations in order to understand the problems they are facing, the coping patterns they are using, and the environmental conditions that may be reinforcing their maladaptive behavior.

In situations where it is not feasible to observe the subject's behavior in everyday settings—as when he or she is institutionalized—an entire family may be asked to meet together in the clinic or hospital where their interactions and difficulties can be observed and studied. In other cases a social worker may obtain relevant data by visiting the subject's home, talking with family members and others who are important to the subject, and observing the stressors and resources in the subject's life situation. In addition to providing important assessment data, this procedure incorporates the "observers" into the therapy program, thereby enhancing the therapy. Jones, Reid, and Patterson (1975) have developed a method for coding and quantifying the observations of a child's behavior at school

and at home. Concrete instances of behavior and interaction can be observed, recorded, and coded, either by trained observers or by the parents themselves. This provides the clinician with information about the stimuli that are controlling the child's interactions, which in turn makes it possible for the clinician to evaluate the quality of the child's interactions and identify the situations that result in behavior problems.

Even in cases where considerable information about the subject's life situation has been collected in structured interviews or in psychological tests, the collection of supplemental observational data is regarded as desirable.

In still other situations where observation in the natural setting is not possible, the clinician may construct or contrive an observational situation that can provide information about the individual's response to a particular situation. For example, an individual who has a phobia for snakes might be placed in a situation where snakelike objects and pictures are presented.

An often-used procedure that enables the clinician to observe the client's behavior directly is *role playing.* The client is instructed to play a part—for example, someone standing up for his or her rights. Role playing a situation like this not only can provide assessment information for the clinician but also can serve as a vehicle for new learning for the client.

Extending the use of observational data a bit further, the clinician may analyze situations with which the subject is likely to be confronted in the future. For example, a patient with little education and a history of chronic unemployment might improve sufficiently to leave the institution but be little better off than before unless treatment has included training in job skills. Thus knowledge of troubled individuals' life situations not only helps in understanding their present maladaptive behavior but is often essential for planning a treatment program that will enable them to meet future challenges in more adaptive ways.

A type of self-observation—which serves as a therapeutic strategy as well as an assessment procedure—is *self-monitoring.* With this technique clients are asked to observe and record their own behavior. Using journals, they record particular behaviors that they are trying to decrease or increase. For example, they might be asked to record the number of times during the week that they were appropriately assertive.

Some self-monitoring techniques involve the use of a "golf counter," which may be worn on the wrist or carried in the pocket and enables the individual to record easily instances of certain behavior. Monitoring one's behavior in this way also has a direct effect on the behavior itself. For example, individuals who record negative behaviors, such as overeating, usually reduce the amount of their food intake over the period of self-observation. Thus the assessment technique of self-monitoring has become a major strategy in the treatment of problem behavior.

Psychological tests. Interviews and behavioral observation are *direct* attempts to determine the individual's beliefs, attitudes, and problems. Psychological tests, on the other hand, are a more *indirect* means of assessing psychological characteristics. Psychological tests are, in essence, standardized sets of procedures or tasks for obtaining samples of behavior: the individual's responses to the standardized stimuli are compared with those of other individuals, usually through established test norms or test score distributions. From these comparisons, the clinician can then draw inferences about the individual's psychological characteristics.[1] Among the characteristics these tests can ascertain are intellectual capacity, motive patterns, personality characteristics, role behaviors, values, level of depression or anxiety, and coping patterns. Though more precise and often more reliable than interviews or observational techniques, psychological tests are far from perfect tools. Often their value depends on the competence of the clinician who interprets them. In general, however, they are useful diagnostic tools for psychologists in much the same way that blood tests or X rays are useful to physicians. In both cases, pathology may be revealed in persons who appear on the surface to be quite normal, or a general impression of "something wrong" can be checked against more precise information. Two general categories of psychological tests are *intelligence tests* and *personality tests*.

1. *Intelligence tests.* There is a wide range of intelligence tests from which the clinician can choose. The Wechsler Intelligence Scale for Children–Revised (WISC–R) and the Stanford-Binet Intelligence Scale are widely used in clinical set-

tings for measuring the intellectual capacity of children. Probably the most commonly used test for measuring adult intelligence is the Wechsler Adult Intelligence Scale–Revised (WAIS–R). It includes both verbal and performance material and consists of eleven subtests. A brief description of two of the subtests—one verbal and one performance—will serve to illustrate the type of functions the WAIS–R measures:

General information. This subtest consists of questions designed to tap the individual's range of information on material that is ordinarily encountered. For example, the individual is asked to do such things as tell how many weeks there are in a year, name the colors in the American flag, and tell who Martin Luther King was.

Picture completion. This subtest consists of 20 cards showing pictures, each with a part missing. The task for the subject is to indicate what is missing. This test is designed to measure the individual's ability to discriminate between essential and nonessential elements in a situation (Wechsler, 1981).

Analysis of scores on the various subtests reveals the individual's present level of intellectual functioning. In addition, the subject's behavior in the test situation may reveal much relevant information. For example, he or she may be very apprehensive about not doing well, may vacillate in responses, may seek continual reassurance from the clinician, or may be so disturbed that concentration on the tasks presented is difficult. These observed behaviors may tell the clinician as much as the actual test scores.

Individual intelligence tests—such as the WISC–R, WAIS–R, and the Stanford-Binet—typically require two to three hours to administer, score, and interpret; in many clinical situations, there is not sufficient time or funding to use these tests in every assessment situation. In cases where intellectual impairment or organic brain damage is suspected to be central to the patient's problem, intelligence testing may be the most crucial diagnostic procedure to include in the test battery. Yet in many clinical settings and for many clinical cases, gaining a thorough understanding of the client's problems and initiating a treatment program do not require knowing the client's IQ; in these cases, intelligence testing would not be recommended.

2. *Personality tests.* There are a great many tests designed to measure characteristics other

---

[1]For those wishing an indepth review of the subject, Graham and Lilly (1984) present a comprehensive guide to the many varieties of psychological testing.

A WAIS test is administered to an adult client. In such test-taking situations, the person's behavior during the test may be as significant as the actual test scores.

People may see many different things in these inkblot pictures; now tell me what you see, what it makes you think of, what it means to you.

The following excerpts are taken from the responses of a subject to the sample inkblot shown here.

than intellectual capacity. It is convenient to group these personality tests into *projective* and *objective* tests.

a) ***Projective tests*** are unstructured in that they rely on various ambiguous stimuli, such as inkblots or pictures rather than questions and answers. Through their interpretations of these ambiguous materials, individuals reveal a good deal about their personal conflicts, motives, coping techniques, and other personality characteristics.

An assumption underlying the use of projective techniques is that in trying to make sense out of vague, unstructured stimuli, individuals "project" their own problems, motives, and wishes into the situation. Thus projective tests are aimed at discovering the ways in which an individual's past learning and self-structure may lead him or her to organize and perceive ambiguous information. Prominent among the many projective tests in common usage are the Rorschach Test, the Thematic Apperception Test (TAT), and sentence-completion tests.

The ***Rorschach Test*** is named after the Swiss psychiatrist Hermann Rorschach, who initiated experimental use of inkblots in personality assessment in 1911. The test utilizes ten inkblot pictures to which the subject responds in succession after being instructed somewhat as follows (Klopfer & Davidson, 1962):

"This looks like two men with genital organs exposed. They have had a terrible fight and blood has splashed up against the wall. They have knives or sharp instruments in their hands and have just cut up a body. They have already taken out the lungs and other organs. The body is dismembered . . . nothing remains but a shell . . . the pelvic region. They were fighting as to who will complete the final dismemberment . . . like two vultures swooping down. . . ."

From this response and other test results, this subject was diagnosed as an antisocial personality with strong hostility.

For several reasons, there has been a decreased use of the Rorschach Test over the past twenty years. The Rorschach can take several hours to administer and interpret, limiting its use to settings with high staff-patient ratio. Furthermore, the results of the Rorschach are often unreliable because of the subjective nature of the test interpretations. In addition, the types of clinical treatments used in mental health facilities generally require more specific behavioral descriptions rather than descriptions of general, often obscure, personality dynamics such as those that typically result from Rorschach Test interpretation.

The Rorschach has been criticized as an instrument with low or negligible validity, but in the hands of a skilled interpreter it has been shown to be quite useful in uncovering certain psychodynamic problems. Furthermore, there have been recent attempts to objectify Rorschach interpretations by clearly specifying the test variables and empirically exploring their relationship to external criteria such as clinical diagnosis (Viglione & Exner, 1981).

The *Thematic Apperception Test (TAT)* was introduced in 1935 by its coauthors, Morgan and Murray of the Harvard Psychological Clinic. It utilizes a series of simple pictures about which the subject is instructed to make up stories. The material is ambiguous and unstructured so that subjects tend to project their own conflicts and worries into it (Bellak, 1975).

Several scoring and interpretation systems have been developed to focus on different aspects of the subject's stories, such as expression(s) of needs (Atkinson, 1958; Winter, 1973), the individual's perception of reality (Arnold, 1962), and analysis of the individual's fantasies (Klinger, 1979). Most often, the clinician simply makes a qualitative and subjective determination of how the story content reflects the individual's underlying traits, motives, and preoccupations.

An example of the way an individual's problems may be reflected in TAT stories is shown in the following story based on Card 1 (a picture of a boy staring at a violin on a table in front of him). The client, David, was a 15-year-old male who had been referred to the clinic by his parents because of their concern about his withdrawal behavior and his poor work at school.

David was generally cooperative during the testing although he remained rather unemotional and unenthusiastic throughout. When he was given Card 1 of the TAT, he paused for over a minute, carefully scrutinizing the card.

"I think this is a . . . uh . . . machine gun . . . yeah, it's a machine gun. The guy is staring at it. Maybe he got it for his birthday or stole it or something." (Pause, The examiner reminded him that he was to make up a story about the picture.)

"OK. This boy, I'll call him Karl, found this machine gun . . . a Browning automatic rifle . . . in his garage. He kept it in his room for protection. One day he decided to take it to school to quiet down the jocks that lord it over everyone. When he walked into the locker hall, he cut loose on the top jock, Amos, and wasted him. Nobody bothered him after that because they knew he kept the BAR in his locker."

It was evident from this story that David was experiencing a high level of frustration and anger in his life. The extent of this anger was reflected in his perception of the violin in the picture as a machine gun—a potential instrument of violence. The clinician inferred that David was feeling threatened not only by people at school but even in his own home where he needed "protection."

This example shows how stories based on TAT cards may provide the clinician with information about the individual's own conflicts and worries, as well as clues to how the individual is handling these problems.

The TAT has been criticized on several grounds in recent years. There is a "dated" quality to the test stimuli: the pictures, developed in the 1930s, appear quaint to many contemporary subjects who have difficulty identifying with the characters in the pictures. Additionally, the TAT can require a great deal of time to administer and interpret. Interpretation of the responses to the TAT is generally subjective and limits the reliability and validity of the test.

Another projective procedure that has proven useful in personality assessment is the *sentence-completion test.* There are a number of such tests designed for children, adolescents, and adults. The material consists of the beginnings of sentences that the subject is asked to complete, as in these examples:

1. I wish _____.
2. My mother _____.
3. Sex _____.
4. I hate _____.
5. People _____.

Sentence-completion tests are somewhat more structured than the Rorschach and most other projective tests. They help examiners pinpoint important clues to the individual's problems, attitudes, and symptoms through the content or the structure of the test responses. Interpretation of the item responses, however, is generally subjective and unreliable. In spite of the fact that the test stimuli or sentence stems are standard, there are usually no norms with which to compare the patient's responses with other subjects or groups.

The projective tests described above provide situations to which an individual responds rather than sampling the individual's own on-

In the Thematic Apperception Test (TAT), patients make up stories based on a series of drawings such as this one. The TAT is a method of revealing to the trained interpreter some of the dominant personality characteristics of the individual.

going thoughts. In an attempt to get a sampling of naturally occurring thoughts, psychologists are experimenting with having individuals carry small electronic "beepers" that produce a signal, such as a soft tone, at unexpected intervals. At each signal, the individual is to write down whatever thoughts the signal interrupted. These thought reports can then be analyzed in various ways. It is possible that this method can eventually be used for some kinds of personality assessment and diagnosis as well as for monitoring progress in psychological therapy (Klinger, 1977).

In sum, projective tests have an important place in many clinical settings, particularly those that attempt to obtain a comprehensive picture of the individual's psychodynamic functioning and have the necessary trained staff to conduct extensive individual psychological evaluations.

The great strengths of projective techniques— their unstructured nature and their focus on the unique aspects of personality—are at the same time their weaknesses, since they make interpretation subjective, unreliable, and difficult to validate. Moreover, projective tests typically require a great deal of time to administer and skill to interpret—both scarce quantities in most clinical settings.

b) *Objective tests* are structured—that is, they typically use questionnaires, self-inventories, or rating scales in which questions are carefully phrased and possible responses are specified. One of the major structured inventories is the ***Minnesota Multiphasic Personality Inventory (MMPI).*** This inventory was developed in 1943 by Hathaway and McKinley and is the most widely used personality test today for both clinical assessment and research in psychopathology (Dahlstrom, Welsh, & Dahlstrom, 1975; Graham, 1978b).

The inventory, a kind of self-report technique, consists of 550 items covering topics ranging from physical condition and psychological states to moral and social attitudes. Subjects are encouraged to answer all items either *true* or *false*. Some sample items follow:

I sometimes keep on at a thing until others lose their patience with me.   T F
Bad words, often terrible words, come into my mind and I cannot get rid of them.   T F
I often feel as if things were not real.   T F
Someone has it in for me.   T F

(Hathaway & McKinley, 1951, p. 28)

The inventory of items for the MMPI was originally administered to a large group of normal individuals (affectionately called the "Minnesota normals") and several groups of psychiatric patients. Answers to all the items were then item-analyzed to see which ones differentiated the various groups. On the basis of the findings, ten clinical scales have been constructed, each consisting of the items that were answered in a particular way by one of the groups. Each of these scales measures tendencies to respond in psychologically deviant ways. Raw scores on these scales are compared with those scores of the normal population and the results are plotted on the MMPI profile (an example of which can be found in the **HIGHLIGHT** on pages 602–3). By drawing a line connecting the scores for the different scales, the clinician can construct a profile that shows how far from normal the patient's performance is on each of the scales. The *Schizophrenia scale*, for example, is made up of the items that schizophrenic patients consistently answered in a particular way. People who score high on this scale, though not necessarily schizophrenic, often show symptoms typical of the schizophrenic population. For example, high scorers on this scale may be withdrawn and shy and have peculiar thoughts; they may have poor contact with reality and in severe cases may have delusions and hallucinations.

The MMPI also includes four validity scales to detect whether the patient has answered the questions in a straightforward, honest manner; extreme endorsement of the items of any of these scales may invalidate the test. In addition

to the validity scales and the ten clinical scales, numerous "special" scales have been devised, four of which have become so widely used for both clinical and research purposes that they are now listed on the MMPI profile form. All the scales listed on the MMPI profile form are given in the **HIGHLIGHT** on page 597.

Clinically, the MMPI is used in several ways to evaluate a patient's personality characteristics and clinical problems. Perhaps the most typical use of the MMPI is as a *diagnostic standard*. That is, the individual's profile pattern is compared with profiles of known patient groups. If the profile fits a particular group, then the diagnostic information that has been collected on prototypical patients in this group can be used as a broad *descriptive diagnosis* of likely behavior, symptoms, etc., for the new patient. Another approach to MMPI interpretation, *content interpretation*, is used to supplement the empirical correlates provided in the above approach. Here, the clinician analyzes the content themes in the individual's response to the items; for example, if the individual endorses a number of items about fears, the clinician might well conclude that the individual is preoccupied with fear.

In spite of its extensive use, the MMPI is not without its critics. Many psychodynamically oriented clinicians feel that the MMPI (like other structured objective tests) is superficial and does not adequately reflect the complexities of the individual taking the test. Some behaviorally oriented critics, on the other hand, criticize the MMPI as being too oriented toward measuring unobservable "mentalistic" constructs such as traits. A more general criticism has been leveled at the datedness of the MMPI itself. The MMPI has been in use since the early 1940s, and even though much of the MMPI interpretive research is much more recent, the item pool and the basic clinical scales have remained the same. In response to this criticism, the publisher of the MMPI is currently updating and broadening the item pool, in addition to collecting new information on clinical groups and providing new normative data. The project is an ongoing one with an expected completion date of the mid-1980s.

Another kind of objective, self-report personality inventory utilizes the statistical technique of *factor analysis* to develop scales. Tests of this

HIGHLIGHT
The scales of the MMPI

Validity scales

Cannot say scale (?)	Measures the total number of unanswered items.
Lie scale (L)	Measures the tendency to claim excessive virtue or to try to present an overall favorable image.
Infrequency scale (F)	Measures a tendency to falsely claim psychological problems.
Defensiveness scale (K)	Measures the tendency to see oneself in an unrealistically positive way.

Clinical scales

Scale 1	Hypochondriasis *(Hs)*	Measures excessive somatic concern and physical complaints.
Scale 2	Depression *(D)*	Measures symptomatic depression.
Scale 3	Hysteria *(Hy)*	Measures hysteroid personality features and the tendency to develop physical symptoms under stress
Scale 4	Psychopathic Deviate *(Pd)*	Measures antisocial tendencies.
Scale 5	Masculinity-feminity *(Mf)*	Measures sex-role conflict.
Scale 6	Paranoia *(Pa)*	Measures suspicious, paranoid ideation.
Scale 7	Psychasthenia *(Pt)*	Measures anxiety and obsessive behavior.
Scale 8	Schizophrenia *(Sc)*	Measures bizarre thoughts and disordered affect accompanying schizophrenia.
Scale 9	Hypomania *(Ma)*	Measures behavior found in manic affective disorder.
Scale O	Social Introversion *(Si)*	Measures social anxiety, withdrawal, and overcontrol.

Special scales

Scale *A*	Anxiety	A factor analytic scale measuring general maladjustment and anxiety.
Scale *R*	Repression	A factor analytic scale measuring overcontrol and neurotic defensiveness.
Scale *Es*	Ego strength scale	An empirical scale measuring potential response to treatment.
Scale *Mac*	MacAndrew addiction scale	An empirical scale measuring addiction proneness.

type are constructed to measure important and relatively independent personality traits, or factors. The goal is to measure one trait at a time with maximum precision and objectivity; a personality profile can then be drawn showing the degree to which several specific traits are characteristic of the individual, as well as their overall pattern. A well-known test of this type is Cattell's Sixteen Personality Factor Questionnaire. A computerized psychological profile based on the "16 PF" is shown in **HIGHLIGHT** on pages 598–99.

Although the 16 PF was derived through factor analytic procedures and represents a solid psychometric measuring instrument based on a great deal of empirical research, the test item content and the derived scales are generally more appropriate for evaluating personality characteristics of normal subjects—for example, in personnel selection—than for clinical patients.

Self-report inventories, such as the MMPI and the 16 PF, have a number of advantages over other types of personality tests. They are cost effective, highly reliable, and objective; and, as we shall see, they can be administered, scored, and interpreted by electronic computer. However, a number of general criticisms have been leveled against the use of self-report inventories. Some clinicians have considered them to be "too mechanistic" to accurately portray the complexity of human beings and their problems. Also, since these tests require the individual to read, comprehend, and answer verbal material, patients who are illiterate or confused will not be able to take the test. Furthermore, the individual's cooperation is required in self-report inventories, and it is possible that the subject may distort his or her answers to create a particular impression. The validity scales of the MMPI are a direct attempt to deal with this last criticism.

A psychological study

In this section we will illustrate psychological assessment through an extensive diagnostic case study of a young man who presented a complicated clinical picture that was substantially clarified through psychological and neuropsychological assessment. This is a very unusual case in several respects: the young man's problems were quite severe and involved both psychological and organic elements; the case involved cross-cultural considerations—the young man was from South America and assessment was done in both English and Spanish (the latter only as necessary); and a number of psychological specialists participated in the assessment study, including a neuropsychologist, a behaviorally oriented clinical psychologist, an Hispanic clinical psychologist, and a psychiatrist.

Esteban, a 21-year-old student from Colombia, South America, had been enrolled in an English language program since late 1979 at a small college in the United States. He had become disruptive in school, evidencing loud, obnoxious behavior in class and quarreling with his roommates (whom he accused of stealing his wallet). After a period of time during which his behavior did not improve, he was expelled in the spring of 1981. The Director of the program indicated that he felt Esteban needed psychological help for his problems, which included not only the behavioral problems but also, reportedly, severe headaches and confused thinking. The Director added that Esteban would be considered

HIGHLIGHT
The 16 PF: A computerized personality report on a convicted murderer

Jerry G., a 34-year-old male who had been convicted of a double murder, was appealing his death penalty on grounds that he had been ordered to commit the killings. The incident occurred as follows.

Mr. G. and two other men planned to commit a robbery at an unoccupied house one evening. However, the plan was altered and the three men stopped two young men on the highway. One of the three, the acknowledged leader, shot the two victims in the back. He then ordered Mr. G. to put the rifle to their backs and "finish them off." In his statement, Mr. G. maintained that the accomplice had threatened to kill him if he did not comply. Mr. G. was convicted of the killings and sentenced to be executed.

In the appeal court, psychological test data that supported Mr. G.'s contention that he was "forced" to shoot the victims were reviewed. It happened that six weeks prior to the incident, Mr. G. had been given a number of psychological tests, including the Sixteen Personality Factor Questionnaire (the 16 PF). Mr. G.'s responses to the questionnaire were submitted for computer analysis. The computer provided both a capsule description of Mr. G.'s personality and a series of charts that attempted to give an overall personality profile. The computer-generated data clearly showed a pattern of serious personality problems.

The court decided to defer the death penalty in this case. The decision was significantly influenced by the psychological test findings. Mr. G., the court contended, was more timid and sensitive to threat than most people and had a personality that could be best described as a "doormat." The court noted, "From the record here it can be seen that G. . . ., with no criminal history, the personality of a doormat, and a problem with alcohol, was not the ringleader in this sordid affair; nor are rehabilitative prospects demonstrably poorer than for those who received imprisonment terms. Our revulsion toward this crime and our lack of sympathy for G. . . . cannot justify executing only him." (Ill. Supreme Court Case 411 NE2d 849, 1982, p. 495)

The 16 PF capsule description and the profile charts (shown at right) confirm the court's sense of Mr. G.'s personality. For instance, Mr. G.'s low dominance score (1), high group-conformity score (8), and high "free-floating anxiety" score (9) all seem to support the defense's case that Jerry was a follower with little capacity to resist the demands of his peers.

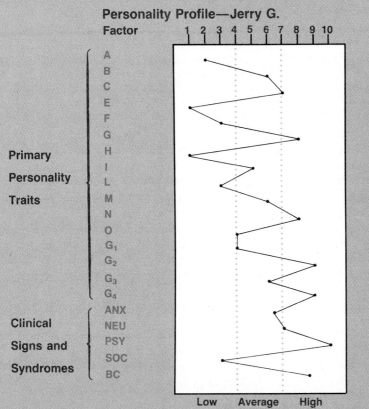

Personality Profile—Jerry G.

Factor		
A		Warmth (2)
B		Intelligence (6)
C		Ego strength (7)
E		Dominance (1)
F		Impulsivity (3)
G		Group conformity (8)
H		Boldness (1)
I		Tender-mindedness (5)
L		Suspiciousness (3)
M		Imagination (6)
N		Shrewdness (8)
O		Guilt proneness (4)
G_1		Rebelliousness (4)
G_2		Self-sufficiency (9)
G_3		Compulsivity (6)
G_4		Free-floating anxiety (9)
ANX		Anxiety (6.3)
NEU		Neuroticism (7.0)
PSY		Psychoticism (10.0)
SOC		Sociopathy (3.0)
BC		Behavior control (7.8)

Primary Personality Traits — Clinical Signs and Syndromes

Scale: 1 2 3 4 5 6 7 8 9 10 — Low   Average   High

TEST-TAKING—Jerry G.

" 'Faking good' attempts are slightly higher than normal. There is little suggestion of the presence of a response set to look bad or to fake anxiety symptoms deliberately. Indications are that he read the items carefully and clearly understood what was required. The random index is within normal limits."

PERSONALITY CAPSULE DESCRIPTION—Jerry G.

"It is likely that his marked submissiveness and passivity lead him to feel a great deal of resentment and unexpressed anger. He is so painfully shy, timid, and cautious that he is virtually unable to take any chances. These extreme withdrawal tendencies make life very difficult for him. He shows very little warmth; indeed, he is markedly reserved. He probably has a history of a 'burnt-child' reaction, that is, of unsatisfactory relationships with others and marked difficulty in gratifying his dependency needs. His self-sufficiency is unusually high, pointing to good work habits and an ability to get things done without depending on others. However, he may be too much of a loner and unable to relate well to others. He appears to be suffering from an unusually high level of free-floating anxiety which may be interfering with his functioning efficiency. He tends to be such a serious, responsible, and sober person that an early family climate is suggested where strong superego demands were made with relatively little dependency gratification. He is well above average with respect to his regard for group conformity. In fact, he may impress others as being overly conscientious and rigidly conventional in his approach to life. He is a good deal more trusting and adaptable than most people, and is an easy person to get along with since he tends not to question other people's motives. He is a shrewd, poised, and sophisticated person with much skill in social relations.

"Above average ego strength and frustration tolerance indicate good potential for handling emotional conflicts and interpersonal relations in an effective manner. Superego introjection is somewhat below average, but not seriously so. He probably has little problem with depression originating in conflict with his superego. He tends to be an accepting person who is respectful of traditions and of the 'establishment.' He does not adopt a critical and radical approach to authority."

for acceptance as a student in another program only if he showed significant improvement in therapy.

Upon hearing of his expulsion, Esteban's parents, who were well-to-do international banking entrepreneurs, flew in from South America and arranged to have him scheduled for a complete physical examination at a well-known medical center in New York. After an extensive medical and neurological examination to determine the source of his headaches and confusion, Esteban was diagnosed as having some "diffuse" brain impairment, but that he was otherwise in good health. His parents then sought a further, more definitive neurological examination. The neurologist at the second hospital recommended a psychological and neuropsychological examination because he suspected that Esteban's mild neurological condition would not account for his extreme psychological and behavioral symptoms. He referred the family to a psychologist for assessment and treatment. Since Esteban was experiencing a number of pressing situational problems—for example, his behavior problems continued, he appeared anxious to find a new English program, and, as we shall see, he had some hard issues to face about his stated career aspirations to be a doctor—the psychologist decided to begin therapy immediately, concurrent with the additional assessment evaluation.

Interviews and behavior observations. Esteban was seen in the initial session with his parents. The interview was conducted in English with some translation into Spanish (mostly by Esteban), since his parents knew little English. Throughout the session Esteban was disorganized and distractible. He had difficulty keeping to the topic being discussed and periodically interrupted his own conversation with seemingly random impulses to show the interviewer papers, books, pamphlets, and the like from his knapsack. He talked incessantly, often very loudly. He was not at all defensive about his problems but talked freely about his symptoms and attitudes. His behavior resembled that of a very hyperactive child—he was excitable, impulsive, and immature. He did not appear to be psychotic; he reported no hallucinations or delusions and was in contact with reality. He related well with the interviewer, seemed to enjoy the session, and expressed an interest in having additional sessions.

During subsequent interviews, Esteban expressed frequent physical complaints such as headaches, tension, and sleeping problems. He reported that he had a great deal of difficulty concentrating on his studies. He couldn't study because he always found other things to do—particularly, talking about religion. He was seemingly outgoing and sociable and had no difficulty initiating conversations with other people. However, he tended to say socially inappropriate things or become frustrated and lose his temper easily. For example, during one family interview, he became enraged and kicked his mother.

Family history.   Esteban's father was a Spanish-Colombian banker in his mid-sixties. He was well-dressed, somewhat passive, though visibly quite warm toward his son. He had had his share of problems in recent years; severe business problems coupled with two heart attacks had brought on a depressive episode that had left him ineffective in dealing with his business. His wife and her brother, an attorney from Madrid, had had to straighten out the business problems. She reported that her husband had had several depressive episodes in the past and that Esteban's moods resembled her husband's in his earlier years.

Esteban's mother was a tense, worried, and somewhat hypochondriacal woman who appeared to be rather domineering. Prior to the first and second interviews, she handed the therapist, in secret, written "explanations" of her son's problems. Her own history revealed that she was unhappy in her marriage and that she lived only for her children, on whom she doted.

Esteban's brother, Juan, was an engineering student at an American university and apparently was doing well academically and socially. He was one year older than Esteban.

Esteban's childhood had been marked with problems. His mother reported that although he had been a good baby—noting that he had been pretty and happy as a small child—he had changed after age 2½. At about that time, he had fallen on his head and was unconscious for awhile; he was not hospitalized. Beginning in the preschool years, he exhibited behavioral problems, including temper tantrums, negativism, and inability to get along with peers. These problems continued when he began school. He frequently refused to go to school, he had periods of aggressive behavior, and he appeared in general to resemble children who are referred to as "hyperactive." It appeared that he was probably overprotected and "infantilized" by his mother.

Esteban was quite close to his brother Juan, with whom he reported he had had extensive homosexual relations when they were growing up. The "darkest day" in Esteban's life was reportedly when Juan broke off the homosexual relationship with him at age 16 and told him to "go and find men." Although he later carried on a platonic relationship with a woman in Colombia, it was never a serious one. Esteban had strong homosexual urges of which he was consciously aware and attempted to control through a growing preoccupation with religion.

Esteban had been in psychotherapy on several occasions since he was 11 years old. After he graduated from high school, he attended law school in Colombia for a quarter, but dropped out because he "wanted to become a doctor instead." (In Colombia, professional schools are combined with college.) He left school, according to his parent's report, because he couldn't adapt. He worked for a time in the family business but had difficulty getting along with other employees and was encouraged to try other work. When that failed, his parents sent him to the United States to study English, rationalizing that Colombia was not as good an environment for him as the United States.

Intelligence testing. Esteban underwent psychological testing to evaluate further the possibility of neurological deficits and to determine if he had the intellectual capabilities to proceed with a demanding academic career. He scored in the borderline to average range of intelligence on the WAIS–R (English version) and on the WAIS (Spanish version). He was particularly deficient in tasks involving practical judgment, common sense, concentration, visual-motor coordination, and concept formation. In addition, on memory tests, he showed a below average memory ability. On memory tests he showed a very poor immediate recall of verbal ideas from paragraphs read aloud (in both English and Spanish). Under most circumstances, individuals showing similar intellectual/neurological deficits are able to live comfortable, fulfilling lives in less complex situations, including the type of

career they choose. It was clear from the test data and Esteban's behavior during testing that his career aspirations—seemingly nurtured by his parents—exceeded his abilities and might well be a factor in much of his frustration.

Personality testing. Esteban was given both the Rorschach Inkblot Test and the MMPI. Both tests have been used extensively with Hispanic subjects. The Rorschach is believed by some to be particularly well suited for cases like Esteban's, perhaps since the test stimuli are relatively unstructured and not culture-bound. Esteban's performance on the Rorschach revealed tension, anxiety, and a preoccupation with morbid topics. He appeared to be overly concerned about his health, prone to depression, indecisive and yet at other times impulsive and careless. His responses were often immature and he showed a strong and persistent ambivalence toward females. In some responses he viewed females in highly aggressive ways—often a fusion of sexual and aggressive images was evident. In general, he demonstrated aloofness and an inability to relate well to other people. Although his Rorschach responses suggested that he could view the world in conventional ways and was probably not psychotic, at times he had difficulty controlling his impulses.

Esteban took the MMPI in both English and Spanish. His MMPI profile was virtually identical in both languages and is given in the **HIGHLIGHT** on page 602–3, along with a computer-based interpretation of his test scores.

Summary of the psychological assessment. Esteban showed mild neurological deficits on neuropsychological testing and a borderline to average level of intellectual ability. He clearly did not have the intellectual capability to pursue a demanding medical career. Difficult or demanding academic tasks placed a great deal of stress on him and resulted in a high degree of frustration. Furthermore, his poor memory made learning complex material difficult.

The MMPI interpretation indicated that Esteban's disorganized behavior and symptomatic patterns reflected a serious psychological disorder. Although he was not currently psychotic, both his past behavior and his test performance suggested that he was functioning marginally and that he showed the potential for personality deterioration in some situations.

HIGHLIGHT

A profile based on the MMPI: Esteban

On the facing page is An MMPI profile chart compiled for Esteban. The "validity scales" are shown in the column at left (the column in which the word *MALE* appears). The "clinical scales" are in the center column. The "special scales" are at right. (The HIGHLIGHT on page 597 describes each of these scales.) Based on the scores you see displayed in the chart, a computer produced the narrative description given below.

Computer-based report

PROFILE VALIDITY

This MMPI profile should be interpreted with caution. There is some possibility that the clinical report is an exaggerated picture of the client's present situation and problems. He is presenting an unusual number of psychological symptoms. This extreme response set could result from poor reading ability, confusion, disorientation, stress, or a need to seek a great deal of attention for his problems.

His test-taking attitudes should be evaluated for the possibility that he has produced an invalid profile. He may be showing a lack of cooperation with the testing or he may be "malingering" by attempting to present a false claim of mental illness. Determining the sources of his confusion, whether conscious distortion or personality deterioration, is important since immediate attention may be required. Clinical patients with this profile are often confused, distractible, and show memory problems. Evidence of delusions and thought disorder may be present. He may be showing a high degree of distress and personality deterioration.

SYMPTOMATIC PATTERN

He is presenting with a mixed pattern of psychological symptoms. This profile shows a pattern of chronic depression and alienation. The client tends to feel quite withdrawn, tense, and anxious. He is having problems concentrating, feels agitated, and is functioning at a very low level of psychological efficiency. He feels apathetic and indifferent and like a passive participant in life. He also feels that he has little energy left over from mere survival to expend on any pleasure in life.

He may be showing signs of serious psychopathology—delusions, problems in thinking, and inappropriate affect. His long-standing lack of achievement and his work behavior have caused him many problems, and he may have serious plans for suicide.

He experiences some conflicts concerning his sex-role identity, appearing somewhat passive and effeminate in his orientation toward life. He may appear somewhat insecure in the masculine role, and he may be uncomfortable in relationships with women. His interests, in general, are more characteristic of women than of men. He tends to be quite passive and submissive in interpersonal relationships, and he tends to make concessions in an effort to avoid confrontation. In addition, he may have low heterosexual drive.

His response content indicates that he is preoccupied with feeling guilty and unworthy, and feels that he deserves to be punished for wrongs he has committed. He feels regretful and unhappy about life, complains about having no zest for life, and seems plagued by anxiety and worry about the future. According to his response content, there is a strong possibility that he has seriously contemplated suicide. A careful evaluation of this possibility is suggested. He views his physical health as failing and reports numerous somatic concerns. He feels that life is no longer worthwhile and that he is losing control of his thought processes. He reports in his response content that he is rather high-strung and believes that he feels things more, or more intensely, than others do. He feels quite lonely and misunderstood at times. The content of his responses indicates that he feels as though he is losing his mind, and that he does not understand things going on around him. The items he endorsed include content suggesting that his thinking is confused and bizarre. He feels that others do not understand him and are trying to control him. He is also tending toward withdrawal into a world of fantasy.

INTERPERSONAL RELATIONS

He has great problems with alienation and social relationships. He feels vulnerable to interpersonal hurt, lacks trust, and may never form close, satisfying relationships. He feels very insecure in relationships and may be preoccupied with guilt and self-defeating behavior.

He appears to be somewhat shy, with some social concerns and inhibitions. He is a bit hypersensitive about what others think of him and is occasionally concerned over his relationships with others. He appears to be somewhat overcontrolled and submissive in personal relationships and social situations, and may have some difficulty expressing his feelings toward others.

The content of this client's MMPI responses suggests the following additional information concerning his interpersonal relations. He views his home situation as unpleasant and lacking in love and understanding. He feels like leaving home to escape a quarrelsome, critical situation, and to be free of family domination.

BEHAVIORAL STABILITY

Individuals with this profile type often lead stormy, chaotic lives and never seem to develop satisfying relationships.

DIAGNOSTIC CONSIDERATIONS

Individuals with this profile tend to have features of both an affective disorder and a thought disorder. In addition, there seems to be a long-standing pattern of maladjustment that is characteristic of people with severe personality disorders. He is likely to be diagnosed as having a Schizophrenic or Major Affective Disorder.

The content of his responses to the MMPI items suggests symptoms (convulsions, paralysis, clumsiness, and double vision) that are associated with neurological dis-

order. Vague pain symptoms, nausea, etc., that are found in neurotic conditions are also present, however. Further neurological evaluation would be needed to make a clear differentiation.

TREATMENT CONSIDERATIONS

Multiple-problem life situations and difficulties forming interpersonal relationships make patients with this profile type poor candidates for relationship-based psychotherapy. Their basic lack of trust and withdrawal would also make psychotherapy difficult. Some outpatients with this profile type seem to benefit from minimal contact treatment, such as brief periodic visits with a directive, supportive therapist. Many need psychotropic medication to control their bizarre thinking or to elevate their mood.

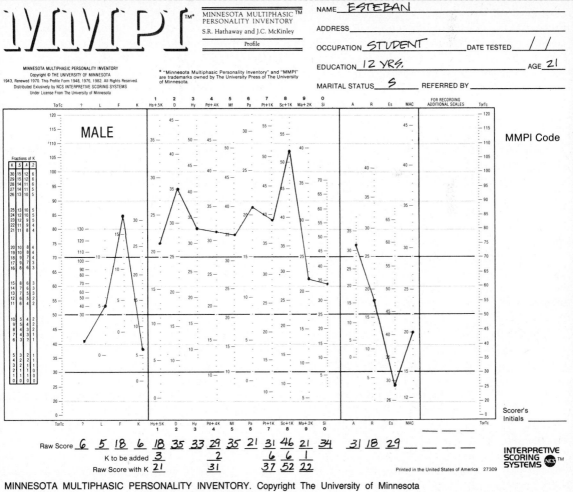

Esteban's most salient psychological problems concerned his tendency to become frustrated and his ready loss of impulse control. He was quite volatile and became upset quite easily. Additionally, Esteban's relative isolation during his early years (due in part to his overprotective mother) did not prepare him to function adequately in many social situations. Another important problem area for Esteban was in psychosexual adjustment. The psychological test results and his personal history clearly indicated a gender-identity confusion.

Within the parameters of DSM-III, Esteban would receive an Axis I diagnosis of *organic personality syndrome* and an Axis II diagnosis of *borderline personality*.

It was concluded that Esteban's chronic psychological problems would require psychological treatment on an intensive and long-term basis. Furthermore, it was recommended that he receive social-skills training and that—rather than a career in medicine—he be encouraged to pursue occupational goals more in keeping with his abilities. Psychotropic medication (Lithium and Mellaril) were prescribed for his affective problems.

A follow-up note. Esteban was seen in psychological therapy twice a week and was kept on medication. He was also seen in a social-skills training program for ten sessions. Through the help of his therapist, he was admitted to a less demanding English program, which seemed more appropriate for his abilities.

For the first six months, Esteban made considerable progress, especially after his behavior became somewhat stabilized as a result of the medications. He became less impulsive and more in control of his anger. He successfully completed the English classes in which he was enrolled. During this period, he lived with his mother, who had taken up a temporary residence near the college. She then returned to Colombia, and Esteban moved into an apartment with a roommate with whom he had increasing difficulty. Several weeks after his mother left, he quit going to therapy and quit taking his medication. He began to frequent local gay bars, at first out of curiosity but later to seek male lovers. At the same time, his preoccupation with religion increased and he moved into a house near campus that was operated by a fundamentalist religious cult. His parents, quite concerned by his overt homosexual behavior (which he described in detail over the phone, for example, asking them to visit the gay bar with him), came back to the States. Realizing that they could not stay permanently to supervise Esteban, they then sought a residential treatment program that would provide him with a more structured living arrangement. All assessment and therapy records were forwarded to those in charge of the residential program.

Integration of assessment data

As assessment data are collected, their significance must be interpreted so that they can be integrated into a coherent "working model" for use in planning or changing treatment.

In a clinic or hospital setting, assessment data are usually evaluated in a staff conference attended by members of the interdisciplinary team (perhaps a clinical psychologist, a psychiatrist, a social worker, and other mental health personnel) who are concerned with the decisions to be made regarding treatment. By putting together all the information they have gathered, they can see whether the findings complement each other and form a definitive clinical picture or whether there are gaps or discrepancies that necessitate further investigation.

At the time of the original assessment, integration of all the data may lead to agreement on a tentative diagnostic classification for the individual—such as *paranoid schizophrenia*. In any case, the findings of each member of the interdisciplinary team, as well as the recommendations for treatment, are entered in the case record, so that it will always be possible to check back and see why a certain course of therapy was undertaken, how accurate the clinical assessment was, and how valid the treatment decision turned out to be.

New assessment data collected during the course of therapy provide feedback on its effectiveness, as well as a basis for making needed modifications in an ongoing treatment program. As we have noted, clinical assessment data are also commonly used in evaluating the final outcome of therapy as well as in comparing the effectiveness of different therapeutic and preventive approaches. Summers (1979), among others,

HIGHLIGHT

Limitations of psychosocial assessment

Despite the need for assessment to understand an individual's problems and to plan appropriate treatment, the assessment process has several limitations and possible risks.

1. *Cultural bias of the instrument or the clinician.* Psychological tests may not elicit valid information from a patient of an ethnic minority, or a clinician from one sociocultural background may have trouble assessing objectively the behavior of an individual from another background (Dahlstrom, 1978; Gynther, 1979).

2. *Theoretical orientation of the clinician.* Assessment is inevitably influenced by the assumptions, perceptions, and theoretical orientation of the clinician. For example, a psychoanalyst and a behaviorist might assess the same behaviors quite differently.

3. *Overemphasis on internal traits.* Many clinicians overemphasize personality traits as the cause of patients' problems without due attention to the possible role of stressors in their life situations.

4. *Insufficient validation.* Many psychological assessment procedures have not been sufficiently validated. For example, unlike many of the personality scales, widely used procedures for behavioral observation and behavioral self-report have not been subjected to strict psychometric validation. The tendency on the part of clinicians to accept the results of these procedures at face value has recently been giving way to a broader recognition of the need for more explicit validation.

5. *Inaccurate data or premature evaluation.* There is always the possibility that some assessment data— and any label or treatment based on them—may be inaccurate. For example, some risk is always involved in making predictions for an individual on the basis of group data or averages. Inaccurate data or premature conclusions not only may lead to a misunderstanding of the patient's problem but may close off attempts to get further information, with possibly grave harm for the patient.

has pointed out the importance of assessing a patient's level of functioning prior to hospital discharge. Too often, individuals who cannot function well outside the mental hospital are released to the community with little or no provision for continuing mental health care.

The decisions made on the basis of assessment data may have far-reaching implications for the persons under study. The staff decision may determine whether a depressed person will be hospitalized or remain with his or her family; whether divorce will be accepted as a solution to an unhappy marriage or a further attempt will be made to salvage the marriage; or whether an accused person will be declared competent to stand trial. Thus a valid decision, based on accurate assessment data, is of far more than theoretical importance. Because of the impact that assessment can have, it is important that those involved keep in mind factors that may limit the accuracy of assessment. Some of these factors are noted in the **HIGHLIGHT** on this page.

The use of computers in assessment

Perhaps the most dramatic innovation in clinical assessment during the last decade has been the increasing sophistication and use of computers in individual assessment. As we have seen, computers are used in assessment both to gather information directly from the individual and to put together and evaluate all the information that has been gathered previously through interviews, tests, and other assessment procedures. By comparing the incoming information with data previously stored in its memory banks, the computer can perform a wide range of assessment tasks. It can supply a diagnosis, indicate the likelihood of certain kinds of behavior, suggest the most appropriate form of treatment, predict the outcome, and print out a summary report concerning the subject. In many of these functions, the computer is actually superior to the individual clinician because it is more efficient at recall of stored material.

In producing test evaluations or making predictions about individuals, the computer can sometimes employ an *actuarial* procedure. Here, descriptions of typical behavior of a large number of individuals with particular patterns of test scores have been stored in the computer. Then, whenever an individual turns up with one of these test score patterns, the appropriate description is printed out in the computer's evaluation. Such descriptions have been written and stored for a number of different test score patterns, most of them based on MMPI scores. Examples of these prepared descriptions appear in the computer evaluations reprinted in the **HIGHLIGHTS** on pages 599 and 602–3. Sometimes the different paragraphs picked up in this way by the computer will have elements that seem inconsistent. This is due to the fact that different parts of the individual's test pattern call up different paragraphs from the computer. The computer simply prints out blindly what has been found to be typical for individuals making similar scores on the various clinical scales. The computer cannot *integrate* the descriptions it picks up, however. This is where the human element comes in: in the clinical use of computers, it is *always* important that a trained professional further interpret and monitor the data.

There are several centers in the country to which clinicians and other professionals can send MMPI score sheets for actuarial interpretations. Some give interpretations with a special focus—for example, to evaluate and make predictions about individuals in a prison setting, or to detect psychological problems in a medical setting, or to make a general psychiatric evaluation.

So far, actuarial systems have been developed with adequate validation for only about twenty discrete personality profiles. This is only about a third of the personality types that might appear in a given clinical setting. To interpret scores that fall outside the computer's "experience tables," the computer is programmed with interpretive statements written by a clinician on the basis of his or her experience with individuals who have had particular test scores. Here the computer takes on the role of an "automated clinician," constructing a clinical report by printing out the statements that are appropriate for the individual's scores.

The essential difference between the actuarial program and the "automated clinician" program is that the first has been more directly and thoroughly validated for personality types; the clinical interpretations of the automated program are based instead on the clinical inference of the program developer. In practice, most computerized personality systems rely heavily on this latter type of information.

Computerized personality assessment is no longer a novelty, but an important, dependable adjunct to clinical evaluation (Johnson et al., 1977). Computer-assisted psychological evaluations are a quick and efficient means of providing the clinician with needed information early in the decision-making process. For example, in some settings, psychological testing can be individually administered via computer wired to a TV console to present the test items. The computer can score and interpret the test items and provide a complete diagnostic report before the client leaves the office. In other settings, test data and paper-and-pencil tests can be sent by mail or data phone to a central processing facility for scoring and interpretation. Factors determining which method of test data collection and processing will be used include the volume of testing done at the clinical facility, the speed with which assessments are completed, and the funding available to spend on psychological assessment. For example, facilities with few new admissions and steady long-term clients may not need an in-house computer assessment system, whereas agencies with a high admission rate and a very limited time for assessment may gain substantially from having test-processing facilities on their premises.

It should be reemphasized that, although computer-based test administration and interpretation are becoming quite widespread, the computer evaluation should be used only by a trained psychological test interpreter who has the final responsibility for the diagnostic study.

Summary

Clinical assessment is one of the most important and complex activities facing the mental health professional. The extent to which a person's problems are understood and appropriately treated depend, largely, on the adequacy of the psychological assessment. The goals of psychological assessment include identifying and describing the individual's symptoms; determining the chronicity and severity of the problem; evaluating the potential causal factors in the person's background; and exploring the personal resources of the individual that might be assets in his or her treatment program.

Interdisciplinary sources of assessment data include both physical evaluation methods and psychosocial assessment techniques. Since many psychological problems have physical components, either as underlying causal factors or as symptom patterns, it is often important to include a medical examination in the psychological assessment. In cases where organic brain damage is suspected, it is important to have neurological tests—such as the EEG, CAT scan, or PET scan—to aid in determining the site and extent of organic brain disorder. In addition, it may be important to have the person take a battery of neuropsychological tests to determine if the underlying brain disorder is affecting his or her behavior.

Psychosocial assessment methods are techniques for gathering relevant psychological information for clinical decisions about patients. The most widely used and most flexible psychosocial assessment methods are the clinical interview and behavior observation. These methods provide a wealth of clinical information. However, they may be subject to extraneous influences that make them somewhat unreliable, and structured interview formats and objective behavior rating scales have been developed to improve their reliability.

Whereas interview and behavior observation attempt to assess directly the individual's beliefs, attitudes, and symptoms, psychological tests attempt to measure these aspects of personality indirectly. Psychological tests include standardized stimuli for collecting behavior samples that can be compared with other individuals through test norms. Two different personality testing approaches have been developed: projective tests, such as the Rorschach, in which unstructured stimuli are presented to the subject who then "projects" meaning or structure on to the stimulus, thereby revealing "hidden" motives, feelings, etc.; and objective tests, or personality inventories, in which the subject is required to read and respond to the itemized statements or questions. Objective personality tests provide a cost effective means of collecting a great deal of personality information rapidly. The MMPI, the most widely used and validated objective personality inventory, provides a number of clinically relevant scales for describing abnormal behavior.

Possibly the most dramatic innovation in clinical assessment in recent years involves the widespread use of computers in the administration, scoring, and interpretation of psychological tests. It is now possible to obtain immediate test interpretation of psychological test results either through a direct computer interactive approach or through data telephone to a main frame computer that interprets tests. In the past few years rapid developments have been taking place in the computer assessment area. It is probable that within the next few years, most clinical assessments will involve computers in some capacity either for administration, scoring, interpretation, or for completing the entire test battery. Of course, mental health professionals will still play a major role in determining the appropriateness and adequacy of the computer diagnostic study.

Biologically based therapies

Carlo, Composition *(1957–58). Carlo (b. 1916) grew up in the Italian province of Verona, where he was put to work as an agricultural worker at the age of 9. As a child, he showed evidence of a solitary nature, preferring in general the company of his dog to that of other people. During the war, he suffered a series of psychological shocks that undermined an already-fragile psychological condition. Subject to delirium and visions of persecution, Carlo entered a psychiatric hospital in 1947. Since 1957, working in a small artist's studio provided by the hospital, he has devoted himself to creating complex, stylized drawings of animals and humans.*

herapy is directed toward modifying maladaptive behavior and fostering adaptive behavior. There are, of course, a great many other approaches to behavior change, such as formal education, political propaganda, and brainwashing. In therapy, however, the primary goal is to help an individual overcome maladaptive patterns and achieve more effective coping behavior.

The concept of therapy is not new. Throughout recorded history, human beings have tried to help each other with problems of living—including mental disorders—in both informal and formal ways. In Chapter 2 we noted the wide range of procedures that have, throughout history, been advocated for helping the mentally disturbed—from exorcism to incarceration and torture, from understanding and kindliness to the most extreme cruelty.

Today both biological and psychological procedures are used in attempts to help individuals overcome psychopathology. In this chapter we shall focus on biological methods that have evolved for the treatment of mental disorders such as the schizophrenias, affective disorders, and disorders in which severe anxiety is central. Then, in the next chapter we shall focus on psychological approaches.

Early attempts at biological intervention

The idea that a disordered mind might be set straight by treatment directed at the body goes back, as we have seen, to ancient times. Beginning with those early "medicine men" who trephined skulls, through to Hippocrates and Kraepelin, and on into the present era, there have always been those who believed that, ultimately, the route to the cure of mental aberration would have to be through alteration of the biological state of the organism. Today, we still have no reliable point-to-point correspondence between behavioral output and particular events in the brain at cellular or subcellular levels. Nonetheless, the dictum "no twisted thought without a twisted molecule," while philosophically and scientifically naive in certain respects, has been deeply internalized by many workers in the field. For them, it is but a small step to conclude that the search for treatment methods should concentrate on finding effective means of rearranging or reconstituting aberrant "molecules"—of changing the presumed physical substrate of abnormal mentality.

However sincere and benign the intent behind the earliest formal methods of treatment for mental disorders, they often in retrospect, seem extreme. The fundamental purpose seems to have been not so much to frighten the person out of his or her madness, but rather either to punish the demon in residence in the patient's body or to alter the patient's physical or biological state, which was presumed to be the underlying cause of the disorder. The latter rationale still forms the basis of biological treatments of the present day, though methods have become more sophisticated and more guided by scientific advances.

Treatments that involve substantial disruption of biological processes have a long history in medicine—witness the former practices of blood-letting, the use of strong purgatives, and the use of many drug compounds now known to be toxic in attempts to treat varied physical ailments. Indeed, it has been said that only within the present century has a random patient with a random illness consulting a random physician gained a better than even chance of not being harmed in the encounter. Even today, as in the chemotherapy treatment of many cancers, it is sometimes necessary to use treatment methods known to exact a heavy cost in terms of the new problems and new dangers they create. In general, however, as more has been learned in the various subfields of medicine, treatment measures have become more benign and less risky. As researchers come to understand scientifically the nature of a disease, they typically are then able to develop biological treatments that are more precisely designed to meet the specific problem. The specificity of the new treatment typically means it has fewer potentially damaging side effects.

Just as the biological sciences are generally far more advanced than the behavioral ones, medical treatment for physical diseases is far more advanced than medical treatment for behavioral disorders. The human brain and mind have yielded their secrets very grudgingly. As a re-

sult, relative to other medical subdisciplines, psychiatry has had a slow and often uncertain development. It should not be surprising, therefore, to find that it has contributed its own array of dubious treatment techniques in the comparatively short history of its recognition as a medical subspecialty. In fact, by 1917, with the discovery by Wagner-Jauregg that general paresis could be curbed by intentionally infecting the patient with malaria (the consequent fevers were lethal to the spirochete), the stage was set for the development of extraordinarily bold and oft-times hazardous ventures in the treatment arena. We shall look at two such treatments that survive to this day: the convulsive therapies and psychosurgery.

Coma and convulsive therapies

Insulin coma therapy, rarely used today, was introduced by Sakel in 1932 as a physiological treatment for schizophrenia. The technique involves administration of increasing amounts of insulin (a hormone that regulates sugar metabolism in the body) on a daily basis until a point is reached at which the patient goes into "shock"—actually hypoglycemic coma, caused by an acute deficiency of glucose (sugar) in the blood. Coma-inducing doses of insulin are administered daily thereafter until the patient has experienced approximately 50 comas, each an hour or more in duration. Comas are terminated by the administration of glucose. This treatment involves profound biological and physiological stress, especially to the cardiovascular and nervous systems. The patient being treated must be closely monitored both during and after the comatose state because of a variety of medical complications that may ensue, including some that are fatal.

Results of insulin coma therapy have been generally disappointing. Where the patient has shown improvement, it has been difficult to determine whether it was due to the experience of the coma or to some other feature associated with the treatment, such as the markedly increased attention of the medical staff. Moreover, patients who do show some improvement tend to be those who would improve readily under other treatment regimens as well; the severe, chronic schizophrenic patient remains for the most part unimproved. Finally, the relapse rate

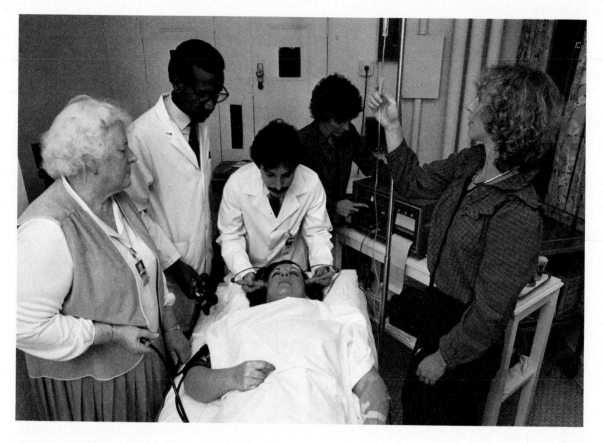

Electroconvulsive therapy (ECT) is administered to a patient.

for those who have improved has been very high. With such a record—and in the face of the marked medical risks—it is hardly surprising that the use of insulin coma as a therapeutic method has largely disappeared (Kalinowski & Hippius, 1969).

Electroconvulsive therapy (ECT) is much more widely used than insulin therapy, mostly because of its seeming effectiveness in alleviating depressive episodes. It was developed after an early observation—erroneous, as it turned out—that schizophrenia rarely occurred in individuals with epilepsy. This observation led to the inference that schizophrenia and epilepsy were somehow incompatible, and that therefore one might be able to cure schizophrenia by inducing convulsions. Various methods of convulsion-induction were tried until 1938 when two Italian physicians, Cerletti and Bini, tried the simplest method of all—that of passing an electric current through the patient's head.

Despite modest variations in the placing of electrodes and the introduction of safeguards, the standard form of bilateral ECT (involving both hemispheres of the brain) remains basically as Cerletti and Bini had determined it: an electric current of approximately 150 volts is passed from one side of the patient's head to the other for up to about one and one-half seconds. The patient immediately loses consciousness and undergoes a marked tonic (extensor) seizure of the muscles, followed by a lengthy series of clonic (contractile) ones of lesser amplitude. Typically, muscle-relaxant premedication is used to prevent violent contractions. In the days before such medication was available, the initial seizure was sometimes so violent as to fracture vertebrae, one of several potential complications of this method of therapy.

After awakening several minutes later, the patient has amnesia for the period immediately preceding the therapy, and is usually somewhat confused for the next hour or so. With repeated treatments, usually administered three times weekly, the patient gradually becomes generally disoriented, a state that clears after termination of treatments. Memory impairment, however, can remain for months (Squire, Slater, & Chase, 1975), or apparently, in some instances, even years (Breggin, 1979).

Normally, a treatment series consists of less than a dozen sessions, although in times past there was widespread overuse of the technique as a means of controlling excited or violent behavior. Today one can still find chronic patients on the "back wards" of mental hospitals whose treatment history includes the inducement of literally hundreds of seizures. The damage created by these excesses is difficult to estimate in precise terms, but it could well be substantial (Breggin, 1979; Palmer, 1981). It is quite possible that each single electroconvulsive treatment administered to a person destroys a varying number of central nervous system neurons.

Objective appraisals of this type of treatment have been curiously ignored by major segments of the psychiatric profession (Breggin, 1979). This would have been more easy to dismiss in the era of the 1940s, because very little else of proven efficacy was then available. It is more difficult to defend the widespread use of the technique at the present time, because effective alternative approaches are abundant. These issues have been discussed at length by Breggin (1979) in what is easily the most comprehensive review of available evidence concerning the potentially damaging effects of ECT. While Breggin's treatise is justifiably criticized for its somewhat biased language and style (e.g., Weiner, 1982), there exists no wholly effective counterargument to his expert review of the evidence. For example, demonstrable brain damage has been found in animals sacrificed immediately after ECT treatment. In short, while there is little doubt about the effectiveness of ECT in alleviating certain disorders—chiefly within the psychotic depressive range (although Breggin disputes even *this* conclusion—a balanced appraisal of the technique requires that it be considered potentially brain-damaging. The appropriate use of the treatment, therefore, should be preceded by a careful assessment of its potential costs and benefits in light of the circumstances attending a particular case. Unfortunately, Breggin noted that such a review is not necessarily routine; this is especially the case, at present, in private psychiatric hospitals, where much ECT is employed.

Responding to these sorts of concerns, the citizens of Berkeley, California, in November 1982 voted overwhelmingly to ban the use of ECT treatment within that city (*Science News*, Nov. 13, 1982), an action that was subsequently judicially overturned. Though the wisdom of holding public elections on such issues may be seriously questioned, the event demonstrates increased citizen awareness and concern about the treatment mental patients receive.

When therapeutic benefits do result from the use of ECT, they sometimes prove to be short-lived, with the patient relapsing back into depression or other disorder. Also, as has been true with some other techniques, the mechanism by which therapeutic effects are brought about has never been adequately explained. Some researchers believe that the therapeutic effect is mediated by induced changes in the biochemistry of brain synapses (Fink, 1979; Fink et al., 1974).

Despite all the questions and controversy, the therapeutic efficacy of ECT, at least in the short term, is well established (Fink, 1979; Scovern & Kilmann, 1980). A dramatic example of the unprecedented early success of ECT that sometimes occured following its introduction is provided in the autobiographical account of Lenore McCall (1947), who suffered a severe depressive disorder in her middle years.

Ms. McCall, a well-educated woman of affluent circumstances and the mother of three children, noticed a feeling of persistent fatigue as the first sign of her impending descent into depression. Too fearful to seek help, she at first attempted to fight off her increasingly profound apathy by engaging in excessive activity, a defensive strategy that accomplished little but the depletion of her remaining strength and emotional reserves.

In due course, she noticed that her mental processes seemed to be deteriorating—her memory appeared impaired and she could concentrate only with great difficulty. Emotionally, she felt an enormous loneliness, bleakness of experience, and increasingly intense fear about what was happening to her mind. She came to view her past small errors of commission and omission as the most heinous of crimes and increasingly withdrew from contact with her husband and children. Eventually, at her husband's and her physician's insistence, she was hospitalized despite her own vigorous resistance. She felt betrayed, and shortly thereafter attempted suicide by shattering a drinking glass and ingesting its fragments; to her great disappointment, she survived.

Ms. McCall thereafter spent nearly four years continuously in two separate mental hospitals, during which she deteriorated further. She was silent and withdrawn, behaved in a mechanical fashion, lost an alarming amount of weight, and underwent a seemingly premature aging process. She felt she emitted an offensive odor. At this time, ECT was introduced into the therapeutic procedures in use at her hospital.

A series of ECT treatments was given to Ms. McCall over a period of about three months. Then, one day, she woke up in the morning with a totally changed outlook: "I sat up suddenly, my heart pounding. I looked around the room and a sweep of wonder surged over me. God in heaven, I'm well. I'm myself. . . ." After a brief period of convalescence, she went home to her husband and children to try to pick up the threads of their lives that had been so painfully severed. She did so, and then wrote the engrossing and informative book from which this history is taken.

Some years ago, a modification in the standard method of administering ECT was introduced. Instead of placing the electrodes on each side of the head in the temple region, thereby causing a transverse flow of current through both cerebral hemispheres, the new procedure involves limiting current flow through only one side of the brain, typically the nondominant (right, for most people) side. This is called *unilateral ECT*, and there is good evidence that it lessens distressing side effects (such as memory impairment) without decreasing therapeutic effectiveness (Daniel & Crovitz, 1983b; Squire, 1977; Squire & Slater, 1978). Unfortunately, it has been estimated that as of the mid-1970s, some 75 percent of psychiatrists who employed ECT still used the original bilateral method exclusively (American Psychiatric Association, 1978). Though this may now be changing in favor of unilateral ECT, we must await further data for confirmation. There is also evidence that the use of a lower-energy pulsating electrical stimulus may produce less mental impairment than the standard treatment (Daniel & Crovitz, 1983a). However, the extent of use of this modification is not known.

ECT is used much less frequently today than heretofore, having yielded to advances in pharmacological approaches. However, it is still employed when other methods prove ineffective, or sometimes as a stopgap measure when slow-acting medication has not yet produced the desired result.

Psychosurgery

In 1935 in Portugal, Moniz introduced a surgical procedure in which the frontal lobes of the brain were severed from the deeper centers underlying them, a technique that eventually evolved into an operation known as *prefrontal lobotomy*. This operation stands as a dubious tribute to the levels to which professionals have sometimes been driven in their search for effective treatments of the psychoses. In retrospect, it seems somewhat surprising that this procedure—which results in permanent brain damage to the patient—won for its originator the Nobel Prize in Medicine for the year 1949.

In the two decades between 1935 and 1955 (when the new antipsychotic drugs became widely available) tens of thousands of mental patients in this country and abroad were subjected to prefrontal lobotomy and related neurosurgical procedures. In fact, in some settings, as many as 50 patients were treated at a facility in a single day (Freeman, 1959)! As is often the case with newly developed techniques of therapy, initial reports of results tended to be enthusiastic, downplaying complications (including a 1 to 4 percent death rate) and undesirable side effects. It was eventually recognized, however, that the "side effects" of psychosurgery could be very undesirable indeed. In some instances they included a permanent inability to inhibit impulses; in others, an unnatural "tranquility," with undesirable shallowness or absence of feeling. By 1951 the Soviet Union had banned all such operations; though rarely performed, they are still permitted by law in the United States and in many other countries.

The advent of the major antipsychotic drugs caused an almost immediate halt in the widespread use of psychosurgical procedures. Such operations are extremely rare today and are used only as a last resort for the intractable psychoses, severely and chronically debilitating obsessive-compulsive disorders, and occasionally for the control of severe pain in cases of terminal illness.

Contemporary psychosurgery, when it is employed, is unquestionably a much more circumspect procedure than was true in the heyday of lobotomies. Today, the permanent damage to the brain has been substantially minimized and therefore fewer detrimental side effects follow. The surgical technique involves the selective destruction of very minute areas; for example, in the "cingulotomy" procedure—which seems to relieve the subjective experience of pain, including "psychic" pain—a very small bundle of nerve fibers connecting the frontal lobes with a deeper structure known as the limbic system is interrupted with virtually pinpoint precision.

Despite these advances, continuing concern has been voiced about such operations, and in the mid-1970s the Congress of the United States called a special national commission to evaluate their effects. The report of that commission indicated some surprisingly beneficial effects that had been achieved with modern psychosurgery—for example, the alleviation of chronic depression—but it also warned that such benefits were often achieved at the expense of the loss of certain cognitive capacities. The commission recommended that cautious exploration of these techniques be continued with selected patients (Culliton, 1976).

The entire debate about psychosurgery has recently received a thorough airing in a fascinating book edited by Elliot Valenstein (1980). The procedures of psychosurgery—and by implication other "brain-disabling" therapies—are examined in relation to the psychiatric, ethical, legal, and social issues they necessarily raise. For example, what meaning can be assigned to the concept of *informed consent* if the patient is so disabled that this radical form of intervention is seriously considered? Or when, if ever, is it justified to employ surgical means to alter human personality? It appears we are finally reaching a level of public awareness and surveillance that will render it increasingly unlikely for these extreme measures to be employed without due consideration, in a context of full disclosure, of the risks as well as the benefits potentially entailed.

Emergence of pharmacological methods of treatment

A long-term goal of medicine has been to discover drugs that can effectively combat the ravages of mental disorder. This goal, one of the pursuits of *pharmacology,* the science of drugs, has until fairly recently remained very elusive. Early efforts in this direction were limited largely to a search for chemical compounds that would have soothing, calming, or sleep-inducing effects. Such drugs, if they could be found, would make it easier to manage distraught, excited, and sometimes violent patients. Little thought was given to the possibility that the status and course of the disorder itself might actually be brought under control by appropriate medication; the focus was on rendering the patient's overt behavior more manageable and thereby making restraint devices such as straitjackets unnecessary.

As the field of psychopharmacology developed, many such compounds were introduced and tried in the mental hospital setting. Almost without exception, however, those that produced the desired calming effects proved to have very serious shortcomings. At effective dosage levels they often produced severe drowsiness if not outright sleep, and many of them were dangerously addicting. On the whole, little real progress was made in this field until the mid-1950s, at which point, as we shall see, a genuine revolution in treatment of the more severe disorders occurred. This breakthrough was followed shortly by the discovery of compounds helpful in the treatment of the less severe, anxiety-based disorders, and eventually by recognition of the therapeutic benefits of lithium salts for affective disorders.

Types of drugs used in therapy

In this section we will trace the discovery of the four types of chemical agents now commonly used in therapy for mental disorders—antipsychotic compounds, antidepressant compounds, antianxiety compounds (minor tranquilizers), and lithium. These drugs are sometimes referred to as *psychotropic* drugs, in that their main effect is on the mental life of the individual. Beyond these drugs, we see new discoveries with growing frequency; a most exciting one is described in the **HIGHLIGHT** on page 616.

Antipsychotic compounds.

The antipsychotic compounds as a group are sometimes called "major tranquilizers," but this term is somewhat misleading. They are used with the major disorders, such as the schizophrenias, but they do more than tranquilize. While they do indeed produce a calming effect on many patients, their unique quality is that of somehow alleviating or reducing the intensity of psychotic symptoms, such as delusions and hallucinations. In some cases, in fact, a patient who is already excessively "tranquil" (e.g., withdrawn or immobile) becomes active and responsive to the environment under treatment by these drugs. The antianxiety compounds, to be described shortly, are by contrast effective in reducing tension without in any way affecting psychotic symptoms.

Although the benefits of the antipsychotic compounds have often been exaggerated, it is difficult to convey the truly enormous influence they have had in altering the environment of the mental hospital. One of the authors, as part of his training, worked several months in the maximum security ward of one such hospital immediately prior to the introduction of this type of medication in 1955. The ward patients fulfilled the oft-heard stereotypes of individuals "gone mad." Bizarreness, nudity, wild screaming, and an ever present threat of violence pervaded the atmosphere. Fearfulness and a near-total preoccupation with the maintenance of control characterized the attitudes of staff. Such staff attitudes were not unrealistic in terms of the frequency of occurrence of serious physical assaults by patients, but they were hardly conducive to the development or maintenance of an effective therapeutic program.

Then, quite suddenly—within a period of perhaps a month—all of this dramatically changed. The patients were receiving antipsychotic medication. The ward became a place in which one could seriously get to know one's patients on a personal level and perhaps even initiate programs of "milieu therapy"[1] and the like, promising reports of which had begun to appear in the professional literature. A new era in hospital treatment had arrived, aided enormously and in many instances actually made possible by the development of these extraordinary drugs.

The beginnings of this development were quite commonplace. For centuries the root of the plant *rauwolfia* (snakeroot) had been used in India for the treatment of mental disorders. In 1943, the *Indian Medical Gazette* reported improvement in manic reactions, schizophrenia, and other types of psychopathology following the use of *reserpine*, a drug derived from rauwolfia. Reserpine was first used in the United States in the early 1950s, after it was found to have a "calming" effect on mental patients (Kline, 1954). Early enthusiasm for the drug was tempered, however, by the finding that it also might produce low blood pressure, nasal congestion, and, perhaps most seriously, severe depression. Reanalysis of this latter finding suggested that the danger of serious depression is mainly for patients with a prior history of depression (Mendels & Frazer, 1974). Reserpine is now used mainly for the control of hypertension.

Meanwhile, the first of the phenothiazine family of drugs, *chlorpromazine* (Thorazine), was being synthesized in the early 1950s by one of the major pharmaceutical houses. It was first marketed at about the same time that reserpine was introduced, and it quickly proved to have virtually the same benefits but fewer undesirable side effects. It soon became the treatment of choice for schizophrenia.

The remarkable early successes reported with chlorpromazine led quickly to a bandwagon effect among other pharmaceutical companies, who began to manufacture and market their own variants of the basic phenothiazine compound. Some of the best known variants are trifluoperazine (Stelazine), promazine (Sparine),

---

[1]In *milieu therapy* the entire facility is regarded as a therapeutic community, and the emphasis is on developing a meaningful and constructive environment in which the patients participate in the regulation of their own activities. Self-reliance and the formation of socially acceptable interpersonal relationships are encouraged.

HIGHLIGHT
Will Alzheimer's disease yield to drug treatment?

The widespread and devastating effects of Alzheimer's disease (formerly called senile dementia), which is increasing in incidence as our population ages, was examined in Chapter 13. It was noted that research has strongly implicated a deterioration of acetycholine-producing cells in the basal forebrain as a primary cause of the disorder. It is suspected that the profound mental deterioration that is the hallmark of the disorder is due to a progressive depletion of the acetylcholine neurotransmitter in brain pathways supporting memory and other vital mental functions. Hence, increasing the availability of acetylcholine in the brain—"artificially," as it were—might deter or even reverse the accompanying dementia.

Unfortunately, at least from this perspective, much of the chemistry of the brain is remarkably well-protected from external interference, and manipulation of this chemistry may require highly indirect pharmacological approaches. Such is the case with brain acetylcholine. However, one drug, physostigmine, is showing considerable promise in this regard. The administration of physostigmine results in the blocking of an enzyme called cholinesterase, a main agent causing the chemical breakdown of acetylcholine. By preventing such breakdown, physostigmine apparently allows for increased concentrations of acetylcholine in the brain pathways that use it for neurotransmission, and thereby improves mental performance in Alzheimer patients.

The presumed action of physostigmine is theoretically tidy; the known facts fit well together. More opaque are observations that a drug called naloxone may benefit the mental functioning of Alzheimer sufferers. So far as is known, naloxone's main effect is to block the action of endorphins, the brain's natural opiates. It is unclear how such an effect would alter acetylcholine levels or improve mental functioning by some other means.

It should be emphasized that work with both of these drugs as they apply to Alzheimer's disease is in very early, experimental stages. Future research could alter the picture dramatically. They are discussed here as illustrative of what the future *might* hold in respect to a disease traditionally considered to be progressive, irreversible, and terminal.

Adapted from an article in the *Chicago Tribune*, April 3, 1983.

---

prochlorperazine (Compazine), thioridazine (Mellaril), perphenazine (Trilafon), and fluphenazine (Prolixin). Currently, too, there are at least six classes of nonphenothiazine antipsychotic compounds available in the United States (Carson, 1984), of which the best known is haloperidol (Haldol). The diversity becomes less bewildering when it is remembered that virtually all of the antipsychotics accomplish a common biochemical effect, namely the blocking of dopamine receptors, as was noted in Chapter 10.

With persistent use or at high dosage, however, all of these preparations have varying degrees of troublesome side effects, such as dryness of mouth and throat, muscular stiffness, jaundice, and a Parkinson-like syndrome involving tremors of the extremities and immobility of the facial muscles. Which side effects develop appears to depend on the particular compound used in relation to the particular vulnerabilities of the treated patient. Many of these side effects are temporary and may be relieved by substitution of another drug of the same class, by a different class of drug, or by reduction in dosage. Also to be noted is that some schizophrenic individuals do not respond to antipsychotic drug therapy and may indeed be made worse by it (Buckley, 1982).

For certain patients, a particularly troublesome side effect of long-term antipsychotic drug treatment is the development of a disfiguring disturbance of motor control, particularly of the facial muscles, known as *tardive dyskinesia*. The disorder is believed to be due to an imbalance in dopamine and acetylcholine activity in the brain, secondary to alterations in receptor sensitivity by antipsychotics and other drugs commonly used in combination to control their side effects.

As yet, there is no completely effective treatment for tardive dyskinesia, and its superficial or "symptomatic" treatment not infrequently worsens the long-range outcome because it necessitates increasing the dosage of the very drugs that, over time, cause the problem (Kucharski & Unterwald, 1981).

Compared to anything we have known before, the effects of antipsychotic compounds in the treatment of schizophrenic disorders are clearly remarkable. At the same time, we must acknowledge that they are not a panacea. Indeed, while the more striking symptoms of schizophrenic psychoses frequently abate with continued use of these drugs, the behavioral residual is usually less than impressive; the patient still does not become the alert, competent person one might hope. Though no longer overtly psychotic, the individual's schizophrenic symptoms often reappear upon withdrawal from the drug. In short, the pharmacologic approach has yet to produce a "cure" for schizophrenia that reliably continues beyond the taking of medication (Berger, 1978).

The range of effects achieved by the antipsychotic drugs may be illustrated by two brief case histories of patients who served as subjects in a clinical research project designed to evaluate differing treatment approaches to the schizophrenias (Grinspoon, Ewalt, & Shader, 1972).

Ms. W. was a 19-year-old, white, married woman who was admitted to the treatment unit as a result of gradually increasing agitation and hallucinations over a three-month period. Her symptoms had markedly intensified during the four days prior to admission, partly as a result of a homosexual seduction she had undergone while under the influence of marijuana. She had had a deprived childhood, but had managed to function reasonably well up to the point of her breakdown.

At the outset of her hospitalization, Ms. W. continued to have auditory and visual hallucinations and appeared frightened, angry, and confused. She believed she had some special, unique relationship with God or the devil. Her thought content displayed loosening of associations, and her affect was inappropriate to this content. Her condition continued to deteriorate for more than two weeks, at which point medication was begun.

Ms. W. was assigned to a treatment group in which the patients were receiving thioridazine (Mellaril). She responded quite dramatically during the first week of treatment. Her behavior became, for the

most part, quiet and appropriate, and she made some attempts at socialization. She continued to improve, but by the fourth week of treatment began to show signs of mild depression. Her medication was increased, and she resumed her favorable course. By the sixth week she was dealing with various reality issues in her life in a reasonably effective manner, and by the ninth week she was spending considerable time at home, returning to the hospital in a pleasant and cheerful mood. She was discharged exactly 100 days after her admission, being then completely free of symptoms.

Mr. S., the eldest of three sons in a fairly religious Jewish family, was admitted to the hospital after developing marked paranoid ideation and hallucinations during his first weeks of college. He had looked forward to going to college, an elite New England school, but his insecurity once on campus caused him to become unduly boastful about his prowess with drinking and women. He stayed up late at night to engage in "bull sessions," and he neglected his studies and other responsibilities. Within ten days he had panicked about his ability to keep up and tried frantically to rearrange his course schedule and his life, to no avail.

His sense of incompetence was transformed over time into the idea that others—including all the students in his dormitory—were against him, and that fellow male students were perhaps flirting homosexually with him. By the time of his referral to the college infirmary, he was convinced the college was a fraud he would have to expose, that the CIA was plotting against him, and that someone was going to kill him. He heard voices and smelled strange odors. He also showed a marked loosening of associations and flat, inappropriate affect. At the time of his transfer to the hospital, he was diagnosed as an acute paranoid schizophrenic.

Mr. S. was assigned to a treatment group receiving haloperidol (Haldol). His initial response to treatment was rapid and favorable, but observers noted that his behavior remained quite immature. Then quite suddenly during the fifth week of treatment, he became very tense, negativistic, and hostile. Thereafter, he gradually became less defiant and angry, and he responded well to a day-care program prescribed by his therapist, although he was nervous and apprehensive about being outside the hospital. He was discharged as improved ten weeks after initiation of his drug therapy.

Three months later Mr. S. was readmitted to the hospital. While he had done well at first, he then had begun to deteriorate, concurrently with his doctor-monitored withdrawal from haloperidol. His behavior showed increasing signs of lack of effective control. He began to set random fires and was described by the investigators as "sociopathic." Two days after his readmission, he signed himself out of the hospital "against medical advice." His parents immediately arranged for his confinement in another hospital, and the investigators subsequently lost contact with him.

Antidepressant compounds.   The antidepressant drugs made their appearance shortly after the introduction of reserpine and chlorpromazine. There are two basic classes of these compounds: the monoamine oxidase (MAO) inhibitors and the tricyclics. While they differ considerably in their chemical makeup, it is currently believed that they accomplish a common biochemical result—namely, that of increasing the concentrations of the neurotransmitters serotonin and norepinephrine at pertinent synaptic sites in the brain (Berger, 1978). In fact, there is current speculation that measurably different types of depression may correlate with differing functional levels of these and possibly other neurotransmitters, and that it may be possible to discover how to use antidepressant drugs in a very selective manner, depending on which neurotransmitter systems they maximally affect (Akiskal, 1979; Maugh, 1981).

Unfortunately, the *etiological* significance of these ideas is complicated by problems similar to those relating excess dopamine activity to schizophrenia (see page 368). For example, the effect of these drugs on neurotransmitter synaptic concentrations occurs quite promptly, whereas the *clinical* effects of the drugs on modifying depressive affect and behavior are often agonizingly delayed. Hence, it seems unlikely that depressive phenomena are directly and uniquely caused by neurotransmitter anomalies corrected by these substances.

Of the two main classes of antidepressants, the tricyclics are by far the more often used. This is largely because the MAO inhibitors are more toxic and require troublesome dietary restrictions; in addition, they are widely believed to have less potent therapeutic effects. Nevertheless, some patients who do not respond favorably to tricyclics will subsequently do well on an MAO inhibitor. A minority of severely depressed patients respond to neither type of antidepressant compound, in which case alternative modes of intervention, such as electroconvulsive therapy, may be tried. Commonly

W*hen first admitted to the hospital, this patient exhibited symptoms of schizophrenia (withdrawal into fantasy and delusions of persecution). Her behavior alternated between spells of crying, agitation, and fearful, unresponding silence (left and top). Treatment included psychotherapy and the use of the drug chlorpromazine to calm her. The patient showed rapid improvement. By the third day, she was dressed in street clothes, and was able to talk animatedly with her psychiatrist (right). After seven weeks, the woman was released. Follow-up treatment included periodic visits to a community health clinic, continuing medication, and the understanding of her husband and family. (Based on Wilson, 1964.)*

used tricyclics are imipramine (Tofranil), amitriptyline (Elavil), and nortriptyline (Aventyl). MAO inhibitors include isocarboxazid (Marplan), phenelzine (Nardil), and tranylcypromine (Parnate).

Antidepressant drugs, particularly tricyclics, continue to be developed, tested, and marketed at a high rate. Among the more recent entrants to the field are amoxapine (Asendin), maprotiline (Ludiomil), and trazodone (Desyrel). Amoxapine is a tricyclic related to certain of the antipsychotic compounds and thus may prove to have a special role in the treatment of schizoaffective disorder. Maprotiline and trazodone are technically not tricyclics at all, but rather tetracyclics; the chemical addition of an extra benzene ring is in each case claimed to reduce problematic side effects. Trazodone, in particular, appears a very promising drug (Moore, 1982).

Pharmacological treatment of depression often produces a dramatic and fully satisfactory result. This is in sharp contrast to the effect of the antipsychotic drugs in merely suppressing schizophrenic symptoms. However, this statement must be tempered with the observation that individuals suffering from severe depressive disorders often respond to any treatment— or even no treatment at all. That is distinctly less true in the case of the schizophrenias.

Antianxiety compounds (the minor tranquilizers). If it is true, as we have observed, that ours is the age of anxiety, it is certainly no less true that ours is also the age of the search for anxiety-reducers. At the present time, literally millions of physician-prescribed pills alleged to contain anxiety- and tension-relieving substances are consumed daily by the American public, to say nothing of the manifold alternative methods people employ to reduce their anxiety—ranging from biofeedback to the practice of ancient Eastern religious rituals—that promise to relieve "uptight" feelings. The nonprescription drug market, which includes traffic in alcoholic beverages, marijuana, and decidedly more problematic substances, has had an unprecedented growth rate since the 1960s—much of it presumably due to the same widespread wish to be somehow relieved of "hassle."

Besides the long-used *barbiturates* (see Chapter 11), which have high addictive potential and a low margin of dosage safety, two additional classes of prescription antianxiety compounds have gained widespread acceptance in recent years. One of these, the propanediols (mostly meprobamate compounds), seems to operate mainly through the reduction of muscular tension, which in turn is experienced by the patient as calming and emotionally soothing. Meprobamate drugs are marketed under the trade names Miltown and Equanil.

The other class of antianxiety compounds is the *benzodiazepines* (see **HIGHLIGHT** on page 621). Up until recently, their use in this country was increasing at an alarming rate; however, thanks to effective public warnings about the addictive potential of these compounds, this trend is now leveling off. Under this rubric are included chlordiazepoxide (Librium), diazepam (Valium), oxazepam (Serax), clorazepate (Tranxene), and flurazepam (Dalmane). In experimental studies on animals, the most striking effect of these compounds has been the recurrence of behavior previously inhibited by conditioned fears but without serious impairment in overall behavioral efficiency. Benzodiazepines, in other words, somehow selectively diminish generalized fear (or anxiety) yet leave adaptive behaviors largely intact. They are thus far superior to many other types of anxiety-reducing chemicals, which tend to produce widespread negative effects on adaptive functioning.

Nevertheless, all of the antianxiety drugs have a basically sedative effect on the organism, and many patients treated with them complain of drowsiness and lethargy. This has been a particular problem among schoolchildren treated with these compounds. Also to be emphasized is that all of these drugs have the potential of inducing dependence when used unwisely or in excess (Bassuk & Schoonover, 1977; Levenson, 1981).

The range of application of the antianxiety compounds is quite broad. They are used in all manner of conditions in which tension and anxiety may be significant components, including anxiety-based and psychophysiologic disorders. They are also used as supplementary treatment in certain neurological disorders in order to control such symptoms as convulsive seizures, but they have little place in the treatment of the psychoses. They are now the most widely prescribed of all of the drugs available to physicians, a fact that has caused concern among

HIGHLIGHT
Chemically induced sleep: Is it worth the risks?

Prescriptions for the benzodiazepine class of antianxiety compounds currently exceed 70 million per year in the United States. Of these, a huge proportion are written for the ostensible purpose of enabling persons to sleep better at night. The most common benzodiazepine prescribed specifically for this purpose is flurazepam (Dalmane). Some 8 million individuals use this general class of drug sometime during any one year, and up to 2 million persons take these pills nightly for more than two months at a time. It is prescribed for many patients hospitalized for physical disease.

Reacting to this overuse, the Institute of Medicine (IOM) of the National Academy of Sciences issued a report outlining the hazards of this remedy for sleeping difficulties—difficulties that in any case they found to be severely overestimated on a routine basis by the persons allegedly suffering from them. Noting that the barbiturates justly deserve their reputation as dangerous drugs, the IOM report indicated that the benzodiazepines may be just as risky, and in some cases more so. For example, flurazepam, while not quite as addicting as the barbiturates, remains in the body in the form of metabolites far longer than do the barbi-

turates, resulting in a build-up of toxic substances in the body that may reach a critical level within a week of regular ingestion of the drug at bedtime. While flurazepam overdose is usually not in itself lethal, it may interact with other drugs, such as alcohol, to produce lethal effects. Because of these readily misunderstood characteristics, the IOM concludes that, overall, flurazepam does not diminish the number of deaths attributable to sleeping pill medication, relative to earlier types of "hypnotic" drugs such as the barbiturates.

A particularly worrisome aspect of this problem is the fact that a certain amount of benign "insomnia" naturally accompanies advancing age. And yet elderly persons receive some 39 percent of all sleeping pill prescriptions. For these individuals there is a real danger that the side effects of these drugs, such as daytime lethargy and clouding of consciousness, may be considered indicators of senile deterioration by family members and even by professional caretakers.

Considering the risks involved in taking these drugs, it seems appropriate to keep in mind an observation of one of the IOM members: losing some sleep now and then is *not* a life-threatening problem (Smith, 1979).

some leaders in the medical and psychiatric fields.

Continuing research on benzodiazepines and related compounds is turning up promising leads that will almost certainly result in important future advances in the treatment of anxiety, as well as other conditions. It is now known that the benzodiazepines produce their effects by chemically binding to specific receptors at neuronal synapses, blocking normal transmission; this suggests that these receptors are implicated in mediating the experience of anxiety. Additionally, since these compounds also have sedative, muscle relaxant and anticonvulsive properties, it might be possible to differentiate specific receptors for each, and to discover variant compounds that will selectively bind to them. In fact, researchers at one of the larger pharmaceutical companies have already discovered a

chemical that appears to counteract anxiety and convulsions without being a muscle relaxant or sedative. Work in this area, recently reviewed by Folkenberg (1982) and by Kolata (1982), has important implications for our basic understanding of brain processes, in addition to its obvious clinical import.

Lithium for the affective disorders.   Lithium is the lightest of the metals. Its simple salts, such as lithium carbonate, were discovered—as early as 1949 by J. Cade in Australia—to be effective in treating manic disorders. Some twenty years passed before this treatment was introduced in the United States. This may have been, in part, for two reasons. First, if not used at the proper dosage, lithium can be very toxic to the individual, causing numerous troublesome side

HIGHLIGHT
Frequently used drugs in the treatment of mental and behavioral disorders

Class	Generic name	Trade name	Used to treat	Effects
Antipsychotic				
a) phenothiazines	chlorpromazine	Thorazine	Psychotic (especially schizophrenic) symptoms such as extreme agitation, delusions, and hallucinations; aggressive or violent behavior.	Somewhat variable in achieving intended purpose of suppression of psychotic symptoms. Side effects, such as dry mouth, are often uncomfortable. In long-term use may produce motor disturbances such as Parkinsonism and tardive dyskinesia.
	thioridazine	Mellaril		
	promazine	Sparine		
	trifluoperazine	Stelazine		
	prochlorperazine	Compazine		
	perphenazine	Trilafon		
	fluphenazine	Prolixin		
b) butyrophenones	haloperidol	Haldol		
c) thioxanthenes	thiothixine	Navane		
	chlorprothixene	Taractan		
Antidepressant				
a) tricyclics	imipramine	Tofranil	Relatively severe depressive symptoms, especially of psychotic severity and unipolar in type.	Somewhat variable in alleviating depressive symptoms, and noticeable effects may be delayed up to three weeks. Multiple side effects—some of them dangerous. Use of MAO inhibitors requires dietary restrictions.
	amitriptyline	Elavil		
	nortriptyline	Aventyl		
	protriptyline	Vivactil		
	doxepin	Sinequan		
b) monoamine oxidase (MAO) inhibitors	isocarboxazid	Marplan		
	phenelzine	Nardil		
	tranylcypromine	Parnate		

effects, such as delirium and convulsions. And yet lithium, if it is to have any notable therapeutic effect, must be used in quantities within the range of potential dangerousness, which varies among different individuals. Thus, at the outset of lithium treatment, the patient's blood levels of lithium must be monitored carefully in relation to observable behavioral effects, in order that the minimum effective dosage can be established.

A second possible reason for the delay in widespread usage of lithium in the United States may have been the simple fact that researchers were skeptical that it was the lithium itself that was producing the beneficial results: the lithium compounds used in treatment are simple inorganic salts that have no known physiological function (Berger, 1978). Lithium, then, is a somewhat peculiar drug.

Its curious qualities notwithstanding, there

Class	Generic name	Trade name	Used to treat	Effects
Antimanic (bipolar)	lithium carbonate	Eskalith Lithane Lithonate Lithotabs Phi-Lithium	Manic episodes and some severe depressions, particularly recurrent ones or those alternating with mania.	Usually effective in resolving manic episodes, but highly variable in effects on depression, probably because the latter is a less homogeneous grouping. Multiple side effects unless carefully monitored; high toxicity potential.
Antianxiety (minor tranquilizers) a) propanediols b) benzodiazepines	meprobamate diazepam chlordiazepoxide flurazepam oxazepam clorazepate	Equanil Miltown Valium Librium Dalmane Serax Tranxene	Nonpsychotic personality problems in which anxiety and tension are prominent features; also used as anticonvulsants and as sleep-inducers (especially flurazepam).	Somewhat variable in achieving intended purpose of tension reduction. Side effects include drowsiness and lethargy. Dependence and toxicity are dangers.
Stimulant	dextroamphetamine amphetamine methylphenidate	Dexedrine Benzedrine Ritalin	Hyperactivity, distractability, specific learning disabilities, and, occasionally, extreme hypoactivity.	Rather unpredictable. When maximally effective, can enable otherwise uneducable children to attend regular schools. Side effects often troublesome, including recently discovered retardation of growth.

can be no doubt at this point concerning lithium's remarkable effectiveness in promptly resolving about 70 percent of all manic states. In addition, as we saw in Chapter 9, lithium is sometimes successful in relieving depressions, although possibly only in those patients who are subject to both manic and depressive episodes—that is, who are bipolar in type (Bassuk & Schoonover, 1977; Berger, 1978; Segal, Yager, & Sullivan, 1976). More recent research, however, suggests that there may be a subclass of *unipolar* depressive patients who benefit from lithium treatment (Coppen, Metcalfe, & Wood, 1982).

The drug has been a boon, especially to those persons who heretofore have experienced repeated bouts with mania and/or depression throughout their adult lives. For many, these cycles can now be modulated or even prevented by regular maintenance doses of lithium—for example, by taking a single tablet each morning and evening. Psychiatry may thus have achieved its first essentially preventive treatment method.

One of Cade's (1949) own cases will serve well as an illustration of the effects of lithium treatment:

Mr. W. B. was a 51-year-old man who had been in a state of chronic manic excitement for five years. So obnoxious and destructive was his behavior that he had long been regarded as the most difficult patient on his ward in the hospital.

He was started on treatment with a lithium compound, and within three weeks his behavior had improved to the point that transfer to the convalescent ward was deemed appropriate. He remained in the hospital for another two months, during which his behavior continued to be essentially normal. Prior to discharge, he was switched to another form of lithium salts, because the one he had been taking had caused stomach upset.

He was soon back at his job and living a happy and productive life. In fact, he felt so well off that, contrary to instructions, he stopped taking his lithium. Thereafter he steadily became more irritable and erratic; some six months following his discharge, he had to cease work. In another five weeks he was back in the hospital in an acute manic state.

Lithium therapy was immediately reestablished, with prompt positive results. In another month Mr. W. B. was pronounced ready to return to home and work, provided he continued taking a prescribed dosage of lithium.

The biochemical basis of the therapeutic effect of lithium is unknown. One well-received hypothesis is that it achieves its effects by limiting the availability of norepinephrine, which functions as a neurotransmitter or modulator at certain synapses in the brain. This effect is opposite that of antidepressant compounds and presumably reduces the individual's ability to process the amount of input typical during a manic state. Of course, this still leaves unexplained the fact that lithium can also alleviate some depressions. An alternative hypothesis is that lithium, being a mineral salt, may have an effect on electrolyte balances, which may also alter the properties of neurotransmission within the brain. So far, however, this connection remains largely speculative. Clearly, the riddle of exactly what occurs will be solved only by more and better research.

Drug therapy for children

Our discussion of the use of drugs in treating maladaptive behavior would be incomplete without some reiteration of their role in the management of childhood disturbances and disorders. We have already addressed this matter to some extent in Chapter 14. While our society has often been too quick to label as deviant, and to proceed to "treat," various annoying or inconvenient behaviors in which children sometimes indulge, it is nevertheless true that *some* children do evidence more or less serious behavior disorders. It is also true that some of them may be helped by judicious use of medication.

Antianxiety, antipsychotic, and antidepressant medications have all been used effectively with children who are, respectively, excessively anxious or "nervous," psychotic, or depressed. Considerable caution must be exercised in the use of these powerful compounds with children, however, in order to be certain that dosage levels are within tolerable limits for a small and as yet biologically immature organism. Not only are excessive blood levels of these drugs physically dangerous, but in some instances they may produce paradoxical reversal effects—that is, the child's problem may become *more* severe (Bassuk & Schoonover, 1977).

We have already mentioned the apparently widespread problem of excessively tranquilized elementary-school pupils. While the diagnostic terms "hyperactivity," "hyperkinesis," "minimal brain dysfunction," and "specific learning disability" have been used somewhat haphazardly in recent years, there appears to be a subset of highly distractable youngsters of normal but unevenly developed cognitive ability who benefit rather dramatically, and paradoxically, from drugs that stimulate the central nervous system. As we saw in Chapter 14, the most widely used of these stimulants are the amphetamines; a closely related compound known as methylphenidate (Ritalin) is also used. In certain instances, these drugs produce a prompt termination of hyperactivity, which typically results in an increase in attention span and in ability to do schoolwork (Sprague, Barnes, & Werry, 1970). Normally, the child thus helped is kept on the drug until he or she reaches adolescence, when hyperactivity tends to diminish by an as yet unknown natural process (Bassuk & Schoonover, 1977).

The danger, of course, is that restless, overactive children will be summarily diagnosed as "hyperkinetic" or "minimally brain damaged" and treated with drugs *whether or not the problem is essentially a physical one.* If such is the case, the option to use less extreme but potentially effective psychological approaches in treating these children may be forgotten (see Chapter 14).

A perspective on pharmacological therapy

Modern psychopharmacology has brought a reduction in the severity and chronicity of many types of psychopathology, particularly the psychoses. It has helped many individuals who would otherwise require hospitalization to function in their family and community setting; it has led to the earlier discharge of those who do require hospitalization and to the greater effectiveness of aftercare programs; and it has made restraints and locked wards largely methods of the past. All in all, pharmacological therapy not only has outmoded more drastic forms of treatment but has led to a much more favorable hospital climate for patients and staff alike (see **HIGHLIGHT** beginning on page 622 for a summary of drugs used in psychopharmacological therapy).

However, there are a number of complications and limitations in the use of psychotropic drugs. Aside from possible undesirable side effects, the problem of matching drug and dosage to the needs of a given individual is often a difficult one, and it is sometimes necessary to change medication in the course of treatment. In addition, as many investigators have pointed out, these drugs tend to alleviate symptoms by inducing biochemical changes rather than bring the individual to grips with personal or situational factors that may be reinforcing maladaptive behaviors. Although the reduction in anxiety, disturbed thinking, and other symptoms may tempt therapists to regard a patient as "recovered," it would seem wise to include psychotherapy in the total program if such gains are to be maintained or improved upon.

The judicious combining of chemical and psychological forms of treatment, however, is a somewhat more complicated challenge than it might at first appear. For example, there may be complex interactions—not all of them necessarily positive in effect—between the two types of influence, such that the potential positive effects of either could be mitigated or compromised by the influence of the other treatment. Research into the problems of combined treatments is still in its infancy, and is characterized by much confusion and contradiction (Hollon & Beck, 1978). Overall, however, there is much reason to be optimistic about the combined use of drugs and psychosocial approaches, especially in the more severe disorders such as schizophrenia (Smith, Glass, & Miller, 1980) and major affective disorder (Klerman & Schechter, 1982).

Other biological therapies

Our still incomplete understanding of the biological bases of mental disorders, particularly the major psychoses, renders the field a fertile one for speculative thought and for continuation of the search for new innovations in biological intervention. By and large, despite the gains described above, the history of these innovations has been a disappointing one; when subjected to rigorous evaluation, most new treatment techniques for which hopeful claims have been made have proven ineffective except by virtue of the power of suggestion—the so-called placebo effect. Nevertheless, it would be folly to condemn out of hand all new proposed therapies: witness, for instance, the unnecessary and unfortunately long delay in the introduction of lithium therapy in the United States. In this section we will review two of the more currently popular of these relatively untried and somewhat maverick biological therapies.

1. *Megavitamin therapy.* In megavitamin therapy treatment includes large dosages of vitamins, particularly niacin (vitamin B_3, nicotinic acid), which have been alleged to have curative properties for schizophrenic patients by correcting certain imbalances in brain biochemistry. In addition, the treatment regimen usually involves large-scale ingestion of other vitamins besides the B group (especially ascorbic acid, vitamin C), as well as various special diets in what is known as the "orthomolecular" approach.

There is no reliable evidence that the orthomolecular approach by itself (that is, without accompanying standard antipsychotic medication) produces any benefit to patients. In fact, an American Psychiatric Association Task Force, charged with conducting an evaluation of this approach, issued the following unusually harsh judgment after a lengthy review of the available evidence:

"In the end the credibility of the megavitamin proponents and the orthomolecular psychiatrists becomes the crucial issue because it is never possible to fully prove or disprove a therapeutic procedure. Rather the theory and practice gain or lose credibility as their premises, methods, and results are examined, and attempts are made at clinical replication by independent investigators. This review and critique has carefully examined the literature produced by megavitamin proponents and by those who have attempted to replicate their basic and clinical work. It concludes that in this regard the credibility of the megavitamin proponents is low.

"Their credibility is further diminished by a consistent refusal over the past decade to perform controlled experiments and to report their new results in a scientifically acceptable fashion.

"Under these circumstances, this Task Force considers the massive publicity which they promulgate via radio, the lay press, and popular books, using catch phrases which are really misnomers like 'megavitamin therapy' and 'orthomolecular treatment' to be deplorable." (Lipton et al., 1973, p. 48)

Despite this harsh judgment, now over a decade old, and the absence of any solid new evidence tending to mitigate its force, megavitamin treatment continues to be strongly advocated by a certain subgroup of practitioners.

2. *Hemodialysis therapy.* In November of 1977, Ervin and Palmour announced that they had isolated a certain peptide molecule from the blood of schizophrenic patients and suggested that this allegedly psychotoxic substance could be removed by hemodialysis—blood purification by means of the artificial kidney machine (*Time*, November 21, 1977). Actually, dialysis treatment of schizophrenia had already been begun some

five years earlier by R. Cade at the University of Florida. Greenberg (1978) reported that Cade and his former colleague Wagemaker claimed recovery or significant improvement for two thirds of treated patients.

At the time of his original report, Greenberg also noted that the National Institute of Mental Health had taken a cautious but interested approach to these claims, pending the results of an independent assessment of efficacy. Those results have recently become available (Schulz et al., 1981). None of the relatively small sample of patients improved with dialysis, and half of them became worse. It seems extremely unlikely, therefore, that this treatment is the long hoped-for panacea. The extensive and unrelievedly disappointing history of announced discoveries of a blood toxin that is responsible for schizophrenia, especially when considered in relation to the unlikelihood of a single factor accounting for the disorder, should make us extremely skeptical of any such future claims.

The failures of megavitamin therapy and hemodialysis, both of which had been introduced by their proponents with considerable fanfare, make a more general and telling point: in this area, as in all of medicine, until treatment efficacy has been confirmed by disinterested and independent investigators, early claims of success should be entertained with appropriate caution. Of course, the very same point applies to the psychosocial therapies, to be discussed in the next chapter.

Summary

Except for the development of electroconvulsive therapy (ECT) beginning in 1938, the biological approach to the treatment of mental disorders, at least on this continent and in Europe, had made little headway until about 1955. Indeed, some of the early biological treatments, such as insulin coma therapy and lobotomy, probably did more harm than good—as did many early medical treatments for purely physical diseases.

The mode of therapeutic action of ECT, which continues to be widely used, is not yet understood. However, there is little doubt of its efficacy for certain patients, especially those suffering from severe depression. Appropriate premedication together with other modifications in technique (e.g., unilateral placement of electrodes) have made this treatment relatively safe and, for the most part, have checked the serious or long-term side effects. Nevertheless, controversy about this method of treatment persists, and there is evidence that it can produce permanent brain damage. Obviously ECT should be used with caution and circumspection, and preferably only after less drastic methods have been tried and failed.

The antipsychotic compound chlorpromazine (Thorazine) became widely available in the mid-1950s, followed shortly by numerous other related (i.e., of the phenothiazine class) and nonrelated antipsychotic compounds of proven effectiveness in diminishing psychotic (especially schizophrenic) symptoms. Thus was initiated a true revolution in the treatment of severe mental disorders—one that, among other things, permanently altered the environment and the function of mental hospitals. Within a short period, too, the antidepressant medications became available to help patients with severe depressions, making it possible in many instances to avoid the use of ECT. Finally, in the late 1960s (after an unaccountable delay in its introduction in this country), the antimanic drug lithium was recognized as having major therapeutic signifi-

cance. With the availability of these three types of drugs, the major psychoses—for the first time in history—now came to be seen as generally and effectively treatable.

Meanwhile, "minor tranquilizers" had been developed that circumvented many of the problems of the barbiturates used earlier in combating excessive tension and experienced anxiety. This extended the benefit of effective drug treatment to many people who were struggling with neurotic problems or with high-stress life circumstances. The meprobamates (e.g., Equanil) were the first of these new antianxiety compounds but were largely superseded by the more potent benzodiazepines (e.g., Valium) for general use.

New biological treatments for mental disorders will doubtless continue to be proposed, but, as in the case of megavitamin therapy, many will prove undeserving of a high degree of confidence. A measure of caution is recommended concerning claims made by the proponents of newly introduced therapies.

Finally, the admittedly impressive gains in biological treatment methods may cause us to lose sight of important psychological processes that may be intrinsic to any mental disorder. In fact, there is some evidence that combinations of biologically and psychologically based approaches may be more successful than either alone, at least with some of the more severe disorders.

Psychologically based therapies

Madge Gill, Dessin *(1951).*
After a difficult, insecure childhood spent in England and Canada, Madge Eades (1884–1961) took up residence in London, where she met her future husband, Thomas Gill, and became interested in the world of spiritualism. She soon became a medium herself, and following a series of personal tragedies took up drawing and painting under the direction of her "spirit guide," MYRNINEREST. Her work frequently centers on a feminine figure whose garments blend into a surrounding design of rich color and intricate detail.

Most of us have experienced a time or situation when we were dramatically helped by a bit of advice from a relative or friend. Or perhaps we made a drastic change in our life-style after a particular experience led to new understanding. As Alexander (1946) pointed out, psychotherapy is not far removed from this sort of familiar experience:

"... Everyone who tries to console a despondent friend [or] calm down a panicky child in a sense practices psychotherapy. He tries by psychological means to restore the disturbed emotional equilibrium of another person. Even these commonsense, everyday methods are based on the understanding of the nature of the disturbance, although on an intuitive and not a scientific understanding.... Methodological psychotherapy to a large degree is nothing but a systematic, conscious application of methods by which we influence our fellow men in our daily life."

Psychotherapy is based on the assumption that, even in cases where physical pathology is present, the individual's perceptions, evaluations, expectations, and coping strategies also play a role in the development of the disorder and will probably need to be changed if recovery is to take place. The belief that individuals with psychological problems *can* change—can learn more adaptive ways of perceiving, evaluating, and behaving—is the conviction underlying all psychotherapy. The goal of psychotherapy, then, is to make this belief a reality.

In general, the goals of psychotherapy can include such steps as (a) changing maladaptive behavior patterns, (b) minimizing or eliminating environmental conditions that may be causing and/or maintaining such behavior, (c) improving interpersonal and other competencies, (d) resolving handicapping or disabling inner conflicts and alleviating personal distress, (e) modifying individuals' inaccurate assumptions about themselves and their world, and (f) fostering a clearcut sense of self-identity. All these are ways of opening pathways to a more meaningful and fulfilling existence.

These goals are by no means easy to achieve. Sometimes an individual's distorted view of the world and unhealthy self-concept are the end products of faulty parent-child relationships reinforced by many years of life experiences. In other instances, inadequate occupational, marital, or social adjustment requires major changes in the person's life situation in addition to psychotherapy. It would be too much to expect that a psychotherapist could in a short time undo the individual's entire past history and prepare him or her to cope with a difficult life situation in a fully adequate manner. But, even in chronic cases, a successful therapeutic experience may enable an individual to gain a new perspective about his or her problems and may provide new behaviors with which to approach the problems more adaptively.

This chapter is devoted to an exploration of the most widely used and accepted contemporary psychological treatment approaches. It has been estimated that there are several hundred "therapeutic approaches" in existence, ranging from psychoanalysis to Zen meditation. Indeed, the last few decades have witnessed a stream of "new therapies"—each winning avid proponents and followers for a time. The "faddism" in the popular literature on self-change might give the casual reader the idea that the entire field of psychotherapy is in constant flux. In reality, the professional field of psychological treatment of emotional disorders has shown an amazing stability. As we shall soon see, the analytic school of psychotherapy is approaching its first century of continuous and widespread application. Despite recent innovations and developments in the analytic method, there is a comfortable consistency between the basic assumptions of contemporary psychoanalysts and their counterparts operating a half century ago. This consistency is also seen in the behavioral treatment approach. Although many new applications and methodological variations have emerged in the past twenty years, the line of development is logically and psychologically consistent with learning principles developed decades ago. Similarly, the client-centered approach to psychological treatment originated in the 1940s; yet, today, over forty years later, client-centered therapy techniques are still widely used with certain types of clients.

In this chapter we shall limit our considerations of psychological therapies to treatment approaches in which individuals, trained in psychological techniques, deliberately establish a therapeutic relationship for the purpose of removing symptoms, altering patterns of behavior, and promoting more effective adjustment by individuals with emotional problems.

Meditation techniques are among the new "therapies" people have used in seeking psychological well-being.

An overview of psychological treatment

Although the techniques discussed in this chapter differ in a number of respects, they all share an orientation that is directed toward change. Affecting the direction and the nature of the change are the individuals involved. Foremost is the person—patient or client—who seeks help and/or receives it for his or her problems. Then there is the person who attempts to bring about change in the client through the use of the special skills he or she has acquired as a therapist. The interaction of these two principals—client and therapist—results in a therapeutic relationship. Most authorities agree that, even though techniques differ, all psychotherapies involve human relationships. This relationship is an important ingredient in treatment. Some theorists have even argued that the therapist's personality is as important to patient improvement as is the therapist's training and background.

Before we turn our attention to the specific psychological intervention techniques, we will attempt to gain perspective by considering more closely the individuals involved in therapy and their relationship.

Who receives psychotherapy?

People who seek psychotherapy vary widely in their types of problems and their motivation to solve them. Perhaps the most obvious candidates for psychological treatment are individuals experiencing sudden and highly stressful situations, people who feel so overwhelmed that they cannot manage the situations on their own. These individuals typically feel quite vulnerable and tend to be open to psychological treatment because they are motivated to alter their present situations. These individuals often respond well to short-term, directive, crisis-oriented treatment (to be discussed in Chapter 18). In situations such as this, the client may gain considerably, in a brief time, from the outside perspective provided by the therapist.

Some individuals enter psychological therapy somewhat as a surprise to themselves. Perhaps they had consulted a physician for their headache or stomach pain, only to be told that there was nothing physically wrong with them. Such individuals, referred on for psychological therapy, may at first resist the idea that their "real" physical symptoms are emotionally based. The resistant attitudes demonstrated by this type of referral underscore the fact that motivation to enter treatment differs widely among psychotherapy clients. Reluctant clients may come from many sources—for example, the alcoholic whose spouse threatens "either therapy or divorce!" or the "uncontrollable" teenager whose parents bring the youth to a clinic rather than to the cycle shop as they promised. Clients who are seeing a therapist under these conditions—in spite of their obvious needs—may not be amenable to therapy at this time, regardless of the good intentions of the referral source.

Many people entering therapy have experienced long-term psychological distress and have had a lengthy history of maladjustment. They may have been experiencing interpersonal problems for some time or may have felt susceptible to low moods that are difficult for them to dispel. Chronic unhappiness and inability to feel confident and secure may finally prompt them to seek outside help. These individuals seek psychological assistance out of despair. They may enter treatment with a high degree of motivation but, as therapy proceeds, their former, persistent patterns of behavior that contributed to their problems in the first place may become resistant forces with which the therapist must contend.

A number of people who enter therapy have problems that would be considered, comparatively speaking, relatively normal. That is, they appear to have achieved success, have financial stability, have generally accepting and loving families, and have accomplished many of their life goals. They enter therapy not out of personal despair or impossible interpersonal involvements, but out of a sense that they have not lived up to their own expectations and realized their own potential. These individuals, partly because their problems are more manageable than the problems of others, may make substantial gains in personal growth. Much of their therapeutic gain can be attributed to their high degree of motivation and personal resources. Individuals who seem to have the best prognosis for personality change, according to some authorities, have been described by the "YAVIS" phenomenon (Schofield, 1964)—they are young, attractive, verbal, intelligent, and successful. Not surprisingly, those who tend to do best in psychotherapy are those who seem to need it least.

Yet psychotherapy is not just for individuals who may have clearly defined problems, high levels of motivation, and an ability to gain ready insight into their behavior. Psychotherapeutic methods of intervention have been applied to a wide variety of chronic problems. Even the severely disturbed psychotic patient may profit from a therapeutic relationship that takes into account his or her level of functioning and maintains therapeutic goals that are within the patient's capabilities.

It should be clear from this brief description of individuals in psychological therapy that there is indeed no "typical" patient, nor, as we shall see, is there a "model" therapy. No form of therapy is applicable to all types of clients, and it appears that all therapies document success with *some* types of individuals. Most authorities agree that client variables, such as extent of the problem and client motivation, are exceedingly important to the outcome of therapy (Bergin, 1978; Garfield, 1978; Rounsaville, Weissman, & Prusoff, 1981). As we shall see, the various therapies have relatively greater success when the therapist takes these characteristics of the client into account in determining the treatment of choice.

Who provides psychotherapeutic services?

Many professionals have traditionally provided advice and counsel to individuals in emotional distress. Physicians have, as ancillary to their role of providing care for the physical problems of their patients, often become trusted advisers in emotional matters as well. In past eras, before the advent of large health maintenance organizations and medical specialization, the family physician was called upon for virtually all health questions. Even today, the medical practitioner—although he or she may have little psychological background and limited time to spend with individual patients—may be called upon to give consultation in psychological matters. Most physicians are trained to recognize psychological problems that are beyond their expertise and to refer the individual to psychological specialists.

Another professional group that deals extensively with the emotional problems of people is the clergy. Members of the clergy are usually in intimate contact with the emotional needs and problems of their congregations. The minister, priest, or rabbi may be the first professional to encounter an individual experiencing emotional crisis. Some clergy actively acquire counseling training and supervised experience in dealing with psychological problems and go on to obtain professional backgrounds, including pastoral counseling degrees. Most limit their counseling to religious matters and spiritual support and do not attempt to provide psychotherapy. Rather, they are trained to recognize problems that require professional management and refer troubled individuals to psychiatrists or psychologists.

Beyond physicians and clergy, the professionals of primary interest to us in this context are those formally trained in the identification and treatment of mental disorders. The three types

HIGHLIGHT
Personnel in psychotherapy

PROFESSIONAL

Clinical psychologist
Ph.D. in psychology with both research and clinical skill specialization. One-year internship in a psychiatric hospital or mental health center. *Or*, Psy.D. in psychology (a professional degree with more clinical than research specialization) plus one-year internship in a psychiatric hospital or mental health center.

Counseling psychologist
Ph.D. in psychology plus internship in a marital or student counseling setting; normally, the counseling psychologist deals with adjustment problems not involving mental disorder.

Psychiatrist
M.D. degree with internship plus residency training (usually three years) in a psychiatric hospital or mental health facility.

Psychoanalyst
M.D. or Ph.D. degree plus intensive training in theory and practice of psychoanalysis.

Psychiatric social worker
B.A., M.S.W., or Ph.D. degree with specialized clinical training in mental health settings.

Psychiatric nurse
R.N. in nursing plus specialized training in care and treatment of psychiatric patients. M.A. and Ph.D. in psychiatric nursing is possible.

Occupational therapist
B.S. in occupational therapy plus internship training with physically or psychologically handicapped, helping them make the most of their resources.

PARAPROFESSIONAL

Community mental health worker
Capable person with limited professional training who works under professional direction (especially crisis intervention).

Alcohol or drug-abuse counselor
Limited professional training but trained in the evaluation and management of alcohol- and drug-addicted persons.

Pastoral counselor
Ministerial background plus training in psychology. Internship in mental health facility as a chaplain.

In both mental health clinics and hospitals, personnel from several fields may function as an interdisciplinary team in therapy—for example, a psychiatrist, a clinical psychologist, a social worker, a psychiatric nurse, and an occupational therapist may work together.

---

of mental health professionals found most often in mental health settings are psychiatrists, clinical psychologists, and psychiatric social workers (see **HIGHLIGHT** on this page). The *psychiatrist* is an M.D. who has had further training—a three-year residency—in dealing with patients in a mental health setting. The medical training of psychiatrists qualifies them for administering somatic therapies such as electroconvulsive therapy and psychotropic medication. In addition, during residency the psychiatric resident receives supervision in psychotherapy. The *clinical psychologist* is a mental health professional who typically has training at the undergraduate level in psychology and has a Ph.D. degree in clinical psychology, with specialization in personality theory, abnormal psychology, psycho-

logical assessment, and psychotherapy. Most clinical psychologists receive broad clinical experience in assessment and psychotherapy in addition to their mental health research training. *Psychiatric social workers* are usually trained in social science at the bachelor's level and may hold an M.A. or Ph.D. from a school of social work. Their graduate training usually involves coursework dealing with family evaluation, psychotherapy, and supervised field experiences.

In any given therapy program, a wide range of medical, psychological, and social-work procedures may be used. Such procedures range from the use of drugs through individual or group psychotherapy and home or job visits aimed at modifying adverse conditions in the client's life situation. Often the latter—as in

The team approach to assessment and treatment brings together a number of mental health professionals. Here a psychologist, a social worker, and members of a community hospital staff watch a videotape and listen to a soundtrack of a child patient.

helping an employer become more understanding and supportive of the client's needs—is as important as treatment directed toward modifying the client's personality makeup and/or behavior.

This willingness to use a variety of procedures is reflected in the growing importance of the *team approach* to assessment and treatment. This approach involves the coordinated efforts of medical, psychological, social work, and other mental health personnel working together as the needs of each case warrant. Also of key importance is the trend toward providing treatment facilities in the community. Instead of considering maladjustment as a private misery of the individual, which in the past often required one's confinement in a distant mental hospital, this approach integrates family and community resources in the treatment.

The therapeutic relationship

The therapeutic relationship is formed out of what both care-seeker and care-giver bring to the therapeutic situation.

The patient's major contribution is his or her motivation. The humanistic assumption—that humans possess an inner drive toward mental and physical health—makes psychotherapy possible. Just as physical medicine, properly used, essentially frees and cooperates with the body's own healing mechanisms, an important ally of the psychotherapist is the individual's own drive toward wholeness and toward the development of unrealized potentialities. Although this inner drive is often obscured in severely disturbed patients, the majority of anxious and confused people are sufficiently discouraged with their situation to be eager to cooperate in any program that holds hope for improvement. Some degree of cooperation by the individual receiving help is considered essential if psychotherapy is to have much chance of success.

Almost as important is the patient's *expectation* of receiving help. This expectancy is often sufficient in itself to bring about some improvement (Frank, 1978). Just as a placebo can lessen pain for the individual who believes it will do so, the individual who expects to be helped by psychotherapy is likely to be helped, almost regardless of the particular methods used by the therapist. Those in the "helping professions" are the first to admit how inexact the state of their art is and how dependent it is on what the "patient" brings to the experience of psychotherapy.

To the "art" of therapy, the therapist brings a variety of professional skills and methods. These methods are alike in that they intend to help individuals see themselves and their situations more objectively—that is, to gain a different perspective. Yet insight and new perspective are only a start and not usually enough alone to bring about the necessary changes in behavior. So besides helping the individual toward a new perspective, most therapy situations also provide a protected setting in which he or she is helped to practice new ways of feeling and acting, gradually developing both the courage and the ability to take responsibility for acting in more effective and satisfying ways in the world.

To bring about such changes, the effective psychotherapist must interact with the patient in a warm and accepting manner to maximize trust and motivation. For this reason, as noted earlier, some theorists have argued that the therapist's personality is as important to the outcome of therapy as his or her training and background. In a comprehensive study of this issue, Parloff et al. (1978) concluded that outcome of therapy was not directly related to the therapist's personality characteristics: however, they concluded that a therapist's own emotional problems may interfere with effective treatment.

Despite general agreement among psychotherapists on these aspects of the client-therapist relationship, professionals can differ in their diagnosis and treatment of psychological disorders. This should not be too surprising, of course. Even in the treatment of physical disorders, we sometimes find that "doctors dis-

agree." In psychopathology, this is even more the case. The differing perspectives on human motivation and behavior outlined in Chapter 3 lead, as might be expected, to quite different diagnoses of what "the problem" is and how the individual should be helped to overcome it. In the balance of this chapter we shall review several of the chief approaches among the many psychological therapies that are being used today in an effort to help individuals overcome psychological problems and lead more satisfying lives. The **HIGHLIGHT** on pages 636–37 provides an overview of some of the key dimensions in this somewhat complex area of study.[1]

Psychodynamic therapy

Psychodynamic therapy is a psychological treatment approach that focuses on individual personality dynamics from a psychoanalytic perspective.[2] Also called *psychoanalytic therapy* or *psychoanalysis* (see Chapter 3) the therapists who practice it are often referred to as *psychoanalysts* or just *analysts*. As developed by Freud, psychoanalytic therapy is an intensive, long-term procedure for uncovering repressed memories, thoughts, fears, and conflicts—presumably stemming from problems in early psychosexual development—and helping the individual come to terms with them in the light of adult reality. It is felt that gaining insight into such repressed material will free individuals from the need to keep squandering their energies on repression and other defense mechanisms. Instead, they can bring their personality resources to bear on consciously resolving the anxieties that prompted the repression in the first place. Freed from this load of threatening material and from the effort of keeping it out of consciousness, they can turn their energies to better personality integration and more effective living.

There are other psychodynamic treatment approaches that do not rigidly adhere to orthodox

[1]Comprehensive but concise descriptions of the major types of psychotherapy may be found in Corsini (1979), Smith (1982), and Weiner (1983).

[2]More extensive treatments of psychodynamic therapy can be found in Greenson's (1967) *The technique and practice of psychoanalysis*, and Langs' (1973) *The technique of psychoanalytic therapy*.

Freudian theory yet are, in part, based on psychoanalytic concepts. We shall examine in some detail Freud's original treatment methods and briefly cover some of the contemporary modifications of psychoanalytic therapy.

Freudian psychoanalysis

Psychoanalysis is a system of therapy that evolved over a period of years during Sigmund Freud's long career. It is not an easy system of therapy to describe, and the problem is complicated by the fact that most people have some more-or-less inaccurate conceptions of it based on cartoons and movies. The best way to begin our discussion is to describe the four basic techniques of this form of therapy: free association, analysis of dreams, analysis of resistance, and analysis of transference. Then we shall note some of the changes that have taken place in psychoanalytic therapy since Freud's time.

1. *Free association.* As we saw in Chapter 3, Freud used hypnosis in his early work to free repressed thoughts from his patients' unconscious (see **HIGHLIGHT** on pages 638–39). Later, he stopped using hypnosis in favor of a more direct method of gaining access to the individual's hidden thoughts and fears—*free association.*

The basic rule of free association is that the individual must say whatever comes into his or her mind, regardless of how personal, painful, or seemingly irrelevant it may be. Usually the patient sits comfortably in a chair or lies in a relaxed position on a couch and gives a running account of all the thoughts, feelings, and desires that come to mind as one idea leads to another. The therapist usually takes a position behind the patient so as not to distract or disrupt the free flow of associations.

Although such a running account of whatever comes into one's head may seem random, Freud did not view it as such; rather, he believed that associations are determined like other events. And, as we have seen, he also thought that the conscious represents a relatively small part of the mind, while the unconscious, like the submerged part of an iceberg, is much the larger portion. The purpose of the free association is to bring to light these long-submerged motives and conflicts. Analytic

HIGHLIGHT
Descriptive comparison of various approaches to psychotherapy

The forms of psychotherapy discussed in this chapter can be classified in a number of ways. Listed below are a few "key dimensions" that will be useful to bear in mind as we examine various approaches to psychotherapy.

1. Individual/group. In individual, or one-to-one, therapy, the therapist treats one person at a time. The effectiveness of such therapies depends to a great extent on the patient-therapist relationship. In group therapy, several persons are treated at the same time in a group setting. Here the interactions and relationships of the group members to one another are important aspects of therapy.

2. Cognitive change/behavior change. Some approaches to psychotherapy focus on changes in the patient's values and other assumptions, on the premise that such cognitive change will lead to more effective behavior. Other approaches focus directly on changing particular behaviors and include chances to

interpretation involves the therapist's "tying" together the patient's often disconnected ideas, beliefs, actions, and so forth into a meaningful explanation to help the patient gain insight into his or her unconscious and possibly maladaptive behavior. The therapist then interprets this material to the individual, guiding him or her toward increased awareness and understanding of these long-repressed feelings.

2. *Analysis of dreams.* Another important procedure for uncovering unconscious material is dream analysis. When a person is asleep, repressive defenses are lowered and forbidden desires and feelings may find an outlet in dreams. For this reason dreams have been referred to as the "royal road to the unconscious." But some motives are so unacceptable to the individual that even in dreams they are not revealed openly but are expressed in disguised or symbolic form. Thus a dream has two kinds of content: *manifest content,* which is the dream as it

develop new skills, on the premise that behavior change will in turn result in cognitive change. Increasingly, today, therapists are working toward both goals.

3. Directive/nondirective. Therapists differ widely with respect to the amount of responsibility they place upon the individual being treated as contrasted with the degree to which they themselves direct the course of therapy. In directive therapy, the therapist takes an "active" role, asking questions and offering interpretations; in nondirective therapy, the major responsibility is placed on the client, and the therapist may simply try to help clients clarify and understand their feelings and values.

4. Inner control of behavior/outer control of behavior. In some instances, psychotherapy is aimed at establishing environmental control of the individual's behavior through planned reinforcement. In other instances, the primary goal of psychotherapy is to change the individual's value assumptions in such a way as to foster the inner cognitive control of behav-ior. Of course, external controls may be used as an emergency measure with the expectation that inner controls will eventually be developed and take over.

5. Brief/long term. Most psychotherapy today is brief, lasting only between 6 and 10 sessions (Butcher & Kolotkin, 1979). Brief approaches to therapy begin with the assumption that the problem is a specific one that will not require a major restructuring of the personality. Relief from particular worries or symptoms is a major goal of the therapy. Long-term therapy, on the other hand, aims at personality reconstruction.

6. Historical focus/here-and-now emphasis. Some approaches to psychological intervention explore patients' early life experiences and attempt to get patients to integrate their childhood feelings, attitudes, and conflicts into their present outlook and perspective. Other treatment approaches focus more on the "here and now" and minimize early experiences. This latter focus often emphasizes present interpersonal relationships and current problem-solving efforts.

appears to the dreamer, and *latent content,* composed of the actual motives that are seeking expression but are so painful or unacceptable that they are disguised.

It is the task of the therapist to uncover these disguised meanings by studying the symbols that appear in the manifest content of the dream. For example, a patient's dream of being engulfed in a tidal wave may be interpreted by the therapist as indicating that the patient feels in danger of being overwhelmed by inadequately repressed fears and hostilities.

3. *Analysis of resistance.* During the process of free association or of associating to dreams, an individual may evidence *resistance*—an unwillingness or inability to talk about certain thoughts, motives, or experiences. For example, a patient may be talking about an important childhood experience and then suddenly switch topics, perhaps stating that "It really isn't that important," or that "It is too absurd to discuss."

Resistance may also be evidenced by the patient's giving a too-glib interpretation of some association, or coming late to an appointment, or even "forgetting" an appointment altogether. Since resistance prevents painful and threatening material from entering awareness, its sources must be sought if the individual is to face the problem and learn to deal with it in a realistic manner.

4. *Analysis of transference.* As patient and therapist interact, the relationship between them may become complex and emotionally involved. Often people carry over and apply to the therapist attitudes and feelings that they had in their relations with a parent or other person close to them in the past, a process known as *transference.* Thus patients may react to their analyst as they did to that earlier person and feel the same hostility and rejection that they felt long ago in relation to the other person.

By recognizing the transference relationship,

HIGHLIGHT
The use of hypnosis in therapy

Hypnosis was known among the ancient Egyptians and other early peoples, but its modern use in psychotherapy dates only from the time of Mesmer, as we saw in Chapter 3. Since that time, there have been periodic fluctuations in the popularity of hypnosis in psychotherapy, and differing viewpoints have arisen concerning the exact nature of hypnotic phenomena. In general, hypnosis may be defined as an altered state of consciousness involving extreme suggestibility. Hypnotic induction procedures are designed to bring about a heightened state of selective attention in which the subject "tunes out" irrelevant stimuli and concentrates solely on the hypnotist's suggestions. The induction of hypnosis and some of its therapeutic uses are briefly outlined below.

1. Induction of hypnosis. Hypnosis may be induced by a variety of techniques, most of which involve the following factors: (a) enlisting the cooperation of the subject and allaying any fears of hypnosis; (b) having the subject assume a comfortable position and relax completely; (c) narrowing and focusing the subject's attention, perhaps by having him or her gaze on some bright object; and (d) directing the subject's activities by means of suggestions. The latter often involves establishing the assumption that normal bodily reactions have in fact come about at the direction of the hyp-

notist. For example, the subject may be directed to gaze upward toward an object and then be told, "your eyelids are starting to feel heavy." This is a normal reaction to the strain of looking upward, but the subject interprets it as being caused by the hypnotist; thus the way is paved for the acceptance of additional suggestions.

2. Recall of buried memories. Traumatic experiences that have been repressed from consciousness may be recovered under hypnosis. This technique was used in treating combat-exhaustion cases during World War II, as we saw in Chapter 5. Under hypnosis, the amnesic soldier could relive his battle experience, thus discharging the emotional tensions associated with it and permitting the experience to be assimilated into his self-structure. Civilian shock reactions involving amnesia may be similarly handled.

3. Age regression. Closely related to memory recall is hypnotic age regression. A hypnotized woman may be told that she is now a six-year-old child again and will subsequently act, talk, and think very much as she did at the age of six years. Regression to the age just preceding the onset of phobias often brings to light the traumatic experiences that precipitated them. Here again reliving the traumatic experience may desensitize the subject to it.

the therapist may provide the individual with the experience of having a "good" father or mother. This may make it possible for the individual to work through the conflict in feelings about the real parent or perhaps to overcome feelings of hostility and self-devaluation that stemmed from the earlier parental rejection. In essence, the pathogenic effects of an undesirable early relationship are counteracted by working through a similar emotional conflict in a therapeutic setting. Since the person's reliving of a pathogenic past relationship in a sense recreates the neurosis in real life, this experience is often referred to as a *transference neurosis*.

It is not possible here to consider at length the complexities of transference relationships,

but it may be stressed that the patient's attitudes toward the therapist do not always follow simple patterns. Often the patient is ambivalent—distrusting the therapist and feeling hostile toward him or her as a symbol of authority, but at the same time seeking acceptance and love. In addition, the problems of transference are by no means confined to the patient, for the therapist may also have a mixture of feelings toward the patient. This phenomenon is known as *countertransference* and must be recognized and handled properly by the therapist in question. For this reason, it is considered important that therapists have a very thorough understanding of their own motives, conflicts, and "weak spots"; in fact, all psychoanalysts themselves undergo

4. Dream induction. Dreams can be induced through hypnosis, although some investigators consider hypnotic dreams to more nearly resemble fantasies than nocturnal dreams. In any event, hypnotic dreams may be used to explore intrapsychic conflicts along the lines of dream analysis worked out by Freud. Perhaps the particular value of such dreams is that the therapist can suggest the theme about which the hypnotic dream should center, using it much like a projective technique in exploring the individual's inner conflicts.

5. Posthypnotic suggestion. One of the hypnotic phenomena most widely used in psychotherapy is posthypnotic suggestion. Here suggestions are made by the therapist during the hypnotic state for behavior to be carried out later in the waking state, with the subject remaining unaware of the source of the behavior. For example, a subject may be told that he or she will no longer have a desire to smoke upon coming out of the hypnotic state. While such suggestions do carry over into the waking state, their duration is usually short. That is, the individual may again experience a desire to smoke in a few hours or a few days. This time factor can be partially compensated for, however, by regular reinforcement of the posthypnotic suggestion in booster sessions.

Some investigators attribute the altered state of consciousness in hypnosis to the subject's strong motivation to meet the demand characteristics of the situation. Barber (1969) has shown that many of the behaviors induced under hypnosis can be replicated in nonhypnotized subjects simply by giving instructions which they are strongly motivated to follow. However, the preponderance of research evidence indicates that behavior induced in hypnotized subjects does differ significantly from that evidenced during simulated hypnosis or role enactment (Diamond, 1974; Fromm & Shor, 1972; Hilgard, 1973, 1974; Miller & Springer, 1974; Nace, Orne, & Hammer, 1974). For example, a number of investigators have offered dramatic evidence that the pain response can be brought almost completely under hypnotic control in many subjects, permitting a degree of pain reduction well beyond that produced in nonhypnotized subjects.

Such drugs as sodium pentothal can be used to produce phenomena similar to those manifested in the hypnotic trance. This form of biological therapy is referred to as *narcoanalysis* or *narcosynthesis.* In Chapter 5 we noted the use of sodium pentothal in the treatment of severe cases of combat exhaustion involving amnesia.

psychoanalysis before they begin independent practice.

Particularly during the early stages, psychoanalytic therapy is directed toward forming hypotheses about unconscious desires and conflicts and helping patients integrate them into the conscious dimension of their personality. However, the new insights patients have achieved about their past problems do not automatically generalize to their present day-to-day relationships. Thus as the therapy progresses toward its terminal phase, it is increasingly directed toward furthering patients' emotional reeducation and helping ensure the generalization of new insights into current real-life situations.

Psychodynamic therapy since Freud

Although some psychoanalysts still adhere to standard long-term psychoanalysis—which may take years—most analysts have worked out modifications in procedure designed to shorten the time and response required. Mann (1973) for example, described what he refers to as "time-limited" psychotherapy. This approach, which focuses on providing symptom relief, follows psychodynamic methods, but is confined to a 12-session treatment course. Probably the most extensive program of short-term psychodynamic therapy, and one which involves a strong research-evaluation component, is that of Strupp and his colleagues (Strupp, 1981; Strupp et al., in press). This therapy, known as *time-limited dynamic psychotherapy*, goes beyond the symptom relief of Mann's program; it aims for lasting modification of the individual's personality structure through the application of psychodynamic principles in therapy that lasts for 25 to 30 sessions.

Other differences in contemporary psychodynamic treatment have evolved also. For example, analytic therapists tend to place more emphasis on current ego functioning and see the ego as a developing and controlling agent in the individual's life (Hartmann, 1958). Thus the individual is seen as more capable of being in control and less dominated by early repressed sexuality than in traditional analysis. Although childhood events are still viewed as important formative experiences, most modern analysts also place more emphasis on patients' current interpersonal relationships and life situations and less on their childhood experiences.

Evaluation of psychodynamic therapy

Despite such modifications, psychodynamic therapy is still commonly criticized for being relatively time-consuming and expensive, for being based on a questionable theory of human nature, for neglecting the patient's immediate problems in the search for unconscious conflicts in the remote past, and for inadequate proof of effectiveness. Because it expects the individual to achieve insight and major personality change, it is also limited in its applicability. For example, it is best suited for persons who are average or above in intelligence and economically well off and who do not suffer from severe psychopathology.

Nevertheless, many individuals do feel that they have profited from psychodynamic therapy—particularly in terms of greater self-understanding, relief from inner conflict and anxiety, and improved interpersonal relationships. Psychodynamically oriented psychotherapy remains the treatment of choice for many individuals who are seeking extensive self-evaluation or an intensive insight into themselves. Even many behavior therapists, when they seek treatment for themselves, select this approach over behavioral methods (Gochman, Allgood, & Geer, 1982).

Behavior therapy

Although the use of conditioning techniques in therapy has a long history, it was not until the 1950s that *behavior therapy* really came into its own.[3] The major reason for the long delay was the dominant position of psychoanalysis in the field of psychological therapy. In recent years, however, the therapeutic potentialities of behavior-therapy techniques have been strikingly demonstrated in dealing with a wide variety of maladaptive behaviors, and there have been literally thousands of research publications dealing with the systematic application of conditioning principles to the modification of maladaptive behavior.

In the behavioristic perspective, as we saw in Chapter 3, the maladjusted person (unless suffering from brain pathology) is seen as differing from other people only in (a) having failed to acquire competencies needed for coping with the problems of living and/or (b) having learned faulty coping patterns that are being maintained by some kind of reinforcement. Thus the behavior therapist specifies in advance the precise maladaptive behaviors to be modified and the adaptive behaviors to be achieved, as well as the specific learning principles or procedures to be utilized.

Instead of exploring past traumatic events or inner conflicts in order to bring about personality change, behavior therapists attempt to modify behavior directly by manipulating environmental contingencies—that is, by the use of reward and punishment. Behavior-therapy techniques seem especially effective in altering maladaptive behavior when the reinforcement is administered immediately following the desired response, and when the person knows what is

---

[3]Two excellent recent volumes dealing with behavior therapy are *Behavior modifications: Principles, issues, and applications*, 2nd ed., by Craighead, Kazdin, and Mahoney (1981) and *Self-management and behavior change*, by Karoly and Kanfer (1982).

expected and why the reinforcement is given. The ultimate goal, of course, is not only to achieve the desired responses but to bring them under the control and self-monitoring of the individual.

We have cited many examples of the application of behavior therapy in earlier chapters. In this section, we shall elaborate briefly on the key techniques of behavior therapy.

Extinction

Since learned behavior patterns tend to weaken and disappear over time if they are not reinforced, often the simplest way to eliminate a maladaptive pattern is to remove the reinforcement for it. This is especially true in situations where maladaptive behavior has been reinforced unknowingly by others.

Billy, a 6-year-old first grader, was brought to a psychological clinic by his parents because he "hated school," and his teacher had told them that his showing-off behavior was disrupting the class and making him unpopular. It became apparent in observing Billy and his parents during the initial interview that both his mother and father were noncritical and approving of everything he did. After further assessment, a three-phase program of therapy was undertaken: (a) the parents were helped to discriminate between showing-off behavior and appropriate behavior on Billy's part; (b) the parents were instructed to show a loss of interest and attention when Billy engaged in showing-off behavior while continuing to show their approval of appropriate behavior; and (c) Billy's teacher was instructed to ignore Billy, insofar as it was feasible, when he engaged in showing-off behavior and to devote her attention at those times to children who were behaving more appropriately.

Although Billy's showing-off behavior in class increased during the first few days of this therapy program, it diminished markedly thereafter when it was no longer reinforced by his parents and teacher. As his maladaptive behavior diminished, he was better accepted by his classmates, which, in turn, helped reinforce more appropriate behavior patterns and change his negative attitude toward school.

Two techniques that rely on the principle of extinction are ***implosive therapy*** and ***flooding.*** Both focus on extinguishing the conditioned avoidance of anxiety-arousing stimuli and can thus be used to treat anxiety disorders. The techniques are roughly similar, except that implosive therapy involves having the client *imagine* an anxiety-arousing situation; flooding, on the other hand, involves placing the client in a real-life anxiety-arousing situation.

In implosion, clients are asked to imagine and relive aversive scenes associated with their anxiety. However, instead of trying to banish anxiety from the treatment sessions, the therapist deliberately attempts to elicit a massive "implosion" of anxiety. This is somewhat reminiscent of psychodynamic approaches because it deals with an internal conceptualization of anxiety. With repeated exposure in a "safe" setting, the stimulus loses its power to elicit anxiety and the neurotic avoidance behavior is extinguished. Hypnosis or drugs may be used to enhance suggestibility under implosive therapy.

In a report of an actual case, Stampfl (1975) described a young woman who could not swim and was terrified of water—particularly of sinking under the water. Although she knew it was irrational, she was so terrified of water "that she wore a life preserver when she took a bath" (p. 66). She was instructed by the therapist to imagine in minute detail taking a bath without a life preserver in a "bottomless" tub, and slipping under the water. Initially, the patient showed intense anxiety, and the scene was repeated over and over. In addition, she was given a "homework" assignment in which she was asked to imagine herself drowning. Eventually, after imagining the worst and finding that nothing happened, her anxiety diminished. After the fourteenth therapy session, she was able to take baths without feelings of anxiety or apprehension; the maladaptive behavior had been effectively extinguished.

Flooding, or *in vivo* procedures, which involve placing the individual in a real-life situation as opposed to a therapeutic setting, may be used with individuals who do not imagine scenes realistically. For example, a client with a phobia of heights may be taken atop a tall building or bridge. This is another means of exposing the client to the anxiety-eliciting stimulus and demonstrating that the feared consequences do not occur. In a study of patients with agoraphobia (fear of open spaces), Emmelkamp and Wessels (1975) concluded that prolonged exposure *in vivo* plainly proved superior to simple reliance on the imagination.

Reports on the effectiveness of implosive therapy and flooding have generally been quite favorable; however, some investigators have reported unfavorable as well as favorable results (Emmelkamp & Wessels, 1975; Mealiea, 1967; Wolpe, 1969b). This appears to be particularly true of flooding *in vivo*. For example, Emmelkamp and Wessels (1975) found that flooding *in vivo* was terrifying for some clients. In one case, the agoraphobic client "hid in a cellar out of fear of being sent into the street for 90 minutes by the therapist" (p. 14).

In general, it would appear that while many patients respond favorably to implosion or flooding, some do not respond, and a few suffer an exacerbation of their phobias. This finding suggests a need for caution in the use of these techniques, particularly since they involve procedures that may be highly traumatic.

Systematic desensitization

The process of extinction can be applied to behavior that is positively reinforced or negatively reinforced (see Chapter 3, pages 70–71). Of the two, behavior that is *negatively reinforced*—reinforced by the successful *avoidance* of a painful situation—is harder to deal with. Since the individual becomes anxious and withdraws at the first sign of the painful situation, he or she never gets a chance to find out whether the expected aversive consequences do in fact come about. In addition, the avoidance is anxiety reducing and hence is itself reinforced.

One technique that has proven especially useful in extinguishing negatively reinforced behavior involves eliciting an antagonistic or competing response. Since it is difficult to feel both pleasant and anxious at the same time, the method of *desensitization* is aimed at teaching the individual to relax or behave in some other way that is inconsistent with anxiety while in the presence (real or imagined) of the anxiety-producing stimulus. It should be pointed out that desensitization is not used *exclusively* to deal with behaviors brought about by negative reinforcement; it can be used for other kinds of behavioral problems as well.

The prototype of this approach is the classic experiment of Jones (1924), in which she successfully eliminated a small boy's conditioned fears of a white rabbit and other furry animals. First she brought the rabbit just inside the door at the far end of the room while the boy, Peter, was eating. On successive days the rabbit was gradually brought closer until Peter could pat it with one hand while eating with the other.

The term *systematic desensitization* has been applied to a specific approach developed by Wolpe (1969; Rachman & Hodgson, 1980). On the assumption that most anxiety-based patterns are, fundamentally, conditioned responses, Wolpe worked out a way to train the client to remain calm and relaxed in situations that formerly produced anxiety. Wolpe's approach is elegant in its simplicity, and the carrying out of his method is equally straightforward.

1. *Training in relaxation.* The first step in therapy is training the individual to relax. This is usually done in the first six sessions and consists of having the individual contract and then gradually relax different muscles until a state of complete relaxation can be achieved at will. The basic technique follows the principles of "progressive relaxation" outlined by Jacobson (1938) and is described in detail by Wolpe (1969). Other techniques that are sometimes used to facilitate complete relaxation include meditation, hypnosis, and drugs.

2. *The construction of hierarchies.* During the early sessions of therapy, time is also spent constructing a hierarchy of the individual's anxieties. This anxiety hierarchy is a list of related stimuli ranked in descending order according to the amount of anxiety they evoke in the client. For example, if a client is overly possessive or jealous of her husband, she describes the situations in which she feels this jealousy. The highest anxiety-producing situation might be observing him at a cocktail party talking intimately with an attractive woman. Further down the list might be hearing him comment favorably about a waitress; the lowest anxiety-evoking stimulus might be noticing him look casually at a young female hitchhiker. In some instances the anxiety is easier to quantify, as in the case of acrophobia (fear of high places) or of a student's examination anxiety; and, of course, anxiety may focus around more than one theme, as when the client shows a variety of phobias.

3. *Desensitization procedure.* When the client has mastered the relaxation techniques and the therapist has established an appropriate anxiety

Desensitization techniques begin by teaching clients to relax through a series of graduated exercises.

hierarchy, the actual process of desensitization begins. While the client relaxes completely in a comfortable chair with closed eyes, the therapist describes a series of scenes, starting with a neutral one, then moving to one at the bottom of the client's anxiety hierarchy and progressing gradually up it. The client, while remaining relaxed, is directed to imagine each situation as it is described. As soon as the client reports experiencing anxiety, the session is terminated. Treatment continues until the client is able to remain in a relaxed state while vividly imagining the scenes that formerly evoked the greatest anxiety.

The usual duration of a desensitization session is about 30 minutes, and the sessions are often given 2 to 3 times per week. The overall therapy program may, of course, take a number of weeks or even months. Kennedy and Kimura (1974) have shown, however, that even patients who have progressed only 25 to 50 percent of the way through their anxiety hierarchy show significant therapeutic gains, as evidenced by a marked reduction in specific avoidance behav-

iors when compared with their pretreatment levels.

Several variants of systematic desensitization have been devised. One variation involves the use of a tape recorder to enable a client to carry out the desensitization process at home. Another utilizes group desensitization procedures—as in "marathon" desensitization groups, in which the entire program is compressed into a few days of intensive treatment. Perhaps the most important variation is *in vivo* desensitization, in which the client is asked to enter real-life situations similar to the ones he or she has just successfully imagined during the desensitization sessions.

Wolpe (1969b) has noted three types of client-related problems that would suggest that desensitization techniques would be an ineffective therapeutic choice: the client demonstrates (a) difficulties in relaxation, (b) misleading or irrelevant hierarchies, and (c) inadequacies of imagery. Desensitization procedures have, however, been used successfully in dealing with a wide range of maladaptive behaviors, including examination anxieties, phobias, anxiety disorders, and certain cases of impotence and frigidity. In particular, desensitization has been highly successful in treating flight phobia (Carr, 1978).

Aversion therapy

This approach involves the modification of undesirable behavior by the old-fashioned method of punishment. Punishment may involve either the removal of positive reinforcers or the use of aversive stimuli, but the basic idea is to reduce the "temptation value" of stimuli that elicit undesirable behavior. The most commonly used aversive stimulus is electric shock, although drugs may also be used. As we shall see, however, punishment is rarely employed as the sole method of treatment.

Apparently the first formal use of *aversion therapy* was made by Kantorovich (1930), who administered electric shocks to alcoholics in association with the sight, smell, and taste of alcohol. Since that time aversion therapy has been used in the treatment of a wide range of maladaptive behaviors, including smoking, drinking, overeating, drug dependence, gambling, sexual variants, and bizarre psychotic behavior. Since we have described the use of aversion therapy in the course of our discussion of abnormal behavior patterns, we shall restrict ourselves here to a review of a few brief examples and principles.

Lovaas (1977) found punishment by electric shock to be effective in extreme cases of severely disturbed autistic children. In one case a 7-year-old autistic boy, diagnosed as severely retarded, had to be kept in restraints 24 hours a day because he would continually beat his head with his fists or bang it against the walls of his crib, inflicting serious injuries. Though it is difficult to understand why punishment should have reduced the frequency of self-destructive behavior, electric shock following such behavior was nevertheless quite effective, bringing about complete inhibition of this maladaptive behavior pattern in a relatively short time (Bucher & Lovaas, 1967).

In earlier chapters we noted that irrational and maladaptive thoughts—obsessions, delusions, and hallucinations—may also be minimized or extinguished by means of electric shock or other aversive control measures.

Nonetheless, electric shock as an aversive stimulus has generally diminished in use in recent years (Harris & Ersner-Hershfield, 1978) because of the ethical problems involved in its use and because the new behaviors induced by it do not automatically generalize to other settings. Also, less dangerous and more effective procedures have been found. The method of choice today is probably differential reinforcement of other responses (DOR), in which behaviors incompatible with the undesired behavior are reinforced. For example, for a child who indulges in antisocial, destructive behavior, positive reinforcement might be used for every sign of constructive play. At the same time, any reinforcement that has been maintaining maladaptive behavior is removed. Lovaas and his colleagues, who reported the successful use of electric shock with autistic children, have themselves recently recommended the use of nonpunitive treatment for self-injurious behavior (Russo, Carr, & Lovaas, 1980).

Aversion therapy is primarily a way of stopping maladaptive responses for a period of time during which there is an opportunity for changing a life-style by encouraging more adaptive alternative patterns that will prove reinforcing in themselves. This point is particularly important, since otherwise the client may simply refrain from maladaptive responses in "unsafe" therapy situations, where such behavior leads to immediate aversive results, but keep making them in "safe" real-life situations, where there is no fear of immediate discomfort.

Modeling

As Bandura (1977b) has pointed out,

"Learning would be exceedingly laborious, not to mention hazardous, if people had to rely solely on the effects of their own actions to inform them what to do. Fortunately, most human behavior is learned observationally through modeling: from observing others one forms an idea of how new behaviors are performed, and on later occasions this coded information serves as a guide for action. Because people can learn from example what to do, at least in approximate form, before performing any behavior, they are spared needless error." (p. 22)

Although reinforcement of modeled behavior can influence whether the observer-learner attends to the model's actions and strengthens the response imitated, observational learning does not seem to require extrinsic reinforcement. Rather, according to Bandura, reinforcement functions as a facilitative condition to learning. Anticipation of a reinforcement may also make the individual more likely to perform the behavior.

As the name implies, modeling involves the learning of skills through imitating another person, such as a parent or a therapist who perform the behavior. A patient may be exposed to behaviors or roles in peers or therapists and encouraged to imitate the desired new behaviors. For example, modeling may be used to promote learning of specific skills, such as self-feeding in the profoundly mentally retarded child, to more complex skills, such as being more effective in social situations for a shy, withdrawn adolescent.

As we have noted, modeling and imitation are used in various forms of behavior therapy. Bandura (1964) found that live modeling combined with instruction and guided participation is the most effective desensitization treatment, resulting in the elimination of snake phobias in over 90 percent of the cases.

Systematic use of positive reinforcement

Systematic programs for the application of positive reinforcement are achieving notable success, particularly in institutional settings. Response shaping, token economies, and behavioral contracting are among the most widely used of such techniques.

1. *Response shaping.* Positive reinforcement is often used in *response shaping;* that is, in establishing a response that is not initially in the individual's behavior repertoire. This technique has been used extensively in working with the behavior problems of children. The following case reported by Wolf, Risley, and Mees (1964) is illustrative:

A 3-year-old autistic boy lacked normal verbal and social behavior. He did not eat properly, engaged in self-destructive behavior such as banging his head and scratching his face, and manifested ungovernable

tantrums. He had recently had a cataract operation, and required glasses for the development of normal vision. He refused to wear his glasses, however, and broke pair after pair.

The technique of shaping was decided upon to counteract the problem of glasses. Initially, the boy was trained to expect a bit of candy or fruit at the sound of a toy noisemaker. Then training was begun with empty eyeglass frames. First the boy was reinforced with the candy or fruit for picking them up, then for holding them, then for carrying them around, then for bringing the frames closer to his eyes, and then for putting the empty frames on his head at any angle. Through successive approximations, the boy finally learned to wear his glasses up to twelve hours a day.

2. *Token economies.* Approval and other intangible reinforcers may be ineffective in behavior-therapy programs, especially those dealing with severely maladaptive behavior. In such instances, appropriate behaviors may be rewarded with tangible reinforcers in the form of tokens that can later be exchanged for desired objects or privileges (Kazdin, 1980). In working with hospitalized schizophrenic patients, for example, Ayllon and Azrin (1968) found that using the commissary, listening to records, and going to movies were considered highly desirable activities by most patients. Consequently, these activities were chosen as reinforcers for socially appropriate behavior. To participate in any of them, the patient had to earn a number of tokens by demonstrating appropriate ward behavior. In Chapter 18 we will describe another successful token economy program with chronic hospitalized patients who had been considered resistant to treatment (Paul, 1982; Paul & Lentz, 1977).

Token economies have been used to establish adaptive behaviors ranging from elementary responses such as eating and making one's bed to the daily performance of responsible hospital jobs. In the latter instance, the token economy resembles the outside world where the individual is paid for his or her work in tokens (money) that can later be exchanged for desired objects and activities.

The use of tokens as reinforcers for appropriate behavior has a number of distinct advantages: (a) the number of tokens earned depends directly on the amount of desirable behavior shown; (b) tokens are not readily subject to sa-

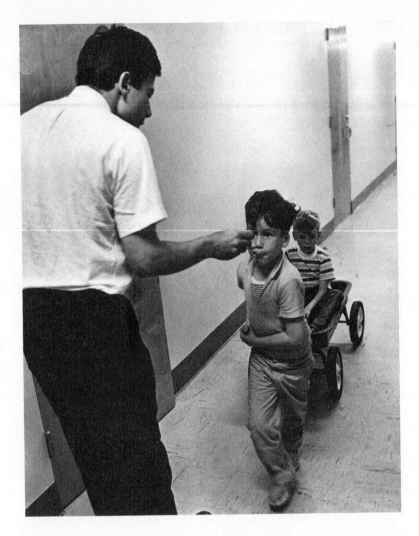

These two autistic boys were enrolled in an intensive behavior-therapy program at the UCLA Neuropsychiatric Institute. Here the boy pulling the wagon is shown receiving immediate positive reinforcement in the form of food for his participation in the activity. Other reinforcement techniques included punishment and modeling.

tiation and hence tend to maintain their incentive value; (c) tokens can reduce the delay that often occurs between appropriate performance and reinforcement; (d) the number of tokens earned and the way in which they are "spent" are largely up to the patient, and (e) tokens tend to bridge the gap between the institutional environment and the demands and system of payment that will be encountered in the outside world.

The ultimate goal in token economies, as in other programs of extrinsic reinforcement, is not only to achieve desired responses but to bring such responses to a level where their adaptive consequences will be reinforcing in their own right—thus enabling natural rather than artificial reward contingencies to maintain the desired be-

havior. For example, extrinsic reinforcers may be used initially to help children overcome reading difficulties, but once the child becomes proficient in reading skills, these skills will presumably provide intrinsic reinforcement as the child comes to enjoy reading for its own sake.

Although their effectiveness has been clearly demonstrated with chronic schizophrenic patients (Paul, 1982), mentally retarded residents in institutional settings, and children, the use of token economies has declined in recent years. In part, this has occurred as a result of reductions in the hospital treatment staffs that are required for effective patient management.

3. *Behavioral contracting.* **Behavioral contracting** is a technique used in some types of psychotherapy and behavior therapy to identify and agree on the behaviors that are to be changed, and to maximize the probability that the behavioral changes will occur and be maintained (Nelson & Mowry, 1976). By definition, a contract is an agreement between two or more parties—such as a therapist and a client, or a parent and a teenager—that governs the nature of the treatment program. The agreement, often in writing, specifies the client's obligations to change, as well as the responsibilities of the other person to provide something the client wants in return, such as tangible rewards, privileges, or therapeutic attention. Behavior therapists frequently make behavioral contracting an explicit focus of treatment, thus helping establish the treatment as a joint enterprise for which both parties have responsibility.

Behavioral contracting can facilitate therapy in several ways: (a) the structuring of the treatment relationship can be explicitly stated, giving the client a clear idea of each person's role in the treatment; (b) the actual responsibilities of the client are outlined along with a system of rewards built in for changed behavior; (c) the limitations of the treatment in terms of the length and focus of the sessions are specified; (d) by agreement, some behaviors may be eliminated from the treatment focus, thereby establishing the "appropriate content" of the treatment sessions; (e) clear treatment goals can be defined; and (f) criteria for determining success or failure in achieving these goals can be built into the program. A classic case of behavioral contracting is described in the HIGHLIGHT on page 648.

Sometimes a contract is negotiated between a disruptive child and the teacher, according to which the child will maintain or receive certain privileges as long as he or she behaves in accordance with the responsibilities set forth in the contract. Usually the school principal is also a party to such a contract to ensure the enforcement of certain conditions which the teacher may not be in a position to enforce, such as removing the child from the classroom for engaging in certain types of misbehavior.

Assertiveness therapy

Assertiveness therapy or training has been used as a method of desensitization as well as a means of developing more effective coping techniques. It appears particularly useful in helping individuals who have difficulties in interpersonal interactions because of conditioned anxiety responses that may prevent them from "speaking up" or even from showing appropriate affection. Such inhibition may lead to continual inner turmoil, particularly if the individual feels strongly about the situation. Assertiveness therapy may also be indicated in cases where individuals consistently allow other people to take advantage of them or maneuver them into situations that they find uncomfortable.

Assertiveness is viewed as the open and appropriate expression of thoughts and feelings, with due regard to the rights of others. Assertiveness training programs typically follow stages in which the desired "assertive" behaviors are first practiced in the therapy setting. Then, guided by the therapist, the individual is encouraged to practice the new, more appropriately assertive behaviors in real-life situations. Often attention is focused on developing more effective interpersonal skills. For example, a client may learn to ask the other person such questions as "Is anything wrong? You don't seem to be your usual self today." Such questions put the focus on the other person without suggesting an aggressive or hostile intent on the part of the speaker. Each act of intentional assertion inhibits the anxiety associated with the situation and therefore weakens the maladaptive anxiety response pattern. At the same time, it tends to foster more adaptive interpersonal behaviors.

Although assertiveness therapy is a highly useful procedure in certain types of situations, it does have limitations. For example, Wolpe (1969b) has pointed out that it is largely irrelevant for phobias involving nonpersonal stimuli. It may also be of little use in some types of interpersonal situations; for instance, if the individual has in fact been rejected by someone, assertive behavior may tend to aggravate rather than resolve the problem. However, in interpersonal situations where maladaptive anxiety can be traced to lack of self-assertiveness, this type of therapy appears particularly effective.

Biofeedback treatment

For many years it was generally believed that voluntary control over physiological processes such as heart rate, galvanic skin response, and

HIGHLIGHT
Behavioral contracting

Candy was a 16-year-old girl who had been admitted to a psychiatric hospital following alleged exhibitionism, drug abuse, truancy from home, and promiscuity (Stuart, 1971a). Candy's parents also complained that she was chronically antagonistic in her verbal exchanges with them and was near failing in her schoolwork. Because of the cost of private psychiatric care, they requested that she be made a ward of the juvenile court. They were advised that their allegations would probably not stand up in court and agreed to let her remain at home under the terms of a behavioral contract.

An initial contract, based on unrealistic parental demands, failed when Candy consistently violated its terms by sneaking out at night. A new, more realistic contract between Candy and her parents was then negotiated, and a monitoring form containing a checklist of chores, curfew conditions, and bonus time for each day of the month was provided. Some of the provisions of this contract were as follows:

"In exchange for the privilege of going out at 7:00 p.m. on one weekend evening without having to ac-

count for her whereabouts Candy must maintain a weekly average of "B" in the academic ratings of all of her classes and must return home by 11:30 p.m.

"In exchange for the privilege of having Candy complete household chores and maintain her curfew Mr. and Mrs. Bremer agree to pay Candy $1.50 on the morning following days on which the money is earned.

"If Candy is 31–60 minutes late she loses the privilege of going out the following day and does forfeit her money for the day." (Stuart, 1971, p. 9)

Behavioral contracting proved to be a constructive means of structuring the interaction between Candy and her parents, and Candy's behavior improved steadily. By removing the issues of privileges and responsibilities from the realm of contention, many intrafamilial arguments were avoided, and those that did occur tended to be tempered by the specified options. Through the contract, privileges such as money and free time were established as effective environmental contingencies in fostering desired behavior (p. 11).

blood pressure was not possible. However, in the early 1960s this view began to change. A number of investigators, aided by the development of sensitive electronic instruments that could accurately measure physiological responses, demonstrated that many of the processes formerly thought to be "involuntary" were modifiable by learning procedures—operant learning as well as classical conditioning. Kimmel (1974) demonstrated that the galvanic skin response could be conditioned by operant learning techniques.

The importance of the autonomic nervous system in the development of abnormal behavior had long been recognized. For example, autonomic arousal is an important factor in anxiety states. Thus many researchers have applied techniques developed in the autonomic conditioning studies in an attempt to modify the "internal environment" of troubled individuals in order to bring about more adaptive behavior—

for instance, to modify heart rates in patients with irregular heartbeat (Weiss & Engel, 1971), to treat stuttering by feeding back information on the electric potential of muscles in the speech apparatus (Lanyon, Barrington, & Newman, 1976), and to reduce lower back pain (Wolf, Nacht, & Kelly, 1982) and chronic headaches (Blanchard et al., in press).

This treatment approach—in which the person is taught to influence his or her own physiological processes—is referred to as *biofeedback.* Several steps are typical in the process of biofeedback treatment: (a) monitoring the physiological response that is to be modified (perhaps blood pressure or skin temperature); (b) converting the information to a visual or auditory signal; and (c) providing a means of prompt feedback—indicating to the subject as rapidly as possible when the desired change is taking place (Blanchard & Epstein, 1978).

For example, in attempts to measure changes

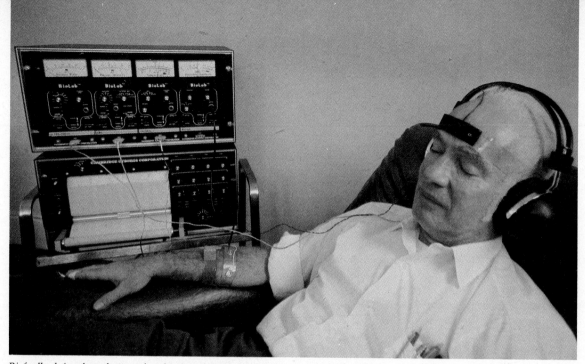

Biofeedback involves the use of sophisticated equipment to provide the subject with information (feedback) so that he or she may modify a given physiological process.

in skin temperature—produced by a constriction of the blood vessels— *thermistors,* which are small thermometers sensitive to temperature changes of about a tenth of a degree, are taped to the subject's skin. Their signal is then amplified and converted to an easily interpreted medium, such as a digital readout display. Given this feedback, the subject may then seek to modify his or her behavior in order to lower the skin temperature.

Biofeedback treatment is a popular treatment approach that requires the investment of large sums of money to purchase complicated equipment and a cadre of semiprofessional biofeedback technicians to perform the treatment. Whether its effectiveness justifies this expense is a difficult question.

Although there is general agreement that many physiological processes can be regulated to some extent by learning, the application of biofeedback procedures to alter abnormal behavior has produced equivocal results. Demonstrations of incidents of clinical biofeedback applications abound, but carefully controlled research has not sufficiently supported earlier clinical impressions of improvement. Blanchard and Young (1973, 1974) pointed out that the effects of biofeedback procedures are generally small

and often do not generalize to situations outside the laboratory, where the biofeedback devices are not present. And two recent, well-controlled studies have failed to show a treatment effect for biofeedback with migraine patients (Kewman & Roberts, 1979) and Raynaud's disease patients (Gugliemi, 1979). In addition, biofeedback had not been shown to be any more effective than relaxation training, leading to the suggestion that biofeedback may simply be a more elaborate means of teaching subjects relaxation (Blanchard & Epstein, 1978; Blanchard et al., 1980; Tarler-Benlolo, 1978).

Thus, with the relatively small effects that biofeedback training produces in many treatment situations, and the findings that other, less expensive behavioral treatments—such as relaxation training (Bradley & Prokop, 1982)—may be just as effective, biofeedback appears not to be the panacea that many had hoped.

Evaluation of behavior therapy

As compared with psychoanalytic and other psychotherapies, behavior therapy appears to have three distinct advantages. First, the treatment approach is precise. The target behaviors to be modified are specified, the methods to be used are clearly delineated, and the results can be readily evaluated (Marks, 1982). Second, the use of explicit principles of learning is a sound basis for effective interventions as a result of their demonstrated scientific validity (Kazdin & Wilson, 1978). Third, the economy of time and costs is quite good. Behavior therapy usually achieves results in a short period of time, since it is generally directed to specific symptoms, leading to faster relief of personal distress for the individual, as well as to lower financial costs. In addition, more people can be treated by a given therapist.

Different kinds of behavior therapy vary in their effectiveness for particular problems: desensitization seems most useful in treating conditioned avoidance responses; aversive techniques in establishing impulse control; and modeling combined with positive reinforcement in the acquisition of complex responses. In addition, behavior therapy techniques are the backbone of modern approaches to the treatment of sexual dysfunctions, discussed in Chapter 12. Like other forms of psychological intervention, behavior therapy has proven somewhat unsuccessful in the treatment of such patterns as childhood autism, schizophrenia, and severe depression, although dramatic results have been shown in some cases by Lovaas (1977) and Paul and Lentz (1977).

Although behavior therapy is not a "cure-all," it has proven effective in the treatment of a wide range of maladaptive behaviors (Kazdin & Wilson, 1978), and typical reports indicate a success rate of well over 50 percent and sometimes as high as 90 percent, depending largely on the type of maladaptive pattern being treated.

Cognitive-behavioral therapy

Early behavior therapists focused on observable behavior. They regarded the inner thoughts of their clients as not really part of the causal chain, and in their zeal to be objective they focused on the relationship between observable behaviors and observable reinforcing conditions.

Thus they were often viewed as mechanistic technicians who simply manipulated their subjects without considering them as people. More recently, however, a number of behavior therapists have reappraised the importance of "private events"—thoughts, perceptions, evaluations, and self-statements—seeing them as processes that mediate the effects of objective stimulus conditions and thus help determine behavior (Mahoney & Arnkoff, 1978).

Homme (1965), a student of Skinner, began this exodus from strict behaviorism in a paper arguing that these private events were behaviors that could be objectively analyzed. He proposed that thoughts be regarded as emitted internal events comparable to emitted external behaviors, and that a technology be developed for modifying thoughts by use of the same principles of learning that were proving so effective in changing outer behavior. These internal, private events he called *coverants,* considering them to be operants of the mind. Following Homme's "coverant behaviorism," many investigators began to apply conditioning principles to covert events, such as thoughts and assumptions.

Cognitive-behavioral therapy, as the term suggests, stems from both cognitive psychology, with its emphasis on the effects of thoughts on behavior, and behaviorism, with its rigorous methodology and performance-oriented focus. At the present time there is no single method of operation in cognitive-behavioral therapy: numerous methods are being developed with varying foci. Two main themes seem to characterize them all, however: (a) the conviction that cognitive processes influence both motivation and behavior, and (b) the use of behavior-change techniques in a pragmatic (hypothesis-testing) manner. That is, the therapy sessions are analogous to experiments in which the therapist and client apply learning principles to alter the client's cognitions, continuously evaluating the effects that the changes in cognitions have on both thoughts and outer behavior. In our discussion we shall focus on three approaches to cognitive-behavioral therapy: the rational-emotive therapy of Ellis, the cognitive therapy of Beck, and stress-inoculation training, as illustrated by the work of Meichenbaum.[4]

---

[4]For an extended discussion of cognitive-behavioral treatment, the following references would be informative: Beck (1976); Foreyt and Rathjen (1978); Goldfried and Davidson (1976); Kendall and Hollon (1979); Lazarus (1971); Mahoney and Arnkoff (1978); Meichenbaum (1977).

Rational-emotive therapy (RET)

One of the earliest behaviorally oriented cognitive therapies was the rational-emotive therapy (RET) of Ellis (1958, 1973, 1975). RET attempts to change the client's basic maladaptive thought processes. In its infancy, RET was viewed skeptically by many professionals who doubted its effectiveness, but it has now become one of the most widely used therapeutic approaches (Garfield & Kurtz, 1976).

Ellis considers the well-functioning individual as one who is behaving rationally and in tune with empirical reality. Unfortunately, many of us have learned unrealistic beliefs and perfectionistic values that cause us to expect too much of ourselves, leading us to behave irrationally and then to feel unnecessarily that we are worthless failures. For example, a person may continually think, "I should be able to win everyone's love and approval" or "I should be thoroughly adequate and competent in everything I do." Such unrealistic assumptions and self-demands inevitably lead to ineffective and self-defeating behavior and then to the emotional response of self-devaluation. The emotional response of self-devaluation is thus the consequence not of real-life events but of an individual's faulty expectations, interpretations, and self-demands.

As a more specific example, consider the case in which a man has a very intense emotional reaction of despair with deep feelings of worthlessness, unlovability, and self-devaluation when he is jilted by his fiancée. With a stronger self-concept and a more realistic picture of both himself and his fiancée, as well as of their actual relationship, his emotional reaction might have been one of relief. It is his interpretation of the situation and of himself rather than the objective situation that has led to his intense emotional reaction. For an idea of how Ellis might diagram such a situation schematically, see the **HIGHLIGHT** on this page.

Ellis (1970) believes that one or more of the core irrational beliefs below are at the root of most psychological maladjustment.

a) One should be loved by everyone for everything one does.
b) Certain acts are awful or wicked, and people who perform them should be severely punished.
c) It is horrible when things are not the way we would like them to be.

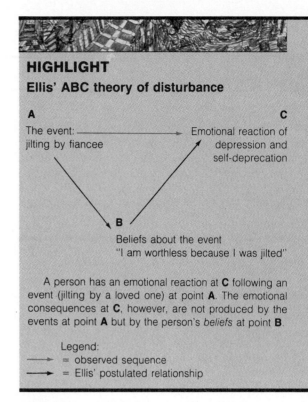

HIGHLIGHT
Ellis' ABC theory of disturbance

A   **C**
The event: ———————————————→ Emotional reaction of
jilting by fiancee   depression and
                                                                   self-deprecation

                                        B
                    Beliefs about the event
                    "I am worthless because I was jilted"

A person has an emotional reaction at **C** following an event (jilting by a loved one) at point **A**. The emotional consequences at **C**, however, are not produced by the events at point **A** but by the person's *beliefs* at point **B**.

Legend:
——→ = observed sequence
——➤ = Ellis' postulated relationship

d) Human misery is produced by external causes, or outside persons, or events rather than by the view that one takes of these conditions.
e) If something may be dangerous or fearsome, one should be terribly upset about it.
f) It is better to avoid life problems if possible than to face them.
g) One needs something stronger or more powerful than oneself to rely on.
h) One should be thoroughly competent, intelligent, and achieving in all respects.
i) Because something once affected one's life, it will indefinitely affect it.
j) One must have certain and perfect self-control.
k) Happiness can be achieved by inertia and inaction.
l) We have virtually no control over our emotions and cannot help having certain feelings.

Irrationality can, however, be viewed in different ways. Arnkoff and Glass (1982) cautioned against an overly simplistic view of irrational behavior as the mere holding of irrational beliefs. Rather, they contend that irrationality may also involve faulty thought processes reflecting a "closed-mindedness" that is more resistant to change than Ellis's view suggests.

The task of rational-emotive therapy is to restructure the individual's belief system and self-evaluation, especially with respect to the irrational "shoulds," "oughts," and "musts" that are preventing a more positive sense of self-worth and a creative, emotionally satisfying, and fulfilling life. Several methods are used.

One way is to *dispute* the person's false beliefs through rational confrontation. For example, the therapist dealing with the case above might ask the young man, "Why should your fiancée's changing her mind mean that *you* are worthless?" Here the therapist would teach the client to identify and dispute the beliefs that were producing the negative emotional consequences.

The rational-emotive therapist also uses behaviorally oriented techniques to bring about changed thoughts and behaviors. Sometimes, for example, homework assignments are given in order to encourage clients to have new experiences and break negative chains of behavior. For example, clients might be instructed to reward themselves by an external reinforcer such as a food treat after working 15 minutes at disputing their beliefs. Another method of self-reinforcement might be through covert statements such as "You are doing a really good job."

In some ways rational-emotive therapy can be viewed as a *humanistic* therapy (to be discussed in the next section) because it takes a clear stand on personal worth and human values. Rational-emotive therapy aims at increasing the individual's feelings of self-worth and clearing the way for self-actualization by removing the false beliefs that have been stumbling blocks to personal growth.

Cognitive-behavioral therapy for depression

Beck's cognitive-behavioral therapy was developed for the treatment of depression (Beck et al., 1979; Hollon & Beck, 1978). One basic assumption underlying this approach is that problems like depression result from patients' illogical thinking about themselves, the world they live in, and the future. These illogical ideas are maintained even in the face of contradictory evidence because the individuals typically engage in self-defeating and self-fulfilling behaviors in

which they (a) *selectively perceive* the world as harmful while ignoring evidence to the contrary; (b) *overgeneralize* on the basis of limited examples—for example, seeing themselves as totally worthless because they were laid off at work; (c) *magnify* the significance of undesirable events—for example, seeing the job loss as the end of the world for them; and (d) engage in *absolutistic*, "all-or-none" thinking—for example, exaggerating the importance of someone's casual comment and perceiving it as final proof of their worthlessness.

In Beck's cognitive-behavioral therapy, however, clients are not persuaded to change their beliefs by debate as in rational-emotive therapy; rather, they are encouraged to gather information about themselves through unbiased experiments that allow them to disconfirm their false beliefs. Together, the therapist and the individual identify the individual's assumptions, beliefs, and expectations and formulate them as hypotheses to be tested. They then design ways in which the individual can check out these hypotheses in the world. These behavioral-disconfirmation experiments are planned to give the individual successful experiences. They are arranged according to difficulty, so that the least difficult tasks will be accomplished successfully before the more difficult ones are attempted (see **HIGHLIGHT** on page 653).

Sometimes the client and the therapist schedule the patient's daily activities on an hour-by-hour basis. Such activity scheduling is an important part of therapy with depressed individuals because by reducing the patient's inactivity, it interrupts the tendency of depressed individuals to ruminate about themselves. An important part of the arrangement is the scheduling of pleasurable events because many depressed patients have lost the capacity for gaining pleasure from their own activities. Both the scheduled pleasurable activities and the rewarding experiences from carrying out the behavioral experiments tend to increase the individual's satisfaction and positive mood.

Besides planning the behavioral assignments, evaluating the results in subsequent sessions, and planning further disconfirmation experiments, there are several other cognitive foci in the therapy sessions. The individual is encouraged to discover underlying assumptions and "automatic thoughts" that may be leading to

HIGHLIGHT

Cognitive-behavioral therapy for a case of depression

Rush, Khatami, and Beck (1975) have reported several cases of successful treatment using cognitive clarification and behavioral assignments for patients with recurring chronic depression. The following case illustrates their approach:

"A 53-year-old white male engineer's initial depressive episode 15 years ago necessitated several month's absence from work. Following medication and psychotherapy, he was asymptomatic up to four years ago. At that time, sadness, pessimism, loss of appetite and weight, and heavy use of alcohol returned.

"Two years later, he was hospitalized for six weeks and treated with lithium and imipramine. He had three subsequent hospitalizations with adequate trials of several different tricyclics. During his last hospitalization, two weeks prior to initiating cognitive-behavioral therapy, he was treated with 10 sessions of ECT. His symptoms were only partially relieved with these various treatments.

"When the patient started cognitive-behavioral therapy, he showed moderate psychomotor retardation. He was anxious, sad, tearful, and pessimistic. He was self-depreciating and self-reproachful without any interest in life. He reported decreased appetite, early morning awakening, lack of sexual interest, and worries about his physical health. Initially he was treated with weekly sessions for 3 months, then biweekly for 2 months. Treatment, terminated after 5 months, consisted of 20 sessions. He was evaluated 12 months after the conclusion of therapy.

"Therapist and patient set an initial goal of his becoming physically active (i.e., doing more things no matter how small or trivial). The patient and his wife kept a separate list of his activities. The list included raking leaves, having dinner, and assisting his wife in apartment sales, etc. His cognitive distortions were identified by comparing his assessment of each activity with that of his wife. Alternative ways of interpreting his experiences were then considered.

"In comparing his wife's resumé of his past experiences, he became aware that he had (1) undervalued his past by failing to mention many previous accomplishments, (2) regarded himself as far more responsible for his "failures" than she did, and (3) concluded that he was worthless since he had not succeeded in attaining certain goals in the past. When the two accounts were contrasted he could discern many of his cognitive distortions. In subsequent sessions, his wife continued to serve as an 'objectifier.'

"In midtherapy, the patient compiled a list of new attitudes that he had acquired since initiating therapy. These included:

1) I am starting at a lower level of functioning at my job, but it will improve if I persist.

2) I know that once I get going in the morning, everything will run all right for the rest of the day.

3) I can't achieve everything at once.

4) I have my periods of ups and downs, but in the long run I feel better.

5) My expectations from my job and life should be scaled down to a realistic level.

6) Giving in to avoidance never helps and only leads to further avoidance.

"He was instructed to re-read this list daily for several weeks even though he already knew the content. The log was continued, and subsequent assumptions reflected in the log were compared to the assumptions listed above.

"As the patient became gradually less depressed, he returned to his job for the first time in 2 years. He undertook new activities (e.g., camping, going out of town) as he continued his log." (pp. 400–01)

The focus of the therapy was on encouraging the patient to restructure his thought content—to reduce the negative self-judgments and to evaluate his actual achievements more realistically. Making and reviewing the list of new attitudes gave the patient more perspective on his life situation, which resulted in an improved mood, less self-blame, and more willingness to risk alternative behavior.

HIGHLIGHT

Stress inoculation therapy to control severe anger

Many clinicians believe that intense anger typically underlies depression. Novaco (1977) employed a stress-inoculation procedure in the treatment of a severely depressed man by focusing on this hypothesized relationship between severe anger and depression.

"The client was a 38-year-old male who had been admitted to the psychiatric ward of a community hospital with the diagnosis of depressive neurosis. Upon admission he was judged to be grossly depressed, having suicidal ruminations and progressive beliefs of worthlessness and inadequacy. He was a credit manager for a national business firm and had been under considerable job pressure. Quite routinely, he developed headaches by midafternoon at work. He had recurrent left anterior chest pain that was diagnosed by a treadmill stress test procedure as due to muscle tension.

"The client had been hospitalized for 3 weeks when the attending psychiatrist referred him to me for the treatment of anger problems. At that time I had initiated a staff training program for the treatment of anger. The principal behavior settings in which problems with anger control emerged were at work, at home, and at church. The client was married and had six children, one of whom was hyperactive.

"Circumstances at work had progressively generated anger and hostility for this man's superiors, colleagues, and supervisees. His anger at work was typically overcontrolled. He would actively suppress his anger and would then periodically explode with a verbal barrage of epithets, curses, and castigations when a conflict arose. At home, he was more impulsively aggressive. The accumulated tensions and frustrations at work resulted in his being highly prone to provocation at home, particularly in response to the disruptive behavior of the children. Noise, disorders, and the frequent fights among the children were high anger elicitors. Unlike his behavior at work, he would quickly express his anger in verbal and physical outbursts. Although not an abusive parent, he would readily resort to physical means and threats of force (e.g., 'I'll knock your goddamn head off') as a way to control the behavior of his children. The children's unruly behavior often became a problem during church services. The client's former training in a seminary disposed him to value family attendance at church, but serious conflict was often the result. In an incident just prior to hospitalization, the client abruptly removed two of his boys from church for creating a disturbance and threatened them to the extent that one ran away. At this point he had begun to realize that he was reacting 'out of proportion,' but

self-defeating tendencies. With this background, the individual is taught to self-monitor his or her thought content and keep challenging its validity.

Stress-inoculation therapy

A third cognitive-behavioral approach to treatment is *stress-inoculation therapy*—a type of self-instructional training focused on altering self-statements that the individual is routinely making in order to restructure his or her characteristic approach to stress-producing situations (Meichenbaum & Cameron, 1982). Like other cognitive-behavioral therapies, stress-inoculation

therapy assumes that the individual's problems result from maladaptive beliefs which are leading to negative emotional states and maladaptive behavior (see **HIGHLIGHT** on pages 654–55).

Stress-inoculation therapy usually involves three stages. In the initial phase, *cognitive preparation*, client and therapist together explore the client's beliefs and attitudes about the problem situation and the self-statements to which they are leading. The focus is on how the individual's self-talk can influence later performance and behavior. Together, the therapist and the client agree on new self-statements that would be more adaptive. Then the second phase of the stress inoculation, *skill acquisition and rehearsal*, is begun. In this phase, more adaptive self-

he felt helpless about instituting the desired changes in behavior.

"During hospitalization, treatment sessions were conducted three times per week for 3½ weeks. Following discharge, follow-up sessions were conducted biweekly for a 2-month period. During these sessions, anger diary incidents were discussed, and there was continued modeling, rehearsal, and practice of coping procedures." (pp. 602–3)

The stress-inoculation program consisted of three phases: (a) In the *cognitive preparation* period, the client was educated about how anger operates—that is, how it is triggered, how to recognize one's anger, how anger affects one's physical state, and what coping strategies can be learned to control anger. He was taught to see anger as an emotional state that was induced by external events but could be altered by his own problem-solving behavior. (b) In the *skill acquisition and rehearsal* period, the therapist modeled effective coping techniques which the client then practiced. For example, he was taught to see possible alternatives to anger in particular situations, thus changing his view about the importance of certain events that had been making him angry. Self-instructions were used to modify his appraisals of anger-pro-

ducing events and to guide his coping behavior when he felt himself becoming angry. He also was given relaxation training. (c) Finally, in the *application and practice* phase, a task-oriented response set was taught in which the client learned to regulate his anger by managing provocative situations in practice sessions. He was given "manageable doses of anger stimuli" in a series of role-play situations, working through a hierarchy of anger-producing situations until the coping skills had been sufficiently learned and rehearsed.

The client's proneness to provocation was evaluated prior to treatment, during treatment, and following treatment by a questionnaire dealing with anger-inducing situations. His behavior was also observed during nine observation periods by a trained clinician. In addition, the client self-monitored his own anger by keeping a diary of anger experiences.

The results were truly dramatic. The client improved on all measures over the course of treatment: antagonism and anger (both overt or restrained) decreased over the period while more positive, constructive behaviors and more relaxed appearance increased. His self-reported anger was also considerably reduced over the three-month period.

statements are learned and practiced. For example, an individual undergoing stress-inoculation therapy for coping with the "feeling of being overwhelmed" would rehearse self-statements such as,

"When fear comes, just pause.
Keep the focus on the present; what is it you have to do?
Label your fear from 0 to 10 and watch it change.
You should expect your fear to rise.
Don't try to eliminate fear totally; just keep it manageable.
You can convince yourself to do it. You can reason fear away.
It will be over shortly.

It's not the worst thing that can happen.
Just think about something else.
Do something that will prevent you from thinking about fear.
Describe what is around you. That way you won't think about worrying." (Meichenbaum, 1974, p. 16)

The third phase of stress-inoculation therapy, *application and practice,* involves applying the new coping strategies in actual situations. This practice is graduated in such a way that the individual is placed in easier situations first and is only gradually introduced to more stressful life situations as he or she feels confident of mastering them.

Stress-inoculation therapy has been successfully employed with a number of clinical problems, especially anxiety (Meichenbaum, 1975); pain (Turk, 1974); and Type A behavior (Jenni & Wollersheim, 1979). This approach is particularly suited to increasing the adaptive capabilities of individuals who have shown a vulnerability to developing problems in certain stressful situations. In addition to its value as a therapeutic technique for identified problems, stress-inoculation therapy may be a viable method for preventing behavior disorders. Although the preventive value of this and other cognitive-behavioral therapy procedures has not been demonstrated by empirical study, many believe that the incidence of maladjustment might be reduced if more individuals' general coping skills were improved (Meichenbaum & Jaremko, 1983).

Evaluation of cognitive-behavioral therapy

A review of research evaluating cognitive-behavioral treatment methods at this time suggests that these approaches to intervention show a great deal of promise in alleviating some behavior problems. Several empirical studies have compared cognitive-behavioral methods with other treatment approaches. Data from these evaluation studies—on Beck's cognitive-behavioral therapy for individuals experiencing depression (Kovacs et al., 1981; McLean & Hakistan, 1979); on rational-emotive therapy (Lipsky, Kassinove, & Miller, 1980); on stress-inoculation procedures (Denicola & Sandler, 1980; Holcomb, 1979; Klepac et al., 1981)—indicate that cognitive-behavioral methods are associated with positive treatment outcomes.

The combining of cognitive and behavioral therapy approaches in practice is growing rapidly. In the next few years, we can expect to see many more studies evaluating the effectiveness of cognitive-behavioral methods as approaches to therapeutic change. There remains disagreement about whether some approaches are "truly" behavioral or "truly" cognitive, and whether or how cognitive change can bring about lasting behavioral change. As such, it is likely that the cognitive-behavioral viewpoint will undergo further theoretical development in the next few years (Kendall, 1982a).

Humanistic-experiential therapies

The *humanistic-experiential* therapies have emerged as significant treatment approaches during the last three decades. To a large extent, they developed in reaction to the psychoanalytic and behavioristic perspectives, which many feel do not accurately take into account either the existential problems or the full potentialities of human beings. In a society dominated by mechanization, computerization, and mass bureaucracy, proponents of the humanistic-experiential therapies see psychopathology as stemming in many cases from problems of alienation, depersonalization, loneliness, and a failure to find meaning and fulfillment in life—problems that are not solved either by delving into forgotten memories or by correcting specific responses.

The humanistic-experiential therapies follow some variant of the general humanistic and existential perspectives spelled out in Chapter 3. They are based on the assumption that we have the freedom to control our own behavior—that we can reflect upon our problems, make choices, and take positive action. Whereas some behavior therapists see themselves as "behavioral engineers," responsible for changing specific behaviors by appropriate modifications in the individual's environment, humanistic-experiential therapists feel that the client must take most of the responsibility for the success of therapy, with the therapist serving as counselor, guide, and facilitator. These therapies may be carried out with individual clients or with groups of clients (see **HIGHLIGHT** on page 657).

Client-centered therapy

The *client-centered,* or *person-centered, therapy* of Carl Rogers (1951, 1961, 1966) actually antedated the strong movement toward behavior therapy that took place in the 1950s and the "humanistic revolution" of the 1960s. It was developed in the 1940s as a truly innovative alternative to psychoanalysis, the only major psychotherapy of the time.

HIGHLIGHT
Group therapy

Treatment of patients in groups first received impetus in the military during World War II, when psychotherapists were in short supply. Group therapy was found to be effective in dealing with a variety of problems, and it rapidly became an important therapeutic approach in civilian life. In fact, all the major systematic approaches to psychotherapy that we have discussed—psychoanalysis, behavior therapy, and so on—have been applied in group as well as individual settings.

Group therapy has traditionally involved a relatively small group of patients in a clinic or hospital setting, using a variety of procedures depending upon the age, needs, and potentialities of the patients and the orientation of the therapists. The degree of structure and of patient participation in the group process varies in different types of groups.

Most often, groups are informal, and many follow the format of encounter groups. Occasionally, however, more or less formal lectures and visual materials will be presented to patients as a group. For example, a group of alcoholic patients may be shown a film depicting the detrimental effects of excessive drinking on the human body, with a group discussion afterwards. While this approach by itself has not proven effective in combating alcoholism, it is often a useful adjunct to other forms of group therapy.

An interesting form of group therapy is *psychodrama*, based on role-playing techniques. The patient, assisted by staff members or other patients, is encouraged to act out problem situations in a theater-like setting. This technique frees the individual to express anxieties and hostilities or relive traumatic experiences in a situation that simulates real life but is more sheltered. The goal is to help the patient achieve emotional catharsis, increased understanding, and improved interpersonal competencies. This form of therapy, developed initially by Moreno (1959),

has proved beneficial for the patients who make up the audience as well as for those who participate on the stage (Sundberg & Tyler, 1962; Yablonsky, 1975).

It may be noted that group therapy may also be nearly completely unstructured, as in activity groups where children with emotional problems are allowed to act out their aggressions in the safety and control of the therapeutic group setting.

Rogers rejected both Freud's view of the primacy of irrational instinct and the therapist's role of prober, interpreter, and director of the therapeutic process. Instead, believing in the natural power of the organism to heal itself, he saw psychotherapy as a process of removing the constraints and hobbling restrictions that often prevent this process from operating. These con-

straints, he believed, grow out of unrealistic demands that people tend to place on themselves when they believe they should not have certain kinds of feelings, such as hostility. By denying that they do in fact have such feelings, they become unaware of their actual "gut" reactions. As they lose touch with their own genuine experience, the result is lowered integration, impaired personal relationships, and various forms of maladjustment.

The primary objective of Rogerian therapy is to resolve this incongruence—to help clients become able to accept and be *themselves*. To this end, the therapist establishes a psychological climate in which clients can feel unconditionally accepted, understood, and valued as persons. In this climate they can begin to feel free for the first time to explore their real feelings and thoughts and to accept hates and angers and "ugly feelings" as parts of themselves. As their self-concept becomes more congruent with their actual experiencing, they become more self-accepting and more open to new experience and new perspectives; in short, they become better integrated people.

In client-centered therapy, also called *nondirective* therapy, it is not the therapist's task to direct the course of therapy. Thus the therapist does not give answers or interpret what the client says or probe for unconscious conflicts or even steer the client onto certain topics. Rather he or she simply listens attentively and acceptingly to what the client wants to talk about, interrupting only to restate in other words what the client is saying. Such restatements, without any judgment or interpretation by the therapist, help the client clarify further the feelings and ideas that he or she is exploring—really to look at them and acknowledge them.

The following excerpt from a counselor's second interview with a young woman will serve to illustrate these techniques of reflection and clarification.

"**Alice:** I was thinking about this business of standards. I somehow developed a sort of a knack, I guess, of—well—habit—of trying to make people feel at ease around me, or to make things go along smoothly. . . .

Counselor: In other words, what you did was always in the direction of trying to keep things smooth and to make other people feel better and to smooth the situation.

Alice: Yes. I think that's what it was. Now the reason why I did it probably was—I mean, not that I was a good little Samaritan going around making other people happy, but that was probably the role that felt easiest for me to play. I'd been doing it around home so much. I just didn't stand up for my own convictions, until I don't know whether I have any convictions to stand up for.

Counselor: You feel that for a long time you've been playing the role of kind of smoothing out the frictions or differences or what not. . . .

Alice: M-hm.

Counselor: Rather than having any opinion or reaction of your own in the situation. Is that it?

Alice: That's it. Or that I haven't been really honestly being myself, or actually knowing what my real self is, and that I've been just playing a sort of false role. Whatever role no one else was playing, and that needed to be played at the time, I'd try to fill it in." (Rogers, 1951, pp. 152–53)

In a survey of trends in psychotherapy and counseling, Rogers was rated one of the most influential psychotherapists among clinical practitioners (Smith, 1982). In addition to his influence in clinical settings, Rogers pioneered in attempting to carry out empirical research on psychotherapy. Using recordings of therapy sessions, he was able to make objective analyses later of what was said, of the client-counselor relationship, and of many aspects of the ongoing processes in these therapy sessions. He was also able to compare a client's behavior and attitudes at different stages of therapy. These comparisons revealed a typical sequence that clients tended to go through. Early sessions were dominated by negative feelings and discouragement. Then, after a time, tentative statements of hope and greater self-acceptance began to appear. Eventually, positive feelings, a reaching out toward others, greater self-confidence, and interest in future plans appeared. This characteristic sequence gave support to Rogers' hypothesis that once freed to do so, individuals have the capacity to lead themselves to psychological health.

Pure client-centered psychotherapy, as originally practiced, is rarely used today, but it opened the way for a variety of humanistically oriented therapies in which the focus is the client's present conscious problems and in which it is assumed that the client is the primary actor in the curative process, with the therapist essentially just the facilitator. The newer humanistic therapies thus accept Rogers' concept of an active self, capable of sound value choices; they also emphasize the importance of a high degree of empathy, genuine warmth, and unconditional positive regard on the part of the therapist. They differ from original client-centered therapy in having found various shortcuts by which the therapist, going beyond simple reflection and clarification, can hasten and help focus the client's search for wholeness. But it is still the client's search and the client's insights that are seen as central in therapy.

Existential therapy

Several important concepts underlie *existential psychotherapy*. The existentialist perspective emphasizes the importance of the human situation as experienced by the individual. Existentialists are deeply concerned about the predicament of humankind, the breakdown of traditional faith, the alienation and depersonalization of the individual in contemporary society, and the lack of meaning in the lives of the individual. But they see individuals as having a high degree of freedom and thus as capable both of doing something about their predicament and of being responsible for doing the best they can. The unique ability of human beings to be aware of, reflect on, and question their existence confronts them with the responsibility for *being*—for deciding what kind of person to become, for establishing their own values, and for actualizing their potentialities.

The application of existential thought to understanding human problems and to helping individuals alter their lives has been recognized over the years by several psychological theorists, including Binswanger (1942) and May, Angel, and Ellenberger (1958). Binswanger, a psychoanalyst, applied the existential frame of reference to his psychoanalytic work and developed a method he referred to as *Daseinanalyse*, or existential analysis. May et al. followed later with what has become a classic work detailing existential analysis. Existential analysts do not limit themselves to an investigation of conscious and subconscious states, as do traditional analysts; rather, they attempt to assist the individual to reconstruct his or her inner world by focusing on the surrounding external reality. Most existential therapists do not strictly follow the methods of Daseinanalyse, but nevertheless accept an existential framework to challenge the patient to experience his or her human feelings.

Existential therapists do not follow any rigidly prescribed procedures, but emphasize the uniqueness of each individual and his or her "way-of-being-in-the-world." They stress the importance of being aware of one's own existence—challenging the individual directly with questions concerning the meaning and purpose of existence—and of the therapeutic encounter—the complex relationship established between two interacting human beings in the therapeutic situation as they both try to be open and "authentic." In contrast to behavior therapy, existential therapy calls for therapists to share themselves—their feelings, their values, and their own existence.

Besides being authentic themselves, it is the task of existential therapists to keep the client responding authentically to the present reality (Havens, 1974; May, 1969). For example, if the client says, "I hate you just like I hated my father," the therapist might respond by saying, "I am not your father, I am me, and you have to deal with me as Dr. S., not as your father." The focus is on the here and now—on what the individual is choosing to do, and therefore be, at this moment. This sense of immediacy, of the urgency of experience, is the touchstone of existential therapy and sets the stage for the individual to clarify and choose between alternative ways of being.

With what types of patients and which clinical problems does existential therapy work best? Like psychodynamic therapy, existential psychotherapy is for the few. It is directed primarily toward the intelligent and verbal individual who appears to be having an existential crisis. The existential treatment approach is believed to work best with individuals who have anxiety-based disorders or personality disorders rather than psychoses. The following case illustrates the type of problem situation that would lend itself to treatment in the existential framework:

A 42-year-old business executive seeks therapy because he feels that life has lost its meaning—he no longer feels that family matters are important to him (his wife is busy starting her career and his only child recently got married and moved to Alaska). Additionally, his work, at which he has had extraordinary success—earning him both financial security and respect—no longer holds meaning for him. He views his days as "wasted and worthless"; he feels both "bored and panicked"; he goes through the motions of the business day feeling "numb", as though he isn't even there. At times, he feels fearful and overwhelmed with a sense of dread that this is all that life has left for him.

Gestalt therapy

The term *gestalt* means "whole," and gestalt therapy emphasizes the unity of mind and body—placing strong emphasis on the need for integration of thought, feeling, and action. *Gestalt therapy* was developed by Frederick (Fritz) Perls (1967, 1969) as a means of teaching clients to recognize the bodily processes and emotional modalities they had been blocking off from awareness. The main goal of gestalt therapy is to increase the individual's self-awareness and self-acceptance.

Although gestalt therapy is commonly used in a group setting, the emphasis is on one individual at a time with whom the therapist works intensively, attempting to help identify aspects of the individual's self or world that are not being acknowledged in awareness. The individual may be asked to act out fantasies concerning feelings and conflicts, or to "be" one part of a conflict while sitting in one chair and then switch chairs to take the part of the "adversary." Often the therapist or other group members will ask questions like, "What are you aware of in your body now?" or "What does it feel like in your gut when you think of that?"

In Perls' approach to therapy, a good deal of emphasis is also placed on dreams:

". . . all the different parts of the dream are fragments of our personalities. Since our aim is to make every one of us a wholesome person, which means a unified person, without conflicts, what we have to do is put the different fragments of the dream together. We have to *re-own* these projected, fragmented parts of our personality, and *re-own* the hidden potential that appears in the dream." (1967, p. 67)

In the following dialogue, taken from the transcript of a "dreamwork seminar," Perls (Fritz) helps a young woman (Linda) discover the meaning of her dream:

"**Linda:** I dreamed that I watch . . . a lake . . . drying up, and there is a small island in the middle of the lake, and a circle of . . . porpoises—they're like porpoises except that they can stand up, so they're like porpoises that are like people, and they're in a circle, sort of like a religious ceremony, and it's very sad—I feel very sad because they can breathe, they are sort of dancing around the circle, but the water, their element, is drying up. So it's like a dying—like

watching a race of people, or a race of creatures, dying. And they are mostly females, but a few of them have a small male organ, so there are a few males there, but they won't live long enough to reproduce, and their element is drying up. And there is one that is sitting over here near me and I'm talking to this porpoise and he has prickles on his tummy, sort of like a porcupine, and they don't seem to be a part of him. And I think that there's one good point about the water drying up, I think—well, at least at the bottom, when all the water dries up, there will probably be some sort of treasure there, because at the bottom of the lake there should be things that have fallen in, like coins or something, but I look carefully and all that I can find is an old license plate . . . That's the dream.

Fritz: Will you please play the license plate?

L: I am an old license plate, thrown in the bottom of a lake. I have no use because I'm no value—although I'm not rusted—I'm outdated, so I can't be used as a license plate . . . and I'm just thrown on the rubbish heap. That's what I did with a license plate, I threw it on a rubbish heap.

F: Well, how do you feel about this?

L: (quietly) I don't like it. I don't like being a license plate—useless.

F: Could you talk about this? That was such a long dream until you come to find the license plate, I'm sure this must be of great importance.

L: (sighs) Useless. Outdated . . . The use of a license plate is to allow—give a car permission to go . . . and I can't give anyone permission to do anything because I'm outdated . . . In California, they just paste a little—you buy a sticker—and stick it on the car on the old license plate (faint attempt at humor). So maybe someone could put me on their car and stick this sticker on me, I don't know . . .

F: Okay, now play the lake.

L: I'm a lake . . . I'm drying up, and disappearing, soaking into the earth . . . (with a touch of surprise) *dying* . . . But when I soak into the earth, I become a part of the earth—so maybe I water the surrounding area, so . . . even in the lake, even in my bed, flowers can grow (sighs) . . . New life can grow . . . from me (cries) . . .

F: You get the existential message?

L: Yes. (sadly, but with conviction) I can paint—I can create—I can create beauty. I can no longer reproduce, I'm like the porpoise . . . but I . . . I'm . . . I . . . keep wanting to say I'm *food* . . . I . . . as water becomes . . . I water the earth, and give life—growing things, the water—they need both the earth and water, and the . . . and the air and the sun, but as the water from the lake, I can play a part in something, and producing—feeding.

F: You see the contrast: On the surface, you find something, some artifact—the license plate, the artificial you—but then when you go deeper, you find the apparent death of the lake is actually fertility. . . .

L: And I don't need a license plate, or a permission, a license in order to . . .

F: (gently) Nature doesn't need a license plate to grow. You don't have to be useless, if you are organismically creative, which means if you are involved.

L: And I don't need permission to be creative . . . Thank you." (Perls, 1969, pp. 81–82)

In gestalt therapy sessions, the focus is on the more obvious elements of the person's behavior. Such sessions are often called "gestalt awareness training," since the therapeutic results of the experience stem from the process of becoming more aware of one's total self and environment. The technique of working through unresolved conflicts is called "taking care of unfinished business." We all go through life, according to Perls, with unfinished or unresolved traumas and conflicts. We carry the excess baggage of these unfinished situations into new relationships and tend to reenact them in our relations with other people. If we are able to complete our past unfinished business, we then have less psychological tension to cope with and can be more realistically aware of ourselves and our world.

Expressing themselves in front of the group, perhaps taking the part of first one and then another fragment of a scene, and denied the use of their usual techniques for avoiding self-awareness, individuals are brought to an "impasse," at which point they must confront their feelings and conflicts. According to Perls, "In the safe emergency of the therapeutic situation, the neurotic discovers that the world does not fall to pieces if he or she gets angry, sexy, joyous, mournful" (1967, p. 331). Thus, individuals find that they can, after all, get beyond impasses on their own.

Evaluation of the humanistic-experiential therapies

The humanistic-experiential therapies have been criticized for their lack of a highly systematized model of human behavior, their lack of agreed-upon therapeutic procedures, and their vagueness about what is supposed to happen between client and therapist. It is these very features,

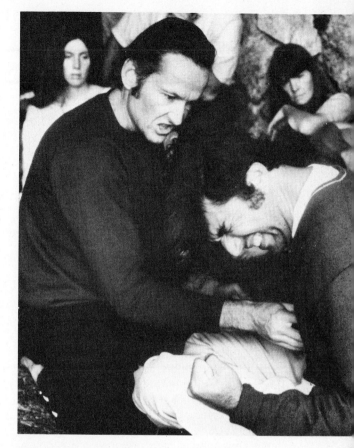

At a gestalt therapy session at Esalen, in Big Sur, California, the leader (left) encourages a member to express his pent-up feelings of anger.

however, that are seen by many proponents of this general approach as contributing to its strength and vitality. Systematized theories can reduce individuals to abstractions, which can result in diminishing their perceived worth and denying their uniqueness as individuals. Because people are so different, we should expect that different techniques would be appropriate for different cases.

In any event, many of the humanistic-experiential concepts—the uniqueness of each individual, the satisfaction that comes from developing and using one's potentials, the importance of the search for meaning and fulfillment, and the human power for choice and self-direction—have had a major impact on our contemporary views of both human nature and psychotherapy.

Therapy for interpersonal relationships

In Chapter 3 we noted the emphasis of the interpersonal perspective on the role of faulty communications, interactions, and relationships in maladaptive behavior. This viewpoint has had an important impact on approaches to therapy—particularly on the behavioristic and humanistic-existential therapies. For example, in behavior therapy we have seen the emphasis on modifying social reinforcements that may be maintaining maladaptive responses; in humanistic-existential therapies we have seen the concern with such problems as lack of acceptance, relatedness, and love in the individual's life.

In many cases, however, disordered interpersonal relationships are at the very center of an individual's problems. Such problems require therapeutic techniques that focus on relationships rather than on individuals. In this section we shall explore the growing fields of couple and family therapy and then examine in some detail the popular interpersonal technique of transactional analysis.

Couple counseling (marital therapy)

The large numbers of couples seeking assistance with problems centering around their relationship have made this a growing field of therapy. Typically the partners are seen together, and therapy focuses on clarifying and improving the interactions and relationships between them. Therapy for only one of the partners has proved less effective for resolving such problems (Gurman & Kniskern, 1978).

Couple counseling includes a wide range of concepts and procedures. Most therapists emphasize mutual need gratification, social role expectations, communication patterns, and similar interpersonal factors. Not surprisingly, happily married couples tend to differ from unhappily married couples in that they talk more to each other, keep channels of communication open,

make more use of nonverbal techniques of communication, and show more sensitivity to each other's feelings and needs. In a recent study comparing distressed versus nondistressed couples, Margolin and Wampold (1981) found that nondistressed couples showed more problem-solving behavior than distressed couples.

Faulty role expectations often play havoc with marital adjustment. For example, Paul (1971) cited the case of a couple who came for marital therapy when the 39-year-old husband was about to divorce his wife to marry a much younger woman. During therapy he broke into sobs of grief as he recalled the death of his Aunt Anna, who had always accepted him as he was and created an atmosphere of peace and contentment. In reviewing this incident, the husband realized that his girlfriend represented his life-long search for another Aunt Anna. This led to a reconciliation with his wife, who was now more understanding of his needs, feelings, and role expectations.

One of the difficulties in couple therapy is the intense emotional involvement of the marital partners, which makes it difficult for them to perceive and accept the realities of their relationship. Often wives can see clearly what is "wrong" with their husbands but not what attitudes and behavior of their own are contributing to the relationship, while husbands tend to have remarkable "insight" into their wives' flaws but not their own. To help correct this problem, videotape recordings have been used increasingly to recapture crucial moments of intense interaction between the partners. By watching these tapes the partners can gain a fuller awareness of the nature of their interactions. Thus a husband may realize for the first time that he tries to dominate rather than listen to his wife and consider her needs and expectations; or a wife may realize that she is continually undermining her husband's feelings of worth and esteem. The following statement was made by a young wife after viewing a videotape playback of the couple's first therapy session:

"See! There it is—loud and clear! As usual you didn't let me express *my* feelings or opinions, you just interrupted me with your own. You're always *telling* me what I think without *asking* me what I think. And I can see what I have been doing in response—withdrawing into silence. I feel like, what's the use of talking."

This insight was shared with the husband, and the couple were able to work out a much more satisfactory marital relationship within a few months.

Other relatively new and innovative approaches to couple therapy include training the partners to use Rogerian nondirective techniques in listening to each other and helping each other clarify and verbalize their feelings and reactions. A mutual readiness to really listen and try to understand what the other one is experiencing—and acceptance of whatever comes out in this process—can be both therapeutic for the individuals and productive of a more open and honest relationship in the future.

Eisler et al. (1974) have used an interesting combination of videotape playbacks and assertiveness therapy.

In one case, a 45-year-old high-school teacher was responding passively and ineffectively to his highly critical wife at the beginning of therapy. By watching videotapes of their interactions, they both received feedback on their roles in the interactions. The husband received training in assertiveness and practiced being more assertive, continuing to watch videotapes of the gradually changing interactions between him and his wife.

In contrast to the videotapes made at the beginning of therapy, those made at the end showed such positive results as improved communication, an increased frequency of expressions of affection and approval, and a marked increase in the amount of smiling in their interactions. Both spouses stated that their posttreatment marital adjustment seemed more satisfying.

Behavior therapy has also been used to bring about desired changes in marital relationships. Here the spouses are taught to reinforce instances of desired behavior while withdrawing reinforcement for undesired behavior (see **HIGHLIGHT** on page 666).

How effective are marital therapies at resolving marital crises and promoting more effective marriages? One recent study involved a five-year follow-up of 320 former marital clients and compared their divorce rates with those of the general population (Cookerly, 1980). In cases in which both partners underwent therapy together, 56.4 percent had remained married for the five-year period; in cases in which other types of marital therapy were used, 29 percent had remained married. All forms of marital therapy showed significantly better results in resolving marital crises and keeping marriages together than did the use of no marital therapy at all.

Family therapy

Therapy for the family group overlaps with marital therapy but has somewhat different roots. Whereas marital therapy developed in response to the large number of clients who came for assistance with marital problems, family therapy had its roots in the finding that many people who had shown marked improvement in individual therapy—often in institutional settings—had a relapse upon their return home. It soon became apparent that many of these people came from disturbed family settings that required modification if they were to maintain their gains.

A pioneer in the field of family therapy has described the problem as follows:

"Psychopathology in the individual is a product of the way he deals with his intimate relations, the way they deal with him, and the way other family members involve him in their relations with each other. Further, the appearance of symptomatic behavior in an individual is necessary for the continued function of a particular family system. Therefore changes in the individual can occur only if the family system changes. . . ." (Haley, 1962, p. 70)

This viewpoint led to an important concept in the field of psychotherapy, namely, that the problem or disorder shown by the "identified patient" is often only a symptom of a larger family problem. A careful study of the family of a disturbed child may reveal that the child is merely reflecting the pathology of the family unit. As a result, most family therapists share the view that the family—not simply the designated person—should be directly involved in therapy if lasting improvement is to be achieved.

Perhaps the most widely used approach to family therapy is the "conjoint family therapy" of Satir (1967). Her emphasis is on improving faulty communications, interactions, and relationships among family members and fostering a family system that better meets the needs of all the family members. The following example shows Satir's emphasis on the problem of faulty communication.

> **"Husband:** She never comes up to me and kisses me. I am always the one to make the overtures.
> **Therapist:** Is this the way you see yourself behaving with your husband?
> **Wife:** Yes, I would say he is the demonstrative one. I didn't know he wanted me to make the overtures.
> **T:** Have you told your wife that you would like this from her—more open demonstration of affection?
> **H:** Well, no you'd think she'd know.
> **W:** No, how would I know? You always said you didn't like aggressive women.
> **H:** I don't, I don't like *dominating* women.
> **W:** Well, I thought you meant women who make the overtures. How am I to know what you want?
> **Th:** You'd have a better idea if he had been able to *tell* you." (Satir, 1967, pp. 72–73)

Marital and family therapies focus on relationships rather than on individuals. In such therapies, the couple or the members of the family group participate together in the process.

Another encouraging approach to resolving family disturbance is called *structured family therapy* (Minuchin, 1974). This approach, based on "systems theory," assumes that the family system itself is more influential than individual personality or intrapsychic conflicts in producing abnormal behavior. It assumes that the family system has contributed to the characteristic behaviors that individual family members have developed; if the family context changes, then the individual members will have a changed experience in the family and will behave differently in accordance with the changed requirements of the new family context. Thus an important goal of structured family therapy is to change the organization of the family in such a way that the family members will behave more positively and supportively toward each other.

Structured family therapy is focused on present interactions and requires an active but not directive approach on the part of the therapist. Initially, the therapist gathers information about the family—a "structural map" of the typical family interaction patterns—by acting like one of the family, and participating in the family interactions as an insider. In this way the therapist discovers whether the family system has rigid or flexible boundaries, who dominates the power structure, who gets blamed when things go wrong, and so on.

Armed with this understanding, the therapist then uses himself or herself as a "change medium" for altering the interaction among the family members. For example, Aponte and Hoffman (1973) report the successful use of structured family therapy in treating an anorexic 14-year-old girl.

Analyzing the communications in the family, the therapists saw a competitive struggle for the father's attention and observed that the girl, Laura, was able to succeed in this competition and get "cuddly" attention from her father by not eating. To bring the hidden dynamics out into the open, they worked at getting the family members to express their desires more directly—in words instead of through hidden behavioral messages. In time, Laura became much more able to verbalize her wishes for affection and gave up the unacceptable and dangerous method of not eating.

Similarly, Minuchin et al. (1975) reported a study in which structured family therapy was

used successfully with families in which children had developed psychophysiologic illnesses. And Stanton and Todd (1976) reported
dramatic improvement rates with its use in several families in which one member was an identified heroin addict.

As with couple problems, maladaptive family
relationships have also been successfully overcome by behavioristically oriented therapies.[5]
Here Huff (1969) has suggested that the task of
the therapist is to reduce the aversive value of
the family for the identified client as well as that
of the client for other family members. "The
therapist does this by actively manipulating the
relationship between members so that the relationship changes to a more positively reinforcing
and reciprocal one" (p. 26).

N. Hurwitz (1974) has elaborated on the role
of the family therapist as an intermediary whose
functions include "interpreter, clarifier, emis-
sary, go-between, messenger, catalyst, mediator, arbitrator, negotiator, and referee" (p. 145).
These role demands are most exacting, and are
commonly shared by cotherapists, one male and
one female.

After reviewing family therapy approaches,
Gurman and Kniskern (1978) concluded that
structured family therapy had had more impressive results than most other experientially and
analytically oriented approaches they had reviewed. In addition, clinical impressions are that
family therapy is effective at reducing family
tensions and promoting more adaptive functioning of individuals in the family. However, the
relative success of family intervention methods
versus individual methods of therapy is an exceedingly difficult area of research. Wellisch and
Trock (1980) found, at a three-year follow-up,
that the previously superior effects of family
therapy had deteriorated; 57 percent of the patients had had to be rehospitalized, as compared
with 20 percent of the individual therapy cases.
We can only speculate about the reasons for this
relatively poor showing for family therapy. If
these results suggest anything, it is perhaps the
simple fact that, for chronic problems, psychotherapy often cannot undo in a short time the
damage of years.

---

[5]A more extended discussion of behaviorally oriented approaches to family therapy can be found in Patterson, Weiss, and
Hops (1976), and Jacobson and Margolin (1979).

Transactional analysis

Eric Berne (1964, 1972) developed a version of
interpersonal therapy based on the notion that
our personalities are composed of three "ego
states"—Child, Adult, and Parent—which correspond roughly to Freud's id, ego, and superego. Our Parent is that part of our personality
we have incorporated from our own parents or
from other parental models whom we have inadvertently learned to emulate. Statements such
as "You shouldn't eat so much" or "Put on a
sweater if you're going outside in the cold" are
examples of our Parent talking. Such statements
may be appropriate when spoken to a child, but
if they are used with a spouse, it may well be
that the speaker is playing too active a Parent
role.

Our Child is that part of us that is a carry-
over from our childhood feelings. "I'll eat as
much as I want, and don't always yell at me!" is
an example of the Child responding to the first
Parent statement above. A Child response to the
second command might be simply to break
down and cry—behavior possibly appropriate
for a real child, but not for a mature adult.

Finally, the Adult in each of us is that part of
us which processes information rationally and
appropriately for the present unique set of circumstances. An adult response to the Parent's
sweater command might be, "I really don't think
it is cold enough for a sweater."

In *transactional analysis*, the therapist analyzes the interactions among group members
(often married couples) and helps the participants understand the ego states in which they
are communicating with each other. As long as
each participant reacts to the other by accepting
the role assigned and responding accordingly—
as a Child, for example, if addressed as a child—
the transactions may continue indefinitely.
Many couples find out that they have been having "complementary" transactions for years, but
that they have always been communicating as
mother to son or father to daughter. However,
when one party decides to stop playing Child to
the spouse's Parent, the game ceases, and conflicts develop that must be worked out. Since
analysis is done in a group setting, other members are encouraged to participate; the method
of their participation often invites analysis of

HIGHLIGHT
Structured behavior therapy for couples

Margolin, Christensen, and Weiss (1975) developed a brief, highly structured form of couple therapy organized around six topics or modules. The sequence takes about ten weeks.

1. Pinpointing contingencies   In an intensive period, the problem behaviors and the conditions maintaining them are identified.

2. Training in communication skills   Several techniques to improve communication, such as paraphrasing and reflecting the partner's feelings, are taught through modeling by the therapist, behavioral rehearsal, and video-feedback.

3. Training in conflict resolution   Partners view videotapes of other couples illustrating good and bad ways to deal with conflicts. Sometimes a poor method such as sidetracking or name-calling is followed by a constructive approach.

4. Formation of utility matrices   Here the partners identify rewards and penalties that they can use in contracts with each other about what they will and will not do.

5. Negotiating and "contingency contracting"   This is one of the most important phases. Practicing their new communication skills, the couple negotiate agreements on behavioral contracts that will provide a more rewarding and less punishing relationship for both of them.

6. Termination and maintenance   Once the agreements go into effect, the therapist helps promptly with any problems that arise to ensure that the learned skills are being practiced and the improved relationship maintained. In fact, throughout the course of the therapy sequence, evening phone contacts supplement the laboratory sessions for obtaining information on the partners' interactions, problems, and use of new skills. Treatment is terminated gradually as the spouses assume their new roles.

Follow-up is an important part of this therapy. The therapist may make weekly telephone contacts for the first weeks following termination. Booster sessions may be scheduled after termination if they are needed.

This form of behavioral marital therapy has been shown to be one of the most effective approaches to improving marriage relationships (Gurman & Kniskern, 1978; Jacobson & Martin, 1976). Moreover, its relatively well-structured modules can be precisely applied and taught readily to beginning therapists. The relatively specific interventions also lend themselves to empirical verification more easily than other, non-behavioral methods; thus research into marital therapy, a previously neglected area, may now be receiving some encouragement. A more recent general exposition of this approach is presented in Weiss and Birchler (1978).

---

how they, in turn, communicate with other people.

Berne characterized many of our social interactions as "games"—not because they are played "for fun," but because they are played according to a set of unspoken rules. In *Games People Play* (1964), he described a number of these, most of which are deadly serious and highly destructive in their effects.

1. *Why Don't You—Yes But (WDYB).* This is considered the prototype game in transactional analysis and involves what is commonly referred to as "gamesmanship" or "one-up-manship." The game is perpetrated by A who adopts a docile stance toward B (the victim) and presents some personal problem in such a way that B is induced to offer advice—for example, to adopt a counterstance of Therapist. Once the advice has been offered, A responds by saying "Yes, but . . . ," and proceeds to add additional information about the problem that renders B's advice erroneous or irrelevant. At this point B may come back with an alternative solution, still believing that A is sincere in offering him or her the Therapist role. A again follows the same procedure and "shoots" B down again. This game may go on for several rounds until B finally realizes he or she has been defeated; at this point, B may assume a self-effacing stance, perhaps acknowledging that A "sure has a tough problem." In this

game, A has perpetrated a transactional role reversal in which he or she has achieved competitive satisfaction at B's expense. A has, so to speak, "put B down."

2. *Wooden Leg.* This game involves the adoption of a "sick" role—much like that in conversion disorders. In essence, the individual asks "What do you expect from a person with a 'wooden leg'?" (a personality deficiency, physical deformity, slum background, or whatever). As we have seen, our society relaxes its demands on persons who are "sick"—who are temporarily or permanently incapable of meeting usual social standards of performance by virtue of some serious misfortune or handicap. It is a "helpless" game played by the Child who wants sympathy but does not really want to get better. The payoff is, "Oh yes, I understand: don't worry, we'll take care of you and give you whatever comfort you need." Of course, this kind of game is maladaptive in that the individual—whether or not he or she actually has the handicap claimed—avoids acquiring the competencies and sense of responsibility needed for independence and self-direction.

3. *Now I've Got You, You Son of a Bitch (NIGYSOB).* This game involves an aggressive payoff in which the perpetrator adopts a self-effacing stance that invites competitive exploitation from the victim. Since there is presumably "a little larceny in all of us," the victim unwisely accepts the proffered role and initiates a program of exploitation. The perpetrator plays along for a while, but at a certain point suddenly reverses his or her stance and reveals the exploitation; with an appropriate show of anger and indignation, the perpetrator assumes his or her justly deserved aggressive position of NIGYSOB. The victim, in turn, is forced into the apologetic and devaluating role of guilty self-effacement.

By analyzing the "games" we play, transactional analysis may make individuals aware of their habitual coping patterns and the consequences these patterns have on interpersonal relationships and life adjustment. In holding up a mirror in which individuals can see their behavior for what it really is, it may reveal how people often unthinkingly manipulate and harm other people as well as themselves.

As an intervention strategy, transactional analysis holds out the possibility of eliminating subterfuges and deceits from our interactions and of achieving more authentic, meaningful, and satisfying personal relationships. However, transactional analysis has not become a "school" of psychotherapy in the sense that psychody-namic therapy or behavior therapy have. Rather its contribution lies in providing some useful techniques that enable individuals to achieve a new understanding of themselves and their behavior in relationships. These techniques may be effectively incorporated in many approaches to psychological treatment.

Integration of therapy approaches

Although an integration of psychoanalysis and learning theory was attempted in the 1950s by Dollard and Miller in their *Personality and Psychotherapy*, the two treatment approaches diverged significantly in the 1960s and 1970s. Recently, a great deal has been written about the possibility of gaining a rapprochement between behavior therapy and other schools of therapy, particularly psychodynamic therapy (Arkowitz & Messer, in press; Marmor & Woods, 1980; Wachtel, 1977, 1982). At first, this trend may seem surprising, given the generally competitive atmosphere and the critical struggles that have traditionally existed between psychoanalysts and behavioral therapists. Early behaviorists were adamant in their criticism of psychoanalysis as inefficient and mystical. The analysts reacted with strong counterarguments, partly in their own defense but also in keeping with their beliefs that behavioral therapies were superficial and treated only symptoms while psychoanalytic treatments sought "deeper" and more permanent cures.

Over the years, however, behavioral and psychoanalytic proponents have had time to become accustomed (or perhaps "desensitized") to each other's criticisms. With the wide dissemination and practice of behavioral methods, it has become apparent to some psychodynamically oriented therapists that behavioral methods are quite effective in the treatment of many anxiety disorders. Similarly, many behaviorally oriented therapists have concluded that it is not simply the application of a *technique* that brings about change in a client. They acknowledge that "relationship" factors are exceedingly important—even when rigorous behavior modification procedures are being used (Lazarus, 1981). In addition, psychotherapy research comparing both treatment methods has generally shown that neither approach has been demonstrated to be superior to the other (Sloane et al., 1975).

Recently, Kendall (1982b) concisely summarized the reasons for the current interest in integrating behavior therapy with other methods. He noted that (a) some behaviorists have concluded that the human organism is multifaceted and that focusing only on "behavior" is not sufficient as a treatment goal; (b) the "less than perfect" success of available therapy methods justifies combining the most successful treatment strategies from all approaches; (c) integrating diverse therapies might inspire a new enthusiasm and promote novel applications of varied treatment methods and perhaps promote new formulations of old problems; and (d) integrating diverse therapy schools would require members of a given school to begin to question the assumptions underlying their treatment approach and would promote a broad reappraisal from different perspectives.

However, according to Kendall, there are inherent problems facing the integrationist position. First, there is no common language uniting the various therapy schools. Second, it is much easier for a trainee to learn a single therapeutic approach than to learn elements of various approaches. Finally, there exist basic conceptual differences that would preclude a fully satisfactory merger between behavior therapy and psychodynamic therapy, such as their different emphases upon etiological factors, treatment goals, and tactical methods.

Further examination of therapeutic methods from the vantage point of alternative viewpoints may, in time, lead to interestingly amalgamated therapeutic approaches. It does not appear at this early point, however, that many of the advocates of the various positions are going to be able to put aside their long identification with particular schools and easily become agents for the "opposition."[6]

---

[6]For further discussions of efforts to integrate various types of therapies, see Apfelbaum (1981) and Ellis (1981).

Evaluation of success in psychotherapy

Competition between individual therapies has tended to obscure the actual success of therapy. Over thirty years ago, Eysenck (1952) shook the field of psychological intervention by citing in his review of evidence on treatment outcomes that people who were simply placed on a waiting list for psychotherapy improved about as much as those who actually received therapy. This pronouncement prompted a flurry of research activity, as well as a thorough reanalysis of the existing data. Reevaluation of therapy-outcome research has painted a very different and more positive picture of the effectiveness of psychotherapy (Bergin & Lambert, 1978; Smith & Glass, 1977).

Problems of evaluation

Evaluating the effectiveness of treatment is a difficult enterprise for several reasons. At best, it is an inexact process, dependent on inexact and inevitably somewhat subjective data. For example, attempts at evaluation generally depend on one or more of the following sources of information: (a) the therapist's impression of changes that have occurred, (b) the patient's reports of change, (c) reports from the patient's family or friends, (d) comparison of pretreatment and posttreatment personality test scores, and (e) measures of change in selected overt behaviors.

Unfortunately, each of these sources has serious limitations. The therapist may not be the best judge of the patient's progress, since any therapist is likely to be biased in favor of seeing himself or herself as competent and successful. Furthermore, therapists can inflate improvement averages by consciously or unconsciously encouraging difficult patients to discontinue therapy. It has also been somewhat facetiously remarked that the therapist often thinks the patient is getting better because he or she is getting used to the patient's symptoms.

The patient, too, is an unreliable source concerning the outcomes of therapy. Patients may not only want to think that they are getting better but may report that they are being helped in an attempt to please the therapist. Family and relatives may also be inclined to "see" the improvement they had hoped for, although they often seem to be more realistic than either the therapist or the patient in their long-term evaluations.

Outside clinical ratings by an independent observer are sometimes used in psychotherapy outcome research to evaluate the progress of a patient; these may be more objective than ratings by those directly involved in the therapy. Another widely used objective measure of patient change is performance on psychological tests. The patient takes a battery of tests before and after therapy and the differences in scores are assumed to reflect progress or deterioration. But although such tests may indeed show changes, they are likely to focus on the particular measures in which the therapist is interested. They are not necessarily valid predictors of how the client will behave in real-life, nor can they give any indication of whether the changes that have occurred are likely to be enduring.

Changes in selected behaviors appear to be the safest measures of outcome, but even this criterion is subject to limitations, for changes in behavior in the therapy situation may not generalize to other situations. In addition, the changes selected reflect the goals of the individual therapist. For example, one therapist may consider therapy "successful" if a patient becomes more manageable on the ward; another, if an individual becomes a more growth-oriented and self-directing person. To complicate matters further, such terms as "recovery," "marked improvement," and "fair improvement" are open to considerable differences in interpretation, and there is always the possibility that spontaneous improvement will be attributed to the particular form of treatment used.

In spite of these difficulties, however, it is possible to study the effectiveness of various treatment approaches separately—determining what procedures work best with various types of individuals (Kendall & Norton-Ford, 1982). In the course of our discussion of abnormal behavior patterns we have mentioned a number of such studies, most of which have demonstrated positive outcomes from psychotherapy.

In this context, it is relevant to ask what happens to people who do not obtain formal treatment. In view of the many ways that people can help each other, it is not surprising that there is often considerable improvement without therapeutic intervention. Some forms of psychopathology, such as manic and depressive psychoses and some types of schizophrenia, appear to run a fairly predictable course with or without treatment, and there are many other instances in which disturbed persons improve over time for reasons that are not apparent.

But even if many emotionally disturbed individuals tend to improve over time without psychotherapy, it seems clear that psychotherapy can often accelerate improvement or ensure desired behavior change that might not otherwise occur (Bergin & Lambert, 1978; Telch, 1981). Most researchers today would agree that psychotherapy is more effective than no treatment. The rate of improvement given in most studies of therapy outcome, regardless of approach, is usually about 70 to 80 percent. Nonetheless, the issue of treatment evaluation remains a vital one—both ethically and practically—if psychologists and other mental health personnel are to be justified in intervening in other persons' lives.

Social values and psychotherapy

The criticism has been raised—from both inside and outside the mental health professions—that psychotherapy can be viewed as an attempt to get people adjusted to a "sick" society rather than to encourage them to work toward its improvement. As a consequence, psychotherapy has often been considered the guardian of the status quo. This issue is perhaps easier for us to evaluate by looking at other cultures; for example, there are frequent allegations that psychiatry is used as a means of political control in the Soviet Union (Faraone, 1982; Zubok, 1980). It has been widely asserted that dissidents in Russia are controlled by placement in mental institutions. Although few people make the claim that psychiatry in the Western World is used to gain control over social critics, there is nevertheless the possibility that therapists are, in some ways, placed in the role of "gatekeeper" of social values. Such charges, of course, bring us back to the question we raised in Chapter 1: What do we mean by "abnormal"? Our answer to that question can only be made in the light of our values.

In a broader perspective, of course, we are concerned with the complex and controversial issue of the role of values in science. For psychotherapy is not a system of ethics but a set of tools to be used at the discretion of the therapist. Thus mental health professionals are confronted with the same kinds of questions that confront scientists in general. Should the physical scientist who helps develop thermonuclear weapons be morally concerned about how they are used? Similarly, should the psychologist or behavioral scientist who develops powerful techniques of behavior control be concerned about how they are used?

Many psychologists and other scientists try to sidestep this issue by insisting that science is value-free—that it is concerned only with gathering "facts," not with how they are applied. But each time therapists decide that one behavior should be eliminated or substituted for another, they are making a value choice. And the increasing social awareness of today's mental health professionals has brought into sharp focus ethical questions concerning their roles as therapists and value models, as well as their roles as agents for maintaining the status quo or fostering social change. Therapy takes place in a context that involves the values of the therapist, the client, and the society in which they live. There are strong pressures on the therapist— from parents, schools, courts, and other social institutions—to help people adjust to "the world as it is." At the same time there are many counterpressures, particularly from young people who are seeking support in their attempts to become authentic persons rather than blind conformists.

The dilemma in which contemporary therapists may find themselves is illustrated by the following case example.

A 15-year-old high-school sophomore is sent to a therapist because her parents have discovered that she has been having sexual intercourse with her boyfriend. The girl tells the therapist that she thoroughly enjoys such relations and feels no guilt or remorse over her behavior, even though her parents strongly disapprove. In addition, she reports that she is quite aware of the danger of becoming pregnant and is very careful to take contraceptive measures.

What is the role of the therapist in such a case? Should the girl be encouraged to conform to her parents' mores and postpone sexual activity until she is older and more mature? Or should the parents be helped to adjust to the pattern of sexual behavior she has chosen? What should be the therapist's goal? It is not unusual to find some individuals being referred for psychological treatment because their behavior, not particularly destructive or disturbing, has caused concern among family members who wish the therapist to "fix" them.

It is apparent that there are diametrically opposed ways of dealing with problems in therapy. Society must enforce conformity to certain norms if it is to maintain its organization and survive. But how does one distinguish between norms that are relevant and those that are irrelevant and outmoded? It is often up to individual therapists to decide what path to take, and this requires value decisions on their part concerning what is best for the individual and for the larger society. Thus, the mental health professional is confronted with the problem of "controlling the controller;" that is, of developing ethical standards and societal safeguards to prevent misuse of the techniques they have developed for modifying individual and group behavior.

Summary

Psychotherapy is aimed at the reduction of abnormal behavior in individuals through psychological means. The goals of psychotherapy include changing maladaptive behavior, minimizing or eliminating stressful environmental conditions, improving interpersonal competencies, resolving personal conflicts, modifying an individual's inaccurate assumptions about himself or herself, and fostering a more positive self-image. Although these goals are by no means easy to achieve, psychological treatment methods have been shown to be generally effective in promoting adaptive psychological functioning in many troubled individuals.

Numerous approaches to psychological treatment ("schools of psychotherapy") have been developed to treat individuals with psychological disorders. One of the oldest approaches to psychological treatment, psychoanalysis or psychodynamic therapy, was originated nearly a century ago by Sigmund Freud. Although complicated systems of psychodynamic treatment have evolved since Freud's time, many features of "orthodox" psychoanalysis today closely resemble Freud's original system. Several other schools of therapy, referred to as neo-Freudian schools, have developed out of the psychoanalytic tradition. These approaches accept some elements of Freudian theory but diverge on key points, such as the length of time to be devoted to therapy or the role of the ego in personality dynamics.

A second major approach to psychological intervention is behavior therapy. Originating over fifty years ago, behavior therapy has come to be used extensively in treating clinical problems. Behavior-therapy approaches make use of a number of techniques such as systematic desensitization, aversion therapy, modeling, reinforcement approaches, assertiveness therapy, and biofeedback. Recently, behavior-therapy methods have been applied to "internal processes," that is thoughts or cognitions, with a great deal of success. Known as cognitive-behavioral therapy, this approach attempts to modify an individual's self-statements in order to change his or her behavior. Cognitive-behavioral methods have been used for a wide variety of clinical problems— from Type A behavior to anger control—and with a range of clinical populations.

Several other psychological treatment methods have been referred to as humanistic-experiential therapies. One of the earliest of these approaches is the person-centered or client-centered therapy of Carl Rogers. This treatment approach, originating in the 1940s, has received broad acceptance and has provided a valuable conceptualization of the patient-therapist interaction as well as specific techniques for generating personal change or personal growth in motivated clients.

In addition to individual treatment approaches, there are psychological treatment methods that are applied in group settings, such as group therapy, or marital or family therapy. These approaches typically assume that a part of the individual's problems lie in his or her interactions with others. Consequently, the focus of treatment is to change ways of interacting among individuals in the social or family context.

In recent years, an attempt has been made to integrate behavior-therapy methods with other psychological treatment approaches, particularly psychodynamic therapy. This effort has resulted from the recognition that elements from both approaches can be used to increase our understanding of the patient and to bring about desired behavior change in troubled patients.

Evaluation of the success of psychotherapy in producing desired behavior change in patients is difficult to determine. However, research in psychotherapy has shown that most treatment approaches are more effective than no treatment at all. Beyond the question of evaluating the success of psychotherapy lies other, larger questions involving the ethical dilemmas posed by therapy. Does psychotherapy encourage conformity to the status quo? Should it do this? These constitute some of the difficult moral and social issues that daily confront mental health professionals.

Contemporary issues in abnormal psychology

Baya, Village au Palmier *(1950?). Baya (b. 1931), was born to a family in the Kabyle tribal group near the north African city of Algiers. Orphaned at the age of 5, she was taken to live in the city proper, where she began to paint and sculpt for her own amusement. In 1950, she married into a traditional Algerian family and immediately ceased her creative efforts. In 1963, a retrospective of her work at the national museum in Algiers induced Baya to begin painting again, but the pieces done since that time have been clearly influenced by popular Algerian art and so cannot be properly considered "Art Brut."*

Over the years, most efforts toward mental health have been largely *restorative,* geared toward helping people only after they have already developed serious problems. Prior to the 1960s, mental health professionals typically did not become involved until *after* an individual had suffered a breakdown; then they often sent such individuals for treatment far away from their home communities, often compounding their distress and disrupting their lives.

Increasingly today, professionals are trying to catch problems *before* they become severe, or better yet to establish conditions in which breakdowns will not occur. However, specific causal factors for many mental disorders are not sufficiently understood to enable explicit preventive programs to be initiated. Efforts toward prevention in the mental health field are still based largely on hypotheses about what works rather than on substantial empirical research. Nonetheless, most professionals in the field believe that preventive efforts are worthwhile. And, in fact, most believe that greater effort needs to be expended toward training professionals in preventive roles and developing more effective research strategies if mental disorder is to be reduced (Murphy & Frank, 1979).

Of course, preventive efforts, like treatment programs, cost money. During periods of economic decline, federal, state, and local governments may reduce their support for such programs. Unfortunately, programs aimed at prevention, because of their long-range scope and their often indirect focus, are perhaps more difficult to justify since they "appear" less cost effective than other programs with direct and explicit outcome criteria.

Where preventive efforts fail and a serious mental health problem develops, today's professionals place more emphasis on the importance of prompt treatment. It is considered to be important, too, that the treatment be in the individual's own community, if possible, so that available family and other familiar supports may be utilized and disruption in the individual's life pattern is reduced. If hospitalization becomes necessary, every effort is taken to prevent the disorder from becoming chronic and to return the individual to the community as soon as possible, with whatever aftercare and continued supportive help that may be needed.

We shall examine, in our final chapter, the

kinds of measures that are being taken to prevent maladaptive behavior or limit its seriousness. Our discussion will begin with a review of preventive strategies. Next, we will explore some timely legal issues related to the care and hospitalization of individuals with mental problems: commitment, deinstitutionalization, and assessment of dangerousness. Closely related to this are the matters of (a) therapist's "duty to warn" others if a client threatens violence and of (b) the use—and some think abuse—of the insanity defense as a plea in capital crimes. Then we shall briefly survey the scope of organized efforts for mental health both in the United States and throughout the world. Finally, we shall conclude the chapter with a consideration of what each of us can do to foster mental health and to help build a good future for all of us.

Perspectives on prevention

In our present discussion we shall utilize the concepts of primary, secondary, and tertiary prevention, which are widely used in public health medicine to describe general strategies of disease prevention. *Primary prevention* is aimed at reducing the possibility of disease and fostering positive health. *Secondary prevention* involves efforts to reduce the impact, duration, or spread of a problem that has already developed—if possible, catching it before it has become serious. *Tertiary prevention* seeks to reduce the long-term consequences to individuals of having had a disorder or serious problem. These preventive strategies, although primarily devised for understanding and control of infectious physical diseases, provide a useful perspective in the mental health field as well.

Primary prevention

In primary prevention we are concerned with two key tasks: seeking out and eradicating conditions that can cause or contribute to mental disorders, and establishing conditions that foster positive mental health. It includes biological, psychosocial, and sociocultural measures. As Kessler and Albee (1975) have noted, "everything aimed at improving the human condition, at making life more fulfilling and meaningful, may be considered to be part of primary prevention of mental or emotional disturbance " (p. 557).

Biological measures. Here primary prevention begins with help in family planning and includes both prenatal and postnatal care. A good deal of current emphasis is being placed on guidance in family planning—how many children to have, when to have them in relation to marital and other family conditions, and even whether to have children at all. Such guidance may include genetic counseling, in which tests for diagnosing genetic defects may be administered to potential parents to assess their risk of having defective children.

Breakthroughs in genetic research have also made it possible to detect and often alleviate genetic defects before a baby is born; when *in utero* treatment is not feasible, such information provides the parents with the choice of having an abortion rather than a seriously defective baby. Continued progress in genetic research may make it possible to identify genetic disorders early or even to correct faulty genes, thus providing humankind with fantastic new power to prevent hereditary pathology.

Psychosocial measures. In regarding normality as "optimal development and functioning" rather than as mere absence of pathology, we imply that the individual will require opportunities for learning needed competencies—physical, intellectual, emotional, and social. As we have seen, failure to develop the skills required for effective problem solving, for handling emotions constructively, and for establishing satisfying interpersonal relationships places the individual at a serious disadvantage in coping with life problems.

A second crucial requirement for psychosocial health is that the individual acquire an accurate frame of reference upon which to build self-identity. We have seen repeatedly that when people's assumptions about themselves or their world are inaccurate, their behavior is likely to be maladaptive. Likewise, inability to find satisfying values that foster a meaningful and fulfilling life constitutes a fertile source of maladjustment and mental disorders.

Psychosocial health measures also require preparation for the types of problems an individual is likely to encounter during given life stages. For example, pregnancy and childbirth usually have a great deal of emotional significance for both parents and may disturb family equilibrium or exacerbate an already disturbed marital situation. Young people who want to marry and have children should have had preparation for the tasks of building a mutually satisfying relationship and helping children develop their potentialities. Similarly, the individual needs to be prepared adequately for other developmental tasks characteristic of given life periods, including old age.

In recent years, psychosocial efforts at primary prevention have been receiving a great deal of attention. The fields of behavioral medicine and, in particular, health psychology, have had substantial influence here. As we saw in Chapter 8, efforts are being made to change the psychological factors underlying life-style patterns—especially in terms of "bad habits" such as smoking, excessive drinking, and poor diet—that may be contributing to the development of both physical and psychological problems.

General sociocultural measures.   The relationship between the individual and the community is a reciprocal one, a fact we sometimes forget in our prizing of individualism. We need autonomy and "space of free movement" to be ourselves, but we also need to belong and contribute to a community. Without a nourishing community, the development of individuals is blighted. At the same time, without responsible, psychologically healthy individuals, the community withers and cannot be a nourishing one. Sociocultural efforts toward primary prevention are focused on making the community as nourishing as possible for the individuals within it.

With our growing realization of the importance of pathological social conditions in producing maladaptive behavior, increased attention is being devoted to creating social conditions that will foster healthy development and functioning in individuals. Efforts to create these conditions are seen in a wide spectrum of social measures ranging from public education and social security to economic planning and social legislation

directed toward ensuring adequate health care for all citizens. Such measures, of course, must take into account the stressors and health problems we are likely to encounter in the future in our rapidly changing society.

Primary prevention through social change in the community is difficult. Although the whole psychological climate can ultimately be changed by a social movement such as the civil rights movement of the 1960s, the "payoff" of such efforts is generally far in the future and may be difficult or impossible to measure. Thus some feel that, to be meaningful, the term *primary prevention* should be reserved for policies in which the initiator clearly specifies (a) how today's program is intended to improve conditions for future health, and (b) how the impact is to be assessed (Kelly, Snowden, & Muñoz, 1977). Of this redefined and delimited concept of primary prevention in the mental health field Kelly and associates have written:

"There are glimmers in the literature that the elusive goal of primary prevention can be realized if long-term impact is an intrinsic element in the work, if systematic factors for personal and social development are the focus, and if people's integration with their community is fostered. In the final analysis, primary prevention requires a radically different kind of psychology, that is, one which commits itself to long-term intervention in people's natural habitat." (1977, p. 333)

Primary preventive measures also include working with individuals who are at special risk, in order to make their environment more supportive and to improve their coping skills. For example, some efforts aimed at deterring high-risk juveniles from smoking or drinking have involved having professional athletes or stars whom the teens respect talk to them either about the dangers or even of their own difficulties with drugs, smoking, etc. Another example of a primary preventive effort is given in the **HIGHLIGHT** on page 676.

Secondary prevention

Secondary prevention emphasizes the early detection and prompt treatment of maladaptive behavior in the individual's family and community setting. Thus it requires a knowledge of the incidence and scope of maladaptive behavior in

HIGHLIGHT
Primary prevention following a crisis

In 1977, 154 people were held hostage at three locations in Washington, D.C., by members of the Hanafi Muslim sect. The largest group of hostages, about 100 people, were subjected to a great deal of humiliation and harassment over the 39-hour period of their confinement, including physical violence, verbal abuse, hunger, physical restraint, and threats of death.

Even before their release, the Health Maintenance Organization to which many of them belonged was making plans for short-term, crisis-oriented, broad-spectrum group therapy, which it offered to all the hostages on release, in most cases in their workplace, which had been the scene of their confinement. Sessions began a few days later and continued twice a week for four weeks, with four groups of about 12 members each. The goal was to prevent existing symptoms from becoming serious, and, where no symptoms had appeared, to forestall or minimize trouble later.

Some of those who accepted the invitation were indeed suffering from symptoms following their ordeal, and therapy was planned to deal directly with each type of symptom. For example,

"in vivo and systematic desensitization were employed for avoidance behaviors; deep muscle relaxation was taught for sleep disturbances, anxiety attacks, multiple somatic complaints, and as a substitute for minor tranquilizers and hypnotic agents; assertion imagery and rational-emotive therapy were used for disturbing images and recurrent irrational thoughts; and assertiveness training and outside referrals were used for disruptive familial relations." (Sank, 1979, p. 336)

One of the women who was experiencing symtpoms at the start of therapy sessions was Shirley, a 47-year-old woman who had been at her desk when several Hanafis burst into the room. She was herded up the stairs with others to the room that was to serve as their prison. On the way she heard screams and saw the bloodied machete that had been used on another employee. The men were separated from the women and roughly bound; several were hu-

miliated. There were times of overwhelming fear when the Hanafi leader came and made grisly threats to individuals and then to the entire group.

After release, Shirley had great trouble returning to the building to work. She also had trouble sleeping and dreamed of the takeover and the bloodied faces and clothes. She cried frequently and suffered from persistent depression and anxiety.

"In the group sessions, Shirley was able to review, along with her co-hostages, the events of the takeover and siege. All were encouraged to speak freely about what had occurred, something they had not been able to do while hostages. Shirley was able to give and get feedback about how she and others had really appeared—how brave, how foolish, how cowardly, and so forth. What were others thinking and feeling then and now? How unique were her postsiege symptoms?

Shirley's aftereffects were not uncommon among the hostages. She reported that the content and availability of the group sessions were extremely helpful to her. She did not feel alone. There was a forum for the expression of her difficulties and a format for dealing with them. It was especially comforting to find the commonality of what she had feared were unique . . . symptoms." (Sank, 1979, p. 337)

The response of the other hostages, too, was highly positive. They appreciated having been sought out and followed professionally whether they seemed to need it or not.

Three months later there was an additional series of sessions for those who still felt the need of help, and approximately a year after the frightening experience an additional session was conducted.

Those in charge of the program felt that offering help through the Health Maintenance Organization and at the scene of the harrowing experience made the help more accessible, less stigmatizing, and more informal than is often the case with psychiatric help. They also felt that their approach had capitalized on a powerful tool in using and strengthening the natural mutual support system of the employees who had suffered the ordeal together and would be continuing to work together in the same building.

specific populations, facilities for the early detection of such behavior, and available treatment facilities in the community.

In secondary prevention, epidemiological studies are particularly important, since they help investigators obtain information about the incidence and distribution of various maladaptive behaviors needing intervention efforts (Dohrenwend & Dohrenwend, 1982). These findings can then be used to suggest what preventive efforts might be most appropriate. For example, various epidemiological studies have shown that certain groups of individuals are at high-risk for mental disorders: including recently divorced people (Bloom et al., 1978), the physically disabled (Freemen, Malkin, & Hastings, 1975), and elderly people living alone (Neugarten, 1977). While findings such as these may be the basis for immediate secondary prevention, they may also aid later in primary prevention by telling us what to look for and where to look—in essence by focusing our efforts in the right direction.

Here we shall look at three interventions that can be used in secondary prevention: crisis intervention, longer-term consulting and educational services, and the use of the mental hospital as a therapeutic community.

Crisis intervention.   Crisis intervention has emerged as a response to a widespread need for immediate help for individuals and families confronted with especially stressful situations (Butcher, Stelmachers, & Maudal, 1983; Golan, 1978; Gorton & Partridge, 1982; Mitchell & Resnik, 1981). Often such people are in a state of acute turmoil and feel overwhelmed and incapable of dealing with the stress by themselves. They do not have time to wait for the customary initial therapy appointment, nor are they usually in a position to continue therapy over a sustained period of time. They need immediate assistance.

To meet this need, two modes of therapeutic intervention have been developed: (a) short-term crisis therapy involving face-to-face discussion, and (b) the telephone "hot line." These forms of crisis intervention are usually handled either by professional mental health personnel or by paraprofessionals—lay persons who have been trained for this work.

1. *Short-term crisis therapy.* The sole concern of short-term crisis therapy is the current problem with which the individual or family is having difficulty. Although medical problems may also require emergency treatment, we are concerned here with personal or family problems of an emotional nature. In such crisis situations the therapist is usually very active, helping clarify the problem, suggesting plans of action, providing reassurance, and otherwise giving needed information and support. In essence, the therapist tries to provide as much help as the individual or family will accept.

If the problem involves psychological disturbance in one of the family members, emphasis is usually placed on mobilizing the support of other family members. Often this enables the person to avoid hospitalization and disruption of family life. Crisis intervention may also involve bringing other mental health or medical personnel into the treatment picture.

Most individuals and families who come for short-term crisis therapy do not continue in treatment for more than one to six sessions. Often, in fact, they come to the therapist or clinic for an "emotional Band-Aid," and after receiving guidance and support in the initial session do not return.

2. *The "hot line."* As we noted in Chapter 9 the Suicide Prevention Center in Los Angeles opened up a whole new approach to dealing with people undergoing crisis. All major cities in the United States and most smaller ones have developed some form of telephone hot line to help individuals undergoing periods of deep stress. While the threat of suicide is the most dramatic example, the range of problems that people call about is virtually unlimited—from breaking up with someone to being on a bad drug "trip." In addition, there are specific hot lines in various communities for rape victims and for runaways who need assistance.

As with other crisis intervention, the person handling hot-line calls is confronted with the problem of rapidly assessing "what's wrong" and "how bad it is." But even if an accurate assessment is possible and the hot-line therapist does everything within his or her power to help the individual—within the confines imposed by the telephone—a distraught caller may hang up without leaving any name, telephone number, or address. This can be a deeply disturbing experience for the therapist—particularly if, for example, the caller has announced that he or she has just swallowed a lethal dose of sleeping pills. Even in less severe cases, of course, the hot-line therapist may never learn whether the caller's problem has been solved. In other instances, however, the caller may be induced to come in for counseling, making more personal contact possible.

For the therapist, crisis intervention is probably the most discouraging of any treatment approach that we have discussed. The urgency of the intervention and the frequent inability to provide any therapeutic closure or follow-up are probably key factors here. Free clinics and crisis centers have reported that their counselors—many of whom are volunteers—tend to "burn out" after a rather short period of time. Despite the high frustration level of this work, however, crisis-intervention therapists fill a crucial need in the mental health field, particularly for the young people who make up the majority of their clients. This need is recognized by the many community mental health centers and general hospitals that provide emergency psychological services, either through hot-lines or walk-in services. For the thousands of individuals in desperate trouble, an invaluable social support is provided by the fact that there is somewhere they can go for immediate help or someone they can call who will listen to their problems and try to help them. Thus, the continuing need for crisis intervention services and telephone hot lines is evident.

Consultation and education of intermediaries.

Often community mental health professionals, such as psychologists and psychiatrists, are able to reach a larger group of individuals in need of psychological attention by working through primary care professionals, such as teachers, social workers, and police personnel.[1] Here the mental health professionals identify a population at risk for the development of psychological disorder and then work with personnel in community institutions who have frequent contact with members of this population. For example, police officers might be trained to direct the individuals involved in a domestic quarrel to seek mental health services rather than settling their differences through violence.

Mental health professionals had originally intended that consultation and education (C & E) be included among the services offered by all community mental health centers. This would have meant that the impact of these centers would have been more indirect—helping individuals experiencing problems by increasing the skill and sensitivity of those who come into contact with them in the community and are in a position to make their lives either more stressful or less so. Currently, however, most community mental health centers provide little such "indirect" service: only about 4 percent of their total effort is devoted to consultation with and education of primary care professionals. Typically, half or more of this involves working with the schools or with other juvenile services; less than a tenth of such consultation time is spent with police and correctional personnel (NIMH, 1978b).

The mental hospital as a therapeutic community.

Most of the traditional forms of therapy that we discussed in Chapters 16 and 17 may, of course, be used in the hospital setting to promote secondary prevention. In addition, in more and more mental hospitals these techniques are being supplemented by an effort to make the hospital environment itself a *therapeutic community* (Gunderson, 1980; Gunn et al., 1978; Jones, 1953; Paul & Lentz, 1977). That is, all the ongoing activities of the hospital are brought into the total treatment program, and the environment or *milieu,* is a crucial aspect of the therapy.

Three general therapeutic principles guide the milieu approach to treatment:

a) Staff expectations are clearly communicated to the patient. Both positive and negative feedback are used to encourage appropriate verbalizations and actions on the part of patients.

b) Patients are encouraged to become involved in all decisions made and all actions taken concerning them. A "do-it-yourself" attitude prevails.

c) All patients belong to social groups on the ward. The experience of group cohesiveness gives each patient group support and encouragement, and the related process of group pressure helps exert control over the patient's behavior.

---

[1]Issues and methods in such consultation and education are discussed in Iscoe, Bloom, and Spielberger (1977); Mann (1978); and Mannino, McLennan, and Shore (1975).

The mental hospital can function as a therapeutic community in which patients are expected to enter into the entire life of the hospital.

In the therapeutic community, as few restraints as possible are placed on the freedom of the patient, and the orientation is toward encouraging patients to take responsibility for their behavior as well as to participate actively in their treatment programs. Open wards permit patients the use of grounds and premises. Self-government programs give them responsibility for managing their own affairs and those of the ward. All hospital personnel are expected to treat the patients as human beings who merit consideration and courtesy. Recent studies have shown that intensive milieu programs significantly benefit nonchronic patients (Gunderson, 1980). Some of the psychotherapeutic aids that may be used are described in the **HIGHLIGHT** on page 680.

The interaction among patients—whether in encounter groups, social events, or other activities—is planned in such a way as to be of therapeutic benefit. In fact, it is becoming apparent that often the most beneficial aspect of the therapeutic community is the interaction among the patients themselves. Differences in social roles and backgrounds may make empathy between staff and patients difficult, but fellow patients have "been there"—they have had similar prob-

lems and breakdowns and have experienced the anxiety and humiliation of being labeled "mentally ill" and hospitalized. Thus constructive and helping relationships frequently develop among patients in a warm, encouraging milieu.

Another highly successful method for helping patients take increased responsibility for their own behavior is the use of *social-learning programs.* These programs use learning principles and techniques such as token economies to shape more socially acceptable behavior (Paul, 1979; Rhoades, 1981).

A persistent danger with hospitalization is that the mental hospital may become a permanent refuge from the world, either because it offers total escape from the demands of everyday living or because it encourages patients to settle into a chronic "sick role" with a permanent excuse for letting other people take care of them (see **HIGHLIGHT** on page 682).

To keep the focus on returning the patient to the community and on preventing the disorder from becoming chronic, hospital staffs try to establish close ties with the family and community and to maintain a "recovery-expectant" attitude. Between 70 and 90 percent of patients labeled as psychotic and admitted to mental hospitals can now be discharged within a few weeks, or at most months.

Even where disorders have become chronic, effective treatment methods are being developed.

In one of the most extensive and well-controlled studies of chronic hospitalized patients, Paul and Lentz (1977) compared the relative effectiveness of three treatment approaches:

a) *Milieu therapy,* focused upon structuring the patient's environment to provide clear communications of expectations, and to get the patient involved in the treatment and participating in the therapeutic community through the group process.

b) *A social-learning treatment program,* organized around learning principles—using a token economy system, with ward staff as reinforcing agents. Undesirable behavior was not reinforced.

c) *Traditional mental hospital treatments,* including chemotherapy, occupational therapy, recreational therapy, activity therapy, and individual or group therapy. No systematic application of milieu therapy or social learning therapy was given to this group.

The treatment project covered a period of six years, with an initial phase of staff training, patient assess-

HIGHLIGHT
Psychotherapeutic aids

There are a number of procedures which have proved of therapeutic value, particularly in hospital settings, but which are usually considered aids or adjuncts to the total therapy program rather than systematic approaches to psychotherapy.

1. **Bibliotherapy.** Books, pamphlets, and other reading material are often of value in helping the patient realize that others have had similar problems and in increasing his or her self-understanding and motivation to improve. Specific reading materials are usually selected in terms of the needs and intellectual abilities of the patient. Related to this type of therapy is the practice of providing patients or prison inmates with the opportunity to take extension or correspondence courses for credit, and in some instances to attend educational institutions.

2. **Audio-visual aids.** Videotape playbacks of excerpts from marital, encounter group, and other forms of therapy are often extremely helpful in reveiwing and integrating critical events and processes in therapy sessions. In addition, there are many fine films dealing with alcoholism, drug abuse, and other maladaptive patterns that can be utilized in overall treatment programs.

3. **Occupational therapy.** This may involve constructive work which contributes to the operation of the hospital or clinic, formal training in actual job skills, or the supervision of the patient in a therapeutic role in helping other patients—often with the expectation that the patient may later become a paraprofessional.

4. **Social events.** Many mental hospitals and clinics have a regular schedule of social events including dances, teas, and "cocktail hours." In some instances patients may operate a closed-circuit television program featuring items of interest to patients. In addition, theatrical productions may be put on by patients. Such social events help the patients feel less isolated and more involved in their environment.

5. **Athletics.** Regularly scheduled athletic events for patient participation may include softball, basketball, and other team sports. Where facilities are available, a physical conditioning program may be worked out to meet individual needs.

6. **Music therapy.** Patients are commonly given opportunities to listen to music and to play an instrument—often as part of a musical group. Traditional music and folk singing have been found especially effective in fostering patient interest and group cohesiveness.

7. **Art therapy.** Painting, clay sculpturing, and other art media may facilitate the communication of feelings and assist in the resolution of inner conflicts, as may creative writing of prose or poetry. In addition, patients commonly experience a sense of pride and accomplishment in their creative productions. In some instances, art exhibitions are held and prizes are awarded, and there may be competition between different hospital or clinic facilities in such exhibitions.

---

ment, and base-line recording, a treatment phase, an aftercare phase, and a long (year and a half) follow-up. The changes targeted included resocialization, the learning of new roles, and the reduction or elimination of bizarre behavior. There were 28 chronic schizophrenic patients in each treatment group, matched for age, sex, socioeconomic level, symptoms, and duration of hospitalization.

The results of the study were quite impressive. Both milieu therapy and social learning therapy produced significant improvement in overall functioning and resulted in more successful hospital releases than the traditional hospital care. However, the behaviorally based social learning program was clearly supe-

rior to the more diffuse program of milieu therapy, as evidenced by the fact that over 90 percent of the released patients from the social learning program remained continuously in the community as compared with 70 percent of the released patients who had had milieu therapy. The figure for the traditional treatment program was less than 50 percent.

Tertiary prevention

Even where hospitalization has successfully modified maladaptive behavior and the patient has learned needed occupational and interpersonal skills, readjustment in the community following release may still be very difficult. Many studies have shown that in the past up to 45 percent of schizophrenic patients have been readmitted within the first year after their discharge. This is where tertiary prevention can play a major role, especially in terms of providing former clients and patients with supportive services that will help them toward long-term psychological well-being.

Today, aftercare programs are helping smooth the transition from insitutional to community life and are markedly reducing the number of relapses. A recent study showed that only 16 percent of patients who received adequate aftercare were readmitted within the first six months as compared with 37 percent for patients not receiving aftercare. By the end of 5 years, more of both groups had been readmitted, but 47 percent of the aftercare group were still in the community, as compared with only 30 percent of the group who had not received aftercare (Glasscote, 1978).

Aftercare is the responsibility of community mental health facilities and personnel as well as of the community as a whole and, of course, the person's family. Its goal is to ensure that released patients will be helped to make an adequate readjustment and return to full participation in their home and community with a minimum of delay and difficulty.

Sometimes aftercare includes a "halfway" period in which the released patient has a gradual return to the outside world. Thus the last decade has seen a trend toward the establishment of *day hospitals* and *halfway houses* for released patients. Since the founding of the first day hospital in Moscow in 1932, there has been a marked growth in this type of facility in Europe and more recently in the United States (Silverman & Val, 1975).

As we have seen, day hospital facilities in community mental health centers may also be used as alternatives to full hospitalization in the beginning. For example, Penk, Charles, and Van Hoose (1978) showed that partial hospitalization in a day treatment setting resulted in as much improvement as full inpatient psychiatric treatment at a lower cost in a group of patients they studied.

Halfway houses are live-in facilities which serve as a home base for former patients as they

A therapy session at a halfway house for drug abuse.

make the transition back to adequate functioning in the community. Typically halfway houses are run not by professional mental health personnel, but by the residents themselves.

In a pilot program with a group of newly released mental patients, Fairweather and his colleagues (1969) demonstrated that these patients could function in the community in a patient-run halfway house. Initially, a member of the research staff coordinated the daily operations of the lodge, but he was shortly replaced by a lay person. The patients were given full responsibility for operating the lodge, for regulating each other's behavior, for earning money, and for purchasing and preparing food.

Forty months after their discharge, a comparison was made of these ex-patients and a comparable group of 75 patients who had been discharged at the same time but had not had the halfway house experience. Whereas most members of the halfway house were able to hold income-producing jobs, to manage their daily lives, and to adjust in the outside world, the majority of those who had not had the halfway house experience were unable to adjust to life on the outside and required rehospitalization.

Similar halfway houses have been established for alcoholics and drug addicts and other per-

HIGHLIGHT
The hospitalization syndrome

Although individuals differ markedly in their response to hospitalization, some who reside in large mental hospitals over long periods of time tend to adopt a passive role, losing the self-confidence and motivation required for reentering the outside world. In fact, a sizable number of chronic patients become adept at manipulating their symptoms and making themselves appear "sicker" than they are in order to avoid the possibility of discharge from the sheltered hospital environment. This pattern is not ordinarily considered to be the result of hospitalization alone, but rather is attributed to an interaction between the patient and the hospital milieu. The following are some of the steps which have been delineated in the development of this hospitalization syndrome or, as it is also called, *social breakdown syndrome.*

1. Deficiency in self-concept. A precondition for the development of the social breakdown syndrome is the presence of severe self-devaluation and inner confusion concerning social roles and responsiblities.

2. Social labeling. During an acute crisis period in the person's life he or she has probably been labeled *psychotic* and perhaps even *dangerous* and has been sent involuntarily to a mental hospital, legally certified as incompetent and lacking in self-control.

3. Induction into the "sick" role. Admission procedures, diagnostic labeling, and treatment by staff members and other patients all too often initiate the individual into the role of a "sick" person—helpless, passive, and requiring care and external control.

4. Atrophy of work and social skills. In institutions that serve primarily as "storage bins" for the emotionally disturbed, basic work and social skills may atrophy through disuse. And during prolonged hospitalization, technological changes in the outside world may contribute to the obsolescence of the individual's work skills.

5. Development of the chronic sick role. Eventually the confused and devaluated patient becomes a full member of the sick community in which passive dependence and "crazy" behavior are not only common but expected.

The staffs of large mental hospitals today are more aware of the pitfalls of chronicity than in the past and are introducing various corrective procedures for remotivation and resocialization, as well as stressing a recovery-expectant attitude.

---

sons attempting to make an adjustment in the community after institutionalization. Such houses may be said to be specialized in the sense that all residents share similar backgrounds and problems, and his seems to contribute to their effectiveness.

One of the chief problems of halfway houses is that of gaining the acceptance and support of community residents. As Denner (1974) has pointed out, this requires educational and other social measures directed toward increasing community understanding, acceptance, and tolerance of troubled people who may differ somewhat from community norms. The viability of such an approach, however, is demonstrated in the example of Gheel—"the town that cares"—which we discussed in Chapter 2 (Aring, 1975a).

Controversial legal issues and the mentally ill

A number of important issues arise related to the legal status of the mentally ill. These issues comprise the subject matter of a field referred to as "forensic psychology" or "forensic psychiatry," and center around the rights of mental patients and/or the right of members of society to be protected from disturbed individuals. For a survey of some of the legal rights that have been gained for the mentally ill over the years, see the **HIGHLIGHT** on page 684.

The issues we shall cover in this section are those that have been the center of controversy in recent years. We shall first review the procedures involved in involuntarily committing disturbed and dangerous individuals to psychiatric institutions. Next, we shall turn to the question of assessing "dangerousness" in disturbed individuals; a related issue here—which has become of key concern to psychotherapists—is the court decision that psychotherapists have a "duty to warn" potential victims of any threatened violence by their patients. We shall examine, too, the controversial "insanity defense" for capital crimes. Finally, we shall examine the issue of deinstitutionalization, or what some have called the premature "dumping" of mental patients into the community.

The commitment process

Individuals with psychological problems or behaviors that are so extreme and severe as to pose a threat to themselves or others may require protective confinement. Those who commit crimes, whether or not they have a psychological disorder, are dealt with primarily through the judicial system—police arrest, court trial, and, if convicted, possibly confinement in a penal institution. Individuals who are judged to be *potentially* dangerous because of their psychological state may, after *civil commitment procedures*, be confined in a mental institution.

The steps in the commitment process vary slightly depending on the state law,[2] the available community mental health resources, and the nature of the problem—for example, commitment procedures will vary depending on whether the problem is one of mental retardation or alcoholism. A distinction should be made here between *voluntary hospitalization* and *involuntary commitment*. In most cases, individuals are placed in mental institutions without court order; that is, they accept voluntary commitment or hospitalization. In these cases they can, with sufficient notice, leave the hospital if they wish. In cases where the individual is believed to be

dangerous or unable to provide for his or her own care, the need for involuntary commitment may arise.

Being "mentally ill" is not sufficient grounds for placing an individual in a mental institution against his or her will. Although procedures vary somewhat from state to state, several conditions beyond mental illness usually must be met before formal commitment can occur (Schwitzgebel & Schwitzgebel, 1980). In brief, the person must be judged to be

a) dangerous to him- or herself;
b) incapable of providing for his or her basic physical needs;
c) unable to make responsible decisions about hospitalization;
d) in need of treatment or care in a hospital.

Typically, filing a petition for a commitment hearing is the first step in the process of committing an individual involuntarily. This petition is usually filed by a concerned person, such as a relative, physician, or mental health professional. When a petition is filed, the judge appoints two examiners to evaluate the "proposed patient." In Minnesota, for example, one examiner must be a physician (not necessarily a psychiatrist); the other can be a psychiatrist or a psychologist. The patient is asked to voluntarily appear for psychiatric examination prior to the commitment hearing. The hearing must be held within 14 days, which can be extended for 30 more days if "good cause" for the extension can be shown. The law requires that the court-appointed examiners interview the patient before the hearing.

If the individual is committed to the mental hospital for treatment, the hospital must report to the court within 60 days as to whether the person needs to be confined even longer. If no report is given by the hospital, the patient must be set free. If the hospital indicates that the individual needs further treatment, then the commitment period becomes indeterminate, subject to periodic reevaluations.

Since the decision to commit an individual is based on the judgments of others about the individual's capabilities and his or her potential for dangerous behavior, the civil commitment process leaves open the possibility of unwar-

---

[2]The examples of the legal procedures for commitment cited in this section are based on Minnesota state law.

HIGHLIGHT

Patient advocacy: important court decisions in establishing patient rights

Several important court decisions in recent years have helped establish certain basic rights for individuals suffering from mental disorders.

Right to treatment
In 1972 a U.S. District Court in Alabama made a landmark decision in the case of *Wyatt* v. *Stickney*. The ruling held that a mentally ill or mentally retarded individual had a right to receive treatment. Since the decision, the State of Alabama has increased its budget for treatment of mental health and mental retardation by 300 percent.

Freedom from custodial confinement
In 1975 the U.S. Supreme Court upheld the principle that patients have a right to freedom from custodial confinement if they are not dangerous to themselves or others and if they can safely survive outside of custody. In the *Donaldson* v. *O'Connor* decision, the defendants were required to pay Donaldson $10,000 for having kept him in custody without providing treatment.

Right to compensation for work
In 1973 a U.S. District Court ruled in the case of *Souder* v. *Brennan* (Secretary of Labor) that a patient in a nonfederal mental institution who performed work must be paid according to the Fair Labor Standards Act. Although a 1976 Supreme Court ruling nullified the part of the lower court's decision dealing with state

hospitals, the ruling still applied to mentally ill and mentally retarded patients in private facilities.

Right to legal counsel at commitment hearings
The State Supreme Court in Wisconsin decided in 1976 in the case of *Memmel* v. *Mundy* that an individual had the right to legal counsel during the commitment process.

Right to live in a community
In 1974, the U.S. District Court decided, in the case of *Stoner* v. *Miller*, that released state mental hospital patients had a right to live in "adult homes" in the community.

Right to refuse treatment
Several court decisions have provided rulings and some states have enacted legislation permitting patients to refuse certain treatments, such as electroconvulsive therapy and psychosurgery.

Right to less restrictive treatment
In 1975 a U.S. District Court issued a landmark decision in the case of *Dixon* v. *Weinberger*. The ruling establishes the right of individuals to receive treatment in less restrictive facilities than mental institutions.

Based on Bernard (1979), National Association for Mental Health (1979), and Mental Health Law Project (1976).

---

ranted violation of a person's civil rights. As a consequence, most states have stringent safeguards in the procedures to assure that any individual who is the subject of a petition for commitment is granted due process, including rights to formal hearings with representation by legal counsel. If there is not time to get a court order for commitment or if there is imminent danger, however, the law allows emergency hospitalization without a formal commitment hearing. In such cases, a physician must sign a statement saying that an imminent danger exists. The patient can then be picked up (usually by the police) and detained under a *hold order*, usually not to exceed 72 hours, unless a petition for commitment is filed within that period.

Involuntary commitment in a psychiatric facility is, in large part, contingent upon a determination that the individual is "dangerous" and needs to be confined out of a need to protect him or herself or society. We will now turn to the important question of evaluating patients in terns of their potential "dangerousness."

Assessment of "dangerousness"

As we have seen, though the majority of psychiatric patients are not considered dangerous and need no special safety precautions, a minority of individuals are violent and require close supervision—perhaps confinement until their "dangerousness" is no longer a problem. The possibility that an individual is dangerous or likely to commit violent acts is, indeed, one of the primary reasons why some individuals are committed to mental institutions—to protect themselves from harm and society from unwanted violence. Rubin (1972) pointed out that approximately 50,000 people a year are kept in preventive confinement, such as maximum security hospitals, and over 400,000 inmates are kept in maximum security prisons because they are believed to be dangerous to society; there is no reason to believe the statistics have changed much since Rubin's study.

The determination that a patient is potentially dangerous is a difficult one to make. Yet, as we will see later, it is a crucial judgment for mental health professionals to make—not only from a therapeutic point of view, to assure that the most appropriate treatment is conducted, but also from a legal point of view. The clinician has clear responsibility in attempting to protect the public from potential violence from the uncontrolled behavior of these patients.

A dramatic incident of a failure to assess the extent of a patient's dangerousness was reported by Gorin (1980, 1982) on the television news program, "60 Minutes":

In December, 1979, Mrs. Eva B. was brutally stabbed to death by her former husband while a police dispatcher listened to her terrified screams over the telephone. Only hours before the stabbing incident occurred, Mr. B., who had attacked Mrs. B. eight times in the past, had been judged by two staff psychiatrists not to be dangerous. He had then been released, as part of his treatment, on a temporary pass from the Pilgrim State Hospital in New York. The hospital staff had released Mr. B. from confinement at this time despite the fact that both the judge and the prosecuting attorney who had been involved in his trial (for attempting to kill his wife) had independently written the New York State Department of Mental Health recommending that Mr. B. be held in the strictest confinement because of his persistent threats against Mrs. B. (Indeed, on two previous occasions, Mr. B. had escaped from the hospital and attempted to kill her.) The judge and attorney had also recommended that Mrs. B. should be warned should Mr. B. be released. Ironically, six hours after she had been murdered, a telegram from the hospital was delivered to Mrs. B.'s home warning her that her husband had not returned from his pass.

Looking beyond what appears to be some failure to follow through on the court's recommendations, this case illustrates a number of difficult yet critical dilemmas involved in trying to identify or predict dangerousness in psychiatric patients.

a) First, it emphasizes the fact that some individuals are capable of uncontrolled violent behavior and hence are potentially dangerous if left unsupervised in the community.

b) It also reflects the dilemma faced by mental health professionals who, attempting to rehabilitate disturbed patients by gradually easing them back into society, must exhibit some degree of trust in these individuals.

c) Finally, and critically, it illustrates the fact that it is very difficult—for professionals and laypersons alike—to accurately appraise "dangerousness" in some individuals.

Attempts to predict "dangerousness."   It is usually an easy matter to determine, after the fact, that an individual has committed a violent act or acts and has demonstrated "dangerous behavior." The difficulty comes when one attempts to determine, in advance, if the individual is going to commit a particular violent act. Assessing a general state of "dangerousness" is not the same thing as predicting whether a violent act *will* occur.

How well do mental health professionals do in predicting "dangerousness"? There are a number of facets to this question. First, the definition of what is "dangerous" is itself unclear. It depends, in large part, upon who is asked. Some individuals have a limited or restrictive definition of what behaviors are dangerous and are willing to tolerate more aggressive behavior than others who view a broader range of behaviors as potentially dangerous. There is greater consensus about the dangerousness of extreme behaviors for example, such as murder, rape, and assault. From the standpoint of society, these kinds of behaviors are condemned as dangerous and viewed as requiring restraint.

Violent acts are particularly difficult to predict because they are apparently determined as much by situational circumstances as they are by the personality traits or "violent predispositions" of the individual. It is, of course, impossible to predict what environmental circumstances are going to occur or if particular circumstances will provoke or instigate aggression on the part of the person.

Mental health professionals typically err on

the conservative side when assessing "violence-proneness" in a patient; that is, they overpredict violence. They consider some individuals more dangerous than they actually are and, in general, predict a greater percentage of clients to be dangerous, requiring protective confinement, than actually become involved in violent acts (Megargee, 1970; Monahan, 1981). Gordon (1977) pointed out that the mental health professional's tendency to overpredict dangerousness places him or her in a "no-lose" situation: If the person commits a violent act, he or she can say, "I told you so"; and if the patient does not commit a violent act, it's because the patient was locked up—"It is just lucky that no one has triggered this person's dangerousness yet" (p. 234).

Methods for assessing potential for "dangerousness."
Evaluating an individual's potential for committing violent acts is difficult because only part of the equation is available for study:

Predisposing personality
+ environmental instigation
= aggressive act

As we have noted, psychologists and psychiatrists usually do not know enough about the environmental circumstances the individual will encounter to evaluate what the "instigation" to aggression will be. Predictions of dangerousness focus, then, primarily on aspects of the individual's personality. The two major sources of personality information are data from personality tests and the individual's previous history. Personality testing is focused on determining whether the individual shows personality traits of hostility, aggressiveness, impulsiveness, poor judgment, etc. Yet many individuals with such characteristics never act upon them. Still, as we noted above, there is a tendency to overpredict the likelihood of aggressive acts. The use of previous history—such as having committed prior aggression, verbalized threats of aggression, having an available means of committing violence (e.g., possession of a gun), etc.—are useful predictors (Monahan, 1981); but, like personality testing, these data only focus on the individual factors and do not account for the situational forces that impinge on the person. The prediction of violence is even more difficult in the case of the "overcontrolled" person who

does not have a history of aggressive behavior. Megargee (1970) studied extensively the "overcontrolled hostile" person who is the epitome of well-controlled behavior but who, on one occasion, loses control and kills another person. Examples of this type of murder are dramatic: the high-school honor student, reportedly civic-minded and fond of helping sick and old people, who is arrested for torturing and killing a three-year-old girl in his neighborhood; or the mild, passive father of four who loses his temper over being cheated by a car dealer and beats the man to death with a tire tool. These examples illustrate the most difficult type of aggressive behavior to predict—the sudden, violent, impulsive act of a seemingly well-controlled and "normal" individual.

The duty-to-warn: Implications of the Tarasoff decision.
What should a therapist do upon learning that one of his or her patients is planning to harm another person? Can the therapist violate the confidence of the therapy and take action to prevent the patient from committing the act? In many states, the therapist not only can violate the confidentiality but is *required by law* to do so—that is, to warn the endangered person of the threat against him/her. The duty-to-warn doctrine was given a great deal of impetus in a California court ruling in the case of *Tarasoff* v. *The Regents of the University of California et al.* (Cal. Reptr. 14, 551 P., 2d 334, 1976). In this case, Prosenjit Poddar was being seen in outpatient psychotherapy by a psychologist at the University Mental Health facility. During the treatment, Mr. Poddar indicated that he intended to kill his former girlfriend, Tatiana Tarasoff, when she returned from vacation. The psychologist, concerned about the threat, discussed the case with his supervisors, and they agreed that Mr. Poddar was dangerous and should be committed for further observation and treatment. They informed the Campus Police, who picked up Mr. Poddar for questioning. The police judged Mr. Poddar to be rational and released him after he promised to leave Ms. Tarasoff alone. Mr. Poddar terminated treatment with the psychologist. About two months later, he killed Ms. Tarasoff. Her parents later sued the University of California and its staff involved in the case for their failure to hospitalize Mr. Poddar and their failure to warn Ms. Tarasoff about the threat to her life.

The court did not find the defendants liable for failing to hospitalize Mr. Poddar; it did, however, find them liable for their failure to warn the victim. In a later analysis of the case, Knapp (1980) said that the court "ruled that difficulty in determining dangerousness does not exempt a psychotherapist from attempting to protect others when a determination of dangerousness exists. The court acknowledged that confidentiality was important to the psychotherapeutic relationship but stated that 'the protective privilege ends where the public peril begins.' " (p. 610).

The "duty-to-warn" ruling in the Tarasoff case, while spelling out a therapist's responsibility in situations where there has been an explicit threat on another's life, left other areas of application unclear. For example, does this ruling apply in cases where a patient threatens to commit suicide? Or when the object of violence is not clearly named, such as when global threats are made? Or would the duty to warn ruling hold up in other states?

Knapp and Vandecreek (1982) pointed out in a follow-up review that subsequent court decisions have not extended the duty to protect to suicidal cases. Furthermore, if the patient does not specifically name an intended victim, then the duty-to-warn does not apply. Regarding the application of the Tarasoff precedent in other states, four out of five of those states having related court cases have upheld the Tarasoff decision and required a duty-to-warn. Interestingly, a Maryland Court decision (*Shaw* v. *Glickman*, 415 A. 2d. 625, MD. Ct. Spec. App. 1980) found that, in Maryland, laws pertaining to privileged communications did not allow the therapist to warn a potential victim—even if a death threat were involved. Thus, a psychotherapist must be fully aware of state laws and judicial precedents in addition to making a determination of potential dangerousness on the part of the patient. The final form of the duty-to-warn doctrine has not fully evolved in the courts; future court decisions will, no doubt, further define the practitioner's responsibility.

The insanity defense

In recent years, the use of the *insanity defense*—"innocent by reason of insanity"—as a defense in capital crime trials has been surrounded by considerable controversy, largely resulting from concerns that criminals may use this plea to avoid criminal responsibility. Actually, the insanity defense has been used in less than 2 percent of cases over time (Fersch, 1980). Yet studies have confirmed the fact that individuals acquitted of crimes by reason of insanity spend less time, on the whole, in the psychiatric hospital than individuals who are actually convicted of crimes spend in prison (Kahn & Raifman, 1981; Pasewark, Pantle, & Steadman, 1982).

Although, historically, the insanity defense has been used infrequently, its use has apparently increased over the past 25 years as the definition of "insanity" has been broadened in the courts. Moreover, much of the controversy over the insanity defense has arisen because it has been used in many highly visible trials. For example, following the assassination attempt on President Reagan's life and the subsequent ruling that the alleged assassin was "insane" at the time, there was a great public outcry over the misuse of the insanity defense. Judging from the media coverage, many people apparently doubt the veracity of the insanity defense, believing instead that it may be contrived to escape justice.

The established precedents defining the insanity defense are:

a) *The M'Naghten Rule* (1843). Under this ruling, people are believed to be sane unless it can be proved that, at the time of committing the act, they were laboring under such a defect of reason (from a disease of the mind) that they did not know the nature and quality of the act they were doing. Or if they did know they were committing the act, they did not know that what they were doing was wrong.

b) *The irresistible impulse* (1887). A second precedent in the insanity defense is the doctrine of the "irresistible impulse." This view holds that accused individuals might not be responsible for their acts, even if they knew that what they were doing was wrong (according to the M'Naghten Rule) if they had lost the power to choose between right and wrong. That is, they could not avoid doing the act in question because they were compelled beyond their will to commit the act (Fersch, 1980).

c) *The Durham Rule*. In 1954, Judge David Bazelon, in a decision of the United States Court of Appeals, broadened the insanity defense further. Bazelon did not believe that the previous precedents allowed for sufficient application of established scientific knowledge of mental illness and proposed a test that would be based on this knowledge. Under this rule, the accused

M'Naghten's trial: the influential case that laid the legal groundwork for the insanity defense.

is "not criminally responsible if his or her unlawful act was the product of mental disease or mental defect." As we have seen, with the expansion of diagnostic classification of mental disorder, a broad range of behaviors can be defined as mental disease or defect. Which mental diseases serve to excuse a defendant from criminal responsibility? Generally, under M'Naghten, psychotic disorders were the basis of the insanity defense; but under the Durham Rule, other conditions (such as personality disorder or dissociative disorder) might also apply. How, then, is guilt or innocence determined? Many authorities believe that the Durham Rule has broadened the insanity defense in such a way as to require of the courts an impossible task—to determine guilt or innocence by reason of insanity on the basis of psychiatric testimony. In many cases, this has involved conflicting testimony, since both prosecution and defense have "their" psychiatric witnesses who are in complete disagreement (Fersch, 1980; Marvit, 1981).

d) *Diminished capacity.* An additional insanity test has been proposed by the New York State Department of Mental Hygiene (1978): "evidence of abnormal mental condition would be admissible to affect the degree of crime for which an accused could be convicted. Specifically, those offenses requiring intent or knowledge could be reduced to lesser included offenses requiring only reckless or criminal neglect." In this insanity defense, the accused would not be declared innocent by reason of insanity, but would be found guilty of a lesser charge, such as criminal negligence instead of murder.

The controversy over the insanity defense has led to much discussion about its reform by professionals in both the mental health and legal fields. Some individuals would like to do away with the insanity defense altogether, while others would prefer a modification of the defense to allow criminal responsibility to be established before the individual's sanity is considered in the case. Several states have revised the insanity defense to "guilty but mentally ill." In these cases, the defendant may be sentenced but placed in a treatment facility rather than in a prison. This two-part judgment would serve to prevent the type of situation where an individual commits a murder; is found not guilty by reason of insanity; is turned over to the mental health facility; the hospital staff find the person rational and in no further need of treatment; and the patient is released to the community after only two months of confinement. Under the "two-part decision" such an individual would ultimately remain in custody of the correctional department. Marvit (1981) suggested this approach might "realistically balance the interest of the mentally ill offender's rights and the community's need to control criminal behavior" (p. 23).

Deinstitutionalization

Originally, as we learned in Chapter 2, asylums or mental hospitals were viewed as the most humane settings for dealing with chronic patients. The individuals who founded the institutions and the society that supported them saw them as "havens" for the retarded or disturbed individual who could not survive in the world on his or her own. Ironically though, as hospitals became overcrowded and hospital staffs overworked, patient care deteriorated. Mental hospitals, founded out of a concern for human welfare, came to be viewed as horrid places. Bassuk and Gerson (1978) noted that "the reform movement, having seen its original objectives apparently accomplished, had ceased to be a significant influence. By early in this century the network of state mental hospitals, once the proud tribute to an era of reform, had largely turned into a bureaucratic morass within which patients were interned, often neglected and sometimes abused" (p. 47).

Recent years have witnessed a period of disenchantment with the large, state mental hospitals designed to treat chronic psychiatric patients. Many authorities have concluded that these institutions serve primarily as "warehouses" for the insane and that they dehumanize individuals rather than treat their problems. It has been recommended by many that some state mental hospitals be permanently closed and their residents returned either to more humane facilities or to their families and the community (Bachrach, 1976). In fact, in a number of cases, the court has decided to close some hospitals.

Paralleling these recommendations is the effort, on the part of many, to develop expanded community resources to provide chronic patients with continued psychiatric care in the local community. Supporters of this effort believe that society should be able to integrate these individuals back into the community and treat patients with the "least restrictive alternative." This movement, referred to as *deinstitutionalization,* has become a focus of controversy in the mental health field today. Some authorities consider the emptying of the hospitals to be a positive expression of society's desire to confer freedom on previously confined individuals, while others speak of the "abandonment" of chronic patients to a cruel and harsh existence.

There has indeed been a significant reduction in hospital populations: from over 559,000 in 1955 to around 150,000 in 1978. A number of factors have interacted to alter the pattern of mental hospital admissions and discharges over the past 25 years. As has been noted in previous chapters, the introduction of the major tranquilizers made it possible for large numbers of patients, who would formerly have required confinement, to be released to the community. The availability of tranquilizing medications led many to believe (falsely) that all mental health problems could be managed with medication. In addition, the changing treatment philosophy and the desire to eliminate mental institutions was accompanied by the belief that society wanted and could financially afford to provide better community-based care for chronic patients outside the large mental hospital.

In the 1960s and 1970s, many advocates for deinstitutionalization could be found: mental hospital reformers saw the movement as an opportunity to rid society of an unwelcome evil; hospital administrators and staff members initially viewed this as a way of lowering the hospital population to manageable numbers; and state governments viewed the movement with favor since it allowed legislatures (ever concerned about budgets) to reduce state funding.

In theory, the movement to close the mental hospitals seemed workable. Many community-based mental health centers were getting under way and could possibly provide continuing care to the residents of hospitals after discharge. Residents would be given welfare funds (supposedly costing the government less than it takes to maintain old-fashioned hospitals) and would be given medication to keep them stabilized until they could obtain continuing care. Many patients would be discharged to home and family while others would be placed in smaller, home-like board and care facilities or nursing homes.

However, many unforeseen problems arose. Many residents of mental institutions had no families or homes to go to; board-and-care facilities were often substandard; the community mental health centers were ill-prepared to provide needed services for chronic patients, particularly on an outpatient basis; many patients had not been carefully selected for discharge and were ill-prepared for community living; many of those who were discharged were not followed up sufficiently or with enough regularity to ensure their successful adaptation outside the hospital. Indeed, countless individuals were discharged to fates that were far more dehumanizing than the conditions in any of the hospitals. The following case illustrates the situation:

Dave B., age 49, had been hospitalized for 25 years in a state mental hospital. When the hospital was scheduled for phase-out, many of the patients, particularly those who were regressed or aggressive, were transferred to another state hospital. Dave was a borderline mentally retarded man who had periodic episodes of psychosis. However, at the time of hospital closing he was not hallucinating and was "reasonably intact." Dave was considered to be one of the "less disturbed" residents since his psychotic behavior was less pronounced and he presented no problem of danger.

He was discharged to a board-and-care facility (actually an old hotel whose clientele consisted mostly of former inpatients). At first, Dave seemed to fit in well at the facility; mostly he sat in his room or in the outside hallway, and he caused no trouble for the caretakers. Two weeks after he arrived he wandered off the hotel grounds and was missing for several days. The police eventually found him living in the city dump. He had apparently quit taking his medication and when he was discovered he was regressed and catatonic. He was readmitted to a state hospital.

Concern over the increasing number of vagrants in New York City prompted the *New York Post* to conclude in an article on psychiatric hospitals that "warehousing" of mental patients no longer took place in state institutions but "in New York streets, transport terminals, flophouses, and shelters for the homeless" (May 10, 1982). The increase in "bag ladies" in major cities was attributed to the premature or inappropriate discharging of patients from psychiatric hospitals. The *Post* article reported that the New York state hospitals, which once held 93,000 patients, in 1982 held only 21,000. It was estimated that 40 percent of the street crime in New York City could be attibuted to former psychiatric patients released from hospitals. Westermeyer (1982a) noted that:

"Patients are returned to the community, armed with drugs to control their illness. The worst aspects of their illnesses may be under control. But many of the patients are not ready to function in society. They need a gradual reintroduction—facilities where someone else can see that they take their drugs, see their psychiatrists, get food, clothing and shelter. Such care is too often more than families can provide and such services are not generally available in a community. As a result, the numbers of bag ladies and men, vagrants and mentally disabled people, living in lonely hotels and dangerous streets, have burgeoned." (p.2)

The extent of problems created by deinstitutionalization is not fully known. The ambiguity comes, in part, from the scarcity of rigorous fol-

low-up data on patients who have been discharged from mental hospitals. There have not been a sufficient number of adequate research studies in this area. Moreover, the research investigations have tended to be difficult to conduct since the patients are transient and are hard to keep track of over time.

It is quite clear that in spite of the problems described above much recent data on patient discharge and outcome status support the deinstitutionalization process. Braun et al. (1981), for example, concluded:

"The most satisfactory studies allow the qualified conclusion that selected patients managed outside the hospital in experimental programs do no worse and by some criteria have psychiatric outcomes superior to those of hospitalized control patients." (p. 747)

However, these same researchers also concluded that deinstitutionalization is likely to be unsuccessful if continuing care in the community is not available or if it is inadequate.

One of the most significant problems in the maintenance of discharged patients outside the hospital involves preventing the individual from developing what has been referred to as the "chronic social breakdown syndrome" (Archer & Gruenberg, 1982). This pattern of maladaptive behavior involves the individual's failing to maintain his or her self-care and social functioning skills at the level he or she attained prior to discharge from the hospital. While maintenance on tranquilizing drugs will help the individual to cope, it is important that assistance be provided to help maintain or attain an adequate social adjustment. This assistance or continuing care in the community can provide the patient with needed structure while he or she is learning new responsibilities and roles that are required in the new living situation.

Some very successful programs designed to reintegrate the chronic patient into the community have been described by Bachrach (1980). All these programs, despite their differences, are based on the following principles:

a) Targeting of chronic patients. The most successful model programs are targeted toward patients who have been persistently and chronically ill.

b) Linkage with other services. The most successful programs incorporate "full spectrum" planning, including treatment and social services.

Deinstitutionalization has been criticized for releasing onto the streets large numbers of people with nowhere to go.

(Archer & Gruenberg, 1982). The underlying premise here is that each day that the patient can spend in the real world is better than none. If short-term rehospitalization is necessary to provide the patient with real-world experiences, then it is a valuable approach to treating mentally ill individuals. Furthermore, the availability of short-term readmission to a hospital can limit the feeling of abandonment that some mental patients may have when they are released into the community. As such, this general pattern of hospital readmission is prevalent today.

Although the population of psychiatric hospitals has diminished significantly over the past three decades, the actual number of hospital admissions has increased (Bassuk & Gerson, 1978). The dramatic increase in the total number of admissions indicates a new trend toward briefer but more frequent hospitalizations for psychiatric patients. About "half of released inpatients are readmitted within a year of discharge" and readmissions to hospitals now exceed first admissions (Bassuk & Gerson, 1978, p. 49).

c) Functional integrity. A successful program generally provides for its patients a full range of services that are usually associated with institutional care.

d) Individually tailored treatment. The treatment program should allow for social-work case management and crisis-intervention services on a 24-hour basis if needed.

e) Cultural or ethnic-group relevance. The successful programs include a consideration of the ethnic or racial characteristics of the population served.

f) Specifically trained staff. Successful programs employ staff members who are apprised of the problems of chronic mental patients living in community settings.

g) Hospital liaison. Since some patients may require readmission to the hospital for brief periods, successful model programs maintain a relationship with the hospital and coordinate readmissions, if necessary.

h) Internal evaluation. The successful programs usually maintain an ongoing self-review program to monitor their functioning on a continuous basis.

Successful community care, according to Bachrach, involves the prospect of readmission to the hospital for short periods if necessary. The importance of short-term hospitalization has been noted by other investigators as well

Organized efforts for mental health

With increasing public awareness of the magnitude and severity of our contemporary mental health problem, governmental, professional, lay organizations and, more recently, business and industrial corporations have joined in a concerted attack on mental disorders—a broad-based attack directed toward better understanding, more effective treatment, and long-range prevention. This trend is apparent not only in our society but also in many other countries. And international as well as national and local organizations and measures are involved.

U.S. efforts for mental health

In the United States, the primary responsibility for dealing with mental disorders fell initially to state and local agencies. During World War II, however, the extent of mental disorders in the United States was brought to public attention when a large number of young men—2 out of every 7 recruits—were rejected for military service for psychiatric reasons. This discovery led to a variety of organized measures for coping with the mental health problem.

The government and mental health.
Aware of the need for more research, training, and services in the field of mental health, Congress in 1946 passed its first comprehensive mental health bill, the National Mental Health Act, which laid the basis for the federal government's present mental health program.

The 1946 bill provided for the establishment of a National Insitute of Mental Health (NIMH) in or near Washington, D.C., to serve as a central research and training center and headquarters for the administration of a grant-in-aid program. The grant-in-aid feature was designed to foster research and training elsewhere in the nation and to help state and local communities expand and improve their own mental health services. New powers were conferred on NIMH in 1956, when Congress, under Title V of the Health Amendments Act, authorized the Institute to provide "mental health project grants" for experimental studies, pilot projects, surveys, and general research having to do with the understanding, assessment, treatment, and aftercare of mental disorders.

As a result of organizational changes since then, the NIMH is now one of three Institutes under the Alcoholism, Drug Abuse, and Mental Health Administration, a division of the Public Health Service. NIMH (a) conducts and supports research on the biological, psychosocial, and sociocultural aspects of mental disorders; (b) supports the training of professional and paraprofessional personnel in the mental health field; (c) assists communities in planning, establishing, and maintaining more effective mental health programs; and (d) provides information on mental health to the public and to the scientific community. Its two companion institutes— the National Institute on Alcohol Abuse and Alcoholism (NIAAA) and the National Institute on Drug Abuse (NIDA)—perform comparable functions in their respective fields (Office of the Federal Register, 1982).

Although the federal government provides leadership and financial aid, the states and localities actually plan and run most NIMH programs. In addition, the states establish, maintain, and supervise their own mental hospitals

and clinics. A number of states have also pioneered, through their own legislation, in the development of community mental health centers, rehabilitation services in the community for ex-patients, and facilities for dealing with alcoholism, drug abuse, and other special mental health problems. In the 1980s, federal support for mental health programs has diminished considerably. Most state and local governments, which were expected to assume much of the support of mental health activities, have not been able to fund programs and facilities at 1960s and 1970s levels. As a result, many programs devoted to mental health training, research, and service have been greatly reduced or even abandoned. As to the future, there is widespread uncertainty about continued financial support for mental health activities.

Professional organizations and mental health.
There are a number of professional organizations in the mental health field. Some of the most influential of these are listed in the **HIGHLIGHT** on pages 694–95.

One of the most important functions of these organizations is to set and maintain high professional and ethical standards within their special areas. This function may include: (a) establishing and reviewing training qualifications for professional and paraprofessional personnel; (b) setting standards and procedures for accreditation of undergraduate and graduate training programs; (c) setting standards for accreditation of clinic, hospital, or other service operations and carrying out inspections to see that the standards are followed; and (d) investigating reported cases of unethical or unprofessional conduct, and taking disciplinary action where necessary.

A second key function of these professional organizations involves communication and information exchange within their fields via meetings, symposia, workshops, refresher courses, the publication of professional and scientific journals, and related activities. In addition, all such organizations sponsor programs of public education as a means of advancing the interests of their professions, drawing attention to mental health needs, and attracting students to careers in their professional fields.

A third key function of professional organizations, which is receiving increasing attention, is that of applying their insights and methods to contemporary social problems. In the 1970s we saw the growing involvement of professional mental health organizations in social problems and even international issues. In 1974, for example, the Board of Trustees of the American Psychiatric Association endorsed the United Nations program for a decade of action to combat racism and racial discrimination and directed that efforts be made to implement this program as it applies to conditions in the United States. In addition, it has tried to call world attention to the use of psychiatric treatment for political dissidents in the Soviet Union. The major professional organizations have also taken strong stands on equal opportunities for women and on the provision of adequate health services for all people.

Composed as they are of qualified personnel, professional mental health organizations are in a unique position to serve as consultants on mental health problems and programs not only on the national level but also on state and local levels. Increasingly, they are establishing a closer liaison with one another as well as with both governmental and voluntary agencies concerned with mental health.

Role of voluntary mental health organizations and agencies.

While professional mental health personnel and organizations can give expert technical advice in regard to mental health needs and programs, real progress in helping plan and implement these programs must come from an informed and concerned citizenry. In fact, it has been repeatedly stated that it has been nonprofessionals who have blazed the trail in the mental health field.

Prominent among the many voluntary mental health agencies is the National Association for Mental Health (NAMH). This organization was founded in 1950 by the merger of the National Committee for Mental Hygiene, the National Mental Health Foundation, and the Psychiatric Foundation; and it was further expanded in 1962 by amalgamation with the National Organization for Mentally Ill Children. Through its national governing body and some 1000 local affiliates, the NAMH works for the improvement of services in community clinics and mental hospitals; it helps recruit, train, and place volunteers for service in treatment and aftercare programs; and it works for enlightened mental health leg-

islation and provision of needed facilities and personnel. It also carries on special educational programs aimed at fostering positive mental health and helping people understand mental disorders.

In addition, the National Association for Mental Health has been actively involved in many court decisions affecting patient rights (NAMH, 1979). In several cases the NAMH has sponsored litigation or served as amicus curiae (friend of the court) in efforts to establish the rights of mental patients to treatment, freedom from custodial confinement, freedom to live in the community, and protection of their confidentiality.

With a program and organization similar to that of the NAMH, the National Association for Retarded Children (NARC) works to reduce the incidence of mental retardation, to seek community and residential treatment centers and services for the retarded, and to carry on a program of education aimed at better public understanding of retarded individuals and greater support for legislation on their behalf. The NARC also fosters scientific research into mental retardation, the recruitment and training of volunteer workers, and programs of community action. On the local level, it is especially interested in forming groups of parents of retarded children in order to help such parents better understand, accept, and deal with their children's limited capabilities.

These and other voluntary health organizations, such as Alcoholics Anonymous, are particularly American in their development of extensive programs of research, service, and training of volunteers financed by donations from interested individuals and foundations. To succeed in their objectives, of course, they need the backing of a wide constituency of knowledgeable and involved citizens.

Mental health resources in private industry.

Personal problems—such as marital distress or other family problems, alcohol or drug abuse, financial difficulties, or job-related stress—can adversely affect employee morale and performance on the job. Psychological difficulties among employees may result in numerous types of job problems such as absenteeism, accident proneness, poor productivity and high job turnover. Many corporations have long rec-

HIGHLIGHT
Professional organizations concerned with mental health

American Psychological Association (APA)
An association of professionally trained psychologists. Its purpose is to advance psychology as a science, as a profession, and as a means of promoting human welfare. It has over 30 divisions concerned with various special areas within psychology, and it establishes and monitors standards for the training and practice of psychologists in mental health work.

American Psychiatric Association (APA)
An association of physicians with training in psychiatry. Its purpose is to further the study of the nature, treatment, and prevention of mental disorders; to help set, improve, and maintain standards of practice and service in mental hospitals, clinics, general hospital psychiatric units, and institutions for the mentally retarded; to further psychiatric research and education; and to foster enlightened views with regard to the social and legal aspects of psychopathology and the role of psychiatry in fostering human welfare.

American Medical Association (AMA)
An association of physicians who are members of constituent state medical associations. In addition to its myriad other functions, it is concerned with mental disorder as a general health problem and with fostering research, education, and legislation to advance comprehensive health efforts in the United States.

American Psychoanalytic Association (APA)
An association of analytically trained psychiatrists. It sets standards for the training of psychoanalysts.

American Sociological Association (ASA)
An association of sociologists, social scientists, and other professional persons interested in research, teaching, and applications of sociology. Its sections on Social Psychology, Medical Sociology, and Criminology have special pertinence to mental health.

National Association of Social Workers (NASW)
An assocation of professionally trained social workers, organized to promote the quality and effectiveness of social work and to foster mental health. It establishes and monitors standards for training and practice, encourages research, and interprets the role of social work in the community.

American Nurses Association (ANA) and National League for Nursing (NLN)
An association of registered nurses concerned with high standards of professional practice (ANA). Two of its clinical committee groups (one on Psychiatric Nursing Practice and one on Maternal and Child Health Nursing) have special mental health concerns. A Coordinating Council unites its program with that of the National League for Nursing, a voluntary organization of professional, semi-professional, and lay persons and of institutions and organizations; the National League is the principal standard-setting group in the nursing field.

American Occupational Therapy Association (AOTA)
A society of registered occupational therapists administering medically supervised activities to physically or

ognized this fact, and yet it has been a relatively recent phenomena to see them act on this knowledge. Today, many companies have expanded the corporation's "obligation" to the employee to include numerous psychological services. Often referred to as employee-assistance programs, these are the means through which corporations can actively provide mental health services to their employees and family members.

One corporation that has pioneered in the development of employee-assistance programs is Control Data Corporation of Minneapolis, Minnesota. Following the implementation of a successful alcoholism treatment program in 1974, Control Data management founded its employee assistance program, the Employee Advisory Resource (known as EAR). This program was initiated to assist employees and their family members in solving personal or job-related problems. The program—modeled after the telephone hotline programs that had been so successful during the 1960s—provides a 24-hour telephone counseling service staffed by approximately 20 EAR counselors. All counselors have been mentally ill persons. It maintains standards of education and training, makes surveys and recommendations on request, and works with its state associations in the preparation and certification of occupational therapy volunteer assistants.

National Rehabilitation Association (NRA)
An assocation of physicians, counselors, therapists, and others (including organizations) concerned with rehabilitation of the physically and mentally handicapped. Reviews existing services and makes recommendations for improved rehabilitation programs.

American Orthopsychiatric Association (AOA)
An organization of psychiatrists, psychologists, social workers, sociologists, and members of other disciplines working in a collaborative approach to the study and treatment of human behavior, primarily in clinical settings. Its focus is on the problems of children. The AOA encourages research and is directly concerned with fostering human welfare.

National Council for Family Relations (NCFR)
Composed primarily of and directed toward practitioners serving couples and families through counseling, therapy, education, and community service. The NCFR fosters research and the application of its findings to practice.

American Association on Mental Deficiency (AAMD)
An interdisciplinary association of physicians, educators, administrators, social workers, psychologists, psychiatrists, and others interested in assisting the

mentally retarded. It works with the American Psychiatric Association in setting standards for hospitals and schools for the mentally retarded.

Council for Exceptional Children (CEC)
Made up largely of professional workers in fields dealing with mentally retarded, physically handicapped, and emotionally disturbed children. It fosters research and its applications, education, and social legislation relating to exceptional children.

American Association for the Advancement of Science (AAAS)
Composed of scientists from many disciplines. Its objectives include furthering the work and mutual cooperation of scientists, improving the effectiveness of science and its contribution to human welfare, and increasing understanding and appreciation of the importance and promise of scientific methods in human progress.

Society for Research in Child Development (SRCD)
An association of psychologists whose aim is to study normal processes of child development. Members are concerned with issues related to improving the welfare of children as well as with encouraging scientific research on developmental processes.

Most of these organizations sponsor national conventions, workshops, symposia, and public educational programs and publish journals in their respective areas. They are also concerned with broad social problems as well as with the special problems in their professional areas.

trained to identify problems and to refer the troubled employee to internal counseling resources or to community agencies. Callers may remain anonymous and the contact is completely confidential. The service is provided at no cost to the employee.

Control Data's EAR has proven to be of help to many employees. During the first five years of operation, over 19,000 employee contacts were recorded. The number of counseling contacts has increased from about 1,550 in the first year to about 5,000 a year at the present time.

Though individuals seek help for a range of problems, the majority of contacts are for legal difficulties, financial problems, alcoholism, and marital stress.

The EAR program provides a number of employee services in addition to the personal counseling and referral program. These include employee educational programs, prevention of future problems, employee relations consultation and employee policy making decisions. The success of the EAR program is reflected in the fact that since 1976 Control Data has assisted over 150 other companies in setting up similar employee assistance programs.

International efforts for mental health

Mental health is a major problem not only in the United States but in the rest of the world as well. Indeed, many of the unfavorable conditions in this country with regard to the causes and treatment of mental disorders are greatly magnified in poorer countries and countries with repressive governments. According to the World Health Organization (WHO, 1978a), 40 million people in the world suffer from severe mental illness, over 80 million from alcohol and drug addiction, mental retardation, and organic brain disorders, and another 80 million suffer from other mental disorders, such as the neuroses. The severity of the world mental health problem is shown in the estimates that mental disorders affect more than 200 million people worldwide.

It was the knowledge of this great problem that served to bring about the formation of several international organizations at the end of World War II. We shall briefly review here the World Health Organization and the United Nations Educational, Scientific, and Cultural Organization (both UN agencies), as well as the World Federation for Mental Health.

The World Health Organization (WHO). The World Health Organization defines health as not simply absence of disease but a positive state of physical, mental, and social well-being. From the first, it has been keenly aware of the close interrelationships between physical, psychosocial, and sociocultural factors—such as the influence of rapid change and social disruption on both physical and mental health; the impossibility of major progress toward mental health in societies where a large proportion of the population suffer from malnutrition, parasites, and disease; and the frequent psychological and cultural barriers to successful programs in family planning and public health.

Formed after World War II as part of the UN system, WHO's earliest focus was on physical diseases; through its efforts dramatic progress has been made toward the conquest of ancient scourges like smallpox and malaria. Over the years, mental health, too, became an increasing concern among the member countries. In response, WHO's present program now integrates mental health concerns with the broad problems of overall health and socioeconomic development that must be faced by member countries (WHO, 1978a). For example, this includes help to both prevent and control mental disorders. Furthermore, it includes efforts to ensure healthy psychosocial development, to protect traditional cultural values and family relationships in the face of rapid industrialization, and to foster community participation in the public health programs.

WHO has headquarters in Geneva and regional offices for Africa, the Americas, Southeast Asia, Europe, the Eastern Mediterranean, and the Western Pacific. Hence its activities extend into areas with diverse physical environments, types of social organization, and mental health facilities. It enters a country only on invitation, helping identify the basic health needs of each country and working with the local authorities to plan and carry out the most useful and appropriate programs. Where possible, it strives to make its services available over a period of several years to ensure continuity and success for the programs that are undertaken.

Another important contribution of WHO has been its International Classification of Diseases, which enables clinicians and researchers in different countries to use a uniform set of diagnostic categories (WHO, 1978b). The American Psychiatric Association's DSM-III classification is coordinated with the WHO classification (ICD-9).

The United Nations Educational, Scientific, and Cultural Organization (UNESCO). The constitution of UNESCO (1945) contains a statement that seems to strike many people with the force of a spiritual conversion: "Since wars begin in the minds of men, it is in the minds of men that the defenses of peace must be constructed." By promoting collaboration among nations through educational, cultural, and scientific channels, UNESCO attempts to foster peace and respect for human rights, with fundamental freedoms for all.

Over 135 countries belong to UNESCO. In general, UNESCO programs are divided into three main areas: (a) *international intellectual co-*

operation aimed at the communication of information and the exchange of ideas among member countries; (b) *operational assistance* through the provision of specialists to advise governments in the planning of educational and other projects and to provide day-by-day assistance in their implementation; and (c) *promotion of peace* through increased knowledge of international problems, emphasis on human rights, and mutual understanding among peoples. On many problems UNESCO works cooperatively with other agencies—sometimes as instigator or catalyst, sometimes as consultant, sometimes as one of several cooperating groups. For example, the use of satellites for educational and mental health purposes was initially arranged by UNESCO.

UNESCO is also working to provide better opportunities for young people to participate actively in the social, economic, and cultural life of their own countries and of the world. It helps in the training of scientists and technicians, as well as in the development of scientific research in developing countries. Thus on many fronts UNESCO is working for the progress of education, culture, and research and for the intellectual and moral unity of humankind in a peaceful world.

The World Federation for Mental Health.
The World Federation for Mental Health was established in 1948 at an international congress of nongovernmental organizations and individuals concerned with mental health. Its purpose is to promote cooperation at the international level between governmental and nongovernmental mental health agencies, and its membership now extends to more than 50 countries. The Federation has been granted consultative status by both WHO and UNESCO, and it assists the UN agencies by collecting information on mental health conditions all over the world.

We have now seen something of the maze of local, national, and international measures that are being undertaken in the mental health field. We can expect these efforts to continue. Furthermore, we can expect to see more and more mental health problems unraveled to reveal discoverable causes and to respond to treatment and prevention by scientific means. Quite simply, many people now believe the statement Julian Huxley (1959) made over two decades ago, that through the advances of modern science and technology "human life [can] gradually be transformed from a competitive struggle against blind fate into a great collective enterprise, consciously undertaken . . . for greater fulfillment through the better realization of human potentialities" (p. 409).

Challenges for the future

We have a long way to go before the dreams of a better world are realized. Many question whether the United States or any other technologically advanced nation can achieve mental health for the majority of its citizens in our time. Racism, poverty, and other social problems that contribute to mental disorder sometimes seem insurmountable.

What happens in the rest of the world affects us also, both directly and indirectly. Worldwide economic instability and shortages and the possibilities of nuclear war and even of destruction of the life-support system of our planet breed widespread anxiety about the future. Our military defenses against perceived threats from other parts of the world absorb vast funds and energy that otherwise might be turned to meeting human and social needs here and elsewhere in the world.

The need for planning

It seems imperative that more effective planning be done at community, national, and international levels before it is too late. Many challenges must be met if we are to create a better world for ourselves and future generations. Without slackening our efforts to meet needs at home, we shall probably find it increasingly essential to participate in international measures toward reducing group tensions and promoting mental health and a better world for people everywhere. At the same time, we can expect that measures undertaken to reduce international conflict and improve the general condition of humankind will make their contribution to our own nation's social progress and mental health. But both kinds of measures will require understanding and moral commitment from concerned citizens.

Unfortunately, some people, including many individuals in positions of power, consider the cost of such social programs too high and their outcomes too remote. Elected officials need to show results before the next election and often feel they cannot afford to work for long-term goals. The 1970s closed on a pessimistic note—a widespread concern about inflation, economic instability, and energy shortages and a generally conservative mood. A sign of this new conservatism was the great taxpayers' revolt in which voters supported extreme tax cuts in state and local funds in spite of appeals that such measures might close off important ongoing social programs. Concerned individuals and organizations may have to increase their efforts if the great gain in the mental health movement made during the last thirty years is to keep its momentum.

To some people in our society, social planning seems contrary to the American way of life and the ideal of individual freedom. Yet as the NIMH (1969) has emphasized:

"Social planning does not imply authoritarian control; a planned society does not mean a closed society. Techniques are now emerging to guarantee that planning will enhance, not diminish, the power and influence of individuals in controlling their destinies and achieving their personal goals. 'Advocacy planning' and 'participatory democracy' provide for the inclusion of all interested groups and individuals in the planning and decision-making process." (p. 117)

In fact, to be planless in our complex, interdependent, and rapidly changing world is to invite—and perhaps ensure—disaster.

The enduring problem of values

We are all concerned not only with *whether* the human race will survive but also with *how*—with the quality of life that will be possible. It will not be enough to preserve human life for a future world of "unsanity" or lockstep regimentation or bare subsistence. For many years we have been creating an increasing part of our own future but often without realizing it and foreseeing only some of the results of our actions. As we increasingly take the future consciously into our own hands, it is critical that we consider the en-

tire range of options open to us and make wise value judgments in choosing among the alternatives.

Why these goals rather than other goals? Why these means rather than other means? The answers to these questions involve value judgments. Although science can specify the conditions that will foster passivity, creativity, or other personality traits, it is our values that determine the kind of children we want to rear, the kind of lives we want to live, and the type of world we want to live in.

Where we lack values for making choices, are confused about our values, or put our faith in false values, the results are likely to be destructive and maladaptive. Although it would be both arrogant and premature to attempt a formulation of universal values, it would appear that we are likely to have to come to grips with the following tentative value assumptions as minimal essentials:

1. A belief in the worth of the individual and of human survival.
2. A belief that personal growth and social progress are possible and worthwhile.
3. A belief in equal justice and in the desirability of opportunities for all persons to fulfill their potentialities.
4. A belief in the value of the "truth" that we try to approach by means of scientific inquiry.
5. A belief in the maxim "love one another" and other basic ethical tenets of the world's religious philosophies.
6. A belief in the right and responsibility of all people to have a voice in decisions that will affect their lives.
7. A belief in humankind as a functional part of the universe with potentialities for evolution that can be fulfilled.
8. A belief in the responsibility of all individuals for carrying forward the progress made by preceding generations and for contributing to the creation of a good future for all.

These value assumptions are not universally accepted, and, being assumptions, they are not subject to proof. They are suggested simply as guidelines that may merit consideration by those who are seeking a new ethic that can match the impact of science on society. If we have no faith in the worth or growth potential of the individual, the possibility or value of greater social justice, or in the potentiality of a meaningful role in the universe for humankind, then these value assumptions will be useless. However, people do not easily adopt the doctrine of despair so vividly portrayed by Shakespeare, that life is

"a tale
Told by an idiot, full of sound and fury,
Signifying nothing." (*Macbeth*, Act V, Scene v)

As we embark upon the great adventure of shaping the future, let us hope that we will learn to change what needs to be changed while preserving what is valid of our heritage from the past. As Haskins (1968) has pointed out, we must be continually aware of the danger that "in embracing new and experimental courses on myriad fronts of movement with the ardor that we must, we do not at the same time discard long-tested values and long-tried adaptive courses, which, if they are lost, will only have, one day, to be rewon—and probably at enormous cost."

This book can go no further toward a value orientation. Beyond this point, we will each be confronted with the challenge of exploring the world of values and making our own value judgments and choices.

The individual's contribution

"Each man can make a difference,
and each man should try."
John F. Kennedy

When students become aware of the tremendous scope of the mental health problem both nationally and internationally and the woefully inadequate facilities for coping with it, they often ask, "What can I do?" This is not an idle question, for much of the progress that has been achieved in the treatment of mental disorders has resulted from the work of concerned citizens. Thus it seems appropriate to suggest a few of the lines of action interested students can profitably take.

Many opportunities in mental health work are open to trained personnel, both professional and paraprofessional. Social work, clinical psychology, psychiatry, and other mental health occupations are rewarding in terms of personal fulfillment. In addition, there are many occupations, ranging from law enforcement to teaching and the ministry, that can and do play key roles in the mental health and well-being of many

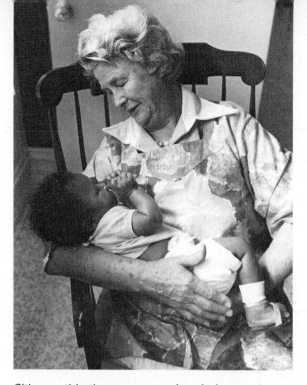

Citizen-participation programs—such as the foster-grandparent programs established in some cities—are one means by which individuals can contribute to the psychological well-being of others.

people. Training in all these fields usually offers individuals opportunities to work in community clinics and related facilities, to gain experience in understanding the needs and problems of people in distress, and to become familiar with community resources.

Citizens can find many ways to be of direct service if they are familiar with national and international resources and programs and invest the effort necessary to learn about their community's special needs and problems. Whatever their roles in life—student, teacher, police officer, lawyer, homemaker, business executive, or trade unionist—their interests are directly at stake. For although the mental health of a nation may be manifested in many ways—in its purposes, courage, moral responsibility, scientific and cultural achievements, and quality of daily life—its health and resources derive ultimately from the individuals within it. In a participatory democracy, it is they who plan and implement its goals.

Besides accepting some measure of responsibility for the mental health of others through the quality of one's own interpersonal relationships, there are several other constructive courses of action open to each citizen, including: (a) serving as a volunteer in a mental hospital, community mental health center, or service organization; (b) supporting realistic measures for ensuring comprehensive health services for all age groups; and (c) working toward improved public education, responsible government, the alleviation of group prejudice, and the establishment of a more sane and harmonious world.

All of us are concerned with mental health for personal as well as altruistic reasons, for we want to overcome the harassing problems of contemporary living and find our share of happiness in a meaningful and fulfilling life. To do so, we may sometimes need the courage to admit that our problems are too much for us. When existence seems futile or the going becomes too difficult, it may help to remind ourselves of the following basic facts, which have been emphasized in the course of the present text.

1. From time to time each of us has serious difficulties in coping with the problems of living.
2. During such crisis periods, we may need psychological and related assistance.
3. Such difficulties are not a disgrace; they can happen to anyone if the stress is sufficiently severe.
4. The early detection and correction of maladaptive behavior is of great importance in preventing the development of more severe or chronic conditions.
5. Preventive measures—primary, secondary, and tertiary—are the most effective long-range approach to the solution of both individual and group mental health problems.

To recognize these facts is essential because statistics show that almost all of us will at some time in our lives have to deal with severely maladaptive behavior or mental disorder either in ourselves or in someone close to us. The interdependence among us and the loss to us all, individually and collectively, when any one of us fails to achieve his or her potential are eloquently expressed in the famous lines of John Donne (1624):

"No man is an island, entire of itself; every man is a piece of the continent, a part of the main. If a clod be washed away by the sea, Europe is less, as well as if a promontory were, as well as if a manor of thy friends or of thine own were: any man's death diminishes me, because I am involved in mankind, and therefore never send to know for whom the bell tolls; it tolls for thee."

Summary

Increasingly today, professionals are trying not only to cure mental health problems but also to prevent them, or at least reduce their effects. Prevention can be viewed as focusing on three levels. *Primary prevention* is aimed at reducing the possibility of disorder and fostering positive mental health efforts. *Secondary prevention* attempts to reduce the impact or duration of a problem that has already occurred. *Tertiary prevention* attempts to reduce the long-term consequences of having had a disorder.

In recent years, several legal controversies concerning the treatment of mental patients have surfaced.

The commitment process and procedures for committing individuals for inpatient care have been reconsidered. Being "mentally ill" is not considered sufficient grounds for commitment. There must be, in addition, evidence that the individual is either dangerous to him- or herself or represents a danger to society. It is not an easy matter, even for trained professionals, to determine in advance if an individual is "dangerous" and likely to cause harm to others. However, professionals must, at times, make such judgments. Recent court rulings have found professionals liable when patients they were treating caused harm to others. The Tarasoff decision held that a therapist has a duty to warn potential victims if his or her patient has threatened to kill another.

Another important issue of "forensic psychology" involves the insanity plea for capital crimes. Many mental health and legal professionals, journalists, and laypersons have questioned the present use of the insanity defense. The original legal precedent, the M'Naghten Rule, held that at the time of committing the act, the accused must have been laboring under such a defect of reason as to not know the nature and quality of the act or to not know that what he or she was doing was wrong. The more recent broadening of the insanity plea, under the Durham rule, has placed more credibility on "scientific knowledge" in that the accused is not "criminally responsible if his or her unlawful act was the product of mental disease or mental defect." This broadening of the insanity plea has led to its use in more and more cases, and decisions often involve conflicting psychiatric testimony. Many people have been questioning the appropriateness of the insanity plea and some experts are recommending changes in it, asking that the individual's guilt or innocence of the crime be established separately from the determination of sanity.

There has been a great deal of legal controversy recently over the release of patients from mental hospitals, or deinstitutionalization, and the failure to provide adequate follow-up of patients in the community. In their zeal to close the large psychiatric institutions, many administrators underestimated the amount of care that would be needed after discharge, and overestimated the community's ability to deal with patients with chronic problems. The result was that some chronic patients were placed in circumstances that required more adaptive abilities than the patients possessed. Recent work in the area of aftercare for former mental patients has provided clearer guidelines for discharge and therapeutic follow-up.

A large number of organizations are concerned and involved with establishing organized efforts for mental health. Several government agencies have mental health as their primary mission. For example, federal agencies such as NIMH, NIDA, and NIAAA are devoted to promoting varied research, training, and service. State and county government agencies may focus their efforts upon *delivery* of mental health services to residents on an inpatient or outpatient basis.

Mental health programming in the United States is also the concern of several professional and mental health organizations, many industrial corporations, and a number of voluntary mental health organizations. In addition, international organizations such as the World Health Organization, the United Nations Educational, Scientific, and Cultural Organization, and the World Federation for Mental Health have contributed to mental health programs worldwide.

Glossary

Many of the key terms that appear in the glossary are page-referenced to passages in the text where the term first receives substantive attention or discussion. A number of other terms commonly encountered in this or other psychology texts are also included; the student is encouraged to make use of this glossary both as a general reference tool and as a study aid for the course in abnormal psychology.

Abnormal. Maladaptive behavior detrimental to the individual and/or the group. (p. 15)

Abnormal psychology. Field of psychology concerned with the study, assessment, treatment, and prevention of abnormal behavior. (p. 14)

Abstinence. Refraining altogether from the use of a particular addictive substance.

Accommodation. The cognitive process whereby new information causes a reorganization of previously existing cognitive maps or structures. (p. 110)

Activation (arousal). Energy mobilization required for organism to pursue its goals and meet its needs.

Actuarial approach. Application of probability statistics to human behavior, as in insurance. (p. 606)

Acute. Term used to describe a disorder of sudden onset and relatively short duration, usually with intense symptoms. (p. 18)

Acute alcoholic hallucinosis. State of alcoholic intoxication characterized by hallucinations. (p. 406)

Acute paranoid disorder. Psychoses characterized by transient and changeable paranoid delusions, usually related to an identifiable stressor and transient in nature. (p. 387)

Acute posttraumatic stress disorder. Disorder in which symptoms develop within six months of extremely traumatic experience instead of entering recovery stage. (p. 163)

Acute schizophrenia. Schizophrenic pattern marked by confusion and intense emotional turmoil; develops suddenly and usually has identifiable precipitating stressors. (p. 349)

Adaptability. Flexibility in meeting changed circumstances or demands.

Adjustive behavior. Behavior by which the individual attempts to deal with stress and meet his or her needs, including efforts to maintain harmonious relationships with the environment.

Adjustment. Outcome of the individual's efforts to deal with stress and meet his or her needs.

Adjustment disorders. Category of disorders in which individual has difficulty adjusting to a common stressor. (p. 156)

Adjustment disorder with depressed mood. Moderately severe affective disorder behaviorally identical to dysthymic disorder or depressed phase of cyclothymic disorder but having an identifiable, though not severe, psychosocial stressor occurring within three months prior to the onset of depression. (p. 306)

Adrenal cortex. Outer layer of the adrenal glands; secretes the adrenal steroids and other hormones.

Adrenal glands. Endocrine glands located at the upper end of the kidneys; consist of inner adrenal medulla and outer adrenal cortex.

Adrenaline. Hormone secreted by the adrenal medulla during strong emotion; causes such bodily changes as an increase in blood sugar and a rise in blood pressure. Also called *epinephrine*. (p. 149)

Advocacy programs. Programs aimed at helping people in underserved populations to obtain aid with which to improve their situations. (p. 577)

Affect. Experience of emotion or feeling. (p. 300)

Affective disorder. Psychosis and related thought disturbances characterized by severe disturbances of feeling or mood. (p. 299)

Aftercare. Follow-up therapy after release from a hospital.

Aggression. Behavior aimed at hurting or destroying someone or something.

Agitation. Marked restlessness and psychomotor excitement.

Agoraphobia. Morbid fear of large, open places.

Alarm and mobilization reaction. First stage of the general-adaptation-syndrome, characterized by the mobilization of defenses to cope with a stressful situation. (p. 154)

Alcoholic. Individual with serious drinking problems, whose drinking impairs life adjustment in terms of health, personal relationships, and/or occupational functioning. (p. 398)

Alcoholic deterioration. Personality deterioration, including impaired judgment, associated with alcoholism.

Alcoholic intoxication. State reached when alcohol content of blood is 0.1 percent or above.

Alcoholism. Dependence on alcohol to the extent that it seriously interferes with life adjustment. (p. 398)

Algophobia. Irrational fear of pain.

Alienation. Lack or loss of relationships to others.

Alpha waves. Brain waves having a frequency of 8 to 12 cycles per second and accompanied by a state of wakeful relaxation.

Alzheimer's disease. The most common form of senile disorder; in some cases Alzheimer's disease may occur well before old age. (p. 505)

Amnesia. Total or partial loss of memory. (p. 217)

Amnestic syndrome. Inability to remember events more than a few minutes after they have occurred coupled with the ability to recall the recent and remote past. (p. 494)

Amniocentesis. A technique that involves drawing fluid from the amniotic sac of a pregnant woman so that the sloughed-off fetal cells can be examined for chromosomal irregularities, including that of Down's syndrome. (p. 523)

Amphetamine. One type of drug that produces a psychologically stimulating and energizing effect. (p. 429)

Analgesia. Insensitivity to pain without loss of consciousness.

Anal stage. In psychoanalytic theory, stage of psychosexual development in which behavior is presumably focused on anal pleasure and activities. (p. 64)

Analytic psychology. The school or system of psychology developed by Carl Jung.

Androgen. Hormones associated with the development and maintenance of male characteristics.

Androgyny. Theoretically, psychologically ideal combination of masculine and feminine traits. (p. 133)

Anesthesia. Loss or impairment of sensitivity (usually to touch but often applied to sensitivity to pain and other senses as well).

Anhedonia. Inability to experience pleasure or joy; believed by some to be a basic characteristic of schizophrenic individuals. (p. 351)

Anomie. State of disregulation of social norms and values.

Anorexia nervosa. Loss or severe diminishment of appetite, apparently of psychogenic origin. (p. 280)

Anoxia. Lack of sufficient oxygen. (p. 520)

Antabuse. Drug used in the treatment of alcoholism.

Anterograde amnesia. Loss of memory for events *following* trauma or shock.

Antianxiety drugs. Drugs which are used primarily for alleviating anxiety.

Antidepressant drugs. Drugs which are used primarily to elevate mood and relieve depression.

Antisocial (psychopathic) personality. Personality disorder involving a marked lack of ethical or moral development. (p. 237)

Anxiety. Generalized feelings of fear and apprehension. (p. 189)

Anxiety attack. Acute episode of intense anxiety. (p. 195)

Anxiety disorder. DSM-III category characterized by chronic anxiety and apprehension. Includes generalized anxiety disorder, panic disorder, obsessive-compulsive disorder, posttraumatic stress disorder, and phobic disorder. (p. 194)

Anxiety disturbance. A childhood disorder marked by over-sensitivity, self-consciousness, unrealistic fears, and a high level of anxiety.

Anxiety hierarchy. Ranking of anxiety-eliciting situations utilized in systematic desensitization therapy.

Anxiety withdrawal. Pattern of childhood maladaptive behaviors involving anxiety and withdrawal. (p. 539)

Aphasia. Loss or impairment of ability to communicate and understand language symbols—involving loss of power of expression by speech, writing, or signs, or loss of ability to comprehend written or spoken language—resulting from brain injury or disease.

Aphonia. Inability to speak above a whisper; a conversion disorder. (p. 215)

Approach-avoidance conflict. Type of stress situation involving both positive and negative features.

Apraxia. Loss of ability to perform purposeful movements.

Arousal. See **Activation.**

Arteriosclerosis. Degenerative thickening and hardening of the walls of the arteries, occurring usually in old age.

Assertiveness training. Behavior therapy technique for helping individuals become more self-assertive in interpersonal relationships. (p. 647)

Assimilation. The cognitive process whereby new information is fitted into previously existing cognitive maps or structures. (p. 110)

Astasia-abasia. Inability to stand or walk without the legs wobbling about and collapsing, although the person has normal control of legs while sitting or lying down; no associated organic pathology. (p. 215)

Ataxia. Muscular incoordination, particularly of the arms and legs. See **Locomotor ataxia.**

At risk. Condition of being considered vulnerable to the development of certain abnormal behaviors. (p. 27)

Atrophy. Wasting away or shrinking of a bodily organ particularly muscle tissue.

Attention deficit disorder. Maladaptive behavior in children characterized by impulsivity, excessive motor activity, and an inability to focus attention for appropriate periods of time; also called *hyperactive syndrome* or *hyperkinetic reaction.* (p. 541)

Attribution theory. Theory by which causes in the behavior of others are interpreted, based on unseen or unrecognized qualities in ourselves. (p. 82)

Autism. Disorder beginning in infancy characterized by inability of child to relate to others or form normal self-concept. (p. 123)

Automated assessment. Psychological test interpretation by electronic computer or some other mechanical means.

Automatic functioning. Unplanned, unconscious reactions to stress. (p. 150)

Autonomic nervous system. The section of the nervous system that regulates the internal organs; consists primarily of ganglia connected with the brain stem and spinal cord and may be subdivided into the sympathetic and parasympathetic systems.

Autonomic reactivity. Individual's characteristic degree of emotional reactivity to stress.

Autonomy. Self-reliance; the sense of being an individual in one's own right.

Autosome. Any chromosome other than those determining sex. (p. 89)

Aversion therapy. Form of behavior therapy in which punishment or aversive stimulation is used to eliminate undesired responses. (p. 644)

Aversive conditioning. Use of noxious stimuli to suppress unwanted behavior.

Aversive stimulus. A stimulus that elicits psychic or physical pain.

Avoidance conditioning. Form of conditioning in which the subject learns to behave in a certain way in order to avoid an unpleasant stimulus. (p. 71)

Avoidant disorder of childhood or adolescence. Disorder in which a child attempts to minimize anxiety by turning inward, withdrawing from others and the world. (p. 559)

Avoidant personality. A personality disorder characterized by hypersensitivity to rejection, limited social relationships, and low self-esteem. (p. 237)

"Bad trip." An unpleasant or traumatic experience while under the influence of a hallucinogenic drug, such as LSD.

Barbiturate. Type of commonly used synthetic sedative drug. (p. 427)

Baseline. In behavior therapy, the initial level of responses emitted by the individual.

Bedlam. Popular contraction of the name of the early London asylum of St. Mary of Bethlehem.

Behavioral assessment. A technique to determine the functional relationships between an individual's behavior and environmental stimuli.

Behavioral contract. Positive-reinforcement technique using a contract, often between family members, stipulating privileges and responsibilities. (p. 646)

Behavioral medicine. A rapidly developing discipline concerned with relations between physical health and the psychological aspects of individuals who have, or are at risk for, physical disease. (p. 273)

Behavioral sciences. The various interrelated disciplines, including psychology, sociology, and anthropology, that focus on human behavior.

Behavior control. Shaping and manipulation of behavior by drugs, persuasion, and other techniques.

Behavior disorder. Synonym for psychological problem.

Behaviorism. School of psychology that formerly restricted itself primarily to study of overt behavior. (p. 68)

Behavior modification. Techniques used to change specific behaviors. (p. 73)

Behavior therapy. Therapeutic procedures based primarily on application of principles of respondent and operant conditioning. (p. 640)

Benign. Of a mild, self-limiting nature; not malignant.

Beta waves. Brain waves having a frequency of 18 to 30 cycles per second and associated with problem solving and feelings of tension.

Biochemical disorders. Disorders involving disturbances in internal chemical regulation.

Biofeedback. Treatment technique by which individuals are taught to change and control internal bodily processes formerly thought to be involuntary (e.g., blood pressure and skin temperature); involves giving the individual immediate feedback about the bodily changes as they occur. (p. 648)

Biogenic amines. Chemicals that serve as neurotransmitters or modulators. (p. 106)

Biological clocks. The 24-hour rhythmic fluctuations in metabolic processes of plants and animals. Also called *circadian cycles.*

Biological viewpoint. An approach to mental disorders emphasizing biological causation. (p. 56)

Bipolar disorder. A manic or depressive episode believed to be a manifestation of an underlying condition predisposing the individual to severe mood swings; has largely replaced the term "manic-depressive psychosis." (p. 301)

Bisexual. A person sexually attracted to both females and males.

Blocking. Involuntary inhibition of recall, ideation, or communication (including sudden stoppage of speech).

Borderline personality. A personality disorder characterized by instability and drastic mood shifts; such individuals are impulsive and at times may appear psychotic. (p. 237)

Brain pathology. Diseased or disordered condition of the brain.

Brainwashing. Extreme form of thought modification and control.

Brain waves. Minute oscillations of electrical potential given off by neurons in the cerebral cortex and measured by the electroencephalograph.

Brief Psychiatric Rating Scale (BPRS). Objective method of rating clinical symptoms that provides scores on eighteen variables (e.g., somatic concern, anxiety, withdrawal, hostility, and bizarre thinking).

Brief psychotherapy. Short-term therapy, usually 8 to 10 sessions, focused upon restoring the individual's functioning and offering emotional support.

Cardiovascular. Pertaining to the heart and blood vessels.

Case study. Assessment information on a specific individual.

Castrating. Refers to any source of injury to or deprivation of the genitals, or more broadly, to a threat to the masculinity or feminity of the individual.

Catalepsy. A condition in which the muscles are waxy and semirigid, tending to maintain the limbs in any position in which they are placed.

Catatonic schizophrenia. Subtype marked by pronounced motor symptoms or stupor or extreme excitement. (p. 354)

Catecholamine. Class of amines sharing a similar chemical structure and involved chiefly in neural transmission.

Catharsis. Discharge of emotional tension associated with repressed traumatic material, e.g., by "talking it out."

CAT scan. See **Computerized axial tomography.**

Causal pattern. Several interacting factors operating together and on each other to cause a result. (p. 95)

Central nervous system (CNS). The brain and spinal cord.

Cerebral arteriosclerosis. Hardening of the arteries in the brain.

Cerebral concussion. Mild head injury that disrupts brain functions.

Cerebral contusion. Brain damage resulting from head injury severe enough to shift brain and compress it against skull.

Cerebral cortex. The surface layers of the cerebrum.

Cerebral hemorrhage. Bleeding into brain tissue from a ruptured blood vessel.

Cerebral laceration. Tearing of brain tissue associated with severe head injury.

Cerebral syphilis. Syphilitic infection of the brain.

Cerebral thrombosis. The formation of a clot or thrombus in the vascular system of the brain.

Cerebrovascular accident (CVA). Blockage or rupture of large blood vessel in brain leading to both focal and generalized impairment of brain function. Also called *stroke*. (p. 509)

Cerebrum. Main part of brain; divided into left and right hemispheres.

Character disorder. See **Personality disorder.**

Chemotherapy. Use of drugs in treatment of mental disorders.

Child abuse. The infliction of physical damage upon a child by parents or other adults.

Child advocacy. Movement concerned with protecting rights and ensuring well-being of children.

Childhood depression. An affective disorder occurring in children often in a masked form, e.g., as acting-out behavior.

Chlorpromazine. One of the major antipsychotic drugs.

Chorea. A pathological condition characterized by jerky, irregular, involuntary movements. See also **Huntington's chorea.**

Chromosomal anomalies. Inherited defects or vulnerabilities caused by irregularities in chromosomes. (p. 97)

Chromosomes. Chainlike structures within cell nucleus that contain genes.

Chronic. Referring to relatively permanent maladaptive pattern or condition. (p. 18)

Chronic schizophrenia. Schizophrenic pattern that develops gradually and tends to be long lasting; also called *process schizophrenia.* (p. 349)

Circadian rhythms. Regular biological cycle of sleep and activity characteristic of each species.

Civil commitment. Procedure whereby an individual certified as mentally disordered can be hospitalized, either voluntarily or against his will.

Classical (respondent) conditioning. Basic form of learning in which a previously neutral stimulus comes to elicit a given response. (p. 70)

Claustrophobia. Irrational fear of small enclosed places.

Client-centered (person-centered) psychotherapy. A nondirective approach to psychotherapy developed chiefly by Carl Rogers and based on his personality theory. (p. 656)

Climacteric. The life period associated with the menopause in women and various related glandular and bodily changes in men.

Clinical-nosological strategy. Approach to classifying behavior problems in which a descriptive class or category is arrived at by examining, through clinical study, the behaviors that appear to define that class. (p. 537)

Clinical picture. Diagnostic picture formed by observation of patient's behavior or by all available assessment data.

Clinical psychologist. Mental health professional with Ph.D. degree or Psy.D. degree in clinical psychology and clinical experience in assessment and psychotherapy. (p. 633)

Clinical psychology. Field of psychology concerned with the understanding, assessment, treatment, and prevention of maladaptive behavior. (p. 15)

Cocaine. A stimulating and pain-reducing psychoactive drug. (p. 431)

Cognition. The act, process, or product of knowing or perceiving.

Cognitive-behavior therapy. A treatment approach in which behavioral methods or learning principles are applied to thought processes (cognitions). (p. 650)

Cognitive derailment ("slippage"). The tendency for thoughts and associations not to follow one another in logical order; believed to be a basic characteristic of schizophrenic disorders.

Cognitive dissonance. Condition existing when new information is contradictory to one's assumptions. (p. 113)

Cognitive map. The network of assumptions that form the individual's "frame of reference" for interpreting and coping with his or her world. (p. 109)

Cognitive mediation. Thought processes in the individual that occur between the stimulus and the response. (p. 228)

Cognitive process (cognition). Mental processes, including perception, memory, and reasoning, by which one acquires knowledge, solves problems, and makes plans.

Cognitive restructuring therapy. A cognitive behavior therapy that aims to alter the individual's false or maladaptive frame of reference.

Collective unconscious. Term used by Carl Jung to refer to that portion of the unconscious which he considered common to all humanity.

Coma. Profound stupor with unconsciousness.

Community mental health. Application of psychosocial and sociocultural principles to the improvement of given environments.

Community psychology. Use of community resources in dealing with maladaptive behavior; tends to be more concerned with community intervention rather than with personal or individual change.

Complex. Group of emotionally toned attitudes, desires, or memories which are partially or totally repressed.

Compulsion. An irrational and repetitive impulse to perform some act. (p. 199)

Compulsive gambling. See **Pathological gambling.**

Compulsive personality. A personality disorder characterized by excessive concern with rules, order, efficiency, and work. (p. 237)

Computer assessment. Use of computers to obtain or interpret assessment data.

Computerized axial tomography (CAT scan). Radiological technique used to locate and assess extent of organic damage without surgery. (p. 586)

Computer model. Use of computer to simulate psychological functioning.

Concordance rates. Rates at which a diagnosis or a trait of one person is predictive of the same diagnosis or trait in relatives. (p. 102)

Concussion. See **Cerebral concussion.**

Conditioned reinforcer. A reinforcer that derives its value from basic unconditioned reinforcers.

Conditioning. Simple form of learning involving stimulus and response. (p. 69) See also **Classical Conditioning** and **Operant Conditioning.**

Conduct disorders. Childhood disorders marked by persistent acts of aggressive or antisocial behavior that may or may not be against the law. (p. 539)

Confabulation. The filling in of memory gaps with false and often irrelevant details. (p. 494)

Confidentiality. Commitment on part of professional person to keep information he or she obtains from a client confidential.

Conflict. Simultaneous arousal of opposing impulses, desires, or motives.

Congenital. Existing at birth or before birth but not necessarily hereditary.

Congenital defect. Genetic defect or environmental condition occurring prior to birth and causing a child to develop a physical or psychological anomaly. (p. 103)

Conscience. The functioning of an individual's system of moral values in the approval or disapproval of his or her own thoughts and actions. Roughly equivalent to Freudian concept of superego. (p. 63)

Consciousness. Awareness of inner and/or outer environment.

Constitution. The relatively constant biological makeup of the individual, resulting from the interaction of heredity and environment. (p. 102)

Consultation. A community intervention approach that aims at helping individuals at risk for disorder by working indirectly through caretaker institutions (e.g., police and teachers).

Contingency. Relationship, usually causal, between two events in which one is usually followed by the other.

Continuous reinforcement. Reward or reinforcement given regularly after each correct response.

Control group. A group of subjects compared with experimental group in assessing effects of independent variables. (p. 24)

Controlled drinking therapy. Behavioral treatment approach aimed at reducing the individual's drinking by self-control methods.

Conversion disorders. Neurotic condition in which symptoms of organic illness appear in the absence of any related organic pathology; previously called *hysteria*. (p. 212)

Convulsion. Pathological, involuntary, muscular contractions.

Corpus callosum. Nerve fibers that connect the two hemispheres of the brain.

Correlation. Relationship of variables to one another suggesting, but not establishing, a causal context. (p. 25)

Corticovisceral control mechanisms. Brain mechanisms that regulate autonomic and other bodily functions.

Counseling psychology. Field of psychology that focuses on helping persons with problems pertaining to education, marriage, or occupation.

Counterconditioning. Relearning by using a particular stimulus to establish a new (and generally more adaptive) response.

Countertransference. Arousal by the client of inappropriate feelings of transference on the part of the analyst during the course of psychoanalytic therapy. (p. 638)

Couple counseling. Treatment for disordered interpersonal relationships involving sessions with both members of the relationship present.

Coverants. Internal, private events, as thoughts and assumptions, to which conditioning principles are applied in cognitive-behavioral therapy. (p. 650)

Covert. Concealed, disguised, not directly observable.

Covert sensitization. A behavioral treatment method for extinguishing undesirable behavior by associating noxious mental images with that behavior.

Cretinism. Condition arising from thyroid deficiency in early life and marked by mental retardation and distinctive physical characteristics. (p. 524)

Criminal responsibility. Legal question of whether an individual should be permitted to use insanity as a defense after having committed some criminal act.

Crisis. Stress situation which approaches or exceeds adaptive capacities of individual or group. (p. 147)

Crisis intervention. Various methods for rendering therapeutic assistance to an individual or group during a period of crisis.

Critical period. Period of development during which organism most needs certain inputs or is most ready for acquisition of a given response. (p. 111)

Cultural-familial mental retardation. Mental retardation resulting from inherited limitation or lack of needed environmental stimulation, with no evidence of brain pathology. (p. 526)

Cultural lag. The tendency for formal conceptions of reality and "appropriate" behavior within a given culture to change more slowly than the actual thinking and actions of a society's members. (p. 150)

Cushing's syndrome. An endocrine disorder resulting from oversecretion of *cortisone* and marked by mood swings, irritability, and other mental symptoms.

Cyclothymic disorder. Mild affective disorder characterized by extreme mood swings of nonpsychotic intensity. (p. 304)

Day hospital. A community-based mental hospital where the patients are treated during the day, returning to their homes at night. (p. 681)

Decompensation. Ego or personality disorganization under excessive stress. (p. 153)

Defense mechanism. See **Ego-defense mechanism.**

Defense-oriented reaction. Reaction involving one's feelings of adequacy and worth rather than objective handling of the stress situation. (p. 150)

Deficiency motivation. Motivation directed primarily toward maintaining or restoring physiological or psychological equilibrium rather than toward personal growth. (p. 117)

Deinstitutionalization. Movement to provide chronic patients with continued psychiatric care in the local community rather than committing them to institutions. (p. 689)

Delinquency. Antisocial or illegal behavior by a minor. (p. 546)

Delirium. State of mental confusion characterized by clouding of consciousness, disorientation, restlessness, excitement, and often hallucinations. (p. 493)

Delirium tremens. Acute delirium associated with prolonged alcoholism; characterized by intense anxiety, tremors, and hallucinations. (p. 405)

Delusion. Firm belief opposed to reality but maintained in spite of strong evidence to the contrary.

Delusion of persecution. False belief that one is being mistreated or interfered with by one's enemies. Often found in schizophrenia.

Delusion system. An internally coherent, systematized pattern of delusions.

Dementia. Severe mental disorder involving impairment of mental ability; not congenital. (p. 494)

Dementia praecox. Older term for schizophrenia. (p. 344)

Demonology. Viewpoint emphasizing supernatural causation of mental disorder, especially "possession" by evil spirits or forces.

Denial of reality. Ego-defense mechanism by means of which the individual protects himself or herself from unpleasant aspects of reality by refusing to acknowledge them. (p. 64)

Dependency. The tendency to rely overly upon others.

Dependent personality. A personality disorder marked by lack of self-confidence and feelings of acute panic or discomfort at having to be alone. (p. 237)

Dependent variable. In an experiment, the factor which the hypothesis predicts will change with changes in the independent variable.

Depersonalization. Loss of sense of personal identity, often with a feeling of being something or someone else.

Depersonalization disorder. A dissociative neurotic disorder, usually occurring in adolescence, in which individuals lose their sense of self and feel unreal or displaced to a different location. (p. 222)

Depression. Emotional state characterized by extreme dejection, gloomy ruminations, feelings of worthlessness, loss of hope, and often apprehension.

Depressive disorder. Neurotic reaction characterized by persistent dejection and discouragement.

Depressive neurosis. Depression of intermediate severity with little or no evidence of personality breakdown or loss of contact with reality. (p. 301)

Depressive stupor. Extreme degree of depression characterized by marked psychomotor underactivity.

Desensitization. Therapeutic process by means of which reactions to traumatic experiences are reduced in intensity by repeatedly exposing the individual to them in mild form, either in reality or in fantasy. (p. 642)

Deterrence. The premise that punishment for criminal offenses will deter that criminal and others from future criminal acts.

Detox. A center or facility for receiving and detoxifying alcohol- or drug-intoxicated individuals.

Detoxification. Treatment directed toward ridding the body of alcohol or other drugs.

Developmental task. A competency that is considered essential to master during a particular life period, e.g., learning to talk during infancy.

Deviant behavior. Behavior which deviates markedly from the average or norm.

Dexedrine. An amphetamine drug; a stimulant used to curb appetite or elevate mood.

Diagnosis. Determination of the nature and extent of a specific disorder.

Diathesis. A predisposition or vulnerability toward developing a given disorder. (p. 96)

Diathesis-stress model. View of abnormal behavior as the result of stress operating on an individual with a biological, psychosocial, or sociocultural predisposition toward developing a specific disorder. (p. 96)

Differential reinforcement of other behavior (DOR). Behavior modification technique for extinguishing undesirable behavior by reinforcing incompatible behaviors.

Dilantin. An anti-convulsant medication often used in controlling epileptic seizures.

Directive therapy. Type of therapeutic approach in which the therapist supplies direct answers to problems and takes much of the responsibility for the progression of therapy.

Discrimination. Learning to interpret and respond differently to two or more similar stimuli. (p. 71)

Diseases of adaptation. Stomach ulcers and other disease conditions resulting from the stresses of life.

Disintegration. Loss of organization or integration in any organized system. (p. 154)

Disorganization. Severely impaired integration.

Disorganized schizophrenia. Subtype representing most severe disintegration of personality and poor prognosis for recovery; characterized by marked incoherence, silly or inappropriate responses. (p. 354)

Disorientation. Mental confusion with respect to time, place, or person.

Displacement. Ego-defense mechanism in which an emotional attitude or symbolic meaning is transferred from one object or concept to another. (p. 64)

Dissociation. Separation or "isolation" of mental processes in such a way that they become split off from the main personality or lose their normal thought-affect relationships.

Dissociative disorder. Psychoneurotic disorder characterized by amnesia, fugue, somnambulism, or multiple personality. (p. 217)

Distress. Negative stress. (p. 142)

Dizygotic (fraternal) twins. Twins that develop from two separate eggs.

DNA. Deoxyribonucleic acid, principal component of genes.

Dominant gene. A gene whose hereditary characteristics prevail in the offspring. (p. 101)

Dopamine. A catecholamine neural transmitter substance.

Double-approach conflict. Type of conflict in which individual is confronted with choosing between two or more desirable alternatives.

Double-avoidant conflict. Type of conflict in which individual is confronted with choosing between two or more aversive alternatives.

Double-bind. Situation in which an individual will be disapproved for performing a given act and equally disapproved if he or she does not perform it. (p. 375)

Down's syndrome. Form of mental retardation associated with chromosomal anomalies. (p. 98)

Dramatization. A defense against anxiety in which the individual engages in attention-getting behavior and self-dramatization. (p. 88)

Dream analysis. Psychotherapeutic technique involving the interpretation of the patient's dreams.

Drive. Internal conditions directing organism toward a specific goal, usually involving biological rather than psychological motives.

Drug abuse. Use of a drug to extent that it interferes with health and/or occupational or social adjustment.

Drug addiction (dependence). Physiological and/or psychological dependence on a drug.

Drug therapy. See **Chemotherapy, Pharmacotherapy.**

DSM-III. Current diagnostic manual of the American Psychiatric Association.

Dual personality. See **Multiple personality.**

Dwarfism. A condition of arrested growth and very short stature.

Dyad. A two-person group.

Dynamic formulation. An integrated evaluation of a patient's traits, attitudes, conflicts, and symptoms that attempts to explain the individual's problem. (p. 585)

Dysfunction. Impairment or disturbance in the functioning of an organ.

Dyslexia. Impairment of the ability to read.

Dyspareunia. Painful coitus in male or female. (p. 452)

Dysrythmias. Abnormal brain-wave patterns. (p. 586)

Dysthymic disorder. Moderately severe affective disorder characterized by extended periods of nonpsychotic depression and brief periods of normal moods. (p. 305)

Echolalia. Meaningless repetition of words by an individual, usually of whatever has been said to that person. (p. 357)

Echopraxia. Repetition of another person's actions or gestures. (p. 357)

Ecology. Relation or interaction between organisms and their physical environment.

Economy, principle of. Theory that the individual meets stress in the simplest way possible. (p. 149)

EEG. See **Electroencephalogram.** (p. 586)

Ego. In psychoanalytic theory, the rational subsystem of the personality which mediates between id and superego demands and reality. More generally, the individual's self-concept. (p. 63)

Egocentric. Preoccupied with one's own concerns and relatively insensitive to the concerns of others.

Ego-defense mechanism (reaction). Type of reaction designed to maintain the individual's feelings of adequacy and worth rather than to cope directly with the stress situation; usually unconscious and reality distorting. (p. 63)

Ego-dystonic homosexuality. Category of "mental disorder" in which individual wishes to change his or her homosexual orientation. (p. 477)

Ego-ideal (self-ideal). The person or "self" the individual thinks he or she could and should be. (p. 110)

Ego involvement. Perception of a situation in terms of its importance to the individual.

Ejaculatory incompetence. A male's inability to ejaculate.

Electra complex. In psychoanalytic theory, an excessive emotional attachment (love) of a daughter for her father. (p. 65)

Electroconvulsive therapy (ECT). Use of electricity to produce convulsions and unconsciousness; also called *electroshock therapy.* (p. 611)

Electroencephalogram (EEG) A recording of the brain waves by an electroencephalograph. (p. 586)

Electrotherapy. Methods of therapy which involve the influence of electric current on the central nervous system.

Embolism. Lodgment of a blood clot in a blood vessel too small to permit its passage.

Emotion. A strong feeling accompanied by physiological changes. (p. 150)

Emotional disturbance. Psychological disorder.

Emotional inoculation. Therapeutic procedures designed to prepare persons who face stress situations, such as surgery, by providing such persons with adaptive techniques.

Emotional insulation. Ego-defense mechanism in which the individual reduces the tensions of need and anxiety by withdrawing into a shell of passivity. (p. 65)

Empathy. Ability to understand and to some extent share the state of mind of another person.

Encephalitis. Inflammation of the brain.

Encopresis. Disorder defined by having bowel movements in one's clothing after the age of 3. (p. 570)

Encounter. Term applied to the interaction between client and therapist (in existential therapy) or between patients (in encounter-group therapy).

Encounter group. Small group designed to provide an intensive interpersonal experience focusing on feelings and group interactions; used in therapy or to promote personal growth.

Endocrine glands. Ductless glands which secrete hormones directly into the lymph or bloodstream.

Endogenous factors. Factors originating within the organism that affect behavior.

Endorphins. Opium-like substances produced in the brain and pituitary gland in response to stimulation; thought to be neurotransmitters. (p. 425)

Energizer. Drug which has a stimulating effect.

Engram. Hypothesized physiological change in nervous system thought to be responsible for memory.

Entrophy. Deterioration and eventual disintegration or death of a living system.

Enuresis. Bed-wetting; involuntary discharge of urine. (p. 567)

Environmental psychology. Field of psychology focusing on the effects of environmental setting on an individual's feelings and behavior.

Enzyme. Catalyst regulating metabolic activities.

Epidemiology. Study of the distribution of physical or mental disorders in a population. (p. 90)

Epilepsy. Group of disorders varying from momentary lapses of consciousness to generalized convulsions.

Epinephrine. Hormone secreted by the adrenal medulla; also called **adrenaline**.

Episodic. Term to describe a disorder that tends to abate and to recur. (p. 18)

Equilibrium. Steady state; balance.

Erectile insufficiency. Inability of male to achieve erection. (p. 451)

Erotic. Pertaining to sexual stimulation and gratification.

Escape learning. Conditioned response in which the subject learns to terminate or escape an aversive stimulus.

Essence. Existential term referring to the fact that one's existence is given but what is made of it is up to the individual and becomes that person's essence.

Essential hypertension. High blood pressure, presumably of a psychological or emotional origin.

Estrogens. Female hormones produced by the ovaries.

Ethnic group. Group of people who are treated as distinctive in terms of culture and group patterns.

Ethnocentrism. Belief that one's own country and race are superior to other countries and races.

Etiology. Causation; the systematic study of the causes of disorders. (p. 94)

Eugenics. The application of methods of selective breeding of human beings with the intent of improving the species.

Euphoria. Exaggerated feeling of well-being and contentment.

Eustress. Positive stress. (p. 142)

Exacerbate. Intensify.

Excitation. Process whereby activity is elicited in a nerve.

Exhaustion and disintegration. Third and final stage in the general adaptation syndrome, in which the organism is no longer able to resist continuing stress; at the biological level may result in death. (p. 154)

Exhibitionism. Public display or exposure of genitals for conscious or unconscious purpose of sexual excitement and pleasure. (p. 464)

Existential anxiety. Anxiety concerning one's ability to find a satisfying and fulfilling way of life.

Existentialism. A view of human beings that emphasizes the individual's responsibility for becoming the kind of person he or she should be. (p. 77)

Existential neurosis. Disorder characterized by feelings of alienation, meaninglessness, and apathy.

Existential therapy. Therapy based on existential concepts, emphasizing the development of a sense of self-direction and meaning in one's existence. (p. 659)

Exogenous. Originating from or due to external causes.

Exorcism. A religiously inspired treatment procedure designed to drive out evil spirits or forces from a "possessed" person.

Expanded consciousness. Sensation caused by psychedelic drugs or meditation in which individual feels the mind is opened to new types of experience.

Experimental group. Group of subjects used to assess effects of independent variables. (p. 24)

Experimental method. Rigorous scientific procedure by which hypotheses are tested. (p. 25)

Experimental neurosis. Neurotic behavior produced in animals by inescapable conflicts and other types of stress.

Extinction. Gradual disappearance of conditioned response when it is no longer reinforced. (p. 71)

Extrapunitive. Characterized by a tendency to evaluate the source of frustrations as external and to direct hostility outward.

Extraversion. Personality type oriented toward the outer world of people and things rather than concepts and intellectual concerns.

Fabrication. Relating imaginary events as if they were true without intent to deceive; confabulation.

Factor analysis. Statistical technique used in identifying and measuring the relative importance of the underlying variables, or factors, which contribute to a complex ability, trait, or form of behavior. (p. 596)

Fading. A technique whereby a stimulus causing some reaction is gradually replaced by a previously neutral stimulus, such that the latter acquires the property of producing the reaction in question.

Familial. Pertaining to characteristics which tend to run in families and have a higher incidence in certain families than in the general population.

Family therapy. Form of interpersonal therapy focusing on relationships within the family.

Fantasy. Daydream; also, an ego-defense mechanism by means of which the individual escapes from the world of reality and gratifies his desires in fantasy achievements. (p. 64)

Faulty genes. Genes containing information that is inimical to healthy development or functioning. (p. 98)

Feedback. Explicit information pertaining to internal physiological processes or to the social consequences of one's overt behavior. (p. 95)

Fetal alcohol syndrome. Observed pattern in infants of alcoholic mothers in which there is a characteristic facial or limb irregularity, low body weight, and behavioral abnormality.

Fetishism. Maladaptive sexual deviation in which an individual achieves sexual gratification by means of some inanimate object or nonsexual part of the body. (p. 462)

Fetus. Embryo after the sixth week following conception.

Field properties. Characteristics of the environment surrounding a living system.

Fixation. Unreasonable or exaggerated attachment to some person or arresting of emotional development on a childhood or adolescent level. (p. 64)

Fixed-interval schedule. Schedule of reinforcement based on fixed period of time after previous reinforced response.

Fixed-ratio schedule. Schedule of reinforcement based on reinforcement after fixed number of nonreinforced responses.

Flashback. The recurrence of a drug experience, usually in a negative manner, without further ingestion of the drug. (p. 434)

Flooding. Anxiety-eliciting technique involving placing the client in a real-life, anxiety-arousing situation. (p. 641)

Folie à deux. A psychotic interpersonal relationship involving two people; e.g., husband and wife both become psychotic with similar or complementary symptomatology. (p. 388)

Follow-up study. Research procedure in which individuals are studied over a period of time or are recontacted at a later time after initial study.

Forcible rape. Act of violence in which sexual relations are forced upon an unwilling partner who is over the age of 18. (p. 474)

Forensic psychiatry. Branch of psychiatry dealing with legal problems relating to mental disorders.

Fraternal twins. Dizygotic twins; fertilized by separate germ cells, thus not having same genetic inheritance. May be of the same or opposite sex.

Free association. Psychoanalytic procedure for probing the unconscious in which individual gives a running account of his every thought and feeling. (p. 62)

Free-floating anxiety. Anxiety not referable to any specific situation or cause.

Frigidity. Inability to experience sexual pleasure or orgasm on the part of the female. Now called *arousal insufficiency* or *orgasmic dysfunction*. (p. 452)

Frontal lobe. Portion of the brain active in reasoning and other higher thought processes.

Frustration. Thwarting of a need or desire.

Frustration tolerance. See **Stress tolerance.**

Fugue. Neurotic dissociative disorder; entails loss of memory accompanied by actual physical flight from one's present life situation to a new environment or less threatening former one. (p. 218)

Functional psychoses. Severe mental disorders attributed primarily to psychological stress.

Furor. Transitory outbursts of excitement or anger during which the individual may be quite dangerous.

Future shock. Condition brought about when social change proceeds so rapidly that the individual cannot cope with it adequately.

Gambling. Wagering on games or events in which chance largely determines the outcome. (p. 442)

Gay. Synonym for "homosexual."

Gender identity. Individual's identification as being male or female.

Gender identity disorder (Transsexualism). Identification of oneself with members of the opposite sex, as opposed to acceptance of one's anatomical sexual identity. (p. 458)

General adaptation syndrome. Reaction of the individual to excessive stress; consists of the alarm reaction, the stage of resistance, and the stage of exhaustion. (p. 154)

Generalization. Tendency of a response that has been conditioned to one stimulus to become associated with other similar stimuli. (p. 71)

Generalized anxiety disorder. Chronic diffuse anxiety and apprehension, possibly punctuated by acute anxiety attacks, stemming from no specific, identifiable threat. (p. 195)

Generalized reinforcer. Reinforcer such as money which may influence a wide range of stimuli and behaviors.

General paresis. Mental disorder associated with syphilis of the brain.

General systems theory. A comprehensive theoretical model embracing all living systems.

Genes. Ultramicroscopic areas of DNA which are responsible for transmission of hereditary traits. (p. 101)

Genetic code. Means by which DNA controls the sequence and structure of proteins manufactured within each cell and also makes exact duplicates of itself.

Genetic counseling. Counseling prospective parents concerning the probability of their having defective offspring as a result of genetic defects.

Genetic inheritance. Potential for development and behavior determined at conception by egg and sperm cells (p. 97).

Genetics. Science of heredity.

Genitalia. Organs of reproduction, especially the external organs.

Genital stage. In psychoanalytic theory, the final stage of psychosexual development involving shift from autoeroticism to heterosexual interest. (p. 64)

Genotype. Genetic characteristics inherited by an individual.

Geriatrics. Science of the diseases and treatment of the aged.

Germ cells. Reproductive cells (female ovum and male sperm) which unite to produce a new individual.

Gerontology. Science dealing with the study of old age.

Gestalt psychology. School of psychology which emphasizes patterns rather than elements or connections, taking the view that the whole is more than the sum of its parts.

Gestalt therapy. Type of psychotherapy emphasizing wholeness of the person and integration of thought, feeling, and action. (p. 660)

Gigantism. Abnormally tall stature resulting from hyperfunctioning of the pituitary.

Glucocorticoids. Adrenocortical hormones involved in sugar metabolism but also having widespread effects on injury-repair mechanisms and resistance to disease; they include hydrocortisone, corticosterone, and cortisone.

Gonads. The sex glands.

Good premorbid schizophrenia. See **Reactive schizophrenia.**

Grand mal epilepsy. Type of epilepsy characterized by generalized convulsive seizures.

Grief work. Necessary period of mourning for an individual to assimilate personal loss into the self-structure and view it as an event of the past.

Group therapy. Psychotherapy with two or more individuals at the same time.

Growth motivation. Motivation directed toward higher-level needs for self-actualization. (p. 117)

Guilt. Feelings of culpability arising from behavior or desires contrary to one's ethical principles. Involves both self-devaluation and apprehension growing out of fears of punishment.

Habit. Any product of learning, whether it is a customary or transitory mode of response.

Habituation. Process whereby an individual's response to the same stimulus lessens with repeated presentations.

Halfway house. Facility which provides aftercare following institutionalization, seeking to ease the individual's adjustment to the community. (p. 681)

Hallucination. Sense perception for which there is no appropriate external stimulus.

Hallucinogens. Drugs or chemicals capable of producing hallucinations. (p. 432)

Hallucinosis. Persistent hallucinations in the presence of known or suspected organic brain pathology. (p. 494)

Hashish. The strongest drug derived from the hemp plant; a relative of marijuana. (p. 435)

Health psychology. Subspecialty within the behavioral-medicine approach that deals with psychology's contributions to diagnosis, treatment, and prevention of behaviorally caused physical illnesses. (p. 273)

Hebephrenic schizophrenia. Type of schizophrenia characterized by severe personality decompensation or disintegration. (p. 354)

Hemiplegia. Paralysis of one lateral half of the body.

Hemophobia. Pathological fear of blood. Also called *hematophobia*.

Heredity. Genetic transmission of characteristics from parents to their children.

Hermaphroditism. Anatomical sexual abnormality in which an individual has sex organs of both sexes.

Heterosexuality. Sexual interest in a member of the opposite sex.

Hierarchy of needs. The concept that needs arrange themselves in a hierarchy in terms of importance or "prepotence," from the most basic biological needs to those psychological needs concerned with self-actualization.

High-risk. Individuals showing great vulnerability to physical or mental disorders. (p. 90)

Histrionic personality. Personality pattern characterized by excitability, emotional instability, and self-dramatization. (p. 237)

Holistic. A systematic approach to science involving the study of the whole or total configuration; the view of human beings as unified psychobiological organisms inextricably immersed in a physical and sociocultural environment. (p. 148)

Homeostasis. Tendency of organisms to maintain conditions making possible a constant level of physiological functioning. (p. 106)

Homosexuality. Sexual preference for member of one's own sex. (p. 477)

Hormones. Chemicals released by the endocrine glands that regulate development of and activity in various bodily organs.

Hostility. Emotional reaction or drive toward the destruction or damage of an object interpreted as a source of frustration or threat.

Humanistic-existential therapy. Type of psychotherapy emphasizing personal growth and self-direction. (p. 656)

Human potential movement. Movement concerned with enrichment of experience, increased sensory awareness, and fulfillment of human potentials.

Huntington's chorea. Incurable disease, presumably of hereditary origin, which is manifested in jerking, twitching movements and mental deterioration.

Hydrocephalus. Organic condition associated with brain damage and mental retardation. (p. 525)

Hydrotherapy. Use of hot or cold baths, ice packs, etc., in treatment.

Hyper-. Prefix meaning *increased* or *excessive*.

Hyperkinetic (hyperactive) reaction. Disorder of childhood characterized by overactivity, restlessness, and distractibility.

Hyperobesity. Extreme overweight; more than 100 pounds over ideal body weight. (p. 438)

Hypertension. High blood pressure. (p. 284)

Hyperventilation. Rapid breathing associated with intense anxiety.

Hypesthesia. Partial loss of sensitivity.

Hypnosis. Trancelike mental state induced in a cooperative subject by suggestion.

Hypnotherapy. Use of hypnosis in psychotherapy.

Hypnotic regression. Process by which a subject is brought to relive, under hypnosis, early forgotten or repressed experiences.

Hypo-. Prefix meaning *decreased* or *insufficient*.

Hypochondriacal delusions. Delusions concerning various horrible disease conditions, such as the belief that one's brain is turning to dust.

Hypochondriasis. Condition dominated by preoccupation with bodily processes and fear of presumed diseases. (p. 207)

Hypomania. Mild form of manic reaction, characterized by moderate psychomotor activity.

Hypothalamus. Key structure at the base of the brain; important in emotion and motivation.

Hypothesis. Statement or proposition, usually based on observation, which is tested in an experiment; may be denied or supported by experimental results but never conclusively proved. (p. 23)

Hysteria. Older term used to include conversion disorders; involves the appearance of symptoms of organic illness in the absence of any related organic pathology.

Hysterical disorder. Disorder characterized by involuntary psychogenic dysfunction of motor, sensory, or visceral processes.

ICD-9. See **International Classification of Diseases.**

Id. In psychoanalytic terminology, the reservoir of instinctual drives; the most inaccessible and primitive stratum of the mind. (p. 62)

Identical twins. Monozygotic twins; developed from a single fertilized egg.

Identification. Ego-defense mechanism in which the individual identifies himself or herself with some person or institution, usually of an illustrious nature. (p. 65)

Ideology. System of beliefs.

Idiot. Older term referring to severe and profound degrees of mental retardation (IQ below 25).

Idiot savant. A mental retardate who can perform unusual mental feats, usually involving music or manipulation of numbers.

Illusion. Misinterpretation of sensory data; false perception.

Imipramine. Antidepressant medication.

Immaturity. Pattern of childhood maladaptive behaviors suggesting lack of adaptive skills. (p. 539)

Implosive therapy. Type of behavior therapy in which desensitization is achieved by eliciting, through the imagination, a massive implosion of anxiety. (p. 641)

Impotence. Inability of male to achieve erection. (p. 451)

Incentive. External inducement to behave in a certain way.

Incest. Sexual relations between close relatives such as father and daughter or brother and sister. (p. 471)

Independent variable. Factor whose effects are being examined in an experiment; it is manipulated in some way while the other variables are held constant.

Index case. In a genetic study, the individual who evidences the trait in which the investigator is interested. Same as *proband*. (p. 102)

Infantile autism. Disorder manifested at birth characterized by inability of child to relate to others or to form a normal relationship to reality. (p. 562)

Inferiority complex. Strong feelings of inadequacy and insecurity which color an individual's entire adjustive efforts.

Inhibition. Conscious restraint of impulse or desire.

Innate. Inborn.

Inner controls. Reality, value, and possibility assumptions which serve to inhibit dangerous or undesirable behavior; could also apply to conditioned avoidance reactions. (p. 110)

Inpatient. Hospitalized patient.

Insanity. Legal term for mental disorder, implying lack of responsibility for one's acts and inability to manage one's affairs.

Insanity defense. "Innocent by reason of insanity" plea used as a legal defense in criminal trials. (p. 687)

Insight. Clinically, the individual's understanding of his or her illness or of the motivations underlying a behavior pattern; in general psychology, the sudden grasp or understanding of meaningful relationships in a situation.

Insight therapy. Type of psychotherapy focusing on helping the patient achieve greater self-understanding with respect to his or her motives, values, coping patterns, and so on.

Insomnia. Difficulty in sleeping.

Inspectionalism. See **Voyeurism.**

Instinct. Inborn tendency to particular behavior patterns under certain conditions in absence of learning; characteristic of species.

Instrumental act. Act directed toward achieving specific goals and meeting needs.

Instrumental (operant) conditioning. Type of conditioning in which the subject is reinforced for making a predetermined response, such as pressing a lever. (p. 70)

Insulin coma therapy. Rarely used physiological treatment for schizophrenia in which the patient receives insulin injections until he or she goes into a coma. (p. 610)

Integration. Organization of parts (psychological, biological functions) to make a functional whole.

Integrative properties. Tendency of living systems to maintain their organization and functional integrity.

Integrity. Quality of being unified and honest with self and others.

Intellectualization. Ego-defense mechanism by which the individual achieves some measure of insulation from emotional hurt by cutting off or distorting the emotional charge which normally accompanies hurtful situations. (p. 65)

Intelligence. Pertaining to ability to learn, reason, and adapt.

Intelligence quotient (IQ). Measurement of "intelligence" expressed as a number or position on a scale. Comparable to term *intellectual level*.

Interdisciplinary (multidisciplinary) approach. Integration of various scientific disciplines in understanding, assessing, treating, and preventing mental disorders. (p. 91)

Intermittent reinforcement. Reinforcement given intermittently rather than after every response.

International Classification of Diseases (ICD-9). System of classification of disorders published by the World Health Organization.

Interpersonal accommodation. A reciprocal process of give and take meant to promote satisfactory interpersonal relationships.

Intrapsychic conflict. Psychoanalytic concept referring to conflict between id, ego, and superego. (p. 63)

Introjection. Incorporation of qualities or values of another person or group into one's own ego structure with a tendency to identify with them and to be affected by what happens to them. (p. 66)

Intromission. Insertion of the penis into the vagina or anus.

Intropunitive. Responding to frustration by tending to blame oneself.

Introspection. Observing (and often reporting on) one's inner experiencing.

Introversion. Direction of interest toward one's inner world of experience and toward concepts rather than external events and objects.

In vivo. Taking place in a real-life situation as opposed to the therapeutic or laboratory setting. (p. 641)

Involutional melancholia (involutional psychotic reaction). Depressive psychotic reaction characterized by depression, agitation, and apprehension.

Ionizing radiation. Form of radiation; major cause of gene mutations.

Isolation. Ego-defense mechanism by means of which contradictory attitudes or feelings which normally accompany particular attitudes are kept apart, thus preventing conflict or hurt.

Jejunal bypass operation. A surgical treatment for extreme obesity which involves disconnecting and bypassing a large portion of the small intestine.

Juvenile delinquency. Legally prohibited behavior committed by minors. (p. 546)

Juvenile paresis. General paresis in children, usually of congenital origin.

Klinefelter's syndrome. Type of mental retardation associated with sex chromosome anomaly.

Korsakoff's psychosis. Psychosis usually associated with chronic alcoholism and characterized by disorientation, gross memory defects, and confabulation. (p. 407)

Labeling. Assigning an individual to a particular diagnostic category, such as schizophrenia.

Lability. Instability, particularly with regard to affect.

Latency stage. In psychoanalytic theory, stage of psychosexual development during which sexual motivations recede in importance and child is preoccupied with developing skills and other activities. (p. 64)

Latent. Inactive or dormant.

Latent content. In psychoanalytic theory, repressed wishes indirectly expressed in the manifest content of dreams. (p. 637)

Latent learning. Learning that becomes evident only after an incentive is introduced.

Law of effect. Principle that responses that have rewarding consequences are strengthened and those that have aversive consequences are weakened or eliminated.

Learning. Modification of behavior as a consequence of experience. (p. 70)

Lesbian. Female homosexual.

Lesion. Anatomically localized area of tissue pathology in an organ.

Lethality scale. Criteria used to assess the likelihood of an individual's committing suicide.

Level of aspiration. Standard by which the individual judges success or failure of his or her behavior. (p. 117)

Libido. In general psychoanalytic terminology, the instinctual drives of the id. In a narrow sense, the drive for sexual gratification. (p. 62)

Life crisis. Stress situation that approaches or exceeds the individual's adjustive capacity.

Life history method. Technique of psychological observation in which the development of particular forms of behavior is traced by means of records of the subject's past or present behavior.

Life-style. The general pattern of assumptions, motives, cognitive styles, and coping techniques that characterize the behavior of a given individual and give it consistency. (p. 110)

Lobotomy. Drastic form of psychosurgery rarely used at present. It involves cutting the nerve fibers that connect the frontal lobes to limbic system.

Locomotor ataxia. Muscular incoordination usually resulting from syphilitic damage to the spinal-cord pathways.

Logic-tight compartments. Form of intellectualization in which contradictory desires or attitudes are "sealed off" in separate areas of consciousness.

Lunacy. Old term roughly synonymous with insanity.

Lycanthropy. The delusion of being a wolf. (p. 37)

Lysergic acid diethylamide-25 (LSD). A potent hallucinogen. (p. 432)

Macrocephalic. Having an abnormally large cranium. (p. 525)

Madness. Nontechnical synonym for severe mental disorder.

Mainstreaming. Placement of mentally retarded children in regular school classrooms to avoid certain negative effects of "special education." (p. 531)

Maintaining cause. Environmental reinforcers or contingencies that tend to maintain maladaptive behavior.

Maintenance strivings. Strivings directed toward maintenance of physiological and psychological equilibrium and integration.

Major affective disorders. Category of affective disorders in which a biological defect or other aberration renders a person liable to experience episodes of a more or less severe affective disorder. (p. 307)

Major depression (Unipolar disorder). A severe affective disorder in which only depressive episodes occur. (p. 301)

Major tranquilizers. Antipsychotic drugs, such as the phenothiazines.

Maladaptive (abnormal) behavior. Behavior which is detrimental to well-being of the individual and/or group.

Maladjustment. A more or less enduring failure of adjustment; lack of harmony with self or environment.

Malinger. To fake illness or disability symptoms consciously. (p. 216)

Malleus Malleficarum. Infamous handbook prepared by two monks dealing with the "diagnosis" and "treatment" of witches and witchcraft.

-mania. Suffix denoting a compulsive or morbid preoccupation with some impulse or activity; e.g., compulsive stealing is called klepto*mania*.

Manic-depressive psychoses. Older term denoting a group of psychotic disorders characterized by prolonged periods of excitement and overactivity (mania) or by periods of depression and underactivity (depression) or by alternation of the two. (p. 309)

Manifest content. In psychoanalytic theory, the apparent meaning of a dream; masks the latent content. (p. 636)

Marathon encounter group. Intensive group experience lasting for 2 or more days with only brief breaks for sleep.

Marijuana. Drug derived from the plant *cannabis indica*; often used in cigarettes called "reefers" or "joints." (p. 435)

Marital schism. Marriage characterized by severe chronic discord which threatens continuation of marital relationship. (p. 129)

Marital skew. Marriage maintained at expense of distorted relationship. (p. 129)

Marital therapy. Therapy directed toward improving communication and interaction between marital partners.

Masked deprivation. Rejection of child by mother; does not involve separation.

Masked disorder. "Masking" of underlying depression or other emotional disturbance by delinquent behavior or other patterns seemingly unrelated to the basic disturbance.

Masochism. Sexual variant in which an individual obtains sexual gratification through infliction of pain. (p. 468)

Mass hysteria. Group outbreak of hysterical reactions.

Masturbation. Self-stimulation of genitals for sexual gratification.

Maternal deprivation. Lack of adequate care and stimulation by the mother or mother surrogate.

Maturation. Process of development and body change resulting from heredity rather than learning. (p. 111)

Medical model. The view of disordered behavior as a symptom of a more basic process, rather than a pattern representing faulty learning. Also associated with approaches to disorder that involve medical ideology, procedures, and rituals—such as the "white coat."

Megalomania. Delusions of grandeur.

Melancoholia. A subset of major depression marked by several symptoms; formerly, a mental disorder characterized by severe depression. (p. 309)

Meninges. Membranes which envelop the brain and spinal cord.

Mental age (MA). A scale unit indicating level of intelligence in relation to chronological age.

Mental deficiency. Synonym for mental retardation; the latter term is now preferred.

Mental disorder. Entire range of abnormal behavior patterns.

Mental illness. Once used synonymously with mental disorder but now ordinarily restricted to psychoses.

Mental retardation. Below-normal intelligence, usually meaning an IQ below 68. (p. 489)

Mescaline. One of the hallucinogenic drugs. (p. 432)

Mesmerism. Theories of "animal magnetism" (hypnosis) formulated by Anton Mesmer.

Methadone. An orally administered narcotic which replaces the craving for heroin and weans the individual from heroin addiction.

Microcephaly. Form of mental retardation characterized by abnormally small cranium and retarded development of brain. (p. 525)

Micturate, micturition. Pertaining to urination.

Migraine headache. Type of psychosomatic disorder characterized by recurrent headaches, usually on one side of head only, and associated with emotional tension.

Mild disorder. Disorder of a low order of severity. (p. 18)

Milieu. The immediate environment, physical or social or both; sometimes used to include the internal state of an organism. (p. 678)

Minimal brain dysfunction (MBD). Controversial term referring to various "soft" neurological signs presumably indicative of malfunctioning of brain. (p. 543)

Minnesota Multiphasic Personality Inventory (MMPI). A widely used and empirically validated personality scale. (p. 595)

Minor tranquilizers. Antianxiety drugs such as the meprobramates and benzodiazepines.

Model. An analogy that helps a scientist order findings and see important relationships among them.

Modeling. Form of learning in which individual learns by watching someone else (the model) perform the desired response. (p. 72)

Model psychoses. Psychoticlike states produced by various hallucinogenic drugs such as LSD.

Moderate disorder. Disorder of an intermediate order of severity. (p. 18)

Modus operandi. Manner or mode of behavior; a criminal's typical pattern of performing crimes.

Mongolism. See **Down's syndrome.**

Monozygotic twins. Identical twins, developed from one fertilized egg.

Moral nihilism. Doctrine which denies any objective or real ground for moral beliefs, and holds that the individual is not bound by obligation to others or society.

Moral therapy. Therapy based on provision of kindness, understanding, and favorable environment; prevalent during early part of 19th century.

Morbid. Unhealthy, pathological.

Morita therapy. Treatment of neuroses involving deprivation of external stimulation and other procedures.

Moron. Term formerly used to refer to mild degrees of mental retardation.

Morphine. Addictive opiate drug.

Motivation. Often used as synonym for drive or activation; implies that the organism's actions are partly determined in direction and strength by its own inner nature.

Motivational selectivity. Influence of motives on perception and other cognitive processes.

Motive. Internal condition which directs action toward some goal; term usually used to include both the drive and the goal to which it is directed.

Motive pattern. Relatively consistent cluster of motives centered around particular strivings and goals. (p. 117)

Multiple personality. Type of dissociative disorder characterized by the development of two or more relatively independent personality systems in the same individual. (p. 220)

Multivariate strategy. Approach to classification of disorders using sophisticated statistical methods to provide behavioral clusters or dimensions for the observed symptoms. (p. 538)

Mutant gene. Gene that has undergone some change in structure.

Mutation. Change in the composition of a gene, usually causing harmful or abnormal characteristics to appear in the offspring.

Mutism. Refusal or inability to speak. (p. 215)

Myxedema. Disorder due to thyroid deficiency in adult life, characterized by mental dullness. (p. 524)

Narcissism. Self-love.

Narcissistic personality. A personality disorder characterized by grandiosity and an exaggerated sense of self-importance; arrogance and exploitation of others which covers up a frail self-concept. (p. 237)

Narcolepsy. Disorder characterized by transient, compulsive states of sleepiness.

Narcotherapy (narcoanalysis, narcosynthesis). Psychotherapy carried on while the patient is in a sleeplike state of relaxation induced by a drug such as sodium pentothal.

Narcotic drugs. Drugs such as morphine which lead to physiological dependence and increased tolerance.

Need. Biological or psychological condition whose gratification is necessary for the maintenance of homeostasis or for self-actualization.

Negativism. Form of aggressive withdrawal which involves refusing to cooperate or obey commands, or doing the exact opposite of what has been requested.

Neologism. A new word; commonly coined by persons labeled as schizophrenic.

Neonate. Newborn infant.

Neoplasm. Tumor.

Nervous breakdown. Refers broadly to lowered integration and inability to deal adequately with one's life situation.

Neurasthenic neurosis. Neurotic disorder characterized by complaints of chronic weakness, easy fatigability, and lack of enthusiasm.

Neurodermatitis. A skin eruption frequently accompanied by intense itching and often considered to be psychosomatically caused.

Neurological examination. Examination to determine presence and extent of organic damage to the nervous system.

Neurology. Field concerned with study of brain and nervous system and disorders thereof.

Neuron. Individual nerve cell.

Neurophysiology. The branch of biology concerned with the functioning of nervous tissue and the nervous system.

Neuropsychological assessment. Use of psychological tests to determine extent of organic brain damage.

Neurosis. Nonpsychotic emotional disturbance characterized by exaggerated use of avoidance behavior and defense mechanisms against anxiety. (p. 187)

Neurosyphilis. Syphilis affecting the central nervous system.

Neurotic nucleus. Basic personality characteristics underlying neurotic disorders.

Neurotic paradox. Failure of neurotic patterns to extinguish despite their self-defeating nature.

Neurotic style. A general personality disposition toward inhibiting certain anxiety-causing behaviors; distinguishable from anxiety, somatoform, and dissociative disorders in that neurotic styles do not manifest themselves in specific, disabling neurotic symptoms. (p. 190)

Neurotransmitters. Chemical substances which transmit nerve impulses from one neuron to another. (p. 106)

Night hospital. Mental hospital in which an individual may receive treatment during all or part of the night while carrying on his usual occupation in the daytime.

Nihilistic delusion. Fixed belief that everything is unreal.

Nomadism. Withdrawal reaction in which the individual continually attempts to escape frustration by moving from place to place or job to job.

Nondirective therapy. An approach to psychotherapy in which the therapist refrains from advice or direction of the therapy. See also **Client-centered psychotherapy.**

Norepinephrine. A catecholamine neurotransmitter substance.

Norm. Standard based on measurement of a large group of persons; used for comparing the scores of an individual with those of others in a defined group.

Normal. Conforming to the usual or norm; healthy.

Normal distribution. Tendency for most members of a population to cluster around a central point or average with respect to a given trait, with the rest spreading out to the two extremes.

NREM sleep. Stages of sleep not characterized by the rapid eye movements that accompany dreaming.

Object-relations. In psychoanalytic theory, viewpoint that emphasizes interpersonal relationships by focusing on internalized "objects" that can have varying conflicting properties. (p. 66)

Obsession. Persistent idea or thought which the individual recognizes as irrational but cannot get rid of. (p. 199)

Obsessive-compulsive disorder. Disorder characterized by persistent intrusion of unwanted desires, thoughts, or actions. (p. 199)

Obsessive-compulsive personality. Personality disorder characterized by excessive concern with conformity and adherence to ethical values.

Occipital lobe. Portion of cerebrum concerned chiefly with visual function.

Occupational therapy. Use of occupational training or activity in psychotherapy.

Oedipus complex. Desire for sexual relations with parent of opposite sex, specifically that of a boy for his mother. (p. 65)

Olfactory hallucinations. Hallucinations involving the sense of smell, as of poison gas.

Operant conditioning. Form of learning in which a particular response is reinforced and becomes more likely to occur. (p. 70)

Operational definition. Defining a concept on the basis of a set of operations that can be observed and measured.

Opium. Narcotic drug which leads to physiological dependence and the building up of tolerance; derivatives are morphine, heroin, paregoric, and codeine. (p. 420)

Oral stage. First stage of psychosexual development in Freudian theory, in which mouth or oral activities are primary source of pleasure. (p. 64)

Organic affective syndrome. Manic or depressive states caused by brain damage. (p. 495)

Organic brain syndromes. Mental disorders associated with organic brain pathology.

Organic delusional syndrome. Delusions or false beliefs caused by known or suspected brain damage. (p. 494)

Organic mental disorders. Mental disorders that occur secondary to damage to the normal brain. (p. 489)

Organic personality syndrome. Change in individual's general personality style or traits caused by brain damage. (p. 495)

Organic viewpoint. Concept that all mental disorders have an organic basis. See **Biological viewpoint.**

Orgasm. Peak sexual tension followed by relaxation.

Outcome research. Studies of effectiveness of treatment.

Outpatient. An ambulatory patient who visits a hospital or clinic for examination and treatment, as distinct from a hospitalized patient.

Ovaries. Female gonads.

Overanxious disorder. Disorder of childhood characterized by chronic anxiety, unrealistic fears, sleep disturbances and exaggerated autonomic responses. (p. 559)

Overcompensation. Type of ego-defense mechanism in which an undesirable trait is covered up by exaggerating a desirable trait. (p. 65)

Overloading. Subjecting organism to excessive stress, e.g., forcing the organism to handle or "process" an excessive amount of information.

Overprotection. Shielding a child to the extent that he or she becomes too dependent on the parent.

Overt behavior. Activities which can be observed by an outsider.

Ovum. Female gamete or germ cell.

Pain cocktail. A concoction of all the medication a pain patient is taking in a single liquid that can be systematically controlled and reduced in strength.

Panic. Severe personality disorganization involving intense anxiety and usually either paralyzed immobility or blind flight. (p. 167)

Panic disorder. Type of anxiety disorder involving recurring periods of acute panic or anxiety. (p. 195)

Paradigm. A model or pattern; in research, a basic design specifying concepts considered legitimate and procedures to be used in the collection and interpretation of data.

Paranoia. Psychosis characterized by a systematized delusional system. (p. 387)

Paranoid personality. Individual showing behavior characterized by projection (as a defense mechanism), suspiciousness, envy, extreme jealousy, and stubbornness. (p. 237)

Paranoid schizophrenia. Subtype of schizophrenic disorder characterized by absurd, illogical, and changeable ideas or hallucinations of grandeur and persecution. (p. 354)

Paranoid state. Transient psychotic disorder in which the main element is a delusion, usually persecutory or grandiose in nature.

Paraphasia. Garbled speech.

Paraphilias. Sexual variant in which unusual objects, rituals, or situations are required for full sexual satisfaction to occur. (p. 460)

Paraprofessional. Individual who has been trained in mental health services, but not at the professional level.

Parasympathetic nervous system. Division of the autonomic nervous system that controls most of the basic metabolic functions essential for life.

Paresis. See **General paresis.**

Paresthesia. Exceptional sensations, such as tingling.

Parkinson's disease (Paralysis agitans). Progressive disease characterized by a masklike, expressionless face and various neurological symptoms such as tremors.

Partial reinforcement. Intermittent reinforcement of a response.

Passive-aggressive personality. Personality pattern characterized by passively expressed aggressiveness. (p. 237)

Path analysis. Statistical technique which takes into account how variables are related to one another through time and how they predict one another. (p. 25)

Pathogenic. Pertaining to conditions which lead to pathology.

Pathological gambling. Addictive disorder in which gambling behavior disrupts the individual's life. (p. 442)

Pathological intoxication. Severe cerebral and behavioral disturbance in an individual whose tolerance to alcohol is extremely low. (p. 404)

Pathology. Abnormal physical or mental condition.

PCP. Phencyclidine; developed as a tranquilizer but not marketed because of its unpredictability. Known on the streets as "angel dust," this drug produces stuporous conditions and, at times, prolonged comas or psychoses. (p. 432)

Pederasty. Sexual intercourse between males via the anus.

Pedophilia. Sexual variant in which an adult engages in or desires sexual relations with a child. (p. 469)

Perception. Interpretation of sensory input.

Perceptual defense. A process in which threatening stimuli are filtered out and not perceived by the organism. (p. 116)

Perceptual filtering. Processes involved in selective attention to aspects of the great mass of incoming stimuli which continually impinge on organism.

Peripheral nervous system. Nerve fibers passing between the central nervous system and the sense organs, muscles, and glands.

Permanent planning. Placing children who are drifting through foster homes back into their original families. (p. 573)

Perseveration. Persistent continuation of a line of thought or activity once it is under way. Clinically inappropriate repetition.

Personality. The unique pattern of traits which characterizes the individual. (p. 233)

Personality disorder. A group of maladaptive behavioral syndromes originating in the developmental years and not characterized by neurotic or psychotic symptoms. (p. 234)

Person-centered therapy. See **Client-centered therapy.**

Pervasive developmental disorder. Severe disorder of childhood marked by deficits in language, perceptual, and motor development; defective reality testing; and inability to function in social situations. Includes *infantile autism* and *symbiotic psychosis*. (p. 562)

Perversion. Deviation from normal.

Petit mal. Relatively mild form of epilepsy involving a temporary partial lapse of consciousness.

PET scan. See **Positron emission tomography.**

Phallic stage. In psychoanalytic theory, the stage of psychosexual development during which genital exploration and manipulation occur. (p. 64)

Phallic symbol. Any object which resembles the erect male sex organ.

Pharmacology. The science of drugs. (p. 614)

Pharmacotherapy. Treatment by means of drugs.

Phenomenological. Referring to the immediate perceiving and experiencing of the individual.

Phenylketonuria (PKU). Type of mental retardation resulting from a metabolic deficiency. (p. 523)

Phobia. Irrational fear; the individual may realize its irrationality but nevertheless be unable to dispel it. (p. 204)

Phobic neurosis. Disorder characterized by intense fear of an object or situation which the individual consciously realizes poses no real danger.

Physiological dependence. Type of drug dependence involving withdrawal symptoms when drug is discontinued.

Pick's disease. Form of presenile dementia.

Pineal gland. Small gland at the base of the brain which helps regulate body's biological clock and may also pace sexual development.

Pituitary gland. Endocrine gland associated with many regulatory functions.

Placebo. An inactive treatment administered in such a way that individual thinks he or she is receiving an active treatment. (p. 275)

Play therapy. Use of play activities in psychotherapy with children.

Pleasure principle. In psychoanalysis, the demand that an instinctual need be immediately gratified regardless of reality. (p. 63)

Polygenic. Action of many genes together in an additive or interactive fashion. (p. 101)

Poor premorbid schizophrenia. See **Process schizophrenia.**

Positive reinforcer. A reinforcer that increases the probability of recurrence of a given response.

Positron emission tomography (PET scan). Scanning technique which measures level of metabolic activity in particular regions of the body. (p. 586)

Posthypnotic amnesia. Subject's lack of memory for the period during which he or she was hypnotized.

Posthypnotic suggestion. Suggestion given during hypnosis to be carried out by the subject after he or she is brought out of hypnosis.

Postpartum disturbances. Emotional disturbances associated with childbirth.

Posttraumatic disorders. Residual symptoms following traumatic experience.

Posttraumatic stress disorders. Category of disorder in which stressor is severe and residual symptoms occur following the traumatic experience. (p. 157)

Precipitating cause. The particular stress which triggers a disorder. (p. 94)

Predisposing cause. Factor which lowers the individual's stress tolerance and paves the way for the appearance of a disorder. (p. 94)

Predisposition. Likelihood that an individual will develop certain symptoms under given stress conditions.

Prefrontal lobotomy. Surgical procedure used before advent of antipsychotic drugs in which frontal lobes of the brain were severed from the deeper centers underlying them, resulting in permanent brain damage. (p. 613)

Prejudice. Emotionally toned conception favorable or unfavorable to some person, group, or idea—typically in the absence of sound evidence.

Premature ejaculation. Inability of male to inhibit ejaculation long enough to satisfy his partner.

Prematurity. Birth of an infant before the end of normal period of pregnancy.

Premorbid. Existing prior to onset of mental disorder.

Prenatal. Before birth.

Presenile dementia. Senile brain deterioration occurring at an early age and accompanied by mental disorder. (p. 505)

Pressure. Demand made on an organism.

Primary cause. Cause without which a disorder would not have occurred. (p. 94)

Primary insufficiency. Dysfunction in which the male has never been able to sustain an erection long enough to have successful intercourse. (p. 451)

Primary orgasmic dysfunction. Inability on the part of a woman to have an orgasm. (p. 452)

Primary prevention. Establishing conditions designed to prevent occurrence of mental disorders. (p. 674)

Primary process. The gratification of an instinctual id demand by means of imagery or fantasy; a psychoanalytic concept. (p. 63)

Primary reaction tendencies. Constitutional tendencies apparent in infancy, such as sensitivity and activity level. (p. 104)

Privileged communication. Freedom from the obligation to report to the authorities information concerning legal guilt revealed by a client or patient.

Proband. In a genetic study, the original individual who evidences the trait in which the investigator is interested. Same as *index case*. (p. 102)

Problem checklist. Inventory used in behavioral assessment to determine an individual's fears, moods, and other problems.

Problem drinker. Behavioral term referring to one who has serious problems associated with drinking. Term is currently preferable to *alcoholic*.

Process (Poor premorbid, Chronic) schizophrenia. Schizophrenic pattern that develops gradually and tends to be long-lasting. (p. 349)

Prognosis. Prediction as to the probable course and outcome of a disorder. (p. 90)

Programmed learning. Method of instruction or learning in which the student is guided through the subject matter step by step.

Projection. Ego-defense mechanism in which individual attributes unacceptable desires and impulses to others. (p. 64)

Projective tests. Any psychological technique for the diagnosis of personality organization utilizing relatively unstructured stimuli which reveal the individual's basic attitudes, conflicts, and so on. (p. 593)

Pseudo-community. Delusional social environment developed by a paranoiac.

Pseudo-mutuality. Relationship among family members that appears to be mutual, understanding, and open, but in fact is not. (p. 375)

Psilocybin. Hallucinogenic drug derived from a mushroom. (p. 432)

Psychedelic drugs. "Mind expanding" drugs, such as LSD, which often result in hallucinations.

Psychedelic therapy. Use of LSD as an adjunct in treatment of severe obsessive or alcoholic individuals.

Psychiatric nursing. Field of nursing primarily concerned with mental disorders.

Psychiatric social worker. Professional having graduate training in social work with psychiatric specialization, typically involving a master's degree. (p. 633)

Psychiatrist. Medical doctor who specializes in the diagnosis and treatment of mental disorders. (p. 633)

Psychiatry. Field of medicine concerned with understanding, assessing, treating, and preventing mental disorders. (p. 15)

Psychic pain. Synonym for *anxiety*.

Psychic trauma. Stressful psychological experience of a severely traumatic nature. (p. 122)

Psychoactive drug. Any drug that primarily affects mental functioning. (p. 398)

Psychoanalysis. Theoretical model and therapeutic approach developed by Freud. (p. 62)

Psychodrama. Psychotherapeutic technique in which the acting of various roles is a cardinal part.

Psychodynamic. A term in psychoanalytic theory referring to the psychic forces and processes developed through the individual's childhood experiences and which influence adult thinking and behavior.

Psychodynamic therapy. Treatment focusing on individual personality dynamics from a psychoanalytic perspective. (p. 635)

Psychogenic. Of psychological origin: originating in the psychological functioning of the individual. (p. 273)

Psychogenic amnesia. Amnesia of psychological origin, common in initial reactions to intolerable traumatic experiences. (p. 217)

Psychogenic pain disorder. A neurotic disorder in which pain is the predominant complaint. (p. 210)

Psychological autopsy. An analytical procedure used to determine whether or not death was self-inflicted.

Psychological need. Need emerging out of environmental interactions, e.g., the need for social approval.

Psychological test. Standardized procedure designed to measure the subject's performance on a specified task.

Psychomotor. Involving both psychological and physical activity.

Psychomotor epilepsy. State of disturbed consciousness in which the individual may perform various actions, sometimes of a homicidal nature, for which he or she is later amnesic.

Psychomotor retardation. Slowing down of psychological and motor functions.

Psychopathic (antisocial) personality. Sociopathic disorder characterized by lack of moral development and inability to show loyalty to other persons or groups. (p. 248)

Psychopathology. Abnormal behavior. (p. 15)

Psychopharmacological drugs. Drugs used in treatment of mental disorders.

Psychophysiologic (Psychosomatic) disorders. Physical disorders in which psychological factors play a major causative role. (p. 274)

Psychosexual development. Freudian view of development as involving a succession of stages, each characterized by a dominant mode of achieving libidinal pleasure.

Psychosexual dysfunction. Inability or impaired ability to experience or give sexual gratification. (p. 450)

Psychosexual variants. See **Variant sexual behavior.**

Psychosis. Severe psychological disorder involving loss of contact with reality and gross personality distortion. Hospitalization is ordinarily required. (p. 301)

Psychosocial. Pertaining to interpersonal interactions and relations which influence the individual's development and/or behavior. (p. 60)

Psychosocial deprivation. Lack of needed stimulation and interaction during early life.

Psychosomatic disorders. See **Psychophysiologic disorders.**

Psychosurgery. Brain surgery used in treatment of functional mental disorders or occasionally to relieve pain.

Psychotherapy. Treatment of mental disorders by psychological methods.

Psychotropic drugs. Drugs whose main effects are mental or behavioral in nature. (p. 615)

Q-sort. A personality inventory in which subject, or clinician, sorts a number of statements into piles according to their applicability to the subject.

Racism. Prejudice and discrimination directed toward individuals or groups because of their racial background.

Random sample. Sample drawn in such a way that each member of population has equal chance of being selected; hopefully representative of population from which drawn.

Rape. An act of violence in which sexual relations are forced upon another person.

Rapport. Interpersonal relationship characterized by a spirit of cooperation, confidence, and harmony.

Rating scale. Device for evaluating oneself or someone else in regard to specific traits.

Rational-emotive therapy. Form of psychotherapy focusing on cognitive and emotional restructuring to foster adaptive behavior.

Rationalization. Ego-defense mechanism in which the individual thinks up "good" reasons to justify his or her actions. (p. 64)

Reaction formation. Ego-defense mechanism in which individual's conscious attitudes and overt behavior are opposite to repressed unconscious wishes. (p. 64)

Reactive (Acute) schizophrenia. Schizophrenic pattern marked by confusion and intense emotional turmoil; normally develops suddenly and has identifiable precipitating stressors. (p. 349)

Reality assumptions. Assumptions which relate to the gratification of needs in the light of environmental possibilities, limitations, and dangers.

Reality principle. Awareness of the demands of the environment and adjustment of behavior to meet these demands. (p. 63)

Reality testing. Behavior aimed at testing or exploring the nature of the individual's social and physical environment; often used more specifically to refer to the testing of the limits of permissiveness of his social environment.

Reality therapy. Form of therapy based on assumption that emotional difficulties arise when an individual violates his or her basic sense of right and wrong.

Recessive gene. Gene which is effective only when paired with an identical gene.

Recidivism. A shift back to one's original behavior (often delinquent or criminal) after a period of treatment or rehabilitation.

Reciprocal inhibition. Technique of desensitization used in behavior therapy in which responses antagonistic to anxiety are paired with anxiety-eliciting stimuli.

Recompensation. Increase in integration or inner organization. Opposite of *decompensation*. (p. 156)

Reentry. Return from the openness of an encounter group to the real world, which is presumably less open and honest.

Referral. Sending or recommending an individual and/or family for psychological assessment and/or treatment.

Regression. Ego-defense mechanism in which the individual retreats to the use of less mature responses in attempting to cope with stress and maintain ego integrity. (p. 65)

Rehabilitation. Use of reeducation rather than punishment to overcome behavioral deficits.

Reinforcement. In classical conditioning, the process of following the conditioned stimulus with the unconditioned stimulus; in operant conditioning, the rewarding of desired responses. (p. 70)

Reinforcing cause. A circumstance tending to maintain behavior that is ultimately maladaptive, as in **secondary gain.** (p. 94)

Rejection. Lack of acceptance of another person, usually referring to such treatment of a child by the parents.

Reliability. Degree to which a test or measuring device produces the same result each time it is used to measure the same thing. (p. 16)

Remission. Marked improvement or recovery appearing in the course of a mental illness; may or may not be permanent.

REM sleep. Stage of sleep involving rapid eye movements (REM), associated with dreaming.

Representative sample. Small group selected in such a way as to be representative of the larger group from which it is drawn. (p. 24)

Repression. Ego-defense mechanism by means of which dangerous desires and intolerable memories are kept out of consciousness. (p. 64)

Reserpine. One of the early antipsychotic drugs, now largely supplanted by newer drugs.

Residual schizophrenia. Category used for persons regarded as recovered from schizophrenia but still manifesting some symptoms. (p. 362)

Resistance. Tendency to maintain symptoms and resist treatment or uncovering of repressed material.

Resistance to extinction. Tendency of a conditioned response to persist despite lack of reinforcement.

Respondent conditioning. See **Classical conditioning.**

Response shaping. Positive reinforcement technique used in therapy to establish a response not initially in the individual's behavioral repertoire. (p. 645)

Reticular activating system (RAS). Fibers going from the reticular formation to higher brain centers and presumably functioning as a general arousal system.

Reticular formation. Neural nuclei and fibers in the brain stem which apparently play an important role in arousing and alerting the organism and in controlling attention.

Retrograde amnesia. Loss of memory for events during a circumscribed period prior to brain injury or damage.

Retrospective study. Research approach which attempts to retrace earlier events in the life of the subject.

Reverse tolerance. Situation in which a decreased amount of some psychoactive drug brings about the effects formerly achieved by a larger dose.

Reynaud's disease. A potentially serious constriction of the small blood vessels of the extremities, cutting off adequate blood flow to them; sometimes considered psychosomatic.

Rigid control. Coping patterns involving reliance upon inner restraints, such as inhibition, suppression, repression, and reaction formation.

Rigidity. Tendency to follow established coping patterns, with failure to see alternatives or extreme difficulty in changing one's established patterns.

Ritalin. A central nervous system stimulant often used to treat hyperactivity in children.

Role. See **Social role.**

Role distortion. Violation of expected role behavior in an undesirable way.

Role obsolescence. Condition occurring when the ascribed social role of a given individual is no longer of importance to the social group.

Role playing. Form of psychotherapy in which the individual acts out a social role other than his or her own or tries out a new role. (p. 591)

Rorschach test. A series of inkblots to which the subject responds with associations that come to mind. Analysis of these productions enables the clinician to infer personality characteristics. (p. 593)

Sadism. Sexual variant in which sexual gratification is obtained by the infliction of pain upon others. (p. 466)

Sample. Group upon which measurements are taken; should normally be representative of the population about which an inference is to be made. (p. 24)

Scapegoating. Displacement of aggression onto some object, person, or group other than the source of frustration.

Schedule of reinforcement. Program of rewards for requisite behavior.

Schizo-affective psychosis. Disorder characterized by schizophrenic symptoms in conjunction with pronounced depression or elation.

Schizoid personality. Personality pattern characterized by shyness, oversensitivity, seclusiveness, and eccentricity. (p. 237)

Schizophrenia. Psychosis characterized by the breakdown of integrated personality functioning, withdrawal from reality, emotional blunting and distortion, and disturbances in thought and behavior. (p. 344)

Schizophreniform disorder. Category of schizophrenic psychosis, usually in an undifferentiated form, of less than six months' duration. (p. 362)

Schizophrenogenic. Qualities in parents that appear to be associated with the development of schizophrenia in offspring; often applied to rejecting, cold, domineering, overprotective mothers or passive, uninvolved fathers. (p. 373)

Schizotypal personality. Personality disorder in which egocentricity, avoidance of others, and eccentricity of thought and perception are distinguishing traits. (p. 237)

Scotophilia. See **Voyeurism.**

Secondary cause. Factor which contributes to a mental illness but which in and of itself would not have produced it, as distinct from the *primary cause.*

Secondary drives. Motives for approval, achievement, etc., as distinguished from basic biological needs. (p. 72)

Secondary gain. Indirect benefit from neurotic or other symptoms. (p. 291)

Secondary insufficiency. Condition in which male has been capable of successful intercourse but is currently dysfunctional. (p. 451)

Secondary prevention. Preventive techniques focusing on early detection and correction of maladaptive patterns within context of individual's present life situation. (p. 674)

Secondary process. Reality-oriented rational processes of the ego. (p. 63)

Secondary reinforcer. Reinforcement provided by a stimulus that has gained reward value by being associated with a primary reinforcing stimulus.

Security. Maintenance of conditions necessary to need gratification.

Sedative. Drug used to reduce tension and induce relaxation and sleep.

Selective vigilance. A tuning of attentional and perceptual processes towards stimuli relevant or central to goal-directed behavior, with decreased sensitivity to stimuli irrelevant or peripheral to this purpose. (p. 116)

Self (ego). The integrating core of the personality which mediates between needs and reality.

Self-acceptance. Being satisfied with one's attributes and qualities while remaining aware of one's limitations.

Self-actualization. Fulfillment of one's potentialities as a human being.

Self-concept. The individual's sense of his or her own identity, worth, capabilities, and limitations.

Self-devaluation. Lowered feelings of worth and self-esteem.

Self-differentiation. Degree to which the individual achieves a sense of unique identity apart from the group.

Self-direction. Basing one's behavior on inner assumptions rather than external contingencies. (p. 110)

Self-esteem. Feeling of personal worth.

Self-evaluation. Way in which the individual views the self, in terms of worth, adequacy, etc.

Self-ideal (Ego-ideal). The person or "self" the individual thinks he or she could and should be. (p. 110)

Self-identity. Individual's delineation and awareness of his or her continuing identity as a person. (p. 109)

Self-instructional training. A cognitive behavioral method aimed at teaching the individual to alter his or her covert behavior.

Self-monitor. To observe and record one's own behavior.

Self-recrimination. Self-condemnation and blame.

Self-reinforcement. Reward of self for desired or appropriate behavior.

Self-statements. Implicit "verbalizations" of what a person is experiencing.

Self-theory. Personality theory which utilizes the self-concept as the integrating core of personality organization and functioning.

Self-worth. The individual's evaluation of himself or herself.

Senile. Pertaining to old age.

Senile dementia. A form of psychosis caused in part by deteriorative brain changes due to aging. (p. 505)

Sensate focus learning. Training to derive pleasure from touching one's partner and being touched by him or her; used in sexual therapy to enhance sexual feelings and help overcome sexual dysfunction. (p. 456)

Sensitivity training group (T-group). One type of small group designed to provide intensive group experience and foster self-understanding and personal growth.

Sensory awareness. Openness to new ways of experiencing and feeling.

Sensory deprivation. Restriction of sensory stimulation below the level required for normal functioning of the central nervous system.

Sentence-completion test. Form of projective technique utilizing incomplete sentences that the subject is to complete, analysis of which enables the clinician to infer personality dynamics. (p. 594)

Separation anxiety disorder. Childhood disorder in which intense and unrealistic fear is experienced when the child is separated from someone on whom he or she feels dependent. (p. 558)

Sequelae. Symptoms remaining as the aftermath of a disorder.

Severe disorder. Disorder of a high degree of severity. (p. 18)

Sex chromosomes. Pair of chromosomes inherited by an individual which determines sex and certain other characteristics. (p. 98)

Sexual deviate. Individual who manifests nonconforming sexual behavior, often of a pathological nature.

Sexual dysfunction. Inability or impaired ability to experience or give sexual gratification.

Shaping. Form of instrumental conditioning; at first, all responses resembling the desired one are reinforced, then only the closest approximations, until finally the desired response is attained. (p. 72)

Sheltered workshops. Workshops where mentally retarded or otherwise handicapped individuals can engage in constructive work in the community.

"Shock" reaction. Transient personality decompensation in the face of sudden acute stress.

Siblings. Offspring of the same parents.

Sick role. Protected role provided by society via medical model for individual suffering from severe physical or mental disorder.

Significant others. In interpersonal theory, parents or others on whom infant is dependent for meeting all physical and psychological needs. (p. 80)

Situational stress reaction (acute). Superficial maladjustment to newly experienced life situations which are especially difficult or trying.

Situational test. Test which measures performance in a simulated life situation.

Social exchange. Model of interpersonal relationships based on the premise that such relationships are formed for mutual need gratification. (p. 81)

Social introversion. A trait characterized by shy, withdrawn, and inhibited behavior.

Socialization. The process by which a child acquires the values and impulse controls deemed appropriate by his or her culture. (p. 110)

Socialized-aggressive disorder. Pattern of childhood maladaptive behaviors involving social maladaption, as stealing, truancy, gang membership. (p. 539)

Social learning programs. Behavioral treatment techniques using learning principles, especially token economies, to help chronic patients assume more responsibility for their own behavior. (p. 679)

Social norms. Group standards concerning behaviors viewed as acceptable or unacceptable.

Social pathology. Abnormal patterns of social organization, attitudes, or behavior; undesirable social conditions which tend to produce individual pathology.

Social role. Behavior expected of individual occupying given position in group. (p. 81)

"Social" self. The facade the individual displays to others as contrasted with the private self.

Social work. Applied offshoot of sociology concerned with the analysis of social environments and providing services which assist the adjustment of the patient in both family and community settings. (p. 15)

Social worker. Person in mental health field with a master's degree in social work (MSW) plus supervised training in clinical or social service agencies.

Sociocultural. Pertaining to broad social conditions which influence the development and/or behavior of individuals and groups.

Socioeconomic status. Position on social and economic scale in community; determined largely by income and occupational level.

Sociogenic. Having its roots in sociocultural conditions.

Sociopathic (Antisocial) personality. Personality disorder involving a marked lack of ethical or moral development. (p. 248)

Sociotherapy. Treatment of interpersonal aspects of the individual's life situation.

Sodium pentothal. Barbiturate drug sometimes used in psychotherapy to produce a state of relaxation and suggestibility.

Sodomy. Sexual intercourse via the anus.

Somatic. Pertaining to the body.

Somatic weakness. Special vulnerability of given organ systems to stress.

Somatization disorder. Neurotic condition beginning before age thirty and continuing for many years characterized by multiple complaints of physical ailments not necessarily involving organic pathology. (p. 207)

Somatotype. Physique or build of a person, as assessed by various theories relating temperament to physical characteristics.

Somnambulism. Sleepwalking.

Spasm. Intense, involuntary, usually painful contraction of muscle or group of muscles.

Spasticity. Marked hypertonicity or continual overcontraction of muscles, causing stiffness, awkwardness, and motor incoordination.

Special vulnerability. Low tolerance for specific types of stress.

Sperm. Male gamete or germ cell.

Split-brain research. Research associated with split-brain surgery, which cuts off transmission of information from one cerebral hemisphere to the other.

Spontaneous recovery (remission). Recovery of a mental patient without treatment or with minimal treatment.

S-R psychologists. Psychologists who emphasize the role of stimulus-response (S-R) connections in learning. Also called *associationists*.

Stage of exhaustion. Third and final stage in the general adaptation syndrome, in which the organism is no longer able to resist continuing stress; may result in death. (p. 154)

Stage of resistance. Second stage of the general adaptation syndrome. (p. 154)

Standardization. Procedure for establishing the expected performance range on a test.

Stanford-Binet. A standardized intelligence test for children.

Startle reaction. Sudden involuntary motor reaction to intense unexpected stimuli; may result from mild stimuli if person is hypersensitive. (p. 170)

Status comparison. A process by which an individual estimates his or her own worth by measuring it against the achievements of others.

Statutory rape. Sexual intercourse with a minor. (p. 474)

Steady states (Homeostasis). Tendency of organism to maintain conditions making possible a constant level of physiological functioning. (p. 106)

Stereotype. A generalized notion of how people of a given race, religion, or other group will appear, think, feel, or act.

Stereotypy. Persistent and inappropriate repetition of phrases, gestures, or acts.

Stimulants. Drugs that tend to increase feelings of alertness, reduce feelings of fatigue, and enable individual to stay awake over sustained periods of time.

Stimulus generalization. The spread of a conditioned response to some stimulus similar to, but not identical with, the conditioned stimulus.

Stress. The internal responses caused by application of a stressor. (p. 142)

Stress-decompensation model. View of abnormal behavior which emphasizes progressive disorganization of behavior under excessive stress.

Stress-inoculation training. A cognitive-behavioral treatment that prepares people to handle stressful situations by altering their attitudes toward themselves and the stressor. (p. 654)

Stress interview. Interview of a subject in which stressors are introduced.

Stressor. Any adjustive demand that requires coping behavior on the part of individual or group. (p. 142)

Stress tolerance (frustration tolerance). Nature, degree, and duration of stress which an individual can tolerate without undergoing serious personality decompensation. (p. 146)

Stroke. See **Cerebrovascular accident.**

Structural therapy. A treatment of autistic children in which the environment is structured to provide spontaneous physical and verbal stimulation to autistic children. (p. 565)

Structured family therapy. Treatment of the entire family by analysis of communication between family members. (p. 664)

Student's disease. Common belief among students of abnormal psychology that they have the symptoms of the disorders they are studying.

Stupor. Condition of lethargy and unresponsiveness, with partial or complete unconsciousness.

Stuttering. Speech disorder characterized by a blocking or repetition of initial sounds of words.

St. Vitus' dance. Hysterical chorea of common occurrence during the Middle Ages. (p. 37)

Sublimation. Ego-defense mechanism by means of which frustrated sexual energy is partially channeled into substitutive activities.

Substance-abuse disorders. Pathological use of a substance for at least a month, resulting in self-injurious behavior. (p. 397)

Substance-dependence disorders. Severe form of substance-use disorder involving physiological dependence on the substance. (p. 397)

Substance-induced organic disorder. Category of disorders based on organic impairment resulting from toxicity or physiologic changes in the brain. (p. 397)

Substance-use disorder. Patterns of maladaptive behavior centered around regular use of substance involved. (p. 397)

Substitution. Acceptance of substitute goals or satisfactions in place of those originally sought after or desired.

Successive approximation. See **Shaping.**

Suicide. Taking one's own life.

Suicidology. The study of the causes and prevention of suicide.

Superego. Conscience; ethical or moral dimensions (attitudes) of personality. (p. 63)

Suppression. Conscious forcing of desires or thoughts out of consciousness; conscious inhibition of desires or impulses.

Surrogate. Substitute parent, child, or mate.

Survey methods. Procedures for obtaining opinions or other data concerning a given population.

Symbol. Image, word, object, or activity that is used to represent something else.

Symbolism. Representation of one idea or object by another.

Sympathetic division. Division of the autonomic nervous system which is active in emergency conditions of extreme cold, violent effort, and emotions.

Symptom. An observable manifestation of a physical or mental disorder.

Syncope. Temporary loss of consciousness resulting from cerebral anoxia.

Syndrome. Group or pattern or symptoms which occur together in a disorder and represent the typical picture of the disorder. (p. 492)

Syphilophobia. Morbid fear of syphilis.

System. An assemblage of interdependent parts, living or nonliving.

Systematic desensitization. A behavior therapy technique for eliminating maladaptive anxiety responses. (p. 72)

Tachycardia. Rapid heartbeat.

Tactual hallucinations. Hallucinations involving the sense of touch, such as feeling cockroaches crawling over one's body.

Tarantism. Type of hysterical dancing occurring in epidemic form during the Middle Ages. (p. 37)

Task-oriented reaction. Realistic rather than ego-defensive approach to stressors. (p. 150)

Tay-Sachs disease. Genetic disorder of lipoid metabolism usually resulting in death by age 3.

Telepathy. Communication from one person to another without use of any known sense organs.

Temporal lobe. Portion of cerebrum located in front of occipital lobe and separated from frontal and parietal lobes by the fissure of Sylvius.

Tension. Condition arising out of the mobilization of psychobiological resources to meet a threat; physically, involves an increase in muscle tonus and other emergency changes; psychologically, is characterized by feelings of strain, uneasiness, and anxiety.

Tertiary prevention. Preventive techniques focusing on short-term hospitalization and intensive aftercare when an emotional breakdown has occurred, with aim of returning individual to his or her family and community setting as soon as possible. (p. 674)

Testes. Male reproductive glands or gonads.

Testosterone. Male sex hormone.

Thematic Apperception Test (TAT). A psychological test composed of a series of pictures based on which the subject makes up a story. Analysis of the story gives the clinician clues about the individual's conflicts, traits, personality dynamics, and so on. (p. 594)

Therapeutic. Pertaining to treatment or healing.

Therapeutic community. The hospital environment used for therapeutic purposes. (p. 678)

Therapy. Treatment; application of various treatment techniques.

Thermistors. Extremely sensitive small thermometers taped to subject's skin to provide feedback during biofeedback training. (p. 649)

Theta wave. Brain wave having a frequency of only 5 to 7 cycles per second.

Threat. Real or imagined danger to individual or group.

Thyroids. Endocrine glands located in neck which influence body metabolism, rate of physical growth, and development of intelligence.

Thyroxin. Hormone secreted by the thyroid glands.

Tic. Intermittent twitching or jerking, usually of facial muscles. (p. 571)

Token economy. Reinforcement technique often used in hospital or institutional settings in which individuals are rewarded for socially constructive behavior with tokens that can then be exchanged for desired objects or activities. (p. 645)

Tolerance. Physiological condition in which increased dosage of an addictive drug is needed to obtain effects previously produced by smaller dose. (p. 397)

Tonic. Pertaining to muscle tension or contraction; muscle tone.

Toxic. Poisonous.

Toxic deliria (psychoses). Severe disturbances in cerebral functions resulting from toxins.

Toxicity. The poisonous nature of a substance. (p. 397)

Trait. Characteristic of individual which can be observed or measured.

Trance. Sleeplike state in which the range of consciousness is limited and voluntary activities are suspended; a deep hypnotic state.

Tranquilizers. Drugs used for antipsychotic purposes and/or reduction of anxiety and tension. See also **Major tranquilizers, Minor tranquilizers.**

Transactional analysis. Form of interpersonal therapy based on interaction of "Child," "Adult," and "Parent" ego states. (p. 655)

Transference. Process whereby client projects attitudes and emotions applicable to another significant person onto the therapist; emphasized in psychoanalytic therapy. (p. 637)

Transient situational disorder. Temporary mental disorder developing under conditions of overwhelming stress, as in military combat or civilian catastrophes.

Transsexualism. Identification of oneself with members of opposite sex, as opposed to acceptance of one's anatomical sexual identity. (p. 458)

Transvestism. Persistent desire to dress in clothing of the opposite sex, often accompanied by sexual excitement. (p. 460)

Trauma. Severe psychological or physiological stressor.

Traumatic. Pertaining to a wound or injury, or to psychic shock.

Traumatic neurosis. See "Shock" reaction.

Treatment contract. Explicit arrangement between therapist and client designed to bring about specific behavioral changes.

Tremor. Repeated fine spastic movement.

Turner's syndrome. Form of mental retardation associated with sex chromosome anomaly.

Unconscious. As used by Freud, psychological material that has been repressed. Also, loss of consciousness; lack of awareness. (p. 63)

Unconscious motivation. Motivation for an individual's behavior of which he or she is unaware.

Underarousal. Inadequate physiological response to a given stimulus.

Undifferentiated schizophrenia. Subtype in which patient either has mixed symptoms or moves rapidly from one subtype to another. (p. 354)

Undoing. Ego-defense mechanism by means of which the individual performs activities designed to atone for his or her misdeeds, thereby, in a sense, "undoing" them. (p. 65)

Unipolar disorder. A severe affective disorder in which only depressive episodes occur, as opposed to *bipolar disorder* in which both manic and depressive processes are assumed to occur. (p. 308)

Unsocialized disturbance of conduct. Childhood disorder in which the child is disobedient, hostile, and highly aggressive.

Vaginismus. An involuntary muscle spasm at the entrance to the vagina that prevents penetration and sexual intercourse. (p. 452)

Validity. Extent to which a measuring instrument actually measures what it purports to measure. (p. 16)

Values. Assumptions concerning good and bad, right and wrong.

Variable. A characteristic or property that may assume any one of a set of different qualities or quantities.

Variant sexual behavior. Behavior in which satisfaction is dependent on something other than a mutually desired sexual engagement with a sexually mature member of the opposite sex. (p. 457)

Vasomotor. Pertaining to the walls of the blood vessels.

Vegetative. Withdrawn or deteriorated to the point where the individual leads a passive, vegetablelike existence.

Verbigeration. Prolonged and monotonous repetition of meaningless words and phrases.

Vertigo. Dizziness.

Vicarious living. Attempt to evade efforts toward self-fulfillment by repressing one's own individuality and identifying with some hero or ideal.

Vicious circle. Chain reaction in which individual resorts to an unhealthy defensive reaction in trying to solve his or her problems, which only serves to complicate them and make them harder to solve.

Virilism. Accentuation of masculine secondary sex characteristics, especially in a woman or young boy, caused by hormonal imbalance.

Viscera. Internal organs.

Visual hallucinations. Hallucinations involving sense of sight.

Voyeurism. Achievement of sexual pleasure through clandestine "peeping," usually watching other persons disrobe and/or engage in sexual activities. (p. 464)

Vulnerabilities. Factors rendering an individual susceptible to behaving abnormally. (p. 93)

Wechsler Intelligence Scale for Children (WISC). A standardized intelligence scale for children.

Withdrawal. Intellectual, emotional, or physical retreat.

Withdrawal disturbance. Disorder of childhood in which the child becomes aloof and detached from a world he or she sees as dangerous.

Withdrawal symptoms. Wide range of symptoms evidenced by addicts when the drug on which they are physiologically dependent is not available. (p. 397)

Word salad. Jumbled or incoherent use of words by psychotic or disoriented individuals.

X chromosome. Sex-determining chromosome: all female gametes contain X chromosomes, and if fertilized ovum has also received an X chromosome from its father it will be female. (p. 98)

XYY syndrome. A chromosomal anomaly in males (presence of an extra Y chromosome) possibly related to impulsive behavior.

Y chromosome. Sex-determining chromosome found in half of the total number of male gametes; uniting with X chromosome always provided by female produces a male offspring. (p. 98)

Zygote. Fertilized egg cell formed by union of male and female gametes.

References

Journal Abbreviations

ACTA PSYCHIATR. SCANDIN.—*Acta Psychiatrica Scandinavica*

AIR UNIVER. QUART. REV.—*Air University Quarterly Review*

AMER. J. DIS. CHILDREN—*American Journal of Disorders in Children*

AMER. J. MED. SCI.—*American Journal of Medical Science*

AMER. J. MENT. DEF.—*American Journal of Mental Deficiency*

AMER. J. NURS.—*American Journal of Nursing*

AMER. J. OCCUPA. THER.—*American Journal of Occupational Therapy*

AMER. J. ORTHOPSYCHIAT.—*American Journal of Orthopsychiatry*

AMER. J. PSYCHIAT.—*American Journal of Psychiatry*

AMER. J. PSYCHOTHER.—*American Journal of Psychotherapy*

AMER. J. PUB. HLTH.—*American Journal of Public Health*

AMER. PSYCHOLOGIST—*American Psychologist*

AMER. SCIEN.—*American Scientist*

ANAL. INTERVEN. DEVELOP. DIS.—*Analysis and Intervention in Developmental Disorders*

ANN. AMER. ACAD. POLIT. SOC. SCI.—*Annals of the American Academy of Political and Social Science*

ANN. N.Y. ACAD. SCI.—*Annals of the New York Academy of Science*

ANNU. REV. PSYCHOL.—*Annual Review of Psychology*

ARCH. GEN. PSYCHIAT.—*Archives of General Psychiatry*

ARCH. INT. MED.—*Archives of Internal Medicine*

ARCH. NEUROL. PSYCHIAT.—*Archives of Neurology and Psychiatry*

BEHAV. ASSESS.—*Behavioral Assessment*

BEHAV. MODIFIC.—*Behavior Modification*

BEHAV. RES. THER.—*Behavior Research and Therapy*

BEHAV. SCI.—*Behavioral Science*

BEHAV. THER.—*Behavior Therapy*

BEHAV. TODAY.—*Behavior Today*

BRIT. J. EDUC. PSYCHOL.—*British Journal of Educational Psychology*

BRIT. J. MED. PSYCHOL.—*British Journal of Medical Psychology*

BRIT. J. OPHTHALMOL.—*British Journal of Ophthalmology*

BRIT. J. PSYCHIAT.—*British Journal of Psychiatry*

BRIT. MED. J.—*British Medical Journal*

BULL. MENNINGER CLIN.—*Bulletin of the Menninger Clinic*

CANADIAN J. PSYCHIAT.—*Canadian Journal of Psychiatry*

CHARACT. & PERS.—*Character and Personality*

CHILD DEVELOP.—*Child Development*

COG. THER. RES.—*Cognitive Therapy and Research*

COMM. MENT. HLTH. J.—*Community Mental Health Journal*

DEVELOP. MED. CHILD NEUROL.—*Developmental Medicine & Child Neurology*

DEVELOP. PSYCHOL.—*Developmental Psychology*

DIS. NERV. SYS.—*Diseases of the Nervous System*

GEN. PSYCHIAT.—*General Psychiatry*

GROUP PSYCHOTHER.—*Group Psychotherapy*

HARVARD ED. REV.—*Harvard Educational Review*

HUMAN DEVELOP.—*Human Development*

INTER. J. FAM. THER.—*International Journal of Family Therapy*

INTER. J. GROUP PSYCHOTHER.—*International Journal of Group Psychotherapy*

INTER. J. PSYCHIAT.—*International Journal of Psychiatry*

INTER. J. PSYCHOANAL.—*International Journal of Psychoanalysis*

J. ABNORM. CHILD. PSYCHOL.—*Journal of Abnormal Child Psychology*

J. ABNORM. PSYCHOL.—*Journal of Abnormal Psychology*

J. ABNORM. SOC. PSYCHOL.—*Journal of Abnormal and Social Psychology*

JAMA—*Journal of the American Medical Association*

J. AMER. ACAD. CHILD PSYCHIAT.—*Journal of the American Academy of Child Psychiatry*

JAP. J. CHILD ADOLES. PSYCHIAT.—*Japanese Journal of Child and Adolescent Psychiatry*

J. APPL. BEH. ANAL.—*Journal of Applied Behavior Analysis*

J. AUTISM DEVEL. DIS.—*Journal of Autism and Developmental Disorders*

J. BEHAV. ASSESS.—*Journal of Behavioral Assessment*

J. BEHAV. RES. EXP. PSYCHIAT.—*Journal of Behavior Research and Experimental Psychiatry*

J. BEHAV. THER. EXP. PSYCHIAT.—*Journal of Behavior Therapy and Experimental Psychiatry*

J. CHILD CLIN. PSYCHOL.—*Journal of Clinical Psychology*

J. CHILD PSYCHOL. PSYCHIAT.—*Journal of Child Psychology and Psychiatry*

J. CLIN. PSYCHOL.—*Journal of Clinical Psychology*

J. CLIN. PSYCHOPATH.—*Journal of Clinical Psychopathology*

J. COMMUNITY PSYCHOL.—*Journal of Community Psychology*

J. COMPAR. PHYSIOL. PSYCHOL.—*Journal of Comparative and Physiological Psychology*

J. CONS. CLIN. PSYCHOL.—*Journal of Consulting and Clinical Psychology*

J. COUNS. PSYCHOL.—*Journal of Counseling Psychology*

J. CRIM. LAW CRIMINOL. POLICE SCI.—*Journal of Criminal Law, Criminology, and Police Science*

J. CRIM. PSYCHOPATH. PSYCHOTHER.—*Journal of Criminal Psychopathology and Psychotherapy*

J. EXPER. ANAL. BEHAV.—*Journal of Experimental Analysis of Behavior*

J. EXPER. CHILD PSYCHOL.—*Journal of Experimental Child Psychology*

J. EXPER. PSYCHOL.—*Journal of Experimental Psychology*

J. EXPER. RES. PERSON.—*Journal of Experimental Research in Personality*

J. GENET. PSYCHOL.—*Journal of Genetic Psychology*

J. GEN. PSYCHOL.—*Journal of General Psychology*

J. GERIAT. PSYCHOL.—*Journal of Geriatric Psychology*

J. HLTH. SOC. BEHAV.—*Journal of Health and Social Behavior*

J. LEARN. DIS.—*Journal of Learning Disabilities*

J. MARR. FAM.—*Journal of Marriage and the Family*

J. MENT. SCI.—*Journal of Mental Science*

J. NERV. MENT. DIS.—*Journal of Nervous and Mental Disease*

J. PEDIAT.—*Journal of Pediatrics*

J. PEDIAT. PSYCHOL.—*Journal of Pediatric Psychology*

J. PERSONAL.—*Journal of Personality*

J. PERS. SOC. PSYCHOL.—*Journal of Personality and Social Psychology*

J. PSYCHIAT.—*Journal of Psychiatry*

J. PSYCHIAT. RES.—*Journal of Psychiatric Research*

J. PSYCHOL.—*Journal of Psychology*

J. PSYCHOSOM. MED.—*Journal of Psychosomatic Medicine*

J. PSYCHOSOM. RES.—*Journal of Psychosomatic Research*

J. SOC. PSYCHOL.—*Journal of Social Psychology*

J. SPEC. ED.—*Journal of Special Education*

J. SPEECH HEAR. DIS.—*Journal of Speech and Hearing Disorders*

J. SPEECH HEAR. RES.—*Journal of Speech and Hearing Research*

MED. J. AUSTRALIA.—*Medical Journal of Australia*

MENT. HLTH. DIG.—*Mental Health Digest*

MENT. HLTH. PROG. REP.—*Mental Health Program Reports*

MENT. HYG.—*Mental Hygiene*

MONOGR. SOC. RES. CHILD DEVELOP.—*Monographs of the Society for Research in Child Development*

N.C. MED. J.—*North Carolina Medical Journal*

NEW ENGL. J. MED.—*New England Journal of Medicine*

N.Y. ST. J. MED.—*New York State Journal of Medicine*

PEDIAT. REV.—*Pediatrics in Review*

PROFESSIONAL PSYCHOL.—*Professional Psychology*

PSYCHIAT. DIG.—*Psychiatry Digest*

PSYCHIAT. QUART.—*Psychiatric Quarterly*

PSYCHIAT. SOC. SCI. REV.—*Psychiatry and Social Science Review*

PSYCHOANAL. QUART.—*Psychoanalytic Quarterly*
PSYCHOANAL. REV.—*Psychoanalytic Review*
PSYCHOL. BULL.—*Psychological Bulletin*
PSYCHOL. REC.—*Psychological Record*
PSYCHOSOM. MED.—*Psychosomatic Medicine*
PSYCH. REP.—*Psychological Reports*
PSYCH. REV.—*Psychological Review*
PSYCH. TODAY—*Psychology Today*
PUBL. MASS. MED. SOC.—*Publication of the Massachusetts Medical Society*
QUART. J. STUD. ALCOHOL.—*Quarterly Journal of Studies in Alcoholism*
SAT. REV.—*Saturday Review*
SCIENTIF. AMER.—*Scientific American*
SCI. J.—*Science Journal*
SCI. NEWS—*Science News*
SCI. NEWSLETTER—*Science Newsletter*
SCI. TECH.—*Science and Technology*
SOCIOL. QUART.—*Sociological Quarterly*
SOC. PSYCHIAT.—*Social Psychiatry*
WORLD MENT. HLTH.—*World Mental Health*

Abel, G. G., Blanchard, E. B., Becker, J. V., & Djenderedjian, A. (1978). Differentiating sexual aggressives with penile measures. *Criminal Justice and Behavior*, **5**, 315–32.

Abrams, R., & Essman, W. B. (1982). *Electroconvulsive therapy: Biological foundations and clinical applications*. Jamaica, NY: SP Medical and Scientific Books.

Abramson, L. Y., Seligman, M. E. P., & Teasdale, J. D. (1978). Learned helplessness in humans: Critique and reformulation. *J. Abnorm. Psychol.*, **87**, 49–74.

Abse, D. W. (1959). Hysteria. In S. Arieti (Ed.), *American handbook of psychiatry* (Vol. 1) pp. 272–92. New York: Basic Books.

Achenbach, T. M. (1966). The classification of children's psychiatric symptoms: A factor-analytic study. *Psychol. Monographs*, **80**, Whole No. 615.

Achenbach, T. M. (1978). The child-behavior profile: I Boys aged 6–11. *J. Cons. Clin. Psychol.*, **46**, 478–88.

Adams, H. E., & Chiodo, J. (1984). Sexual deviations. In H. E. Adams & P. B. Sutker (Eds.), *Comprehensive handbook of psychopathology*. New York: Plenum.

Adams, H. E., & Sturgis, E. T. (1977). Status of behavioral reorientation techniques in the modification of homosexuality: A review. *Psychol. Bull.*, **84**, 1171–88.

Adams, M. S. & Neel, J. V. (1967). Children of incest, *Pediatrics*, **40**, 55–62.

Adler, A. (1943). Neuropsychiatric complications in victims of Boston's Cocoanut Grove disaster. *JAMA*, **123**, 1098–1101.

Agras, S., Sylvester, D., & Oliveau, D. (1969). The epidemiology of common fears and phobias. Unpublished manuscript.

Agras, W. S. (1982). Behavioral medicine in the 1980's: Non random connections. *J. Cons. Clin. Psychol.*, **50**(6), 820–40.

Akil, H., Watson, S., Sullivan, S., & Barchas, J. D. (1978). Enkephalin-like material in normal human cerebrospinal fluid: Measurement and levels. *Life Sciences*, **23**, 121–26.

Akiskal, H. S. (1979). A biobehavioral approach to depression. In R. A. Depue (Ed.), *The psychobiology of depressive disorders: Implications for the effects of stress*. New York: Academic Press.

Akiskal, H. S., & McKinney, W. T., Jr. (1975). Overview of recent research in depression: Integration of ten conceptual models into a comprehensive clinical frame. *Arch. Gen. Psychiat.*, **32**(3), 285–305.

Alander, R., & Campbell, T. (1975, Spring). An evaluation of an alcohol and drug recovery program: A case study of the Oldsmobile Experience. *Human Resource Management*, 14–18.

Al-Anon. (1971). *Al-Anon—Family treatment tool in alcoholism*. New York: Al-Anon Family Group Headquarters, Inc.

Alexander, B. (1981). Behavioral approaches to the treatment of bronchial asthma. In C. K. Prokop & L. A. Bradley

(Eds.), *Medical psychology: Contributions to behavioral medicine*. New York: Academic Press.

Alexander, B. K., & Hadaway, P. F. (1982). Opiate addiction: The case for an adaptive orientation. *Psychol. Bull.*, **92**(2), 367–81.

Alexander, F. (1946). Individual psychotherapy. *Psychosom. Med.*, **8**, 110–15.

Alexander, F. (1950). *Psychosomatic medicine*. New York: Norton.

Alexander, S. (1974, July 8). Under the rock. *Newsweek*, **84**(2), 35.

Allerton, W. S. (1970). Psychiatric casualties in Vietnam. *Roche Medical Image and Commentary*, **12**(8), 27.

Allridge, P. (1970). Hospitals, madhouses, and asylums: Cycles in the care of the insane. *Brit. J. Psychiat.*, **134**, 321–34.

Amcoff, S. (1980). The impact of malnutrition on the learning situation. In H. M. Sinclair & G. R. Howat (Eds.), *World nutrition and nutrition education*. New York: Oxford University Press.

Amenson, C. S., & Lewinsohn, P. M. (1981). An investigation into the observed sex difference in prevalence of unipolar depression. *J. Abnorm. Psychol.*, **90**, 1–13.

American Association on Mental Deficiency (AAMD). (1973). *Manual on terminology and classification in mental retardation* (Rev. ed.). H. J. Grossman (Ed.). Special Publication Series No. 2, 11 +. Washington, DC.

American Medical Association. (1982, June 30). *The alcoholism report*, Vol. X, No. 17.

American Medical Association, Committee on Alcoholism and Drug Dependency. (1969). *The illness called alcoholism*. Chicago: AMA.

American Medical Association, Department of Mental Health. (1968a). The crutch that cripples: Drug dependence, Part I. *Today's Health*, **46**(9), 11–12; 70–72.

American Medical Association, Department of Mental Health. (1968b). The crutch that cripples: Drug dependence, Part II. *Today's Health*, **46**(10), 12–15; 73–75.

American Psychiatric Association. (1968). *Diagnostic and statistical manual of mental disorders* (2nd ed.). Washington, DC: APA.

American Psychiatric Association. (1972). Classification of mental retardation. Supplement to the *Amer. J. Psychiat.*, **128**(11), 1–45.

American Psychiatric Association, (1978). Task Force on Electroconvulsive Therapy. *Report: Electroconvulsive therapy*. Washington: American Psychiatric Association.

American Psychiatric Association. (1980). *Diagnostic and statistical manual of mental disorders* (3rd ed.). Washington, DC: Author.

American Psychological Association. (1970). Psychology and mental retardation. *Amer. Psychologist*, **25**, 267–68.

American Psychological Association. (1981). *Ethical Principles of Psychologists*. Washington, DC: American Psychological Association.

Anchin, J. C., & Kiesler, D. J. (Eds.). (1982). *Handbook of interpersonal psychotherapy*. New York: Pergamon.

Andersen, B. L. (1983). Primary orgasmic dysfunction: Diagnostic considerations and review of treatment. *Psychol. Bull.*, **93**, 105–36.

Andrasik, F., Blanchard, E. B., Arena, J. G., Teders, S. J., Teevan, R. C., & Rodichok, L. D. (1982). Psychological functioning in headache sufferers. *Psychosomatic Medicine*, **44**, 171–82.

Andrasik, F., Holroyd, K. A., & Abell, T. (1979). Prevalence of headache within a college student population: A preliminary analysis. *Headache*, **20**, 384–87.

Andreasen, N. C. (1982). Concepts, diagnosis and classification. In E. S. Paykel (Ed.), *Handbook of affective disorders*. New York: Guilford Press.

Andreasen, N. C., & Grove, W. M. (1982). The classification of depression: Traditional versus mathematical approaches. *Amer. J. Psychiat.*, **139**, 45–52.

Andreasen, N. C., Olsen, S. A., Dennert, J. W., & Smith, M. R. (1982a). Ventricular enlargement in schizophrenia: Definition and prevalence. *Amer. J. Psychiat.*, **139**, 292–96.

Andreasen, N. C., Olsen, S. A., Dennert, J. W., & Smith,

M. R. (1982b). Ventricular enlargement in schizophrenia: Relationship to positive and negative symptoms. *Amer. J. Psychiat.*, **139**, 297–302.

Andrews, G., & Harvey, R. (1981). Does psychotherapy benefit neurotic patients? A reanalysis of the Smith, Glass, and Miller data. *Arch. Gen. Psychiat.*, **38**, 1203–08.

Angst, J. (1980). Clinical typology of bipolar illness. In R. H. Belmaker, & H. M. van Praag (Eds.), *Mania: An evolving concept.* New York: Spectrum.

Anonymous. (1977). The animal school. *Adolescence: The prevention and treatment of emotional disturbances.* Morganton, N. C.: Broughton Hospital, p. 4.

Anthony, E. J. (1978). Concluding comments on treatment implications. In L. C. Wynne, R. L. Cromwell & S. Matthysse (Eds.), *The nature of schizophrenia: New approaches to research and treatment.* (pp. 481–84). New York: Wiley.

Apfelbaum, B. (1981). Integrating psychoanalytic and behavior therapy. *Amer. Psycholog.*, **36**(7), 796–97.

Apfelberg, B., Sugar, C., & Pfeffer, A. Z. (1944). A psychiatric study of 250 sex offenders. *Amer. J. Psychiat.*, **100**, 762–70.

Aponte, H., & Hoffman, L. (1973). The open door: A structural approach to a family with an anorectic child. *Family Process*, **12**, 1–44.

Archer, J. and Gruenberg, E. (1982). The chronically mentally disabled and "deinstitutionalized." *Annual Review of Public Health*, **3**, 445–68.

Archibald, H. C., & Tuddenham, R. D. (1965). Persistent stress reaction after combat. *Arch. Gen. Psychiat.*, **12**(5), 475–81.

Arieti, S. (1974). An overview of schizophrenia from a predominantly psychological approach. *Amer. J. Psychiat.*, **131**(3), 241–49.

Arieti, S. (1982). Individual psychotherapy. In E. S. Paykel (Ed.), *Handbook of affective disorders.* New York: Guilford Press.

Arieti, S., & Bemporad, J. R. (1980). The psychological organization of depression. *Amer. J. Psychiat.*, **137**, 1360–65.

Aring, C. D. (1974). The Gheel experience: Eternal spirit of the chainless mind! *JAMA*, **230**(7), 998–1001.

Aring, C. D. (1975a). Gheel: The town that cares. *Family Health*, (1975), **7**(4), 54–55; 58; 60.

Aring, C. D. (1975b). Science and the citizen. *Scientif. Amer.*, **232**(1), 48–49; 52–53.

Arkowitz, H., & Messer, S. B. (Eds.). (In press). *Psychoanalytic and behavior therapy: Is integration possible?* New York: Plenum.

Arnkoff, D. B., & Glass, C. R. (1982). Clinical cognitive constructs: Examination, evaluation, and elaboration. In P. C. Kendall (Ed.), *Advances in cognitive-behavioral research and therapy* (Vol. 1, pp. 2–30). New York: Academic Press.

Arnold, L. E. (1973). Is this label necessary? *Journal of School Health*, **43**(8), 510–14.

Arnold, L. E. (1978). *Helping parents help their children.* New York: Brunner/Mazel.

Arnold, M. B. (1962). *Story sequence analysis: A new method of measuring motivation and predicting achievement.* New York: Columbia University Press.

Aronson, E. (1973). The rationalizing animal. *Psych. Today*, **6**(12), 46–50, 52.

Atkeson, B. M., Calhoun, K. S., Resick, P. A., & Ellis, E. M. (1982). Victims of rape: Repeated assessment of depressive symptoms. *J. Cons. Clin. Psychol.*, **50**, 96–102.

Atkeson, B. M., & Forehand, R. (1978). Parent behavior training for problem children: An examination of studies using multiple outcome measures. *J. Abnorm. Child Psychol.*, **6**, 449–60.

Atkinson, J. W. (Ed.). (1958). *Motives in fantasy, action, and society.* Princeton, N.J.: Van Nostrand.

Averill, J. R. (1973). Personal control over aversive stimuli and its relationship to stress. *Psychol. Bull.*, **80**(4), 286–303.

Ayllon, T., & Azrin, N.H. (1968). *The token economy: A motivational system for therapy and rehabilitation.* New York: Appleton-Century-Crofts.

Bachrach, A. J., Erwin, W. J., & Mohr, J. P. (1965). The control of eating behavior in an anorexic by operant condi-

tioning techniques. In L. P. Ullmann & L. Krasner (Eds.), *Case studies in behavior modification,* New York: Holt, Rinehart.

Bachrach, L. L. (1976). *Deinstitutionalization: An analytic review and sociological perspective.* U.S. Department of Health, Education, and Welfare. National Institute of Mental Health, Washington, DC: U.S. Government Printing Office.

Bachrach, L. L. (1980). Overview: Model programs for chronic patients. *Amer. J. Psychiat.*, **132**, 1023–31.

Bagley, C. (1969). Incest behavior and incest taboo. *Social Problems*, **16**(4), 505–19.

Bagley, C. (1973). Occupational class and symptoms of depression. *Social Science and Medicine*, **7**(5), 327–40.

Baker, L., & Lyen, K. R. (1982). Anorexia nervosa. In M. Winick (Ed.), *Adolescent nutrition.* New York: Oxford University Press.

Bales, R. F. (1946). Cultural differences in rates of alcoholism. *Quart. J. Stud. Alcohol.*, **6**, 480–99.

Bandura, A. (1964). *Principles of behavior modification.* New York: Holt, Rinehart & Winston.

Bandura, A. (1969). *Principles of behavior modification.* New York: Holt, Rinehart & Winston.

Bandura, A. (1973). *Aggression: A social learning analysis.* Englewood Cliffs, N.J.: Prentice-Hall.

Bandura, A. (1974). Behavior theory and the models of man. *Amer. Psychologist*, **29**(12), 859–69.

Bandura, A. (1977a). Self-efficacy: Toward a unifying theory of behavioral change. *Psychol. Rev.*, **84**(2), 191–215.

Bandura, A. (1977b). *Social learning theory.* Prentice-Hall.

Bandura, A. (1978). The self-system in reciprocal determinism. *Amer. Psychologist*, **33**(4), 344–58.

Bandura, A., & Walters, R. H. (1963). *Social learning and personality development.* New York: Holt, Rinehart & Winston.

Bannister, D. (1971). Schizophrenia: Carnival mirror of coherence. *Psych. Today*, **4**(8), 66–69; 84.

Bannister, G., Jr. (1975). Cognitive and behavior therapy in a case of compulsive gambling. *Cognitive therapy and research.* **1**, 223–27.

Barahal, R. M., Waterman, J., & Martin, H. P. (1981). The social cognitive development of abused children. *J. Cons. Clin. Psychol.*, **49**(4), 508–16.

Barber, T. X. (1969). *Hypnosis: A scientific approach.* New York: Van Nostrand Reinhold.

Barchas, J., Akil, H., Elliott, G., Holman, R., & Watson, S. (1978, May 26). Behavioral neurochemistry: Neuroregulators and behavioral states. *Science*, **200**, 964–73.

Bard, M. (1966). The price of survival for cancer victims. *Transaction*, **3**(3), 10–14.

Barkley, R. A., & Cunningham, C. E. (1979). The effects of methylphenidate on the mother-child interaction of hyperactive children. *Arch. Gen. Psychiat.*, **36**, 201–11.

Barlow, D. H. (1974). The treatment of sexual deviation: Toward a comprehensive behavioral approach. In K. S. Calhoun, H. E. Adams, & K. M. Mitchell (Eds.), *Innovative treatment methods in psychopathology.* New York: Wiley Interscience Series.

Barlow, D. H., & Abel, G. G. (1976). Sexual deviation. In W. E. Craighead, A. E. Kazdin, & M. J. Mahoney (Eds.), *Behavior modification: Principles, issues, and applications.* Boston: Houghton Mifflin.

Barlow, D. H., & Agras, W. S. (1973). Fading to increase heterosexual responsiveness in homosexuals. *J. Appl. Beh. Anal.*, **6**, 355–66.

Barlow, D. H., Reynolds, E. J., & Agras, W. S. (1973, April). Gender identity change in a transsexual. *Arch. Gen. Psychiat.*, **28**(4), 569–76.

Barry, H., III. (1982). Cultural variations in alcohol abuse. In I. Al-Issa (Ed.), *Culture and psychopathology.* Baltimore: University Park Press.

Bartak, L. (1978). Educational approaches. In M. Rutter & E. Schopler (Eds.), *Autism: A reappraisal of concepts and treatment.* New York: Plenum.

Bartak, L., & Rutter, M. (1973). Special education treatment of autistic children: A comparative study, I. *J. Child Psychol. Psychiat.*, **14**, 161–79.

Bartemeier, L. H., Kubie, L. S., Menninger, K. A., Romano, J., & Whitehorn, J. C. (1946). Combat exhaustion. *J. Nerv. Ment. Dis.*, **104**, 385–89, 489–525.

Bartrop, R. W., Lazarus, L., Luckhurst, E. et al. (1977). Depressed lymphocyte function after bereavement. Lancet, 1, 834–36.

Basedow, H. (1927). The Australian aboriginal. London: Adelaide.

Bassuk, E. L., & Gerson, S. (1978). Deinstitutionalization and mental health services. Scientific American, 238(2), 46–53.

Bassuk, E. L., & Schoonover, S. C. (1977). The practitioner's guide to psychoactive drugs. New York: Plenum.

Bateson, G. (1959). Cultural problems posed by a study of schizophrenic process. In A. Auerback (Ed.), Schizophrenia: an integrated approach. New York: Ronald Press.

Bateson, G. (1960). Minimal requirements for a theory of schizophrenia, Arch. Gen. Psychiat., 2, 477–91.

Baucom, D. H. (1983). Sex role identity and the decision to regain control among women: A learned helplessness investigation. J. Pers. Soc. Psychol., 44, 334–43.

Baumrind, D. (1971). Current patterns of parental authority. Develop. Psychol., 4(1), 1–103.

Baumrind, D. (1975). Early socialization and the discipline controversy. Morristown, N. J.: General Learning Press.

Bazell, R. J. (1973, Feb. 23). Drug abuse: Methadone becomes the solution and the problem. Science, 179(4975), 772–75.

Beard, G. M. (1905). A practical treatise on nervous exhaustion (neurasthenia), its symptoms, nature, sequences, treatment (5th ed.). New York: E. B. Treat.

Beck, A. (1976). Cognitive therapy and emotional disorders. New York: International Universities Press.

Beck, A. T. (1967). Depression: Causes and treatment. Philadelphia: University of Pennsylvania Press.

Beck, A. T. (1971). Cognition, affect, and psychopathology. Arch. Gen. Psychiat., 24(6), 495–500.

Beck, A. T., Beck, R., & Kovacs, M. (1975). Classification of suicidal behaviors: I. Qualifying intent and medical lethality. Amer. J. Psychiat., 132(3), 285–87.

Beck, A. T., Laude, R., & Bohnert, M. (1974). Ideational components of anxiety neurosis. Arch. Gen. Psychiat., 31(3), 319–25.

Beck, A. T., Rush, A. J., Shaw, B., & Emery, G. (1979). Cognitive therapy of depression: A treatment manual. New York: Gilford Press.

Beck, L., Langford, W. S., Mackay, M., & Sum, G. (1975). Childhood chemotherapy and later drug abuse and growth curve: A follow-up study of 30 adolescents. Amer. J. Psychiat., 132(4), 436–38.

Becker, J. (1977). Affective disorders. Morristown, N. J.: General Learning Press.

Becker, J., & Altrocchi, J. (1968). Peer conformity and achievement in female manic-depressives. J. Abnorm. Psychol., 73(6), 585–89.

Becker, W. C. (1964). Consequences of different kinds of parental discipline. In M. L. Hoffman & L. W. Hoffman (Eds.), Review of child development research (Vol. 1). New York: Russell Sage Foundation.

Beckman, L. J. (1978). Self-esteem of women alcoholics. Journal of Studies on Alcohol, 3, 491–98.

Beers, C. (1970). A mind that found itself. (Rev. ed.) New York: Doubleday.

Behar, D., & Stewart, M. A. (1982). Aggressive conduct disorder of children. Acta Psychiatr. Scandin., 65(3), 210–20.

Belgian Consulate. (1982). Washington, DC. Personal communication.

Bell, A. O. (1974). Homosexualities: Their range and character. In J. K. Cole and R. Dienstbier (Eds.), Nebraska symposium on motivation, 1973 (pp. 1–26). Lincoln, Neb.: University of Nebraska Press.

Bell, A. P., & Weinberg, M. S. (1978). Homosexualities: A study of diversity among men and women. New York: Simon & Schuster.

Bell, A. P., Weinberg, M. S., & Hammersmith, S. K. (1981). Sexual preference: Its development in men and women. Bloomington: Indiana University Press.

Bell, E., Jr. (1958). The basis of effective military psychiatry. Dis. Nerv. System, 19, 283–88.

Bellak, L. (1975). The Thematic Apperception Test, the Children's Apperception Test, and the Senior Apperception Technique in clinical use (3rd ed.). New York: Grune & Stratton.

Bellak, L. (1979). Introduction: An idiosyncratic overview. In L. Bellak (Ed.), Disorders of the schizophrenic syndrome. New York: Basic Books.

Bellman, M. (1966). Studies on encopresis. Acta Paediatrica Scandanovica Suppl., 170, 121.

Belsky, J., & Steinberg, L. D. (1978). The effects of day care: A critical review. Child Develop., 49, 929–49.

Bem, D. J. (1972). Self-perception theory. In L. Berkowitz (Ed.), Advances in experimental social psychology (Vol. 6). New York: Academic Press.

Bemis, K. M. (1978). Current approaches to the etiology and treatment of anorexia nervosa. Psychol. Bull., 85, 593–617.

Bender, L. (1973). The life course of children with schizophrenia. Amer. J. Psychiat., 130(7), 783–86.

Benedict, R. (1934). Anthropology and the abnormal J. Gen. Psychol., 10, 59–82.

Bengelsdorf, I. S. (1970, Mar. 5). Alcohol, morphine addictions believed chemically similar. Los Angeles Times, II, 7.

Benjamin, H. (1966). The transsexual phenomenon. New York: Julian Press.

Benjamin, L. S. (1974). Structural analysis of social behavior. Psychol. Rev., 81, 392–425.

Benjamin, L. S. (1976a). A reconsideration of the Kety and associates study of genetic factors in the transmission of schizophrenia. Amer. J. Psychiat., 133, 1129–33.

Benjamin, L. S. (1976b). A reply to a rebuttal. Amer. J. Psychiat. 133, 1466.

Benjamin, L. S. (1977). Structural analysis of a family in therapy. J. Cons. Clin. Psychol., 45, 391–406.

Benjamin, L. S. (1979). Use of structural analysis of social behavior (SASB) and Markov chains to study dyadic interactions. J. Abnorm. Psychol., 88, 303–13.

Benjamin, L. S. (1982). Use of structural analysis of social behavior (SASB) to guide intervention in psychotherapy. In J. C. Anchin & D. L. Kiesler (Eds.), Handbook of interpersonal psychotherapy. New York: Pergamon.

Bennett, A. E. (1947). Mad doctors. J. Nerv. Ment. Dis., 106, 11–18.

Bentler, P. M., & Prince, C. (1969). Personality characteristics of male transvestites. III. J. Abnorm. Psychol., 74(2), 140–43.

Bentler, P. M., & Prince, C. (1970). Psychiatric symptomology in transvestites. J. Clin. Psychol., 26(4), 434–35.

Bentler, P. M., Shearman, R. W., & Prince, C. (1970). Personality characteristics of male transvestites. J. Clin. Psychol., 126(3), 287–91.

Beres, D., & Obers, S. J. (1950). The effects of extreme deprivation in infancy on psychic structure in adolescence. In R. S. Eissler et al. (Eds.), The psychoanalytic study of the child. Vol. 5. New York: International University Press.

Berg, A. (1954). The sadist. O. Illner & G. Godwin (trans.) New York: Medical Press of New York.

Berger, P. A. (1978). Medical treatment of mental illness. Science, 200, 974–81.

Berger, R. J. (1970). Morpheus descending. Psych. Today, 4(1), 33–36.

Bergin, A. E., & Lambert, M. J. (1978). The evaluation of therapeutic outcomes. In S. L. Garfield & A. E. Bergin (Eds.), Handbook of psychotherapy and behavior change: An empirical analysis. New York: Wiley.

Bergler, E. (1947). Analysis of an unusual case of fetishism. Bull. Menninger Clin., 2, 67–75.

Bergsma, D. (Ed.). (1974). Medical genetics today (National Foundation Series). Baltimore: Johns Hopkins University Press.

Berk, S. N., Moore, M. E., & Resnick, J. H. (1977). Psychosocial factors as mediators of acupuncture therapy. J. Cons. Clin. Psychol., 45, 612–19.

Berman, E. (1975, August). Tested and documented split personality: Veronica and Nelly. Psychology Today, 78–81.

Bernard, J. L. (1979). Reply to Siegal. Amer. Psychologist, 34(3), 280–82.

Berne, E. (1964). Games people play: The psychology of human relationships. New York: Grove Press.

Berne, E. (1972). *What do you say after you say hello?* New York: Grove Press.

Bettelheim, B. (1943). Individual and mass behavior in extreme situations. *J. Abnorm. Soc. Psychol.,* 38, 417–52.

Bettelheim, B. (1955). *Truants from life: The rehabilitation of emotionally disturbed children.* New York: Free Press.

Bettelheim, B. (1959, Mar.). Joey: A "mechanical boy." *Scientif. American,* 200, 116–27.

Bettelheim, B. (1960). *The informed heart.* New York: Free Press.

Bettelheim, B. (1967). *The empty fortress.* New York: Free Press.

Bettelheim, B. (1969). Laurie. *Psych. Today,* 2(12), 24–25; 60.

Bettelheim, B. (1974). *A home for the heart.* New York: Alfred A. Knopf.

Bibring, E. (1953). The mechanism of depression. In P. Greenacre (Ed.), *Affective disorders.* New York: International University Press.

Bieber, I., Dain, H., Dince, P., Drellech, M., Grand, H., Grundlach, R., Kremer, M., Ritkin, A., Wilbur, C., & Bieber, T. (1962). Quote from *Homosexuality: A psychoanalytic study.* New York: Basic Books, Inc.

Bijou, S. W. (1966). A functional analysis of retarded development. In N. R. Ellis (Ed.), *International review of research in mental retardation.* (Vol. 1). New York: Academic Press.

Biklen, D. (1976). Advocacy comes of age. *Exceptional Children,* 42, 308–13.

Binstock, J. (1974). Choosing to die: The decline of aggression and the rise of suicide. *The Futurist,* 8(2), 68–71.

Binswanger, L. (1942). *Grundformen und Erkenntnis Menschlichen Daseing.* Zurich: Max Nichans.

Biran, M., & Wilson, G. T. (1981). Treatment of phobic disorders using cognitive and exposure methods: A self-efficacy analysis. *J. Cons. Clin. Psychol.* 49, 886–99.

Bird, B. L., Cataldo, M. F., & Parker, L. (1981). Behavioral medicine for muscular disorders. In S. M. Turner, K. S. Calhoun, & H. E. Adams (Eds.), *Handbook of clinical behavior therapy.* New York: Wiley.

Birns, B., & Bridger, W. (1977). Cognitive development and social class. In J. Wortis (Ed.), *Mental retardation and developmental disabilities* (Vol. 9, pp. 203–33). New York: Brunner/Mazel.

Blacker, K. H., Jones, R. T., Stone, G. C., & Pfefferbaum, D. (1968). Chronic users of LSD: The "acidheads." *Amer. J. Psychiat.,* 125(3), 97–107.

Blair, C. D., & Lanyon, R. I. (1981). Exhibitionism: Etiology and treatment. *Psychol. Bull.,* 89, 439–63.

Blake, G. (1967, Jan. 26). Community treatment plan aids delinquents. Five year experiment. *Los Angeles Times,* 1; 6.

Blanchard, E. B., & Andrasik, F. (1982). Psychological assessment and treatment of headache: Recent developments and emerging issues. *J. Cons. Clin. Psychol.,* 50(6), 859–79.

Blanchard, E. B., Andrasik, F., Ahles, T. A., Teders, S. J., & O'Keefe, D. (1980). Migraine and tension headache: A metaanalytic review. *Behavior Therapy,* 11, 613–31.

Blanchard, E. B., Andrasik, F., Neff, D. F., Teders, S. J., Pallmeyer, T. P., Arena, J. G., Jurish, S. E., Saunders, N. L., & Rodichok, L. D. (1983). Sequential comparisons of relaxation training and biofeedback in the treatment of three kinds of chronic headache or, The machines may be necessary some of the time. *Behav. Res. Ther.*

Blanchard, E. B., & Epstein, L. H. (1978). *A biofeedback primer.* Reading, Mass: Addison-Wesley.

Blanchard, E. B., Miller, S. T., Abel, G. G., Haynes, M. R., & Wicker, R. (1979). Evaluation of biofeedback in treatment of borderline essential hypertension. *J. Appl. Beh. Anal.,* 12, 99–109.

Blanchard, E. B., & Young, L. D. (1973). Self-control of cardiac functioning: A promise as yet unfulfilled. *Psychol. Bull.,* 79, 145–63.

Blanchard, E. B., & Young L. D. (1974). Clinical applications of biofeedback training: A review of evidence. *Arch. Gen. Psychiat.,* 30, 573–89.

Blaney, P. H. (1977). Contemporary theories of depression: Critique and comparison, *J. Abnorm. Psychol.,* 86(2), 203–23.

Blatt, S. J., D'Afflitti, J. P. & Quinlan, D. M. (1976). Experiences of depression in normal young adults. *J. Abnorm. Psychol.,* 85, 383–89.

Blatt, S. J., Quinlan, D. M., Chevron, E. S., McDonald, C., & Zuroff, D. (1982). Dependency and self-criticism: Psychological dimensions of depression. *J. Cons. Clin. Psychol.* 50, 113–24.

Blau, A., Slaff, B., Easton, K., Welkowitz, J., Springarn, J., & Cohen, J. (1963). The psychogenic etiology of premature births. *Psychosom. Med.,* 25, 201–11.

Blau, D. (1970). The course of psychiatric hospitalization in the aged. *J. Geriat. Psychol.,* 3(2), 210–23.

Bleeker, E. (1968). Many asthma attacks psychological. *Sci. News,* 93(17), 406.

Bleuler, E. (1950). *Dementia praecox or the group of schizophrenias.* New York: International Universities Press. (Originally published in 1911.)

Bleuler, M. (1974). Offspring of schizophrenics. *Schizophrenia Bull.,* 8, 93–107.

Bleuler, M. (1978). The long-term course of schizophrenic psychoses. In L. C. Wynne, R. L. Cromwell, & S. Matthysse (Eds.), *The nature of schizophrenia: New approaches to research and treatment.* (pp. 631–36). New York: Wiley.

Bloch, H. S. (1969). Army clinical psychiatry in the combat zone—1967–1968. *Amer. J. Psychiat.,* 126, 289–98.

Block, A. A., & Chambliss, W. J. (1981). *Organizing crime.* New York: Elsevier.

Bloom, B. L., Asher, S. J., & White, S. W. (1978). Marital disruption as a stressor: A review and analysis. *Psychol. Bull.,* 85, 867–94.

Bluemel, C. S. (1948). *War, politics, and insanity.* Denver: World Press.

Bluestone, H., & McGahee, C. L. (1962). Reaction to extreme stress. *Amer. J. Psychiat.,* 119, 393–96.

Blum, R. (1969). *Society and drugs* (Vol. 1) San Francisco: Jossey-Bass.

Blumenthal, J. A., Williams, R. B., Jr., Kong, Y., Schonberg, S. M., & Thompson, L. W. (1978). Type A behaviors pattern and coronary atherosclerosis. *Circulation,* 58(4), 634–39.

Blumer, D., & Benson, D. F. (1975). Personality changes with frontal and temporal lobe lesions. In D. F. Benson & D. Blumer (Eds.), *Psychiatric aspects of neurological disease* (pp. 151–70). New York: Grune & Stratton.

Bockhoven, J. S. (1972). *Moral treatment in community mental health.* New York: Springer.

Boehm, G. (1968). At last—a nonaddicting substitute for morphine? *Today's Health,* 46(4), 69–72.

Bolen, D. W., & Boyd, W. H. (1968). Gambling and the gambler. *Arch. Gen. Psychiat.,* 18(5), 617–30.

Bolen, D. W. Caldwell, A. B., & Boyd, W. H. (1975, June). *Personality traits of pathological gamblers.* Paper presented at the Second Annual Conference on Gambling, Lake Tahoe, Nevada.

Boll, T. J. (1978). Diagnosing brain impairment. In B. B. Wolman, (Ed.), *Clinical diagnosis of mental disorders: A handbook.* New York: Plenum.

Boll, T. J. (1980). The Halstead-Reitan neurophysiology battery. In S. B. Filskov & T. J. Boll (Eds.), *Handbook of neurophysiology.* New York: Wiley Interscience Series.

Bolls, R. C., & Fanselow, M. S. (1982). Endorphins and behavior. *Annu. Rev. Psychol.,* 33, 87–101.

Borg, W. R., & Ascione, F. R. (1982). Classroom management in elementary mainstreaming classrooms. *J. Educ. Psychol.,* 74, 84–95.

Borkovec, T. D. (1970). Autonomic reactivity to sensory stimulation in psychopathic, neurotic, and normal juvenile delinquents. *J. Cons. Clin. Psychol.,* 35, 217–22.

Borus, J. F. (1974). Incidence of maladjustment in Vietnam returnees. *Arch. Gen. Psychiat.,* 30(4), 554–57.

Boucher, J. (1981). Memory for recent events in autistic children. *J. Autism Devel. Disorders,* 11(3), 293–301.

Bourne, P. G. (1970). Military psychiatry and the Vietnam experience. *Amer. J. Psychiat.,* 127(4), 481–88.

Bowen, M. (1959). Family relationships in schizophrenia. In A. Auerback (Ed.), *Schizophrenia: An integrated approach.* New York: Ronald Press.

Bowen M. (1960). A family concept of schizophrenia. In D. D. Jackson (Ed.), *The etiology of schizophrenia*, New York: Basic Books.

Bowers, M., Jr. (1965). The onset of psychosis—A diary account. *Psychiatry*, **28**, 346–58.

Bowlby, J. (1960). Separation anxiety. *Inter. J. Psychoanal.*, **41**, 89–93.

Bowlby, J. (1973). Separation: Anxiety and anger. *Psychology of attachment and loss series*. (Vol. 3). New York: Basic Books.

Boyd, J. H., & Weissman, M. M. (1982). Epidemiology. In E. S. Paykel (Ed.), *Handbook of affective disorders*. New York: Guilford Press.

Boyd, W. H., & Bolen, D. W. (1970). The compulsive gambler and spouse in group psychotherapy. *Inter. J. Group Psychother.*, **20**, 77–90.

Braden, W., Stillman, R. C., & Wyatt, R. J. (1974). Effects of marijuana on contingent negative variation and reaction times. *Arch. Gen. Psychiat.*, **31**(4), 537–41.

Bradley, L. A., & Prokop, C. K. (1981). The relationship between medical psychology and behavioral medicine. In C. K. Prokop & L. A. Bradley (Eds.), *Medical psychology: Contributions to behavioral medicine*. New York: Academic Press.

Bradley, L. A., & Prokop, C. K. (1982). Research methods in contemporary medical psychology. In P. C. Kendall & J. N. Butcher (Eds.), *Handbook of research methods in clinical psychology*. New York: Wiley Interscience.

Braff, D. L., Silverton, L., Sacuzzo, D. P., & Janowsky, D. S. (1981). Impaired speed of visual information processing in marijuana intoxication. *Amer. J. Psychiat.*, **138**(5), 613–17.

Braginsky, B. M., & Braginsky, D. D. (1974). The mentally retarded: Society's Hansels and Gretels. *Psych. Today*. **7**(10), 18; 20–21; 24; 26; 28–30.

Braginsky, B. M., Braginsky, D. D., & Ring, K. (1969). *Methods of madness: The mental hospital as a last resort*. New York: Holt, Rinehart, and Winston.

Brandel, S. K. (1980). Refugees: New dimensions to an old problem *Communique*. Washington, DC: Overseas Development Council.

Brandsma, J. M., Maultsby, M. C., & Welsh, R. J. (1980). *Outpatient treatment of alcoholism: A review and comparative study*. Baltimore: University Park Press.

Brantley, P., & Sutker, P. B. (1983). Antisocial personalities. In P. Sutker & H. Adams (Eds.), *Comprehensive handbook of psychopathology*. New York: Plenum.

Braun, P., Kochansky, G., Shapiro, R., Greenberg, S., Gudeman, J. E., Johnson, S., & Shore, M. (1981). Overview: Deinstitutionalization of psychiatric patients, a critical review of outcome studies. *Amer. J. Psychiat.*, **138**(6), 736–49.

Brebner, A., Hallworth, H. J., & Brown, R. I. (1977). Computer-assisted instruction programs and terminals for the mentally retarded. In P. Mittler (Ed.), *Research to practice in mental retardation* (Vol. 2, pp. 421–26). Baltimore: University Park Press.

Brecksville V. A. Medical Center. (1981). *Annual report for 1981: Gambling treatment program*. Cleveland, OH.

Breggin, P. R. (1979). *Electroshock: Its brain-disabling effects* New York: Springer.

Brehm, S. S. (1976). *The application of social psychology to clinical practice*. New York: Halsted Press.

Brenner, M. H. (1973). *Mental illness and the economy*. Cambridge, MA: Harvard University Press.

Bridges, F. A., & Cicchetti, D. (1982). Mothers' ratings of the temperament characteristics of Down Syndrome infants. *Develop. Psychol.*, **18**, 238–44.

Brodey, W. M. (1959). Some family operations and schizophrenia. *Arch. Gen. Psychiat.*, **1**, 379–402.

Brodie, E. B. (1981). Can mother-infant interaction produce vulnerability to schizophrenia? *J. Nerv. Ment. Dis.*, **169**(2), 72–81.

Brodie, H. K. H., Gartrell, N., Doering, C., & Rhue, T. (1974). Plasma testosterone levels in heterosexual and homosexual men. *Amer. J. Psychiat.*, **131**(1), 82–83.

Bromberg, W. (1937). *The mind of man*. New York: Harper.

Brooks, D. N. (1974). Recognition, memory, and head injury. *Journal of Neurology, Neurosurgery, & Psychiatry*, **37**(7), 794–801.

Brown, B. (1974, Apr. 29). Depression roundup. *Behav. Today*. **5**(17), 117.

Brown, G. W. (1972). Life-events and psychiatric illness: Some thoughts on methodology and causality. *J. Psychosom. Res.*, **16**(5), 311–20.

Brown, G. W., & Harris, T. (1978). *Social origins of depression*. London: Tavistock Publications.

Brown, J. F., & Menninger, K. A. (1940). *Psychodynamics of abnormal behavior*. New York: McGraw-Hill.

Brown, R. I. (1977). An integrated program for the mentally handicapped. In P. Mittler (Ed.), *Research to practice in mental retardation* (Vol. 2, pp. 387–88). Baltimore: University Park Press.

Browne, E. G. (1921). *Arabian medicine*. New York: Macmillan.

Bruch, H. (1973). *Eating disorders: Obesity, anorexia nervosa and the person within*. New York: Basic Books.

Bruch, H. (1978). *The golden cage: The enigma of anorexia nervosa*. Cambridge, Mass.: Harvard University Press.

Bry, B. H., McKeon, P., & Pandina, R. J. (1982). The extent of drug use as a function of number of risk factors. *J. Abnorm. Psychol.*, **91**(4), 273–79.

Bryan, T. H. (1974). Learning disabilities: A new stereotype. *J. Learn. Dis.*, **7**(5), 46–51.

Buber, M. (1957). Distance and relation. *Psychiatry*, **20**, 97–104.

Bucher, B., & Lovaas, O. I. (1967). Use of aversive stimulation in behavior modification. In M. R. Jones (Ed.), *Miami symposium on the prediction of behavior 1967: Aversive stimulation* (pp. 77–145). Coral Gables: University of Miami Press.

Buchsbaum, M. S., Murphy, D. L., Coursey, R. D., Lake, C. R., & Zeigler, M. G. (1978). Platelet monoamine oxidase, plasma dopamine betahydroxylase and attention in a "biochemical high-risk" sample. In L. C. Wynne, R. L. Cromwell, & S. Matthysse (Eds.), *The nature of schizophrenia: New approaches to research and treatment* (pp. 387–96). New York: Wiley.

Buckley, P. (1982). Identifying schizophrenic patients who should not receive medication. *Schizophrenia Bulletin*, **8**, 429–32.

Buckner, H. T. (1970). The transvestic career path. *Psychiatry*, **33**(3), 381–89.

Budoff, M. (1977). The mentally retarded child in the mainstream of the public school: His relation to the school administration, his teachers, and his age-mates. In P. Mittler (Ed.), *Research to practice in mental retardation*. (Vol. 2, pp. 307–13). Baltimore: University Park Press.

Budzynski, T. (1974). In M. Schneider, Some cheering news about a very painful subject. *The Sciences*, **14**(4), 6–12.

Bukstel, L. H., & Kilmann, P. R. (1980). Psychological effects of imprisonment on confined individuals. *Psychol. Bull.*, **88**(2), 469–93.

Bullard, D. M., Glaser, H. H., Heagarty, M. C., & Pivcheck, E. C. (1967). Failure to thrive in the neglected child. *Amer. J. Orthopsychiat.*, **37**, 680–90.

Bumbalo, J. H., & Young, D. E. (1973). The self-help phenomenon. *Amer. J. Nurs.*, **73**, 1588–91.

Burgess, A. W., & Holmstrom, L. (1974). Rape trauma syndrome. *Amer. J. Psychiat.*, **131**. 981–86.

Burgess, A. W., & Holmstrom, L. (1976). Coping behavior of the rape victim. *Amer. J. Psychiat.*, **133**, 413–18.

Burks, H. L., & Harrison, S. I. (1962). Aggressive behavior as a means of avoiding depression. *Amer. J. Orthopsychiat.*, **32**, 416–22.

Burns, G. W. (1972). *The science of genetics*. New York: Macmillan.

Burnstein, M. H. (1981). Child abandonment: Historical, sociological, and psychological perspectives. *Child Psychiat. Human Develop.*, **11**, 213–21.

Burquist, B. (1981). The violent girl. *Adolescence*, **16**(64), 749–64.

Burros, W. M. (1974). The growing burden of impotence. *Family Health*, **6**(5), 18–21.

Buss, A., & Plomin, R. (1975). *A temperament theory of personality development.* New York: Wiley.

Buss, A. H. (1966). *Psychopathology.* New York: Wiley.

Butcher, J. N., & Kolotkin, R. (1979). Evaluation of outcome in brief psychotherapy. *Psychiatric Clinics of North America,* 3(1), 157–69.

Butcher, J. N., & Pancheri, P. (1976). *Handbook of international MMPI research.* Minneapolis: University of Minnesota Press.

Butcher, J. N., Stelmachers, Z., & Maudal, G. R. (1983). Crisis intervention and emergency psychotherapy. In I. Weiner (Ed.), *Clinical methods in psychology* (2nd ed.). New York: John Wiley and Sons.

Byassee, J. E. (1977.) Essential hypertension. In R. B. Williams, Jr. & W. D. Gentry (Eds.), *Behavioral approaches to medical treatment* (pp. 113–37). Cambridge MA: Ballinger.

Bychowski, G. (1950). On neurotic obesity. *Psychoanal. Rev.,* 37, 301–19.

Cade, J. F. J. (1949). Lithium salts in the treatment of psychotic excitement. *Medical Journal of Australia,* 36 (part II): 349–352.

Cadoret, R. J. (1978). Evidence for genetic inheritance of primary affective disorder in adoptees. *Amer. J. Psychiat.,* 135, 463–66.

Caffey, E. M. Galbrecht, C. R., & Klett, C. J. (1971). Brief hospitalization and aftercare in the treatment of schizophrenia. *Arch. Gen. Psychiat.,* 21(1), 81–86.

Cameron, N. (1959). Paranoid conditions and paranoia. In S. Arieti (Ed.), *American handbook of psychiatry.* New York: Basic Books.

Cameron, N., & Margaret, A. (1949). Experimental studies in thinking. I. Scattered speech in the responses of normal subjects to incomplete sentences. *J. Exper. Psychol.,* 39(5), 617–27.

Cameron, N., & Margaret, A. (1951). *Behavior pathology.* Boston: Houghton Mifflin.

Campbell, D. (1926). *Arabian medicine and its influence on the Middle Ages.* New York: Dutton.

Cannon, W. B. (1942). "Voodoo" death. *American Anthropologist,* 44(2), 169–81.

Cantor, D. (1982, Apr. 26). Psychoanalysis gains new strengths, admirers. Cited in *Behav. Today,* 3.

Cantwell, D. P., Mattison, R., Russell, A. T., & Will, L. (1979). A comparison of DSM II and DSM III in the diagnosis of childhood disorders, *Arch. Gen. Psychiat.,* 36, 1227–28.

Cappell, H. D., & Pliner, P. L. (1973). Volitional control of marijuana intoxication: A study of the ability to "come down" on command. *J. Abnorm. Psychol.,* 82(3), 428–34.

Caputo, D. V., & Mandell, W. (1970). Consequences of low birth weight. *Develop. Psychol.,* 3(3), 363–83.

Carlson, G., & Goodwin, F. K. (1973). The stages of mania: A longitudinal analysis of the manic episode. *Arch. Gen. Psychiat.,* 28(2), 221–28.

Carothers, J. C. (1947). A study of mental derangement in Africans, and an attempt to explain its peculiarities more especially in relation to the African attitude of life. *J. Ment. Sci.,* 93, 548–97.

Carothers, J. C. (1951). Frontal lobe function and the African. *J. Ment. Sci.,* 97, 12–48.

Carothers, J. C. (1953). The African mind in health and disease. In *A study of ethnopsychiatry.* Geneva: World Health Organization, No. 17.

Carothers, J. C. (1959). Culture, psychiatry, and the written word. *Psychiatry,* 22, 307–20.

Carpenter, W. T., & Strauss, J. S. (1979). Diagnostic issues in schizophrenia. In L. Bellak (Ed.), *Disorders of the schizophrenic syndrome.* New York: Basic Books.

Carr, A. T. (1971). Compulsive neurosis: Two psychophysiological studies. *Bulletin of the British Psychological Society,* 24, 256–57.

Carr, J. E. (1978). Behavior therapy and the treatment of flight phobia. *Aviation, Space and Environmental Medicine,* 49(9), 1115–19.

Carruthers, M., (1980). Hazardous occupations and the heart. In C. L. Cooper & R. Payne (Eds.), *Current concerns in occupational stress.* New York: Wiley.

Carson, R. C. (1969). *Interaction concepts of personality.* Chicago: Aldine.

Carson, R. C. (1971). Disordered interpersonal behavior. In W. A. Hunt (Ed.), *Human behavior and its control* (pp. 134–57). Cambridge, MA: Schenkman (Distributed by General Learning Press, Morristown, N.J.).

Carson, R. C. (1979). Personality and exchange in developing relationships. In R. L. Burgess & T. L. Huston (Eds.), *Social exchange in developing relationships.* New York: Academic Press.

Carson, R. C. (1984). The schizophrenias. In H. E. Adams & P. B. Sutker (Eds.), *Comprehensive handbook of psychopathology.* New York: Plenum.

Carson, T. P., & Adams, H. E. (1981). Affective disorders: Behavioral perspectives. In S. M. Turner, K. S. Calhoun, H. E. Adams (Eds.,), *Handbook of clinical behavior therapy.* New York: Wiley.

Carson, T. P., & Carson, R. C. (1984). The affective disorders. In H. E. Adams, & P. B. Sutker (Eds.), *Comprehensive handbook of psychopathology.* New York: Plenum.

Carstens, C. (1982). Behavioral treatment of functional dysphagia in a 12-year-old boy. *Psychosomatics,* 23(2), 195–96.

Castiglioni, A. (1946). *Adventures of the mind.* New York: Knopf.

Cautela, J. R. (1967). Covert sensitization. *Psych. Rep.,* 20, 459–68.

Cavallin, H. (1966). Incestuous fathers: A clinical report. *Amer. J. Psychiat.,* 122(10), 1132–38.

Celentano, D. D., & McQueen, D. V. (1978). Comparison of alcoholism prevalence rates obtained by survey and indirect estimators. *J. Studies on Alcohol,* 39, 420–34.

Centerwall, W. R., & Centerwall, S. A. (1961). Phenylketonuria (Folling's disease): The story of its discovery. *Journal of the History of Medicine,* 16, 292–96.

Chaiken, J. M., & Chaiken, M. R. (1982). *Varieties of criminal.* National Institute of Justice. U.S. Department of Justice. Washington, DC: U.S. Government Printing Office.

Chalfant, J. C., & Scheffelin, M. A. (1969). *Central processing dysfunctions in children: A review of research.* INNDS monogr. no. 9. Washington, DC: U.S. Government Printing Office.

Chambers, R. E. (1952). Discussion of "Survival factors. . . ." *Amer. J. Psychiat.,* 109, 247–48.

Chapman, L. J., & Chapman, J. P. (1980). Scales for rating psychotic and psychotic-like experiences as continua. *Schizophrenia Bull.,* 6, 476–89.

Charney, F. L. (1979). Inpatient treatment programs. In W. H. Reid (Ed.), *The psychopath: A comprehensive study of antisocial disorders and behaviors.* New York: Brunner/Mazel.

Chaves, J. F., & Barber, T. X. (1973). Needles and knives: Behind the mystery of acupuncture and Chinese meridians. *Human Behavior,* 2(1), 18–24.

Chesney, M. A., Eagleston, J. R., & Rosenman, R. H. (1981). Type A behavior: Assessment and intervention. In C. K. Prokop & L. A. Bradley (Eds.), *Medical psychology: Contributions to behavioral medicine.* New York: Academic Press.

Chesno, F. A., & Kilmann, P. R. (1975). Effects of stimulation on sociopathic avoidance learning. *J. Abnorm. Psychol.,* Apr. 84(2), 144–50.

Chess, S., Thomas, A., & Birch, H. G. (1965). *Your child is a person.* New York: Viking.

Chesser, E. (1971). *Strange loves: The human aspects of sexual deviation.* New York: William Morrow.

Chodoff, P. (1970). The German concentration camp as a psychological stress. *Arch. Gen. Psychiat.,* 22(1), 78–87.

Chodoff, P. (1972). The depressive personality: A critical review. *Arch. Gen. Psychiat.,* 27(2), 666–73.

Christensen, D., & Rosenthal, R. (1982). Gender and nonverbal decoding skill as determinants of interpersonal expectancy effects. *J. Pers. Soc. Psychol.,* 42, 75–87.

Christenson, R. M., Walker, J. I., Ross, D. R., & Maultbie, A. A. (1981). Reactivation of traumatic conflicts. *Amer. J. Psychiat.,* 138, 984–85.

Christie, B. L. (1981). Childhood enuresis: current thoughts on causes and cures. *Social Work Health Care,* 6(3), 77–90.

Christodorescu, D., Collins, S., Zellingher, R., & Tautu, C. (1970). Psychiatric disturbances in Turner's syndrome: Report of three cases. *Psychiatrica Clinica*, 3(2), 114–24.

Churchill, W. (1967). *Homosexual behavior among males: A cross-cultural and cross-species investigation.* New York: Hawthorne.

Claeson, L. E., & Malm, U. (1973). Electro-aversion therapy of chronic alcoholism. *Behav. Res. Ther.*, 11(4), 663–65.

Clancy, H., & McBride, G. (1969). The autistic process and its treatment. *J. Child Psychol. Psychiat.*, 10(4), 233–44.

Clark, G. R. Kivitz, M. S., & Rosen, N. (1969). Program for mentally retarded. *Sci. News*, 96, 82.

Clarke, J. (1961). The precipitation of juvenile delinquency. *J. Ment. Sci.*, 107, 1033–34.

Clayton, P. J. (1982). Bereavement. In E. S. Paykel (Ed.), *Handbook of affective disorders.* New York: Guilford Press.

Clement, P. (1970). Elimination of sleepwalking in a seven-year-old boy. *J. Cons. Clin. Psychol.*, 34(1), 22–26.

Clements, S. D. (1966). *Minimal brain dysfunction in children—Terminology and identification.* Washington, DC: HEW.

Climent, C. E., Rollins, A., Ervin, F. R., & Plutchik, R. (1973). Epidemiological studies of women prisoners, I: medical and psychiatric variables related to violent behavior. *Amer. J. Psychiat.*, 130(9), 985–90.

Cline, V. B., Croft, R. G., & Courrier, S. (1973). Desensitization of children to television violence. *J. Pers. Soc. Psychol.*, 27, 360–65.

Cloninger, C. R., & Guze, S. (1970). Psychiatric illness and female criminality: The role of sociopathy and hysteria in the antisocial woman. *Amer. J. Psychiat.*, 127(3), 303–11.

Coates, T. J., Perry, C., Killen, J., & Slinkard, L. A. (1981). Primary prevention of cardiovascular disease in children and adolescents. In C. K. Prokop & L. A. Bradley (Eds.), *Medical psychology: Contributions to behavioral medicine.* New York: Academic Press.

Coates, T. J., & Thoreson, C. E. (1981). Treating sleep disorders: Few answers, some suggestions, and many questions. In S. M. Turner, K. S. Calhoun, & H. E. Adams (Eds.), *Handbook of clinical behavior therapy.* New York: Wiley.

Cockayne, T. O. (1864–1866). *Leechdoms, wort cunning, and star craft of early England.* London: Longman, Green, Longman, Roberts & Green.

Cohen, F. (1981). Stress and bodily illness. *Psychiatric Clinics of North America*, 4(2), 269–86.

Cohen, J., & Hansel, M. (1956). *Risk and gambling: A study of subjective probability.* New York: Philosophical Library.

Cohen, M., Seghorn, T., & Calmas, W. (1969). Sociometric study of the sex offender. *J. Abnorm. Psychol.* 74(2), 249–55.

Cohen, S. (1976). The use of psychedelics as adjuncts to psychotherapy. In U. Binder, A. Binder, & B. Rimland (Eds.), *Modern therapies.* New York: Prentice-Hall.

Cohen, S. L., & Fiedler, J. E. (1974). "Content analysis of multiple messages in suicide notes". *Life-Threatening Behavior*, 4(2), 75–95.

Cohen, S. M., Allen, M. G., Pollin, W., & Hrubec, Z. (1972). Relationship of schizo-affective psychosis to manic depressive psychosis and schizophrenia. *Arch. Gen. Psychiat.*, 26(6), 539–46.

Cole, J. O. (1974). Depression. *Amer. J. Psychiat.*, 131(2), 204–5.

Cole, S. O. (1975). Hyperkinetic children: The use of stimulant drugs evaluated. *Amer. J. Orthopsychiat.*, 45(1), 28–37.

Coleman, J. C. (1973). Life stress and maladaptive behavior. *Amer. J. Occupa. Ther.*, 27(4), 169–80.

Commission of Inquiry into the Non-Medical Use of Drugs. (1970). *Interim report.* Ottawa, Canada: Crown.

Comstock, G., Chaffee, S., Katzman, N., McCombs, M., & Roberts, D. (1978). *Television and human behavior.* New York: Columbia University Press.

Cookerly, J. R. (1980). Does marital therapy do any lasting good? *J. Marital and Family Ther.*, 6(4), 393–97.

Cooper, A. J. (1969). A clinical study of "coital anxiety" in male potency disorders. *J. Psychosom. Res.*, 13(2), 143–47.

Cooper, J. E., Kendell, R. E., Gurland, B. J., Sharpe, L., Copeland, J. R. M., & Simon, R. (1972). *Psychiatric diagnosis in New York and London.* London: Oxford University Press.

Coopersmith, S. (1967). *The antecedents of self-esteem.* San Francisco: Freeman.

Copeland, J. (1968). Aspects of mental illness in West African students. *Soc. Psychiat.*, 3(1), 7–13.

Coppen, A., Metcalfe, M., & Wood, K. (1982). Lithium. In E. S. Paykel (Ed.), *Handbook of affective disorders.* New York: Guilford Press.

Corsini, R. (Ed.). (1979). *Current psychotherapies.* (2nd Ed.) Itasca, NY: Peacock.

Coryell, W., & Winokur, G. (1982). Course and outcome. In E. S. Paykel (Ed.), *Handbook of affective disorders.* New York: Guilford Press.

Cotler, S. B. (1971). The use of different behavioral techniques in treating a case of compulsive gambling. *Behavior Therapy*, 2, 579–81.

Covi, L., Lipman, R. S., Derogatis, L. R., Smith, J. E., III, & Pattison, J. H. (1974). Drugs and group psychotherapy in neurotic depression. *Amer. J. Psychiat.*, 131(2), 191–97.

Cox, D. J., Freundlich, A., & Meyer, R. G. (1975). Differential effectiveness of electromyographic feedback, verbal relaxation instructions, and medication placebo with tension headaches. *J. Cons. Clin. Psychol.*, 43, 892–98.

Coyne, J. C. (1976). Depression and the response of others. *J. Abnorm. Psychol.*, 55(2), 186–93.

Coyne, J. C., Aldwin, C., & Lazarus, R. S. (1981). Depression and coping in stressful episodes. *J. Abnorm. Psychol.*, 90, 439–47.

Coyne, J. C., & Holroyd, K. (1982). Stress, coping and illness: A transactional perspective. In T. Millon, C. Greene, & R. Meagher (Eds.), *Handbook of clinical health psychology.* New York: Plenum.

Craighead, W. E., Kazdin, A. E., & Mahoney, M. J. (1981). *Behavior modification: Principles, issues, and applications.* Boston: Houghton Mifflin.

Cravioto, J., & de Licardie, E. R. (1975). Environmental and nutritional deprivation in children with learning disabilities. In W. M. Cruickshank & D. P. Hallahan (Eds.), *Perceptual and learning disabilities in children* (Vol. 2): *Research and Theory.* Syracuse, New York: Syracuse University Press.

Creasy, M. R., & Crolla, J. A. (1974, Mar. 23). Prenatal mortality of trisomy 21 (Down's syndrome). *Lancet*, 1(7856), 473–74.

Crichton, R. (1959). *The great imposter.* New York: Random House.

Crisp, A. H. (1977). The prevalence of anorexia nervosa and some of its associations in the general population. In S. Kasl & F. Reichsman (Eds.), *Advances in psychosomatic medicine: Vol 9. Epidemiologic studies in psychosomatic medicine* (pp. 38–47). Basel, Switzerland: S. Karger.

Crisp, A. H., Douglas, J. W. B., Ross, J. M., & Stonehill, E. (1970). Some developmental aspects of disorders of weight. *J. Psychosom. Res.*, 14, 313–20.

Crisp, A. H., Palmer, R. L., & Kalury, R. S. (1976). How common is anorexia nervosa? A prevalence study. *Brit. J. Psychiat.*, 218, 519–54.

Crockett, D., Clark, C., & Klonoff, H. (1981). Introduction—an overview of neuropsychology. In S. B. Filskov & T. J. Boll (Eds.), *Handbook of clinical neuropsychology.* New York: Wiley.

Crook, T., & Eliot, J. (1980). Parental death during childhood and adult depression: A critical review of the literature. *Psychol. Bull.*, 87, 252–59.

Culliton, B. J. (1970, Jan. 24). Pot facing stringent scientific examination. *Sci. News*, Jan. 24, 97(4), 102–5.

Culliton, B. J. (1976). Psychosurgery: National Commission issues surprisingly favorable report. *Science*, 194, 299–301.

Cummings, C., Gordon, J. R., & Marlatt, G. A. (1980). Relapse: Prevention and prediction. In W. R. Miller (Ed.), *The addictive behaviors.* New York: Pergamon Press.

Curlee, J. (1969). Alcoholism and the "empty nest." *Bull. Menninger Clin.*, 33(3), 165–71.

Custer, R. L. (1982). An overview of compulsive gambling. In P. A. Carone, S. F. Yolles, S. N. Kieffer & L. W. Krinsky

(Eds.), *Addictive disorders update*. New York: Human Sciences.

Dahlstrom, W. G. (1978, Aug.). *Minority status and MMPI scores: MMPI score patterns and background characteristics of black adults.* Paper presented at the meeting of the American Psychological Association, Toronto.

Dahlstrom, W. G., Welsh, G. S., & Dahlstrom, L. E. (1975). *An MMPI handbook: Research applications (Vol. 2).* Minneapolis: University of Minnesota Press.

Daniel, W. F., & Crovitz, H. F. (1983a). Acute memory impairment following electroconvulsive therapy: 1. Effects of electrical stimulus and number of treatments. *Acta Psychiatrica Scandinavica,* 67, 1–7.

Daniel, W. F., & Crovitz, H. F. (1983b). Acute memory impairment following electroconvulsive therapy: 2. Effects of electrode placement. *Acta Psychiatrica Scandinavica,* 67, 57–68.

Darbonne, A. R. (1969). Suicide and age: A suicide note analysis. *J. Cons. Clin. Psychol.,* 33, 46–50.

Davenport, W., (1965). Sexual patterns and their regulation in a society of the Southwest Pacific. In F. Beach (Ed.), *Sex and behavior.* New York: Wiley.

Davidson, A. D. (1979a, Spring). Coping with stress reactions in rescue workers: A program that worked. *Police Stress.*

Davidson, A. D. (1979b) Personal communication.

Davidson, W. S. (1974). Studies of aversive conditioning for alcoholics: A critical review of theory and research methodology. *Psychol. Bull.,* 81(9), 571–81.

Davidson, W. S., & Seidman, E. (1974). Studies of behavior modification and juvenile delinquency: A review, methodological critique, and social perspective. *Psychol. Bull.,* 81(12), 998–1011.

Davis, J. M. (1976). Overview: Maintenance therapies in psychiatry: Affective disorder (Vol. 2). *Amer. J. Psychiat.,* 133(1), 1–13.

Davis, J. M. (1978). Dopamine theory of schizophrenia: A two-factor theory. In L. C. Wynne, R. L. Cromwell, & S. Matthysse (Eds.), *The nature of schizophrenia; New approaches to research and treatment* (pp. 105–15). New York: Wiley.

Davis, M. H., Saunders, D. R., Creer, T. L., & Chai, H. (1973). Relaxation training facilitated by biofeedback apparatus as a supplemental treatment in bronchial asthma. *J. Psychosom. Res.,* 17(2), 121–28.

Davison, G. C. (1976). Homosexuality: The ethical challenge. *J. Cons. Clin. Psychol.,* 44(2), 157–62.

Davison, G. C. (1978). Not can but ought: The treatment of homosexuality. *J. Cons. Clin. Psychol.,* 46(1), 170–2.

Day, G. (1951, May 12). The psychosomatic approach to pulmonary tuberculosis. *Lancet,* 6663.

De Beauvoir, S. (1970, Feb. 9). The terrors of old age. *Newsweek,* 54.

DeFazio, V. J., Rustin, S., & Diamond, A. (1975). Symptom development in Vietnam era veterans. *Amer. J. Orthopsychiat.,* 45(1), 158–63.

DeFrancis, V. (1969). *Protecting the child victim of sex crimes committed by adults.* Denver: Children Division, American Humane Association.

DeMyer, M. K., Hingtgen, J. N., & Jackson, R. K. (1981). Infantile autism reviewed: A decade of research. *Schizophrenia Bull.* 7(3), 388–451.

Denicola, J., & Sandler, J. (1980). Training abusive parents in child management and self-control skills. *Behav. Ther.,* 11, 263–70.

Denner, B. (1974). Returning madness to an accepting community. *Comm. Ment. Hlth, J.,* 10(2), 163–72.

Depue, R. A., & Monroe, S. M. (1978). The unipolar-bipolar distinction in the depressive disorders. *Psychol. Bull.,* 85, 1001–29.

Depue, R. A., Slater, J. F., Wolfstetter-Kausch, H., Klein, D., Goplerud, E., & Farr, D. (1981). A behavioral paradigm for identifying persons at risk for bipolar disorder: A conceptual framework. *J. Abnorm. Psychol.,* 90, 381–437.

Deur, J. I., & Parke, R. D. (1970). Effects of inconsistent punishment on aggression in children. *Develop. Psychol.,* 2, 403–11.

Deutsch, A. (1946). *The mentally ill in America.* New York: Columbia University Press.

Devroye, A. (1973). Incest: Bibliographical review (French). *Acta Psychiatrica Belgica,* 73(6), 661–712.

De Young, M. (1982). Innocent seducer and innocently seduced? The role of the child incest victim. *J. Clin. Child Psychol.,* 11, 56–60.

Diamond, B. L. (1969). Sirhan B. Sirhan: A conversation with T. George Harris. *Psych. Today,* 3(4), 48–56.

Diamond, M. J. (1974). Modification of hypnotizability: A review. *Psychol. Bull.,* 81(3), 180–98.

Dickens, B. M., Doob, A. N., Warwick, O. H., & Winegard, W. C. (1982). *Report of the Committee of Enquiry into Allegations concerning Drs. Linda and Mark Sobell.* Toronto: Addiction Research Foundation.

Diller, L., & Gordon, W. A. (1981). Interventions for cognitive deficits in brain-injured adults. *J. Cons. Clin. Psychol.,* 49, 822–34.

Dinitz, S., & Conrad, J. P. (1980). The dangerous two percent. In D. Shichor & D. H. Kelly (Eds.), *Critical issues in juvenile delinquency.* Lexington, MA.: Lexington Books.

Dixen, J., & Jenkins, J. O. (1981). Incestuous child sexual abuse: A review of treatment strategies. *Clin. Psychol. Rev.,* 1, 211–22.

Doane, J., West, K., Goldstein, M. J., Rodnick, E., & Jones, J. (1981). Parental communication deviance and affective style as predictors of subsequent schizophrenia spectrum disorders in vulnerable adolescents. *Arch. Gen. Psychiat.,* 38, 679–85.

Dobrokhotova, T. A. (1968). On the pathology of the emotional sphere in tumorous lesion of the frontal lobes of the brain. *Zhurnal Nevropatologii i Psikhiartrii,* 68(3), 418–22.

Dogoloff, L. I. (1980). Prospect of the 1980's: Challenge and response. *Drug Enforcement,* 7(1), 2–3.

Dohrenwend, B. P. (1979). Stressful life events and psychopathology: Some issues of theory and method. In J. F. Barrett, R. M. Rose & G. L. Klerman (Eds.), *Stress and mental disorder* (pp. 1–15). New York: Raven Press.

Dohrenwend, B. P., & Dohrenwend, B. S. (1974). Social and cultural influences on psychopathology. *Annu. Rev. Psychol.,* 25, 417–52.

Dohrenwend B. P., & Dohrenwend, B. S. (1982). Perspectives on the past and future of psychiatric epidemiology: The 1981 Rema Lapouse Lecture. *Amer. J. Public Health,* 72(1), 1271–79.

Dohrenwend, B. P., Dohrenwend, B. S., Gould, M. S., Link, B., Neugebauer, R., & Wunsch-Hitzig, R. (1980). *Mental illness in the United States: Epidemiological estimates.* New York: Praeger.

Dohrenwend, B. P., & Egri, G. (1981). Recent stressful life events and episodes of schizophrenia. *Schizophrenia Bull.,* 7, 12–23.

Dole, V. P., & Nyswander, M. (1967). The miracle of methadone in the narcotics jungle. *Roche Report,* 4(11), 1–2; 8; 11.

Dole, V. P., Nyswander, M., & Warner, A. (1968). Successful treatment of 750 criminal addicts. *JAMA,* 206, 2709–11.

Doleschal, E., & Klapmuts, N. (1974, Jan. 21). New criminology. *Behav. Today,* 5(3), 18–19.

Doleys, D. M. (1979). Assessment and treatment of childhood enuresis. In R. J. Finch & P. C. Kendall (Eds.), *Clinical treatment and research in child psychopathology.* New York: Spectrum Publications.

Dollard, J. & Miller, N. E. (1950). *Personality and psychotherapy.* New York: McGraw-Hill.

Donne, J. (1624). Meditation XVII. *Devotions upon emergent occasions.* London.

Donoghue, E. C., Abbas, K. A., & Gal, E. (1970). The medical assessment of mentally retarded children in hospital. *Brit. J. Psychiat.,* 117(540), 531–32.

Dooley, D., & Catalano, R. (1980). Economic change as a cause of behavioral disorder. *Psychol. Bull.,* 87, 450–68.

Dorfman, D. D. (1978). The Cyril Burt question: New findings. *Science,* 201, 1177–86.

Downing, R. W., & Rickels, K. (1974). Mixed anxiety-depression: Fact or myth? *Arch. Gen. Psychiat.,* 30(3), 312–17.

Draguns, J. G. (1979). Culture and personality. In A. J. Marsella, R. Tharp, & T. Cibowrowski (Eds.), *Perspectives in cross-cultural psychology*. New York: Academic Press.

Drake, R. E., & Wallach, M. A. (1979). Will mental patients stay in the community: A social psychological perspective. *J. Cons. Clin. Psychol.*, 47(2), 285–94.

Dreger, R. M., Lewis, P. M., Rich, T. A., Miller, K. S., Reid, M. P., Overlade, D. C., Taffel, C., & Flemming, E. L. (1964). Behavioral classification project. *J. Consult. Psychol.*, 28, 1–13.

Drug Enforcement Administration, Department of Justice. (1979). *Controlled Substance Inventory List*. Washington, D.C.

Dunbar, F., (1943). *Psychosomatic diagnosis*. New York: Harper & Row.

Dunbar, F. (1954). *Emotions and bodily changes* (4th ed.). New York: Columbia University Press.

Dunn, F. M., & Howell, R. J. (1982). Relaxation training and its relationship to hyperactivity in boys, *J. Clin. Psychol.*, 38(1), 92–100.

Dunner, D. L., & Hall, K. S. (1980). Social adjustment and psychological precipitants in mania. In R. H. Belmaker, & H. M. van Praag (Eds.), *Mania: An evolving concept*. New York: Spectrum.

Durkheim, E. (1951). *Suicide: A study in sociology*. Trans. J. A. Spaulding & G. Simpson. Ed. G. Simpson. New York: Free Press, 1951. Originally published 1897.

Dvoredsky, A. E., & Stewart, M. A. (1981). Hyperactivity followed by manic-depressive disorders: Two case reports. *J. Clin. Psychiat.*, 42(5), 212–14.

Earl, H. G. (1965). 10,000 children battered and starved: Hundreds die. *Today's Health*, 43(9), 24–31.

Earl, H. G. (1966). Head injury: The big killer. *Today's Health*. 44(12), 19–21.

East, W. N. (1946). Sexual offenders. *J. Nerv. Ment. Dis.*, 103, 626–66.

Eastman, C. (1976). Behavioral formulations of depression. *Psychol. Rev.*, 83, 277–91.

Edwards, C. C. (1973). What you can do to combat high blood pressure. *Family Health*, 5(11), 24–26.

Edwards, R. P., Alley, G. R., & Snider, W. (1971). Academic achievement and minimal brain dysfunction. *J. Learn. Dis.*, 4(3), 134–38.

Efron, V., Keller, M., & Gurioll, C. (1974). *Statistics on consumption of alcohol and on alcoholism*. New Brunswick, NJ: Rutgers Center of Alcohol Studies.

Egbert, L., Battit, G., Welch, C., & Bartlett, M. (1964). Reduction of postoperative pain by encouragement and instruction of patients. *New Engl. J. Med.*, 270, 825–27.

Egeland, B., & Brunnquell, D. (1979). An at-risk approach to the study of child abuse: Some preliminary findings. *J. Amer. Acad. Child Psychiat.*, 18, 219–35.

Egeland, B., Cicchetti, D., & Taraldson, B. (1976, Apr. 26). Child abuse: A family affair. *Proceedings of the N. P. Masse Research Seminar on Child Abuse*, 28–52. Paper presented Paris, France.

Ehrhardt, A. A., & Meyer-Bahlburg, H. F. L. (1981). Effects of prenatal sex hormones on gender-related behavior. *Science*, 211, 1312–18.

Eisenberg, L. (1971). Principles of drug therapy in child psychiatry with special reference to stimulant drugs. *Amer. J. Orthopsychiat.*, 4(3). 371–79.

Eisler, R. M., Miller, P. M., Hersen, M., & Alford, H. (1974). Effects of assertive training on marital interaction. *Arch. Gen. Psychiat.*, 30(5), 643–49.

Eitinger, L. (1961). Pathology of the concentration camp syndrome. *Arch. Gen. Psychiat.*, 5, 371–79.

Eitinger, L. (1962). Concentration camp survivors in the postwar world. *Amer. J. Orthopsychiat.*, 32, 367–75.

Eitinger, L. (1964). *Concentration camp survivors in Norway and Israel*. New York: Humanities Press.

Eitinger, L. (1969). Psychosomatic problems in concentration camp survivors. *J. Psychosom. Res.*, 13, 183–90.

Eitinger, L. (1973, Sept.). A follow-up study of the Norwegian concentration camp survivors: Mortality and morbidity. *Israel Annals of Psychiatry and Related Disciplines*, 11, 199–210.

Elkind, D. (1967). Middle-class delinquency. *Mental Hygiene*, 51, 80–84.

Elkind, D., & Weiner, I. B. (1978). *Development of the child*. New York: Wiley.

Ellinwood, E. H. (1971). Assault and homicide associated with amphetamine abuse. *Amer. J. Psychiat.*, 127(9), 90–95.

Ellis, A. (1958). Rational psychotherapy. *J. Gen. Psychol.*, 59, 35–49.

Ellis, A. (1970). *Reason and emotion in psychotherapy*. New York: Lyle Stuart.

Ellis, A. (1973). Rational-emotive therapy. In R. J. Corsini (Ed.), *Current psychotherapies*. Itasca, Ill.: Peacock Publishers.

Ellis, A. (1975). Creative job and happiness: The humanistic way. *The Humanist*, 35(1), 11–13.

Ellis, A. (1977). The treatment of a psychopath with rational therapy. In S. J. Morse & R. I. Watson (Eds.), *Psychotherapies: A comparative casebook*. New York: Holt, Rinehart & Winston.

Ellis, A. (1981). Misrepresentation of behavior therapy by psychoanalysts. *Amer. Psycholog.*, 36(7), 798–99.

Ellis, E. M., Atkeson, B. M., & Calhoun, K. S. (1982). An examination of differences between multiple- and single-incident victims of sexual assault. *J. Abnorm. Psychol.*, 91, 221–24.

Ellison, K. (1977). Personal communication.

Emmelkamp, P. M. G., & Wessels, H. (1975). Flooding in imagination vs. flooding in vivo: A comparison with agoraphobics. *Behav. Res. Ther.*, 13(1), 7–15.

Enders, L. J., & Flinn, D. E. (1962). Clinical problems in aviation medicine: Schizophrenic reaction, paranoid type. *Aerospace Medicine*, 33, 730–32.

Engel, G. (1961). Is grief a disease? *Psychosom. Med.*, 23, 18–23.

Engel, G. L., (1962). *Psychological development in health and disease*. New York: Saunders.

Engel, G. L. (1977). The need for a new medical model: A challenge for biomedicine. *Science*, 196, 129–36.

Engelhardt, D. M. (1974). Pharmacologic basis for use of psychotropic drugs: An overview. *N.Y. St. J. Med.*, 74(2), 360–66.

English, C. J. (1973). Leaving home: A typology of runaways. *Society*, 10(5), 22–24.

Epstein, H. (1979). *Children of the holocaust: Conversations with sons and daughters of survivors*. New York: Putnam.

Epstein, S., & Fenz, W. D. (1962). Theory and experiment on the measurement of approach-avoidance conflict. *J. Abnorm. Soc. Psychol.*, 64(1), 97–112.

Epstein, S., & Fenz, W. D. (1965). Steepness of approach and avoidance gradients in humans as a function of experience: Theory and experiment. *J. Exper. Psychol.*, 70(1), 1–12.

Erlenmeyer–Kimling, L., & Cornblatt, B. (1978). Attentional measures in a study of children at high risk for schizophrenia. In L. C. Wynne, R. L. Cromwell, & S. Matthysse (Eds.), *The nature of schizophrenia: New approaches to research and treatment* (pp. 359–65). New York: Wiley.

Ernst, P., Beran, B., Badash, D. Kosovsky, R., & Kleinhauz, M. (1977). Treatment of the aged mentally ill: Further unmasking of the effects of a diagnosis of chronic brain syndrome, *Journal of the American Geriatric Society*, 10, 466–69.

Eron, L. D., Huesmann, L. R., Lefkowitz, M. M., & Walder, L. O. (1974). How learning conditions in early childhood—including mass media—relate to aggression in late adolescence. *Amer. J. Orthopsychiat.*, 44(3), 412–23.

Eron, L. D., & Peterson, R. A. (1982). Abnormal behavior: Social approaches. In M. R. Rosenzweig & L. W. Porter (Eds.), *Annu. Rev. of Psychol.* 33, 231–65.

Erwin, W. J. (1977). A 16-year follow-up of a case of severe anorexia nervosa. *J. Behav. Ther. Exp. Psychiat.*, 8, 157–60.

Evans, R. B. (1969). Childhood parental relationships of homosexual men. *J. Cons. Clin. Psychol.*, 33(2), 129–35.

Eysenck, H. J. (1952). The effects of psychotherapy: An evaluation. *Journal of Consulting Psychology*, 16, 319–24.

Eysenck, H. J. (1960). *Behaviour therapy and the neuroses*. London: Pergamon Press.

Eysenck, H. J. (1976) The learning theory model of neurosis: A new approach. *Behav. Res. Ther.*, 14, 251–67.

Eysenck, H. J., Wakefield, J. A., & Friedman, A. (1983). Diagnosis and clinical assessment: The DSM III. In M. R. Rosenzweig & L. W. Porter (Eds.), *Annual review of psychology*, **34**, 167–83.

Fabrega, H. (1981). Cultural programming of brain-behavior relationships. In J. R. Merikangas (Ed.), *Brain-behavior relationships*. Lexington, MA.: D. C. Heath.

Fairet, J. P. (1822). *De l'hypocondrie et du suicide*. Paris: Caroullebois. Libraire de la Société de Médecine.

Fairweather, G. W., Sanders, D. H., Maynard, H., & Cressler, D. L. (1969). *Community life for the mentally ill: An alternative to institutional care*. Chicago: Aldine.

Falls, H. F. (1970). Ocular changes in Down's syndrome help in diagnosis. *Roche Report*, **7**(16), 5.

Faraone, S. (1982). Psychiatry and political repression in the Soviet Union. *Amer. Psychologist*, **37**(10), 1105–12.

Farber, I. E., Harlow, H. F., & West, L. J. (1956). Brainwashing, conditioning, and DDD (debility, dependency and dread). *Sociometry*, **19**, 271–85.

Farberow, N. L. (1974). *Suicide*. Morristown, N. J.: General Learning Press.

Farberow, N. L. (1975). Cultural history of suicide. In N. L. Farberow (Ed.), *Suicide in different cultures*. Baltimore: University Park Press. pp. 1–15.

Farberow, N. L., & Litman, R. E. (1970). A comprehensive suicide prevention program. Suicide Prevention Center of Los Angeles, 1958–1969. Unpublished final report DHEW NIMH Grants No. MH 14946 & MH 00128. Los Angeles.

Farberow, N. L., Shneidman, E. S., & Leonard, C. (1963). Suicide among general medical and surgical hospital patients with malignant neoplasms. Veterans Administration, Dept. of Medicine and Surgery. *Medical Bulletin* MB–9, Feb. 25, 1963, 1–11.

Farberow, N. L., & Simon, M. D. (1975). Suicide in Los Angeles and Vienna. In N. L. Farberow (Ed.), *Suicide in different cultures*. Baltimore: University Park Press. pp. 185–204.

Faretra, G. (1981). A profile of aggression from adolescence to adulthood: An 18-year follow-up of psychiatrically disturbed and violent adolescents. *Amer. J. Orthopsychiat.*, **51**, 439–53.

Faris, R. E. L., & Dunham, H. W. (1939). *Mental disorders in urban areas*. Chicago: University of Chicago Press. (Reprinted, 1965).

Farley, F. H., & Farley, S. V. (1972). Stimulus seeking motivation and delinquent motivation among institutionalized delinquent girls. *J. Cons. Clin. Psychol.*, **39**, 94–97.

Feighner, J. P., Robins, E., Guze, S. B., Woodruff, R. A., Winokur, G., & Muñoz, R. (1972). Diagnostic criteria for use in psychiatric research. *Arch. Gen. Psychiat.*, **26**, 57–63.

Feild, H. S. (1978). Attitudes toward rape: A comparative analysis of police, rapists, crisis counselors, and citizens. *J. Pers. Soc. Psychol.*, **36**, 156–79.

Feingold, B. F. (1977). Behavioral disturbances linked to the ingestion of food additives. *Delaware Medical Journal*, **49**, 89–94.

Feinsilver, D. (1970). Communication in families of schizophrenic patients. *Arch. Gen. Psychiat.*, **22**(2), 143–48.

Feldman, R., & Weisfeld, G. (1973). An interdisciplinary study of crime. *Crime and Delinquency*. **19**(2), 150–62.

Felton, B. J., & Shinn, M. (1981). Ideology and practice of deinstitutionalization. *J. Social Issues*, **37**(3), 158–72.

Fenna, D. et al. (1971). Ethanol metabolism in various racial groups. *Canadian Medical Association Journal*, **105**, 472–75.

Fenz, W. D. (1971). Heart rate responses to a stressor: A comparison between primary and secondary psychopaths and normal controls. *J. Exper. Res. Person.*, **5**(1), 7–13.

Fenz, W. D., & Velner, J. (1970). Physiological concomitants of behavior indexes in schizophrenia. *J. Abnorm. Psychol.*, **76**(1), 27–35.

Fersch, E. A., Jr., (1980). *Psychology and psychiatry in courts and corrections*. New York: Wiley.

Ferster, C. B. (1973). A functional analysis of depression. *Amer. Psychologist*, **28**(10), 857–70.

Fetterman, J. L. (1949). *Practical lessons in psychiatry*. Springfield, IL,: Charles C. Thomas.

Feuerstein, R. (1977). Mediated learning experience: A theoretical basis for cognitive modifiability during adolescence. In P. Mittler (Ed.), *Research to practice in mental retardation* (Vol. 2, pp. 105–16). Baltimore: University Park Press.

Field, M. J. (1960). *Search for security: An ethnopsychiatric study of rural Ghana*. Evanston: Northwestern University Press.

Filskov, S. B., & Goldstein, S. G. (1974). Diagnostic validity of the Halstead-Reitan Neuropsychology battery. *J. Cons. Clin. Psychol.*, **42**, 383–88.

Filskov, S. B., Grimm, B. H., & Lewis, J. A. (1981). Brainbehavior relationships. In S. B. Filskov & T. J. Boll (Eds.), *Handbook of clinical neuropsychology*. New York: Wiley.

Filskov, S. B., & Locklear, E. (1982). A multidimensional perspective on clinical neuropsychology research. In P. C. Kendall & J. N. Butcher (Eds.), *Handbook of research methods in clinical psychology*. New York: Wiley.

Fine, R. (1979). *A history of psychoanalysis*. New York: Columbia University Press.

Fink, M. (1979). *Convulsive therapy: Theory and practice*. New York: Raven Press.

Fink, M., Kety, S., McGaugh, I., & Williams, T. A. (Eds.), (1974). *Psychobiology of convulsive therapy*. New York: Wiley.

Finkelstein, B. (1968). Offenses with no apparent motive. *Dis. Nerv. Sys.*, 1968, **29**(5), 310–14.

Fischer, W. F. (1970). *Theories of anxiety*. New York: Harper & Row.

Fish, B. (1975). Biologic antecedents of psychosis in children. In D. X. Freedman (Ed.), *Biology of the major psychoses*. New York: Raven.

Fishburne, P. M., Abelson, H. I., & Cisin, I. (1980). *National survey on drug abuse; Main finding: 1979*. Rockville, MD: National Institute of Drug Abuse.

Fleischman, M. J. (1981). A replication of Patterson's "Intervention for boys with conduct problems," *J. Cons. Clin. Psychol.*, **49**(3), 342–51.

Folkenberg, J. (1982). "For the first time, we may have a reasonable understanding of the biochemistry of anxiety." *ADAMHA News*, **8**, 1–4.

Fontana, A. F., & Dowds, B. N., (1975). Assessing treatment outcomes. *J. Nerv. Ment. Dis.*, **161**, 221–30.

Forehand, R., Rogers, T., McMahon, R. J., Wells, K. C., & Griest, D. L. (1981). Teaching parents to modify child behavior problems: An examination of some follow-up data. *J. Pediat. Psychol.*, **6**(3), 313–32.

Foreyt, J., & Rathjen, D. (Eds.), (1978). *Cognitive behavior therapy: Research and application*. New York: Plenum Press.

Forgac, G. E., & Michaels, E. J. (1982). Personality characteristics of two types of male exhibitionists. *J. Abnorm. Psychol.*, **91**, 287–93.

Forgione, A. G. (1976). The use of mannequins in the behavioral assessment of child molesters: Two case reports. *Behav. Ther.*, **7**, 678–85.

Forgus, R. H., & DeWolfe, A. S. (1974). Coding of cognitive input in delusional patients. *J. Abnorm. Psychol.*, **83**(3), 278–84.

Forssman, H., & Akesson, H. O., (1965). Mortality in patients with Down's syndrome. *Journal of Mental Deficiency Research*, **9**, 146–61.

Fox, R. E. (1976). Family therapy. In I. Weiner (Ed.), *Clinical methods in psychology*. New York: Wiley.

Frances, A. (1980). The DSM-III personality disorders section: A commentary, *Amer. J. Psychiat.*, **137**(9), 1050–54.

Frank, J. D. (1978). *Persuasion and Healing* (2nd ed.). Baltimore: John Hopkins University Press.

Frankel, A. S. (1970). Treatment of a multisymptomatic phobic by a self-directed, self-reinforced imagery technique: A case study. *J. Abnorm. Psychol.*, **76**, 496–99.

Frankl, V. E. (1963). *Man's search for meaning* (Rev. ed.). Boston: Beacon Press.

Freedman, A. M., Kaplan, H. I., & Sadock, B. J. (1976). *Modern synopsis of comprehensive textbook of psychiatry* (2nd ed.). Baltimore: Williams & Wilkins.

Freedman, B., & Chapman, L. J. (1973). Early subjective experience in schizophrenic episodes. *J. Abnorm. Psychol.*, **82**(1), 46–54.

Freedman, M. (1975). Homosexuals may be healthier than straights. *Psych. Today*, **8**(10), 28–32.

Freeman, R. D., Malkin, S. F., & Hastings, J. O. (1975). Psychosocial problems of deaf children and their families: A comparative study. *American Annals of the Deaf*, **120**, 391–405.

Freeman, T. (1960). On the psychopathology of schizophrenia. *J. Ment. Sci.*, **106**, 925–37.

Freeman, W. (1959). Psychosurgery. In S. Arieti (Ed.), *American handbook of psychiatry* (Vol. 2, pp. 1521–40). New York: Basic Books.

Freud, A. (1946). *Ego and the mechanisms of defense*. New York: International Universities Press.

Friar, L. R., & Beatty, J. (1976). Migraine: Management by trained control of vasoconstriction. *J. Cons. Clin. Psychol.*, **44**, 46–53.

Friedman, J. H., (1974). Woman's role in male impotence. *Medical Aspects of Human Sexuality*, **8**(6), 8–23.

Friedman, M., & Rosenman, R. (1959). Association of specific overt behavior pattern with blood and cardiovascular findings. *JAMA*, **169**, 1286.

Friedman, P. (1948). The effects of imprisonment. *Acta Medica Orientalia*, Jerusalem, 163–67.

Friedman, P. (1949). Some aspects of concentration camp psychology. *Amer. J. Psychiat.*, **105**, 601–5.

Friedman, P., & Linn, L. (1957). Some psychiatric notes on the Andrea Doria disaster, *Amer. J. Psychiat.*, **114**, 426–32.

Friedman, R., & Iwai, J. (1976). Genetic predisposition and stress-induced hypertension. *Science*, **193**, 161–92.

Friedrich, W., Einbender, A. J., & Luecke, W. J. (1983). Cognitive and behavioral characteristics of physically abused children. *J. Cons. Clin. Psychol.*, **51**(2), 313–14.

Fromm, E., & Shor, R. E. (1972). *Hypnosis: Research developments and perspectives*. Chicago: Aldine.

Fuller, G. D. (1978). Current status of biofeedback in clinical practice. *Amer. Psychologist*, **33**(1), 39–78.

Fulmer, R. H., & Lapidus, L. B. (1980). A study of professed reasons for beginning and continuing heroin use. *Inter. J. Addictions*, **15**, 631–45.

Furlong, W. B. (1971). How "speed" kills athletic careers. *Today's Health*, **49**(2), 30–33; 62; 64; 66.

Gager, N., & Schurr, C., (1976). *Sexual assault: Confronting rape in America*. New York: Grosset & Dunlap.

Gajzago, C., & Prior, M. (1974). Two cases of "recovery" in Kanner syndrome. *Arch. Gen. Psychiat.*, **31**(2), 264–68.

Gal, P. (1959). Mental disorders of advanced years. *Geriatrics*, **14**, 224–28.

Ganzer, V. J., & Sarason, I. G. (1973). Variables associated with recidivism among juvenile delinquents. *J. Cons. Clin. Psychol.*, **40**(1), 1–5.

Garb, J. R., & Stunkard, A. J. (1974). Effectiveness of a self-help group in obesity control: A further assessment. *Arch. Int. Med.*, **134**, 716–20.

Garfield, S. L. (1978). Research on client variables in psychotherapy. In S. L. Garfield and A. E. Bergin (Eds.), *Handbook of psychotherapy and behavior change: An empirical analysis*. New York: Wiley.

Garfield, S. L., & Kurtz, R. (1976). Clinical psychologists in the 1970s. *Amer. Psychologist*, **31**, 1–9.

Garmezy, N. (1978a). Current status of other high-risk research programs. In L. C. Wynne, R. L. Cromwell, & S. Matthysse (Eds.), *The nature of schizophrenia: New approaches to research and treatment*. New York: Wiley.

Garmezy, N. (1978b). DSM III: Never mind the psychologists; Is it good for the children? *The Clinical Psychologist*, **31**, 1–6.

Garmezy, N. (1978c). Observations of high-risk research and premorbid development in schizophrenia. In L. C. Wynne, R. L. Cromwell, & S. Matthysse (Eds.), *The nature of schizophrenia: New approaches to research and treatment*. New York: Wiley.

Gartner, A., & Riessman, F. (1974). Is there a new work ethic? *Amer. J. Orthopsychiat.*, **44**(4), 563–67.

Gaw, A. C., Chang, L. W., & Shaw, L. (1975). Efficacy of acupuncture on osteoarthritic pain: A controlled, double-blind study. *New Engl. J. Med.*, **293**, 375–78.

Gebhard, P. H. (1965). Situational factors affecting human sexual behavior. In F. Beach (Ed.), *Sex and behavior*. New York: Wiley.

Gebhard, P. H., Gagnon, J. H., Pomeroy, W. B., & Christenson, C. V. (1965). *Sex offenders: An analysis of types*. New York: Harper & Row.

Geisz, D., & Steinhausen, H. (1974). On the "psychological development of children with hydrocephalus." (German) *Praxis der Kinderpsychologie und Kinderpsychiatrie*, **23**(4), 113–18.

Gelles, R. J. (1978). Violence toward children in the United States. *Amer. J. Orthopsychiat.*, **48**, 580–90.

German, W. J. (1959). Initial symptomatology in brain tumors. *Connecticut Medicine*, **23**, 636–37.

Geschwind, N. (1975). The borderland of neurology and psychiatry: Some common misconceptions. In D. F. Benson & D. Blumer (Eds.), *Psychiatric aspects of neurological disease* (pp. 1–9). New York: Grune & Stratton.

Gesell, A. (1953). Human infancy and the embryology of behavior. In A. Weider (Ed.), *Contributions toward medical psychology*. New York: Ronald.

Gibson, H. B. (1974). Morita therapy and behavior therapy. *Behav. Res. Ther.*, **12**(4), 347–55.

Gilbert, J. G., & Lombardi, D. N. (1967). Personality characteristics of young male narcotic addicts. *J. Couns. Psychol.*, **31**, 536–38.

Gillberg, C., & Schaumann, H. (1981). Infantile autism and puberty. *J. Autism and Develop. Disorders*, **11**(4), 365–71.

Ginsberg, G. L., Frosch, W. A., & Shapiro, T. (1972). The new impotence. *Arch. Gen. Psychiat.*, **26**(3), 218–20.

Glasscote, R. (1978). What programs work and what programs do not work for chronic mental patients? In J. A. Talbott (Ed.), *The chronic mental patient: Problems, solutions and recommendations for a public policy*. Washington, DC: American Psychiatric Association.

Glasser, R. (1971). *365 days*. New York: Braziller.

Gleser, G., & Sacks, M. (1973). Ego defenses and reaction to stress: A validation study of the Defense Mechanisms Inventory. *J. of Cons. Clin. Psychol.*, **40**(2), 181–87.

Glow, R. A. (1981). Treatment alternatives for hyperactive children—A comment on "problem children" and stimulant drug therapy. *Austral. J. Psychiat.*, **15**(2), 123–28.

Glueck, S., & Glueck, E. (1968). *Non-delinquents in perspective*. Cambridge: Harvard University Press.

Glueck, S., & Glueck, E. T. (1969). Delinquency prediction method reported highly accurate. *Roche Reports*, **6**(15), 3.

Gochman, S. I., Allgood, B. A., & Geer, C. R. (1982). A look at today's behavior therapists. *Professional Psychol.*, **13**(5), 605–9.

Golan, N. (1978). *Treatment in crisis situations*. New York: The Free Press.

Golden, C. J. (1978). *Diagnosis and rehabilitation in clinical neuropsychology*. Springfield, IL: Charles C. Thomas.

Golden, C. J., Graber, B., Blose, I., Berg, R., Coffman, J., & Bloch, S. (1981). Differences in brain densities between chronic alcoholic and normal control patients. *Science*, **211**(30), 508–10.

Golden, C. J., MacInnes, W. D., Ariel, R. N., Ruedrich, S. L., Chu, C-C., Coffman, J. A., Graber, B., & Bloch, S. (1982). Cross-validation of the ability of the Luria-Nebraska Neuropsychological Battery to differentiate chronic schizophrenics with and without ventricular enlargement. *J. Cons. Clin. Psychol.*, **50**, 87–95.

Golden, C. J., Moses, J. A., Fishburne, F. J., Engum, E., Lewis, G. P., Wisniewski, A. M., Conley, F. K., Berg, R. A., & Graber, B. (1981). Cross-validation of the Luria-Nebraska Neuropsychological Battery for the presence, lateralization, and location of brain damage. *J. Cons. Clin. Psychol.*, **49**, 491–507.

Golden, D. A., & Davis, J. G. (1974). Counseling parents after the birth of an infant with Down's syndrome. *Children Today*, **3**(2), 7–11.

Goldfarb, A. (1974). *Aging and the organic brain syndrome*. Fort Washington, PA: McNeill Labs.

Goldfarb, R. L. (1974). American prisons: Self-defeating concrete. *Psych. Today*, **7**(8), 20; 22; 24; 85; 88–89.

Goldfried, M., & Davidson, G. (1976). *Clinical behavior therapy*. New York: Holt, Rinehart & Winston.

Goldfried, M. R. (1980). Toward the delineation of therapeutic change principles. *Amer. Psychologist*, **35**, 991–99.

Goldfried, M. R., Lineham, M. M., & Smith, J. L. (1978). Reduction of test anxiety through cognitive restructuring. *J. Cons. Clin. Psychol.*, **46**(1), 32–39.

Goldfried, M. R., & Merbaum, M. (Eds.), (1973). *Behavior change through self control*. New York: Holt, Rinehart and Winston.

Goldman, M. S., Williams, D. L., & Klisz, D. K. (1983). Recoverability of psychological functioning following alcohol abuse: Prolonged spatial-visual dysfunction in older alcoholics. *J. Cons. Clin. Psychol.*, **51**(3), 370–78.

Goldsmith, W., & Cretekos, C. (1969). Unhappy odysseys: Psychiatric hospitalization among Vietnam returnees. *Amer. J. Psychiat.*, **20**, 78–83.

Goldstein, A., et al. (1974, Mar. 4). Researchers isolate opiate receptor. *Behav. Today*, **5**(9), 1.

Goldstein, M. J., & Palmer, J. O. (1975). The case of George P. Adapted from *The experience of anxiety: A casebook*, Second Edition. Cambridge: Oxford University Press.

Goldstein, M. J., Rodnick, E. H., Jones, J. E., McPherson, S. R., & West, K. L. (1978). Family precursors of schizophrenia spectrum disorders. In L. C. Wynne, R. L. Cromwell, & S. Matthysse (Eds.), *The nature of schizophrenia: New approaches to research and treatment*. New York: Wiley Medical.

Goodman, J. (1972). A case study of an "autistic-savant": Mental function in the psychotic child with markedly discrepant abilities. *J. Child Psychol. Psychiat.*, **13**(4), 267–78.

Goodwin, D. W. (1976). *Is alcoholism hereditary?* New York: Oxford University Press.

Goodwin, D. W. (1979). Alcoholism and heredity. *Arch. Gen. Psychiat.*, **36**, 57–61.

Goodwin, D. W., Schulsinger, F., Hermansen, L., Guze, S. B., & Winokur, G. (1973). Alcohol problems in adoptees raised apart from alcoholic biological parents. *Arch. Gen. Psychiat.*, **28**(2), 238–43.

Goodwin, D. W., Schulsinger, F., Moller, N., Hermansen, L., Winokur, G., & Guze, S. B. (1974). Drinking problems in adopted and nonadopted sons of alcoholics. *Arch. Gen. Psychiat.*, **31**(2), 164–69.

Gordon, R. (1977). A critique of the evaluation of Patuxent Institution, with particular attention to the issues of dangerousness and recidivism. *Bulletin of the American Academy of Psychiatry and the Law*, **5**, 210–55.

Gorin, N. (1980). Looking out for Mrs. Berwid. *Sixty Minutes*. (Narrated by Morley Safer.) New York: CBS Television News.

Gorin, N. (1982). It didn't have to happen. *Sixty Minutes*. (Narrated by Morley Safer.) New York: CBS Television News.

Gorton, J., & Partridge, R. (Eds.). (1982). *Practice and management of psychiatric emergency care*. St. Louis, MO.: Mosby.

Gosslin, C. C., & Eysenck, S. B. G. (1980). The transvestite "double image:" A preliminary report. *Personality and Individual Differences*, **1**, 172–73.

Gossop, M. (1981). *Theories of neurosis*. New York: Springer-Verlag.

Gottesman, I. I., & Shields, J. (1972). *Schizophrenia and genetics*. New York: Academic Press.

Gottesman, I. I., & Shields, J. (1976). A critical review of recent adoption, twin, and family studies of schizophrenia: Behavioral genetics perspectives. *Schizophrenia Bull.* **2**, 360–401.

Gottfredson, M. T., Hindelang, M. J., & Parisi, N. (1978). *Sourcebook of criminal justice statistics*. Washington, DC: Statistics Service.

Gottheil, E., Thornton, C. C., Skoloda, T. E., & Alterman, A. I. (1982). Follow-up of abstinent and non-abstinent alcoholics. *Amer. J. Psychiat.*, **139**(5), 560–65.

Gottlieb, J. (1981). Mainstreaming: Fulfilling the promise? *Amer. J. Ment. Def.*, **86**, 115–26.

Gottschalk, L. A., Haer, J. L., & Bates, D. E. (1972). Effect of sensory overload on psychological state: Changes in social alienation—personal disorganization and cognitive-intellectual impairment. *Arch. Gen. Psychiat.*, **27**(4), 451–56.

Graham, D. L., & Cross, W. C. (1975). Values and attitudes of high school drug users. *Journal of Drug Education*, **5**, 97–107.

Graham, J. R. (1978a). *MMPI characteristics of alcoholics, drug abusers and pathological gamblers*. Paper presented at the 13th Annual Symposium on Recent Developments in the Use of the MMPI. Puebla, Mexico, March, 1978.

Graham, J. R. (1978b). *The Minnesota Multiphasic Personality Inventory*. In B. B. Wolman (Ed.), *Clinical diagnosis of mental disorders: A handbook*. New York: Plenum.

Graham, J. R., & Lilly, R. S. (1984). *Psychological testing*. Englewood Cliffs, NJ: Prentice-Hall.

Gralnick, A. (1942). Folie a deux—The psychosis of association: A review of 103 cases and the entire English literature, with case presentations. *Psychiat. Quart.*, **14**, 230–63.

Grant, L., Sweetland, H. L., Yager, J., & Gerst, M. (1981). Quality of life events in relation to psychiatric symptoms. *Arch. Gen. Psychiat.*, **38**(3), 335–39.

Grant, V. W. (1953). A case study of fetishism. *J. Abnorm. Soc. Psychol.*, **48**, 142–49.

Gray, S. W., & Ramsey, B. K. (1982). The early training project: A life-span view. *Human Develop.*, **25**, 48–57.

Green, A. (1978). Self-destructive behavior in battered children, *Amer. J. Psychiat.*, **135**, 579–82.

Green, L., & Warshauer, D. (1981). Note on the "paradoxical" effect of stimulant drugs on hyperactivity with reference to the rate-dependency effect, *J. Nerv. Ment. Dis.*, **169**(3), 196–98.

Green, R. (1974). *Sexual identity conflict in children and adults*. New York: Basic Books.

Greenacre, P. (1945). Conscience in the psychopath. *Amer. J. Orthopsychiat.*, **15**, 495–509.

Greenberg, J. (1978). Dialysis: Aid for schizophrenia? *APA Monitor*, **9**, 8.

Greene, M. H., Brown, B. S., & Dupont, R. L. (1975). Controlling the abuse of illicit methadone in Washington, D.C. *Arch. Gen. Psychiat.*, **32**(2), 221–26.

Greene, M. H., & Dupont, R. L., (1974). Heroin addiction trends. *Amer. J. Psychiat.*, **131**(5), 545–50.

Greenfield, J. C., & Wolfson, J. M. (1935). Microcephalia vera. *Arch. Neurol. Psychiat.*, **33**, 1296–1316.

Greenson, R. R. (1967). *The technique and practice of psychoanalysis (Vol. 1)*. New York: International Universities Press.

Greer, S. (1964). Study of parental loss in neurotics and sociopaths. *Arch. Gen. Psychiat.*, **11**(2), 177–80.

Gregory, I., & Rosen, E. (1965). *Abnormal psychology*. Philadelphia: W. B. Saunders.

Gresham, F. M. (1982). Misguided mainstreaming: The case for social skills training with handicapped children. *Exceptional Children*, **48**, 422–33.

Griest, D. L., & Wells, K. C. (1983). Behavioral family therapy with conduct disorders in children. *Behav. Ther.*, **14**, 37–53.

Griest, J. H., Gustafson, D. H., Stauss, F. F., Rowse, G. L., Laughren, T. P., & Chiles, J. A. (1974). Suicide risk prediction: A new approach. *Life-Threatening Behavior*, **4**(4), 212–23.

Grinker, R. R. (1969). An essay on schizophrenia and science. *Arch. Gen. Psychiat.*, **20**, 1–24.

Grinker, R. R., & Spiegel, J. P. (1945). *War neuroses*. Philadelphia: Blakiston.

Grinspoon, L., Ewalt, J. R., & Shader, R. I. (1972). *Schizophrenia: Pharmacotherapy and psychotherapy*. Baltimore: Williams & Wilkins Co.

Gross, G., & Huber, G. (1973). Zur prognose der schizophenier. *Psychiatria Clinica*, **6**(1), 1–16.

Groth, A. N., & Birnbaum, H. J. (1978). Adult sexual orientation and attraction to underage persons. *Arch. Sexual Behav.*, **7**, 175–81.

Groth, A. N., Burgess, A. W., & Holmstrom, L. L. (1977). Rape: Power, anger, and sexuality. *Amer. J. Psychiat.*, **134**, 1239–43.

Grove, W. M. (1982). Psychometric detection of schizotypy. *Psychol. Bull.*, **92**, 27–38.

Grunebaum, H., & Perlman, M. S. (1973). Paranoia and naivete. *Arch. Gen. Psychiat.*, **28**(1), 30–32.

Guerra, F. (1971). *The pre-columbian mind*. New York: Seminar Press.

Gugliemi, R. S. (1979). *A double-blind study of the effectiveness of skin temperature biofeedback as a treatment for Raynaud's disease*. Unpublished doctoral dissertation, University of Minnesota.

Gunderson, J. G. (1980). A reevaluation of milieu therapy for nonchronic schizophrenic patients. *Schizophrenia Bull.*, **6**(1), 64–69.

Gunn, J., Robertson, G., Dell, S., & Way, C. (1978). *Psychiatric aspects of imprisonment*. New York: Academic Press.

Gunther, J. (1949). *Death be not proud*. New York: Harper.

Gurland, B., & Kuriansky, J. (1978). Some observations on British and American concepts of schizophrenia. In L. C. Wynne, R. L. Cromwell, & S. Matthysse (Eds.), *The nature of schizophrenia: New approaches to research and treatment* (pp. 686–89). New York: Wiley.

Gurman, A. S., & Kniskern, D. P. (1978). Research on marital and family therapy: Progress, perspective and prospect. In S. L. Garfield & A. E. Bergin (Eds.), *Handbook of psychotherapy and behavior change*. New York: Wiley.

Guthrie, P. D. (1975, May 25). California copes with change. *Los Angeles Times*, May 25, 1975, IV, 5.

Guze, S. B., Goodwin, D. W., & Crane, J. B. (1969). Criminality and psychiatric disorders. *Arch. Gen. Psychiat.*, **20**, 592–97.

Gynther, M. D. (1979). Ethnicity and personality. In J. N. Butcher (Ed.), *New directions in MMPI research*. Minneapolis: University of Minnesota Press.

Hafner, H. (1968). Psychological disturbances following prolonged persecution. *Soc. Psychiat.*, **3**(3), 80–88.

Hagan, J. W., & Huntsman, N. J. (1971). Selective attention in mental retardation. *Develop. Psychol.*, **5**(1), 151–60.

Hague, M., Ellerstein, N. S., Gundy, J. H., Shelov, S. P., Weiss, J. C., McIntire, M. S. Olness, K. N., Jones, D. J., Heagarty, M. C., & Starfield, B. H. (1981). Parental perceptions of enuresis: A collaborative study. *Amer. J. Dis. Children*, **135**(9), 809–11.

Halberstam, M. (1972). Can you make yourself sick? A doctor's report on psychosomatic illness. *Today's Health*, **50**(12), 24–29.

Haley, J. (1959). The family of the schizophrenic: A model system. *J. Nerv. Ment. Dis.* **129**, 357–74.

Haley, J. (1962). Whither family therapy. *Family Process*, **1**, 69–100.

Haley, S. A. (1978). Treatment implications of post-combat stress response syndromes for mental health professionals. In C. R. Figley (Ed.), *Stress disorders among Vietnam veterans*. New York: Brunner/Mazel.

Hall, J. C., Bliss, M., Smith, K., & Bradley, A. (1970). Suicide gestures, attempts found high among poor. *Psychiatric News*, July 1, 1970, 20.

Hall, R. C. W., Gardner, E. R., Stickney, S. K., LeCann, A. F., & Popkin, M. K. (1978). Physical illness presenting as psychiatric disease. *Arch. Gen. Psychiat.*, **35**, 1315–20.

Hall, R. C. W., Popkin, M. K., Devaul, R. A., Faillace, L. A., & Stickney, S. K. (1980). Physical illness manifesting as psychiatric disease: Analysis of a state hospital inpatient population. *Arch. Gen. Psychiat.*, **37**, 989–95.

Hallworth, H. J. (1977). Computer-assisted instruction for the mentally retarded. In P. Mittler (Ed.), *Research to practice in mental retardation* (Vol. 2, pp. 419–20). Baltimore: University Park Press.

Halmi, K. A., Falk, J. R., & Schwartz, E. (1981). Binge-eating and vomiting: A survey of a college population. *Psychological Medicine*, **11**, 697–706.

Hamburg, D. A., Elliott, G. R., & Parron, D. L. (Eds.). (1982). *Health and behavior: Frontiers of research in the biobehavioral sciences*. Washington, DC: National Academy Press.

Hammen, C. L., & Peters, S. D. (1977). Differential responses to male and female depressive reactions. *J. Cons. Clin. Psychol.*, **45**, 994–1001.

Hammen, C. L., & Peters, S. D. (1978). Interpersonal consequences of depression: Responses to men and women enacting a depressed role. *J. Abnorm. Psychol.*, **87**(3), 322–32.

Hanerton, J. L., Canning, N., Ray, M., & Smith, S. (1975). A cytogenetic survey of 14,069 newborn infants: Incidence of chromosome abnormalities. *Clinical Genetics*, **8**, 223–43.

Haney, B., & Gold, M. (1973). The juvenile delinquent nobody knows. *Psychol. Today*, **7**(4), 48–52; 55.

Hanson, D. R., & Gottesman, I. I. (1976). The genetics, if any, of infantile autism and childhood schizophrenia. *Journal of Autism and Childhood Schizophrenia*, **6**, 209–34.

Hanson, D. R., Gottesman, I. I., & Meehl, P. E. (1977). Genetic theories and the validation of psychiatric diagnoses: Implications for the study of children of schizophrenics. *J. Abnorm. Psychol.*, **86**(6), 575–88.

Harburgh, E., Erfurt, J. C., Hauenstein, L. S., Chape, C., Schull, W. J., & Schork, M. A. (1973). Socioecological stress, suppressed hostility, skin color, and black-white male blood pressure: Detroit, *Psychosom. Med.*, **35**, 276–96.

Harding, W. M., Zinberg, N. E., Stelmack, S. M., & Barry, M. (1980). Formerly-addicted-noncontrolled opiate users. *Inter. J. Addictions*, **15**, 47–60.

Hare, R. D. (1968). Psychopathy, autonomic functioning and the orienting response. *J. Abnorm. Psychol.*, **73**(Monogr. Suppl. 3, part 2), 1–24.

Hare, R. D. (1970). *Psychopathy: Theory and research*. New York: Wiley, 1970.

Harlow, H. (1969). A brief look at autistic children. *Psychiat. Soc. Sci. Rev.*, **3**(1), 27–29.

Harlow, J. M. (1868). Recovery from the passage of an iron bar through the head. *Publ. Mass. Med. Soc.*, **2**, 327.

Harris, S. L., & Ersner-Hershfield, R. (1978). Behavioral suppression of seriously disruptive behavior in psychotic and retarded patients: A review of punishment and its alternatives. *Psychol. Bull.*, **85**, 1352–75.

Hartmann, E. (1968). Longitudinal studies of sleep and dream patterns in manic-depressive patients. *Arch. Gen. Psychiat.*, **19**, 312–29.

Hartmann, H. (1958). *Ego psychology and the problem of adaptation*. New York: International Universities Press.

Haskins, C. P. (1968). *Report to the president, 1966–1967*. Washington, DC: Carnegie Institute.

Hathaway, S. R., & McKinley, J. C. (1951). *The Minnesota multiphasic personality inventory* (Rev. ed.). New York: Psychological Corporation.

Hatzenbuehler, L. C., & Schroeder, H. E. (1978). Desensitization procedures in the treatment of childhood disorders. *Psychol. Bull.*, **85**, 831–44.

Hausman, W., & Rloch, D. M. (1967). Military psychiatry. *Arch. Gen. Psychiat.*, **16**, 727–39.

Havens, L. L. (1974). The existential use of the self. *Amer. J. Psychiat.*, **131**(1), 1–10.

Havighurst, R. J. (1969). Suicide and education. In E. S. Shneidman (Ed.), *On the nature of suicide*. San Francisco: Jossey-Bass.

Hawk, A. B., Carpenter, W. T., & Strauss, J. S. (1975). Diagnostic criteria and five-year outcome in schizophrenia. *Arch. Gen. Psychiat.*, **32**(3), 343–47.

Hayes, T. A., Panitch, M. L., & Barker, E. (1975). Imipramine dosage in children: A comment on "Imipramine and electrocardiographic abnormalities in hyperactive children." *Amer. J. Psychiat.*, **132**(5), 546–47.

Haywood, H. C., Meyers, C. E., & Switsky, H. N. (1982). Mental retardation. In M. R. Rosenzweig & L. W. Porter (Eds.), *Annu. Rev. Psychol.*, **33**.

Hazlett, B. (1971, Mar. 2). Two who played with death—and lost the game. *Los Angeles Times*, II, 1; 5.

Hearst, E. D., Cloninger, C. R., Crews, E. L., & Cadoret, R. J. (1974). Electrosleep therapy: A double-blind trial. *Arch. Gen. Psychiat.*, **30**(4), 463–66.

Heaton, R. K., & Pendleton, M. G. (1981). Use of neuropsychological tests to predict adult patient's everyday functioning. *J. Cons. Clin. Psychol.*, **49**(6), 807–21.

Heaver, W. L. (1943). A study of forty male psychopathic

personalities before, during and after hospitalization. *Amer. J. Psychiat.*, **100**, 342–46.

Hecaen, H., & Albert, M. L. (1975). Disorders of mental functioning related to frontal lobe pathology. In D. F. Benson, & D. Blumer (Eds.), *Psychiatric aspects of neurological disease* (pp. 137–49). New York: Grune & Stratton.

Hechtman, L., Weiss, G., & Perlman, T. (1980). Hyperactives as young adults: Self esteem and social skills. *Canadian J. Psychiat.*, **25**(6), 478–83.

Hedblom, J. H. (1973). Dimensions of lesbian experience. *Archives of Sexual Behavior*, **2**(4), 329–41.

Heider, F. (1958). *The psychology of interpersonal relations.* New York: Wiley.

Hekimian, L. J., & Gershon, S. (1968). Characteristics of drug abusers admitted to a psychiatric hospital. *JAMA.* **205**(3), 125–30.

Heller, K., Sher, K. J., & Benson, C. S. (1982). Problems associated with risk of overprediction in studies of offspring of alcoholics: Implications for prevention. *Clin. Psychol. Rev.*, **2**, 183–200.

Helzer, J. E., Robins, L. N., Taibleson, M., Woodruff, R. A., Jr., Reich, T., & Wish, E. D. (1977). Reliability of psychiatric diagnosis: A methodological review. *Arch. Gen. Psychiat.*, **34**, 129–33.

Hendin, H. (1975). Student suicide: Death as a life-style. *J. Nerv. Ment. Dis.*, **160**(3), 204–19.

Hennigan, K. M., Del Rosario, M. L., Heath, L., Cook, T. D., Wharton, J. D., & Calder, B. J. (1982). Impact of the introduction of television on crime in the United States: Empirical findings and theoretical implications. *J. Pers. Soc. Psychol.*, **42**(3), 461–77.

Herman, J. L. (1981). *Father-daughter incest.* Cambridge, MA: Harvard University Press.

Herrenkohl, R. C., Herrenkohl, E. C., & Egolf, B. P. (1983). Circumstances surrounding the occurrence of child maltreatment. *J. Cons. Clin. Psychol.*, **51**(3), 424–31.

Hersen, M., & Eisler, R. M. (1976). Social skills training. In W. E. Craighead, A. E. Kazdin, & M. J. Mahoney (Eds.), *Behavior modification: Principles, issues, and applications.* Boston: Houghton Mifflin.

Herzog, D. B., & Rathbun, J. M. (1982). Childhood depression: Developmental considerations. *Amer. J. Dis. Children*, **136**(2), 15–20.

Heston, L. (1966). Psychiatric disorders in foster home reared children of schizophrenic mothers. *Brit. J. Psychiat.*, **112**, 819–25.

Hetherington, E. M. (1973). Girls without fathers. *Psych. Today*, **6**(9), 47; 49–52.

Hetherington, E. M., Cox, M., & Cox, R. (1978, May). *Family interaction and the social, emotional and cognitive development of children following divorce.* Symposium on The family: Setting priorities, Institute for Pediatric Service, Johnson & Johnson Baby Food Company. Washington, DC.

Hewitt, L. E., & Jenkins, R. L. (1946). *Fundamental patterns of maladjustment: The dynamics of their origin. A statistical analysis based upon five hundred case records of children examined at the Michigan Child Guidance Institute.* Springfield: State of Illinois.

Hilgard, E. R. (1973). The domain of hypnosis: With some comments on alternative paradigms. *Amer. Psychologist*, **28**(11), 972–82.

Hilgard, E. R. (1974). Weapon against pain: Hypnosis is no mirage. *Psych. Today*, **8**(6), 120–22; 126; 128.

Hill, A. L. (1975). Investigation of calendar calculating by an idiot savant. *Amer. J. Psychiat.*, **132**(5), 557–59.

Hill, C. V., Greer, W. E., & Felsenfeld, O. (1967). Psychological stress, early response to foreign protein, and blood cortisol in vervets. *Psychosom. Med.*, **29**, 279–83.

Hill, D. (1968). Depression: Disease, reactions, or posture? *Amer. J. Psychiat.*, **125**(4), 445–57.

Hine, F. R. (1971). *Introduction to psychodynamics: A conflict-adaptational approach.* Durham, NC: Duke University Press.

Hine, F. R., Carson, R. C., Maddox, G. L., Thompson, R. J., & Williams, R. B. (1983). *Introduction to behavioral science in medicine.* New York: Springer-Verlag.

Hine, F. R., Pfeiffer, E., Maddox, G. L., Hein, P. L., & Friedel, R. O. (1972). *Behavioral science: A selective view.* Boston: Little, Brown.

Hiroto, D. S., & Seligman, M. E. P. (1975). Generality of learned helplessness in man. *J. Pers. Soc. Psychol.*, **31**(2), 311–27.

Hirsch, J. (1972). Can we modify the number of adipose cells? *Postgraduate Medicine*, **51**, 83–86.

Hirsch, S. et al. (Eds.). (1974). *Madness network news reader.* San Francisco: New Glide Publications. Poem entitled "Self-knowledge" from VISIONS OF A MADMAN by P. G. Harrison.

Hirsch, S. R., & Leff, J. P. (1975). *Abnormalities in parents of schizophrenics.* London: Oxford University Press.

Hirst, W. (1982). The amnesic syndrome: Descriptions and explanations. *Psychol. Bull.*, **91**, 435–60.

Hodgson, R. J., & Rachman, S. (1972). The effects of contamination and washing in obsessional patients. *Behav. Res. Ther.*, **10**(2), 111–17.

Hoffman, A. (1971). LSD discoverer disputes "chance" factor in finding. *Psychiatric News*, **6**(8), 23–26.

Hoffman, J. L. (1943). Psychotic visitors to government offices in the national capital. *Amer. J. Psychiat.*, **99**, 571–75.

Hogan, R., Mankin, D., Conway, J., & Fox, S. (1970). Personality correlates of undergraduate marijuana use. *J. Cons. Clin. Psychol.*, **35**(1), 58–73.

Hokanson, J. E., & Burgess, M. (1962). The effects of three types of aggression on vascular process. *J. Abnorm. Soc. Psychol.*, **64**, 446–49.

Hokanson, J. E., Sacco, W. P., Blumberg, S. R., & Landrum, G. C. (1980). Interpersonal behavior of depressed individuals in a mixed-motive game. *J. Abnorm. Psychol.*, **89**, 320–33.

Holcomb, W. (1979). *Coping with severe stress: A clinical application of stress-inoculation therapy.* Unpublished doctoral dissertation, University of Missouri-Columbia.

Holden, C. (1975). Prisons: faith in "rehabilitation" is suffering a collapse. *Science*, **188**(4190), 815–17.

Hollon, S. (1979, Apr.). *Status and efficacy of behavior therapies for depression: Comparisons and combinations with alternative approaches.* Paper presented at conference on Research Recommendations for the Behavioral Treatment of Depression, University of Pittsburgh.

Hollon, S., & Beck, A. T. (1978). Psychotherapy and drug therapy: Comparisons and combinations. In S. L. Garfield & A. E. Bergin (Eds.), *Handbook of psychotherapy and behavior change* (pp. 437–90). New York: Wiley.

Hollt, V., Dum, J., Blasig, J., Schubert, J. P., & Herz, A. (1975). Comparison of in vivo and in vitro parameters of opiate receptor binding in naive and tolerant dependent rodents. *Life Sciences*, **16**, 1823–28.

Holmes, L. B., Moser, H. W., Halldorsson, S., Mack, C., Pant, S., & Matzilevich, B. (1972). *Mental retardation: An atlas of diseases with associated physical abnormalities.* New York: Macmillan.

Holmes, T. H., & Masuda, M. (1974). Life change and illness susceptibility. In B. P. Dohrenwend & B. S. Dohrenwend (Eds.), *Stressful life events: Their nature and effects* (pp. 45–72). New York: Wiley.

Holmes, T. H., & Rahe, R. H. (1967). The social readjustment rating scale. *J. Psychosom. Res.*, **11**(2), 213–18.

Holmes, T. S., & Holmes, T. H. (1970). Short-term intrusions into the life style routine. *J. Psychosom. Res.*, **14**(2), 121–32.

Holmstrom, L., & Burgess, A. W. (1975). Assessing trauma in the rape victim. *Amer. J. Nurs.*, **75**, 1288.

Holroyd, K. A., & Andrasik, F. (1978). Coping and the self-control of chronic tension headache. *J. Cons. Clin. Psychol.*, **46**, 1036–45.

Holroyd, K. A., Andrasik, F., & Westbrook, T. (1977). Cognitive control of tension headache. *Cognitive Therapy and Research*, **1**, 121–33.

Holvey, D. N., & Talbott, J. H. (Eds.). (1972). *The Merck manual of diagnosis and therapy* (12th ed.). Rahway, N.J.: Merck, Sharp, & Dohme Research Laboratories.

Homans, G. C. (1961). *Social behavior: Its elementary forms*. New York: Harcourt Brace Jovanovich.

Homer, L. E. (1974). The anatomy of a runaway. *Human Behavior*, **3**(4), 37.

Homme, L. E. (1965). Perspectives in psychology: Control of coverants, the operants of the mind (Vol. 24). *Psychol. Rec.*, **15**, 501–11.

Hook, E. B. (1980). Genetic Counseling Dilemmas: Down Syndrome, Paternal Age, and Recurrence Risk after Remarriage. *Amer. J. Medical Genetics*, **5**, 145–51.

Hooker, E. (1957). The adjustment of the male overt homosexual. *Journal of Projective Techniques*, **21**, 18–31.

Hooker, E. (1962). The homosexual community. In *Proceedings of the XIV International Congress of Applied Psychology* (Vol. II). *Personality research*. Copenhagen: Munksgaard.

Hoover, E. L. (1973). Lesbianism: Reflections of a "straight" woman. *Human Behavior*, **2**(10), 9.

Horowitz, M. J. (1969a). Flashbacks: Recurrent intrusive images after the use of LSD. *Amer. J. Psychiat.*, **126**(4), 147–51.

Horowitz, M. J. (1969b). Psychic trauma. *Arch. Gen. Psychiat.*, **20**, 552–59.

Horowitz, M. J., & Solomon, G. F. (1978). Delayed stress response syndromes in Vietnam veterans. In C. R. Figley (Ed.), *Stress disorders among Vietnam veterans: Theory, research, and treatment*. New York: Brunner/Mazel.

Horton, D. (1943). The functions of alcohol in primitive societies: a cross-cultural study. *Quart. J. Stud. Alcohol.*, **4**, 199–320.

Horton, P. C., Louy, J. W., & Coppolillo, H. P. (1974). Personality disorder and transitional relatedness. *Arch. Gen. Psychiat.*, **30**(5), 618–22.

Hoshino, Y. et al. (1980). Early symptoms of autism in children and their diagnostic significance, *Jap. J. Child Adoles. Psychiat.*, **21**(5), 284–99.

Hotchkiss, S. (1978). The realities of rape. *Human Behavior*, **7**, 18–23.

Householder, J., Hatcher, R., Burns, W., & Chasnoff, I. (1982). Infants born to narcotic addicted mothers. *Psychol. Bull.*, **92**(2), 453–68.

Howes, M. J., & Hokanson, J. E. (1979). Conversational and social responses to depressive interpersonal behavior. *J. Abnorm. Psychol.*, **88**, 625–34.

Hsu, L. K. G. (1980). Outcome of anorexia nervosa. *Arch. Gen. Psychiat.*, **37**, 1041–46.

Huff, F. W. (1969). A learning theory approach to family therapy. *The Family Coordinator*, **18**(1), 22–26.

Hunter, E. J. (1976). The prisoner of war: Coping with the stress of isolation. In R. H. Moos (Ed.), *Human adaptation: Coping with life crises*. Lexington MA: D.C. Heath & Company.

Hunter, E. J. (1978). The Vietnam POW veteran: Immediate and long-term effects. In C. R. Figley (Ed.), *Stress disorders among Vietnam veterans*. New York: Brunner/Mazel.

Hunter, E. J. (1981). *Wartime stress: Family adjustment to loss* (USIU Report No. TR-USIU-81-07). San Diego, CA: United States International University.

Hurd, P. D., Johnson, C. A., Pechacek, T., Bast, L. P., Jacobs, D. R., & Luepker, R. V. (1980). Prevention of cigarette smoking in seventh grade students. *J. Behav. Med.*, **3**, 15–28.

Hurley, J. R. (1965). Parental acceptance-rejection and children's intelligence. *Merrill-Palmer Quart.*, **11**(1), 19–32.

Hurwitz, N. (1974). The family therapist as intermediary. *The Family Coordinator*, **23**(2), 145–58.

Hurwitz, T. D. (1974). Electroconvulsive therapy: A review. *Comprehensive Psychiatry*, **15**(4), 303–14.

Huxley, A. (1954). *The doors of perception*. New York: Harper & Row.

Huxley, A. (1965). Human potentialities. In R. E. Farson (Ed.), *Science and human affairs*. Palo Alto, Calif.: Science and Behavior Books.

Huxley, J. (1953). *Evolution in action*. New York: Harper & Row.

Huxley, J. (1959). The future of man. *Bulletin of the Atomic Scientists*, **15**, 402–9.

Hyatt, R., & Rolnick, N. (Eds.). (1974). *Teaching the mentally handicapped child*. New York: Behavioral Publications.

Iacono, W. G., Tuason, V. B., & Johnson, R. A. (1981). Dissociation of smooth-pursuit and saccadic eye tracking in remitted schizophrenics: An ocular reaction time task that schizophrenics perform well. *Arch. Gen. Psychiat.*, **38**, 991–96.

Ikemi, Y., Ago, Y., Nakagawa, S., Mori, S., Takahashi, N., Suematsu, H., Sugita, M., & Matsubara, H. (1974). Psychosomatic mechanism under social changes in Japan. *J. Psychosom. Res.*, **18**(1), 15–24.

Ironside, R., & Batchelor, I. R. C. (1945). The ocular manifestations of hysteria in relation to flying. *Brit. J. Ophthalmol.*, **29**, 88–98.

Isaacson, R. L. (1970). When brains are damaged. *Psych. Today*, **3**(4), 38–42.

Iscoe, I., Bloom, B. L., & Spielberger, C. D. (Eds.), (1977). *Community psychology in transition*. Washington, DC: Hemisphere.

Itard, J. (1932). *The wild boy of Aveyron*. (G. Humphrey & M. Humphrey, Trans.). New York: Century. (Original work published in Paris, 1799.)

Jaco, E. G. (1960). *The social epidemiology of mental disorders*. New York: Russell Sage Foundation.

Jacob, T. (1975). Family interaction in disturbed and normal families: A methodological and substantive review. *Psychol. Bull.*, Jan. **82**(1), 33–65.

Jacobs, P. A., Brunton, M., & Melville, M. M. (1965). Aggressive behavior, mental sub-normality, and the XYY male. *Nature*, **208**, 1351–52.

Jacobson, E. (1938). *Progressive relaxation*. Chicago: University of Chicago Press.

Jacobson, N. S., & Margolin, G. (1979). *Marital therapy: Strategies based on social learning and behavior exchange principles*. New York: Brunner/Mazel.

Jacobson, N. S., & Martin, B. (1976). Behavioral marriage therapy: Current status. *Psychol. Bull.*, **83**, 540–56.

James, A. L., & Barry, R. J. (1981). General maturational lag as an essential correlate of early onset psychosis. *J. Autism Devel. Dis.*, **11**(3), 271–83.

James, W. (1890). *The principles of psychology* (Vols. 1 & 2). New York: Holt.

Janis, I. L. (1958). *Psychological stress: Psychoanalytic and behavioral studies of surgical patients*. New York: Wiley.

Janis, I. L., & Leventhal, H. (1965). Psychological aspects of physical illness and hospital care. In B. B. Wolman (Ed.), *Handbook of clinical psychology* (pp. 1360–77). New York: McGraw-Hill.

Janis, I. L., Mahl, G. F., Kagan, J., & Holt, R. R. (1969). From *Personality: Dynamics, development, and assessment*. New York: Harcourt Brace Jovanovich, Inc.

Janowsky, D. S., El-Yousef, M. K., & Davis, J. M. (1974). Interpersonal maneuvers of manic patients. *Amer. J. Psychiat.*, **131**(3), 250–55.

Janowsky, D. S., Leff, M., & Epstein, R. (1970). Playing the manic game. *Arch. Gen. Psychiat.*, **22**, 252–61.

Jarvik, L. F., Klodin, V., & Matsuyama, S. S. (1973). Human aggression and the extra Y chromosome: fact or fantasy? *Amer. Psychologist*, **28**(8), 674–82.

Jarvik, M. E. (1967). The psychopharmacological revolution. *Psych. Today*, **1**(1), 51–58.

Jeffrey, D. B., & Katz, R. C. (1977). *Take it off and keep it off: A behavioral program for weight loss and healthy living*. Englewood Cliffs, N.J.: Prentice-Hall.

Jeffery, R. W., Wing, R. R., & Stunkard, A. J. (1978). Behavioral treatment of obesity: The state of the art, 1978. *Behavior Therapy*, **9**, 189–99.

Jellinek, E. M. (1952). Phases of alcohol addiction. *Quart. J. Stud. Alcohol.*, **13**, 673–78.

Jellinek, E. M. (1971). Phases of alcohol addiction, In G. D. Shean (Ed.), *Studies in abnormal behavior* (pp. 86–98). Chicago: Rand McNally.

Jenkins, C. D. (1974, June 22). Behavior that triggers heart attacks. *Sci. News*, **105**(25), 402.

Jenkins, R. L. (1968). The varieties of children's behavioral problems and family dynamics. *Amer. J. Psychiat.*, **124**(10), 134–39.

Jenkins, R. L. (1969). Classification of behavior problems of children. *Amer. J. Psychiat.*, **125**(8), 68–75.

Jenkins, R. L. (1970). Diagnostic classification in child psychiatry. *Amer. J. Psychiat.*, **127**(5), 140–41.

Jennet, B. et al. (1976). Predicting outcome in individual patients after severe head injury. *Lancet*, **1**, 1031.

Jenni, M. A., & Wollersheim, J. P. (1979). Cognitive therapy, stress-management training and the type A behavior pattern. *Cog. Ther. Res.*, **3**(1), 61–73.

Jensen, J. E. (1983, Mar. 23). Subcommittee on investigations and oversight of the Committee on Science and Technology. United States Congress, Letters to Drs. Mark and Linda Sobell.

Johnson, C. A., & Katz, R. C. (1973). Using parents as change agents for their children: A review. *J. Child Psychol. Psychiat.*, **14**(3), 181–200.

Johnson, H. R., Myhre, S. A., Riwalcaba, R. H. A., Thuline, H. C., & Kelley, V. C. (1970). Effects of testosterone on body image and behavior in Klinefelter's syndrome: A pilot study. *Develop. Med. Child Neurol.*, **12**(4), 454–60.

Johnson, J. (1969). The EEG in the traumatic encephalography of boxers. *Psychiatrica Clinica*, **2**(4), 204–11.

Johnson, J. H., Williams, T. A., Giannetti, R. A., & Schmidt, L. J. (1977). Strategies for the successful introduction of computer technology in a mental health care setting—the problem of change. *Conference Proceedings, National Computer Conference* (Vol. 46), Monode, NJ: AFIPS Press.

Johnston, L. D., Bachman, J. G., & O'Malley, P. M. (1979). *1979 highlights: Drugs and the nation's high school students: Five year national trends*. Rockville, MD: National Institute on Drug Abuse.

Joint Commission on the Mental Health of Children. (1968). Position statement: Statement of the American Orthopsychiatric Association on the work of the Joint Commission on the Mental Health of Children. *Amer. J. Orthopsychiat.*, **38**(3), 402–9.

Joint Commission on the Mental Health of Children. (1970). Crisis in child mental health: Challenge for the 1970's. New York: Harper & Row.

Jones, E. E., & Davis, K. E. (1965). From acts to dispositions: The attribution process in person perception. In L. Berkowitz (Ed.), *Advances in experimental social psychology* (Vol. 2). New York: Academic Press.

Jones, K. L., & Smith, B. W. (1975). The fetal alcohol syndrome. *Teratology*, **12**, 1–10.

Jones, K. L., Smith, B. W., & Hanson, J. W. (1976). Fetal alcohol syndrome: A clinical delineation. *Ann. N.Y. Acad. Sci.*, **273**, 130–37.

Jones, M. (1953). *The therapeutic community*. New York: Basic Books.

Jones, M. C. (1924). A laboratory study of fear: The case of Peter. *Pedagogical Seminary*, **31**, 308–15.

Jones, M. C. (1968). Personality correlates and antecedents of drinking patterns in adult males. *J. Cons. Clin. Psychol.*, **32**(1), 2–12.

Jones, M. C. (1971). Personality antecedents and correlates of drinking patterns in women. *J. Cons. Clin. Psychol.*, **36**(1), 61–69.

Jones, R. A. (1977). *Self-fulfilling prophecies: Social, psychological, and physiological effects of expectancies*. Hillsdale, NJ: Erlbaum Associates.

Jones, R. R., Reid, J. B., & Patterson, G. R. (1975). Naturalistic observation in clinical assessment. In P. M. Reynolds (Ed.), *Advances in psychological assessment* (Vol. 3). San Francisco: Jossey-Bass.

Jordan, H. A., & Levitz, L. S. (1975). Behavior modification in a self-help group. *Journal of the American Dietetic Association*, **62**, 27–29.

Judd, L., & Mandell, A. (1968). Chromosome studies in early infantile autism. *Arch. Gen. Psychiat.*, **18**(4), 450–57.

Kaada, B., & Retvedt, A. (1981). Enuresis and hyperventilation response in the EEG, *Develop. Med. Child Neurol.*, **23**(5), 591–99.

Kadushin, A. (1967). Reversibility of trauma: A follow-up study of children adopted when older. *Social Work*, **12**(4), 22–23.

Kagan, J. (1973). In. B. Pratt (Ed.), Kagan counters Freud, Piaget theories on early childhood deprivation effects. *APA Monitor*, 1973, **4**(2), 1;7.

Kagan, J., Kearsley, R. B., & Zelazo, P. R. (1976, February). *The effects of infant day-care on psychological development*. Symposium on The effect of early experience on child development, American Association for the Advancement of Science. Boston.

Kahana, B., & Kahana, E. (1970). Changes in mental status of elderly patients in age-integrated and age-segregated hospital milieus. *J. Abnorm. Psychol.*, **75**, 177–81.

Kahn, M. W., & Raifman, L. (1981). Hospitalization versus imprisonment and the insanity plea. *Criminal Justice and Behavior*, **8**(4), 483–90.

Kahn, R. L. (1969). Stress: from 9 to 5. *Psych. Today* **3**(4), 34–38.

Kaiser Foundation Health Plan, Inc. (1970). *Planning for health*. Summer, 1–2.

Kales, A., Paulson, M. J., Jacobson, A., & Kales, J. (1966). Somnambulism: Psychophysiological correlates. *Arch. Gen. Psychiat.*, **14**(6), 595–604.

Kalinowski, L. B., & Hippius, H. (1969). *Pharmacological, convulsive and other somatic treatments in psychiatry*. New York: Grune & Stratton.

Kallmann, F. J. (1952). Twin and sibship study of overt male homosexuality. *American Journal of Human Genetics*, June **4**(2), 136–46.

Kallmann, F. J. (1958). The use of genetics in psychiatry. *J. Ment. Sci.*, **104**, 542–49.

Kallmann, F. J. (1961). Genetic factors in aging: Comparative and longitudinal observations on a senescent twin population. In P. H. Hoch & J. Zubin (Eds.), *Psychopathology of aging* (pp. 227–47). New York: Grune & Stratton.

Kanner, L. (1943). Autistic disturbances of effective content. *Nervous Child*, **2**, 217–40.

Kantorovich, F. (1930). An attempt at associative reflex therapy in alcoholism. *Psychological Abstracts*, **4282**.

Kaplan, H. S. (1974). *The new sex therapy*. New York: Brunner/Mazel.

Kaplan, H. S. (1975). *The illustrated manual of sex therapy*. New York: Quadrangle/The New York Times Book Company.

Kaplan, L. J., & Kessler, D. (Eds.), (1976). *An economic analysis of crime*. Springfield, Il: Charles C. Thomas Co.

Kaplun, D., & Reich, R. (1976). The murdered child and his killers. *Amer. J. Psychiat.*, **133**(7), 809–13.

Karnes, M. B., Teska, J. A., & Hodgins, A. S. (1970). The effects of four programs of classroom intervention on the intellectual and language development of 4-year-old disadvantaged children. *Amer. J. Orthopsychiat.*, **40**, 58–76.

Karnosh, L. J. (with collaboration of Zucker, E. M.). (1945). *Handbook of psychiatry*. St. Louis: C. V. Mosby.

Karoly, P., & Kanfer, F. H. (1982). *Self-management and behavior change*. New York: Pergamon Press.

Karon, B. P., & Vandenbos, G. R. (1981) *Psychotherapy of schizophrenia: Treatment of choice*. New York: Jason Aronson.

Kashani, J. H., Cantwell, D. P., Shekim, W. O., & Reid, J. C. (1982). Major depressive disorder in children admitted to an inpatient community mental health center. *Amer. J. Psychiat.*, **139**(6), 671–72.

Kashani, J. H., Hiodges, K. K., Simonds, J. F., & Hilderbrand, E. (1981a). Life events and hospitalization in children: A comparison with a general population. *Brit. J. Psychiat.*, **139**, 221–25.

Kashani, J. H., Husain, A., Shekim, W. O., Hodges, K. K., Cytryn, L., McKnew, D. H. (1981b). Current perspectives on childhood depression: An overview. *Amer. J. Psychiat.*, **138**(2), 143–53.

Kashani, J. H., Venzke, R., & Millar, E. A. (1981). Depression in children admitted to hospital for orthopaedic procedures. *Brit. J. Psychiat.*, **138**, 21–25.

Katkin, E. S., & Obrist, P. A. (1978). An inaccurate picture. *Amer. Psychologist, 33,* 963.

Katz, M. M., Sanborn, K. O., Lowery, H. A., & Ching. J. (1978). Ethnic studies in Hawaii: On psychopathology and social deviance. In L. C. Wynne, R. L. Cromwell, & S. Matthysse (Eds.), *The nature of schizophrenia: New approaches to research and treatment* (pp. 572–85). New York: Wiley.

Katz, M. M., Waskow, E. E., & Olsson, J. (1968). Characteristics of the psychological state produced by LSD. *J. Abnorm. Psychol., 73*(1), 1–14.

Kaufman, I., Frank, T., Heims, L., Herrick, J., Reiser, D., & Willer, L. (1960). Treatment implications of a new classification of parents of schizophrenic children. *Amer. J. Psychiat., 116,* 920–24.

Kaufmann, W. (1973). *Without guilt and justice: From decidophobia to autonomy.* New York: Peter H. Wyden.

Kay, E. J., Lyons, A., Newman, W., Mankin, D., & Loeb, R. C. (1978). A longitudinal study of personality correlates of marijuana use. *J. Cons. Clin. Psychol., 46,* 470–1.

Kazdin, A. E. (1980). *Behavior modification in applied settings.* (2nd ed.). Homewood, IL: Dorsey.

Kazdin. A. E., & Wilson, G. T. (1978). *Evaluation of behavior therapy: Issues, evidence and research strategies.* Cambridge, MA: Ballinger.

Kelly, J. G., Snowden, L. R., & Muñoz, R. F. (1977). Social and community interventions. *Ann. Rev. Psychol., 28,* 323–61.

Kempe, R., & Kempe, H. (1979). *Child Abuse.* London: Fontana/Open Books.

Kendall, P. C. (1981). Cognitive-behavioral interventions with children. In B. Lahey & A. E. Kazdin (Eds.), *Advances in clinical child psychology* (Vol. 4). New York: Plenum.

Kendall, P. C. (1982a). Cognitive processes and procedures in behavior therapy. In C. M. Franks, G. T. Wilson, P. C. Kendall, & K. D. Brownell, (Eds.), *Annual Review of Behavior Therapy* (Vol. 8). New York: Guilford Press.

Kendall, P. C. (1982b). Integration: Behavior therapy and other schools of thought. *Behav. Ther., 13,* 559–71.

Kendall, P. C., & Bemis, K. M. (1983). Thought and action in psychotherapy: The cognitive-behavioral approaches. In M. Hersen, A. E. Kazdin & A. S. Bellack, (Eds.), *The clinical psychology handbook.* New York: Pergamon.

Kendall, P. C., Deardorff, P. A., & Finch, A. J. (1977). Empathy and socialization in first and repeat juvenile offenders and normals. *J. Abnorm. Psychol., 5,* 93–97.

Kendall, P. C., & Finch, A. J. (1976). A cognitive-behavioral treatment for impulse control: A case study. *J. Cons. Clin. Psychol., 44,* 852–57.

Kendall, P. C., & Finch, A. J. (1978). A cognitive-behavioral treatment for impulsivity: A group comparison study. *J. Cons. Clin. Psychol., 46,* 110–18.

Kendall, P. C., & Hollon, S. D. (Eds.), (1979). *Cognitive behavioral intervention: Theory, research and procedures.* New York: Academic Press.

Kendall, P. C., & Norton-Ford, J. D. (1982). Therapy outcome research methods. In P. C. Kendall & J. N. Butcher (Eds.), *Handbook of research methods in clinical psychology.* New York: Wiley.

Kendler, K. S., & Davis, K. L. (1981). The genetics and biochemistry of paranoid schizophrenia and other paranoid psychoses. *Schizophrenia Bull., 7,* 689–709.

Kendler, K. S., & Gruenberg, A. M. (1982). Genetic relationship between paranoid personality disorder and the "schizophrenic" spectrum disorders. *Amer. J. Psychiat., 139*(9), 1185–86.

Kendler, K. S., Gruenberg, A. M., & Strauss, J. M. (1981). An independent analysis of the Copenhagen sample of the Danish adoption study of schizophrenia: II. The relationship between schizotypal personality disorder and schizophrenia. *Arch. Gen. Psychiat., 38,* 982–84.

Kendler, K. S., & Tsuang, M. T. (1981). Nosology of paranoid schizophrenia and other paranoid psychoses. *Schizophrenia Bull., 7,* 594–610.

Keniston, K. (1977, Nov. 28). Meeting the needs of children: I, The necessity of politics. *Christianity and Crisis* (pp. 247–48).

Kennedy, J. F. (1963). Message from the President of the United States relative to mental illness and mental retardation. *Amer. Psychologist, 18,* 280–89.

Kennedy, T. D., & Kimura, H. K. (1974). Transfer, behavioral improvement, and anxiety reduction in systematic desensitization. *J. Cons. Clin. Psychol., 42*(5), 720–28.

Kernberg, O. F. (1975). *Borderline conditions and pathological narcissism.* New York: Jason Aronson.

Kernberg, O. F. (1976). *Object relations theory and clinical psychoanalysis.* New York: Jason Aronson.

Kessler, M., & Albee, G. W. (1975). Primary prevention. *Ann. Rev. Psychol., 26,* 557–91.

Kety, S. S., Rosenthal, D., Wender, P. H., Schulsinger, F., & Jacobsen, B. (1978). The biologic and adaptive families of adopted individuals who become schizophrenic: Prevalence of mental illness and other characteristics. In L. C. Wynne, R. L. Cromwell, & S. Matthysse (Eds.), *The nature of schizophrenia: New approaches to research and treatment* (pp. 25–27) New York: Wiley.

Kewman, D., & Roberts, A. H. (1979). Skin temperature biofeedback and migraine headaches. Paper presented at the Annual Conference of the Biofeedback Society of America, San Diego.

Keys, A., Brožek, J., Henschel, A., Mickelson, O., & Taylor, H. L. (1950). *The biology of human starvation.* Minneapolis: University of Minnesota Press.

Kidson, M., & Jones, I. (1968). Psychiatric disorders among aborigines of the Australian Western Desert. *Arch. Gen. Psychiat. 19,* 413–22.

Kidson, M. A. (1973). Personality and hypertension. *J. Psychosom. Res., 17*(1), 35–41.

Kiersch, T. A. (1962). Amnesia: A clinical study of ninety-eight cases. *Amer. J. Psychiat., 119,* 57–60.

Kiester, E., Jr. (1974). Explosive youngsters: What to do about them. *Today's Health, 52*(1), 49–53; 64–65.

Kiev, A. (1972). *Transcultural psychiatry.* New York: Free Press.

Kiloh, L. G. (1982). Electroconvulsive therapy. In E. S. Paykel (Ed.), *Handbook of affective disorders.* New York: Guilford Press.

Kilpatrick, D. G., Sutker, P. B., Roitch, J. C., & Miller, W. C. (1976). Personality correlates of polydrug users. *Psych. Rep. 38,* 311–17.

Kimmel, H. D. (1974). Instrumental conditioning of autonomically mediated responses. *Amer. Psychologist, 29,* 325–35.

King, C. A., & Young, R. D. (1981). Peer popularity and peer communication patterns: Hyperactivity versus active but normal boys. *J. Abnorm. Child Psychol., 9*(4), 464–82.

King, L. J., Murphy, G., Robins, L., & Darvish, H. (1969). Alcohol abuse: A crucial factor in the social problems of Negro men. *Amer. J. Psychiat., 125*(12), 96–104.

Kingsley, R. G., & Wilson, G. T. (1977). Behavior therapy for obesity: A comparative investigation of long-term efficacy. *J. Cons. Clin. Psychol., 45,* 288–98.

Kinney, D. K., & Jacobsen, B. (1978). Environmental factors in schizophrenia: New adoption study evidence. In L. C. Wynne, R. L. Cromwell, & S. Matthysse (Eds.), *The nature of schizophrenia: New approaches to research and treatment* (pp. 38–51). New York: Wiley.

Kinsey, A. C., Pomeroy, W. B., & Martin, C. E. (1948). *Sexual behavior in the human male.* Philadephia: W. B. Saunders.

Kinsey, A. C., Pomeroy, W. B., & Martin, C. E. (1953). *Sexual behavior in the human female.* Philadelphia: W. B. Saunders.

Kinston, W., & Rosser, R. (1974). Disaster: Effects on mental and physical state. *J. Psychosomatic Research, 18,* 437–56.

Kinzie, J. D., & Bolton, J. M. (1973, July). Psychiatry with the aborigines of West Malaysia. *Amer. J. Psychiat., 130*(7), 769–73.

Kirkpatrick, C., & Kanin, E. J. (1957). Male sexual aggression on a university campus. *American Sociological Review, 22,* 52–58.

Kirsh, E. S. (1974). Narcotics overdosage. *Hospital Medicine, 10,* 8–10, 12, 17–24.

Kirstein, L., Prusoff, B., Weissman, M., & Dressler, D. M. (1975). Utilization review of treatment for suicide attempters. *Amer. J. Psychiat., 132*(1), 22–27.

Klagsbrun, F. (1976). *Too young to die: Youth and suicide.* Boston: Houghton Mifflin.

Klepac, R. K., Hauge, G., Dowling, J., & McDonald, M. (1981). Direct and generalized effects of three components of stress-inoculation for increased pain tolerance. *Behav. Ther.*, **12**, 417–24.

Klerman, G. L. (1982). Practical issues in the treatment of depression and mania. In E. S. Paykel (Ed.), *Handbook of affective disorders*. New York: Guilford Press.

Klerman, G. L., & Izen, J. E. (1977). The effects of bereavement and grief on physical health and general well-being. In S. Kasl & F. Reichsman (Eds.), *Advances in psychosomatic medicine: Vol. 9. Epidemiologic studies in psychosomatic medicine* (pp. 63–104). Basel, Switzerland: S. Karger.

Klerman, G. L., & Schechter, G. (1982). Drugs and psychotherapy. In E. S. Paykel (Ed.), *Handbook of affective disorders*. New York: Guilford Press.

Kline, N. S. (1954). Use of *Rauwolfia serpentina* in neuropsychiatric conditions. *Ann. N.Y. Acad. Sci.*, **54**, 107–32.

Klinger, E. (1979). Modes of normal conscious flow. In K. S. Pope & J. L. Singer (Eds.), *The stream of consciousness: Scientific investigations into the flow of human experience*. New York: Plenum.

Klopfer, B., & Davidson, H. (1962). *The Rorschach technique: An introductory manual*. New York: Harcourt Brace Jovanovich, Inc.

Knapp, S. (1980). A primer on malpractice for psychologists. *Professional Psychology*, **11**(4), 606–12.

Knapp, S., & Vandecreek, L. (1982). Tarasoff: Five years later. *Professional Psychology*, **13**(4), 511–16.

Knittle, J. L., Timmers, K. I., & Katz, D. P. (1982). Adolescent obesity. In M. Winick (Ed.), *Adolescent nutrition*. New York: Oxford University Press.

Knowles, J. H. (1977). Editorial. *Science*, **198**, 1103–04.

Kobasa, S. C. (1979). Stressful life events, personality, and health: An inquiry into hardiness. *J. Pers. Soc. Psychol.*, **37**(1), 1–11.

Koch, R. (1967). The multidisciplinary approach to mental retardation. In A. A. Baumeister (Ed.), *Mental retardation: Appraisal, education, and rehabilitation*. Chicago: Aldine.

Kohn, M. L. (1973). Social class and schizophrenia: A critical review and a reformulation. *Schizophrenia Bulletin*, No. 7, 60–79.

Kolata, G. B. (1981a). Clues to the cause of senile dementia: Patients with Alzheimer's disease seem to be deficient in a brain neurotransmitter. *Science*, **211**, 1032–33.

Kolata, G. B. (1981b). Fetal alcohol advisory debated. *Science*, **214**, 642–46.

Kolata, G. B. (1982). New valiums and anti-valiums on the horizon. *Science*, **216**, 604–5.

Kolodny, R. C., Masters, W. H., Hendrys, J., & Toro, G. (1971). Plasma testosterone and the semen analysis in male homosexuals. *New Engl. J. Med.*, **285**(21), 1170–74.

Konopka, G. (1964). Adolescent delinquent girls. *Children*, **11**(1), 21–26.

Konopka, G. (1967). Rehabilitation of the delinquent girl. *Adolescence*, **2**(5), 69–82.

Kora, T., & Ohara, K. (1973). Morita therapy. *Psych. Today*, **6**(10), 63–68.

Kormos, H. R. (1978). The nature of combat stress. In C. R. Figley (Ed.), *Stress disorders among Vietnam veterans*. New York: Brunner/Mazel.

Koss, M. P., & Oros, C. J. (1982). Sexual experiences survey: A research instrument investigating sexual aggression and victimization. *J. Cons. Clin. Psychol.*, **50**, 455–57.

Kovacs, M., & Beck, A. T. (1977). An empirical clinical approach towards a definition of childhood depression. In J. G. Schulterbrand & A. Raskin (Eds.), *Depression in children: Diagnosis, treatment and conceptual models*. New York: Raven Press.

Kovacs, M., Rush, A. J., Beck, A. T., & Hollon, S. D. (1981). Depressed outpatients treated with cognitive therapy or pharmacotherapy: A one year follow-up. *Arch. Gen. Psychiat.*, **38**, 33–39.

Kraepelin, E. (1883). *Compendium der psychiatrie*. Leipzig: Abel.

Kraepelin, E. (1937). *Clinical psychiatry* (6th ed.). New York: Macmillan. Originally published 1899.

Krafft-Ebing, R. V. (1950). *Psychopathica sexualis*. New York: Pioneer Publications.

Kraines, S. H. (1948). *The therapy of the neuroses and psychoses* (3rd ed.). Philadelphia: Lea & Febiger.

Krech, D. (1966). *Environment, heredity, brain, and intelligence*. Paper presented to the Southwestern Psychological Association. Arlington, TX.

Krech, D., Rosenzweig, M. R., & Bennett, E. L. (1962). Relations between brain chemistry and problem-solving among rats raised in enriched and impoverished environments. *J. Compar. Physiol. Psychol.*, **55**, 801–7.

Kringlen, E. (1967). *Heredity and environment in the functional psychosis: An epidemiological-clinical twin study*. Oslo: Universitsforlaget.

Kringlen, E. (1978). Adult offspring of two psychotic parents, with special reference to schizophrenia. In L. C. Wynne, R. L. Cromwell, & S. Matthysse (Eds.), *The nature of schizophrenia: New approaches to research and treatment* (pp. 9–24). New York: Wiley.

Krohn, M. D., Akers, R. L., Radosevich, M. J., & Lanza-Kaduce, L. (1980). Social status and deviance. *Criminology*, **18**(3), 303–18.

Krug, S. E. (1982). The use of the 16PF in an Illinois Supreme Court Ruling. Personal Correspondence.

Krugman, S., & Ward, R. (1973). *Infectious diseases of children and adults*. St. Louis: Mosby.

Krystal, H. (1968). *Massive psychic trauma*. New York: International Universities Press.

Kübler-Ross, E. (1975). *Death: The final stage of growth*. Englewood Cliffs, NJ: Prentice-Hall.

Kucharsky, L. T., & Unterwald, E. M. (1981). Symptomatic treatment of tardive dyskinesia: A word of caution. *Schizophrenia Bull.*, **7**, 571–73.

Kuechenmeister, C. A., Linton, P. H., Mueller, T. V., & White, H. B. (1977). Eye tracking in relation to age, sex, and illness. *Arch. Gen. Psychiat.*, **34**, 578–79.

Kuhn, T. S. (1962). *The structure of scientific revolutions*. Chicago: University of Chicago Press.

Kunnes, R. (1973). Double dealing in dope. *Human Behavior*, Oct. **2**(10), 22–27.

Kurdek, L. A., Blisk, D., & Siesky, A. E. (1981). Correlates of children's long-term adjustment to their parents' divorce. *Develop. Psychol.*, **17**, 565–79.

Kurland, H. D. (1967). Extreme obesity: A psychophysiological disorder. *Psychosomatics*, **8**, 108–11.

Kushner, F. H. (1973). All of us bear the scars. *U.S. News & World Report*, **74**(16), 41.

Kushner, M. (1968). The operant control of intractable sneezing. In C. D. Spielberger (Ed.), *Contributions to general psychology: Selected readings for introductory pscyhology*. New York: Ronald Press.

Lader, M., & Mathews, A. (1970). Physiological changes during spontaneous panic attacks. *J. Psychosom. Res.*, **14**(4), 377–82.

Laing, R. D. (1967, Feb. 3). Schizophrenic split. *Time*, 56.

Laing, R. D. (1969). *The divided self*. New York: Pantheon.

Laing, R. D. (1971). Quoted in J. S. Gordon, Who is mad? Who is sane? R. D. Laing: In search of a new psychiatry. *Atlantic*, **227**(1), 50–66.

Laing, R. D., & Esterson, A. (1964). *Sanity, madness, and the family*. London: Tavistock.

Lamb, H. R., & Grant. R. W. (1982). The mentally ill in an urban county jail. *Arch. Gen. Psychiat.*, **39**(1), 17–22.

Lamson, B. (1980). Sexual arousal of heterosexual, homosexual, and bisexual women. Unpublished master's thesis, University of Georgia.

Landesman-Dwyer, S. (1981). Living in the community. *Amer. J. Ment. Def.*, **86**, 223–34.

Lang, P. (1970). Autonomic control. *Psych. Today*, **4**(5), 37–41.

Lang, P. J., Stroufe, L. A., & Hastings, J. E. (1967). Effects of feedback and instructional set on the control of cardiac-rate variability. *J. Exp. Psychol.*, **75**, 425–31.

Langer, E. J., & Abelson, R. P. (1974). A patient by any other name . . . ; Clinician group difference in labeling bias. *J. Cons. Clin. Psychol.* **42**(1), 4–9.

Langner, T. S., Gersten, J. C., Greene, E. L., Eisenberg, J. G., Herson, J. H., & McCarthy, E. D. (1974). Treatment of psychological disorders among urban children. *J. Cons. Clin. Psychol.*, 42(2), 70–79.

Langs, R. J. (1973). *The technique of psychoanalytic therapy. Vol. 1: The initial contact, theoretical framework, understanding the patient's communications, the therapist's interventions.* New York: Aronson.

Lanyon, R. I., Barrington, C. C., & Newman, A. C. (1976). Modification of stuttering through EMG biofeedback: A preliminary study. *Behavior therapy*, 7, 96–103.

Latham, C., Holzman, P. S., Manschreck, T. C., & Tole, J. (1981). Optokinetic nystagmus and pursuit eye movements in schizophrenia. *Arch. Gen. Psychiat.*, 38, 997–1003.

Lazarus, A. (1971). *Behavior therapy and beyond.* New York: McGraw-Hill.

Lazarus, A. A. (1981). *The practice of multimodal therapy.* New York: McGraw-Hill.

Lazarus, A. P. (1968). Learning theory in the treatment of depression. *Behav. Res. Ther.*, 8, 83–89.

Leary, T. (1957). *Interpersonal diagnosis.* New York: Ronald.

Lebedev, B. A. (1967). Corticovisceral psychosomatics. *Inter. J. Psychiat.*, 4(3), 241–46.

Lebra, W. (Ed.). (1976). Culture-bound syndromes, ethnopsychiatry and alternate therapies. In *Mental health research in Asia and the Pacific* (Vol. 4). Honolulu: University Press of Hawaii.

Leeman, C. P., & Mulvey, C. H. (1974). Brief psychotherapy of the dependent personality: Specific techniques. *Psychonometrics*, 25, 36–42.

Leff, M. J., Roatch, J. F., & Bunney, W. E., Jr. (1970). Environmental factors preceding the onset of severe depressions. *Psychiatry*, 33(3), 298–311.

Lefkowitz, M. M., & Burton, N. (1978). Childhood depression: A critique of the concept. *Psychol. Bull.*, 85, 716–26.

Lefkowitz, M. M., Eron, L. D., Walder, L. O., & Huesmann, L. R. (1977). *Growing up to be violent: A longitudinal study of the development of aggression.* New York: Pergamon Press.

Lefkowitz, M. M., Huesmann, L. R., Walder, L. O., Eron, L. D. (1973). Developing and predicting aggression. *Sci. News*, 103(3), 40.

Lehmann, H. E. (1967). Psychiatric disorders not in standard nomenclature. In A. M. Freedman, H. I. Kaplan, & H. S. Kaplan (Eds.), *Comprehensive textbook of psychiatry.* Baltimore, Md.: Williams & Wilkins.

Lehmann, H. E. (1968). Clinical perspectives on anti-depressant therapy. *Amer. J. Psychiat.*, 124(11, Suppl.), 12–21.

Leiblum, S. R., & Pervin, L. A. (1980). *Principles and practice of sex therapy.* New York: Guilford Press.

Leiderman, P. H., & Leiderman, G. F. (1974). Affective and cognitive consequences of polymatric infant care in the East African highlands. In A. Pick (Ed.), *Minnesota symposium on child development* (Vol. 8). Minneapolis: University of Minnesota Press.

Lemert, E. M. (1962). Paranoia and the dynamics of exclusion. *Sociometry*, 25, 2–25.

Lennard, H. L., & Bernstein, A. (1969). *Patterns in human interaction.* San Francisco: Jossey-Bass.

Leon, G. (1976). Current directions in the treatment of obesity. *Psychol. Bull.*, 83, 557–78.

Leon, G. L. (1983). *Treating eating disorders: Obesity, anorexia nervosa and bulimia.* Lexington, MA: Lewis.

Leon, G. L., Butcher, J. N., Kleinman, M., Goldberg, A., Almagor, M. (1981). Survivors of the holocaust and their children: Current status and adjustment. *J. Pers. Soc. Psychol.*, 41(3), 503–16.

Leon, G. R., & Chamberlain, K. (1973). Emotional arousal, eating patterns, and body image as differential factors associated with varying success in maintaining a weight loss. *J. Cons. Clin. Psychol.*, 40, 474–80.

Leon, G. R., Eckert, E. D., Teed, D., & Buckwald, H. (1978). Changes in body image and other psychological factors after intestinal bypass surgery for massive obesity.

Leon, G. R. & Roth, L. (1977). Obesity. Psychological causes, correlations and speculations. *Psychol. Bull.*, 84, 117–39.

Leonard, A. G. (1906). *The lower Niger and its tribes.* London: Barnes & Noble.

Leonard, C. V. (1974). Depression and suicidality. *J. Cons. Clin. Psychol.*, 42(1), 98–104.

Lettieri, D. J., Sayers, M., & Pearson, H. W. (Eds.), (1980). *Theories on drug abuse: Selected contemporary perspectives.* Rockville, MD: National Institute on Drug Abuse.

Levenson, A. J. (1981). *Basic psychopharmacology.* New York: Springer.

Levenson, R. W., Sher, K. J., Grossman, L. M., Newman, J., & Newlin, D. B. (1980). Alcohol and stress response dampening: Pharmacological effects, expectancy and tension reduction. *J. Abnorm. Psychol.*, 89(4), 528–38.

Levin, S. (1949). Brain tumors in mental hospital patients. *Amer. J. Psychiat.*, 105, 897–900.

Levine, M. D. (1976). Children with encopresis: A descriptive analysis. *Pediatrics*, 56, 412.

Levine, M. D., & Bakow, H. (1975). Children with encopresis: A study of treatment outcomes. *Pediatrics*, 58, 845.

Levitt, L. P. (1974, Apr. 1). *Illinois State Plan for the Prevention, Treatment, and Control of Alcohol Abuse and Alcoholism (Vol. 1): Objectives—Plan of Action—Basic Data.* Department of Mental Health and Developmental Disabilities, State of Illinois.

Levy, L., & Rowitz, L. (1974). Mapping out schizophrenia. *Human Behavior*, 3(5), 39–40.

Levy, S. M. (1976). Schizophrenic symptomatology: Reaction or strategy? A study of contextual antecedents. *J. Abnorm. Psychol.*, 85, 435–45.

Lewinsohn, P. M. (1974). A behavioral approach to depression. In R. J. Friedman & M. M. Katz (Eds.), *The psychology of depression: Contemporary theory and research.* New York: Halstead Press.

Lewinsohn, P. M., & Graf, M. (1973). Pleasant activities and depression. *J. Cons. Clin. Psychol.*, 41(2), 261–68.

Lewinson, T. S. (1940). Dynamic disturbances in the handwriting of psychotics; with reference to schizophrenic, paranoid, and manic-depressive psychoses. *The American Journal of Psychiatry*, 97, 102–35.

Lewis, J. M., Rodnick, E. H., & Goldstein, M. J. (1981). Intrafamilial interactive behavior, communication deviance, and risk for schizophrenia. *J. Abnorm. Psychol.*, 90, 448–57.

Lewis, M. S., & Griffin, P. A. (1981). An explanation for the season of birth effect in schizophrenia and certain other diseases. *Psychol. Bull.*, 89, 589–96.

Lewis, N. D. C. (1941). *A short history of psychiatric achievement.* New York: Norton.

Lewis, W. C. (1974). Hysteria: The consultant's dilemma. *Arch. Gen. Psychiat.*, 30(2), 145–51.

Lexow, G. A., & Aronson, S. S. (1975). Health advocacy: A need, a concept, a model. *Children Today*, 4(1), 2–6; 36.

Liberman, R. P., & Raskin, D. E. (1971). Depression: A behavioral formulation. *Arch. Gen. Psychiat.*, 24(6), 515–23.

Libet, J. M., & Lewinsohn, P. M. (1973). Concept of social skill with special reference to the behavior of depressed persons. *J. Cons. Clin. Psychol.*, 40(2), 304–12.

Lichy, M. H. (1982). Assessment of client functioning in residential settings. In M. Miraba (Ed.), *The chronically mentally ill; Research and services.* New York: SP Medical and Scientific Books.

Lidz, T. (1968). The family, language, and the transmission of schizophrenia. In D. Rosenthal & S. S. Kety (Eds.), *The transmission of schizophrenia* (pp. 175–84). Elmsford, NY: Pergamon Press.

Lidz, T. (1973). *The origin and treatment of schizophrenoid disorders.* New York: Basic Books.

Lidz, T. (1978). Egocentric cognitive regression and the family setting of schizophrenic disorders. In L. C. Wynne, R. L. Cromwell, & S. Matthysse (Eds), *The nature of schizophrenia: New approaches to research and treatment* (pp. 526–33). New York: Wiley.

Lidz, T., Fleck, S., & Cornelison, A. R. (1965). *Schizophrenia and the family.* New York: International University Press.

Lieberman, L. M. (1982). The nightmare of scheduling. *J. Learn. Dis.*, 15, 57–58.

Liem, J. H. (1974). Effects of verbal communications of parents and children: A comparison of normal and schizophrenic families. *J. Cons. Clin. Psychol.*, 42, 438–50.

Liem, J. H. (1980). Family studies of schizophrenia: An update and commentary. *Schizophrenia Bull.*, **6**, 429–55.

Lievens, P. (1974). The organic psychosyndrome of early childhood and its effects on learning. *J. Learn. Dis.*, **7**(10), 626–31.

Life. (1951). The kid with the bad eye. **30**(5), pp. 17–21.

Lifton, R. J. (1972). The "Gook syndrome" and "numbed warfare." *Sat. Rev.*, **55**(47), 66–72.

Liljefors, I., & Rahe, R. H. (1970). An identical twin study of psychosocial factors in coronary heart disease in Sweden. *Psychosom. Med.*, **32**(5), 523–42.

Lindzey, G. (1967). Some remarks concerning incest, the incest taboo, and psychoanalytic theory. *Amer. Psychologist*, **22**(12), 1051–59.

Lipsky, M. J., Kassinove, H., & Miller, N. J. (1980). Effects of rational-emotive therapy, rational role reversal and rational-emotive imagery on the emotional adjustment of community mental health center patients. *J. Cons. Clin. Psychol.*, **48**, 366–74.

Lipton, E. L., Steinschneider, A., & Richmond, J. B. (1966). Psychophysiologic disorders in children. In L. W. Hoffman & M. L. Hoffman (Eds.), *Review of child development research* (pp. 169–220). Russell Sage Foundation.

Lipton, M. A., Ban, T. A., Kane, F. J., Levine, J., Loren, R., & Wittenborn, R. (1973). *Megavitamin and orthomolecular therapy in psychiatry*. APA Task Force on Vitamin Therapy in Psychiatry. Washington: American Psychiatric Association.

Lipton, S. (1943). Dissociated personality: A case report. *Psychiatric Quarterly*, **17**, 35–36.

Livingood, J. M. (Ed.). (1972). *National Institute of Mental Health Task Force on Homosexuality: Final report and background papers*. Rockville, MD.: National Institute of Mental Health.

Livingston, J. (1974, Mar.). Compulsive gamblers: A culture of losers. *Psych. Today*, 51–55.

Lloyd, R. W., Jr., & Salzberg, H. C. (1975). Controlled social drinking: An alternative to abstinence as a treatment goal for some alcohol abusers. *Psychol. Bull.*, **82**, 815–42.

Lobitz, W. C., & Lobitz, G. K. (1978). Clinical assessment in the treatment of sexual dysfunctions. In J. LoPiccolo & L. LoPiccolo (Eds.), *Handbook of sex therapy* (pp. 85–102). New York: Plenum Press.

Lombroso-Ferrero, G. (1911). *Criminal man*. New York: Putnam's.

Loney, J., Langhorne, J. E., & Paternite, C. E. (1978). An empirical basis for subgrouping the hyperkinetic/minimal brain dysfunction syndrome. *J. Abnorm. Psychol.*, **87**, 431–41.

Loper, R. G., Kammeier, M. L., & Hoffman, H. (1973). MMPI characteristics of college freshmen males who later became alcoholics. *J. Abnorm. Psychol.*, **82**, 159–62.

LoPiccolo, J. (1978). Direct treatment of sexual dysfunction. In J. LoPiccolo & L. LoPiccolo (Eds.), *Handbook of sex therapy* (pp. 1–17). New York: Plenum Press.

LoPiccolo, J., & LoPiccolo, L. (Eds.) (1978). *Handbook of sex therapy*. New York: Plenum Press.

Loranger, A. W., Oldham, J. M., & Tulis, E. H. (1982). Familial transmission of DSM-III borderline personality disorder. *Arch. Gen. Psychiat.*, **39** (7), 795–99.

Lorenz, V. C., & Shuttlesworth, D. E. (1983). The impact of pathological gambling on the spouse of the gambler. *J. Community Psychol.*, **11**, 67–76.

Lorr, M., & Klett, C. J. (1968). Cross-cultural comparison of psychotic syndromes. *J. Abnorm. Psychol.*, **74**(4), 531–43.

Los Angeles Times. (1970, Apr. 1). Prostitute's diary aids in syphilis hunt. III, 16.

Los Angeles Times. (1973, Sept. 30). A transvestite's plea for understanding and tolerance. IV, 7.

Lothstein, L. M. (1982). Sex reassignment surgery: Historical, bioethical, and theoretical issues. *Amer. J. Psychiat.*, **139**, 417–26.

Lovaas, O. I. (1977). *The autistic child: Language development through behavior modification*. New York: Halsted Press.

Lovaas, O. I., Schaeffer, B., & Simmons, J. Q. (1974). In O. I. Lovaas & B. D. Bucker (Eds.), *Perspectives in behavior modification with deviant children*. Englewood Cliffs, N.J.: Prentice-Hall.

Lovibond, S. H., & Caddy, G. R. (1970). Discriminated aversive control in the moderation of alcoholics' drinking behavior. *Behavior Therapy*, **1**, 437–44.

Lubin, B. (1976). Group therapy. In I. Weiner (Ed.), *Clinical methods in psychology*. New York: Wiley.

Lubinsky, D. Tellegen, A., & Butcher, J. N. (1983). Masculinity, femininity, and androgyny viewed and assessed as distinct concepts. *J. Pers. Soc. Psychol.*, **44**, 428–39.

Lucas, A. R., Duncan J. W., & Piens, V. (1976). The treatment for anorexia nervosa. *Amer. J. Psychiat.*, **133**, 1034–38.

Ludwig, A. O., & Ranson, S. W. (1947). A statistical follow-up of treatment of combat-induced psychiatric casualties. I and II. *Military Surgeon*, **100**, 51–62, 169–75.

Lund, S. N. (1975). *Personality and personal history factors of child abusing parents*. Unpublished doctoral dissertation, University of Minnesota.

Lykken, D. T. (1957). A study of anxiety in the sociopathic personality. *J. Abnorm. Soc. Psychol.*, **55**(1), 6–10.

Lyle, O. E., & Gottesman, I. I. (1977). Premorbid psychometric indicators of the gene for Huntington's disease. *J. Cons. Clin. Psychol.*, **45**, 1011–22.

Lynch, H. T., Harlan, W. L., & Dyhrberg, J. S. (1972). Subjective perspective of a family with Huntington's chorea. *Arch. Gen. Psychiat.*, **27**(1), 67–72.

Lynch, J. J. (1977). *The broken heart*. New York: Basic Books, Inc.

MacDonald, A. D. (1964). Intelligence in children of very low birth weight. *British Journal of Preventive Social Medicine*, **18**, 59–75.

MacDonald, M. R., & Kuiper, N. A. (1983). Cognitive-behavioral preparations for surgery: Some theoretical and methodological concerns. *Clin. Psychol. Rev.*, **3**, 27–39.

MacFarlane, J. W., Allen, L., & Honzik, M. P. (1954). *A developmental study of the behavior problems of normal children between 21 months and 14 years*. Berkeley: University of California Press.

MacLusky, N. J., & Naftolin, F. (1981). Sexual differentiation of the central nervous system. *Science*, **211**, 1294–1303.

MacMillan, D. L., & Keogh, B. K. (1971). Normal and retarded children's expectancy for failure. *Develop. Psychol.*, **4**(3). 343–48.

Magaro, P. A. (1980). *Cognition in schizophrenia and paranoia*. Hillsdale, NJ: Laurence Erlbaum Associates.

Magaro, P. A. (1981). The paranoid and the schizophrenic: The case for distinct cognitive style. *Schizophrenia Bull.*, **7**, 632–61.

Magrab, P. R. (1982). Services for children: Challenge for the 1980's. *J. Pediat. Psychol.*, **7**(2), 105–10.

Mahler, M. (1976). *On human symbiosis and the vicissitudes of individuation*. New York: Library of Human Behavior.

Mahoney, G., Glover, A., & Finger, I. (1981). Relationship between language and sensorimotor development of Down syndrome and nonretarded children. *Amer. J. Ment. Def.*, **86**, 21–27.

Mahoney, M., & Arnkoff, D. (1978). Cognitive and self-control therapies. In S. Garfield & A. Bergin (Eds.), *Handbook of psychotherapy and behavior change: An empirical analysis*. New York: Wiley.

Mahoney, M. J. (1974). *Cognition and behavior modification*. Cambridge, Mass.: Ballinger.

Main, M., & Weston, D. R. (1981). The quality of the toddler's relationship to mother and to father: Related to conflict behavior and the readiness to establish new relationships. *Child Develop.*, **52**, 932–40.

Maisch, H. (1972). *Incest*. New York: Stein & Day.

Makita, K. (1973). The rarity of "depression" in childhood. *Acta Psychiatrica*, **40**, 37–44.

Malamud, N. (1975). Organic brain disease mistaken for psychiatric disorder: A clinicopathologic study. In D. F. Benson & D. Blumer (Eds.), *Psychiatric aspects of neurological disease* (pp. 287–307). New York: Grune & Stratton.

Malatesta, V. J., Sutker, P. B., & Treiber, F. A. (1981). Sensation seeking and chronic public drunkenness. *J. Cons. Clin. Psychol.*, **49**, 292–94.

Malinowski, B. (1927). *Sex and repression in savage society.* New York: Humanities.

Mann, J. (1973). *Time-limited psychotherapy.* Cambridge, MA: Harvard University Press.

Mann, P. A. (1978). *Community psychology: Concepts and applications.* New York: The Free Press.

Mannino, F. V., McLennan, B. W., & Shore, M. F. (1975). *The practice of mental health consultation.* New York: Gardner.

Marchant, R., Howlin, P., Yule, W., & Rutter, M. (1974). Graded change in the treatment of the behavior of autistic children. *J. Child Psychol. Psychiat.*, **15**(3), 221–27.

Margolese, M. S., & Janigen, O. (1973). Androsterone/etiocholanolone ratios in male homosexuals. *Brit. Med. J.*, **3**, 207–10.

Margolin, G., Christensen, A., & Weiss, R. L. (1975). Contracts, cognition, and change: A behavioral approach to marriage therapy. *The Counseling Psychologist*, **5**(3), 15–26.

Margolin, G., & Wampold, B. E. (1981). Sequential analysis of conflict and accord in distressed and non-distressed marital partners. *J. Cons. Clin. Psychol.*, **49**(4), 554–67.

Mariotto, M. J. (1979). Observational assessment systems use for basic and applied research. *J. Behav. Assess.*, **1**(3), 239–50.

Marks, I. (1978). Behavioral psychotherapy of adult neurotics. In S. L. Garfield & A. E. Bergin (Eds.), *Handbook of psychotherapy and behavior change: An empirical analysis.* New York: Wiley.

Marks, I. M. (1982). Toward an empirical clinical science: Behavioral psychotherapy in the 1980's. *Behav. Ther.*, **13**, 63–81.

Marlatt, G. A., & Gordon, J. R. (1980). Determinents of relapse: Implications for the maintenance of behavior change. In P. Davidson & S. Davidson (Eds.), *Behavioral medicine: Changing health lifestyles.* New York: Brunner/Mazel.

Marmor, J., & Woods, S. M. (Eds.). (1980). *The interface between psychodynamic and behavior therapies.* New York: Plenum.

Marsella, A. J. (1980). Depressive experience and disorder across cultures. In H. C. Triandis, & J. Draguns (Eds.), *Handbook of cross-cultural psychology* (Vol. 6). Boston: Allyn & Bacon.

Marshall, W. L. (1974). A combined treatment approach to the reduction of multiple fetish-related behaviors. *J. Cons. Clin. Psychol.*, **42**(4), 613–16.

Martin, G. I., & Zaug, P. J. (1975). Electrocardiographic monitoring of enuretic children receiving therapeutic doses of imipramine. *Amer. J. Psychiat.*, **132**(5), 540–42.

Marvit, R. C. (1981). Guilty but mentally ill—an old approach to an old problem. *The Clinical Psychologist*, **34**(4), 22–23.

Mash, E. J., Handy, L. C., & Hamerlynck, L. A. (1976). *Behavior modification approaches to parenting.* New York: Brunner/Mazel.

Maslow, A. H. (Ed.). (1954/1970). *Motivation and personality.* New York: Harper & Row.

Maslow, A. H. (1962). *Toward a psychology of being.* New York: Van Nostrand.

Maslow, A. H. (1969). Toward a humanistic biology. *Amer. Psychologist*, **24**(8), 734–35.

Maslow, A. H. (1971). *Farther reaches of human nature.* Escalen Institute Book Publishing Program, New York: Viking Press.

Masserman, J. H. (1961). *Principles of dynamic psychiatry* (2nd ed.). Philadelphia: W. B. Saunders Company.

Masters, W. H., & Johnson, V. E. (1966). *Human sexual response.* Boston: Little, Brown.

Masters, W. H., & Johnson, V. E. (1970). *Human sexual inadequacy.* Boston: Little, Brown.

Masters, W. H., & Johnson, V. E. (1975). *The pleasure bond: A new look at sexuality and commitment.* Boston: Little, Brown.

Masters, W. H., & Johnson, V. E. (1979). *Homosexuality in perspective.* Boston: Little, Brown.

Matarazzo, J. D. (1983). The reliability of psychiatric and psychological diagnosis. *Clin. Psychol. Rev.* **3**, 103–45.

Matson, J. L. (1981). Use of independence training to teach shopping skills to mildly mentally retarded adults. *Amer. J. Ment. Def.*, **86**, 178–83.

Matsunaga, E., Tonomura, A., Hidetsune, O., & Yasumoto, K. (1978). Reexamination of paternal age effect in Down's syndrome. *Human Genetics*, **40**, 259–68.

Mattes, J. A., & Gittelman, R. (1981). Effects of artificial food colorings in children with hyperactive symptoms: A critical review and results of a controlled study. *Arch. Gen. Psychiat.*, **38** (6), 714–18.

Matthews, K. A. (1982). Psychological perspectives on the type A behavior pattern. *Psychol. Bull.*, **91**(2), 293–323.

Maugh, T. M. (1981). Biochemical markers identify mental states. *Science*, **214**, 39–41.

Maurer, R., Cadoret, R. J., & Cain, C. (1980). Cluster analysis of childhood temperament data on adoptees. *Amer. J. Orthopsychiat.*, **50**, 522–34.

Maurer, R. G., & Stewart, M. A. (1980). Attention deficit without hyperactivity in a child psychiatry clinic, *J. Clin. Psychiat.*, **41**(7), 232–33.

May, R. (1969). *Love and will.* New York: Norton.

May, R., Angel, E., & Ellenberger, H. S. (Eds.). (1958). *Existence: A new dimension in psychiatry and psychology.* New York: Basic Books.

Mayer, C. L., & Scheffelin, M. (1975). State-wide planning for special education in California. *J. Learn. Dis.*, **8**(4), 50–54.

Mayer-Gross, W. (1944). Arteriosclerotic, senile, and presenile psychoses. *J. Ment. Sci.*, **90**, 316–27.

Mays, J. A. (1974, Jan. 16). High blood pressure, soul food. *Los Angeles Times*, II, 7.

McAdoo, W. G., & DeMyer, M. K. (1978). Personality characteristics of parents. In M. Rutter & E. Schopler (Eds.). *Autism: A reappraisal of concepts and treatment.* New York: Plenum.

McAlister, A., Puska, P., Koskela, K., Pallonen, U., & Maccoby, N. (1980). Mass communication and community organization for public health education. *Amer. Psychologist*, **35**, 375–79.

McCall, L. (1961). *Between us and the dark* (originally published in 1947). Summary in W. C. Alvarez, *Minds that came back.*

McClelland, D. C. (1979). Inhibited power motivation and high blood pressure in men. *J. Abnorm. Psychol.*, **88**(2), 182–90.

McClelland, D. C., Davis, W. N., Kalin, R., & Wanner, E. (1972). *The drinking man.* New York: The Free Press.

McCombie, S. L. (1976). Characteristics of rape victims seen in crisis intervention. *Smith College Studies in Social Work*, **46**, 137–58.

McCord, W., & McCord, J. (1964). *The psychopath: An essay on the criminal mind.* New York: Van Nostrand Reinhold.

McDavid, J. W., & Harari, H. (1968). *Social psychology: Individuals, groups, societies.* New York: Harper & Row.

McEwen, B. S. (1981). Neural gonadal steroid actions. *Science*, **211**, 1303–11.

McGarvey, B., Gabrielli, W. F., Bentler, P. M., & Mednick, S. A. (1981). Rearing, social class, education, and criminality: A multiple indicator model. *J. Abnorm. Psychol.*, **90**, 354–64.

McGlannan, F. K. (1975). Learning disabilities: The decade ahead. *J. Learn. Dis.*, **8**(2), 56–59.

McLean, P. D., & Hakistan, A. R. (1979). Clinical depression: Comparative efficacy of outpatient treatments. *J. Cons. Clin. Psychol.*, **47**, 818–36.

McLemore, C. W. & Benjamin, L. S. (1979). Whatever happened to interpersonal diagnosis: A psychological alternative to DSM III. *Amer. Psychologist*, **34**, 17–34.

McNeil, T. F., & Kaij, L. (1978). Obstetrical factors in the development of schizophrenia: Complications in the births of preschizophrenics and in reproduction by schizophrenic parents. In L. C. Wynne, R. L. Cromwell, & S. Matthysse (Eds.), *The nature of schizophrenia: New approaches to research and treatment*. New York: Wiley.

Mead, M. (1949). *Male and female*. New York: Morrow.

Mealiea, W. L., Jr. (1967). *The comparative effectiveness of systematic desensitization and implosive therapy in the elimination of snake phobia*. Unpublished doctoral dissertation, University of Missouri.

Mechanic, D. (1962). *Students under stress*. New York: Free Press.

Medea, A., & Thompson, K. (1974). *Against rape*. New York: Farrar, Straus, and Giroux.

Mednick, S. A. (1978). Berkson's fallacy and high-risk research. In L. C. Wynne, R. L. Cromwell, & S. Matthysse (Eds.), *The nature of schizophrenia: New approaches to research and treatment* (pp. 442–52). New York: Wiley.

Mednick, S. A., & Schulsinger, F. (1968). Some premorbid characteristics related to breakdown in children with schizophrenic mothers. In D. Rosenthal & S. S. Kety (Eds.), *The transmission of schizophrenia* (pp. 267–91). Oxford: Pergamon.

Mednick, S. A., Schulsinger, F., Teasdale, T. W., Schulsinger, H., Venables, P., & Rock, D. (1978). Schizophrenia in high risk children: Sex differences in predisposing factors. In G. Serban (Ed.), *Cognitive defects in the development of mental illness*. New York: Brunner/Mazel.

Meehl, P. E. (1962). Schizotaxia, schizotypy, schizophrenia. *Amer. Psychologist, 17*, 827–38.

Meehl, P. E. (1978). Theoretical risks and tabular asterisks: Sir Karl, Sir Ronald, and the slow progress of soft psychology. *J. Cons. Clin. Psychol., 46*, 806–34.

Megargee, E. I. (1966). Undercontrolled and overcontrolled personality types in extreme antisocial aggression. *Psychological Monographs, 80* (Whole No. 611).

Megargee, E. I. (1970). The prediction of violence with psychological tests. In C. D. Spielberger (Ed.), *Current topics in clinical and community psychology* (Vol. 2). New York: Academic Press.

Meichenbaum, D. (1974). *Cognitive behavior modification*, General Learning Corporation, 16.

Meichenbaum, D. (1975). A self-instructional approach to stress management: A proposal for stress-inoculation training. In C. Spielberger & I. Sarason (Eds.), *Stress and anxiety* (Vol. 2). New York: Wiley.

Meichenbaum, D., (1977). *Cognitive-behavior modification*. New York: Plenum.

Meichenbaum, D., & Cameron, R. (1982). Cognitive-behavior therapy. In G. T. Wilson & C. M. Franks (Eds.), *Contemporary behavior therapy: Conceptual and empirical foundations*. New York: Guilford.

Meichenbaum, D., & Cameron, R. (1983). Stress innoculation training: Toward a general paradigm for training coping skills. In D. Meichenbaum & M. E. Jaremko (Eds.), *Stress reduction and prevention* (pp. 115–54). New York: Plenum.

Meichenbaum, D., and Goodman, J. (1971). Training impulsive children to talk to themselves: A means of developing self-control. *J. Abnorm. Psychol., 77*, 115–26.

Meichenbaum, D., & Jaremko, M. E. (1983). *Stress reduction and prevention*. New York: Plenum.

Meichenbaum, D., Turk, D., & Burstein, S. (1975). The nature of coping with stress. In I. Sarason & C. Spielberger (Eds.), *Stress and anxiety* (Vol. 2). New York: Wiley.

Meiselman, K. C. (1978). *Incest*. San Francisco: Jossey-Bass.

Meissner, W. W. (1978). *The paranoid process*. New York: Jason Aronson.

Meissner, W. W. (1981). The schizophrenic and the paranoid process. *Schizophrenia Bull., 7*, 611–31.

Melges, F. T., & Bowlby, J. (1969). Types of hopelessness in psychopathological process. *Arch. Gen. Psychiat., 20*, 690–99.

Mellor, C. S. (1970). First rank symptoms of schizophrenia. *Brit. J. Psychiat., 117*, 15–23.

Mellsop, G., Varghese, F., Joshua, S., & Hicks, A. (1982). The reliability of axis II of DSM-III. *Amer. J. Psychiat., 139*(10), 1360–61.

Meltzer, H. Y. (1979). Biochemical studies in schizophrenia. In L. Bellak (Ed.), *The schizophrenic syndrome*. New York: Basic Books.

Melville, K. (1973a). Capital punishment. *The Sciences, 13*(4), 20–22.

Melville, K. (1973b). Changing the family game. *The Sciences, 13*(3), 17–19.

Mendels, J., & Frazer, A. (1974). Brain biogenic amine depletion and mood. *Arch. Gen. Psychiat., 30*, 447–51.

Mendlewicz, J. (1980). X-linkage of bipolar illness and the question of schizoaffective illness. In R. H. Belmaker, & H. M. van Praag (Eds.), *Mania: An evolving concept*. New York: Spectrum.

Mendlewicz, J., & Rainer, J. D. (1977). Adoption study supporting genetic transmission in manic-depressive illness. *Nature, 268*, 327–29.

Menninger, K. (1938). *Man against himself*. New York: Harcourt, Brace.

Menninger, K. (1945). *The human mind* (3rd ed.). New York: Knopf.

Menninger, K. (1948). Diagnosis and treatment of schizophrenia. *Bulletin of the Menninger Clinic, 12*, 101–04.

Menninger, W. C. (1948). *Psychiatry in a troubled world*. New York: Macmillan.

Mental Health Law Project. (1976, June). *Summary of Activities*, Vol. II, No. 2.

Merbaum, M. (1977). Some personality characteristics of soldiers exposed to extreme war stress: A follow-up study of post-hospital adjustment. *J. Clin. Psychol., 33*, 558–62.

Merbaum, M., & Hefez, A. (1976). Some personality characteristics of soldiers exposed to extreme war stress. *J. Cons. Clin. Psychol., 44*(1), 1–6.

Meyer, R. E., & Mirin, S. M. (1979). *The heroin stimulus: Implications for a theory of addiction*. New York: Plenum.

Mezzich, J. E., Coffman, G. A., & Goodpaster, S. M. (1982). A format for DSM III diagnostic formulation: Experience with 1111 consecutive cases. *Amer. J. Psychiat., 139*, 591–96.

Miller, J. P. (1974). Relax! The brain machines are here. *Human Behavior. 3*(8), 16–23.

Miller, J. P. (1975, Spring). Suicide and adolescence. *Adolescence, 10*(37), 11–24.

Miller, M. L., Chiles, J. A., & Barnes, V. B. (1982). Suicide attempts within a delinquent population. *J. Cons. Clin. Psychol., 50*, 491–98.

Miller, R. (1970). Does Down's syndrome predispose children to leukemia? *Roche Report, 7*(16), 5.

Miller, R. R., & Springer, A. D. (1974). Implications of recovery from experimental amnesia. *Psych. Rev., 81*(5), 470–73.

Miller, W. R. (1978). Behavioral treatment of problem drinkers: A comparative outcome study of three controlled drinking therapies. *J. Cons. Clin. Psychol., 46*, 74–86.

Miller, W. R. (1979). Problem drinking and substance abuse: Behavioral perspectives. In N. Krasnegar (Ed.). *Behavioral approaches to analysis and treatment of substance abuse*.

Miller, W. R., & Caddy, G. R. (1977). Abstinence and controlled drinking in the treatment of problem drinking. *Journal of Studies on Alcohol, 38*, 986–1003.

Miller, W. R., & Muñoz, R. F. (1976). *How to control your drinking*. Englewood Cliffs, N.J.: Prentice-Hall.

Miller, W. R., & Orr, J. (1980). Nature and sequence of neuropsychological deficits in alcoholics. *J. Studies on Alcohol, 41*(3), 325–37.

Millon T. (1981). *Disorders of personality: DSM III, Axis II*. New York: Wiley.

Milner, K. O. (1949). The environment as a factor in the aetiology of criminal paranoia, *J. Ment. Sci., 95*, 124–32.

Mindham, R. H. S. (1982). Tricyclic antidepressants and amine precursors. In E. S. Paykel (Ed.), *Handbook of affective disorders*. New York: Guilford Press.

Minuchin, S. (1974). *Families and family therapy*. Cambridge, MA: Harvard University Press.

Minuchin, S., Baker, L., Rosman, B., Liebman, R., Milman, L., & Todd, T. (1975). A conceptual model of psychosomatic illness in children. *Arch. Gen. Psychiat.*, **32**, 1031–38.

Mischel, W. (1968). *Personality and assessment*. New York: Wiley.

Mischel, W. (1973). Toward a cognitive social learning reconceptualization of personality. *Psychol. Rev.*, **80**(4), 252–83.

Mishler, E. G., & Waxler, N. E. (1968). *Interaction in families: An experimental study of family processes and schizophrenia*. New York: Wiley.

Mitchell, J. T., & Resnik, H. L. P. (1981). *Emergency response to crisis*. Bowie, MD: Robert J. Brady.

Mittler, P. (Ed.). (1977). *Research to practice in mental retardation* (3 Volumes). Baltimore: University Park Press.

Moffitt, T. E., Gabrielli, W. F., Mednick, S. A., & Schulsinger, F. (1980). Socioeconomic status, I.Q. and delinquency, *J. Abnorm. Psychol.*, **90**(2), 152–56.

Monahan, J. (1981). *Predicting violent behavior: An assessment of clinical techniques*. Beverly Hills: Sage Publications, Inc.

Money, J. (1974). Prenatal hormones and postnatal socialization in gender identity differentiation. In J. K. Cole & R. Dienstbier (Eds.), *Nebraska symposium on motivation, 1973*. (pp. 221–95). Lincoln, Neb.: University of Nebraska Press.

Money, J. (1980). *Love and love sickness: The science of sex, gender difference, and pair-bonding*. Baltimore: Johns Hopkins University Press.

Money, J. & Alexander, D. (1969). Psychosexual development and absence of homosexuality in males with precocious puberty. *J. Nerv. Ment. Dis.*, **148**(2), 111–23.

Money, J., & Ehrhardt, A. A. (1972). *Man & woman, boy & girl: Differentiation and dimorphism of gender identity*. Baltimore: Johns Hopkins University Press.

Monnelly, E. P., Woodruff, R. A., & Robins, L. N. (1974). Manic depressive illness and social achievement in a public hospital sample. *Acta Psychiatr. Scandin.*, **50**, 318–25.

Montenegro, H. (1968). Severe separation anxiety in two preschool children: Successfully treated by reciprocal inhibition. *J. Child Psychol. Psychiat.*, **9**(2), 93–103.

Moody, S., & Graham, V. (1978, Nov. 26). Why? *Sunday Sun Times*, pp. 8–10.

Moore, D. F. (Ed.). (1982, Aug.). New antidepressants. *Psychopharmacology Update*, **3**, Asheville, NC: Appalachian Hall.

Mora, G. (1967). Paracelsus' psychiatry. *Amer. J. Psychiat.*, **124**, 803–14.

Moran, E. (1970). Gambling as a form of dependency. *British Journal of Addiction*, **64**, 419–28.

Moreno, J. L. (1959). Psychodrama. In S. Arieti et al. (Eds.), *American handbook of psychiatry* (Vol. 2). New York: Basic Books.

Morishima, A. (1975). His spirit raises the ante for retardates. *Psych. Today*, **9**(1), 72–73.

Morrison, J. (1980). Adult psychiatric disorders in parents of hyperactive children. *Amer. J. Psychiat.*, **137**(7), 825–27.

Morrison, J. R. (1973). Catatonia: Retarded and excited types. *Arch. Gen. Psychiat.*, **28**(1), 39–41.

Morrison, J. R. (1974). Catatonia: Prediction of outcome. *Comprehensive Psychiatry*, **15**(4), 317–24.

Mucha, T. F., & Reinhardt, R. F. (1970). Conversion reactions in student aviators. *Amer. J. Psychiat.*, **127**, 493–97.

Munro, J. F., & Duncan, L. J. P. (1972). Fasting in the treatment of obesity. *The Practitioner*, **208**, 493–98.

Murase, T., & Johnson, F. (1974). Naikan, Morita, and western psychotherapy. *Arch. Gen. Psychiat.*, **31**(1), 121–28.

Murphy, G. E. (1973). Suicide and the right to die. *Amer. J. Psychiat.*, **130**(4), 472–73.

Murphy, H. B. (1968). Cultural factors in the genesis of schizophrenia. In D. Rosenthal & S. S. Kety (Eds.), *The transmission of schizophrenia* (pp. 137–52). Elmsford, NY: Pergamon Press.

Murphy, H. B. (1978). Cultural influences on incidence, course, and treatment response. In L. C. Wynne, R. L. Cromwell, & S. Matthysse (Eds.), *The nature of schizophrenia:*

New approaches to research and treatment (pp. 586–94). New York: Wiley.

Murphy, H. B. M., & Hall, B. (1972). Chronicity, community and culture. Paper presented at the Colloque sur traitments au long cours des états psychotiques, Paris, France.

Murphy, J. M. (1976). Psychiatric labeling in cross-cultural perspective. *Science*, **191**(4231), 1019–28.

Murphy, L. B., & Frank, C. (1979). Prevention: The clinical psychologist. *Ann. Rev. Psychol.*, **30**, 173–207.

Murphy, P. V. (1970, Dec. 13). Crime and its causes—A need for social change. *Los Angeles Times*, H, 1–2.

Murphy, S., Nichols, J., Eddy, R., & Umphress, A. (1971). Behavioral characteristics of adolescent enuretics. *Adolescence*, **6**(21), 1–18.

Murray, D. C. (1973). Suicidal and depressive feelings among college students. *Psych. Rep.*, **33**(1), 175–81.

Murray, H. A. (1938). *Explorations in personality*. New York: Oxford University Press.

Nace, E. P., Orne, M. T., & Hammer, A. G. (1974). Posthypnotic amnesia as an active psychic process. *Arch. Gen. Psychiat.*, **31**(2), 257–60.

Nagaraja, J. (1974). Somnambulism in children: Clinical communication. *Child Psychiatry Quarterly*, **7**(1), 18–19.

Napoleon N., Chassin, L., & Young, R. D. (1980). A replication and extension of "Physical attractiveness and mental illness." *J. Abnorm. Psychol.*, **89**, 250–53.

Nardini, J. E. (1952). Survival factors in American prisoners of war of the Japanese. *Amer. J. Psychiat.*, **109**, 241–48.

Nardini, J. E. (1962). Psychiatric concepts of prisoners of war confinement. The William C. Porter Lecture—1961. *Military Medicine*, **127**, 299–307.

Nathan, P. E. (1977). An overview of behavioral treatment approaches. In G. A. Marlatt & P. E. Nathan (Eds.), *Behavioral approaches to alcoholism*. New Brunswick, N.J.: Rutgers Center of Alcohol Studies.

National Association for Mental Health. (1971). NAMH supports repeal of homosexual status. *Psychiatric News*, **6**(3), 1.

National Association for Mental Health. (1979, Mar. 23). Bulletin #103.

National Center for Health Statistics. (1982). Washington, DC: U.S. Government Printing Office.

National Institute of Drug Abuse. (1976). *Marijuana and health, 3rd annual report to Congress from the Secretary of Health, Education, and Welfare*. Washington, D.C.: U.S. Government Printing Office.

National Institute of Drug Abuse. (1981). *Trend report: January 1978-September 1980*. Data from Client Oriented Data Acquisition Program (CODAP)(Series E, No. 24). Washington, DC: U.S. Department of Health and Human Services.

National Institute of Mental Health. (1969). *The mental health of urban America*. Washington, DC: U.S. Government Printing Office.

National Institute of Mental Health. (1970). United States Department of Health, Education, and Welfare. Mental Health Publication No. 5027. Washington, DC: U.S. Government Printing Office.

National Institute of Mental Health. (1971). Amphetamines approved for children. *Sci. News*, **99**(4), 240.

National Institute of Mental Health. (1976, Apr. 20). Rising suicide rate linked to economy. *Los Angeles Times*, VIII, 2; 5.

National Institute of Mental Health. (1978a, Oct.). *Third report on alcohol and health*. Washington, DC: U.S. Government Printing Office.

National Institute of Mental Health. (1978b). *Indirect services* (Statistical Note #147). Washington, DC: U.S. Government Printing Office.

National Institute of Mental Health. (1979). *Crisis intervention program for disasters in small communities*. Washington, DC: U.S. Government Printing Office.

National Institute on Alcohol Abuse and Alcoholism. (1978). *Report*. Washington, DC: U.S. Government Printing Office.

Neale, J. M., & Oltmanns, T. F. (1980). *Schizophrenia*. New York: Wiley.

Nelson, H. (1969, Oct. 6). Study compares drug dangers. *Los Angeles Times*, I, 3; 25.

Nelson, H. (1971, Jan. 26). County suicide rate up sharply among young. *Los Angeles Times*, II, 1.

Nelson, H. (1973, Mar. 27). High blood pressure found in third of adults in survey. *Los Angeles Times*, II, 1; 3.

Nelson, H. (1974, Apr. 29). How to be successfully fired. *Behav. Today*, 5(17), 118–19.[a]

Nelson, Z. P., & Mowry, D. D. (1976). Contracting in crisis intervention. *Community Mental Health Journal*, 12, 37–43.

Nemiah, J. C. (1961). The case of Mary S. *Foundations of psychopathology*. Cambridge: Oxford University Press.

Nemiah, J. C. (1967). Obsessive-compulsive reaction. In A. M. Freedman & H. I. Kaplan (Eds.), *Comprehensive textbook of psychiatry*. Baltimore: Williams & Wilkins.

Neugarten, B. L. (1974, Sept.). Age groups in American society and the rise of the young-old. *The Annals of the American Academy of Political and Social Science*, 415, 187–98.

Neugarten, B. L. (1977). Personality and aging. In J. E. Birren & K. W. Schaie (Eds.), *Handbook of the psychology of aging*. New York: Van Nostrand.

Newman, L. E. & Stoller, R. J. (1974). Nontranssexual men who seek sex reassignment. *Amer. J. Psychiat.*, 131(4), 437–41.

Newman, M. G. & Cates, M. S. (1977). *Methadone treatment in narcotic addiction*. New York: Academic Press.

New York Post (1982, May 10). City streets now "warehouse" the mentally ill.

New York State Department of Mental Hygiene. (1978). *The insanity defense in New York*. New York: The New York Department of Mental Hygiene.

Niederland, W. G. (1968). Clinical observations of the survivor syndrome. *Inter. J. Psychoanal.*, 49, 313–16.

Nielsen, J., Bjarnason, S., Friedrich, U., Froland, A., Hansen, V. H., & Sorensen, A. (1970). Klinefelter's syndrome in children. *J. Child Psychol. Psychiat.*, 11(2), 109–20.

Noble, E. P. (Ed.). (1979). Alcohol and health: Technical support document. Third special report to the U.S. Congress. (DHEW Publication No. ADM79-832). Washington, DC: U.S. Government Printing Office.

Notman, N.T. & Nadelson, C. C. (1976). The rape victim: Psychodynamic considerations. *Amer. J. Psychiat.*, 133(4), 408–13.

Novaco, R. W. (1977). Stress inoculation: A cognitive therapy for anger and its application to a case of depression. *Journal of Counseling and Clinical Psychology*, 45, pp. 600–8.

Nurnberger, J. I., & Gershon, E. S. (1982). Genetics. In E. S. Paykel (Ed.), *Handbook of affective disorders*. New York: Guilford Press.

Nurnberger, J., Roose, S. P., Dunner, D. S., & Fieve, R. R. (1979). Unipolar mania: A distinct clinical entity? *Amer. J. Psychiat.*, 136, 1420–23.

O'Brien, D. (1979, March). Mental anguish: An occupational hazard. *Emergency*, 61–64.

O'Connell, P. (1976, Nov.). Trends in psychological adjustment: Observations made during successive psychiatric follow-up interviews of returned Navy-Marine Corps POWs (R. Spaulding, Ed.). *Proceedings of the 3rd Annual Joint Meeting Concerning POW/MIA matters*, San Diego, Calif., 16–22.

O'Dell, S. (1974). Training parents in behavior modification: A review. *Psychol. Bull.*, 81(7), 418–33.

Office of the Federal Registry. (1982). *The United States Government Manual 1982/1983*. National Archives and Records Service. Washington, DC: Government Printing Office.

Offir, C. (1974). Old people's revolt—"At 65, work becomes a four-letter word." *Psych. Today*, 7(10), 40.

Offit, A. K. (1981). *Night thoughts: Reflections of a sex therapist*. New York: Congdon & Lattés.

Okura, K. P. (1975). Mobilizing in response to a major disaster. *Comm. Ment. Hlth. J.*, 2(2), 136–44.

Olds, S. (1970). Say it with a stomach ache. *Today's Health*, 48(11), 41–43; 88.

O'Leary, K. D. (1980). Pills or skills for hyperactive children, *J. Appl. Beh. Anal.*, 13(1), 191–204.

O'Leary, S., & Steen, P. L. (1982). Subcategorizing hyperactivity: The Stony Brook Scale. *J. Cons. Clin. Psychol.*, 50(3), 426–32.

Ollendick, T. H. (1981). Self-monitoring and self-administered overcorrection.: The modification of nervous tics in children. *Behav. Modific.*, 5(1), 75–84.

O'Neill, M., & Kempler, B. (1969). Approach and avoidance responses of the hysterical personality to sexual stimuli. *J. Abnorm. Psychol.*, 74, 300–305.

Onyehalu, A. S. (1981). Identity crisis in adolescence. *Adolescence*, 16, 629–32.

Opler, M. K., & Singer, J. L. (1959). Ethnic differences in behavior and psychopathology. *Inter. J. Social Psychiat.* 2, 11–23.

Oros, C. J., & Koss, M. P. (1978, Aug.). Women as rape victims. Paper presented at the American Psychological Association Annual Meeting, Toronto.

Osgood, C. E., & Luria, Z. (1954). A blind analysis of a case of multiple personality using the semantic differential. *J. Abnorm. Soc. Psychol.*, 49, 579–91.

Osgood, C. E., Luria, Z., Jeans, R. E., & Smith, S. W. (1976). The three faces of Evelyn: A case report. *J. Abnorm. Psychol.*, 85, 249–70.

Ossofsky, H. J. (1974). Endogenous depression in infancy and childhood. *Comprehensive Psychiatry*, 15(1), 19–25.

Öst, L-G., & Hugdahl, K. (1981). Acquisition of phobias and anxiety response patterns in clinical patients. *Behav. Res. & Ther.*, 19, 439–47.

Ostfeld, A. M., & D'Atri, D. A. (1977). Rapid sociocultural change and high blood pressure. In S. Kasl & F. Reichsman (Eds.), *Advances in psychosomatic medicine: Vol. 9. Epidemiologic studies in psychosomatic medicine* (pp. 20–37). Basel, Switzerland: S. Karger.

Overall, J. E., & Hollister, L. E. (1982). Decision rules for phenomenological classification of psychiatric patients, *J. Cons. Clin. Psychol.*, 50(4), 535–45.

Owens, C. E. (1980). *Mental health and Black offenders*. Lexington, MA: Lexington Books.

Paine, R.S. (1969). *Minimal brain dysfunction*. National Project on Learning Disabilities. Public Health Service Publication No. 2015. Washington, DC: U.S. Government Printing Office.

Palazzoli, M.S. (1978). *Self-starvation: From individual to family therapy in the treatment of anorexia nervosa*. New York: Jason Aronson.

Palmer, R. L. (Ed.). (1981). *Electroconvulsive therapy: An appraisal*. New York: Oxford University Press.

Parker, G. (1975). Psychological disturbance in Darwin evacuees following cyclone Tracy. *Medical J. Australia*, 1, 650–52.

Parkes, C. M., Benjamin, B., & Fitzgerald, R. G. (1969, Mar. 22). Broken heart: A statistical study of increased mortality among widowers. *Brit. Med. J.*, Mar. 22, 1969, 1, 740–43.

Parkin, M. (1974). Suicide and culture in Fairbanks: A comparison of three cultural groups in a small city of interior Alaska. *Psychiatry*, 37(1), 60–67.

Parloff, M. B., Waskow, I. E., & Wolfe, B. (1978). Research on therapist variables in relation to process and outcome. In S. L. Garfield & A. E. Bergin (Eds.), *Handbook of psychotherapy and behavior change*. New York: Wiley.

Pasewark, R. A., Pantle, M. L., & Steadman, H. J. (1982). Detention and rearrest rates of persons found not guilty by reason of insanity and convicted felons. *American J. Psychiat.*, 139(7), 892–97.

Paternite, C. E., & Loney, J. (1980). Childhood hyperkinesis: Relationships between symptomatology and home environment. In C. K. Whelan & B. Henker (Eds.), *Hyperactive children: The social ecology of identification and treatment*. New York: Academic Press.

Patterson, G. R. (1979). Treatment for children with conduct problems: A review of outcome studies. In S. Feshbach & A. Fraczek (Eds.), *Aggression and behavior change: Biological and social processes*. New York: Praeger.

Patterson, G. R., Weiss, R. L., & Hops, H. (1976). Training of marital skills. In H. Leitenberg (Ed.), *Handbook of behavior modification and behavior therapy*. New York: Prentice-Hall.

Paul, G. L. (1979). New assessment systems for residential treatment, management, research and evaluation: A symposium, *J. Behavior, Assess.*, 1(3), 181–84.

Paul, G. L. (1982). The development of a "transportable" system of behavioral assessment for chronic patients. Invited address. University of Minnesota. Minneapolis: Minnesota.

Paul, G. L., & Lentz, R. J. (1977). *Psychosocial treatment of chronic mental patients: Milieu versus social-learning programs.* Cambridge, MA: Harvard University Press.

Paul, N. (1971, May 31). The family as patient. *Time*, 60.

Pauly, I. B. (1968). The current status of the change of sex operation. *J. Nerv. Ment. Dis.*, 147(5), 460–71.

Pausnau, R. O., & Russell, A. T. (1975). Psychiatric resident suicide: An analysis of five cases. *Amer. J. Psychiat.*, 132(4), 402–6.

Pavlov, I. P. (1928). [*Lectures on conditioned reflexes*] (W. H. Gantt, trans.). New York: International Publishers.

Paykel, E. S. (1973). Life events and acute depression. In J. P. Scott & E. C. Senay (Eds.), *Separation and depression*, (pp. 215–36). Washington: American Association for the Advancement of Science.

Paykel, E. S. (Ed.). (1982a). *Handbook of affective disorders.* New York: Guilford Press.

Paykel, E. S. (1982b). Life events and early environment. In E. S. Paykel (Ed.), *Handbook of affective disorders.* New York: Guilford Press.

Paykel, E. S., Hallowell, C., Dressler, D. M., Shapiro, D. L., & Weissman, M. M. (1974). Treatment of suicide attempters. *Arch. Gen. Psychiat.*, 31(4), 487–91.

Paykel, E. S., Prusoff, B. A., & Myers, J. K. (1975). Suicide attempts and recent life events. *Arch. Gen. Psychiat.*, 32(3), 327–33.

Payne, J. H., Dewind, L. T., & Commons, R. R. (1963). Metabolic observations in patients with jejunocolic shunts. *American Journal of Surgery*, 106, 273–89.

Payne, R. L. (1975). Recent life changes and the reporting of psychological states. *J. Psychosom. Res.*, 19(1), 99–103.

Peck, M. A., & Schrut, A. (1971). Suicidal behavior among college students. *HSMHA Health Reports*, 86(2), 149–56.

Pelham, W. E., Schnedler, R. W., Bologna, N. C., & Contreras, J. A. (1980). Behavioral and stimulant treatment of hyperactive children: A therapy study with methylphenidate probes in a within subject design. *J. Appl. Beh. Anal.*, 13(2), 221–36.

Pemberton, D. A., & Benady, D. R. (1973). Consciously rejected children. *Brit. J. Psychiat.*, 123(576), 575–78.

Pendery, M. L. Maltzman, I. M., & West, L. J. (1982). Controlled drinking by alcoholics? New findings and a reevaluation of a major affirmative study. *Science*, 217(9), 169–74.

Penk, W. E., Charles, H. L., & Van Hoose, T. A. (1978). Comparative effectiveness of day hospital and inpatient psychiatric treatment. *J. Cons. Clin. Psychol.*, 46, 94–101.

Penk, W. E., Rabinowitz, R., Roberts, W. R., Patterson, E. T., Dolan, M. P., & Atkins, H. E. (1981). Adjustment differences among male substance abusers varying in degree of combat experience in Vietnam. *J. Cons. Clin. Psychol.*, 49(3), 426–37.

Penrose, L. S. (1963). *Biology of mental defect* (3rd ed.). New York: Grune & Stratton.

Perlberg, M. (1979, April). Adapted from Trauma at Tenerife: The psychic aftershocks of a jet disaster. *Human Behavior*, 49–50.

Perls, F. S. (1967). Group vs. individual therapy. *ETC: A review of general semantics.* 34, 306–12.

Perls, F. S. (1969). *Gestalt therapy verbatim.* Lafayette, California: Real People Press. Reprinted by permission.

Perris, C. (1979). Recent perspectives in the genetics of affective disorders. In J. Mendlewicz, & B. Shopsin (Eds.), *Genetic aspects of affective illness.* New York: SP Medical & Scientific.

Perris, C. (1982). The distinction between bipolar and unipolar affective disorders. In E. S. Paykel (Ed.), *Handbook of affective disorders.* New York: Guilford Press.

Perry, T. (1970). The enigma of PKU. *The Sciences*, 10(8), 12–16.

Pert, C. B., & Snyder, S. H. (1973, Mar. 9). Opiate receptor: Demonstration in nervous tissue. *Science*, 179(4077), 1011–14.

Pervin, L. A. (1978). *Current controversies and issues in personality.* New York: Wiley.

Peters, J. J. (1976). Children who are victims of sexual assault and the psychology of offenders. *Amer. J. Psychother.*, 30, 398–421.

Peterson, D. R. (1961). Behavior problems of middle childhood. *J. Consult. Psychol.*, 25, 205–9.

Peterson, G. C. (1978). Organic brain syndrome: Differential diagnosis and investigative procedures. *Psychiatric Clinics of North America*, 1, 21–36.

Peto, A. (1972). Body image and depression. *Inter. J. Psychoanal.*, 53(2), 259–63.

Pfeffer, C. R. (1981). The family system of suicidal children. *Amer. J. Psychother.*, 35, 330–41.

Phillips, G. B., Castelli, W. P., Abbott, R. D., & McNamara, P. M. (1983). Association of hyperestrogenemia and coronary heart disease in men in the Framingham cohort. *Amer. J. Medicine*, 74, 863–69.

Piaget, J. (1970). *Genetic epistemology.* New York: Columbia University Press.

Pitt, B. (1982). Depression and childbirth. In E. S. Paykel (Ed.), *Handbook of affective disorders.* New York: Guilford Press.

Plater, F. (1664). *Praxeos medical Tomi tres.* (Basil 1656), *Histories and Observations.* London: Culpeper and Cole.

Plato, (n.d.) *The laws* (Vol. 5). G. Burges (Trans.). London: George Bell & Sons.

Pliner, P. L., & Cappell, H. D. (1974). Modification of affective consequences of alcohol: A comparison of social and solitary drinking. *J. Abnorm. Psychol.*, 83(4), 418–25.

Plotkin, R. (1981). When rights collide: Parents, children and consent to treatment, *J. Pediat. Psychol.*, 6(2), 121–30.

Poland, B. J., & Lowry, R. B. (1974). The use of spontaneous abortuses and stillbirths in genetic counseling. *Amer. J. Obstetrics and Gynecology*, 118, 322–26.

Polich, J. M., Armor, D. J., & Braiker, H. B. (1981). *The course of alcoholism: Four years after treatment.* New York: Wiley Interscience.

Pollack, J. H. (1968). Five frequent mistakes of parents. *Today's Health*, 46(5), 14–15; 26–29.

Pollak, J. M. (1979). Obsessive-compulsive personality: A review. *Psychol. Bull.*, 86(2), 225–41.

Pollin, W., Allen, M. G., Hoffer, A., Stabenau, J. R., & Hrubec, Z. (1969). Psychopathology in 15,909 pairs of veteran twins. *Amer. J. Psychiat.*, 126, 597–609.

Polner, M. (1968). Vietnam War stories. *Transaction*, 6(1), 8–20.

Polvan, N. (1969). Historical aspects of mental ills in Middle East discussed. *Roche Reports*, 6(12), 3.

Popkin, M. K., Stillner, V., Osborn, L. W., Pierce, C. M., & Shurley, J. T. (1974). Novel behaviors in an extreme environment. *Amer. J. Psychiat.*, 131(6), 651–54.

Post, F. (1944). Some problems arising from a study of mental patients over the age of sixty years. *J. Ment. Sci.*, 90, 554–65.

Post, R. M. (1975). Cocaine psychoses: A continuum model. *Amer. J. Psychiat.*, 132(3), 225–31.

Poznanski, E., & Zrull, J. P. (1970). Childhood depression. *Arch. Gen. Psychiat.*, 23(1), 8–15.

Poznanski, E. O. (1973). Children with excessive fears. *Amer. J. Orthopsychiat.*, 43(3), 428–38.

Prange, A. J. (1973). The use of drugs in depression: Its practical and theoretical aspects. *Psychiatric Annals*, 3, 56–75.

Pratt, B. (1972). Studies reveal alcoholism differs in males and females. *APA Monitor*, 3(7), 1.

President's Commission on Law Enforcement and Administration of Justice. (1967). Katzenbach, N. D. (Chairman), *The challenge of crime in a free society.* Washington, DC: U.S. Government Printing Office.

President's Commission on Mental Health. (1978). *Report to the President.* Washington, DC: U.S. Government Printing Office.

President's Committee on Mental Retardation. (1970). *The decisive decade.* Washington, D.C.: U.S. Government Printing Office.

Pringle, M. L. K. (1965). *Deprivation and education*. New York: Humanities Press.

Prinz, R. J., Connor, P. A., & Wilson, C. C. (1981). Hyperactive and aggressive behaviors in childhood: Intertwined dimensions. *J. Abnorm. Child Psychol.*, **9**(2), 191–202.

Prizant, B. M., & Duchan, J. F. (1981). The functions of immediate echolalia in autistic children. *J. Speech Hear. Dis.*, **46**(3), 241–49.

Project Dawn Drug Enforcement Agency. (1977). *Drug Abuse Warning Network: Project DAWN V.*, May 1976–April 1977.

Project Dawn Drug Enforcement Agency. (1980). Drug Abuse Warning Network: Project DAWN, May 1979–April 1980.

Provence, S., & Lipton, R. C. (1962). *Infants in institutions*. New York: International University Press.

Prusoff, B., & Klerman, G. L. (1974). Differentiating depressed from anxious neurotic outpatients. *Arch. Gen. Psychiat.*, **30**(3), 302–9.

Puska, P. (1983, Feb./Mar.). Television can save lives. *World Health*. Geneva, Switzerland: Magazine of the World Health Organization, 8–11.

Puska, P., Tuomiehto, J., Salonen, J., Neittaanmäki, L., Maki, J., Virtamo, J., Nissinen, A., Koskela, K., & Takalo, T. (1979). Changes in coronary risk factors during a comprehensive five-year community programme to control cardiovascular diseases (North Karelia Project). *Brit. Med. J.*, **2**, 1173–78.

Quay, H. C. (1965). Psychopathic personality as pathological stimulation seeking. *Amer. J. Psychiat.*, **122**(2), 180–83.

Quay, H. C. (1979). Classification. In H. C. Quay & J. S. Wherry (Eds.), *Psychopathological disorders of childhood*. New York: Wiley.

Rabin, A. I., Doneson, S. L., & Jentons, R. L. (1979). Studies of psychological functions in schizophrenia. In L. Bellak (Ed.), *The schizophrenic syndrome*. New York: Basic Books.

Rabkin, J. G. (1972). Opinions about mental illness: A review of the literature. *Psychol. Bull.*, **77**(3), 153–71.

Rabkin, J. G. (1979). Criminal behavior of discharged mental patients: A critical appraisal of the research. *Psychol. Bull.*, **86**(1), 1–27.

Rabkin, J. G., & Struening, E. L. (1976). Life events, stress, and illness. *Science*, **194**, 1013–19.

Rachman, S. & Hodgson, R. (1980). *Obsessions and compulsions*. Englewood Cliffs, NJ: Prentice-Hall.

Rachman, S. J. (1978). *Fear and courage*. San Francisco, Calif.: Freeman.

Rae-Grant, Q. (1981, Nov. 2). High human price of pot smoking starting to show. *Behav. Today*, 4–5.

Rahe, R. H. (1974). Life change and subsequent illness reports. In K. E. Gunderson & R. H. Rahe (Eds.), *Life stress and illness*. Springfield, IL: Thomas.

Rahe, R. H., & Arthur, R. J. (1978). Life change and illness studies: Past history and future directions. *Human Stress*, **4**, 3–15.

Rahe, R. H., & Lind, E. (1971). Psychosocial factors and sudden cardiac death. *J. Psychosom. Res.*, **15**(1), 19–24.

Rao, A. V. (1970). A study of depression as prevalent in South India. *Transcultural Psychiat. Research Rev.*, **7**, 116–20.

Rapoport, J. L., & Ferguson, H. B. (1981). Biological validation of the hyperkinetic syndrome. *Dev. Med. Child Neurol.*, **23**(5), 667–82.

Raskin, A. (1974). A guide for drug use in depressive disorders. *Amer. J. Psychiat.*, **131**(2), 181–85.

Rees, T. P. (1957). Back to moral treatment and community care. *J. Ment. Scien.*, **103**, 303–13. In H. B. Adams "Mental illness" or interpersonal behavior? *Amer. Psychologist*, 1964, **19**, 191–97.

Regional Research Institute for Human Services. (1978). *Overcoming barriers to planning for children in foster care*. U.S. Department of Health, Education, and Welfare.

Reice, S. (1974). Editorial. *Family Health*, **6**(4), 4.

Reiss, A. J., Jr. (1976). Settling the frontiers of a pioneer in American criminology: Henry McKay. In J. F. Short, Jr. (Ed.) *Delinquency, crime and society*. Chicago: University of Chicago Press.

Rekers, G. A., Lovaas, O. I., & Low, B. (1975). The behavioral treatment of a "transsexual" preadolescent boy. *J. Abnorm. Psychol.*, **2**(1), 99–116.

Rentzel, L. (1972). *When all the laughter died in sorrow*. New York: Saturday Review Press.

Retterstol, N. (1975). Suicide in Norway. In N. L. Farberow (Ed.). *Suicide in different cultures*. (pp. 77–94). Baltimore: University Park Press.

Revitch, E., & Weiss, R. G. (1962). The pedophiliac offender. *Dis. Nerv. Sys.*, **23**, 73–78.

Reynolds, D. K., & Farberow, N. L. (1976). *Suicide: Inside and out*. Berkeley: University of California Press.

Rhoades, L. J. (1981). *Treating and assessing the chronically mentally ill: The pioneering research of Gordon L. Paul*. U.S. Department of Health and Human Services. Public Health Service. (Library of Congress Catalog #81-600097). Washington, DC: U.S. Government Printing Office.

Ribble, M. A. (1944). Infantile experience in relation to personality development. In J. McV. Hunt (Ed.), *Personality and the behavior disorders* (Vol. 2, pp. 621–51). New York: Ronald.

Ribble, M. A. (1945). Anxiety in infants and its disorganizing effects. In N. D. C. Lewis & B. L. Pacella (Eds.), *Modern trends in child psychiatry*. New York: International University Press.

Rice, R. D. (1977). Neurophysiological development in premature infants following stimulation. *Develop. Psychol.*, **13**, 69–76.

Rieder, R. O. (1973). The offspring of schizophrenic parents: A review. *J. Nerv. Ment. Dis.*, **157**(3), 179–90.

Rieder, R. O. (1979). Children at risk. In L. Bellak (Ed.), *The schizophrenic syndrome*. New York: Basic Books.

Rimm, D. C., & Lefebvre, R. C. (1981). Phobic disorders. In S. M. Turner, K. S. Calhoun, & H. E. Adams (Eds.), *Handbook of clinical behavior therapy*. New York: Wiley.

Rinkel, M. (1966). Psychedelic drugs. *Amer. J. Psychiat.*, **122**(6), 1415–16.

Ritchie, P. L. (1975). *The effect of the interviewer's presentation on some schizophrenic symptomatology*. Unpublished doctoral dissertation, Duke University.

Ritvo, E., & Ornitz, E. (1970). A new look at childhood autism points to CNS disease. *Roche Report*, **7**(18), 6–8.

Ritzler, B. A. (1981). Paranoia—prognosis and treatment: A review. *Schizophrenia Bull.*, **7**, 710–28.

Roberts, A. H., Erikson, R. V., Riddle, M., & Bacon, J. G. (1974). Demographic variables, base rates, and personality characteristics associated with recidivism in male delinquents. *J. Cons. Clin. Psychol.*, **42**(6), 833–41.

Roberts, W. R., Penk, W. E., Gearing, M. L., Rabinowitz, R., Dolan, M. P., & Patterson, E. T. (1982). Interpersonal problems of Vietnam combat veterans with symptoms of posttraumatic stress disorder. *J. Abnorm. Psychol.*, **91**(6), 444–50.

Robins, L. N. (1970). The adult development of the antisocial child. *Seminars in Psychiatry*, **2**(4), 420–34.

Robinson, H., Kirk, R. F., Jr., Frye, R. F., & Robertson, J. T. (1972). A psychological study of patients with rheumatoid arthritis and other painful diseases. *J. Psychosom. Res.*, **16**(1), 53–56.

Robinson, N. M., & Robinson, H. B. (1976). *The mentally retarded child* (2nd ed.). New York: McGraw-Hill.

Robinson, P. W., Newby, T. J., & Ganzell, S. L. (1981). A token system for a class of underachieving, hyperactive children, *J. Appl. Beh. Anal.*, **14**(3), 307–15.

Robinson, S., & Winnik, H. Z. (1973). Severe psychotic disturbances following crash diet weight loss. *Arch. Gen. Psychiat.*, **29**(4), 559–62.

Rodin, J. (1974). *Obesity and external responsiveness*. Paper presented at the meeting of the Eastern Psychological Association, Philadelphia, April 1974.

Rodin, J., & Langer, E. J. (1977). Long-term effects of a control-relevant intervention with the institutionalized aged. *J. Pers. Soc. Psychol.*, **35**, 897–902.

Rodman, D. H., & Collins, M. J. (1974). A community residence program: an alternative to institutional living for the mentally retarded. *Training School Bulletin*, **71**(1), 41–48.

Roe, A., Burks, B. S., & Mittelmann, B. (1945). Adult adjustment of foster children of alcoholic and psychotic parentage and the influence of the foster home. *Memorial Section on Alcohol Studies*, No. 3., New Haven: Yale University Press.

Roff, J. D. (1974). Adolescent schizophrenia: Variables related to differences in long-term adult outcome. *J. Cons. Clin. Psychol.*, **42**(2), 180–83.

Roff, J. D., & Knight R. (1981). Family characteristics, childhood symptoms, and adult outcome in schizophrenia. *J. Abnorm. Psychol.*, **90**, 510–20.

Rogers, C. R. (1951). *Client-centered therapy*. Boston: Houghton Mifflin.

Rogers, C. R. (1959). A theory of therapy personality, and interpersonal relationships as developed in the client-centered framework. In S. Koch (Ed.), *Psychology: A study of a science, Vol. 3*. (pp. 184–256). New York: McGraw-Hill.

Rogers, C. R. (1961). *On becoming a person: A client's view of psychotherapy*. Boston: Houghton Mifflin.

Rogers, C. R. (1966). Client-centered therapy. In S. Arieti et al. (Eds.), *American handbook of psychiatry* (Vol. 3). New York: Basic Books.

Rohrer, J. H. (1961). Interpersonal relations in isolated small groups. In B. E. Flaherty (Ed.), *Psychophysiological aspects of space flight*. New York: Columbia University Press.

Romo, M., Siltanen, P., Theorell, T., & Rahe, R. H. (1974). Work behavior, time urgency, and life dissatisfactions in subjects with myocardial infarction: A cross-cultural study. *J. Psychosom. Res.*, **18**(1), 1–8.

Rooth, G. (1974). Exhibitionists around the world. *Human Behavior*, **3**(5), 61.

Rorvik, D. M. (1970, Apr. 7). Do drugs lead to violence? *Look*, 58–61.

Rose, A., & Burks, B. (1968). Roundup of current research: Is the child really the father of the man? *Trans-action*, **5**(6), 6.

Rosen, D. H. (1970). The serious suicide attempt: Epidemiological and follow-up study of 886 patients. *Amer. J. Psychiat.*, **127**(6), 64–70.

Rosen, G. (1967). Emotion and sensibility in ages of anxiety. *Amer. J. Psychiat.*, **124**, 771–84.

Rosen, H., & Kiene, H. E. (1946). Paranoia and paranoiac reaction types. *Diseases of the Nervous System*, **7**, 330–37.

Rosenhan, D. L. (1973). On being sane in insane places. *Science*, **179**(4070), 365–69.

Rosenthal, D. (Ed.). (1963). *The Genain quadruplets*. New York: Basic Books.

Rosenthal, D. (1970). *Genetic theory and abnormal behavior*. New York: McGraw-Hill.

Rosenthal, D., Wender, P. H., Kety, S. S., Welner, J., & Schulsinger, F. (1971). The adopted-away offspring of schizophrenics. *Amer. J. Psychiat.*, **128**(3), 307–11.

Rosenthal, S. H. (1972). Electrosleep: A double-bind clinical study. *Biological Psychiatry*, **4**(2), 179–85.

Rosenthal, S. H., & Wulfsohn, N. L. (1970). Electrosleep—A clinical trial. *Amer. J. Psychiat.*, **127**(4), 533–34.

Rosenzweig, M. R., Krech, D., Bennett, E. L., & Diamond, M. C. (1968). Modifying brain chemistry and anatomy by enrichment or impoverishment of experience. In G. Newton & S. Levine (Eds.), *Early experience and behavior*. Springfield, IL: Charles C. Thomas.

Ross, A. O., & Pelham, W. E. (1981). Child psychopathology. *Annu. Rev. Psychol.* **32**, 243–78.

Ross, M. (1974). This doctor will self-destruct . . . . *Human Behavior*, **3**(2), 54.

Ross, M. (1975). Suicide among physicians. *Tufts Medical Alumni Bulletin*, **34**, (3).

Rossman, P. (1973). The pederasts. *Society*, **10**(3), 28–32; 34–35.

Rosten, R. A. (1961). Some personality characteristics of compulsive gamblers. Unpublished dissertation, UCLA.

Roth, M., & Mountjoy, C. Q. (1982). The distinction between anxiety states and depressive disorders. In E. S. Paykel (Ed.), *Handbook of affective disorders*. New York: Guilford Press.

Rothbart, M. K. (1981). Measurement of temperament in infancy. *Child Develop.* **52**, 569–78.

Rounsaville, B. J., Weissman, M. M., & Prusoff, B. A. (1981). Psychotherapy with depressed outpatients: Patient and process variables as predictors of outcome. *Amer. J. Psychiat.*, **138**, 67–74.

Rubin, B. (1972). Prediction of dangerousness in mentally ill criminals. *Arch. Gen. Psychiat.*, **25**, 392–407.

Rubin, R. T., Reinisch, J. M., & Haskett, R. F. (1981). Postnatal gonadal steroid effects on human behavior. *Science*, **211**, 1318–24.

Rudestam, K. E. (1971). Stockholm and Los Angeles: A cross-cultural study of the communication of suicidal intent. *J. Cons. Clin. Psychol.*, **36**(1), 82–90.

Runcie, J., & Thompson, T. J. (1970), Prolonged starvation—A dangerous procedure? *Brit. Med. J.*, **3**, 432–35.

Rush, A. J., Beck, A. T., Kovacs, M., & Hollon, S. (1977). The comparative efficacy of cognitive therapy and imipramine in the treatment of depressed out-patients. *Cognitive Therapy and Research*, **1**(1), 17–37.

Rush, A. J., Khatami, M., & Beck, A. T. (1975). Cognitive and behavior therapy in chronic depression. *Behavior Therapy*, **6**, 398–404.

Russell, J. B. (1972). *Witchcraft in the middle ages*. Ithaca, NY: Cornell University Press.

Russell, S. (1975). The development and training of autistic children in separate training centres and in centres for retarded children. *Special Publication No. 6*. Victoria: Mental Health Authority.

Russell, W. L. (1941). A psychopathic department of an American general hospital in 1808. *Amer. J. Psychiat.*, **98**, 229–37.

Russo, D. C., Carr, E. G., & Lovaas, O. I. (1980). Self-injury in pediatric populations. In J. Ferguson & C. B. Taylor (Eds.), *Comprehensive handbook of behavioral medicine. Volume 3: Extended applications and issues*. Holliswood, NY: Spectrum Publications.

Rutter, M. (1972). Maternal deprivation reconsidered. *J. Psychosom. Res.*, **16**(4), 241–50.

Rutter, M. (1977). Surveys to answer questions: Some methodological considerations. In P. J. Graham (Ed.), *Epidemiological approaches in child psychiatry*. New York: Academic Press.

Rutter, M. (1978). Diagnosis and definition. In M. Rutter & E. Schopler (Eds.), *Autism: A reappraisal of concepts and treatment*. New York: Plenum.

Rutter, M., & Schopler, E. (Eds.). (1978). *Autism: A reappraisal of concepts and behavior*. New York: Plenum.

Rutter, M., Yule, W., & Graham, P. (1973). Enuresis and behavioral deviance: Some epidemiological considerations. In I. Kolvin, R. C. MacKeith, & S. R. Meadow (Eds.), *Bladder control and enuresis*. Philadelphia: J. B. Lippincott.

Ryckman, R. M. (1978). *Theories of personality*. New York: D. Van Nostrand.

Ryle, A. (1969). *Student Casualties*. London: Penguin.

Sachar, E. J., Gruen, P. H., Altman, N., Langer, G., & Halpern, F. S. (1978). Neuroendocrine studies of brain dopamine blockade in humans. In L. C. Wynne, R. L. Cromwell, & S. Matthysse (Eds.), *The nature of schizophrenia: New approaches to research and treatment* (pp. 95–104). New York: Wiley.

Sack, R. L. & Miller, W. (1975). Masochism: A clinical and theoretical overview. *Psychiatry*, **38**(3), 244–57.

Safer, D. J., & Allen, R. P. (1973, May 2). Stimulant drugs said to suppress height, weight. *Psychiatric News*, May 2, 1973, **8**(9), 9.

Salzman, L. (1968). Obsessions and phobias. *Inter. J. Psychiat.*, **6**, 451–68.

Sank, L. I. (1979). Community disasters: Primary prevention and treatment in a Health Maintenance Organization. *Amer. Psychologist*, **34**(4), 334–38.

Sanson, A. V. (1980). Classification of hyperactive symptoms. *Med. J. Australia.*, **1**(8), 375–76.

Sanua, V. D. (1969). Sociocultural aspects. In L. Bellak & L.

Loeb (Eds.), *The schizophrenic syndrome*. New York: Grune & Stratton.

Sarbin, T. R., & Juhasz, J. B. (1967). The historical background of the concept of hallucination. *Journal of the History of the Behavioral Sciences, 3*, 339–58.

Sarbin, T. R., & Mancuso, J. C. (1970). Failure of a moral enterprise: Attitudes of the public toward mental illness. *J. Cons. Clin. Psychol., 35*, 159–73.

Sarbin, T. R., & Mancuso, J. C. (1980). *Schizophrenia: Medical diagnosis or moral verdict*. New York: Pergamon.

Sargent, D. A. (1973, June 16). Loss of identity in prison. *Sci. News, 103*(24), 390.

Sargent, M. (1982a, July 16). Schizophrenic quads not identically ill, studies show. *ADAMHA News, 8*(13), 4–5.

Sargent, M. (1982b, Dec. 3). Researcher traces Alzheimer's disease eight generations back in one family. *ADAMHA News, 8*(23), 3.

Sarvis, M. A. (1962). Paranoid reactions: Perceptual distortion as an etiological agent. *Arch. Gen. Psychiat., 6*, 157–62.

Sasaki, M., & Hara, Y. (1973). Paternal origin of the extra chromosome in Down's syndrome. *Lancet, 2*(7840), 1257–58.

Satir, V. (1967). *Conjoint family therapy* (Rev. ed.). Palo Alto: Science and Behavior Books.

Satterfield, J. H., Satterfield, B. T., & Cantwell, D. P. (1981). Three year multimodal treatment study of 100 hyperactive boys. *J. Pediat, 98*(4), 650–55.

Saul, L. J. (1945). Psychological factors in combat fatigue. *Psychosom. Med., 7*, 257–72.

Sawyer, J. B., Sudak, H. S., & Hall, S. R. (1972, Winter). A follow-up study of 53 suicides known to a suicide prevention center. *Life-Threatening Behavior, 2*(4), 227–38.

Saxbe, W. (1974, Aug. 28). Cited in Ostrow, R. J. Soaring crime rate is severe, setback: Saxbe warns U.S. *Los Angeles Times*, I, 1; 12.

Schaar, K. (1974). Suicide rate high among women psychologists. *APA Monitor, 5*(7), 1; 10.

Schaefer, H. H. (1971). Accepted theories disproven. *Sci. News, 99*(11), 182.

Schaefer, J. M. (1974). Drunkenness and culture stress: A holocultural test. *Transcultural Psychiatric Research Review, 11*, 127–29.

Schaefer, J. M. (1977, August 30). Firewater myths revisited: Towards a second generation of ethanol metabolism studies. Paper presented at Cross-cultural Approaches to Alcoholism. Physiological variation: Invited Symposium. NATO Conference Os, Bergen, Norway.

Schaefer, J. M. (1978). Alcohol metabolism reactions among the Reddis of South India. *Alcoholism: Clinical and experimental research, 2*(1), 61–69.

Schalock, R. L., Harper, R. S., & Carver, G. (1981). Independent living placement: Five years later. *Amer. J. Ment. Def., 86*, 170–77.

Schanche, D. A. (1974, Aug.). The emotional aftermath of "the largest tornado ever." *Today's Health, 52*(8), 16–19; 61; 63–64.

Scharfman, M., & Clark, R. W. (1967). Delinquent adolescent girls: Residential treatment in a municipal hospital setting. *Arch. Gen. Psychiat., 17*(4), 441–47.

Schild, S. (1972). Parents of children with PKU. *Children Today, 1*(4), 20–22.

Schlieffer, S. T., Keller, S. E., McKegney, F. P., et al. (1980, Mar.). Bereavement and lymphocyte function. Paper presented at meeting of the American Psychiatric Association, San Francisco, CA.

Schmauk, F. J. (1970). Punishment, arousal, and avoidance learning in sociopaths. *J. Abnorm. Psychol., 76*(3), 325–35.

Schneider, K. (1959). *Clinical psychopathology*. New York: Grune & Stratton.

Schneider, S. (1978). Attitudes toward death in adolescent offspring of holocaust survivors. *Amer. J. Orthopsychiat., 13*, 575–83.

Schofield, W. (1964). *Psychotherapy: The purchase of friendship*. Englewood Cliffs, NJ: Prentice-Hall.

Schopler, E. (1978). Changing parental involvement in behavioral treatment. In M. Rutter & Schopler (Eds.), *Autism:*

A reappraisal of concepts and treatment. New York: Plenum Press.

Schowalter, J. E. (1980). Tics. *Pediat. Rev., 2*, 55–57.

Schreibman, L., & Koegel, R. L. (1975). Autism: A defeatable horror. *Psych. Today, 8*(10), 61–67.

Schuckit, M. A. (1980). Self-rating of alcohol intoxication by young men with and without family histories of alcoholism. *J. of Studies on Alcohol, 41*, 242–49.

Schuckit, M. A., & Rayses, U. (1979). Ethanol ingestion: Differences in blood acetaldehyde concentrations in relatives of alcoholics and controls. *Science, 203*, 54–55.

Schulsinger, F. (1980). Biological psychopathology. *Ann. Rev. Psychol., 31*, 583–606.

Schulterbrandt, J. D., & Raskin, A. (Eds.). (1977). *Depression in children: Diagnosis, treatment and conceptual models*. New York: Raven Press.

Schulz, S. C., van Kammen, D. P., Balow, J. E., Flye, M. W., & Bunney, W. E. (1981). Dialysis in schizophrenia: A double-blind evaluation. *Science, 211*, 1066–68.

Schumer, F. (1983). *Abnormal psychology*. Lexington, MA: D. C. Heath.

Schwab, J. J. (1970). Comprehensive medicine and the concurrence of physical and mental illness. *Psychosomatics, 11*(6), 591–95.

Schwartz, B. (1968). The effect in Philadelphia of Pennsylvania's increased penalties for rape and attempted rape. *J. Crim. Law, Criminol. Police Sci., 59*(4), 509–15.

Schwartz, C. C., & Myers, J. K. (1977). Life events and schizophrenia: I. Comparison of schizophrenics with a community sample. *Arch. Gen. Psychiat., 34*, 1238–41.

Schwartz, D. A. (1963). A review of the "paranoid" concept. *Gen. Psychiat., 8*, 349–61.

Schwartz, G. E. (1978). Psychobiological foundations of psychotherapy and behavior change. In S. L. Garfield & A. E. Bergin (Eds.), *Handbook of psychotherapy and behavior change* (2nd ed. pp. 63–99). New York: Wiley.

Schwartz, H. (1975, May 25). Danger ahead in get-tough policy. *Los Angeles Times*, IV, 5.

Schwartzman, J. (1974, May). The individual, incest, and exogamy. *Psychiatry, 37*, 171–80.

Schwitzgebel, R. L., & Schwitzgebel, R. K. (1980). *Law and psychological practice*. New York: Wiley.

Scovern, A. W., & Kilmann, P. R. (1980). Status of electroconvulsive therapy: A review of the outcome literature. *Psycholog. Bull., 87*, 260–303.

Sears, R. R. (1961). Relation of early socialization experiences to aggression in middle childhood. *J. Abnorm. Soc. Psychol., 63*, 466–92.

Sears, R. R., Maccoby, E. E., & Levin, H. (1957). *Patterns of child rearing*. New York: Harper & Row.

Segal, D. S., Yager, J., & Sullivan, J. L. (1976). *Foundations of biochemical psychiatry*. Boston: Butterworth.

Seiden, R. H. (1974). Suicide: preventable death. *Public Affairs Report. 15*(4), 1–5.

Seidl, F. W., (1974). Community oriented residential care: The state of the art. *Child Care Quarterly, 3*(3), 150–63.

Seidler, G. (1980, Mar./Apr.). U.S. faces another heroin epidemic. *U.S. J. Drug and Alcohol Dependence*, 1–2.

Seixas, F. A., & Cadoret, R. (1974, Apr. 15). What is the alcoholic man? *New York Academy of Sciences*, Apr. 15, 1974, *223*, 13–14.

Seligman, M. E. P. (1973). Fall into hopelessness. *Psych. Today, 7*(1), 43–47; 48.

Seligman, M. E. P. (1975). *Helplessness: On depression, development, and death*. San Francisco: W. H. Freeman.

Seligman, M. E. P., & Hager, M. (Eds.). (1972). *Biological boundaries of learning*. New York: Appleton-Century-Crofts.

Selkin, J. (1975). Rape. *Psychology Today, 8*(8), 70–72.

Selkin, J., & Loya, F. (1979). Issues in the psychological autopsy of controversial public figures. *Professional Psychology, 10*(1), 87–93.

Selling, L. S. (1943). *Men against madness*. New York: Garden City Books.

Selye, H. (1976a). *Stress in health and disease*. Woburn, MA: Butterworths.

Selye, H. (1976b). *The stress of life* (2nd ed.). New York: McGraw-Hill.

Senay, E. C., & Redlich, F. C. (1968) Cultural and social factors in neuroses and psychosomatic illnesses. *Social Psychiatry*, 3(3), 89–97.

Sergovich, F., Valentine, G. H., Chen, A. T., Kinch, R., & Smout, M. (1969). Chromosomal aberrations in 2159 consecutive newborn babies. *New Engl. J. Med.*, 280(16), 851–54.

Serrano, A. C., Zuelzer, M. B., Howe, D. D., & Reposa, R. E. (1979). Ecology of abusive and nonabusive families, *J. Amer. Acad. Child Psychiat.*, 18, 167–75.

Sgroi, S. M. (1977). Sexual molestation of children: The last frontier in child abuse. In S. Chess & A. Thomas (Eds.)., *Annual progress in child psychiatry and child development: 1976.* New York: Brunner/Mazel.

Shakow, D. (1969). On doing research in schizophrenia. *Arch. Gen. Psychiat.*, 20(6), 618–42.

Shapiro, A. K., & Morris, L. A. (1978). The placebo effect in medical and psychological therapies. In S. L. Garfield & A. E. Bergin (Eds.) *Handbook of psychotherapy and behavior change* (2nd ed., pp. 369–410). New York: Wiley.

Shapiro, D. (1965). *Neurotic styles.* New York: Basic Books.

Shapiro, S. (1968). Maturation of the neuroendocrine response to stress in the rat. In G. Newton, & S. Levine (Eds.), *Early experience and behavior.* Springfield, Il: Charles S. Thomas.

Shatan, C. F. (1978). Stress disorders among Vietnam veterans: The emotional content of combat continues. In C. R. Figley (Ed.), *Stress disorders among Vietnam veterans: Theory, research and treatment.* New York: Brunner/Mazel.

Sheldon, W. H. (with the collaboration of C. W. Dupertuis & E. McDermott). (1954). *Atlas of men.* New York: Harper & Row.

Sherrod, B. (1968). *Dallas Times Herald* n.d. Quoted in D. Bolen & W. H. Boyd, Gambling and the gambler. *Arch. Gen. Psychiat.*, 18(5), 617–30.

Sherwin, I., & Geschwind, N. (1978). Neural substrates of behavior. In A. M. Nicholi (Ed.), *The Harvard guide to modern psychiatry* (pp. 59–80). Cambridge, MA: Harvard University Press.

Shields, P. E., Emerson, M. G., & Mount, M. K. (1979). A descriptive study of employees returning to work after treatment for alcoholism. *Technical Report.* Control Data Corp.

Shimkunas, A. M. (1972). Demand for intimate self-disclosure and pathological verbalizations in schizophrenia. *J. Abnorm. Psychol.*, 80, 197–205.

Shneidman, E. S. (1969). Fifty-eight years. In E. S. Shneidman (Ed.), *On the nature of suicide* (pp. 1–30). San Francisco: Jossey-Bass.

Shneidman, E. S., & Farberow, N. L. (Eds.). (1957). *Clues to suicide.* New York: McGraw-Hill.

Shneidman, E. S., Parker, E., & Funkhouser, G. R. (1970). You and death. *Psych. Today*, 4(3), 67–72.

Shoemaker, M. E., & Paulson, T. L. (1976). Group assertion training for mothers: A family intervention strategy. In E. J. Mash, L. C. Handy, & L. A. Hamerlynck (Eds.), *Behavior modification approaches to parenting.* New York: Brunner/Mazel.

Shur, E., & Hare, E. (1983). Age-prevalence and the season of birth effect in schizophrenia: A response to Lewis and Griffin. *Psychol. Bull.*, 93, 373–77.

Siegelman, M. (1974, Jan.). Parental background of male homosexuals and heterosexuals. *Archives of Sexual Behavior*, 3, 3–18.

Siegler, M., Osmond, H., & Newell, S. (1968). Models of alcoholism. *Quart. J. Stud. Alcohol.*, 29(3–A), 571–91.

Sigal, J. J., Silver, D., Rakoff, V., & Ellin, B. (1973, Apr.). Some second-generation effects of survival of the Nazi persecution. *Amer. J. Orthopsychiat.*, 43(3), 320–27.

Sigerist, H. E. (1943). *Civilization and disease.* Ithaca, NY: Cornell University Press.

Siggers, W. W. (1979). The role of the psychologist in advocacy for the handicapped. *Professional Psychology*, 10(1), 80–86.

Silberstein, R. M., & Irwin, H. (1962). Jean-Marc-Gaspard Itard and the savage of Aveyron: An unsolved diagnostic problem in child psychiatry. *J. Amer. Acad. Child Psychiat.*, 1(2), 314–22.

Silverman, W. H., & Val, E. (1975). Day hospital in the context of a community mental health program. *Comm. Ment. Hlth. J.*, 11(1), 82–90.

Silverstein, A. B., Legutki, G., Friedman, S. L., & Takayama, D. L. (1982). Performance of Down syndrome individuals on the Stanford-Binet Intelligence Scale. *Amer. J. Ment. Def.*, 86, 548–51.

Simon, W. (1975). Male sexuality: The secret of satisfaction. *Today's Health*, 53(4), 32–34; 50–52.

Singer, J., & Singer, I. (1978). Types of female orgasm. In J. LoPiccolo & L. LoPiccolo (Eds.), *Handbook of sex therapy* (pp. 175–86). New York: Plenum Press.

Singer, J. E., (1980). Traditions of stress research: Integrative comments. In I. G. Sarason & C. D. Spielberger (Eds.), *Stress and anxiety* (Vol. 7, pp. 3–10). Washington, D.C.: Hemisphere.

Singer, M., & Wynne, L. C. (1963). Differentiating characteristics of the parents of childhood schizophrenics, childhood neurotics and young adult schizophrenics. *Amer. J. Psychiat.*, 120, 234–43.

Singer, M., & Wynne, L. C. (1965a). Thought disorder and family relations of schizophrenics. III. Methodology using projective techniques. *Arch. Gen. Psychiat.*, 12, 182–200.

Singer, M., & Wynne, L. C. (1965b). Thought disorder and family relations of schizophrenics. IV. Results and implications. *Arch. Gen. Psychiat.*, 12, 201–12.

Singer, M. T., Wynne, L. C. & Toohey, M. I. (1978). Communication disorders and the families of schizophrenics. In L. C. Wynne, R. L. Cromwell, & S. Matthysse (Eds.), *The nature of schizophrenia: New approaches to research and treatment.* (pp. 499–511). New York: Wiley.

Sizemore, C. C., & Pittillo, E. S. (1977). *I'm Eve.* Garden City, NY: Doubleday.

Skigen, J., & Solomon, J. R. (1978). Community resources and facilities for the elderly patient with organic mental disease. *Psychiatric Clinics of North America*, 1, 169–77.

Skinner, B. F. (1948). *Walden two.* New York: Macmillan.

Skinner, B. F. (1971). *Beyond freedom and dignity.* New York: Knopf.

Skinner, B. F. (1974). *About behaviorism.* New York: Knopf.

Sklar, L. S., & Anisman, H. (1981). Stress and cancer. *Psychol. Bull.*, 89(3), 369–406.

Slater, E. T. O. (1944). Genetics in psychiatry. *J. Ment. Sci.*, 90, 17–35.

Slater, J. & Depue, R. A. (1981). The contribution of environmental events and social support to serious suicide attempts in primary depressive disorder. *J. Abnorm. Psychol.*, 90, 275–85.

Sloane, R. B., Staples, F. R., Cristol, A. H., Yorkston, N. J., & Whipple, K. (1975). *Psychotherapy versus behavior therapy.* Cambridge, MA: Harvard University Press.

Small, G. W., & Nicholi, A. M., Jr. (1982, Sept. 18). Cited in Herbert, W., An epidemic in the works. *Science News*, 122, 188–90.

Small, I. F., & Small, J. G., (1971). Sex and the passive-aggressive personality. *Medical Aspects of Human Sexuality*, 5(12), 78–89.

Small, J. G. (1966). The organic dimensions of crime. *Arch. Gen. Psychiat.*, 55(1), 82–89.

Smith, D. (1982). Trends in counseling and psychotherapy. *Amer. Psycholog.*, 37(7), 802–9.

Smith, G. F., & Berg, J. M. (1976). *Down's anomaly.* New York: Churchill Livingstone (Distributed by Longman, Inc.).

Smith, M. L., & Glass, G. V. (1977). Meta-analysis of psychotherapy outcome studies. *Amer. Psychologist*, 32, 752–60.

Smith, M. L., Glass, G. V., & Miller, T. I. (1980). *The benefits of psychotherapy.* Baltimore: Johns Hopkins University Press.

Smith, R. J. (1978). *The psychopath in society.* New York: Academic Press.

Smith, R. J. (1979). Study finds sleeping pills overprescribed. *Science*, 204, 287–88.

Smith, R. L. (1968). Strange tales of medical imposters. Today's Health, 1968, 46(10), 44–47; 69–70.

Snortum, J. R., Marshall, J. E., Gillespie, J. E. McLaughlin, J. P., & Mosberg, L. (1969). Family dynamics and homosexuality. Psych. Rep., 24(3), 763–70.

Snyder, M., Tanke, E. D., & Berscheid, E. (1977). Social perception and interpersonal behavior: On the self-fulfilling nature of social stereotypes. J. Pers. Soc. Psychol., 35(9), 656–66.

Snyder, S. H. (1978). Dopamine and schizophrenia. In L. C. Wynne, R. L. Cromwell & S. Matthysse (Eds.), The nature of schizophrenia: New approaches to research and treatment (pp. 87–94). New York: Wiley.

Sobell, M. B., & Sobell, L. C. (1973). Alcoholics treated by individualized behavior therapy: One year treatment outcome. Behav. Res. Ther., 11(4), 599–618.

Sobell, M. B., & Sobell, L. C. (1978). Behavioral treatment of alcohol problems. New York: Plenum.

Solomon, J. (1972). Why gamble? A psychological profile of pathology. The Sciences, 12(6), 20–21.

Soni, S. D., & Rockley, G. J. (1974). Socio-cultural substrates of folie à deux. Brit. J. Psychiat., 125(9), 230–35.

Sontag, L. W., Steele, W. G., & Lewis, M. (1969). The fetal and maternal cardiac response to environmental stress. Human Develop., 12, 1–9.

Sosowsky, L. (1980). Explaining the increased arrest rate among mental patients: A cautionary note. Amer. J. Psychiat., 137, 1602–4.

Spanos, N. P. (1978). Witchcraft in histories of psychiatry: A critical analysis and an alternative conceptualization. Psychol. Bull., 85(2), 417–39.

Spence, J. T., & Helmreich, R. L. (1978). Masculinity and femininity: Their psychological dimensions, correlates, & antecedents. Austin, TX: University of Texas Press.

Spitz, R. A. (1945). Hospitalization: An inquiry into the genesis of psychiatric conditions of early childhood. In R. S. Eissler, A. Freud, H. Hartman, & E. Kris (Eds.), The psychoanalytic study of the child (Vol. 1) New York: International Universities Press.

Spitz, R. A. (1946). Anaclitic depression. In Psychoanalytic study of the child (Vol. 2). New York: International Universities Press.

Spitzer, R. L., Skodol, A. E., Gibbon, M., & Williams, J. B. W. (1981). DSM-III case book. Washington, DC: American Psychiatric Association.

Spitzer, R. L., Skodol, A. E., Gibbon, M., & Williams, J. B. W. (1983). Psychopathology: A case book. New York: McGraw-Hill.

Sprague, R. L., Barnes, K. R., & Werry, J. S. (1970). Methylphenidate and thioridazine: Learning reaction time, activity, and classroom behavior in disturbed children. Amer. J. Orthopsychiat., 40, 615–28.

Spring, B. J., & Zubin, J. (1978). Attention and information-processing as indicators of vulnerability to schizophrenic episodes. In L. C. Wynne, R. L. Cromwell & S. Matthysse (Eds.), The nature of schizophrenia: New approaches to research and treatment (pp. 366–75). New York: Wiley.

Squire, L. R. (1977). ECT and memory loss. Amer. J. Psychiat., 134, 997–1001.

Squire, L. R., & Slater, P. C. (1978). Bilateral and unilateral ECT: Effects on verbal and nonverbal memory. Amer. J. Psychiat., 135, 1316–20.

Squire, L. R., Slater, P. C., & Chase, P. M. (1975). Retrograde amnesia: Temporal gradient in very long-term memory following electroconvulsive therapy. Science, 187, 77–79.

Stabenau, J. R., Tupin, J., Werner, M., & Pollin, W. (1965). A comparative study of families of schizophrenics, delinquents, and normals. Psychiatry, 28, 45–59.

Stainbrook, E. J. (1977). Depression: The psychological context. In G. Usdin (Ed.), Depression: Clinical, biological and psychological perspectives (pp. 28–51). New York: Brunner/Mazel.

Stampfl, T. G. (1975). Implosive therapy: Staring down your nightmares. Psych. Today. 8(9), 66–68; 72–73.

Stanely, E. J., & Barter, J. T. (1970). Adolescent suicidal behavior. Amer. J. Orthopsychiat., 40(1), 87–96.

Stanton, M.D., & Todd, T. C. (1976, June). Structural family therapy with heroin addicts: Some outcome data. Paper presented at the Society for Psychotherapy Research, San Diego.

Stare, F. J., Whelan, E. M., & Sheridan, M. (1980). Diet and hyperactivity: Is there a relationship?, Pediatrics, 6(4), 521–25.

Stein, J. (1970). Neurosis in contemporary society: Process and treatment. Belmont, Calif.: Brooks/Cole.

Stein, M. (1981). A biopsychosocial approach to immune function and medical disorders. Psychiatric Clinics of North America, 4(2), 203–21.

Steiner, C. (1977). Games alcoholics play. New York: Ballantine.

Steinmann, A., & Fox, D. J. (1974). The male dilemma: How to survive the sexual revolution. New York: Jason Aronson.

Stene, J., Stene, E., Stengel-Rutkowski, S., & Murken, J. D. (1981). Paternal age and Down's syndrome, data from prenatal diagnoses (DFG). Human Genetics, 59, 119–24.

Stephan, W. G. (1973). Parental relationships and early social experiences of activist male homosexuals and male heterosexuals. J. Abnorm. Psychol., 82(3), 506–13.

Stephens, J. H., Astrup, C., & Mangrum, J. C. (1966). Prognostic factors in recovered and deteriorated schizophrenics. Amer. J. Psychiat., 122(10), 1116–21.

Stephens, R., & Cottrell, E. (1972). A follow-up study of 200 narcotic addicts committed for treatment under the narcotic addict rehabilitation act. British Journal of Addiction, 67, 45–53.

Stern, M. P. (1979). The recent decline in ischemic heart disease mortality. Ann. Internal Med., 9(4), 630–40.

Stern, R. L. (1947). Diary of a war neurosis. J. Nerv. Ment. Dis., 106, 583–86.

Stern, R. S., Lipsedge, M. S., & Marks, I. M. (1973). Obsessive ruminations: A controlled trial of thought-stopping technique. Behav. Res. Ther., 11(4), 659–62.

Stewart, A. L., & Brook, R. H. (1983). Effects of being overweight. Amer. J. Pub. Hlth, 73(2), 171–78.

Stewart, M. A., Deblois, C. S., Meardon, J. & Cummings, C. (1980). Aggressive conduct disorder of children: The clinical picture. J. Nerv. Ment. Dis., 168(10), 604–10.

Stierlin, H. (1973). A family perspective on adolescent runaways. Ment. Hlth. Dig., 5(10), 1–4.

Stoller, R. J. (1974). Sex and gender (Vol. 1): The development of masculinity and femininity. New York: Jason Aronson.

Stone, S. (1937). Psychiatry through the ages. J. Abnorm. Soc. Psychol., 32, 131–60.

Strage, M. (1971). VD: The clock is ticking. Today's Health, 49(4), 16–18; 69–71.

Strange, R. E., & Brown, D. E., Jr. (1970). Home from the wars. Amer. J. Psychiat., 127(4), 488–92.

Strategy Council on Drug Abuse. (1979). Federal strategy for drug abuse and drug traffic (No. 052-003-00640-5). Washington, DC: U.S. Government Printing Office.

Strauss, T. S. (1979). Social and cultural influences on psychopathology. Annu. Rev. Psychol. 30(4). 397–415.

Strayer, R., & Ellenhorn, L. (1975). Vietnam veterans: A study exploring adjustment patterns and attitudes. Journal of Social Issues, 31, 81–93.

Strayhorn, J. M. (1982). Foundations of clinical psychiatry. Chicago: Year Book Medical Publishers.

Streissguth, A. P. (1976). Maternal alcoholism and the outcome of pregnancy: A review of the fetal alcohol syndrome. In M. Greenblatt & M. A. Schuckit (Eds.), Alcoholism: Problems in Women and Children. New York: Grune & Stratton.

Strine, G. (1971, Mar. 30). Compulsive gamblers pursue elusive dollar forever. Los Angeles Times, III, 1; 6.

Stroebe, M. S., & Stroebe, W. (1983). Who suffers more? Sex differences in health risks of the widowed. Psychol. Bull., 93(2), 279–301.

Strupp, H. H. (1981). Toward a refinement of time-limited dynamic psychotherapy. In S. H. Budman (Ed.), Forms of brief therapy. New York: Guilford Press.

Strupp, H., Sandell, J. A., Waterhouse, G. J., O'Malley, S. S., & Anderson, J. L. (In press). Short term dynamic therapies for depression: therapy and research. In J. Rush (Ed.), *Short term psychotherapies for the depressed patient: Cognitive, behavioral, interpersonal and psychodynamic approaches.*

Stuart, R. B. (1967). Behavioral control of overeating. *Beh. Res. Ther.,* **5,** 357–65.

Stuart, R. B. (1971a). Behavioral contracting within the families of delinquents. *Journal of Behavior Therapy and Experimental Psychiatry,* **2,** 1–11.

Stuart, R. B. (1971b). A three-dimensional program for the treatment of obesity. *Beh. Res. Ther.,* **9,** 177–86.

Stunkard, A., D'Aquili, E., Fox, S., & Filion, R. D. L. (1972). Influence of social class on obesity and thinness in children. *JAMA,* **221,** 579–84.

Sturgis, E. T., & Adams, H. E. (1978). The right to treatment: Issues in the treatment of homosexuality. *J. Cons. Clin. Psychol.,* **46**(1), 165–69.

Sturgis, E. T., & Meyer, V. (1981). Obsessive-compulsive disorders. In S. M. Turner, K. S. Calhoun, & H. E. Adams (Eds.), *Handbook of clinical behavior therapy.* New York: Wiley.

Su, C. V., Lin, S., Wang, Y. T., Li, C. H., Hung, L. H., Lin, C. S., & Lin, B. C. (1978). Effects of B-endorphin on narcotic abstinence syndrome in man. *Taiwan I Hoven Hui Tsa Chih,* **77,** 133–41.

Suinn, R. M. (1977). Type A behavior pattern. In R. B. Williams, Jr., & W. D. Gentry (Eds.), *Behavioral approaches to medical treatment* (pp. 55–56). Cambridge, MA: Ballinger.

Sulkunen, P. (1976). Drinking patterns and the level of alcohol consumption: An international overview. In R. I. Gibbons et al. (Eds.), *Research advances in alcohol and drug problems. Vol. 3.* New York: Wiley.

Sullivan, H. S. (1953). *The interpersonal theory of psychiatry.* H. S. Perry & M. L. Gawel (Eds.). New York: Norton.

Sullivan, H. S. (1956). *Clinical studies in psychiatry.* New York: Norton.

Sullivan, J. P., & Batareh, G. J. (1973). Educational therapy with the severely retarded. *The Training School Bulletin,* **70**(1), 5–9.

Summers, F. (1979). Characteristics of new patient admissions to aftercare. *Hospital and Community Psychiatry,* **30**(3), 199–202.

Summit, R., & Kryso, J. (1978). Sexual abuse of children: A clinical spectrum. *Amer. J. Orthopsychiat.,* **48,** 237–51.

Sundberg, N. D., & Tyler, L. E. (1962). *Clinical psychology.* New York: Appleton-Century-Crofts.

Surwit, R. S., Shapiro, D., & Good, M. I. (1978). Comparison of cardiovascular biofeedback, neuromuscular biofeedback, and meditation in the treatment of borderline essential hypertension. *J. Cons. Clin. Psychol.,* **46,** 252–53.

Suter, B. (1976). Suicide and women. In B. B. Wolman & H. H. Krauss (Eds.), *Between survival and suicide* (pp. 129–61). New York: Gardner.

Sutherland, E. H. & Cressey, D. R. (1966). *Principles of criminology* (7th ed.). Philadelphia: Lippincott.

Sutherland, S., & Scherl, D. J. (1970). Patterns of response among victims of rape. *Amer. J. Orthopsychiat.,* **40,** 503–11.

Sutker, P. B., & Archer, R. P. (1984). Drug abuse and dependency disorders: Psychopathology and deviance. In H. E. Adams & P. B. Sutker (Eds.), *Comprehensive handbook of Psychopathology.* New York: Plenum.

Sutker, P. B., Archer, R. P., & Kilpatrick, D. G. (1979). Sociopathy and antisocial behavior: Theory and treatment. In S. M. Turner, K. S. Calhoun, & H. E. Adams (Eds.), *Handbook of clinical behavior therapy.* New York: Wiley.

Sutker, P. B., & Moan, C. E. (1973). A psychosocial description of penitentiary inmates. *Arch. Gen. Psychiat.,* **29**(5), 663–67.

Swanson, D. W. (1968). Adult sexual abuse of children: The man and circumstances. *Dis. Nerv. Sys.,* **29**(10), 677–83.

Swanson, D. W., Bohnert, P. J., & Smith, J. A. (1970). *The paranoid.* Boston: Little, Brown.

Swanson, D. W., & Dinello, F. A. (1970). Severe obesity as a habituation syndrome. *Arch. Gen. Psychiat.,* **22,** 120–27.

Switzer, E. (1974). Female sexuality. *Family Health,* **6**(3), 34–36; 38.

Symonds, M. (1976). The rape victim: Psychological patterns of response. *Amer. J. Psychoanalysis,* **36**(1), 27–34.

Szasz, T. S. (1961). *The myth of mental illness.* New York: Harper & Row.

Szasz, T. S. (1963). *Law, liberty, and psychiatry.* New York: Macmillan.

Szasz, T. S. (1970). *The manufacture of madness.* New York: Harper & Row.

Szasz, T. S. (1976). The ethics of suicide. In B. B. Wolman & H. H. Krauss (Eds.), *Between survival and suicide* (pp. 163–85). New York: Gardner.

Tanna, V. L. (1974). Paranoid states: A selected review. *Comprehensive Psychiatry,* **15**(6), 453–70.

Tarjan, G., & Eisenberg, L. (1972, May). Some thought on the classification of mental retardation in the United States of America. *Amer. J. Psychiat.,* Supplement, **128**(11), 14–18.

Tarjan, G., Wright, S. W., Eyman, R. K., & Keeran, C. V. (1973). Natural history of mental retardation: some aspects of epidemiology. *Amer. J. Ment. Def.,* **77**(4), 369–79.

Tarler-Beniolo, L. (1978). The role of relaxation in biofeedback training: A critical review of the literature. *Psychol. Bull.,* **85**(4), 727–55.

Tarver, S. G., & Hallahan, D. P. (1974). Attention deficits in children with learning disabilities: A review. *J. Learn. Dis.,* **7**(9), 560–69.

Tasto, D. L. & Hinkle, J. E. (1973). Muscle relaxation treatment for tension headaches. *Beh. Res. Ther.,* **11,** 347–50.

Tavel, M. E. (1962). A new look at an old syndrome: Delirium tremens. *Arch. Int. Med.,* **109,** 129–34.

Taves, I. (1969). Is there a sleepwalker in the house? *Today's Health,* **47**(5), 41; 76.

Telch, M. J. (1981). The present status of outcome studies: A reply to Frank. *J. Cons. Clin. Psychol.,* **49**(3), 472–75.

Templer, D. I., & Lester, D. (1974). Conversion disorders: A review of research findings. *Comprehensive Psychiatry,* **15**(4), 285–94.

Terkel, S. (1970). *Hard times: An oral history of the Great Depression.* New York: Pantheon.

Thacher, M. (1978, Apr.). First steps for the retarded. *Human Behavior.*

Theodor, L. H., & Mandelcorn, M. S. (1973). Hysterical blindness: A case report and study using a modern psychophysical technique. *J. Abnorm. Psychol.,* **82**(3), 552–53.

Thibaut, J. W., & Kelley, H. H. (1959). *The social psychology of groups.* New York: Wiley.

Thiel, H., Parker, D., & Bruce, T. A. (1973). Stress factors and the risk of myocardial infarction. *J. Psychosom. Res.,* **17**(1), 43–57.

Thienes-Hontos, P., Watson, C. G., & Kucala, T. (1982). Stress disorder symptoms in Vietnam and Korean war veterans. *J. Cons. Clin. Psychol.,* **50**(4), 558–61.

Thigpen, C. H., & Cleckley, H. M. (1957). *Three Faces of Eve.* New York: McGraw-Hill.

Thomas, A., & Chess, S. (1977). *Temperament and development.* New York: Brunner/Mazel.

Thompson, K. C., & Hendrie, H. C. (1972). Environmental stress in primary depressive illness. *Arch. Gen. Psychiat.,* **26**(2), 130–2.

Thompson, N. L., Jr., & McCandless, B. R. & Strickland, B. R. (1971). Personal adjustment of male and female homosexuals and heterosexuals. *J. Abnorm. Psychol.,* **78**(2), 237–40.

Thompson, N. L., Jr., Schwartz, D. M., McCandless, B. R., & Edwards, D. A. (1973). Parent-child relationships and sexual identity in male and female homosexuals and heterosexuals. *J. Cons. Clin. Psychol.,* **41**(1), 120–27.

Thompson, R. J., & O'Quinn, A. N. (1979). *Developmental disabilities: Etiologies, manifestations, diagnoses, and treatments.* New York: Oxford University Press.

Thorndike, E. L. (1913) *The psychology of learning.* New York: Teachers College.

Thornton, W. E., & Thornton, B. P. (1974). Narcotic poisoning: A review of the literature. *Amer. J. Psychiat.,* **131**(8), 867–69.

Tienari, P. (1968). Schizophrenia in monozygotic male twins.

L

In D. Rosenthal & S. S. Kety (Eds.), *The transmission of schizophrenia* (pp. 27–36). Oxford: Pergamon.

Time. (1951, Jan. 22). Young man with a gun. pp. 19–20.

Time. (1952, Dec. 22). Billy's last words.

Time. (1966, June 17). From Shocks to stop sneezes. *Time*, p. 72.

Time. (1974, Apr. 22). Alcoholism: New victims, new treatment. **103**(16), pp. 75–81.

Time. (1975, June 30). The crime wave. **105**(27), 12–20.

Time. (1977, July 25). Night of terror. **110**(4), pp. 12–22.

Time. (1977, Oct. 10). Did TV make him do it? **110**(15), 87–88.

Time. (1980, Sept. 1). Suicide belt. **116**(9), 56.

Time. (1981, May 4). Stomping and whomping galore, pp. 73–74.

Time. (1983, Apr. 18). Ailing schoolgirls. **121**(16), 52.

Tinbergen, N. (1974). Ethology and stress disease. *Science*, **185**(4145), 20–27.

Tittle, C. R., Villemez, W. J., & Smith, D. A. (1978). The myth of social class and criminality: An empirical assessment of the empirical evidence. *Amer. Sociological Rev.*, **43**, 643–56.

Tizard, B., & Rees, J. (1975). The effect of early institutional rearing on the behavior problems and affectional relationships of four-year-old children. *J. Child Psychol. Psychiat.*, **16**(1), 61–73.

Toffler, A. (1970). *Future shock.* New York: Random House.

Tollison, C. D., & Adams, H. E. (1979). *Sexual disorders.* New York: Gardner Press.

Tollison, C. D., Adams, H. E. & Tollison, J. W. (1979). Cognitive and physiological measurement of sexual arousal in homosexual, bisexual, and heterosexual males. *J. Behav. Assess.*, **1**, 305–14.

Toolan, J. M. (1981). Depression and suicide in children: An overview. *Amer. J. Psychother.*, **35**(3), 311–22.

Torrey, E. F. (1973). Is schizophrenia universal? An open question. *Schizophrenia Bulletin*, Winter **7**, 53–59.

Torrey, E. F. (1980). Epidemiology. In L. Bellak (Ed.), *Disorders of the schizophrenic syndrome.* New York: Basic Books.

Traub, E. (1974, April.) "What can happen if you're an overprotective parent". *Today's Health Magazine.*

Travis, J. H. (1933). Precipitating factors in manic-depressive psychoses. *Psychiat. Quart.*, **7**, 411–18.

Tripp, C. A. (1975). *The homosexual matrix.* New York: McGraw-Hill.

Trotter, S. (1975). Labeling: It hurts more than it helps. *APA Monitor*, **6**(1), 5.

Tseng, W. S. (1973). The development of psychiatric concepts in traditional Chinese medicine. *Arch. Gen. Psychiat.*, **29**(4), 569–75.

Tsuang, M. T., Fowler, R. C., Cadoret, R. J., & Monnelly, E. (1974). Schizophrenia among first-degree relatives of paranoid and nonparanoid schizophrenics. *Comprehensive Psychiatry*, **15**(4), 295–302.

Tuckman, J., Kleiner, R., & Lavell, M. (1959). Emotional content of suicide notes. *Amer. J. Psychiat.* **116**, 59–63.

Tuohy, W. (1967, July 30). Drugs fight shell shock in Vietnam. *Los Angeles Times*, F, pp. 12–13.

Tuohy, W. (1968, Dec. 1). Combat fatigue: U.S. lessens its toll in Vietnam. *Los Angeles Times*, A, p. 1.

Turk, D. (1974). *Cognitive control of pain: A skills training approach.* Unpublished manuscript, University of Waterloo, Ontario, Canada.

Turner, R. Dopkeen, L., & Labreche, G. (1970) Marital status and schizophrenia: A study of incidence and outcome. *J. Abnorm. Psychol.*, **76**(1), 110–16.

Turner, R. K., & Taylor, P. D. (1974). Conditioning treatment of nocturnal enuresis in adults: Preliminary findings. *Behav. Res. Ther.*, **12**(1), 41–52.

Tymchuk, A. J., Knights, R. M., & Hinton, G. G. (1970). The behavioral significance of differing EEG abnormalities in children with learning and/or behavior problems. *J. Learn. Dis.*, **3**(11), 547–52.

Uchida, I. A. (1973). Paternal origin of the extra chromosome in Down's syndrome. *Lancet.* **2**(7840), 1258.

Uhlenhuth, E. (1973, Feb. 7). Free therapy said to be helpful to Chicago train wreck victims. *Psychiatric News*, **8**(3), 1, 27.

Uhlenhuth, E. H., & Paykel, E. S. (1973). Symptom intensity and life events. *Arch. Gen. Psychiat.*, **28**(4), 473–77.

Ulleland, C. N. (1972). The offspring of alcoholic mothers. *Ann. N.Y. Acad. Sci.*, **197**, 167–69.

Ullmann, L. P., & Krasner, L. (1975). *Psychological approach to abnormal behavior* (2nd ed.). Englewood Cliffs, NJ: Prentice-Hall.

Ullmann, M., & Gruen, A. (1961). Behavioral changes in patients with strokes, *Amer. J. Psychiat.*, **117**, 1004–9.

Ulmar, G. (1971). Adolescent girls who steal. *Psychiat., Diag.*, **32**(3), 27–28.

Uniform Crime Reports. (1981). Federal Bureau of Investigation. U.S. Dept. of Justice. Washington, DC: U.S. Government Printing Office.

Uniform Crime Reports. (1982). *Federal Bureau of Investigation, U.S. Dept. of Justice.* Washington, DC: U.S. Government Printing Office.

United Nations. (1959, Nov. 20). *Declaration of the rights of a child.* Adopted by the General Assembly of the United Nations.

United Nations Educational, Scientific, & Cultural Organization. (1945). *Constitution.* Paris: UNESCO.

United Press International. (1982, Oct. 24). 'Tylenol hysteria' hits 200 at football game. *Chicago Tribune*, Sec. 1, p. 4.

U.S. Department of Health and Human Services. (1980). *Third Annual Report: Drug abuse prevention, treatment and rehabilitation in the fiscal year 1980.* Washington, DC: U.S. Government Printing Office.

U.S. Department of Health, Education and Welfare. (1971). Physical damage of pot yet unproven, says HEW. *Psychiatric News.* **6**(7), 3.

U.S. Department of Health, Education and Welfare. (1971). National health survey. *Roche Report*, **1**(9), 2.

U.S. Department of Health, Education and Welfare. (1974). *Alcohol and health.* Morris E. Chafetz, Chairman of the Task Force. Washington, DC: U.S. Government Printing Office.

U.S. Department of Health, Education and Welfare. (1978). *The alcoholism report: The authoritative newsletter for professionals.* Washington, DC: U.S. Government Printing Office, **7**(3), 2.

U.S. Department of Justice. (1982, Oct/Nov.). Prisoners at mid-year 1982. *Bureau of Justice's Statistical Bulletin*, 1–4.

U.S. News & World Report. (1973, May 14). How the POW's fought back. **74**(20), pp. 46–52; 110–15.

U.S. News & World Report. (1975, May 12). More kids on the road—Now it's the "throwaways." **78**(19), pp. 49–50.

U.S. News & World Report. (1982, Aug. 30). Anorexia: The starving disease epidemic, **93**, pp. 47–48.

Ursano, R. J., Boydstun, J. A., & Wheatley, R. D., (1981). Psychiatric illness in U.S. air force Vietnam prisoners of war: A five-year follow-up, *Amer. J. Psychiat.* **138**(3), 310–14.

Vaillant, G. E. (1975). Sociopathy as a human process: A viewpoint. *Arch. Gen. Psychiat.*, **32**(2), 178–83.

Valenstein, E. S. (Ed.). (1980). *The psychosurgery debate: Scientific, legal, and ethical perspectives.* San Francisco: W. H. Freeman.

Vallacher, R. R. Wegner, D. M., & Hoine, H. (1980). A postscript on application. In D. M. Wegner & R. R. Vallacher (Eds.), *The self in social psychology.* New York: Oxford University Press.

Vandereycken, W. (1982). Paradoxical strategies in a blocked sex therapy. *Amer. J. Psychother.*, **36**, 103–8.

Vaughn, C. E., & Leff, J. P. (1976). The influence of family and social factors on the course of psychiatric illness: A comparison of schizophrenic and depressed neurotic patients. *Brit. J. Psychiat.*, **129**, 125–37.

Vaughn, C. E., & Leff, J. P. (1981). Patterns of emotional response in relatives of schizophrenic patients. *Schizophrenia Bull.*, **7**, 43–44.

Viglione, D. J., & Exner, J. E. (1983). Current research on the Comprehensive Rorschach System. In J. N. Butcher & C. D. Spielberger (Eds.), *Advances in personality assessment* (Vol. 4). New York: Lawrence Erlbaum and Associates Publishing.

Viscott, D. S. (1970). A musical idiot savant. *Psychiatry, 33*(4), 494–515.

Volavka, J., Davis, L. G., & Ehrlich, Y. H. (1979). Endorphins, dopamine, and schizophrenia. *Schizophrenia Bull., 5*, 227–39.

Volpe, A., & Kastenbaum, R. (1967). TLC. *Amer. J. Nurs., 67*, 100–3.

von Zerssen, D. (1982). Personality and affective disorders. In E. S. Paykel (Ed.), *Handbook of affective disorders.* New York: Guilford Press.

Wachtel, P. L. (1977). *Psychoanalysis and behavior therapy: toward an integration.* New York: Basic Books.

Wachtel, P. L. (1982). What can dynamic therapies contribute to behavior therapy? *Behav. Ther., 13*, 594–609.

Wagner, G. (1981). Methods for differential diagnosis of psychogenic and organic erectile failure. In G. Wagner, & R. Green (Eds.), *Impotence: Physiological, psychological, surgical diagnosis and treatment.* New York: Plenum.

Wagner, G., & Green, R. (1981). (Eds.). *Impotence: Physiological, psychological, surgical diagnosis and treatment.* New York: Plenum.

Wahler, R. G. (1980). The insular mother: Her problems in parent-child treatment. *J. Appl. Beh. Anal., 13*, 207–19.

Wahler, R. G., Hughey, J. B., & Gordon, J. S. (1981). Chronic patterns of mother-child coercion: Some differences between insular and noninsular families. *Anal. Interven. Develop. Dis., 1*, 145–56.

Walinder, J. (1968). Transsexualism: Definition, prevalence, and sex distribution. *Acta Psychiatr. Scandin., 203*, 255–58.

Wallerstein, J. S., & Kelly, J. B. (1979). *Children of divorce: Preventions in parent-child relationships.*

Walsh, T. B. (1980). The endocrinology of anorexia nervosa. *Psychiatric Clinics of North America, 3*(2), 299–312.

Ward, A. J. (1978). Early childhood autism and structural therapy: Outcome after 3 years. *J. Cons. Clin. Psychol., 46*, 586–87.

Warnes, H. (1973). The traumatic syndrome. *Ment. Hlth. Dig., 5*(3), 33–34.

Warrington, E. K., & Weiskrantz, L. (1973). An analysis of short-term and long-term memory defects in man. In J. A. Deutsch (Ed.), *The psychological basis of memory.* New York: Academic Press.

Watkins, C., Gilbert, J. E., & Bass, W. (1969). The persistent suicidal patient. *Amer. J. Psychiat., 125*, 1590–93.

Watson, A. A. (1973). Death by cursing—A problem for forensic psychiatry. *Medicine, Science and the Law, 13*(3), 192–94.

Watson, C. G., Kucala, T., Angulski, G., & Brunn, C. (1982). Season of birth and schizophrenia: A response to the Lewis and Griffin critique. *J. Abnorm. Psychol., 91*, 120–25.

Watson, J. B., & Rayner, R. (1920). Conditioned emotional reactions. *J. Exper. Psychol., 3*, 1–14.

Watson, S., & Akil, H. (1979). Endorphins: Clinical issues. In R. Pickens & L. Heston (Eds.), *Psychiatric factors in drug abuse.* New York: Grune and Stratton.

Weary, G., & Mirels, H. L. (1982). *Integrations of clinical and social psychology.* New York: Oxford University Press.

Wechsler, D. (1981). *Manual for the Wechsler Adult Intelligence Scale.* New York: Psychological Corporation.

Weinberg, M., & Williams, C. J. (1974). *Male homosexuals: Their problems and adaptations in three societies.* New York: Oxford University Press.

Weiner, H. (1977). *Psychobiology and human disease.* New York: Elsevier.

Weiner, H. F., Thaler, M., Reiser, M. F., & Mirsky, I. A. (1957). Etiology of duodenal ulcer: I. Relation of specific psychological characteristics to rate of gastric secretion (Serum pepsenogen). *Psychosom. Med., 19*, 1–10.

Weiner, I. B. (1983). Clinical methods in psychology (2nd ed.). New York: Wiley.

Weiner, R. (1982). Another look at an old controversy. *Contemporary Psychiat., 1*, 61–62.

Weinraub, M., & Frankel, J. (1977). Sex differences in parent-infant interaction during free play, departure, and separation. *Child Develop., 48*, 1240–48.

Weisenberg, M. (1977). Pain and pain control. *Psychol. Bull., 84*, 1008–44.

Weiss, E., & English, O. S. (1943). *Psychosomatic medicine.* Philadelphia: W. B. Saunders.

Weiss, G. (1981). Controversial issues of the pharmacotherapy of the hyperactive child. *Canadian J. Psychiat., 26*(6), 385–92.

Weiss, G., Hechtman, T., Perlman, T., Hopkins, J., & Wener, A. (1979). Hyperactives as young adults: A controlled prospective ten-year follow-up of 75 children. *Arch. Gen. Psychiat., 36*, 675–81.

Weiss, J. M. (1974, Apr. 6). Cited in Depressing situations. *Sci. News, 105*(14) p. 224.

Weiss, R. L., & Birchler, G. R. (1978). Adults with marital dysfunction. In M. Hersen & A. Bellack (Eds.), *Behavior therapy in the psychiatric setting.* Baltimore: Williams & Williams.

Weiss, S. M., Herd, J. A., & Fox, B. H. (1981). *Perspectives on behavioral medicine.* New York: Academic Press.

Weiss, T., & Engel, B. T. (1971). Operant conditioning of heart rate in patients with premature ventricular contractions. *Psychosomatic Medicine, 33*, 301–21.

Weissman, M. M., Fox, K., & Klerman, G. L. (1973). Hostility and depression associated with suicide attempts. *Amer. J. Psychiat., 130*(4), 450–55.

Weissman, M. M., Klerman, G. L., Rounsaville, B. J., Chevron, E. S., & Neu, C. (1982). Short-term interpersonal psychotherapy (IPT) for depression: Description and efficacy. In J. C. Anchin, & D. J. Kiesler (Eds.), *Handbook of interpersonal psychotherapy.* New York: Pergamon Press.

Weissman, M. M., Pottenger, M., Kleber, H., Ruben, H. L., Williams, D., & Thompson, D. (1977). Symptom pattern in primary and secondary depression. *Arch. Gen. Psychiat., 34*, 854–62.

Weitzman, E. D., & Luce, G. (1970). Biological rhythms: Indices of pain, adrenal hormones, sleep, and sleep reversal. In NIMH, *Behavioral sciences and mental health.* Washington, DC: Govt. Printing Office.

Wekstein, L. (1979). *Handbook of suicidology: Principles, problems, and practice.* New York: Brunner/Mazel.

Wellisch, D. K., & Trock, G. K. (1980). A three-year follow-up of family therapy. *Inter. J. Fam. Ther., 2*(3), 169–75.

Wells, C. E. (1979). Diagnosis of dementia. *Psychosomatics, 20*, 517–22.

Wells, C. F., & Stuart, I. R. (Eds.). (1981). *Self-destructive behavior in children and adolescents.* New York: Van Nostrand Reinhold.

Wender, P. H. (1972). In R. Cancro, Genetics of schizophrenia: Some misconceptions clarified. *Roche Report, Frontiers of Psychiatry, 2*(4), 1–2; 8.

Wender, P. H., Rosenthal, D. Kety, S. S., Schulsinger, F., & Weiner, J. (1974). Cross-fostering: A research strategy for clarifying the role of genetic and experiential factors in the etiology of schizophrenia. *Arch. Gen. Psychiat., 30*(1), 121–28.

Werry, J. S. (1979). The childhood psychosis. In H. C. Quay and J. S. Werry (Eds.). Psychopathological disorders of childhood. New York: Wiley.

Werry, J. S., & Quay, H. C. (1971). The prevalence of behavior symptoms in younger elementary school children. *Amer. J. Orthopsychiat., 41*, 136–43.

Wertham, F. (1949). *The show of violence.* New York: Doubleday.

West, J. (1976). *The woman said yes: Encounters with life and death.* New York: Harcourt Brace Jovanovich.

Westermeyer, J. (1982a). Bag ladies in isolated cultures, too. *Behavior Today, 13*(21), pp. 1–2.

Westermeyer, J. (1982b). *Poppies, pipes and people: Opium and its use in Laos,* Berkeley, CA: University of California Press.

Wetli, C. B., & Wright, R. K. (1979). Death caused by recreational cocaine use. *JAMA, 241*(23), 2519–22.

Whalen, C. K., & Henker, B. (1976). Psychostimulants and children: A review and analysis. *Psychol. Bull.*, **83**, 1113–30.

White, A. D. (1896). *A history of the warfare of science with theology in Christendom*. New York: Appleton.

White, R. B., Davis, H. K., & Cantrell, W. A. (1977). Psychodynamics of depression: Implications for treatment. In G. Usdin (Ed.), *Depression: Clinical, biological and psychological perspectives* (pp. 308–38). New York: Brunner/Mazel.

Whitehead, W. E., Winget, C., Fedoravicius, A. S., Wooley, S., & Blackwell, B. (1982). Learned illness behavior in patients with irritable bowel syndrome and peptic ulcers. *Digestive Diseases and Sciences*, **27**, 202–08.

Whitehouse, P. J., Price, D. L., Struble, R. G., Clark, A. W., Coyle, J. T., & DeLong, M. R., (1982) Alzheimer's disease and senile dementia: Loss of neurons in the basal forebrain. *Science*, **215**, 1237–39.

Whitwell, J. R. (1936). *Historical notes on psychiatry*. London: H. K. Lewis.

Widom, C. S. (1977). A methodology for studying noninstitutionalized psychopaths. *J. Cons. Clin. Psychol.*, **45**, 674–83.

Wiggins, J. S. (1982). Circumplex models of interpersonal behavior in clinical psychology. In P. C. Kendall & J. N. Butcher (Eds.), *Handbook of research methods in clinical psychology*. New York: Wiley Interscience.

Wikler, A. (1973). Dynamics of drug dependence: Implications of a conditioning theory for research and treatment. *Arch. Gen. Psychiat.*, **28**(5), 611–16.

Wilbur, R. S. (1973, June 2). In S. Auerbach (Ed.), POWs found to be much sicker than they looked upon release. *Los Angeles Times*, Part I, p. 4.

Williams, C. L. (in press). The provision of mental health services to Southeast Asian refugees.

Williams, J. A., Koegel, R. L. & Egel, A. L. (1981). Response-reinforcer relationships and improved learning in autistic children. *J. Appl. Beh. Anal.*, **14**(1), 53–60.

Williams, R. B., Jr. (1977). Headache. In R. B. Williams, Jr. & W. D. Gentry (Eds.), *Behavioral approaches to medical treatment* (pp. 41–53). Cambridge Mass.: Ballinger.

Williams, R. B., Jr., & Gentry, W. D. (Eds.). (1977). *Behavioral approaches to medical treatment*. Cambridge. MA: Ballinger.

Wilsnack, S. C. (1973a). Feminity by the bottle, *Psych. Today*, **6**(11), 39–43; 96.

Wilsnack, S. C. (1973b). Sex role identity in female alcoholism, *J. Abnorm. Psychol.*, **82**(2), 253–61.

Wilson, J. R. (1964). *The mind*. New York: Time-Life, Inc.

Wing, L. (1980). Childhood autism and social class: A question of selection. *Brit. J. Psychiat.*, **137**, 410–17.

Wing, L. K. (1976). Diagnosis, clinical description and prognosis. In L. Wing (Ed.), *Early childhood autism*. London: Pergamon Press.

Wing, S., & Manton, K. G. (1983). The contribution of hypertension to mortality in the U.S.: 1968, 1977. *Amer. J. Public Health*, **73**(2), 140–44.

Winick, M. (1976). (Ed.) *Malnutrition and brain development*. New York: Oxford University Press.

Winick, M., & Rosso, P. (1973). Effects of malnutrition on brain development. *Biology of Brain Dysfunction*, **1**, 301–17.

Winokur, G., Clayton, P. J., & Reich, T. (1969). *Manic depressive illness*. St Louis: Mosby.

Winokur, G., & Pitts, F. N. (1964). Affective disorder: Is reactive depression an entity? *J. Nerv. Ment. Dis.*, **138**, 541–47.

Winokur, G., Reich, T., Rimmer, J., & Pitts, F. N., Jr. (1970). Alcoholism. III: diagnosis and familial psychiatric illness in 259 alcoholic probands. *Arch. Gen. Psychiat.*, **23**(2), 104–11.

Winsberg, B. G., Goldstein, S., Yepes, L. E., & Perel, J. M. (1975). Imipramine and electrocardiographic abnormalities in hyperactive children. *Amer. J. Psychiat.*, **132**(5), 542–45.

Winter, D. G. (1973). *The power motive*. New York: Free Press.

Winters, K. C., Weintraub, S., & Neale, J. M. (1981). Va-

lidity of MMPI code types in identifying DSM-III schizophrenics, unipolars, and bipolars. *J. Cons. Clin. Psychol.*, **49**, 486–87.

Witkin, H. A. et al. (1976). Criminality in XYY and XXY men. *Science*, **193**(4253), 547–55.

Witzig, J. S. (1968). The group treatment of male exhibitionists. *Amer. J. Psychiat.* **125**, 75–81.

Wolf, M., Risley, T., & Mees, H. (1964). Application of operant conditioning procedures to the behavior problems of an autistic child. *Behavior Research and Therapy*, **1**, 305–12.

Wolf, S. L., Nacht, M., & Kelly, J. L. (1982). EMG feedback training during dynamic movement for low back pain patients. *Behav. Ther.*, **13**, 395–406.

Wolff, H. G. (1948). *Headache and other head pain*. Cambridge: Oxford University Press.

Wolff, H. G. (1950). Life stress and cardiovascular disorders. *Circulation*, **1**, 187–203.

Wolff, H. G. (1960). Stressors as a cause of disease in man. In J. M. Tanner (Ed.), *Stress and psychiatric disorder*. London: Oxford University Press.

Wolff, P. H. (1972). Ethnic differences in alcohol sensitivity. *Science*, **175**, 449–50.

Wolff, W. M., & Morris, L. A. (1971). Intellectual personality characteristics of parents of autistic children. *J. Abnorm. Psychol.*, **77**(2), 155–61.

Wolkind, S. N. (1974). The components of "affectionless psychopathy" in institutionalized children. *J. Child Psychol. Psychiat.*, **15**(3), 215–20.

Wolpe, J. (1969a). For phobia: A hair of the hound. *Psych. Today*, **3**(1), 34–37.

Wolpe, J. (1969b). *The practice of behavior therapy*. New York: Pergamon.

Woodruff, R. A., Guze, S. B., & Clayton, P. J. (1972). Anxiety neurosis among psychotic patients. *Comprehensive Psychiatry*, **13**, 165–70.

Woodruff, R. A., Guze, S. B., Clayton, P. J., & Carr, D. (1973). Alcoholism and depression. *Arch. Gen. Psychiat.*, **28**(1), 97–100.

World Health Organization (1974, Oct. 25). In W. Tuohy, World health agency zeroes in on suicide. *Los Angeles Times*, VI, 1–3.

World Health Organization (1975). *Schizophrenia: A multi-national study*. Geneva: World Health Organization.

World Health Organization (1978a, April). *Report of the director-general*. Geneva: World Health Organization.

World Health Organization (1978b). *Mental disorders: Glossary and guide to their classification in accordance with the ninth revision of the International Classification of Diseases*. Geneva: World Health Organization.

World Health Organization. (1979). *International classification of diseases*. (9th ed.) (ICD-9). Geneva: World Health Organization.

Worthington, E. R. (1978). Demographic and pre-service variables as predictors of post-military adjustment. In C. R. Figley (Ed.), *Stress disorders among Vietnam veterans*. New York: Brunner/Mazel.

Wortis, J. (1972, May). Comments on the ICD classification of mental retardation. *Amer. J. Psychiat.*, Supplement, **128**(11), 21–24.

Wortis, J. (Ed.). (1973). *Mental retardation and developmental disabilities: An annual review* (Vol. 5). New York: Brunner/Mazel.

Wright, L., Schaefer, A. B., & Solomons, G. (1979). *Encyclopedia of pediatric psychology*. Baltimore: University Park Press.

Wunsch-Hitzig, R., Gould, M. S., & Dohrenwend, B. P (1980). Hypotheses about the prevalence of clinical maladjustment in children in the United States. In S. Salzinger, J. Antrobus, & J. Glick (Eds.), *The ecosystem of the "sick" child: implications for classification and intervention for disturbed and mentally retarded children*. New York: Academic Press.

Wynne, L. C., Roohey, M. L., & Doane, J. (1979). Family studies. In L. Bellak (Ed.), *The schizophenic syndome*. New York: Basic Books.

Wynne, L. C., Ryckoff, I. M., Day, J., & Hirsch, S. I. (1958). Pseudomutuality in the family relations of schizophrenics. *Psychiatry*, **21**, 205–20.

Yablonsky, L. (1962). *The violent gang*. New York: Macmillan.
Yablonsky, L. (1975). Psychodrama lives. *Human Behavior*, 4(2), 24–29.
Yap, P. M. (1951). Mental diseases peculiar to certain cultures: A survey of comparative psychiatry. *J. Ment. Sci.*, 97(3), 313.
Yarden, P. E. (1974). Observations on suicide in chronic schizophrenics. *Comprehensive Psychiatry*, 15(4), 325–33.
Yates, A. (1981). Narcissistic traits in certain abused children. *Amer. J. Orthopsychiat.*, **51**, 55–62.
Yerbury, E. C., & Newell, N. (1943). Genetic and environmental factors in psychoses of children. *Amer. J. Psychiat.*, **100**, 599–605.
Yolles, S. F. (1967, April). Quote from "Unraveling the mystery of schizophrenia." *Today's Health*.
Yolles, S. (1969, Sept. 26). Cited in Pop drugs: The high as a way of life. *Time*, **94**(13), p. 74.

Zahn, T. P., Rapoport, J. L., & Thompson, C. L. (1980). Autonomic and behavioral effects of dextroamphetamine and placebo in normal and hyperactive boys, *J. Abnorm. Child Psychol.*, 8(2), 145–60.
Zigler, E., Abelson, W. D., Trickett, P. K., & Seitz, V. (1982). Is an intervention program necessary in order to improve economically disadvantaged children's IQ scores? *Child Develop.*, **53**, 340–48.
Zilberg, N. J., Weiss, D. S., & Horowitz, M. (1982). Impact of events scale: A cross validation study and some empirical evidence supporting a conceptual model of stress response syndromes. *J. Cons. Clin. Psychol.*, **50**(3), 407–14.
Zilbergeld, B., & Evans, M. (1980, Jan.). The inadequacy of Masters and Johnson. *Psych. Today*, 29–43.
Zilboorg, G., & Henry, G. W. (1941). *A history of medical psychology*. New York: Norton.
Zimbardo, P. G. (1973). A field experiment in autoshaping. In C. Ward (Ed.), *Vandalism*. London: Architectural Press.

Zimbardo, P. G., Haney, C., Banks, W. C., & Jaffe, D. (1975). The psychology of imprisonment: Privation, power, and pathology. In D. Rosenhan & P. London (Eds.), *Theory and research in abnormal psychology* (2nd ed., pp. 270–87). New York: Holt, Rinehart & Winston.
Zimring, F. (1979). *American Youth Violence*. Chicago: University of Chicago Press.
Zinberg, N. E. (1980). The social setting as a control mechanism in intoxicant use. In D. J. Lettieri, M. Sayers, & H. W. Pearson (Eds.), *Theories on drug abuse: Selected contemporary perspectives*. Rockville, MD: National Institute on Drug Abuse.
Zis, A. P., & Goodwin, F. K. (1982). The amine hypothesis. In E. S. Paykel (Ed.), *Handbook of affective disorders*. New York: Guilford Press.
Zitrin, A., Hardesty, A. S., Burdock, E. I., & Drossman, A. K. (1976). Crime and violence among mental patients. *Amer. J. Psychiat.*, **133**(2), 142–49.
Zola, I. K. (1966). Culture and symptoms—An analysis of patients' presenting complaints. *American Sociological Review*, **31**, 615–30.
Zubin, J. (1978). Concluding comments. In L. C. Wynne, R. L. Cromwell, & S. Matthysse (Eds.), *The nature of schizophrenia*. New York: Wiley.
Zubok, B. (1980). Russian psychiatry and the maintenance of the social order. Invited Address. Department of Psychiatry, University of Minnesota Medical School.
Zucker, S. H., and Altman, R. (1973). An on-the-job training program for adolescent trainable retardates. *Training School Bulletin*, **70**(2), 106–10.
Zuckerman, M. (1972). *Manual and research report for the Sensation Seeking Scale (SSS)*. Newark, DE: University of Delaware.
Zuckerman, M. (1978). Sensation seeking and psychopathy. In R. D. Hare and D. Schalling (Eds.), *Psychopathic behavior: Approaches to research*, New York: Wiley.
Zung, W. W. K. (1969). A cross-cultural survey of symptoms in depression. *Amer. J. Psychiat.*, **126**(1), 116–21.
Zung, W. W. K. & Green, R. L., Jr. (1974). Seasonal variations of suicide and depression. *Gen. Psychiat.*, **30**(1), 89–91.

Acknowledgments

Photo credits

Details of each photograph used as a chapter opener are repeated throughout the chapter. A detail from each chapter will also be an element of one of the composites used in the part openers.

All photographs not credited are the property of Scott, Foresman.

Front and back cover, front endsheet: Collection de l'Art Brut, Lausanne
Chapter 1: 4 Collection de l'Art Brut, Lausanne 7 Peter Thomas/Tom Stack & Assoc. 8 The British Library 9 The Tate Gallery, London 10 Culver Pictures 11 The Trustees of Sir John Soane's Museum 13 James H. Karales/Peter Arnold 21 Tom Damman/NYT Pictures 25 Bohdan Hrynewych/Stock, Boston **Chapter 2:** 30 Collection de l'Art Brut, Lausanne 32 The Bettmann Archive 34 The British Library 37 The Pierpont Morgan Library 39(t) The Bettmann Archive 39(b) The Tate Gallery, London 40 Sven Nackstrand/Gamma-Liaison 42(l) Historical Pictures Service, Chicago 42(r) The Bettmann Archive 44 Historical Pictures Service, Chicago 45 Culver Pictures 47 Bulloz 48(tl,r) National Library of Medicine, Bethesda, Maryland 48(bl) Historical Pictures Service, Chicago 51(l,c) Historical Pictures Service, Chicago 51(r) The Bettmann Archive **Chapter 3:** 54 Collection de l'Art Brut, Lausanne 57 Historical Pictures Service, Chicago 58 P. Chock/Stock, Boston 61 Historical Pictures Service, Chicago 66(l) UPI 66(r) Wide World 67(l) Association for the Advancement of Psychoanalysis of the Karen Horney Psychoanalytic Institute and Center 67(cl) New York University 67(cr) UPI 67(r) Courtesy Dr. Margaret S. Mahler 68 The Bettmann Archive 69(l) UPI 69(c) Courtesy Dr. B. F. Skinner 69(r) Courtesy Dr. Albert Bandura 71 Charles Biasiny-Rivera 73(l) Stockphotos, Inc. 73(c) N. Wayne Hansen 73(r) Bonnie Griffith/The Picture Cube 78(tl,bl,tr) The Bettmann Archive 78(br) Hugh Wilkerson 82(l) Jon Erikson 82(r) William Alanson White Psychiatric Foundation 84 Institute for Intercultural Studies/Library of Congress 85(t) Victor Englebert 85(bl) Philip Jon Bailey/The Picture Cube 85(br) Rick Smolan 86(tl) Michael O'Brien/Archive 86(tr) Bruno Barbey/Magnum 86(bl) Rhoda Sidney/Leo de Wys 86(br) David R. Frazier 87(tl) Evelyn Jones/Taurus 87(tr) Paul Knipping/Leo de Wys 87(bl,br) Rick Smolan **Chapter 4:** 92 Collection de l'Art Brut, Lausanne 94 Wide World 99(both) Frank Johnston/*The Washington Post*/Woodfin Camp 101 Theatre Collection; Museum of the City of New York 103(both) Freund-/Globe Photos 107(l) Wallace Kirkland, LIFE Magazine © 1945 Time, Inc. 107(r) Bill Gillette/Stock, Boston 111 Panuska/DPI 115(l) Burt Glinn/Magnum 115(r) Leonard Freed/Magnum 118(tl) Phil & Loretta Hermann/Tom Stock & Assoc. 118(bl) Rhoda Sidney/Leo de Wys 118(r) © Joel Gordon 119 UPI 125(t) Eric Roth/The Picture Cube 125(b) Bill Gallery/Stock, Boston 128(t) Eugene Richards/The Picture Cube 128(b) Ethan Hoffman/Archive 134 Ethan Hoffman/Archive 135(both) Dr. Philip G. Zimbardo **Chapter 5:** 140 Collection de l'Art Brut, Lausanne 143(l) Cary Wolinsky/Stock, Boston 143(r) Joan Liftin/Archive 144 Martha Cooper 145 Charles Harbutt/Archive

Literary, Figures, and Tables

14: Hirsch, S. et al. (Eds.). *Madness network news reader*. San Francisco: New Glide Publications, 1974. Poem entitled "Self-knowledge" from VISIONS OF A MADMAN by P. G. Harrison. Reprinted by permission of the author. **19, 20:**American Psychiatric Association, *Diagnostic and statistical manual of mental disorders*, Third Edition. Washington, D.C.: APA, 1980. Reprinted by permisson. **46:**Karnosh, L. J. (with collaboration of Zucker, E. M.). *Handbook of psychiatry*. St. Louis: C. V. Mosby, 1945. Reprinted by permission. **100:**Chicago Tribune Graphic: "Chromosome Abnormalities" from *Chicago tribune*, Feb. 6, 1983. Reprinted by permission. **124:**Traub, E. Quote from "What can happen if you're an overprotective parent" by E. Traub. *Today's Health* (April 1974), 52(4), 40–43; 67–69, published by the American Medical Association. **127:**Haley, J. The family of the schizophrenic: A model system. *Journal of Nervous and Mental Disease*, 1959, 129, 357–74. Copyright © 1959 by The Williams & Wilkins Co., Baltimore. Reprinted by permission. **149:**"Social Readjustment Rating Scale (SRRS)" by T. H. Holmes and R. H. Rahe from *Journal of psychosomatic research*, Vol. 11, No. 2, 1967. Copyright © 1967, Pergamon Press, Ltd. Reprinted by permission. **155:**Figure 1.3 "Selye's General Adaptation Syndrome" from *Stress* by Tom Cox. Copyright © 1978 by Tom Cox. Reprinted by permission of Macmillan, London and Basingstoke. **158–159:**Terkel, S. *Hard times: An oral history of the Great Depression*. Copyright © 1970 by Studs Terkel. Reprinted by permission of Pantheon Books, a Division of Random House, Inc. and Elaine Greene Ltd. **159–60:**Janis, I. L., Mahl, G. F., Kagan, J., & Holt, R. R. From *Personality: Dynamics, development, and assessment*. Published by Harcourt Brace Jovanovich, Inc., 1969. Reprinted by permission. **171:**Bartemeier, L. H., Kuble, L. S., Menninger, K. A., Romano, J., & Whitehorn, J. C. Combat exhaustion. *Journal of Nervous and Mental Disease*, 1946, 104, 385–89; 489–525. Published by The Williams & Wilkins Co. Copyright 1946 and reprinted by permission of The Smith Ely Jelliffe Trust. **171–72:**Stern, R. L. Diary of a war neurosis. *Journal of Nervous and Mental Disease*, 1947, 106, 583–86. Published by the Williams & Wilkins Co. Copyright 1947 and reprinted by permission of The Smith Ely Jelliffe Trust. **177:**Shatan, C. F. Stress disorders among Vietnam veterans: The emotional content of combat continues. From *Stress disorders among Vietnam veterans: Theory, research and treatment*, edited by Charles R. Figley, Ph.D. Copyright © 1978 by Charles R. Figley. Reprinted by permission of Brunner/Mazel, Publishers. **177:**Archibald, H. C., & Tuddenham, R. D. Persistent stress reaction after combat. *Arch. Gen. Psychiat.*, 1965, 12(5), 475–81. **179:**From "Reactivation of Traumatic Conflicts" by Randall M. Christenson, John Ingram Walker, Donald R. Ross, and Allan A. Maltrie from *American Journal of psychiatry*, Vol. 138:7, pp. 984–85, 1981. Copyright © 1981, the American Psychiatric Association. **180:**Nardini, J. E. Survival factors in American prisoners of war of the Japanese. Reprinted from The *American Journal of Psychiatry*, volume 109, pages 241–48, 1952. Copyright 1952, the American Psychiatric Association. **191:**From *Psychopathology: a case book* by Robert L. Spitzer, et al. Copyright © 1983 by McGraw-Hill, Inc. Reprinted by permission. **208–9:**Menninger, K. A. *The human mind* (3rd ed.). New York: Knopf, 1945. From pages 139–140 in *The Human Mind*, by Karl Menninger. Copyright 1930, 1937, 1945, and renewed 1958, 1965 by Karl Menninger. Reprinted by permission of Alfred A. Knopf, Inc. **218–19:**Masserman, J. H. *Principles of dynamic psychiatry* (2nd ed.). Philadelphia: W. B. Saunders Company, 1961. Reproduced by permission of the author and publisher. **220–21:**Osgood, C. E., Luria, Z., Jeans, R. F., & Smith, S. W. The three faces of Evelyn: A case report. *Journal of Abnormal Psychology*, 1976, Vol. 85, pp. 249–70. Copyright © 1976 by the American Psychological Association. Reprinted by permission. **221–22:**Lipton, S. Dissociated personality: A case report. *Psychiatric Quarterly*, 1943, 17, 35–36. Reprinted by permission of Human Science Press, 72 Fifth Avenue, New York, N.Y. 10011. **228–29:**Frankel, A. S. Treatment of a multisymptomatic phobic by a self-directed, self-reinforced imagery technique: A case study. Reprinted from the *Journal of Abnormal Psychology*, 1970, Vol. 76, pp. 496–99, "Treatment of a Multisymptomatic Phobic by a Self-Directed, Self-Reinforced Imagery Technique" by A. S. Frankel, by permission of the American Psychological Association. **234–35:**American Psychiatric Association, *Diagnostic and statistical manual of mental disorders*, Third Edition. Washington, D.C.: APA, 1980. Reprinted by permission. **237–38, 239, 240–41, 241–42:**Spitzer, R. L., Skodol, A. E., Gibbon, M. and William, J. B. W., *DSM-III case book*. Washington, D.C.: American Psychiatric Association, 1981. Reprinted by permission. **250:**Bluemel, C. S. *War, politics, and insanity*. Denver: World Press, 1948. Reprinted by

Name index

Reverse tolerance, 425, 436
Reward and punishment: and antisocial personality, 255; in conditioning, 70–71, 258; in therapy, 640, 645–47
Rhythm test, 589
Rights: of children, 576–78; of homosexuals to treatment, 478, 479; of patients, 683–85, 693; of prisoners, 269; of society, 684–87; to suicide, 338–40
Rigidity, 126, 130, 289, 513; and affective disorders, 319; in anxiety reaction, 201–3; in personality disorders, 237, 243–44, 246; and psychoses, 373, 375, 390, 392, 394, 512, 513
Risk-taking, 193, 242
Ritalin, 422, 544, 545, 623, 624
Ritualistic behavior, 357
Role obsolescence, 514
Role playing, 591, 655, 657
Roles: and alcoholism, 408–9; disorder-engendering, 134–35; and expectations, 662; and schizophrenia, 370–71, 375, 380–81; sex (see Sex roles); sick (see Sick role); social-, 81, 82, 133, 514, 515, 662, 682, 690; in transactional analysis, 665–67
Rorschach test, 586, 593–94, 601, 607
Rubella, 520, 521
Ruminations, 202
Runaways, 473, 549, 550–51, 553, 554, 557, 677

On Sacred Disease, 34
Sadism, 457, 460, 456–68, 487
Sadness, 302, 308
St. Vitus's dance, 37, 216
Salpêtrière Hospital, 47, 61
Samaritans, 337
Sample, in research, 22, 23, 24, 29, 587
Sara and Maud case, 221–22
Scales of MMPI, 596, 597, 606, 607
Scapegoating, 177
Schizoaffective disorder, 313–14, 362
Schizoid personality disorder, 235, 237, 238–40, 242, 270
Schizophrenia, 7, 18, 22, 72, 239, 343–86, 395, 495, 586, 596; in childhood, 536, 538, 542; defining, 353–54; and environment, 88, 348–49, 363, 366, 367; factors in, 362–85, 626; and faulty parenting, 123, 127–28, 129, 345–49, 373–78; and Genain family, 345–49, 356, 363, 373–74, 375, 379; and genetic factors, 100, 102, 363, 366–67; incidence of, 345, 356, 359, 363, 366, 384; and other psychoses, 300, 323–24, 391; and season of birth, 95, 370; and sexual variants, 466, 468, 470; similarity of, to drug effects, 433; therapy and prognosis, 356, 385–86, 610–11, 615–18, 619, 622, 625–26, 650, 669, 680, 681; types of, 354–62; writings of, 352, 354–56, 361
Schizophrenia Bulletin, 362
Schizophrenia scale of MMPI, 596, 597
Schizophreniform disorder, 362
Schizophrenogenic parents, 373–74
Schizotypal personality disorder, 237, 239, 270, 362, 366, 370
"School phobia," 166
Science News, 612
Scotophilia (See Voyeurism)
Seashore's Test, 589
Season-of-birth phenomenon, 95, 370
Seconal, 422, 428
Secondary drives, 72
Secondary gains, 205, 209, 210, 216, 291, 379, 547
Secondary insufficiency, 451
Secondary prevention, 674, 675, 677–80, 700
Secondary process, 63
Secondary thought processes, 350
Security, need for, 99, 113, 198

Sedatives (See Barbiturates)
Seductive behavior, 239, 240, 485
"Selective forgetting," 152
Selective vigilance, 116
Self: in autism, 564; as a determinant, 109–16, 136; in personality disorders, 242; sense of loss of, 222–23; and schizophrenia, 351; in therapy, 660–61
Self-acceptance, 658, 660
Self-accusation, 321
Self-actualization (See Actualization)
Self-centeredness (See Egocentricism)
Self-concept, 76, 80, 83, 159, 165; in childhood disorders, 547, 560, 564; and hospitalization, 108, 682; and mental retardation, 528; in personality disorders, 249; and schizophrenia, 378; and sexual variants, 458–59, 464, 465, 475, 485; and therapy, 651, 658
Self-confidence, 209, 242, 418, 558, 658, 682
Self-consciousness, 572
Self-control: and alcohol usage, 414–15, 417–18, 447; and drug abuse, 421, 424, 436, 447; and gambling, 445; and weight loss, 442
Self-criticism, 303, 306, 322
Self-defeating behavior (See Anxiety-based disorders)
Self-devaluation, 135, 153, 257, 638; and affective disorders, 323; and aging, 512; and depression, 303; through hospitalization, 682; and neuroses, 190; in paranoia and schizophrenia, 379, 380, 393; and sexual variants or dysfunctions, 455, 486; and suicide, 328; and therapy, 651
Self-direction, 73, 75, 76, 77, 110, 113, 202, 227, 661, 667
Self-efficacy, 418
Self-esteem, 65, 110, 114, 124, 135, 141, 240, 242, 589; and affective disorders, 310, 317, 321, 322; and alcoholism, 408–9; and childhood disorders, 546, 568; inflated, 310, 321, 400; for mentally retarded, 529–30, 531; and paranoia, 390, 392; and suicide, 329
Self-fulfilling prophecy, 82, 518, 584
Self-fulfillment, 76, 77, 81, 189, 224
Self-help program, for dieting, 441
Self-hypnosis, 361
Self-ideal, 110
Self-identity, 76, 109, 114, 242, 513, 527, 630, 674
Self-image, 80, 144, 409, 512, 542, 670
Self-instructions, in therapy, 544
Selfishness, 78, 125, 130
Self-monitoring, 572, 587, 591–92, 641, 655
Self-mutilation, 241–42, 357, 468–69
Self-pity, 108, 181
Self-punishment, 216
Self-regulating systems, 95
Self-reinforcement, 652
Self-report inventory, 586, 587, 590, 595–98, 605
Self-report schedule, 590
Self-statements, 654–55, 671
Self-structure, deficient, 379
Self-system, 80
Semantic Differential Technique, 220, 221
Senile dementia, 57, 90, 466, 470, 492, 494, 505, 615
Sensate focus, 456
Sensation-seeking, 249, 254
Sensorimotor area of brain, 493
Sensory strip of brain, 491, 493
Sensory symptoms, in conversion reactions, 213–15
Sentence-completion tests, 593, 594
Separation: marital, 149, 157, 160–61, 185, 254, 261, 290, 299, 328, 375, 553; parental, 121, 129–30, 254, 548–49, 558–59

Separation anxiety disorder, 558–59
Separation-individuation, 67
Serax, 620, 623
Serotonin, 316, 618
Severe affective disorders, 307–14
Severe mental retardation, 489, 519, 520, 521, 523, 525, 526, 528, 529, 531, 533, 644
Sex and Repression in Savage Society, 84
Sex-change surgery, 114, 458, 459, 460
Sex chromosomes, 98, 100
Sex drive, 62, 63, 68, 224, 457
Sex-linked genetic disorders, 100, 315
Sex roles, 133, 135, 454–55; and addiction, 408, 426; and sexual variants, 457, 458, 465; and suicide, 331
Sexual behavior, 68, 448–87; and affective disorders 300, 304, 310, 653; and alcohol, 402, 405, 406–7; assessment of, 590; and brain disorders, 470, 471, 491, 551; conflicts and guilt over, 65–66, 453, 454; and delinquency, 123, 551, 552; and development, 68; and drugs, 421, 422, 426, 431, 432, 436, 453; dysfunctions in, 149, 449–57, 650; involving assault or nonconsent, 464–76; and paranoia, 394; and personality disorders, 465, 466, 470, 472; and psychoanalytic model, 63–65, 68; and schizophrenia, 371, 374, 379; and reassignment surgery, 114, 458, 459, 460; and roles, 133, 135, 454–55, 457, 458, 465; and stress, 466; variants, 457–77; victimless variants of, 457, 458–64, 477–86, 487
Sexual dysfunctions, 149, 449–57, 650
Sexual phobia, 228–29
Sexual variants, 457–87; exhibitionism, 457, 460, 464–66, 470, 487; fetishism, 457, 460, 462–64, 467, 468, 487; homosexuality, 362, 394, 457, 458, 468, 469, 499, 601, 604; incest, 346, 359, 371, 374, 457, 471–74, 485, 487; 553; masochism, 457, 460, 467, 468–69, 487; pedophilia, 74, 457, 460, 469–70, 487; rape, 457, 471, 474–76, 477, 487 (see also Rape); sadism, 457, 460, 466–68, 487; and transsexualism, 458–60, 476; transvestism, 457, 458, 460–62, 463, 487; treatment for, 476–77, 479; voyeurism, 457, 460, 464, 487
Shaping, 72, 74
Shared paranoid disorder, 387, 388
Shaw v. Glickman, 687
"Shell shock" (See Combat, reactions to)
Shock stage, of trauma, 163, 166
Short-term crisis therapy, 677
Shyness, 462, 464, 465, 485, 539, 558, 559, 560, 579, 596, 645
Siblings: and alcoholism, 407–8; and incest, 472, 473; and incidence of manic-depressive reactions, 314; and incidence of schizophrenia, 102, 363, 366; and psychophysiologic disorders, 288
Sick role, 108, 667, 679, 682; in combat reactions, 176; for gambling, 444; in neuroses, 205, 209, 211–12, 216, 217
Significant others, 80, 114; in childhood disorders, 558–59; and suicide, 337, 338
"Silent abusers," 428
"Silent treatment," 113, 114
Simple deterioration in Alzheimer's dementia, 507
Sinequan, 622
Skill acquisition and rehearsal, 654–55
Sleep and sleep disturbances: in adjustment disorders, 159; in affective disorders, 300, 304, 307, 308, 309, 310, 314, 316, 341; and aging, 621; and alcohol or drug usage, 405, 407, 430; and brain disorders, 493; in childhood disorders, 558, 559, 570; deprivation, 106; drugs for, 422, 427–28, 614, 621,

Feedback, please!

We need your reactions and ideas if *Abnormal Psychology and Modern Life* is to serve you and others better. What did you like best and least? What would you like to have more or less of? How could it have been handled better? Please jot down your suggestions, cut out this page, fold and tape or staple it, and mail it to us. No postage is needed.

Many thanks!
The authors

For every chapter that you read, please make a check mark on each line to indicate your evaluation of it. It is ideal if you can do this as soon as you finish reading each chapter.

Chapter	Informational Value			Interest		
	high	average	low	high	average	low
1 Abnormal behavior in our times						
2 Historical views of abnormal behavior						
3 Biological, psychosocial, and sociocultural viewpoints						
4 Causal factors in abnormal behavior						
5 Stress and adjustment disorders						
6 Anxiety-based disorders (neuroses)						
7 Personality disorders and crime						
8 Psychological factors and physical illness						
9 Affective disorders and suicide						
10 Schizophrenic disorders and paranoia						
11 Substance-use and other addictive disorders						
12 Psychosexual disorders and variants						
13 Organic mental disorders and mental retardation						
14 Behavior disorders of childhood and adolescence						
15 Clinical assessment						
16 Biologically based therapies						
17 Psychologically based therapies						
18 Contemporary issues in abnormal psychology						

What did you like best about *Abnormal Psychology and Modern Life?*

How could *Abnormal Psychology and Modern Life* **be improved?**

Your name and address (if you wish)

_____

_____

Size of your psychology class _____

Male _____ Female _____ Age _____

Were you in a discussion section? _____

Your course grade _____

Besides the text, did you use:

Will you take more psychology? _____

Student's Guide to accompany Abnormal

Your probable major _____

Psychology and Modern Life 7th _____

School _____

Other supplementary material _____

fold here

Overall evaluation of *Abnormal Psychology and Modern Life* 7th

All things considered, how does *Abnormal Psychology and Modern Life* compare to texts you have used in other courses?

*much
better*   *better*   *about
average*   *worse*   *much
worse*

Would you recommend its continued use at your school?

_____ Definitely yes
_____ Yes
_____ Uncertain
_____ No
_____ Definitely no

fold here

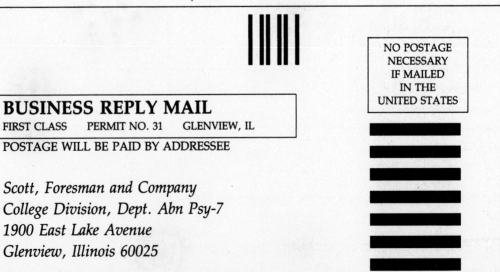

BUSINESS REPLY MAIL

FIRST CLASS   PERMIT NO. 31   GLENVIEW, IL

POSTAGE WILL BE PAID BY ADDRESSEE

Scott, Foresman and Company
College Division, Dept. Abn Psy-7
1900 East Lake Avenue
Glenview, Illinois 60025

NO POSTAGE
NECESSARY
IF MAILED
IN THE
UNITED STATES

cut page out

DSM-III Classification*

Disorders Usually First Evident in Infancy, Childhood, or Adolescence

Mental retardation
Mild mental retardation
Moderate mental retardation
Severe mental retardation
Profound mental retardation
Unspecified mental retardation

Attention deficit disorder
with hyperactivity
without hyperactivity
residual type

Conduct disorder
undersocialized, aggressive
undersocialized, nonaggressive
socialized, aggressive
socialized, nonaggressive
atypical

Anxiety disorders of childhood or adolescence
Separation anxiety disorder
Avoidant disorder of childhood or adolescence
Overanxious disorder

Other disorders of infancy, childhood, or adolescence
Reactive attachment disorder of infancy
Schizoid disorder of childhood or adolescence
Elective mutism
Oppositional disorder
Identity disorder

Eating disorders
Anorexia nervosa
Bulimia
Pica
Rumination disorder of infancy
Atypical eating disorder

Stereotyped movement disorders
Transient tic disorder
Chronic motor tic disorder
Tourette's disorder
Atypical tic disorder
Atypical stereotyped movement disorder

Other disorders with physical manifestations
Stuttering
Functional enuresis
Functional encopresis
Sleepwalking disorder
Sleep terror disorder

Pervasive developmental disorders
Infantile autism
Childhood onset pervasive developmental disorder
Atypical

From the *Diagnostic and statistical manual of mental disorders, Third Edition.* Washington, D.C.: American Psychiatric Association, 1980. Reprinted by permission.

Axis II **Specific developmental disorders**
Developmental reading disorder
Developmental arithmetic disorder
Developmental language disorder
Developmental articulation disorder
Mixed specific developmental disorder
Atypical specific developmental disorder

Organic Mental Disorders

Section 1. Organic mental disorders in whose etiology or pathophysiological process is listed below.

Dementias arising in the senium and presenium
Primary degenerative dementia, senile onset
with delirium
with delusions
with depression
uncomplicated
Primary degenerative dementia, presenile onset
Multi-infarct dementia

Substance-induced
Alcohol
intoxication
idiosyncratic intoxication
withdrawal
withdrawal delirium
hallucinosis
amnestic disorder
Dementia associated with alcoholism
Barbiturate or similarly acting sedative or hypnotic
intoxication
withdrawal
withdrawal delirium
amnestic disorder
Opioid
intoxication
withdrawal
Cocaine
intoxication
Amphetamine or similarly acting sympathomimetic
intoxication
delirium
delusional disorder
withdrawal
Phencyclidine(PCP) or similarly acting arylcyclohexylamine
intoxication
delirium
mixed organic mental disorder
Hallucinogen
hallucinosis
delusional disorder
affective disorder
Cannabis
intoxication
delusional disorder
Tobacco
withdrawal

Caffeine
intoxication
Other or unspecified substance
intoxication
withdrawal
delirium
dementia
amnestic disorder
delusional disorder
hallucinosis
affective disorder
personality disorder
atypical or mixed organic mental disorder

Section 2. Organic brain syndromes whose etiology or pathophysiological process is either noted as an additional diagnosis or is unknown.
Delirium
Dementia
Amnestic syndrome
Organic delusional syndrome
Organic hallucinosis
Organic affective syndrome
Organic personality syndrome
Atypical or mixed organic brain syndrom

Substance Use Disorders

Alcohol abuse
Alcohol dependence (Alcoholism)
Barbiturate or similarly acting sedative or hypnotic abuse
Barbiturate or similarly acting sedative or hypnotic dependence
Opioid abuse
Opioid dependence
Cocaine abuse
Amphetamine or similarly acting sympathomimetic abuse
Amphetamine or similarly acting sympathomimetic dependence
Phencyclidine (PCP) or similarly acting arylcyclohexylamine abuse
Hallucinogen abuse
Cannabis abuse
Cannabis dependence
Tobacco dependence
Other, mixed or unspecified substance abuse
Other specified substance dependence
Unspecified substance dependence
Dependence on combination of opioid and other non-alcohol substance
Dependence on combination of substances, excluding opioids and alcohol

Schizophrenic Disorders

Schizophrenia
disorganized
catatonic
paranoid
undifferentiated
residual